MW01200976

Ethics
Theory and Contemporary Issues
Tenth Edition

Andrew Fiala
California State University, Fresno, Professor of Philosophy

Barbara MacKinnon
University of San Francisco, Professor of Philosophy, Emerita

Australia • Brazil • Canada • Mexico • Singapore • United Kingdom • United States

Ethics: Theory and Contemporary Issues,
Tenth Edition
Andrew Fiala/Barbara MacKinnon

SVP, Product: Cheryl Costantini

VP, Product: Thais Alencar

Portfolio Product Director: Laura Ross

Portfolio Product Manager: Vanessa Manter

Product Assistant: Vivian Graham

Learning Designer: Rebecca Shuman

Senior Content Manager: Michelle Ruelos Cannistraci

Digital Project Manager: Jennifer Chinn

Senior Director, Product Marketing: Neena Bali

Product Marketing Manager: Danielle Dornbusch

Content Acquisition Analyst: Deanna Ettinger

Production Service: Lumina Datamatics Ltd.

Designer: Sarah Cole

Cover Image Source: Jacques-Louis David; iStock.com/kieferpix; iStock.com/Hydromet; iStock.com/Cimmerian; iStock.photo/vchal; JGI/Blend Images/Thinkstock; iStock.com/ EvanTravels; imageBROKER/Alamy Stock Photo; Proxima Studio/Shutterstock.com

Copyright © 2024 Cengage Learning, Inc. ALL RIGHTS RESERVED.

No part of this work covered by the copyright herein may be reproduced or distributed in any form or by any means, except as permitted by U.S. copyright law, without the prior written permission of the copyright owner.

Unless otherwise noted, all content is Copyright © Cengage Learning, Inc.

Previous edition(s): © 2018, © 2015, © 2012

For product information and technology assistance, contact us at
**Cengage Customer & Sales Support, 1-800-354-9706
or support.cengage.com.**

For permission to use material from this text or product, submit all requests online at **www.copyright.com**.

Library of Congress Control Number: 2023908346

ISBN: 978-0-357-79853-9

Cengage
200 Pier 4 Boulevard
Boston, MA 02210
USA

Cengage is a leading provider of customized learning solutions. Our employees reside in nearly 40 different countries and serve digital learners in 165 countries around the world. Find your local representative at **www.cengage.com.**

To learn more about Cengage platforms and services, register or access your online learning solution, or purchase materials for your course, visit **www.cengage.com.**

Printed at CLDPC, USA, 05-23

Brief Contents

Contents

Preface

We live in a rapidly changing and contentious time. There are conflicts of value all around us and serious debates about contemporary issues, including health care, abortion, euthanasia, biotechnologies, social justice, racial and economic inequality, global poverty, gender and sexuality, crime and punishment, war and peace, environmentalism, and our treatment of animals. In the background of these issues are conflicting theories of ethics. This book provides an overview of ongoing and perennial discussions about ethical theory, while also showing how ethical judgment might apply to a variety of contemporary issues. It is intended for students who are learning to think critically about ethics and who want to learn more about contemporary moral questions. Readers of this book will obtain a comprehensive introduction to ethics in theory and practice. We hope that readers will gain critical thinking skills and a deeper understanding of moral issues that can be employed in their own lives.

This, the tenth edition, is a significant revision of this well-known and widely used textbook, which was originally authored by Barbara MacKinnon more than thirty years ago. As in previous revisions, all of the information in the chapters on applied topics has been updated. This edition also brings to the forefront significant issues of concern for contemporary readers. This includes more focus on social justice, inclusivity, and diversity—in both the applied chapters and in the chapters focused on moral theories and the history of philosophy. The book reflects the changing social, political, and legal landscape in which we live. It includes, for example, a new chapter on Health Care Ethics, which allows us to discuss ethical issues associated with public health (with

the COVID-19 pandemic in the forefront). It also includes a substantially revised and updated discussion of abortion (in light of changing law) and a significant update to issues related to feminism, marriage equality, and transgender persons. In addition to featuring new and neglected voices, and addressing a number of new topics, the book has also undergone a substantial revision in terms of structure, format, and learning design.

New to This Edition

Learning Aids

The book continues to emphasize student learning through clear summaries, engaging examples, and helpful study tools. We continue to include review exercises, bolded key terms, and discussion cases. In this edition, we have paid further attention to student learning by clarifying learning outcomes and mapping them across the text. These learning outcomes form the basis of another new feature, **Chapter Summaries** at the end of each chapter. In addition, two other new features have been added to each chapter. Each chapter begins with an engaging opening vignette based on real-world issues followed by **"What Do You Think?" questions** intended to generate thought (and which could be used in classroom discussion). In the middle of each chapter, we have inserted a quick multiple-choice **"Knowledge Check" quiz**, intended to reinforce student learning.

Chapter Updates

The tenth edition includes up-to-date and detailed information about a variety of topics. Each chapter has been revised to reflect new scholarship and current data. In the first half of the book, which focuses on ethical theory (Chapters 1–9), this revision includes significant updates in thinking about and presenting the work of historical figures, in a way that is responsive to new and emerging scholarship in the history of philosophy.

Major changes occurred especially in the second half of the book (the "Ethics / Contemporary Issues" section, Chapters 10–20). In these chapters on applied topics, extensive updates and new research are included with regard to empirical matters. These chapters have been updated in light of changing facts in the world and in the law, and in social and political institutions. They also reflect technological innovations and new ethical challenges. We have revised the structure and organization of these chapters including writing an entirely new chapter (Chapter 10) on **Health Care Ethics**. This chapter contains discussion of ethical issues that arose during the COVID-19 pandemic, as well as ongoing and emerging issues in health care. As part of these changes, we have merged the chapters on abortion and euthanasia. The abortion section has been extensively revised in light of the changing legal status of abortion in the aftermath of the U.S. Supreme Court's *Dobbs* decision.

Some further structural changes were made, including a reshuffling of chapters that allowed us to group chapters together under a couple of general themes. The chapters on Health Care Ethics (Chapter 10), Abortion and Euthanasia (Chapter 11), and Biotechnology and Bioengineering (Chapter 12) are grouped under the general theme of **Bioethics**. The chapters on Equality and Discrimination (Chapter 13), Economic Justice (Chapter 14), Global Justice and Globalization (Chapter 15), and Sexual Morality (Chapter 16) are found within a general section on **Social Justice**. We have gathered the chapters on Punishment and the Death Penalty (Chapter 17) and Peace, Violence, and War (Chapter 18) in a section on **Social Order and Violence**. And finally, we have grouped the chapters on Environmental Ethics (Chapter 19) and Animal Ethics and Beyond (Chapter 20) under the general heading of **The Nonhuman**.

The following highlights specific changes for each chapter

Chapter 1: Ethics and Ethical Reasoning

›› New opening vignette: "Living and Dying Well: The Case of Socrates"

›› New discussion of "critical theory of ethics"

›› New readings from G. E. Moore, E. O. Wilson, and Naomi Zack

Chapter 2: Religion and Global Ethics

›› New opening vignette: "The Challenge of Global Ethics"

›› Revised discussion of human rights

›› New reading from Eleanor Roosevelt

Chapter 3: Ethical Relativism

›› New opening vignette: "Cultural Competence"

›› Revised discussion of pluralism (including American pragmatism and Alain Locke)

›› New readings from Alain Locke and Anita Superson

Chapter 4: Egoism, Altruism, and the Social Contract

›› New opening vignette: "Community Service"

›› New discussions of empathy, compassion, and care ethics

›› New reading from Virginia Held

Chapter 5: Utilitarianism

›› New opening vignette: "Population Pressures"

›› New discussion of John Stuart Mill's views of race and women

Chapter 6: Deontological Ethics

›› New opening vignette: "Conscientious Objection"

›› New discussion of Kant's views of race and women (and Charles Mills's reinterpretation of Kant)

›› New reading from Charles Mills

Chapter 7: Natural Law and Human Rights

›› New opening vignette: "The Rights of Refugees"

›› Updated discussion of *summum bonum* (highest good)

›› New discussion of slavery and gender from the standpoint of natural law, including new discussion of Mary Wollstonecraft and Frederick Douglass

Chapter 8: Virtue Ethics

›› New opening vignette: "Vaccine Virtues and Vices"

›› New discussion of Aristotle on slavery and gender hierarchy

>> New readings from Alasdair MacIntyre and Lisa Tessman

Chapter 9: Feminist Thought and the Ethics of Care

>> New opening vignette: "Rights and Equality for Women"

>> Restructured and revised to include discussions of gender essentialism, transgender issues, and intersectionality

>> Updated history of feminism

>> Updated discussions of violence against women, pornography, and honor killings

>> New reading from bell hooks

Chapter 10: Health Care Ethics

>> An entirely new chapter includes: basic principles of health care ethics, public health, rationing, paternalism, health equity, and other new topics

>> New opening vignette: "COVID-19 Pandemic, Masking, and Vaccine Mandates"

>> New readings from Onora O'Neill, Anita Silvers, John Harris, Kai Nielsen, John David Lewis, Norman Daniels, and Wendy Rogers

Chapter 11: Abortion and Euthanasia

>> This is a new chapter that combines previously separate chapters on abortion and euthanasia (and that builds on ideas in the health care ethics chapter)

>> New opening vignette: "The End of *Roe v. Wade*"

>> Extensive updates on legal issues

>> New readings from Mary Anne Warren, Ronald Dworkin et al., and *Dobbs v. Jackson* (2022)

Chapter 12: Biotechnology and Bioengineering

>> New opening vignette: "Genetic Engineering"

>> Updated details about CRISPR gene editing, new biotech, the disabilities perspective

>> New reading from Rosemarie Garland-Thomson

Chapter 13: Equality and Discrimination

>> New opening vignette: "Black Lives Matter"

>> New and updated topics: critical race theory and bans on CRT, anti-racism, intersectionality, and reparations

>> Also including new discussion of W. E. B. Du Bois, Supreme Court affirmative action cases, and police brutality

>> New reading from Ibram X. Kendi

Chapter 14: Economic Justice

>> New opening vignette: "Loan Forgiveness"

>> New and updated coverage of loan forgiveness, eviction moratorium, and other issues

>> Updates on economic data: wage and wealth gaps including racial/gender gaps

Chapter 15: Global Justice and Globalization

>> New opening vignette: "Global Poverty"

>> New and updated coverage of global reparations, decolonization, Indigenous peoples, global poverty, inequality, refugees, and immigration—as well as updated discussion of Peter Singer

>> New readings from Krushil Watene and José Jorge Mendoza

Chapter 16: Sexual Morality

>> New opening vignette: "Ethical Pornography?"

>> New and updated coverage of Plato's views of sex and love, hedonism and asceticism, affirmative consent, sex work, and LGBTQ+ issues, including transgender issues and marriage equality, and new authors discussed: Talia Bettcher, J. K. Rowling, Loren Cannon, and Carole Pateman

>> New readings from Carole Pateman and Jessica Flanigan

Chapter 17: Punishment and the Death Penalty

>> New opening vignette: "Decriminalization and Sentencing Reform"

>> New and updated information on sentencing reform, death penalty abolitionism, crime rates, incarceration rates, racial disparities, and racial profiling

Chapter 18: Peace, Violence, and War

>> New opening vignette: "War in Ukraine"

>> Updated coverage and information on positive/negative peace, structural violence, drone warfare, torture, and war crimes

>> New authors discussed including Jane Addams, James Lawson, Francisco de Vitoria, and Hugo Grotius

>> New readings from James Lawson and Larry May

Chapter 19: Environmental Ethics

>> New opening vignette: "The Costs of Climate Change"

>> New and updated coverage of forest fires, climate change data, environmental justice, ecosystem services, ecofeminism, discrimination and racism in the history of environmentalism, and Dakota Access Pipeline protests

>> New authors discussed including Winona LaDuke, Leah Thomas, and Greta Thunberg

>> New reading from Greta Thunberg

Chapter 20: Animal Ethics—and Beyond

>> New opening vignette: "Hunting and Eating"

>> Updated data and coverage of endangered species, animal agriculture, animal experimentation, animal welfare legislation, as well as a new topic on nonhuman sentience (including AI and extraterrestrial life)

>> New authors discussion including Gary Francione, Bob Fischer, Kant on extraterrestrial life, J. J. C. Smart, and Michael Dorf

>> New reading from Michael Dorf

Focus on Inclusivity and Diversity

This new edition focusers significantly on inclusivity and diversity. We have sought to include new and diverse voices among the authors we discuss and the primary sources included in the text. We have revised and updated case studies and discussion questions with this in mind. And we have explicitly addressed racial, economic, gender, and religious issues that arise in the history of philosophy. At the same time, we remain committed to a rigorous and comprehensive approach to ethical theory and applied topics. To this end, issues of inclusivity and diversity are often left as questions for student to discuss, as they reflect on case studies, discussion questions, and the theories and frameworks discussed in the text. We believe that this revision provides a current and cutting-edge learning opportunity that will resonate with today's students.

A Revised Approach to Primary Sources

This edition includes some familiar readings from previous editions and some new additions. This revision is focused more on shorter reading excerpts, rather than including longer primary source documents. This allows us to include more primary source material, featuring a broader range of authors. In some cases, older readings have been shortened to make room for new readings. In general, we have included more short excerpts by a more diverse set of authors, including emerging voices. Still included from previous editions are readings from classical authors in ethical theory such as Plato, Kant, Mill, Aristotle, and Aquinas. We have added in those chapters readings from G. E. Moore, Alain Locke, Naomi Zack, Anita Superson, Virginia Held, Charles Mills, Alasdair MacIntyre, Lisa Tessman, and bell hooks. The applied chapters include familiar mainstays of applied ethics such as Judith Thomson on abortion, James Rachels on euthanasia, Leon Kass on biotechnology, and Peter Singer on global poverty. We continue to feature authors added in previous editions, including John Lachs on relativism, Hilde Lindemann on feminism, Bertha Alvarez Manninen on abortion, the U.S. Supreme Court *Obergefell* decision, Naomi Zack on Black Lives Matter, Iris Marion Young's "Five Faces of Oppression," Pope Francis and Ayn Rand on economic issues, Michelle Alexander on the New Jim Crow, Tom Regan on animal rights, the Transhumanist declaration, Andrew Fitz-Gibbon on peace, and Garrett Hardin on global poverty. In addition, we have added a number of new authors in those applied chapters: Onora O'Neill, Anita Silvers, John Harris, Kai Nielsen, John David Lewis, Norman Daniels, and Wendy Rogers (in the Health Care Ethics chapter), Mary Anne Warren and Ronald Dworkin (in the chapter on Abortion and Euthanasia), Rosemarie Garland-Thomson on velvet eugenics in the chapter on Biotechnology, Ibram X. Kendi on anti-racism in the chapter on Equality and Discrimination, Krushil Watene and José Jorge Mendoza in the chapter on Global Justice, Carole Pateman and Jessica Flanigan in the chapter on Sexual Morality, James Lawson and Larry May in the chapter on War and Peace, Greta Thunberg in the chapter on Environmental Ethics, and Michael Dorf in the chapter on Animals and Beyond.

Our hope is that this wider array of shorter readings will be more useful for students and instructors. Each primary source reading is introduced with discussion questions that could be used in class or in online discussion forums.

Organization of the Text

The theory chapters in Part I (Chapters 1–9) present detailed summaries of the theories and major concepts, positions, and arguments.

The contemporary issues chapters in Part II (Chapters 10–20) include summaries of:

>> current social conditions and recent events, with special emphasis on their relevance to students' lives;

>> conceptual issues, such as how to define key words and phrases (e.g., *cloning*, *terrorism*, and *distributive justice*);

>> arguments and suggested ways to organize an ethical analysis of each topic; and

>> tables outlining possible moral positions, linked to normative theories and key authors.

Throughout this text, we seek to engage readers by posing challenging ethical questions and then offering a range of possible answers or explanations. The aim is to present more than one side of each issue so that students can decide for themselves what position they will take. This also allows instructors more latitude to emphasize specific arguments and concepts and to direct the students' focus as they see fit.

Where possible throughout the text, the relation of ethical theory to the practical issues is indicated. For example, one distinction used throughout the text is between consequentialist and non-consequentialist considerations and arguments. The idea is that if students are able to first situate or categorize a philosophical reason or argument, then they will be better able to evaluate it critically in their thinking and writing. Connections to related concepts and issues in other chapters are also highlighted throughout the text to help students note similarities and contrasts among various ethical positions.

Features of the Text

We have sought to make this tenth edition of *Ethics: Theory and Contemporary Issues* the most comprehensive and up-to-date ethics text available. It combines theory and issues, text and readings, as well as current empirical information about contemporary moral problems. It is designed to be flexible, user-friendly, current, pedagogically helpful, and balanced.

>> The flexible structure of the text allows instructors to emphasize only those theories and applied ethical topics that best suit their courses.

>> The text is user-friendly, while at the same time philosophically reliable. It employs pedagogical aids throughout and at the end of each chapter, and provides extensive examples from current events and trends. The exposition challenges students with stimulating questions and is interspersed with useful diagrams, charts, and headings.

>> The text not only provides up-to-date coverage of developments in the news and in scientific journals but also on ethical issues as they are discussed in contemporary philosophy.

>> It offers a balanced collection of readings, including both the ethical theories and contemporary sources on the issues.

>> It includes diverse voices and emerging issues, which will be of interest for current students.

>> *Ethics: Theory and Contemporary Issues*, Tenth Edition, is accompanied by a broad range of online and textual tools that amplify its teachability and give instructors specific pedagogical tools for different learning styles.

To aid both instructor and student, each chapter contains the following pedagogical aids:

>> **Learning Outcomes**: An updated list of learning objectives at the beginning of each chapter that are mapped to headings in the text. These learning outcomes are intended to help the reader know what they are supposed to be learning as they read.

>> **"What Do You Think?"**: Each chapter begins with an opening vignette with discussion questions based on real-world issues. These are intended to give readers something concrete to think about as they begin the chapter. They may be useful for in-class discussions.

>> **Knowledge Check**: A quick multiple-choice quiz is provided in the middle of each chapter, intended to help students summarize and check their understanding.

>> **"Moral Approaches" Tables**: Most chapters include a table outlining moral positions, which are intended to summarize conclusions and connections on multiple sides of the argument, while also providing an indication of which side of the argument the authors discussed in the chapter may agree with.

>> **Key Terms**: Key terms appear in bold to draw the reader's attention.

>> **Chapter Summary**: The end of each chapter contains an extended summary of key concepts and issues written in clear, accessible prose. These detailed summaries provide students with a thorough grounding in the theory and practical application of philosophical ethics.

>> **Primary Source Readings**: Each chapter includes several short reading excerpts. These excerpts begin with study questions, which readers can use to guide their reading and which may also for the basis of in-class discussion. In most cases, we have opted for shorter excerpts, while trying to cover a range of perspectives.

>> **Review Exercises**: Review exercises at the end of each chapter can be used as a final check on what the reader has learned. These can also be used for exam and quiz questions, or for homework and discussion.

>> **Discussion Cases**: Discussion cases follow each chapter in Part II (the applied topics chapters). These cases are intended to put the reader's learning to work in problem-solving, critical thinking, and ethical decision-making. These case studies can be used to provide opportunities for class or group discussion.

>> **Glossary**: A glossary of definitions of key terms and definitions is provided at the end of the book.

Course Solutions

Online Learning Platform: MindTap

Today's leading online learning platform, *MindTap* for Fiala/Mackinnon, *Ethics: Theory & Contemporary Issues, Tenth Edition*, gives you complete control of your course to craft a personalized, engaging learning experience that challenges students, builds confidence, and elevates performance.

MindTap introduces students to core concepts from the beginning of your course using a simplified learning path that progresses from understanding to application and delivers access to eTextbooks, study tools, auto-graded assessments, and performance analytics.

Use *MindTap* for Fiala/Mackinnon, *Ethics: Theory & Contemporary Issues, Tenth Edition* as-is, or personalize it to meet your specific course needs. You can also easily integrate *MindTap* into your Learning Management System (LMS).

MindTap Instructor Features

MindTap for Fiala/Mackinnon, *Ethics: Theory & Contemporary Issues, Tenth Edition*, today's most innovative online learning platform, powers your students from memorization to mastery. *MindTap* gives you complete control of your course to provide engaging content, challenge every individual, and build student confidence.

Boost Comprehension with Improved Learning Design

Students focus and better comprehend key learnings through a Learning Path divided into groups of short activities, all anchored to a single concept. Built on proven learning research and theory, *MindTap* presents concepts by pairing assessment and content in a visually captivating format that helps students maintain their focus and reduces distraction when completing activities.

Provide Full Course Access On the Go

Offer your students the flexibility they need to fit learning into their day—wherever they are. Compatible with smartphones and tablets, the Cengage mobile app enables students to complete activities and assignments, read and listen to their eTextbook online and offline, receive due date reminders, and study anytime, anywhere, with tools like flashcards, quizzes, and more. Keep students connected and engaged to your course, even on the go.

MindTap Student Features

Learn on your terms with *MindTap* for Fiala/Mackinnon, *Ethics: Theory & Contemporary Issues, Tenth Edition*.

Instant Access in Your Pocket

Take advantage of the free mobile app Cengage Read to learn on your terms. Read or listen to your eTextbook online or offline, anywhere, anytime from your smartphone or tablet.

MindTap Helps You Succeed in Class

Track your scores and stay motivated to achieve your goals. The *MindTap* Green Dot tool keeps you focused along the way. Your Personal Study Plan delivers performance reports and opportunities to review and retake completed assignments based on your learning needs.

MindTap activities and assessments support you in expanding your knowledge of ethics and philosophy and gain mastery of the text's themes and concepts. Here are some of the activities and assessments you will find in the Fiala/Mackinnon, *Ethics: Theory & Contemporary Issues, Tenth Edition MindTap*:

›› **Ethical Dilemma: What Do You Think?** This new activity tasks you with reading a short ethical dilemma and then answering a polling question to indicate your opinion about the issue. This activity is designed to get you thinking about the theories you will encounter in the chapter and may be used to foster class discussion (online or in-person).

›› **Check Your Understanding:** This activity offers focused instruction covering the most important concepts in each chapter. Revised feedback includes

robust explanations on why answers are right or wrong with rejoinders that connect to the relevant sections of the eBook for review and remediation.

›› **Chapter Quiz:** Assess your knowledge of a chapter's themes and concepts with a twenty-question multiple-choice quiz. Chapter Quizzes have been updated for accuracy and alignment with the tenth edition.

›› **Gale College Collection:** Access the full text of many of the primary source readings referenced in your textbook through the Gale College Collection.

MindTap also includes a variety of other tools that support philosophy teaching and learning:

›› The Philosophy Toolbox collects tutorials on using *MindTap* and researching and writing academic papers, including citation information and tools, that instructors can use to support students in the writing process.

To learn more, go to https://www.cengage.com/mindtap.

Instructor Resources

Additional instructor resources for this product are available online on the Instructor Companion Site. Instructor assets include an Instructor Manual, PowerPoint slides, a Solution and Answer Guide, Educator's Guide, Transition Guide, and a test bank powered by Cognero compatible with multiple learning management systems. Sign up or sign in at www.cengage.com to search for and access this product and its online resources.

The Instructor Manual includes information about all activities and assessments available for each chapter, a chapter outline, chapter summary, key terms with definitions, and suggestions for lectures and classroom activities including questions for further thought, critical thinking writing prompts, and activities that may be conducted in an on-ground, hybrid, or online modality.

The PowerPoint Lecture Slides are closely tied to the Instructor Manual, providing ample opportunities for generating classroom discussion and interaction. They offer ready-to-use, visual outlines of each chapter that may be easily customized for your lectures.

The **Solution and Answer Guide** provides answers to the chapter review exercises along with notes for facilitating discussions.

The **Educator's Guide** describes the content and activities available in the accompanying *MindTap* course.

The **Transition Guide** provides a chapter-by-chapter list that highlights content changes and updates in the new edition of the textbook and courseware design.

The **Test Bank**, offered in Blackboard, Moodle, Desire2Learn, and Canvas formats, contains multiple-choice and essay questions for each chapter. Import the test bank into your LMS to edit and manage questions and to create tests.

Cengage Learning Testing, powered by Cognero, is a flexible online system that allows instructors to author, edit, and manage test bank content online. Instructors can create multiple test versions and instantly deliver them through their learning management system right to the classroom.

About the Authors

Andrew Fiala, PhD, is professor of philosophy and director of the Ethics Center at California State University, Fresno, a large public university in California's agricultural heartland, the San Joaquin Valley. He has been teaching ethical theory and applied ethics courses for more than two decades. He inherited this book from Barbara MacKinnon, PhD, who retired from the University of San Francisco, where she was a professor of philosophy. Barbara MacKinnon guided the text through seven editions. Andrew Fiala joined the team for the eighth edition. In each subsequent revision, he has tried to remain true to the spirit of Barbara MacKinnon's text, which includes lively prose, engaging examples, and careful analysis.

Acknowledgments

We wish to thank the many people who have made valuable suggestions for improving the tenth edition of the text, including Jacqueline Alvarez, Merced College; Erik Baldwin, Indiana University Northwest; Cynthia Boyce, Lincoln Trail College; Michael Emerson, Northwestern Michigan College; Jennifer Harrison, Warren County Community College; Sean Hayden, Tennessee Wesleyan University; Valerie Holliday, Baton Rouge Community College; R. Scacci, Warren County Community College and Catherine Zusky.

Throughout previous editions and revisions, Barbara MacKinnon has offered her heartfelt thanks to the students in her classes at the University of San Francisco. Over the years, they have contributed greatly to this text by challenging her to keep up with the times and to make things more clear and more interesting. She also appreciates the support of her husband and fellow philosopher, Edward MacKinnon. She dedicates this book to her two wonderful daughters, Jennifer and Kathleen. Andrew Fiala is thankful for Barbara Mackinnon's hard work throughout the previous editions of this book and for the opportunity to transform his classroom teaching experience into a useful text for teaching ethics.

We also wish to acknowledge the many professional people from Cengage and its vendors who have worked on this edition, including Vanessa Manter, Senior Product Manager; Rebecca Shuman, Learning Designer; Michelle Ruelos Cannistraci, Senior Content Manager, Sarah Cole, Art Director; and Vivian Graham, Product Assistant.

History of Ethics Timeline

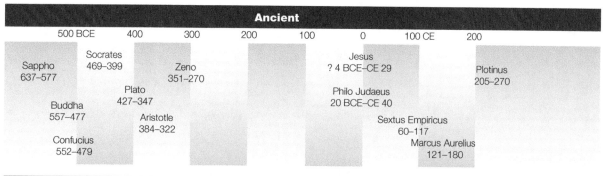

Ancient

500 BCE	400	300	200	100	0	100 CE	200

Sappho
637–577

Socrates
469–399

Zeno
351–270

Jesus
? 4 BCE–CE 29

Plotinus
205–270

Plato
427–347

Buddha
557–477

Aristotle
384–322

Philo Judaeus
20 BCE–CE 40

Confucius
552–479

Sextus Empiricus
60–117

Marcus Aurelius
121–180

Medieval

CE 300	400	500	600	700	800	900	1000	1100	1200	1300

Augustine
345–400

Boethius
480–524

Mohammed
570–632

Anselm
1033–1109

Aquinas
1224–1274

Abelard
1079–1142

Scotus
1265–1308

Avicebron
1021–1058

Ockham
1285–1347

Maimonides
1135–1204

Avicenna
980–1037

Averroes
1126–1198

Modern

1500	1600	1700	1800	1900	2000

Bacon
1561–1626

Locke
1632–1704

Hume
1711–1776

Kierkegaard
1813–1851

G. E. Moore
1873–1958

Martha Nussbaum
b. 1947–

Hobbes
1588–1679

Leibniz
1646–1716

Kant
1724–1804

Marx
1818–1883

Rawls
1921–2002

Judith Butler
b. 1956–

Spinoza
1632–1677

Hegel
1770–1831

Nietzsche
1844–1900

Habermas
1929–

Nick Bostrom
b. 1973–

Rousseau
1712–1778

Mill
1806–1873

Sartre
1905–1979

Singer
b. 1946–

Gandhi
1869–1948

Noddings
1929–2022

Wollstonecraft
1759–1797

de Beauvoir
1908–1986

Charles Mills
1951–2021

Bentham
1748–1832

James
1846–1910

Judith Jarvis Thomson
1929–2020

Dewey
1859–1952

Virginia Held
b. 1929–

Alain Locke
1885–1954

Alasdair MacIntyre
b. 1929–

W. E. B. Dubois
1869–1963

1

Ethics and Ethical Reasoning

Learning Outcomes

After reading this chapter, you should be able to:

1.1 Explain the difference between normative ethics and metaethics.

1.2 Explain the difference between normative and descriptive claims.

1.3 Decide whether naturalistic explanations of ethics commit the naturalistic fallacy.

1.4 Define key terms: intuitionism, emotivism, objectivism, and subjectivism.

1.5 Differentiate between instrumental and intrinsic values.

1.6 Explain sound and valid arguments as well as some fallacies of reasoning.

1.7 Evaluate consequentialist and nonconsequentialist approaches to ethics.

Living and Dying Well: The Case of Socrates

Socrates was sentenced to death for two crimes: impiety and corrupting the youth. He denied that he was guilty of these crimes, a claim that was widely shared by his followers, including Plato. As Socrates sat in prison awaiting his execution, his friend Crito approached him with a plan to escape. Socrates rejected Crito's plan and the idea of escaping. Socrates maintained that as a good man, he was obliged to remain in prison and allow his execution to be carried out. Among the arguments that Socrates made were the following. First, he

Jacques-Louis David

claimed that it is wrong to respond to injustice with injustice and that it is wrong to return evil for evil. To escape would be wrong. And Socrates thinks that two wrongs don't make a right. Second, he maintained that honor and goodness are more important than life itself. He put it this way: "It is not merely living that matters but, rather, living well." Socrates was eventually put to death by the city of Athens.

What Do You Think?

1. Is Socrates correct to suggest that it is wrong to return evil for evil and that two wrongs don't make a right?

2. Do you agree with the idea that living well is more important than merely living?

3. What would you do if you were wrongly convicted of a crime and sentenced to death? Would you try to escape? Do you think Socrates was wise to refuse to escape?

4. What basic principles or virtues guide your thinking about these issues?

Introduction

This is a book about ethics. It provides an overview of questions that arise in thinking about what it means to live well. The philosophical study of ethics asks the fundamental question of what it means to live a good life. As you will see, this question leads to further questions and ongoing disputes about the meaning of morality and about how moral theories apply to concrete issues. We hope that in thinking critically about the controversies and arguments that occur here, you will be on your way to answering the questions of ethics for yourself. We also hope that you will have a better understanding of what others believe and why they might believe the way they do.

The book has two major sections. In the first nine chapters, we focus on theoretical questions. In the second half of the book, we explore a number of practical or applied issues. The first half of the book is theoretical and historical. In this part, we consider many important philosophical theories, while also exploring and critiquing the thinking of key authors in the philosophical tradition. In the second half of the book, we take what we've learned about ethical theory and apply it to challenging issues of contemporary concern.

Our goal throughout is to inspire critical thinking about values. Critical thinking is not easy. But philosophers agree with Socrates that "the unexamined life is not worth living." We live better when we understand what we believe and why we believe it. This is true within the lives of individuals. You will live better if you think critically about your own values. Critical thinking also has a social benefit. Society is better off when we are able to think critically about what we value, why we value it, and why we disagree.

Why Study Ethics?

It is clear that we often disagree about questions of value. Should vaccinations be required? Should same-sex marriage be legal? Should abortion be legal? Should drugs such as marijuana be legalized? Should we torture terrorists in order to get information from them? Should we eat animals or use them in medical experiments? These sorts of questions are sure to expose divergent ideas about what is right or wrong.

Discussions of these sorts of questions often devolve into unreasonable name-calling, foot-stomping, and other questionable argument styles. The philosophical study of ethics aims to produce good arguments that provide reasonable support for our opinions about practical topics. We also want to be self-critical in our thinking and argumentation. If someone says that abortion should (or should not) be permitted, they need to explain why this is so. It is not enough to say that abortion should not be permitted because it is wrong or that women should be allowed to choose abortion because it is wrong to limit women's choices. To say that these things are wrong is merely to reiterate that they should not be permitted. Such an answer *begs the question*. Circular, question-begging arguments are fallacious. We need further argument and information to know *why* abortion is wrong or *why* limiting free choice is wrong. We need a theory of what is right and wrong, good or evil, justified, permissible, and unjustifiable, and we need to understand how our theory applies in concrete cases. The first half of this book will discuss various theories and concepts that can be used to help us avoid begging the question in debates about ethical issues. The second half looks in detail at a number of these issues.

It is appropriate to wonder, at the outset, why we need to do this. Why isn't it sufficient to simply state your opinion and assert that "x is wrong (or evil, just, permissible, etc.)"? One answer to this question is that such assertions do nothing to solve the deep conflicts of value that we find in our world. We know that people disagree about abortion, same-sex marriage, animal rights, and other issues. If we are to make progress toward understanding each other, if we are to make progress toward establishing some consensus about these topics, then we have to understand *why* we think certain things are right and others are wrong. We need to make arguments and give reasons in order to work out our own conclusions about these issues and in order to explain our conclusions to others. This effort to understand, explain, and argue about values was important to Socrates and his philosophical followers. It remains important for human beings today. This is especially true in a world that includes a growing appreciation for diversity and the need to critically examine the assumptions of our legal, moral, and political systems.

One important feature of the philosophical study of values is that it is up to us to figure out what is right or wrong, good or evil. It is insufficient to appeal to custom or authority in deriving our conclusions about moral issues. While it may be appropriate for children to simply obey their parents' decisions, adults should strive for more than conformity and obedience to authority. Sometimes our parents, teachers, and other adults are wrong—or they disagree among themselves. Sometimes the law is wrong—or laws conflict—or we come into conflict with the law, as in the case of Socrates. And sometimes religious authorities are wrong—or those authorities do not agree. To appeal to authority on moral issues, we would first have to decide which authority is to be trusted and believed. Which religion provides the best set of moral rules? Which set of laws in which country is to be followed? Even within the United States, there are ongoing legal conflicts with regard to many issues. Some states have legalized marijuana and physician-assisted suicide, others have not. Some states continue to use the death penalty, others do not. Abortion continues to be a contentious legal issue. We disagree about public health measures. And we disagree about issues involving race, gender, and sexuality. The world's religions also disagree about a number of issues: for example, the status of women, the permissibility of abortion, and whether war is justifiable. And members of the same religion or denomination may disagree among themselves about these issues. To begin resolving these conflicts, we need critical philosophical inquiry into basic ethical questions. In Chapter 2, we discuss the world's diverse religious traditions and ask whether there is a set of common ethical ideas that is shared by these traditions. In this chapter, we clarify what ethics is and how ethical reasoning should proceed.

What is Ethics?

On the first day of an ethics class, we often ask students to write one-paragraph answers to the question, "What is ethics?"

How would you answer? Over the years, there have been significant differences of opinion among our students on this issue. Some have argued that ethics is a

highly personal thing, a matter of private opinion. Others claim that our values come from family upbringing. Other students think that ethics is a set of social principles, the codes of one's society or particular groups within it, such as medical or legal organizations. Some write that many people get their ethical beliefs from their religion.

One general conclusion can be drawn from these students' comments: We tend to think of ethics as the set of values or principles held by individuals or groups. I have my ethics and you have yours; groups—professional organizations and societies, for example—have shared sets of values. We can study the various sets of values that people have. This could be done historically and sociologically. Or we could take a psychological interest in determining how people form their values. But philosophical ethics is a critical enterprise that asks whether any particular set of values or beliefs is better than any other. We compare and evaluate sets of values and beliefs, giving reasons for our evaluations. We ask questions such as, "Are there good reasons for preferring one set of values over another?" In this text, we examine ethics from a critical or evaluative standpoint. This examination will help you come to a better understanding of your own values and the values of others.

Ethics is a branch of *philosophy*. It is also called *moral philosophy*. In general, philosophy is a discipline or study in which we ask—and attempt to answer—basic questions about key areas or subject matters of human life and about pervasive and significant aspects of experience. Some philosophers, such as Plato and Kant, have tried to do this systematically by interrelating their philosophical views in many areas. According to Alfred North Whitehead, "Philosophy is the endeavor to frame a coherent, logical, necessary system of general ideas in terms of which every element of our experience can be interpreted."[1] Some contemporary philosophers have given up on the goal of building a system of general ideas, arguing instead that we must work at problems piecemeal, focusing on one particular issue at a time. For instance, some philosophers might analyze the meaning of the phrase *to know,* while others might work on the morality of lying. Some philosophers are optimistic about our ability to address these problems, while others are more skeptical because they think that the way we analyze the issues and the conclusions we draw will always be influenced by our background, culture, and habitual ways of thinking. Most agree, however, that these problems are worth wondering about and caring about.

We can ask philosophical questions about many subjects. In the philosophical study of **aesthetics**, philosophers ask basic or foundational questions about art and objects of beauty: what kinds of things do or should count as art (rocks arranged in a certain way, for example)? Is what makes something an object of aesthetic interest its emotional expressiveness, its peculiar formal nature, or its ability to reveal truths that cannot be described in other ways? In the philosophy of science, philosophers ask whether scientific knowledge gives us a picture of reality as it is, whether progress exists in science, and whether the scientific method discloses truth. Philosophers of law seek to understand the nature of law itself, the source of its authority, the nature of legal interpretation, and the basis of legal responsibility. In the philosophy of knowledge, called **epistemology**, we try to answer questions about what we can know of ourselves and our world, and what it means to know something rather than just to believe it. In each area, philosophers ask basic questions about the particular subject matter. This is also true of moral philosophy.

> Ethics, or moral philosophy, asks basic questions about the good life, about what is better and worse, about whether there is any objective right and wrong, and how we know it if there is.

Normative Ethics vs. Metaethics

1.1 Explain the difference between normative ethics and metaethics.

One objective of ethics is to help us decide what is good or bad, better or worse. This is generally called **normative ethics**. Normative ethics defends a thesis about what is good, right, or just. Normative ethics can be distinguished from **metaethics**. Metaethical inquiry asks questions about the nature of ethics, including

the meaning of ethical terms and judgments. Metaethical questions include metaphysical questions about the very objects of ethics. **Metaphysics** is the study of ultimate reality. It asks about what exists, what is real, and about the meaning, purpose, and function of life, the universe, and everything. Important questions here include whether there really is something called "the good," whether evil exists, as well as related questions about the nature of the soul and the meaning and purpose of life. We might also wonder whether there is one answer to these kinds of questions or whether we are left with **relativism**, which is the claim that there is no single answer to them. As you can imagine, some of these issues overlap with religion. Questions about the relation between philosophical ethics and religion—as we discuss in Chapter 2—are metaethical. Theoretical questions about ethical relativism—as discussed in Chapter 3—are also metaethical. The other chapters in Part I are more properly designated as normative theory. These chapters present accounts of what is good or evil, just or unjust. Major normative theories discussed here include: **utilitarianism** (the idea that we ought to promote the greatest happiness for the greatest number), **Kantian deontology** (the idea that moral duty should be focused on universal rules that are not concerned with consequences or outcomes), **natural law** (the idea that moral laws are found in nature and discernible by reason), and **virtue ethics** (the idea that focuses on character traits and good habits). In Part I, we will also discuss **egoism** and the **social contract theory**, **care ethics**, and the critical lens of **feminism**.

Ethical and Other Types of Evaluation

1.2 Explain the difference between normative and descriptive claims.

"That's great!" "Now, this is what I call a delicious meal!" "That play was wonderful!" All of these statements express approval of something. They do not tell us much about the meal or the play, but they do imply that the speaker thought they were good. These are *evaluative* statements. Ethical statements or judgments are also *evaluative*. They tell us what the speaker believes is good or bad. They do not simply *describe* the object of the judgment—for example, as an action that occurred at a certain time or that affected people in a certain way. They go further and express a positive or negative regard for it. Of course, factual matters are relevant to moral evaluation. For example, factual judgments about whether capital punishment has a deterrent effect might be relevant to our moral judgments about it. So also would we want to know the facts about whether violence can ever bring about peace; this would help us judge the morality of war. Because ethical judgments often rely on such *empirical* information, ethics is often indebted to other disciplines such as sociology, psychology, and history. Thus, we can distinguish between empirical or **descriptive claims**, which state factual beliefs, and evaluative judgments, which state whether such facts are good or bad, just or unjust, right or wrong. Evaluative judgments are also called **normative judgments**. Moral judgments are evaluative because they "place a value," negative or positive, on some action or practice, such as capital punishment.

We also evaluate people, saying that a person is good or evil, just or unjust. Because these evaluations also rely on beliefs in general about what is good or right, they are also normative. For example, the judgment that a person is a hero or a villain is based on a normative theory about good or evil sorts of people.

> Descriptive (empirical) judgment: Capital punishment acts (or does not act) as a deterrent.
> Normative (moral) judgment: Capital punishment is justifiable (or unjustifiable).

"That is a good knife" is an evaluative or normative statement. However, it does not mean that the knife is morally good. In making ethical judgments, we use terms such as *good, bad, right, wrong, obligatory*, and *permissible*. We talk about what we ought or ought not to do. These are evaluative terms. *But not all evaluations are moral in nature.* We speak of a good knife without attributing moral goodness to it. In so describing the knife, we are probably referring to its practical usefulness for cutting. Other evaluations refer to other systems of values. When people tell us that a law is legitimate or unconstitutional, that is a legal judgment. When we read that two articles of clothing ought not to be worn together, that is an aesthetic judgment. When religious leaders tell members of their communities what they ought to do, that is a religious matter. When a community teaches people to bow before elders or use eating utensils in a certain way, that is a matter of custom. These various normative or evaluative judgments appeal to practical, legal, aesthetic, religious, or customary norms for their justification.

How do other types of normative judgments differ from moral judgments? Some philosophers believe that it is a characteristic of moral "oughts" in particular that they override other "oughts," such as aesthetic ones. In other words, if we must choose between what is aesthetically pleasing and what is morally right, then we ought to do what is morally right. In this way, morality may also take precedence over the law and custom. The doctrine of civil disobedience relies on this belief, because it holds that we may disobey certain laws for moral reasons. Although moral evaluations differ from other normative evaluations, this is not to say that there is no relation between them. In fact, moral reasons often form the basis for certain laws. But law—at least

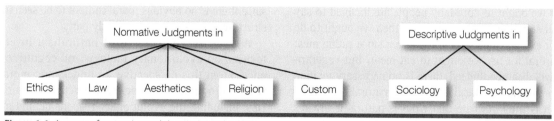

Figure 1-1 An array of normative and descriptive judgments.

in the United States—results from a variety of political compromises. We don't tend to look to the law for moral guidance. And we are reluctant to think that we can "legislate morality," as the saying goes. Of course, there is still an open debate about whether the law should enforce moral ideas in the context of issues such as same-sex marriage or abortion.

There may be moral reasons supporting legal arrangements—considerations of basic justice, for example. We may also think that some laws are practically useful, or that they were created by wise and virtuous individuals. But there remains an open question about the normative status of law. The descriptive fact that law exists is different from the normative question of whether the law is good and ought to be obeyed. Similar questions hold for aesthetic matters. Specific forms of art exist as a descriptive fact; but there are open normative questions about whether those art forms are beautiful or good—or what they are good for. Consider, for example, the question of the value of modern art, graffiti as an art form, or the status of rock or rap music. We will not consider aesthetic judgments further here. But we should note that ethics is not the only area in which we make normative judgments and in which there are normative disagreements.

Sociobiology and the Naturalistic Fallacy

1.3 Decide whether naturalistic explanations of ethics commit the naturalistic fallacy.

The distinction between descriptive and normative claims is a central issue for thinking about ethics. We often confuse these issues in our ordinary thinking, in part because we think that what we ordinarily do is what we ought to do. Many people are inclined to say that if something is natural to us, then we ought to do it. For example, one might argue that since eating meat is natural for us, we ought to eat meat. But vegetarians will disagree. Indeed, there is no necessary relation between what is ethical and what is natural or customary. It is thus not true that what is natural is always good. But people often make the mistake of confusing

facts of nature and value judgments. Most of the time, we are not attentive to the shift from facts to values, the shift from *is* to *ought*. Consider an example used by the eighteenth-century philosopher David Hume, who noticed that incest appears to be quite natural—animals do it all the time. But human beings condemn incest. If it is natural, why do we condemn it? Hume pointed out the problem of deriving an *ought* from an *is*; philosophers after Hume named the rule against simplistically deriving an *ought* from an *is* **Hume's law**. From this perspective, it is not logical, for example, to base our ideas about how we ought to behave from a factual account of how we actually do behave. This logical mistake was called the **naturalistic fallacy** by G. E. Moore, an influential philosopher of the early twentieth century. Moore maintained that moral terms such as *good* are names for nonempirical properties that cannot be reduced to some other natural thing. Moore claimed that to attempt to define *good* in terms of some mundane or natural thing such as pleasure is to commit a version of this fallacy. The problem is that we can ask whether pleasures are actually good. Just because we desire pleasure does not mean that it is good to desire pleasure. As Moore suggested, there is always an open question about whether what is natural is also good.

Now, not everyone agrees that appeals to nature in ethics are fallacious. There are a variety of naturalistic approaches to thinking about ethics. One traditional approach to ethics is called **natural law** ethics (which we discuss in detail in Chapter 7). Natural law ethics focuses on human nature and derives ethical precepts from an account of what is natural for humans. Natural law ethicists may argue, for example, that human body parts have natural functions and that by understanding these natural functions, we can figure out certain moral ideas about sexuality or reproduction. Opponents might argue that this commits the naturalistic fallacy, since there is no obvious moral content to be seen in the structure and function of our body parts.

A more recent version of naturalism in ethics focuses on evolutionary biology and cognitive science. From this perspective, to understand morality, we need to understand the basic functions of our species, including the evolutionary reasons behind moral behavior. We also need to understand how our brains function in order to explain how pleasure works, why some people are psychopathic, and why we struggle to balance egoistic and altruistic motivations. One version of this naturalism is known as **sociobiology**—an idea that was introduced by the biologist E. O. Wilson (we have an excerpt from Wilson in the primary source readings for this chapter).[2] "If the brain evolved by natural selection, even the capacities to select particular esthetic judgments and religious beliefs must have arisen by the same mechanistic process," Wilson explained.[3] The basic idea of sociobiology is that human behaviors result from the pressures of natural selection. Understanding human morality involves understanding the adaptive advantage of certain behaviors, which can be studied by comparing human behaviors with the behavior of other social animals—from insects to chimpanzees.

Figure 1-2 Does animal behavior provide a guide for human ethical behavior?

Jeannette Katzir Photog/Shutterstock.com

Sociobiology attempts to understand altruism, for example, in terms of evolutionary processes. From this perspective, altruistic concern develops through natural selection because altruistic animals will help each other survive. Biologist Richard Dawkins explains a related idea in terms of "the selfish gene." Dawkins's idea is that our genes use our altruistic and other behaviors to spread themselves. Thus, when we cooperate within groups that share a genetic endowment, we help to preserve the group and help to disseminate our shared genetic characteristics, often in competition with rival genetic groups.[4]

In discussing sociobiology and interpreting biological evidence, we must be careful, however, not to anthropomorphize.[5] When we look at the natural world, we often interpret it in anthropomorphic terms, seeing in animals and even in genes themselves the motivations and interests that human beings have. In other words, we must be careful that our value judgments do not cloud or confuse our description of the facts.

While the naturalistic approach of sociobiology is provocative and insightful, we might still worry that it commits the naturalistic fallacy. Just because altruistic behavior is natural and useful in the evolutionary struggle for survival does not mean that it is good, just, or right. To see this, let us return to Hume's example of incest. Incest might be useful as a method for disseminating our genetic material—so long as the negative problems associated with inbreeding are minimized. We do inbreed animals in this way in order to select for desirable traits. But it is still appropriate to ask whether incest is morally permissible for human beings—the question of *ought* might not be settled by what *is*.

Ethical Terms

You might have wondered what the difference is between calling something "right" and calling it "good." Consider the ethical meaning for these terms. Right and wrong usually apply to actions, as in "You did the right thing," or "That is the wrong thing to do." These terms prescribe things for us to do or not to do. On the other hand, when we say that something is morally good, we may not explicitly recommend doing it. However, we do recommend that it be positively regarded. Thus, we say things such as "Peace is good, and distress is bad." It is also interesting that with "right" and "wrong" there seems to be no in-between; it is either one or the other. However, with "good" and "bad" there is room for degrees, and some things are thought to be better or worse than others.

Other ethical terms require careful consideration. For example, when we say that something "ought" or "ought not" to be done, there is a sense of urgency and obligation. We can refrain from doing what we ought to do, but the obligation is still there. On the other hand, there are certain actions that we think are permissible but that we are not obligated to do. Thus, one may think that there is no obligation to help someone in trouble, though it is "morally permissible" (i.e., not wrong) to do so and even "praiseworthy" in some cases. Somewhat more specific ethical terms include *just* and *unjust* and *virtuous* and *vicious*.

To a certain extent, which set of terms we use depends on the particular overall ethical viewpoint or theory we adopt. This will become clearer as we discuss and analyze the various normative theories in this first part of the text.

Ethics and Reasons

When we evaluate something as right or wrong, good or bad, we appeal to certain norms or reasons. If someone claims that affirmative action is unjustified, for example, they should give reasons for this conclusion. It is not sufficient for them to say that this is just how they feel (although we'll discuss a theory of ethics that appeals to emotion in a moment). Some sort of argument is also required. And this argument ought to appeal to reasons, principles, norms, ideas, and concepts that are not merely based in feeling. Philosophical ethics asks us to interrogate our feelings in light of these norms and concepts. Perhaps the person feels that affirmative action is somehow unfair. Again, we will seek an explanation and argument about why affirmative action is unfair. As we push the matter further, we seek an explanation of *why* it might be unfair and what constitutes fairness and unfairness. Of course, there is an open and complicated argument about affirmative action (we will examine this in detail in Chapter 13). This means that other people

may "feel" differently about affirmative action—and the proponents of affirmative action will be asked to explain why they feel this way and how their understanding of affirmative action connects to an argument that justifies the practice.

Reason-giving is essential in philosophical ethics. However, this does not mean that making ethical judgments is and must be purely rational. We might be tempted to think that good moral judgments require us to be objective and not let our feelings, or emotions, enter into our decision-making. Yet this assumes that feelings always get in the way of making good judgments. Sometimes this is surely true, as when we are overcome by anger, jealousy, or fear and cannot think clearly. Biases and prejudice may stem from such strong feelings. We think prejudice is wrong because it prevents us from judging rightly. But emotions can often aid good decision-making. We may, for example, simply feel the injustice of a certain situation or the wrongness of someone's suffering. Furthermore, our caring about some issue or person may, in fact, direct us to more carefully examine the ethical issues involved. However, some explanation of why we hold a certain moral position is still required. Simply to say "X is just wrong" without explanation, or to merely express strong feelings or convictions about "X," is not sufficient.

Intuitionism, Emotivism, Subjectivism, Objectivism

1.4   Define key terms: intuitionism, emotivism, objectivism, and subjectivism.

Philosophers differ on how we know what is good. They also differ on the question of whether moral judgments refer to something objective or whether they are reports of subjective opinions or dispositions.

To say that something is good is often thought to be different from saying that something is yellow or heavy. The latter two qualities are empirical, known by our senses. However, good or goodness is held to be a nonempirical property, said by some to be knowable through intuition. A position known as **intuitionism** claims that our ideas about ethics rest on some sort of intuitive knowledge of ethical truths. This view is associated with G. E. Moore, whom we discussed earlier.[6] Another philosopher, W. D. Ross, thinks that we have a variety of "crystal-clear intuitions" about basic values. These intuitions are clear and distinct beliefs about ethics, which Ross explains using an analogy with mathematics: just as we see or intuit the self-evident truth of "2 + 2 = 4," we also see or intuit ethical truths: for example, that we have a duty to keep our promises. As Ross explains,

> Both in mathematics and in ethics we have certain crystal-clear intuitions from which we build up all that we can know about the nature of numbers and the nature of duty…we do not read off our knowledge of particular branches of duty from a single ideal of the good life, but build up our ideal of the good life from intuitions into the particular branches of duty.[7]

A very important question is whether our intuitions point toward some objective moral facts in the world or whether they are reports of something subjective. A significant problem for intuitionism is that people's moral intuitions seem to differ. Unlike the crystal-clear intuitions of mathematics—which are shared by all of us—the intuitions of ethics are not apparently shared by everyone.

Another view, sometimes called **emotivism**, maintains that when we say something is good, we are showing our approval of it and recommending it to others rather than describing it. This view is associated with the work of twentieth-century philosophers such as A. J. Ayer and C. L. Stevenson. But it has deeper roots in a theory of the moral sentiments, such as we find in eighteenth-century philosophers Adam Smith and David Hume. Hume maintains, for example, that reason is "the slave of the passions," by which he means that the ends or goals we pursue are determined by our emotions, passions, and sentiments. Adam Smith maintains that human beings are motivated by the experience of pity, compassion, and sympathy for other human beings. For Smith, ethics develops out of natural sympathy toward one another, experienced by social beings like ourselves.

Emotivism offers an explanation of moral knowledge that is subjective, with moral judgments resting on subjective experience. One version of emotivism makes ethical judgments akin to expressions of approval or disapproval. In this view, to say "murder is wrong" is to express something like "murder—yuck!" Similarly, to say "courageous self-sacrifice is good" is to express something like "self-sacrifice—yay!" One contemporary author, Leon Kass, whom we encounter in Chapter 12, argues that there is wisdom in our experiences of disgust and repugnance—that our emotional reactions to things reveal deep moral insight. Kass focuses especially on the "yuck factor" that many feel about advanced biotechnologies such as cloning.

One worry, however, is that our emotions and feelings of sympathy or disgust are variable and relative. Our own emotional responses vary, depending on our moods; and these responses vary among and between individuals. Emotional responses are relative to culture and even to the subjective dispositions of individuals. Indeed, our own feelings change over time and are not reliable or sufficient gauges of what is going on in the external world. The worry here is that our emotions merely express internal or subjective responses to things and that they do not connect us to an objective and stable source of value.

Other moral theories aim for more objective sources for morality. From this standpoint, there must be objective reasons that ground our subjective and emotional responses to things. Instead of saying that the things we desire are good, an **objectivist** about ethics will argue that we ought to desire things that are good—with an emphasis on the goodness of the thing-in-itself apart from our subjective responses. This idea can also be called **moral realism**, which is the idea that there are ethical facts and that moral judgments can be said to be true or false. The ancient Greek philosopher Plato was an objectivist, who thought that "the Good" was an ideal being that could be known by thought. Objectivists hold that values have an objective reality—that they are objects available for knowledge—as opposed to **subjectivists**, that is, those who affirm **subjectivism** in ethics, which is the claim that value judgments merely express subjective opinion. Plato thought that we could compare our subjective moral opinions with "the Good" and that it was possible to find the truth of morality. Similar to Plato, those who ground morality in God are objectivists, as are those who defend some form of natural law ethics, which focuses on essential or objective features of bodies and their functions. Interestingly, the approach of sociobiology tends not to be objectivist in this sense. Although the sociobiologist bases their study of morality on objective facts in the world, the sociobiologist does not think that moral judgments represent moral facts. Instead, as Michael Ruse puts it,

> Objective ethics, in the sense of something written on tablets of stone (or engraven on God's heart) external to us, has to go. The only reasonable thing that we, as sociobiologists, can say is that morality is something biology makes us believe in, so that we will further our evolutionary ends.[8]

Instrumental and Instrinsic Goods

1.5   Differentiate between instrumental and intrinsic values.

One important distinction made in thinking about ethics is the distinction between **intrinsic** and **instrumental** goods. Instrumental goods are things that are useful as instruments or tools—we value them as means toward some other end. Intrinsic goods are things that have value in themselves or for their own sake. For example, we might say that life is an intrinsic good and fundamentally valuable. But food is an instrumental good because it is a means or tool that is used to support life. From Ruse's perspective, morality itself is merely an instrumental good that is used by evolution for other purposes. Morality is, from this perspective, simply a tool that helps the human species to survive. The selfish gene hypothesis of Richard Dawkins understands individual human beings instrumentally, as carriers of genetic information: "We are survival machines—robot vehicles blindly programmed to serve the selfish molecules known as genes."[9] This runs counter to our usual moral view, which holds that human beings have intrinsic or inherent value. The idea that some things have intrinsic value is common to a variety of approaches that claim that ethics is objective. The intrinsic value of a thing is supposed to be an objective fact about it, which has no relation to our subjective response to that thing. Claims about intrinsic value show up in arguments about human rights and about the environment. Do human beings, ecosystems, or species have intrinsic value, or is the value of these things contained within our subjective responses and in their instrumental uses? This question shows us that the metaethical theories are connected to important practical issues.

► **Knowledge Check**   Answers appear at the end of the chapter.

1. **True/False:** Moral realists suggest that ethical judgments are entirely subjective.

2. **True/False:** Authors such as Hume and Moore suggest that it is a fallacy to move directly from an "is" claim to an "ought" claim.

3. Questions about issues in moral epistemology and about the metaphysical presuppositions of ethics are best described as the concerns of:
   a. Normative theory
   b. Metaethics
   c. Sociobiology
   d. Descriptive Claims

4. Emotivism would agree with which of the following:
   a. The truth of an ethical judgment is known by comparing that judgment with an ideal ethical object.
   b. The faculty of intuition provides us with access to ethical truth.
   c. Ethical judgments are actually subjective feelings.
   d. Morality is based upon objective facts.

Ethical Reasoning and Arguments

1.6   Explain sound and valid arguments as well as some fallacies of reasoning.

It is important to know how to reason well in thinking or speaking about ethical matters. This is helpful not only in trying to determine what to think about controversial ethical matters but also in arguing for something you believe is right and in critically evaluating positions held by others.

The Structure of Ethical Reasoning and Argument

To be able to reason well in ethics, you need to understand what constitutes a good argument. We can do this by looking at an argument's basic structure. This is the structure not only of ethical arguments about what is good or right but also of arguments about what is the case or what is true.

Suppose you are standing on the shore and a person in the water calls out for help. Should you try to rescue that person? You may or may not be able to swim. You may or may not be sure you could rescue the person. In this case, however, there is no time for reasoning, as you would have to act promptly. On the other hand, if this were an imaginary case, you would have to think through the reasons for and against trying to rescue the person. You might conclude that if you could actually rescue the person, then you ought to try to do it. Your reasoning might go as follows:

> Every human life is valuable.
> Whatever has a good chance of saving such a life should be attempted.
> My swimming out to rescue this person has a good chance of saving their life.
> Therefore, I ought to do so.

Or you might conclude that you could not save this person, and your reasoning might go like this:

> Every human life is valuable.
> Whatever has a good chance of saving such a life should be attempted.
> In this case, there is no chance of saving this life because I cannot swim.
> Thus, I am not obligated to try to save them (although, if others are around who can help, I might be obligated to try to get them to help).

Some structure like this is implicit in any ethical argument, although some are longer and more complex chains than the simple form given here. One can recognize the reasons in an argument by their introduction through key words such as *since*, *because*, and *given that*. The conclusion often contains terms such as *thus* and *therefore*. The reasons supporting the conclusion are called **premises**. In a sound argument, the premises are true and the conclusion follows from them. In the case presented earlier, then, we want to know whether you can save this person and also whether his life is valuable. We also need to know whether the conclusion actually follows from the premises. In the case of the earlier examples, it does. If you say you ought to do what will save a life and you can do it, then you ought to do it. However, there may be other principles that would need to be brought into the argument, such as whether and why one is always obligated to save someone else's life when one can.

To know under what conditions a conclusion actually follows from the premises, we would need to analyze arguments in much greater detail than we can do here. Suffice it to say, however, that the connection is a logical connection—in other words, it must make rational sense. You can improve your ability to reason well in ethics first by being able to pick out the reasons and the conclusion in an argument. Only then can you subject them to critical examination in ways we suggest here.

Evaluating and Making Good Arguments

Ethical reasoning can be done well or done poorly. Ethical arguments can be constructed well or constructed poorly. A good argument is a **sound argument**. It has a **valid** form in which the conclusion actually follows from the premises, and the premises or reasons given for the conclusion are true. An argument is poorly constructed when it is fallacious or when the reasons on which it is based are not true or are uncertain. An ethical argument always involves some claim about values—for example, that saving a life is good. These value-based claims must be established through some theory of values. Part I of this book examines different theories that help establish basic values.

Ethical arguments also involve conceptual and factual matters. Conceptual matters are those that relate to the meaning of terms or concepts. For example, in a case of lying, we would want to know what lying actually is. Must it be verbal? Must one have an intent to deceive? What is deceit itself? Other conceptual issues central to ethical arguments may involve questions such as, "What constitutes a 'person'?" (in arguments over abortion) and "What is 'cruel and unusual punishment'?" (in death penalty arguments, for example). Sometimes, differences of opinion about an ethical issue are a matter of differences not in values but in the meaning of the terms used.

Ethical arguments often also rely on factual claims. In our example, we might want to know whether it was actually true that you could save the drowning person. In arguments about the death penalty, we may want to know whether such punishment is a deterrent. In such a case, we need to know what scientific studies have found and whether the studies themselves were well grounded. To have adequate factual grounding, we will want to seek out a range of reliable sources of information and be open-minded. The chapters in Part II of this book include factual material that is relevant to ethical decisions about the topics under consideration.

It is important to be clear about the distinction between facts and values when dealing with moral conflict and disagreement. We need to ask whether we disagree about the values involved, about the concepts and terms we are employing, or about the facts connected to the case.

There are various ways in which reasoning can go wrong or be fallacious. We began this chapter by considering the fallacy of **begging the question** or **circular argument**. Such reasoning draws on the argument's conclusion to support its premises, as in "abortion is wrong because it is immoral." Another familiar problem of argumentation is the **ad hominem** fallacy. In this fallacy, people say something like, "That can't be right because just look who is saying it." They look at the source of the opinion rather than the reasons given for it. You can find out more about these and other fallacies from almost any textbook in logic or critical thinking.

You also can improve your understanding of ethical arguments by making note of a particular type of reasoning that is often used in ethics: **arguments from analogy**. In this type of argument, one compares familiar examples with the issue being disputed. If the two cases are similar in relevant ways, then whatever

one concludes about the first familiar case one should also conclude about the disputed case. For example, Judith Jarvis Thomson (who shows up in Chapter 11's discussion of abortion) once asked whether it would be ethically acceptable to "unplug" someone who had been attached to you and who was using your kidneys to save his life. If you say that you are justified in unplugging, then a pregnant woman is also justified in doing the same with regard to her fetus. The reader is prompted to critically examine such an argument by asking whether or not the two cases were similar in relevant ways—that is, whether the analogy fits.

Finally, we should note that giving reasons to *justify* a conclusion is also not the same as giving an *explanation* for why one believes something. Someone might explain that they do not support euthanasia because that was the way they were brought up or that they oppose the death penalty because they cannot stand to see someone die. To justify such beliefs, one would need rather to give reasons that show not why one does, in fact, believe something but why one *should* believe it. Nor are rationalizations justifying reasons. They are usually reasons given after the fact that are not one's true reasons. *Rationalizations* are usually excuses, used to explain away bad behavior. These false reasons are given to make us look better to others or ourselves. To argue well about ethical matters, we need to examine and give reasons that support the conclusions we draw.

Ethical Theory

Good reasoning in ethics usually involves either implicit or explicit reference to an ethical theory. An *ethical theory* is a systematic exposition of a particular view about what are the nature and basis of good or right. The theory provides reasons or norms for judging acts to be right or wrong; it provides a justification for these norms. These norms can then be used as a guide for action. We can diagram the relationship between ethical theories and moral decision-making as follows.

We can think of the diagram as a ladder. In practice, we can start at the ladder's top or bottom. At the top, at the level of theory, we can start by clarifying for ourselves what we think are basic ethical values. We then move downward to the level of principles generated

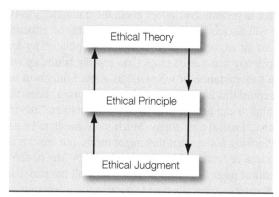

Figure 1-3 The relation between theory, principle, and judgment.

from the theory. The next step is to apply these principles to concrete cases. We can also start at the bottom of the ladder, facing a particular ethical choice or dilemma. We can work our way back up the ladder, thinking through the principles and theories that implicitly guide our concrete decisions. Ultimately and ideally, we come to a basic justification, or the elements of what would be an ethical theory. If we look at the actual practice of thinking people as they develop their ethical views over time, the movement is probably in both directions. We use concrete cases to reform our basic ethical views, and we use the basic ethical views to throw light on concrete cases.

An example of this movement in both directions would be if we start with the belief that pleasure is the ultimate value and then find that applying this value in practice leads us to do things that are contrary to common moral sense or that are repugnant to us and others. We may then be forced to look again and possibly alter our views about the moral significance of pleasure. Or we may change our views about the rightness or wrongness of some particular act or practice on the basis of our theoretical reflections. Obviously, this sketch of moral reasoning is quite simplified. Feminists and others have criticized this model of ethical reasoning, partly because it claims that ethics is governed by general principles that are supposedly applicable to all ethical situations. Does this form of reasoning give due consideration to the particularities of individual, concrete cases? Can we really make a general judgment about the value of truthfulness or courage that will help us know what to do in particular cases in which these issues play a role?

Types of Ethical Theory

1.7 Evaluate consequentialist and nonconsequentialist approaches to ethics.

In Part I of this book, we consider the following types of moral theory: *egoism* and *contractarianism*, *utilitarianism*, *deontological ethics*, *natural law*, *virtue ethics*, and *feminist ethics*. These normative theories differ in terms of what they say we should look at in making moral judgments about actions or practices. For example, does it matter morally that I tried to do the right thing or that I had a good motive? Surely it must make some moral difference, we think. But suppose that in acting with good motives I violate someone's rights. Does this make the action a bad action? We would probably be inclined to say yes. Suppose, however, that in violating someone's rights, I am able to bring about a great good. Does this justify the violation of rights? Some theories judge actions in terms of their motive, some in terms of the character or nature of the act itself, and others in terms of the consequences of the actions or practices.

We often appeal to one of these types of reason. Take a situation in which I lie to a person, Jim. We can make the following judgments about this action. Note the different types of reasons given for the judgments.

> That was good because you intended to make Jim happy by telling him a lie that was intended to improve his self-esteem—or it was bad because you meant to deceive him and do him harm. (Motive)
> That was good because it is good to make people happy—or it was bad because it is always wrong to tell a lie. (Act)
> That was good because it really did help Jim develop his self-esteem—or it was bad because it caused Jim to believe things about himself that were not true. (Consequences)

Figure 1-4 Three focal points of moral judgment.

Although we generally think that a person's motive is relevant to the overall moral judgment about their action, we tend to think that it reflects primarily on our moral evaluation of *the person*. We also have good reasons to think that the results of actions matter morally. Those theories that base moral judgments on consequences are called **consequentialist** or sometimes **teleological** moral theories (from the Greek root *telos*, meaning "goal" or "end"). Those theories that hold that actions can be right or wrong regardless of their consequences are called **nonconsequentialist** or **deontological** theories (from the Greek root *deon*, meaning "duty").

One moral theory we will examine is *utilitarianism*. It provides us with an example of a consequentialist moral theory in which we judge whether an action is better than alternatives by its actual or expected results or consequences; actions are then judged in terms of the promotion of human happiness. Kant's moral theory, which we will also examine, provides us with an example of a nonconsequentialist theory, according to which acts are judged right or wrong independently of their consequences; in particular, acts are judged by whether they conform to requirements of rationality and human dignity. The other ethical theories that we will examine stress human nature as the source of what is right and wrong. Some elements of these theories are deontological and some teleological. So, also, some teleological theories are consequentialist in that they advise us to produce some good. But if the good is an ideal, such as virtue or self-realization, then such theories differ from consequentialist theories such as utilitarianism. As anyone who has tried to put some order to the many ethical theories knows, no theory completely and easily fits one classification, even those given here. Feminist theories of care provide yet another way of determining what one ought to do (see Chapter 9).

CRITICAL THEORY OF ETHICS

As you will see in Chapter 9, feminism is not only understood in relation to a normative ethic of care. It also provides a critical lens that asks questions about normative ethics in general, and indeed about the normative theories we will discuss in what follows. Some feminist criticisms go so far as to "repudiate extant moral philosophy as a hopelessly masculinist project, necessarily bound up with the subordination of women," as Amia Srinivasan has described this kind of project.[10] But Srinivasan claims that feminism can also be employed to "rehabilitate" the tradition of moral philosophy. Much more needs to be said in thinking about what this might mean. But we can use the idea of "critical theory" to explain this. The notion of a critical theory of ethics might extend all the way back to Socrates—who asked us to continually interrogate our assumptions about life and ethics. In the nineteenth and twentieth centuries, critical theory came to mean a theory that is focused on contradictions in our theorizing, including especially social contradictions involving oppression and exclusion of women, minorities, and members of marginalized groups.

Feminism can be understood as a critical theory in this sense. There are other related and interconnected critiques of moral theory that are articulated from a standpoint that is concerned about race, ethnicity, class, ability, and so on. One way of articulating this critical approach is to understand it as a critique of "ideal theory," as Charles Mills has explained. Mills, a Black philosopher who died in 2021, suggested that the Western academic tradition of moral philosophy has often made a number of racialized assumptions about people and about society in articulating an account of ethics—and that this tradition has often ignored the reality of oppression.[11] For example, Mills suggested in his influential book *The Racial Contract* that the social contract idea that is a central concept in European ethical and political philosophy is hopelessly entangled with the oppressive racial politics of modern European history—including colonialism and slavery.[12] In developing this kind of approach, Naomi Zack has argued that we need a "critical reading" of the tradition of moral philosophy that makes explicit the fact that philosophical ethics is often articulated from the vantage point of social and political elites (as you'll see in the reading excerpt included below).[13]

In the chapters that follow, we have attempted to provide some insights that come from such a critical vantage point. We will point out, as we proceed, some of the blind spots in the Western tradition of moral philosophy when it comes to gender and race. In Part I, as we consider major normative theories, we will also consider issues of race and gender in the works of philosophers such as Aristotle, John Stuart Mill, and Immanuel Kant. In Part II, we examine several concrete ethical issues, including a number that involve complicated questions about race, gender, class, ability, and so on. As we proceed, we will apply various ethical theories in order to understand how these normative theories analyze these various issues from different perspectives and sometimes reach different conclusions about what is morally right or wrong, better or worse.

Can Ethics be Taught?

It would be interesting to know just why some college and university programs require their students to take a course in ethics. Does this requirement stem from a belief that a course in ethics or moral philosophy can actually make people good?

When asked whether ethics can be taught, students have given a variety of answers. "If it can't be taught, then why are we taking this class?" a student wondered. Another student responded, "Look at the behavior of certain corporate executives who have been found guilty of criminal conduct. They surely haven't learned proper ethical values." Still others disagreed with both views. Although certain ideals or types of knowledge can be taught, ethical behavior cannot be taught because it is a matter of individual choice, they said.

Plato thought that ethics could be taught. He argues that "All evil is ignorance." In other words, we do what is wrong because we do not know or believe it is wrong; and if we truly believe that something is right, we should necessarily do it. Now, we are free to disagree with Plato by appealing to our own experience. If I know that I should not have that second piece of pie, does this mean that I will not eat it? Ever? Plato might attempt to convince us that he is right by examining or clarifying what he means by the phrase *to know*. If we were really convinced with our whole heart and mind that something is wrong, then we might be highly likely (if not determined) not to do it. However, whether ethics courses should attempt to convince students of such things is surely debatable.

Another aspect of the problem of teaching ethics concerns the problem of motivation. If one knows

something to be the right thing to do, does there still remain the question of why we should do it? One way to motivate people to be ethical may be to show them that it is in their own best interest to do the right thing.

Most moral philosophers think that a course on ethics is ethically useful. It should help students understand the nature of ethical problems and help them think critically about ethical matters by providing conceptual tools and skills. It should enable them to form and critically analyze ethical arguments. It is up to the individual, however, to use these skills to reason about ethical matters. A study of ethics should also lead students to respect opposing views because it requires them to analyze carefully the arguments that support views contrary to their own. It also provides opportunities to consider the reasonableness of at least some viewpoints that they may not have considered.

In this opening chapter, we have learned something about what the philosophical study of ethics is. We have considered a few metaethical issues. We have provided a description of ethical reasoning and arguments. We have briefly considered the nature of ethical theories and the role they play in ethical reasoning. We will examine these theories more carefully in the chapters to come, and we will see how they might help us analyze and come to conclusions about particular ethical issues.

Let us return, now, to the vignette with which we began: the story of Socrates and his argument against escaping from prison and avoiding execution. In this chapter, we've begun to outline some key questions that we'd need to answer to evaluate his case. In order to evaluate whether Socrates is correct to suggest that it is wrong to return evil for evil, we would need a moral theory to guide us. We also need a moral theory to guide us in deciding what counts as living well (and dying well). Behind these theories of right and wrong, good and evil, are metaethical questions. The case of Socrates is interesting and complicated—and good people may disagree about the question of whether he should have escaped. The same is true for the issues we will consider in the second half of this book: public health, abortion, euthanasia, economic justice, animal ethics, biotechnology, racial justice, crime and punishment, war and peace, and so on. Each of these issues presents us with complex questions about the nature of morality and the proper source of moral judgment.

Chapter Summary

1.1 What is the difference between normative ethics and metaethics?

Normative theories provide some definite answer to the question of what is good, evil, just, or unjust. Utilitarianism and natural law are kinds of normative theory. Metaethical theories take a step back, asking questions about the sources of our norms. Metaethics ask questions about how we know what is good, whether the good is objective or subjective, and so on.

1.2 How can we distinguish between normative and descriptive claims?

Normative claims use verbs such as "should" and "ought." These claims say that something is right or wrong, good or bad. Descriptive claims focus on facts rather than values.

1.3 Do naturalistic explanations of ethics commit the naturalistic fallacy?

The naturalistic fallacy suggests that you cannot simply go from an "is" (a descriptive claim) to an "ought" (a normative claim). Some people attempt to provide a naturalistic explanation of ethics (e.g., the theory known as sociobiology). The question is whether sociobiological approaches to ethics are able to tell us how we ought to behave or whether they are merely descriptive. Also note that "natural law" theories of ethics can be distinguished from the naturalistic approach of sociobiology.

1.4 What is the meaning of key terms such as intuitionism, emotivism, objectivism, and subjectivism?

Intuitionism is a metaethical theory that claims we have a faculty of ethical intuition that sees, perceives, or knows the good; and that the good has intrinsic value that cannot be reduced to some other kind of value.

Emotivism is a metaethical theory that holds that ethical judgments are expressions of emotion (e.g., that these judgments are like saying "yuck" or "yay").

Objectivism maintains that values are not merely matters of opinion but rather that values exist as facts or realities "out there" in the world.

Subjectivism denies the truth of objectivism, maintaining instead that values are matters of opinion grounded in some fact that exists in the objective world.

1.5 What is the difference between instrumental and intrinsic values?

Instrumental value describes the value of a thing in terms of its usefulness to us as a tool or instrument. Intrinsic value focuses on the non-instrument value of a thing (relate to inherent value or value "in itself").

1.6 What is a sound (and valid) argument? What is a fallacy?

In a valid argument, the truth of the conclusion necessarily follows from the truth of the premises. Sound arguments are valid arguments whose premises (and conclusion) are actually true. A fallacy is a weak or bad argument. In this chapter, we described some fallacies such as begging the question (arguing in a circle) and ad hominem arguments (personal attacks).

1.7 How can we evaluate consequentialist and nonconsequentialist approaches to ethics?

Consequentialist theories focus on producing good outcomes. One example is utilitarianism, which focuses on creating the greatest happiness for the greatest number of people. Nonconsequentialist theories are more concerned with motives, intentions, and the nature of specific acts. Kantian deontology and natural law are forms of nonconsequentialist theories. To evaluate these different approaches to ethics, we need to decide what matters most: outcomes or intentions. One reason to think that intentions matter is because we often do not have control over outcomes. But we often think that the mere intention to do good is insufficient unless some good outcome actually occurs.

Primary Source Readings

The reading selections for this chapter focus on some of the metaethical issues discussed in this chapter. The first comes from David Hume's *Treatise of Human Nature,* first published in 1739. The excerpt from Hume discusses the problem of deriving normative claims from descriptive claims, the problem of deriving an *ought* from an *is,* with a particular focus on the question of the morality of incest. The second is an excerpt on emotivism from C. L. Stevenson, a philosopher associated with the Anglo-American tradition in twentieth-century philosophy. Following that, we have an excerpt from G. E. Moore's *Principia Ethica* in which he discusses the unique and irreducible idea of good, while explaining how the "naturalistic fallacy" occurs when we try to reduce the good to something else. After Moore, we have an excerpt from E. O. Wilson that provides some insight into a sociobiological approach to thinking about ethics—what Wilson calls here a "naturalistic" understanding of ethics. Finally, we have an excerpt from Naomi Zack that opens the question of the need for a "critical reading" of the tradition of moral philosophy.

Reading 1-1   Ethical Judgments and Matters of Fact* | David Hume

Study Questions

As you read the excerpt, please consider the following questions:

1. How does Hume employ the fact of animal incest to advance his argument that morality does not consist merely of "matters of fact" and that morality is not merely an "object of reason"?
2. Explain Hume's idea that morality is a matter of feelings and sentiments.
3. Why does Hume have a problem with deducing an *ought* from an *is*?

I would fain ask any one, why incest in the human species is criminal, and why the very same action, and the same relations in animals have not the smallest moral turpitude and deformity? If it be answered, that this action is innocent in animals, because they have not reason sufficient to discover its turpitude; but that man, being endowed with that faculty which ought to restrain him to his duty, the same action instantly becomes criminal to him; should this be said, I would reply, that this is evidently arguing in a circle. For before reason can perceive this turpitude, the turpitude must exist; and consequently is independent of the decisions of our reason, and is their object more properly than their effect. According to this system, then, every animal, that has sense, and appetite, and will; that is, every animal must be susceptible of all the same virtues and vices, for which we ascribe praise and blame to human creatures. All the difference is, that our superior reason may serve to discover the vice or virtue, and by that means may augment the blame or praise: But still this discovery supposes a separate being in these moral distinctions, and a being, which depends only on the will and appetite, and which, both in thought and reality, may be distinguished from the reason. Animals are susceptible of the same relations, with respect to each other, as the human species, and therefore would also be susceptible of the same morality, if the essence of morality consisted in these relations. Their want of a sufficient degree of reason may hinder them from perceiving the duties and obligations of morality, but can never hinder these duties from existing; since they must antecedently exist, in order to their being perceived.

Reason must find them, and can never produce them. This argument deserves to be weighed, as being, in my opinion, entirely decisive.

Nor does this reasoning only prove, that morality consists not in any relations, that are the objects of science; but if examined, will prove with equal certainty, that it consists not in any *matter of fact*, which can be discovered by the understanding. This is the *second* part of our argument; and if it can be made evident, we may conclude, that morality is not an object of reason. But can there be any difficulty in proving, that vice and virtue are not matters of fact, whose existence we can infer by reason? Take any action allowed to be vicious: Willful murder, for instance. Examine it in all lights, and see if you can find that matter of fact, or real existence, which you call *vice*. In which-ever way you take it, you find only certain passions, motives, volitions and thoughts. There is no other matter of fact in the case. The vice entirely escapes you, as long as you consider the object. You never can find it, till you turn your reflection into your own breast, and find a sentiment of disapprobation, which arises in you, towards this action. Here is a matter of fact; but it is the object of feeling, not of reason. It lies in yourself, not in the object. So that when you pronounce any action or character to be vicious, you mean nothing, but that from the constitution of your nature you have a feeling or sentiment of blame from the contemplation of it. Vice and virtue, therefore, may be compared to sounds, colours, heat and cold, which, according to modern philosophy, are not qualities in objects, but perceptions in the mind: And this discovery in morals, like that other in physics, is to be regarded as a considerable advancement of the speculative sciences; though, like that too, it has little or no influence on practice. Nothing can be more real, or concern us more, than our own sentiments of pleasure and uneasiness; and if these be favourable to virtue, and unfavourable to vice, no more can be requisite to the regulation of our conduct and behaviour.

I cannot forbear adding to these reasonings an observation, which may, perhaps, be found of some importance. In every system of morality, which I have hitherto met with, I have always remarked, that the author proceeds for some time in the ordinary way of reasoning, and establishes the being of a God, or makes observations concerning human affairs; when of a sudden I am surprised to find, that instead of the usual copulations of propositions, *is*, and *is not*, I meet with no proposition that is not connected with an *ought*, or an *ought not*. This change is imperceptible; but is, however, of the last consequence. For as this *ought*, or *ought not*, expresses some new relation or affirmation, it is necessary that it should be observed and explained; and at the same time that a reason should be given, for what seems altogether inconceivable, how this new relation can be a deduction from others, which are entirely different from it. But as authors do not commonly use this precaution, I shall presume to recommend it to the readers; and am persuaded, that this small attention would subvert all the vulgar systems of morality, and let us see, that the distinction of vice and virtue is not founded merely on the relations of objects, nor is perceived by reason.

From David Hume, *A Treatise on Human Nature* (1739; Project Gutenberg, 2010), bk. III, pt. 1, sec. 1, http://www.gutenberg.org/files/4705/4705-h/4705-h.htm

* Title supplied by the editor.

Reading 1-2   Emotivism and Ethics | C. L. Stevenson

Study Questions
As you read the excerpt, please consider the following questions:

1. What does Stevenson mean when he says that ethical judgments are used to create an influence?

2. How does the example of stealing illustrate Stevenson's understanding of the meaning of ethical terms?

3. What does he mean by the "emotive meaning" of ethical terms?

Doubtless there is always *some* element of description in ethical judgments, but this is by no means all. Their major use is not to indicate facts, but to *create an influence*. Instead of merely describing people's interests, they *change* or *intensify* them. They recommend an interest in an object, rather than state that the interest already exists.

For instance: When you tell a man that he oughtn't to steal, your object isn't merely to let him know that people disapprove of stealing. You are attempting, rather, to get *him* to disapprove of it. Your ethical judgment has a quasi-imperative force which, operating through suggestion, and intensified by your tone of voice, readily permits you to begin to *influence*, to *modify*, his interests. If in the end you do not succeed in getting *him* to disapprove of stealing, you will feel that you've failed to convince him that stealing is wrong. You will continue to feel this, even though he fully acknowledges that you disapprove of it, and that almost everyone else does. When you point out to him the consequences of his actions—consequences which you suspect he already disapproves of—these *reasons* which support your ethical judgment are simply a means of facilitating your influence. If you think you can change his interests by making vivid to him how others will disapprove of him, you will do so; otherwise not....

The emotive meaning of a word is a tendency of a word, arising through the history of its usage, to produce (result from) *affective* responses in people. It is the immediate aura of feeling which hovers about a word. Such tendencies to produce affective responses cling to words very tenaciously....

Strictly speaking, then, it is impossible to define "good" in terms of favourable interest if emotive meaning is not to be distorted. Yet it is possible to say that "This is good" is *about* the favourable interest of the speaker and the hearer or hearers, and that it has a pleasing emotive meaning which fits the words for use in suggestion....

A word must be added about the moral use of "good." This differs from the above in that it is about a different kind of interest. Instead of being about what the hearer and speaker *like*, it is about a stronger sort of approval. When a person *likes* something, he is pleased when it prospers, and disappointed when it doesn't. When a person *morally approves* of something, he experiences a rich feeling of security when it prospers, and is indignant, or "shocked" when it doesn't. These are rough and inaccurate examples of the many factors which one would have to mention in distinguishing the two kinds of interest. In the moral usage, as well as in the non-moral, "good" has an emotive meaning which adapts it to suggestion.

From C. L. Stevenson, *Facts and Values* (New Haven, CT: Yale University Press, 1963).

Reading 1-3 Good, Yellow, and the Naturalistic Fallacy | G. E. Moore

Study Questions

As you read the excerpt, please consider the following questions:

1. What does Moore mean when he says that good cannot be defined?

2. Explain Moore's analogy with "yellow." How does that help explain his conception of "good"?

3. What does Moore mean by "the naturalistic fallacy"?

If I am asked "What is good?" my answer is that good is good, and that is the end of the matter. Or if I am asked "How is good to be defined?" my answer is that it cannot be defined, and that is all I have to say about it. But disappointing as these answers may appear, they are of the very last importance....

My point is that "good" is a simple notion, just as "yellow" is a simple notion; that, just as you cannot, by any manner of means, explain to anyone who does not already know it, what yellow is, so you cannot explain what good is. Definitions of the kind that I was asking for, definitions which describe the real nature of the object or notion denoted by a word, and which do not merely tell us what the word is used to mean, are only possible when the object or notion in question is something complex.... But yellow and good, we say, are not complex: they are notions of that simple kind, out of which definitions are composed and with which the power of further defining ceases....

Consider yellow, for example. We may try to define it, by describing its physical equivalent; we may state what kind of light-vibrations must stimulate the normal eye, in order that we may perceive it. But a moment's reflection is sufficient to shew that those light-vibrations are not themselves what we mean by yellow. They are not what we perceive. Indeed, we should never have been able to discover their existence, unless we had first been struck by the patent difference of quality between the different colours. The most we can be entitled to say of those vibrations is that they are what corresponds in space to the yellow which we actually perceive.

Yet a mistake of this simple kind has commonly been made about "good." It may be true that all things which are good are also something else, just as it is true that all things which are yellow produce a certain kind of vibration in the light. And it is a fact, that Ethics aims at discovering what are those other properties belonging to all things which are good. But far too many philosophers have thought that when they named those other properties they were actually defining good; that these properties, in fact, were simply not "other," but absolutely and entirely the same with goodness. This view I propose to call the "naturalistic fallacy"....

From George Edward Moore, *Principia Ethica* (Cambridge University Press, 1903).

Reading 1-4   The Social Conquest of Earth | E. O. Wilson

Study Questions

As you read the excerpt, please consider the following questions:

1. How does Wilson use the conflict between group and individual selection to explain moral conflicts?

2. Why do you think Wilson suggests that what he calls "the naturalistic understanding" of ethics does not lead to "absolute precepts"?

3. Do you agree with Wilson's claim that his naturalistic approach can be used to rule out certain activities we would call evil such as genocide and slavery?

The dilemma of good and evil was created by multilevel selection, in which individual selection and group selection act together on the same individual but largely in opposition to each other. Individual selection is the result of competition for survival and reproduction among members of the same group. It shapes instincts in each member that are fundamentally selfish with reference to other members. In contrast, group selection consists of competition between societies, through both direct conflict and differential competence and exploiting the environment. Group selection shapes instincts that tend to make individuals altruistic toward one another (but not toward members of other groups). Individual selection is responsible for much of what we call sin, while group selection is responsible for the greater part of virtue. Together they have created the conflict between the poorer and better angels of our nature.

In the search for ultimate causes of the human condition, the distinction between levels of natural selection applied to human behavior is not perfect. Selfish behavior, perhaps including nepotism-generating kin selection, can in some ways promote the interests of the group through invention and entrepreneurship.... Group selection in its turn promoted the genetic interests of individuals with privilege and status as rewards for outstanding performance on behalf of the tribe.

Nevertheless, an iron rule exists in genetic social evolution. It is that selfish individuals beat altruistic individuals, while groups of altruists beat groups of selfish individuals. The victory can never be complete; the balance of selection pressures cannot move to either extreme. If individual selection were to dominate, societies would dissolve. If groups selection were to dominate, human groups would come to resemble ant colonies....

The naturalistic understanding of morality does not lead to absolute precepts and sure judgments, but instead warns against basing them blindly on religious and ideological dogma. When such precepts are misguided, which is often, it is usually because they are based on ignorance. Some important factor or other was unintentionally omitted during the formulation....

There is a principle to be learned by studying the biological origins of moral reasoning. It is that outside the clearest ethical precepts, such as the condemnation of slavery, child abuse, and genocide, which all will agree should be opposed everywhere without exception, there is a larger gray domain inherently difficult to navigate. The declaration of ethical precepts and judgments made from them requires a full understanding of why we care about the matter one way or the other, and that includes the biological history of the emotions engaged....

I have no doubt that in many cases, perhaps the great majority, the precepts shared by most societies today will stand the test of biology-based realism. Others, such as the ban on artificial conception, condemnation of homosexual preference and forced marriages of adolescent girls, will not. Whatever the outcome, it seems clear that ethical philosophy will benefit from the reconstruction of its precepts based on both science and culture.

From Edward O. Wilson, *The Social Conquest of Earth* (New York: Norton, 2012).

Reading 1-5   Ethics, Mores, and Race | Naomi Zack

Study Questions

As you read the excerpt, please consider the following questions:

1. How does Zack explain the difference between group mores and philosophical ethics?
2. What is the significance of Zack's claim that the Western tradition, beginning with Plato, is elitist?
3. What does Zack mean when she suggests that we need a "critical reading" of the philosophical tradition?

Part of the difference between ethics and mores is a distinction between individual and group. Philosophers have concentrated on the hearts, minds, and actions of individuals, whereas ethos/mores and the morality arising from them are group based. Individual perspectives can accommodate greater abstraction than group perspectives. In their rhetorical address to individuals as readers, Western philosophers have been able to construct abstract and ideal ethical systems, requiring for their validation only the comprehension and agreement of individuals, who do not have to be in the same place and time as either one another or the philosopher being read. Moral systems in society, by contrast, are closely tied to understanding and agreement within groups, occurring at the same time, often defined by place. Mores and morals are thus concretely historical, compared to ethics. Mores need not be ethical and ethics does not require a foundation in mores....

Independently of the subject of race, philosophers have little consensus about competing ethical systems, so the philosophical results of "integrating" race into the rest of philosophical ethical/moral discourse would likely be inconclusive. Still, we might be able to see what different ethical/moral systems and traditions could contribute to the subject of race at this time....

But of course, before the discussion concerning race can be moved ahead in this way, ethics itself, as distinct from mores, has to be an attractive enterprise with basic assumptions and methods that all principled parties can accept. For the public, this is a matter of conscience, social change, and rhetoric. For philosophers and those in other humanistic disciplines who address race, what could begin as a fruitful theoretical issue might quickly encounter skepticism about the possibility of using Western philosophical ethics for racial liberatory purposes. Beginning with Plato, Western moral philosophy seems to have been elitist on exactly those grounds that later came to be the grounds of modern race, with its attendant white racial supremacy. So why should intellectuals who are people of color make use of a system of thought that was used to exclude people of color from the goods of human life?

The answer is that the system of thought cannot be appropriated just exegetically but requires a critical reading, an inquiry in search of philosophical egalitarianism. Along the way, it should be possible to show how certain theoretical gaps or omissions enabled professional moral philosophers to propound elevated and seemingly egalitarian theories that were compatible with inequality and injustice in the world. The inquiry here is not a matter of pointing out hypocrisy or other kinds of disconnections between theory and practice, but discovering the inadequacies of some otherwise good moral theories.

From *The Ethics and Mores of Race: Equality after the History of Philosophy, with a New Preface* (Lanham, MD: Rowman & Littlefield Publishers, 2015).

Review Exercises

1. Determine whether the following statements about the nature of ethics are true or false. Explain your answers.

   a. Ethics is the study of why people act in certain ways.

   b. The solution to moral conflicts and ethical disputes is to accurately describe the way the world actually is.

   c. The statement "Most people believe that cheating is wrong" is an ethical evaluation of cheating.

2. Label the following statements as either *normative* (N) or *descriptive* (D). If normative, label each as *ethics* (E), *aesthetics* (A), *law* (L), *religion* (R), or *custom* (C).

   a. One ought to respect one's elders because it is one of God's commandments.

   b. Twice as many people today, as compared to ten years ago, believe that the death penalty is morally justified in some cases.

   c. It would be wrong to put an antique chair in a modern room.

   d. People do not always do what they believe to be right.

   e. I ought not to turn left here because the sign says "No Left Turn."

   f. We ought to adopt a universal health insurance policy because everyone has a right to health care.

3. Discuss the differences between the ideas that ethics is subjective and that it is objective.

4. Explain emotivism and intuitionism in ethical theory.

5. Discuss the advantages and disadvantages of using naturalistic explanations in ethics.

6. As they occur in the following statements, label the reasons for the conclusion as appeals to the *motive* (M), the *act* (A), or the *consequences* (C).

   a. Although you intended well, what you did was bad because it caused more harm than good.

   b. We ought always to tell the truth to others because it is right to tell the truth.

   c. Although it did turn out badly, you did not want that, and thus you should not be judged harshly for what you caused.

Knowledge Check Answer Key

1. **False.** Moral realists do not suggest that ethical judgments are subjective; rather, they maintain that ethical judgments point toward objective facts.

2. **True.** Hume and Moore suggest it is fallacious to move directly from an "is" to an "ought."

3. **b.** Questions about issues in moral epistemology and about the metaphysical presuppositions of ethics are best described as the concerns of metaethics.

4. **c.** Emotivism would agree that ethical judgments are actually subjective feelings.

2 Religion and Global Ethics

Learning Outcomes

After reading this chapter, you should be able to:

2.1 Describe the challenge of developing a global ethical perspective in a world that is religiously diverse.

2.2 Explain how the idea of universal human rights is linked to secularism, cosmopolitanism, and the European Enlightenment.

2.3 Evaluate the divine command theory of ethics.

2.4 Explain the idea of the Golden Rule.

2.5 Articulate how the problem of evil and free will create challenges for religious ethics.

2.6 Differentiate between secular/humanistic and religious approaches to ethics.

2.7 Explain the critique of modern secular values using the concept of Eurocentrism.

The Challenge of Global Ethics

Human beings are diverse. We speak different languages and organize our lives around different cultural practices and religious beliefs. Is it possible for us to achieve consensus about ethics? A number of attempts have been made to articulate a unifying set of global moral principles. The United Nations was founded on one such attempt. Through the collaborative work of Eleanor Roosevelt and other leaders, the UN's Universal Declaration of Human Rights was adopted in 1948 by the nations

CBW / Alamy Stock Photo

of the world. More recently, the Parliament of the World's Religions has adopted a "Global Ethic" (endorsed by the Parliament in 1993). These documents and organizations maintain that there is a common set of values that should be shared by all human beings. But human beings continue to disagree and argue about ethics. We also disagree about the proper method for discovering a global ethic. Philosophers typically maintain that we should consult reason and appeal to rational arguments in order to discover universal values. But religious people also turn to faith. And some skeptics believe that it is impossible to achieve consensus about morality in a religiously and culturally diverse world.

What Do You Think?

1. Is there a unifying set of moral rules?

2. What values would you include as key values in a "global ethic"?

3. Is morality dependent on religious faith? Or can ethical principles be discovered by reason without appealing to religion?

4. Are there basic principles that would allow us to "agree to disagree" and coexist despite our diversity?

Introduction

In this chapter, we will consider two key issues in thinking about ethics: global diversity and religion. There are two related questions to be considered in this chapter. Is there some set of values that could unite the world, despite the diversity of laws, culture, and religions? And what can a consideration of religion contribute to the study of ethics? One significant idea in thinking about global ethics is the idea of human rights. But as we'll see, there are significant questions about idea of human rights, including the question of how human rights are grounded and defended. One traditional approach to human rights suggests that these rights are granted to us by God. But does the idea of human rights depend upon a religious point of view? Could human rights be defended from a secular or non-religious point of view? And how should we think about human rights in a world that includes diverse religious traditions?

The topics address here are returned to in other chapters. We discuss relativism in more detail in the next chapter (Chapter 3). We also consider the question of global ethical responsibility in more detail in Chapter 15. In the present chapter, we bring up traditional questions about religion, including the question of "the divine command" theory of ethics, and the metaphysical questions of freedom of the will. We will consider whether the Golden Rule ("do unto others as you would have them do unto you") is a useful idea for developing a global ethic. The approach of this book is non-religious and secular, which means that we will not offer any specifically religious answers to the questions we raise here. But that secular approach is not without its critics. One critical objection discussed in this chapter is whether modern secular approaches to ethics are Eurocentric.

The topics discuss here are contentious. People disagree about religion, human rights, and ethics. These disputes rest upon deep disagreements about fundamental things. The goal of this chapter is to dig into the roots of these disagreements and to provide critical insight into what people disagree about and why. There are no easy answers here, which can be frustrating. But it might help to know that the questions raised in this chapter are part of a long conversation about ethics that extends from Socrates through the founding of the United Nations and beyond.

Human Rights, Identity, and Diversity

2.1 Describe the challenge of developing a global ethical perspective in a world that is religiously diverse.

We live in an increasingly integrated world. With the click of the mouse, you can instantly interact with people from a variety of cultures and religions. It is inspiring to see how well we human beings get along despite our differences. But diversity—especially religious diversity—can create tension and difficulty.

Religious tension has become a major concern. Religious fundamentalists of various denominations have asserted the supremacy of their preferred religious texts, traditions, and interpretations. Politicians have asserted claims of cultural and religious supremacy. Some religious people have resorted to violence in defense of their faith. Other religious people proclaim that religion ought to be tolerant and peaceful, despite the intolerance of some radicals.

One solution to religious tension is respect for persons grounded on basic claims about human rights, including the right to freedom of religious belief (we discuss human rights in more detail in Chapter 7). The idea of religious freedom is enshrined in the First Amendment to the Constitution of the United States. Religious freedom is also featured in international agreements and institutions. In 1948, the United Nations' member nations ratified the Universal Declaration of Human Rights, which lays out a set of basic moral principles. The nations of the world are supposed to share these principles despite our vast cultural, religious, and political differences. The preamble to the UN Declaration begins by affirming the "inherent dignity" and "inalienable rights" of all members of the human family. It explains that disregard for these rights has resulted in barbarous acts that outrage "the moral conscience of mankind." It continues, "the advent of a world in which human beings shall enjoy freedom of speech and belief and freedom from fear and want has been proclaimed as the highest aspiration of the common people." It goes on to state that the purpose of the United Nations is to promote universal respect for human rights and fundamental freedoms.[1]

The UN Declaration was created in the aftermath of the Second World War under the leadership of Eleanor Roosevelt, who said in 1948, "the future must see the broadening of human rights throughout the world."[2] The Declaration aims for global agreement about basic rights, the inherent dignity of human beings, and "equal rights for men and women," with the broader goals of fostering world peace and harmony. As ongoing religious and cultural disputes illustrate, however, there are outstanding disagreements about the nature of these basic rights. In Eleanor Roosevelt's day, there was a difficult and emerging conflict between democratic nations and totalitarian nations. This conflict involved claims about freedom of speech, freedom of the press, and freedom of religion. The UN document asserts the importance of freedom of speech and freedom of religion. Article 18 of the UN Declaration explicitly states, "Everyone has the right to freedom of thought, conscience and religion; this right includes freedom to change his religion or belief, and freedom, either alone or in community with others and in public or private, to manifest his religion or belief in teaching, practice, worship and observance."

But does freedom of speech run up against a limit when such speech defames important religious figures (say, when a cartoonist draws a caricature of a saint or prophet)? Does freedom of speech hit a limit when such speech advocates for practices and social arrangements that are viewed by religious people as immoral (say, when it advocates abortion, same-sex marriage, or other practices that some religious people reject)? In some parts of the world, freedom of religion is viewed as leading to apostasy and blasphemy, which are a punishable offense. In previous centuries, Christians burned witches and heretics alive. And today, in some countries, blasphemy and apostasy are punishable by death. One famous example of this is the *fatwa,* or religious decree, announced by the Iranian cleric and supreme leader Ayatollah Ruhollah Khomeini, which called for the death of novelist Salman Rushdie in 1989 for writing a novel the Ayatollah considered blasphemous. According to the US Commission on International Religious Freedom, in 2017 there were eighty-four countries around the world that have laws against blasphemy. This includes countries like Iran but also Italy, India, and Indonesia.[3] Ireland was once on this list, but it abolished its blasphemy law in 2020.

Of course, freedom of speech means that it is possible to say insulting things about religion and religious groups. A controversial example occurred when Donald Trump was running for president. Trump was asked if Islam was at war with the West. He replied by saying, "I think Islam hates us." He continued: "We have to be very vigilant and very careful. And we can't allow people coming into this country who have this hatred of the United States."[4] After he was elected president, the Trump administration instituted a ban on travel from certain Muslim countries. This led to legal challenges, which went all the way up to the US Supreme Court. The Trump "Muslim Ban," as it was called by critics, was revoked by President Joe Biden in January 2021. Of course, all of this is contentious and quarrelsome, which shows us why it is important to think carefully and critically about religion, ethics, and political life.

This example reminds us of the ongoing challenge of religious diversity. Should the law restrict the freedom of members of certain religions? Are some religions un-American or otherwise illiberal? Are some religions hateful and intolerant?

Scholars of religion will remind us that these kinds of questions represent an unfortunate tendency to deal in gross overgeneralizations when it comes to religion. To say, as then-candidate Trump did, that "Islam hates us" is to fail to understand the global and historical complexity of Islam. There are about two billion followers of Islam on earth, including millions of Muslim citizens of the United States and other Western nations. Islam is internally diverse, as is Christianity, as are other religions. The world's religious traditions have developed across the centuries. This development includes ongoing arguments about the meaning of religious texts and traditions. As rival interpretations developed, the world's religions have evolved in different ways in different places. And religions continue to evolve.

To say that a particular religion (or religion in general) is hateful or intolerant is to deal in stereotypes and caricatures that ignore the cultural and historical diversity of religion. It makes little sense to generalize about an entire religion hating "us" (or loving "us," for that matter; and we might also ask who is the "us" that is loved or hated). Moreover, people are often confused about what we are talking about when using the term *religion*. Religion is a family resemblance concept, which includes a variety of things. Religion is often understood as a set of beliefs—a faith. This could include ideas about God (or Allah or some other name for the divine). But some "religions" are not primarily focused on the divine. Buddhism and Confucianism tend to be less theologically oriented than Christianity or Islam. And beyond the question of theology, religion is about culture and identity. Religion includes practices, rituals, and rules of behavior. It is about what we eat (or don't eat), how we celebrate life (and mourn death), and who we love (and how we marry). Thus, the idea of freedom of thought, conscience, and religion that is enshrined in the UN Declaration of Human Rights includes also the freedom to engage in rituals, practices, and behaviors that are, broadly speaking, "religious." And again, it is worth emphasizing that the world's religious traditions are internally diverse. This diversity extends to include all of the diverse cultural practices that are associated with religion. Some Muslim women cover their hair; others do not. Some Christians wear crosses around their necks; others do not. Some Sikh men grow their beards; others do not. Some Jews avoid nonkosher food; others do not. Some Hindus are strict vegetarians; other are not. And so on. The idea of religious freedom allows

for divergent religious beliefs, practices, and identities. This freedom applies within religious traditions and among them.

While the example of Islam in the United States has been in the forefront, religious diversity is a challenge across the globe and throughout history. There have been clashes among Sikhs, Hindus, and Muslims in India, between Tibetan Buddhists and Chinese forces in Tibet, and between Israelis and Palestinians. And in previous centuries, Christians engaged in colonialism at the expense of indigenous peoples and native religions. Christian sects also fought against one another, while Jews were persecuted and exterminated by Christians in Europe. Each of these conflicts is unique. But one prevailing theme is the clash of values in which the basic ideas of freedom of expression and respect for religious diversity conflict with rigid religious intolerance and religious bigotry.

Religious differences continue to be flashpoints for conflict with regard to the topics to be discussed in the second half of this book. There are religious disputes about health care, abortion, euthanasia, the death penalty, and war. One approach to these issues might be broadly described as either **libertarian** or **liberal**. These terms have a complicated history and application in economics, political philosophy, and ethics (see Chapter 14 for more details). But the basic point is to emphasize freedom of choice and toleration. Now, from some religious perspectives, the basic ideas of toleration and freedom of religion may be seen as immoral. If religious salvation depends on conformity to some orthodox set of beliefs, then it would be wrong to tolerate the unorthodox. And as we've seen, there are nations that prohibit blasphemy in an effort to defend religious orthodoxy. Furthermore, it might be that the ideas we find in the First Amendment to the American Constitution or in the UN Declaration only make sense within the context of Western secular democracies. Are these values shared by the world's diverse religious people and faiths? And which set of values is more fundamental: the secular value of respect for religious liberty or the sectarian values that are often dear to the religious faithful?

This points to the important question of how ethics relates to religion. While recent events continue to bring these matters to the forefront, there are deep historical precedents for this discussion. Socrates—the father of the Western philosophical tradition—ran into trouble with the religious and political authorities of Athens. Socrates asked people how they defined moral terms, trying to understand ideas such as justice, courage, love, and friendship. But his philosophical inquiries were tinged with skepticism. He questioned traditional religion, traditional political authority, and conventional wisdom. He called himself a "gadfly," by which he meant that he buzzed around Athens, nipping at and probing things. He believed that his effort would help Athenians understand morality and help to make them virtuous. Many Athenians found Socrates to be offensive and even immoral. Some viewed him as a dangerously subversive figure. Eventually, he was brought to court and formally charged with not believing in the gods of the city and with corrupting its youth. Many suspected him of being an atheist. As a result, he was sentenced to death.

Freedom, Cosmopolitanism, and the European Enlightenment

2.2 Explain how the idea of universal human rights is linked to secularism, cosmopolitanism, and the European Enlightenment.

The story of Socrates demonstrates the controversial nature of philosophical inquiry and the complicated relationship between philosophy and religion. If it is difficult for us to imagine how Socrates could have been sentenced to death for asking questions about Athenian morality and religion, it is because we are used to extensive freedom when it comes to religion and morality. Europeans and Americans tend to believe that the freedom enjoyed in this part of the world is unique—a product of a distinctly Western tradition of tolerance and pluralism. However, we should be careful when making sweeping generalizations about history. There have been many tolerant and open-minded epochs in the history of the world. The Buddhist emperor Ashoka is known for sponsoring a tolerant regime, as is the Muslim emperor Akbar. And under Confucianism, China was tolerant toward a variety of religious perspectives.

China proclaimed an "Edict of Toleration" in 1692, which permitted Christian missionary work—at around the same time that Protestants were still being persecuted in Europe. Indeed, at the time, the philosopher Leibniz and other Europeans praised China and Confucianism for its open and tolerant spirit.

World history includes a number of freethinkers—both within the lineage that follows after Socrates and in others of the world's traditions. Nonetheless, much of our terminology for understanding these sorts of issues is rooted in Western thinking. The terms *philosophy*, *politics*, and *ethics* come to us from the Greek language. And philosophers, historians, and political theorists often still tend to tell a Eurocentric or Western-focused story about the development of tolerance, liberty, and individual rights.

That standard story often begins with Socrates, his trial and execution, and the development of his ideas by his student Plato, and Plato's student Aristotle. One of Socrates's other followers was Diogenes the Cynic, a free spirit who refused to conform to social conventions and had an antagonistic relationship with the authorities of his time. One ancient legend explains that when Alexander the Great was a young man, about to embark on his conquest of the ancient world, he went to see Diogenes, who was lounging in the sun. After demanding that the young prince stop blocking his sunbath, Diogenes asked Alexander what he was up to. Alexander explained that he was about to depart with his armies to conquer the world. Diogenes asked, "Then what?" and Alexander said that he supposed he would relax after that. Diogenes said, "Why not sit in the sun with me now and relax, and save yourself all of the trouble?" When the astonished Alexander asked Diogenes where he was from, Diogenes replied, "I am a cosmopolitan," which means a citizen of the world.

In this anecdote, Diogenes displays skepticism toward conventional authority, while asserting his freedom and claiming independence from any particular nation or culture—values that have come to be associated with the Western philosophical approach. This approach emphasizes individual freedom over traditional hierarchies and universal morality over local customs and traditions. Like Diogenes, it makes a **cosmopolitan** claim: it aspires to a single moral community of humanity not bound by national, cultural, or, in many cases, religious traditions. And it questions many things we take for granted.

While it is true that there are a variety of differences across the globe, including vast religious differences, the cosmopolitan perspective holds that certain ethical principles are universally valuable, such as respect for life and liberty. In the Western world, ideas have been institutionalized in the laws of the modern nation-state. And a growing body of international law, including the UN Declaration, emphasizes a set of basic ideas about individual liberties and human rights.

Although we've noted that toleration and freedom are not uniquely Western values, the usual historical account emphasizes the development of these values during the seventeenth and eighteenth centuries in Europe. This era is known as **the Enlightenment**. It is the period during which many of the philosophers we'll discuss in the book were active: Locke, Hume, Kant, Bentham, and others. These philosophers tended to think that liberty and tolerance were key values. They were optimistic that history was developing in a progressive direction. They thought that progress would occur through the employment of human reason. And they were interested in discovering common values and learning from other cultures. Also during this time, many philosophical ideas were put into practice in revolutionary politics, as was the case in the American and French revolutions.

The American Revolution can be seen to begin with a famous phrase from the Declaration of Independence: "We hold these truths to be self-evident, that all men are created equal, that they are endowed by their Creator with certain unalienable Rights, that among these are Life, Liberty and the pursuit of Happiness." Drawing on the natural law tradition as developed by John Locke (see Chapter 7), the Declaration enshrines individual liberties at the core of American society. The Constitution of the United States goes further, detailing areas of individual liberty on which government must not intrude. The most important example, for our purposes, is the First Amendment to the Constitution, which reads, "Congress shall make no law respecting an establishment of religion, or prohibiting the free exercise thereof; or abridging the freedom of speech, or of the press; or

the right of the people peaceably to assemble, and to petition the Government for a redress of grievances." The First Amendment makes religious liberty the law of the land (in the so-called "free exercise" clause), while also prohibiting government from getting involved in religion (in the so-called "establishment clause"). The American system can thus be seen to explicitly reject the kind of society that executed Socrates, where an "established" state religion allowed the authorities to punish (by death) speech perceived to be blasphemous. We've come a long way from ancient Athens.

It should not be surprising that philosophers emphasize individual liberty. Philosophical speculation involves wide-ranging inquiry into an ever-expanding set of topics. We cannot philosophize properly unless we are free to question, argue, and think. Nor is it surprising that philosophical reflection on morality points in a cosmopolitan direction. When Jefferson claims that "all men are created equal," he implies that inalienable rights—of life, liberty, and the pursuit of happiness—are the endowment of all people, from all cultures (despite the sexist language that uses the word "men" for what we should properly call "humanity").

A quick glance at world history or today's newspaper makes it clear that no such consensus exists. For a long time, even in the United States, there was substantial disagreement about whether all "men" really were created equal. Slavery was taken for granted by the generation that wrote the US Constitution. Women were not permitted to vote. And religious diversity in the early American republic was limited to toleration among a few Christian denominations. Toleration did not extend, for example, to include the Mormons (the Church of Latter-Day Saints), who migrated to Utah in pursuit of the freedom to worship. Nor did it extend to include the native peoples who were the victims of American colonial expansion. Even after slavery was abolished, Americans continued to disagree about the status of women and what racial equality should look like. It took decades of long struggle for women to gain the right to vote. And Americans are still struggling to come to terms with the racist history of slavery and Native American genocide. This struggle involves an effort to understand the role that religion played in creating structures of oppression—and role of religion in opposing oppression. In the global context, these issues are far from resolved.

Philosophical freedom can lead to conflicts with authority, especially religious authorities. At around the same time that the American revolutionaries were fighting in the name of liberty, the German philosopher Immanuel Kant defined enlightenment in terms of freedom. He thought that progress would occur when we were permitted freedom to argue and when we were courageous enough to use this freedom to imagine ways to improve society. Kant wrote,

> Enlightenment is man's emergence from his self-incurred immaturity. Immaturity is the inability to use one's own understanding without the guidance of another. This immaturity is self-incurred if its cause is not lack of understanding, but lack of resolution and courage to use it without the guidance of another. The motto of enlightenment is therefore: *Sapere Aude!* (dare to know): "Have courage to use your own understanding!"[5]

Kant thought that history would develop in a cosmopolitan direction, with European nations forming a confederation based on shared moral ideas. This federation—an idea that foreshadowed the development of the United Nations—would ensure perpetual peace. It would take two long centuries of war and misery for Europe and the rest of the world to finally achieve Kant's idea. And the idea still seems a bit naive, given remaining cultural and religious differences across the globe.

Religion, Civic Life, and Civil Disobedience

Like Socrates, Kant advocated gradual reform through public argument about morality, politics, and religion. This philosophical approach can seem naive when faced with entrenched and powerful unjust systems, such as slavery, serfdom, colonialism, and apartheid. What if the rulers simply have no interest in listening to the ruled?

After Kant, a variety of thinkers and activists—from Henry David Thoreau to Mohandas K. Gandhi to Martin Luther King Jr.—concluded that principled resistance to an unjust system required something

more than argument. Rather than advocate the violent overthrow of the regime, these thinkers called for **civil disobedience**, the open, nonviolent refusal to obey an unjust law, with the intent of accepting the penalty and arousing the conscience of the community as a whole. King developed his ideas about nonviolent civil disobedience from his study of Gandhi, the Indian political activist and religious leader who advocated **ahimsa** (nonviolence) as a key to the struggle for Indian independence. King also drew inspiration from Jesus and from Socrates. King argues in his "Letter from Birmingham Jail" that Socrates and other philosophers are gadflies who nonviolently point out conflicts within society. In King's era, those conflicts were focused on racial injustice, as well as poverty and the war in Vietnam. In a sense, King is an heir to the Enlightenment dream, by which individuals and societies strive to achieve moral maturity through rational inquiry. Like Socrates, King expresses faith in logical questioning of accepted dogmas as a means of overcoming injustice. And like Kant, King also sees his efforts in explicitly cosmopolitan terms, as a quest for universal justice. But King combined philosophical critique with nonviolent civil disobedience. It is important to note, however, that advocates of civil disobedience criticize existing traditions and institutions while also demonstrating a kind of loyalty to those traditions and institutions: they break the law—and accept punishment—as a way of pointing out injustices and failures in the system. The critical stance and civil disobedience of the Civil Rights Movement were not merely negative. It had the positive goal of helping the United States realize the full promise of its founding documents, while remaining faithful to the deals of American political, moral, and religious ideology.

This last point is particularly important to bear in mind as we consider the relationship between philosophical inquiry and religious traditions and institutions. Sometimes, it might seem that the most serious impediment to free-ranging philosophical criticism is religion—especially those forms of religious belief that want to limit freedom in the name of conformity to the will of God. With regard to morality, it is often thought that what is required is obedience to God's commandments, laws, prophets, and the institutions that have developed to defend and disseminate the faith. (We will hear more about this view of

Bob Fitch/Take Stock/The Image Works

Figure 2-1 Martin Luther King Jr. in his Atlanta office, standing in front of a portrait of Mohandas K. Gandhi.

morality in the next section.) And it may seem that philosophy has nothing to offer a faith-centered worldview, that it has no interest in the sacred, and views human life in exclusively secular terms.

It is true that contemporary philosophy tends to be secular in its orientation. A 2020 survey of over 1,700 English-speaking philosophers indicates that 19 percent of the philosophers surveyed accept or lean toward *theism* (belief in the existence of God or gods), while 67 percent accept or lean toward atheism; the remainder affirm agnosticism or some other alternative.[6] It is also worth noting that there are a growing number of secular and nonreligious people in general. A report from 2021 indicates that in the United States, 63 percent of people identify as Christian, while 29 percent claim that they have no religious affiliation (the remaining population belong to other religions).[7] Similar trends have been reported in other countries.

It is impossible to draw a firm line dividing philosophy and religion. For most of human history, the two subjects have been deeply intertwined or even indistinguishable. Both are concerned with the most fundamental questions of human existence: Why are we here? What is the meaning of life? How should we treat one another? And both have frequently challenged ruling powers and conventional ways of thinking. The example of Martin Luther King is a case in point; King was a devout Baptist minister who also thought that philosophical critique was necessary to make moral progress. King drew his primary inspiration from Jesus's teachings on poverty, tolerance, and love. He also valued Socrates's example. It is not necessarily true that philosophical ethics is atheistic or opposed to religious belief. The philosophers mentioned here—Socrates, Locke, and Kant—remained committed to some form of theistic belief.

Religion remains at the center of many of the applied ethical topics that we will discuss later in this text, as noted above. Religious perspectives on such topics are not easy to categorize as "liberal" or "conservative." Religion is not one thing. There are a variety of sects and denominations, just as there are a variety of religious people who belong to these sects and denominations. And this reminds us of the importance of religious liberty. Religious liberty along with the freedom of philosophical inquiry are essential in a world that includes a wide variety of people who disagree about religious, political, and moral questions.

Ethics, Religion, and Divine Command Theory

2.3 Evaluate the divine command theory of ethics.

Many people get their ethical or moral views from their religion. Although religions include other elements, most do have explicit or implicit requirements or ideals for moral conduct. In some cases, they contain explicit rules or commandments. The Ten Commandments, for example, includes rules such as "Honor thy father and mother" and "Thou shalt not kill." Some religions recognize and revere saints or holy people who model key virtues. And most religions have a long history of internal arguments and interpretations about the nature and content of moral law.

Most contemporary philosophers, however, believe that ethics does not necessarily require a religious grounding. Rather than relying on holy books or religious revelations, philosophical ethics uses reason and experience to determine what is good and bad, right and wrong, better and worse. In fact, even those people for whom morality is religiously based may want to examine some of their views using reason. They may want to examine various interpretations of their religious principles for internal consistency or coherence. Or they may want to know whether elements of their religious morality—some of its rules, for example—are good or valid ones given that other people have different views of what is right and wrong, and given that the problems of contemporary times may be different from those of the past.

If right and wrong can only be grounded in religious belief, then nonbelievers could not be said to have moral views or make legitimate moral arguments. But in a pluralistic society, religious believers need to engage in constructive dialogue with nonbelievers and evaluate their claims. In fact, religious believers regularly make moral judgments that are not based strictly on their religious views but rather on reflection and common sense.

Thinking further about religious morality also raises challenges to it. A key element of many religious moralities is the view that certain things are good for us to do because this is what God wants. This conception is often referred to as the **divine command theory**. The idea is that certain actions are right because they are what God wills. The reading at the end of this chapter from Plato's dialogue *Euthyphro* examines this view. In this dialogue, Socrates asks whether things are good because they are approved by the gods or whether the gods approve of them because they are good. To say that actions are good simply because they are willed or approved by the gods or God seems to make morality arbitrary. God could decree anything to be good—lying or treachery, for example. It seems more reasonable to say that lying and treachery are bad, and for this reason, the gods or God condemns or disapproves of them and we should also. One implication of this view is that morality has a certain independence; if so, we should be able to determine whether certain actions are right or wrong in themselves and for what reason.

This argument does not imply, however, that religion cannot provide a motivation or inspiration to be moral. Many believe that if life has some eternal significance in relation to a supreme and most perfect being, then we ought to take life and morality extremely seriously. This is

not to say that the only reason religious persons have for being moral or doing the morally right thing is so that they will be rewarded in some life beyond this one. Such a view might be seen to undermine morality, since it suggests that we should be good only if we are "bribed" to do so. Rather, if something is morally right, then this is itself a reason for doing it. Thus, the good and conscientious person is the one who wants to do right simply because it is right.

Questions about the meaning of life, however, often play a significant role in a person's thoughts about the moral life. Some people might even think that atheists have no reason to be moral or to be concerned with doing the morally right thing. However, this is not necessarily so. For example, a religious person may be inclined to disregard the moral stakes of what occurs in this life, if they think of it as fleeting and less important than the afterlife. And an atheist who believes that this life is all there is may in fact take this life more seriously and care more about living morally. Furthermore, religious and nonreligious people live together in contemporary society and have pressing practical reasons to think clearly and reason well about morality.

For at least three reasons, we should all seek to develop our moral reasoning skills. First, we should be able to evaluate critically our own or other views of what is thought to be good and bad or just and unjust, including religious views. Second, believers of various denominations as well as nonbelievers ought to be able to discuss moral matters together. Third, the fact that many of us live in organized secular communities, cities, states, and countries requires that we be able to develop and rely on widely shared reason-based views on issues of justice, fairness, and moral ideals. This is especially true in political communities with some separation of church and state, where no state religion is mandated, and where one has freedom to practice a chosen religion or practice no religion at all. In these settings, it is important to have nonreligiously based ways of dealing with moral issues. This is one goal of philosophical ethics.

The Russian novelist Fyodor Dostoevsky provides the kernel of one argument that is often used in defense of divine command ethics. Dostoevsky's writings express the famous claim that, "If God is dead, then everything is permissible."[8] This idea articulates the worry that if there were no God, then there would be no morality. There are two concerns here: one about

Giulio Origlia/Getty Images

Samir Hussein/Getty Images

Figure 2-2 Pope Francis and the Dalai Lama represent the wide range of religious diversity in the world.

religion as the source of morality and another about religion as providing a motivation for morality. The first concern is that without God as a source for morality, there would be no eternal, absolute, or objective basis for morality. We will deal with the first concern in more detail in Chapter 3 when we consider **relativism**, which is the claim that there are no eternal, absolute, or objective values. Theists often hold that God is the source of moral law, provided through the words of a prophet, such as Moses, who receives the moral law directly from God. Some theists worry that if that prophetic origin of morality is denied, we are left without any objective moral principles. Most of the rest of the first half of this book focuses on providing an account of values that avoids this criticism; the ethical theories we will study try to provide reasons and justifications for ethical principles without reference to God.

The second concern is that without a divine judge who punishes us or rewards us in the afterlife, there would be no motivation to be ethical. A version of this concern led Kant to postulate God and immortality as necessary for morality—so that we might at least hope that moral actions would be rewarded (and immoral actions would be punished) in an afterlife. In response, atheists might argue that the demands, rewards, and punishments of human social life are sufficient to provide motivation to be ethical. We turn to the issue of motivation in our discussion of egoism in Chapter 4. In that chapter, we consider a story from Plato about Gyges, a man who can literally get away with murder. If you were able to do whatever you wanted without fear of getting caught, would you commit immoral deeds? Or do you think that we need some idea of a God who observes our deeds and punishes us or rewards us accordingly?

One of the most important problems for defenders of divine command ethics is the fact of religious diversity. Even if we agree with Dostoevsky that God is required for ethics, we still have to figure out which God or religious story is the one that provides the correct teaching about morality. Saying that ethics is based in religion does not really help us that much because we must also determine which religion is the correct one. Given the incredible amount of religious diversity in the world, it is easy to see that the divine command approach is not really very helpful without a much broader inquiry into the truth of various religions.

Figure 2-3 Bishop Barbara Harris is among the diverse faith leaders of the world.

Peter Southwick/AP Photo

The problem of diversity holds even within specific religious traditions. This problem was recognized at the time of Socrates and Plato. Plato asks us to consider which versions of the Greek religious stories are the correct or proper ones. The same consideration applies to contemporary religions. Not only do we have to determine which religion is correct, we also have to determine which version of this religion is the correct one. Consider, for example, that Christianity includes a range of denominations: Eastern Orthodox, Roman Catholic, and Protestant (which includes a range of groups from Mennonites and Quakers to Methodists, Presbyterians, and Southern Baptists). Similar diversity can be found within Islam, Judaism, and the religious traditions that come out of South Asia. Even if we think that ethics comes from God, how can we decide which account of God's commands is the correct one? The philosophical approach reminds us that we would have to use reason and experience—including especially our own human insight into ethics—to decide among the world's religious traditions.

Pluralism and the Golden Rule

2.4 Explain the idea of the Golden Rule.

One approach to resolving the problem of diversity is to look for common ground among the world's cultural and religious traditions. This general idea is known as **religious pluralism**. A more specific philosophical view is often called **value pluralism**, which argues that there are multiple and conflicting goods in the world, which cannot be reduced to some other good. (We will discuss pluralism again when we deal with relativism in Chapter 3.) Pluralists about religion often make a different sort of argument. Religious pluralists, such as John Hick, claim that there is a common core of ideas found among the world's religious traditions. As Hick puts it, quoting the Islamic poet Rumi, "the lamps are many, but the light is one."[9]

The usual candidate for this common core among religions is something like the **Golden Rule**: "Do unto others as you would have them do unto you" or "treat others as you would like to be treated." Many people have claimed that each of the world's religious and cultural systems includes something like the Golden Rule. John Hick argues that "all the great traditions teach the moral ideal of generous goodwill, love, compassion, epitomized in the Golden Rule."[10] The Tibetan Buddhist leader, the Dalai Lama, put it this way: "All of the different religious faiths, despite their philosophical differences, have a similar objective. Every religion emphasizes human improvement, love, respect for others, sharing other people's suffering. On these lines every religion has more or less the same viewpoint and the same goal."[11] The reading from Gandhi that follows at the end of this chapter makes a similar point.

A related point is made in the reading excerpt from Eleanor Roosevelt, which emphasizes what she calls "brotherly love." This expression may seem a bit old-fashioned since it uses gendered language—and today we might say "neighborly love" instead. Whatever we call it, this kind of love is another way of describing the idea that we should love our neighbors as ourselves (which is another formulation of the Golden Rule). Eleanor Roosevelt was, by the way, a great advocate for the rights of women as well as for civil rights for African Americans—and she was the chairperson of the committee that drafted the UN Declaration of Human Rights. Of further interest to us here is the fact that Roosevelt understood human rights and the idea of neighborly love in a way that was extended globally and that also included nonreligious people. She thought that both religious and nonreligious people can understand the importance of these ideas.

The religious pluralist idea is a friendly and optimistic one; it hopes to be able to reconcile the world's religious traditions around an ethical core. Indeed, there is some evidence for such a convergence in the existence of interfaith organizations that promote religious diversity and pluralism. One example of this is the Parliament of the World's Religions, a group dedicated to creating peaceful and harmonious relations among the world's religions—as we discussed in the opening vignette. The Parliament says, in *Towards a Global Ethic*: "We must treat others as we wish others to treat us. We make a commitment to respect life and dignity, individuality and diversity, so that every person is treated humanely, without exception."[12]

Unfortunately, this hopeful reconciliation must ignore much; the very deep differences that exist among religions, the fact of apparently immoral elements in some religious traditions, the reality of religious conflict, and the moral importance of our deep differences over metaphysical questions. As religion scholar Stephen Prothero suggests, the idea that all religions are basically the same "is a lovely sentiment but it is dangerous, disrespectful, and untrue."[13]

Consider for example, the Hindu idea of *dharma*, which is a complex concept that refers to laws of natural order, justice, propriety, and harmony. The idea of dharma is connected to the traditional Indian caste system. Now, there are parallels between the idea of destiny and caste in India and medieval Christian ideas about natural law and the great chain of being. But the differences between these ideas are as important as the similarities. The end goal of Hindu ethics is to attain some form of self-realization and

Figure 2-4 In this image, American painter Norman Rockwell imagined that the common idea of all the world's cultures and religions was the Golden Rule: "Do unto others as you would have them do unto you."

connection with the eternal soul of Brahman. While this may sound like the kind of insight and beatification (or holiness) that occurs in Christian unity with God, the differences are again quite important. God and Brahman are not simply synonyms, and self-realization in Hindu tradition is quite different from beatification in Christianity.

Other differences and similarities exist among the world's traditions. For example, charity, gifts, almsgiving, and hospitality are important values in most religious traditions. But these ideas manifest themselves in different ways. Islam emphasizes *zakat*, or alms-giving, as one of its five pillars. This includes a universal duty to build a just society, help the poor, and eliminate oppression. While this sounds quite a bit like the idea of charity and tithing in the Christian tradition, *zakat* may be more important and more obligatory than mere charity—closer to a tax than a gift. And in Islam, there is another related idea, *sadaqah*, which connotes voluntary charity as opposed to mandatory alms-giving. For Indigenous peoples of the Pacific Northwest, the *potlatch* is an important ritual and tradition of gift-giving. The potlatch is a well-known example of "give-away" ceremonies practiced by many Native American tribes.[14] These ceremonies involve practices of gratitude, friendship, and gift-giving that help express and reinforce communal values, while also connecting participants to a larger tradition and cosmology. But the *potlatch* is different from *zakat*, which is different from other practices of charity and hospitality in other traditions. There are similarities, to be sure. But the differences are as important and pervasive as the similarities.

Optimistic religious pluralists want to reduce all of these differences to common values such as love, compassion, and the Golden Rule. But it is easy to see that religious ethics is not simply about love and compassion. If all the world's religions agree about compassion, love, and the Golden Rule, how do we explain holy wars and religious violence? If all religions are basically variations on the theme of love and compassion, how do we explain religious texts and ideas that are not very compassionate? Would a purely compassionate and loving God destroy the earth with a flood, threaten punishment in Hell, or require gruesome tests of faith? Would compassionate and loving religious believers stone adulterers and LGBTQ+ people

and burn witches alive? While interpreters of religion can explain these things in various ways, the specific details of religious ethics and interpretation matter as much as the general principle of compassion or love.

The Problem of Evil and Free Will

2.5 Articulate how the problem of evil and free will creates challenges for religious ethics.

A further ethical question arises in the context of thinking about religion and ethics: the **problem of evil**. This issue provides a concrete example of the problem of religious diversity, since different religions will deal with the problem of evil in different ways. How do we explain the presence of suffering and evil in the world? Buddhists explain that life is characterized by suffering, or *dukkha*—a term that can also be translated as pain, stress, or even disease. They explain that suffering comes from attachment to the fleeting goods of this world and from wrongful actions. Christians also struggle with the problem of evil. But for Christians, the existence of evil creates a metaphysical problem. How can evil exist in a world that is supposedly created by a benevolent and all-powerful God? The Christian tradition developed elaborate **theodicies**, or

---

▶ **Knowledge Check**   Answers appear at the end of the chapter.

1. Which clause of the First Amendment to the US Constitution guarantees that there is no official state religion?

    a. The right to bear arms

    b. The free exercise clause

    c. The establishment clause

    d. The right to petition

2. What is the name for the era in which modern philosophers were attempting to articulate a secular approach to ethics?

    a. The medieval period

    b. The Cold War

    c. The End of History

    d. The Enlightenment

3. The divine command theory holds which of the following two ideas (pick two)?

    a. All men are created equal.

    b. Ethical principles are grounded in God.

    c. God is just and merciful.

    d. God provides a motivation for ethical behavior.

4. Which concept implies that there are multiple and conflicting goods in the world, which cannot be reduced to some other good?

    a. Pluralism

    b. The Golden Rule

    c. Human rights

    d. Brotherly love

arguments that attempt to justify God as all-powerful and all-knowing, despite the problem of evil. Important thinkers such as Augustine and Leibniz responded to this problem by focusing on sin and on freedom of the will. For Augustine, **original sin** is passed down from Adam to the rest of us. Leibniz clarifies that God provided us with free will so that we might choose between good and evil and argues that the best of all possible worlds is one that contains both freedom and the related possibility of evil.

Humanistic philosophers have subjected these sorts of disputes to skeptical criticism. How do we know that all life is suffering and that suffering is caused by attachment (as Buddhists suggest)? How do we know that there is a God, that this God created freedom, and that original sin is passed down (as Christians suggest)? The metaphysical complexities introduced by religion point toward mysteries and paradoxes that give humanistic philosophers reasons to be skeptical.

Consider the question of free will. If we are not free, then we are not responsible for our actions—in which case, the enterprise of moral philosophy begins to seem shaky. As the well-known atheist author Sam Harris explains,

> Morality, law, politics, religion, public policy, intimate relationships, feelings of guilt and personal accomplishment—most of what is distinctly human about our lives seems to depend upon our viewing one another as autonomous persons, capable of free choice….Without free will, sinners and criminals would be nothing more than poorly calibrated clockwork, and any conception of justice that emphasized punishment (rather than deterring, rehabilitating, or merely containing them) would appear utterly incongruous.[15]

Despite this admission, Harris denies the idea of free will—based on a natural scientific account of human physiology, brain function, and other material conditions—while still arguing that morality makes sense. (We will read a brief excerpt from Harris regarding religion at the end of this chapter.) Philosophers have pondered the problem of free will for millennia. Some deny that there is free will in an entirely deterministic universe. Others have argued that free will remains compatible with determinism.

Free will is a puzzle even within Christianity, where there are questions about how much freedom we can have in a universe that is created by an omnipotent (all-powerful) and omniscient (all-knowing) God. Different Christian denominations have different ideas about this issue, with some emphasizing the idea of predestination, by which God ordains things in advance, and others responding to this issue differently. Other religions have responded to the problem of free will in a variety of ways. Buddhists and Hindus have a different conception of freedom and the problem of free will than Christians do—although there are differences even within these vast and complex traditions. But Buddhists, at least, do not believe in a God who punishes evil. Rather, they believe that suffering results from the laws of *karma,* the law of continuity between causes and effects: bad deeds lead to suffering and good ones lead to reward—whether in this life or the next. Whether the idea of karma is compatible with free will is an open question. The Confucian and Taoist traditions also maintain that human beings have the freedom to choose. But Confucianism holds that such free choices are constrained by destiny or fate, while the Taoists emphasize freedom experienced in harmony with nature. In these Chinese traditions, there is, again, no God who judges or punishes.

As noted, the idea of religious pluralism focuses on the ethical "core" of the world's religions. But it is difficult to see how such radically different ideas could converge. As Stephen Prothero acknowledges, "the world's religious traditions do share many ethical precepts. . . . The Golden Rule can be found not only in the Christian Bible and the Jewish Talmud but also in Confucian and Hindu books."[16] But the Golden Rule is a very weak common link. Philosophers have also subjected the Golden Rule to criticism. One problem for the Golden Rule is that if it tells us to love our neighbors as ourselves, we need a definition of "neighbors." Does this mean we should love only those who are related to us—our coreligionists, for example? Or do we have obligations to distant human beings and future generations who do not live in our geographic (or temporal) neighborhood? Even if we all accept the Golden Rule as a basic moral starting point, there are still very difficult questions of application. How does the Golden Rule apply to sexual ethics, abortion, euthanasia, or the death penalty? And what does the Golden Rule tell us to do about evil? Should we punish evildoers? Or should we follow Jesus, who explained that in addition to loving our neighbors, we should love our enemies and refrain from returning evil for evil? The problem of responding to wrongdoing and evil is a complex moral issue, one that is subject to multiple interpretations even within specific religious traditions. Different traditions—even different sects and denominations within the same tradition—give divergent answers about these applied ethical issues, including the very deep question of where evil comes from and how we should deal with it.

We will see that the normative theories defended by philosophers also suffer from a similar problem: they appear to conflict and can be applied in various ways. But the conflicts among the different theories in philosophical ethics may be easier to reconcile, since philosophical arguments are usually not subject to the same ambiguities of interpretation and translation that tend to plague ancient scriptural sources.

It may be possible to imagine a pluralistic convergence of the world's religions around certain key moral principles and central human values. However, until this convergence occurs, we will have to find some way to coexist despite our differences. The challenge of coexistence is exacerbated by our growing diversity. As more and different religious people (and nonreligious people) come to share life in common in our cosmopolitan world, we have to find some set of values that can allow us to live together even though we disagree about religion.

Secular Ethics and Toleration

2.6 Differentiate between secular/humanistic and religious approaches to ethics.

The effort to find ways to coexist despite our religious differences gives rise to **secular ethics**. *Secular* means "based in this world or this age" (as opposed to the eternal and otherworldly focus of religion). When we say that an ethical idea or theory is secular, we mean that it is divorced from any source in religion. A secular ethic can develop out of religious conflict, as members of different religious groups agree to coexist despite their differences. Indeed, this is how the secular system that we currently have in the Western world developed through

the course of several centuries of religious wars beginning with the Protestant Reformation.

By the end of the seventeenth century, European philosophers of the Enlightenment era were arguing that public **toleration** of religious diversity was necessary. A hallmark of secularism is the idea of freedom of religion and toleration of religious diversity. For many, the progress of **secularization** is a central aspect of modernization: as cultures and polities modernize, they also become more secular. One recent study concludes that secularization "suggests a trend, a general tendency toward a world in which religion matters less and various forms of secular reason and secular institutions matter more. It is a trend that has been expected at least since modernity and has been given quasi-scientific status in sociological studies advancing a secularization thesis."[17] While this same study presents a somewhat critical perspective on the secularization thesis, the idea does help to explain much of recent history, including the spread of secular cosmopolitan ideas such as those we find in the UN document discussed at the outset of this chapter. Of course, religious fundamentalism—whether it be Christian, Muslim, Jewish, Hindu, or the like—still remains a potent force, with some religious leaders arguing for the subordination of women, arguing against scientific naturalism, and trying to defend traditional ideas from previous centuries.

One of the most important Western philosophical sources for thinking about secularism is John Locke, who is discussed in greater detail in Chapter 7. In the 1680s, Locke published his influential "Letter Concerning Toleration," which has served as an important touchstone. Locke argues that the state should tolerate religious dissenters. For Locke, religious belief must be a matter of inward persuasion, which is not amenable to the use of force. Locke's basic point is that force is simply not effective to produce genuine religious belief. If that's the case, then political efforts to establish conformity of belief by the use of coercion will ultimately be ineffective. Locke goes on to argue that spiritual and civil authorities must operate in wholly different spheres—the former through persuasion and conversion and the latter through laws backed by coercive force. Religions are to be left alone to deal with spiritual issues. And the state is supposed to focus only on issues related to public order.

This argument forms the basis of the constitutional doctrine that is often called "separation of church and state."

Locke's ideas had a significant impact on Jefferson and the other founders of the United States—and they have gone on to influence ethical and political thought, including the ideas found in the UN Declaration of Human Rights. The question of toleration and religion has also been taken up by a number of important philosophers. The influential American political philosopher John Rawls has argued that societies need to work to develop "overlapping consensus" among people who adhere to divergent religious and moral worldviews. He calls these deeply held worldviews "comprehensive doctrines." According to Rawls, societies should focus on agreement in the political realm, instead of trying to force a deeper agreement about these comprehensive moral and religious ideas. This leads to a theory of political justice that Rawls calls "political liberalism," as well as a basic conception of human rights that emphasizes toleration for religious diversity. Rawls's goal is to find a way to establish peaceful coexistence in a just society among people who disagree about the highest good. Overlapping consensus about political issues would leave us with something like a secular ethic: a system of values and fair rules that can be agreed on by people who come from quite different religious traditions or by people who have no religion at all. (Rawls's influential theory of justice is discussed in greater detail in Chapter 14.)

In contrast to Rawls's view, there are some who have a more radical understanding of the term *secular* that equates it with atheism. Some religious people denounce "secular humanism" as nothing more than atheism. One of the most influential proponents of the idea of secular humanism, Paul Kurtz, has worked hard to clarify that secular humanism can remain open to religious believers, even though it is grounded in a nonreligious approach to ethics. Kurtz has recently focused on what he calls "neo-humanism," which is an attempt to reconcile atheists and religious believers around a global ethics. Kurtz's "Neo-Humanist Manifesto" states, "The challenge facing humankind is to recognize the basic ethical principle of planetary civilization—that every person on the planet has equal dignity and value as a person, and this transcends the limits of national, ethnic, religious, racial, or linguistic boundaries or identities."[18] Kurtz's idea hearkens back to the Enlightenment ideal of a cosmopolitan world grounded in shared ethical values. It also appears to have much in common with religious cosmopolitanism of the sort associated with the Parliament of the World's Religion.

Criticisms of Secularism and Global Ethics

2.7 Explain the critique of modern secular values using the concept of Eurocentrism.

The dream of global consensus around secular principles may seem like an appealing solution to centuries of violent conflict and contention over religion. But it remains an open question whether this is possible. One significant problem is that some religious people reject any taint of secularism on doctrinal grounds. For religious believers who think that God requires absolute obedience to divine commandments, or that those commandments must be embodied in the laws of the state, a secular ethic that does not explicitly embrace God as the source of morality will appear to be morally suspect and blasphemous.

Such responses can present advocates of tolerance with a problem called the **paradox of toleration**. The paradox revolves around the question of whether there is a good reason to tolerate those who are intolerant or those who reject the very idea of toleration. Some defenders of toleration simply bite the bullet here and admit that there are limits to toleration. Locke, for example, did not extend toleration to atheists or to Catholics. He thought atheists were untrustworthy since they did not believe in God, and he thought that Catholics were too loyal to Rome to be trusted. Although Locke defended toleration, he clearly thought that there were some people who could not be tolerated. We've come a long way since the time of Locke. But the rise of new fundamentalist movements within such religions as Judaism, Christianity, and Islam has posed new challenges for the idea of tolerance. (**Fundamentalism** is characterized by rigid adherence to a literal interpretation of religious doctrines and a reaction against compromise with secularism and modernity.) The political philosopher Jürgen Habermas argues that "a fundamentalism that leads to a practice of intolerance is incompatible with the democratic constitutional state."[19]

He concludes, "in multicultural societies, the national constitution can tolerate only forms of life articulated within the medium of such non-fundamentalist traditions."[20] Habermas is saying that we cannot tolerate those who reject liberal-democratic principles of toleration on fundamentalist religious grounds. Indeed, it is not difficult to imagine circumstances in which religious fundamentalists violate the shared principles of secular ethics. What do we do about religious pacifists who refuse to serve in the military or pay their taxes, pastors who think it is acceptable for thirteen-year-old girls to be married to older men, or religious communities that mutilate the genitals of their daughters? And what of religious groups who get involved in democratic politics to advance intolerant agendas—or who may be explicitly opposed to democracy itself? In many cases, even those who want to embrace religious diversity will have to say that there are ethical limits to what they are willing to tolerate in terms of religious belief and practice.

A further problem is that secularization, cosmopolitanism, and modernization sometimes appear to spring directly from the post-Reformation philosophy and politics of the West. One charge against secular and cosmopolitan ethics is that it is Eurocentric, meaning that it is an idea that makes sense only within the context of European culture and history. As the sociologist of religion José Casanova explains, "Cosmopolitanism remains a faithful child of the European Enlightenment."[21]

A significant point of such a criticism has to do with the role of political and economic power. According to this way of thinking, European culture, with its emphasis on individualism and the separation of church and state, spread across the world along with European colonial power. While some may think that this is a progressive development, critics will view it as an imposition of European culture and values that come at the expense of alternative ideas about morality and politics. A related criticism develops from Karl Marx's critique of "bourgeois morality" as the product of a certain strand of European thinking, associated with the ruling class. (Marxists, by the way, tend to view religion as "the opiate of the people," that is, as a drug that reconciles oppressed people to the injustices of the social order by promising an otherworldly reward.) More recently, scholars such as Enrique Dussel have expanded this critical perspective to argue that **Eurocentrism** is at the heart of continual cultural

divisions and economic inequalities that plague the globe (as we discuss in more detail in Chapter 16). An influential Latin American philosopher, Dussel critiques the traditional Anglo-American and European approach to philosophy and ethics. For Dussel, European philosophy begins with conquest—as the colonial conquests of the Americas, Asia, and Africa coincide with the dawning of European Enlightenment.[22] Dussel suggests there may be a connection between European imperialism and European ethics—that moral ideas about a variety of topics from sex and gender to individualism and human rights, to the use of drugs and the morality of war, have a lot to do with the economic and political power structures at work in the world.

The approaches to ethics that we are discussing in this book can appear to be Eurocentric. From this standpoint, one might argue that the approach of this book reflects the biases of a predominantly Christian and European worldview. Indeed, the main normative traditions discussed in this book—utilitarianism, virtue ethics, natural law, and Kantian deontology—are rooted in the ideas of European philosophers.

In response, one might admit that even though understanding ethics in an objective and universal fashion, without reference to religion, is a goal that is widely shared by many in the Western world, this goal is not uniquely Christian or European. Indeed, it is one shared by many people around the world. As Amartya Sen and others have pointed out, the move toward philosophical and cosmopolitan ethics is also deeply rooted in non-Western intellectual traditions. It is true that we must be sensitive to the diverse cultural and religious starting points from which we begin reflecting on ethics. But this does not mean that we should not attempt to move beyond narrow allegiances and prejudices toward a broader, more impartial, and more objective perspective—that is, toward a cosmopolitan and pluralist point of view that would incorporate the insights of the world's great moral and religious traditions. Whether we can attain this goal is an open question. In Chapter 3, we confront this problem more directly as a question of relativism. The question of that chapter will be whether there really is such a thing as a universal, objective point of view or whether we are hopelessly stuck within a perspective and worldview that we inherit from our culture or religion.

Chapter Summary

2.1 How would you describe the challenge of developing a global ethical perspective in a world that is religiously diverse?

After reading this chapter, you should have some idea of the broad diversity of religious perspectives. But you should also have some idea about those who hope for a pluralistic convergence (say around the Golden Rule). While diversity is a challenge, organizations such as the Parliament of the World's Religions are aiming to find common ground.

2.2 How is the idea of universal human rights linked to secularism, cosmopolitanism, and the European Enlightenment?

Documents such as the UN Declaration of Human Rights aim to find common ground. The idea of developing a cosmopolitan consensus about rights and values is an ancient one. One important component of this is religious liberty, which is often understood as a secular value.

2.3 How do philosophers evaluate the divine command theory of ethics?

Since the time of Plato, philosophers have questioned whether ethics comes from God's command or whether ethical values have some independent existence or value. Some think that there can be no morality without God. But philosophers have suggested that there may be some other basis for morality.

2.4 What is the Golden Rule, and why is it important?

The Golden Rule tells us to love our neighbors as ourselves. It is found in many religious and cultural traditions. It is often considered as a focal point for the effort to develop a global ethic.

2.5 How does the problem of evil and free will create challenges for religious ethics?

The problem of evil asks why the omniscient and omnipotent God is not able to prevent evil. One solution to this problem is to invoke the idea of free will, such that evil is not God's fault but rather is the fault of those who misuse their freedom. Free will seems to be assumed by those who think human beings can be held responsible for doing good and avoid evil. But free will remains problematic—both within religious worldviews and within the deterministic worldview of natural science.

2.6 What is the difference between secular/humanistic and religious approaches to ethics?

Secular systems of value attempt to ground ethics in values that are not religious. This usually attempts to include diverse religious people through overlapping consensus or within some system of toleration and religious liberty. But sometimes secularism can seem to be anti-religious and atheistic. And some religious people may disagree about the importance of finding common ground in a secular system of values.

2.7 How can we explain the Eurocentric critique of modern secular values?

Some critics of modernity and secularism will claim that these ideas were created by Europeans and only make sense from within a European/Christian (and North American) worldview. Saying these values are Eurocentric implies that they are imposed on non-Europeans or that non-European people do not fully embrace them. In response, defenders of secularism can explain that non-European cultures do embrace these values and that there are efforts to find global consensus about shared values.

Primary Source Readings

The first reading for this chapter is from Plato, who offers a critique of religious ethics in his dialogue *Euthyphro*. In the dialogue, Socrates discusses religion with Euthyphro, a young man who claims to know what piety demands. Socrates suggests that the idea of what is good is somehow prior to our understanding of what religion requires. Following this is a short excerpt from an essay by Sam Harris that outlines a contemporary argument against religion and the need to evolve beyond religion. The next reading is from Mohandas K. Gandhi, who argues for a pluralistic convergence of religious ideas. In this essay, Gandhi considers the idea that the world's religions converge around a common ethical core. We conclude with an excerpt from a book written by Eleanor Roosevelt in 1938, where she connects the idea of human rights and hope for peace with an idea of brotherly love that transcends religion.

Reading 2-1 Euthyphro | Plato

Study Questions

As you read the excerpt, please consider the following questions:

1. Do the gods have different conceptions about what is good and evil, just and unjust? Why does this pose a problem for Euthyphro's account?
2. Which comes first: being pious or being loved by the gods?
3. What does Socrates suggest is yet needed to give a definition of piety or goodness?

Euthyphro. Piety . . . is that which is dear to the gods, and impiety is that which is not dear to them.

Socrates. Very good, Euthyphro; you have now given me the sort of answer which I wanted. But whether what you say is true or not I cannot as yet tell, although I make no doubt that you will prove the truth of your words.

Euthyphro. Of course.

Socrates. Come, then, and let us examine what we are saying. That thing or person which is dear to the gods is pious, and that thing or person which is hateful to the gods is impious, these two being the extreme opposites of one another. Was not that said?

Euthyphro. It was.

Socrates. And well said?

Euthyphro. Yes, Socrates, I thought so; it was certainly said.

Socrates. And further, Euthyphro, the gods were admitted to have enmities and hatreds and differences?

Euthyphro. Yes, that was also said.

Socrates. And what sort of difference creates enmity and anger? Suppose for example that you and I, my good friend, differ about a number; do differences of this sort make us enemies and set us at variance with one another? Do we not go at once to arithmetic, and put an end to them by a sum?

Euthyphro. True.

Socrates. Or suppose that we differ about magnitudes, do we not quickly end the differences by measuring?

Euthyphro. Very true.

Socrates. And we end a controversy about heavy and light by resorting to a weighing machine?

Euthyphro. To be sure.

Socrates. But what differences are there which cannot be thus decided, and which therefore make us angry and set us at enmity with one another? I dare say the answer does not occur to you at the moment, and therefore I will suggest that these enmities arise when the matters of difference are the just and unjust, good and evil, honourable and dishonourable. Are not these the points about which men differ, and about which when we are unable satisfactorily to decide our differences, you and I and all of us quarrel, when we do quarrel?

Euthyphro. Yes, Socrates, the nature of the differences about which we quarrel is such as you describe.

Socrates. And the quarrels of the gods, noble Euthyphro, when they occur, are of a like nature?

Euthyphro. Certainly they are.

From Plato, *Euthyphro*, trans. B. Jowett (Project Gutenberg, 2008). http://www.gutenberg.org/files/1642/1642-h/1642-h.htm

Socrates. They have differences of opinion, as you say, about good and evil, just and unjust, honourable and dishonourable: there would have been no quarrels among them, if there had been no such differences—would there now?

Euthyphro. You are quite right.

Socrates. Does not every man love that which he deems noble and just and good, and hate the opposite of them?

Euthyphro. Very true.

Socrates. But, as you say, people regard the same things, some as just and others as unjust—about these they dispute; and so there arise wars and fightings among them.

Euthyphro. Very true.

Socrates. Then the same things are hated by the gods and loved by the gods, and are both hateful and dear to them?

Euthyphro. True.

Socrates. And upon this view the same things, Euthyphro, will be pious and also impious?

Euthyphro. So I should suppose.

Socrates. Then, my friend, I remark with surprise that you have not answered the question which I asked. For I certainly did not ask you to tell me what action is both pious and impious: but now it would seem that what is loved by the gods is also hated by them. And therefore, Euthyphro, in thus chastising your father you may very likely be doing what is agreeable to Zeus but disagreeable to Cronos or Uranus, and what is acceptable to Hephaestus but unacceptable to Heré, and there may be other gods who have similar differences of opinion.

Euthyphro. But I believe, Socrates, that all the gods would be agreed as to the propriety of punishing a murderer: there would be no difference of opinion about that.

Socrates. Well, but speaking of men, Euthyphro, did you ever hear any one arguing that a murderer or any sort of evil-doer ought to be let off?

Euthyphro. I should rather say that these are the questions which they are always arguing, especially in courts of law: they commit all sorts of crimes, and there is nothing which they will not do or say in their own defence.

Socrates. But do they admit their guilt, Euthyphro, and yet say that they ought not to be punished?

Euthyphro. No; they do not.

Socrates. Then there are some things which they do not venture to say and do: for they do not venture to argue that the guilty are to be unpunished, but they deny their guilt, do they not?

Euthyphro. Yes.

Socrates. Then they do not argue that the evil-doer should not be punished, but they argue about the fact of who the evil-doer is, and what he did and when?

Euthyphro. True.

Socrates. And the gods are in the same case, if as you assert they quarrel about just and unjust, and some of them say while others deny that injustice is done among them. For surely neither God nor man will ever venture to say that the doer of injustice is not to be punished?

Euthyphro. That is true, Socrates, in the main.

Socrates. But they join issue about the particulars—gods and men alike; and, if they dispute at all, they dispute about some act which is called in question, and which by some is affirmed to be just, by others to be unjust. Is not that true?

Euthyphro. Quite true.

Socrates. Well then, my dear friend Euthyphro, do tell me, for my better instruction and information, what proof have you that in the opinion of all the gods a servant who is guilty of murder, and is put in chains by the master of the dead man, and dies because he is put in chains before he who bound him can learn from the interpreters of the gods what he ought to do with him, dies unjustly; and that on behalf of such a one a son ought to proceed against his father and accuse him of murder. How would you show that all the gods absolutely agree in approving of his act? Prove to me that they do, and I will applaud your wisdom as long as I live.

Euthyphro. It will be a difficult task; but I could make the matter very clear indeed to you.

Socrates. I understand; you mean to say that I am not so quick of apprehension as the judges: for to them you will be sure to prove that the act is unjust, and hateful to the gods.

Euthyphro. Yes indeed, Socrates; at least if they will listen to me.

Socrates. But they will be sure to listen if they find that you are a good speaker. There was a notion that came into my mind while you were speaking; I said to myself: "Well, and what if Euthyphro does prove to me that all the gods regarded the death of the serf as unjust, how do I know anything more of the nature of piety and impiety? For granting that this action may be hateful to the gods, still piety and impiety are not adequately defined by these distinctions, for that which is hateful to the gods has been shown to be also pleasing and dear to them." And therefore, Euthyphro, I do not ask you to prove this; I will suppose, if you like, that all the gods condemn and abominate such an action. But I will amend the definition so far as to say that what all the gods hate is impious, and what they love pious or holy; and what some of them love and others hate is both or neither. Shall this be our definition of piety and impiety?

Euthyphro. Why not, Socrates?

Socrates. Why not! Certainly, as far as I am concerned, Euthyphro, there is no reason why not. But whether this admission will greatly assist you in the task of instructing me as you promised, is a matter for you to consider.

Euthyphro. Yes, I should say that what all the gods love is pious and holy, and the opposite which they all hate, impious.

Socrates. Ought we to enquire into the truth of this, Euthyphro, or simply to accept the mere statement on our own authority and that of others? What do you say?

Euthyphro. We should enquire; and I believe that the statement will stand the test of enquiry.

Socrates. We shall know better, my good friend, in a little while. The point which I should first wish to understand is whether the pious or holy is beloved by the gods because it is holy, or holy because it is beloved of the gods.

Euthyphro. I do not understand your meaning, Socrates.

Socrates. I will endeavour to explain; we speak of carrying and we speak of being carried, of leading and being led, seeing and being seen. You know that in all such cases there is a difference, and you know also in what the difference lies?

Euthyphro. I think that I understand.

Socrates. And is not that which is beloved distinct from that which loves?

Euthyphro. Certainly.

Socrates. Well; and now tell me, is that which is carried in this state of carrying because it is carried, or for some other reason?

Euthyphro. No; that is the reason.

Socrates. And the same is true of what is led and of what is seen?

Euthyphro. True.

Socrates. And a thing is not seen because it is visible, but conversely, visible because it is seen; nor is a thing led because it is in the state of being led, or carried because it is in the state of being carried, but the converse of this. And now I think, Euthyphro, that my meaning will be intelligible; and my meaning is, that any state of action or passion implies previous action or passion. It does not become because it is becoming, but it is in a state of becoming because it becomes; neither does it suffer because it is in a state of suffering, but it is in a state of suffering because it suffers. Do you not agree?

Euthyphro. Yes.

Socrates. Is not that which is loved in some state either of becoming or suffering?

Euthyphro. Yes.

Socrates. And the same holds as in the previous instances; the state of being loved follows the act of being loved, and not the act the state.

Euthyphro. Certainly.

Socrates. And what do you say of piety, Euthyphro: is not piety, according to your definition, loved by all the gods?

Euthyphro. Yes.

Socrates. Because it is pious or holy, or for some other reason?

Euthyphro. No, that is the reason.

Socrates. It is loved because it is holy, not holy because it is loved?

Euthyphro. Yes.

Socrates. And that which is dear to the gods is loved by them, and is in a state to be loved of them because it is loved of them?

Euthyphro. Certainly.

Socrates. Then that which is dear to the gods, Euthyphro, is not holy, nor is that which is holy loved of God, as you affirm; but they are two different things.

Euthyphro. How do you mean, Socrates?

Socrates. I mean to say that the holy has been acknowledged by us to be loved of God because it is holy, not to be holy because it is loved.

Euthyphro. Yes.

Socrates. But that which is dear to the gods is dear to them because it is loved by them, not loved by them because it is dear to them.

Euthyphro. True.

Socrates. But, friend Euthyphro, if that which is holy is the same with that which is dear to God, and is loved because it is holy, then that which is dear to God would have been loved as being dear to God; but if that which is dear to God is dear to him because loved by him, then that which is holy would have been holy because loved by him. But now you see that the reverse is the case, and that they are quite different from one another. For one (theophiles) is of a kind to be loved because it is loved, and the other (oston) is loved because it is of a kind to be loved. Thus you appear to me, Euthyphro, when I ask you what is the essence of holiness, to offer an attribute only, and not the essence—the attribute of being loved by all the gods. But you still refuse to explain to me the nature of holiness. And therefore, if you please, I will ask you not to hide your treasure, but to tell me once more what holiness or piety really is, whether dear to the gods or not (for that is a matter about which we will not quarrel); and what is impiety?

Euthyphro. I really do not know, Socrates, how to express what I mean. For somehow or other our arguments, on whatever ground we rest them, seem to turn round and walk away from us.

Reading 2-2   Letter to a Christian Nation | Sam Harris

Study Questions

As you read the excerpt, please consider the following questions:

1. Why does Harris suggest that it is a "ludicrous obscenity" to raise children to believe that they are Christian, Muslim, or Jewish?

2. What kind of evolutionary purpose may religion have served?

3. Is religion an impediment to building a global society?

One of the greatest challenges facing civilization in the twenty-first century is for human beings to learn to speak about their deepest personal concerns—about ethics, spiritual experience, and the inevitability of human suffering—in ways that are not flagrantly irrational.

We desperately need a public discourse that encourages critical thinking and intellectual honesty. Nothing stands in the way of this project more than the respect we accord religious faith.

. . . .

If we ever do transcend our religious bewilderment, we will look back upon this period in human history with horror and amazement. How could it have been possible for people to believe such things in the twenty-first century? How could it be that they allowed their societies to become so dangerously fragmented by empty notions about God and Paradise?

. . . .

Clearly, it is time we learned to meet our emotional needs without embracing the preposterous. We must find ways to invoke the power of ritual and to mark those transitions in every human life that demand profundity—birth, marriage, death—without lying to ourselves about the nature of reality. Only then will the

---

Sam Harris, *Letter to a Christian Nation* (New York: Knopf, 2006), pp. 87–89.

practice of raising our children to believe that they are Christian, Muslim, or Jewish be widely recognized as the ludicrous obscenity that it is. And only then will we stand a chance of healing the deepest and most dangerous fractures in our world.

. . . .

It is important to realize that the distinction between science and religion is not a matter of excluding our ethical intuitions and spiritual experiences from our conversation about the world; it is a matter of our being honest about what we can reasonably conclude on their basis. There are good reasons to believe that people like Jesus and the Buddha weren't talking nonsense when they spoke about our capacity as human beings to transform our lives in rare and beautiful ways. But any genuine exploration of ethics or the contemplative life demands the same standards of reasonableness and self-criticism that animate all intellectual discourse.

As a biological phenomenon, religion is the product of cognitive processes that have deep roots in our evolutionary past. Some researchers have speculated that religion itself may have played an important role in getting large groups of prehistoric humans to socially cohere. If this is true, we can say that religion has served an important purpose. This does not suggest, however, that it serves an important purpose now. There is, after all, nothing more natural than rape. But no one would argue that rape is good, or compatible with a civil society, because it may have had evolutionary advantages for our ancestors. That religion may have served some necessary function for us in the past does not preclude the possibility that it is now the greatest impediment to our building a global civilization.

Reading 2-3   Religion and Truth | Mohandas K. Gandhi

Study Questions

As you read the excerpt, please consider the following questions:

1. How does Gandhi describe "the religion that underlies all religions"?
2. Why does Gandhi think that *ahimsa* (nonviolence) and self-purification are important?
3. What is the one unifying element of the world's diverse religions, according to Gandhi?

By religion, I do not mean formal religion, or customary religion, but that religion which underlies all religions, which brings us face to face with our Maker.

Let me explain what I mean by religion. It is not the Hindu religion which I certainly prize above all other religions, but the religion which transcends Hinduism, which changes one's very nature, which binds one indissolubly to the truth within and which ever purifies. It is the permanent element in human nature which counts no cost too great in order to find full expression and which leaves the soul utterly restless until it has found itself, known its Maker and appreciated the true correspondence between the Maker and itself.

I have not seen Him, neither have I known Him. I have made the world's faith in God my own, and as my faith is ineffaceable, I regard that faith as amounting to experience. However, as it may be said that to describe faith as experience is to tamper with truth, it may perhaps be more correct to say that I have no word for characterizing my belief in God.

There is an indefinable mysterious Power that pervades everything. I feel it, though I do not see it. It is this unseen Power which makes itself felt and yet defies all proof, because it is so unlike all that I perceive through my senses. It transcends the senses. But it is possible to reason out the existence of God to a limited extent.

From Mohandas K. Gandhi, *All Men Are Brothers* (Lausanne, SA: UNESCO, 1969). Reprinted by permission of Navajivan Trust.

I do dimly perceive that whilst everything around me is ever-changing, ever-dying, there is underlying all that change a Living Power that is changeless, that holds all together, that creates, dissolves, and re-creates. That informing Power or Spirit is God. And since nothing else I see merely through the senses can or will persist, He alone is.

And is this Power benevolent or malevolent? I see it as purely benevolent. For I can see that in the midst of death life persists, in the midst of untruth truth persists, in the midst of darkness light persists. Hence I gather that God is Life, Truth, Light. He is Love. He is the Supreme God.

I know, too, that I shall never know God if I do not wrestle with and against evil even at the cost of life itself. I am fortified in the belief by my own humble and limited experience. The purer I try to become the nearer to God I feel myself to be. How much more should I be near to Him when my faith is not a mere apology, as it is today, but has become as immovable as the Himalayas and as white and bright as the snows on their peaks?

This belief in God has to be based on faith which transcends reason. Indeed, even the so-called realization has at bottom an element of faith without which it cannot be sustained. In the very nature of things it must be so. Who can transgress the limitations of his being? I hold that complete realization is impossible in this embodied life. Nor is it necessary. A living immovable faith is all that is required for reaching the full spiritual height attainable by human beings. God is not outside this earthly case of ours. Therefore, exterior proof is not of much avail, if any at all. We must ever fail to perceive Him through the senses, because He is beyond them. We can feel Him, if we will but withdraw ourselves from the senses. The divine music is incessantly going on within ourselves, but the loud senses drown the delicate music, which is unlike and infinitely superior to anything we can perceive or hear with our senses.

But He is no God who merely satisfies the intellect, if He ever does. God to be God must rule the heart and transform it. He must express Himself in even the smallest act of His votary. This can only be done through a definite realization more real than the five senses can ever produce. Sense perceptions can be, often are, false

and deceptive, however real they may appear to us. Where there is realization outside the senses it is infallible. It is proved not by extraneous evidence but in the transformed conduct and character of those who have felt the real presence of God within. Such testimony is to be found in the experiences of an unbroken line of prophets and sages in all countries and climes. To reject this evidence is to deny oneself.

To me God is Truth and Love; God is ethics and morality; God is fearlessness. God is the source of Light and Life and yet He is above and beyond all these. God is conscience. He is even the atheism of the atheist. . . . He transcends speech and reason. . . . He is a personal God to those who need His personal presence. He is embodied to those who need His touch. He is the purest essence. He simply *is* to those who have faith. He is all things to all men. He is in us and yet above and beyond us. . . . He is long-suffering. He is patient but He is also terrible. . . . With Him ignorance is no excuse. And withal He is ever forgiving for He always gives us the chance to repent. He is the greatest democrat the world knows, for He leaves us "unfettered" to make our own choice between evil and good. He is the greatest tyrant ever known, for He often dashes the cup from our lips and under the cover of free will leaves us a margin so wholly inadequate as to provide only mirth for Himself. . . . Therefore Hinduism calls it all His sport.

To see the universal and all-pervading Spirit of Truth face to face one must be able to love the meanest of creation as oneself. And a man who aspires after that cannot afford to keep out of any field of life. That is why my devotion to truth has drawn me into the field of politics; and I can say without the slightest hesitation, and yet in all humility, that those who say that religion has nothing to do with politics do not know what religion means.

Identification with everything that lives is impossible without self-purification; without self-purification the observance of the law of *ahimsa* must remain an empty dream; God can never be realized by one who is not pure of heart. Self-purification therefore must mean purification in all walks of life. And purification being highly infectious, purification of oneself necessarily leads to the purification of one's surroundings.

But the path of self-purification is hard and steep. To attain to perfect purity one has to become absolutely passion-free in thought, speech and action; to rise above the opposing currents of love and hatred, attachment and repulsion. I know that I have not in me as yet that triple purity, in spite of constant, ceaseless striving for it. That is why the world's praise fails to move me, indeed it very often stings me. To conquer the subtle passions seems to me to be far harder than the physical conquest of the world by the force of arms.

I am but a poor struggling soul yearning to be wholly good—wholly truthful and wholly non-violent in thought, word and deed; but ever failing to reach the ideal which I know to be true. It is a painful climb, but the pain of it is a positive pleasure to me. Each step upward makes me feel stronger and fit for the next.

I am endeavouring to see God through service of humanity, for I know that God is neither in heaven, nor down below, but in every one.

Indeed religion should pervade every one of our actions. Here religion does not mean sectarianism. It means a belief in ordered moral government of the universe. It is not less real because it is unseen. This religion transcends Hinduism, Islam, Christianity, etc. It does not supersede them. It harmonizes them and gives them reality.

Religions are different roads converging to the same point. What does it matter that we take different roads, so long as we reach the same goal? In reality, there are as many religions as there are individuals.

If a man reaches the heart of his own religion, he has reached the heart of the others too.

So long as there are different religions, every one of them may need some distinctive symbol. But when the symbol is made into a fetish and an instrument of proving the superiority of one's religion over others', it is fit only to be discarded.

After long study and experience, I have come to the conclusion that: (1) all religions are true; (2) all religions have some error in them; (3) all religions are almost as dear to me as my own Hinduism, in as much as all human beings should be as dear to one as one's own close relatives. My own veneration for other faiths is the same as that for my own faith; therefore no thought of conversion is possible.

God has created different faiths just as He has the votaries thereof. How can I even secretly harbour the thought that my neighbour's faith is inferior to mine and wish that he should give up his faith and embrace mine? As a true and loyal friend, I can only wish and pray that he may live and grow perfect in his own faith. In God's house there are many mansions and they are equally holy.

Let no one even for a moment entertain the fear that a reverent study of other religions is likely to weaken or shake one's faith in one's own. The Hindu system of philosophy regards all religions as containing the elements of truth in them and enjoins an attitude of respect and reverence towards them all. This of course presupposes regard for one's own religion. Study and appreciation of other religions need not cause a weakening of that regard; it should mean extension of that regard to other religions.

It is better to allow our lives to speak for us than our words. God did not bear the Cross only 1,900 years ago, but He bears it today, and He dies and is resurrected from day to day. It would be poor comfort to the world if it had to depend upon a historical God who died 2,000 years ago. Do not then preach the God of history, but show Him as He lives today through you.

I do not believe in people telling others of their faith, especially with a view to conversion. Faith does not admit of telling. It has to be lived and then it becomes self-propagating.

Divine knowledge is not borrowed from books. It has to be realized in oneself. Books are at best an aid, often even a hindrance.

I believe in the fundamental truth of all great religions of the world. I believe that they are all God-given, and I believe that they were necessary for the people to whom these religions were revealed. And I believe that, if only we could all of us read the scriptures of the different faiths from the standpoint of the followers of those faiths, we should find that they were at the bottom all one and were all helpful to one another.

Belief in one God is the corner-stone of all religions. But I do not foresee a time when there would be only one religion on earth in practice. In theory, since there is one God, there can be only one religion. But in practice, no two persons I have known have had the same identical conception of God. Therefore, there will, perhaps, always be different religions answering to different temperaments and climatic conditions.

I believe that all the great religions of the world are true more or less. I say "more or less" because I believe that everything that the human hand touches, by reason of the very fact that human beings are imperfect, becomes imperfect. Perfection is the exclusive attribute of God and it is indescribable, untranslatable. I do believe that it is possible for every human being to become perfect even as God is perfect. It is necessary for us all to aspire after perfection, but when that blessed state is attained, it becomes indescribable, indefinable. And, I, therefore, admit, in all humility, that even the Vedas, the Koran and the Bible are imperfect word of God and, imperfect beings that we are, swayed to and fro by a multitude of passions, it is impossible for us even to understand this word of God in its fullness.

I do not believe in the exclusive divinity of the Vedas. I believe the Bible, the Koran and the Zend Avesta, to be as much divinely inspired as the Vedas. My belief in the Hindu scriptures does not require me to accept every word and every verse as divinely inspired....I decline to be bound by any interpretation, however learned it may be, if it is repugnant to reason or moral sense.

Reading 2-4   This Troubled World | Eleanor Roosevelt

Study Questions

As you read the excerpt, please consider the following questions:

1. What does Roosevelt have in mind with regard to "brotherly love" as a solution to the troubles of this world?

2. Is her idea of brotherly love a religious idea?

3. How might Roosevelt's thinking as explained here be linked to her advocacy of the idea of universal human rights?

We can establish no real trust between nations until we acknowledge the power of love above all other power. We cannot cast out fear and therefore we cannot build up trust. Perfectly obvious and perfectly true, but we are back again to our fundamental difficulty—the education of the individual human being, and that takes time. We cannot sit around a table and discuss our difficulties until we are able to state them frankly. We must feel that those who listen wish to get at the truth and desire to do what is best for all. We must reach a point where we can recognize the rights and needs of others, as well as our own rights and needs.

I have a group of religious friends who claim that the answer to all these difficulties is a great religious revival. They may be right, but great religious revivals which are not simply short emotional upheavals lifting people to the heights and dropping them down again below the place from which they rose, mean a fundamental change in human nature. That change will come to some people through religion, but it will not come to all that way, for I have known many people, very fine people, who had no formal religion. So the change must come to some, perhaps, through a new code of ethics, or an awakening sense of responsibility for their brothers, or a discovery that whether they believe in a future life or not, there are now greater enjoyments and rewards in this world than those which they have envisioned in the past.

I would have people begin at home to discover for themselves the meaning of brotherly love.... We will have to want peace, want it enough to pay for it, pay for it in our own behavior and in material ways. We will have to want it enough to overcome our lethargy and go out and find all those in other countries who want it as much as we do.

From Eleanor Roosevelt, *This Troubled World* (New York: Kinsey and Company, 1938).

Some time we must begin, for where there is no beginning there is no end, and if we hope to see the preservation of our civilization, if we believe that there is anything worthy of perpetuation in what we have built thus far, then our people must turn to brotherly love, not as a doctrine but as a way of living. If this becomes our accepted way of life, this life may be so well worth living that we will look into the future with a desire to perpetuate a peaceful world for our children. With this desire will come a realization that only if others feel as we do, can we obtain the objectives of peace on earth, good will to men.

Review Exercises

1. If you could develop a global ethic, what would its basic values be?

2. Describe the challenge of developing a global ethical perspective in light of religious and national differences.

3. What is the history of the idea of universal human rights? How is this history susceptible to the charge that it is Eurocentric?

4. Explain arguments in favor of the divine command theory of ethics, as well as arguments against that theory. Is it true that if there were no God, then everything would be permitted?

5. Is the humanistic or secular approach to ethics better than religious approaches to ethics? How so? Is the humanistic or secular approach antagonistic to religion?

6. What does Socrates mean when he says in *Euthyphro* that the holy or pious is holy or pious because it is loved by the gods? Do you agree with his argument?

7. Are you optimistic about our ability to develop a global ethical consensus across our national and religious differences? Why or why not?

8. Do you think that all religions are pointing in a similar direction, or are there irreconcilable differences among them?

9. What is the value of love, compassion, and the Golden Rule—is this a religious idea or can nonreligious people affirm it?

Knowledge Check Answer Key

1. **b.** The free exercise clause refers to the section of the First Amendment to the US Constitution that guarantees there is no official state religion.

2. **d.** The Enlightenment is the name for the era in which modern philosophers were attempting to articulate a secular approach to ethics.

3. **b and d.** The divine command theory posits that ethical principles are grounded in God and that God provides a motivation for ethical behavior.

4. **a.** Pluralism is the concept that implies that there are multiple and conflicting goods in the world, which cannot be reduced to some other good.

3 Ethical Relativism

Cultural Competence

In some cultures, epilepsy is viewed as a spiritual malady. But according to Western medicine, epilepsy is a neurological disorder that can usually be treated with anti-seizure medications. This divergent way of thinking about a disease such as epilepsy can lead to a clash of cultural and ethical ideals. An influential example of this problem was examined by Anne Fadiman in her book *The Spirit Catches You and You Fall Down*.[1] Fadiman explores the case of Lia Lee, a child who was diagnosed with epilepsy. The child's family was Hmong (an ethnic group with roots in Southeast Asia). They had recently relocated to California from a refugee camp in Thailand. According to the traditional wisdom of Hmong culture, Lia's condition was spiritual—a case of "the spirit catching you and you fall down." The child's Western doctors viewed Lia's condition differently and wanted to treat her with medication. Miscommunication and misunderstanding caused difficulties. Eventually the child died. This tragic case has become an often-cited example of the challenge of *cultural competence*. Doctors need to do a better job of understanding the cultural, religious, and ethical beliefs of their patients. But one wonders where cultural competence ends and cultural relativism begins. Is there an answer to the question of how we ought to understand and treat epilepsy? Or are we left with a clash of values and divergent norms?

imageBROKER/Alamy Stock Photo

What Do You Think?

1. Are ethical disagreements inevitable given the diversity of culture, religion, and morality?
2. Can you imagine some values that could (or should) be shared, even in a case like the one described here?
3. How important is cultural competency? In health care? In education? In legal structures?
4. Is cultural competency a form of relativism?

Introduction

Chapter 2 introduced the difficulty of trying to discover a set of universal values that are valid for people who come from diverse religious and cultural backgrounds. This points toward the problem of relativism. Relativism means that our judgments about ethics are relative to (or dependent on) something else. Cultural relativism holds that ethical judgments are relative to cultural contexts. Individualistic versions of relativism hold that judgments about morality are relative to an individual's point of view. In saying that judgments are relative to individuals or cultures, we mean that they are a function of, or dependent on, what those individuals or cultures happen to believe. Relativism can be based on **epistemological** claims about what we know. Relativism can also be based on a claim about the nature of values (as discussed in Chapter 1). The epistemological approach maintains that knowledge about values is derived from or dependent on a cultural context or worldview. A metaphysical approach claims that there are no absolute, transcendent, or universal values. For the metaphysical relativist, there are only individual perspectives and culturally defined values—there are no absolute or objective values.

Relativism is a very difficult metaethical issue. It asks us to consider how we know things in the realm of morality. And it asks us to consider the ultimate nature or reality of moral values. The belief that guides this text—indeed, the belief that guides most philosophical discussions of ethics—is that better and worse choices can be made, and that morality is not simply a matter of what we feel to be morally right or wrong; nor is morality simply a matter of what our culture tells us. If this were not the case, there would not seem to be much point in studying ethics. The purpose of studying ethics, as noted in Chapter 1, is to improve one's ability to make good ethical judgments. If ethical relativism were true, then this purpose could not be achieved.

Descriptive versus Metaethical Ethical Relativism

3.1 Describe the difference between descriptive relativism and metaethical relativism.

Ethical relativism is a kind of skepticism about ethical reasoning—it is skeptical of the idea that there are right and wrong answers to ethical questions. There are some good reasons why we might be skeptical about the existence of universal or objective values (or that we can know what the objective or universal values are). One reason for skepticism is the empirical and historical fact that different cultures disagree about moral values. As a descriptive fact, relativism appears to be true: it is evident that there are different ideas about ethics at large in the world. What we call **descriptive ethical relativism** is the factual or descriptive claim that there are different ideas about values.

In support of descriptive relativism, we might list some of the ways that cultures vary with regard to morality. Some societies hold bribery to be morally acceptable, but other societies condemn it. Views on appropriate sexual behavior and practices vary widely. Some societies believe that cannibalism, the eating of human flesh, is good because it ensures tribal fertility or increases manliness. Some groups of the Inuit, the Indigenous native peoples of northern Canada and Alaska, believed that it was appropriate to abandon their elderly when they could no longer travel with the group, whereas other groups once practiced ritual strangulation of the old by their children. The anthropologist Ruth Benedict documented the case of a Native American group that believed it was justified in killing an innocent person for each member of the group who had died. This was not a matter of revenge but a way of fighting death. In place of bereavement, the group felt relieved by the second killing.[2]

There are a variety of examples of descriptive relativism. In some countries, it is acceptable for women to wear short skirts; in others, women are expected to cover their legs and hair. Indeed, relativism shows up in the language we use to describe contested practices. Consider the practice of cutting women's genitals. Those who are sympathetic to the practice might call it *female circumcision*. But that practice is illegal in other societies, which condemn it by calling it *female genital mutilation* (as we discuss in Chapters 9 and 12). You should be able to think of many other examples of such differences.

Descriptive relativism might appear to lead to a normative rule of thumb, that "when in Rome," we should "do as the Romans do." This saying originated from a discussion between Augustine and Ambrose—two important Christian saints of the fourth century. Augustine noticed that the Christians in Rome fasted on a different day than the Christians in Milan. Ambrose explained that when in Rome, he does what the Romans do. In many cases, it does appear to be wise to go along with local practices. The issue of the appropriate day for fasting is a minor point, and it is easy enough to "go along" with such minor details. But should we also go along with local practices that could include slavery, female genital mutilation, child sacrifice, or cannibalism?

Different cultures do have different values. But it might still be the case that some of these cultures are wrong about certain values. Recall the "fact/value" distinction discussed in Chapter 1. Just because something is a fact of the world (as descriptive relativism is a fact) does not mean that it is a good thing. It is possible that we *ought* to strive to overcome our cultural differences. And it is possible that some cultures (or individuals) are wrong—despite the fact that cultures and individuals vary in their moral judgments. We want to say, for example, that cultures that practice slavery (as the United States did until the 1860s) are wrong to do so. The mere fact

that cultures disagree about values should not immunize cultures from moral criticism. But to say that a culture is wrong, we need an objective or nonrelativist account of the values that would allow us to criticize that culture.

A stronger version of relativism goes beyond merely descriptive relativism and claims that there are no objective or absolute values that would allow us to make such criticisms. We call this version of relativism **metaethical relativism**. Metaethical relativism holds that there are no universal or objective norms (or that human beings cannot know such objective values). Rather, from this point of view, values are simply the beliefs, opinions, practices, or feelings of individuals and cultures. In saying that values are "relative" to individuals or societies, we mean that they are a function of, or dependent on, what those individuals or societies do, in fact, believe. According to metaethical relativism, there is no objective right and wrong. The opposite point of view, that there is an objective right and wrong, is often called **objectivism**, or sometimes simply nonrelativism.

We can understand more about ethical relativism by comparing ethics with science. Most people believe that the natural sciences (biology, chemistry, physics, geology, and their modern variants) tell us things about the natural world. Throughout the centuries, and in modern times, in particular, science seems to have made great progress in uncovering the nature and structure of our world. Moreover, science seems to have a universal validity. Regardless of a person's individual temperament, background, or culture, the same natural world seems accessible to all who sincerely and openly investigate it. Modern science is thought to be governed by a generally accepted method and seems to produce a gradually evolving common body of knowledge. Although this is the popular view of science, philosophers hold that the situation regarding science is much more complex and problematic. And it is possible for there to be relativism with regard to theories of the natural world. Not everyone agrees, for example, that Western biomedicine holds all the answers to good health. Nevertheless, it is useful to compare the ordinary view of science as providing objective truth about the physical world with common understandings of morality.

Morality, in contrast to science, does not seem so objective. Not only is there no general agreement about what is right and wrong, but some people doubt that ethical judgments are the sorts of things about which we could agree. Some people think of morality as a matter of subjective opinion. This is basically the conclusion of ethical relativism: morality is simply a function of the moral beliefs that people have. There is nothing beyond this. Specifically, no category of objective moral truth or reality exists that is comparable to that which we seem to find in the world of nature investigated by science.

Individual versus Cultural Relativism

3.2 Evaluate key concepts such as objectivism, subjectivism, nihilism, skepticism, and moral realism.

In further exploring the nature of ethical relativism, we should note that it has two basic and different forms. According to one form, called personal or **individual relativism** (also called **subjectivism**), ethical judgments and beliefs are the expressions of the moral outlook and attitudes of individual persons. Rather than being objective, such judgments are subjective. I have my ethical views, and you have yours; neither my views nor yours are better or more correct. I may believe that a particular war was unjust, and you may believe it was just. Someone else may believe that all war is wrong. According to this form of relativism, because no objective right or wrong exists, no particular war can be said to be really just or unjust, right or wrong, nor can *all* wars. We each have our individual histories that explain how we have come to hold our particular views or attitudes. But they are just that—our own individual views and attitudes. We cannot say that they are correct or incorrect because to do so would assume some objective standard of right and wrong against which we could judge their correctness. Such a standard does not exist, according to ethical relativism.

According to some versions of individual ethical relativism, moral judgments are similar to expressions of taste. We each have our own individual tastes. I like certain styles or foods, and you like others. Just as no taste can be said to be correct or incorrect, so also no ethical view can be valued as better than any other. My saying that this war is or all wars are unjust is, in effect,

my expression of my dislike of or aversion to war. This is similar to the theory of ethics called emotivism, which we discussed in Chapter 1.

The second form of ethical relativism, called social or **cultural relativism**, holds that ethical values vary from society to society and that the basis for moral judgments lies in these social or cultural views. For an individual to decide and do what is right, he or she must look to the norms of the society. People in a society may, in fact, believe that their views are the correct moral views. And it is possible to consult experts and authorities within a society who provide arguments and explanations about what is right or wrong. Those authorities and experts may also correct, judge, and evaluate individual members of a society; and so, the values of a society are not merely subjective. In this sense, there are conventions or social agreements about ethics. But ethics is *merely conventional*, according to relativism. Moreover, a cultural relativist holds that no society's views or conventions are better than any other in a transcultural sense. In other words, cultural relativism holds that moral expertise and ethical authority are only defined within (or internal to) a society or culture. Relativism holds that there is no such thing as a set of universal moral truths that could be used to evaluate a culture or that is external to cultural conventions. According to cultural relativism, it is not possible to say that any culture is better or worse than any other—since there is no such thing as better or worse in a transcultural or objective sense.

Skepticism, Nihilism, and Pluralism

While it is obvious that different cultures or societies often have different views about what is morally right and wrong, ethical relativism goes further. For the stronger versions of ethical relativism, what is morally right or wrong depends entirely on what society holds as right or wrong. In its strongest forms, relativism is a kind of skepticism or even nihilism.

Skeptical relativists often make an epistemological claim about the limits of human knowledge. **Skepticism** denies that it is possible to know that there are transcultural values. Nihilists often go even further. **Nihilism** maintains that universal or objective values do not exist. As Gilbert Harman puts it, nihilism is "the doctrine that there are no moral facts, no moral truths, and no moral knowledge."[3] And even though we might claim that there are moral truths and moral knowledge defined within our own culture, those truths and knowledge claims are merely conventional—a product of the social world in which we live.

One author often associated with relativism is Friedrich Nietzsche. Nietzsche maintains that words like *good* and *evil* are defined by different people based on their own perspectives on the world. Indeed, Nietzsche is often viewed as a proponent of **perspectivism**, the idea that there are only perspectives on the world—and nothing beyond these perspectives. Nietzsche also thinks that moral judgments reflect power relations and basic instinctual needs. For example, those who are in power tend to call themselves "good" because they instinctively view themselves as superior to those who are less powerful. As Nietzsche explains, "It is our needs that interpret the world; our drives and their For and Against. Every drive is a kind of lust to rule; each one has its perspective that it would like to compel all the other drives to accept as a norm."[4] For Nietzsche, there is no truth beneath these perspectives, instincts, and drives other than the "will to power." Such a strong version of relativism makes it quite difficult to judge or criticize across cultural divides.

A weaker version of relativism holds that there are some abstract and basic norms or values that are shared but that these abstract values are expressed in different cultures in different ways. Thus, different cultures may share the idea that "life should be valued," for example, but they will disagree about what counts as "life" and what counts as "valuing life." It might be that both human and animal lives count, and so no animal lives can be taken in order to support human beings. Or it might be that some form of ritual sacrifice could be justified as a way of valuing life.

One version of this kind of "weak relativism" or "soft universalism" is the "capabilities approach" to ethics and human welfare—as developed by the economist Amartya Sen and the philosopher Martha Nussbaum. Nussbaum maintains that there are certain central features of human flourishing or human well-being, including life, bodily health, bodily integrity, and so on. See Table 3-1 for Nussbaum's list of capabilities. But she

Jose Luis Cereijido/EPA/Newscom

Figure 3-1 Philosopher Martha C. Nussbaum during an event at Oveido University in Spain.

admits the possibility of "multiple realization" of these basic capabilities. As Nussbaum explains, "each of the capabilities may be concretely realized in a variety of different ways, in accordance with individual tastes, local circumstances, and traditions."[5] Nussbaum's approach leads to a sort of **pluralism**. Nussbaum writes that "legitimate concerns for diversity, pluralism, and personal freedom are not incompatible with the recognition of universal norms; indeed, universal norms are actually required if we are to protect diversity, pluralism, and freedom, treating each human being as an agent and an end."[6] But critics will argue that so long as there is no universal agreement about the specific sorts of values that count for human flourishing and an ethical life, we are still left with a kind of relativism.

Nussbaum is not the first author to attempt to articulate a kind of value pluralism that is somewhere in the middle between subjectivism and objectivism. This has long been a concern for American philosophers. We see it in the writings of authors such as William

Table 3-1   Nussbaum's Central Capabilities[7]

1. Life
2. Bodily health
3. Bodily integrity
4. Senses, imagination, and thought
5. Emotions
6. Practical reason
7. Affiliation
8. Other species
9. Play
10. Control over one's environment: political and material

James and John Dewey, philosophers who are part of a movement called *pragmatism* that tended to view philosophical problems in pluralistic and practical terms. Among the authors of the pragmatist tradition, it is worth mentioning Alain Locke, a Black philosopher and social critic who is often described as "the father of the Harlem Renaissance." Locke studied philosophy at Harvard and in Europe, earning a PhD in philosophy from Harvard in 1918. Among his contributions is a defense of value pluralism (we have an excerpt from his work in the primary source readings for this chapter). Locke also articulated a theory of cultural relativism that attempted to be sensitive to the difficult task of understanding cultures. This includes recognizing the internal complexity of cultural formations and the way that cultures interact with one another. Locke thought that a sensitive approach to cultural relativism and value pluralism could help to promote social peace. He explained in a 1935 essay entitled "Cultural Relativism and Ideological Peace" that relativism "contradicts value dogmatism and counteracts value bigotry without destroying the sense of active loyalty."[8] He continued, "cultural relativism … can become a very constructive philosophy by way of integrating values and value systems that might otherwise never react to one another, of, if they did, would do so only in opposition, rivalry, and conflict."[9] Locke's vision of the world was cosmopolitan and democratic. He hoped that in the future

Figure 3-2 Alain Locke, "Father of the Harlem Renaissance."

Alfred Eisenstaedt/The LIFE Picture Collection/Shutterstock

there would be cultural "reciprocity" that would put an end to "cultural superiority" and "imperialism."[10]

Reasons Supporting Ethical Relativism

3.3 Evaluate the arguments in favor of relativism.

There are many reasons for believing that ethical relativism is true. We will first summarize the three most commonly given reasons and then evaluate their related arguments.[11]

The Diversity of Moral Views

One reason most often given to support relativism is the existence of moral diversity among people and cultures. In fields such as science and history, investigation tends to result in general agreement despite the diversity among scientists. But we have not come to such agreement in ethics. Philosophers have been investigating questions about the basis of morality since ancient times. With sincere and capable thinkers pursuing such a topic for millennia, one would think that some agreement would have been reached. But this seems not to be the case. It is not only on particular issues such as abortion that sincere people disagree but also on basic moral values or principles.

Tolerance, Open-Mindedness, and Cultural Competence

Related to the fact of diversity is the desire to be tolerant and open-minded. Often people maintain relativism in an attempt to refrain from judging and condemning others. One worry here is **ethnocentrism**, the tendency to view your own culture as superior to others. Since we know that there are problems with regard to ethnocentrism and bias in judging, we may want to prevent these problems by espousing relativism. From this perspective, the idea is that since there are a variety of cultures with different values, we are in no place to judge which culture is right and which is wrong. Furthermore, a defender of relativism may argue that those who try to judge are being ethnocentric, closed-minded, and intolerant. This may be connected to the effort to develop **cultural competence**, the desire to understand and relate to the cultural values of other people. But sometimes, the desire not to be judgmental can lead us to conclude that there are no right answers and no objective values.

Moral Uncertainty

Another reason to believe that what relativism holds is true is the great difficulty we often have in knowing what is the morally right thing to believe or do. Often we don't know what is morally most important. For example, we do not know whether it is better to help one's friend or do the honest thing in a case in which we cannot do both. Perhaps helping the friend is best in some circumstances, but being honest is best in others. We are not sure which is best in a particular case. Furthermore, we cannot know for sure what will happen down the line if we choose one course over another. Each of us is also aware of our personal limitations and the subjective viewpoint that we bring to moral judging. Thus, we distrust our own judgments. We then generalize and conclude that all moral judgments are simply personal and subjective viewpoints. In this case, our uncertainty leads us to affirm a more general skepticism.

▶ Knowledge Check   Answers appear at the end of the chapter.

1. Which of the following best describes metaethical relativism?

    a. It is the idea that it is always wrong to judge others.

    b. It is the idea that there are no universal or objective norms.

    c. It is the idea that different cultures should not disagree about morality.

    d. It is the idea that moral values are real and objective.

2. Which idea denies that objective moral values exist?

    a. Ethnocentrism

    b. Cultural competence

    c. Unconscious bias

    d. Nihilism

3. Friedrich Nietzsche's form of relativism is sometimes called

    a. The capabilities approach

    b. Perspectivism

    c. Slave morality

    d. Ethnocentrism

4. Which of the following suggests that it is good to understand other people's cultures?

    a. Cultural competence

    b. Cultural imperialism

    c. Social welfare

    d. Social justice

Situational Differences

Finally, people and situations, cultures and times differ in significant ways. The situations and living worlds of different people vary so much that it is difficult to believe that the same things that would be right for one would be right for another. In some places, overpopulation or drought is a problem; other places have too few people or too much water. In some places, people barely have access to the basic necessities of life; in other places, food is plentiful and the standard of living is high. Some individuals are healthy, while others are seriously ill. Some are more outgoing, while others are more reserved. How can the same things be consistently right or wrong under such different circumstances and for such different individuals? It seems unlikely, then, that any moral theory or judgment can apply in a general or universal manner. We thus tend to conclude that they must be relative to the particular situation and circumstance and that no objective or universally valid moral good exists.

Are These Reasons Convincing?

3.4 Evaluate the arguments against relativism.

Let us consider possible responses by a nonrelativist or objectivist to the preceding three points.

The Diversity of Moral Views

We can consider the matter of diversity of moral views from two different perspectives. First, we can ask, how widespread and deep is the disagreement? Second, we may ask, what does the fact of disagreement prove?

How Widespread and Deep Is the Disagreement?

If two people disagree about a moral matter, does this always amount to a moral disagreement? For example, Tyler says that we ought to cut down dramatically on carbon dioxide emissions, while Jordan says that we do not have a moral obligation to do this. This looks like a basic moral disagreement, but it actually may result from differences in their factual, rather than ethical, beliefs. (See Table 3-2) Tyler may believe that the current rate of carbon emissions is causing and will cause dramatically harmful global climate effects,

such as rising sea levels and more severe weather. Jordan may see no such connection because she believes that scientists' assessments and predictions are in error. If they did agree on the factual issues, then Tyler and Jordan might agree to a moral conclusion about climate change—say, if it turns out that they both agree on the basic moral obligation to do what we can to improve the current human condition and prevent serious harm to existing and future generations.

Many apparent moral disagreements are not moral disagreements at all but disagreements about factual or other beliefs. But suppose that at least some of them are about moral matters. Suppose that we do disagree about the relative value, for example, of health and peace, honesty and generosity, or about what rights people do and do not have. It is this type of disagreement that the moral relativist would need to make his or her point.

What Would Disagreement about Basic Moral Matters Prove?

In past years, we have asked students in our ethics classes to tell us in what year George Washington died. A few brave souls venture a guess: 1801, or at least after 1790? No one is sure. Does this disagreement or lack of certitude prove that he did not die or that he died on no particular date? Belief that he did die and on a particular date is consistent with differences of opinion and with uncertainty. So also in ethics: people can disagree about what constitutes the right thing to do and yet believe that there is a right thing to

Figure 3-3 Arguments over moral matters often stem from factual disagreements, such as whether CO_2 emissions from cars and other sources are causing catastrophic climate change.

iStockphoto.com/David Parsons

Table 3-2   Example of a Disagreement about Carbon Emissions

Basic Moral Agreement	Factual Disagreement	Different Moral Conclusions
We ought not to harm.	CO_2 emissions harm.	We ought to reduce emissions.
We ought not to harm.	CO_2 emissions do not harm.	We need not reduce emissions.

do. "Is it not because of this belief that we try to decide what is right and worry that we might miss it?" the nonrelativist would ask.

Or consider the supposed contrast between ethics and science. Although a body of knowledge exists on which those working in the physical sciences agree, those at the forefront of these sciences often profoundly disagree. Does such disagreement prove that no objectivity exists in such matters? If people disagree about whether the universe began with a "big bang" or about what happened in its first millisecond, does this prove that no answer is to be found, even in principle, about the universe's beginning? Not necessarily.

Tolerance, Open-Mindedness, Cultural Competence

3.5 Differentiate between relativism and a commitment to tolerance.

While some people think that relativism goes hand in hand with tolerance and open-mindedness, it is not necessarily true that these things are mutually implied. It is possible to hold that since there are a variety of different cultures, we should simply ignore the other cultures or show them no respect whatsoever. If relativism holds that there are no universal norms that tell us how to deal with cross-cultural interaction, then tolerance and open-mindedness themselves must be seen as culturally relative values, no more legitimate than intolerance or aggression. Moreover, if Nietzsche is correct that the moral world consists of perspectives and struggles for power, there is no good reason to remain open-minded and tolerant. Indeed, relativism might be used to support the use of power in order to defend and expand your own worldview or perspective when it comes into conflict with others.

Often the advocates of tolerance, open-mindedness, and cultural competence are suggesting that those values are good and that everyone ought to cultivate them. To say that doctors, teachers, or lawyers ought to be more aware of the cultural differences of their patients, pupils, and clients is to make a claim about a set of values that are supposed to be objective. Indeed, those who argue in defense of toleration and open-mindedness will often claim that it is wrong to be intolerant or closed-minded. Are these claims supposed to be objectively true? Or would an advocate of toleration be willing to say that we should even tolerate those who are not tolerant or open-minded?

At this point, we might want to consider a significant problem that is often raised as an objection to relativism, which is that it prevents us from engaging in cultural critique. In the essay excerpted below, Louis Pojman points out that there are two forms of this concern. First, relativism implies that we cannot critique cultures and cultural practices that are obviously wrong, and, second, that relativism leaves us without any way of evaluating the work of reformers. If values are relative, there is no basis for critique or reform. In a more recent essay also excerpted below, Anita Superson argues that this is a problem for movements like feminism. In order to articulate a critique of rape or oppression in general, as Superson argues, we appear to need an objective standard of criticism. And as Susan Moller Okin has pointed out, defenders of patriarchal practices can use cultural relativism as a way of avoiding critique. Okin notes that this is a problem that holds for all kinds of cultural criticism. But she notes in particular that defenders of patriarchal cultures will often say, "But this is our culture" as a way of justifying "the continued infringement of women's rights."[12] The challenge considered by Okin and Superson is how to be sensitive to cultural difference while still being committed to cultural critique.

Moral Uncertainty

Let us examine the point that moral matters are complex and difficult to determine. Because of this, we are often uncertain about what is the morally best thing to do. For example, those who "blow the whistle" on unscrupulous employers or coworkers must find it difficult to know whether they are doing the right thing when they consider the potential costs to themselves and others around them. However, this sort of dilemma is not strictly a question of relativism but of skepticism. Skepticism is the view that it is difficult, if not impossible, to know something. However, does the fact that we are uncertain about the answer to some question, even a moral question, prove that it lacks an answer? One reason for skepticism might be the belief that we can see things only from our own perspective and thus, in ethics and other inquiries, can never know things as they are. This is a form of subjectivism (as defined earlier). The nonrelativist could argue that in our very dissatisfaction with not knowing and in our seeking to know what we ought to do, we behave as though we believe that a better or worse choice can be made.

In contrast, matters of science and history often eventually get clarified and settled. We can now look up the date of George Washington's death (1799), and scientists gradually improve our knowledge in various fields. "Why is there no similar progress in ethical matters?" relativists might respond. Answers to that question will depend on a variety of issues, including our ideas about ethical theory (as discussed in the first half of this book) and our ideas about progress on social issues (as discussed in the second half). The fact of continued disagreement about moral theory and moral issues reminds us that ethical inquiry is different from inquiry in history and the social sciences or in the natural sciences.

Situational Differences

Do dramatic differences in people's life situations make it unlikely or impossible for them to have any common morality? Suppose that health is taken as an objective value. Is it not the case that what contributes to the health of some is different from what contributes to the health of others? Insulin injections are often good for the diabetic but not for the nondiabetic. A nonrelativist might reply as follows: even though the good in these specific cases differs, there is still a general value—health—that is the goal. Similarly, justice involves "giving to each his or her due"; but what is due people is not always strictly the same. Those who work hard may deserve something different from those who do not, and the guilty deserve punishment that the innocent do not. These different applications of justice do not mean that justice is not an objective moral value. (See Table 3-3.)

One reason situational differences may lead us to think that no objective moral value is possible is that we may be equating objectivism with what is sometimes called **absolutism**. Absolutism is the view that moral rules or principles have no exceptions and are context-independent. One example of such a rule is "Stealing is always wrong." According to absolutism, situational differences such as whether or not a person is starving would make no difference to moral conclusions about whether that person is justified in stealing food—if stealing is wrong.

However, an objectivist who is not an absolutist can argue that although there are some objective goods—for example, health or justice—what is good in a concrete case may vary from person to person and circumstance to circumstance. They could hold that stealing might be justified in some circumstances because it is necessary for life, an objective good, and

Table 3-3   Example of Applying Values to Situational Differences

Objective Value	Situational Differences	Different Moral Conclusions
Health	Diabetic	Insulin injections are good.
Health	Nondiabetic	Insulin injections are not good.
Justice	Works hard	Deserves reward
Justice	Does not work hard	Does not deserve reward

a greater good than property. Opposing absolutism does not necessarily commit one to a similar opposition to objectivism.

One result of this clarification should be the realization that what is often taken as an expression of relativism is not necessarily so. Consider this statement: "What is right for one person is not necessarily right for another." If the term *for* means "in the view of," then the statement simply states the fact that people do disagree. It states that "What is right in the view of one person is not what is right in the view of the other." However, this is not yet relativism. Relativism goes beyond this in its belief that this is all there is. Relativists will claim that there only are various points of view and that there is no way to reconcile what's right for one person with what's right for another. Similarly, if *for* is used in the sense "Insulin injections are good for some people but not for others," then the original statement is also not necessarily relativistic. It could, in fact, imply that health is a true or objective good and that what leads to it is good and what diminishes it is bad. For ethical relativism, on the other hand, there is no such objective good.

Is Relativism Self-Contradictory?
One significant argument against relativism is that it is self-contradictory. If relativists claim that all values or truths are relative, then it is possible to ask whether the claim of relativism is itself merely a relative truth or value judgment. But it might be that such an argument against relativism sets up a **straw man**, an easy-to-defeat version of the opposing position. The philosopher Richard Rorty argued that there are no relativists in the sense that is aimed at by this sort of an argument. Rorty explains,

> Relativism is the view that every belief on a certain topic, or perhaps about any topic, is as good as every other. No one holds this view. Except for the occasional cooperative freshman, one cannot find anybody who says that two incompatible opinions on an important topic are equally good. The philosophers who get called "relativists" are those who say that the grounds for choosing between such opinions are less algorithmic than had previously been thought.[13]

Rorty does not claim that any belief is as good as any other. Instead, he says that it is not so easy to figure out what is better or worse—as he puts it here, there are no "algorithms" that can be used to give precise answers about these things. His version of relativism attempts to avoid the charge of self-contradiction by connecting relativism to skepticism. Rorty has described his approach to things as "pragmatism" or "anti-foundationalism," by which he means that we find ourselves in the middle of things without access to any final account of ultimate reality or absolute values. For pragmatists such as Rorty, our judgments about things (including our judgment about ideas such as relativism) are provisional and embedded in contexts, cultures, and ways of life.

A related objection holds that a relativist has no way to define the group or perspective to which things are relative. With which group should my moral views coincide: my country, my state, my family, or myself and my peers? And how would we decide? Different groups to which I belong may have different moral views. Moreover, if a society changes its views, does this mean that morality changes? If 52 percent of its people once supported some war but later only 48 percent did, does this mean that earlier the war was just but it became unjust when the people changed their minds about it?

One problem that individual relativism faces is whether its view accords with personal experience. According to individual relativism, it seems that I should turn within and consult my moral feelings to solve a personal moral problem. This is often just the source of the difficulty, however; for when I look within, I find conflicting feelings. I want to know not how I *do* feel but how I *ought* to feel and what I *ought* to believe. But the view that there is something I possibly ought to believe would not be relativism.

As we saw above, a problem for both types of relativist lies in the implied belief that relativism is a more tolerant position than objectivism. The cultural relativist can hold that people in a society should be tolerant only if tolerance is one of the dominant values of their society. The claim that all people should be tolerant cannot be an objective or transcultural value, according to relativism. We can also question whether there is any reason for an individual relativist to be tolerant, especially if being tolerant means not just putting up with others who disagree with us but also listening to their positions and arguments. Why should I listen to another who disagrees with me? If ethical relativism is true, it cannot be because the other person's moral views may be better than mine in an objective sense, for there is no objectively better position. Objectivists might argue that their position provides a better basis for both believing that tolerance is an objective and transcultural good and that we ought to be open to others' views because they may be closer to the truth than ours are.

Relativism is sometimes simply a kind of intellectual laziness or a lack of moral courage. Rather than attempting to give reasons or arguments for my own position, I may hide behind some statement such as, "What is good for some is not necessarily good for others." I may say this simply to excuse myself from having to think about or be critical of my own ethical positions. Those who hold that there is an objective right and wrong may also do so uncritically. They may simply adopt the views of their parents or peers without evaluating those views themselves.

The major difficulty with an objectivist position is the problem it has in providing an alternative to the relativist position. The objectivist should give us reason to believe that there is an objective good. To pursue this problem in a little more detail, we will briefly examine two issues discussed by contemporary moral philosophers. One is the issue of the reality of moral value—**moral realism**; the other concerns the problem of deciding among plural goods—**moral pluralism**.

Moral Realism

Realism is the view that there exists a reality independent of those who know it. Most people are probably realists in this sense about a variety of things. We think, for example, that the external world is real in the sense that it actually exists, independently of our awareness of it. If a tree falls in the woods and no one is there, the event is still real and it still makes a sound. The sound waves are real, even if the subjective perception of them depends on a variety of contingent factors.

Now compare this to the situation regarding ethics. If I say that an act—say, saving a drowning child—is good, then what is the object of my moral judgment? Is there some real existing fact of goodness that I can somehow sense in this action? I can observe the act and its surrounding context. But in what sense, if any, do I observe the goodness of the act itself? The British philosopher G. E. Moore (discussed in Chapter 1) held that goodness is a specific quality that attaches to people or acts.[14] According to Moore, although we cannot observe the goodness of an act (we cannot hear, touch, taste, or see it), we intuit its presence. Philosophers like Moore have had difficulty explaining both the nature of the quality and the particular intuitive or moral sense by which we are supposed to perceive it.

Some moral philosophers who seek to support a realist view of morality attempt to explain moral reality as a relational matter—perhaps as a certain fit between actions and situations or actions and our innate sensibilities.[15] For example, because of innate human sensibilities, some say, we would not be able to approve of torturing the innocent. The problem, of course, is that not everyone agrees. To continue with this example, some people would be willing to torture an innocent person if they thought that by doing so they could elicit information about a terrorist attack or send a message to frighten would-be terrorists. And some activities that we might describe as torture—starvation, sleep deprivation, even beatings—can be viewed as valuable in religious contexts, in cultural initiation rituals, and even in hazing that occurs on sports teams or in fraternities. Moral realists will claim that such disagreements can be resolved by consulting the real objects of morality that are supposed to make judgments about good and evil true. But relativists wonder whether there are any actual or objective qualities of actions that are intuited in the same way by all observers, just as they doubt that moral truth rests on objective moral reality.

Moral Pluralism

3.6 Evaluate value pluralism.

Another problem nonrelativists or objectivists face is whether the good is one or many. According to some theories, there is one primary moral principle by which we can judge all actions. However, suppose this were not the case, that there were instead a variety of equally valid moral principles or equal moral values. For example, suppose that autonomy, justice, well-being, authenticity, and peace were all equally valuable. In this case, we would have a plurality of values. One version of pluralism is grounded in the claim that human beings are different and diverse, and that they should be allowed to flourish in their own way. As John Lachs explains in the essay that follows at the end of the chapter, "sanity and toleration demand that we allow each person to pursue his own, possibly unique form of fulfillment."[16] Nussbaum's capabilities approach, discussed earlier, is a kind of pluralism, as is Alain Locke's view. Nussbaum suggests that a common set of basic goods can be realized in multiple ways in different cultural contexts. And Locke insisted that tolerance and reciprocity were foundational values in a peaceful democratic world, which would in turn allow us to develop a reasonable pluralism.

Another version of value pluralism is W. D. Ross's account of what he calls *prima facie* duties. According to Ross, there are a variety of duties as seen in Table 3-4. To say that these duties are **prima facie** (which means "at first face" or "on first look") means that they are duties that are important and valuable at first blush, all other things being equal. It might be, however, that these duties conflict—because there are more than one of them. The fact of a plurality of goods or duties means that there will be conflicts of values.

The difficulty of this pluralistic account is that we face a problem when we are forced to choose between competing duties or values. For example, what do we do when we've made a promise to someone (and have a duty of fidelity) but that promise conflicts with the opportunity to do something good for someone else (in order to fulfill the duty of beneficence)? In such cases when duties or values conflict, we may be forced simply to choose one or the other for no reason or on the basis of something other than reason. Whether some rational and nonarbitrary way exists to make such decisions is an open question. Whether ultimate choices are thus subjective or can be grounded in an assessment of what is objectively best is a question not only about how we do behave but also about what is possible in matters of moral judgment.

Pluralism about morality may be understood as a form of relativism, which holds that there is no single objective or universal standard. In response, pluralists might hold that there are several equally plausible standards of value. But—as we saw in our discussion of religious pluralism in Chapter 2—it is possible for a pluralist to hold that there is some sort of convergence toward something unitary and universal in the realm of values. It might be that there is a hierarchy of values. But genuine pluralism points toward a sort of equality among values, which does not admit to a hierarchical organization of duties.

In subsequent chapters, we will examine several major ethical theories—utilitarianism, deontology, natural law theory, and the ethics of care. These theories are articulated from an objectivist or nonrelativist standpoint: defenders of these theories claim that the theory presents a substantive definition of what is good. But the problem of relativism returns as soon as we ask whether there is some way to compare or unite these normative theories—or whether we are left with incompatible accounts of the good.

Table 3-4   Ross's Prima Facie Duties[17]

1. Fidelity
2. Reparation
3. Gratitude
4. Beneficence
5. Non-maleficence
6. Justice
7. Self-improvement

Chapter Summary

3.1 What is the difference between descriptive relativism and metaethical relativism?

Descriptive relativism makes an empirical claim about the fact of diversity. Metaethical relativism makes a claim about the nature of value and moral judgment. Descriptive relativism is true: there is cultural diversity. But metaethical relativism is contentious and opens up complicated questions about the nature of value and moral judgment.

3.2 How might we evaluate key concepts such as objectivism, subjectivism, nihilism, skepticism, and moral realism?

Objectivism holds that values are objective, which can be understood in terms of the claim that moral judgments can be either true or false in comparison with some objective standard. Subjectivism denies that there are objective moral values, rather locating moral judgment in the opinions of individuals. Nihilism is the claim that there are no objective moral values. Skepticism suggests that we cannot know the objective source of value. And moral realism holds that there are in fact real, actual moral values. To evaluate these claims, you would need to consider epistemological and metaphysical ideas about the "reality" of value and about what we can know about value judgments. You might also want to see what kinds of practical results would follow from these concepts.

3.3 What are some of the arguments in favor of relativism?

Some relativists argue from the fact of diversity (from descriptive relativism) to the skeptical problem of how we might know objective values. Other arguments in favor of relativism develop from a concern to avoid ethnocentrism and a desire to be tolerant. Metaethical relativism depends on a metaphysical account of value, with most relativists denying that there is any reality to the supposed realm of value.

3.4 What are some of the arguments against relativism?

Relativism may be self-contradictory insofar as it claims something like "it is true that there is no truth. . . ." Relativism is also problematic if we want positive arguments about universal values and if we want to be able to criticize or reform cultural practices. Relativism is not necessarily connected with tolerance, since it is not possible to give an affirmative argument about tolerance from within a relativist point of view.

3.5 What's the difference between relativism and a commitment to tolerance?

Advocates of tolerance typically affirm the idea that tolerance itself is good. And the value of tolerance is often used to criticize cultures and practices that are intolerant. Relativism does not maintain that tolerance is good—rather, it is either a statement about the fact of diversity (i.e., descriptive relativism) or it is a metaphysical or epistemological claim about the fact that there are no objective values (or that we cannot know them).

3.6 How might we evaluate value pluralism?

Value pluralism is the idea, associated with authors such as Alain Locke, Martha Nussbaum, and even W. D. Ross that holds that it is not possible to reduce moral judgments to some singular, universal, or absolute claim about what is good. Sometimes value pluralism is very similar to relativism. But in other cases, as in Nussbaum's, it is related to the claim that there a few typical items on a list of values, or, as in Ross's case, that there is a set of prima facie values.

3.7 How might you defend your own ideas about relativism and how it is related to ethical judgment?

In order to defend a thesis about relativism, you would need to distinguish between descriptive relativism and metaethical relativism. You would also need to define key terms and standpoints—such as whether you are thinking about skepticism with regard to value or whether you are focused on something else, such as a nihilistic rejection of all value claims. A thesis about relativism would also need to consider whether and how relativism can be of use in thinking about issues such as cultural competence, tolerance, ethnocentrism, and so on.

Primary Source Readings

The first essay excerpted here is from Alain Locke. Published in 1935, in this essay Locke argues about the need to find a middle ground between subjectivity and objectivism. In the next reading excerpt, Pojman argues against relativism, suggesting that relativism and tolerance are not necessarily linked. In the following reading, John Lachs offers a defense of a form of relativism that is pluralistic and tolerant and that is grounded in a claim about the diversity of human nature. This section concludes with an excerpt on feminist metaethics and relativism published by Anita Superson in 2017. Superson suggests that relativism makes critique impossible.

Reading 3-1   Values and Imperatives | Alain Locke

Study Questions

As you read the excerpt, please consider the following questions:

1. Why does Locke suggest that values are not abstract, disembodied, or absolute?

2. What do you suppose Locke means when he calls for us to focus on a "functional" analysis of values?

3. Do you agree with Locke that "value pluralism" will not result in "value-anarchy"?

All philosophies, it seems to me, are in ultimate derivation philosophies of life and not of abstract, disembodied "objective" reality; products of time, place and situation, and thus systems of timed history rather than timeless eternity.…

To my thinking, the gravest problem of contemporary philosophy is how to ground some normative principle or criterion of objective validity for values without resort to dogmatism and absolutism on the intellectual plane, and without falling into their corollaries, on the plane of social behavior and action, of intolerance and mass coercion. This calls for a functional analysis of value norms and a search for normative principles in the immediate context of valuation.…

What seems most needed is some middle ground between these extremes of subjectivism and objectivism. The natural distinctions of values and their functional criteria surely lie somewhere in between the atomistic relativism of a pleasure-pain scale and the colorless, uniformitarian criterion of logic—the latter more of a straightjacket for value qualities than the old intellectualist trinity of Beauty, Truth and Good. Flesh and blood values may not be as universal or objective as logical truths and schematized judgments, but they are not thereby deprived of some relative objectivity and universality of their own.

At the same time that it takes sides against the old absolutism and invalidates the summum bonum principle; this type of value pluralism does not invite the chaos of value-anarchy or the complete laissez faire of extreme value individualism. It rejects equally trying to reduce value distinctions to the flat continuum of a pleasure-pain economy or to a pragmatic instrumentalism of ends-means relations. Of course, we need the colorless, common-denominator order of factual reality and objectivity (although that itself serves a primary value as a mechanism of the coordination of experience), but values simply do not reduce to it. To set values over against facts does not effectively neutralize values. Since we cannot banish our imperatives, we must find some principle of keeping them within bounds. It should be possible to maintain some norms as functional and native to the process of experience,

"Values and Imperatives," from *The Works of Alain Locke*, ed. Charles Molesworth (Oxford, UK: Oxford University Press, 2012).

without justifying arbitrary absolutes, and to uphold some categoricals without calling down fire from heaven....

However, no one can sensibly expect a sudden or complete change in our value behavior from any transformation, however radical, in our value theory.

Relativism will have to slowly tame the wild force of our imperatives. There will be no sudden recanting of chronic, traditional absolutisms, no complete undermining of orthodoxies, no huge, overwhelming accessions of tolerance. But absolutism is doomed in the increasing variety of human experience.

Reading 3-2   Who's to Judge? | Louis Pojman

Study Questions

As you read the excerpt, please consider the following questions:

1. How does Pojman link ethnocentrism (what he calls "ethnocentricism") to relativism?

2. How does Pojman explain the connection (or lack thereof) between cultural relativism and the idea of tolerance?

3. Why does Pojman think we are entitled to judge other cultures?

Today we condemn ethnocentricism, the uncritical belief in the inherent superiority of one's own culture, as a variety of prejudice tantamount to racism and sexism.... This rejection of ethnocentrism in the West has contributed to a general shift in public opinion about morality, so that for a growing number of Westerners, consciousness-raising about the validity of other ways of life has led to a gradual erosion of belief in moral *objectivism*, the view that there are universal moral principles, valid for all people at all times and climes.

Recognizing the importance of our social environment in generating customs and beliefs, many people suppose that ethical relativism is the correct ethical theory. Furthermore, they are drawn to it for its liberal philosophical stance. It seems to be an enlightened response to the sin of ethnocentricity, and it seems to entail or strongly imply an attitude of tolerance towards other cultures....

Tolerance is certainly a virtue, but is this a good argument for it? I think not. If morality simply is relative to each culture then if the culture does not have a principle of tolerance, its members have no obligation to be tolerant.... From a relativistic point of view there is no more reason to be tolerant than to be intolerant, and neither stance is objectively morally better than the other.

Not only do relativists fail to offer a basis for criticizing those who are intolerant, but they cannot rationally criticize anyone who espouses what they might regard as a heinous principle. If, as seems to be the case, valid criticism supposes an objective or impartial standard, relativists cannot morally criticize anyone outside their own culture. Adolf Hitler's genocidal actions, so long as they are culturally accepted, are as morally legitimate as Mother Teresa's works of mercy....

The relativist may argue that in fact we don't have an obvious impartial standard from which to judge. "Who's to say which culture is right and which is wrong?" But this seems to be dubious. We can reason and perform thought experiments in order to make a case for one system over another. We may not be able to *know* with certainty that our moral beliefs are closer to the truth than those of another culture or those of others within our own culture, but we may be *justified* in believing that they are. If we can be closer to the truth regarding factual or scientific matters, why can't we be closer to the truth on moral matters? Why can't a culture simply be confused or wrong about its moral perceptions?...

"Who's to Judge?", by Louis Pojman. From *Vice and Virtue in Everyday Life*, 6e, Sommers & Sommers. © 2003 Cengage Learning. Reprinted by permission of Gertrude "Trudy" Pojman.

To take such a stand is not to commit the fallacy of ethnocentricism, for we are seeking to derive principles through critical reason, not simply uncritical acceptance of one's own mores....

So...."Who's to judge what's right or wrong?" the answer is: *We are*. We are to do so on the basis of the best reasoning we can bring forth and with sympathy and understanding.

Reading 3-3   Relativism and Its Benefits | John Lachs

Study Questions

As you read the excerpt, please consider the following questions:

1. What does Lachs mean when he says that values are about "who we are"?

2. How is Lachs's account of the variety of human natures connected to his defense of tolerance?

3. What are the benefits of relativism, as imagined by Lachs?

There is a relativism that many candid and tolerant minds spontaneously believe. Human nature is various: this variety, due to biological, social and psychological conditions, must be construed not as a threat or an evil, but as a God-given bounty of being. A variety of natures implies a variety of perfections. Only the egotist, committed to seeing pale replicas of himself everywhere in the world, would want to impose the same values and the same mode of behavior on every living soul. Sanity and toleration demand that we allow each person to pursue his own, possibly unique form of fulfillment; if we had even a vestige of Christian love, we would rejoice in seeing the growth of any man toward his goal.

Values vary with the individual's nature. The good, therefore, is not a question of what we think or how we feel but of who we are. A person's nature, though not unchanging, is perfectly definite. This makes it possible for him to progress in self-knowledge. It also renders the goals that would fulfill him definable and his values precise. These values may differ from the ideal of the next man, but they are not less vital or legitimate.

Would moral or social anarchy not flow if we acted as though this view were true? Not in the least. If the nature of the individual determines his values, similar natures yield similar commitments. The fact that human beings live in cooperative societies is the best evidence that their natures are similar or at least compatible. This is assured by processes of socialization which are, on occasion, so successful that even people left free to do precisely what they want continue to do their usual, useful tasks. What little self-realization there may be that interferes with the fulfillment of others can be readily controlled by threats or a measure of force. In an orchestra each instrument plays its own tune; is this reason for saying that there is anarchy in the pit? The fact that values are individual does not entail that people must fail to agree on common goods and goals.

Consider the benefits that would accrue if we could make this relativism generally accepted. The view is a secular variant of the beautiful thought of many theologians that even the least of his creatures has dignity and justification in the eyes of God. If sincerely believed, this thought could transform the soul. It would help allay our suspicion of all things alien. It could render us more modest and loving by showing the monstrous egotism displayed in judging another. As a result, we may develop a more tolerant and helpful attitude toward life-styles and values different from those we like or admire: we could then begin to appreciate moral variety or the bounty of fulfillment and perfection open to humans....

John Lachs, "Relativism and Its Benefits," in *Soundings: An Interdisciplinary Journal* 56: 3 (Fall 1973), pp. 312–322.

Reading 3-4   On Relativism | Anita Superson

Study Questions

As you read the excerpt, please consider the following questions:

1. Why does Superson suggest that feminist critique may need to be more absolutist than relativist to have "any bite"?

2. What does Superson suggest about the relationship between relativism and tolerance?

3. What might Superson mean when she suggests defending universal values but "in a non-partriarchal way"?

Why would feminists endorse moral relativism? If rape, or more generally, oppression is morally wrong, it would seem that it is wrong universally, and that there is some fact about it that explains its wrongness. Indeed, for any feminist claims about oppression to have any bite, it would seem that moral absolutism must be true.

One of the main reasons why some feminists have hesitations about moral absolutism is the worry about judging other cultures and tolerance. Since women have been judged throughout history according to patriarchal standards ... some feminists believe that we should refrain from judging women any further. A common belief is that if we are moral relativist, the only judgments we can legitimately make are ones about persons in our own culture who fail to live up to the culture's moral code. Additionally, Western feminists have been accused of unfairly judging women in other cultures while not pointing the finger at women in their own culture for participating in patriarchal practices...

Having said all this, however, it is false that moral relativism necessarily endorses tolerance, since it is an open question whether any particular moral code endorses tolerance. Thus this is not a good reason for feminists to favor relativism over absolutism. Additionally, Margaret Urban Walker argues that it is possible to criticize prevailing moral standards while recognizing that morality is culturally and socially situated. Walker believes that we justify and critique morality from the standpoint of our own society's moral perspective, rather than from the standpoint of an objective,

universal standard, in a way that is sensitive to the standpoint of the nonprivileged in our society....

Another reason feminists might shy away from moral absolutism is their belief that it can lead to moral imperialism, having moral standards, particularly ones grounded in patriarchy, dictated for all. To avoid moral imperialism, some feminists endorse multiculturalism, the view that minority cultures should be protected by special group rights or privileges. But other feminists such as Susan Moller Okin urge that feminists should be skeptical about multiculturalism because it is often at odds with the basic tenets of feminism—that women should not be disadvantaged by their sex, that they have human dignity equal to that of men, and that they should have the same opportunity as men to live fulfilling and freely chosen lives....

But this raises a third concern that feminists have about moral absolutism, namely, how do we defend universal values in a non-patriarchal way? How do we show, non-paternalistically, that some practices are objectively bad for women?...

Most feminists also believe that we have made feminist progress, politically, socially, and economically, though we still have a way to go. Were moral relativism true there could be no feminist moral progress, since progress implies a standard by which we measure improvement.

Anita Superson, "Feminist Metaethics," in Ann Garry, Serene J. Khader, Alison Stone, eds., *The Routledge Companion to Feminist Philosophy* (New York: Routledge, 2017).

Review Exercises

1. Are there universal, objective moral values? Or are you convinced that relativism is true?

2. What is the difference between individual relativism (subjectivism) and social or cultural relativism?

3. What is the difference between the descriptive claim that people do differ in their moral beliefs and the metaethical theory of relativism?

4. Do toleration, open-mindedness, and cultural competence depend on a commitment to cultural relativism?

5. How would you know whether a moral disagreement was based on a basic difference in moral values or a disagreement about facts? As an example, consider the issue of climate change discussed in the chapter. Are there other examples you can think of?

6. What is moral realism? How does your understanding about the reality of the external world differ from your intuitions about morality?

7. Why might social critics such as feminists be in favor of or against relativism?

Knowledge Check Answer Key

1. **b.** Metaethical relativism is best described as the idea that there are no universal or objective norms.

2. **d.** Nihilism is the idea that denies that objective moral values exist.

3. **b.** Friedrich Nietzsche's form of relativism is sometimes called perspectivism.

4. **a.** Cultural competence suggests that it is good to understand other people's cultures.

4 Egoism, Altruism, and the Social Contract

Learning Outcomes

After reading this chapter, you should be able to:

4.1 Describe differences between descriptive (or psychological) egoism and ethical egoism.

4.2 Define key terms: altruism, empathy, compassion, love.

4.3 Explain criticisms of altruism and the importance of reciprocal altruism.

4.4 Explain the challenge posed by the prisoner's dilemma.

4.5 Describe how the social contract provides a solution to problems of egoism.

4.6 Discuss how egoism is connected to laissez-faire capitalism and economics.

4.7 Evaluate the conflict between impartiality, egoism, and care.

4.8 Defend your own ideas about egoism, altruism, and the social contract.

Community Service

In many schools, colleges, and universities, students are encouraged and even required to engage in altruistic community service projects. Elementary school students participate in fundraisers and food drives; older students give blood and engage in other humanitarian activities. Often these projects are part of a deliberate effort to teach kindness, develop compassion, and promote concern for the needy. At the university level, service projects are frequently coordi-

iStock.com/kieferpix

nated by clubs, fraternities, and sororities. And some universities have "service learning" courses in which students get credit for participating in service projects. But if you get credit for it, is it really altruistic? Some students engage in these activities in a deliberate effort to pad their résumés. A record of community service is viewed as a plus on college and scholarship applications. And job seekers often brag about their volunteer service. Some critics of service learning might complain that there is something wrong about people engaging in altruistic behavior for selfish reasons. But others may argue in response that required service can help to teach people the value of altruism, kindness, and compassion.

What Do You Think?

1. Is it a good idea that schools and universities promote community service?
2. Is it really altruistic service if it is required?
3. Is it wrong for people to engage in service activities as a way of padding a résumé?
4. Can community service help people learn the value of altruism even if they are motivated to participate for egoistic reasons?

Introduction

4.1 Describe differences between descriptive (or psychological) egoism and ethical egoism.

Morality seems to require that individuals overcome egoism. In some cases, we even seem to think that individuals should sacrifice their own selfish interests for the benefit of others. Moral traditions tend to praise altruists and condemn egoists. In the Christian tradition, the parable of the Good Samaritan provides a memorable illustration that explores the idea of loving your neighbor as yourself. This idea is not unique to Christianity. The Jewish sage Rabbi Hillel said, in the first century BCE, "Do not do to others that which is hateful." Other traditions similarly emphasize the importance of altruism, love, and compassion. One of the five pillars of Islam is *almsgiving*, which means giving to the needy. Sikhism includes the idea of *seva*, which means selfless, voluntary service. Buddhists focus on the importance of compassion for all sentient beings. And even in secular morality, it is common to say, as Paul Kurtz does, that altruism is "intrinsic to the good life."[1]

Altruism means, most basically, concern for the well-being of others. Some versions of altruism may even appear to hold that truly self-sacrificial behavior is the peak of moral development. Unlike altruists, egoists are primarily concerned with their own well-being. Sometimes egoists are purely selfish, even to the point of being willing to take advantage of others. But less selfish defenders of egoism may claim that egoism is not about taking advantage or being uncaring. Rather, egoism may be a descriptive thesis about human behavior, which claims that even apparently altruistic behavior is ultimately motivated by self-interest. From this perspective, people behave altruistically because they hope to gain something in return, even behaving altruistically in hopes of developing social relations of cooperation, which are valuable in the long run. A further form of egoism holds that we would all be better off if people just looked out for themselves and left other people alone. From an egoistic perspective, social rules can be understood as resulting from agreements among rational and self-interested individuals. That idea is known as the **social contract theory,** which posits that we join together and obey a common set of rules out of a kind of "enlightened self-interest."

Popular culture is full of examples of the conflict between egoism and altruism. Television programs like *Survivor* create circumstances in which people are forced to forge short-term alliances to maximize their own self-interest. The film and book *The Hunger Games* shows us a life-and-death competition in which children struggle for survival in a war of all against all. In these contexts, egoism is to be expected and altruism is an exceptional and heroic virtue.

Disagreements about ethics and political life often rest on divergent ideas about human nature. We wonder whether people are basically egoistic or altruistic, whether we are motivated by self-interest or are able to genuinely concern ourselves with the interests of others. Our conception of social organizations, politics, and the law often is often determined by what we think about the motives of individuals. Are individuals basically cooperative or competitive? Are they motivated primarily by egoistic or altruistic concerns? Should social organizations be set up to minimize the dangers of an inevitable cutthroat competition? Or is there a more cooperative and altruistic basis for social cooperation?

To think about these issues, we need to consider a basic empirical question: Are people essentially selfish and primarily motivated by self-interest, or are they altruistic and motivated by concern for others? We also have to ask a normative question: Is selfishness good or bad? These two concerns illustrate two different versions or meanings of egoism and altruism. One version is descriptive and answers the empirical question. According to this idea, egoism (or altruism) is a theory that describes what people are like. Simply put, **descriptive egoism** holds that people are basically self-centered or selfish; that is, they primarily pursue their own self-interest. Often referred to as **psychological egoism,** it is a theory about how people behave or why they do what they do.

Egoism is opposed to altruism. Altruism is often viewed as pure concern for the well-being of others. Sometimes altruism is thought to require entirely unselfish behavior, even to the point at which we sacrifice ourselves for others. But a broader conception of altruism involves a variety of what psychologists call **pro-social behaviors**—that is, behaviors that are not primarily self-interested and that are motivated by basic concern for others.

Empathy, Compassion, and Love

4.2 Define key terms: altruism, empathy, compassion, love.

The empirical question of whether human beings are motivated by self-interest or by non-self-interested concern for others is not easy to answer. How do we really know what motivates others? Indeed, are you sure that you know what motivates *you* all of the time? Scientists have examined this question from various perspectives. Psychological studies, including accounts of developmental psychology, can give us some insight into what actually motivates people. These studies are connected to other studies that explore our capacity for empathy, compassion, and love.

It's worth distinguishing these ideas here: **empathy** is the psychological capacity to understand what someone else is experiencing; **compassion** builds on that capacity and includes the desire to help alleviate

suffering; while **love** appears to be more about intimacy and attachment. These distinctions are slippery, of course. Some varieties of love point in the direction of compassion and altruism. This is the idea behind so-called "brotherly love," which we discussed in Chapter 2 in relation to Eleanor Roosevelt, and which we might call, in a more inclusive formulation, "neighborly love" or even "universal love." Of course, love can also be narrowly focused on a closed circle of intimacy. Or love may grow beyond that narrow focus in a more universal direction. Altruistic behavior may be motivated and understood in various ways. It might be motivated by a narrow concern for our friends and loved ones. Or it might come from a more general compassion—from the desire to help those who are suffering or even from a kind of universal love. In evaluating altruistic behaviors, we also ought to consider the question of motivation.

Another line of inquiry looks at pro-social behavior from an evolutionary perspective. It turns out that pro-social cooperation produces an evolutionary advantage, especially in social species of animals such as our own. Individuals who cooperate with others tend to be able to pass on their genes better than selfish egoists and those who cheat. This is especially true when we cooperate with and support those who are related to us. Our genes get passed on when we are altruistic toward our close relations, helping those who share our genes to survive. This might explain why parents are willing to sacrifice for their own children—but not so willing to sacrifice for children to whom they are not related. It might also explain why we may be more willing to help a cousin than a stranger. Such an evolutionary explanation points toward instinctive forces that lie below the surface of our more explicit motivations and intentions.

Of course, an account of human behavior that is solely focused on the ways that pro-social behavior functions in evolutionary contexts fails to consider the subjective side of experience and human freedom. Sometimes our motivations and intentions run at cross-purposes to attitudes and behaviors that provide evolutionary advantage. Furthermore, it is possible to ask a normative question with regard to the descriptive science of pro-social behavior. We may be instinctively motivated to help those to whom we are more closely

Pictorial Press Ltd/Alamy Stock Photo

Figure 4-1 Films such as *The Hunger Games* illustrate conflicts between egoism and altruism.

related. But should we really help our close relations and only our close relations? The term **nepotism** is used to condemn those who show favoritism to their close relations. Maybe we should ignore everyone else and focus only on our own needs and interests. Or maybe we should focus our concern more broadly on humanity at large, possibly even extending moral concern to members of other species.

The Debate about Egoism and Altruism

4.3 Explain criticisms of altruism and the importance of reciprocal altruism.

We must, then, ask a moral question with regard to the empirical science of egoism and altruism. *Should* we be motivated by self-interest, or *should* we be concerned with the well-being of others? As a normative theory, **ethical egoism** holds that it is good for people to pursue their own self-interest. Some versions of ethical egoism also hold that altruism is misguided and wrong. In this view, people should pursue their own self-interest, while minding their own business and ignoring others. In defense of this idea, ethical egoists may argue that altruism breeds dependency and undermines the self-esteem of those who receive benefits and gifts from do-gooder altruists.

Various authors have defended egoism. One of the most influential is the novelist and essayist Ayn Rand. Rand's ideas are especially influential among political conservatives in the United States. Former U.S. congressman Paul Ryan (Mitt Romney's vice-presidential running mate in 2012 and Speaker of the House of Representatives in 2016) reportedly gave copies of Ayn Rand's books to his staff.[2] Rand's works are also admired by Donald Trump and by leading figures in Silicon Valley, including the late Steve Jobs and Peter Thiel.[3] Congressman Ryan explained that his reading of Ayn Rand was "the reason I got involved in public service."[4] The fans of Rand's philosophy tend to hold to a libertarian ideology that admires entrepreneurial spirit and which emphasizes laissez-faire capitalism and limited government intervention (these political and economic issues are discussed in more detail in Chapter 14).

A fiercely individualistic émigré from Bolshevik Russia, Ayn Rand thought that altruism was pernicious. She argued that altruistic morality "regards man as a sacrificial animal" and that altruism "holds that man has no right to exist for his own sake, that service to others is the only justification of his existence, and that self-sacrifice is his highest moral duty, virtue and value." Her argument goes on to present the altruistic idea of self-sacrifice as a kind of death wish: "altruism holds *death* as its ultimate goal and standard of value—and it is logical that renunciation, resignation, self-denial, and every other form of suffering, including self-destruction, are the virtues it advocates."[5]

While Rand condemns altruism, most mainstream moralists tend to hold that altruism is better than egoism. Altruistic morality tends to praise the idea of setting self-interest aside and attending to the needs of others. The basic principle of altruism is outlined in the Golden Rule—that you should "do unto others as you would have them do unto you." Another version of this idea focuses on the importance of love, saying that you should love your neighbor as yourself. Or as Rabbi Hillel put it, as we stated earlier, "Do not do to others that which is hateful."

Some argue that the moral point of view is one that involves some basic level of altruism. While altruists need not go to the extremes that Rand criticizes—in advocating suicidal self-sacrifice, for example—most people

Figure 4-2 Ayn Rand (1905–1982) was a well-known proponent of egoism.

tend to think that pro-social and cooperative behavior are morally praiseworthy. Indeed, philosophers such as Kurt Baier, James Sterba, and Alan Gewirth have argued in various ways that egoism is basically inconsistent. As Gewirth explains, the egoist's moral claims do not apply to all other people in the same way that they apply to himself.[6] Baier explains that one of our "most widely held moral convictions" is that "in certain circumstances it is morally wrong to promote one's own best interest or greatest good."[7] The prevailing tendency in moral theory aims toward overcoming egoism and learning to develop an altruistic (or at least impartial and non-self-interested) point of view. Philosophers and moral psychologists have made this argument. It has also been articulated eloquently by the Dalai Lama, who said:

> Ultimately, humanity is one and this small planet is our only home, If we are to protect this home of ours, each of us needs to experience a vivid sense of universal altruism."[8]

A further issue is the question of how social cooperation is supposed to occur. Defenders of altruism can argue that there is something natural about developing and nurturing caring relationships with others—perhaps grounded in an account of natural family bonds or group belonging. It may appear to be more difficult for egoists to explain how self-interested egoists can avoid brutal and counterproductive competition and develop a system of cooperation. But cooperation can be explained as paying off in terms of self-interest. From the perspective of egoism, it is rational for self-interested persons to cooperate, since cooperation tends to produce good outcomes for those who cooperate. One way of describing this is in terms of **reciprocal altruism**, which holds that altruistic behavior makes sense for self-interested persons when it is repaid in kind. A more elaborate development of reciprocal altruism is found in the social contract theory, which holds that it is in each person's self-interest to join with others in a social contract that helps us each to maximize our self-interest in community with others. We discuss the social contract theory in more detail toward the end of this chapter.

Psychological Egoism

What Is Psychological Egoism?

Psychological egoism is a descriptive theory about our motivations and interests. In one interpretation, it might be taken to say that people are basically selfish. Here, psychological egoism holds that people usually or always act for their own narrow and short-range self-interest. But a different formulation of this theory asserts that although people do act for their own self-interest, this self-interest is to be understood more broadly and as being more concerned with long-term outcomes. Thus, we might distinguish between acting selfishly and acting in our own self-interest.

In the broader view, many things are in a person's interest: good health, satisfaction in a career or work, prestige, self-respect, family, and friends. Moreover, if we really wanted to attain these things, we would need to avoid shortsighted selfishness. For example, we would have to be self-disciplined in diet and lifestyle to be healthy. We would need to plan long-term for a career. And we would need to be concerned about others and not be overbearing if we wanted to make and retain friends.

Everett Collection Inc/Alamy Stock Photo

However, a friendly egoist does not actually need to be concerned about others but only to *appear* to be concerned. In this view, doing good to others would be not for the sake of others but, rather, to enable one to call on those friends when they are needed. This would be helping a friend not for the friend's sake but for one's own sake.

Putting the matter in this way also raises another question about how to formulate this theory. Is psychological egoism a theory according to which people always act in their own best interests? Or does it hold that people are always motivated by the desire to attain their own best interests? The first version would be easily refuted; we notice that people do not always do what is best for them. They eat too much, choose the wrong careers, waste time, and so forth. This may be because they do not have sufficient knowledge to be good judges of what is in their best interests. Or it may be because of a phenomenon known as **weakness of will**. For example, I may want to lose weight or get an *A* in a course but may fail to do what I have to do in order to achieve my goal. Philosophers have puzzled over this problem, which is also called the problem of **akrasia** (a Greek term for weakness of will). This is a complex issue in moral psychology; to treat it adequately would take us beyond what we can do here.[9] But the basic concern is why we fail to do the things we know we ought to do. If we really know what we ought to do, it might seem that we would never fail to do it.

On the other hand, it might be true that people always do what they *think* is best for them. Another version of psychological egoism asserts that human beings act for the sake of their own best interests. In this version, the idea is not that people sometimes or always act in their own interests, but that this is the only thing that ultimately motivates people. If they sometimes act for others, it is only because they think that it is in their own best interests to do so. A stronger version of psychological egoism asserts that people cannot do otherwise than act for the sake of their own interests. But how would we know this? We know how people act, but how could we show that they cannot act otherwise?

Is Psychological Egoism True?

Some of our most cherished social values may involve more selfish motivation than we generally like to admit.

Consider the following story about Abraham Lincoln.[10] It is reported that one day as he was riding in a coach over a bridge, he heard a mother pig squealing. Her piglets were drowning after having fallen into the creek and she could not get them out. Lincoln supposedly asked the coachman to stop, waded into the creek, and rescued the piglets. When his companion cited this as an example of unselfishness, Lincoln responded that it was not for the sake of the pigs that he acted as he did. Rather, it was because he would have no peace later when he recalled the incident if he did not do something about it now. In other words, although it seemed unselfish, his action was self-centered. Advocates for psychological egoism often draw on such accounts of underlying selfish motivations to bolster their arguments.

But how are we to evaluate the claims of psychological egoism? As a theory about human motivation, it is difficult, if not impossible, to prove. How do we assess the motivations of people? We cannot just assume that apparently altruistic individuals are acting for the sake of the selfish satisfaction they receive from what they do. Nor can we ask them, for individuals are often poor judges of what actually motivates them. We commonly hear or say to ourselves, "I don't know why I did that!"

Furthermore, it is difficult to distinguish different sources of our motivations. Are we innately egoistic or altruistic—that is, are we born with a tendency toward egoism or altruism? Or do our cultural values contribute to our egoistic (or altruistic) tendencies? For example, we might consider differences in socialization between boys and girls. It might be that female children are expected to be altruistic and caring, while male children are taught to be independent and self-motivated. And it might be that these differences in socialization are also dependent on other cultural differences, with boys and girls from different cultures growing up with divergent dispositions toward altruism or egoism.

Leaving aside the issue of socialization, suppose that people do, in fact, get satisfaction from helping others. This is not the same thing as acting for the purpose of getting that satisfaction. What psychological egoism needs to show is not that people get satisfaction from what they do, but that achieving such satisfaction is their aim. Now, we can find at least some examples in our own actions to test this theory. Do we read the book to get satisfaction or to learn something? Do we pursue that career opportunity because of the satisfaction that we think it will bring or because of the nature of the opportunity? Do we volunteer to help the sick or the needy because we think it will give us personal satisfaction or because we think it will actually help someone? The opening vignette of this chapter asked you to consider this question in the context of community service: do we engage in volunteer and service projects because we want to help others or because we want to pad our résumés?

There are deep psychological conundrums about our motivations. Perhaps we believe we are acting selflessly but actually find our egos inflating with pride as we consider our good deeds. Does this make us egoistic? Or is it just the nature of mixed motivations and the complexity of moral and social life? Our lives involve many such confusions and complexity. One has to do with the problem of directly aiming at satisfaction, pleasure, or happiness. Henry Sidgwick described this as the **paradox of hedonism**: "The impulse toward pleasure, if too predominant, defeats its own aim."[11] We probably have a better chance of being happy if we do not aim at happiness itself, but obtain happiness while pursuing other worthwhile objects. We often discover happiness along the way, as a by-product of good activities. And sometimes we experience joy and pride at engaging in altruistic projects. This experience of happiness does not necessarily prove that our actions are egoistic.

Psychological egoism, as a theory about human motivation, is especially difficult to prove. It also can't be disproved or falsified. Even if it were shown that we *often* act for the sake of our own interest or satisfaction, that is not enough to prove that psychological egoism is true. According to this theory, we must show that people *always* act to promote their own interests. Next, we need to consider whether this has any relevance to the normative question of how we *ought* to act.

Ethical Egoism

What Is Ethical Egoism?

Ethical egoism is a normative theory. It is a theory about what we *ought* to do, how we *ought* to act. As with psychological egoism, we can formulate ethical egoism in different ways. One version is *individual*

ethical egoism. According to this version, I ought to look out only for my own interests. I ought to be concerned about others only to the extent that this concern also contributes to my own interests. A slightly broader formulation of ethical egoism, sometimes called *universal ethical egoism*, maintains that people ought to look out for and seek only their own best interests. As in the individual form, in this second version, people ought to help others only when and to the extent that it is in their own best interests to do so. It is possible to explain cooperation from this perspective as a kind of *reciprocal altruism*: we cooperate because we each see that it is in our own self-interest to cooperate. As the saying goes, I'll scratch your back if you scratch mine. If this is an entirely egoistic idea, then what I really want is to get my back scratched (something I cannot do for myself), and I realize that in order to get what I want, I have to give you something you want in return. This can also be understood as a kind of *enlightened self-interest* that understands the importance of cooperative activity in a world in which we maximize our own self-interest by cooperating with others.

Is Ethical Egoism a Good Theory?

We can evaluate ethical egoism in several ways. We will consider its grounding in psychological egoism and its consistency or coherence. We will also consider how it explains social cooperation in the social contract theory as well as its derivation from economic theory. Finally, we will consider its conformity to commonsense moral views.

Grounding in Psychological Egoism Let us consider first whether psychological egoism, if true, would provide a good foundation for ethical egoism. It might be that we should affirm ethical egoism because people are basically and unavoidably egoistic. But recall the discussion of the naturalistic fallacy in Chapter 1: it is not clear that we can derive the *value* of ethical egoism from the *fact* of psychological egoism. If people were in fact always motivated by their own interests, would that be a good reason to hold that they *ought* to be so motivated? It seems superfluous to tell people that they ought to do what they always do anyway or will do, no matter what. One would think that at least sometimes one of the functions of moral language is to try to motivate ourselves or others to do what we are not inclined to do. For example, I might tell myself that even though I could benefit by cheating on a test, it is wrong, and so I should not do it.

Furthermore, the fact that we do behave in a certain way seems a poor reason for believing that we ought to do so. If people always cheated, would that make cheating right? Thus, although it may at first seem reasonable to rely on a belief about people's basic selfishness to prove that people ought to look out for themselves alone, this seems far from convincing.

Consistency or Coherence Universal ethical egoism may be inconsistent or incoherent. Ethical egoism holds that everyone ought to seek their own best interests. But could anyone consistently support such a view? Wouldn't this mean that we would want our own best interests served and, at the same time, be willing to allow that others serve their interests—even to our own detriment? If food was scarce, then I would want enough for myself, and yet, at the same time, I would have to say that I should not have it for myself when another needs it to survive. This view seems to have an internal inconsistency. We might compare it to playing a game in which I can say that the other player ought to block my move, even though, at the same time, I hope that they do not do so.

The Prisoner's Dilemma

4.4 Explain the challenge posed by the prisoner's dilemma.

A serious problem plaguing agreements that are made among egoists is the temptation to cheat. If I agree to scratch your back after you scratch mine, what guarantee do you have that I will follow through on my promise once I've gotten my back scratched? If we are both convinced that human beings are basically egoistic, then you will suspect that I will cheat (and I'll suspect that you will cheat), in which case it will be difficult to cooperate. For this reason, there is a worry that egoism will lead to conflict and war. To prevent this from happening, even egoists might agree that we need

something external to ourselves to guarantee that we do not renege on our promises. This is the basis for the development of the social contract, which can be interpreted as an agreement made by self-interested persons who want to establish a legal system that ensures promises are kept and that prevents cheating by egoists.

The problem for egoism can be clarified with reference to a thought experiment known as **the prisoner's dilemma**. Imagine that the police arrest two suspects, X and Y. The cops have the prisoners in two separate rooms. They offer each prisoner the following deal: If you betray the other suspect, you will go free instead of getting a twenty-year term in prison; but if you both betray each other, you will each end up with ten years in prison. On the other hand, if both prisoners keep their mouths shut and refuse to betray each other, there will be no conviction and they will both go free. The choices look like this (Table 4-1):

For the prisoners, the best option is if they coordinate their choices and both refuse to betray each other. But if the prisoners suspect each other of being self-interested egoists, they will not trust each other. Each will suspect the other of betrayal in pursuit of a better deal. And so it is likely that self-interested prisoners will end up with less-than-optimal outcomes. Each prisoner will suspect the other of operating out of self-interested motives that will lead to cheating and reneging on prior promises. The prisoner's dilemma thought experiment is often used as a model to show why we need some larger structure to ensure that we do not break our promises. It might be that morality itself provides that larger structure: if we would just agree to comply with the dictates of morality, we would be able to guarantee cooperation. But if there are egoists who would break moral rules when they think that they can get away with it, we might need

Table 4-1 The Choices in the Prisoner's Dilemma

	Y betrays X	Y does not betray X
X betrays Y	Each ends up with 10 years	X goes free; Y gets 20 years
X does not betray Y	Y goes free; X gets 20 years	Each goes free

something stronger than morality—we might need an enforcement mechanism, that is, something like a legal and political system that helps to guarantee cooperation. It is possible, then, that rational, self-interested individuals would agree to something like a social contract.

The Social Contract

4.5 Describe how the social contract provides a solution to problems of egoism.

A justification of the legal system can be grounded in the rational self-interest of human beings. The idea of the social contract is that it is rational for self-interested individuals to join together and submit to the rule of law in order to ensure that promises are kept and that social cooperation will occur. This idea has been very influential in political philosophy, where it is associated with ideas found in Thomas Hobbes, John Locke, Jean-Jacques Rousseau, and others. As a political theory, it sometimes appeals to a historical circumstance in which individuals come together and agree to a system of law. Of course, it unlikely that there is an actual historical event when the social contract was formed. And critics of the idea will point out that most actual states were not formed by consent and agreement. Indeed, history shows us that states often result from conquest and war—and even in states that have moments of consent and agreement (as in the American Constitutional Convention), there are some who are excluded (enslaved people, women, and others) from the original contract situation. In moral theory, the idea of the social contract theory is not necessarily concerned with the founding of a legal system. Rather, it is an attempt to explain how and why egoists can agree to a set of moral principles that limit them in pursuing their own self-interest. Moral versions of the social contract idea are sometimes called *contractarianism* or *contractualism*. There are subtle differences between these ideas. But the basic thought it that morality is the result of an agreement among people, whether these contractors are viewed as self-interested egoists seeking to maximize self-interest or as free and rational beings who understand the importance of trust, promise-keeping, and other moral goods. One important point about this approach to morality is that it differs from other approaches such as the divine command theory, which hold that there is a transcendent source of morality, or from the natural law theory, which holds that moral principles are woven into the structure of the world.

▶ **Knowledge Check**   Answers appear at the end of the chapter.

1. Psychological egoism is the claim that people should only love themselves. (True/False)

2. Which of the following is false?

    a. Compassion is the desire to help alleviate the suffering of others.

    b. The ability to understand what others are experiencing is called empathy.

    c. Pro-social behaviors are generally altruistic.

    d. Nepotism occurs when we refuse to give preference to those we love.

3. A theory that says that we ought only to pursue our self-interest is called

    a. Ethical egoism

    b. The Golden Rule

    c. The paradox of hedonism

    d. Descriptive egoism

4. What is the point of the prisoner's dilemma?

    a. To explain how to escape from the jail of our own consciousness

    b. To demonstrate the importance of equality and fairness in criminal justice

    c. To show that noncooperative egoists can end up with worse outcomes

    d. To demonstrate how akrasia ("weakness of will") causes crime

One influential version of the social contract idea is found in the writings of the seventeenth-century English philosopher Thomas Hobbes. Hobbes holds that individuals are self-interested; that is, they seek to fulfill their interests and desires and above all seek self-preservation. Hobbes maintains that in the state of nature, individuals would be equal in terms of strength, since even weak individuals can band together with others or use sneak attacks to overpower stronger individuals. Conflict arises when these equally powerful individuals seek the same thing. The competing individuals will thereby become enemies. As a result, the state of nature will be one of war, of all against all, and the results, as Hobbes describes them, are quite bleak.

> In such condition there is no place for industry, because the fruit thereof is uncertain, and consequently, not culture of the earth, no navigation, nor the use of commodities that may be imported by sea, no commodious building, no instruments of moving and removing such things as require much force, no knowledge of the face of the earth, no account of time, no arts, no letters, no society, and which is worst of all, continual fear and danger of violent death, and the life of man, solitary, poor, nasty, brutish, and short.[12]

The solution is peace via an agreement in which one gives up as much liberty "as against other men, as he would allow other men against himself."[13] For Hobbes, the social contract is an agreement to give up certain things to better secure one's own self-interest. Thus, individuals will agree to certain rules, which would be in each individual's best interest to accept and obey. To secure the peace and ensure that these rules are obeyed, Hobbes believes that an absolute sovereign ruler is required.

Hobbes's social contract theory is based on the desire of each person to secure their own advantage while agreeing to social rules enforced by a sovereign; it is a view of how society should function and thus both a political and a moral position. Other versions of the social contract idea were proposed by philosophers such as Locke and Rousseau. Contemporary moral and political theories also appeal to contract ideas, such as those found in the works of Thomas Scanlon, David Gauthier,

and John Rawls.[14] Gauthier's idea is that we should imagine basic moral rules that rational, self-interested parties would voluntarily agree to. Gauthier suggests that rational, self-interested agents would recognize the need for mutual restraint: it is in the interest of self-interested agents to agree to restrain the unbridled pursuit of self-interest. John Rawls imagines an ideal form of the social contract. He asks what rational self-interested people would agree to, in terms of justice, if these self-interested contractors did not know whether they were young or old, rich or poor, male or female, able-bodied or disabled. If this "veil of ignorance" were in place, Rawls suggests, the contractors would set up a system that was fair to everyone. Rawls's influential ideas are considered in more detail in Chapter 14.

Connections with Economic Theory

4.6 Discuss how egoism is connected to laissez-faire capitalism and economics.

One argument for ethical egoism is taken from economic theory—for example, that proposed by Adam Smith. He and other proponents of **laissez-faire capitalism** (a form of capitalism with minimal government regulation or intervention) argue that self-interest provides the best economic motivation. The idea is that when the profit motive or individual incentives are absent, people will either not work or not work as well. If it is my land or my business, then I will be more likely to take care of it than if the profits go to others or to the government. In addition, Smith believes that in a system in which each person looks out for their own economic interests, the general outcome will be best, as though an "invisible hand" were guiding things.[15]

Although this is not the place to go into an extended discussion of economic theory, it is enough to point out that not everyone agrees on the merits of laissez-faire capitalism. Much can be said for the competition that it supports, but it does raise questions, for example, about the breakdown of "winners" and "losers" in such a competition. Is it acceptable if the same individuals, families, or groups consistently win or lose, generation after generation? What if there are many more economic "losers" and a few extremely wealthy "winners"?

And what about those with innate or inherited disadvantages that prevent them from competing? Is care for these people a community responsibility? Recent community-oriented theories of social morality stress just this notion of responsibility and oppose laissez-faire capitalism's excessive emphasis on individual rights.[16] (Further discussion of capitalism can be found in Chapter 14.) In any case, a more basic question can be asked about the relevance of economics to morality. Even if an economic system worked well or efficiently, would this prove that morality ought to be modeled on it? Is not the moral life broader than the economic life? Are all human relations economic relations?

Furthermore, the argument that everyone ought to seek their own best interests because this contributes to the general well-being is not ethical egoism at all—since self-interest is merely used here as a means to pursuing a broader collective value. As we will come to see more clearly when we examine it, this is a form of utilitarianism (see Chapter 5).

Impartiality, Egoism, and Care

4.7 Evaluate the conflict between impartiality, egoism, and care.

In assessing ethical egoism, it is reasonable to ask whether it makes sense if we understand morality as requiring that we take up an impartial vantage point. As we'll see in subsequent chapters, most normative theories emphasize some form of impartiality, whether in utilitarianism, Kantian deontology, or natural law. Impartiality is connected to ideas such as justice, fairness, and equality. The basic idea is that in making moral judgments we should attempt to be unbiased, neutral, or disinterested. From a moral vantage point that takes these values seriously, it would be wrong to make exceptions for yourself or to pursue your own self-interest at the expense of others. This is also true when considering virtue ethics. Virtues are not merely good because they are good for you.

This seems to point to the conclusion that some elements of ethical egoism are contrary to commonsense morality. Of course, a philosophical approach to ethics raises questions about what counts as commonsense

morality and how commonsense morality might be grounded. But let's assume for the moment that commonsense morality includes basic virtues such as honesty, loyalty, and fairness; and that there are basic moral rules such as "don't lie," "don't cheat," and "treat people fairly." Among the basic elements of commonsense morality, we would probably also include the value of love, compassion, and care. We mentioned at the outset that the world's religious traditions tend to argue in favor of altruistic behavior. And most—if not all—religious and cultural traditions include prohibitions on lying and cheating, as well as a call for fairness and justice.

From this commonsense vantage point, self-serving actions are simply wrong. It is wrong to lie or cheat in order to gain a personal advantage and it is wrong to treat people unfairly. Critics of ethical egoism will worry that egoism seems to assume that anything is all right as long as it serves an individual's best interests (and so long as one could get away with it). Cheating and lying would be permitted so long as they served one's interests. When not useful to one's interest, virtues such as honesty and loyalty would have no value. Ethical egoists could argue on empirical or factual grounds that lying and cheating are not in one's best interests because liars and cheats typically get caught. Similarly, they might argue that the development of virtues is often in one's own best interest when those virtues are valued by a particular culture or society. For example, if I am known for being honest or loyal, this may enable me to more readily get what I want. But is such a strategic and egoistic commitment to loyalty or honesty the same thing as valuing loyalty or honesty for its own sake?

Egoists may respond to this objection by claiming that a kind of commonsense morality will emerge from egoism: that self-interested egoists will mostly agree to be honest, loyal, and fair. Perhaps this would occur through the "invisible hand" of the market, the enforcement mechanisms of the social contract, and the way that "enlightened self-interest" leads us to cooperate.

Furthermore, part of the intuitive appeal of egoism may derive from the sense that people ought to take better care of themselves—and stop worrying so much about being fair, impartial, and compassionate to others. By having a high regard for ourselves, we increase our self-esteem. We then depend less on others and more on ourselves. We might also be stronger and happier. These are surely desirable traits. Some altruists, moreover, might be too self-effacing. They might be said to lack a proper regard for themselves. There is also some truth in the view that unless one takes care of oneself, one is not of much use to others. This view implies not ethical egoism, however, but again a form of utilitarianism because it makes a claim about the general utility of self-regard and self-esteem.

But let's suppose that a person cares for no one but themselves, refusing to consider the needs of others and ignoring the demands of fairness, impartiality, and justice. Would you consider that person to be a moral person? Can we think of that person as even operating in the moral realm? It is possible to imagine a person who does not lie, does not cheat, and who talks a lot about justice—but who does so only for self-interested reasons. This person may understand that in social settings it is not smart to lie because lies usually get exposed, that cheaters often get punished, and that people get praised for talking about justice. It is likely that this person is not operating in the realm of morality—but is merely focused on *prudence*, making shrewd judgments about what serves their self-interest. But morality seems to imply more than prudence. Moral people don't avoid lying merely because they worry that lies may be exposed; they also believe that lying is wrong and that others have a right to know the truth. Moral people don't avoid cheating because they are afraid of punishment; they also think that cheating is wrong. And moral people don't talk about justice to impress others; they actually believe that justice is important.

Taking the moral point of view appears to involve being able to see beyond ourselves and our own interests. It may also mean that we attempt to see things from another's point of view; or even that we attempt to be impartial. Morality seems to require that moral rules apply equally to all, or that we have to give reasons why some persons are treated differently than others.

Care Ethics and the Challenge of Impartiality

The idea of morality as impartiality raises a number of interesting questions. We usually do not think that we have to justify treating those close to us differently and more favorably than others. But this is often condemned as nepotism, an immoral (and sometimes illegal) preference for one's own friends and relations. Is it really wrong to care more for our own children or friends than we do for strangers? Or should we aspire to be impartial and treat everyone equally?

This points us toward some of the questions that can be raised about the importance of impartiality and whether impartiality is required in order to be moral. As we mentioned at the outset, most cultural and religious traditions emphasize the idea of compassion and love. These ideas can sometimes be interpreted as impartial concern for the well-being of others—a kind of universal love or universal altruism. But love can also be narrowly oriented toward the suffering of concrete others.

The apparent conflict between impartial altruistic concern and concrete, focused love has been a subject of concern for ethicists who focus on the importance of nurture and care. **Care ethics** (also called the ethics of care) developed in the past several decades in connection with a feminist critique of ideas such as impartiality. Some feminists have claimed that the ethical ideal of impartiality, neutrality, and disinterested judgment tends to emphasize a certain "masculine" paradigm of moral development and a conception of justice that does not account for the lived experience of women. (See Chapter 9 for further treatment of this issue.) Virginia Held explains that the ethics of care grows out of a critique of a certain European ideal in which men were viewed as impartial actors in the public realm and women were relegated to the private sphere. She says, "The ethics of care rejects the model that became dominant in the West in the seventeenth and eighteenth centuries as democratic states replaced feudal society: a public sphere of mutually disinterested equals coexisting with a private sphere of female caring and male rule. The ethics of care advocates care as a value for society as well as household."[17] Held further explains that some cultures and religious traditions do not emphasize such a divide between public impartiality and private care, noting specifically that a "less sharp split" can be found in Confucian culture. (We have an excerpt from Held in the primary source readings for this chapter.)

For care ethicists, the dichotomy between egoism and altruism may be understood as a kind of false dilemma. Care ethicists tend to think that human beings are "relational." We find ourselves born into a world of caregivers: our mothers, fathers, grandparents, and others who care for us. We are related to these others or "in relation" before we even develop an "ego." And in most cases, we will grow to develop new relationships of care in relation to our friends, lovers, spouses, and children. In these relationships, the need for care is obvious; and it is much less obvious that we have a choice in the matter about whether we want to be altruistic or egoistic. According to the critical vantage point of care ethics, to claim that there is a choice in the matter is to misunderstand human nature—and to adopt a vantage point that privileges the experience of men in a patriarchal society who, as members of the public sphere, have often had much more choice than women when it comes to the question of who they care for and how much. The same point can be made with regard to impartiality: the impartial vantage point may make sense for men in the public sphere of a patriarchal culture, but it is less easy to adopt for women who are confined to the private sphere where relations of care predominate.

Feminists and care ethicists have noted that these conflicts are not easily resolved. As Lisa Tessman explains, "Feminist critics of impartiality have typically defended *both* partialist moral requirements that arise within particular relationships, *and* requirements to respond to the needs of distant strangers—whether as a matter of justice or a matter of care."[18] Maybe we could try to bring care and impartiality together. But the difficulty is found in conflicts that result when we are asked to choose between impartiality and concrete relationships of care. Consider one of the kinds of examples that Tessman discusses: whether to use your resources to support the well-being of your own child or to support a common educational fund that supports all children in your community. One the one hand, you have a special obligation to care for your own child; on the other hand, you have an obligation of impartial justice to focus equally on the well-being of all children.

A related case is considered by Virginia Held. Held imagines a devoted teacher who has a positive impact on a large number of students. Should that teacher spend more time at school, helping children they are not related to—or should they spend more time at home caring for their own children? Held points out that there is a conflict here in terms of how we prioritize our relationships and moral obligations. She explains, "When relationships are valuable, moral recommendations based on them may conflict with moral recommendations that would be made from the point of view of impartiality."[19]

We might also note that in caring for our own children or close friends, we experience pleasure, pride, and satisfaction. Could this be a kind of egoism or nepotism? Is it wrong to base our decisions on our selfish interest in the well-being of our children or friends? Finally, let's note a further worry that could be articulated from a feminist vantage point, which is that in patriarchal cultures, women are encouraged (or even forced) to ignore or subvert their own self-interest. Does this mean that feminists should embrace egoism and focus entirely on their own self-interest? Likely not. But there is room for discussion here about the importance for feminists and care ethicists of values such as self-sufficiency, autonomy, individualism, and even egoism.

Why Be Moral?

Let us assume now, as we conclude this chapter, that morality does involve altruism, considering other people's points of view and treating people equally or impartially and that morality involves compassion, empathy, care, and other topics we've discussed in this chapter. Why should anyone embrace these ideas, especially when it is not in their self-interest to do so? In other words, are there any reasons we can give to show why one should be moral in this sense? One reason we might provide is to say that behaving in this way is just what being moral means. But how can we explain why we ought to do what we ought to do?

We could argue that it is generally better for people to have and follow moral rules. Without such rules, our social lives would be pretty wretched. As Hobbes suggests, a life of egoism in the state of nature would be one of constant conflict and war. And so, we might argue that the social contract provides us with an answer to the question of why be moral: the answer is that we ought to abide by the agreements of the contract because those agreements are in our self-interest.

However, this does not answer the question of why I should be moral when it is not in my best interests to do so—or why and whether it would ever be moral to break that social contract.

If you were trying to convince someone as to why they should be moral, how would you do it?

You might tell the individual that being virtuous is to one's own advantage. You might recall some of the advice from Benjamin Franklin's *Poor Richard's Almanac*.[20] "A stitch in time saves nine." "Observe all men, thyself most." "Spare and have is better than spend and crave." Many of the moral aphorisms put forward by motivational speakers and self-help gurus are focused on maximizing self-interest. These are the self-interested counsels of a practical morality. It turns out that most virtues are usually in our own best interests. It is in our interest to be temperate, courageous, thrifty, kind, honest, and so on—because these virtues help us live a stable life in a world that we share with others. Indeed, it does appear to be in our interests to be altruistic, since concern for others is often reciprocated.

You might also appeal to fear of punishment, reprisal, and social condemnation that would follow from breaking moral rules. But as we've seen, this may be merely appeal to our prudential self-interest. If you are not honest, you will not be trusted. If you steal, you risk being punished. But are there other non-prudential reasons to be moral?

This is an ancient question. In a famous discussion from Plato's *Republic*, we encounter a situation in which someone is able to do whatever they want without fear of punishment. This is the story of "Gyges Ring." The tale tells of a shepherd named Gyges, who comes into possession of a ring that makes him invisible. He proceeds to use his invisibility to take what he wants from others. Plato asks us to consider whether we would do the same if, like Gyges, we could get away with it. Is not getting caught and avoiding punishment the only reason that people do the right thing? Plato's own solution involves a complex argument about the objective reality of moral goodness. He suggests that if we truly understand "the good," then it would be obvious to us why we ought to be moral.

There are other reasons you might offer to convince someone to be moral. You might make the point that altruism, compassion, and a concern for justice are ennobling. Even when it involves sacrifice for a cause, being a moral person gives one a certain dignity, integrity, and self-respect. Only humans are capable of being moral, you might say, and human beings cannot flourish without being moral. You can give more thought to this question when you read about Immanuel Kant's moral theory in Chapter 6. For Kant, human dignity and worth is wholly bound up with being able to act for moral reasons. Kant, like others we will discuss in what follows, also thinks that there is a close link between rationality and morality. The ancient version of this idea can be traced back to Plato and the Greeks, who suggested that knowing the good gives us a reason to do the good. This idea also provides the root of the natural law tradition, which we discuss in Chapter 7. The natural law tradition teaches that there is a moral order and structure in reality that can be known by us and that the most basic principle of morality is, as Thomas Aquinas put it, "the good is to be done and pursued and evil is to be avoided."[21] Of course, we still need to figure out exactly what the good is—and there is often a disagreement between altruists and egoists about this question. A different approach, as found in the utilitarian approach to morality, provides an argument against egoism. John Stuart Mill simply stated that one person's happiness counts exactly as much as every other person's (we'll examine this in more detail in Chapter 5). Mill takes this to be a moral truth that helps to show why egoists who make exceptions for themselves are mistaken about the very idea of morality. While thinking about this claim, we might bear in mind the egoist's claim that it is more rational to focus on our own self-interest and that if each of us simply pursued our own self-interest, we would all be better off. Is this right? And in this formulation, doesn't the egoist make an appeal to some claims that may in fact appeal to a notion of the common good? In conclusion, it is worth continuing to ask yourself what it means to be moral, why we should be moral, and whether morality requires us to overcome egoism.

Chapter Summary

4.1 How can we describe differences between descriptive (or psychological) egoism and ethical egoism?

Descriptive (psychological) egoism is an account of how we behave and what motivates us: it claims that we are motivated by self-interest. Ethical egoism builds on this idea, claiming that it is good for us to pursue our own self-interest.

4.2 How can we define the key terms altruism, empathy, compassion, and love?

Altruism is behavior and concern that are oriented toward others. Empathy is a psychological ability to understand other people's experience. Compassion is found when we are motivated to alleviate other people's suffering. Love is based on intimacy, although some forms of love (Christian agape) aim beyond intimacy toward universal concern.

4.3 What are some criticisms of altruism, and how do we explain the importance of reciprocal altruism?

Some critics of altruism (e.g., Ayn Rand) argue that altruism requires self-sacrifice. Reciprocal altruism grows out of enlightened self-interest as cooperative behavior, often described as "you scratch my back, I'll scratch yours."

4.4 What is the prisoner's dilemma, and how does it pose a challenge for egoism?

The prisoner's dilemma is a thought experiment that asks us to consider how egoists can end up with bad outcomes if they do not cooperate. It tends to point toward the need for reciprocal altruism or something like the social contract.

4.5 How does the social contract provide a solution to problems of egoism?

The social contract is found in political theory and in moral theories such as contractarianism. These ideas suggest that rational self-interest can lead us to agree to obey a common system of morality and law.

4.6 How is egoism connected to laissez-faire capitalism and economics?

Laissez-faire capitalism is based on the idea that if everyone seeks to maximize their own self-interest, the economy will grow and produce good outcomes for most of us.

4.7 How can we evaluate the conflict between impartiality, egoism, and care?

Moral traditions tend to encourage altruism and discourage egoism. And some argue that morality requires us to rise above egoism and become impartial. It might be that egoism is merely focused on prudence—and is not really a moral point of view. In order to evaluate this conflict, we would need to consider how important impartiality is in our understanding of morality. And thinking about this, we might want to keep in mind the criticism of impartiality that is sometimes made by feminists—and the alternative idea of an ethics of care.

4.8 How would you defend your own ideas about egoism, altruism, and the social contract?

After reading this chapter, you should be able to defend your own thinking about the importance of egoism (both as a descriptive account of human behavior and as a normative theory). You should be able to explain what you think about altruism, empathy, compassion, and love. And you should have some idea about whether the contractarian approaches are useful.

Primary Source Readings

In the first reading, Plato's characters in *The Republic* explore the contention that we always act in our own interests—one of the reasons given in support of an egoist theory. Plato offers a thought experiment involving Gyges's magic ring to help us think about what we would really do if no one was looking. In the second reading, the English philosopher Thomas Hobbes provides an answer to the question of what people would do if they were not regulated by social rules. He argues not only that all human beings tend to pursue their own safety and interests—but also why it is rational for self-interested individuals to create a social contract that furthers the goal of self-protection. In the next excerpt, psychologist Steven Pinker offers an evolutionary explanation of the importance of altruism that has some resonance with our discussion of sociobiology in Chapter 1. Finally, we have an excerpt from Virginia Held, a well-known proponent of feminist care ethics. She asks us to consider whether too much of a focus on the conflict between egoism and altruism might be misplaced.

Reading 4-1 The Ring of Gyges | Plato

Study Questions

As you read the excerpt, please consider the following questions:

1. What view of morality is described using the story of the ring of Gyges?
2. How does this story describe the difference between appearing just and being just?
3. According to the story, what do parents (and religions, myths, and poetry) teach their children and us about morality?

Glaucon (to Socrates). They say that to do injustice is, by nature, good; to suffer injustice, evil; but that the evil is greater than the good. And so when men have both done and suffered injustice and have had experience of both, not being able to avoid the one and obtain the other, they think that they had better agree among themselves to have neither; hence there arise laws and mutual covenants; and that which is ordained by law is termed by them lawful and just. This they affirm to be the origin and nature of justice;—it is a mean or compromise, between the best of all, which is to do injustice and not be punished, and the worst of all, which is to suffer injustice without the power of retaliation; and justice, being at a middle point between the two, is tolerated not as a good, but as the lesser evil, and honoured by reason of the inability of men to do injustice. For no man who is worthy to be called a man would ever submit to such an agreement if he were able to resist; he would be mad if he did. Such is the received account, Socrates, of the nature and origin of justice.

Now that those who practise justice do so involuntarily and because they have not the power to be unjust will best appear if we imagine something of this kind: having given both to the just and the unjust power to do what they will, let us watch and see whither desire will lead them; then we shall discover in the very act the just and unjust man to be proceeding along the same road, following their interest, which all natures deem to be their good, and are only diverted into the path of justice by the force of law. The liberty which we are supposing may be most completely given to them in the form of such a power as is said to have been possessed by Gyges the ancestor of Croesus the Lydian. According to the tradition, Gyges was a shepherd in the service of the king of Lydia; there was a great storm, and an earthquake made an opening in the earth at the

From Plato, *The Republic*, bk. 2, in *The Dialogues of Plato*, 3rd ed., trans. B. Jowett (Oxford, UK: Oxford University Press, 1892), pp. 357–369.

place where he was feeding his flock. Amazed at the sight, he descended into the opening, where, among other marvels, he beheld a hollow brazen horse, having doors, at which he stooping and looking in saw a dead body of stature, as appeared to him, more than human, and having nothing on but a gold ring; this he took from the finger of the dead and reascended. Now the shepherds met together, according to custom, that they might send their monthly report about the flocks to the king; into their assembly he came having the ring on his finger, and as he was sitting among them he chanced to turn the collet of the ring inside his hand, when instantly he became invisible to the rest of the company and they began to speak of him as if he were no longer present. He was astonished at this, and again touching the ring he turned the collet outwards and reappeared; he made several trials of the ring, and always with the same result—when he turned the collet inwards he became invisible, when outwards he reappeared. Whereupon he contrived to be chosen one of the messengers who were sent to the court; where as soon as he arrived he seduced the queen, and with her help conspired against the king and slew him, and took the kingdom. Suppose now that there were two such magic rings, and the just put on one of them and the unjust the other; no man can be imagined to be of such an iron nature that he would stand fast in justice. No man would keep his hands off what was not his own when he could safely take what he liked out of the market, or go into houses and lie with any one at his pleasure, or kill or release from prison whom he would, and in all respects be like a God among men. Then the actions of the just would be as the actions of the unjust; they would both come at last to the same point. And this we may truly affirm to be a great proof that a man is just, not willingly or because he thinks that justice is any good to him individually, but of necessity, for wherever any one thinks that he can safely be unjust, there he is unjust. For all men believe in their hearts that injustice is far more profitable to the individual than justice, and he who argues as I have been supposing, will say that they are right. If you could imagine any one obtaining this power of becoming invisible, and never doing any wrong or touching what was another's, he would be thought by the lookers-on to be a most wretched idiot, although they would praise him to one another's faces,

and keep up appearances with one another from a fear that they too might suffer injustice. Enough of this.

Now, if we are to form a real judgment of the life of the just and unjust, we must isolate them; there is no other way; and how is the isolation to be effected? I answer: Let the unjust man be entirely unjust, and the just man entirely just; nothing is to be taken away from either of them, and both are to be perfectly furnished for the work of their respective lives. First, let the unjust be like other distinguished masters of craft; like the skilful pilot or physician, who knows intuitively his own powers and keeps within their limits, and who, if he fails at any point, is able to recover himself. So let the unjust make his unjust attempts in the right way, and lie hidden if he means to be great in his injustice (he who is found out is nobody): for the highest reach of injustice is, to be deemed just when you are not. Therefore I say that in the perfectly unjust man we must assume the most perfect injustice; there is to be no deduction, but we must allow him, while doing the most unjust acts, to have acquired the greatest reputation for justice. If he have taken a false step he must be able to recover himself; he must be one who can speak with effect, if any of his deeds come to light, and who can force his way where force is required by his courage and strength, and command of money and friends. And at his side let us place the just man in his nobleness and simplicity, wishing, as Aeschylus says, to be and not to seem good. There must be no seeming, for if he seem to be just he will be honoured and rewarded, and then we shall not know whether he is just for the sake of justice or for the sake of honours and rewards; therefore, let him be clothed in justice only, and have no other covering; and he must be imagined in a state of life the opposite of the former. Let him be the best of men, and let him be thought the worst; then he will have been put to the proof; and we shall see whether he will be affected by the fear of infamy and its consequences. And let him continue thus to the hour of death; being just and seeming to be unjust. When both have reached the uttermost extreme, the one of justice and the other of injustice, let judgment be given which of them is the happier of the two.

Socrates. Heavens! my dear Glaucon, I said, how energetically you polish them up for the decision, first one and then the other, as if they were two statues.

Glaucon. I do my best. And now that we know what they are like there is no difficulty in tracing out the sort of life which awaits either of them. This I will proceed to describe; but as you may think the description a little too coarse, I ask you to suppose, Socrates, that the words which follow are not mine.—Let me put them into the mouths of the eulogists of injustice: They will tell you that the just man who is thought unjust will be scourged, racked, bound—will have his eyes burnt out; and, at last, after suffering every kind of evil, he will be impaled: Then he will understand that he ought to seem only, and not to be, just; the words of Aeschylus may be more truly spoken of the unjust than of the just. For the unjust is pursuing a reality; he does not live with a view to appearances—he wants to be really unjust and not to seem only—

> "His mind has a soil deep and fertile,
> Out of which spring his prudent counsels."

In the first place, he is thought just, and therefore bears rule in the city; he can marry whom he will, and give in marriage to whom he will; also he can trade and deal where he likes, and always to his own advantage, because he has no misgivings about injustice; and at every contest, whether in public or private, he gets the better of his antagonists, and gains at their expense, and is rich, and out of his gains he can benefit his friends, and harm his enemies; moreover, he can offer sacrifices, and dedicate gifts to the gods abundantly and magnificently, and can honour the gods or any man whom he wants to honour in a far better style than the just, and therefore he is likely to be dearer than they are to the gods. And thus, Socrates, gods and men are said to unite in making the life of the unjust better than the life of the just.

Adeimantus. Socrates, you do not suppose that there is nothing more to be urged?

Socrates. Why, what else is there?

Adeimantus. The strongest point of all has not been even mentioned.

Socrates. Well, then, according to the proverb, "Let brother help brother"—if he fails in any part do you assist him; although I must confess that Glaucon has already said quite enough to lay me in the dust, and take from me the power of helping justice.

Adeimantus. Nonsense. But let me add something more: There is another side to Glaucon's argument about the praise and censure of justice and injustice, which is equally required in order to bring out what I believe to be his meaning. Parents and tutors are always telling their sons and their wards that they are to be just; but why? not for the sake of justice, but for the sake of character and reputation; in the hope of obtaining for him who is reputed just some of those offices, marriages, and the like which Glaucon has enumerated among the advantages accruing to the unjust from the reputation of justice. More, however, is made of appearances by this class of persons than by the others; for they throw in the good opinion of the gods, and will tell you of a shower of benefits which the heavens, as they say, rain upon the pious; and this accords with the testimony of the noble Hesiod and Homer, the first of whom says, that the gods make the oaks of the just—

> "To bear acorns at their summit, and bees in the middle;
> And the sheep are bowed down with the weight of their fleeces,"[1]

and many other blessings of a like kind are provided for them. And Homer has a very similar strain; for he speaks of one whose fame is—

> "As the fame of some blameless king who, like a god,
> Maintains justice; to whom the black earth brings forth
> Wheat and barley, whose trees are bowed with fruit, And
> his sheep never fail to bear, and the sea gives him fish."[2]

Still grander are the gifts of heaven which Musaeus and his son[3] vouchsafe to the just; they take them down into the world below, where they have the saints lying on couches at a feast, everlastingly drunk, crowned with garlands; their idea seems to be that an immortality of drunkenness is the highest meed of virtue. Some extend their rewards yet further; the posterity, as they say, of the faithful and just shall survive to the third and fourth generation. This is the style in which they praise justice. But about the wicked there is another strain; they bury them in a slough in Hades, and make them carry water in a sieve; also while they are yet living they bring them to infamy, and inflict upon them the punishments which Glaucon described as the portion of the just who are reputed to be unjust; nothing else does their invention supply. Such is their manner of praising the one and censuring the other.

Once more, Socrates, I will ask you to consider another way of speaking about justice and injustice, which is not confined to the poets, but is found in prose writers. The universal voice of mankind is always declaring that justice and virtue are honourable, but grievous and toilsome; and that the pleasures of vice and injustice are easy of attainment, and are only censured by law and opinion. They say also that honesty is for the most part less profitable than dishonesty; and they are quite ready to call wicked men happy, and to honour them both in public and private when they are rich or in any other way influential, while they despise and overlook those who may be weak and poor, even though acknowledging them to be better than the others. But most extraordinary of all is their mode of speaking about virtue and the gods: they say that the gods apportion calamity and misery to many good men, and good and happiness to the wicked. And mendicant prophets go to rich men's doors and persuade them that they have a power committed to them by the gods of making an atonement for a man's own or his ancestor's sins by sacrifices or charms, with rejoicings and feasts; and they promise to harm an enemy, whether just or unjust, at a small cost; with magic arts and incantations binding heaven, as they say, to execute their will. And the poets are the authorities to whom they appeal, now smoothing the path of vice with the words of Hesiod—

"Vice may be had in abundance without trouble; the way is smooth and her dwelling-place is near. But before virtue the gods have set toil,"[4]

and a tedious and uphill road: then citing Homer as a witness that the gods may be influenced by men; for he also says—

"The gods, too, may be turned from their purpose; and men pray to them and avert their wrath by sacrifices and soothing entreaties, and by libations and the odour of fat, when they have sinned and transgressed."[5]

And they produce a host of books written by Musaeus and Orpheus, who were children of the Moon and the Muses—that is what they say—according to which they perform their ritual, and persuade not only individuals, but whole cities, that expiations and atonements for sin may be made by sacrifices and amusements which fill a vacant hour, and are equally at the service of the living and the dead; the latter sort they call mysteries, and they redeem us from the pains of hell, but if we neglect them no one knows what awaits us.

And now when the young hear all this said about virtue and vice, and the way in which gods and men

regard them, how are their minds likely to be affected, my dear Socrates,—those of them, I mean, who are quickwitted, and, like bees on the wing, light on every flower, and from all that they hear are prone to draw conclusions as to what manner of persons they should be and in what way they should walk if they would make the best of life? Probably the youth will say to himself in the words of Pindar—

"Can I by justice or by crooked ways of deceit ascend a loftier tower which may be a fortress to me all my days?"

For what men say is that, if I am really just and am not also thought just, profit there is none, but the pain and loss on the other hand are unmistakeable. But if, though unjust, I acquire the reputation of justice, a heavenly life is promised to me. Since then, as philosophers prove, appearance tyrannizes over truth and is lord of happiness, to appearance I must devote myself. I will describe around me a picture and shadow of virtue to be the vestibule and exterior of my house; behind I will trail the subtle and crafty fox, as Archilochus, greatest of sages, recommends. But I hear some one exclaiming that the concealment of wickedness is often difficult; to which I answer, Nothing great is easy. Nevertheless, the argument indicates this, if we would be happy, to be the path along which we should proceed. With a view to concealment we will establish secret brotherhoods and political clubs. And there are professors of rhetoric who teach the art of persuading courts and assemblies; and so, partly by persuasion and partly by force, I shall make unlawful gains and not be punished. Still I hear a voice saying that the gods cannot be deceived, neither can they be compelled. But what if there are no gods? or, suppose them to have no care of human things—why in either case should we mind about concealment? And even if there are gods, and they do care about us, yet we know of them only from tradition and the genealogies of the poets; and these are the very persons who say that they may be influenced and turned by "sacrifices and soothing entreaties and by offerings." Let us be consistent then, and believe both or neither. If the poets speak truly, why then we had better be unjust, and offer of the fruits of injustice; for if we are just, although we may escape the vengeance of heaven, we shall lose the gains of injustice; but, if we are unjust, we shall keep the gains, and by our sinning and praying, and praying and sinning, the gods will be propitiated, and we shall not be punished. "But there is a world below in which either we or our posterity will suffer for our unjust deeds." Yes, my friend, will be the reflection, but there are mysteries and atoning deities, and these have great power. That is what mighty cities declare; and the children of the gods, who were their poets and prophets, bear a like testimony.

On what principle, then, shall we any longer choose justice rather than the worst injustice? when, if we only unite the latter with a deceitful regard to appearance, we shall fare to our mind both with gods and men, in life and after death, as the most numerous and the highest authorities tell us. Knowing all this, Socrates, how can a man who has any superiority of mind or person or rank or wealth, be willing to honour justice; or indeed to refrain from laughing when he hears justice praised? And even if there should be some one who is able to disprove the truth of my words, and who is satisfied that justice is best, still he is not angry with the unjust, but is very ready to forgive them, because he also knows that men are not just of their own free will; unless, peradventure, there be some one whom the divinity within him may have inspired with a hatred of injustice, or who has attained knowledge of the truth—but no other man. He only blames injustice who, owing to cowardice or age or some weakness, has not the power of being unjust. And this is proved by the fact that when he obtains the power, he immediately becomes unjust as far as he can be.

The cause of all this, Socrates, was indicated by us at the beginning of the argument, when my brother and I told you how astonished we were to find that of all the professing panegyrists of justice—beginning with the ancient heroes of whom any memorial has been preserved to us, and ending with the men of our own time— no one has ever blamed injustice or praised justice except with a view to the glories, honours, and benefits which flow from them. No one has ever adequately described either in verse or prose the true essential nature of either of them abiding in the soul, and invisible to any human or divine eye; or shown that of all the things of a man's soul which he has within him, justice is the greatest good, and injustice the greatest evil. Had this been the universal strain, had you sought to persuade us of this from our youth upwards, we should not have been on the watch to keep one another from doing wrong, but every one would have been his own watchman, because afraid, if he did wrong, of harbouring in himself the greatest of evils. I dare say that Thrasymachus and others would seriously hold the language which I have been merely repeating, and words even stronger than these about justice and injustice, grossly, as I conceive, perverting their true nature. But I speak in this vehement manner, as I must frankly confess to you, because I want to hear from you the opposite side; and I would ask you to show not only the superiority which justice has over injustice, but what effect they have on the possessor of them which makes the one to be a good and the other an evil to him. And please, as Glaucon requested of you, to exclude reputations; for unless you take away from each of them his true reputation and add on the false, we shall say that you do not praise justice, but the appearance of it; we shall think that you are only exhorting us to keep injustice dark, and that you really agree with Thrasymachus in thinking that justice is another's good and the interest of the stronger, and that injustice is a man's own profit and interest, though injurious to the weaker. Now as you have admitted that justice is one of that highest class of goods which are desired indeed for their results, but in a far greater degree for their own sakes—like sight or hearing or knowledge or health, or any other real and natural and not merely conventional good—I would ask you in your praise of justice to regard one point only: I mean the essential good and evil which justice and injustice work in the possessors of them. Let others praise justice and censure injustice, magnifying the rewards and honours of the one and abusing the other; that is a manner of arguing which, coming from them, I am ready to tolerate, but from you who have spent your whole life in the consideration of this question, unless I hear the contrary from your own lips, I expect something better. And therefore, I say, not only prove to us that justice is better than injustice, but show what they either of them do to the possessor of them, which makes the one to be a good and the other an evil, whether seen or unseen by gods and men.

Socrates. Sons of an illustrious father, that was not a bad beginning of the Elegiac verses which the admirer of Glaucon made in honour of you after you had distinguished yourselves at the battle of Megara—

"'Sons of Ariston,' he sang, 'divine offspring of an illustrious hero.'"

The epithet is very appropriate, for there is something truly divine in being able to argue as you have done for the superiority of injustice, and remaining unconvinced by your own arguments. And I do believe that you are not convinced—this I infer from your general character, for had I judged only from your speeches I should have mistrusted you. But now, the greater my confidence in you, the greater is my difficulty in knowing what to say. For I am in a strait between two; on the one hand I feel that I am unequal to the task; and my inability is brought home to me by the fact that you were not satisfied with the answer which I made to Thrasymachus, proving, as I thought, the superiority which justice has over injustice. And yet I cannot refuse to help, while breath and speech remain to me; I am afraid that there would be an impiety in being present when justice is evil spoken of and not lifting up a hand in her defence. And therefore I had best give such help as I can.

Glaucon and the rest entreated me by all means not to let the question drop, but to proceed in the investigation. They wanted to arrive at the truth, first, about the nature of justice and injustice, and secondly, about their relative advantages. I told them, what I really thought, that the enquiry would be of a serious nature, and would require very good eyes. Seeing then, I said, that we are no great wits, I think that we had better adopt a method which I may illustrate thus; suppose that a short-sighted person had been asked by some one to read small letters from a distance; and it occurred to some one else that they might be found in another place which was larger and in which the letters were larger—if they were the same and he could read the larger letters first, and then proceed to the lesser—this would have been thought a rare piece of good fortune.

Adeimantus. Very true. But how does the illustration apply to our enquiry?

Socrates. I will tell you. Justice, which is the subject of our enquiry, is, as you know, sometimes spoken of as the virtue of an individual, and sometimes as the virtue of a state.

Adeimantus. True.

Socrates. And is not a State larger than an individual?

Adeimantus. It is.

Socrates. Then in the larger the quantity of justice is likely to be larger and more easily discernible. I propose therefore that we enquire into the nature of justice and injustice, first as they appear in the State, and secondly in the individual, proceeding from the greater to the lesser and comparing them.

Adeimantus. That is an excellent proposal.

Notes

1. Hesiod, *Works and Days*, p. 230.
2. Homer, *Od*, xix, p. 109.
3. Eumolpus.
4. Hesiod, *Works and Days*, p. 287.
5. Homer, *Iliad*, ix, p. 493.

Reading 4-2 Self-Love | Thomas Hobbes

Study Questions

As you read the excerpt, please consider the following questions:

1. In what ways are people equal and unequal? Which is more significant?
2. What does Hobbes mean when he says that nature has given everyone a right to all? What is the result of this?
3. Beyond society and its rules, is there any right or wrong, or just or unjust, according to Hobbes?

There be in animals, two sorts of *motions* peculiar to them: one called vital; begun in generation, and continued without interruption through their whole life; such as are the *course* of the *blood*, the *pulse*, the *breathing*, the *concoction, nutrition, excretion*, etc. to which motions there needs no help of imagination: the other is *animal motion*, otherwise called *voluntary motion*; as to *go*, to *speak*, to *move* any of our limbs, in such manner as is first fancied in our minds. That sense is motion in the organs and interior parts of man's body, caused by the action of the things we see, hear, etc.; and that fancy is but the relics of the same motion, remaining after sense. . . . And because *going, speaking*, and the like *voluntary motions*, depend always upon a precedent thought of *whither, which way*, and *what*; it is evident, that the imagination is the first internal beginning of all voluntary motion. And although unstudied men do not conceive any motion at all to be there, where the thing moved is invisible; or the space it is moved in is, for the shortness of it, insensible; yet that doth not hinder, but that such motions are. For let a space be never so little, that which is moved over a greater space, whereof that little one is part, must first be moved over that. These small beginnings of motion, within the body of man, before they appear in walking, speaking, striking, and other visible actions, are commonly called ENDEAVOR.

This endeavor, when it is toward something which causes it, is called APPETITE, or DESIRE; the latter, being the general name; and the other oftentimes restrained to signify the desire of food, namely *hunger* and *thirst*. And when the endeavor is fromward something, it is generally called AVERSION. These words, *appetite* and *aversion*, we have from the Latins; and they both of them signify the motions, one of approaching, the other of retiring. . . . For nature itself does often press upon men those truths, which afterwards, when they look for somewhat beyond nature, they stumble at. For the schools find in mere appetite to go, or move, no actual motion at all: but because some motion they must acknowledge, they call it metaphorical motion; which is but an absurd speech: for though words may be called metaphorical; bodies and motions cannot.

That which men desire, they are also said to LOVE: and to HATE those things for which they have aversion. So that desire and love are the same thing; save that by desire, we always signify the absence of the object; by love, most commonly the presence of the same. So also by aversion, we signify the absence; and by hate, the presence of the object.

Of appetites and aversions, some are born with men; as appetite of food, appetite of excretion, and exoneration, which may also and more properly be called aversions, from somewhat they feel in their bodies; and some other appetites, not many. The rest, which are appetites of particular things, proceed from experience, and trial of their effects upon themselves or other men. For of things we know not at all, or believe not to be, we can have no further desire, than to taste and try. But aversion we have for things, not only which we know have hurt us, but also that we do not know whether they will hurt us, or not.

Those things which we neither desire, nor hate, we are said to *contemn*; CONTEMPT being nothing else but an immobility, or contumacy of the heart, in resisting the action of certain things; and proceeding from that the heart is already moved otherwise, by other more potent objects; or from want of experience of them.

And because the constitution of a man's body is in continual mutation, it is impossible that all the same things should always cause in him the same appetites, and aversions: much less can all men consent, in the desire of almost any one and the same object.

But whatsoever is the object of any man's appetite or desire, that is it which he for his part calleth *good*: and the object of his hate and aversion, *evil*; and of his *contempt, vile* and inconsiderable. For these words of good, evil, and contemptible, are ever used with relation to the person that useth them: there being nothing simply and absolutely so; nor any common rule of good and evil, to be taken from the nature of the objects themselves. . . .

Felicity of this life consisteth not in the repose of a mind satisfied. For there is no such *finis ultimus*, utmost aim, nor *summum bonum*, greatest good, as is spoken of in the books of the old moral philosophers. Nor can a man any more live, whose desires are at an end, than he, whose senses and imaginations are at a stand. Felicity is a continual progress of the desire, from one object to another; the attaining of the former, being still but the way to the latter. The cause whereof is, that the object of man's desire, is not to enjoy once only, and for one instant of time; but to assure for ever, the way of his future desire. . . .

So that in the first place, I put for a general inclination of all mankind, a perpetual and restless desire of power after power, that ceaseth only in death. And the cause of this, is . . . that a man . . . cannot assure the power and means to live well, which he hath present, without the acquisition of more. . . .

Nature hath made men so equal, in the faculties of the body, and mind; as that though there be found one man sometimes manifestly stronger in body, or of quicker mind than another; yet when all is reckoned together, the difference between man, and man, is not so considerable, as that one man can thereupon claim to himself any benefit, to which another may not pretend, as well as he. For as to the strength of body, the weakest has strength enough to kill the strongest, either by secret machination, or by confederacy with others, that are in the same danger with himself.

And as to the faculties of the mind, setting aside the arts grounded upon words, and especially that skill of proceeding upon general, and infallible rules, called science; which very few have, and but in few things; as being not native faculty, born with us; nor attained, as prudence, while we look after somewhat else, I find yet a greater equality amongst men, than that of strength. For prudence, is but experience; which equal time, equally bestows on all men, in those things they equally apply themselves unto. That which may perhaps make such equality incredible, is but a vain conceit of one's own wisdom, which almost all men think they have in a greater degree, than the vulgar; that is, than all men but themselves, and a few others, whom by fame, or for concurring with themselves, they approve. For such is the nature of men, that howsoever they may acknowledge many others to be more witty, or more eloquent, or more learned; yet they will hardly believe there be many so wise as themselves; for they see their own wit at hand, and other men's at a distance. But this proveth rather that men are in that point equal, than unequal. For there is not ordinarily a greater sign of the equal distribution of any thing, than that every man is contented with his share.

From this equality of ability, ariseth equality of hope in the attaining of our ends. And therefore if any two men desire the same thing, which nevertheless they cannot both enjoy, they become enemies; and in the way to their end, which is principally their own conservation, and sometimes their delectation only, endeavor to destroy, or subdue one another. And from hence it comes to pass, that where an invader hath no more to fear, than another man's single power; if one plant, sow, build, or possess a convenient seat, others may probably be expected to come prepared with forces united, to dispossess, and deprive him, not only of the fruit of his labor, but also of his life, or liberty. And the invader again is in the like danger of another.

And from this diffidence of one another, there is no way for any man to secure himself, so reasonable, as anticipation; that is, by force, or wiles, to master the persons of all men he can, so long, till he see no other power great enough to endanger him: and this is no more than his own conservation requireth, and generally allowed. Also because there be some, that taking pleasure in contemplating their own power in the acts of conquest, which they pursue farther than their security requires; if others, that otherwise would be glad to be at ease within modest bounds, should not by invasion increase their power, they would not be able, long time, by standing only on their defense, to subsist. And by consequence, such augmentation of dominion over men being necessary to a man's conservation, it ought to be allowed him.

Again, men have no pleasure, but on the contrary a great deal of grief, in keeping company, where there is no power able to overawe them all. For every man looketh that his companion should value him, at the same rate he sets upon himself: and upon all signs of contempt, or undervaluing, naturally endeavors, as far as he dares, (which amongst them that have no common power to keep them in quiet, is far enough to make them destroy each other), to extort a greater value from his contemners, by damage; and from others, by the example.

So that in the nature of man, we find three principal causes of quarrel. First, competition; secondly, diffidence; thirdly, glory.

The first, maketh men invade for gain; the second, for safety; and the third, for reputation. The first use violence, to make themselves masters of other men's persons, wives, children, and cattle; the second, to defend them; the third, for trifles, as a word, a smile, a different opinion, and any other sign of undervalue, either direct in their persons, or by reflection in their kindred, their friends, their nation, their profession, or their name.

Hereby it is manifest, that during the time men live without a common power to keep them all in awe, they are in that condition which is called war; and such a war, as is of every man, against every man. For WAR, consisteth not in battle only, or the act of fighting; but in a tract of time, wherein the will to contend by battle is sufficiently known: and therefore the notion of time, is to be considered in the nature of war; as it is in the nature of weather. For as the nature of foul weather, lieth not in a shower or two of rain; but in an inclination thereto of many days together: so the nature of war, consisteth not in actual fighting; but in the known disposition thereto, during all the time there is no assurance to the contrary. All other time is PEACE.

Whatsoever therefore is consequent to a time of war, where every man is enemy to every man; the same is consequent to the time, wherein men live without security, than what their own strength, and their own invention shall furnish them withal. In such condition, there is no place for industry; because the fruit thereof is uncertain: and consequently no culture of the earth; no navigation, nor use of the commodities that may be imported by sea; no commodious building; no instruments of moving, and removing, such things as require much force; no knowledge of the face of the earth; no account of time; no arts; no letters; no society; and which is worst of all, continual fear, and danger of violent death; and the life of man, solitary, poor, nasty, brutish, and short....

It may peradventure be thought, there was never such a time, nor condition of war as this; and I believe it was never generally so, over all the world: but there are many places, where they live so now. For the savage people in many places of America, except the government of small families, the concord whereof dependeth on natural lust, have no government at all; and live at this day in that brutish manner, as I said before. Howsoever, it may be perceived what manner of life there would be, where there were no common power to fear, by the manner of life, which men that have formerly lived under a peaceful government, use to degenerate into, in a civil war.

But though there had never been any time, wherein particular men were in a condition of war one against another; yet in all times, kings, and persons of sovereign authority, because of their independency, are in continual jealousies, and in the state and posture of gladiators; having their weapons pointing, and their eyes fixed on one another; that is, their forts, garrisons, and guns upon the frontiers of their kingdoms; and continual spies upon their neighbors; which is a posture of war. But because they uphold thereby, the industry of their subjects; there does not follow from it, that misery, which accompanies the liberty of particular men....

From Thomas Hobbes, *Leviathan*, in *The English Works of Thomas Hobbes*, ed. Sir William Molesworth (London: John Bohn, 1839), pp. 2:38–41, 85.

Reading 4-3   Altruism in Nature | Steven Pinker

Study Questions

As you read the excerpt, please consider the following questions:

1. How does Pinker explain the evolution of compassionate and marital love?

2. What is "nepotistic altruism" and how does Pinker suggest it evolves?

3. What is "reciprocal altruism" and how is it explained in evolutionary terms?

There are several reasons why organisms may evolve a willingness to do good deeds. They may help other creatures while pursuing their own interests, say, when they form a herd that confuses predators or live off each other's by-products. This is called mutualism, symbiosis, or cooperation. Among humans, friends who have common tastes, hobbies, or enemies are a kind of symbiont pair. The two parents of a brood of children are an even better example. Their genes are tied up in the same package, their children, so what is good for one is good for the other, and each has an interest in keeping the other alive and healthy. These shared interests set the stage for compassionate love and marital love to evolve.

And in some cases organisms may benefit other organisms at a cost to themselves, which biologists call altruism. Altruism in this technical sense can evolve in two main ways. First, since relatives share genes, any gene that inclines an organism toward helping a relative will increase the chance of survival of a copy of itself that sits inside that relative, even if the helper sacrifices its own fitness in the generous act. Such genes will, on average, come to predominate, as long as the cost to the helper is less than the benefit to the recipient discounted by their degree of relatedness. Family love—the cherishing of children, siblings, parents, grandparents, uncles and aunts, nieces and nephews, and cousins—can evolve. This is called nepotistic altruism.

Altruism can also evolve when organisms trade favors. One helps another by grooming, feeding, protecting, or backing him, and is helped in turn when the needs reverse. This is called reciprocal altruism, and it can evolve when the parties recognize each other, interact repeatedly, can confer a large benefit on others at small cost to themselves, keep a memory for favors offered or denied, and are impelled to reciprocate accordingly. Reciprocal altruism can evolve because cooperators do better than hermits or misanthropes. They enjoy the gains of trading their surpluses, pulling ticks out of one another's hair, saving each other from drowning or starvation, and baby-sitting each other's children. Reciprocators can also do better over the long run than the cheaters who take favors without returning them, because the reciprocators will come to recognize the cheaters and shun or punish them. The demands of reciprocal altruism can explain why the social and moralistic emotions evolved. Sympathy and trust prompt people to extend the first favor. Gratitude and loyalty prompt them to repay favors. Guilt and shame deter them from hurting or failing to repay others. Anger and contempt prompt them to avoid or punish cheaters. And among humans, any tendency of an individual to reciprocate or cheat does not have to be witnessed firsthand but can be recounted by language. This leads to an interest in the reputation of others, transmitted by gossip and public approval or condemnation, and a concern with one's own reputation.

"The Blank Slate [Discover Magazine 10/2002]," adapted from *The Blank Slate: The Modern Denial of Human Nature* by Steven Pinker.

Reading 4-4   Egoism, Altruism, and Care | Virginia Held

Study Questions

As you read the excerpt, please consider the following questions:

1. What do you think Held means when she says that the ethics of care is not meant to support the traditional subordination of women?

2. Why does Held suggest that the ethics of care shows that the framework that focuses on egoism versus altruism is "misplaced"?

3. What does Held mean by claiming that the ethics of care is not about "self-sacrifice"?

One of the frequent criticisms made of the ethics of care, including by feminists, is that it is too conservative, even reactionary. It is thought by some to reinforce women's traditional roles of taking care of others, and it is criticized for not lending itself to major social change....

As Carol Gilligan's recent work shows . . . and as many of us defending the ethics of care have been saying for some time, the view of the ethics of care as supporting the traditional subordination of women is seriously mistaken. What could be more revolutionary than upsetting the gender hierarchy of patriarchy in the most basic ways we think about how we ought to live and what we ought to do? Not revolutionary in the traditional way, perhaps, of shooting people who stand in the way. But revolutionary in the real way of changing how people think and feel about the most important questions they face. The ethics of care asks for the transformations of society, politics, law, economic activity, the family, and personal relations away from the assumptions of patriarchy and toward the world of caring and the kind of justice caring calls for.

Moral philosophers who try to develop the ethics of care often seek the values embedded in practices of care, the actual labor of taking care of children and others in need of care as we all are at various times in our lives and in various ways. Practices of care call for sensitivity, empathy, trust, and especially responsiveness to need. They cultivate the development of trust and mutual consideration. Care relies on the insights and motivations of the emotions as well as on reason. It values especially caring relations, not simply the dispositions of individual persons. In contrast with the model of the "liberal individual" of the dominant moral and political theories, it conceptualizes persons as relational. It especially understands how the whole framework of self versus other, of egoism versus altruism, is misplaced for much of human life already, and how it could and should be reduced rather than expanded in applicability....

Care should not be understood as self-sacrifice. Egoism versus altruism is the wrong way to interpret the issues. Yes, the interests of a given caregiver and care receiver will sometimes conflict, but for the most part we do not pit our own interests against those of others in this context. We want what will be good for both or all of us together. We want our children and others we care for, and those who care for us, to do well along with ourselves, and for the relations between us to be good ones. The dominant assumption that the issues being considered are always about the self versus others or the self versus the universal "all others" needs to be revised in this context and then extended.

From Virginia Held, "The Ethics of Care as Normative Guidance: Comment on Gilligan." *Journal of Social Philosophy* 45: 1 (Spring 2014), pp. 107–115.

Review Exercises

1. Explain the basic difference between psychological egoism and ethical egoism.

2. Explain how reciprocal altruism is connected to enlightened self-interest.

3. Is psychological egoism true, and what must be shown to prove its truth?

4. How is psychological egoism supposed to provide support for an argument for ethical egoism? What is one problem for this argument?

5. Summarize the arguments regarding the consistency or inconsistency of ethical egoism.

6. In what sense does the argument for ethical egoism based on economics support not egoism but utilitarianism—in other words, the view that we ought to do what is in the best interest of all or the greatest number?

7. Explain how the prisoner's dilemma can be used in discussions of egoism and cooperative endeavor.

8. How does the social contract provide a response to the challenge of egoism?

9. How would care ethicists respond to the debate about egoism and altruism?

10. How does the discussion of evolution (in Pinker) inform our understanding of the conflict between egoism and altruism?

Knowledge Check Answer Key

1. **False.** Psychological egoism is not normative; rather, it describes egoistic self-regard.

2. **d.** Nepotism occurs when we refuse to give preference to those we love.

3. **a.** Ethical Egoism

4. **c.** To show that noncooperative egoists can end up with worse outcomes

5 Utilitarianism

Learning Outcomes

After reading this chapter, you should be able to:

5.1 Explain the differences between utilitarianism and egoism as kinds of consequentialism.

5.2 Provide an overview of John Stuart Mill's defense of utilitarianism.

5.3 Articulate ways that utilitarianism is related to hedonism and Epicureanism.

5.4 Identify key components of the utilitarian assessment of pleasure: intensity, duration, fruitfulness, and likelihood.

5.5 Describe the trolley problem and how it exemplifies the challenge of utilitarianism.

5.6 Explain the difference between act utilitarianism and rule utilitarianism.

5.7 Defend your own thesis regarding the value of utilitarianism.

Population Pressures

In 2019, the global population exceeded 7.7 billion people. The United Nations predicts that by 2030 the global population will increase to 8.5 billion, with the population growing to 9.7 billion by 2050.[1] The increase in human population during the past couple of centuries has been explosive. This growing population has created problems including overcrowding, soil depletion, overfishing, pollution, and climate change. Industrialization and technology have led

iStock.com/Hydromet

to massive use of carbon-based fuels, which contribute to global climate change. If the world's population keeps growing at the current pace—and if the growing human population eats, drives, and consumes at current rates—we may be headed for a worldwide environmental and humanitarian crisis. The United Nations has concluded, "should the global population reach 9.6 billion by 2050, the equivalent of almost three planets could be required to provide the natural resources needed to sustain current lifestyles."[2] Some argue that we should take steps to limit consumption, population growth, or both. Population control might include morally controversial technologies such as abortion. And proposals to limit consumption may impinge on our freedom. On the one hand, each of us wants the freedom to reproduce, spend, and consume as we wish. On the other, the cumulative effect of individual choices can lead to less happiness for all—as the overall increase in population and pollution may decrease opportunities and life prospects for everyone.

What Do You Think?

1. Is human population growth a problem?

2. Should we take steps to limit population growth? What kinds of steps?

3. Should the primary focus of ethics and social policy be the well-being of everyone, or should it be the rights and freedoms of individuals?

4. Do you think it is possible to promote general happiness for everyone (including future generations) without violating the liberty of some people?

Introduction

When we think about issues from a perspective that takes into account the general happiness of everyone, we are adopting a utilitarian point of view. Utilitarianism asks us to focus our moral concern on creating good outcomes for as many people as possible. Since it is concerned with outcomes, utilitarianism is a form of consequentialism.

Large social engineering projects are often grounded in utilitarian concerns. Consider the effort in China to control population growth by limiting reproduction to one child per family. This policy officially ended in 2015. But it was in place for about twenty-five years. Critics of the policy argued that it violated a fundamental right to reproduce. But the policy could be justified on utilitarian grounds as being in the interest of the majority—including future generations. An important question here is whether limitations on basic rights may be justified by the larger utilitarian concerns of social policy.

One virtue of utilitarianism is that it is responsive to empirical conditions and "facts on the ground." Utilitarian efforts to maximize good consequences require that we adjust our policies in light of changing circumstances. The one-child policy created outcomes that rippled across Chinese society, including, for example, a shift in family structure and gender ratios. As the Chinese government has adjusted its population policies, it has struggled to manage costs and benefits. An important question here is whether morality should be focused on complex and changing consequences or whether it should be concerned with abstract and invariable moral principles that are not focused on consequences.

Utilitarian reasoning can be used to justify a variety of actions and policy decisions. How do we justify speed limits on the highways? It might seem that each of us should be free to go as fast as we want. However, unbridled speed would result in more accidents, which not only kill people but also slow the rest of us down. Speed limits satisfy the utilitarian goal of maximizing the greatest happiness for the greatest number. Some will be unhappy because they can't drive 100 mph. But when we each drive at 65 mph and arrive safely, we are each more likely to be better off. Some may be less happy because they are forced to drive more slowly, but overall, more of us are happier. A similar kind of thing occurred during the COVID-19 pandemic, when cities shut down, schools moved online, and masks were required in order to slow the spread of the disease. Defenders of civil liberties argued that all this was a violation of their freedom. But public health officials justified these shutdowns and mask mandates in the name of the greater good of public health. (We will discuss this case in more detail in Chapter 10.)

Some uses of utilitarian reasoning are controversial because they seem to run counter to our intuitions about basic principles of right and wrong. Consider, for example, the use of torture in interrogations of terror suspects. If a terrorist had planted a bomb in a public place that would threaten to kill thousands of innocent people, would it be justifiable to torture the terrorist to force them to reveal the location of the bomb? On the one hand, some assert that torture is never permissible because it violates basic moral principles. The United Nations Convention Against Torture defines it as "any act by which severe pain or suffering, whether physical or mental, is intentionally inflicted on a person for such purposes as obtaining from him or a third person information or a confession."[3] On the other hand, suppose, for example, that torture could save many lives. Would it then be justified? Former vice president Dick Cheney maintained that "enhanced interrogation techniques" including waterboarding (a process that simulates drowning) produced useful information. According to the *New York Times,* the CIA waterboarded terror suspect Khaled Sheikh Mohammed 183 times.[4] In a speech on the tenth anniversary of the September 11 terror attacks, Cheney claimed that by waterboarding terrorists such as Mohammed, information was extracted that led to the assassination of Osama bin Laden.[5] Cheney and other members of the Bush administration justified torture on utilitarian grounds. Their view is shared by many. A Pentagon study of "the ethics of troops on the front line" during the American war in Iraq found that 41 percent said that "torture should be allowed to save the life of a soldier or Marine," and about the same number said that it "should be allowed to gather important information from insurgents."[6] From a utilitarian standpoint, it may make good sense to inflict pain on someone to prevent pain that would be inflicted on a greater number of others. From the same standpoint, however, one may argue that practices such as torture cause greater

harm than good—by extracting false confessions and lowering a country's standing with potential allies. In any event, the question remains: Does a good end justify an otherwise objectionable means?

Weighing Consequences

5.1 Explain differences between utilitarianism and egoism as kinds of consequentialism.

Utilitarianism encourages us to engage in a kind of cost–benefit analysis in which we analyze the benefits and costs of different choices. Whichever has the greater net benefit is the best alternative. Such an approach begins with the belief that we can measure and compare the risks and benefits of various actions. The idea is that actions are morally better or worse depending on whether they produce pleasure or pain or, more abstractly, on how they affect human well-being and happiness. Unlike egoism, utilitarianism focuses on the *sum* of individual pleasures and pains. It is not my pleasures or pains that matter, but the cumulative happiness of a number of people.

Another aspect of utilitarianism is the belief that each of us counts equally. Peter Singer, an influential contemporary defender of utilitarianism, derives utilitarianism from the basic idea that each person's interests ought to be given equal consideration. Related to this is the idea that "my own interests cannot count for more, simply because they are my own, than the interests of others."[7] The basic procedure for utilitarianism is to add up the interests of everyone who is affected by an action without privileging the interests of anyone in particular. Utilitarianism is thus opposed to racist or sexist ideas, for example, which often hold that the interests of some people matter more than the interests of others.

Utilitarianism suggests that we ought to consider the totality of consequences of a policy or action. Forms of utilitarianism will differ depending on how we understand what sorts of consequences or interests matter. Complexities arise in defining key concepts such as happiness, interest, and well-being. Singer, for example, wants to focus on *interests* instead of pleasures or happiness. This indicates that it is possible that some pleasures are not really in our interest. For example, drug use can produce pleasure, but it is not in anyone's

Figure 5-1 Utilitarianism focuses on the greatest happiness for the greatest number of people.

Annie Owen/Robert Harding World Imagery/Corbis

long-term interest to be addicted to cocaine or heroin. We might also focus on people's *preferences*—that is, what people themselves state that they prefer. But again there is an important question of whether our preferences actually coordinate with our interests—or can we prefer things that are not in our interest? In different terms, we might wonder whether pleasure is a good thing or whether genuine happiness can be reduced to pleasure. In any case, utilitarians have to provide an account of what matters when we try to add up benefits and harms—whether it is subjective feeling, taste, and preference, or whether it is something deeper and more objective such as well-being or other interests (in health, longevity, fulfillment, accomplishment, etc.).

Utilitarianism has to provide an account of *whose* interests or happiness matters. Jeremy Bentham, one of the founding fathers of utilitarianism, extended his utilitarian concern in a way that included all suffering beings, including nonhuman animals. Peter Singer would agree. He is well-known as an advocate of animal welfare. Like Bentham, he claims that the interests of nonhuman animals ought to be taken into account. (We discuss the issue of animal ethics further in Chapter 20.)

One important point to bear in mind when discussing utilitarianism is that utilitarians generally do not think that actions or policies are good or bad in themselves. Rather, for the utilitarian, the goodness or badness of an action is solely a function of its consequences. Thus, even killing innocent people may be acceptable if it produces an outcome that saves a greater number of others from harm.

Historical Background

5.2 Provide an overview of John Stuart Mill's defense of utilitarianism.

Jeremy Bentham and John Stuart Mill

The classical formulation of utilitarian moral theory is found in the writings of Jeremy Bentham (1748–1832) and John Stuart Mill (1806–1873). Jeremy Bentham was an English-born student of law and the leader of a radical movement for social and legal reform based on utilitarian principles. His primary published work was *Introduction to the Principles of Morals and Legislation* (1789). The title indicates his aim: to take the same principles that provide the basis for morals as a guide for the formation

and revision of law. Bentham believed that the same principles guided both social and personal morality.

James Mill, the father of John Stuart Mill, was an associate of Bentham's and a supporter of his views. John Stuart was the eldest of James's nine children. He was educated in the classics and history at home. By the time he was twenty, he had read Bentham and had become a devoted follower of his philosophy. The basic ideas of utilitarian moral theory are summarized in Mill's short work *Utilitarianism*, in which he sought to dispel the misconception that morality has nothing to do with usefulness or utility or that morality is opposed to pleasure. Mill was also a strong supporter of personal liberty, and in his pamphlet *On Liberty* he argued that the only reason for society to interfere in a person's life was to prevent them from doing harm to others. People might choose wrongly, but he believed that allowing bad choices was better than government coercion. Liberty to speak one's own opinion, he believed, would benefit all. However, it is not clear that utility is always served by promoting liberty. Nor is it clear what Mill would say about cases in which liberty must be restricted to promote the general good, as in the case of speed limits or airport security rules. But Mill's interest in public policy and legislation is made clear

Figure 5-2 A portrait of the utilitarian philosopher John Stuart Mill (1806–1873).

The Print Collector/Alamy Stock Photo

from the fact that he served in the British Parliament from 1865 to 1868.

The original utilitarians were liberal, progressive, empiricist, and optimistic. They believed that social policy ought to work for the good of all persons, not just the upper class. They believed that when interests of various persons conflicted, the best choice was that which promoted the interests of the greater number. The utilitarians were progressive in that they questioned the status quo. For example, they believed that if the contemporary punishment system was not working well, it ought to be changed. Social programs should be judged by their usefulness in promoting the greatest happiness for the greatest number. Observation would determine whether a project or practice succeeded in this goal. Thus, utilitarianism is part of the empiricist tradition in philosophy, which holds that we know what is good only by observation or by appeal to experience. Bentham and Mill were also optimists. They believed that human wisdom and science would improve the lot of humanity. Mill wrote in *Utilitarianism*, "All the grand sources of human suffering are in a great degree, many of them almost entirely, conquerable by human care and effort."[8]

Mill's Views on Race and Women

Of course, Mill and Bentham were products of their time and had some views that we would criticize today. But they were generally interested in an egalitarian worldview. Bentham and Mill were both critical, for example, of slavery. And Mill is well known as an advocate of improved relations between the sexes. In his essay *The Subjection of Women*, Mill criticized the treatment of women in his era, which did not allow them to develop their talents and contribute to the good of society. Consistent with these views, he also supported the right of women to vote. Later in life he married his longtime companion and fellow liberal Harriet Taylor. But Mill was a product of his times. He worked for the British East India Company, and in some of his writings, he defended British imperialism on vaguely utilitarian grounds. He claimed it was good for those who were colonized, since he thought that in being colonized, they would be "civilized." This view—sometimes called "the white man's burden"—has been criticized by opponents of colonialism and imperialism. One scholar has described Mill as a "tolerant imperialist."[9] He justified his imperialism

by claiming (in utilitarian fashion) that it was good for those who were educated and improved by the British. Mill's views of slavery were more obviously progressive. He was not sympathetic to the slavery of his time, which he described in 1850 as "cruelty, tyranny, and wanton oppression."[10] He condemned slavery as follows: "I have yet to learn that anything more detestable than this has been done by human beings in any part of the earth."[11]

The Principle of Utility

The basic moral principle of utilitarianism is called the **principle of utility** or the **greatest happiness principle**. As John Stuart Mill explained it, "actions are right in proportion as they tend to promote happiness, wrong as they tend to produce the reverse of happiness."

Utilitarianism is a form of consequentialism. It focuses on the consequences of actions. Egoism is also a form of consequentialism. But unlike egoism, utilitarianism focuses on the consequences for all persons impacted by an action. Consider the diagram used to classify moral theories provided in Chapter 1.

According to classical utilitarian moral theory, when we evaluate human acts or practices, we consider neither the nature of the acts or practices nor the motive for which people do what they do. As Mill puts it, "He who saves a fellow creature from drowning does what is morally right, whether his motive be duty or the hope of being paid for his trouble."[12] It is the result of one's action—that a life is saved—that matters morally. According to utilitarianism, we ought to decide which action or practice is best by considering the likely or actual consequences of each alternative. For example, over the years, people have called for a suicide barrier—a net that would catch would-be jumpers—on the Golden Gate Bridge in San Francisco, California, to prevent people from using it jump to their deaths. Nearly 2,000 people have jumped from the bridge to their deaths, and work has begun on a suicide barrier that will cost over $200 million when finally completed.[13]

Figure 5-3 Three focal points of moral judgment.

Building a suicide barrier on a bridge is neither good nor bad in itself, according to utilitarianism. Nor is it sufficient that people supporting the building of such a barrier be well intentioned. The main thing that matters for the utilitarian is whether, by erecting such a barrier, we would actually increase happiness by preventing suicides. And the useful outcome of preventing suicide must be weighed against the costs of such a project, in a kind of cost-benefit analysis.

Pleasure and Happiness

5.3   Articulate ways that utilitarianism is related to hedonism and Epicureanism.

Of course, there is an open question about whether suicide is good or bad. Some will argue that there is something inherently or intrinsically wrong with suicide. The deontologist Immanuel Kant provides this sort of argument, as you will see in Chapter 6, maintaining that suicide is wrong in principle. But utilitarians cannot argue that suicide is intrinsically wrong—since they do not focus on the intrinsic rightness or wrongness of acts. Instead, utilitarians have to consider the impact of suicide on the happiness of all those it affects.

Since utilitarians reject the idea that certain acts are intrinsically good or evil, they are open to experimentation and evidence. And they are open to various ways of conceiving the goodness of consequences. Any sort of consequences might be considered good—for example, power, fame, or fortune. However, classical utilitarianism is a *pleasure* or *happiness* theory, meaning that it tends to reduce all other goods to some form of pleasure or happiness. Utilitarianism was not the first such theory to appear in the history of philosophy. Aristotle's ethics, as we shall see in Chapter 8, also focuses on happiness, although it is different from utilitarianism in its focus on virtue. Closer to utilitarianism is the classical theory that has come to be known as **hedonism** (from *hedon*, the Greek word for pleasure) or **Epicureanism** (named after Epicurus, 341–270 bce). Epicurus held that the good life was the pleasant life. For him, this meant avoiding distress and desires for things beyond one's basic needs. Bodily pleasure and mental delight and peace were the goods to be sought in life.

Utilitarians believe that pleasure or happiness is the good to be produced. As Bentham puts it, "Nature has placed mankind under the governance of two sovereign masters, *pain* and *pleasure*. It is for them alone to point out what we ought to do, as well as to determine what we shall do."[14] Things such as fame, fortune, education, and freedom may be good, but only to the extent that they produce pleasure or happiness. In philosophical terms, they are **instrumental goods** because they are useful for attaining the goals of happiness and pleasure. Happiness and pleasure are the only **intrinsic goods**— that is, the only things good in themselves.

In this explanation of utilitarianism, you may have noticed the seeming identification of pleasure and happiness. In classical utilitarianism, there is no difference between pleasure and happiness. Both terms refer to a kind of psychic state of satisfaction. However, there are different types of pleasure of which humans are capable. According to Mill, we experience a range of pleasures or satisfactions from the physical satisfaction of hunger to the personal satisfaction of a job well done. Aesthetic pleasures, such as the enjoyment of watching a beautiful sunset, are yet another type of pleasure. We also can experience intellectual pleasures such as the peculiar satisfaction of making sense out of something. Mill's theory includes the idea that there are higher, uniquely human pleasures—as we will explain below.

In Mill's view, we should consider the range of types of pleasure in our attempts to decide what the best action is. We also ought to consider other aspects of the pleasurable or happy experience. According to the greatest happiness or utility principle, we must measure, count, and compare the pleasurable experiences likely to be produced by various alternative actions in order to know which is best.

Calculating the Greatest Amount of Happiness

5.4   Identify key components of the utilitarian assessment of pleasure: intensity, duration, fruitfulness, and likelihood.

Utilitarianism is not an egoistic theory. As we noted in Chapter 4's presentation on egoism, those versions of egoism that said we ought to take care of ourselves because this works out better for all in the long run are actually versions of utilitarianism, not egoism. Some philosophers have called utilitarianism *universalistic* because it is the happiness or pleasure of all who are affected by an action or practice that is to be considered. We are not just to consider our own good, as in egoism, nor just the good of others, as in altruism. Sacrifice may be good, but not in itself. As Mill puts it, "A sacrifice which does not increase or tend to increase the sum total of happiness, (utilitarianism) considers as wasted."[15] Everyone affected by some action is to be counted equally. We ourselves hold no privileged place, so our own happiness counts no more than that of others. I may be required to do what displeases me but pleases others. Thus, in the following scenario, Act B is a better choice than Act A:

> Act A makes me happy and two other people happy.
> Act B makes me unhappy but five others happy.

In addition to counting each person equally, Bentham and his followers identified five elements that are used to calculate the greatest amount of happiness: the net amount of pleasure or happiness, its intensity, its duration, its fruitfulness, and the likelihood of any act to produce it.[16]

Pleasure Minus Pain Almost every alternative that we choose produces unhappiness or pain as well as happiness or pleasure for ourselves, if not for others. Pain is intrinsically bad, and pleasure is intrinsically good. Something that produces pain may be accepted, but only if it causes more pleasure overall. For instance, if the painfulness of a punishment deters an unwanted behavior, then we ought to punish, but no more than is necessary or useful. When an act produces both pleasure or happiness and pain or unhappiness, we can think of each moment of unhappiness as canceling out a moment of happiness so that what is left to evaluate is the remaining or *net* happiness or unhappiness. We are also to think of pleasure and pain as coming in bits or moments. We can then calculate this net amount by adding and subtracting units of

pleasure and displeasure. This is a device for calculating the greatest amount of happiness even if we cannot make mathematically exact calculations. The following simplified equation indicates how the net utility for two acts, A and B, might be determined. We can think of the units as either happy persons or days of happiness:

> Act A produces 12 units of happiness and 6 of unhappiness (12 − 6 = 6 units of happiness).
> Act B produces 10 units of happiness and 1 of unhappiness (10 − 1 = 9 units of happiness).

On this measure, Act B is preferable because it produces a greater net amount of happiness, namely, 9 units compared with 6 for Act A.

Intensity Moments of happiness or pleasure are not all alike. Some are more intense than others. The thrill of some exciting adventure—say, running river rapids—may produce a more intense pleasure than the serenity we feel standing before a beautiful vista. All else being equal, the more intense the pleasure, the better. All other factors being equal, if I have an apple to give away and am deciding which of two friends to give it to, I ought to give it to the friend who will enjoy it most. In calculations involving intensity of pleasure, a scale is sometimes useful. For example, we could use a positive scale of 1 to 10 degrees, from the least pleasurable to the most pleasurable. In the following scenario, then, Act B is better (all other things being equal) than Act A, even though Act A gives pleasure to thirty more people; this result is because of the greater intensity of pleasure produced by Act B:

> Act A gives forty people each mild pleasure (40 × 2 = 80 degrees of pleasure).
> Act B gives ten people each intense pleasure (10 × 10 = 100 degrees of pleasure).

Duration Intensity is not all that matters regarding pleasure. The more serene pleasure may last longer. This also must be factored in our calculation. The longer lasting the pleasure, the better, all else being equal. Thus, in the following scenario, Act A is better than Act B because it gives more total days of pleasure or happiness. This is so even though it affects fewer people (a fact that raises questions about how the number of people counts in comparison to the total amount of happiness):

> Act A gives three people each eight days of happiness (3 × 8 = 24 days of happiness).
> Act B gives six people each two days of happiness (6 × 2 = 12 days of happiness).

Fruitfulness A more serene pleasure from contemplating nature may or may not be more fruitful than an exciting pleasure such as that derived from running rapids. The fruitfulness of experiencing pleasure depends on whether it makes us more capable of experiencing similar or other pleasures. For example, the relaxing event may make one person more capable of experiencing other pleasures of friendship or understanding, whereas the thrilling event may do the same for another. The fruitfulness depends not only on the immediate pleasure, but also on the long-term results. Indulging in immediate pleasure may bring pain later on, as we know only too well after overindulging in sweets or alcohol. So also the pain today may be the only way to prevent more pain tomorrow. The dentist's work on our teeth may be painful today, but it makes us feel better in the long run by providing us with pain-free meals and undistracted, enjoyable mealtime conversations.

Likelihood If before acting we are attempting to decide between two available alternative actions, we must estimate the likely results of each before we compare their net utility. If we are considering whether to go out for some sports competition, for example, we should consider our chances of doing well. We might have greater hope of success trying something else. It may turn out that we ought to choose an act with lesser rather than greater beneficial results if the chances of it happening are better. It is not only the chances that would count, but also the size of the prize. In the following equation, A is preferable to B. In this case,

"A bird in the hand is worth two in the bush," as the old saying goes:

> Act A has a 90 percent chance of giving eight people each five days of pleasure (40 days × 0.90 = 36 days of pleasure).
> Act B has a 40 percent chance of giving ten people each seven days of pleasure (70 days × 0.40 = 28 days of pleasure).

Quantity versus Quality of Pleasure

Bentham and Mill are in agreement that the more pleasure or happiness, the better. However, there is one significant difference between them. According to Bentham, we ought to consider only the *quantity* of pleasure or happiness brought about by various acts: how much pleasure, to how many people, how intense it is, how long-lasting, how fruitful, and how likely the desired outcome will occur. Consider Bentham's own comment on this point: The "quantity of pleasure being equal, pushpin (a children's game) is as good as poetry."[17] The aesthetic or intellectual pleasure that one might derive from reading and understanding a poem is no better in itself than the simple pleasure of playing a mindless game.

Mill agreed with Bentham that the greater amount of pleasure and happiness, the better. But Mill believed that the *quality* of the pleasure should also count. In his autobiography, Mill describes a personal crisis in which he realized that he had not found sufficient place in his life for aesthetic experiences; he realized that this side of the human personality also needed developing and that these pleasures were significantly different from others. This experience and his thoughts about it may have led him to focus on the quality of pleasures. Some are intrinsically better than others, he believed. For example, intellectual pleasures are more valuable in themselves than purely sensual pleasures. Although he does not tell us how much more valuable they are, he clearly believed this greater value ought to be factored into our calculation of the "greatest amount of happiness." Although I may not always be required to choose a book over food (e.g., I may now need the food more than the book), the intellectual pleasures that might be derived from reading the book are of a higher quality than the pleasures gained from eating.

Mill attempts to prove or show that intellectual pleasures are better than sensual ones. We are to ask people who have experienced a range of pleasures whether they would prefer to live a life of a human, despite all its disappointments and pains, or the life of an animal, which is full of pleasures but only sensual pleasures. He believes that people generally would choose the former. They would prefer, as he puts it, "to be a human being dissatisfied than a pig satisfied; better to be Socrates dissatisfied than a fool satisfied."[18] Socrates was often frustrated in his attempts to know certain things. He struggled to get a grasp on true beauty and true justice. Because human beings have greater possibilities for knowledge and achievement, they also have greater

potential for failure, pain, and frustration. The point of Mill's argument is that the only reason we would prefer a life of fewer net pleasures (the dissatisfactions subtracted from the total satisfactions of human life) to a life of a greater total amount of pleasures (the life of the pig) is that we value something other than the *amount* (quantity) of pleasures; we value the *kind* (quality) of pleasures as well.[19] When considering this argument, you might ask yourself two questions. First, would people generally prefer to be Socrates than a pig? Second, if Mill is correct in his factual assessment, then what does this fact prove? Could it be that people are mistaken about what kinds of pleasures are the best, as Socrates himself often implied? This points us back to the question of whether happiness is merely a subjective preference or whether happiness resides in a more objective standard.

▶ Knowledge Check   Answers appear at the end of the chapter.

1. Utilitarianism is a non-consequentialist theory of ethics (True/False).

2. What might a utilitarian say about an activity such as torture?

   a. That torture might be justifiable if it produces a good outcome such as preventing a terrorist attack.

   b. That torture can only be justified if it is not lethal.

   c. That there is a fundamental prohibition against torture grounded in the idea of human rights.

   d. That there is something wrong with the character and personality of those who torture others.

3. Which of the following is a primary concern for utilitarianism?

   a. Cultivating the talents of geniuses at the expense of everyone else.

   b. Developing an account of intrinsic good that ignores questions of instrumental value.

   c. Maximizing pleasure and happiness for everyone while minimizing pain.

   d. Trying to create short and intense pleasure, while ignoring long-run consequences.

4. What is the point of Mill's discussion of Socrates and the pig?

   a. Mill was trying to show why utilitarianism can be useful in evaluating how humans behave toward animals.

   b. Mill was trying to justify meat-eating by claiming that Socrates was a carnivore.

   c. Mill was attempting to prove that the experience of animals matters in carrying out the utilitarian calculus.

   d. Mill was trying to explain the importance of qualitative differences in pleasure and happiness.

Evaluating Utilitarianism

The following are just some of the many considerations raised by those who wish to determine whether utilitarianism is a valid moral theory.

Application of the Principle

One reaction that students often have to calculating the greatest amount of happiness is that this theory is too complex. When we consider all of the variables concerning pleasure and happiness that are to be counted when trying to estimate the "greatest amount of pleasure or happiness," the task of doing so looks extremely difficult. We must consider how many people will be affected by alternative actions, whether they will be pleased or pained by them, how pleased or pained they will be and for how long, and the likelihood that what we estimate will happen, will, in fact, come to be. In addition, if we want to follow Mill rather than Bentham, we must consider whether the pleasures will be the lowlier sensual pleasures, the higher more intellectual pleasures, or something in between. However, in reality, we may at any one time have to consider only a couple of these variables, depending on their relevance to the moral question we are considering.

The point of this criticism is that no one can consider all of the variables that utilitarianism requires us to consider: the probable consequences of our action to all affected in terms of duration, intensity, fruitfulness, likelihood, and type or quality of pleasure. It also requires us to have a common unit of measurement of pleasure. (Elementary units called *hedons* have been suggested.) The difficulty is finding a way to reduce pleasures of all kinds to some common or basic unit of measurement. A utilitarian could respond to these criticisms by arguing that while this complexity indicates that no one can be a perfect judge of utility, we do make better judgments if we are able to consider these variables. No moral theory is simple in its application.

A more difficult problem in how to apply the principle of utility comes from Mill's specific formulation of it. It may well be that in some cases, at least, one cannot both maximize happiness and make the greatest number of people happy. Thus, one choice may produce 200 units of happiness—but for just one person. The other alternative might produce 150 units of happiness, 50 for each of three people. If the maximization of overall happiness is taken as primary, we should go with the first choice; if the number of people is to take precedence, we should go with the second choice. Most readings of Mill, however, suggest that he would give preference to the overall maximization of utility. In that case, how the happiness was distributed (to one versus three) would not, in itself, count.

Utilitarianism and Personal Integrity

A more substantive criticism of utilitarianism concerns its universalist and maximizing agenda—that we should always do that which maximizes overall happiness. Many critics have noted that utilitarian theory does not allow us to privilege our own happiness over that of others. Nor can we privilege the happiness of those we love. In determining what to do, I can give no more weight to my own projects or my own children than other people's similar projects or their children. For some philosophers, the idea that I must treat all persons equally is contrary to common sense, which tells us that we ought to care for our own children more than we care for the children of distant others. Utilitarians might respond that we should probably give more attention to our own projects and our own children, but only because this is likely to have better results overall. We know better how to promote our own projects and have more motivation to do so. Thus, giving preference to ourselves will probably be more effective.

A further objection maintains that there is something wrong if utilitarianism requires us to not give preference to ourselves and to our own personal moral commitments. Utilitarianism appears to be an affront to our personal integrity.[20] The idea is that utilitarianism seems to imply that I am not important from my own point of view. However, a utilitarian might respond that it is important that people regard themselves as unique and give due consideration to their own interests because this will probably have better consequences both for these individuals and the broader society.

Ends and Means

A second criticism concerns utilitarianism's consequentialist character. You may have heard the phrase "The end justifies the means." People often utter this phrase with a certain amount of disdain. Utilitarianism, as a consequentialist moral theory, holds that it is the consequences or ends of our actions that determine whether particular means to them are justified. This seems to lead to conclusions that are contrary to commonsense morality. For example, wouldn't it justify punishing or torturing an innocent person, a "scapegoat," in order to prevent a great evil or to promote a great good? Or could we not justify on utilitarian grounds the killing of some individuals for the sake of the good of a greater number, perhaps in the name of population control? Or could I not make an exception for myself from obeying a law, alleging that it is for some greater long-term good? Utilitarians might respond by noting that such actions or practices will probably do more harm than good, especially if we take a long-range view. In particular, they might point out that practices allowing the punishment of known innocents would undermine the legitimacy and deterrent effect of the law—and thus reduce overall utility.

The Trolley Problem

5.5 Describe the trolley problem and how it exemplifies the challenge of utilitarianism.

One particular problem for utilitarianism is exemplified by what has come to be called the trolley problem.[21] According to one version of this scenario, imagine you find yourself beside a train track, on which a trolley is speeding toward a junction. On the track ahead of the trolley are five workers who will all be killed if the trolley continues on its current course. You have access to a switch, and if you pull it, the trolley will be diverted onto another track where it will kill only one worker. According to utilitarianism, if nothing else is relevant, you would not only be permitted but *required* to pull the switch, which would result in one death and five lives saved. From a utilitarian standpoint, it is obvious that you should pull the switch, since not pulling the switch would result in greater net loss of life. Now, compare this scenario with another. In this case, you find yourself on a bridge over a single trolley track with the five workers below you. Next to you on the bridge is a very large man. The only way to stop the trolley in this case is to push the big fellow off the bridge and onto the tracks ahead of the workers. Would you be permitted to do this? In both cases, five lives would be saved and one lost. But are the cases the same morally? It would seem that according to utilitarianism, in which only the results matter, the cases would be morally the same. However, it is the intuition of most people that the second case is significantly different. You can't kill one person to save five. To take another example, it seems clear that a doctor who has five patients needing organ transplants to save their lives should not be permitted to take those organs out of another healthy patient and thereby killing the healthy patient.

It is important to note that versions of the trolley problem have been employed by psychologists to probe human decision-making procedures. Some of this research examines how different parts of the brain are involved in different ways of making decisions that involve moral dilemmas.[22] This sort of research investigates the psychological sources of our decisions—whether emotional responses predominate, whether we actually calculate costs and benefits, and whether we tend to feel bound to abstract moral rules. One study used a virtual reality version of the trolley problem to pursue this question. It found that 89 percent of people chose the utilitarian option when confronted with a 3D virtual reality representation of a run-away boxcar that threatened to crash into a group of people.[23] One issue exposed by these sorts of studies is that people respond differently when confronted with the choice of doing something (pulling the lever to divert the train into the group of people) or not doing something (allowing the train to crash into the group). One conclusion of this sort of research is that sometimes there are conflicts in how we actually react and how we think we *should* react to morally fraught situations. Other inquiries have considered whether utilitarian calculation involves a sort of "coldness" that runs counter to empathy and other emotional responses.[24] Another study by Daniel Bartels and David Pizarro concludes, "participants who indicated greater endorsement of utilitarian solutions had higher scores on measures of psychopathy, Machiavellianism, and life meaninglessness."[25] This potentially disturbing connotation of utilitarian reasoning appears to follow from the fact that the utilitarian

© Cengage Learning

Figure 5-4 The trolley problem asks us to consider whether the numbers count and whether there is a difference between doing and allowing.

decision—to kill one in order to save others—asks us to overcome an emotional or instinctual aversion to harming others. And yet it might be that—from the utilitarian point of view—this is exactly what we should do in order to bring about greater happiness for the greatest number. The psychological research into the dilemmas generated by utilitarianism is interesting. But the normative or moral question remains. Moral philosophy is not merely interested in the psychological question of how we react in these situations, it is also concerned with the question of how we *ought* to react.

Act and Rule Utilitarianism

5.6 Explain the difference between act utilitarianism and rule utilitarianism.

Utilitarianism may appear to justify any action just so long as it has better consequences than other available actions. Therefore, cheating, stealing, lying, and breaking promises may all seem to be justified, depending on whether they maximize happiness in some particular case. In response to this type of criticism, contemporary utilitarians often focus on general rules instead of on individual acts. The version of utilitarianism that focuses on rules is usually called **rule utilitarianism**. This is contrasted with **act utilitarianism**, which focuses solely on the consequences of specific individual acts.

Both are forms of utilitarianism. They are alike in requiring us to produce the greatest amount of happiness for the greatest number of people. They differ in what they believe we ought to consider in estimating the consequences. Act utilitarianism states that we ought to consider the consequences of *each act separately*. Rule utilitarianism states that we ought to consider the consequences of the act performed as a *general practice*.[26]

Take the following example. Ariel is considering whether to keep or break her promise to go out to dinner with Brandon. She believes that if she breaks this promise in order to do something else with other friends, then Brandon will be unhappy—but she and the other friends will be happier. According to act utilitarianism, if the consequences of her breaking the promise are better than keeping it, she ought to break it.

> Act utilitarianism: Consider the consequences of some particular act such as keeping or breaking one's promise.

A rule utilitarian, on the other hand, would tell Ariel to consider what the results would be if everyone broke promises or broke them in similar situations. The question "What if everyone did that?" is familiar to us. According to rule utilitarianism, Ariel should ask what the results would be if breaking promises in similar circumstances became a general practice or a general rule that people followed. It is likely that trust in promises would be weakened. This outcome would be bad, she might think, because if we could not trust one another to keep promises, we would generally be less capable of making plans and relating to one another—two important sources of human happiness. So, even if there would be no general breakdown in trust from just this one instance of promise-breaking, Ariel should still probably keep her promise according to rule utilitarian thinking.

> Rule utilitarianism: Consider the consequences of some practice or rule of behavior—for example, the practice of promise-keeping or promise-breaking.

Another way to understand the method of reasoning used by the rule utilitarian is the following: I should ask what would be the best practice. For example, regarding promises, what rule would have the better results when people followed it? Would it be the rule or practice "Never break a promise made"? At the other end of the spectrum would be the rule or practice "Keep promises only if the results of doing so would be better than breaking them." (This actually amounts to a kind of act utilitarian reasoning.) However, there might be a better rule yet, such as: "Always keep your promise unless doing so would have very serious harmful consequences." If this rule was followed, people would generally have the benefits of being able to say, "I promise," and have people generally believe and trust them. The fact that the promise would not be kept in some limited circumstances would probably not do great harm to the practice of making promises.

Some utilitarians go further and ask us to think about sets of rules. It is not only the practice of promise-keeping that we should evaluate, but also a broader set of related practices regarding truthfulness and bravery and care for children (for example). Moreover, we should think of these rules as forming a system in which there are rules for priority and stringency. These rules would tell us which practices are more important and how important they are compared to the others.

We should then do what the best system of moral rules dictates, where *best* is still defined in terms of the maximization of happiness.[27]

Which form of utilitarianism is better is a matter of dispute. Act utilitarians can claim that we ought to consider only what will or is likely to happen if we act in certain ways—not what *would* happen if we acted in certain ways but will not happen because we are not going to so act. Rule utilitarians can claim that acts are similar to one another and so can be thought of as practices. My lying in one case to get myself out of a difficulty is similar to another person's lying in other cases to get themselves out of difficulties. Because we should make the same judgments about similar cases (for consistency's sake), we should judge this act by comparing it with the results of the actions of everyone in similar circumstances. We can thus evaluate the general practice of "lying to get oneself out of a difficulty." You can be the judge of which form of utilitarian reasoning is more persuasive.

"Proof" of the Theory

One of the best ways to evaluate a moral theory is to examine carefully the reasons that are given to support it. Being an empiricist theory, utilitarianism must draw its evidence from experience. This is what Mill does in his attempt to prove that the principle of utility is the correct moral principle. His argument is as follows: Just as the only way in which we know that something is visible is its being seen, and the only way we can show that something is audible is if it can be heard, so also the only proof that we have that something is desirable is its being desired. Because we desire happiness, we thus know it is desirable or good. In addition, Mill holds that happiness is the only thing we desire for its own sake. All else we desire because we believe it will lead to happiness. Thus, happiness or pleasure is the only thing good in itself or the only intrinsic good. All other goods are instrumental goods; in other words, they are good insofar as they lead to happiness. For example, reading is not good in itself but only insofar as it brings us pleasure or understanding (which is either pleasurable in itself or leads to pleasure).

There are two main contentions in this argument. One is that good is defined in terms of what people desire. The other is that happiness is the only thing desired for itself and is the only intrinsic good. Critics have pointed out that Mill's analogy among what is visible, audible, and desirable does not hold up under analysis. In all three words, the suffix means "able to be," but in the case of *desirable*, Mill needs to prove not only that we can desire happiness (it is able to be desired), but also that it is *worth* being desired. Furthermore, just because we desire something does not necessarily mean that we *ought* to desire it or that it is good. There is a risk of the naturalistic fallacy (as defined in Chapter 1) here. Is this a case of illegitimately deriving an *ought* from an *is*?

Mill recognizes the difficulty of proving matters in ethics and that the proofs here will be indirect rather than direct. On the second point, Mill adds a further comment to bolster his case about happiness. He asserts that this desire for happiness is universal and that we are so constructed that we can desire nothing except what appears to us to be or to bring happiness. You may want to consider whether these latter assertions are consistent with his empiricism. Does he know these things from experience? In addition, Mill may be simply pointing to what we already know rather than giving a proof of the principle. You can find out what people believe is good by noticing what they desire. In this case, they desire to be happy or they desire what they think will bring them happiness.[28]

Utilitarianism is a highly influential moral theory that also has had significant influence on a wide variety of policy assessment methods. It can be quite useful for evaluating alternative health care systems, for example. Whichever system brings the most benefit to the most people with the least cost is the system that we probably ought to support. Although Mill was perhaps too optimistic about the ability and willingness of people to increase human happiness and reduce suffering, there is no doubt that the ideal is a good one. Nevertheless, utilitarianism has difficulties, some of which we have discussed here. You will know better how to evaluate this theory when you can compare it with those treated in the following chapters.

Chapter Summary

5.1 How can we explain the differences between utilitarianism and egoism as kinds of consequentialism?

Utilitarianism and egoism are both concerned with outcomes and consequences. However, while egoism is concerned with promoting good consequences for an individual ego, utilitarianism is focused on promoting the greater happiness for the greater number, which may in fact include some unhappiness for some individuals.

5.2 What are key ideas found in John Stuart Mill's defense of utilitarianism?

Mill formulated the principle of utility, which said that we should promote the greatest happiness for the greatest number of people. He was also interested in qualitative differences that exist between mere animalistic happiness and a more sophisticated human form of happiness. Mill extended his ideas toward a view that included rights for women and a critique of slavery.

5.3 How is utilitarianism related to hedonism and Epicureanism?

Hedonists, like Epicurus, are focused on pleasure. But rather than asserting that animalistic pleasure is the primary good, utilitarianism builds on the Epicurean focus on higher, human goods. As consequentialist theories, Epicureanism, hedonism, and utilitarianism are not primarily concerned with abstract and invariable moral principles.

5.4 What are the key ideas of the utilitarian assessment of pleasure, including intensity, duration, fruitfulness, and likelihood?

The utilitarian calculus involves weighing the pros and cons of an action with a focus on intensity (how intense is the pleasure or pain?), duration (how long will it last?), fruitfulness (how likely is it to generate other pleasures or pains?), and likelihood (how likely is pleasure or pain to occur?)

5.5 What is the trolley problem, and how does it exemplify the challenge of utilitarianism?

The trolley problem is a thought experiment that asks us to consider whether the numbers matter. There are variations of the basic setup, but the problem asks us to weigh the happiness of some against the happiness of others. In general, for utilitarianism, the numbers matter, and there is a correct answer, which is to kill one in order to save five people. The "challenge" is that decisions such as this are not easy, and some philosophers will maintain that this is a problem for utilitarianism, that is, that it downplays the complexity of moral life by insisting on a simplistic calculation of outcomes.

5.6 How can we explain the difference between act utilitarianism and rule utilitarianism?

Act utilitarianism focuses the utilitarian calculus on a distinct deed or single activity, asking whether this deed or activity tends to produce more (or less) happiness. Rule utilitarianism extends the utilitarian calculus in a way that asks whether the rule or principle generally promotes the greatest happiness for the greatest number.

5.7 How might you defend your own thesis regarding the value of utilitarianism?

Among the reasons to embrace utilitarianism is the fact that it takes consequences seriously. This also means that it is responsive to the empirical world and that the conclusions of the theory may change as conditions change. But this empirical and consequential basis also provides a focal point for critique. Different theories of ethics will claim that utilitarianism is, in a sense, too flexible and too responsive to the world. Such a non-consequentialist (and nonutilitarian) theory will insist that actions are good or evil based on some quality of the act itself or the intention behind the act. Utilitarianism is not concerned with the intrinsic value of the act itself; nor is it much concerned with intentions.

Primary Source Reading

The reading selection in this chapter is from the classical work *Utilitarianism* by John Stuart Mill. Mill considers the importance of happiness—and the need to consider the happiness of others. His work remains one of the important touchstones for thinking about utilitarianism.

Reading 5-1   Utilitarianism | John Stuart Mill

Study Questions

As you read the excerpt, please consider the following questions:

1. How does Mill describe the basic moral standard of utilitarianism?
2. How does he defend himself against those who accuse utilitarianism of being a crass pleasure theory similar to Epicureanism?
3. How do we know that happiness is a good in itself or as an end?

What Utilitarianism Is

The creed which accepts as the foundation of morals "utility" or the "greatest happiness principle" holds that actions are right in proportion as they tend to promote happiness; wrong as they tend to produce the reverse of happiness. By happiness is intended pleasure and the absence of pain; by unhappiness, pain and the privation of pleasure. To give a clear view of the moral standard set up by the theory, much more requires to be said; in particular, what things it includes in the ideas of pain and pleasure, and to what extent this is left an open question. But these supplementary explanations do not affect the theory of life on which this theory of morality is grounded—namely, that pleasure and freedom from pain are the only things desirable as ends; and that all desirable things (which are as numerous in the utilitarian as in any other scheme) are desirable either for pleasure inherent in themselves or as means to the promotion of pleasure and the prevention of pain.

Now such a theory of life excites in many minds, and among them in some of the most estimable in feeling and purpose, inveterate dislike. To suppose that life has (as they express it) no higher end than pleasure—no better and nobler object of desire and pursuit—they designate as utterly mean and groveling, as a doctrine worthy only of swine, to whom the followers of Epicurus were, at a very early period, contemptuously likened; and modern holders of the doctrine are occasionally made the subject of equally polite comparisons by its German, French, and English assailants.

When thus attacked, the Epicureans have always answered that it is not they, but their accusers, who represent human nature in a degrading light, since the accusation supposes human beings to be capable of no pleasures except those of which swine are capable. If this supposition were true, the charge could not be gainsaid, but would then be no longer an imputation; for if the sources of pleasure were precisely the same to human beings and to swine, the rule of life which is good enough for the one would be good enough for the other. The comparison of the Epicurean life to that of beasts is felt as degrading, precisely because a beast's pleasures do not satisfy a human being's conceptions of happiness. Human beings have faculties more elevated than the animal appetites and, when once made conscious of them, do not regard anything as happiness which does not include their gratification. I do not, indeed, consider the Epicureans to have been by any means faultless in drawing out their scheme of consequences from the utilitarian principle. To do this in any sufficient manner, many Stoic, as well as Christian, elements require to be included. But there is no known Epicurean theory of life which does not assign to the pleasures of the intellect, of the feelings and imagination, and of the moral sentiments a much higher value as pleasures than to those of mere sensation. It must be admitted, however, that utilitarian writers in general have placed the superiority of mental over bodily pleasures chiefly in the greater permanency, safety, uncostliness, etc., of the former—that is, in their circumstantial advantages rather than in their intrinsic nature. And on all these points utilitarians have fully proved their case; but they might have taken the other and, as it may be called, higher ground with entire consistency. It is quite compatible with the principle of utility to recognize the fact that some kinds of pleasure are more desirable and more valuable than others. It would be absurd that, while in estimating all other things quality is considered as well as quantity, the estimation of pleasure should be supposed to depend on quantity alone.

Some Pleasures Are Better than Others*

If I am asked what I mean by difference of quality in pleasures, or what makes one pleasure more valuable than another, merely as a pleasure, except its being greater in amount, there is but one possible answer. Of two pleasures, if there be one to which all or almost all who have experience of both give a decided preference, irrespective of any feeling of moral obligation to prefer it, that is the more desirable pleasure. If one of the two is, by those who are competently acquainted with both, placed so far above the other that they prefer it, even though knowing it to be attended with a greater amount of discontent, and would not resign it for any quantity of the other pleasure which their nature is capable of, we are justified in ascribing to the preferred enjoyment a superiority in quality so far outweighing quantity as to render it, in comparison, of small account.

Now it is an unquestionable fact that those who are equally acquainted with and equally capable of appreciating and enjoying both do give a most marked preference to the manner of existence which employs their higher faculties. Few human creatures would consent to

---

From John Stuart Mill, *Utilitarianism* (London: Parker, Son, and Bourn, 1863), Chapters 2 and 4.

* Heading added by the editor.

be changed into any of the lower animals for a promise of the fullest allowance of a beast's pleasures; no intelligent human being would consent to be a fool, no instructed person would be an ignoramus, no person of feeling and conscience would be selfish and base, even though they should be persuaded that the fool, the dunce, or the rascal is better satisfied with his lot than they are with theirs. They would not resign what they possess more than he for the most complete satisfaction of all the desires which they have in common with him. If they ever fancy they would, it is only in cases of unhappiness so extreme that to escape from it they would exchange their lot for almost any other, however undesirable in their own eyes. A being of higher faculties requires more to make him happy, is capable probably of more acute suffering, and certainly accessible to it at more points, than one of an inferior type; but in spite of these liabilities, he can never really wish to sink into what he feels to be a lower grade of existence. We may give what explanation we please of this unwillingness; we may attribute it to pride, a name which is given indiscriminately to some of the most and to some of the least estimable feelings of which mankind are capable; we may refer it to the love of liberty and personal independence, an appeal to which was with the Stoics one of the most effective means for the inculcation of it; to the love of power or to the love of excitement, both of which do really enter into and contribute to it; but its most appropriate appellation is a sense of dignity, which all human beings possess in one form or other, and in some, though by no means in exact, proportion to their higher faculties, and which is so essential a part of the happiness of those in whom it is strong that nothing which conflicts with it could be otherwise than momentarily an object of desire to them. Whoever supposes that this preference takes place at a sacrifice of happiness— that the superior being, in anything like equal circumstances, is not happier than the inferior—confounds the two very different ideas of happiness and content. It is indisputable that the being whose capacities of enjoyment are low has the greatest chance of having them fully satisfied; and a highly endowed being will always feel that any happiness which he can look for, as the world is constituted, is imperfect. But he can learn to bear its imperfections, if they are at all bearable; and

they will not make him envy the being who is indeed unconscious of the imperfections, but only because he feels not at all the good which those imperfections qualify. It is better to be a human being dissatisfied than a pig satisfied; better to be Socrates dissatisfied than a fool satisfied. And if the fool, or the pig, are of a different opinion, it is because they only know their own side of the question. The other party to the comparison knows both sides.

It may be objected that many who are capable of the higher pleasures occasionally, under the influence of temptation, postpone them to the lower. But this is quite compatible with a full appreciation of the intrinsic superiority of the higher. Men often, from infirmity of character, make their election for the nearer good, though they know it to be the less valuable; and this no less when the choice is between two bodily pleasures than when it is between bodily and mental. They pursue sensual indulgences to the injury of health, though perfectly aware that health is the greater good. It may be further objected that many who begin with youthful enthusiasm for everything noble, as they advance in years, sink into indolence and selfishness. But I do not believe that those who undergo this very common change voluntarily choose the lower description of pleasures in preference to the higher. I believe that, before they devote themselves exclusively to the one, they have already become incapable of the other. Capacity for the nobler feelings is in most natures a very tender plant, easily killed, not only by hostile influences, but by mere want of sustenance; and in the majority of young persons it speedily dies away if the occupations to which their position in life has devoted them, and the society into which it has thrown them, are not favorable to keeping that higher capacity in exercise. Men lose their high aspirations as they lose their intellectual tastes, because they have not time or opportunity for indulging them; and they addict themselves to inferior pleasures, not because they deliberately prefer them, but because they are either the only ones to which they have access or the only ones which they are any longer capable of enjoying. It may be questioned whether anyone who has remained equally susceptible to both classes of pleasures ever knowingly and calmly preferred the lower, though many, in all ages, have broken down in an ineffectual attempt to combine both.

From this verdict of the only competent judges, I apprehend there can be no appeal. On a question which is the best worth having of two pleasures, or which of two modes of existence is the most grateful to the feelings, apart from its moral attributes and from its consequences, the judgment of those who are qualified by knowledge of both, or, if they differ, that of the majority among them, must be admitted as final. And there needs be the less hesitation to accept this judgment respecting the quality of pleasures, since there is no other tribunal to be referred to even on the question of quantity. What means are there of determining which is the acutest of two pains, or the intenser of two pleasurable sensations, except the general suffrage of those who are familiar with both? Neither pains nor pleasures are homogeneous, and pain is always heterogeneous with pleasure. What is there to decide whether a particular pleasure is worth purchasing at the cost of a particular pain, except the feelings and judgment of the experienced? When, therefore, those feelings and judgment declare the pleasures derived from the higher faculties to be preferable in kind, apart from the question of intensity, to those of which the animal nature, disjoined from the higher faculties, is susceptible, they are entitled on this subject to the same regard.

The Moral Standard

I have dwelt on this point as being a necessary part of a perfectly just conception of utility or happiness considered as the directive rule of human conduct. But it is by no means an indispensable condition to the acceptance of the utilitarian standard; for that standard is not the agent's own greatest happiness, but the greatest amount of happiness altogether; and if it may possibly be doubted whether a noble character is always the happier for its nobleness, there can be no doubt that it makes other people happier, and that the world in general is immensely a gainer by it. Utilitarianism, therefore, could only attain its end by the general cultivation of nobleness of character, even if each individual were only benefited by the nobleness of others, and his own, so far as happiness is concerned, were a sheer deduction from the benefit. But the bare enunciation of such an absurdity as this last renders refutation superfluous.

According to the greatest happiness principle, as above explained, the ultimate end, with reference to and for the sake of which all other things are desirable—whether we are considering our own good or that of other people—is an existence exempt as far as possible from pain, and as rich as possible in enjoyments, both in point of quantity and quality; the test of quality and the rule for measuring it against quantity being the preference felt by those who, in their opportunities of experience, to which must be added their habits of self-consciousness and self-observation, are best furnished with the means of comparison. This, being according to the utilitarian opinion the end of human action, is necessarily also the standard of morality, which may accordingly be defined "the rules and precepts for human conduct," by the observance of which an existence such as has been described might be, to the greatest extent possible, secured to all mankind; and not to them only, but, so far as the nature of things admits, to the whole sentient creation....

Of What Sort of Proof the Principle of Utility Is Susceptible

It has already been remarked that questions of ultimate ends do not admit of proof, in the ordinary acceptation of the term. To be incapable of proof by reasoning is common to all first principles, to the first premises of our knowledge, as well as to those of our conduct. But the former, being matters of fact, may be the subject of a direct appeal to the faculties which judge of fact—namely, our senses and our internal consciousness. Can an appeal be made to the same faculties on questions of practical ends? Or by what other faculty is cognizance taken of them?

Questions about ends are, in other words, questions [about] what things are desirable. The utilitarian doctrine is that happiness is desirable, and the only thing desirable, as an end; all other things being only desirable as means to that end. What ought to be required of this doctrine, what conditions is it requisite that the doctrine should fulfill—to make good its claim to be believed?

The only proof capable of being given that an object is visible is that people actually see it. The only proof that a sound is audible is that people hear it; and so of the other sources of our experience. In like manner, I apprehend, the sole evidence it is possible to produce that anything is desirable is that people do actually desire it. If the end which the utilitarian doctrine proposes to itself were not, in theory and in practice, acknowledged to be an end, nothing could ever convince any person that it was so. No reason can be given why the general happiness is desirable, except that each person, so far as he believes it to be attainable, desires his own happiness. This, however, being a fact, we have not only all the proof which the case admits of, but all which it is possible to require, that happiness is a good, that each person's happiness is a good to that person, and the general happiness, therefore, a good to the aggregate of all persons. Happiness has made out its title as one of the ends of conduct and, consequently, one of the criteria of morality.

But it has not, by this alone, proved itself to be the sole criterion. To do that, it would seem, by the same rule, necessary to show, not only that people desire happiness, but that they never desire anything else. Now it is palpable that they do desire things which, in common language, are decidedly distinguished from happiness. They desire, for example, virtue and the absence of vice no less really than pleasure and the absence of pain. The desire of virtue is not as universal, but it is as authentic a fact as the desire of happiness. And hence the opponents of the utilitarian standard deem that they have a right to infer that there are other ends of human action besides happiness, and that happiness is not the standard of approbation and disapprobation.

Happiness and Virtue

But does the utilitarian doctrine deny that people desire virtue, or maintain that virtue is not a thing to be desired? The very reverse. It maintains not only that virtue is to be desired, but that it is to be desired disinterestedly, for itself. Whatever may be the opinion of utilitarian moralists as to the original conditions by which virtue is made virtue, however they may believe (as they do) that actions and dispositions are only virtuous because they promote another end than virtue, yet this being granted, and it having been decided, from considerations of this description, what is virtuous, they

not only place virtue at the very head of the things which are good as means to the ultimate end, but they also recognize as a psychological fact the possibility of its being, to the individual, a good in itself, without looking to any end beyond it; and hold that the mind is not in a right state, not in a state conformable to utility, not in the state most conducive to the general happiness, unless it does love virtue in this manner—as a thing desirable in itself, even although, in the individual instance, it should not produce those other desirable consequences which it tends to produce, and on account of which it is held to be virtue. This opinion is not, in the smallest degree, a departure from the happiness principle. The ingredients of happiness are very various, and each of them is desirable in itself, and not merely when considered as swelling an aggregate. The principle of utility does not mean that any given pleasure, as music, for instance, or any given exemption from pain, as for example health, is to be looked upon as means to a collective something termed happiness, and to be desired on that account. They are desired and desirable in and for themselves; besides being means, they are a part of the end. Virtue, according to the utilitarian doctrine, is not naturally and originally part of the end, but it is capable of becoming so; and in those who live it disinterestedly it has become so, and is desired and cherished, not as a means to happiness, but as a part of their happiness.

To illustrate this further, we may remember that virtue is not the only thing originally a means, and which if it were not a means to anything else would be and remain indifferent, but which by association with what it is a means to comes to be desired for itself, and that too with the utmost intensity. What, for example, shall we say of the love of money? There is nothing originally more desirable about money than about any heap of glittering pebbles. Its worth is solely that of the things which it will buy; the desires for other things than itself, which it is a means of gratifying. Yet the love of money is not only one of the strongest moving forces of human life, but money is, in many cases, desired in and for itself; the desire to possess it is often stronger than the desire to use it, and goes on increasing when all the desires which point to ends beyond it, to be compassed by it, are falling off. It may, then, be said truly that money is desired not for the sake of an end, but as part of the end. From being a means to happiness, it has come to be itself a principal ingredient of the individual's conception of happiness. The same may be said of the majority of the great objects of human life: power, for example, or fame, except that to each of these there is a certain amount of immediate pleasure annexed, which has at least the semblance of being naturally inherent in them—a thing which cannot be said of money. Still, however, the strongest natural attraction, both of power and of fame, is the immense aid they give to the attainment of our other wishes; and it is the strong association thus generated between them and all our objects of desire which gives to the direct desire of them the intensity it often assumes, so as in some characters to surpass in strength all other desires. In these cases the means have become a part of the end, and a more important part of it than any of the things which they are means to. What was once desired as an instrument for the attainment of happiness has come to be desired for its own sake. In being desired for its own sake it is, however, desired as part of happiness. The person is made, or thinks he would be made, happy by its mere possession; and is made unhappy by failure to obtain it. The desire of it is not a different thing from the desire of happiness any more than the love of music or the desire of health. They are included in happiness. They are some of the elements of which the desire of happiness is made up. Happiness is not an abstract idea but a concrete whole; and these are some of its parts. And the utilitarian standard sanctions and approves their being so. Life would be a poor thing, very ill provided with sources of happiness, if there were not this provision of nature by which things originally indifferent, but conducive to, or otherwise associated with, the satisfaction of our primitive desires, become in themselves sources of pleasure more valuable than the primitive pleasures, both in permanency, in the space of human existence that they are capable of covering, and even in intensity.

Virtue, according to the utilitarian conception, is a good of this description. There was no original desire of it, or motive to it, save its conduciveness to pleasure, and especially to protection from pain. But through the association thus formed it may be felt a good in itself, and desired as such with as great intensity as any other good; and with this difference between it and the love of money, of power, or of fame—that all of these may, and often do, render the individual noxious to the other members of the society to which he belongs, whereas there is nothing which makes him so much a blessing to them as the cultivation of the disinterested love of virtue. And consequently, the utilitarian standard, while it tolerates and approves those other acquired desires, up to the point beyond which they would be more injurious to the general happiness than promotive of it, enjoins and requires the cultivation of the love of virtue up to the greatest strength possible, as being above all things important to the general happiness.

Happiness the Only Intrinsic Good

It results from the preceding considerations that there is in reality nothing desired except happiness. Whatever is desired otherwise than as a means to some end beyond itself, and ultimately to happiness, is desired as itself a part of happiness, and is not desired for itself until it has become so. Those who desire virtue for its own sake desire it either because the consciousness of it is a pleasure, or because the consciousness of being without it is a pain, or for both reasons united; as in truth the pleasure and pain seldom exist separately, but almost always together—the same person feeling pleasure in the degree of virtue attained, and pain in not having attained more. If one of these gave him no pleasure, and the other no pain, he would not love or desire virtue, or would desire it only for the other benefits which it might produce to himself or to persons whom he cared for.

We have now, then, an answer to the question, of what sort of proof the principle of utility is susceptible. If the opinion which I have now stated is psychologically true—if human nature is so constituted as to desire nothing which is not either a part of happiness or a means of happiness—we can have no other proof, and we require no other, that these are the only things desirable. If so, happiness is the sole end of human action, and the promotion of it the test by which to judge all human conduct; from whence it necessarily follows that it must be the criterion of morality, since a part is included in the whole.

Review Exercises

1. State and explain the basic idea of the principle of utility or the greatest happiness principle.

2. What does it mean to speak of utilitarianism as a consequentialist moral theory?

3. What is the difference between intrinsic and instrumental good? Give examples of each.

4. Which of the following statements exemplify consequentialist reasoning? Can all of them be given consequentialist interpretations if expanded? Explain your answers.

   a. Honesty is the best policy.

   b. Eduardo has the right to know the truth.

   c. What good is going to come from giving money to a homeless person on the street?

   d. There is a symbolic value present in personally giving something to another person in need.

   e. It is only fair that you give him a chance to compete for the position.

   f. If I do not study for my ethics exam, it will hurt my GPA.

   g. If you are not honest with others, you cannot expect them to be honest with you.

5. Is utilitarianism a hedonist moral theory? Why or why not?

6. Using utilitarian calculation, which choice in each of the following pairs is better, X or Y?

   a. X makes four people happy and me unhappy.
      Y makes me and one other person happy and three people unhappy.

   b. X makes twenty people happy and five unhappy.
      Y makes ten people happy and no one unhappy.

   c. X will give five people each two hours of pleasure. Y will give three people each four hours of pleasure.

   d. X will make five people very happy and three people mildly unhappy. Y will make six people moderately happy and two people very unhappy.

7. What is Mill's argument for the difference in value between intellectual and sensual pleasures?

8. Which of the following is an example of act utilitarian reasoning, and which is an example of rule utilitarian reasoning? Explain your answers.

   a. If I do not go to the meeting, others will not go either. If that happens, there would not be a quorum for the important vote, which would be bad. Thus, I ought to go to the meeting.

   b. If doctors generally lied to their patients about their diagnoses, patients would lose trust in their doctors. Because that would be bad, I should tell this patient the truth.

   c. We ought to keep our promises because it is a valuable practice.

   d. If I cheat here, I will be more likely to cheat elsewhere. No one would trust me then. So I should not cheat on this test.

Knowledge Check Answer Key

1. **True.** Utilitarianism is a non-consequentialist theory of ethics.

2. **a.** A utilitarian's response to an activity such as torture is that it might be justifiable if it produces a good outcome such as preventing a terrorist attack.

3. **c.** Maximizing pleasure and happiness for everyone while minimizing pain is a primary concern for utilitarianism.

4. **d.** In his discussion of Socrates and the pig, Mill was trying to explain the importance of qualitative differences in pleasure and happiness.

Deontological Ethics

Learning Outcomes

After reading this chapter, you should be able to:

6.1 Explain how deontology is a non-consequentialist approach to ethics.

6.2 Describe different deontological approaches to ethics.

6.3 Explain the difference between hypothetical and categorical imperatives.

6.4 Describe two formulations of the categorical imperative.

6.5 Apply Kantian reasoning to a variety of cases in the real world.

6.6 Evaluate the difference between perfect and imperfect duties.

6.7 Defend your own thesis with regard to the value of deontological ethics.

Conscientious Objection

Are you obligated to obey an unjust law or to comply with a policy that you think is immoral? On the one hand, it seems that morality requires us to refuse to apply policies that are immoral. If that's the case, we may have a duty of conscientious objection or conscientious refusal. But on the other hand, there might be chaos if everyone chose which laws they were going to obey. Society seems to function better if everyone simply obeys the law. While we may think that we only have a moral

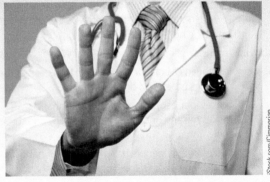

iStock.com/Cimmerian

duty to obey just laws, we might be concerned with the general consequences of disobedience. This issue comes up in a variety of contexts. Soldiers who disagree with the morality of a war may think they should refuse to fight. Health-care professionals who believe that certain practices are immoral may refuse to participate in those practices. And those who disagree with the policies of their government may want to stop paying their taxes. Conscientious objection is connected to the general idea of civil disobedience, which we discussed in Chapter 2. The American Transcendentalist thinker Henry David Thoreau refused to pay his taxes in the 1840s, claiming that he did not want to support slavery and what he viewed as an unjust war. A century later, Martin Luther King Jr. and others in the American Civil Rights Movement engaged in acts of civil disobedience, while opponents of the war in Vietnam of war refused to serve in the armed forces. Philosopher John Rawls reflected on this sort of thing, explaining that conscientious refusal could be justified when our "natural duty" to avoid doing "grave injustice" outweighs our duty to obey.[1] But if everyone refused to pay their taxes and broke laws they disagreed with, this could cause significant social problems. Fundamental questions arise here. What is our duty? Who or what should we obey? And do the consequences of disobedience matter?

What Do You Think?

1. Do we always have a duty to obey the law—even an unjust law?

2. Are you concerned about the consequences of disobedience, especially if it becomes widespread?

3. Does the context matter? For example, whether it is a soldier or a nurse who refuses? And what about tax refusers such as Thoreau?

4. How do we know what our duty is, especially when there is an apparent conflict between the duty to obey the law and the duty to avoid supporting injustice?

Introduction

6.1 Explain how deontology is a non-consequentialist approach to ethics.

An approach to ethics that emphasizes duty is best described as a deontological theory. The word *deontology* means "theory of duty" (the Greek word *deon* means "duty"). Deontological ethics focuses on duties, obligations, and rights. The term deontological was coined by the utilitarian philosopher Jeremy Bentham, who described it as "knowledge of what is right or proper."[2] Bentham thought that deontology points in the direction of the principle of utility. But contemporary philosophers use the term deontological to indicate a contrast with the utilitarian focus on the consequences of actions. Instead of focusing on consequences, deontological ethics focuses on duties and obligations: things we ought to do regardless emphasize of the consequences. One way of describing this is to say that deontological theories the *right* over the *good*, by which we mean that deontology focuses on right actions and right intentions, while downplaying the importance of the goods or benefits that are produced by these actions.

While utilitarian ethics focuses on producing the greatest happiness for the greatest number, deontological ethics focuses on what makes us worthy of happiness. This was an important idea for the philosopher Immanuel Kant, as well as for the Stoics and others who emphasize

duty. Rather than focusing on what makes us happy, Kant suggested that we should focus on what makes us think we deserve to be happy, which for Kant means obeying the moral law and doing our duty. As Kant explained, morality "is not properly the doctrine of how we are to make ourselves happy but of how we are to become worthy of happiness."[3] For Kant, morality is not a "doctrine of happiness" or set of instructions on how to become happy. Rather, it is the "rational condition of happiness." Kant maintains that there are certain things we ought *not* do, even if these things would produce the greatest happiness for the greatest number. Kant also suggests that morality should be focused on respecting the dignity and worth of persons. In Kant's language, we have a duty to respect persons as "ends in themselves," rather than viewing them as means to be used in the production of happiness.

The Ethics of Duty

6.2 Describe different deontological approaches to ethics.

In this chapter, we will primarily focus on the moral theory of Immanuel Kant (1724–1804). Kant was a German philosopher who is now regarded as a central figure in the history of modern philosophy. Modern philosophy itself is sometimes divided into pre-Kantian and post-Kantian periods. Although he is renowned for his moral philosophy, he wrote on a variety of matters including science, geography, beauty, and war and peace. Kant was a firm believer in the ideas of the Enlightenment (as discussed in Chapter 2), especially reason and freedom, and he was also a supporter of the American Revolution.

One of Kant's lasting ideas is what he calls "the categorical imperative," which can be understood in simple terms as Kant's basic idea of the moral law. We will explain this further in what follows. But let's note here at the outset that Kant gives a clear idea of what morality requires. One formulation of the categorical imperative goes as follows: *Always treat humanity, whether in your own person or that of another, never simply as a means but always at the same time as an end.* This principle requires respect for humanity that is not primarily concerned with consequences. We don't respect persons because it is useful but, rather, because it is right. In general, deontological ethics is less concerned with outcomes than with motives (such as respect) and the logic and principles that guide action.

This concern with the basic structure of moral principles is an important feature of Kant's deontological theory. But critics have argued that his focus on abstraction may be part of the reason he failed to critically interrogate the racist and sexist assumptions of his time. There is an interesting and evolving debate among scholars about the question of what Kant meant by key terms such as "humanity" and "person," and whether he thought that women and non-Europeans were to be included among those who were worthy of respect.[4] This scholarship shows that Kant—like other men of his generation—tended to view the world in a hierarchical fashion. As we discuss Kant and deontological ethics in general, it is worth asking who exactly counts as a person who is worthy of respect. And it is worth considering how deontological principles can be applied to concrete issues including racism, sexism, and other topics of contemporary concern.

There are a variety of deontological theories. Divine command ethics, as discussed in Chapter 2, is deontological in the sense that obedience to God's command is a duty that must be followed no matter what the consequences. The biblical story of Abraham and Isaac (in Genesis 22) provides an example of duty. Out of obedience to God's command, Abraham is willing to sacrifice his own son. In this story, religious duty must be done despite the consequences and the unhappiness that is produced.

This episode shows us one of the problems for divine command ethics—a problem that has been recognized since Socrates discussed it with Euthyphro in Plato's dialogue (see Chapter 2). How is morality related to God's commands? And how are we to know that it is, in fact, God who commands us and not the voice of our culture or our own selfish motives or even mental illness? The Abraham and Isaac episode famously prompted Kant to suggest that Abraham should have questioned God as follows: "That I ought not to kill my good son is quite certain. But that you, this apparition, are God—of that I am not certain, and never can be, not even if this voice rings down to me from heaven."[5] For Kant, the commands of ethics are clear, certain, and without exception—and they do not include the command to kill our own children. In response to this sort of criticism, the Danish philosopher Søren Kierkegaard suggested that the story of Abraham shows us that there may be religious duties that transcend the duties of ethics. Kant rejects such a claim. For Kant, moral duties are universal and absolute, and we should use our knowledge of morality to criticize and interpret religious stories and ideas.

Another form of deontological ethics can be found in the ancient Greek and Roman philosophy of **Stoicism**. The Stoics emphasized doing your duty and playing your part as determined by the natural order of things. Rather than struggling against *external* circumstances that we cannot control, the Stoics argue that the key to morality and happiness is *internal*, a matter of how we orient our will and intentions. According to this view, duty is its own reward. Epictetus, a Stoic philosopher who died in 135 CE, explains, "As Zeus has ordained, so act: if you do not act so, you will feel the penalty, you will be punished. What will be the punishment? Nothing else than not having done your duty: you will lose the character of fidelity, modesty, propriety. Do not look for greater penalties than these."[6]

The typical image of a Stoic is of a sternly disciplined, courageous, and emotionally composed individual who acts solely for the sake of duty—and whose commitment to obedience and duty infuses every part of life. We often associate Stoic ethics with the kind of courageous and selfless obedience to duty that is typical of soldiers. This image of military service and duty was embodied in the Roman Stoic emperor Marcus Aurelius, who describes the life of Stoic duty as follows: "It is thy duty to order thy life well in every single act; and if every act does its duty, as far as is possible, be content; and no one is able to hinder thee so that each act shall not do its duty."[7] He imagines someone objecting to the rigors of duty by claiming that some external circumstances stand in the way of the fulfillment of duty. But he replies, "Nothing will stand in the way of thy acting justly and soberly and considerately." As Marcus explains elsewhere, "it is thy business to do thy duty like a soldier in the assault on a town."[8] The basic idea of Stoicism is that we can control our own intentions and actions, even when we cannot control the consequences and external circumstances. From this standpoint, you fulfill your moral obligation by doing what you know is right, even if the external world makes that difficult.

Although Immanuel Kant admired the Stoics' emphasis on "strength of the soul,"[9] he also believed they underestimated the difficulty of being moral. One problem is that we are confused about moral duty—because we often confuse moral duties with other, more practical concerns, including the concerns of happiness. To clarify this, Kant focused on the logical and rational structure of duty itself—apart from considerations of happiness, prudence, or the natural order of things.

Another more modern sort of deontological approach to ethics can be found in discussions of human rights. Accounts of human rights typically claim that respect for human rights helps to define our duties. To say that someone has a right to freedom of speech, for example, creates a duty to respect that right. And a state that violated that right would be disrespecting that right, even if the state claimed that censorship was being used in pursuit of good consequences and the greater good. We'll discuss this further in the next chapter, where we'll consider human rights as connected with the idea of natural law. But let's note here that Kantian ethics has some affinity with natural law theory. Kant's own approach is more complicated—as we'll see here. But Kant's focus on autonomy and respect for persons can be used to help us understand the idea of human rights.[10]

While it is easy enough to state in general that there are duties and obligations that we ought to fulfill, it is more difficult to establish exactly what those duties and obligations are. In the opening vignette for this chapter, we saw how this issue arises with regard to obedience to unjust laws. Further questions arise, such as the following. Is patriotism an obligation—and does it include patriotism to an unjust or corrupt state? Is the duty to our parents and ancestors primary, as it is in the morality of Confucius? Do we have obligations of compassion and concern for all sentient beings, as many Buddhists argue? These questions remind us that deontological ethics might need to be supplemented with a broader theory of "the good," which tells us how the theory of duty should apply to personal, social, and political affairs. Indeed, this criticism of deontological ethics was noted by John Stuart Mill, who criticized Kant for defining a theory of duty that was so abstract that it could not rule out immoral actions.

As we turn to a more detailed discussion of Kant, bear this accusation in mind. Is Kant's conception of duty too abstract? Or does the Kantian theory help to specify our duties in sufficient detail to avoid this charge?

Figure 6-1 The story of Abraham and Isaac is an example of how religious duties may conflict with ethical duties.

iStockphoto.com/Duncan Walker

Immanuel Kant

6.3 Explain the difference between hypothetical and categorical imperatives.

Two of the main questions that Kant believed philosophy should address are: "What can I know?" and "What ought I do?"[11] While Kant's theory of knowledge is important and influential, our concern here is his moral philosophy.

One way to begin your examination of Kant's moral theory is to think about how he would answer the question, "What gives an act moral worth?" It is not the consequences of the act, according to Kant, that matters most. Suppose, for example, that I try to do what is right by complimenting a person on their achievements. Through no fault of my own, my action ends up hurting that person because they misunderstand my effort. According to Kant, because I intended and tried to do what I thought was right, I ought not be blamed for things having turned out badly. The idea is that we generally ought not to be blamed or praised for what is not in our control. The consequences of our acts are not always in our control, and things do not always turn out as we want. However, Kant believed that our motives are in our control. We are responsible for our intention to do good or bad, and thus it is for this that we are held morally accountable.

Kant also objected to basing morality on the consequences of our actions for another reason. To make morality a matter of producing certain states of affairs, such as happy experiences, seems to approach morality backwards. In such a view, actions and even human beings could be thought of as merely having *use value*. We would be valued to the extent that we were instrumental in bringing about what itself was of greater value, namely, happy states or experiences. However, in Kant's view, we should not be used in this way, for we are rational beings or *persons*. Persons have intrinsic or inherent value, according to Kant, not mere instrumental value. The belief that *people ought not to be used*, but ought to be regarded as having the highest intrinsic value, is central to Kant's ethics, as is having *a motive to do what is right*. As we shall see in the next two sections, Kant uses this second idea to answer the question: "What gives an act moral worth?"

What Is the Right Motive?

Kant believed that an act has moral worth only if it is done with a right intention or motive.[12] He referred to this as having a "good will." Kant writes that the only thing that is unconditionally good is a good will. Everything else needs a good will to make it good. Without a right intention, such things as intelligence, wit, and control of emotions can be bad and used for evil purposes. Having a right intention means doing what is right (or what one believes to be right) just because it is right. In Kant's words, it is to act "out of duty," out of a concern and respect for the moral law. Kant was not a relativist. He believed that there is a right and a wrong thing to do, whether or not we know or agree about it.

To explain his views on the importance of a right motive or intention, Kant provides the example of a shopkeeper who does the right thing, who charges her customers a fair price and charges the same to all. But what is her motive? Kant discusses three possible motives: (1) The shopkeeper's motive or reason for acting might be because it is a good business practice

Figure 6-2 A portrait of Immanuel Kant (1724–1804).

Georgios Kollidas/Alamy Stock Photo

to charge the same to all. It is in her own best interest that she do this. Although not necessarily wrong, this motive is not praiseworthy. (2) The shopkeeper might charge a fair and equal price because she is sympathetic toward her customers and is naturally inclined to do them good. Kant said that this motive is also not the highest. We do not have high moral esteem or praise for people who simply do what they feel like doing, even if we believe they are doing the right thing. (3) If the shopkeeper did the right thing just because she believed it was right, however, then this act would be based on the highest motive. We have a special respect, or even a moral reverence, for people who act out of a will to do the right thing, especially when this comes at great cost to themselves. An act has moral worth only when it is motivated by concern for the moral law.

Now, we do not always *know* whether our acts are motivated by self-interest, inclination, or pure respect for morality. Also, we often act from mixed motives. We are more certain that the motive is pure, however, when we do what is right even when it is not in our best interest (when it costs us dearly) and when we do not feel like doing the right thing. In these cases, we can know that we are motivated by concern to do the right thing because the other two motives are missing. Moreover, this ability to act for moral reasons, while resisting other inclinations, is one reason that human beings have a unique value and dignity. The person who says to himself, "I feel like being lazy (or mean or selfish), but I am going to try not to because it would not be right," is operating out of the motive of respect for morality itself. This ability to act for moral reasons or motives, Kant believes, is one part of what gives human beings dignity and worth.

What Is the Right Thing to Do?

For our action to have moral worth, according to Kant, we must not only act out of a right motivation but also do the right thing. Consider again the diagram of the three focal points of moral judgment that we used in Chapter 1.

Figure 6-3 Three focal points of moral judgment.

As noted earlier, Kant does not believe that morality is a function of producing good consequences. We may do what has good results, but if we do so for the wrong motive, then that act has no moral worth. However, it is not only the motive that counts for Kant. We must also do what is right. The act itself must be morally right. Both the act and the motive are morally relevant. In Kant's terms, we must act not only "out of duty" (have the right motive) but also "according to duty" or "as duty requires" (do what is right). How then are we to know what is the right thing to do? Once we know this, we can try to do it just because it is right.

To understand Kant's reasoning on this matter, we need to examine the difference between what he calls a **hypothetical imperative** and a **categorical imperative**. First of all, an imperative is simply a form of statement that tells us to do something, for example, "Stand up straight" and "Close the door" and also "You ought to close the door." Some, but only some, imperatives are moral imperatives. Other imperatives are hypothetical. For example, the statement "If I want to get there on time, I ought to leave early" does not embody a moral "ought" or a moral imperative. What I ought to do in that case is a function of what I happen to want—to get there on time—and of the means necessary to achieve this—leaving early. Moreover, I can avoid the obligation to leave early by changing my goals. I can decide that I do not need or want to get there on time. Then I need not leave early. These ends may be good or bad. Thus, the statement "If I want to harm someone, then I ought to use effective means" also expresses a hypothetical "ought." These "oughts" are avoidable, or, as Kant would say, contingent. They are contingent or dependent on what I happen to want or the desires I happen to have, such as to please others, to harm someone, to gain power, or to be punctual.

These oughts are also quite individualized. What I ought to do is contingent or dependent on my own individual goals or plans. These actions serve as means to whatever goals I happen to have (or whatever goals my particular community or society happens to approve). Other people ought to do different things than I because they have different goals and plans. For example, I ought to take introduction to sociology because I want to be a sociology major, while you ought to take a course on the philosophy of Kant because you have chosen to be a philosophy major. These are obligations only for those who have these goals or desires. Think of them in this form: "If (or because) I want X, then I ought to do Y." Whether I ought to do Y is totally contingent or dependent on my wanting X.

Moral obligation, on the other hand, is very different in nature. Kant believed that we experience moral obligation as something quite demanding. If there is something I morally ought to do, I ought to do it no matter what—whether or not I want to, and whether or not it fulfills my desires and goals or is approved by my society. Moral obligation is not contingent on what I or anyone happens to want or approve. Moral oughts are thus, in Kant's terminology, unconditional or necessary. Moreover, whereas hypothetical oughts relate to goals we each have as individuals, moral oughts stem from the ways in which we are alike as persons, for only persons are subject to morality. This is because persons are rational beings, and only persons can act from a reason or from principles. These oughts are thus not individualized but universal as they apply to all persons. Kant calls moral oughts *categorical imperatives* because they tell us what we ought to do no matter what, under all conditions, or categorically.

It is from the very nature of categorical or moral imperatives, as unconditional and universally binding, that Kant derives his views about morality. In fact, he uses the term *the categorical imperative* to describe the basic moral principle by which we determine what we ought and ought not to do.

The Categorical Imperative

6.4 Describe two formulations of the categorical imperative.

The categorical imperative, Kant's basic moral principle, is comparable in importance for his moral philosophy to the principle of utility for utilitarians. It is Kant's test for right and wrong. Several formulations of the categorical imperative are found in Kant's writings. We will concentrate on just two and call them the first and second forms of the categorical imperative. The others, however, do add different elements to our understanding of his basic moral principle and will be mentioned briefly.

The First Form

Recall that moral obligation is categorical; that is, it is unconditional and applies to all persons as persons rather than to persons as individuals. It is in this sense universal. Moreover, because morality is not a matter of producing good consequences of any sort (be it happiness, knowledge, or peace), the basic moral principle will be formal, without content. It will not include reference to any particular good. Knowing this, we are on the way to understanding the first form of the categorical imperative, which simply requires that we do only what we can accept or will that everyone do. Kant's own statement of it is basically the following:

> Act only on that maxim that you can will as a universal law.

In other words, whatever I consider doing, it must be something that I can consistently will or accept that all others do. To will something universally is similar to willing it as a law, for a law by its very nature has a degree of universality. By *maxim*, Kant means a description of the action or policy that I will put to the test. This is expressed in the form of a rule or principle. For example, I might want to know whether "being late for class" or "giving all my money to homeless people" describes a morally permissible action. I need only formulate some maxim or rule and ask whether I could will that everyone follow that maxim. For example, I might ask whether I could will the universal maxim or general rule, "Whenever I have money to spare, I will give it to those homeless people." However, this needs further clarification.

How do I know what I can and cannot will as a universal practice? As a rational being, I can only will what is noncontradictory. What do we think of a person who says that it is both raining and not raining here now? It can be raining here and not there, or now and not earlier. But it is either raining here or it is not. It cannot be both. So also we say that a person who wants to "have his cake and eat it, too" is not being rational. "Make up your mind," we say. "If you eat it, it is gone."

How I know whether I can will something universally without contradiction can be explained by using one of Kant's own examples. He asks us to consider whether it is morally permissible for me to "make a lying or false promise in order to extricate myself from some difficulty." Thus, I would consider the maxim, "Whenever I am in some difficulty that I can get out of only by making a lying or false promise, I will do so." To know whether this would be morally acceptable, it must pass the test of the categorical imperative. If I were to use this test, I would ask whether I could will that sort of thing for all. I must ask whether I could will a general practice in which people who made promises—for example, to pay back some money—could make the promises without intending to keep them. If people who generally made such promises did so falsely, then others would know this and would not believe the promises. Consider whether you would lend money to a woman if she promised to pay you back but you knew she was lying. The reasoning is thus: If I tried to will a general practice of false promise-making, I would find it impossible to do so because by willing that promises could be false, I would also will a situation in which it would be impossible to succeed in making a lying promise. Everyone would know that all promises were potential lies. No one could then make a promise, let alone a false promise, because no one would believe them. Part of being able to make a promise is to have it believed. The universal practice of false promise-making is self-contradictory and could not exist. If everyone made such lying promises, no one could!

Now consider an example such as that of the notorious Tuskegee syphilis experiments, in which Black men were used as medical test subjects without their full knowing consent (we discuss this example further in Chapter 10 in the context of racism and social justice concerns in health care). Using Kant's categorical imperative to test this, one would see that if it were a general practice for researchers to lie to their subjects in order to convince them to participate in experiments, they would not be able to get people to participate. A general practice of deceiving potential research subjects would undermine the credibility of all researchers. The only way a particular researcher could successfully lie would be if most other researchers told the truth. Only then could the researcher expect prospective subjects to believe the lie (since the research subjects would generally tend to believe that researchers were telling the truth). But it is easy to see that in this case the lying researcher is behaving in a way that makes an exception to the universal rule. Like false promising, a universal practice in which researchers lied to their prospective subjects is self-contradictory

and cannot be willed with consistency. Therefore, lying to prospective research subjects fails the test of the categorical imperative and is morally impermissible.

In some ways, Kant's basic moral principle, the categorical imperative, is a principle of fairness. I should not do what I am not able to will that everyone do. For me to succeed in making a lying promise, others must generally make truthful promises so that my lie will be believed. This would be to treat myself as an exception. But this is not fair. In some ways, the principle is similar to the so-called Golden Rule, which requires us only to do unto others what we would be willing for them to do unto us. However, it is not the same, for Kant's principle requires our not willing self-canceling or contradictory practices, whereas the Golden Rule requires that we appeal in the final analysis to what we would or would not like to have done to us. Kant explains that the Golden Rule

> cannot be a universal law, for it does not contain the principle of duties to oneself, nor of the duties of benevolence to others (for many a one would gladly consent that others should not benefit him, provided only that he might be excused from showing benevolence to them), nor finally that of duties of strict obligation to one another, for on this principle the criminal might argue against the judge who punishes him, and so on.[13]

To explain, the Golden Rule is only about what I or you like or don't like (what we would have others "do unto us"). But this fails to get us to the level of universal duty that is central to Kant's moral theory.

The Second Form

The first form of Kant's categorical imperative requires universalizing one's contemplated action or policy. In the second form, we are asked to consider what constitutes proper treatment of persons as persons. According to Kant, one key characteristic of persons is their ability to set their own goals. Persons are autonomous (from the Greek *auto*, meaning "self," and *nomos*, meaning "rule" or "law"). They are literally self-ruled, or at least capable of being self-ruled. As persons, we choose our own life plans, what we want to be, our friends, our college courses, and so forth. We have our own reasons for doing so. We believe that although our choices are influenced by our circumstances and by the advice and opinions of others, we knowingly allow ourselves be so influenced, and thus, these choices are still our own choices. In this way, persons are different from things. Things cannot choose what they wish to do. We decide how we shall use things. We impose our own goals on things, using wood to build a house and a pen or computer to express our ideas. It is appropriate to use things for our ends, but it is not appropriate to use persons as though they were things purely at our disposal and without wills of their own. Kant's statement of this second form of the categorical imperative is as follows:

> Always treat humanity, whether in your own person or that of another, never simply as a means but always at the same time as an end.

This formulation tells us how we ought to treat ourselves as well as others, namely, as ends rather than merely as means. Kant believes that we should treat persons as having value in themselves and not just as having instrumental value. People are valuable, regardless of whether they are useful or loved or valued by others. We should not simply use others or let ourselves be used. Although I may in some sense use a woman—for example, to paint my house—I may not *simply* use her. The goal of getting my house painted must be shared by the painter, who is also a person and not just an object to be used by me for my own ends. She must know what is involved in the project. I cannot lie to manipulate her into doing something to which she otherwise would not agree. And she must agree to paint the house voluntarily rather than be coerced into doing it. These and similar requirements are necessary for treating another person as an end rather than merely as a means to my ends or goals.

We can use this second form of the categorical imperative to evaluate the examples we considered for the first form. The moral conclusions should be the same whether we use the first or second form. Kant believes that in lying to another person—for example, saying that we will pay back money when we have no intention of doing so—we would be attempting to manipulate another person against that person's will. (Others are presumably unwilling to just give us the money.)

▶ Knowledge Check   Answers appear at the end of the chapter.

1. Deontology is a consequentialist theory of ethics (True/False).

2. Which of the following is NOT true?
    a. Deontological theories tend to emphasize the rightness of actions and intentions rather than the good they produce.
    b. Deontology is a concept that focuses on duty.
    c. Deontological theories are focused on finding ways to make people happy.
    d. The idea of human rights can be understood in deontological terms.

3. What might Kant say about the morality of lying?
    a. That lying is justifiable, if it is done for the greater good.
    b. That lying is justifiable, if it makes the liar happy.
    c. That lying is wrong because it is disrespectful of persons.
    d. That lying is wrong because it tends to produce unhappiness in the long run.

4. Which of the following (pick two) express two versions of the categorical imperative?
    a. Pursue your own self-interest and reciprocate with those who help you.
    b. Only act according to a rule that can be universalized.
    c. Always show respect to rational beings.
    d. Give love to those who need it.

This would violate the requirement not to use persons. Similarly, in the Tuskegee experiments, the deceptive researchers used the subjects as means to an end rather than as ends in themselves.

We noted that Kant provided more formulations of his categorical imperative than the two discussed here. In another of these formulations, Kant relies on his views about nature as a system of everything that we experience because it is organized according to laws. Thus, he says that we ought always to ask whether some action we are contemplating could become a universal law of nature. The effect of this version is to emphasize morality as universal and rational, for nature necessarily operates according to coherent laws. Other formulations of the categorical imperative stress autonomy. We are to ask whether we could consider ourselves as the author of the moral practice that we are about to accept. We are subject to both the moral law and its author because it flows from our own nature as a rational being. Another formulation amplifies what we have here called the second form of the categorical imperative. This formulation points out that our rationality makes us alike as persons, and together, we form a community of persons. He calls the community of rational persons a **kingdom of ends**— that is, a kingdom in which all persons are authors as well as subjects of the moral law. Thus, we ask whether the action we are contemplating would be fitting for and promote such a community. These formulations of the categorical imperative involve other interesting elements of Kant's philosophy, but they also involve more than we can explore here.

Evaluating Kant's Moral Theory

6.5 Apply Kantian reasoning to a variety of cases in the real world.

There is much that is appealing in Kant's moral philosophy, particularly its central aspects—its focus on motives, its emphasis on fairness, its aim of consistency, and its basic idea of treating persons as autonomous and morally equal beings. Kant's deontological approach is quite different from that exemplified by utilitarianism, with its emphasis on the maximization of happiness and the production of good consequences. To more fully evaluate Kant's theory, consider the following aspects of his thought.

The Nature of Moral Obligation

One of the bases on which Kant's moral philosophy rests is his view of the nature of moral obligation. He believes that moral obligation is real and strictly binding. According to Kant, this is how we generally think of moral obligation. If there is anything that we morally ought to do, we simply ought to do it. Thus, this type of obligation is unlike that which flows from what we ought to do because of the particular goals that we each have as individuals. To evaluate this aspect of Kant's moral philosophy, you must ask yourself whether this is also what you think about the nature of moral obligation. This is important for Kant's moral philosophy because acting out of respect for the moral law is required for an action to have moral worth. Furthermore, being able to act out of such a regard for morality is also the source of human dignity, according to Kant.

The Application of the Categorical Imperative

Critics such as John Stuart Mill (as noted previously) have pointed out problems with the universalizing form of the categorical imperative. For example, some have argued that when using the first form of the categorical imperative, there are many things that I could will as universal practices that would hardly seem to be moral obligations. I could will that everyone write their names on the top of their test papers. If everyone did that, it would not prevent anyone from doing so. There would be no contradiction involved if this were a universal practice. Nevertheless, this would not mean that people have a moral obligation to write their names on their test papers. A Kantian might respond that to write your name on your test paper is an example of a hypothetical, not a categorical, imperative. I write my name on my paper because I want to be given credit for it. If I can will it as a universal practice, I then know it is a morally permissible action. If I cannot will it universally, it is impermissible or wrong. Thus, the categorical imperative is actually a negative test—in other words, a test for what we should not do, more than a test for what we ought to do. Whether or not this is a satisfactory response, you should know that this is just one of several problems associated with Kant's universalizing test.

Concern for the universality of moral rules is not unique to Kantian ethics. We saw in Chapter 5 that rule utilitarianism is focused on the general utility of rules.

Although Kantians and rule utilitarians are both interested in universalized rules, there is a difference in how Kantian and rule utilitarian reasoning proceeds. Rule utilitarians require that we consider what the *results* would be if some act we are contemplating were to be a universal practice. Reasoning in this way, we ask what would be the results or consequences of some general practice, such as making false promises, or whether one practice would have better results than another. Although in some sense Kant's theory requires that we consider the possible consequences when universalizing some action, the determinant of the action's morality is not whether it has good or bad consequences, but whether there would be anything contradictory in willing the practice as a universal law. Because we are rational beings, we must not will contradictory things.

The second form of the categorical imperative also has problems of application. In the concrete, it is not always easy to determine whether one is using a person—for example, what is coercion and what is simply influence, or what is deception and what is not. When I try to talk a friend into doing something for me, how do I know whether I am simply providing input for my friend's own decision-making or whether I am crossing the line and becoming coercive? Moreover, if I do not tell the whole truth or withhold information from another person, should this count as deception on my part? Although these are real problems for anyone who tries to apply Kant's views about deceit and coercion, they are not unique to his moral philosophy. Theories vary in the ease of their use or application. Difficulty of application is a problem for most, if not all, moral philosophies.

Duty

Some of the language and terminology found in Kant's moral theory can sound harsh to modern ears. Duty, obligation, law, and universality may not be the moral terms most commonly heard today. Yet if one considers what Kant meant by duty, the idea may not seem so strange to us. Kant was not advocating any particular moral code or set of duties held by any society or group. Rather, duty is what reason tells us is the right thing to do. However, Kant might acknowledge that there is a streak of *absolutism* in his philosophy. Absolutists think that morality consists of a set of exceptionless rules. Kant does, at times, seem to favor absolutism. He provides examples in

which it seems clear that he believes it is always wrong to make a false promise or to lie deliberately. There is even one example in which Kant suggests that if a killer comes to the door asking for someone they intend to kill, you must tell the truth. But Kant's moral theory provides only one exceptionless rule, and that is given in the categorical imperative. We are never permitted to do what we cannot will as a universal law or what violates the requirement to treat persons as ends in themselves. Even with these two tests in hand, it is not always clear just how they apply. Furthermore, they may not give adequate help in deciding what to do when they seem to produce contradictory duties, as in the conflict between telling the truth and preserving a life.

Moral Equality and Impartiality

One positive feature of Kant's moral theory is its emphasis on the moral equality of all persons, which is implied in his view that the nature of moral obligation is universally binding. We should not make exceptions for ourselves; we should only do what we can will for all. Moral obligation and morality itself flow from our nature as rational and autonomous persons. Morality is grounded in the ways in which we are alike as persons, rather than the ways in which we are different as individuals. This provides a source for those who want to argue for moral equality and equal moral rights. If we do not treat others as equal persons, we are disrespecting them. If we are not willing to make the same judgment for cases similar to our own, or if we are not willing to have the same rules apply to all, we can be accused of hypocrisy. When we criticize hypocrisy, we act in the spirit of Kant.

Another feature of Kant's moral philosophy is its spirit of impartiality. For an action to be morally permissible, we should be able to will it for all. However, persons differ in significant ways. Among these are differences in gender, race, age, and talents. In what way does morality require that all persons be treated equally, and in what way does it perhaps require that different persons be treated differently in light of relevant differences?[14]

Some critics have wondered about Kant's stress on the nature of persons as rational and autonomous beings. It might be that human beings are not best conceived as rational autonomous beings, such as Kant describes. He seems to forget our emotions and our dependency on relationships. But Kant might reply that we often have no control over how we feel and thus that our feelings should not be a key element of our moral lives. He might also argue that it is the common aspects of our existence as persons, and not the ways in which we are different and unique, that give us dignity and are the basis for the moral equality that we possess. In short, even if we are often not fully autonomous or rational, we ought to consider ourselves as autonomous and rational—and treat others as if they were autonomous and rational—for this is the source of human dignity.

Kant's Views of Race and Women

Before we conclude our evaluation of Kant's ethical theory, it is important to note that Kant was a man of his times who held objectionable views of women and non-White people. Kant is correctly regarded as a philosophical innovator, who changed the way we think about ourselves and our place in the cosmos. His moral theory is complex and important. But Kant's innovations did not include a revision of the widely held sexist and racist ideas of his time. As mentioned at the outset of this chapter, Kant's views of women and non-European peoples reflected a hierarchical view of human nature. He thought that rationality—which was crucial to his moral theory as the focal point of respect and autonomy—was a rare achievement of European men. He suggested, in an early work, *Observations on the Feeling of the Beautiful and the Sublime* (1764), that women were incapable of attaining to the highest level of moral (and aesthetic) development. In that same text, Kant disparaged non-White people as inferior. Kant's views were influenced by his reading of David Hume (whom we discussed in Chapter 1)—and were common among the men of his generation, including members of the founding generation of the United States. Some defenders of Kant point out that his thinking about race and gender seems to have evolved over time and that in later texts (from the 1790s) he seems to have provided an incipient argument against slavery.

Some of the details of this debate may only be of interest to devoted scholars of Kant and the European Enlightenment. But the question of his racism and sexism is an important topic, worth considering as we evaluate his moral theory.[15] In thinking about this topic, it is worth considering whether Kant's cultural views

undermine the abstract and universalizing aims of his theory. Critics will argue that by focusing on the abstract logic of morality, as Kant does, he turns a blind eye to the inequality and oppression of the real world. But can we defend the ideal version of his deontological theory, while being more sensitive to how his thinking could be used to argue against issues such as racism and sexism?

It may be possible to develop a critique of racism and sexism that is grounded in Kantian deontology. Indeed, Charles Mills—a Black American philosopher—has offered such a reappropriation of Kant, suggesting that it is possible to use a "deracialized" Kantian theory of morality to articulate an anti-racist social and moral theory.[16] (We include an excerpt from Mills's work in the primary source readings for this chapter.) Mills explains that he is interested in "a Kantian discourse reshaped by the realities of racial subordination."[17] That would be a way of using Kant to argue against racism—and sexism. For example, we could argue (as Kant himself failed to do) that respect for persons ought to include respect for women and non-White persons, who ought to be considered as rational beings and end-in-themselves. We could insist that the idea of humanity be explicitly universalized so that it includes all human beings of all genders and races. And we could also argue, using the first version of Kant's categorical imperative, that slavery, racial injustice, and the subordination of women are wrong—since the maxims of those behaviors cannot be universalized.

Perfect and Imperfect Duties

6.6 Evaluate the difference between perfect and imperfect duties.

Before concluding our presentation of Kant, let's consider an important distinction that he makes between perfect and imperfect duties. In his attempt to explain his views, Kant provides us with several examples. We have already considered one of these: making a false promise. His conclusion is that we should not make a false or lying promise, both because we could not consistently will it for all and because it violates our obligation to treat persons as persons and not to use them only for our own purposes. Kant calls such duties **perfect duties** (they are sometimes described as *necessary* duties). As the term suggests, perfect duties

MPI/Archive Photos/Getty Images

Figure 6-4 Could Kantian principles be used to generate an argument against slavery, racism, or sexism?

are absolute. We can and should absolutely refrain from making false or lying promises. From the perspective of the first form of the categorical imperative, we have a perfect duty not to do those things that could not even exist and are inconceivable as universal practices. Using the second form of the categorical imperative, we have a perfect duty not to do what violates the requirement to treat persons as ends in themselves.

However, some duties are more flexible. Kant calls these duties **imperfect duties** (sometimes also called *meritorious* duties). Consider another example he provides: egoism. Ethical egoism is the view that we may rightly seek only our own interest and help others only to the extent that doing so also benefits us (see Chapter 4). Is this a morally acceptable philosophy of life? Using the first form of Kant's categorical imperative to test the morality of this practice, we must ask whether we could will that everyone was an egoist. If I try to do this, I would need to will that I was an egoist as well as others, even in those situations when I needed others' help. In those situations, I must allow

that they not help me when it is not in their own best interest. But being an egoist myself, I would also want them to help me. In effect, I would be willing contradictories; that they help me (I being an egoist) and that they not help me (they being egoists). Although Kant admits that a society of egoists could indeed exist, no rational person could will it, for a rational person does not will contradictories. We have an imperfect or meritorious duty, then, not to be egoists but to help people for their own good and not just for ours. However, just when to help others and how much to help them are a matter of some choice. There is a certain flexibility here. One implication of this view is that there is no absolute duty to give one's whole life to helping others. We, too, are persons and thus have moral rights and also can at least sometimes act for our own interests.

The same conclusion regarding the wrongness of egoism results from the application of the second form of the categorical imperative. If I were an egoist and concerned only about myself, I might argue that I was not thereby committed to using other people. I would simply leave them alone. But according to Kant, such an attitude and practice would still be inconsistent with the duty to treat others as persons. As persons, they also have interests and plans, and to recognize this, I must at least sometimes and in some ways seek to promote their ends and goals. Thus, avoiding egoism appears to be an imperfect duty, according to Kant's theory. The distinction between perfect and imperfect duties will have implications for handling conflicts among different duties. Perfect duties will take precedence over imperfect ones; we cannot help some by violating the rights of others.

Variations on Kant and Deontology

Just as there are contemporary versions of and developments within the utilitarian tradition, there are also many contemporary versions of Kantian and deontological moral theory. One is found in the moral philosophy of W. D. Ross, who also held that there are things we ought and ought not do regardless of the consequences.[18] We discussed Ross in Chapter 3 in relation to pluralism. According to Ross, we have duties not only of beneficence, but also to keep promises, pay our debts, and be good friends and parents and children. Contrary to Kant, Ross believed that we can know through moral intuition in any instance what we ought to do. Sometimes, we are faced with a conflict of moral duties. It seems intuitive that we ought to be both loyal and honest, but we cannot be both. We have *prima facie*, or conditional duties, of loyalty and honesty. In case of conflicting duties, according to Ross, we have to consider which duty is the stronger—that is, which has the greater balance of rightness over wrongness. In choosing honesty in some situations, however, one does not negate or forget that one also has a duty to be loyal. Obvious problems arise for such a theory. For example, how does one go about determining the amount of rightness or wrongness involved in some action? Don't people have different intuitions about the rightness or wrongness of any particular action? This is a problem for anyone who holds that intuition is the basis for morality.

This discussion of Ross and the possibility of conflicting duties takes us back to the question of conscientious objection with which we began this chapter. It might be that a fundamental conflict arises in this context. On the one hand, we have a duty to obey the law of the land; on the other hand, we have a duty to obey the moral law. Kant himself faced this dilemma. In his famous essay "What Is Enlightenment?" (1984), Kant broached the topic. His conclusion was, "argue as much as you like about whatever you like, but obey."[19] He advocated for the public use of reason and freedom of critical speech. But he still maintained that those who disagreed with state policies should nonetheless obey the law. In this regard, Kant's views are different from those of Thoreau, Martin Luther King, Jr., and others who defend the idea of conscientious objection.[20]

One of the most noted contemporary versions of Kant's moral philosophy is found in the political philosophy of John Rawls. In *A Theory of Justice*, Rawls applies some aspects of Kantian principles to issues of social justice. Rawls thinks that there are natural duties—not to be cruel, to help others, and what he calls a natural duty of justice, which includes a duty to support just institution and comply with them. But as we saw in the opening vignette, Rawls suggests, unlike Kant, that there may be a conflict of duties between obedience to the law and what a "natural duty" to avoid being an agent of grave injustice. Rawls unique contribution to ethics and politics is found in his idea of justice as fairness, as topic we discuss in more detail in Chapter 14. To know what is fair, we must put ourselves imaginatively in the position of a group of free and equal rational beings who are choosing principles of justice for their society. In thinking of persons as free and equal rational beings in order to develop principles of justice, Rawls is securely in the Kantian tradition of moral philosophy. Kant also stresses autonomy. It is this aspect of our nature that gives us our dignity as persons. Kant's categorical imperative also involves universalization. We must do only those things that we could will that everyone do. It is only a short move from these notions of autonomy and universalization to the Rawlsian requirement to choose those principles of justice that we could accept no matter which position in society we happen to occupy.

Kantian and other versions of deontology continue to be influential. And as we mentioned above, despite concerns about Kant's views of race and gender, scholars such as Charles Mills have found it useful to extend Kant's ideas to a critique of racism and sexism. You will be able to better evaluate the Kantian theory as you see aspects of it applied to issues in Part Two of this text.

Chapter Summary

6.1 How is deontology a non-consequentialist approach to ethics?

Deontological ethics focuses on duties. These duties are supposed to be required of us despite the consequences. Unlike a utilitarian approach that focuses on producing the greatest happiness for the greatest number, deontological theories are not concerned with maximizing happiness.

6.2 How can we describe different deontological approaches to ethics?

Deontology means "theory of duty." Kantian deontology emphasizes the universality of the moral law and our duty to respect persons and the moral law. Other deontological theories describe duty in related ways. Stoicism focuses on doing your duty within the natural order of things (and is connected in this way to natural law theory). Divine command ethics can also be described as based on a duty to obey God's commands. W. D. Ross provided an account of duty that allowed for the possibility of conflicting duties.

6.3 What is the difference between hypothetical and categorical imperatives?

These are key concepts in Kant's account of ethics. Hypothetical imperatives are based on a presupposition about what we are aiming at. Hypothetical imperatives rules for obtaining some purpose. In this sense, they are about the means to be taken for some end and are thus connected with prudence. The categorical imperative is Kant's way of describing the moral law. It tells us what we ought to do, without regard for any particular purpose. The categorical imperative is not focused on thinking about means toward ends; rather, it provides a moral guide for thinking about any particular set of means and ends.

6.4 What are the two formulations of the categorical imperative?

The first formulation of the categorical imperative tells us to act only on those maxims (rules of action) that can logically be universalized. This formulation asks us to imagine that the rule applies universally. The second formulation specifies that we should respect persons as ends in themselves and not use them only as a means.

6.5 How might we apply Kantian reasoning to cases in the real world?

Kant discusses four cases. He argues against suicide from self-love. He argues that it is wrong to make a lying promise. He says we have a duty to develop our talents. And he suggests that charity is a good thing. In each case, he applies his two versions of the categorical imperative, asking whether the maxim of action can be universalized and whether it respects persons. In the chapter, we also discussed some other examples, including Kant's view

on conscientious objection: he contends that we should argue but obey. We also discussed how Kant's views might provide an argument against slavery (although Kant does not himself make that argument)—and how scholars such as Charles Mills suggest that Kantian ethics could be used to argue against racism and sexism.

6.6 How can we evaluate the difference between perfect and imperfect duties?

Perfect duties are necessary and absolute. For example, it is always wrong in Kant's view to make a lying promise. Imperfect duties are less absolute and more flexible. For example, while Kant suggest that there is a duty to be charitable, there is some flexibility about how charity ought to occur. In order to evaluate the difference between these types of duty, we would need to ask whether the obligation is something that permits some variation in its implementation (in which case it is an imperfect duty) or whether there is a strict and universal requirement (in which case it is a perfect duty).

6.7 How might you defend your own thesis with regard to the value of deontological ethics?

One virtue of deontological ethics is its non-consequentialist focus on duty. For those who want clear prescriptions and a theory of ethics that is universal, deontology is of value. Kantian deontology offers a logical analysis of the universality of the moral law that also tells us that we should respect persons as ends in themselves. This approach can provide clear answers to a number of moral questions. But a critic who wants moral judgment to be responsive to changing circumstances may suggest that the strictness of the Kantian approach is its fatal flaw. Moreover, while Kant's approach (and that of other deontological theories) separates happiness from duty in a way that asks us to become worthy of happiness, an approach to morality that is interested in happiness and pleasure may find the Kantian approach to be too abstract and demanding.

Primary Source Readings

The reading selection in this chapter from Kant's *Fundamental Principles of the Metaphysic of Morals* contains the key elements of his moral philosophy. As the title implies, Kant is trying to establish the foundations of morality. He begins by claiming that the only thing that is good without qualification is a good will. He goes on to explain duty and the categorical imperative, while applying these ideas to some basic examples.

We follow this reading from Kant with a short excerpt from Charles Mills's article on "Black Radical Kantianism." In this article, Mill argues for a reinterpretation of Kant that applies Kantian ideas to a critique of racism.

Reading 6-1   Fundamental Principles of the Metaphysic of Morals | Immanuel Kant

Study Questions
As you read the excerpt, please consider the following questions:

1. How does Kant state his basic moral principle?
2. What is the difference between a rule of skill, a counsel of prudence, and a command of morality?
3. Explain how Kant uses the categorical imperative in his four examples. Make sure you understand his application of both forms of the categorical imperative.

The Good Will*

Nothing can possibly be conceived in the world, or even out of it, which can be called good without qualification, except a good will. Intelligence, wit, judgment, and the other *talents* of the mind, however they may be named, or courage, resolution, perseverance, as qualities of temperament, are undoubtedly good and desirable in many respects; but these gifts of nature may also become extremely bad and mischievous if the will which is to make use of them, and which, therefore, constitutes what is called *character*, is not good. It is the same with the *gifts of fortune*. Power, riches, honor, even health, and the general well-being and contentment with one's condition which is called *happiness*, inspire pride, and often presumption, if there is not a good will to correct the influence of these on the mind, and with this also to rectify the whole principle of acting and adapt it to its end. The sight of a being who is not adorned with a single feature of a pure and good will, enjoying unbroken prosperity, can never give pleasure to an impartial rational spectator. Thus a good will appears to constitute the indispensable condition even of being worthy of happiness.

There are even some qualities which are of service to this good will itself, and may facilitate its action, yet which have no intrinsic unconditional value, but always presuppose a good will, and this qualifies the esteem that we justly have for them, and does not permit us to regard them as absolutely good. Moderation in the affections and passions, self-control and calm deliberation are not only good in many respects, but even seem to constitute part of the intrinsic worth of the person; but they are far from deserving to be called good without qualification, although they have been so unconditionally praised by the ancients. For without the principles of a good will, they may become extremely bad, and the coolness of a villain not only makes him far more dangerous, but also immediately makes him more abominable in our eyes than he would have been without it.

From Immanuel Kant, *Fundamental Principles of the Metaphysic of Morals*, trans. Thomas Kingsmill Abbott (1879; Project Gutenberg 2004), secs. 1 and 2, http://www.gutenberg.org/ebooks/5682

* Heading added by the editor.

* Some notes have been deleted and the remaining ones renumbered.

A good will is good not because of what it performs or effects, not by its aptness for the attainment of some proposed end, but simply by virtue of the volition, that is, it is good in itself, and considered by itself is to be esteemed much higher than all that can be brought about by it in favour of any inclination, nay even of the sum total of all inclinations. Even if it should happen that, owing to special disfavour of fortune, or the niggardly provision of a step-motherly nature, this will should wholly lack power to accomplish its purpose, if with its greatest efforts it should yet achieve nothing, and there should remain only the good will (not, to be sure, a mere wish, but the summoning of all means in our power), then, like a jewel, it would still shine by its own light, as a thing which has its whole value in itself. Its usefulness or fruitlessness can neither add nor take away anything from this value. It would be, as it were, only the setting to enable us to handle it the more conveniently in common commerce, or to attract to it the attention of those who are not yet connoisseurs, but not to recommend it to true connoisseurs, or to determine its value....

Acting from Duty

We have then to develop the notion of a will which deserves to be highly esteemed for itself, and is good without a view to anything further, a notion which exists already in the sound natural understanding, requiring rather to be cleared up than to be taught, and which in estimating the value of our actions always takes the first place, and constitutes the condition of all the rest. In order to do this we will take the notion of duty, which includes that of a good will, although implying certain subjective restrictions and hindrances. These, however, far from concealing it, or rendering it unrecognizable, rather bring it out by contrast, and make it shine forth so much the brighter. I omit here all actions which are already recognized as inconsistent with duty, although they may be useful for this or that purpose, for with these the question whether they are done from duty cannot arise at all, since they even conflict with it. I also set aside those actions which really conform to duty, but to which men have no direct inclination, performing them because they are impelled thereto by some other inclination. For in this case we can readily distinguish whether the action which agrees with duty is done from duty, or from a selfish view. It is much harder to make this distinction when the action accords with duty, and the subject has besides a direct inclination to it. For example, it is always a matter of duty that a dealer should not overcharge an inexperienced purchaser, and wherever there is much commerce the prudent tradesman does not overcharge, but keeps a fixed price for every one, so that a child buys of him as well as any other. Men are thus honestly served; but this is not enough to make us believe that the tradesman has so acted from duty and from principles of honesty: his own advantage required it; it is out of the question in this case to suppose that he might besides have a direct inclination in favour of the buyers, so that, as it were, from love he should give no advantage to one over another. Accordingly the action was done neither from duty nor from direct inclination, but merely with a selfish view.

On the other hand, it is a duty to maintain one's life; and, in addition, every one has also a direct inclination to do so. But on this account the often anxious care which most men take for it has no intrinsic worth, and their maxim has no moral import. They preserve their life *as duty requires*, no doubt, but not *because duty requires*. On the other hand, if adversity and hopeless sorrow have completely taken away the relish for life; if the unfortunate one, strong in mind, indignant at his fate rather than desponding or dejected, wishes for death, and yet preserves his life without loving it—not from inclination or fear, but from duty—then his maxim has a moral worth.

To be beneficent when we can is a duty; and besides this, there are many minds so sympathetically constituted that without any other motive of vanity or self-interest, they find a pleasure in spreading joy around them, and can take delight in the satisfaction of others so far as it is their own work. But I maintain that in such a case an action of this kind, however proper, however amiable it may be, has nevertheless no true moral worth, but is on a level with other inclinations, e.g., the inclination to honour, which, if it is happily directed to that which is in fact of public utility and accordant with duty, and consequently honourable, deserves praise and encouragement, but not esteem. For the maxim wants the moral import, namely, that such actions be done *from duty*, not from inclination. Put the case that the mind of that philanthropist were clouded by sorrow of his own, extinguishing all sympathy with the lot of others, and that while he still has the power to benefit others in distress he is not touched by their trouble because he is absorbed with his own; and now suppose that he tears himself out of this dead insensibility, and performs the action without any inclination to it, but simply from duty, then first has his action its genuine moral worth. Further still; if nature has put little sympathy in the heart of this or that man; if he, supposed to be an upright man, is by temperament cold and indifferent to the sufferings of others, perhaps because in respect of his own he is provided with the special gift of patience and fortitude, and supposes, or even requires, that others should have the same—and such a man would certainly not be the meanest product of nature—but if nature had not specially framed him for a philanthropist, would he not still find in himself a source from whence to give himself a far higher worth than that of a good-natured temperament could be? Unquestionably. It is just in this that the moral worth of the character is brought out which is incomparably the highest of all, namely, that he is beneficent, not from inclination, but from duty.

To secure one's own happiness is a duty, at least indirectly; for discontent with one's condition under a pressure of many anxieties and amidst unsatisfied wants might easily become a great temptation to *transgression of duty.*...

It is in this manner, undoubtedly, that we are to understand those passages of Scripture also in which we are commanded to love our neighbour, even our enemy. For love, as an affection, cannot be commanded, but beneficence for duty's sake; even though we are not impelled to it by any inclination, nay, are even repelled by a natural and unconquerable aversion. This is *practical* love, and not *pathological*, a love which is seated in the will, and not in the propensions of sense, in principles of action and not of tender sympathy; and it is this love alone which can be commanded.

The second proposition[1] is: That an action done from duty derives its moral worth, *not from the purpose* which is to be attained by it, but from the maxim by which it is determined, and therefore does not depend on the realization of the object of the action, but merely on the *principle of volition* by which the action has

taken place, without regard to any object of desire. It is clear from what precedes that the purposes which we may have in view in our actions, or their effects regarded as ends and springs of the will, cannot give to actions any unconditional or moral worth. In what then can their worth lie, if it is not to consist in the will and in reference to its expected effect? It cannot lie anywhere but in the *principle of the will* without regard to the ends which can be attained by the action. For the will stands between its *a priori* principle which is formal, and its *a posteriori* spring which is material, as between two roads, and as it must be determined by something, it follows that it must be determined by the formal principle of volition when an action is done from duty, in which case every material principle has been withdrawn from it.

Respect for the Moral Law

The third proposition, which is a consequence of the two preceding, I would express thus: *Duty is the necessity of acting from respect for the law*. I may have inclination for an object as the effect of my proposed action, but I cannot have respect for it, just for this reason, that it is an effect and not an energy of will. Similarly, I cannot have respect for inclination, whether my own or another's; I can at most if my own, approve it; if another's, sometimes even love it; i.e., look on it as favorable to my own interest. It is only what is connected with my will as a principle, by no means as an effect—what does not subserve my inclination, but overpowers it, or at least in case of choice excludes it from its calculation—in other words, simply the law of itself, which can be an object of respect, and hence a command. Now an action done from duty must wholly exclude the influence of inclination, and with it every object of the will, so that nothing remains which can determine the will except objectively the *law*, and subjectively *pure respect* for this practical law, and consequently the maxim[2] to follow this law even to the thwarting of all my inclinations.

Thus the moral worth of an action does not lie in the effect expected from it, nor in any principle of action which requires to borrow its motive from this expected effect. For all these effects—agreeableness of one's condition, and even the promotion of the happiness of others—could have been also brought about by other causes, so that for this there would have been no need of the will of a rational being; it is in this, however, alone that the supreme and unconditional good can be found. The preeminent good which we call moral can therefore consist in nothing else *than the conception of law* in itself, *which certainly is only possible in a rational being*, in so far as this conception, and not the expected effect, determines the will. This is a good which is already present in the person who acts accordingly, and we have not to wait for it to appear first in the result.[3]

The Categorical Imperative

But what sort of law can that be, the conception of which must determine the will, even without paying any regard to the effect expected from it, in order that this will may be called good absolutely and without qualification? As I have deprived the will of every impulse which could arise to it from obedience to any law, there remains nothing but the universal conformity of its actions to law in general, which alone is to serve the will as a principle, i.e., *I am never to act otherwise than so that I could also will that my maxim should become a universal law*. Here now, it is the simple conformity to law in general, without assuming any particular law applicable to certain actions, that serves the will as its principle, and must so serve it, if duty is not to be a vain delusion and a chimerical notion. The common reason of men in its practical judgments perfectly coincides with this, and always has in view the principle here suggested. Let the question be, for example: May I when in distress make a promise with the intention not to keep it? I readily distinguish here between the two significations which the question may have: Whether it is prudent, or whether it is right, to make a false promise. The former may undoubtedly often be the case. I see clearly indeed that it is not enough to extricate myself from a present difficulty by means of this subterfuge, but it must be well considered whether there may not hereafter spring from this lie much greater inconvenience than that from which I now free myself, and as, with all my supposed cunning, the consequences cannot be so easily foreseen but that credit once lost may be much more injurious to me than any mischief which I seek to avoid at present, it should be considered whether it would not be more prudent to act herein according to a universal maxim, and to make it a habit to promise nothing except with the intention of keeping

it. But it is soon clear to me that such a maxim will still only be based on the fear of consequences. Now it is a wholly different thing to be truthful from duty, and to be so from apprehension of injurious consequences. In the first case, the very notion of the action already implies a law for me; in the second case, I must first look about elsewhere to see what results may be combined with it which would affect myself. For to deviate from the principle of duty is beyond all doubt wicked; but to be unfaithful to my maxim of prudence may often be very advantageous to me, although to abide by it is certainly safer. The shortest way, however, and an unerring one, to discover the answer to this question whether a lying promise is consistent with duty, is to ask myself, Should I be content that my maxim (to extricate myself from difficulty by a false promise) should hold good as a universal law, for myself as well as for others? and should I be able to say to myself, "Every one may make a deceitful promise when he finds himself in a difficulty from which he cannot otherwise extricate himself"? Then I presently become aware that while I can will the lie, I can by no means will that lying should be a universal law. For with such a law there would be no promises at all, since it would be in vain to allege my intention in regard to my future actions to those who would not believe this allegation, or if they over hastily did so would pay me back in my own coin. Hence my maxim, as soon as it should be made a universal law, would necessarily destroy itself.

I do not therefore need any far-reaching penetration to discern what I have to do in order that my will may be morally good. Inexperienced in the course of the world, incapable of being prepared for all its contingencies, I only ask myself: Canst thou also will that thy maxim should be a universal law? If not, then it must be rejected, and that not because of a disadvantage accruing from it to myself or even to others, but because it cannot enter as a principle into a possible universal legislation, and reason extorts from me immediate respect for such legislation. I do not indeed as yet discern on what this respect is based (this the philosopher may inquire), but at least I understand this, that it is an estimation of the worth which far outweighs all worth of what is recommended by inclination, and that the necessity of acting from pure respect for the practical law is what constitutes duty, to which every other motive must give place, because it is the condition of a will being good in itself, and the worth of such a will is above everything.

Thus then, without quitting the moral knowledge of common human reason, we have arrived at its principle. And although no doubt common men do not conceive it in such an abstract and universal form, yet they always have it really before their eyes, and use it as the standard of their decision....

Moral and Nonmoral Imperatives

Everything in nature works according to laws. Rational beings alone have the faculty of acting according *to the conception of laws*, that is according to principles, i.e., have a will. Since the deduction of actions from principles requires *reason*, the will is nothing but practical reason. If reason infallibly determines the will, then the actions of such a being which are recognised as objectively necessary are subjectively necessary also; i.e., the will is a faculty to choose *that only* which reason independent of inclination recognises as practically necessary, i.e., as good. But if reason of itself does not sufficiently determine the will, if the latter is subject also to subjective conditions (particular impulses) which do not always coincide with the objective conditions; in a word, if the will does not in itself completely accord with reason (which is actually the case with men), then the actions which objectively are recognised as necessary are subjectively contingent, and the determination of such a will according to objective laws is obligation, that is to say, the relation of the objective laws to a will that is not thoroughly good, is conceived as the determination of the will of a rational being by principles of reason, but which the will from its nature does not of necessity follow.

The conception of an objective principle, in so far as it is obligatory for a will, is called a command (of reason), and the formula of the command is called an Imperative.

All imperatives are expressed by the word *ought* (or *shall*), and thereby indicate the relation of an objective law of reason to a will, which from its subjective constitution is not necessarily determined by it (an obligation). They say that something would be good to do or to forbear, but they say it to a will which does not always do a thing because it is conceived to be good to do it. That is practically *good*, however, which determines the

will by means of the conceptions of reason, and consequently not from subjective causes, but objectively, that is, on principles which are valid for every rational being as such. It is distinguished from the *pleasant*, as that which influences the will only by means of sensation from merely subjective causes, valid only for the sense of this or that one, and not as a principle of reason, which holds for every one.[4]

A perfectly good will would therefore be equally subject to objective laws (viz., of good), but could not be conceived as *obliged* thereby to act lawfully, because of itself from its subjective constitution it can only be determined by the conception of good. Therefore no imperatives hold for the Divine will, or in general for a *holy* will; *ought* is here out of place, because the volition is already of itself necessarily in unison with the law. Therefore imperatives are only formulae to express the relation of objective laws of all volition to the subjective imperfection of the will of this or that rational being, e.g., the human will.

Now all imperatives command either *hypothetically* or *categorically*. The former represent the practical necessity of a possible action as means to something else that is willed (or at least which one might possibly will). The categorical imperative would be that which represented an action as necessary of itself without reference to another end, that is, as objectively necessary.

Since every practical law represents a possible action as good, and on this account, for a subject who is practically determinable by reason as necessary, all imperatives are formulae determining an action which is necessary according to the principle of a will good in some respects. If now the action is good only as a *means to something else*, then the imperative is *hypothetical*; if it is conceived as good in itself and consequently as being necessarily the principle of a will which of itself conforms to reason, then it is *categorical*.

Thus the imperative declares what action possible by me would be good, and presents the practical rule in relation to a will which does not forthwith perform an action simply because it is good, whether because the subject does not always know that it is good, or because, even if it know this, yet its maxims might be opposed to the objective principles of practical reason.

Accordingly the hypothetical imperative only says that the action is good for some purpose, *possible* or *actual*. In the first case it is a *problematical*, in the second an *assertorical* practical principle. The categorical imperative which declares an action to be objectively necessary in itself without reference to any purpose, that is, without any other end, is valid as an *apodictic* (practical) principle.

Whatever is possible only by the power of some rational being may also be conceived as a possible purpose of some will; and therefore the principles of action as regards the means necessary to attain some possible purpose are in fact infinitely numerous. All sciences have a practical part consisting of problems expressing that some end is possible for us, and of imperatives directing how it may be attained. These may, therefore, be called in general imperatives of skill. Here there is no question whether the end is rational and good, but only what one must do in order to attain it. The precepts for the physician to make his patient thoroughly healthy, and for a poisoner to ensure certain death, are of equal value in this respect, that each serves to effect its purpose perfectly. Since in early youth it cannot be known what ends are likely to occur to us in the course of life, parents seek to have their children taught a *great many things*, and provide for their skill in the use of means for all sorts of arbitrary ends, of none of which can they determine whether it may not perhaps hereafter be an object to their pupil, but which it is at all events possible that he might aim at; and this anxiety is so great that they commonly neglect to form and correct their judgment on the value of the things which may be chosen as ends.

There is *one* end, however, which may be assumed to be actually such to all rational beings (so far as imperatives apply to them, viz., as dependent beings), and, therefore, one purpose which they not merely may have, but which we may with certainty assume that they all actually have by a natural necessity, and this is *happiness*. The hypothetical imperative which expresses the practical necessity of an action as means to the advancement of happiness is *assertorical*. We are not to present it as necessary for an uncertain and merely possible purpose, but for a purpose which we may presuppose with certainty and *a priori* in every man, because it belongs to his being. Now skill in the choice of means to his own greatest well-being may be called *prudence*,[5] in the narrowest sense. And thus the imperative which refers to the choice of means to

one's own happiness, that is, the precept of prudence, is still always *hypothetical*; the action is not commanded absolutely, but only as means to another purpose.

Finally, there is an imperative which commands a certain conduct immediately, without having as its condition any other purpose to be attained by it. This imperative is *categorical*. It concerns not the matter of the action, or its intended result, but its form and the principle of which it is itself a result; and what is essentially good in it consists in the mental disposition, let the consequence be what it may. This imperative may be called that of *morality*.

There is a marked distinction also between the volitions on these three sorts of principles in the dissimilarity of the obligation of the will. In order to mark this difference more clearly, I think they would be most suitably named in their order if we said they are either *rules* of skill, or *counsels* of prudence, or *commands* (laws) of morality. For it is law only that involves the conception of an unconditional and objective necessity, which is consequently universally valid; and commands are laws which must be obeyed, that is, must be followed, even in opposition to inclination. Counsels, indeed, involve necessity, but one which can only hold under a contingent subjective condition, viz., they depend on whether this or that man reckons this or that as part of his happiness; the categorical imperative, on the contrary, is not limited by any condition, and as being absolutely, although practically, necessary may be quite properly called a command. We might also call the first kind of imperatives *technical* (belonging to art), the second *pragmatic*[6] (belonging to welfare), the third moral (belonging to free conduct generally, that is, to morals).

Now arises the question, how are all these imperatives possible? This question does not seek to know how we can conceive the accomplishment of the action which the imperative ordains, but merely how we can conceive the obligation of the will which the imperative expresses. No special explanation is needed to show how an imperative of skill is possible. Whoever wills the end wills also (so far as reason decides his conduct) the means in his power which are indispensably necessary thereto....

We shall therefore have to investigate *a priori* the possibility of a categorical imperative, as we have not in this case the advantage of its reality being given in experience, so that (the elucidation of) its possibility should be requisite only for its explanation, not for its establishment. In the meantime it may be discerned beforehand that the categorical imperative alone has the purport of a practical law; all the rest may indeed be called principles of the will but not laws, since whatever is only necessary for the attainment of some arbitrary purpose may be considered as in itself contingent, and we can at any time be free from the precept if we give up the purpose; on the contrary, the unconditional command leaves the will no liberty to choose the opposite, consequently it alone carries with it that necessity which we require in a law....

In this problem we will first inquire whether the mere conception of a categorical imperative may not perhaps supply us also with the formula of it, containing the proposition which alone can be a categorical imperative; for even if we know the tenor of such an absolute command, yet how it is possible will require further special and laborious study; which we postpone to the last section.

When I conceive a hypothetical imperative in general, I do not know beforehand what it will contain, until I am given the condition. But when I conceive a categorical imperative I know at once what it contains. For as the imperative contains, besides the law, only the necessity of the maxim[7] conforming to this law, while the law contains no condition restricting it, there remains nothing but the general statement that the maxim of the action should conform to a universal law, and it is this conformity alone that the imperative properly represents as necessary.

There is therefore but one categorical imperative, namely this: *Act only on that maxim whereby thou canst at the same time will that it should become a universal law.*

Now if all imperatives of duty can be deduced from this one imperative as from their principle, then although it should remain undecided whether what is called duty is not merely a vain notion, yet at least we shall be able to show what we understand by it and what this notion means.

Applying the Categorical Imperative

Since the universality of the law according to which effects are produced constitutes what is properly called *nature* in the most general sense (as to form), that is the existence of things so far as it is determined by

general laws, the imperative of duty may be expressed thus: *Act as if the maxim of thy action were to become by thy will a Universal Law of Nature.*

We will now enumerate a few duties, adopting the usual division of them into duties to ourselves and to others, and into perfect and imperfect duties.[8]

1. A man reduced to despair by a series of misfortunes feels wearied of life, but is still so far in possession of his reason that he can ask himself whether it would not be contrary to his duty to himself to take his own life. Now he inquires whether the maxim of his action could become a universal law of nature. His maxim is: From self-love I adopt it as a principle to shorten my life when its longer duration is likely to bring more evil than satisfaction. It is asked then simply whether this principle of self-love can become a universal law of nature. Now we see at once that a system of nature of which it should be a law to destroy life by the very feeling which is designed to impel to the maintenance of life would contradict itself, and therefore could not exist as a system of nature; hence that maxim cannot possibly exist as a universal law of nature and consequently would be wholly inconsistent with the supreme principle of all duty.

2. Another finds himself forced by necessity to borrow money. He knows that he will not be able to repay it, but sees also that nothing will be lent to him, unless he promises stoutly to repay it in a definite time. He desires to make this promise, but he has still so much conscience as to ask himself: Is it not unlawful and inconsistent with duty to get out of a difficulty in this way? Suppose however that he resolves to do so: then the maxim of his action would be expressed thus: When I think myself in want of money, I will borrow money and promise to repay it, although I know that I never can do so. Now this principle of self-love or of one's own advantage may perhaps be consistent with my whole future welfare; but the question now is, Is it right? I change then the suggestion of self-love into a universal law, and state the question thus: How would it be if my maxim were a universal law? Then I see at once that it could never hold as a universal law of nature, but would necessarily contradict itself. For supposing it to be a universal law that every one when he thinks himself in a difficulty should be able to promise whatever he pleases, with the purpose of not keeping his promise, the promise

itself would become impossible, as well as the end that one might have in view in it, since no one would consider that anything was promised to him, and would ridicule all such statements as vain pretences.

3. A third finds in himself a talent which with the help of some culture might make him a useful man in many respects. But he finds himself in comfortable circumstances, and prefers to indulge in pleasure rather than to take pains in enlarging and improving his happy natural capacities. He asks, however, whether his maxim of neglect of his natural gifts, besides agreeing with his inclination to indulgence, agrees also with what is called duty. He sees then that a system of nature could indeed subsist with such a universal law, though men (like the South Sea islanders) should let their talents rust, and resolve to devote their lives merely to idleness, amusement, and propagation of their species, in a word to enjoyment; but he cannot possibly will that this should be a universal law of nature, or be implanted in us as such by a natural instinct. For, as a rational being, he necessarily wills that his faculties be developed, since they serve him for all sorts of possible purposes, and have been given him for this.

4. A fourth, who is in prosperity, while he sees that others have to contend with great wretchedness and that he could help them, thinks: What concern is it of mine? Let every one be as happy as heaven pleases or as he can make himself; I will take nothing from him nor even envy him, only I do not wish to contribute anything either to his welfare or to his assistance in distress! Now no doubt if such a mode of thinking were a universal law, the human race might very well subsist, and doubtless even better than in a state in which every one talks of sympathy and good will, or even takes care occasionally to put it into practice, but on the other side, also cheats when he can, betrays the rights of men or otherwise violates them. But although it is possible that a universal law of nature might exist in accordance with that maxim, it is impossible to will that such a principle should have the universal validity of a law of nature. For a will which resolved this would contradict itself, inasmuch as many cases might occur in which one would have need of the love and sympathy of others, and in which by such a law of nature, sprung from his own will, he would deprive himself of all hope of the aid he desires.

These are a few of the many actual duties, or at least what we regard as such, which obviously fall into two classes on the one principle that we have laid down. We must be *able to will* that a maxim of our action should be a universal law. This is the canon of the moral appreciation of the action generally. Some actions are of such a character, that their maxim cannot without contradiction be even *conceived* as a universal law of nature, far from it being possible that we should *will* that it should be so. In others this intrinsic impossibility is not found, but still it is impossible to *will* that their maxim should be raised to the universality of a law of nature, since such a will would contradict itself. It is easily seen that the former violate strict or rigorous (inflexible) duty; the latter only laxer (meritorious) duty. Thus it has been completely shown how all duties depend as regards the nature of the obligation (not the object of the action) on the same principle.

If now we attend to ourselves on occasion of any transgression of duty, we shall find that we in fact do not will that our maxim should be a universal law, for that it is impossible for us; on the contrary we will that the opposite should remain a universal law, only we assume the liberty of making an exception in our own favour or (just for this time only) in favour of our inclination. . . .

The will is conceived as a faculty of determining oneself to action *in accordance with the conception of certain laws*. And such a faculty can be found only in rational beings. Now that which serves the will as the objective ground of its self-determination is the *end*, and if this is assigned by reason alone, it must hold for all rational beings. On the other hand, that which merely contains the ground of possibility of the action of which the effect is the end, this is called the *means*. The subjective ground of the desire is the *spring*, the objective ground of the volition is the *motive*; hence the distinction between subjective ends which rest on springs, and objective ends which depend on motives that hold for every rational being. Practical principles are *formal* when they abstract from all subjective ends, they are *material* when they assume these, and therefore particular springs of action. The ends which a rational being proposes to himself at pleasure as *effects* of his actions (material ends) are all only relative, for it is only their relation to the particular desires of the subject that gives them their worth, which therefore cannot furnish principles universal and necessary for all rational beings and for every volition, that is to say practical laws. Hence all these relative ends can give rise only to hypothetical imperatives.

Persons as Ends

Supposing, however, that there were something *whose existence has in itself* an absolute worth, something which being *an end in itself*, could be a source of definite laws, then in this and this alone would lie the source of a possible categorical imperative, i.e., a practical law. Now I say, man and generally any rational being exists as an end in himself, *not merely as a means* to be arbitrarily used by this or that will, but in all his actions, whether they concern himself or other rational beings, must always be regarded at the same time as an end. All objects of the inclinations have only a conditional worth, for if the inclinations and the wants founded on them did not exist, then their object would be without value. But the inclinations themselves being sources of want, are so far from having an absolute worth for which they should be desired, that on the contrary it must be the universal wish of every rational being to be wholly free from them. Thus the worth of any object which *is to be acquired* by our action is always conditional. Beings whose existence depends not on our will but on nature's, have nevertheless, if they are irrational beings, only a relative value as means, and are therefore called *things*; rational beings on the contrary, are called *persons*, because their very nature points them out as ends in themselves, that is as something which must not be used merely as means, and so far therefore restricts freedom of action (and is an object of respect). These, therefore, are not merely subjective ends whose existence has a worth for us as an effect of our action, but *objective ends*, that is things whose existence is an end in itself; an end moreover for which no other can be substituted, which they should subserve *merely* as means, for otherwise nothing whatever would possess *absolute worth*; but if all worth were conditioned and therefore contingent, then there would be no supreme practical principle of reason whatever.

If then there is a supreme practical principle or, in respect of the human will, a categorical imperative, it must be one which, drawn from the conception of that which is necessarily an end for every one because it is *an end in itself*, constitutes an objective principle of will, and can therefore serve as a universal practical law. The foundation of this principle is: *rational nature exists as an end in itself*. Man necessarily conceives his own existence as being so; so far then, this is a *subjective* principle of human actions. But every other rational being regards its existence similarly, just on the same rational principle that holds for me:[9] so that it is at the same time an objective principle, from which as a supreme practical law all laws of the will must be capable of being deduced. Accordingly the practical imperative will be as follows: *So act as to treat humanity, whether in thine own person or in that of any other, in every case as an end withal, never as a means only....*

We will now inquire whether this can be practically carried out.

To abide by the previous examples:

First, under the head of necessary duty to oneself: He who contemplates suicide should ask himself whether his action can be consistent with the idea of humanity *as an end in itself*. If he destroys himself in order to escape from painful circumstances, he uses a person merely as a *means* to maintain a tolerable condition up to the end of life. But a man is not a thing, that is to say, something which can be used merely as means, but must in all his actions be always considered as an end in himself. I cannot, therefore, dispose in any way of a man in my own person so as to mutilate him, to damage or kill him. (It belongs to ethics proper to define this principle more precisely, so as to avoid all misunderstanding, for example, as to the amputation of the limbs in order to preserve myself; as to exposing my life to danger with a view to preserve it, etc. This question is therefore omitted here.)

Secondly, as regards necessary duties, or those of strict obligation, towards others: He who is thinking of making a lying promise to others will see at once that he would be using another *man merely as a means*, without the latter containing at the same time the end in himself. For he whom I propose by such a promise to use for my own purposes cannot possibly assent to my mode of acting towards him, and therefore cannot himself contain the end of this action. This violation of the principle of humanity in other men is more obvious if we take in examples of attacks on the freedom and property of others. For then it is clear that he who transgresses the rights of men intends to use the person of others merely as means, without considering that as rational beings they ought always to be esteemed also as ends, that is, as beings who must be capable of containing in themselves the end of the very same action.[10]

Thirdly, as regards contingent (meritorious) duties to oneself: It is not enough that the action does not violate humanity in our own person as an end in itself, it must also *harmonize with it*. . . . Now there are in humanity capacities of greater perfection which belong to the end that nature has in view in regard to humanity in ourselves as the subject; to neglect these might perhaps be consistent with the *maintenance* of humanity as an end in itself, but not with the advancement of this end.

Fourthly, as regards meritorious duties towards others: The natural end which all men have is their own happiness. Now humanity might indeed subsist although no one should contribute anything to the happiness of others, provided he did not intentionally withdraw anything from it; but after all, this would only harmonize negatively, not positively, with *humanity as an end in itself*, if everyone does not also endeavor, as far as in him lies, to forward the ends of others. For the ends of any subject which is an end in himself ought as far as possible to be my ends also, if that conception is to have its full effect with me.

Notes

1. The first proposition was that to have moral worth an action must be done from duty.

2. A *maxim* is the subjective principle of volition. The objective principle (i.e., that which would also serve subjectively as a practical principle to all rational beings if reason had full power over the faculty of desire) is the practical *law*.

3. It might here be objected to me that I take refuge behind the word *respect* in an obscure feeling instead of giving a distinct solution of the question by a concept of the reason. But although respect is a feeling, it is not a feeling *received* through influence, but is *self-wrought* by a rational concept, and, therefore, is specially distinct from all feelings of the former kind, which may be referred either to inclination or fear. What I recognise immediately as a law for me, I recognise with respect. This merely signifies the consciousness that my will is *subordinate* to a law, without the intervention of other influences on my sense. The immediate determination of the will by the law, and the consciousness of this is called *respect*, so that this is regarded as an *effect* of the law on the subject, and not as the *cause* of it. Respect is properly the conception of a work which thwarts my self-love. Accordingly it is something which is considered neither as an object of inclination nor of fear, although it has something analogous to both. The *object* of respect is the *law* only, and that, the law which we impose on *ourselves*, and yet recognise as necessary in itself. As a law, we are subjected to it without consulting self-love; as imposed by us on ourselves, it is a result of our will. In the former respect it has an analogy to fear, in the latter to inclination. Respect for a person is properly only respect for the law (of honesty, & c.), of which he gives us an example. . . .

4. The dependence of the desires on sensations is called inclination, and this accordingly always indicates a *want*. The dependence of a contingently determinable will on principles of reason is called an *interest*. This, therefore, is found only in the case of a dependent will which does not always of itself conform to reason; in the Divine will we cannot conceive any interest. But the human will can also *take an interest* in a thing without therefore acting *from interest*. The former signifies the *practical* interest in the action, the latter the *pathological* in the object of the action. The former indicates only dependence of the will on principles of reason in themselves; the second, dependence on principles of reason for the sake of inclination, reason supplying only the practical rules how the requirement of the inclination may be satisfied. In the first case the action interests me; in the second the object of the action (because it is pleasant to me). We have seen in the first section that in an action done from duty we must look not to the interest in the object, but only to that in the action itself, and in its rational principle (viz., the law).

5. The word *prudence* is taken in two senses: in the one it may bear the name of knowledge of the world, in the other that of private prudence. The former is a man's ability to influence others so as to use them for his own purposes. The latter is the sagacity to combine all these purposes for his own lasting benefit. This latter is properly that to which the value even of the former is reduced, and when a man is prudent in the former sense, but not in the latter, we might better say of him that he is clever and cunning, but, on the whole, imprudent.

6. It seems to me that the proper signification of the word *pragmatic* may be most accurately defined in this way.

For *sanctions* are called pragmatic which flow properly, not from the law of the states as necessary enactments, but from *precaution* for the general welfare. A history is composed pragmatically when it teaches prudence, that is, instructs the world how it can provide for its interests better, or at least as well as the men of former time.

7. A maxim is a subjective principle of action ... the principle on which the subject acts; but the law is the objective principle valid for every rational being, and is the principle on which it *ought to act* that is an imperative.

8. It must be noted here that I reserve the division of duties for a *future metaphysic of morals*; so that I give it here only as an arbitrary one (in order to arrange my examples). For the rest, I understand by a perfect duty, one that admits

no exception in favour of inclination, and then I have not merely external but also internal perfect duties.

9. This proposition is here stated as a postulate. The ground of it will be found in the concluding section.

10. Let it not be thought that the common: *quod tibi non vis fieri*, etc., could serve here as the rule or principle. For it is only a deduction from the former, though with several limitations; it cannot be a universal law, for it does not contain the principle of duties to oneself, nor of the duties of benevolence to others (for many a one would gladly consent that others should not benefit him, provided only that he might be excused from showing benevolence to them), nor finally that of duties of strict obligation to one another, for on this principle the criminal might argue against the judge who punishes him, and so on.

Reading 6-2   "Black Radical Kantianism" | Charles W. Mills

Study Questions
As you read the excerpt, please consider the following questions:

1. Why might Mills suggest that there is a need for a Kantian theory that is "reshaped by the realities of racial subordination"?

2. What are the key principles of Kantian thought that Mills suggests we ought to "deracialize" and reconsider?

3. What do you think Mills means when he speaks of "black radical Kantianism"?

My own project in recent years has become the articulation of a "black radical liberalism" that draws on what are standardly judged to be the "radical" strains of Afro-modern thought—black Marxism, black nationalism, and black feminism—while incorporating their key insights into a modified and radicalized liberal framework. And a "black radical Kantianism" is supposed to be a key element of this proposed synthesis, though not in the sense of documenting the actual uptake of Kant by black radical theorists . . . but in the sense of demonstrating how classic themes in this literature can illuminatingly be translated into a Kantian discourse reshaped by the realities of racial subordination. So the agenda is both descriptive and prescriptive, looking at the fortunes of "personhood" as a general liberal category under illiberal circumstances, and suggesting a "Kantian" reconstruction as a de-ghettoizing approach for bringing together these segregated conversations.

Why Kant, though? To begin with, there is the strategic argument from Kant's rise to centrality in contemporary Western normative theory over the last half-century. With the demise or at least considerable diminution in significance of the utilitarian liberalism (Jeremy Bentham, James and John Stuart Mill, Henry Sidgwick) that was hegemonic from the early 1800s to the mid-twentieth century, it is deontological/contractarian liberalism that is now most influential. . . . Immanuel Kant is now regarded not merely as the most important ethicist of modernity, but as one of its most significant normative political theorists also. So a racially informed engagement with this body of discourse would have the virtues of being in dialogue with what is now the central strand in Western ethico-political theory: Afro-modern political thought in conversation with Euro-modern political thought. But second, in addition to these strategic considerations (and perhaps more importantly), the key principles and ideals of Kant's ethico-political thought are, once deracialized, very attractive: the respect for the rights of individual persons, the ideal of the *Rechtsstaat* [i.e., the rule of law—ed.] (admittedly somewhat modified from Kant's own version), and the vision of a global cosmopolitan order of equals. The problem, in my opinion, has been less Kant's own racism (since it is simply bracketed by most contemporary Kantians) than the failure to rethink these principles and ideals in the light of a modernity structured by racial domination. And that brings me to the third point. In contrast with, say, a dialogue between European and Asian political traditions, which at least for long periods of time developed largely separately from one another, the Euro-modern

and the Afro-modern traditions are intimately and dialectically linked. As emphasized at the start, the latter develops in specific contestation of the former, involving both resistance to and rejection of its crucial tenets insofar as they rationalize and justify Euro-domination, while nonetheless sometimes seeking to appropriate and modify others for emancipatory ends. So developing a "black radical Kantianism" as a self-conscious enterprise should be not merely instrumentally and intrinsically valuable, but illuminative of a counter-hegemonic normative system already present in Afro-modern thought. . . .

From Charles W. Mills, "Black Radical Kantianism" *Res Philosophica*, Vol. 95, No. 1, January 2018, pp. 1–33.

Review Exercises

1. Explain why we might not want to locate an action's moral worth in its consequences.

2. When Kant refers to "a good will" or "good intention," does he mean wishing others well? Explain.

3. What does Kant mean by "acting out of duty"? How does the shopkeeper exemplify this?

4. What is the basic difference between a categorical and a hypothetical imperative? In the following examples, which are hypothetical and which are categorical imperatives? Explain your answers.

   a. If you want others to be honest with you, then you ought to be honest with them.

   b. Whether or not you want to pay your share, you ought to do so.

   c. Because everyone wants to be happy, we ought to consider everyone's interests equally.

   d. I ought not to cheat on this test if I do not want to get caught.

5. How does the character of moral obligation lead to Kant's basic moral principle, the categorical imperative?

6. Explain Kant's use of the first form of the categorical imperative to argue that it is wrong to make a false promise. (Make sure that you do not appeal to the bad consequences as the basis of judging it wrong.)

7. According to the second form of Kant's categorical imperative, would it be morally permissible for me to agree to be someone's slave or to kill myself? Explain.

8. What is the practical difference between a perfect and an imperfect duty?

9. How can we use Kantian ideas to argue against racism and sexism?

Knowledge Check Answer Key

1. **False.** Deontology is a non-consequentialist approach to ethics.

2. **c.** Deontological theories are focused on duties and obligations and emphasize the *right* over the *good*.

3. **c.** Kant might say that lying is wrong because it is disrespectful of persons.

4. **b and c.** Only act according to a rule that can be universalized and always show respect to rational beings express two versions of the categorical imperative.

7 Natural Law and Human Rights

Learning Outcomes

After reading this chapter, you should be able to:

7.1 Explain how natural law theory is related to the law of peoples and norms of international law.

7.2 Identify the contributions to natural law theory made by key thinkers such as Cicero, Thomas Aquinas, and John Locke.

7.3 Explain the importance of teleology for thinking about natural law.

7.4 Describe how natural law theory is related to the idea of natural rights and the idea of human rights.

7.5 Clarify how natural law arguments are grounded in claims about the essence of human nature that resist relativism.

7.6 Defend your own thesis with regard to the value of natural law theory and the idea of human rights.

The Rights of Refugees

In the summer of 2022, the United Nations estimated that a record 100 million people had been forcibly displaced from their homes within the past year.[1] These refugees come from an array of countries: Ethiopia, Burkina Faso, Myanmar, Nigeria, Afghanistan, the Democratic Republic of the Congo, and Ukraine. Many of these people are fleeing violence, war, and oppression. But people are also forced from their homes by floods, storms, and other natural disasters. Refugees are quite vulnerable

PAUL RATJE/AFP/Getty Images

since they are often left without the protection of their previous home government. The United Nations has a number of documents and agreements that explicitly call for the protection of refugees, beginning with the 1948 UN Declaration of Human Rights, which states (Article 14), "Everyone has the right to seek and to enjoy in other countries asylum from persecution." One of the most important of rights of refugees is the right not to be forcibly returned to a home country, where they might face torture, imprisonment, or death. In international law this is called the right of *non-refoulement*. Other rights include the right not to be punished for illegally entering a country of refuge, as well as the right to housing, education, free movement, and the right to work. But refugees create challenges for countries that receive them, including how to house them and provide for their care and protection. And some people fear an influx of foreigners who may not assimilate. These challenges have led to many well-publicized crises. One of these occurred at the southern border of the United States in 2021, when more than ten thousand Haitian refugees camped out under a bridge in Del Rio, Texas. The U.S. government refused entry for many of these refugees. By 2022, the United States had forcibly returned at least twenty thousand refugees to Haiti, where they must contend with disease, poverty, violence, and political turmoil.[2] The Trump and Biden administrations defended the deportation of Haitian refugees as a matter of public safety. Human rights organizations decried it as a violation of human rights and international law.

What Do You think?

1. Do refugees have a right to take refuge? Should they be protected against refoulement?
2. Do you agree that refugees have a right to education, housing, freedom of movement, and work?
3. What is the basis for your thinking about these rights? And about human rights in general?
4. Can you imagine good reasons for denying refugees the right to asylum? Do you agree with the U.S. policy of forcibly deporting Haitian refugees?

Introduction

7.1 Explain how natural law theory is related to the law of peoples and norms of international law.

In 1776, Thomas Jefferson wrote in the Declaration of Independence, "We hold these truths to be self-evident, that all men are created equal, that they are endowed by their Creator with certain inalienable rights, that among these are life, liberty and the pursuit of happiness."[3] Jefferson had read the work of English philosopher John Locke, who had written in his *Second Treatise on Government* that all human beings were of the same species, born with the same basic capacities.[4] Locke argues that because all humans have the same basic nature, they should be treated equally. This argument should sound familiar from our previous discussion of Kant and deontology. Kant emphasizes respect for human persons as ends in themselves. Locke and Jefferson fill in this abstract idea with a list of natural human rights, including the right to life and liberty. Locke also thought that there was a natural right to own property, while Jefferson thought that there was a right to the pursuit of happiness. These natural rights are supposed to be grounded in self-evident truth.

This self-evidence is found in "the Laws of Nature and Nature's God," as the first sentence of the Declaration of Independence puts it.

Discussions of human rights remain important today. We saw in Chapter 2 that the United Nations issued a Universal Declaration of Human Rights, which began by asserting "the inherent dignity and...the equal and inalienable rights of all members of the human family." These rights are said to be shared by all human beings, regardless of cultural, religious, or political differences. But in reality, respecting and upholding human rights is not always a simple task for societies and governments, including that of the United States. Our opening discussion in this chapter, of the rights of refugees, reminds us how complicated this can be. But despite this complication, there is a growing sense in the world that there is a set of common global norms that ought to guide domestic and international life. Some of these norms have been codified into international law and show up in documents such as the UN Declaration of Human Rights. These norms can be used to criticize the behavior of states, including their legal systems. It is common to say that these norms are based on a system of "natural law" that transcends any give system of civil law (what is sometimes called "positive law").

Consider another example of how the natural law and the idea of human rights can be used. Following the 2001 terrorist attacks on the World Trade Center and the Pentagon, and with the U.S. invasion of Afghanistan, questions arose about the legal status and treatment of individuals captured by the U.S. forces. In our discussion of utilitarianism in Chapter 5, we mentioned that the U.S. government endorsed the use of torture (referred to as "enhanced interrogation techniques") for some of these individuals. This would seem to be a violation of Article 5 of the UN Declaration of Human Rights, which states, "No one shall be subjected to torture or to cruel, inhuman or degrading treatment or punishment."

Furthermore, since 2004, many of these suspected terrorists have been transferred to a prison at Guantanamo Bay in Cuba, a U.S. naval base on the southeastern side of the island. (The United States still holds a lease to this land because of the 1903 Cuban–American Treaty.) It was thought that these individuals were members, supporters, or sympathizers of Al-Qaeda or the Taliban. It was said that these prisoners were not part of any army of any state and thus not prisoners of war but, rather, "enemy combatants" not covered by any of the protections of the Geneva Conventions. These individuals were not given the protections of U.S. laws. And they were denied such basic human rights as knowing the charges against them and being allowed to defend themselves in court. This treatment would seem to violate Article 6 of the UN Declaration, which states, "Everyone has the right to recognition everywhere as a person before the law."

In recent years—and after intense legal and humanitarian scrutiny of Guantanamo's detainment policies—many hundreds of the detainees have been sent back to their countries of origin. Some were finally allowed lawyers, although not of their own choosing. U.S. courts have also ruled that the detainees must be given trials in U.S. military, rather than civilian, courts. As of mid-2022, fewer than 40 prisoners still remained in the Guantanamo detention facility, at a cost of over $500 million per year.[5] The U.S. has been working to process these prisoners. But some seem doomed to be held indefinitely, since even when they are cleared for release, there are no countries that are willing to accept them. Some of these prisoners went on a hunger strike in 2013 to protest their treatment.

Figure 7-1 Detainees in a holding area at Camp X-Ray at Guantanamo Bay, Cuba.

Shane McCoy/WireImage/Getty Images

Prison officials force-fed them—by inserting feeding tubes up their noses. Critics argued that it was a violation of international law and a human rights violation to force-feed prisoners in this way.[6]

In this and many other contemporary situations, we may ask what is meant by "human rights"—and does every person possess such rights, even enemy combatants? This is one of the fundamental questions addressed in this chapter.

A related question is how the idea of rights applies in situations in which there is no legal or political system to enforce them. Is there a system of "natural law" that is more fundamental than the positive laws of any particular legal or political system? While the idea of natural law is an ancient one, the concept has been an object of renewed interest, especially now that we are aware that states can commit crimes against their own people, including war crimes and genocide. If there is something that we might call natural law, we would suppose that it would at least include a law against genocide.

Figure 7-2 Child labor seems to be a human rights violation.

The Nuremberg trials were trials of Nazi war criminals held in Nuremberg, Germany, from 1945 to 1949. There were thirteen trials in all. In the first trial, Nazi leaders were found guilty of violating international law by starting an aggressive war. Nine of them, including Hermann Goering and Rudolf Hess, were sentenced to death. In other trials, defendants were accused of committing atrocities against civilians. Nazi doctors who had conducted medical experiments on those imprisoned in the death camps were among those tried. Their experiments maimed and killed many people, all of whom were unwilling subjects. For example, experiments for the German air force were conducted to determine how fast people would die in very thin air. Other experiments tested the effects of freezing water on the human body. The defense contended that the military personnel, judges, and doctors were only following orders from

their superiors in the Nazi regime. However, the prosecution argued successfully that even if the experimentation did not violate the defendants' own laws, they were still "crimes against humanity." The idea was that a law more basic than civil laws exists—a moral law—and these doctors and others should have known what this basic moral law required. (We discuss war crimes further in Chapter 18.)

The idea that the basic moral law can be known by human reason is a central tenet of natural law theory. Some treatments of human rights also use human nature as a basis. According to this view, human rights are those things that we can validly claim because they are essential for human beings to function well. These natural human rights are the same for all human beings, since, on this theory, all human beings share a common essence or human nature.

Natural Law Theory

The **natural law theory** is a theory of ethics that holds that there are moral laws found in nature and discernable by the use of reason. The way the term is used in discussions of ethics should not be confused with those other "laws of nature" that are the generalizations of natural science. The laws of natural science are *descriptive* laws. They describe how nature behaves. For example, gases expand with their containers and when heat is applied. Boyle's law about the behavior of gases does not tell gases how they *ought* to behave. In fact, if gases were found to behave differently from what we had so far observed, the laws would be changed to match this new information. Simply put, scientific laws are descriptive generalizations of fact.

Moral laws, on the other hand, are *prescriptive* laws. They tell us how we *ought* to behave. The natural law is the moral law written into nature itself. What we ought to do, according to this theory, is determined by considering certain aspects of nature. In particular, we ought to examine our nature as human beings to see what is essential for us to function well as members of our species. We look to certain aspects of our nature to know what is good and what we ought to do.

Civil law is also prescriptive. As an expression of the moral law, however, natural law is supposed to be more basic or higher than the laws of any particular society. Although laws of particular societies vary and change over time, the natural law is supposed to be universal and stable. In *Antigone*, an ancient Greek tragedy by Sophocles, the protagonist disobeys the king and buries her brother's body—thereby breaking the law of her monarchical society. She does so because she believes that she must follow a higher law, which requires that her brother be buried. In the play, Antigone loses her life for obeying this higher law. In the Nuremberg trials, prosecutors also argued that there was a higher law that all humans should recognize—one that takes precedence over national laws and customs.

People today sometimes appeal to this moral law in order to claim that civil laws ought to be reformed. This is the basic idea behind the theory of civil disobedience and conscientious refusal as outlined and practiced by Henry David Thoreau, Mohandas K. Gandhi, and Martin Luther King Jr. (as discussed in Chapter 2 and in the opening vignette of Chapter 6). When Thoreau was imprisoned for not paying taxes that he thought were used for an unjust war, he defended his actions by appealing to a system of rights and wrongs that is superior to the civil law. In his famous essay "Civil Disobedience," he writes, "Must the citizen ever for a moment, or in the least degree, resign his conscience to the legislator? Why has every man a conscience, then? I think that we should be men first, and subjects afterward. It is not desirable to cultivate a respect for the law, so much as for the right."[7] In suggesting that "the right" is more important than "the law," Thoreau is pointing toward the idea of natural law, which provides us with a source of morality that transcends the civil law.

Historical Origins

7.2 Identify the contributions to natural law theory made by key thinkers such as Cicero, Thomas Aquinas, and John Locke.

The tradition of natural law ethics is a long one. Aristotle was among the first to develop a complex ethical philosophy based on the view that certain actions are right or wrong because they are suited to or go against human nature (we discuss Aristotle in more detail in Chapter 8).

Aristotle had a profound influence on the medieval Christian philosopher and Dominican friar Thomas Aquinas (1224–1274). Aquinas is often credited as a primary source for natural law ethics.

The natural law idea can also be found in a variety of other ancient Greek thinkers, especially the Stoics, who held that we have a duty to obey the basic laws of nature. (The Stoics were discussed in Chapter 6.) The key moral principle for the Stoics was to "follow nature." This means that nature has a goal or *telos* for human beings, which we ought to pursue. They also believed that there are laws to which all people are subject, no matter what their local customs or conventions. Early Roman jurists believed that a common element existed in the codes of various peoples: a *jus gentium*, or "law of peoples."

One of the most important of the Roman authors associated with the natural law tradition is Cicero (106–43 BCE). In his *Republic*, Cicero explained the natural law as follows:

> True law is right reason conformable to nature, universal, unchangeable, eternal, whose commands urge us to duty, and whose prohibitions restrain us from evil. Whether it enjoins or forbids, the good respect its injunctions, and the wicked treat them with indifference. This law cannot be contradicted by any other law, and is not liable either to derogation or abrogation. Neither the senate nor the people can give us any dispensation for not obeying this universal law of justice. It needs no other expositor and interpreter than our own conscience. It is not one thing at Rome, and another at Athens; one thing today, and another tomorrow; but in all times and nations this universal law must forever reign, eternal and imperishable. It is the sovereign master and emperor of all beings. God himself is its author, its promulgator, its enforcer. And he who does not obey it flies from himself, and does violence to the very nature of man. And by so doing he will endure the severest penalties even if he avoid the other evils which are usually accounted punishments.[8]

Cicero's point is that the natural law transcends time and place: it is eternal and imperishable, the same today and tomorrow, the same in Rome as in Athens. Moreover, he maintains that the natural law comes from God himself. It is not surprising that Cicero and his ideas had a profound impact, for example, on Thomas Jefferson and the authors of the founding documents of the United States.

During the medieval period, Greek and Roman philosophy died out in Western Europe, although these ideas were preserved in the East, especially in the work of Islamic scholars. Medieval Islamic and Christian traditions tended to think that morality was primarily derived from scripture. Greek and Roman ideas eventually reentered European culture and were distilled and connected to Christianity by Aquinas. Aquinas's goal was to find a way to synthesize faith and reason, to connect the insights of reason with the commands of faith. While the natural law tradition is often connected to religion, it is not merely a version of divine command theory, since it holds that reason can discover the moral law independent of scripture.

Aquinas was a theologian who held that the natural law is part of the divine law or plan for the universe. The record of much of what he taught can be found in his work the *Summa Theologica* (an excerpt is provided in the reading selection at the end of this chapter).[9] Aquinas maintains that "the natural law shares in the eternal law." He recognizes that this may make it seem that there is no need for human law. But Aquinas argues that particular human laws are a reflection or incomplete manifestation of the divine law. Aquinas indicated his debt to Cicero by quoting him several times in his discussions of law and justice. For example, "Human law originally sprang from nature. Then things became customs because of their rational benefit. Then fear and reverence for law validated things that both sprang from nature and were approved by custom."[10] The point here is that human laws reflect both the natural law and the developed expression of these laws in the customs and positive laws made by humans.

Echoing the views of Aristotle, Aquinas held that the moral good consists in following the innate tendencies of our nature. We are biological beings. Because we tend by nature to grow and mature, we ought to preserve our being and our health by avoiding undue risks and doing what will make us healthy. Furthermore, as sentient animals, we can know our world through the physical senses. We ought to use our senses of touch, taste, smell, hearing, and sight; we ought to develop and

Portrait of Thomas Aquinas/Italian School, (17th century)/ARNOLDO MONDADORI EDITORE (AMBROSIANA)/Pinacoteca Ambrosiana, Milan, Italy/Bridgeman Images

Figure 7-3 A portrait of Thomas Aquinas (1225–1274).

make use of these senses to appreciate those aspects of existence that they reveal to us. We ought not to do things that injure these senses. Like many nonhuman animals, we reproduce our kind through intercourse. This is what nature means for us to do, according to this version of natural law theory. (See further discussion of this issue in Chapter 16.)

Unique to persons are the specific capacities of knowing and choosing freely. Thus, we ought to treat ourselves and others as beings that are capable of understanding and free choice. Those things that help us pursue the truth, such as education and freedom of public expression, are good. Those things that hinder pursuit of the truth are bad. Deceit and lack of access to the sources of knowledge are morally objectionable simply because they prevent us from fulfilling our innate natural drive or orientation to know the way things are.[11] Moreover, whatever enhances our ability to choose freely is good. A certain amount of self-discipline, options from which to choose, and reflection on what we ought to choose are among the things that enhance freedom. To coerce people and to limit their possibilities of choosing freely are examples of what is inherently bad or wrong.

Finally, natural law theory argues that we ought to find ways to live well together, for this is a theory that emphasizes the interconnectedness of human beings in which no person is an island. We are social creatures by nature. Thus, the essence of natural law theory is that we ought to further the inherent ends of human nature and not do what frustrates human fulfillment or flourishing. These ideas can be developed into a concern for social justice, including care for impoverished people and persons with disabilities, the right to decent work and living conditions, and even the right to health care.

After Aquinas and throughout the modern period of European history, the idea of natural law and natural right became more widespread and more secular. One of the important authors who developed ideas about the natural law was Hugo Grotius, a Dutch jurist who was working during the early part of the seventeenth century. Grotius explained the development of natural law from out of human nature as follows:

> For the mother of right, that is, of natural law, is human nature; for this would lead us to desire mutual society, even if it were not required for the supply of other wants; and the mother of civil laws, is obligation by mutual compact; and since mutual compact derives its force from natural law, nature may be said to be the grandmother of civil laws.[12]

Grotius is known as one of the founders of international law. His ideas about international law had a practical application, for example, in his discussion of the rules of war. Grotius maintained that there was a common law among nations, which was valid even in times of war. We will return to this topic in Chapter 18, where we will discuss the *just war theory*. Note that the idea of natural law may give us grounds to criticize the treatment of the prisoners at Guantanamo Bay, the case we discussed above. If we think that all human beings have basic rights and that these rights exist even in time of war, perhaps we ought to provide these rights to the prisoners at Guantanamo. And, with reference to this chapter's opening vignette, it is worth noting that

Grotius also explains the idea of a right to asylum and refuge. He stated, "Those who have been driven from their homes have the right to acquire a permanent residence in another country, in submission to the government there in authority."[13] He connects this right with a right to hospitality, including the right to "temporary sojourn" in a foreign land.

Evaluating Natural Law Theory

7.3 Explain the importance of teleology for thinking about natural law.

Natural law theory has many appealing characteristics. Among them are its belief in the objectivity of moral values and the notion of the good as human flourishing. Natural law is also appealing insofar as it links ethical principles to a more general account of reality. Using philosophical terminology, we might say that the virtue of natural law is its explicit connection with metaphysics and ontology, by which we mean that natural law is based on an account of what exists, where it comes from, and what its meaning and purpose is. This part of the theory—the focus on meaning and purpose—can be described as an account of teleology. The important idea here is that the world is supposed to be organized in such a way that human beings have a basic set of aims, purposes, ends, or functions. Reason can discern these values, which are found in the very nature of reality. In traditional versions of the natural law theory, this ontological and teleological approach includes an account of the *summum bonum* (the highest, most complete and perfect good). For Aquinas, this was connected to an account of the place of humanity within the order of the created universe. And while this is typically a religious idea, natural law is unlike some versions of divine command theory. Philosophical natural law theories emphasize that reason provides a key (as opposed to more dogmatic appeal to scripture or revelation). Natural law holds that reason is able to discern the natural order of things and understand the moral structures built into reality. For traditional natural law theory, what reason shows us is that life is organized teleologically: it has a purpose and function. Again, for traditional natural law theorists such as Aquinas, this purpose is to know God and find your place within the God-created order. Unlike some contemporary human rights theories (which we discuss further below), natural law theories want to locate our rights within a larger metaphysical account of where these rights come from and what we are supposed to do with our rights. To explain this, we might point out that natural law is not merely about a permission or limitation on interference (as rights are sometimes conceived); rather, natural law also gives us an obligation. As Aquinas says, good is to be done and evil is to be avoided. In order to know what we ought to do, we need also to know what the good is.

Various criticisms of the theory have also been advanced, including the following.

First, according to natural law theory, we are to determine what we ought to do by deciphering the moral law as it is written into nature—specifically, human nature. One problem that natural law theory must address concerns our ability to read nature. The moral law is supposedly knowable by human reason. But in fact, people have disagreed about what counts as natural and reasonable. The fact of cultural relativism (which we discussed in Chapter 3) makes this clear. People have also disagreed about the highest good (or *summum bonum*). Not only do they disagree about what the highest good might be, but they also disagree that there is even such a thing as the *summum bonum*. Thomas Hobbes made this point in *Leviathan* (Chapter 11) when he said, "there is no such *finis ultimus*, utmost aim, nor *summum bonum*, greatest good, as is spoken of in the books of the old moral philosophers."

A further problem is that traditional natural law theory has picked out highly positive traits of human nature: the desire to know the truth, to choose the good, and to develop as healthy mature beings. Not all views of the essential characteristics of human nature have been so positive, however. Some philosophers have depicted human nature as deceitful, evil, and uncontrolled. This is why Hobbes argued that we need a strong government. Without it, he wrote, life in a state of nature would be "nasty, brutish, and short." (We discussed Hobbes in Chapter 4.) A further problem is that if nature is taken in the broader sense—meaning *all* of nature—and if a natural law as a moral law were based on this, the general approach might even endorse

such theories as **social Darwinism**. This view holds that because the most fit organisms in nature are the ones that survive and dominate, so also the most fit should endure in human society and the weaker ought to perish. When applied to capitalist economic and social organization, social Darwinism could be used to explain why the wealthy dominate the lower classes. This idea was popularized at the end of the nineteenth century and was used to defend hierarchical social organization as a "natural" outcome of the struggle for survival. While this idea applied modern scientific theory (Darwinian biology) to explain and justify inequality and domination, the question of unequal social organization has a deeper historical connection with natural law. In the ancient world, slavery and the subordination of women were taken for granted as a "natural" feature of the human world (as we discuss further later in this chapter).

Another question for natural law theory is the following: Can the way things are by nature provide the basis for knowing how they *ought* to be? On the face of it, this may not seem right. Just because something exists in a certain way does not necessarily mean that it is good. Floods, famine, and disease all exist, but that does not make them good. And slavery was once taken for granted as "natural," along with the subordination of women. But these apparently natural facts may not be natural at all—and even if domination and oppression are common and frequent in the history of the world, this does not make the right. As we saw in Chapter 1, in our discussion of the naturalistic fallacy and Hume's law, it is not easy to derive an *ought* from an *is*. Evaluations cannot simply be derived from factual matters. Other moral philosophers have agreed. Henry Veatch, for example, worried that natural law and the related idea of natural rights were undermined by this problem: "the entire doctrine of natural rights and natural law would appear to rest on nothing less than a patent logical fallacy."[14]

In response to this objection, defenders of natural law might claim that what they are really focused on is a set of basic or intrinsic goods. Or they may deny, as Ralph McInerny has, that there is anything fallacious about deriving an ought from an is: "The concern not to infer value from fact, Ought from Is, is a symptom of false fastidiousness. Worse, it is to take at face value one of the most fundamental errors of modern moral thought."[15] According to McInerny, the value of things is connected to the purpose and function of those things. McInerny maintains that natural law makes best sense in a theistic framework, where the purpose of things is embedded in these things by God. Other authors have clarified that natural law is connected to a theory of basic goods that are known self-evidently: "They cannot be verified by experience or deduced from any more basic truths through a middle term. They are self-evident."[16] This idea of self-evident moral principles and basic goods fits with Jefferson's language in the Declaration: "We hold these truths to be self-evident...."

A standard criticism of this idea would question whether any truths are self-evident in this way. And returning to Hume's problem of deriving an ought from an is, we can still ask (as G. E. Moore did) how we make the leap from fact to value. When we know something to be a fact, that things exist in a certain way, it still remains an open question whether this fact is good. One response for the natural law theory is to state that nature is **teleological**, that it has a certain directedness. The Thomistic approach grounds this directedness in God. But it is possible to develop this idea from a nontheistic point of view. In Aristotle's terms, we could say that things move or develop toward some natural goal, their final purpose. If we were going to defend natural law theory, we would have to be able to explain human nature in terms of its innate potentialities and the goals of human development. Yet from the time of the scientific revolution of the seventeenth century, such final purposes have become suspect. One could not always observe nature's directedness, and it came to be associated with discredited notions of nonobservable spirits directing things from within. If natural law theory does depend on there being purposes in nature, it must be able to explain where these purposes come from and how we can know what they are.

Consider one possible explanation of the source of whatever purposes there might be in nature. Christian philosophers have long maintained that nature manifests God's plan for the universe. For Aristotle, however, the universe is eternal; it always existed and was not created by God. His concept of God was that of

a most perfect being toward which the universe is in some way directed. According to Aristotle, there is an order in nature, but it did not come from the mind of God. For Christian philosophers such as Augustine and Thomas Aquinas, however, nature has the order it does because the universe was created after a divine plan. Nature not only is intelligible but also exists for a purpose that was built into it. Some natural law theorists follow Aquinas on this, whereas others either follow Aristotle or abstain from judgments about the source of the order in nature. But can we conceive of an order in nature without a divine orderer? This depends on what we mean by order in nature. If it is taken in the sense of a plan, this implies that it has an author. However, natural beings may simply develop in certain ways as a result of chance or evolutionary adaptation, while, in reality, there is no plan.

Evolutionary theory thus presents a challenge to natural law theory. If the way that things have come to be is the result of many chance variations, there are no purposes, plans, or preordained functions in nature. The biological and anthropological sciences tend to undermine the idea that there is a universal human nature, since individuals and species vary and change over time. If we wanted to defend natural law theory in the context of contemporary biology, we would have to find natural bases and norms for behavior. One such Darwinian version of natural law has been defended by Larry Arnhart, who argues that human beings have a "natural moral sense" and that "modern Darwinian biology supports this understanding of the ethical and social nature of human beings by showing how it could have arisen by natural selection through evolutionary history."[17]

Natural Rights and Human Rights

7.4 Describe how natural law theory is related to the idea of natural rights and the idea of human rights.

As we saw at the beginning of this chapter, the idea that moral requirements may be grounded in human nature is central to the theory of natural rights. John Locke provided a theory of natural rights that Thomas Jefferson drew on in the Declaration of Independence.

According to Locke, certain things are essential for us as persons. Among these are life itself, as well as liberty and the ability to pursue those things that bring happiness. These are said to be rights not because they are granted by some state, but because they are important for us as human beings or persons. They are thus moral rights first, though they may need to be enforced by societal institutions and laws.

A central feature of the Declaration's statement of our inalienable rights is the idea that these rights are self-evidently true. These rights are supposed to be known by the light of reason with as much clarity as the truths of mathematics. One apparent problem for natural rights claims is that not everyone agrees about rights. Consider the problem of slavery and the issue of equality for women. For centuries of U.S. history, it was not self-evidently true to a majority of citizens that non-White people and women were entitled to equal rights. In response to this problem, defenders of natural rights will argue that experience and education are required to show us what is true. No one is born knowing the truths of mathematics or ethics—and people can be mistaken about these truths. We learn these things over time. Indeed, cultures and traditions develop (even the traditions of mathematics). John Finnis, for example, explains self-evident truth as follows: "The important thing about a self-evident proposition is that people (with the relevant experience and understanding of terms) *assent* to it without needing the proof of argument."[18] Thus, in this view, Jefferson might mean that people with relevant experience and understanding will agree that we have the inalienable rights he enumerates in the Declaration (although such agreement continues to be a problem in our diverse, pluralistic culture).

Throughout the eighteenth century, political philosophers often referred to the laws of nature in discussions of natural rights. For example, Voltaire wrote that morality has a universal source. It is the "natural law...which nature teaches all men" what they should do.[19] The Declaration of Independence was influenced by the writings of jurists and philosophers who believed that a moral law is built into nature. Thus, in the first section, it asserts that the colonists were called on "to assume among the powers of the earth, the separate and equal station, to which the Laws of Nature and of Nature's God entitle them."[20]

Today, various international codes of human rights, such as the UN's Universal Declaration of Human Rights and the Geneva Conventions' principles for the conduct of war, contain elements of a natural rights tradition. These attempt to specify rights that all people have simply by virtue of being human, regardless of their country of origin, race, or religion.

One problem that arises in thinking about all of this is the question of whether there is a difference between "natural rights" and "human rights." For many people these terms are more or less synonymous. But some scholars have argued that the idea of natural rights is more closely related to the idea of natural law than is the idea of human rights. In the thinking of Locke and Jefferson, the notion of rights was grounded in a worldview that includes a creator who endows us with these rights. This worldview looks very similar to the worldview of the traditional natural law theory. Locke made this explicit in his *Second Treatise of Government*:

> The state of nature has a law of nature to govern it, which obliges every one: and reason, which is that law, teaches all mankind, who will but consult it, that being all equal and independent, no one ought to harm another in his life, health, liberty, or possessions: for men being all the workmanship of one omnipotent, and infinitely wise maker; all the servants of one sovereign master, sent into the world by his order, and about his business; they are his property, whose workmanship they are, made to last during his, not one another's pleasure.[21]

But in the twentieth and twenty-first centuries, the assertion of "human rights" has often been made without grounding it in a religious or metaphysical worldview. The UN Declaration of Human Rights does not invoke the idea of a creator. Instead, it speaks of inherent dignity and inalienable rights without appealing to a religious idea or metaphysical system of natural law that grounds these ideas. Here, for example, is the first clause of the UN Declaration;

> Whereas recognition of the inherent dignity and of the equal and inalienable rights of all members of the human family is the foundation of freedom, justice and peace in the world.

Notice that this statement makes a quasi-consequentialist argument about the importance of recognizing human dignity—that it is essential for freedom, justice, and peace.

Also consider how Article 1 of the UN Declaration uses language that is reminiscent of Locke and Jefferson but without invoking a creator:

> All human beings are born free and equal in dignity and rights. They are endowed with reason and conscience and should act towards one another in a spirit of brotherhood.

This statement speaks of an endowment of reason without explaining where this endowment comes from.

Evaluating Natural Rights and Human Rights Theory

One of the virtues of the idea of human rights is that it is now part of our widely accepted moral vocabulary. Unlike Kantian deontology, ordinary people frequently make use of the language of rights. It is quite common to view moral conflicts and atrocities from the perspective of rights. When we claim that a fundamental value

is at risk or has been damaged, we are likely to say that our rights have been violated. Of course, it remains an open question as to what we mean by the term "rights."

In some cases, rights are merely defined as "civil rights," which implies that these are rights that belong to us because of our membership in a political system. Civil rights include, for example, the right to vote. Non-citizens do not have that right within our community. Of course, we may think every human being has a basic human right to have the civil right to vote within their own community. But even this is up for debate. For example, should prisoners or parolees have the right to vote? This often depends on the jurisdiction in which they are imprisoned or paroled. But would it be a human rights violation to deny a prisoner the right to vote? Or is this merely a matter of positive law to be determined according to some specific account of how civil rights are distributed within a political community? Related to this question is another question about whether and to

---

► **Knowledge Check**   Answers appear at the end of the chapter.

1. What is another name for the highest good?
   a. Summa Theologica
   b. Summa Cum Laude
   c. Summum Malum
   d. Summum Bonum

2. Which of the following is true with regard to Thomas Aquinas?
   a. He based his ethical system entirely on a divine command theory.
   b. He was interested in finding a way to unite faith and reason.
   c. He was an atheist who denied that there was a moral law.
   d. He denied reason in order to make room for faith.

3. What is the meaning of "nature" in the natural law theory of morality?
   a. Natural law morality provides a descriptive account of the laws that structure physical

reality, such as the law governing the expansion of gases.
   b. Natural law morality is naturalistic in the sense that it asks us to behave according to our animal nature and in accord with the idea that is known as social Darwinism.
   c. Natural law morality offers a normative theory that tells us what we ought to do, based on an account of natural purposes and functions.
   d. Natural law is a fallacy that is based on the attempt to withdraw from the world of what is into the dream world of what we imagine.

4. What did Jefferson say about natural rights?
   a. They were self-evident and inalienable.
   b. They were created by the state.
   c. The idea of natural rights was fallacious since in nature there really are no rights.
   d. Natural rights gave the strong the authority to do whatever they can get away with.

what extent our rights actually are "inalienable." Is the death penalty a human rights violation? Or have murderers somehow give up their right to life? (We'll discuss this further in Chapter 17.)

As mentioned above, there is some confusion about the distinction between natural rights and human rights. Defenders of natural rights may claim that the virtue of the theory is the way it is grounded in something like natural law and religious traditions. But the more contemporary human rights approach seeks a language of rights that is more inclusive and less sectarian. Rather than invoking a creator who grants us our rights, the human rights tradition simply states that we have inherent dignity and inalienable rights. Some will see this as a virtue of the human rights theory—since it allows for a more inclusive approach to the idea that seems better suited for a cosmopolitan and secular world. But critics will claim that when human rights are divorced from some basis in natural law and natural right, the concept begins to become incoherent.

This worry reflects a famous criticism of natural rights that comes from the utilitarian philosopher Jeremy Bentham: "Natural rights is simple nonsense: natural and imprescriptible rights, rhetorical nonsense—nonsense upon stilts."[22] Bentham thought that there were no rights outside of the legal and political system. Bentham worried that the idea of natural rights was a perversion of language—since there were no "rights" in nature. Bentham also worried that when people made declarations about the "rights of man" (as happened during the French Revolution), this only invited destructive revolutions and anarchy. While Locke, Jefferson, and Hobbes used the idea of natural rights to argue that states were founded on an underlying social contract (which we also discussed in Chapter 4), Bentham thought the social contract was also a fiction. According to Bentham, governments develop through a long history involving habit and force. And he thought the ethical goal was to make sure that the legal system pointed in the direction of general happiness—not to postulate rights, which could lead to revolution against the legal system.

A more troubling critique was presented by Alasdair MacIntyre in the 1980s. He claimed that every attempt at providing a defense of natural rights had failed. He said, "The truth is plain: there are no such rights, and belief in them is one with belief in witches and unicorns."[23] MacIntyre makes this point with regard to a general failure in metaethical theory to resolve the dispute among intuitionists, emotivists, and others who claim divergent sources of moral insight. MacIntyre continues by saying that those who claim that our rights are "self-evident" are deluded. "We know that there are no self-evident truths," he states.[24] An obvious fact supports this claim: we disagree about who has which rights. The example we started with assumes, for example, that refugees have rights. But do they? Not everyone seems to agree.

This fact poses a significant problem for a natural rights theory: that not everyone agrees on what human nature requires or which natural rights are central. In the UN's 1948 Declaration, the list of rights includes welfare rights and rights to food, clothing, shelter, and basic security. Just what kinds of things can we validly claim as human rights? Freedom of speech? Freedom of religion? Freedom of assembly? Housing? Clean air? Friends? Work? Income? Health care? Many of these are listed in a range of treaties and other documents that nations have adopted. However, an account of human rights requires more than lists. A rationale for what constitutes a human right is necessary in order to determine which rights should be protected or promoted. This is also something that a natural rights theory should help provide—perhaps by deriving the rights we are supposed to have from some more basic set of rights. Perhaps we think that the right to life, liberty, and happiness is fundamental and self-evident. But then we would need to describe how the right to work, education, or health care can be grounded in one of those other self-evident rights. The problem with merely stipulating a list of rights is that we need a justification for the list and basic rights—and the list that is derived from that basic list. But since different people come up with different lists, there is the danger of disagreement and the possibility of relativism.

One fundamental disagreement has to do with the question of whether our rights are basically negative prohibitions against interference or whether we have a more "positive" right to sustenance, care, and nourishment. Some contemporary philosophers argue that the basic rights that society ought to protect are not welfare rights, such as rights to food, clothing, and shelter, but only liberty rights, such as the right not to be interfered with in our daily lives.[25] (See further discussion of negative and positive rights in the section on socialism in Chapter 14.) The conflict between positive and negative rights remains a problem to be solved for a theory of human rights.

A theory of human rights is typically connected to a theory of human nature, as discussed previously in relation to natural law. A significant problem arises, however, in terms of human beings who are not "natural" or "normal," and with regard to nonhuman animals. Do people with cognitive disabilities or human fetuses have the same rights as adult human beings? Do nonhuman animals—especially those with advanced cognitive capacities, such as chimpanzees—have rights? These questions will return in our discussions of abortion and animal welfare in Chapters 11 and 17. But it is important to note here that considerations of rights raise complex questions about what sorts of creatures possess these rights. An account of rights that focuses on human nature will have to be careful to consider how human nature is expressed in fetuses and in people with disabilities. And if the concept of rights is to be restricted only to human beings, the defender of the concept of rights will have to explain the importance of the distinction between humans and our nonhuman relatives.

Finally, we should note that not all discussions of human rights are focused on human nature. John Stuart Mill argued that rights were related to general utility: "To have a right, then, is, I conceive, to have something which society ought to defend me in the possession of. If the objector goes on to ask, why it ought? I can give him no other reason than general utility."[26] For Mill, rights language provides a strong assertion of those values that promote the greatest happiness for the greatest number. Another example is found in the writings of Walter Lippmann, one of the most influential political commentators of the twentieth century, who held a rather utilitarian view that we ought to agree that there are certain rights because these provide the basis for a democratic society, and it is precisely such a society that works best. It is not that we can prove that such rights as freedom of speech or assembly exist; we simply accept them for pragmatic reasons because they provide the basis for democracy.[27]

The notion of rights can be and has been discussed in many different contexts. Among those treated in this book are issues of animal rights (Chapter 20), economic rights (Chapter 14), fetal rights (Chapter 11), women's rights (Chapter 9), equal rights and discrimination (Chapter 13), and war crimes (Chapter 18).

Slavery and Gender from the Vantage Point of Natural Law and Natural Rights

One objection that critics may make with regard to natural law and natural rights theory is that these approaches have been connected with ideas that we find to be morally outrageous. Aristotle, for example, thought that slavery could be justified in that it was in accord with nature (a point we will explore further in the next chapter). And it is worth noting that some of the greatest proponents of natural law and natural rights themselves owned slaves and defended colonialism. John Locke was involved in authoring, in 1669, "The Fundamental Constitutions of Carolina," which included the following: "Every freeman of Carolina shall have absolute power and authority over his negro slaves." Locke also likely endorsed the enslavement of Native American people who were defeated by the British in war, although the scholarship on Locke and his views of slavery and colonialism continues to generate scholarly debate.[28] And in subsequent centuries, proponents of the idea of natural rights nonetheless defended slavery. It is worth noting here that Thomas Jefferson enslaved over six hundred people. Defenders of Jefferson will argue that he eventually argued for the gradual emancipation of enslaved people. But the fact remains that he did not take action to free his own slaves.[29]

It is worth noting that natural law arguments can be made against slavery. An important figure here is Francisco Vitoria (1486–1546), a theologian influenced by Aquinas and the idea of natural law. Vitoria argued in the 1530s against Spanish colonialism by claiming that "the Indians" were not natural slaves. Nonetheless, Vitoria allowed for the use of war against native peoples who attacked the Spanish as they expanded into the Americas. While he did not justify this by appealing to the claim that the native peoples of the Americas were natural slaves, he did suggest that the Spanish were justified in fighting against the natives if they resisted the Spanish conquest. His justification of this was based on natural law arguments connected with the idea of a law of peoples that allows for justified warfare. He claimed that if the Indians attacked first, the Spanish were justified in fighting in response.[30]

Centuries later, abolitionists appealed to natural law and natural right arguments to make the case against slavery. Among these was Lysander Spooner (1808–1887), an American abolitionist who wrote in 1845 that slavery is "entirely contrary to natural right" and "entirely destitute of authority from natural law."[31] And Frederick Douglass pointed out the hypocrisy of slavery by invoking the basic American idea of natural rights in his famous Fourth of July speech in 1852 ("What to the Slave is the Fourth of July?"):

> You declare, before the world, and are understood by the world to declare, that you "hold these truths to be self-evident, that all men are created equal; and are endowed by their Creator with certain inalienable rights; and that, among these are, life, liberty, and the pursuit of happiness"; and yet, you hold securely, in a bondage which, according to your own Thomas Jefferson, "is worse than ages of that which your fathers rose in rebellion to oppose," a seventh part of the inhabitants of your country.[32]

A related problem arises in thinking about how the history of natural law and natural rights theories have been involved in patriarchal domination of men over women. Aristotle again provides a source: he thought that women were naturally inferior to men. The natural law tradition continued for long centuries to assume that there was a natural hierarchy in which men were entitled to rule over women. This idea influenced the thinking of Locke, as well as Jean-Jacques Rousseau. Rousseau's writings were, however, criticized by Mary Wollstonecraft, whose *Vindication of the Rights of Woman* (1792) is an important touchstone for feminism (which we'll discuss further in Chapter 9).

Wollstonecraft maintains that Rousseau and others are wrong to infer from the female's "natural" weakness in comparison with the male that women are lacking in value or rights. One significant problem is that

John Opie/Wikimedia Commons

Figure 7-4 Mary Wollstonecraft (1759–1797) argued for women's rights.

the supposed weakness of women can be understood as the result of an oppressive patriarchal culture—and is not natural at all. Wollstonecraft also says that there is a flaw in the tradition, which holds that "the rights of humanity" are confined to "the male line from Adam downwards."[33] Wollstonecraft's turn of phrase here is instructive: she focuses on the rights of humanity instead of the phrase "rights of man" that was typical of her era.

Natural law arguments were traditionally used in support of gender inequality. It was thought to be natural for fathers to rule within the family and for men to rule over women. Women have historically not been given equal rights with men. In the United States, women were not all granted the right to vote until 1920 with the ratification of the Nineteenth Amendment to the Constitution. Women around the globe are still struggling for this basic right. The women of Kuwait only gained the right to vote in 2005. The inequality of women and denial of women's rights are manifest in other parts of social, political, and economic life across the globe: achievement gaps, wage gaps, lack of access to health care, reproductive issues, control of sexuality, and so on. We consider these issues in more detail in subsequent chapters.

These discussions of inequality and violations of rights make one wonder whether our rights really are *self-evident* if people continue to disagree about them. On the one hand, the natural law and natural rights view suggests that our rights are self-evident. But those very ideas have been used to deny rights to enslaved people and to women. Defenders of the natural law and natural rights approach will argue that we are becoming more enlightened and that we are better now at understanding the true nature of things. But critics of natural law may argue that there is a fatal flaw in an approach that allowed for slavery and the oppression of women.

Is There a Human Nature?

7.5 Clarify how natural law arguments are grounded in claims about the essence of human nature that resist relativism.

Natural law and the idea of natural human rights presume that there is a common core to the human experience—that we are endowed with basic capacities, that we share common purposes, and that we value and enjoy a common set of intrinsic goods. In short, natural law and human rights rest on an objective account of human nature. One way of putting this is to say that human nature is discovered by us through the use of reason—and that human nature is not created by us or constructed by society. Let's return, as we conclude this chapter, to the statement from the UN Declaration of Human Rights that we cited at the beginning. This document says that all human beings are "endowed with reason and conscience." But this kind of essentializing language points toward some very deep philosophical questions. Is it true that all human beings possess reason and conscience? How are these ideas defined in different places, times, and cultures? And does this mean that those beings who lack reason and conscience are not fully human and not worthy of respect?

These kinds of questions may prompt some to think that there is simply no such thing as human nature. The history of humanity shows us that human beings have disagreed about who counts as fully human. In the twentieth century, existentialists such as Jean-Paul Sartre argued that there was no essential human nature.

As Sartre puts it, "existence precedes essence," which means that through the course of our lives we create our own nature or essence. More recent authors—who are often described as "postmodernists"—have made this argument in even stronger terms. Richard Rorty put the criticism of human nature this way:

> There is nothing deep inside each of us, no common human nature, no built-in human solidarity, to use as a moral reference point. There is nothing to people except what has been socialized into them. . . . Simply by being human we do not have a common bond. For all we share with all other humans is the same thing we share with all other animals—the ability to feel pain.[34]

This skepticism about human nature might point toward a broader conception of what matters morally. In Rorty's view, as expressed here, what seems to matter is mere sentience, the ability to suffer and feel pain. This might provide a source of broad "solidarity" with all suffering beings that downplays the importance of those features of "human nature" that were often held up as the essential defining feature of humanity: rationality, autonomy, and so on. But is that enough of a foundation for us to speak of human rights?

Defenders of natural law ethics worry that if we deny that there is a human essence, we will end up with a kind of relativism. From the standpoint of natural law, a denial of a common human nature will appear as relativism and skepticism that prevent us from establishing universal moral rules. As Craig Boyd has argued in defense of natural law and against the sorts of criticism made by people like Sartre and Rorty, "Natural law requires, as a presupposition, that human beings have enduring, identifiable natures, which in turn requires some kind of realism."[35] From this standpoint, the hope is that by grounding morality in objective or "realist" claims, we can discover basic principles and moral ideals that will be shared by all of us—and which we can use to criticize unjust and immoral practices such as slavery. As you reflect on natural law ethics, one of the most fundamental questions is whether there is an enduring and identifiable human nature or whether the complexity and changeable history of the human experience undermines the very idea of a shared human nature.

Chapter Summary

7.1 How is natural law theory related to the law of peoples and the norms of international law?

The idea that there is a law of peoples or a set of international laws points beyond the particular (or positive) laws of a given state or regime. Rather, there is supposed to be a transcendent law that could be used to criticize the laws of any particular country or government. Key thinkers in the natural law tradition, such as Grotius, were interested in developing systems of international law. This idea has evolved into contemporary ideas about universal human rights and the emerging system of international agreements and international laws.

7.2 What were the contributions that Cicero, Aquinas, and Locke made to natural law theory?

Cicero was an ancient Roman thinker whose approach is associated with Stoicism. The Stoics encouraged us to "follow nature." Cicero suggested that the natural law was both reasonable and eternal—as opposed to the changing and capricious laws of particular governments.

Aquinas is a key thinker in Medieval European Christianity. He attempted to bring faith and reason together in a systematic way. And like the ancient philosophers, Aquinas thought that reason could help us to discern the moral law found in God-created nature.

John Locke is a modern thinker who helped inspire the social contract idea that political law was grounded in the natural rights of the governed, including the right to life, liberty, and property. Locke's thinking inspired Jefferson and others, who made use of natural rights arguments.

7.3 How is the idea of teleology import in understanding natural law theory?

Natural law theory maintains that the universe is structured according to aims, ends, purposes, and functions. This is connected to a metaphysical and ontological account of reality. Reason can discern these purposes and functions. And morality is defined in connection with the goal of actualizing these aims and behaving according to a plan or system that organizes the cosmos. In some cases, this includes an account of the summum bonum or highest good, which provides us with an overarching goal or purpose.

7.4 How does natural law theory relate to the idea of natural rights and the idea of human rights?

The natural law tradition suggests that reason can discern moral structure in nature, since nature is organized according to a system of purposes and functions that clarify what we ought to do and how we should behave. The idea of natural rights develops out of this idea, claiming that our rights are self-evident, as a natural endowment. Both natural law and natural rights traditions are connected to a metaphysical theory that was typically religious. Human rights theories develop out of this approach, usually attempting to assert human rights without invoking any particular sectarian point of view.

7.5 How are natural law arguments grounded in claims about the essence of human nature that resist relativism?

The teleological account of the universe that is typical of natural law claims that human beings can be understood in terms of a basic set of purposes, functions, and ends. These functions help to define the human essence. Morality, according to natural law, should be directed toward helping us fulfill our function or purpose. This idea runs counter to a certain skepticism about human nature that is typical of relativism. Relativists tend to deny that there is any given human essence. Thus natural law offers a response to relativism. But one objection to natural law may be to raise the problem of relativism and the question of whether there is any real human essence.

7.6 How might you defend your own thesis with regard to the value of natural law theory and the idea of human rights?

A virtue of natural law theory and the idea of natural rights is that it grounds morality in a set of claims about reality that are supposed to be knowable and even self-evident. This approach is often further grounded in a metaphysical account of ultimate reality and the meaning and purpose of human life. Human rights theory is less metaphysical; but it also typically offers an account of self-evident claims about human nature. For those who want a clear account of morality grounded in self-evident truth, natural law and human rights theories will be of use. However, others will reject this approach in light of skeptical questions about what is self-evident and in light of the kinds of problems raised by relativism. Moreover, critics of the theory may argue that its defenders often had moral views that we no longer believe (such as about the inequality of women or the defense of slavery). Defenders of the theory may suggest in response that it has been improved and perfected and that it is no longer used to justify inequality and slavery. Indeed, arguments against slavery and the inequality of women have often been grounded in claims about basic human rights.

Primary Source Readings

The reading selections here from Thomas Aquinas and John Locke include discussions of the grounding of morality and rights in human nature. First, Aquinas explains how natural law is grounded in logical principles and an account of our natural inclinations. Then John Locke explains how natural law and natural rights are created by a benevolent God.

Reading 7-1   On Natural Law | Thomas Aquinas

Study Questions

As you read the excerpt, please consider the following questions:

1. How does one determine whether something is good or evil, according to Aquinas? Give some of his examples.

2. What is the natural function of the human as human? How is this related to natural law? To virtue?

3. How does Aquinas believe that we should decide which laws are just?

Whether Natural Law Contains Many Precepts or Only One

In the human context, the precepts of natural law relate to activities in a way similar to first principles in demonstrations. But there are many indemonstrable first principles. Therefore there are many precepts of natural law.

As was previously stated, precepts of natural law relate to practical reason just as the first principles of demonstration relate to speculative reason, both being self-evident. However, something is said to be self-evident in two ways: one intrinsically self-evident, the other evident to us. A particular proposition is said to be intrinsically self-evident when the predicate is implicit in the subject, although this proposition would not be self-evident to someone ignorant of the definition of the subject. For instance, this proposition "man is rational" is self-evident by its very nature since saying "human" entails saying "rational." Nevertheless this proposition is not self-evident to one who does not know what a man is. . . .

[Now] that which is primary in apprehension is being, the understanding of which is included in anything whatsoever that is apprehended. Accordingly, the first indemonstrable principle is that one cannot simultaneously affirm and deny something. This is founded in the understanding of being and non-being and in this principle all

From Thomas Aquinas, *Summa Theologica* (1265–1272), First Part of the Second Part (*Prima Secundæ Partis*), trans. Edward MacKinnon.

others are founded, as stated in *Metaphysics IV*. Just as being is the first thing that falls under simple apprehension, so also the good is the first thing that falls under the apprehension of practical reason which is ordered to action. Every agent acts for an end, which is understood as a good. Accordingly, the first principle of practical reason is the one based on the concept of the good: Good is what everything desires. This, accordingly, is the first principle of law: Good is to be done and evil avoided. All the other precepts of natural law are based on this. All concern what is to be done or avoided, because practical reason naturally apprehends what is the human good.

Good has the nature of an end while evil has a contrary nature. Accordingly, every thing for which a man has a natural inclination is naturally apprehended as a good and consequently something to be pursued, while anything contrary to this is to be avoided as evil. Therefore the ordering of the precepts of natural law stems from the order of natural inclinations. In the first place, there is the inclination of man towards natural good, an inclination shared by all substances inasmuch as they naturally desire self-preservation. The consequence of this inclination is that whatever preserves human life and avoids obstacles is a matter of natural law. Secondly, there is in man a more specialized inclination following the natural bent he shares with other animals. Accordingly these things are said to pertain to natural law that "nature has taught to all animals," such as the mating of male and female, education of children, and similar things. Thirdly, there is in man an inclination toward good based on reason, something proper only to man. Thus man has a natural inclination to know the truth about God, and that he should live in society. On this ground, those things that stem from this inclination are also a matter of natural law. Thus, man should overcome ignorance and should not offend fellow members of society, and similar considerations.

Whether All Acts of Virtue Are Prescribed by Natural Law

All those things to which man is inclined by nature pertain to natural law. Everything naturally inclines to operations that are appropriate to its form, as fire toward heating. Since a rational soul is the proper form of humans the natural inclination of a man is to act according to reason. And this is acting virtuously. In this respect, all virtuous acts pertain to natural law. Each person's reason naturally tells him to act virtuously. However, if we speak of virtuous acts in themselves, or according to their proper species, then not all virtuous acts are matters of natural law. For many things accord with virtue, though nature lacks an initial inclination. It is through rational inquisition that men come to know which things conduce to living well.

Whether There Is One Natural Law for All

As was said previously, those things towards which man is naturally inclined pertain to natural law. Among such things it is distinctively human for a man to act in accord with reason. Reason inclines us to proceed from the common to the particular (as shown in *Physics I*). In this regard there is a difference between speculative and practical reason. Speculative reason is concerned in the first instance with things that are necessary, or could not be otherwise. Thus truth is easily found in proper conclusions just as in common principles. But practical reason is concerned with contingent matters involving human activity. Therefore, if there is some necessity in common principles, there is increasing error the further we descend to particular conclusions. In speculative reason, there is the same degree of truth in principles and conclusions, although the truth of the conclusion may not be as well known to many as the principles are, for they are common conceptions. In activities, however, there is not the same degree of truth or practical rectitude, among all people concerning conclusions, but only concerning principles. Even those people who share the same rectitude concerning conclusions do not share the same knowledge.... With regard to the proper conclusions of practical reason, all do not share the same truth or rectitude. Even those that do share equal truth are not equally known. For everyone, it is right and true to act in accord with reason. From this principle follows a quasi-proper conclusion, that debts should be paid. This is true as a general rule. However, it may happen to be harmful in a particular case, and consequently unreasonable to give goods back, if for example someone is intending to attack the homeland. Thus, uncertainty increases the more we descend to particulars. Thus if it is claimed that goods are to be restored with certain precautions, or under certain conditions, then the more detailed the conditions are, the more uncertainty increases, even to the degree that it is not clear whether or not they should be restored.

Accordingly, we claim that first principles of natural law are the same for all, but in rectitude and knowledge.

However, the quasi conclusions from these principles are for the most part the same for all both in rectitude and knowledge, though in a few cases there can be a deficit both with respect to rectitude because of some particular impediments (just as things naturally generated and corrupted are deficient in a few cases because of obstacles) and there can also be a deficit in knowledge. The reason for this is that some people have their reason perverted by passion, which may be due to bad customs or to a defective natural disposition....

Whether Every Law Fashioned by Humans Is Derived from Natural Law

But it should be recognized that something can be deviant from natural law in two ways. The first is as a conclusion from principles; the other as a determination of some common generalities. The first mode is similar to the practice of the sciences, where conclusions are produced by deduction from principles. The second mode, however, is more like what occurs in the arts, where common forms are tailored to special cases. A carpenter, for example, must determine the common form of a home to be this or that particular shape. Therefore, some things are derived from the common principle of natural law in the form of conclusions. Thus the prohibition of murder is derived from the general principle that evil should not be done. Other things, however, have the form of a determination. Natural law requires punishment for the evildoer, but whether he receives this or that penalty is a particular determination of natural law. Both forms, accordingly, are found in human law. However, determinations of the first mode are not only contained in human law, but they also have force through natural law. The second mode, however, derive their force only from human law....

In every being that is for (or oriented toward) an end it is necessary that its form has a determinate proportionality to the end, as the form of a saw is geared towards cutting as is clear in *Physics II*. Anything that is ruled and measured should have a form proportioned to its ruler and measure. Now human law has both, because it is something ordered to an end; and it has a rule or measure regulated or measured by a higher measure, which is both divine law and the law of nature, as previously explained. The end of human law is the well-being of humans ... accordingly, ... the first condition of law posits three things: That it accords with religion, inasmuch as it is proportioned to divine law; that it fosters discipline, inasmuch as it is proportional to natural law; and that it advances well-being inasmuch as it is proportional to human needs.

Reading 7-2   Second Treatise of Civil Government | John Locke

Study Questions

As you read the excerpt, please consider the following questions:

1. What two things characterize human beings in their natural state, according to Locke?
2. Why, according to Locke, do we need civil government?
3. According to Locke, was there ever really an existing state of nature as he describes it?

Of the State of Nature

To understand political power aright, and derive it from its original, we must consider what estate all men are naturally in, and that is, a state of perfect freedom to order their actions, and dispose of their possessions and persons as they think fit, within the bounds of the law of Nature, without asking leave or depending upon the will of any other man.

A state also of equality, wherein all the power and jurisdiction is reciprocal, no one having more than another, there being nothing more evident than that creatures of the same species and rank, promiscuously born to all the same advantages of Nature, and the use

---

From John Locke, *Second Treatise of Civil Government* (London: Routledge and Sons, 1887).

of the same faculties, should also be equal one amongst another, without subordination or subjection, unless the lord and master of them all should, by a manifest declaration of his will, set one above another, and confer on him, by an evident and clear appointment, an undoubted right to dominion and sovereignty....

But though this be a state of liberty, yet it is not a state of license; though man in that state have an uncontrollable liberty to dispose of his person or possessions, yet he has not liberty to destroy himself, or so much as any creature in his possession, but where some nobler use than its bare preservation calls for it. The state of Nature has a law of Nature to govern it, which obliges every one, and reason, which is that law, teaches all mankind who will but consult it, that being all equal and independent, no one ought to harm another in his life, health, liberty or possessions; for men being all the workmanship of one omnipotent and infinitely wise Maker; all the servants of one sovereign Master, sent into the world by His order and about His business; they are His property, whose workmanship they are made to last during His, not one another's pleasure. And, being furnished with like faculties, sharing all in one community of Nature, there cannot be supposed any such subordination among us that may authorize us to destroy one another, as if we were made for one another's uses, as the inferior ranks of creatures are for ours. Every one as he is bound to preserve himself, and not to quit his station willfully, so by the like reason, when his own preservation comes not in competition, ought he as much as he can to preserve the rest of mankind, and not unless it be to do justice on an offender, take away, or impair the life, or what tends to the preservation of the life, the liberty, health, limb, or goods of another.

And that all men may be restrained from invading other's rights, and from doing hurt to one another, and the law of Nature be observed, which willeth the peace and preservation of all mankind, the execution of the law of Nature is in that state put into every man's hands, whereby every one has a right to punish the transgressors of that law to such a degree as may hinder its violation. For the law of Nature would, as all other laws that concern men in this world, be in vain if there were nobody that in the state of Nature had a power to execute that law, and thereby preserve the innocent and restrain offenders; and if any one in the state of Nature may punish another for any evil he has done, every one may do so. For in that state of perfect equality, where naturally there is no superiority or jurisdiction of one over another, what any may do in prosecution of that law, every one must needs have a right to do.

And thus, in the state of Nature, one man comes by a power over another, but yet no absolute or arbitrary power to use a criminal when he has got him in his hands, according to the passionate heats, or boundless extravagancy of his own will, but only to retribute to him so far as calm reason and conscience dictate, what is proportionate to his transgression, which is so much as may serve for reparation and restraint. For these two are the only reasons why one man may lawfully do harm to another, which is that we call punishment. In transgressing the law of Nature, the offender declares himself to live by another rule than that of reason and common equity, which is that measure God has set to the actions of men for their mutual security, and so he becomes dangerous to mankind; the tie which is to secure them from injury and violence being slighted and broken by him, which being a trespass against the whole species, and the peace and safety of it, provided for by the law of Nature, every man upon this score, by the right he hath to preserve mankind in general, may restrain, or where it is necessary, destroy things noxious to them, and so may bring such evil on any one who hath transgressed that law, as may make him repent the doing of it, and thereby deter him, and, by his example, others from doing the like mischief. And in this case, and upon this ground, every man hath a right to punish the offender, and be executioner of the law of Nature....

From these two distinct rights (the one of punishing the crime, for restraint and preventing the like offence, which right of punishing is in everybody, the other of taking reparation, which belongs only to the injured party) comes it to pass that the magistrate, who by being magistrate hath the common right of punishing put into his hands, can often, where the public good demands not the execution of the law, remit the punishment of criminal offences by his own authority, but yet cannot remit the satisfaction due to any private man for the damage he has received. That he who hath suffered the damage has a right to demand in his own name, and he alone can remit. The damnified person has this power of appropriating to himself the goods or service of the offender by right of self-preservation, as every man has a power to punish the crime to prevent its being committed again, by the right he has of preserving all mankind, and doing all reasonable things he can in order to that end. And thus it is that every man in the state of Nature has a power to kill a murderer, both to deter others from doing the like injury (which no reparation can compensate) by the example of the punishment that attends it from everybody, and also to secure men from the attempts of a criminal who, having renounced reason, the common rule and measure God hath given to mankind, hath, by the unjust violence and slaughter he hath committed upon one, declared war against all mankind, and therefore may be destroyed as a lion or a tiger, one of those wild savage beasts with whom men can have no society nor security. And upon this is grounded that great law of Nature, "Whoso sheddeth man's blood by man shall his blood be shed." And Cain was so fully convinced that every one had a right to destroy such a criminal, that, after the murder of his brother, he cried out, "Every one that findeth me shall slay me," so plain was it writ in the hearts of all mankind.

By the same reason may a man in the state of Nature punish the lesser breaches of that law, it will, perhaps, be demanded, with death? I answer: Each transgression may be punished to that degree, and with so much severity, as will suffice to make it an ill bargain to the offender, give him cause to repent, and terrify others from doing the like. Every offence that can be committed in the state of Nature may, in the state of Nature, be also punished equally, and as far forth, as it may, in a commonwealth. For though it would be beside my present purpose to enter here into the particulars of the law of Nature, or its measures of punishment; yet it is certain there is such a law, and that too as intelligible and plain to a rational creature and a studier of that law as the positive laws of commonwealths, nay, possibly plainer; as much as reason is easier to be understood than the fancies and intricate contrivances of men, following contrary and hidden interests put into words; for

truly so are a great part of the municipal laws of countries, which are only so far right as they are founded on the law of Nature, by which they are to be regulated and interpreted.

To this strange doctrine—viz., That in the state of Nature every one has the executive power of the law of Nature, I doubt not but it will be objected that it is unreasonable for men to be judges in their own cases, that self-love will make men partial to themselves and their friends; and, on the other side, ill-nature, passion, and revenge will carry them too far in punishing others, and hence nothing but confusion and disorder will follow, and that therefore God hath certainly appointed government to restrain the partiality and violence of men. I easily grant that civil government is the proper remedy for the inconveniencies of the state of Nature, which must certainly be great where men may be judges in their own case, since it is easy to be imagined that he who was so unjust as to do his brother an injury will scarce be so just as to condemn himself for it. But I shall desire those who make this objection to remember that absolute monarchs are but men; and if government is to be the remedy of those evils which necessarily follow from men being judges in their own cases, and the state of Nature is therefore not to be endured, I desire to know what kind of government that is, and how much better it is than the state of Nature, where one man commanding a multitude has the liberty to be judge in his own case, and may do to all his subjects whatever he pleases without the least question or control of those who execute his pleasure? and in whatsoever he doth, whether led by reason, mistake, or passion, must be submitted to? which men in the state of Nature are not bound to do one to another. And if he that judges, judges amiss in his own or any other case, he is answerable for it to the rest of mankind.

It is often asked as a mighty objection, where are, or ever were, there any men in such a state of Nature? To which it may suffice as an answer at present, that since all princes and rulers of "independent" governments all through the world are in a state of Nature, it is plain the world never was, nor never will be, without numbers of men in that state. I have named all governors of "independent" communities, whether they are, or are not, in league with others; for it is not every compact that puts an end to the state of Nature between men, but only this one of agreeing together mutually to enter into one community, and make one body politic; other promises and compacts men may make one with another, and yet still be in the state of Nature. The promises and bargains for truck, &c., between the two men in Soldania, or between a Swiss and an Indian, in the woods of America, are binding to them, though they are perfectly in a state of Nature in reference to one another for truth, and keeping of faith belongs to men as men, and not as members of society....

Review Exercises

1. What is the difference between the scientific laws of nature, the positive laws of political life, and the natural law?

2. In what way is natural law theory teleological?

3. What specific natural capacities are singled out by natural law theorists? How do these determine what we ought to do, according to the theory?

4. How is Aquinas's approach to natural law connected to his theological views?

5. How is natural law connected with Stoicism?

6. Describe the basic idea of rights according to early natural rights theorists such as Locke, including where they come from and how we know we have them.

7. Give examples of what sorts of rights we are supposed to have according to the theories of natural rights and human rights? What is the problem with merely stipulating a list of rights?

8. What is the difference between natural/human rights and civil rights?

9. Explain the criticism of natural law from the perspective of those who deny the idea of "human nature."

10. How have critics of slavery and proponents of women's rights advanced our understanding of human rights and natural law?

Knowledge Check Answer Key

1. **d.** Summum Bonum is another name for the highest good.

2. **b.** Thomas Aquinas was interested in finding a way to unite faith and reason.

3. **c.** Natural law morality offers a normative theory that tells us what we ought to do, based on an account of natural purposes and functions.

4. **a.** Jefferson asserted that natural rights are self-evident and inalienable.

8 Virtue Ethics

Learning Outcomes

After reading this chapter, you should be able to:

8.1 Explain how virtue ethics differs from other approaches to ethics.

8.2 Describe some key virtues and apply them to concrete situations.

8.3 Explain how the idea of the golden mean functions in virtue ethics.

8.4 Explain how virtues are connected to an account of the functions or purposes of human life.

8.5 Analyze the idea of eudaimonia and what it means within Aristotle's theory of virtue.

8.6 Evaluate Aristotle's moral philosophy in comparison with other virtue theories.

8.7 Defend your own thesis with regard to the value of virtue ethics.

Vaccine Virtues and Vices

When NBA star Kyrie Irving announced that he would not be getting a COVID-19 vaccination, some fans turned against him, claiming that he let his team down by refusing to get the jab. But Senator Ted Cruz came to his defense, claiming in a tweet, "Kyrie is showing great courage."[1] This dispute leads us to wonder about a virtue such as courage. Is it courageous to refuse to get vaccinated? Or does courage require us to get the jab? And are there other virtues than courage that are needed in a pandemic?

Bagus Production/Shutterstock

During the pandemic, related questions of virtue arose with regard to the kinds of virtues that are generally emphasized in different cultures. In East Asian countries such as China, South Korea, Japan, and Vietnam, the death rate was significantly lower than in countries like Brazil and the United States.[2] A number of causal factors help explain this: public health infrastructure, trust in government, the degree of political freedom, and the relative age of the population. But a widely discussed issue was a difference in culture and virtue.[3] Some argue that in societies influenced by Confucianism, people responded to the pandemic with a set of virtues that are useful in social emergencies. A Confucian approach to virtue emphasizes filial piety (respect for elders), humaneness (benevolence), and propriety (courtesy). These virtues appear to be helpful when lockdowns, quarantines, and masking are needed to contain an outbreak of disease that can kill older people. On the other hand, so the argument goes, these virtues are less important in Western societies, where individual liberty, nonconformity, and the sort of courage ascribed to Kyrie Irving are emphasized. Of course, we want to avoid stereotyping and overgeneralizing here. Respect for elders is also a virtue in Western traditions, as are compassion and courtesy; and people in Asia also value liberty. But the question nonetheless arises about whether some sets of virtues work better in a pandemic. And beneath this concern is a deeper question about whether there is one set of virtues common to all human beings or whether there are competing or rival accounts of virtue.

What Do You Think?

1. What kinds of virtues are important in a public health crisis and in other social emergencies?
2. Is it courageous to refuse to get vaccinated?
3. Are there different accounts of virtue that are relative to different cultures?
4. Is there one common set of virtues for all human beings?

Introduction

8.1 Explain how virtue ethics differs from other approaches to ethics.

Virtue ethics is concerned with questions about character, habits, attitudes, and dispositions. Virtue ethicists ask questions about particular virtues such as courage and about how these virtues combine in a good and happy life. Often, this involves looking at role models and exemplars of virtue.

Consider the story of Pat Tillman, a successful NFL player who gave up his NFL career to serve in the Army. Tillman played safety for the Arizona Cardinals. After the September 11 attacks in 2001, Tillman turned down a $3.6 million contract offer and enlisted. He qualified to become an Army Ranger. His unit served in Iraq and in Afghanistan, where he was killed, by accident, by members of his own platoon during a firefight. Tillman's death prompted a number of controversies. The Army initially informed Tillman's family and the public that he had been killed by enemy fire, in an apparent effort to preserve the image of Tillman as a war hero. (Among other awards, he posthumously received the Army's Silver Star for Valor.) A subsequent book about Tillman claimed that he was not a supporter of the Iraq War and was critical of President George W. Bush.[4] Nonetheless,

Tillman remains a model of virtue and courage. Senator John McCain used Tillman's story to explain the virtues of citizenship and patriotism in his book *Character Is Destiny*.[5] What is remarkable about Tillman is his willingness to sacrifice a lucrative football career for life and death as an Army Ranger. He seemed to embody virtues—such as courage, loyalty, self-sacrifice, and patriotism—that are often mourned as deficient or absent in contemporary society. Do you agree with this assessment? Is Tillman a hero? And how is his courage similar or different to that of Kyrie Irving?

When thinking about virtue, it is useful to think about the people you admire. Whether it is a relative, a coworker, a friend, or some celebrity, it is helpful to consider the traits that make those people good. We usually admire people who are courageous, kind, honest, generous, loyal, diligent, temperate, fair, modest, and hospitable. Such traits of character are traditionally known as *virtues*.

Virtues and Everyday Life

8.2 Describe some key virtues and apply them to concrete situations.

The theories that we have treated so far in this text are concerned with how we determine the right action to take or policy to establish. The focus on virtue takes a different approach to morality. Rather than asking what we ought to *do*, virtue ethics asks how we ought to *be*. Virtue ethics is concerned with those traits of character, habits, tendencies, and dispositions that make a person good. When some or all of the traits mentioned above are unusually well developed in a person, that person may be regarded as a hero or even as a saint. Such an idea of perfection is found in the familiar phrase "paragon of virtue," which points in the direction of someone who is flawless or perfect. One version of virtue ethics is focused on thinking about saints and heroes as paradigms or exemplars of human excellence.

In a well-known article on the topic, Susan Wolf described a moral saint as "a person whose every action is as good as possible, that is, who is as morally worthy as can be."[6] But Wolf goes on to argue that moral saints are not especially happy, since the demands of saintly perfection might include self-sacrifice. At issue here is a definition of happiness. Virtue ethics tends to hold that happiness is something different from pleasure. Pat Tillman's life and death were not particularly pleasant— he suffered through Army Ranger training and then was killed at the age of twenty-seven. But perhaps there is something more important than pleasure. At any rate, even if it is difficult and unpleasant to become a hero or a saint, the virtue tradition maintains that people live better when they possess most or all of the virtues. People can also exhibit bad character traits. For example, they can be cowardly, dishonest, tactless, careless, boorish, stingy, vindictive, disloyal, lazy, or egotistical. Another word for bad traits such as these is *vice*. An ethics focused on virtue encourages us to develop the good traits and get rid of the bad ones, that is, to develop our virtues and eliminate our vices.

The ethical issues that are treated in the second half of this text are generally controversial social issues: the death penalty, abortion, and terrorism, for example. Virtue ethics seems more personal. It involves not so much asking which side of some social issue one should support as what kind of person one should be. Virtues can help us make good decisions in tough situations. But they also serve us on a daily basis. Virtues such as courage, loyalty, honesty, and fairness show up in our interactions with relatives, friends, and coworkers. We often think about virtues when we consider how our behavior serves as a good (or bad) model for our children, students, and colleagues.

John Cordes/Icon SMI/ZUMA/Corbis

Figure 8-1 Pat Tillman is looked to as a model of virtue.

Virtue ethics can be useful in thinking about the applied issues discussed in the second half of the text. As we saw in our opening discussion, it is possible that some virtues are more useful socially than others. And different cultures and societies may emphasize different virtues. Virtues also depend, in part, on our roles and help us fulfill the requirements of our roles: so soldiers ought to be courageous and strong, while teachers ought to be patient and kind. Virtue ethics encourages us to consider the question of how a soldier's virtues might differ from those of a teacher. Some of the applied topics we will discuss have connections with questions about the virtues of various vocations and roles. In thinking about euthanasia and physician-assisted suicide, for example, issues arise regarding the proper virtues of health-care providers. In thinking about the morality of abortion, we might think about proper virtues of parents and lawmakers, as well as doctors. In thinking about the morality of war, we consider the virtues we associate with military service.

There will be overlap among the virtues found in different vocations. But different roles require different character traits and habits. This reminds us that virtue ethics has a pluralistic aspect. There are many different virtues that can be emphasized and integrated in various ways in the life of an individual. Moreover, virtuous people tend to be responsive to the unique demands of various situations; they do the right thing, at the right time, in the right way, exhibiting a sort of "practical wisdom" that is sensitive to context. From the standpoint of utilitarianism or deontology, which wants clearly defined rules and principles for action, virtue ethics can seem imprecise and vague. But an asset of virtue ethics may be its sensitivity to context and its recognition of plurality in morals.

Although we probably do not use the term *virtuous* as frequently today as in times past, we still understand the essence of its meaning. A virtuous person is a morally good person, and virtues are good traits. Another word that is useful in understanding virtue is *excellence*. The virtues are those things that make us excellent; they allow us to manifest our highest potential. There is more than one thing that makes us excellent. Indeed, virtues are often described in the plural—as a list of qualities that lead to living well. Loyalty is a virtue, and so is honesty. A moral philosophy that concentrates on the notion of virtue is called a *virtue ethics*. For virtue ethics, the moral life is about developing good *character*. It is about determining the ideals for human life and trying to embody these ideals in one's own life. The virtues are ways in which we embody these ideals. For example, if we consider honesty to be such an ideal, then we ought to try to become honest persons.

Aristotle

Aristotle was born in 384 BCE in Stagira in northern Greece. His father was a physician for King Philip of Macedonia. Around age seventeen, he went to study at Plato's Academy in Athens. Aristotle traveled for several years and then for two or three years was the tutor to Alexander, Philip's young son who later became known as Alexander the Great. In 335 BCE, Aristotle returned to Athens and organized his own school, called the Lyceum. There he taught and wrote almost until his death thirteen years later, in 322 BCE.[7] Aristotle is known not only for his moral theory, but also for writings in logic, biology, physics, metaphysics, art, and politics. The basic notions of his moral theory can be found in his *Nicomachean Ethics*, named for his son Nicomachus.[8]

As noted in Chapter 7, Aristotle was one of the earliest writers to ground morality in nature, and specifically in *human* nature and an account of the highest good (i.e., the *summum bonum* we also discussed in Chapter 7). His theory of ethics stressed the notion of virtue and how virtue was connected to happiness (*eudaimonia* in Greek), which was for Aristotle the highest good. For Aristotle, virtue was an excellence of some sort. Our word *virtue* originally came from the Latin *vir* and referred to strength or manliness.[9] In Aristotle's Greek, the term for virtue was *arete*, a word that can also be translated as "excellence." When we are virtuous (or excellent), we flourish, thrive, and attain happiness.

According to Aristotle, there are two basic types of virtue (or excellence): intellectual virtues and moral virtues. Intellectual virtues are excellences of mind, such as the ability to understand and reason and judge well. Moral virtues, on the other hand, dispose us to act well. These virtues are learned by repetition. For instance, by practicing courage or honesty, we become more courageous and honest. Just as repetition in playing a musical instrument makes playing easier, repeated acts of honesty make it easier to be honest. The person who has the virtue of honesty finds it easier to be honest than the person who does not have the virtue. It becomes habitual or second nature to them. The same thing applies to the opposite of virtue, namely, vice. The person who lies and lies again finds that lying is easier and telling the truth is more difficult. One can have bad moral habits (vices) as well as good ones (virtues). Just like other bad habits, bad moral habits are difficult to change or break. And like other good habits, good moral habits take practice to develop.

Virtue as a Mean

8.3 Explain how the idea of the golden mean functions in virtue ethics.

Aristotle's philosophy outlines a variety of particular virtues including courage, temperance, justice, pride, and magnanimity. However, Aristotle also provides a unifying framework for understanding virtue in general, as a mean between extremes. This idea is occasionally known as the **golden mean** (and should not be confused with the Golden Rule, which we've discussed in previous chapters). By saying that virtue is a *mean*, we are using the word with reference to how it is used in mathematics, where the *mean* is the average. (The term *mean* here should also not be confused with the idea of using someone as a *means*, as we discussed in Chapter 6 in relation to Kant's theory of ethics.)

To better understand the idea that virtue is a mean, take the following example. The virtue of courage can be understood as a mean or middle between the two extremes of deficiency and excess. The virtue of courage has to do with fear. When facing danger or challenges, we should have neither too much fear—which makes us unable to act—nor too little fear—which makes us take reckless or foolish risks. Too little fear leaves us "foolhardy"; too much fear is called "cowardice." The virtue of courage is having just the right amount of fear, depending on what is appropriate for us as individuals and for the circumstances we face. So, too, the other virtues can be seen as means between extremes (as indicated in Table 8-1).

Different authors have offered different lists of virtues and corresponding vices. For the Greek tradition, following Plato, there were four basic or **cardinal virtues**: prudence (or wisdom), justice, temperance, and courage. Questions arise about which traits count as virtues and how these virtues are related to corresponding vices. For example, we might want to count loyalty and honesty as virtues. If loyalty is a virtue, is it also a middle between two extremes? Can there be such

a thing as too little or too much loyalty? What about honesty? Too much honesty might be seen as undisciplined openness, and too little as deceitfulness.

Not all virtues may be rightly thought of as means between extremes. For example, if justice is a virtue, could there be such a thing as being too just? It is important to note that virtue ethics still maintains that some things are simply wrong and not amenable to explanation in virtue terminology. For example, murder is wrong; there is no right time for murder or right amount of murder.

Nature, Human Nature, and the Human Good

8.4 Explain how virtues are connected to an account of the functions or purposes of human life.

Aristotle was a close observer of nature. In fact, in his writings, he mentions some five hundred different kinds of animals.[10] He noticed that seeds of the same sort always grew to the same mature form. He opened developing eggs of various species and noticed that these organisms manifested a pattern in their development even before birth. Tadpoles, he might have said, always follow the same path and become frogs, not turtles. So also with other living things. Acorns always become oak trees, not elms. He concluded that there was an order in nature. It was as if natural beings, such as plants and animals, had a principle of order within them that directed them toward their goal—their mature final form. This view can be called a *teleological* view, from *telos*, the Greek word for "goal," because of its emphasis on a goal embedded in natural things. It was from this conclusion that Aristotle developed his notion of the good. You might also notice that the idea of a natural goal, purpose, or function showed up in the discussion of natural law (in Chapter 7).

According to Aristotle, "the good is that at which all things aim." Good things are things that fulfill some purpose, end, or goal. Thus, the good of the shipbuilder is to build ships. The good of the lyre player is to play well. The traits that allow for good shipbuilding or lyre-playing will be somewhat different. But good

Table 8-1 Virtue as a Mean between Two Extremes

	Deficit (Too Little)	Virtue (the Mean)	Excess (Too Much)
Fear	Foolhardiness	Courage	Cowardice
Giving	Illiberality	Liberality	Prodigality
Self-Regard	Humility	Pride	Vanity
Pleasures	(No Name Given)	Temperance	Profligacy

shipbuilders and good lyre players will share certain virtues, such as intelligence and creativity. Aristotle asks whether there is anything that is the good of the human being—not as shipbuilder or lyre player, but simply as human. To answer this question, we must first think about what it is to be human. According to Aristotle, natural beings come in kinds or species. From their species flow their essential characteristics and certain key tendencies or capacities. For example, a squirrel is a kind of animal that is, first of all, a living being. It develops from a young to a mature form. It is a mammal and therefore has other characteristics of mammals. It is bushy-tailed, can run along telephone wires, and gathers and stores nuts for its food. From the characteristics that define a squirrel, we also can know what a *good* squirrel is. A good specimen of a squirrel is one that is effective, successful, and functions well. It follows the pattern of development and growth it has by nature. A good squirrel does, in fact, have a bushy tail and good balance, and knows how to find and store its food. It would be a bad example of a squirrel if it had no balance, couldn't find its food, or had no fur and was sickly. It would have been better for the squirrel if its inherent natural tendencies to grow and develop and live as a healthy squirrel had been realized.

Aristotle thought of human beings as natural beings with a specific human nature. Human beings have certain specific characteristics and abilities that we share as humans. Unlike squirrels and acorns, human beings can choose to act in the service of their good or act against it. But just what is their good? Aristotle recognized that a good eye is a healthy eye that sees well. A good horse is a well-functioning horse, one that is healthy and able to run and do what horses do. What about human beings? Is there something comparable for the human being as human? Is there some good for humans as humans?

Eudaimonia and the Highest Good

8.5   Analyze the idea of eudaimonia and what it means within Aristotle's theory of virtue.

Just as we can tell what the good squirrel is from its own characteristics and abilities as a squirrel, the same should be true for the human being. For human beings

to function well or flourish, they should perfect their human capacities. If they do this, they will be functioning well as human beings. They will also be happy, for a being is happy to the extent that it is functioning well. Aristotle believed that the ultimate good of humans is happiness, blessedness, or prosperity. This is what Aristotle viewed as the *summum bonum*, the supreme or highest good. The Greek word for this sort of happiness is **eudaimonia**. *Eudaimonia* is not to be confused with pleasure. Indeed, the virtues are often at odds with pleasure. A coward who is afraid of danger is reluctant to experience pain. And a courageous person may have to forgo pleasure and submit to pain—including the pain of being killed. Aristotle warned that pleasure can distract us from what is good. Thus, Aristotle's account of *eudaimonia* aims at a kind of happiness that is deeper and longer lasting than mere pleasure. The term *eudaimonia* gives us a clue about this. The *eu-* prefix means "good," and *daimonia* is related to the Greek word for "spirit" or "soul." Thus, Aristotle's idea is that virtue produces the happiness of having a good soul or spirit, which fulfills essential human functions or purposes.

Aristotle is thus interested in the question of what our human functions or purposes might be. Human beings have much in common with what we might call "lower" forms of beings (and Aristotle assumed that there was a kind of hierarchy in nature). For example, we are living, just as plants are. Thus, we take in material from outside us for nourishment, and we grow from an immature to a mature form. We have senses of sight, hearing, and so forth, as do the higher animals. We are social animals as well, who must live in groups together with other human beings. Since human beings have various functions or purposes, there are various types of virtue. For example, the virtues of social life help us fulfill our function as social beings. The moral or social virtues would include honesty, loyalty, and generosity.

But is there anything unique to humans, an essentially human function or purpose? Aristotle believed that it is our "rational element" that is peculiar to us. The good for humans, then, is living in accord with this rational element. Our rational element has two different functions: one is to know, and the other is to guide choice and action. We must develop our ability to know the world and the truth. We must also choose wisely. In doing this, we will be functioning well, specifically as humans. Thus, in addition to social or moral virtues, there are also intellectual virtues, which help us fulfill our function as intelligent animals. According to Aristotle, these virtues include practical knowledge, scientific knowledge, and practical wisdom. It is not surprising that Aristotle—who was a philosopher and a student of Plato—thought that the intellectual virtues were more important than the other virtues, since they help us fulfill our uniquely human capacities.

Aristotle on Slavery and Gender Hierarchy

As mentioned above, Aristotle assumed that there was hierarchy built into nature. Human beings are more advanced than animals. And even among humans, Aristotle assumed there was a natural hierarchy, with men above women, and free persons above enslaved persons. This hierarchical worldview was common in the ancient world. And in a sense, Aristotle's views reflect the social world in which he found himself. In that world, slavery was taken for granted, along with the subordination of women. Aristotle's theory also involves other hierarchical structures. In his *Politics*, Aristotle explains that the household (the place of family life and the household economy) was naturally inferior to or subordinated to the larger form of social organization called the *polis* (the Greek word for city or state). Women and slaves were confined to the household—to the realm of private life. And the realm of the political (the world of the *polis*) was a place for male citizens.

Aristotle explained his thinking in *Politics* as follows:

> As between the sexes, the male is by nature superior and the female inferior, the male ruler and the female subject. And the same must also necessarily apply in the case of mankind as a whole; therefore, all men that differ as widely as the soul does from the body and the human being from the lower animal. These are by nature slaves, for whom to be governed by this kind of authority is advantageous.... For he is by nature a slave who is capable of belonging to another.[11]

This last idea, Aristotle's notion that there are "slaves by nature," has provoked outrage. Aristotle appears to suggest that some human beings are naturally inferior and are justifiably enslaved. Aristotle's account of slavery is not racialized in the way that slavery was in modern European and American history, although he did make a distinction between Greeks and "barbarians." Rather, he suggested that "natural slaves" were intellectually and morally inferior—a claim that was more about ability than race. For people who are unable to govern themselves, Aristotle said slavery is both "expedient and just."[12]

This kind of thing may lead us to think twice about the very idea of virtue ethics. Is virtue ethics too focused on the kind of virtues that are particular to roles and one's position within the social hierarchy? Virtue ethics does not provide us with a theory of universal human rights that could be used to critique the idea of slavery or the subordination of women. Aristotle's approach suggests that a woman's virtue will be different from a man's and a slave's virtue will be different from a citizen's. His idea is that virtues are defined by the aims, functions, and purposes of these various natural and social roles. This view has a certain plausibility that reflects the idea that virtues are determined in relation to roles and social position. Of course, today we would not defend the idea that a virtuous slave ought to obey their master. But there are hierarchical roles and virtues in modern culture found in family life, educational institutions, and the military. To what extent are obedience and submissiveness still a virtue in modern life? Aristotle is not the only ancient thinker to suggest that there could be a kind of virtue for slaves that was different from other sorts of virtues. The Apostle Paul said in more than one place in the Christian Bible that wives should submit to their husbands, that children should obey their fathers, and that slaves should obey their masters.[13] But noting that this idea was common in the ancient world does not mean that it is good or acceptable. And it leads us to wonder about the issue of historical and cultural relativism, which we discussed in previous chapters. What kind of moral theory— and what kind of theory of virtue—would we need in order to argue against slavery and the subordination of women?

Along these lines, it is worth noting that Aristotle reserved the highest happiness and good (the *summum bonum*) for free males. Toward the end of *Nicomachean Ethics*, Aristotle claimed that the ultimate good was for human beings to develop the capacity for contemplation that is associated with the life of the mind and philosophy. Contemplation is an activity that utilizes our intellectual virtues. In a sense, these are our highest capacities, and when we engage in the activity of contemplation, we are as free and godlike as a human being can be. While this is an inspiring idea of human flourishing, in Aristotle's social world, this highest level of human development was only possible for free men; it was not available for women or for those Aristotle called natural slaves. And again, we should ask ourselves whether this is reasonable or acceptable. Are there some human beings who not able to attain the highest stage of moral and intellectual development? Or is there a different theory—or an improved virtue theory—that might provide a more inclusive account of human flourishing and the highest good?

One suggestion along these lines has been provided by philosopher Lisa Tessman (we include a short excerpt from her in the primary source readings for this chapter).

Tessman points out the limits of his theory by reminding us that Aristotle "never intended the *polis* to be an inclusive one."[14] She suggests that in response, we may need a different conception of virtue than Aristotle had. Instead of celebrating obedience and conformity to hierarchy, we might claim that compassion, solidarity, and rebelliousness are also important virtues. We might even make inclusivity into a virtue. Tessman explains, "a trait that contributes to one's own well-being cannot count as morally praiseworthy if it detracts from the flourishing of an inclusive social collectivity."[15] According to Tessman's critical reinterpretation of Aristotle, it would be odd to speak of happiness or flourishing in a society based on hierarchy, domination, and oppression—things that Aristotle simply took for granted.

As we conclude this critical encounter with Aristotle, it is impossible to deny that Aristotle's account has had an important and lasting influence on virtue ethics and on Western philosophy in general. But it is easy to see that some of his ideas can no longer to be taken literally in the modern world. Indeed, authors like Tessman have provided an extensive critique of Aristotle

▶ **Knowledge Check**   Answers appear at the end of the chapter.

1. Which of the following is NOT a primary concern of virtue ethics?

   a. Habits

   b. Character

   c. Prohibitions

   d. Happiness

2. Which of the following provides a useful synonym for the term "virtue"?

   a. Potentiality

   b. Actuality

   c. Purity

   d. Excellence

3. Aristotle would agree with which of the following?

   a. Eudaimonia is the highest good.

   b. Ethics rests on a set of divine commandments.

   c. There are no purposes or functions found in nature.

   d. Slavery ought to be abolished.

4. Which of the following best demonstrates the idea of virtue as a mean?

   a. Courage is a saintly virtue that requires self-sacrifice.

   b. Courage is located between rashness and cowardice.

   c. Courage is only required of soldiers and police.

   d. Courage is a male virtue that does not apply to women.

that seeks to extend the insights of Aristotle's account of virtue and happiness in ways that Aristotle would not have imagined.[16] But the general account provided by Aristotle—that focuses on the connection between virtue, teleology, happiness, and the highest good—continues to inform our thinking about ethics.

Cross-Cultural and Contemporary Virtue Ethics

8.6   Evaluate Aristotle's moral philosophy in comparison with other virtue theories.

Versions of virtue ethics can also be found in other traditions. The Confucian tradition in China is often described as a virtue tradition. This tradition traces its roots back to Confucius (551–479 BCE), whose role in Chinese philosophy was similar to the role Socrates played in Greek philosophy—as founding character and touchstone for later authors who want to reflect on virtue and wisdom. Unlike Socrates, however, who was something of a rough-mannered outsider to the elite social scene of Athens, Confucius was viewed as a model of courtly gentility and decorum. The Confucian tradition emphasizes two main virtues, *jen* (or *ren*) and *li*. *Jen* is often translated as "humaneness" or "compassion." *Li* is often translated as "propriety," "manners," or "culture." Along with this is the virtue of *xiào*, which is often translated as "filial piety" or "family reverence." Confucian ethics aims toward a synthesis of these virtues, seeking to describe a life oriented around compassion, courtesy, and respect for parents and elders. In the *Analects* of Confucius, this is explained in various ways. Consider the following advice attributed to Confucius:

> A youth, when at home, should be filial, and, abroad, respectful to his elders. He should be earnest and truthful. He should overflow in love to all, and cultivate the friendship of the good. When he has time and opportunity, after the performance of these things, he should employ them in polite studies.[17]

Confucius advises young people to be polite and respectful, earnest and truthful, and to overflow with love. Similar advice holds for others who are at different stages of life's journey. Confucius also holds that there are specific virtues for those inhabiting different roles: for fathers, brothers, sons, and government officials. As is true of most of the other traditions of the ancient world, the primary focus here is on male roles; women's roles were defined in subordination to the male.

Other traditions emphasize different forms of virtue. Hinduism emphasizes five basic moral virtues or *yamas*: nonviolence (*ahimsa*), truthfulness, honesty, chastity, and freedom from greed.[18] Hinduism also includes mental virtues to be perfected in meditation and yogic practice: calmness, self-control, self-settledness, forbearance, faith, and complete concentration, as well as the hunger for spiritual liberation.[19] Buddhism shares with Hinduism an emphasis on both intellectual and moral virtues. The "noble eightfold path" of Buddhism includes moral virtues such as right speech, right action, and right livelihood, as well as intellectual virtues of understanding and mindfulness.[20] Christian virtue ethics includes similar moral virtues, as well as what Thomas Aquinas called the "theological virtues." In the Christian tradition, the four cardinal moral virtues are prudence, justice, temperance, and fortitude, while the three theological virtues are faith, hope, and love. It is easy to see that there is overlap among these different traditions in terms of the virtues required for a good life, despite some clear differences. The common thread that links them as traditions of *virtue ethics* is the idea that habits and character traits matter, along with sustained philosophical reflection on the reasons they matter.

Various contemporary moral philosophers have also stressed the importance of virtue.[21] For example, Philippa Foot has developed a contemporary version of virtue ethics. She believes that the virtues are "in some general way, beneficial. Human beings do not get on well without them."[22] According to Foot, virtues provide benefits both to the virtuous person and to their community, just as vices harm both the self and the community. Think of courage, temperance, and wisdom, for example, and ask yourself how persons having these virtues might benefit others as well as themselves. Some virtues such as charity, however, seem to benefit mostly others. But this makes sense for social virtues, which help us fulfill our function as social beings. However, there is an open question about which beneficial

Figure 8-2 Statue of Confucius in Shanghai, China.

iStockphoto.com/destiger-photo

character traits are to be thought of as moral virtues and which are not. Wit or powers of concentration benefit us, but we would probably not consider them to be *moral* virtues.

Foot also asks whether virtue is best seen in the intention that guides an action or in the execution of an action. Think of generosity. Does the person who intends to be generous but cannot seem to do what helps others really possess the virtue of generosity? Or rather, is it the person who actually does help who has the virtue? Foot believes that virtue is also something we must choose to develop and work at personifying. Furthermore, following Aristotle, Foot argues that the virtues are *corrective*. They help us be and do things that are difficult for us. For example, courage helps us overcome natural fear. Temperance helps us control our desires. Since people differ in their natural inclinations, they also differ in what virtues would be most helpful for them to develop. Foot's view is just one example of

how the notion of virtue continues to be discussed by moral philosophers.

Evaluating Virtue Ethics

One question that has been raised for virtue ethics is how we determine which traits are virtues, and whether they are so in all circumstances. Are there any universally valuable traits? Wherever friendship exists, loyalty would seem necessary, although the form it might take would vary according to time and place. Honesty also seems necessary for good human relations. We might also start with Aristotle's own list of virtues, which reflected what were considered the primary civic virtues of his day. But Aristotle's society included slavery and gender hierarchy. One wonders whether it makes sense to speak of virtuous slave-masters or whether the submissive traits of women in patriarchal cultures are really virtuous. Similar problems occur as we consider differences among civilizations. Are the virtues of Confucian culture the same (or better or worse) than the virtues of Muslim, Christian, or Hindu cultures?

Contemporary moral philosopher Alasdair MacIntyre believes that virtues depend at least partly on the practices of a culture or society. A warlike society will value heroic virtues, whereas a peaceful and prosperous society might think of generosity as a particularly important virtue.[23] However, these must also be virtues specific to human beings as humans, for otherwise one could not speak of "human excellences." But this is just the problem. What is it to live a full human life? Can one specify this apart from what it is to live such a life in a particular society or as a particular person? The problem here is not only how we know what excellences are human excellences, but also whether there are any such traits that are ideal for all persons, despite differences in gender, social roles, and physical and mental capacities. MacIntyre has suggested that we also ought to be aware that a virtue tradition may involve a circle of ideas that may be incommensurable with the circle of ideas found in other traditions. One of the examples he considers to make this point is the difference between Aristotelian and Confucian traditions.[24] This contrast reflects the discussion with which we began this chapter. It might be that Asian cultures influenced by Confucius emphasize a different set of virtues than are emphasized in Western traditions. Are these traditions incommensurable, or is there some way to synthesize and connect them?

A further problem with regard to virtue is the question of the degree of effort and discipline required to be virtuous. Who manifests the virtue of courage the most—the person who, as Foot puts it, "wants to run away but does not or the one who does not even want to run away?"[25] We generally believe that we ought to be rewarded for our moral efforts, and thus, the person who wants to run away, but does not, seems more praiseworthy. On the other hand, possession of the virtue of courage is supposed to make it easier to be brave. Aristotle's approach also directs our attention to the importance of moral education, good friends, and other social supports. We develop our habits, character, and virtues as a result of moral education. Thus, those who are raised in supporting social environments should find it easier to be virtuous. Part of Foot's own answer to this dilemma involves the distinction between those fears for which we are in some way responsible and those that we cannot help. Thus, a person who has led a timid life and has avoided confronting their fears may have contributed to their lack of courage in some way by the choices they have made and the kinds of activities they have engaged in.

Foot also addresses the question of whether someone who does something morally wrong—say, robs a bank or commits a murder—and does so courageously, demonstrates the virtue of courage. She suggests that the solution to this problem requires a larger account of human flourishing and the good. A villain who acts "courageously" is not truly courageous, or as Foot puts it, "in him, courage is not a virtue."[26] The point here is that virtues should not be considered in isolation. Rather, virtues are supposed to be beneficial and part of an account of human happiness.

This last point returns us to Lisa Tessman's critique of Aristotle and to a significant concern about what counts as happiness or *eudaimonia*. Tessman's critique asks us to consider as a central question of virtue ethics the question of happiness for whom and under what circumstances? Tessman points out that Aristotle's theory is limited by the way he uncritically accepts the assumptions of a world that includes slavery and the subordination of women.

She argues that we need a different account of society, virtue, happiness, and human flourishing that is more inclusive and that affirms the value of the kinds of virtues that are useful in liberatory struggles. She also suggests that the very idea of virtue can be warped when it is used to describe life within oppressive social systems. Consider, as an example, the submissiveness of an enslaved person in a slave society. That might be a coping mechanism for an enslaved person—but is it really a virtue? And yet to encourage resistance and rebellion may ask too much of a person who may be tortured or killed if they resist. Tessman further explains the idea of "burdened virtues," which are the kinds of virtues that appear in contexts in which people suffer from oppression. Anger is one example she discusses. In non-oppressive circumstances, it may be wise to encourage moderation and restraint of anger. But for those living in oppressive conditions, anger may be an important part of their resistance to oppression, even though it can create anxiety and undermine happiness. This is complicated by the fact that anger may prompt a backlash from those on the top of the oppressive hierarchy. This kind of analysis reminds us that the social circumstances matter as we try to construct an account of virtue and flourishing.

We can also ask whether virtue ethics is really a distinct type of ethics. Consider two of the other theories we have discussed: utilitarianism (Chapter 5) and deontology (Chapter 6). The concept of virtue is not foreign to Mill or Kant. However, for both of them, it is secondary. Their moral theories tell us how we ought to decide what to *do*. Doing the right thing—and with Kant, for the right reason—is primary. However, if the development of certain habits of action or tendencies to act in a certain way will enable us to do good more easily, then they would surely be recognized by these philosophers as good. Utilitarians would encourage the development of those virtues that would be conducive to the maximization of happiness. If temperance in eating and drinking will help us avoid the suffering that can come from illness and drunkenness, this virtue ought to be encouraged and developed in the young. So also with other virtues. According to a Kantian, we should develop habits and virtues that would make it more likely that we act fairly (according to universalizable maxims) and treat people as ends rather than simply as means.

When evaluating the virtue ethics tradition developed by Aristotle, we should also consider a more specific criticism of it introduced by Kant. Kant argues that Aristotle's notion of virtue as a mean between two vices—the golden mean—is simply false. Kant writes that "it is incorrect to define any virtue or vice in terms of mere degree," which "proves the uselessness of the Aristotelian principles that virtue consists in the middle way between two vices."[27] Kant rejects the idea that there is a gradation of behaviors or dispositions from one extreme (or vice) to the other with virtue in the middle. Rather, for Kant, some things are praiseworthy and others are wrong, and do not vary by degrees on a continuum. Kant suggests that the Aristotelian idea of the golden mean simply confuses us and distracts us from thinking about why a given virtue is good. Bearing this argument in mind, it is worth considering whether the idea of virtue as a mean between vices really makes sense of the way we ordinarily understand virtues such as courage and vices like cowardice. Is this idea genuinely helpful to us in identifying the nature of virtue?

In virtue ethics, the primary goal is to be a good person. Now, a critic of virtue ethics might argue that *being* good is only a function of being *inclined* to do good. However, ethics appears to require not only a habitual inclination toward good deeds, but also actually doing good. Is what matters the deed or the inclination to carry it out? If what really matters are the actions and deeds, then virtue is simply one aspect of an action-oriented moral philosophy such as consequentialism. However, virtue ethics does have a somewhat different emphasis. It is an ethics whose goal is to determine what is essential to being a well-functioning or flourishing human person. Virtue ethics stresses an ideal for humans or persons. As an ethics of ideals or excellences, it is an optimistic and positive type of ethics. One problem that virtue ethics may face is what to say about those of us who do not meet the ideal. If we fall short of the virtuous model, does this make us bad or vicious? As with all moral theories, many questions concerning virtue remain to engage and puzzle us.

Chapter Summary

8.1 How does virtue ethics differ from other approaches to ethics?

Virtue ethics focuses on character traits, habits, and dispositions. It is not focused, as utilitarianism is, on producing overall social happiness. Nor is it focused on prohibitions, duties, or rights such as we find in deontological theories and in accounts of human rights. Rather, virtue ethics is interested in the character traits that help us flourish. In order to explain this, virtue ethics clarifies how virtues are connected to purposes, roles, and functions, including an account of human flourishing.

8.2 What are some key virtues, and how can they be applied to concrete situations?

We've seen that there are a variety of virtues. The Greeks emphasized four cardinal virtues: wisdom, justice, temperance, and courage. The Confucian tradition emphasized three virtues: courtesy, benevolence, and respect for elders. And there are other traditions that emphasize different kinds of virtue. These virtues can be applied in different ways. We discussed how courage may be something to admire in a soldier but also how it could be used to describe those who refuse vaccinations. We even discussed the question of whether a villain could be courageous. The challenge of applying virtues is that we must also clarify the specific circumstances, the vocational and institutional roles of individuals, and a general view of human flourishing.

8.3 How does the idea of the golden mean function in virtue ethics?

The "mean" of virtue ethics is found in the middle, with virtue lying somewhere between two "vices"—a vice of deficiency and a vice of excess. For example, courage is a mean between two extremes: rashness/foolhardiness (excessive fearlessness) and cowardice/timidity (too much fear). Another example is pride, which is found in the middle between humility (a deficiency of pride) and vanity (excessive pride).

8.4 How are virtues connected to an account of the functions or purposes of human life?

Virtues are excellences, habits, and traits that help us perform our functions well and fulfill our purposes. This is what it means to say that virtue theory is teleological. The Greek word *telos* means purpose or goal. In order to figure out which virtues we ought to cultivate, we need an account of the overall goal or purpose (*telos*) of life. Aristotle's account focuses on two sets of virtues—intellectual and moral (or social) virtues. This account is connected to an account of two general areas that define the purpose or function of human life. We are rational social animals. Thus, we ought to develop social virtues, as well as virtues of intellectual life that lead us toward the good of contemplation.

8.5 Analyze the idea of *eudaimonia* and what it means within Aristotle's theory of virtue.

Eudaimonia is a Greek word that can be translated as happiness or flourishing. Aristotle suggests that when we are virtuous, we will be happy. This does not mean that life will be pleasant. Eudaimonia is not pleasure. Rather, it is the kind of happiness that comes from fulfilling your purpose and developing virtuous character traits.

8.6 How can we evaluate Aristotle's moral philosophy in comparison with other virtue theories?

Aristotle's theory provides an ancient model that has been an important point of reference for the subsequent development of Western moral philosophy. Aristotle, however, is an ancient thinker whose writings contain the idea that women and "natural slaves" should be subordinate. These ideas can be criticized from the vantage point of a more universal account of human rights or from the standpoint of a virtue theory (such as Tessman's) that emphasizes a more inclusive social theory. Nonetheless, Aristotle's general account of virtue as a mean and his way of connecting virtue to a teleological account of human flourishing and the *summum bonum* provide a useful model. Aristotle is not the only virtue ethicist. There are other virtue traditions. We discussed Hindu and Confucian traditions in this chapter. It turns out that there are divergent ways of explaining the key virtues for a good life.

8.7 How might you defend your own thesis with regard to the value of virtue ethics?

One useful aspect of virtue ethics is its focus on commonsense moral terms such as courage, honesty, compassion, and so on. We generally understand how these terms function in our moral lives. It is also natural to focus on moral heroes and exemplars. And it is easy to understand that there are differences in the way that virtues manifest in different roles and vocations. Virtue ethics explains this by encouraging us to understand ethics as teleological, that is, oriented around purposes and functions. This theory is useful in ordinary life, and it also reminds us to think about the big questions of human flourishing and the highest good. But we might have some worries about this approach. One objection may be that ancient virtue traditions tend to have an unacceptable account of human nature built on a hierarchical worldview. Another problem arises when we compare virtue traditions. There remains an open question as to whether there is one overarching account of human nature that can help us define virtue in general or whether there are divergent virtues that are found within different worldviews.

Primary Source Readings

The main reading selection for this chapter is from Aristotle's *The Nicomachean Ethics*. We also include short excerpts from Alasdair MacIntyre's influential book *After Virtue* and from Lisa Tessman's book *Burdened Virtues*. Aristotle's text is foundational to the Western philosophical tradition. In this excerpt, Aristotle explains what virtue is, how it is related to the highest human good, to human functioning, and how it is a mean between extremes. The excerpt from MacIntyre raises the question of whether there is one account of virtue or many. In the excerpt from her book, Tessman suggests that virtue is necessary for happiness but not sufficient, while raising the problem of flourishing and virtue under adverse conditions.

Reading 8-1   The Nicomachean Ethics | Aristotle

Study Questions

As you read the excerpt, please consider the following questions:

1. What is virtue, and how do we acquire it?
2. How is virtue a mean? Explain this by using some of Aristotle's examples.
3. Why is it so difficult to be virtuous?

The Nature of the Good*

Every art and every scientific inquiry, and similarly every action and purpose, may be said to aim at some good. Hence the good has been well defined as that at which all things aim. But it is clear that there is a difference in the ends; for the ends are sometimes activities, and sometimes results beyond the mere activities. Also, where there are certain ends beyond the actions, the results are naturally superior to the activities.

As there are various actions, arts, and sciences, it follows that the ends are also various. Thus health is the end of medicine, a vessel of shipbuilding, victory of strategy, and wealth of domestic economy. It often happens that there are a number of such arts or sciences which fall under a single faculty, as the art of making bridles, and all such other arts as make the instruments of horsemanship, under horsemanship, and this again as well as every military action under strategy, and in the same way other arts or sciences under other faculties. But in all these cases the ends of the architectonic arts or sciences, whatever they may be, are more desirable than those of the subordinate arts or sciences, as it is for the sake of the former that the latter are themselves sought after. It makes no difference to the argument whether the activities themselves are the ends of the actions, or something else beyond the activities as in the above mentioned sciences.

If it is true that in the sphere of action there is an end which we wish for its own sake, and for the sake of which we wish everything else, and that we do not desire all things for the sake of something else (for, if that is so, the process will go on ad infinitum, and our desire will be idle and futile) it is clear that this will be the good or the supreme good. Does it not follow then that the knowledge of this supreme good is of great importance for the conduct of life, and that, if we know it, we shall be like archers who have a mark at which to aim, we shall have a better chance of attaining what we want? But, if this is the case, we must endeavour to comprehend, at least in outline, its nature, and the science or faculty to which it belongs....

Happiness: Living and Doing Well

As every knowledge and moral purpose aspires to some good, what is in our view the good at which the political science aims, and what is the highest of all practical goods? As to its name there is, I may say, a general agreement. The masses and the cultured classes agree in calling it happiness, and conceive that "to live well" or "to do well" is the same thing as "to be happy." But as to the nature of happiness they do not agree, nor do the masses give the same account of it as the philosophers. The former define it as something visible and palpable, e.g. pleasure, wealth, or honour; different people give different definitions of it, and often the same person

From Aristotle, *The Nicomachean Ethics*, trans. J. E. C. Welldon (London: Macmillan, 1892), bks. 1 and 2.

* Heading added by the editor.
* Some notes omitted; the remaining notes renumbered.

gives different definitions at different times; for when a person has been ill, it is health, when he is poor, it is wealth, and, if he is conscious of his own ignorance, he envies people who use grand language above his own comprehension. Some philosophers[1] on the other hand have held that, besides these various goods, there is an absolute good which is the cause of goodness in them all. . . .

The Function of a Person

Perhaps, however, it seems a truth which is generally admitted, that happiness is the supreme good; what is wanted is to define its nature a little more clearly. The best way of arriving at such a definition will probably be to ascertain the function of Man. For, as with a flute-player, a statuary, or any artisan, or in fact anybody who has a definite function and action, his goodness, or excellence seems to lie in his function, so it would seem to be with Man, if indeed he has a definite function. Can it be said then that, while a carpenter and a cobbler have definite functions and actions, Man, unlike them, is naturally functionless? The reasonable view is that, as the eye, the hand, the foot, and similarly each several part of the body has a definite function, so Man may be regarded as having a definite function apart from all these. What then, can this function be? It is not life; for life is apparently something which Man shares with the plants; and it is something peculiar to him that we are looking for. We must exclude therefore the life of nutrition and increase. There is next what may be called the life of sensation. But this too, is apparently shared by Man with horses, cattle, and all other animals. There remains what I may call the practical life of the rational part of Man's being. But the rational part is twofold; it is rational partly in the sense of being obedient to reason, and partly in the sense of possessing reason and intelligence. The practical life too may be conceived of in two ways,[2] viz., either as a moral state, or as a moral activity: but we must understand by it the life of activity, as this seems to be the truer form of the conception.

The function of Man then is an activity of soul in accordance with reason, or not independently of reason. Again the functions of a person of a certain kind, and of such a person who is good of his kind e.g. of a harpist and a good harpist, are in our view generically the same, and this view is true of people of all kinds without exception, the superior excellence being only an addition to the function; for it is the function of a harpist to play the harp, and of a good harpist to play the harp well. This being so, if we define the function of Man as a kind of life, and this life as an activity of soul, or a course of action in conformity with reason, if the function of a good man is such activity or action of a good and noble kind, and if everything is successfully performed when it is performed in accordance with its proper excellence, it follows that the good of Man is an activity of soul in accordance with virtue or, if there are more virtues than one, in accordance with the best and most complete virtue. But it is necessary to add the words "in a complete life." For as one swallow or one day does not make a spring, so one day or a short time does not make a fortunate or happy man. . . .

Virtue

Virtue or excellence being twofold, partly intellectual and partly moral, intellectual virtue is both originated and fostered mainly by teaching; it therefore demands experience and time. Moral[3] virtue on the other hand is the outcome of habit. . . . From this fact it is clear that no moral virtue is implanted in us by nature; a law of nature cannot be altered by habituation. Thus a stone naturally tends to fall downwards, and it cannot be habituated or trained to rise upwards, even if we were to habituate it by throwing it upwards ten thousand times; nor again can fire be trained to sink downwards, nor anything else that follows one natural law be habituated or trained to follow another. It is neither by nature then nor in defiance of nature that virtues are implanted in us. Nature gives us the capacity of receiving them, and that capacity is perfected by habit.

Again, if we take the various natural powers which belong to us, we first acquire the proper faculties and afterwards display the activities. It is clearly so with the senses. It was not by seeing frequently or hearing frequently that we acquired the senses of seeing or hearing; on the contrary it was because we possessed the senses that we made use of them, not by making use of them that we obtained them. But the virtues we acquire by first exercising them, as is the case with all the arts, for it is by doing what we ought to do when we have learnt the arts that we learn the arts themselves; we become e.g. builders by building and harpists by playing the harp. Similarly it is by doing just acts that we become just, by doing temperate acts that we become temperate, by doing courageous acts that we become courageous. The experience of states is a witness to this truth, for it is by training the habits that legislators make the citizens good. This is the object which all legislators have at heart; if a legislator does not succeed in it, he fails of his purpose, and it constitutes the distinction between a good polity and a bad one.

Again, the causes and means by which any virtue is produced and by which it is destroyed are the same; and it is equally so with any art; for it is by playing the harp that both good and bad harpists are produced and the case of builders and all other artisans is similar, as it is by building well that they will be good builders and by building badly that they will be bad builders. If it were not so, there would be no need of anybody to teach them; they would all be born good or bad in their several trades. The case of the virtues is the same. It is by acting in such transactions as take place between man and man that we become either just or unjust. It is by acting in the face of danger and by habituating ourselves to fear or courage that we become either cowardly or courageous. It is much the same with our desires and angry passions. Some people become temperate and gentle, others become licentious and passionate, according as they conduct themselves in one way or another way in particular circumstances. In a word moral states are the results of activities corresponding to the moral states themselves. It is our duty therefore to give a certain character to the activities, as the moral states depend upon the differences of the activities. Accordingly the difference between one training of the habits and another from early days is not a light matter, but is serious or rather all-important.

Deficiency and Excess

The first point to be observed then is that in such matters as we are considering deficiency and excess are equally fatal. It is so, as we observe, in regard to health and strength; for we must judge of what we cannot see by the evidence of what we do see. Excess or deficiency of gymnastic exercise is fatal to strength. Similarly an excess or deficiency of meat and drink is fatal to health, whereas a suitable amount produces, augments and sustains it. It is the same then with temperance, courage, and the other virtues. A person who avoids and is afraid of everything and faces nothing becomes a coward; a person who is not afraid of anything but is ready to face everything becomes foolhardy. Similarly he who enjoys every pleasure and never abstains from any pleasure is licentious; he who eschews all pleasures like a boor is an insensible sort of person. For temperance and courage are destroyed by excess and deficiency but preserved by the mean state.

Again, not only are the causes and the agencies of production, increase and destruction in the moral states the same, but the sphere of their activity will be proved to be the same also. It is so in other instances which are more conspicuous, e.g. in strength; for strength is produced by taking a great deal of food and undergoing a great deal of labour, and it is the strong man who is able to take most food and to undergo most labour. The same is the case with the virtues. It is by abstinence from pleasures that we become temperate, and, when we have become temperate, we are best able to abstain from them. So too with courage; it is by habituating ourselves to despise and face alarms that we become courageous, and, when we have become courageous, we shall be best able to face them.

The Nature of Virtue

We have next to consider the nature of virtue.

Now, as the qualities of the soul are three, viz. emotions, faculties and moral states, it follows that virtue must be one of the three. By the emotions I mean desire, anger, fear, courage, envy, joy, love, hatred, regret, emulation, pity, in a word whatever is attended by pleasure or pain. I call those faculties in respect of which we are said to be capable of experiencing these emotions, e.g. capable of getting angry or being pained or feeling pity. And I call those moral states in respect of which we are well or ill-disposed towards the emotions, ill-disposed e.g. towards the passion of anger, if our anger be too violent or too feeble, and well-disposed, if it be duly moderated, and similarly towards the other emotions.

Now neither the virtues nor the vices are emotions; for we are not called good or evil in respect of our emotions but in respect of our virtues or vices. Again, we are not praised or blamed in respect of our emotions; a person is not praised for being afraid or being angry, nor blamed for being angry in an absolute sense, but only for being angry in a certain way; but we are praised or blamed in respect of our virtues or vices. Again, whereas we are angry or afraid without deliberate purpose, the virtues are in some sense deliberate purposes, or do not exist in the absence of deliberate purpose. It may be added that while we are said to be moved in respect of our emotions, in respect of our virtues or vices we are not said to be moved but to have a certain disposition.

These reasons also prove that the virtues are not faculties. For we are not called either good or bad, nor are we praised or blamed, as having an abstract capacity for emotion. Also while Nature gives us our faculties, it is not Nature that makes us good or bad, but this is a point which we have already discussed. If then the virtues are neither emotions nor faculties, it remains that they must be moral states.

The nature of virtue has been now generically described. But it is not enough to state merely that virtue is a moral state, we must also describe the character of that moral state.

It must be laid down then that every virtue or excellence has the effect of producing a good condition of that of which it is a virtue or excellence, and of enabling it to perform its function well. Thus the excellence of the eye makes the eye good and its function good, as it is by the excellence of the eye that we see well. Similarly, the excellence of the horse makes a horse excellent and good at racing, at carrying its rider and at facing the enemy.

If then this is universally true, the virtue or excellence of man will be such a moral state as makes a man good and able to perform his proper function well. We have already explained how this will be the case, but another way of making it clear will be to study the nature or character of this virtue.

Virtue as a Mean

Now in everything, whether it be continuous or discrete, it is possible to take a greater, a smaller, or an equal amount, and this either absolutely or in relation to ourselves, the equal being a mean between excess and deficiency. By the mean in respect of the thing itself, or the absolute mean, I understand that which is equally distinct from both extremes; and this is one and the same thing for everybody. By the mean considered relatively to ourselves I understand that which is neither too much nor too little; but this is not one thing, nor is it the same for everybody. Thus if 10 be too much and 2 too little we take 6 as a mean in respect of the thing itself; for 6 is as much greater than 2 as it is less than 10, and this is a mean in arithmetical proportion. But the mean considered relatively to ourselves must not be ascertained in this way. It does not follow that if 10 pounds of meat be too much and 2 be too little for a man to eat, a trainer will order him 6 pounds, as this may itself be too much or too little for the person who is to take it; it will be too little e.g. for Milo,[4] but too much for a beginner in gymnastics. It will be the same with running and wrestling; the right amount will vary with the individual. This being so, everybody who understands his business avoids alike excess and deficiency; he seeks and chooses the mean, not the absolute mean, but the mean considered relatively to ourselves.

Every science then performs its function well, if it regards the mean and refers the works which it produces to the mean. This is the reason why it is usually said of successful works that it is impossible to take anything from them or to add anything to them, which implies that excess or deficiency is fatal to excellence but that the mean state ensures it. Good...artists too, as we say, have an eye to the mean in their works. But virtue, like Nature herself, is more accurate and better than any art; virtue therefore will aim at the mean;—I speak of moral virtue, as it is moral virtue which is concerned with emotions and actions, and it is these which admit of excess and deficiency and the mean. Thus it is possible to go too far, or not to go far enough, in respect of fear, courage, desire, anger, pity, and pleasure and pain generally, and the excess and the deficiency are alike wrong; but to experience these emotions at the right times and on the right occasions and towards the right persons and for the right causes and in the right manner is the mean or the supreme good, which is characteristic of virtue. Similarly there may be excess, deficiency, or the mean, in regard to actions. But virtue is concerned with emotions and actions, and here excess is an error and deficiency a fault, whereas the mean is successful and laudable, and success and merit are both characteristics of virtue.

It appears then that virtue is a mean state, so far at least as it aims at the mean. Again, there are many different ways of going wrong; for evil is in its nature infinite, to use the Pythagorean[5] figure, but good is finite. But there is only one possible way of going right. Accordingly the former is easy and the latter difficult; it is easy to miss the mark but difficult to hit it. This again is a reason why excess and deficiency are characteristics of vice and the mean state a characteristic of virtue.

"For good is simple, evil manifold."[6]

Virtue then is a state of deliberate moral purpose consisting in a mean that is relative to ourselves, the mean being determined...by reason, or as a prudent man would determine it.

It is a mean state *firstly as lying* between two vices, the vice of excess on the one hand, and the vice of deficiency on the other, and secondly because, whereas the vices either fall short of or go beyond what is proper in the emotions and actions, virtue not only discovers but embraces that mean.

Accordingly, virtue, if regarded in its essence or theoretical conception, is a mean state, but, if regarded from the point of view of the highest good, or of excellence, it is an extreme.

But it is not every action or every emotion that admits of a mean state. There are some whose very name implies wickedness, as e.g. malice, shamelessness, and envy, among emotions, or adultery, theft, and murder, among actions. All these, and others like them, are censured as being intrinsically wicked, not merely the excesses or deficiencies of them. It is never possible then to be right in respect of them; they are always sinful.

Right or wrong in such actions as adultery does not depend on our committing them with the right person, at the right time or in the right manner; on the contrary it is sinful to do anything of the kind at all. It would be equally wrong then to suppose that there can be a mean state or an excess or deficiency in unjust, cowardly, or licentious conduct; for, if it were so, there would be a mean state of an excess or of a deficiency, an excess of an excess and a deficiency of a deficiency. But as in temperance and courage there can be no excess or deficiency because the mean is, in a sense, an extreme, so too in these cases there cannot be a mean or an excess or deficiency, but, however the acts may be done, they are wrong. For it is a general rule that an excess or deficiency does not admit of a mean state, nor a mean state of an excess or deficiency.

But it is not enough to lay down this as a general rule; it is necessary to apply it to particular cases, as in reasonings upon actions, general statements, although they are broader..., are less exact than particular statements. For all action refers to particulars, and it is essential that our theories should harmonize with the particular cases to which they apply.

Some Virtues

We must take particular virtues then from the catalogue[7] *of virtues*.

In regard to feelings of fear and confidence, courage is a mean state. On the side of excess, he whose fearlessness is excessive has no name, as often happens, but he whose confidence is excessive is foolhardy, while he whose timidity is excessive and whose confidence is deficient is a coward.

In respect of pleasures and pains, although not indeed of all pleasures and pains, and to a less extent in respect of pains than of pleasures, the mean state is temperance..., the excess is licentiousness. We never find people who are deficient in regard to pleasures; accordingly such people again have not received a name, but we may call them insensible.

As regards the giving and taking of money, the mean state is liberality, the excess and deficiency are prodigality and illiberality. Here the excess and deficiency take opposite forms; for while the prodigal man is excessive in spending and deficient in taking, the illiberal man is excessive in taking and deficient in spending.

(For the present we are giving only a rough and summary account *of the virtues*, and that is sufficient for our purpose; we will hereafter determine their character more exactly.[8])

In respect of money there are other dispositions as well. There is the mean state which is magnificence; for the magnificent man, as having to do with large sums of money, differs from the liberal man who has to do only with small sums; and the excess corresponding to it is bad taste or vulgarity, the deficiency is meanness. These are different from the excess and deficiency of liberality; what the difference is will be explained hereafter.

In respect of honour and dishonour the mean state is highmindedness, the excess is what is called vanity, the deficiency littlemindedness. Corresponding to liberality, which, as we said, differs from magnificence as having to do *not with great but* with small sums of money, there is a moral state which has to do with petty honour and is related to highmindedness which has to do with great honour; for it is possible to aspire to honour in the right way, or in a way which is excessive or insufficient, and if a person's aspirations are excessive, he is called ambitious, if they are deficient, he is called unambitious, while if they are between the two, he has no name. The dispositions too are nameless, except that the disposition of the ambitious person is called ambition. The consequence is that the extremes lay claim to the mean or intermediate place. We ourselves speak of one who observes the mean sometimes as ambitious, and at other times as unambitious; we sometimes praise an ambitious, and at other times an unambitious person. The reason for our doing so will be stated in due course, but let us now discuss the other virtues in accordance with the method which we have followed hitherto.

Anger, like other emotions, has its excess, its deficiency, and its mean state. It may be said that they have no names, but as we call one who observes the mean gentle, we will call the mean state gentleness. Among the extremes, if a person errs on the side of excess, he may be called passionate and his vice passionateness, if on that of deficiency, he may be called impassive and his deficiency impassivity.

There are also three other mean states with a certain resemblance to each other, and yet with a difference. For while they are all concerned with intercourse in speech and action, they are different in that one of them is concerned with truth in such intercourse, and the others with pleasantness, one with pleasantness in amusement and the other with pleasantness in the various circumstances of life. We must therefore discuss these states in order to make it clear that in all cases it is the mean state which is an object of praise, and the extremes are neither right nor laudable but censurable. It is true that these mean and extreme states are generally nameless, but we must do our best here as elsewhere to give them a name, so that our argument may be clear and easy to follow....

Why It Is So Difficult to Be Virtuous

That is the reason why it is so hard to be virtuous; for it is always hard work to find the mean in anything, e.g. it is not everybody, but only a man of science, who can find the mean or centre[9] of a circle. So too anybody can get angry—that is an easy matter—and anybody can give or spend money, but to give it to the right persons, to give the right amount of it and to give it at the right time and for the right cause and in the right way, this is not what anybody can do, nor is it easy. That is the reason why it is rare and laudable and noble to do well. Accordingly one who aims at the mean must begin by departing from that extreme which is the more contrary to the mean; he must act in the spirit of Calypso's[10] advice,

"Far from this smoke and swell keep thou thy bark,"

for of the two extremes one is more sinful than the other. As it is difficult then to hit the mean exactly, we must take the second best course,[11] as the saying is, and choose the lesser of two evils, and this we shall best do in the way that we have described, *i.e. by steering clear of the evil which is further from the mean*. We must also observe the things to which we are ourselves particularly prone, as different natures have different inclinations, and we may ascertain what these are by a consideration of our feelings of pleasure and pain. And then we must drag ourselves in the direction opposite to them; for it is by removing ourselves as far as possible from what is wrong that we shall arrive at the mean, as we do when we pull a crooked stick straight.

But in all cases we must especially be on our guard against what is pleasant and against pleasure, as we are not impartial judges of pleasure. Hence our attitude towards pleasure must be like that of the elders of the people in the Iliad towards Helen, and we must never be afraid of applying the words they use; for if we dismiss pleasure as they dismissed Helen, we shall be less likely to go wrong. It is by action of this kind, to put it summarily, that we shall best succeed in hitting the mean.

Notes

1. Aristotle is thinking of the Platonic "ideas."

2. In other words life may be taken to mean either the mere possession of certain faculties or their active exercise.

3. The student of Aristotle must familiarize himself with the conception of intellectual as well as of moral virtues, although it is not the rule in modern philosophy to speak of the "virtues" of the intellect.

4. The famous Crotoniate wrestler.

5. The Pythagoreans, starting from the mystical significance of number, took the opposite principles of "the finite"... and "the infinite"... to represent good and evil.

6. A line—perhaps Pythagorean—of unknown authorship.

7. It would seem that a catalogue of virtues ... must have been recognized in the Aristotelian school. Cp. *Eud. Eth.* ii. Chapter 3.

8. I have placed this sentence in a parenthesis, as it interrupts the argument respecting the right use of money.

9. Aristotle does not seem to be aware that the centre ... of a circle is not really comparable to the mean ... between the vices.

10. *Odyssey*, pp. xii, 219, and 200; but it is Odysseus who speaks there, and the advice has been given him not by Calypso but by Circe (ibid. pp. 101–110).

11. The Greek proverb means properly "we must take to the oars, if sailing is impossible."

Reading 8-2   After Virtue | Alasdair MacIntyre

Study Questions

As you read the excerpt, please consider the following questions:

1. Why might MacIntyre suggest that there may be a single unified account of the virtues?

2. What differences exist among virtue traditions?

3. If there is to be a unified account of the virtues, what would be required?

One response to the history which I have narrated so far might well be to suggest that even within the relatively coherent tradition of thought which I have sketched there are just too many different and incompatible conceptions of a virtue for there to be any real unity to the concept or indeed to the history. Homer, Sophocles, Aristotle, the New Testament and medieval thinkers differ from each other in too many ways. They offer us different and incompatible lists of the virtues; they give a different rank order of importance to different virtues; and they have different and incompatible theories of the virtues. If we were to consider later Western writers on the virtues, the list of differences and incompatibilities would be enlarged still further; and if we extended our enquiry to Japanese, say, or American Indian cultures, the differences would become greater still. It would be all too easy to conclude that there are a number of rival and alternative conceptions of the virtues, but even within the tradition which I have been delineating, no single core conception....

... The most striking contrast with Aristotle's catalogue is to be found neither in Homer's nor in our own, but in the New Testament's. For the New Testament not only praises virtues of which Aristotle knows nothing—faith, hope and love—and says nothing about virtues such as phronesis which are crucial for Aristotle, but it praises at least one quality as a virtue which Aristotle seems to count as one of the vices relative to magnanimity, namely humility. Moreover, since the New Testament quite clearly sees the rich as destined for the pains of Hell, it is clear that the key virtues cannot be available to them; yet they are available to slaves....

... Without an overriding conception of the telos of a whole human life, conceived as a unity, our conception of certain individual virtues has to remain partial and incomplete....

From Alasdair MacIntyre, *After Virtue*, 3rd ed. (Notre Dame, IN: Notre Dame University Press, 2007), Chapter 14.

... Unless there is a telos which transcends the limited goods of practices by constituting the good of a whole human life, the good of a human life conceived as a unity, it will both be the case that a certain subversive arbitrariness will invade the moral life and that we shall be unable to specify the context of certain virtues adequately....

... There is at least one virtue recognized by the tradition which cannot be specified at all except with reference to the wholeness of a human life—the virtue of integrity or constancy.... This notion of singleness of purpose in a whole life can have no application unless that of a whole life does....

... Is it rationally justifiable to conceive of each human life as a unity, so that we may try to specify each such life as having its good and so that we may understand the virtues as having their function in enabling an individual to make of his or her life one kind of unity rather than another?

Reading 8-3   Burdened Virtues | Lisa Tessman

Study Questions

As you read the excerpt, please consider the following questions:

1. Why does Tessman suggest that virtue is a necessary but not sufficient condition for flourishing?

2. What does Aristotle mean when he says that it is "nonsense" to speak of a victim on "the rack" as happy—and how does that apply to Tessman's concern with oppression?

3. Why does Tessman suggest that virtues that are found in "conditions of great adversity" may be disconnected from flourishing?

While I have obviously seen some liberatory value in eudaimonistic virtue ethics, here I will highlight the presence of a fundamental problem with applying a eudaimonistic virtue ethics such as Aristotle's. The problem arises because of an assumption of his that I believe to be correct: that virtue is necessary but not sufficient for eudaimonia or flourishing. This fact creates a tension whenever those conditions that, in addition to virtue, are necessary for flourishing, are actually absent. This typically happens under the adverse circumstances created by oppression, where the external or background conditions necessary for flourishing will tend to be lacking or diminished. Furthermore, under these conditions it may frequently be the case that a trait (say, courage) necessary for flourishing will require a sacrifice of something else (say, one's physical or psychological health) that is also necessary for flourishing. Under these conditions, the project of identifying and developing the virtues and the venture of aiming at a flourishing life may not coincide, as they usually do in, say, Aristotle's ethics. Aristotle's discussions of virtue usually take for granted that the background conditions for virtue are being met: luck has been sufficiently good, material needs have been fulfilled, enough leisure time has been available, no great adversity is presenting itself. He does consider how things change under adversity or tragedy, but (aside from some attention to war) he does not focus on systemic sources of adversity that would cause some people's lives to be predictably fraught with terrible conditions. Under conditions that are difficult but not terrible, one can talk about the virtues that "shine through" (*Nicomachean Ethics* 1100b30) adversity. But when conditions are truly disastrous, talk of the virtues becomes irrelevant for eudaimonia, since eudaimonia is simply out of reach; according to Aristotle, one is "talking nonsense" if one describes the "victim on the rack" as happy, no matter how virtuous he may be (*Nicomachean Ethics* 1153b19–21)....

How, under conditions of oppression, does one determine what the virtues are? Aristotle cannot provide much guidance in answering this question.... Much contemporary work in virtue ethics assumes that one can work toward identifying the virtues by beginning

From Lisa Tessman, *Burdened Virtues: Virtue Ethics for Liberatory Struggles* (Oxford, UK: Oxford University Press, 2005).

with the concept of flourishing and then asking which traits are conducive to or constitutive of flourishing. This would work well if virtue were both necessary and sufficient for flourishing. It also works in a rough sort of a way even if virtue is insufficient for flourishing, as long as it is also the case most of the time that everything else that is necessary for flourishing—such as the right material conditions—obtains. But, under conditions of great adversity, the necessary background conditions for flourishing tend not to obtain. Oftentimes, then, there will be traits that should be counted as virtues but whose bearers will nevertheless be unable to flourish.

Review Exercises

1. What is the basic difference between virtue ethics and other types of ethics we have studied?

2. According to Aristotle, what is the difference between intellectual and moral virtue?

3. Explain the importance of character and habits in virtue ethics.

4. Give a list of some virtues and related vices; explain how these virtues contribute to *eudaimonia*.

5. According to Aristotle, how is virtue a mean between extremes? Give some examples.

6. Are there virtues that are excellences for all human beings, or are virtues dependent on our roles or our culture?

7. What does Aristotle say about slavery and gender hierarchy?

8. What kinds of virtues might be needed in a more egalitarian society than the one Aristotle lived in?

9. Who most exemplifies the virtue of courage—the person who finds it difficult to be brave or the person who finds it easy to be courageous?

10. Can a virtue such as courage be used to describe the actions of a villain (can a bad person really be courageous)?

Knowledge Check Answer Key

1. **c.** Deontological theories focus on prohibitions, while virtue ethics is primarily concerned with habits, character, and happiness.

2. **d.** Excellence is a synonym for the term "virtue."

3. **a.** Aristotle would agree that eudaimonia is the highest good.

4. **b.** Courage is located between rashness and cowardice best demonstrates the idea of virtue as a mean.

9 Feminist Thought and the Ethics of Care

Learning Outcomes

After reading this chapter, you should be able to:

9.1 Describe the importance of feminist thought for ethical inquiry.

9.2 Explain feminist criticisms of traditional views about ethics and moral development.

9.3 Evaluate the ethics of care.

9.4 Distinguish between the several versions or "waves" of feminism.

9.5 Analyze feminist critiques of gender, race, and other intersectional identities.

9.6 Explain the problem of violence against women.

9.7 Defend your own ideas about the importance of feminist ethics and the ethics of care.

Rights and Equality for Women

In 2022, protests broke out in Iran in reaction against modesty laws that require women to cover their hair with a *hijab*. These protests were prompted by the death in police custody of a young woman, Mahsa Amini, who had exposed too much of her hair. In protest, some women cut their hair in public; others burned their *hijabs*.[1] As police cracked down, nearly fourteen thousand people were arrested and almost three hundred were killed.[2] At about the same time, the U.S. women's soccer team won a lawsuit in which they maintained that the players on the U.S. men's team were paid about four times more than women players.[3] This disparity existed despite the fact that the U.S. women's team was much more successful than the men's team, having won four World Cups and four Olympic gold medals. Another related issue involved the case of Brittney Griner, a WNBA star and Olympic gold medalist who was arrested in Russia and sentenced to nine years in prison for drug possession. Commentators pointed out that Griner and other women basketballers played in Russia to earn extra cash because of the huge disparities between the earnings of WNBA players and male NBA players. Others wondered whether Griner's case was also influenced by the fact that she is Black and lesbian.[4]

YASIN AKGUL/Getty Images

These are the kinds of issues that are of concern for feminists, who point out the need for continuing struggles for women's liberation and equality. Feminism provides a critical lens on social and political inequalities involving women. This includes critiques of oppressive, patriarchal systems that aim to control women's bodies. It also includes critiques of inequities and unfairness involving women in legal, economic, social, academic, athletic, cultural, and other spheres. Feminism also involves a critique of the idea of gender, as it is traditionally understood, while also asking us to consider how gender and gender inequality are connected to other issues involving race, culture, religion, sexuality, economics, and politics.

What Do You Think?

1. How important to you is the struggle for women's liberation and equality?
2. What kinds of issues involving the inequality of women are most important for you?
3. Would you be willing to go to jail, as the protesters in Iran have, in protesting for women's rights?
4. How do race, culture, religion, and sexuality impact our thinking about women's issues?

Introduction

9.1 Describe the importance of feminist thought for ethical inquiry.

In this chapter, we will discuss the broad critical theory of feminism. We will also discuss the ethics of care, which has developed in relation to feminist critiques of other forms of normative theory. Feminism may be understood as a theoretical inquiry focused on the ways women are empowered or disempowered by cultural, social, legal, political, and philosophical ideas and ideologies. Feminism also has a practical aim. As defined by Noëlle McAfee, it is "both an intellectual commitment and a political movement that seeks justice for women and the end of sexism in all forms."[5] In this regard, feminism may also be understood as a focal point for topics in applied ethics such as reproductive rights, economic inequality, and other topics that will be discussed in detail in the second half of this book. It should be obvious that feminism is not only a concern for women; all people who care about the well-being of women are also feminist. Feminism in ethical theory offers a critique of traditional approaches to ethics, which are primarily focused on values such as autonomy, impartiality, and neutrality. While it is useful to invoke these traditional moral values in criticizing women's oppression, some feminists worry that these sorts of values are themselves morally problematic. This criticism argues that values such as autonomy,

impartiality, and neutrality are patriarchal values, distinctively stressed by male-dominant cultures, which downplay the importance of concrete caring relationships. Such caring relationships are more typical of the private sphere and family life—those parts of life that have traditionally been viewed as feminine, as opposed to the masculine and patriarchal public sphere. (The terms "patriarchal" and "patriarchy" generally mean a system oriented toward "rule by the father" or more generally ruled by men.)

As a critical normative theory, feminism asks us to consider how the concerns of women and questions involving gender have been treated by more traditional normative theories. Feminism might, for example, prompt us to ask what natural law theory, utilitarianism, Kantian deontology, or virtue ethics have to say about women and gender. We've addressed this concern in prior chapters in our accounts of those normative theories. But we might say in summary that traditional normative theories in the Western philosophical tradition have often failed to adequately address the concerns of women, and have in many cases supported patriarchal points of view that were harmful to women. As we noted in our chapter on virtue ethics, for example, Aristotle viewed women as inferior to men. Feminist critique offers a remedy for that kind of patriarchal judgment that begins from the basic assumption that women are fully human and equal to men in moral worth and dignity.

More recent versions of feminism also call into question the supposed dichotomy between masculine and female points of view, offering a broad critique of gender norms, the so-called gender binary, and gender essentialism. In this context, feminism is linked to a broad inquiry into the meaning of gender, sex, and sexuality. In this chapter and what follows we will generally use the term "sex" to refer to something biological, connected to genitalia, chromosomes, and other physical features; "gender" is a term that is typically used to refer to cultural or social notions, such as what it means to be masculine or feminine as defined within culture. This distinction (the "sex/gender distinction") points us to the complicated fact that gender is a social and cultural concept that changes over time and that has been mapped onto biological sex in various ways. This idea is captured in a well-known phrase of Simone de Beauvoir's, "One is not born, but becomes a woman."[6] One must learn what it means to be a woman, and this depends on context. A further concern is the fact that human biological sex is variable: people's chromosomes and genitalia do not fit neatly into a binary account of sex. Any simplistic account of what it means to be a woman or a man will be called into question by trans and intersex people, for example. We discuss issues that impact transgender individuals and community in more detail in Chapter 15, where we also note that there is an ongoing debate between feminists and trans theorists. One of the focal points of that debate is the question of whether feminism ought to also focus on the concerns of trans women or whether there is another theory—perhaps "transfeminism"—that applies better to the concerns of trans people and that can extend feminism to include the concerns of trans people.[7]

Within applied ethics, feminism focuses our attention on topics involving women and gender. These issues include the reproductive rights of women, violence against women, sexual morality, gender discrimination including unequal pay for women, and related issues involving gender. Many of these topics are discussed in more detail in the second half of this book. Finally, let's also note by way of introduction that while feminism is understood as a critical theory that offers a critique of more traditional theories of ethics, it can also have a more affirmative focus that celebrates the success of women and the value of women's lives and experience. The ethics of care, which we discuss here, is one example of a theory of ethics that seeks to promote what

some call "women's ways" of knowing, valuing, and experiencing the world.

Gender in Moral Reasoning and the Ethics of Care

9.2 Explain feminist criticisms of traditional views about ethics and moral development.

The critique of traditional moral concepts such as autonomy and impartiality has led some feminists to develop a normative theory known as "the ethics of care" or "care ethics." This theory developed in the past half century out of a feminist critique of traditional normative theories such as utilitarianism and deontology. At one point, this was described as a "feminine" approach to morality, since "caring" was associated with traditional notions of femininity and women were often expected to act as caregivers. But as we'll see here, feminism asks us to reconsider the stereotype of women as feminine caregivers (and the related stereotype of men as impartial and autonomous judges). As the critique of gender has developed, care ethics has also evolved beyond its original focus on care and relationships as specifically feminine values.

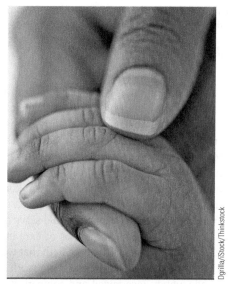

Figure 9-1 Care ethics focuses our attention on relationships of dependence and care.

We discussed care ethics in Chapter 4, where we considered it as a kind of altruism. There we noted that care ethics focuses on the importance of concrete relationships and that that focus may be in conflict with a more universal or impartial moral point of view. Care ethics is often more sympathetic to the role that emotions such as empathy and compassion play in our moral lives. It is also concerned with reflecting the embodied experience of people in ethical relationships. Thus, care ethics is less concerned with formulating abstract principles. And in this way, it is interested in the moral significance of a variety of topics involving "embodied relationality" that are often neglected by traditional moral theories.[8] These topics might include giving birth, dying, grieving, loving, working, creating, teaching, and caregiving. In Chapter 4, we included an excerpt from Virginia Held, one of the leading philosophers working on care ethics. Let's quote Held again here, in order to get a sense of how she understands the ethics of care.

> The central focus of the ethics of care is on the compelling moral salience of attending to and meeting the needs of the particular others for whom we take responsibility. Caring for one's child, for instance, may well and defensibly be at the forefront of a person's moral concerns. The ethics of care recognizes that human beings are dependent for many years of their lives, that the moral claim of those dependent on us for the care they need is pressing, and that there are highly important moral aspects in developing the relations of caring that enable human beings to live and progress.[9]

Held does not mention gender or feminism in this explanation of the ethics of care. But in focusing on caring for children, we can see the connection—since traditionally it was "women's work" to care for children. This idea has changed quite a bit in recent decades, as women have pursued work and careers outside of the home and as some men have opted to stay at home and care for children. Nonetheless, there remains a cultural norm and expectation that women should serve as caregivers. The proponents of the ethics of care build on that idea, and have gone on to argue both that women's unpaid (and often unchosen) caregiving work should be more adequately recognized and compensated, and that moral theory should emphasize the importance of caregiving as a basic moral good.

This theory developed out of critical feminist work in psychology and social science. One important source of the contemporary discussions of gender differences in moral perspectives and moral reasoning was sparked by the work of psychologist Carol Gilligan, beginning in the 1970s.[10] Gilligan interviewed both male and female subjects about various moral dilemmas and found that the females she interviewed had a different view than the males of what was morally required of them. They used a different moral language to explain themselves, and their reasoning involved a different moral logic. Gilligan concluded that males and females have different kinds of ethics. The ensuing debate, which will be discussed here, has focused on whether there is a distinctively feminine morality. One significant question is whether the idea that there is a female approach to

Figure 9-2 Carol Gilligan is an important feminist scholar.

Neil Turner/Alamy

ethics helps or hinders the cause of reducing violence against women, and whether it helps or hinders the effort to promote liberty and equality for women.

In Carol Gilligan's studies from the 1970s, a hypothetical situation was posed to two eleven-year-old children, Jake and Amy.[11] This situation is known as the "Heinz dilemma" because it featured a hypothetical person named Heinz. A man's wife was extremely ill and in danger of dying. A certain drug might save her life, but the man (Heinz) could not afford it, in part because the druggist had set an unreasonably high price for it. The question was whether the man should steal the drug. Jake answered by trying to figure out the relative value of the woman's life and the druggist's right to his property. He concluded that the man should steal the drug because he calculated that the woman's life was worth more. Amy was not so sure. She wondered what would happen to both the man and his wife if he stole the drug. "If he stole the drug, he might save his wife then, but if he did, he might have to go to jail, and then his wife might get sicker again."[12] She said that if the husband and wife talked about this, they might be able to think of some other way out of the dilemma.

One interesting thing about this case is the very different ways in which the two children tried to determine the right thing to do in this situation. The boy used a calculation in which he weighed and compared values from a neutral standpoint. The girl spoke about the possible effects of the proposed action on the two individuals and their relationship. Her method did not give the kind of definitive answer that is apparent in the boy's method. When researchers examined this and similar cases, they speculated that these differences in moral reasoning may be the result of sex or gender.[13]

Another representative example also seems to show a gender difference in moral reasoning.[14] In explaining how they would respond to a moral dilemma about maintaining one's moral principles in the light of peer or family pressure, two teen subjects responded quite differently. The case was one in which the religious views of each teen differed from those of their parents. The male said that he had a right to his own opinions, though he respected his parents' views. The female said that she was concerned about how her parents would react to her views. "I understand their fear of my new religious ideas." However, she added,

"they really ought to listen to me and try to understand my beliefs."[15] Although the male and female subjects reached similar conclusions, they used different reasoning. They seemed to have two decidedly different orientations or perspectives. The male spoke in terms of an individual's right to their own opinions, while the female talked of the need for the particular people involved to talk with and come to understand one another. These and similar cases raise questions about whether a gender difference actually exists in the way people reason about moral matters.

Several contrasting pairs of terms are associated with or can be used to describe feminine and masculine ethical perspectives, according to the sort of analysis inspired by Gilligan and her work. Gilligan's initial research supposed that these different ethical perspectives could be traced to differences in sex and gender. But we ought to be careful about essentializing this kind of analysis. Perhaps we could use the terms "feminine" and "masculine" to describe this difference—but that also risks claiming that there is some essential defining trait to masculine or feminine points of view. So it might be better to call one perspective a "caring" perspective and another a "disinterested" or "impartial" perspective. These are listed in Table 9-1.

Table 9-1 Comparing Care with Impartial Ethical Perspectives

Caring Ethical Perspective	Impartial Ethical Perspective
Traditionally "feminine"	Traditionally "masculine"
Personal	Impersonal
Partial	Impartial
Private	Public
Natural	Contractual
Feeling	Reason
Compassionate	Fair
Concrete	Universal
Responsibility	Rights
Relationship	Individual
Solidarity	Autonomy

In analyzing this list of opposed values, we ought to think carefully about the claim that care is a typically female or feminine moral perspective. Does this mean that all women are more caring than men? Or that men cannot be caring? And does it mean that women cannot value autonomy or impartiality? By assigning gender stereotypes to the divergent ethical perspectives, we risk reinforcing pernicious (and false) conceptions about gender and sex.

Consider, for example, the idea of *relatedness*. One traditional approach might claim that women are supposedly more concerned about particular people and their relations and how they will be affected by some action. In this view, feminine morality is highly personal. On this account, women are partial to their particular loved ones and think that one's primary moral responsibility is to these people. It is the private and personal natural relations of family and friends that are the model for other relations. From this point of view, women are supposed to stress the concrete experiences of this or that event and are concerned about the real harm that might befall a particular person or persons. The primary moral obligation is to prevent harm and to help people. Women are supposed to be better able to empathize with others and are supposed to be concerned about how they might feel if certain things were to happen to them. They supposedly believe that moral problems can be solved by talking about them and by trying to understand others' perspectives. Caring and compassion are key virtues. The primary moral obligation is not to turn away from those in need.

But do those traditional gendered ideas actually account for the diversity of women's lived experience? Could it be that women were thought to be focused on private relationships of care because they were, at one time, confined to the private sphere and not allowed to exercise autonomous moral judgment in the public sphere? And does such a gendered understanding of moral judgment continue to reinforce institutions that exclude women—or suggest that women are better suited for caring professions such as nursing or teaching, and that they ought not be lawyers or soldiers? You can see that there are substantial objections, from a feminist perspective, for any account of morality that suggests that women and men have an essentially different approach to moral reasoning.

And yet feminists have articulated and supported the idea of the ethics of care. One of the most influential figures in the ethics of care is Nel Noddings, whose book *Caring: A Feminine Approach to Ethics and Moral Education* was published in 1984.[16] The subtitle of the book makes it clear that she is associating care with a feminine approach to ethics. Noddings spent her career defending and explaining her ideas about care ethics. This approach includes an account of how caring relationships are important from the standpoint of evolution—as a mother's care for her children promotes their survival and emotional and moral health. Indeed, Noddings maintains that we all have a natural desire to be cared for—and that we have the ability to provide care. This is true whether we are male or female, even though evolution and culture tend to make us think that care is more female than male. Noddings emphasizes that care is not a voluntary act of free and equal parties who enter into social contracts. Rather, we find ourselves already embedded in family and social contexts that create networks of care. These networks and relationships are not primarily governed by abstract rules; rather, they depend on the needs and relations of the individuals. So for Noddings, care is two-sided: it involves a complex interplay between the carer and the cared-for. For Noddings, caring means listening attentively and seeing lovingly. It involves what she describes as motivational displacement, where the needs of the other overwhelm us, as in a mother's physical reaction to the crying of her infant child. Noddings thinks that the deep connections of care are psychologically and morally important for human flourishing and that society would be better if it promoted caring relationships through education and institutional design.

The supposedly typical *masculine moral perspective* contrasts sharply with the supposed feminine value care. The "masculine" approach to ethics is more focused on fairness, justice, and rights than on relationships and care for the needy. It appears to demand that we ought to adopt a universal and impartial standpoint in moral reasoning. An impartial kind of utilitarianism asks, for example, about the overall effects of some action and whether the good effects, when all are considered, outweigh the bad. On this account, moral decisions ought to be made impersonally or from some unbiased and detached point of view. The moral realm would then, in many ways, be similar to the public domain of law and contract. The law must not be biased and must treat everyone equally. In this view, moral thinking involves a type of universalism that recognizes the equal moral worth of all persons, both in themselves and before the law. People ought to keep their promises because this is the just thing to do and helps create a reliable social order. Morality is a matter of doing one's duty, keeping one's agreements, and respecting other people's rights. Impartiality and respectfulness are key virtues. The primary obligation is not to act unfairly.

What are we to make of the view that there are two very different sorts of morality: one that focuses on care and relation (and is typically viewed as "feminine") and another that focuses on impartiality and universality (and that is viewed as "masculine")? In focusing on this difference, Carol Gilligan was taking aim at one of the dominant points of view about moral development, namely, that of the psychologist Lawrence Kohlberg.[17] According to Kohlberg, the highest stage of moral development is the stage in which an adult can be governed not by social pressure, but by personal moral principles and a sense of justice. Based on these principles, adults come to regard other people as moral equals and manifest an impartial and universal perspective. In his own research, Kohlberg found that women did not often reach this stage of development. He thus judged them to be morally underdeveloped or morally deficient. Gilligan pointed out that his conclusions were based on an all-male sample, as he worked out his theory.[18] The problem was that after deriving his principles from male subjects, he then used them to judge both male and female moral development.

Gilligan and Kohlberg were not the first psychologists to believe a difference existed between men's and women's views of morality. Sigmund Freud held that women "show less sense of justice than men, that they are less ready to submit to the great exigencies of life, that they are more often influenced in their judgments by feelings of affection or hostility...."[19] According to Freud, women were morally inferior to men. Instead of being able to establish themselves as separate people living in society and adapting to its rules, girls remained in the home, attached to their mothers. Thus, girls developed a capacity for personal relations and intimacy, while their male counterparts developed a sense of separateness

and personal autonomy. The idea was that women base their morality on concerns about personal relations, while men base their morality on rules that can reconcile the separate competing individuals in society.[20] Believing that a focus on personal relations rather than a sense of justice was a lesser form of morality, Freud and others thought that women were morally inferior to men.

In mentioning Kohlberg and Freud here, we see the need for feminist critique. At one point it was common for male psychologists and philosophers to provide theories of morality and development that failed to account for the experience of women and that tended to reflect the gender norms of their time and culture. Gilligan and other feminists worked to expose the flaw in this method. They also sought to open the conversation about morality and moral development in a way that accounted both for the experience of women and for the problem of exclusion and bias in moral theory.

Is There a Gender Difference in Morality?

Several questions ought to be asked about the theory that women and men exhibit a different type of moral perspective and moral reasoning. First, is this contention true? Is it an empirical fact that men and women manifest a different type of moral thinking? Second, if it is a fact, how are we to explain it? What may be the source or cause of this difference? Third, if there is a difference, is one type of moral thinking higher or more developed or better than the other? We might also wonder whether the attempt to distinguish between male and female forms of moral experience serves the feminist goal of helping women or whether it simply reiterates traditional gender stereotypes.

To determine whether there is, in fact, a difference between the moral language and logic of males and females, we need to rely on empirical surveys and studies. We have already described some of the earlier findings of Carol Gilligan in this regard. Her conclusions in more recent studies have varied somewhat.[21] For example, her later research finds some variation in moral reasoning among both men and women. According to these findings, while both men and women sometimes think in terms of a justice perspective, few men think in terms of a care perspective. Being able to take one perspective rather than the other, she wrote, is much like being able to see the

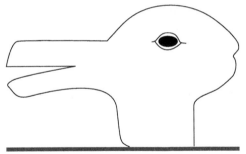

Figure 9-3 The Duck–Rabbit.

following well-known line drawing figure (Figure 9-3) as a rabbit or as a duck. One's perspective affects how one sees the figure.

Gilligan explains, with regard to ethics, that if one has a justice perspective, one will see that "the *self* as moral agent stands as the figure against a ground of social relationships, judging the conflicting claims of self and others against a standard of equality or equal respect." She continues to explain that if one has a care perspective, one will see that "the *relationship* becomes the figure, defining self and others. Within the context of relationship, the self as a moral agent perceives and responds to the perception of need."[22] In this more recent work, Gilligan studied "educationally advantaged North American adolescents and adults" and found that two-thirds had one or the other orientation as their primary focus. Still, she found sex differences in the results. "With one exception, all of the men who focused, focused on justice. The women divided, with roughly one-third focusing on justice and one-third on care" (the other third had a hybrid approach).[23] In this study, women did not always have the care perspective as their focus—but without the women in the study, the care focus would have been almost absent.

Other theorists are not so sure about what the evidence shows. For example, Catherine Greeno and Eleanor Maccoby believe that any difference between men's and women's morality can be accounted for by social status and experience, rather than gender. Using other studies, they point out that in many cases, those who exhibit so-called feminine morality have been housewives and women who lack higher education. They found that career women showed types of

moral reasoning similar to those of men.[24] The question of whether women do exhibit a unique type of moral language and logic will need to be decided by those who study the empirical data. And, of course, you can examine your own experience to see whether the males and females you know seem to reason differently when discussing moral issues. You might also want to consider how the results of such studies might be impacted if they included nonbinary or gender-fluid people in their samples.

The Sources of Feminine Morality

At least three distinct types of explanation address a possible difference between masculine and feminine morality. One proposes differences in the psychosexual development of the two sexes; a second points to biological differences; and a third gives a social, cultural, or educational explanation.

We have already described something of the Freudian account of the effects of psychosexual development on male and female moral thinking. A few more points may be added. According to this view, males and females have different concepts of the self and their gender identities; this concept is influenced by their development in relation to their mothers and fathers. As they grow up, females develop a sense of being connected with their mothers, whereas males find themselves being different from their mothers. According to Nancy Chodorow, who amplifies Freud's theory, development of the self and one's sense of individuality depends on being able to separate oneself from others. Thus males, who tend to separate themselves from their mothers, come to have a sense of self as independent, whereas females do not develop the sense of separate selves and rather see themselves as attached or connected to others. From this developmental situation, males and females supposedly develop different senses of morality—males develop a morality associated with separation and autonomy, and females develop a morality with relationships and interdependence. According to traditional views such as Kohlberg's, mature moral thinking involves being able to be detached and see things from some impartial perspective. Judging from a care perspective means that one cannot judge dispassionately or without bias, and this was deemed to be a moral defect. However, as we have seen, this traditional view of care ethics has been criticized by feminists and others.

A second account of the source of differences in masculine and feminine morality is exemplified by the writings of Caroline Whitbeck, who locates it, at least in part, in women's and men's biology, that is, in the difference in their reproductive capacities and experiences. In pregnancy, labor, and childbirth, women experience certain feelings of dependency and contingency.[25] They do not have full control of their bodies. They experience weakness and pain. They feel themselves participating in "species life" at its most primitive level. Because of their own feelings during this time, they can sympathize more readily with the infant's or child's feelings of helplessness and dependency.

Some will claim that female caring and nurturing spring naturally from the intimate and sympathetic relation that mothers are supposed to have toward their children. A naturalistic explanation of this might maintain that there is some instinctive orientation toward nurturance in women that is ultimately a matter of biology and physiology. It might be, however, that culture and socialization also matter. Girls and women are taught to exhibit nurturing behaviors by a culture that expects them to be nurturers and caregivers. This points to the idea that mothering is not only a biological phenomenon but also a social and cultural one. Although some women bear children, it is not necessary that they rear them. Still, because they do give birth to and nurse infants, women have generally come to be the primary child-rearers. And yet cultural norms have evolved in recent decades in the Western world, as women pursue careers and fathers have stayed home to care for children. It is also important to note that LGBTQ+ individuals and couples conceive and rear children, which calls into question traditional accounts of the gendered norms involved in caring for children.

It is from the elements of so-called maternal practice that women's morality arises, according to the third view (i.e., the cultural or social view of care and femininity).[26] Sara Ruddick suggests, for example, that maternal practice results in "maternal thinking," which is the "vocabulary and logic of connections" that arise from women "acting in response to demands of their children."[27] She believes that maternal thinking is not simply a kind of feeling that comes naturally to women, but a purposeful way of thinking and acting. It involves finding ways to preserve, develop, and promote one's children. Infants are extremely vulnerable and will not survive if they do not have the basics of food, clothing, and shelter. Children must be safeguarded from the many dangers of life. They need help in growing—physically, socially, and morally. Particular virtues are required for a mother to be able to satisfy the needs of her children. Among those described by Ruddick are humility (for one cannot do everything), cheerfulness combined with realism, and love and affection. Mothers also need to guard against certain negative traits and feelings, for example, feelings of hopelessness and possessiveness. According to this view, it is because they spend much of their lives mothering that women develop a morality consistent with this experience. And cultural norms tend to reinforce the value of care and nurturance for women. Traditional cultures tend to praise caregiving women and celebrate mothering, while questioning the femininity of women who don't exemplify the maternal virtues. Maternal morality stresses relationships and the virtues that are necessary for mothering. One does not necessarily have to be a biological mother, however, both to engage in mothering and to develop maternal ethics, according to this viewpoint. Just because men and some women do not give birth does not mean that they cannot be parents and develop the outlook required for this practice.

Until recently, maternal practice has principally been women's work. But this social norm is changing as some men are more involved in child-rearing, and as the traditional heterosexual idea of family life has evolved to include same-sex couples and single parents, along with the idea of marriage equality (which we discuss in more detail in Chapter 16). Cultural norms of masculinity and femininity have evolved, as more mothers work outside of the home and more fathers serve as caregivers within the home.

Evaluating Gender-Specific Approaches to Morality

Many questions remain concerning these three explanations of gender differences in morality. Some are factual or empirical questions, for they ask whether something is or is not the case. Do women in fact think and act in the ways described above? Are they more likely to do so than men? Does giving birth or rearing children cause those involved in these practices to think in a certain way and to have a certain moral perspective? As we've noted, those questions are complicated by changing conceptions of who raises children and changing notions of sex, sexuality, marriage, and family life.

We should also note that gender norms manifest in diverse ways in different cultures, racial and ethnic groups, and in diverse religious traditions. Feminists have been at the forefront of raising questions about sex, sexuality, diversity, and what is called "intersectionality." We discuss intersectionality in more detail in Chapter 13, but it is a useful concept here, as we are asking whether there are important or essential differences between men and women. An intersectional approach focuses on the network, web, or intersection of identities that make up an individual's identity and experience, including the various ways that people are oppressed or discriminated against in different ways depending on gender, sexual orientation, race, class, education, religion, and other social roles. With this complexity of identities in mind, questions about gender would also have to be connected to questions about race, class, religion, sexual orientation, and other categories. Is the experience of morality the same or different for Black women, Latina women, Asian women, and White women? Or for rich women and poor women? Or for Muslim women, Jewish women, Hindu women, and Christian women? Or for straight women, lesbian women, or trans women? In asking these kinds of question, we return to the problem of essentialism, which we mentioned previously. It turns out that gender is not one essential thing; rather, it is interwoven with a variety of identities and commitments. And even within a given cultural, racial, or economic worldview, the experiences of individual women will be different.

This critique of essentialism has long been part of feminist thought. For early feminists, one of the problems to be confronted was the fact that women were categorized and subjected to an image of femininity that was imposed on them by a patriarchal social structure.

But one risk of an approach that rejects essentialism that has also been noted by feminists is that if feminism is defined as a movement that seeks to empower women, end the oppression of women, and improve the lives of women—then it seems important to have a common idea of who (or what) women are and what it means to support their liberation.[28] The issues raised here are complex. We cannot resolve them here. But you may want to pause to think about this set of questions about intersectionality and essentialism for yourself. Is there one thing that is common to all women? And if not, then what should the focus of feminism be?

The Ethics of Care

9.3 Evaluate the ethics of care.

Let's return now to the question of care ethics. There is a great deal of appeal and suggestiveness in the theory of the ethics of care. Morality does appear to involve concrete relations of care. And the altruist focus of care ethics is a useful rejoinder to egoism (as we discussed in Chapter 4). It is also useful to compare this type of relational, caring morality with more traditional theories, such as utilitarianism and deontology, to see how different the perspectives are as exemplified by the theories. Whether one way of judging morally is *better* than the other is, of course, an open question. As we have seen, there has been a tradition of thought that says that the so-called feminine morality—an ethics of care focused on particular relations—is a lower-level morality. When we consider the (masculine) sources of this tradition, we find many reasons to criticize it. Perhaps, on the contrary, it is the ethics of care that provides a better moral orientation. For example, instead of judging war in terms of whether the overall benefits outweigh the costs, we may do well to think about the particular people involved—for example, that every soldier is someone's daughter, son, sister, brother, mother, or father. Or perhaps the two orientations are complementary. Perhaps a justice orientation is the minimum that morality requires. We could then build on this minimum and, for example, temper justice with care and mercy. On the other hand, the care orientation may be the more basic one, and justice concerns could then be brought in to determine how best to care.

If specific feminine and masculine virtues parallel these ethical orientations, another question arises. Would it not be possible and good for both men and women to develop both sets of virtues? If these virtues are described in a positive way—say, caring and not subservience—would they not be traits that all should strive to possess? These traits might be simply different aspects of the human personality, rather than the male or female personality. They would then be human virtues and human perspectives, rather than male or female virtues and perspectives. In this view, an ethics of fidelity, care, and sympathy would be just as important for human flourishing as an ethics of duty, justice, and acting on principle. While there would be certain moral virtues that all people should develop, other psychological traits could also vary according to temperament and choice. Individuals would be free to manifest, according to their own personalities, any combination of positive moral characteristics. These sets of characteristics and virtues could be synthesized, in various ways, and people would be free to adopt the masculine and feminine traits that suit their personality, interests, and inclination. And here we might again consider what gender fluidity might contribute to this conversation. Could we imagine different people at different stages in their life's journey focusing on different sets of values, for example, being more caring when rearing children while being more impartial when working in the public sphere? Could it be that gender norms and expectation are episodic in this way and relational?

Not all feminist writers are supportive of the ethics of care. While most would agree that one can describe a particular type of morality that exhibits the characteristics said to belong to an ethics of care, these writers question whether all aspects of such an ethics of care are good. For example, care ethics seems to be based on relations between unequals. The mother–child relation is such a relation. The dependency in the relation goes only one way. One does all (or most of) the giving, and the other all (or most of) the receiving. This may tend to reinforce or promote a one-sided morality of self-sacrifice and subjugation.

It may reinforce the view that women ought to be the ones who sacrifice and help and support others, chiefly children and men.

This critique has been articulated by a number of feminist authors including Catharine MacKinnon, who said, "Women value care because men have valued us according to the care we give them."[29] Building on MacKinnon's argument, Amanda Cawston and Alfred Archer explain:

> According to feminist critics, care ethics offers an ethical ideal that will entrench the oppression of women rather than challenge it. The basic criticism is that care ethics endorses an ideal of self-sacrifice that is harmful to the aims of the feminist movement.[30]

This criticism also tends to hold that care ethics rests on stereotypes about female and male behavior, which tend to reinforce male dominance. If we think that men are impartial while women are not, this may lead us to think twice about assigning women to positions of authority where impartiality is required. Furthermore, as we've explained, the firm binary distinction between the genders is problematic, as is the claim that there is some essential feature of femininity or masculinity. To be blunt, we might note that some women are not all that caring, and some men are quite caring. The differences may be described in terms such as masculine and feminine—but in reality, this gendered terminology does not map accurately onto actual differences among diverse individuals. Furthermore, these supposed differences may only be cultural differences. It might be the case in Western cultures that women are more caring and men are more impartial. But this may not be true in other cultures. Michael Slote, a prominent defender of care ethics, notes that in African cultures, both men and women exhibit caring behaviors; he also argues that "there are very strong elements of care thinking in both Confucian and Buddhist thought." Slote concludes that this shows that "the ethics of care can and should be regarded as a potential overall human morality, rather than as something just about, or at most only relevant to, women."[31] If this is right, it might be useful to imagine a defense of care ethics that goes beyond gender.

Feminist Thought

9.4 Distinguish between the several versions or "waves" of feminism.

Feminism can be defined as a political movement that seeks justice for women and an end to sexism in all forms. This movement has included a concerted effort on behalf of equal rights for women. Feminism is also a theoretical focal point in philosophy that is concerned with exposing sexism in the history of philosophy and that articulates the concerns of women. It has also evolved to include theoretical questions about gender, sex, sexuality, and the importance of these concepts in thought, institutional structures, and political life. The history of feminism includes those who are primarily concerned with promoting women's equality and rights, those who want to raise the value of women's unique characteristics, and those who raise questions about what it means to be a woman (and about gender in

general). This way of describing the history of feminism corresponds to the notion of "waves" of feminism often used in feminist history. The first wave (in the eighteenth, nineteenth, and early twentieth centuries) was about women's equality and rights—as manifest, for example, in women's suffrage movements. In the United States, first-wave feminism culminated in the passage of the Nineteenth Amendment to the U.S. Constitution, which gave women the right to vote in 1920. The second wave (in the middle of the twentieth century) was focused on articulating what it means to be a woman and with "women's liberation" understood in connection to social and cultural issues such as access to birth control, equal pay, and a critique of sexism in culture, in educational institutions, in religion, and in political life. The third wave (in the late twentieth and twenty-first centuries) opens up larger philosophical questions about sex, sexuality, and gender, including a recognition of the complexity of gender, sex, and sexuality as they are influenced by and made manifest in culture, race, and

▶ **Knowledge Check**   Answers appear at the end of the chapter.

1. Feminism can be described as:

    a. A theory explaining why women are inferior to men and deserve to be subordinated.

    b. An empirical account of female biology, physiology, and psychology.

    c. A critical theory of patriarchal ideas and social structures.

    d. A social, legal, and political system in which women rule over men.

2. Which of the following is NOT typical of the "caring" (or feminine) approach to ethics?

    a. A focus on concrete relationships

    b. A focus on private life

    c. A focus on feelings such as empathy

    d. A focus on impartiality

3. Which of the following is true?

    a. Aristotle and other traditional moral theorists tended to neglect women and devalue the female perspective.

    b. Carol Gilligan agreed with Freud and Kohlberg that the female approach to moral reasoning was inferior.

    c. All feminists support the idea of care ethics, suggesting that it helps to empower women.

    d. Noddings and other care ethicists modeled their theory on Kantian principles.

4. What is the difference between sex and gender, as explained in this chapter?

    a. Sex is biological, while gender is cultural.

    b. Sex is cultural, while gender is essential.

    c. Sex is fluid, while gender is binary.

    d. Sex is reproductive, while gender is speculative.

other intersectional identities. This is a rough-and-ready historical overview. The concerns of the "waves" overlap. And some have even suggested that a fourth wave of feminism has emerged in the digital age.

The First Wave

At any rate, the history of feminism begins with those who have stressed women's rights and equality. Among the earliest and most important examples is Mary Wollstonecraft, who advocated for women's rights in *A Vindication of the Rights of Women* (1792). In that text Wollstonecraft stated:

> There must be more equality established in society, or morality will never gain ground, and this virtuous equality will not rest firmly even when founded on a rock, if one-half of mankind be chained to its bottom by fate, for they will be continually undermining it through ignorance or pride.[32]

Wollstonecraft's plea for equality was connected to a critique of the idea that women were by nature weak, irrational, and emotional. Wollstonecraft argued that women were not naturally inferior to men but rather that their social situation had in many ways made them so. It was a society that subordinates women that taught women negative moral traits such as cunning and vanity, she insisted. Wollstonecraft's argument in favor of women's equality was taken up by suffragettes who sought political equality and the right to vote. In 1848, for example, the Seneca Falls Convention had met in the United States with a focus on women's rights, under the leadership of Elizabeth Cady Stanton, Lucretia Mott, and others. The Seneca Falls Convention made a Declaration of Sentiments that stated, "We hold these truths to be self-evident; that all men and women are created equal." Elizabeth Cady Stanton explained in her speech at the convention, "We are assembled to protest against a form of government existing without the consent of the governed—to declare our right to be free as man is free."[33] That convention was organized and led by women, but the movement had male supporters. Frederick Douglass, a man who escaped from slavery and went on to become a famous advocate for the abolition of slavery, spoke at the Seneca Falls Convention and signed the Declaration of Sentiments. Reflecting on the work of the convention, Douglass noted that there were important parallels between the abolition of slavery and the call for women's equality. He explained:

> In respect to political rights, we hold woman to be justly entitled to all we claim for man. We go farther, and express our conviction that all political rights which it is expedient for man to exercise, it is equally so for women. All that distinguishes man as an intelligent and accountable being, is equally true of woman; and if that government is only just which governs by the free consent of the governed, there can be no reason in the world for denying to woman the exercise of the elective franchise, or a hand in making and administering the laws of the land. Our doctrine is, that "Right is of no sex."[34]

At about this time, the utilitarian philosopher John Stuart Mill and his wife Harriet Taylor Mill also made important contributions to this movement. In 1851, Harriet Taylor Mill published an essay, "The Enfranchisement of Women," which gave voice to the women's suffrage movement in North America and in Europe. She wrote of "an organized agitation on a new question," explaining: "This question is, the enfranchisement of women; their admission, in law and in fact, to equality in all rights, political, civil, and social, with the male citizens of the community."[35] This idea was discussed further in a book, *The Subjection of Women*, published by John Stuart Mill 1869. As we've noted, this "first wave" of feminism culminated in women obtaining the legal right to vote in the United States and elsewhere. By 1948, the United Nations included an explicit statement about women in its Declaration of Human Rights (which, as we saw in Chapter 2, was the result of the efforts of Eleanor Roosevelt, another important figure in the women's rights movement). The Preamble to the UN Declaration affirms its commitment to "the dignity and worth of the human person and in the equal rights of men and women."[36]

The Second Wave

As formal political rights were granted to women in Western nations during the early and middle part of the twentieth century, the so-called second wave of feminism began to appear. Simone de Beauvoir's *The Second Sex* (1949) became a classic text for what has been called a "second wave" of feminists (the first wave being the nineteenth-century women's rights advocates).[37] Beauvoir is an important existentialist philosopher, as well as a key figure in the history of feminism. Women, she argues, are a "second sex" because they are regarded always in terms of being an "other" to the primary male sex. In an existentialist vein, she stressed the need for women to be independent selves and free to establish their own goals and projects. Various other writers in the history of the women's movement stressed the importance of raising women's consciousness so that they might understand how women's experience is shaped by social and cultural norms. This involves helping women become aware of how certain social circumstances leave women with second-class status, while encouraging women to examine the various ways they have been oppressed and subordinated in their personal, professional, and political lives. The movement's aim was not only to raise consciousness but also to act politically to bring about further social, legal, economic, and political equality of women. Thus, for example, they sought the passage of the Equal Rights Amendment (ERA) to the U.S. Constitution. Although the ERA passed both houses of the U.S. Congress in 1972, it failed to receive enough support in the states in order to be ratified. The original congressional authorization expired in 1982. Since 1982, members of the U.S. Congress have continued to reintroduce the ERA at each new session of the Congress. Second-wave feminism included a focus on reproductive rights for women, including access to birth control and to abortion (as we'll discuss in more detail in later chapters). It also included a critique of sexism in social relationships, in marriage, and in the workplace. Another of the influential authors of this wave of feminism was Betty Friedan, whose book *The Feminine Mystique* (1963) was widely read in the United States, where it was first published, and elsewhere. Friedan argued, among other things:

It is time to stop giving lip service to the idea that there are no battles left to be fought for women in America, that women's rights have already been won. It is ridiculous to tell girls to keep quiet when they enter a new field, or an old one, so the men will not notice they are there. In almost every professional field, in business and in the arts and sciences, women are still treated as second-class citizens. It would be a great service to tell girls who plan to work in society to expect this subtle, uncomfortable discrimination—tell them not to be quiet, and hope it will go away, but fight it. A girl should not expect special privileges because of her sex, but neither should she "adjust" to prejudice and discrimination.[38]

The Third Wave

9.5 Analyze feminist critiques of gender, race, and other intersectional identities.

The so-called third wave of feminism has responded to the diverse experiences of individuals as they confront sexism and gender discrimination. We mentioned above the growing recognition of the importance of intersectional identity. Consider, for example, that a Black woman's experience of sexism in the workplace may be quite different from a White woman's experience. One of the important authors who has articulated this concern is bell hooks (who has chosen to not use capital letters in her pen name, as a way of protesting against dominant cultural norms and expectations). As a Black woman, hooks articulated the sense that feminism had often neglected the concerns of non-White women. In response to this, hooks (Figure 9-4) argued in her 1981 book *Ain't I A Woman* that feminism ought to be committed to "the liberation of all people."[39] The title of hooks's book is taken from a famous speech by Sojourner Truth, a Black woman who escaped from slavery in the 1820s. In the 1850s, Truth gave a speech at a women's rights convention where she contrasted the treatment of Black women and White women and asked the assembled White women to notice her plight by asking "Ain't I a woman?" (We have a short excerpt from bell hooks's book in the primary source readings for this chapter).

Karjean Levine/Archive Photos/Getty Images

Figure 9-4 bell hooks argues against oppression in all of its forms.

While hooks is critical of racism among White feminists, her goal is to eliminate racism, sexism, and other forms of oppression. In another work, she explains:

> Individuals who fight for the eradication of sexism without supporting struggles to end racism or classism undermine their own efforts. Individuals who fight for the eradication of racism or classism while supporting sexist oppression are helping to maintain the cultural basis of all forms of group oppression.[40]

In response to the critical perspective offered by hooks and others, feminists have engaged in further efforts to understand structures of domination and oppression and to respond to intersectional complexities. This includes a growing awareness among Western feminists of the range of women's experiences in diverse cultures. Women's issues will be different in Iran, Pakistan, Israel, and in the United States or Europe, depending on religious, cultural, and even generational differences. Women in the Western world who are concerned with liberty and equality for women in

the rest of the world have become more aware of the need to listen to women in the developing world and to appreciate the unique cultural situations that structure their lives, including in diverse religious traditions and in Indigenous cultures. One prominent feminist who has been working on international women's issues is the philosopher Martha Nussbaum (whose work we touched on in Chapter 3). Nussbaum points out that cultures are dynamic and internally complex. Nonetheless, she argues that it is still important to clarify abstract moral principles, provided they are grounded in empirical reality. She explains that although feminist philosophy has often been "skeptical of universal moral normative approaches," feminism can make universal claims that "need not be insensitive to difference or imperialistic."[41] Nussbaum's own work on gender issues in India exemplifies the approach she champions; criticism must be grounded in local practices and based on the needs and interests of the women whose lives are characterized by the specifics of the local context.

Other recent feminist discussions point to a further critique of abstract moral principles. These discussions are often concerned with the sheer complexity of gender terms and sexuality. One prominent author associated with third-wave feminism is Judith Butler (Figure 9-5), whose work is influenced by post-structuralist philosophy and what is often called *queer theory*—which aims to deconstruct traditional norms for thinking about gender and sexuality. In her most influential book, *Gender Trouble*, Butler discusses such figures as hermaphrodites and drag queens in order to elucidate the ways in which gender norms are socially constructed and "performed," in an attempt to liberate gender and sexuality from strict social conventions. As might be expected, this approach has implications for sexual morality and the issue of transgender rights (as we'll discuss in Chapter 12). This concern with deep philosophical questions about gender, sex, and sexuality is connected to Wollstonecraft's original inquiry into the way that the notion of femininity and female virtue was constructed by the social norms of the European society in which she lived. It can also be found in the work of authors like de Beauvoir, Friedan, and hooks, as we've noted. And as the complexities

AP Images/dapd/Thomas Lohnes

Figure 9-5 Feminist philosopher and queer theorist Judith Butler.

of gender, sex, and sexuality have become more apparent—including the intersectional diversity that becomes apparent when race, class, religion, and culture are included—it is clear that more careful and critical reflection is needed.

Feminist Ethics

Many of these forms of feminist moral thought may be said to advance a *feminist ethics*, distinguishable from an ethics of care (which is sometimes called *feminine ethics*, because of its focus on feminine virtues).[42] Writers who explore feminist ethics often focus on analyzing the causes of women's subordination and oppression and systematic violence against women. Feminist ethicists are also engaged in strategies for eliminating this violence and oppression. In this, they have an explicitly political orientation.

The political activist side of feminism may be directed at local and national issues, such as the Equal Rights Amendment mentioned previously. It might also have a global focus. At the international level, women have worked together to raise the status of women around the world and seek ways to better the conditions under which they live. International conferences have brought women together from all nations to discuss their problems and lend each other support.

One initiative is the effort to provide small loans to women in impoverished areas (so-called microfinancing) so that they can stabilize their financial and family lives. Other focuses of activism include reproductive health, preventing violence against women, and educating women in an effort to equalize literacy rates and life prospects. Of course, such international and cross-cultural work requires sensitivity and awareness of the problems of cultural relativism and religious diversity.

Some feminists point out that traditional philosophy is among the causes of women's oppression. Traditional moral philosophy has not been favorable to women. It has tended to support the view that women should develop "women's virtues," such as modesty, humility, and subservience—which are often to their detriment. For example, Aristotle held that women are inferior to men not only because of certain biological phenomena having to do with heat in the body but also because they lack certain elements of rationality. According to Aristotle, free adult males could rule over slaves, women, and children because of the weakness in their "deliberative" faculties. In the case of women, while they have such a faculty, Aristotle claims it is "without authority."[43] In *Emile*, Jean-Jacques Rousseau's work on the education of the young, the French philosopher advances a quite different type of ideal education for the protagonist Emile than for Emile's wife-to-be, Sophie. Because morality is different for men and women, the young of each sex ought to be trained in different virtues, according to Rousseau. Emile is to be trained in virtues such as justice and fortitude, while Sophie is to be taught to be docile and patient.[44] With this history of male-dominant moral philosophy in mind, it is easy to see why some feminists may be reluctant to affirm traditional notions about feminine virtues, since these are associated with a long history of the subordination of women.

Even contemporary moral philosophers have not given women and women's concerns their due, according to many feminist writers. They have not been interested in matters of the home and domesticity. They have tended to ignore issues such as the "feminization of poverty," the use of reproductive technologies, sexual harassment, and violence against and sexual abuse of women. It is mainly with women writing on these topics in contemporary ethics that they have gained some respectability as topics of genuine philosophical interest. So also have the issues of female oppression and subordination become topics of wider philosophical interest.

Evaluation of Feminist Thought and the Ethics of Care

We have already pointed out some of the critical questions that have been raised about the ethics of care. As we have seen, some writers point out that care does not always come naturally to women, and not all women are good mothers or good nurturers. Moreover, men may also exhibit these characteristics, and some cultures emphasize care as a primary value for both men and women. However, supporters of the ethics of care may reply that their theory of the importance of care does not depend on any essential claim about gender. Rather, care ethicists might conceive their project as advance care in opposition to more traditional values, such as impartiality and universality. Of course, one might reply that those traditional values—impartiality, universality, and justice—are crucially important. Indeed, those values have often been of use in the women's rights movement, which has argued for women's equality and access for women to civil and political rights.

In addition, many critics of care ethics contend that the promotion of so-called feminine traits may not be of benefit to women and may reinforce their subservient position in society. Defenders of care ethics might respond that it is not such "feminine" virtues as obedience, self-sacrifice, silence, and service that define an ethics of care. Rather, such an ethics tells us from what perspective we are to judge morally, namely, from the perspective of specific persons in relation to each other, susceptible to particular harms and benefits.

Can an ethics of care free itself from the negative associations of traditional femininity? Can feminist ethicists support an ethics of care while also seeking to promote women's equality? It is clear, at least, that women cannot be restricted to traditionally subservient roles if they are to be treated equally and fairly in both the public realm and the realm of the home and family.

What these discussions have also suggested is that we can no longer maintain that one ethics exists for the home and the private realm (an ethics of care and relationships)

and another ethics for work or the public realm (an ethics of justice and fairness and impartiality). "Neither the realm of domestic, personal life, nor that of non-domestic, economic and political life, can be understood or interpreted in isolation from the other," writes feminist political philosopher Susan Moller Okin.[45] These two realms not only overlap, Okin argues, but also can and should exemplify the values and virtues of each other. Elements of altruism and concern for particular, concrete individuals have a place in the political as well as the domestic realm. Furthermore, when feminists say "the personal is political," they mean that "what happens in the personal life, particularly in relations between the sexes, is not immune from the dynamic of *power*, which has typically been seen as a distinguishing feature of the political."[46] These relations should thus also be restrained by considerations of fairness and justice.

One further question arises about the ethics of care. While such an ethics describes an ideal context for ethical decision making, it does not tell us how we are to determine what will help or harm particular individuals. It does not in itself say what constitutes benefit or harm. It gives no rules for what we are to do in cases of conflict of interest, even among those to whom we are partial, or what to do when we cannot benefit all. It seems to give little definitive help for knowing what to do in cases where we must harm some to benefit others. Supporters of care ethics may respond that by setting the context for ethical decision making, an ethics of care has already done something valuable, for it thus provides a balance to the otherwise one-sided traditional ethics of the impersonal and universal. Perhaps this is a valuable minimum achievement. Or perhaps care ethics, with its emphasis on human connectedness, has an even more central role to play in today's ethical and political discussions. As Gilligan notes,

> By rendering a care perspective more coherent and making its terms explicit, moral theory may facilitate women's ability to speak about their experiences and perceptions and may foster the ability of others to listen and to understand. At the same time, the evidence of care focus in women's moral thinking suggests that the study of women's development may provide a natural history of moral development in which care is ascendant, revealing the ways in which creating and sustaining responsive connection with others becomes or remains a central moral concern.[47]

Feminism and the ethics of care remain important focal points for moral theory, which includes the question of whether we can talk about care without falling prey to old-fashioned and traditional notions of femininity and female virtue. But there is an open question about the extent to which a more traditional set of values (impartiality, justice, etc.) is of use in the struggle for women's rights and equality. It is worth asking whether it is possible to achieve some synthetic view that combines those traditionally masculine values with the values emphasized by care ethics.

Violence Against Women and Other Issues

9.6   Explain the problem of violence against women.

As we conclude this chapter, let's consider a few of the concrete issues that involve women and are a concern for feminism. We will discuss these kinds of issues in more detail in subsequent chapters. But let's note here that one of the most important concerns of feminist ethics (understood, again, as an ethical concern for the well-being, equality, and flourishing of women) is violence against women and ongoing inequalities and oppression. As we noted in the opening vignette for this chapter, this became a concern in 2022, as protests broke out and violence ensued in Iran over the question of women's rights and Iranian modesty laws. Ten years earlier, another notorious example occurred in Pakistan when a 15-year-old schoolgirl, Malala Yousafzai (Figure 9-6), was shot in the head by Taliban assassins as she waited for a bus. The Taliban targeted Malala because she had spoken out in defense of the right of girls to attend school. Malala recovered from her wounds and went on to become an international advocate for the rights of girls and women. In 2014, she became the youngest person ever to receive the Nobel Peace Prize. When asked if she was a feminist, she responded, "I'm a feminist," and said that we all should be feminists because "feminism is another word for equality."[48]

North Americans may like to imagine that violence against women is only a problem in other parts of

Figure 9-6 Women holding signs in support of Malala Yousafzai in 2012 in Islamabad, Pakistan.

the globe. But in the United States, there is still a significant amount of violence against women. A 2022 report indicates that in 2020 (the last year for which complete data was available), more than two thousand women were murdered by men and that 89 percent of those murders were committed by someone known to the victim.[49] This kind of violence often afflicts women in marginalized communities. In response, there have been active movements to end gender violence focused on women in those communities. One notable example is Missing and Murdered Indigenous Women (MMIW), which has been active in Canada, the United States, and in Latin America in responding to historic injustices against Indigenous women, while also sounding the alarm about contemporary violence. In the United States, the MMIW movement has pointed out that Indigenous women are much more likely to suffer violence. The U.S. Bureau of Indian Affairs states: "Native American and Alaska Native rates of murder, rape, and violent crime are all higher than the national averages. When looking at missing and murdered cases, data shows that Native American and Alaska Native women make up a significant portion of missing and murdered individuals."[50]

Violence against women became a focal point in 2016 in the United States, as the Obama White House brought forward a "1 is 2 Many" campaign, which was intended to reduce violence against women. According to data provided by that campaign, one in five women will be sexually assaulted in college, one in nine teenage girls will be forced to have sex, and one in ten teens will be hurt on purpose by someone they are dating.[51] To combat the problem of sexual assault and date rape, the state of California enacted legislation in 2014 that requires "affirmative consent" for sex—popularly known as the "yes means yes" law. We will discuss this further in Chapter 16 in connection with sexual morality. We will also discuss in that chapter the Me Too movement, which evolved in the past few years as women spoke out against powerful men who engaged in sexual harassment and rape.

Some feminists have argued that violence against women is also connected to pornography and the general objectification of women that takes place in popular culture. Andrea Dworkin made this point in the 1980s in her book *Pornography: Men Possessing Women*, where she argued that pornography encourages men to view women's bodies as commodities to be possessed and abused.[52] Dworkin and others point out that defenders of pornography often make claims about freedom of speech that fail to take into account the way that women are victimized by pornography and sexual violence. Some authors have also suggested that another insidious form of violence against women occurs through a cultural obsession with female beauty, which fuels the epidemic of eating disorders and the growing use of cosmetic surgery to "perfect" the female body.[53] Naomi Wolf links this to the rise of pornography;

"the influence of pornography on women's sexual sense of self has now become so complete that it is almost impossible for younger women to distinguish the role pornography plays in creating their idea of how to be, look and move in sex from their own innate sense of sexual identity."[54] It might be, however, that pornography is a celebration of sexuality, which empowers women. Pro-sex or sex-positive feminists such as Wendy McElroy argue that pornography benefits women both personally and politically. From McElroy's perspective, the point is to make sure that sex work is free of coercion, which respects women by affording them the freedom to choose as individuals to participate or not.[55] This dispute reminds us that feminism, like other approaches to moral theory, is subject to diverse interpretations. We discuss debates about pornography and sex work in more detail in Chapter 16.

While the charge about the degrading and violent aspects of pornography has been made by Western feminists, a similar argument against the general sexual objectification of women comes from defenders of traditional roles for women and rules of modesty. While this argument has been made in a variety of cultural contexts, the most prominent current discussion involves rules governing the use of veiling in Muslim cultures. Defenders of the veil, or *hijab*, argue that modest dress protects women from being publicly harassed or molested, often quoting a passage from the Qur'an (33:59), which states that modest dress for women will ensure that they are not abused. Similar ideas are found in other cultures and religious traditions, including in some ultra-Orthodox Jewish communities and in conservative Christian communities. Critics argue that women should be free from molestation regardless of how they dress. From this perspective, the problem is not what women wear or how they behave, but a male-dominated culture in which men seek to regulate and control women.

The problem of violence against women is a global issue. Nicholas Kristof and Sheryl WuDunn have chronicled the problem in their book (and documentary) *Half the Sky*. Across the world, rape and sex slavery threaten the well-being of women. In some cases, women are denied access to medical care and resources simply because they are women. Female fetuses are aborted because of a cultural bias toward male offspring. Girls' genitals are cut in a practice that some call ritual "circumcision" but critics call **female genital mutilation** or FGM. While cultural relativists might be reluctant to judge such cases (as discussed in Chapter 3), feminists focus on the harm that FGM causes to girls and women. Even worse than FGM is the fact that girls and women are often liable to be killed simply because of their gender. Kristof and WuDunn conclude:

> It appears that more girls have been killed in the last fifty years, precisely because they were girls, than men were killed in all the battles of the twentieth century. More girls are killed in this routine "gendercide" in any one decade than people were slaughtered in all the genocides of the twentieth century.[56]

A significant problem is "honor killing." In some cultures, when a woman has done something that the culture considers shameful, the male members of the family feel justified in killing her. In some places, rape is "punished" by killing the woman who has been raped or by forcing the rape victim to marry her rapist. Related to this are violence related to disputes about dowries and even accusations of witchcraft. Robert Paul Churchill has explored the issue of honor killing in his book *Women in the Crossfire*, which chronicles and criticizes the tendency of men to kill women in the name of something like family honor. Churchill points out that in many cultures, "women become trapped in and subjected to terror and deadly violence as a consequence of the ways men vie with one another for honor and status within a form of extreme patriarchy." He continues:

> The hierarchical patriarchies in which honor killings occur sustain and replicate themselves through the systematic and structural victimization of women and girls. Women are permanent potential victims, whose lives are disposable should men believe it necessary to kill to maintain their status as honorable men and to uphold the honor of the extended family, and through it, patriarchy itself.[57]

The data on violence against women is tragic and disheartening for those who are concerned with the well-being of women. The United Nations reports that in 2020, forty-seven thousand women and girls were killed by intimate partners or family members.[58] The data on violence against women are difficult to collect and analyze. But one data set referred to in the UN's report indicates that in India, there were six to eight thousand honor killings every year between 2016 and 2020. In addition, every year in India there are hundreds of murders of women related to witchcraft accusations and to disputes about dowries. As we conclude this appalling account of gender-related violence, we should also point out that there is a significant problem of violence against trans people, including especially trans women. The Human Rights Campaign noted at the end of 2022 that in 2021, there were fifty fatalities involving trans people and thirty-four murders of trans people in 2022.[59]

While the mainstream of Western culture now holds that women deserve to be treated equally and that violence against women and trans persons is wrong, it is clear that there is still a long way to go in terms of actualizing this idea both in the Western world and internationally. The World Economic Forum tracks gender disparities across the globe in four categories (economic opportunity, educational attainment, health outcomes, and political empowerment of women). In a 2022 report, they note that at the current rate of progress, it will take 132 years for there to be global parity in these areas.[60] Countries that rank the best in terms of gender parity on this scale include Iceland, Finland, Norway, and New Zealand.[61] The United Kingdom is ranked twenty-second, Canada is twenty-fifth, and the United States is ranked at twenty-seventh. The last four countries in this ranking were Iran, the Democratic Republic of the Congo, Pakistan, and Afghanistan. Among issues of concern for nations in the developed world such as the United States is a remaining gender pay gap. In 2022, women only earned 83 percent of what men earned.[62] Some of this inequality may be explained in terms of the kinds of careers that women and men choose, or in connection with time taken off by women to raise children and provide care for loved ones. But the pay gap continues to be a significant point of concern—as in the example we discussed in the opening vignette about the unequal pay of male and female athletes in the United States. One bit of good news about the status women in the United States is the fact that women seem to be doing better than men in terms of educational attainment. An analysis from the Brookings Institution about this in 2022 states: "In every U.S. state, young women are more likely than their male counterparts to have a bachelor's degree. The education gender gap emerges well before college, however: girls are more likely to graduate high school on time and perform substantially better on standardized reading tests than boys (and about as well in math)."[63] Of course, in response to this kind of data, one might wonder why boys are falling behind and what we can do to support them. We might also wonder, as we conclude this chapter, about the ways that class, race, and other markers of identity factor into these various and remaining inequalities and disparities.

Chapter Summary

9.1 How can we describe the importance of feminist thought for ethical inquiry?

Feminism offers a point of view that is concerned with the liberation of women. One concern of feminism is the critique of traditional normative theories, which have tended to marginalize women and ignore their concerns. Feminism directs our attention to this lack in traditional normative theory. It also directs our attention to concrete issues of concern for women such as violence against women.

9.2 How can we explain feminist criticisms of traditional views about ethics and moral development?

Feminists have pointed out that traditional values such as impartiality, universality, and abstract rationality are associated with patriarchal systems of thought. This was reflected in debates about moral development in the twentieth century. Kohlberg's theory tended to prioritize the "male" or "masculine" point of view, which was held to be focused on abstract rules and impartiality. Carol Gilligan criticized Kohlberg's theory by noting that Kohlberg ignored the voices of girls and women. Gilligan suggested that female moral development may be different from the male, thus opening the door to questions about the importance of care, empathy, and other values that are less abstract and impartial.

9.3 How might we evaluate the ethics of care?

Care ethics developed in the twentieth century as a "feminine" alternative to the "masculine" paradigm of traditional moral theory—building on insights found in Gilligan's work and in the work of other feminists,

such as Nel Noddings. Care ethics emphasizes the importance of concrete relations, the private sphere, feelings like compassion and empathy, and specific structures of caregiving and being cared for. Some feminists advocated that this should be considered as a significant alternative to traditional moral theory. But some feminists criticized that idea, suggesting both that the ethics of care tends to assume traditional notions of masculinity and femininity, and that it risks reaffirming the subordination of women by suggesting, for example, that women ought to be focused on so-called women's work and the caring professions. Subsequent developments in care ethics have responded to this critique by noting that there is no essential biological difference between the male and female points of view and by also recognizing that care is manifest in diverse ways in different cultures.

9.4 How can we distinguish between the several versions or "waves" of feminism?

The first wave (in the nineteenth and early twentieth centuries) was focused on equality and civil rights for women (including the right to vote). It included authors like Mary Wollstonecraft and Harriet Taylor Mill, as well as activists such as Elizabeth Cady Stanton. The second wave developed in the latter half of the twentieth century in the work of authors such as Simone de Beauvoir and Betty Friedan, who were interested in broader questions of culture and social equality. The third wave developed a broader critique of gender, sex, and sexuality, as well as an awareness of the need for feminists to address issues from an intersectional perspective.

9.5 How can we analyze feminist critiques of gender, race, and other intersectional identities?

One of the concerns of more contemporary feminists is to attend to the complexities of gender, sex, and sexuality and the way that these issues are connected to race, class, ethnicity, and other identities. bell hooks provides an example of a Black feminist who was critical of the lack of diverse voices in feminism. Judith Butler and others offered a further level of complexity by arguing that gender is a social construct that is not simply understood in terms of traditional views of sex and sexuality. This set of worries has led feminists to question the so-called gender binary and to consider, among other things, the concerns of trans women. In addition to these complex issues, feminists are also still concerned with traditional women's rights issues including civil and political rights and the ongoing problem of violence against women.

9.6 How can we understand the problem of violence against women?

Violence against women includes sexual violence such as rape, as well as honor crimes, female genital mutilation, and domestic violence. Violence against women persists in the developed world, as well as in developing countries—although its manifestation involves cultural differences. In Iran, for example, a concern is modesty laws regulating hair covering.

In North America, activists are working on issues involving missing and murdered Indigenous women. There are also questions about pornography, sexual harassment, and violence against trans women and trans persons. One way of understanding this issue is to connect it to patriarchal ideas about women's bodies as objects of male control and domination.

9.7 How can you defend your own ideas about the importance of feminist ethics and the ethics of care?

To defend a thesis about these issues, a student should clarify what they think about the feminist critique of traditional moral theory and what they think about the feminist critique of traditional notions of moral development and psychology. A student would also need to clarify whether they think that care ethics provides a useful addition to moral theory from a feminist point of view or whether it seems beholden to traditional concepts of femininity and masculinity. A student would also need to consider how race, class, and religion introduce different concerns and complications into the conversation—along with the larger question about how we understand and define sex and gender. Finally, a student would need to consider how they might respond to questions about civil and political rights, inequalities between men and women, and the problem of gender-based violence.

Primary Source Readings

This chapter's reading selections begin with an excerpt from bell hooks's 1981 book *Ain't I a Woman*, where she discusses the connections between feminism and race and articulates a form of Black feminism. After that, we have a brief excerpt from Nel Noddings, a key proponent of care ethics; the excerpt is from her book *Caring*, first published in 1984. Following that we have an excerpt from Annette Baier that provides a critique of the traditional emphasis on justice that is derived from her reading of Carol Gilligan's account of moral development. The final excerpt is from Hilde Lindemann, in which she explains feminist ethics in connection with the idea that gender is about power and norms.

Reading 9-1   Ain't I A Woman? | bell hooks

Study Questions

As you read the excerpt, please consider the following questions:

1. What does hooks suggest about the relation between racism and sexism?

2. What does hooks conceive of as the larger goal of feminism?

3. Why does hooks continue to affirm feminism even though she suggests that it may include racism?

Although the women's movement motivated hundreds of women to write on the woman question, it failed to generate in depth critical analyses of the black female experience. Most feminists assumed that problems black women faced were caused by racism—not sexism. The assumption that we can divorce the issue of race from sex, or sex from race, has so clouded the vision of American thinkers and writers on the "woman" question that most discussions of sexism, sexist oppression, or woman's place in society are distorted, biased, and inaccurate. We cannot form an accurate picture of woman's status by simply calling attention to the role assigned females under patriarchy. More specifically, we cannot form an accurate picture of the status of black women by simply focusing on racial hierarchies....

Many women have found that neither the struggle for "social equality" nor the focus on an "ideology of woman as an autonomous being" are enough to rid society of sexism and male domination. To me feminism is not simply a struggle to end male chauvinism or a movement to ensure that women will have equal rights with men; it is a commitment to eradicating the ideology of domination that permeates Western culture on various levels—sex, race, and class, to name a few—and a commitment to reorganizing U.S. society so that the self-development of people can take precedence over imperialism, economic expansion, and material desires....

It is a contradiction that white females have structured a women's liberation movement that is racist and excludes many non-white women. However, the existence of that contradiction should not lead any woman to ignore feminist issues. Oftentimes I am asked by black women to explain why I would call myself a feminist and by using that term ally myself with a movement that is racist. I say, "The question we must ask again and again is how can racist women call themselves feminists." It is obvious that many women have appropriated feminism to serve their own ends, especially those white women who have been at the forefront of the movement; but rather than resigning myself to this appropriation I choose to reappropriate the term "feminism," to focus on the fact that to be "feminist" in any authentic sense of the term is to want for all people, female and male, liberation from sexist role patterns, domination, and oppression.

From bell hooks, *Ain't I a Woman* (New York: Routledge, 2015).

Reading 9-2   Caring | Nel Noddings

Study Questions

As you read the excerpt, please consider the following questions:

1. How does relatedness figure into ethics?

2. Is the caring approach to ethics that Noddings describes one that only women can enjoy?

3. How does caring connect with subjectivity in ethics and the idea of universality?

Ethical caring, the relation in which we do meet the other morally, will be described as arising out of natural caring—that relation in which we respond as one-caring out of love or natural inclination. The relation of natural caring will be identified as the human condition that we, consciously or unconsciously, perceive as "good." It is that condition toward which we long and strive, and it is our longing for caring—to be in that special relation—that provides the motivation for us to be moral. We want to be *moral* in order to remain in the caring relation and to enhance the ideal of ourselves as one-caring....

...In recognition of the feminine approach to meeting the other morally—our insistence on caring for the other—I shall want to preserve the uniqueness of human encounters. Since so much depends on the subjective experience of those involved in ethical encounters, conditions are rarely "sufficiently similar" for me to declare that you must do what I do. There is, however, a fundamental universality in our ethics, as there must be to escape relativism. The caring attitude, that attitude which expresses our earliest memories of being cared for and our growing store of memories of both caring and being cared for, is universally accessible. Since caring and the commitment to sustain it form the universal heart of the ethic, we must establish a convincing and comprehensive picture of caring at the outset.

Another outcome of our dependence on an ethical ideal is the emphasis on moral education. Since we are dependent on the strength and sensitivity of the ethical ideal—both our own and that of others—we must nurture that ideal in all of our educational encounters. I shall claim that we are dependent on each other even in the quest for personal goodness. How good *I* can be is partly a function of how *you*—the other—receive and respond to me. Whatever virtue I exercise is completed, fulfilled, in you. The primary aim of all education must be nurturance of the ethical idea....

...I shall strike many contrasts between masculine and feminine approaches to ethics and education and, indeed, to living. These are not intended to divide men and women into opposing camps. They are meant, rather, to show how great the chasm is that already divides the masculine and feminine in each of us and to suggest that we enter a dialogue of genuine dialectical nature in order to achieve an ultimate transcendence of the masculine and feminine in moral matters....

...When I look at my child—even one of my grown children—and recognize the fundamental relation in which we are each defined, I often experience a deep and overwhelming joy. It is the recognition of and longing for relatedness that form the foundation of our ethic, and the joy that accompanies fulfillment of our caring enhances our commitment to the ethical ideal that sustains us as one-caring.

From Nel Noddings, *Caring* (Berkeley: University of California Press, 1984), pp. 1–6.

Reading 9-3   The Need for More Than Justice | Annette Baier

Study Questions

As you read the excerpt, please consider the following questions:

1. Why does Baier, following Gilligan, suggest that a focus on rights, justice, and autonomy is insufficient?
2. How is Gilligan's emphasis on interdependency supposed to provide an alternative to justice?
3. Why does Baier see as the antidote to "patriarchal poison"?

The main complaint about the Kantian version of a society with its first virtue justice, construed as respect for equal rights to formal goods such as having contracts kept, due process, equal opportunity including opportunity to participate in political activities leading to policy and law-making, to basic liberties of speech, free association and assembly, religious worship, is that none of these goods do much to ensure that the people who have and mutually respect such rights will have any other relationships to one another than the minimal relationship needed to keep such a "civil society" going....

Gilligan reminds us that noninterference can, especially for the relatively powerless, such as the very young, amount to neglect, and even between equals can be isolating and alienating. On her less individualist version of individuality, it becomes defined by responses to dependency and to patterns of interconnexion, both chosen and unchosen. It is not something a person has, and which she then chooses relationships to suit, but something that develops out of a series of dependencies and interdependencies, and responses to them....

The moral tradition which developed the concept of rights, autonomy and justice is the same tradition that provided "justifications" of the oppression of those whom the primary right-holders depended on to do the sort of work they themselves preferred not to do. The domestic work was left to women and slaves, and the liberal morality for right-holders was surreptitiously supplemented by a different set of demands made on domestic workers. As long as women could be got to assume responsibility for the care of home and children, and to train their children to continue the sexist system, the liberal morality could continue to be the official morality, by turning its eyes away from the contribution made by those it excluded....

It is however also true that the moral theories that made the concept of a person's rights central were not just the instruments for excluding some persons, but also the instruments used by those who demanded that more and more persons be included in the favored group. Abolitionists, reformers, women, used the language of rights to assert their claims to inclusion in the group of full members of a community. The tradition of liberal moral theory has in fact developed so as to include the women it had for so long excluded, to include the poor as well as rich, blacks and whites, and so on.... So we should not be wholly ungrateful for those male moral theories, for all their objectionable earlier content. They were undoubtedly patriarchal, but they also contained the seeds of the challenge, or antidote, to this patriarchal poison....

It is clear, I think, that the best moral theory has to be a cooperative product of women and men, has to harmonize justice and care. The morality it theorizes about is after all for all persons, for men and for women, and will need their combined insights.

Annette Baier, "The Need for More Than Justice," Canadian Journal of Philosophy, supplementary vol. 13, ed. Marshal Hanen and Kai Nielsen (Calgary: University of Calgary Press, 1988), pp. 41–56.

Reading 9-4   What Is Feminist Ethics? | Hilde Lindemann

Study Questions

As you read the excerpt, please consider the following questions:

1. What does Lindemann mean when she claims that feminism is about power and gender?
2. What does it mean to say that gender is a norm and not a natural fact?
3. What are the two moral commitments of feminism, according to Lindemann?

My own view is that feminism isn't—at least not directly—about equality, and it isn't about women, and it isn't about difference. It's about power. Specifically, it's about the social pattern, widespread across cultures and history, that distributes power asymmetrically to favor men over women. This asymmetry has been given many names, including the subjugation of women, sexism, male dominance, patriarchy, systemic misogyny, phallocracy, and the oppression of women. A number of feminist theorists simply call it gender, and ... I will too.

Most people think their gender is a natural fact about them, like their hair and eye color.... But gender is a *norm*, not a fact. It's a prescription for how people are supposed to act; what they must or must not wear;

how they're supposed to sit, walk, or stand; what kind of person they're supposed to marry; what sorts of things they're supposed to be interested in or good at; and what they're entitled to. And because it's an *effective* norm, it creates the differences between men and women in these areas.

Gender doesn't just tell women to behave one way and men another, though. It's a *power* relation, so it tells men that they're entitled to things that women aren't supposed to have, and it tells women that they are supposed to defer to men and serve them. It says, for example, that men are supposed to occupy positions of religious authority and women are supposed to run the church suppers. It says that mothers are supposed to take care of their children but fathers have more important things to do. And it says that the things associated with femininity are supposed to take a back seat to the things that are coded masculine....

Gender, then, is about power. But it's not about the power of just one group over another. Gender always interacts with other social markers—such as race, class, level of education, sexual orientation, age,

religion, physical and mental health, and ethnicity—to distribute power unevenly among women positioned differently in the various social orders, and it does the same to men....

Feminist ethics is *normative* as well as descriptive. It's fundamentally about how things ought to be.... Feminist ethicists differ on a number of normative issues, but as the philosopher Alison Jaggar has famously put it, they all share two moral commitments: "that the subordination of women is morally wrong and that the moral experience of women is worthy of respect." The first commitment—that women's interests ought not systematically to be set in the service of men's—can be understood as a moral challenge to power under the guise of gender. The second commitment—that women's experience must be taken seriously—can be understood as a call to acknowledge how that power operates. These twin commitments are the two normative legs on which any feminist ethics stands.

Hilde Lindemann, *Invitation to Feminist Ethics* (New York: McGraw-Hill, 2006), pp. 2–3, 6–16.c.

Review Exercises

1. What is feminism and how is it related to philosophical inquiries into sex and gender?

2. What are some limitations of traditional approaches to ethics when viewed from the vantage point of feminism?

3. Identify and explain some supposed differences between masculine and feminine ethical perspectives, as articulated by Carol Gilligan's work.

4. How is Carol Gilligan's work to be understood in relation to the work of Lawrence Kohlberg or Freud?

5. What are the basic features of the ethics of care?

6. What criticisms of care ethics have been articulated by feminists?

7. What is the primary focal point of the so-called first wave of feminism, and who are some of its key thinkers?

8. What is the significance of intersectionality for feminism, and how is it related to the critical perspective provided by an author such as bell hooks?

9. How do issues involving trans persons and the queer theory of Judith Butler connect to the concerns of feminism?

10. What are some of the concerns feminists might have about pornography, violence against women, and economic inequality?

Knowledge Check Answer Key

1. **c.** Feminism can be described as a critical theory of patriarchal ideas and social structures.

2. **d.** A focus on impartiality is not typical of the "caring" (or feminine) approach to ethics.

3. **a.** Aristotle and other traditional moral theorists tended to neglect women and devalue the female perspective.

4. **a.** Sex is biological, while gender is cultural.

10 Health Care Ethics

Learning Outcomes

After reading this chapter, you should be able to:

10.1 Describe basic topics and methods of studying bioethics.

10.2 Discuss the philosophical complexity of "health."

10.3 Describe how basic principles of bioethics show up in codes and institutions.

10.4 Explain how autonomy applies in thinking about advance directives and paternalism.

10.5 Explain how beneficence might be applied in evaluating cosmetic surgery.

10.6 Evaluate the opioid epidemic using the concept of non-maleficence.

10.7 Apply the concept of justice to the problem of rationing health care.

10.8 Defend a thesis about the right to health care.

10.9 Critically evaluate ethical issues involved in the COVID-19 pandemic.

COVID-19 Pandemic, Masking, and Vaccine Mandates

At the end of 2019, a novel coronavirus appeared in Wuhan, China, that caused pneumonia-like respiratory symptoms. By March 2020, the World Health Organization (WHO) declared that the disease known as COVID-19 had become a pandemic.[1] Human societies took radical steps to prevent the spread of a disease that had killed over 6.5 million people globally by the end of the summer of 2022.[2] Businesses closed, travel was restricted, and schools began teaching online. In some parts of the world, there was a near total quarantine. In other

JEFF DEAN/AFP/Getty Images

places, people were required to wear masks and engage in "social distancing." Vaccines were developed and made available toward the end of 2020, becoming widely available in 2021. Some institutions required vaccination. Throughout this period, there was substantial backlash against these public health efforts. Businesses pushed back against the disruption of shutdowns. Parents and students complained about online schooling and mask mandates. And a number of people simply refused to get vaccinated.

Proponents of proactive public health measures argued that vaccinations and other steps were necessary to save lives. Critics complained about violations of their liberty. And people worried about the negative consequences of shutdowns including economic impacts, the loss of learning, and loneliness and despair. In the background were disinformation and polarization regarding the science of preventing and predicting disease. Different nations and American states made different choices in responding to the pandemic, which caused further confusion. The disease continued to spread and the virus mutated. By May 2022, there were one million deaths from COVID-19 in the United States.[3] A study published that month estimated that nearly half of COVID-19 deaths could have been prevented if 100 percent of adults had been quickly and fully vaccinated.[4] As this public health crisis was unfolding, ethicists debated whether vaccinations should be mandatory and whether the societal response to COVID-19 was morally justifiable.

What Do You Think?

1. How should society balance the concern for liberty with the desire to promote public health?

2. Should people be forced to get vaccinated in a pandemic or to wear a mask?

3. Who should be in charge of public health: cities, states, or federal/international agencies?

4. Do individuals have a personal obligation to take steps to prevent spreading disease?

Introduction

10.1 Describe basic topics and methods of studying bioethics.

In the first half of this book, we looked at ethical theory including metaethical problems and a variety of normative theories. In the second half of the book, we consider concrete problems in applied ethics. In these chapters, we will apply different normative theories to specific cases. As we'll see in each case, the details matter. But we can also formulate general approaches and conclusions based on common themes.

In this chapter, we'll discuss health care ethics. This chapter is connected to the next one, where we consider abortion and euthanasia, and to the one that immediately follows, where we look at other biotechnologies such as cloning, genetic screening, enhancement technologies, and so on. In general, these three chapters can be considered under the general idea of "bioethics." **Bioethics** is the application of ethical judgment to topics involving life and living things. This includes issues in health care and medicine (which we discuss in this chapter), as well as issues arising in thinking about birthing and dying (which we consider in the next). Bioethics also involves ethical questions about our use of technology to tinker with, fix, enhance, and engineer living things (Chapter 12). Bioethics can also include other issues involving nonhuman animals—such as the question of using animal experimentation in biomedical research. It may also extend to include concern for environmental ethics. We consider the nonhuman world in much more detail in the last two chapters of the book (Chapters 19 and 20).

Our focus in this chapter is ethical issues that arise in thinking about human health, broadly construed. Sometimes this field of inquiry is referred to as medical ethics. These two terms—health care and medicine—are sometimes viewed as synonyms. But for our purposes here, we will understand health care as the very broad concern for human health. This includes public health measures and preventative care as well as therapeutic care.

As you can see, *care* is an idea that is central to this topic. We discussed "care ethics" (or "the ethics of care") in Chapter 4 in connection with altruism and a relational approach to ethics; and in Chapter 9, we also considered the idea in connection with feminism and a "feminine" approach to morality. One of the important features of care ethics is found in the relationship between caregiver and cared-for. This relationship is unique in each case.

You will understand the point if you have ever been a caregiver or someone cared-for. In the first case, say, when caring for a sick or injured person, you understand that what matters are the changing needs, interests, and experiences of the person in need of care. And in the second case, when being cared for, you might recognize how unique and complicated these relationships are, involving all kinds of social and psychological issues—from feelings of gratitude and resentment to complex relationships of dependence and mutuality. A central question of care ethics is about what those relationships should look like. And often the answer, in specific cases, is "it depends."

When we focus on the details of particular cases, we are engaged in what some scholars call **casuistry**. This term is associated with medieval moral reasoning, and sometimes it is viewed as little more than sophistry—as a process of quibbling over minor details. But casuistry is basically an approach to moral reasoning that employs practical reasoning to resolve case studies. The root of the term "casuistry" is "case." A case study–based approach to thinking about things begins with the details of the case. The case is then considered in relationship with other similar cases. Paradigms are examined and analogies are employed. Basic principles and larger ideas may be appealed to. And the point is to come up with some reasonable conclusion about the specific case. We will engage in a quite a bit of case study analysis in the second half of the book. As you will see, there are case studies discussed throughout these chapters. And each chapter concludes with some cases and examples that you can discuss and consider. You may have engaged in this kind of reasoning in other areas of study. The case study approach is quite common, for example, in business and in discussions of business ethics.

One worry about an overemphasis on case studies, however, is that we can end up stuck in the immediacy of the details. Another worry is that an approach that is focused entirely on the details of specific cases does not tell us how to resolve dilemmas or what to do when our intuitions about a given case conflict. Indeed, one worry is that an overemphasis on case studies leaves our intuitions intact without critically questioning them. Thus,

we might reach decisions based on prejudice, ignorance, or misinformed judgment. Furthermore, by focusing too much on the details, we may fail to look for larger patterns, and this may prevent us from thinking critically about larger principles.

In other words, an approach to health care ethics that is entirely focused on the concrete needs of those who are cared for and the specific details of individual cases seems too narrow. We should also wonder whether there are general themes and principles that should be understood and applied in thinking about health care. We might then apply basic normative theories to the topic. This application may begin with the distinction between consequentialist and non-consequentialist approaches to ethics. Consequentialist theories such as utilitarianism will be concerned with promoting good outcomes. The basic idea of utilitarianism is to cultivate the greatest happiness for the greatest number of people. When applied to health care, this idea can help us respond to questions about who should be cared for and how much. This approach can help us, for example, think about how we can best distribute medical resources. On the other hand, a non-consequentialist approach may focus our attention on questions about rights, autonomy, and respect. These kinds of values may impose limits on what we might do in pursuit of good outcomes. From this standpoint, we might say that health care ethics should be guided—and limited—by the need to respect the wishes and best interests of those we care for. Thus, consent is an important idea in health care ethics: treatments and therapies can only be administered if the patient agrees to them.

We might also use the language of rights to discuss health care. Some will say that health care is a fundamental right and that society has an obligation to provide for that right. The Constitution of the World Health Organization maintains, for example:

Health is a state of complete physical, mental and social well-being and not merely the absence of disease or infirmity. The enjoyment of the highest attainable standard of health is one of the fundamental rights of every human being without distinction of race, religion, political belief, economic or social condition.[5]

Of course, it is one thing to state that people have a right to complete physical, mental, and social well-being, and it is another to connect that to policies and procedures in the messy world of actual health care. Does this mean that everyone has a right to any health care procedure they want, even if it is dangerous and expensive? We will return to the question of rights below.

Defining Health

10.2 Discuss the philosophical complexity of "health."

Now let's pause to consider the WHO's definition of health as a state of complete physical, mental, and social well-being. This definition of health appears to be bland and uncontroversial, as well as overly broad and unattainable. When has any person or society ever experienced a state of complete physical, mental, and social well-being? It turns out that "health" is a complex normative concept or ideal that opens the door to complex philosophical, social, and ethical questions. What exactly is complete physical, mental and social well-being? That conception is quite broad. It might include a variety of disparate issues: access to clean drinking water, remedies for food insecurity, suicide prevention, campaigns to end smoking, obesity reduction, and even public safety measures such as gun control or anti-poverty policies, and so on. It makes sense to speak of "social health" or "a healthy economy." But how are these things related to problems like sore throats and stomachaches? Furthermore, any idea of "well-being" likely includes a variety of normative assumptions about what counts as a good and valuable life. Jonathan Metzl, a psychiatrist, points out that health "is a term replete with value judgments, hierarchies, and blind assumptions that speak as much about power and privilege as they do about well-being. Health is a desired state, but it is also a prescribed state and an ideological position."[6] Consider one of the examples that Metzl and other authors included in his book *Against Health* discuss to make his point, our image of what an ideal body should look like. There has been what Kathleen LeBesco describes as a "fat panic" associated with

Christopher Lane/Contour by Getty Images

Figure 10-1 How do we measure health?

the so-called "obesity epidemic."[7] It is true that obesity can be linked to health problems. But is our obsession with lean bodies and our fear of fat really about health; or is it about something else, maybe aesthetics, sex, marketing, or some other value that is not really about health? The point is this: our determination of what counts as a healthy body will include a variety of judgments and values that go beyond some simple, objective determination of health and well-being.

In this chapter, we will not focus on economic or social health, although we will discuss economic and social issues in passing. Instead, we will focus more narrowly on physical health, while also considering mental health. But even if we focus on physical health, things become complicated. With regard to physical health, we might wonder, for example, what exactly counts as healthy or sick. This connects to what we consider as a disability or disease. Is color-blindness a disease? Is nearsightedness or myopia a disability? And what about presbyopia, the inability to focus on near objects, that typically occurs in old age? And how do those syndromes compare to total blindness? There is a spectrum of abilities and disabilities. And some things that may seem to be a disease or disability may in fact be "normal." Presbyopia is normal and natural: it is normal for adults to need reading glasses in their forties or fifties. It turns out, the idea of what counts as "normal" or "normal function"—important ideas in thinking about health—is somewhat variable and depends on a variety of circumstances. And what is normal in terms of abilities (and in evaluating disabilities) also depends on the values and structures of the social world. In a world that ignores the difference between red and green, color-blindness may not even be noticed. In a world where people typically died before reaching fifty years old (as they did until a few hundred years ago), presbyopia would be a rare condition. And if your social world did not require reading or working with close/near objects, presbyopia would be irrelevant. On the other hand, in a world that has braille and computers that can read texts out loud, blindness may be less disabling than it would be in a world without those technologies.

Of course, it would be easier if health were a simple fact that is objective and measurable. It might be convenient if the numbers on a scale could tell exactly how healthy we are. But numbers are subject to interpretation. Is two hundred pounds a lot or a little, when it comes to weight, healthy or unhealthy? Well, that depends, doesn't it? Other objective measures might be suggested. Perhaps we might attempt to measure health in terms of longevity. But is a society in which people live to sixty-five a healthy one—or should we aspire to have everyone live to be 100? How do we determine the right age? And what if we are able to keep 80- and 90-year-old people alive, but their quality of life is severely diminished? And how do we measure *quality of life*, anyway? The point here is that health cannot be reduced to some simple set of objective measurements. Health also involves qualitative evaluation and context-dependent interpretation. Of course, we are familiar with the idea of measuring health in numerical terms. In addition to being weighed, when you go to the doctor, you also have your temperature taken. When your temperature is above a certain point (typically 98.6 degrees Fahrenheit), you have fever and are sick. But even this simple measurement of temperature needs interpretation

and context. A woman's temperature varies throughout her menstrual cycle, and these variations can be used to determine fertility. There is also a circadian rhythm (daily variation) to human temperature: our temperatures tend to be lower in the middle of the night, for example. More complex phenomena are subject to more complicated interpretations about what is healthy. Let's return to the question of weight. Is it healthy to be above or below a certain number of pounds? Wrestlers, bodybuilders, and fashion models lose weight intentionally. Religious devotees and political prisoners may also engage in fasts and hunger strikes. But is this healthy? And how do we distinguish that kind of weight loss from eating disorders that are classified as diseases such as anorexia nervosa or bulimia?

At some point, physiological occurrences are subject to social, cultural, and moral interpretation and judgment. In Chapter 3, we discussed the issue of "cultural competence" in health care and how diverse cultures may approach different "diseases." The example discussed in Chapter 3 involved culturally divergent understandings of what was going on in the case of a Hmong girl with epilepsy. As discussed in Anne Fadiman's book *The Spirit Catches You and You Fall Down*, in the culture of the girl's parents, epilepsy was viewed as a spiritual disorder; the doctors treating the girl viewed it as a medical problem. This spiritual understanding of epilepsy is not unique to the Hmong culture described in Fadiman's book. In the European tradition, epilepsy was often thought to be the result of witchcraft or demonic possession. One recent study has suggested that Socrates may have suffered from epilepsy, attributing the "sign" or voice that he heard in his head and his tendency to fall into a trance to a mild kind of nonconvulsive temporal lobe seizure.[8] Science, culture, and religion intertwine in thinking about disease and health, which is why cultural competence is an important feature of medical care.

The questions raised in connection with the idea of cultural competence are especially complicated and controversial with regard to mental health, sexuality, and gender. Consider, for example, issues involving sexuality. In the middle of the twentieth century, "homosexuality" was considered to be a mental disorder and listed as such in the *Diagnostic and Statistical*

Manual of Mental Disorders of the American Psychiatric Association (APA). But in the 1970s and '80s, the mental health establishment revised its understanding of sexuality and came to view "sexual orientation" as involving a variety of identities that lie on a spectrum. This change in medical understanding may seem like the distant past for students in the twenty-first century. But some religions continue to view homosexuality as a disorder that needs to be cured by so-called "conversion therapy." The APA maintains (in a policy statement from 2018) that conversion therapy is unethical.[9] A similar and related conversation is ongoing with regard to transgender rights. States such as Texas, Alabama, Arkansas, and Arizona have banned certain "gender-affirming" procedures for children under eighteen. The former governor of Arizona, Doug Ducey, explained that he signed legislation as a "common-sense" measure intended to delay "any irreversible gender reassignment surgery until the age of 18."[10] Critics of the legislation claimed that it "would harm transgender youth for whom age-appropriate, gender-affirming care is medically necessary."[11] Behind the political debate is a question about what counts as reasonable and medically necessary health care—and what counts as health.

As we conclude this discussion, consider how complicated the question of health becomes when we think about it from the standpoint of public health. One value from the standpoint of public health is "health optimization," finding a balance that promotes the best or optimal health for the most people. But it turns out that this depends on what we mean by health. During the COVID-19 pandemic, there was a vigorous debate about what kind of response was needed, and this debate involved disputes about what were the most important values. For many, the crucial goal was to prevent the disease from killing people, especially those with vulnerable immune systems and "comorbidities" (i.e., elderly people, people with disabilities, and others such as patients undergoing chemotherapy). In an effort to prevent the disease from spreading and killing people, there were widespread "shutdowns." Schools and businesses went online, public events were cancelled, travel was discouraged, and so on. But critics of shutdowns argued that there were health risks from the shutdowns

including economic collapse, loss of learning, and mental health disorders caused by loneliness and dislocation. The debate between opponents and proponents of shutdowns was often about what counts as public health (at least when it was not merely a political shouting match). In pursuit of public health, should we focus our attention primarily on preventing contagious diseases from spreading? Should we also be worried about economic issues? Or mental health issues? Or education? And we might wonder whether our focus should be on those who are most vulnerable or on the well-being of those who are less vulnerable. This reminds us that "health" and health care are complex topics that are in need of careful and critical thought.

Basic Principles and Codes of Bioethics

10.3 Describe how basic principles of bioethics show up in codes and institutions.

Let's return to the question of using case studies in bioethics. It seems that it is insufficient simply to focus on the details of cases. In order to promote critical thought that is not lost in those details, scholars have explained the kinds of basic principles that may be appealed to in thinking about ethics in health care. A variety of values and lists of basic principles have been described and articulated in thinking about bioethics and health care. In this section, we will consider some lists of principles and codes that have been proposed as guides for ethics in health care.

The idea that doctors and researchers need ethical guidance is an ancient one. Among the most famous documents in the history of medicine is the Hippocratic oath, a text associated with the ancient Greek physician Hippocrates. Ancient doctors swore this oath, in the name of Apollo, Asclepius, and other healing gods, promising that they would practice medicine ethically. A physician who swore the Hippocratic oath promised not to cause abortion, not to practice euthanasia, to avoid sexual relations with patients, and to keep information in confidence. (Of course, we continue to debate the ethics of abortion and euthanasia, as we will discuss in much more detail in the next chapter.) One idea associated with the Hippocratic oath is the idea of avoiding harm. The phrase *primum non nocere* (first, do no harm) is connected with the oath and with the practice of ancient medicine. This phrase and the very idea of a professional oath are a reminder that the knowledge possessed by doctors and other health care professionals can be dangerous. Those who know how to cure injury or disease may also know how to cause these things. The double-sided nature of medicine is found in another ancient symbol of the medicinal arts, *the caduceus.*[12] The caduceus is a staff with two serpents intertwined about it. You may have seen this symbol on a badge, emblem, or sign. Sometimes the staff has wings. Sometimes there is only one snake. But the meaning is fairly obvious. Snakes are venomous. They can be dangerous. But in the caduceus the snakes are tamed and turned to good use. The symbolic idea is that the physician's knowledge must also be turned in the right direction. This is why the idea "first, do no harm" is central. Oaths, codes, and legal regulations exist in order to make sure that health care professionals use their knowledge for good purposes.

With this reference to the ancient Greeks in mind, it is worth noting that there has always been a significant connection between medicine and philosophy. Socrates often made arguments that employed medical analogies. For example, he once suggested that what we ultimately need is a "physician of the soul" who can help us figure out the difference between good and evil.[13] And he described the practice of philosophy as a kind of midwifery that helps us give birth to truth, knowledge, and virtue.[14] The philosophical inquiry into good and evil, virtue and knowledge, has obvious implications for the question of what counts as health, as discussed above and for how we understand and construct codes of ethics that govern health care.

Leaving the ancient world behind, let's consider more recent developments. One influential document meant to guide bioethical practice is "The Belmont Report." This document was produced in the United States in the 1970s by the National Commission for the Protection of Human Subjects of Biomedical and Behavioral Research. Three values are highlighted in the report: respect for persons, beneficence, and justice.[15] Respect for persons focuses on issues such as consent, in accord with

©Stock Montage/Getty Images

Figure 10-2 Hippocrates (ca. 460–377 BCE) was a Greek physician, known as the "father of medicine."

the basic idea that the autonomy of persons should be respected; and that people with "diminished autonomy" should be afforded special protection. Beneficence includes both working toward the well-being of people and protecting people from harm. Justice is focused on fair and equitable distributions of harms and benefits (including an awareness of past injustices). Other statements, declarations, and international agreements have proposed other related versions of bioethical principles. For example, the Helsinki Declaration was adopted by the World Medical Association in the 1960s and updated most recently in 2013.

Some of these documents and codes emerge as a response to atrocities and ethical failures. The Helsinki Declaration has been described as an attempt to respond to the atrocities committed by Nazi doctors during the Second World War. It built on a prior document, the Nuremburg Code, that developed out of the Nazi war crimes tribunals after the war. That document emphasizes, for example, the importance of informed consent for participation in biomedical experiments. One of the most basic principles of the Nuremberg Code is the idea of voluntary, uncoerced, and informed consent. The Code explains:

> The voluntary consent of the human subject is absolutely essential. This means that the person involved should have legal capacity to give consent; should be situated as to be able to exercise free power of choice, without the intervention of any element of force, fraud, deceit, duress, over-reaching, or other ulterior form of constraint or coercion, and should have sufficient knowledge and comprehension of the elements of the subject matter involved as to enable him to make an understanding and enlightened decision.[16]

Implied in this principle is the belief that persons are autonomous, and that autonomy ought to be respected and protected even if it means that we cannot do certain types of research on people that may seem to be beneficial. And implicit in this is the idea that there may be some people in some situations who are not freely able to consent—prisoners, for example, or people with disabilities.

It is worth noting the kinds of atrocities that Nazi doctors like the notorious Josef Mengele were involved in, as a reminder and a warning of how things can go terribly wrong in the world of bioethics. Nazi doctors were involved in mass sterilizations as well as a variety of unethical experimentation including procedures done without anesthesia. Ultimately, some doctors participated in or facilitated the project of mass murder in the death camps—a practice that was used against vulnerable populations (e.g., people with disabilities) and was described as "euthanasia" and connected to the idea of eugenics. This project turned genocidal and the machinery of murder was turned against racial and ethnic groups that were deemed unfit to live. Six million Jews were killed in this fit of anti-Semitic atrocity. Josef Mengele and a staff of other doctors were part of the group that chose who would live and die during the "selection" process at the concentration camp Auschwitz. Mengele evaded capture and fled to South America after the war. Other doctors were captured and put on trial as war criminals. Some were executed.

The case of the Nazi doctors is among the most notorious in history. It is a sobering reminder of the double-sided nature of medicine—and of the need for ethical and legal regulation of health care. Other atrocities have also prompted the medical and scholarly community to reassess their ethical framework and commitments. The Belmont Report was created, in part, as a response to the notorious Tuskegee Syphilis Experiment.

Between 1932 and 1972, experiments were conducted in Tuskegee, Alabama, in which 390 poor and illiterate Black men who had syphilis were followed in order to determine the progress of the disease, whether it was always fatal, and how it was spread. The researchers even failed to give the men penicillin treatment for syphilis when it became available in the early 1940s. The study was ended in 1972 when it became public and a source of major controversy. These men had not been treated with respect but had been exploited and used for the purpose of obtaining information. Moreover, they were taken advantage in the context of racial inequalities. The experiment was condemned as racist. And it became clear that the American medical establishment needed ethical guidance actions. The Belmont Report was one response.

As we've mentioned here, one significant issue is that it is possible to take advantage of and exploit vulnerable people—prisoners, racial minorities, children, people with disabilities, elderly people, and so on. This

Figure 10-3 The Tuskegee Syphilis experiment is widely viewed as an example of unethical research.

National Archives and Records Administration

kind of exploitation seems especially egregious if we believe that the heart of health care is care for those who are vulnerable. The Helsinki Declaration makes that clear, stating: "Some groups and individuals are particularly vulnerable and may have an increased likelihood of being wronged or of incurring additional harm. All vulnerable groups and individuals should receive specifically considered protection."[17] The Helsinki Declaration, the Nuremburg Code, and the Belmont Report are documents that specifically address the question of bioethical research, that is, research involving human subjects. These days, there is extensive training for those who are doing such research. Universities that do that kind of research will have an Institutional Review Board (IRB) that supervises and approves research protocols. And training is required even for students who are assisting on research projects. If you are a student in the biosciences or in psychology or some other field that does human subjects research, you will likely encounter the codes and documents we've discussed here when you are trained in the ethics of this kind of research. And while the IRB supervises such research, there is another body that supervises research involving nonhuman animals, often called the Institutional Animal Care and Use Committee (IACUC). We will not discuss animal research in the present chapter, but we take it up again in Chapter 20 within a larger consideration of animal welfare and animal rights concerns.

The basic ideas and principles outlined in these documents are also more broadly applicable to issues in health care. Obviously, there is a connection between biomedical research and medicine and health care: research is used to study disease and test therapeutic responses. But health care also involves hands-on treatment of sick and injured people, as well as preventive care, and more broadly public health projects. There may be some differences between the field of human subjects research and the application of that research in specific cases. Consider, for example, the different kinds of interests and obligations that might arise in thinking about the case of vaccinations during a pandemic. First, researchers will begin developing vaccines in labs. They may use animal models (supervised by an IACUC). Then at some point, they will want to test their vaccine in humans (research that would be supervised by an IRB).

The vaccine would then need to be approved by a government agency such as the Food and Drug Administration. And then when the vaccine becomes available, it will need to be administered by doctors, nurses, and clinics, who have an obligation to care for their patients. There may also be public health infrastructure such as the national Centers for Disease Control and Prevention (in the United States) and also state-level public health agencies, who may have a slightly different set of obligations involving maximizing distributions of vaccine and ensuring that vulnerable populations are well served. At each level there are ethical questions and concerns. And, as mentioned, the focal point of ethical concern may shift as we move from one part of the process to the next.

So far, we have discussed several basic principles that emerge out of the codes and agreements governing biomedical research: respect for persons, beneficence, justice, care for the vulnerable, and a concern that public health officials are fairly distributing and maximizing public health outcomes. Scholars have suggested various lists of bioethical principles. One such influential list has been provided by Tom Beauchamp and James Childress, who add non-maleficence to the values listed in the Belmont Report.[18] Non-maleficence is the idea of "doing no harm." They thus suggest four main values: autonomy, beneficence, non-maleficence, and justice. Other lists expand on these ideas in various ways. We've seen that informed consent is an important idea, which may be connected to respect for autonomy. Respect for persons could also be expanded to plausibly include confidentiality or privacy, as well as honesty. Others might suggest adding a principle such as health optimization for individuals (focused on helping people live the longest and healthiest lives possible) or health maximization when thinking about public health (focused on making sure that the population is as healthy as can be).[19] In the case of health maximization, we might describe this as utilitarian concern for "general welfare."

We will consider these values in more detail in what follows. But let's pause to note that these principles are offered, in part, as a way to explain or apply the key values found in the different normative theories that we discussed in the first part of this book. Utilitarian

Table 10-1 Basic Principles of Health Care Ethics

Autonomy	Concern to protect people's right to choose and freedom from coercion; connected with the practice of obtaining voluntary, informed consent and with the virtue of honesty in health care
Beneficence	Concern to provide beneficial care to individuals that is in the best interest of the person cared for; could become paternalistic if beneficence occurs without consent
Non-Maleficence	Concern to avoid causing harm ("do no harm"); imposes a limit on harmful and risky procedures
Distributive Justice	Concern to distribute the benefits of health care across populations; may include addressing inequalities in health and access to health care
Human Rights	Concern to respect and support human rights in health care; associated with the claim that people have a right (or are entitled) to health care
Health Maximization	Utilitarian concern to promote the greatest health for the greatest number of people; typically, a focus of public health policies
Care for the Vulnerable	Focus on the special needs of those who are most vulnerable; connected with the "ethics of care" and care for those who are dependent, disabled, lacking in autonomy, or otherwise vulnerable

theories are focused on producing good outcomes—and can thus be linked to the value of beneficence as well as the idea of health maximization. Care ethics is also obviously concerned with beneficence, while focusing on relationships of dependence and care. Kantian deontology emphasizes respect for persons. The natural law theory can be used to support respect for the rights of persons. Throughout these theories there are concerns for justice such as fairness, equality, and equitable distribution of goods. And virtue ethics traditions typically include ideas such as honesty among the list of key virtues.

In work in applied ethics generally, there is an ongoing conversation about which theories to apply in specific cases, how these principles apply, and what we ought to do when there is a conflict of duties or commitments. We will see this process unfold in each of the chapters in the rest of this book. One way to describe this process is to suggest that we find ourselves with lists of "prima facie" duties. These are values that are duties "on the face of it" or at first appearance, which is taken to mean that each is valuable but they may in some cases conflict. We discussed this idea in connection with the work of the philosopher W. D. Ross in

prior chapters. As we discussed in Chapter 3, Ross provides us with a list of several prima facie duties: fidelity, reparation, gratitude, beneficence, non-maleficence, justice, and self-improvement. Some of the values in this list overlap with values discussed in bioethics. No matter what list we come up with, the challenge is what we do when there is a conflict of values, that is, when prima facie values come into conflict with one another.

Let's make this concrete and return to the case of pandemic restrictions and vaccination requirements. On the one hand, we might think that respect for autonomy means that individuals should be respected in their right to choose or not choose to be vaccinated or to wear a mask. But autonomy is not the only value. Beneficence might push us in the direction of requiring a mask or vaccination for the good of the person who is being required to get a shot or wear a mask. We may also be concerned with something like health maximization, when we consider the issue from the standpoint of public health, and conclude that masks and vaccines should be required not only for the good of the individual but also because of a concern for general welfare. We might also be especially concerned with the health impacts of the pandemic on the most vulnerable people—elderly people or people with other underlying diseases, disabilities, and comorbidities—and so encourage vaccines and masking for the good of those vulnerable people.

As you can see in this example, the application of these principles does not necessarily provide us with a definitive answer. It turns out there are different kinds of answers that emerge from the application of these various kinds of principles. We'll see that this kind of pluralistic or open-ended result is often found in the applied ethics challenges we discuss here. Some students of ethics may despair at this point, thinking that what we discover here is that there are no answers. But that skeptical and despairing conclusion can be tempered by the following insight. It is difficult to come to a final conclusion about these topics because these things are quite complicated; but it seems fairly obvious that some answers are simply wrong and cannot be justified in light of the values and principles we are discussing here. It would be wrong, for example, to kidnap people and use them in experimental vaccine research. There is universal agreement that the Nazi medical experiments were evil and that the Tuskegee Syphilis Experiment was racist and wrong. The good news is that there is broad consensus among the professional bioethics community in condemning these sorts of unethical research projects. But there are remaining challenges. These challenges include contemporary cases of unfair treatment and inequities in health care. And there are many cases in which we have conflicting goods and genuine moral dilemmas.

A dilemma occurs when there are two good things in conflict with one another. For example, there may be a conflict between the value of honesty and the value of beneficence. Imagine a case in which a medical professional or caregiver knows information but considers withholding it for the sake of the patient. Perhaps they worry that they may cause the patient to panic if they disclose that information. This is a genuine dilemma insofar as it involves a conflict of two important values. It is worth noting that sometimes in moral reasoning in ordinary life, we may think there is a dilemma when actually there is not. Rushworth Kidder pointed out, in his book *How Good People Make Tough Choices*, that there is an important difference between a *dilemma* (which he calls a "right v. right" situation) and a

temptation (which is a "right v. wrong" situation).[20] With a temptation, we know (or ought to know) what the right answer is, but we are tempted by the wrong answer. Let's imagine a different case in which the caregiver withholds key information because they want to manipulate the patient for selfish reasons. Perhaps they want the patient to have an expensive and unnecessary surgical procedure in order to profit from it. Here we have an immoral situation that is not an actual dilemma. It is not a dilemma when we are confronted with a choice between informed consent (which is the right thing to do) and taking advantage of a vulnerable person (which is wrong). By clarifying basic principles to be used in moral reasoning, it is easier to see when an actual dilemma occurs—and to distinguish genuine dilemmas from immoral decisions.

As we conclude our discussion of the codes and principles of bioethics, let's consider one further important point about how moral judgment is organized and occurs in the real world of bioethics. We've already mentioned the work of IRBs and IACUCs on university campuses and in research facilities. These organizations are guided by legal regulations and written codes of ethics. It is reassuring to know that there are legal regulations and ethical codes that guide the behavior of researchers, doctors, nurses, clinics, and hospital. These laws and codes provide explicit guidelines in many cases. Health care establishments typically require training, certification, and ongoing education in ethics. And most organizations have ethics committees that are consulted in thinking about challenging cases. Typically, the members of a hospital ethics committee will include doctors, nurses, social workers, lawyers, clergy (in religious hospitals), and maybe even a philosopher with expertise in biomedical ethics. These committees function in ways that are similar to what occurs on IRBs and IACUCs—they approve procedures and protocols and provide consultation when difficult and complex ethical decisions must be made. Again, in the background of those decisions and consultations is a code of ethics. In some cases, codes of ethics include a punitive component. Doctors or nurses who violate the codes can be sanctioned by the professional organizations to which they belong. There are also legal requirements and the possibility of criminal and civil liability.

Codes of ethics are also found in a variety of professions—from journalism to business and the law. There are also committees and regulatory agencies in many fields, as well as professional and legal sanctions that help to "police" ethics in various professions. But in health care settings, the issues are literal matters of life and death, and so the punishments and the nature of judgment can be intense and severe. Society has an interest in regulating the medical establishment and ensuring that health care is provided in ethical ways.

Current Issues

And now let's consider each value in turn in a bit more detail, while outlining important ideas and questions connected with each—and applying basic principles to specific cases and contemporary concerns. For our purposes here, we will apply seven key values: autonomy, beneficence, non-maleficence, distributive justice, human rights, as well as health maximization and care for the vulnerable (which we will combine in one section). As we shall see, each of these values involves

some complex questions. And they must be balanced with one another in thinking about cases and controversies. Among the cases we will discuss here are issues related to: paternalism and informed consent, advance directives, cosmetic surgery, organ donation, opioid addiction, pandemic restrictions, health care insurance, care for the needy, the risk of eugenics, and questions about social justice in health care distributions. The rest of the chapter is divided into sections that consider a key value and apply it to thinking about cases.

Autonomy: Informed Consent, Advance Directives, and Paternalism

10.4 Explain how autonomy applies in thinking about advance directives and paternalism.

Autonomy focuses our attention on the importance of self-rule, self-control, self-regulation, and self-determination. This is a central idea in Kantian approaches to ethics.[21] Kant emphasized the importance

---

► **Knowledge Check**   Answers appear at the end of the chapter.

1. Which of the following is *not* typically a consideration of bioethics?

   a. Moral questions arising in the context of clinical medical practice

   b. Moral questions about how to grow the economy and share wealth

   c. Moral questions about how to promote and maximize public health

   d. Moral questions about how human subjects are used in research

2. The idea of doing no harm (*primum non nocere*) is associated with which of the following?

   a. Autonomy

   b. Utility

   c. The caduceus

   d. Non-maleficence

3. What is the difference between beneficence and health maximization?

   a. Beneficence is focused on the well-being of individual patients, while health maximization is a concern of public health.

   b. Beneficence is concerned with avoiding harm, while health maximization is concerned with increasing health.

   c. Beneficence tells us to support growth and reproduction, while health maximization instructs us to regulate growth and limit reproduction.

   d. Beneficence is focused on consequences, while health maximization is focused on virtues.

4. Informed consent is associated with which value?

   a. Utility

   b. Beneficence

   c. Justice

   d. Autonomy

The Washington Post/The Washington Post/Getty Images

Figure 10-4 The case of Henrietta Lacks indicates some basic problems involving consent.

of rational, free will. He suggested that a human being's capacity for rational autonomy was the source of human dignity and worth. He argued that autonomous rational beings were to be respected as "ends-in-themselves" and not used merely as a means for some instrumental purpose. A related idea can be found in the natural rights and human rights tradition, where it is often explained in terms of a fundamental right to liberty. But utilitarian thinkers, such as John Stuart Mill, also understood liberty as an important social and political value.

As we've mentioned, there are some egregious historical cases in which doctors have blatantly violated the autonomy of patients and research subjects. We might add to our list of violations the case of Henrietta Lacks. Henrietta Lacks was a young Black mother with an aggressive form of cancer. Tissue samples were taken without her consent, which then became widely used in biomedical research. This case exploded into the public mind when a popular book was published in 2010, *The Immortal Life of Henrietta Lacks*. At issue was not only the use of samples from Lacks's body without her

consent but also the fact that she was a Black woman and received treatment in the 1950s during the era of Jim Crow. The cases pointed to social justice concerns about the degree to which women, racial minorities, and poor people are able to access and control their own health care and medical information.

In order to prevent this kind of exploitation, the bioethical principle of autonomy emerged as an important safeguard against exploitation and abuse. In practice, this has become standardized in the idea of informed consent, which is now a central feature of health care ethics. But there are cases and circumstances in which informed consent becomes problematic. One typical problem arises when people lack the education, information, or psychological capacity to rationally decide. This becomes obvious in end-of-life situations involving people with significant cognitive impairment (we'll discuss this further in a moment and in the next chapter). One solution to this problem is found in the use of *advance directives* and *living wills* through which patients express their preferences and wishes in anticipation of a future scenario in which they were to become incapacitated and unable to explicitly consent to care. This is an important feature of contemporary medical practice. Advance directives and living wills are an important component in end-of-life situations and in conversations about euthanasia (as we'll see in the next chapter). And even the "organ donation card" that many people have—even young people—is a kind of advance directive providing consent in advance to have one's organs donated to another in case of death. But advance directives are only useful to the extent that a patient has some such document on file and has discussed their wishes with loved ones. And even if a written declaration exists, there is an open question about whether one can actually predict in advance what one would want.

A related question arises in the context of "ordinary" health care. One wonders whether people are truly informed, rational, and autonomous when making medical decisions. Consider, for example, when you receive a diagnosis and plan for care at the dentist's office. The dentist shows you the x-ray and explains your options. And then you are asked to consent. But how much do you actually know about dentistry? What kind of skill do you have in reading x-rays and evaluating the pros and cons of a care plan? It is also worth considering the circumstances involved when asked to make decisions about care. Pain and anxiety can inhibit rational decision-making. And if you are in a hurry or worried about money, that can also have an impact. When health care decisions are especially complicated and stressful—as in the case of choosing a treatment plan for cancer, for example—the idea of rational, informed, autonomous consent may seem especially problematic. Of course, the health care organization will ask you to sign off on a certain procedure. Care cannot proceed with your "consent." But how autonomous are you, really, when deciding about life-saving treatments?

These kinds of concerns have been brought up from the standpoint of critical theories of ethics and society, which challenge both the very idea of autonomy and the reality of informed consent in social contexts. Some worry that there can be subtle (and not-so-subtle) coercion in the background of our decision-making processes. Consider, for example, a case in which a teenage girl is pressured by her father with regard to an abortion decision. That kind of case directs our attention to at least two different structures of authority, autonomy, power, and value. On the one hand, there is a gender-based issue involving a woman's right to choose and the girl's sense of bodily control. But this case also includes another set of issues involving age and parental authority. Generally, it is the parents who must consent to medical procedures on behalf of their minor children. But such an approach becomes controversial in the case of sexual, psychological, and other health care. And in some states, teenagers do not need parental consent for abortion care. But even if this is true, how autonomous is a teenage girl when facing a reproductive health care crisis that may also involve a crisis in her family life?

In response to these kinds of concerns, one might suggest that autonomy is overrated. In one sense, the doctor knows better than we do what's in our best interest. Consider the dentist case again. The dentist has studied oral health, has viewed hundreds of x-rays, and has treated many patients. Surely the dentist knows better than you do what ought to be done. And if you are anxious, in a hurry, or worried about money, the dentist may be better situated psychologically to make a rational decision about your care. This leads us to the idea of paternalism. **Paternalism** literally means to act like a "father." It implies that "father knows best." That's a metaphor, of course, but the idea is that those with relevant knowledge and expertise are better positioned to make decisions. In political situations, this might also include political power and legal authority to make decisions. Defenders of autonomy will bristle at the idea of paternalism, as it seems to point in the direction of violations of liberty. Critics of the COVID-19 pandemic restrictions often seemed to reject the paternalism of state public health authorities in the name of autonomy.

But paternalism also involves the idea that the expert or authority is taking action in our own best interest. Again, the metaphor of a father can explain this. A good father may restrict his child's liberty—say by enforcing a rule about bedtime or some dietary rule. But the father does not do this in order to harm or exploit his child. Rather, it is intended for the benefit of the child and comes from a perspective of benevolent care that is connected with the fact that the father has more experience and expertise than the child, and is better situated to make good decisions. In some cases, paternalism in health care can be justified in the same way and understood in connection with the basic value of beneficence. This comes up in discussions of honesty and truth telling in medical practice. Informed consent and respect for autonomy point in the direction of full disclosure: to fully consent to care you would need to know the truth. But is truth telling always good? And are doctors (or parents or other paternal figures) ever justified in lying or refusing to divulge information? What if knowing the truth would cause discomfort or anxiety? It is easy to imagine cases of justifiable and benevolent paternalism. Imagine, for example, a case in which nurses restrain and sedate a delusional patient who is trying to remove a respirator or some other life-saving device. Is that kind of case different from a case in which a patient refuses chemotherapy or even asks for assistance in ending their own life (as in the case of physician-assisted suicide, which we discuss in the next chapter)? And how is the restraint of a delusional patient different from the case of mandatory vaccination?

There may be some reason to think that paternalism can be defended in some cases. But there are obvious reasons to be suspicious of paternalism in the context of health care for competent adults. One reason to emphasize autonomy is that it is useful as a strong institutional safeguard that prevents those egregious kinds of cases in which doctors exploit and abuse patients. We also tend to think that individuals have a better sense of who they are, what they value, and how they want to live (and die). In this sense, autonomy is not only about informed consent in particular choices. Rather, it is about the existential condition of having a meaningful life. Autonomy also encourages us to recognize that individuals will bear the burdens of their health care choices. The doctor provides treatment but the patient has to live with the consequences. One useful suggestion for negotiating the apparent conflict between paternalism and autonomy is that health care professionals and patients need to be viewed as partners engaged in a discussion about means and ends. Patients establish their own life choices involving long-term and short-term goals. Health care professionals are experts who understand the best ways to achieve those goals and the costs and benefits of various choices.[22]

Beneficence and Cosmetic Surgery

10.5 Explain how beneficence might be applied in evaluating cosmetic surgery.

Our discussion of paternalism points toward the idea of beneficence. Health care providers are supposed to provide beneficial care. Paternalists might suggest that beneficial care ought to be provided even in cases in which informed consent is lacking (say, to save the life of the patient). And so the principle of beneficence could be used to support paternalism. But the basic focus of beneficence is not paternalism but to ensure that health care is focused primarily on the well-being of the patient. Beneficence is a basic idea connected to altruistic concern for others (as discussed in Chapter 3). The English term comes from Latin roots that literally mean "doing good" (*bene-* means "good" and *-ficus* mean "doing or producing"). It should be familiar to English speakers from the word "benefit." A benefit is something that is good for us. Beneficence thus means that health care should be of benefit for the client or patient. This also means that other concerns (such as the profit or convenience of the physician) are irrelevant. In our account of health care ethics here, we are considering beneficence as a narrowly focused principle that is concerned with doing good for the patient, as distinguished from a utilitarian concern for the greater social good. As mentioned, beneficence may imply the idea of non-maleficence (doing no harm). There is a kind of cost–benefit analysis to be employed in thinking about benefits and harms. In biomedical settings, the idea is that health care professionals should be healing patients and not harming them. And beyond healing, there may also be an idea of preventive care and a holistic approach to health care that aims to provide people with health broadly construed. Thus, in the case of dentistry, a semiannual cleaning and checkup is beneficial since it prevents damage and long-term harm.

This idea seems fairly easy to understand. But a moment's reflection shows that it is not always obvious what counts as beneficial. End-of-life situations come to mind as cases in which it is unclear what counts as beneficent care. Is it to a patient's benefit to be kept alive on artificial life-support machinery, or could there be cases in which death is actually beneficial? We'll discuss that further in the next chapter. Here, let's consider another case that prompts philosophical inquiry, the case of cosmetic surgery (also called aesthetic surgery or plastic surgery). A useful distinction might be made here between *therapy* and *enhancement* (which we discuss in more detail in Chapter 12): therapeutic interventions return people to normal function, while enhancements aim beyond normal function. A therapeutic usage of cosmetic surgery would occur, for example, in the case of reconstructive breast surgery after mastectomy. Women with breast cancer may have all or part of the breast tissue removed (as well as other treatments). And once the cancer is defeated, they may choose to have their breast reconstructed in order to return to a "normal" appearance. It would seem that this could be understood as a beneficial procedure that would count as therapeutic. But what about other cosmetic surgeries? Is nontherapeutic breast augmentation beneficial? And what about the range of other surgeries and procedures that have become popular: from Botox treatments and hair transplants to buttock implants and leg-lengthening surgeries. Leg lengthening involves having your femurs broken and stretched by a process involving a titanium implant that is gradually expanded.[23] The procedure is expensive and painful, but it can help a person gain several inches in height. If a patient requests this surgery and is informed about the risks and the pain, the principle of autonomy would suggest that it is acceptable. But is it really beneficial? Maybe patient satisfaction provides a key to answering this question. If the patient is happy after the procedure, is that enough to make it clear that the procedure is beneficial? And what about steroids for bodybuilders? That can help to produce short-term muscle gain, but it may also cause long-term harm including liver and cardiac damage. But if the user is satisfied and consents to those long-term risks, is that sufficient? One might defend the procedure by focusing on autonomy and patient satisfaction, while still questioning whether it is actually beneficial.

On one very narrow definition of beneficence, as long as the patient is healthy in the immediate aftermath of a procedure, no harm has been done. A somewhat broader focus would take in long-term harms and benefits. But a broader conception of beneficence would also focus on overall well-being including psychological, social, and economic well-being. One significant concern in the literature on the ethics of cosmetic surgery is the problem of psychological problems that are sometimes experienced by those who seek cosmetic surgery, including "body dysmorphic disorder" (BDD). This occurs when people obsessively focus on perceived flaws in their appearance. In our culture, where social media influencers establish standards of beauty, some people will feel pressure to conform to these standards. In some cases, this can even result in an "addiction" to plastic surgery. Some authors suggest that BDD is a "counterindication" for cosmetic surgery. One problem is that if a patient suffers from BDD, the surgical procedure may not actually solve their perception of flawed appearance. They may pursue further surgeries or may seek to retaliate against physicians.[24] This last point is a reminder that there are also self-interested reasons for health care providers to focus on ethical care.

Non-Maleficence and the Opioid Epidemic

10.6 Evaluate the opioid epidemic using the concept of non-maleficence.

Non-maleficence is complementary to beneficence. In one sense, these two concepts inform the idea of a cost–benefit analysis that seeks to establish a balance between harms and benefits. But non-maleficence may also be conceived as a kind of absolute prohibition on causing harm, formulated as the requirement to "do no harm" (*primum non nocere*). As mentioned before, this basic idea is important because the knowledge and expertise possessed by doctors and nurses can be used to deliberately inflict harm. And there are atrocities such as the case of Nazi doctors, where this principle was cruelly ignored. Non-maleficence may simply tell us never to behave in this way and to always avoid inflicting harm. Certainly, non-maleficence would prohibit malicious cruelty. Other cases are less clear-cut. Some beneficial treatments may also cause harm, due to side effects, possible infections, and so on. In those cases, we would probably want to engage in cost–benefit analysis and think about those possible harms in relation to the benefit we are hoping for or expect. This way of balancing the concerns of beneficence and non-maleficence is obviously complex and dependent on tolerance for risk, the degree of certainty of our predictions, and so on. One risk-averse idea would be to err on the side of caution when imposing possible harms. In other contexts, this risk-averse strategy is sometimes referred to as a "precautionary principle." A precautionary principle may suggest avoiding actions that have any risk of causing harm, according to the old adage "better safe than sorry." But there are also risks from being too cautious.

Another concern is negligence. Negligence also causes harm. But negligence is different from malice. In cases of negligence, harm is not deliberately done; rather, the harm results from a kind of non-doing, that is, from neglecting to do something you should have done. One way to explain this application of non-maleficence is to connect it to the idea of "due care." Problems occur when health care professionals are careless and expose people to unnecessary risks. This also occurs in a number of other professional and social settings. An obvious example involves leaving dangerous items (say, a loaded gun or a poison) unprotected and easily accessible. A person who leaves a dangerous item unprotected did not actively do anything to put the gun or poison into the hands of another person. But if a child were to harm themselves with this dangerous object, the person who left that item unprotected has nonetheless contributed to that harm. They were negligent in a duty of due care.

In thinking about non-maleficence, the idea of *harm* is a central concern. This may seem to be an obvious concept with an objective definition. But harm is philosophically complicated. Not all painful things are harmful, for example (as you'll understand if you pause to consider the old adage "no pain, no gain"). Dental work is not pleasant and may cause some pain, but we would not ordinarily describe dentistry as harmful. The definition of harm depends on the circumstance, as well as on the intentions of the agents involved in the action. If a dentist drilled your teeth out of some malicious and sadistic intention to cause pain, that would be harmful: the dentist in such a case would intend to cause you harm for their own selfish purpose. The experience of

the patient also seems to matter. Consider the issue of organ donation. It would ordinarily be harmful to remove an organ from a living body. But in the case of a brain-dead person, organ removal would no longer be considered a harm. One question here is whether the donor had agreed in advance for their organs to be donated to others in such a circumstance. That's a concern we encountered in thinking about autonomy. But if they had not agreed and their organs were harvested anyway (or their cells were used without their consent, as in the case of Henrietta Lacks), there is an interesting question about who exactly would be harmed in such a case. The unwilling donor no longer exists, so how can they be harmed? There is a complex philosophical literature on the topic of "posthumous harm" (i.e., harms that occur after we are dead).[25] But assuming that consent is in place and the donor is brain-dead, we would assume that the donor's body would not be harmed since it will not experience the procedure or feel pain. Or would it? It turns out that the question of whether to administer anesthesia to the bodies of organ donors is subject to an ongoing conversation among medical professionals.[26]

In the next chapter, we will discuss two further controversial issues that involve questions of harm: abortion and euthanasia. With regard to abortion, a significant question is whether a fetus is a kind of being that can be harmed. And at the end of life, it is possible that allowing a patient to die (passive euthanasia) or even actively helping them die (active euthanasia) may not be a situation in which death is understood as harmful. We'll leave these questions here for further discussion in the next chapter.

An interesting conceptual question arises in thinking about non-maleficence as focused on a negative prohibition. Non-maleficence does not tell us what to do; rather, it tells us what to avoid. This may seem straightforward. So, it seems simple enough to say that physicians ought not prescribe medications or surgical procedures that cause harm. But as we saw in the case of cosmetic surgery, the line to be drawn is not always clear. Let's consider another example, in connection with opioid prescriptions. Pain relief would seem to be a fundamental concern of health care. But we also know that drug addiction is a serious problem—and that opioid abuse has become a public health concern. The Centers for Disease Control and Prevention (CDC) reports that there were more than 107,000 deaths from drug overdoses in 2021.[27] These numbers include illicit drugs such as cocaine and methamphetamine. But the largest proportion of those deaths was from opioids such as fentanyl: over 80,000 of those deaths were opioid related. This is not to say that those deaths from opioids were the direct result of medically necessary pain management. But the problem is that some patients will take advantage of health care providers to obtain prescriptions (say, by seeing more than one doctor). There is a resale market for prescription opioids. And there is the risk of addiction, which can lead to a negative cycle and increased risk for overdose death. Thus, health care professionals ought to be focused on the risk of abuse and addiction when prescribing opioids, in accord with the idea of avoiding harm. Indeed, protocols exist that regulate and limit opioid prescriptions with the intention of reducing potential harm. Some critics have worried, however, that in the effort to prevent harm, there may be a tendency to under-prescribe useful pain management drugs. The solution would seem to seek to balance non-maleficence with beneficence: the need to prevent harm must be balanced with the need to provide pain management.[28]

The question of opioid prescriptions erupted into the news in recent years, as a major corporation, Purdue Pharmaceuticals, was sued by a number of states for billions of dollars in damages for contributing to the opioid crisis. Purdue Pharma was the manufacturer of OxyContin, a prescription opioid that was widely abused. The drug company aggressively marketed the drug to doctors, seeking to increase prescriptions—and profits.[29] As a result of the lawsuits, the firm declared bankruptcy in 2019. Scholars have used this example as a case study in non-maleficence.[30] There are larger social questions here about public health and the responsibilities of corporations and institutions involved in the health care industry. But a basic consideration must be non-maleficence: pharmaceutical companies and others involved in the health care industry have a responsibility to reduce or avoid harm and to take steps to mitigate harm when it occurs. Consider another, related example that is often cited in case studies in

business ethics, the case of the Tylenol recall that occurred in 1982. Someone had tampered with Tylenol in the Chicago area, resulting in the poisoning deaths of seven people. Johnson and Johnson, the manufacturer of the drug, voluntarily recalled all Tylenol from store shelves across the country. This resulted in a significant cost to the company. Business ethics textbooks cite this as a case of a corporation taking ethical responsibility in the face of a crisis. The drug company had a responsibility to "do no harm," we might say, and if their product was harming people, they ought to take precautionary steps to stop the harm from occurring. As a result of that case, new drug and product packaging regulations were enacted that prevented tampering. Those kinds of regulations can also be understood from the vantage point of non-maleficence. Food and drug producers have an obligation to ensure that their products are tamperproof as a harm reduction strategy.

Justice, Equity, and Rationing

10.7   Apply the concept of justice to the problem of rationing health care.

As we've discussed, justice is an idea that is found in most codes and sets of principles guiding health care ethics. Justice is, like other ethical concepts, a complicated idea. One important conception of justice tells us that we ought to treat similar cases in similar ways. There is a basic principle of equality involved here, which we will discuss in more detail in Chapter 13. The ideal of treating similar cases in equal or similar ways is linked to an ideal of fairness or impartiality. It would be unfair, for example, if a rich person got better treatment than a poor person—in a hospital, a school, or a court of law. The basic idea is that it is wrong to treat people differently, unless there is some good reason to give them unequal treatment. It is easy to see how this idea of justice would apply in health care settings.

Imagine two patients arriving in the emergency room, each with the same injury but one is rich and the other is poor. It would be unjust of the physician to treat the rich person better than the poor person. A similar conclusion would hold that it would be unjust to provide differential treatment to people based on race, ethnicity, religious affiliation, sexual identity, gender, and so on. The idea of justice can be linked to what we might call "non-discrimination in health care," which aims to provide equitable and unbiased health care. This is linked to the importance of what is called **health equity** or "equitable health care." In subsequent chapters, we will connect the notions of equity, equality, and non-discrimination to the idea of "social justice." The basic idea is there should be equitable distributions of health and health care in society for all people without regard for race, gender, disability status, and so on. The CDC explains health equity as follows:

> Health equity is achieved when every person has the opportunity to "attain his or her full health potential" and no one is "disadvantaged from achieving this potential because of social position or other socially determined circumstances." Health inequities are reflected in differences in length of life; quality of life; rates of disease, disability, and death; severity of disease; and access to treatment.[31]

With this is mind it is worth noting that in the United States there remain many inequalities in the distribution of health and health care. The CDC points toward disparities in terms of cancer rates, the rate of chronic diseases, oral health, tobacco use, and other areas in which there are differences between populations that reflect racial, ethnic, and economic differences. Consider for example, life expectancy. In the United States, according to a projection from the Kaiser Family Foundation based on data from 2020, overall life expectancy was 77.3 years.[32] But for Black people, life expectancy was only 71.8 years. White people had a life expectancy of 77.6 years, while for Hispanic people it was 78.8 years. When gender was included, these disparities were more glaring. Life expectancy for Black males was only 68 years. Data regarding infant mortality, pregnancy-related mortality, diabetes, HIV death, heart disease, and other indicators were also worse for Black people than for White people. These racial disparities indicate the need for continued work on social justice in health care. Furthermore, it is likely that, as Anita Silvers put it, "health is good for justice, and justice is good for health."[33] People will be healthier when society treats everyone fairly and distributes health care equitably; and a society with healthier people will also be a more just society (we have an excerpt from Silvers among the primary source readings for this chapter).

Of course, the goal of fairness, equity, and justice can still leave us with questions and possible dilemmas. What about age and the problem of ageism? Or the problem of ableism and discrimination against people with disabilities? Is it wrong to discriminate in health care based on age or disability? For example, is an 80-year-old who is suffering from cognitive decline entitled to the same care in an emergency as an otherwise healthy 30-year-old? Let's say there is a car accident and each of these two hypothetical patients has a similar life-threatening injury that requires emergency surgery—but there is only one operating room available. Which patient should go into surgery first? The principle of nondiscrimination might seem to suggest that in the name of impartiality we should flip a coin. And it would seem unjust and discriminatory to operate on the 30-year-old first if the only reason we help them first is because they are younger. Would it be "ageist" (unjust discrimination because of age) if we chose the 30-year-old on the assumption that the 80-year-old was nearer to death, anyway, due to their advanced age? If this were an actual case, other factors might help us decide, such as the likelihood of success, the question of consent, and so on. But in general, the principle of justice encourages us to avoid partiality and bias.

The imagined example we just considered is a case of *rationing* health care. Rationing occurs when there are not enough resources to serve all needs, and some decisions must be made about distributing or allocating those resources. Decisions about rationing may occur in thinking about organ donation, for example. In the United States, there is an ongoing shortage of donor organs, with over one hundred thousand people on the waiting list for a donated organ.[34] If there are not enough hearts, livers, and other donor organs to go around (bearing in mind the complexity of harvesting organs and matching them to needy recipients), some ethically appropriate decision-making procedure must be devised for deciding who gets a needed organ.

Rationing is a matter of "distributive justice" in health care. There are various theories of distributive

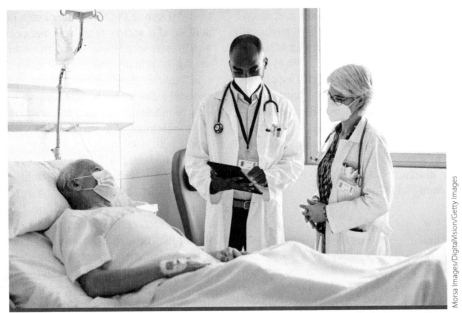

Morsa Images/DigitalVision/Getty Images

Figure 10-5 Does age matter when rationing health care?

justice and frameworks for establishing just distributions. One idea may focus on need. Another focus may be to create and support equality. Some may suggest a lottery system is fair. Or perhaps we ought to focus on giving care to those who are first in line or who have been waiting the longest for care. Others may want to leave distributions up to the vicissitudes of the market, with high-quality health care going to those who can afford it. In the background is a question about "procedural justice," which puts our attention on some fair procedure for making decisions about allocations and distributions. The question of rationing becomes very difficult in cases where there are complex differences among those who are on the receiving end of the distribution process. If everything were equal—say we were deciding who to treat among two similarly situated 30-year-olds—then maybe a coin flip would be a fair procedure for deciding. But things are rarely equal in that way. Needs are different, as is the prognosis for successful recovery. One principle of rationing may be to help the neediest patients first (we'll take this up later when we discuss care for the vulnerable). But sometimes in attending to those most in need, we can end

up neglecting easy-to-fix problems of larger numbers of people who are less needy. And what about those who are waiting for care? Will they be forced to wait longer each time a needier person shows up and jumps the queue for care?

Another concern is the matter of "social worth." If one of those in need of care were a successful businessperson with a large family to support but the other was unemployed and had no family to support, would that make a difference in how we think about allocating medical resources? This may seem to be a reasonable question from the standpoint of a kind of superficial utilitarianism. But ethicists generally reject the idea of social worth as a legitimate focal point of moral judgment. The Organ Procurement and Transplantation Network maintains, in its code of ethics, that social worth should not be considered when allocating organs. They explain, "considering one person more useful to society than another, based on prevailing social values, may be a matter of opinion or good fortune in the random distribution of natural and socially cultivated talents and abilities."[35] To use social worth as a criterion risks introducing bias, prejudice, and subjective opinion into the distributive process. And it seems to neglect the inherent value, dignity, or worth of individuals (as we might put it from a Kantian or natural law standpoint). It is worth noting that if we reject social worth as a criterion for health care allocations, this also appears to preclude a focus on wealth and market-based allocations. It does not seem ethical, from this perspective, to allow disparities in wealth to influence health care distributions. And so there may appear to be something unjust about a society in which wealthy people get better care and live longer than people who live in poverty.

The topic of health care rationing came to the fore during the COVID-19 pandemic, especially when surges of illness put a strain on limited health care resources. Consider, for example, the question of who should receive vaccines first, as the production of vaccine slowly geared up. When COVID vaccines first became available, the decision was made to provide them to frontline workers (doctors and nurses) as well as those most at risk (e.g., elderly people and those with other underlying health conditions). This may seem unfair or unjust, since it seems to violate the principle of equality. But is unequal treatment justified in this case due to the unique circumstances of the groups that got vaccines first?

Or consider the question of who should be put on a ventilator and who should be allowed to die if there were not enough ventilators to go around. One typical suggestion for a "ventilator triage" protocol was to save the most lives and the most life-years.[36] This means that if such a decision must be made, it might be justifiable to use scarce medical resources to support younger people who are more likely to survive than to use these ventilators on older or sicker people with less hope for survival. This may sound harsh—and ageist or ableist. And again, it seems to violate the idea or equality as well as the idea that the neediest people should be helped first. But is it really unjust to focus lifesaving procedures on those who have the most life-years to gain?

The idea of "life-year maximization" can be compared with some other ideas about rationing health care. One idea is known as "fair innings," a metaphor taken from baseball and cricket that can be linked to the idea of an age cutoff. The argument is basically that there is a certain number of years (or innings) that are expected in order to have a "fair share" of life's goods and experiences. Those who have not yet had a chance to play their fair share of innings should be aided first, while those who have had a fair share of life should go to the back of the distribution line. One problem with the fair innings argument is that it is exceedingly difficult to figure out where to draw the line. Is seventy years long enough for a fair chance at life? What criteria would we employ to draw the line there, and would it really be reasonable to say that we ought to help a 65-year-old before helping a 75-year-old? Also, an age cutoff does not seem to help in considering allocations for those who are younger than that cutoff. Again, if we draw a line at year seventy, how would that help us in making a choice between 30-year-old and a 28-year-old? The fair innings approach does not seem to help us much in that case. It can also be accused of being ageist insofar as it suggests that the life of a younger person is more worth saving than that of an older person. The philosopher John Harris has discussed this at length, arguing that it would be very difficult to draw a line in a way that is not ageist (we have an excerpt from Harris at the end of this chapter).[37] A similar argument could be employed if we used disability as a way of drawing a line. Should we put people with disabilities to the back of the distribution line while focusing our lifesaving attention on those who are able-bodied and more likely to survive? That seems to be a kind of ableism that discriminates against people with disabilities.

The question of health care rationing becomes even more complicated when we think about social and cultural differences that manifest in emergencies and pandemics. For example, there were geographic and regional differences during the COVID-19 pandemic that resulted in different rates of illness and death. State public health departments competed for scarce resources including ventilators, personal protective equipment, and vaccines. This had the potential to result in unequal outcomes across state borders. Small states with smaller budgets were in competition with bigger states to obtain medical supplies, which meant that money and power influenced the distribution process.[38] If we think that equality, rationality, and fairness are a part of justice, then this kind of free market distribution process appears to be unjust, since it seems to imply that people in small states will suffer while people in bigger states might have better outcomes. This kind of disparity is also problematic when thinking about global distributions of health care. During the COVID-19 pandemic, different countries had different access to vaccines, personal protective equipment, and so on.[39] Global justice would seem to require more equitable distributions across national borders.

Human Rights and the Right to Health Care

10.8 Defend a thesis about the right to health care.

Another way to explain the idea of justice is to say that it is giving people what they deserve. Only criminals *deserve* to be punished, which is why it is unjust to punish innocent people. And students who perform well *deserve* to get good grades. In health care settings, we might say that sick and injured people *deserve* to be cared for. Does that mean that sick and injured people have a *right* to be cared for or that they are *entitled* to be cared for? As we mentioned at the beginning of this chapter, the World Health Organization states that "the enjoyment of the highest attainable standard of health is one of the fundamental rights of every human being."[40] But how is that right supposed to be administered? What kinds of social systems would need to be created in order to ensure that this right to health care is respected?

This question is especially relevant as we think about social disparities in health outcomes and about inequities in access to health care and medical insurance. During the past couple of decades in the United States, there has been an ongoing debate about health care and medical insurance. Some advocate for "universal health care," the idea that everyone should have equal access to decent health care, which is to be provided in some way by the government. Others would prefer to leave the private health care and insurance markets alone, so that consumers may decide how much risk and coverage they are willing to pay for.

In 2010, the Affordable Care Act (sometimes called "Obamacare" because it was proposed during Barack Obama's presidency) became law. This law expanded insurance coverage while also requiring that individuals obtain insurance. The law created insurance markets/exchanges, and it allowed young adults to remain on their parents' insurance. One issue that the law sought to address was the problem of denials of coverage for those with preexisting conditions. It is easy to imagine that in seeking to maximize profits, an insurance program might be reluctant to cover people they know to be very sick—since that coverage could prove to be costly in the long run. Would such a denial of service be a kind of discrimination against people who are ill or disabled? But how would we remedy that problem? Would we force healthy people to pay for a system that cares for those who are sick?

There has been an ongoing debate about the specifics of the Affordable Care act. Republicans in the United States have typically sought to "overturn Obamacare," as this effort has been described. The effort has included challenges to the ACA law at the level of the Supreme Court, with details still being worked out. But the more general question here is whether people have a right to health care (and health insurance) and whether society should support a general kind of health insurance, or whether health care is an individual choice that is best left up to the open market. On the left, people such as Senator Bernie Sanders of Vermont have argued in favor of "heath care for all," while claiming that "health care is a human right, not a privilege."[41] Senator Sanders has offered a proposal to bolster the Affordable Care Act by expanding Medicare and creating "Medicare for all." Medicare is the federal system of health insurance provided for people over age sixty-five (and which is also available to some younger people with disabilities). Medicare for all would expand this system more broadly and create what is called a "single-payer" system, one in which there is a single health care system that pays for everything. But Republican critics of this idea have branded it as "socialism." They argue against the idea of a government program that provides health care to everyone, warning that it would be expensive and inefficient. In his State of the Union address in 2020, President Trump described the idea as a "socialist takeover of our healthcare system," saying also, "We will never let socialism destroy American healthcare."[42] The political and rhetorical use of the term socialism here is worth thinking about (we will examine socialism in more detail in Chapter 14). Senator Bernie Sanders has described himself as a "democratic socialist," and proposals for universal health care can reasonably be described as socialist. The idea is for there to be a comprehensive social system that would support health care for everyone. Critics of such as system, such as President Trump, use the word "socialism" as a pejorative, assuming that socialized health care is negative.

Apart from the political debate, there is a fundamental question in this debate about justice, rights, and outcomes. Defenders of universal health care believe that everyone has an equal right to health care. The philosopher Kai Nielsen has gone so far as to argue that when societies can afford it, quality health care should be free and openly available to all (we have an excerpt from Nielsen at the end of this chapter).[43] Given this, it is not surprising that Nielsen has also defended socialism, claiming that it is better at promoting democracy, equality, and autonomy than free market capitalism.[44] But Nielsen's argument in support of universal health care need not be connected to a more radical effort to create socialism in every part of the economy. Rather, the focus here is on the question of whether all individuals, regardless of socioeconomic status, have a right to quality health care. Not only is there a right to health care, from Nielsen's point of view, but people would be healthier and public health would increase if there were some system of free, universal health care. In defense of this point of view, a further critique is made, which is that there is something unjust about a society that has drastically different health outcomes that result from a system in which affluent people pay for high-quality care, while poor and working-class people end up with lesser-quality care.

In response, opponents question the efficiency of a system of universal health care. They also claim that individuals have a fundamental right to choose with regard to health care. This right includes the right to choose not to pay into a system of insurance. A further point has been made by John David Lewis, that in a system based on the idea of a right to health care, this

right will infringe on the rights of doctors and health care institutions. If you have a right to health care, does this then mean that a doctor has an obligation to provide it to you? Lewis suggests that rights ought to be understood *negatively*—as projects against violations of liberty. But to claim that others have a right to health care creates a *positive* duty to help, which may seem to violate the liberty of health care providers. As he says, "There is no right to medical care, because there is no right to coerce medical professionals to provide it."[45] (We have an excerpt from Lewis in the readings for this chapter.) Lewis and other opponents of universal health care do not want to force people into a government-run system because, as they claim, the market would be more efficient and because this would allow people to choose for themselves how much care/coverage they want to pay for, how much risk they are willing to take, and how much assistance they want to provide for those in need. In response, an author such as Nielsen may suggest that this focus on negative rights in health care seems to misunderstand the nature of justice in health care. Liberty should be balanced with equality, from this perspective, and as Nielsen suggests, society may have an obligation to treat health as a basic need.

As might be expected, it is possible to imagine a middle ground between the free market libertarianism of Lewis and the egalitarian socialism of Nielsen in the debate about the right to health care. Such a middle position has been defended by Norman Daniels, who articulates a "liberal" approach to the topic that builds on the work of the philosopher John Rawls (whom we discuss in detail in Chapter 14). The basic idea of "liberal" here involves a combination of both liberty and equality. For Daniels (and Rawls), one important question is the issue of fairness. Daniels suggests that health is a "primary good" that ought to be fairly distributed and that health care institutions are among the basic institutions of society that ought to help equalize "the natural lottery." The problem of the natural lottery is that people end up with disparate health outcomes through no fault of their own—they inherit genetic tendencies toward disease, or contract a disease, or end up with an injury, or they happen to be lucky and have good genes or the good fortune to avoid injury. Health care institutions should help people

Table 10-2 Outline of Moral Approaches to the Right to Health Care

	Free Market	Liberal	Socialism
Thesis	No right to health care; no obligation to provide health care	Basic fairness and minimal health care; but also allow individual choice	Free access to universal health care for all people
Corollaries and Implications	Rights understood negatively as protections against interference; no positive duty to provide health or health care	Justice as fairness aiming to create minimal equality; may allow for inequities so long as basic health is assured	There is a positive right to health; health is viewed as a basic good to which all people are entitled
Connections with Moral Theory	*Libertarian* focus on negative rights; *consequentialist* focus on "efficiencies" of the market	*Non-consequentialist* concern for *fairness* that balances *equality* and *liberty* (choice); *consequentialist* focus on base-level health and health care	*Deontological* focus on the basic *right to health care*; *consequentialist* concern for well-being and public health
Relevant Authors	John David Lewis	Norman Daniels (and John Rawls)	Kai Nielsen

respond to those vicissitudes. But for Daniels, the goal is not complete equality. He describes the ideal of equality of health as a "futile goal of eliminating or leveling all natural differences among persons."[46] Rather, the point is to provide equitable and fair access to health care to help remedy the obvious and undeserved inequalities that result when people end up with the bad luck of bad health. At minimum, we should want to help everyone achieve a basic level of normal function. Daniels suggests, "meeting health needs has the goal of promoting normal functioning: it concentrates on a specific class of obvious disadvantages and tries to eliminate them."[47] On Daniels's account, in achieving this goal, we could still allow for a range of options or tiers of health care.[48] This would obviate the objection raised by defenders of the free market, who worry that a state-run universal system of health care would take away individual choice. On this hybrid model, there would be some minimal amount of care provided for everyone. But people may want to purchase supplemental insurance or pursue health care options that they pay for on their own. This may seem to be something like what the Affordable Care Act provides—but Daniels has offered a

critique of that law that suggests that it does not really go far enough in redressing the inequalities and lack of health coverage found in American society.[49] Daniels requires that minimal care be provided that promotes "normal function" for everyone at the most basic tier of health care coverage; but he also allows freedom of choice beyond that, so long as those choices do not adversely affect those on the bottom tier. (We have an excerpt from Daniels among the primary sources for this chapter.)

Health Maximization, Care for the Vulnerable, and Pandemic Restrictions

10.9 Critically evaluate ethical issues involved in the COVID-19 pandemic.

The idea of health maximization is a focus of public health policy. It is important to note that the concerns of public health will be somewhat different than the concerns of individual clinical care.[50] Paternalistic violations of individual autonomy could be supported, for example, in the name of public health. The basic idea would be that we could violate the liberty of some people in order to maximize the overall health of the population. Laws that require seat belts, motorcycle helmets, or that prohibit tobacco are justified in this way, as paternalistic requirements designed to promote safety and public health.

There is a philosophically significant question about the very idea of public health, what it means and how we measure it. Is public health something that is metaphysically distinct from the health of individuals, or is it merely the quantitative or aggregate result we get when adding up the health of various individuals? And when we try to evaluate public health, should we be focused on the health of those who are most needy and vulnerable, or should we be focused on those who are healthiest? In the literature on public health, there are various ways of speaking about and measuring health maximization. For example, one focus might be mortality rates. But preventing death is not the only concern of public health. Another significant concern is quality of life, which includes preventing disease and disability. Thus, in addition to focusing on life-years, scholars focus on "quality adjusted life-years" (QALY) or "disability adjusted life-years" (DALY). But these measurements have provoked some criticism. How do we measure the quality of life, and what counts as a disability? Would a blind person who lived for one hundred years have a better or worse life than a sighted person who died at age fifty? And wouldn't any assessment of quality of life in this case also depend on the kind of society the person lived in? In a society with schools for the blind, widespread use of braille, and other resources, blindness may not be as much of an impairment as in a society without those supports. Quality of life measurements also depend on socioeconomic status. How would we compare the quality of life of a rich blind person to that of a poor sighted person? Critics of QALY and DALY metrics will point out that there are often cultural, social, and other biases woven into these measurements.[51]

And yet these kinds of comparative measurements are important for any cost–benefit analysis involving public health. Consider the difference between two societies. Imagine that in one society (let's call it "Society A"), 25 percent of the people live very long lives, often reaching one hundred years of age; another 50 percent die at a younger age, say in their sixties; and the remaining 25 percent often die in their youth. In Society A, these differences are related to a number of factors, including wealth, race, and disability status. What would we think if we learned that it is the wealthy, White, and able-bodied in Society A who live longest, while people who are poor, non-White, and have disabilities tend to die younger? Now contrast that with another society (let's call it "Society B"), in which nearly 100 percent of the people live to be about sixty-five but in which no one lives much longer than that. Imagine that in Society B, most resources are used to prevent early death, to provide equitable access to health care, and to support people with chronic diseases and disabilities. Which society is doing better with regard to public health? This caricatured example is used to make the point that any judgment about public health will involve a complex judgment about what counts as health maximization—and that this relates to issues in social justice, as well as to questions about what we understand as "healthy." Is a society in which some live long lives but people with disabilities die early a healthy society? On the other hand, is a society in which there are more persons with disabilities a healthy one? In answering these questions, you might want to consider a claim made by Anita Silvers (in the excerpt we include in the primary source readings): "In a just society, broad-based access to health support likely will maintain at-risk individuals whose lives would be lost in an unjust society."[52] Silvers asks us to consider whether in a more just society, there may be more people who are not healthy. Perhaps such a society would include more people like Anita Silvers herself, a polio survivor who was left with partial quadriplegia as a result of her illness. After her childhood disease, she went on to become a respected scholar and a prominent member of the American Philosophical Association. To survive polio requires substantial societal and health care support. Does health maximization involve spending societal resources on vulnerable polio survivors? Or is it supposed to be focused on maximizing longer, healthier lives for those who are not so vulnerable?

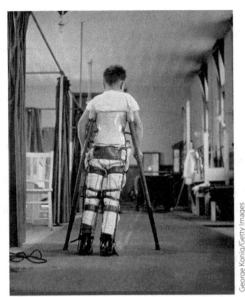

George Konig/Getty Images

Figure 10-6 What are our obligations to vulnerable people?

Health maximization is basically a utilitarian question of how to produce "the greatest health for the greatest number of people" (in a formulation that slightly modifies John Stuart Mill's "greatest happiness" principle). This is one notion of distributive justice, which tells us that the best distribution of health care would be one that maximizes overall health or what we might call "aggregate population health."[53] As we've just indicated, there are complexities in how we understand and measure aggregate population health. With that in mind, let's consider a serious problem in bioethics, the idea of eugenics.

Eugenics is the idea of creating good genes or improving the genetic stock of humanity. We will discuss eugenics again in our chapter on biotechnology (Chapter 12), where it will be examined in connection with genetic screening and other reproductive technologies. Some bioethicists support the use of these kinds of biotechnologies as a reasonable exercise of reproductive autonomy. But there are obvious eugenic consequences of reproductive technologies that screen out diseases and prevent people with disabilities from being born. The notion of eugenics has been widely discredited by bioethicists because eugenics as a social movement resulted in obvious atrocities. In the twentieth century,

eugenic policies included programs that were justified in the name of "public health" that aimed at preventing "unhealthy" people from reproducing. In practice, this often had racist and class-based application: it was people of color, and people who were poor or had mental illness, who were viewed as a drag on the public health system and who were, in some cases, forcibly sterilized. In the United States, sixty thousand people were forcibly sterilized; in Nazi Germany, there were four hundred thousand victims of this procedure.[54] Beyond forced sterilization, an even worse atrocity occurred in Nazi Germany with the extermination of undesirable people.

One way to prevent this kind of atrocity is to emphasize autonomy and respect for the dignity and worth of human beings. It is easy to see how a utilitarian concern for public health that is not constrained by respect for autonomy and dignity could end up in atrocity. Vulnerable people—sick people, people with disabilities, and so on—can be costly. One very simplistic and crass utilitarian approach to public health would suggest that in the name of public health we should not support vulnerable people.

In response, we might add an additional limitation to any notion of health maximization, which is that there are special duties and obligations to care for the vulnerable. We mentioned earlier that the Helsinki Declaration and other codes and documents emphasize the importance of care for vulnerable individuals or communities. Building on this account, one might suggest that public health and health maximization should be focused on those who are most vulnerable and most in need of care. Wendy Rogers has examined this idea in an essay entitled "Vulnerability and Bioethics," where she reminds us that the bioethical principles of autonomy, beneficence, and non-maleficence can be appealed to in order to protect vulnerable people in clinical settings. She argues that this protection must also be extended into the concerns of public health: "Within public health practice, vulnerable populations have been identified as those who are more likely to suffer from an increased burden of ill health and therefore require extra support or protection."[55] She explains that vulnerability includes economic and racial/ethnic features, as well as gender and ability or disability status. For example, she considers the vulnerability of "homeless persons," explaining that homeless people are vulnerable to physical injury and violence, as well as exposure to infectious diseases and inadequate nutrition. And homeless people generally do not have access to health care, while also suffering from social stigma and discrimination.[56] (We have a short excerpt from Rogers in the primary source readings for this chapter.)

The basic idea of caring for vulnerable people can be understood in terms of the oft-cited aphorism (attributed to a number of diverse sources): "We should judge a society by how it treats its most vulnerable members." A limited version of this idea has been explored and defended by the philosopher John Rawls. Rawls's theory of justice is a kind of social contract theory that imagines the kind of principles of justice that rational and unbiased people might agree to. One of Rawls's basic notions is called "the difference principle." This idea allows for social inequalities as long as they help the least advantaged members of society. The basic idea is that some inequalities are acceptable as long as those on the bottom of the social pyramid are doing well enough and are not further disadvantaged by those inequalities. But as critics of Rawls have pointed out, his theory does not really attend to the special needs of the most vulnerable people, that is, those with disabilities, the sick, and the aged. Martha Nussbaum has offered an extended critique of Rawls that notes that "Classic social contract doctrines, even Rawls's very subtle and morally sensitive such doctrine, cannot adequately handle these problems of justice for and to the disabled, or the related problems of care for dependents that the existence of disabled and elderly people in our societies creates."[57] The basic problem is that when social contract theorists like Rawls imagine a just society, they typically fail to take into account the reality of illness, dependency, and the need for care. They also fail to recognize that caring for others is a fundamental part of living. And on some accounts, caregiving is essential to living well, since some of life's most important and memorable moments occur when caring for children, for aged parents, or for those who are sick or disabled. Sometimes the critique of the failure to recognize the importance of caregiving is articulated as a feminist concern. Caregiving has often been viewed as "women's work" and has been devalued. Nussbaum is an example of an author who articulates this feminist critique, claiming that the devaluation

of caregiving that occurs in relation to gender roles is a source of significant injustice. She also emphasizes, deriving from her idea of "the capabilities approach" (which we discussed in Chapter 3), that care for those with special needs is an important part of any decent and just society. Nussbaum explains:

> Health care and other forms of care are, for real people, central goods making well-being possible.... More generally, care for children, elderly people, and people with mental and physical disabilities is a major part of the work that needs to be done in any society, and in most societies it is a source of great injustice. Any theory of justice needs to think about the problem from the beginning, in the design of the basic institutional structure, and particularly in its theory of the primary goods.[58]

Thus, Nussbaum would suggest that health care systems need to think more carefully about the social importance of care. This is a central idea that is emphasized from the standpoint of "care ethics," in which relationships are prioritized along with a concern for dependency, vulnerability, and precariousness.[59] From this point of view, public health maximization ought to be associated with a complementary principle of special care for vulnerable people, and we might judge the health of a society in terms of how it helps and supports those with special needs. Nussbaum explains, in a chapter where she focuses on caring for children and adults with mental impairments, "Children and adults with mental impairments are citizens. Any decent society must address their needs for care, education, self-respect, activity, and friendship."[60]

As we conclude this chapter, let's return to the case with which we began: the COVID-19 pandemic. Many of the issues we have discussed in this section and throughout the chapter showed up in the COVID health crisis. The question of distributing vaccines and ventilators was often focused on the need to help the vulnerable. Elderly people and people with comorbidities were able to access vaccines earlier than younger, less vulnerable people. But when there were scarce resources and the need to ration supplies of ventilators, protocols were proposed that might place vulnerable people at risk. We discussed the issue of rationing previously.

Here we might also emphasize the challenge created by the pandemic of people who were psychologically damaged by the pandemic due to isolation and anxiety, as well as those who have been afflicted by "long COVID" (long-term disability inflicted by the disease). Returning to the issue of QALY and DALY measurements discussed above, it is worth asking what matters most in thinking about the response to pandemic. Is mere survival enough? Gross mortality rates do inform us about the success or failure of public health efforts to curtail the pandemic. But we should also be interested in the effect of those public health efforts on the quality of life of everyone, including the mental health of those who experienced anxiety, loneliness, and depression. Finally, even as society got a handle on the disease through the use of vaccines and other prophylactics, there is still an open question about how well we are doing in supporting those who have been disabled by long COVID. In July 2021, for example, long COVID was recognized as a disability under guidance offered from the U.S. Department of Health and Human Services.[61] This means that people suffering from it can gain protections that apply to other people with disabilities.

As we conclude, let's consider one of the most controversial policies associated with the pandemic: the idea of **quarantine**, which is a period of isolation intended to prevent the spread of contamination.[62] The word "quarantine" comes from the Italian word for forty. A quarantine was supposed to last for forty days. Forty days was an important number in the European Middle Ages, associated, in the Bible, with a mystical process of purification. It rained for forty days and nights during Noah's flood. Moses wandered for forty years in the desert. And Jesus fasted for forty days. Today, quarantines typically do not last for forty days. Rather, isolation periods are based on scientific knowledge about the infectiousness of various diseases. The incubation period for COVID-19 was first thought to be fourteen days, so people who were infected with the disease were encouraged to self-quarantine or isolate themselves for two weeks. Later, as knowledge of the disease increased and vaccinations became available and other health protocols were created, the self-quarantining period was reduced to less than one week. Quarantines may not seem controversial when viewed from the standpoint of

public health. The goal is to prevent infected people from spreading the disease. This is easily justified by appealing to utilitarian reasoning: to defend the health of the majority, some people's liberty is limited. Of course, this seems to run counter to the idea of autonomy and basic principles of liberty and human rights. And so, during the COVID-19 pandemic, protests broke out repeatedly as people refused to comply with public health regulations that restricted their liberty, even including protests against wearing a face mask. We might note that face masking is quite different from quarantining. A face mask mandate is a minimally invasive restriction that allows people to go about their business. It does not require other restrictions of travel, work, or activity. But again, some protestors suggested that even this minimal restriction was an unjustified infringement on their personal liberty. It is worth asking whether mask mandates are more or less restrictive than other public health restrictions we've discussed here, including seat belt laws and prohibitions on tobacco.

Quarantines are, of course, much more restrictive. During the COVID-19 crisis, there were different kinds of quarantines practiced in different parts of the world at different times. Different cities, states, countries, and regions were isolated in different ways, and people were forced to stay home for periods of time that varied. This may have seemed unfair, especially if you live in a state, country, or city that had more or less restrictive regulations than some other place. Another ethical concern is about healthy people in the quarantine zone who are not yet infected. It may seem odd to lock healthy people into a closed environment with infected people. But that is what happened in some cases, as healthy passengers on cruise ships were prevented from disembarking when there were cases of COVID-19 onboard. But staying in close proximity to those who are infected puts those healthy people at risk. This would seem to violate the basic principle of non-maleficence—since we may end up harming those healthy people. A committed utilitarian might argue in the name of the greater good that some healthy people's rights may be infringed and their well-being may be put at risk. But what if a healthy person disagrees? Would a healthy person in quarantine be wrong to try to escape? And what if some of the noninfected people were also particularly vulnerable, say if they suffered from some disease that increased their likelihood of dying if they were to contract the disease? If such a person got infected, would they have a right to sue the public health officials who put them at risk for damages?

It turns out that quarantines are not as easy to justify as we might think. Bioethicist George Annas has argued that quarantine is an "arbitrarily draconian" measure and a "relic of the past that has outlived its usefulness."[63] And yet, during the COVID-19 pandemic,

we saw quarantines unfolding all around us. In the future, when another pandemic arises, it is easy to imagine public health officials responding in similar ways. And so the questions discussed here will continue to be of interest. How can we maximize public health, and how can we protect vulnerable people while also respecting autonomy and human rights? That question, along with the other questions and issues discussed in this chapter, demonstrates the ongoing need for careful and critical attention to health care ethics.

Chapter Summary

10.1 What are some basic topics and methods for studying bioethics?

Bioethics is the application of ethical judgments to topics involving life. It includes health care ethics, as well as issues involving animals and other living things. Important topics include end-of-life issues, questions about reproduction (including abortion), as well as issues involving animal rights and biomedical research. One important method used in bioethics and in health care ethics is the case-study approach (sometimes called *casuistry*). This method considers the details of specific cases while trying to resolve problems and dilemmas. But this method should not merely focus on details of the cases; it should also apply basic principles and the moral theories we've discussed in the first part of the text including consequentialism, deontology, human rights theory, natural law, and care ethics

10.2 Why is health a philosophically complex idea?

Health is a basic concept in thinking about health care ethics. But health is not merely a straightforwardly objective concept. It also contains a normative or evaluative element. There are objective measures of health such as weight, temperature, and so on. But these measurements require interpretation. A similar interpretive effort is needed in order to understand what counts as a disability or disease. There are social components of health and disease as well. And various impairments will be more or less "disabling" depending on social, economic, and cultural factors.

A very broad conception of health (found in the World Health Organization's constitution) describes health as complete physical, mental, and social well-being. But this broad conception opens the concept to include social health (and issues like poverty). It also establishes an ideal of complete well-being that may be unrealistic or unattainable.

10.3 How do basic principles of bioethics show up in codes and institutions?

The history of bioethics begins with the Hippocratic oath. In more recent decades, a number of codes and declarations were created, often in response to atrocities that were committed by doctors and scientists. These codes and declarations have established basic principles that guide medical, health care, and research practice. There is a complex system of ethical supervision in place in health care institutions and labs. The goal of these codes and ethics advisory boards is to ensure that biomedical practice is ethical and that atrocities do not occur. These codes and ethics institutions can also offer advice and guidance in dealing with specific cases and ethical dilemmas that occur in health care practice. A number of basic principles have been proposed in these codes. Typically, this includes respect for autonomy, beneficence, non-maleficence, justice, and utilitarian or distributive concerns. We have also added in our list of values to be considered, respect for human rights, health maximization, and care for the vulnerable.

10.4 How does autonomy apply in thinking about advance directives and paternalism?

Autonomy is self-control. Respect for autonomy focuses on the importance of voluntary and informed consent. In ordinary circumstances, a medical patient or research subject should give explicit consent based on an understanding of what they are consenting to. But in some cases, this is difficult or impossible to achieve, as in cases of incapacitation. Advance directives are documents that express consent in advance. These documents are used in end-of-life care situations. Paternalism occurs when someone acts on our behalf, taking beneficent action. In some cases (again, for example, when we are incapacitated), doctors and loved ones may decide on an action done for our benefit. But in general, paternalism is limited by the value of autonomy. It is presumed that it is usually better to allow patients to decide for themselves rather than to paternalistically intervene on their behalf.

10.5 How can beneficence be applied in evaluating cosmetic surgery?

Beneficence is focused on concern for the well-being of the patient. There are questions in thinking about beneficence, especially at the end of life with regard to euthanasia. One set of distinctions that is useful in thinking about beneficence is that between therapies and enhancements: therapies return us to normal function, while enhancements take us beyond normal function. Cosmetic surgery is often therapeutic. The case of breast reconstruction after mastectomy is an example. But cosmetic surgery can also be an enhancement. Patients may request cosmetic enhancements (such as leg-lengthening surgery). But it is an open question whether such a painful and risky procedure is beneficent, even if a patient consents.

10.6 How can you use the concept of non-maleficence to evaluate the opioid epidemic?

Non-maleficence is the idea of "doing no harm." It means that health care professionals and institutions should avoid causing harm, while exercising "due care." A variety of questions can be raised about non-maleficence including the difference between malice and neglect. This concept can be applied to the opioid addiction epidemic, which has caused significant harm including a number of deaths, in connection with a cost–benefit analysis. Pain relief is beneficent and opioids can help mitigate pain. But the benefit of opioids must be balanced with the risk of addiction, abuse, and overdose. Health care institutions typically have protocols for prescribing opioids that are focused on harm reduction. But, as discussed, pharmaceutical companies have been held liable for the harm caused by opioids they manufactured and promoted. In general, those involved in the health care industry, including corporations, have an obligation to avoid harm and to take steps to mitigate harm when it does occur.

10.7 How can you apply the concept of justice to the problem of rationing health care?

Justice involves treating people fairly and equally. This is the basic idea of "social justice" and "health equity" or "equitable health care." It is unjust to discriminate against people (and treat them unfairly or unequally) in health care settings. As discussed, there are many inequities in the current health care system that involve different health outcomes based on race, gender, economics, and so on. Ideally, people would be treated fairly and equitably. But this becomes complicated if decisions about rationing scarce medical resources must be made. Various ideas for rationing were mentioned (first in line, a lottery, a focus on need, etc.). One significant challenge is rationing health care to those of different ages, with different disability status or life expectancy. We discussed the concept of "fair innings" and the problem of drawing a line or age cutoff for rationing. Problems were discussed including the possibility of ableism and ageism in a system of rationing. Justice requires that we treat people fairly and equitably, but schemes for rationing scarce medical resources pose questions about fairness and equity.

10.8 How might you defend a thesis about the right to health care?

The idea of human rights has been employed in discussions of health care ethics. Some claim that there is a fundamental right to health care. Others argue that there is no such right because there is no positive duty to provide health care to others. In the first case, one could argue in defense of the idea of universal health care, claiming that everyone has a right to high-quality health care. In the second case, those who argue against the right to universal health care prefer a system that allows people to choose their own health care in an open and free market. Some argue for a middle path that provides basic health care for everyone that guarantees a baseline of health and normal functioning while also allowing people the choice to buy coverage and care according to their own interests and desires. In the chapter, we discussed these various options as either libertarian, socialist, or liberal. In order to defend a thesis about the right to health care, you would need to consider whether you think that the idea of human rights includes this particular right; you would also need to consider the extent of care and the value of liberty and choice in health care policy.

10.9 How can you critically evaluate ethical issues involved in the COVID-19 pandemic?

In discussing issues that were involved in the COVID-19 pandemic, all of the principles of health care ethics could be employed including autonomy, beneficence, non-maleficence, and justice. We also focused on the idea of health maximization (seeking to maximize public health) and the idea of special concern for vulnerable individuals and communities. With regard to masking, quarantines, and vaccinations, the general goal of public health maximization would point toward support of these practices, including the possibility of a mandate or requirement for masking, isolation, and vaccination. But this mandate runs up against a limit of autonomy: it can seem paternalistic and a violation of liberty to force people to get vaccines or to remain in isolation. One could also argue against vaccines, quarantines, and social/economic shutdowns from the standpoint of non-maleficence. Critics argue that these things are harmful and that the harm caused by an economic shutdown cannot be justified in terms of the suggested benefit. Defenders of those practices would disagree, claiming that there are important gains in terms of public health from those prevention strategies. Finally, defenders of such policies can also argue that these policies help to protect vulnerable people (older people and people with underlying health conditions or disabilities), who were more likely to die from the disease.

Primary Source Readings

In the primary source readings for this chapter, we have excerpts from a number of important authors who address topics we've discussed here. We begin with Onora O'Neill, an important British philosopher whose work is grounded in Kantian ethics. In this essay, she considers the dilemma that seems to arise in thinking about autonomy and paternalism in cases involving people with impaired capacity. Following that, we have an excerpt from Anita Silvers, who asks us to consider what we mean by health and how it connects to justice. John Harris then discusses the question of fair innings and the difficulty of drawing a line without becoming ageist. Then we have three related excerpts discussing the question of universal health care from Kai Nielsen, John David Lewis, and Norman Daniels (each of whom have been discussed in the chapter). This collection of primary source excerpts concludes with an excerpt from Australian philosopher Wendy Rogers, who considers the idea of vulnerability in thinking about bioethics.

Reading 10-1   Paternalism and Partial Autonomy | Onora O'Neill

Study Questions

As you read the excerpt, please consider the following questions:

1. Why does O'Neill suggest that autonomy cannot be the only concern of medical ethics?

2. Why is consenting "opaque," as O'Neill describes it?

3. Why does O'Neill think that it is difficult to establish clear guidelines that distinguish between unacceptable paternalism and respect for autonomy?

When cognitive or volitional capacities, or both, are lacking or impaired, autonomous action is reduced or impossible. Autonomy is lacking or incomplete for parts of all lives (infancy, early childhood), for further parts of some lives (unconsciousness, senility, some illness and mental disturbance) and throughout some lives (severe retardation). Since illness often damages autonomy, concern to respect it does not seem a promising fundamental principle for medical ethics. Medical concern would be strangely inadequate if it did not extend to those with incomplete autonomy....

Human autonomy is limited and precarious in many contexts, and the consent given to others' actions and projects is standardly selective and incomplete. All consent is consent to some proposed action or project under certain descriptions. When we consent to an action or project we often do not consent even to its logical implications or to its likely results (let alone its actual results), nor to its unavoidable corollaries and presuppositions. Put more technically, consenting . . . is opaque. When we consent, we do not necessarily "see through" to the implications of what we consent to and consent to these also. When a patient consents to an operation he or she will often be unaware of further implications or results of that which is consented to. Risks may not be understood and post-operative expectations may be vague. But the opacity of patients' consent is not radically different from the opacity of all human consenting....

Various forms of manipulation and of questionable paternalism fail to meet these requirements. Patients are manipulated if they are "made offers they cannot refuse," given their actual cognitive and volitional capacities. For example, patients who think they may be denied further care or discharged without recourse if they refuse proposed treatment may be unable to refuse it. To ensure that "consent" is not manipulated, available alternatives may have to be spelled out and refusal of treatment shown to be a genuine option. "Consent" which is achieved by relying on misleading or alarmist descriptions of prognosis or uninformative accounts of treatment and alternatives does not show genuine respect. Only patients who are quite unable to understand or decide need complete paternalist protection. When there is a relationship of unequal power, knowledge or dependence, as so often between patients and doctors, avoiding manipulation and unacceptable paternalism demands a lot....

We find that we are left without a single boundary-line between acceptable and unacceptable medical practice. What we have are patterns of reasoning which yield different answers for different patients and for different proposals for treatment. One patient can indeed be expected to come to an informed and autonomous (if idiosyncratic) decision; another may be too confused to take in what his options are. A third may be able to understand the issues but too dependent or too distraught to make decisions. Attempts to provide uniform guidelines for treating patients as persons, respecting their autonomy and avoiding unacceptable medical paternalism are bound to be insensitive to the radical differences of capacity of different patients.

Onora O'Neill, "Paternalism and Partial Autonomy." *Journal of Medical Ethics* 10: 4 (December 1984), pp. 173–178.

Reading 10-2   Equitable Personal Healthiness | Anita Silvers

Study Questions

As you read the excerpt, please consider the following questions:

1. How does Silvers connect health and justice?

2. Why does Silvers say that just societies do not necessarily manifest higher aggregated levels of health than unjust ones?

3. How does her idea of equitable personal healthiness help to account for differences of age, disability status, and other factors?

Bioethicists and other health-policy scholars often seem to view health and justice as symbiotic.... Bioethicists believe that securing social justice will make us healthier. Injustice is manifested in the denial of important goods such as health and education to those who deserve and need them. Thus, without committing to any specific theory of justice, we can expect that more citizens in just societies will have access to the material resources needed to achieve and sustain good health, and to the educational resources needed to understand the importance of maintaining health, than in unjust societies.

Further, a just society is organized to promote the good of citizens collectively, whereas an unjust society ignores the good of the many and serves only the few. We thus can anticipate that just societies are likely to pursue broad public health initiatives for their citizens, seeking to improve conditions for all types of citizens, whereas unjust societies focus on health issues of importance to the most influential citizens, if they cultivate public health at all. Similarly, just societies will promote health-care research equity. For example, in a just society the principles regulating drug development and testing will ensure that therapies benefit women as positively as men, and that remedies for illnesses prevalent in minority or powerless populations are sought as energetically as for the illnesses of large or influential populations. In sum, we can postulate that larger proportions of the citizenry of just societies will live in conditions that improve health than will the citizenry of unjust societies. Parenthetically, although more citizens will be healthier in just societies than in unjust ones, just societies will not necessarily manifest higher aggregated levels of health than unjust ones. In a just society, broad-based access to health support likely will maintain at-risk individuals whose lives would be lost in an unjust society. To illustrate, a society where the concern to improve everyone's health creates programs that prevent polluted urban air may maintain the lives of more sufferers of serious respiratory disorders than a society in which only the powerful have access to clean air. A society where dialysis is available without regard to age or cause of kidney failure is likely to maintain the lives of more elderly diabetics than one that denies this lifesaving treatment to whatever groups cannot meet the eligibility qualifications to have more years of life. And a society where fragile neonates are treated regardless of their prospects of disability is likely to increase the proportion of disabled children in its population....

The standard of justice in health care is not "the nation's health," although a depressed level of aggregated health may be a sign of neglect of the welfare of many citizens. Equitable personal healthiness, at levels appropriate to facilitate different individuals' securing of their own variety of goods, is what we should expect of a just system.

Anita Silvers, "Bedside Justice and Disability: Personalizing Preserving Impartiality," in *Medicine and Social Justice: Essays on the Distribution of Health Care*, First Edition, ed. Rosamond Rhodes et al. (Oxford, UK: Oxford University Press, 2002), pp. 235–247.

Reading 10-3 Ageism and Fair Innings | John Harris

Study Questions

As you read the excerpt, please consider the following questions:

1. What does Harris think about the importance of a person's desire to stay alive?

2. What point is Harris making in discussing the notion of fair innings?

3. Harris concludes here by focusing on developing sufficient resources to postpone death. How does that point toward a different conclusion than the fair innings argument?

I am inclined to believe that where two individuals both equally wish to go on living for as long as possible our duty to respect this wish is paramount. It is, as I have suggested, the most important part of what is involved in valuing the lives of others. Each person's desire to stay alive should be regarded as of the same importance and as deserving the same respect as that of anyone else, irrespective of the quality of their life or its expected duration.

This would hold good in all cases in which we have to choose between lives, except one. And that is where one individual has had a fair innings and the other not. In this case, while both equally wish to have their lives further prolonged one, but not the other, has had a fair innings. In this case, although there is nothing to choose between the two candidates from the point of view of their respective will to live and both would suffer the injustice of having their life cut short when it might continue, only one would suffer the further injustice of being deprived of a fair innings—a benefit that the other has received.

It is sometimes said that it is a misfortune to grow old, but it is not nearly so great a misfortune as not to grow old. Growing old when you don't want to is not half the misfortune that is not growing old when you do want to. It is this truth that the fair innings argument captures. So that while it remains true, as the anti-ageist argument asserts, that the value of the unelapsed possible lifespan of each person who wants to go on living is equally valuable however long that span may be, the question of which person's premature death involves the greater injustice can be important. The fair innings argument points to the fact that the injustice done to someone who has not had a fair innings when they lose out to someone who has is significantly greater than in the reverse circumstances. It is for this reason that in the hopefully rare cases where we have to choose between candidates who differ only in this respect that we should choose to give as many people as possible the chance of a fair innings....

So long as people want to live out the rest of their lives, however long this may be, or looks like being, then they should be given the best chance we can give them of doing so and we should not choose between such people on any other grounds, but treat each as an equal. The most moral and the most honorable way of dealing with the difficulties and anomalies that remain is to try to ensure that we have sufficient resources to devote to postponing death, wherever and whenever we can, whether for long or for short periods, so that we do not have to choose between people invidiously.

John Harris, *The Value of Life: An Introduction to Medical Ethics* (New York: Taylor & Francis, 1990).

Reading 10-4   The Right to Health Care | Kai Nielsen

Study Questions

As you read the excerpt, please consider the following questions:

1. What exactly does Nielsen mean when he claims that there is a right to health care?
2. Nielsen suggests that the equal right to health care does not mean that everyone should be treated exactly alike. What does that mean?
3. What does Nielsen think about the importance of the ability of a patient to pay for health care?

If we genuinely believe in moral equality, we will want to see come into existence a world in which all people capable of self-direction have, and have as nearly as is feasible equally, control over their own lives and can, as far as the institutional arrangements for it obtaining are concerned, all live flourishing lives where their needs and desires as individuals are met as fully as possible and as fully and extensively as is compatible with the possibility being open to everyone alike...

The following are healthcare needs which are also basic needs: being healthy and having conditions treated which impede one's functioning well or which adversely affect one's well-being or cause suffering. These are plainly things we need. Where societies have the economic and technical capacity to do so, as these societies plainly do, without undermining other equally urgent or more urgent needs, these health needs, as basic needs, must be met, and the right to have such medical care is a right for everyone in the society regardless of her capacity to pay. This just follows from a commitment to moral equality into an equality of condition. Where we have the belief, a belief which is very basic in non-fascistic modernizing societies, that each person's good is to be given equal consideration, it is hard not to go in that way, given a plausible conception of needs and reasonable list of needs based on that conception. If there is the need for some particular regime of care and the society has the resources to meet that need, without undermining structures protecting other at least equally urgent needs, then, *ceteris paribus*, the society, if it is a decent society, must do so. The commitment to more equality—the commitment to the belief that the life of each person matters and matters equally—entails, given a few plausible empirical premises, that each person's health needs will be the object of an equal regard. Each has an equal claim, *prima facie*, to have her needs satisfied where this is possible. That does not, of course, mean that people should all be treated alike in the sense of their all getting the same thing. Not everyone needs flu shots, braces, a dialysis machine, a psychiatrist, or a triple bypass. What should be equal is that each person's health needs should be the object of equal societal concern since each person's good should be given equal consideration.... Everyone should have their health needs met where possible. Moreover, where the need is the same, they should have (where possible), and where other at least equally urgent needs are not thereby undermined, the same quality treatment. No differentiation should be made between them on the basis of their ability to pay.... There should, in short, where this is possible, be open and free medical treatment of the same quality and extent available to everyone in the society.

Kai Nielsen, "Autonomy, Equality, and a Just Health Care System." *International Journal of Applied Philosophy* 4: 3 (Spring 1989), pp. 39–44.

Reading 10-5   No Right to Health Care | John David Lewis

Study Questions

As you read the excerpt, please consider the following questions:

1. How does Lewis connect the notion of a right to health care to a duty to provide that care for others?

2. Why does Lewis suggest that health care is not a right but a responsibility?

3. What is the worry that Lewis has about coercion being used against doctors and other medical professionals?

The greatest motivation behind calls for government control of medicine today may be found in the idea that medical care is an individual right, to be provided by the state. Such a claim is powerful precisely because it is moral in nature; it demands that doctors, other medical professionals, and taxpayers accept the moral duty to provide medical care to others because they need it. . . .

If medical care is a right, then every member of the medical profession is bound—and may be required by law—to provide such care, at terms set by the government, whether they agree or not. Further, every citizen of means will be bound to finance such care for others, through taxation. But is this moral claim correct? Those who oppose such government interventions generally see medical care not as a right, but as a personal responsibility for each individual, to be purchased voluntarily from wiling producers. If so, then no one may properly demand medical services as a right—or be coerced into providing such services.

These two positions are in deep conflict in America today. This essay will expand upon each, and show they are founded upon diametrically opposed views of individual rights, which are at moral and conceptual odds with each other. A conclusion follows: claims to medical care as a right are historically recent, are not consistent with the rights set forth either in the Declaration of Independence or the U.S. Constitution, and are logically contradictory. Acceptance of these claims, however, has greatly empowered the growth of the welfare state, and has hastened the decline in freedom for everyone while dramatically increasing medical costs. . . .

I start with a particular claim about the concept of rights: a right is a moral principle that identifies and prescribes the freedom of the individual in a society under law. A right defines the scope of individual freedom against which others may not infringe. The grounding of rights is found in the nature and identity of the individual, not in wishes or needs belonging to a group. . . .

There is no right to medical care, because there is no right to coerce medical professionals to provide it. . . . To claim a right to medical care is to claim nothing less than a right to run the lives of those who must provide the care. The "duties" invoked may be in direct opposition to the goals of doctors and other medical professionals, each of whom made a commitment to pursue medicine as a career across decades. It is because they made this commitment that they are now to be placed under state control. This highlights the deep opposition between the egoistic conception of rights as freedom from coercion, and the altruistic conception of rights as imposing duties on others.

John David Lewis, "There Is No Right to Healthcare," in *Medical Ethics*, 2nd ed., ed. Michael Boylan (New York: Wiley-Blackwell, 2013), pp. 275–282.

Reading 10-6 How Equal Must Our Rights to Health Care Be? | Norman Daniels

Study Questions

As you read the excerpt, please consider the following questions:

1. What does Daniels think about the notion of a tiered system of health care?
2. What kinds of objections does Daniels consider with regard to allowing wealthy people to purchase better care?
3. What is Daniels concerned about when he worries that some forms of tiering could leave poor people behind?

How equal must our rights to health care be? Specifically, must everyone receive exactly the same kinds of health-care services and coverage, or is fairness in health care compatible with a "tiered" system? . . .

The primary social obligation is to assure everyone access to a tier of services that effectively promotes normal functioning and thus protects equality of opportunity. Since health care is not the only important good, resources to be invested in the basic tier are appropriately and reasonably limited, for example, by democratic decisions about how much to invest in education or job training as opposed to health care. Because of their very high "opportunity costs," there will be some beneficial medical services that it will be reasonable not to provide in the basic tier, or to provide only on a limited basis, for example, with queuing. . . .

In a society that permits significant income and wealth inequalities, some people will want to buy coverage for these additional services. Why not let them? After all, we allow people to use their after-tax income and wealth as they see fit to pursue the "quality of life" and opportunities they prefer. The rich can buy special security systems for their homes. They can buy safer cars. They can buy private schooling for their children. Why not allow them to buy supplementary health care for their families?

One objection to allowing a supplementary tier is that its existence might undermine the basic tier either economically or politically. It might attract better-quality providers away from the basic tier, or raise costs in the basic tier, reducing the ability of society to meet its social obligations. The supplementary tier might undermine political support for the basic tier, for example, by undercutting the social solidarity needed if people are to remain committed to protecting opportunity for all. These objections are serious, and where a supplementary tier undermines the basic tier in either way, economically or politically, priority must be given to protecting the basic tier. In principle, however, it seems possible to design a system in which the supplementary tier does not undermine the basic one. . . .

A second objection is not to tiering itself but to the structure of inequality that results. Compare two scenarios. In one, the most people are adequately served by the basic tier and only the best-off groups in society have the means and see the need to purchase supplementary insurance. . . . In the second, the poorest groups can complain that they are left behind by others in society even in the protection of their health. In the first, the majority has less grounds for reasonable resentment or regret. . . . If the basic tier is not undermined by higher tiers, and if the structure of the inequality that results is not objectionable, then it is difficult to see why some tiering should not be allowed.

Norman Daniels, "Is There a Right to Health Care? And If So, What does It Encompass?," in *A Companion to Bioethics*, 2nd ed., eds. Helga Kuhse and Peter Singer (New York: Wiley-Blackwell, 2009), pp. 362–372.

Reading 10-7   Vulnerability and Bioethics | Wendy Rogers

Study Questions

As you read the excerpt, please consider the following questions:

1. What are the two notions of vulnerability that Rogers describes?

2. Why does Rogers suggest that a focus on consent is not sufficient when it comes to vulnerability?

3. How is a concern for vulnerability connected to the idea of solidarity in Rogers's thinking?

Vulnerability is a critical concept in bioethics. The fields of research ethics and public health ethics rely on the concept to identify individuals or groups who require special attention or increased protection compared with an unspecified norm, while attention to vulnerability is implicit within many accounts of clinical ethics. As we have seen, there is a dual notion of vulnerability operating within bioethics. The concept has been recognized as universally applicable: as embodied beings we are all vulnerable in the face of health threats, decreased capacities, and our changing circumstances over time. Simultaneously, there is widespread recognition that extra duties of protections are owed to the especially vulnerable. This has led to something of a theoretical impasse, since these two classes of vulnerability are not well distinguished in either the bioethical or philosophical literature. In turn, lacking such clarity makes it difficult to identify the vulnerable and respond to their needs in morally defensible ways.

By taking vulnerability seriously, by attempting to understand just what it is that we identify when we find a person or group to be vulnerable, there is potential to provide a major reorientation or shift within bioethics. . . . Bioethics has been strongly shaped by research ethics and the ethics of the clinical encounter. This has led to a focus on certain key concepts, particularly respect for autonomy and informed consent, and how these can be protected within the confines of the consultation or the research ethics review process. This is an important task as there is no doubt that, absent such protections, vulnerable individuals are harmed in various

ways. However, we need a deeper understanding of vulnerability in order to grasp the significance of, and respond to specific vulnerabilities of patients or research participants or populations. A serious focus on vulnerability will both allow us and force us to look beyond the often procedural issue of informed consent to broader issues such as vulnerability arising from the structure of the research enterprise or the shape and direction of the research agenda. Addressing vulnerability is more than just a matter of improving consent procedures—it includes questioning the nature of the research itself.

A focus within bioethics on vulnerability highlights our common humanity and may thereby offer grounds for increased attention to community and solidarity. . . . We can, however, build on social justice approaches in public health to develop our understanding of the links between vulnerability and solidarity. As biological and social beings, we share much vulnerability—to ill health, to bad luck, to natural and man-made disasters. Although these and other vulnerabilities are not equally distributed, none of us are invulnerable. We all have some experience and understanding of what it is to feel vulnerable. Appealing to our shared inherent vulnerability is one way of grounding solidarity as a value in bioethics in a way that may avoid a divisive us or them mentality and go beyond self-interest or prudential concerns.

Wendy Rogers, "Vulnerability and Bioethics," in *Vulnerability: New Essays in Ethics and Feminist Philosophy*, eds. Catriona Mackenzie, Wendy Rogers, and Susan Dodds (Cambridge, UK: Cambridge University Press, 2014).

Review Exercises

1. Why does the study of bioethics tend to focus on case studies (sometimes called casuistry), and what does this mean for moral judgment?

2. How many basic principles of bioethics are there? Compare and contrast different lists of principles (including the list provided in this chapter).

3. What is health? How are social and cultural factors connected to judgments about health?

4. What kinds of cultural and social factors are at play in thinking about the COVID-19 pandemic from a health care and public health perspective?

5. Explain how codes of ethics have evolved and are used in health care and research.

6. Can a code of ethics or list of principles help us solve ethical dilemmas?

7. Imagine some cases in which benevolent paternalism comes into conflict with respect for autonomy. How would you resolve such a dilemma?

8. How do you think we should respond to cases in which rationing is needed? What rule or criterion would you apply?

9. Is there a right to health and health care? If so, how much and at what cost? If not, why not?

10. Explain why eugenics might be a problem if we focus only on health maximization.

Discussion Cases

1. Privacy, minors, and parents. A 15-year-old girl is taken to a pediatrician by her mother with a fever and flu-like symptoms. After some tests, the doctor determines that the girl has a sexually transmitted disease. In a private consultation, the doctor informs the girl that she has an STD. In that conversation, the teen explains that her mother does not know that she is sexually active. She begs the doctor not to disclose the diagnosis. In the state where this occurs, minors are permitted to receive this kind of health care without parental consent. The girl's mother, however, demands further information about her daughter, about why certain medications are being prescribed, and so on. She explains to the doctor that she loves her daughter and wants the best for her and that in order to help the girl, she has a right to know what the diagnosis is.

Does the mother have the right to know about her daughter's diagnosis and treatment? Would it matter if the girls were younger or older? How can we apply the values of autonomy and beneficence in this case?

2. Organ transplants for people with disabilities and older adults. Some studies show that access to organ transplantation may involve inequities. For example, if an adult with an intellectual disability needs an organ transplant, they may be less likely to receive one.[64] A well-known case involved Sandra Jensen, who had Down syndrome. Sandra needed a heart-lung transplant, but in the selection process she was discriminated against because of her

disability. Eventually, Sandra received a transplant in 1996, the first person with Down syndrome to receive such a transplant. A more recent case involved Charlotte Woodward, another woman with Down syndrome who received a heart transplant. Different American states have different laws governing discrimination in organ transplants. This led to the introduction of a federal law, The Charlotte Woodward Organ Transplant Discrimination Prevention Act, in the U.S. Congress intended to prevent this kind of discrimination. Similar discrimination may exist with regard to age. As the population ages, more older people are in need of organs such as kidneys. This has led to proposals such as "old for old," a slogan meant to indicate that older people in need of transplant should get older organs (from older donors) that may be less healthy.[65] The idea is that a younger donor kidney would go to a younger recipient who is likely to live longer. What kinds of criteria should be used for determining who gets a donated organ? Would it be discriminatory to establish criteria the took into account a recipient's age or disability status? What about the idea of "old for old"—is that an acceptable principle?

3. Dying alone during COVID. During the COVID-19 pandemic, many hospitals and nursing homes insisted on isolating their patients, including those who were dying. This procedure was justified out of the desire to prevent the spread of this contagious disease. This justification gained further support when medical supplies and hospital beds were in high demand and hospitals were worried about being swamped and overwhelmed with patients. Patients who died of COVID-19 were often isolated and prevented from being in the presence of their loved ones. Not only was this hard on patients who were already suffering and nearing death, but it was also difficult for grieving family members. Cell phones and video links were used to connect grieving families to their dying kin. But many died without getting a final chance to touch the skin of a wife, a father, or a child. In response, a few nurses and bioethicists have protested against what they see as overly restrictive visitation policies, policies that are obviated by the development of vaccines, efficient air filters, and other techniques that can minimize transmission.[66] And even then, one wonders whether a family member should be allowed to risk a visit to a loved one, so long as they understand the risk. Is it paternalistic to prevent people from visiting loved ones dying of infectious diseases such as COVID-19? Does a utilitarian concern for the greater good justify the idea of isolating those who are dying of COVID-19? What other values could be employed in thinking about this case?

4. Truth, lying, and caring. A physician, Daniela Lamas, wrote a column in the *New York Times* expressing regret for telling a dying patient the truth about his impending death.

The patient had been living in denial of the underlying disease until he ended up in the intensive care unit. He wanted to go home. But Dr. Lamas told him bluntly, "You're dying." The man was distraught. He soon died. In her column, Dr. Lamas wondered whether she did the right thing in telling the truth. She wrote, "I know that I added to my patient's pain in the last hours of his life. I wish that I had done it differently. I could have paused and told him that yes, he was going to go home. I could have simply been there with him and said nothing at all. That small kindness might have done more for him than the truth."[67] In response to this column, another doctor, Kenneth Prager, wrote a letter to *The Times* in which he explained that a "sizeable minority" of patients do not want to hear the truth. He explained, "While patients have a right to know, they also have a right not to know. And by telling patients in denial about their impending death—what they don't want to hear—physicians may violate an ancient dictum of medical ethics: First, do no harm."[68]

Is Dr. Prager right? Do patients who are in denial about their disease have a right not to know? Can truth telling be connected to non-maleficence in the way he suggests? Or is it always right to tell the truth? And what do you think about Dr. Lamas's claim that lying or remaining silent would have been a "small kindness"—does that imply that lying can be part of beneficent care?

Knowledge Check Answer Key

1. **b.** Moral questions about how to grow the economy and share wealth is typically not a consideration of bioethics.

2. **d.** Non-maleficence is associated with the idea of doing no harm (*primum non nocere*).

3. **a.** Beneficence is focused on the well-being of individual patients, while health maximization is a concern of public health.

4. **d.** Autonomy is a value associated with informed consent.

11 Abortion and Euthanasia

Learning Outcomes

After reading this chapter, you should be able to:

11.1 Explain the conflict between pro-life and pro-choice points of view.

11.2 Evaluate moral and ontological issues involved in thinking about abortion.

11.3 Evaluate the application of moral theories to different kinds of euthanasia.

11.4 Explain social justice and feminist concerns that arise in thinking about abortion and euthanasia.

11.5 Summarize the legal dispute in the United States about the right to privacy.

11.6 Analyze how double effect reasoning might apply in thinking about euthanasia and abortion.

11.7 Defend a thesis about abortion and euthanasia.

The End of *Roe v. Wade*

In 2022, the U.S. Supreme Court issued a ruling, *Dobbs v. Jackson*, that overturned *Roe v. Wade*. The *Roe* case was decided in 1973. It had established the right to abortion in the United States. *Dobbs* eliminated that right. After *Dobbs* was decided, a number of American states quickly enacted laws restricting abortion. Opponents of abortion viewed this as the culmination of a long struggle to eliminate abortion. Abortion rights advocates saw the *Dobbs* decision as a defeat for women's rights. The debate about abortion concerns a conflict between those who defend privacy and autonomy, and those who think that abortion is an unjustifiable form of killing. It is easy to see that this conflict connects to other issues such as euthanasia.

SHAWN THEW/EPA/Corbis

Abortion has long been a subject of controversy in the United States and elsewhere. In 2018, for example, Ireland passed a referendum that legalized abortion there within the first twelve weeks of pregnancy.[1] And while some American states are prohibiting abortion, some states in Mexico have recently legalized the procedure.[2] Some defenders of abortion rights argue that a fetus is not yet a person and that abortion is thus not really an act of homicide. Others argue that even if a fetus is a person, a mother's right to choose trumps the fetus's right to life. On the other side are those who claim that "life begins at conception," which is meant to imply that a fetus is a person with a right to life, even at a very early stage of development. In the background of this debate are spiritual, philosophical, and legal questions about personhood, liberty, and the rights of women. Our answers to those questions can have implications for a variety of other issues involving gender, sexuality, reproduction, and end-of-life decisions.

What Do You Think?

1. Do women have a fundamental right to choose to have an abortion?
2. What kinds of beings have a basic right to life?
3. Should abortion be legal or illegal?
4. How does your thinking about abortion connect to your thinking about end-of-life decisions and other issues involving privacy?

Introduction

11.1 Explain the conflict between pro-life and pro-choice points of view.

In the previous chapter, we discussed general principles of bioethics as well as some concrete issues in medical ethics including the importance of values such as respect for autonomy, concern for well-being, avoiding harm, and a concern for justice. We introduced the topics of euthanasia and abortion in that chapter. Here we focus on these two topics in much more detail. The moral issues involved in thinking about abortion and euthanasia are interconnected. Among the issues we will discuss here are conceptual and ontological questions about the beginning and end of life, as well as a concern for autonomy, consent, and choice.

With regard to the beginning of life there are difficult, complicated, and contentious questions, such as the following: Is a fetus the kind of being that possesses rights or personhood? When in the course of development does a fetus become a person or obtain rights? What is the nature of the relationship between the mother and the fetus? And whose rights are more important—the mother or the fetus—when there is a conflict? With regard to the end of life there are equally difficult, complicated, and contentious questions, such as the following: When does human life end? What are the conditions that make life worth living? Is it ever morally justifiable to allow someone to die or to actively bring about their death? And what are the moral obligations of friends, family, and caregivers when people are suffering and in pain?

Pro-Choice and Pro-Life

As we begin, let's clarify a very basic distinction between pro-choice and pro-life points of view. This distinction often appears in popular discussion of these kinds of topics. These two points of view are not strictly parallel: each focuses on a different part of a complex issue. With regard to abortion, the pro-choice side focuses on the rights of women. It can be connected to the idea of autonomy as found among the basic principles of medical ethics—and the right to privacy as found in legal discussions. Pro-choice is not "pro-abortion." One can support the right to choose without claiming that abortions ought to happen. Nor does the pro-choice argument claim that abortion is a good or optimal outcome. Rather, the pro-choice side of the argument is often described as defending "abortion rights" or "reproductive rights." Notice that we might have a right to something but not ever choose to exercise that right. In the United States, for example, there is a "right to bear arms,"

Figure 11-1 Pro-choice v. pro-life.

located in the Second Amendment to the Constitution. This does not mean you must own or carry a weapon. Rather, it means if you choose to own a gun, the government cannot prevent you from doing so. Similar reasoning applies to the concept of "abortion rights" on the pro-choice side of the argument. The basic idea is that pregnant women should be free to choose to have abortions. In many cases, this choice is a tragic one involving a conflict of values: abortion occurs in the context of unwanted pregnancy, but pregnancy is usually viewed as a good thing.[3] And it is entirely possible for a defender of the pro-choice point of view to say, "I don't think I would ever choose to have an abortion myself, but I think women should have the right to choose for themselves." In teaching this topic for decades, we have often heard students make that kind of claim. Notice that the focus of this pro-choice claim is on the general idea of a woman's right to choose. The pro-choice point of view is thus often connected to other claims about women's rights and respect for the autonomy of women, which is why the topic of abortion rights has often been an area of concern for feminists. Keeping this in mind can help explain slogans such as "my body, my choice" that are found on the pro-choice side of the argument. One of the leading abortion rights groups in the United States is NARAL, Pro-Choice America (NARAL is an acronym that stands for "National Association to Repeal Abortion Laws"). As NARAL Pro-Choice America explains on their website:

> The right to choose abortion is essential to ensuring a woman can decide for herself if, when and with whom to start or grow a family. We'll never stop fighting to protect and expand this fundamental human right.[4]

On the other side of the debate is the pro-life position. This approach is focused on defending the "right to life" of the fetus by opposing abortion. As we shall see in this chapter, there are complicated questions about the moral status of the fetus. This even includes a dispute about what we should call a human fetus. The pro-life approach often avoids the term "fetus," speaking instead of "the child" or "the baby"—and thereby implying that the developing fetus is really a human person. In what follows, we will use the word

"fetus"—as this is the preferred terminology in medicine and in philosophical accounts of abortion. The pro-life point of view typically claims that the fetus has a "right to life." The basic anti-abortion argument made on the pro-life side is that to end a pregnancy involves destroying a fetus, and since, from this perspective, a fetus has a right to life, this is an egregious violation that amounts to murder. Organizations that argue and advocate against abortion often describe the right to life as beginning at the point of conception. The National Right to Life Committee (NRLC) is one of the oldest and most active anti-abortion groups in the United States. On its website, the NRLC explains its opposition to abortion by maintaining, among other things, that millions of "unborn babies" are killed each year, as follows:

> The life of a baby begins long before he or she is born. A new individual human being begins at fertilization, when the sperm and ovum meet to form a single cell. If the baby's life is not interrupted, he or she will someday become an adult man or woman. Worldwide, millions of unborn babies are killed each year.[5]

Notice the language used in that passage speaks of unborn babies, not fetuses. And notice the implication of the idea that life begins at fertilization (or conception). This means that any intervention that destroys a human embryo, even early on in the process of gestation, is morally problematic. We'll discuss this issue further in Chapter 12 in connection with arguments about in vitro fertilization and other reproductive technologies. The word "embryo" is typically employed in medical discussions of the early stages of pregnancy and fetal development. Again, notice that in discussions of abortion, our choice of language can indicate a normative commitment. Is a fertilized ovum a "baby" or an "embryo"?

The terminological complexities connected with abortion include several other issues that we should think carefully about. One involves the question of the procedure itself. For our purposes here, we will be considering abortion as a voluntary termination of pregnancy. This helps us distinguish abortion from miscarriage (although we should note that sometimes a miscarriage is described as a "spontaneous abortion").

But even the word abortion comes with moral connotations. Some view this procedure as an evil and terrible thing; they may also turn the word abortion into an insult, for example, calling doctors who perform abortions "abortionists" (which is usually used in a negative sense). In response to this, some want to avoid the term entirely, speaking instead of "termination" of pregnancy. Another issue involves what we choose to call the person who is carrying the fetus. Although it is typical to speak of "mothers" and "pregnant women," some have suggested that we ought instead to speak of "pregnant persons." The later choice of language aims to be inclusive of trans people and those who do not conform to traditional gender norms. Furthermore, in speaking of pregnant "persons," we may find it easier to think about conflicts of rights between persons— since one way of conceiving abortion rights focuses on a conflict of rights between a fetus and the pregnant person whose uterus is gestating it. But that kind of clinical language may appear to be cold and even offensive from the perspective of those who prefer to speak of "mothers" and "wombs" instead of pregnant persons and gestating uteruses. The legal world continues, for the most part to speak of mothers and women (as we see in court cases such as *Roe v. Wade* and *Dobbs v. Jackson*). And in focusing on pregnant *women*, the issue becomes more obviously one of concern for feminists. Of course, language and culture are in flux. For our purposes here, we've chosen to speak primarily of pregnant women and mothers, although we also occasional use the phrase "pregnant person." Do you agree with this choice of language? What do you think we ought to call a person with a uterus who is pregnant? And what do you think we ought to call the entity contained within that uterus?

These terminological questions point toward deeper ontological and moral questions. The word **ontology** means theory of being. The ontological question with regard to abortion is whether we are talking about a clump of cells that belongs entirely to the mother, a separate and independent being, an unborn child, or something else. This question is reflected in whether we choose to call this thing an embryo, a fetus, a baby, or a person. In our discussion here, we will use the term "person" to refer to an entity who is worthy of moral consideration. When we ask whether a fetus is a person,

we are asking whether this entity has a certain kind of ontological and moral value. Similar moral and ontological questions hold with regard to ethical questions at the end of life. Is a brain-dead human body a person? Do we call such a body "kept alive" by machinery a "corpse"? And is this machinery really keeping the person "alive"—or is the person already dead despite the fact that the body appears to be alive?

There are terminological disputes involved in the conversation about the end of life. The word "euthanasia" literally means "good death." But some deny that death can ever be good. Could there be cases in which it would better to be dead—or to be killed? In some contexts, this is described as "mercy killing." But philosophers and the law have tended to avoid that term. A related terminological concern is what we call it when a doctor prescribes lethal medication that is taken by the patient at home. Philosophers have tended to call this "physician-assisted suicide." But the word "suicide" has moral and legal connotations. For example, insurance policies may not cover suicide. And although it is common to say that people "commit suicide," some argue that this linguistic formulation carries a negative connotation—since we "commit crimes" but rarely use the word "commit" to describe something positive (although some people do encourage us to "commit random acts of kindness"). Some advocates seek to avoid the term suicide and speak instead of "aid in dying" or "death with dignity." In California, the law that made assisted suicide legal was called "The End of Life Option." The legislation states, "death resulting from the self-administration of an aid-in-dying drug is not suicide, and therefore health and insurance coverage shall not be exempted on that basis."[6] What do you think we ought to call it when a person takes lethal medication to end their life—have they "committed suicide" or merely availed themselves of aid in dying?

Now let's consider how pro-choice and pro-life points of view might connect to discussions of euthanasia and what we call here physician-assisted suicide. In general, pro-choice thinkers will want to allow people to decide for themselves, while the pro-life position will argue against euthanasia and assisted suicide. A pro-choice approach to these topics will argue that individuals should be free to choose how and when they die. There are complexities here involving autonomy and consent.

These complexities arise especially in cases involving disability and impairment. But the presumption of a pro-choice approach to the end of life is that autonomy matters. If a patient provides autonomous consent to a procedure that ends their life, then that life-ending procedure can be justified. There are a variety of ways that this can happen. A patient could explicitly request a life-ending procedure. In the case of assisted suicide, this occurs when a patient asks a doctor to prescribe lethal medication and then takes that medicine themselves. There are also legal and medical documents known as living wills and advance directives, in which patients indicate their preferences for end-of-life care. In some cases, consent becomes murky—such as when someone suffers brain damage and there is no advance directive. But pro-choice thinking applied to the end of life will generally be in favor of the right to choose to "die with dignity." In response, opponents of euthanasia and assisted suicide will argue that those kinds of choices ought not be made by us and that we should focus on "living with dignity," as it is sometimes put, rather than helping people die.

The link between abortion and euthanasia has been made by pro-choice authors such as Judith Jarvis Thomson and Ronald Dworkin. Dworkin explained the link by connecting the pro-choice idea to an argument against governmental tyranny. He wrote:

> People who dread being kept alive, permanently unconscious or sedated beyond sense, intubated and groomed and tended as vegetables, think this condition degrades rather than respects what has been intrinsically valuable in their own living. Others disagree: They believe, about euthanasia as about abortion, that mere biological life is so inherently precious that nothing can justify deliberately ending it. The disagreement, once again, is an essentially religious or spiritual one, and a decent government, committed to personal integrity and freedom, has no business imposing a decision. Dictating how people should see the meaning of their own lives and deaths is a crippling, humiliating form of tyranny.[7]

In 1997, when the Supreme Court was considering cases involving physician-assisted suicide, Dworkin and a group of well-known philosophers made arguments in favor of the practice in an amicus (friend of the court) brief known as "The Philosophers' Brief" (an excerpt is included in the readings for this chapter). These philosophers conclude: "In a free society, individuals must be allowed to make those decisions for themselves, out of their own faith, conscience, and convictions."[8]

On the other hand, the pro-life position is typically opposed to both euthanasia and physician-assisted suicide. The basic idea here is that life is good and death is bad. This leads to the normative claim that it is wrong to kill or to help someone end their own life. In some cases, this idea is connected to a comprehensive pro-life point of view that has been described as a "consistent ethic of life." Such a comprehensive approach is opposed to all kinds of killing: suicide, euthanasia, abortion, the death penalty, and war. This idea is closely associated with the teachings of the Roman Catholic Church. The idea was described in detail by Pope John Paul II in his text *The Gospel of Life* (1995), where he stated his opposition to "whatever is opposed to life itself, such as any type of murder, genocide, abortion, euthanasia, or willful self-destruction, whatever violates the integrity of the human person."[9] This pro-life position is quite broad in its scope. It involves opposition to slavery, prostitution, and anything that is not supportive of "life," even including the working conditions of the poor. This idea has been reiterated by more recent Catholic thinkers, including Pope Francis.

Of course, there is disagreement about "life issues" within and among religious perspectives. Christians disagree about abortion and about euthanasia.[10] And when we consider the breadth of world religions, we find a wide diversity of thinking about these topics. Rabbi Dayna Ruttenberg explained that Judaism offers a different take on abortion. In an article she wrote as the U.S. Supreme Court was overturning *Roe v. Wade*, she explained, "many of us working to protect the right to abortion are doing so because of our religious commitments, not despite them."[11] She explains further:

> Abortion laws that enshrine specific Christian concepts—"fetal personhood," for example, or the notion that life begins at conception—trample over other understandings of when life begins. That doesn't affect just Jews, but also Muslims, atheists, agnostics, and plenty of Christians who support reproductive freedom.[12]

The pro-life idea can be articulated without appeal to religion. Typically, this kind of argument is made from within a point of view that might be connected to the normative theory known as "natural law" (which we discuss in Chapter 7). One of the texts included in the readings for this chapter makes this kind of argument. J. Gay-Williams says, "Every human being has a natural inclination to continue living." And, "Euthanasia does violence to this natural goal of survival. It is literally acting against nature because all the processes of nature are bent toward the end of bodily survival."[13]

Of course, not everyone who is pro-life with regard to abortion or euthanasia will also be opposed to war and the death penalty—and vice versa. There may be cases in which a pro-life approach would allow for justifiable killing, say killing in self-defense. But once we open the door to thinking about exceptions such as justification for killing in self-defense, we may end up thinking about possible exceptions in the case of abortion or euthanasia. Would an exception to the prohibition on abortion be permitted in a case where pregnancy threatened a woman's life or reproductive health? And in the case of euthanasia, what about an exception in the case of debilitating pain?

There are challenges for thinking about a consistent and comprehensive pro-life position. What qualifies as "life"? And what do we do when there are conflicting ideas about life or about whose rights have priority? There are also challenges for thinking about whether there are any limits to the pro-choice point of view. Can a person consent to anything and everything? Or are there moral limits to choice and to consent?

Table 11-1 Outline of Moral Approaches to Pro-Choice and Pro-Life Arguments Regarding Abortion and Euthanasia

	Pro-Choice	Moderate Choice	Pro-Life
Thesis	Pregnant woman is free to terminate pregnancy as she wishes; voluntary euthanasia and physician-assisted suicide ought to be permitted.	Early abortion is permissible, but late-term abortions are morally problematic; there may be limits on when death can be consented to.	Abortion is prohibited, with possible exceptions for cases of rape, incest, or threat to the mother's health; euthanasia is wrong even if there is consent.
Corollaries and Implications	Fetus is not a person and/or a woman's right trumps any rights a fetus might have; there are situations in which death with dignity is better than life with suffering or disability.	Moral status of the fetus may change during the course of a pregnancy; euthanasia choices should include discussions of mental health and palliative care.	Fetus is a person based on a claim such as "life begins at conception"; anti-euthanasia argument may maintain that suffering is good and that we do not have a "right to die."
Connections with Moral Theory	Emphasis is on rights, autonomy, and control in birthing or dying; consequentialist focuses on benefits of abortion/euthanasia as well as preventing harms and suffering; possible connection with feminist concern for women's rights.	Conflict of rights may exist between the mother's right to choose and the fetus's developing right to life; judgments about consequences may depend on the stage of pregnancy and the degree of suffering at the end of life.	Focus is on the fetus's right to life and the basic idea that life is good; consequentialist argument celebrates benefits of family life or appeal to natural law ideas about reproduction, pregnancy, and natural death.
Relevant authors	Mary Anne Warren Peter Singer	Judith Jarvis Thomson Ronald Dworkin	Don Marquis J. Gay-Williams

Moral Approaches to Abortion

11.2 Evaluate moral and ontological issues involved in thinking about abortion.

Some arguments about abortion focus on questions about the moral or ontological status of the fetus. These are questions about whether the fetus is a human being or a person and whether the fetus has inherent value or rights, including a right to life. But there are also arguments about abortion for which the question of the moral status of the fetus is not essential. We'll look first at arguments that do not concern themselves primarily with questions about the fetus. Then we'll consider the moral status of the fetus in more detail.

Utilitarian and Consequentialist Approaches to Abortion

Arguments that focus on something other than the moral status of the fetus tend to be consequentialist in nature and broadly utilitarian. Arguments in support of abortion rights often cite the bad consequences that may result from a continued pregnancy—for example, the loss of a job or other opportunities for the pregnant person, the suffering of the future child, the burden of caring for a child under difficult circumstances, and other economic, psychological, and social consequences. Some utilitarian arguments against abortion also cite the loss of potential happiness and future social contributions of the being who is aborted.

These kinds of arguments consider the likely consequences of alternative decisions—for the fetus, for the mother, and for others involved. Among the kinds of consequences to consider are health risks and benefits, positive or negative mental or psychological consequences, and financial and social results of the alternative choices. For example, a pregnant woman might consider questions such as these: What would be the effect on her of having the child versus ending the pregnancy? What are the consequences to any others affected? Would the child, if born, be likely to have a happy or unhappy life, and how would one determine this? How would an abortion or the child's birth affect their family, other children, the biological father, the grandparents, and other people?

Notice that the issue of whether the fetus is a person or a human being is not the primary concern when arguing from this type of consequentialist perspective. Abortion at a later stage of pregnancy might have different effects on people than at an earlier stage, and it might also have different effects on the fetus in terms of whether it might experience pain. It is the effects on everyone involved—the mother, the fetus, and others—that count in utilitarian thinking. Utilitarians may evaluate the moral and ontological status of the fetus in various ways. Those various evaluations may affect the outcome of the utilitarian calculation—depending on how much weight we give to the fetus, its future experience, and so on. Also notice that on utilitarian or consequentialist grounds, abortion sometimes would be permissible and sometimes not; it would depend on the consequences. Moral judgments about abortion will be better or worse, according to this view, depending on the adequacy of the prediction of consequences.

Critics of utilitarian reasoning often complain that utilitarianism disregards fundamental questions of rights. A critic may point out that if we do not take the right to life seriously, then utilitarian reasoning may condone the taking of any life if the overall consequences of doing so are good. This is indeed a possible outcome of utilitarian reasoning—a point that is often made clear in "trolley problem" scenarios that ask us to think about sacrificing or killing one person for the benefit of a number of others (we discuss the trolley problem in Chapter 6). One version of utilitarianism focuses on the consequences of individual acts. An act utilitarian would ask whether in a specific case, the overall benefits of an abortion decision outweigh the particular harms involved. A different sort of reasoning can be found in rule utilitarianism. A rule utilitarian must consider which overall set of rules or practices regarding abortion would be best. Would the rule "No one should have an abortion" be likely to maximize happiness? Would the rule "No one should have an abortion unless the pregnancy threatens the mother's health or well-being" have better consequences overall? There are other, broader questions worth considering from this perspective. We might ask how the practice of abortion when the fetus has certain abnormalities might affect our more general treatment of people with physically or mental disabilities: if fewer persons with disabilities are born, would this impact the way they are viewed by society? Or how would a restrictive abortion policy affect women's health as well as their ability to participate as equal human beings, enjoying jobs and other opportunities? Whichever practice or rule is likely to have the better net result—that is, more good consequences and fewer bad ones—is the best practice or rule to follow.

In any case, some critics of the utilitarian approach would argue that the moral status of the fetus, such as whether it is the kind of being that has a right to life, is, in fact, essential to moral decisions about abortion. Others would insist that we address the matter of the rights of the pregnant woman (or others) and the problem of conflicts of rights.

Rights-Based Approaches to Abortion

Some arguments about abortion consider the rights of persons but still maintain that the moral status of the fetus is irrelevant. It is irrelevant in the sense that whether or not we think of the fetus as a person with full moral rights, that point is not definitive for thinking about the morality of abortion. An influential article on abortion by Judith Jarvis Thomson—an excerpt of which appears at the end of this chapter—presents such an argument. Thomson assumes, for the purpose of argument, that the fetus is a person from early on in pregnancy. But her conclusion is that abortion is still justified, even if the fetus is a person with a right to life (and she assumes it is also permissible if the fetus is not a person).[14] This is why the argument does not turn on what we say about the moral status of the fetus.

The question Thomson poses is whether the pregnant woman has an obligation to sustain the life of the fetus by providing it with the use of her body. To have us think about this, she asks us to consider an imaginary scenario. Suppose, she says, that you wake up one morning and find yourself attached through various medical tubes and devices to a famous violinist. You find out that during the night, you have been kidnapped and "hooked up" to this violinist by a group of classical music enthusiasts. The violinist has severe kidney problems, and the only way that his life can be saved is through being attached to another person—so that the

other person's kidneys will do the work of purifying his blood for some fixed period of months, until his own kidneys have recovered. The question Thomson poses is this: Would you be morally permitted or justified in "unplugging" the violinist, even though doing so would result in his death? Thomson argues that you would be justified, in particular because you have not consented to devote your body and your time to saving the violinist's life. She goes on to argue that this example has an analogy to abortion, most obviously in cases of pregnancies resulting from rape.

Thomson extends her argument beyond the case of rape, using other analogies to help make her point about other pregnancies that occur, for example, in the case of failed birth control. One would only have a responsibility to save the violinist (or nurture the fetus) if one had agreed to do so. The consent that Thomson has in mind is a deliberate and planned choice. She argues that although it would be generous of you to save the life of the violinist (or the fetus), you are not obligated to do so. Her point is that no one has a right to use your body, even to save their own life, unless you consent to do so. Thomson published her argument in 1971 before *Roe v. Wade* legalized abortion in the United States. Her argument reflects the concerns of feminists who were arguing at that time that women have the same right to bodily integrity and choice as men do. A woman's body ought not to be used against her will for whatever purposes by others, even noble purposes such as the nurturing of children. Critics of this argument point out that it may apply at most to abortion in cases of rape, where consent is not given, but that in other cases, a woman may be said to implicitly consent to a pregnancy if she engaged in intercourse knowing that it might result in pregnancy. One response to this is that we do not always consider a person to have consented to unintended and chance consequences of their actions. Thomson argues that, in the end, it is the woman's right to choose whether to allow her body to be used or not—in the case of rape or in other cases of accidental pregnancy.

The Ontological and Moral Status of the Fetus

Rights-based and utilitarian arguments about abortion do not necessarily depend on what we say about the moral status of the fetus. Thomson's argument is meant to apply whether or not we think that the fetus is a person. But other arguments hold that the question of the fetus's ontological and moral status is crucial. What kind of value or moral status does the developing fetus have? Does it have a different moral status in various stages of development? If so, when does the status change, and why? Further questions may include how to weigh its value or rights in comparison to other values or the rights of others. At bottom, these questions point toward the ontological and moral status of the fetus. The ontological question asks what sort of being the fetus is. Is it merely a part of its mother, belonging entirely to her since it is located within her body? Or is it a unique and distinct being despite the fact that it is entirely dependent on the mother's body? The ontological question is connected to the moral question of the moral status of the being. What we want to know is both what kind of a being the fetus is and what sort of value that kind of being has.

A significant challenge for thinking about the moral status of the fetus is the fact that fetuses change and develop over time. So, we may have to acknowledge the importance of stages of development. In which case, we must ask: (1) *What* is present? (2) *When* is this present (at what stage)? and (3) *Why* is this significant? Different people will draw moral lines at different places within this developmental continuum. In what follows, we'll briefly consider five possible ways to draw such a line: at conception, when a heartbeat is present, when the brain develops, when quickening occurs, at the point of viability. We will also consider a sixth issue, the question of potentiality. And in the background of each of these issues (with the exception of viability) is the fact that the fetus is supported by, contained within, and entirely dependent on the body of a pregnant person. Defenders of abortion argue that this background condition—of dependence—is sufficient to prove that the fetus is not yet a person. But opponents of abortion claim that what matters is something about the fetus itself, and not the fact that it is dependent on another person's body.

1. Conception or Fertilization Conception, or the stage at which the sperm penetrates and fertilizes the

ovum, is the time at which many opponents of abortion say that the fetus has full moral status. The reason usually given for this claim is that at conception the fetus receives its full genetic makeup, from the combination of sperm and egg.[15] One argument for taking this stage as morally significant appears to be based on an ontological argument that goes something like this: If the being that is born at the end of a pregnancy is a human being or person, and if there is no substantial change in its constitution from its initial form, then it is the same being all the way through the stages of development. Otherwise, we would be implying that different beings are succeeding one another during this process.

Critics of this position often point out that although fetal development is continuous, the bare genetic material present at conception is not enough to constitute a person at that point. In this early stage, the cells are *totipotent*, which means they can become skin cells, heart cells, or many other types of cells.[16] There is no structure or differentiation at this point of development, nothing that resembles a person in this initial form. The fertilized egg is not even clearly an individual. For example, consider what happens in the case of identical twinning. Before implantation, identical twins are formed by the splitting of cells in the early embryo. Each resulting twin has the same genetic makeup. Now, what are we to think of the original embryo? Those who support conception as the crucial time at which we have a being with full moral status and rights must explain how there can be an individual at conception, at least in the case of identical twinning.

2. Heartbeat If we move forward in the gestation of a fetus, one developmental milestone is fetal heartbeat. Some restrictive abortion laws focus on fetal heartbeat and draw a line there, stipulating that abortion is not permitted after fetal heartbeat can be detected. These restrictions typically draw that line at around six weeks of fetal development. This focal point is linked to an intuitive sense that something that has a heartbeat is alive.

Critics of this approach point out that even though there may be rhythmic motion detectable at six weeks, this is not really the beating of a fully developed heart. Rather, it is motion in the place at which the heart will eventually develop. The rhythmic pulsing is not detectable by a stethoscope at this point, but requires advanced ultrasound technology. Furthermore, the importance of heartbeat is debatable. And it is an open question about whether the heart is a relevant focal point at which to draw a moral line. Consider how this works in end-of-life considerations where the issue of heartbeat returns. It is possible that brain-dead bodies can be kept "alive" through artificial heart machines. And we generally do not think that people whose hearts have stopped beating are fully dead, since we can apply CPR and get their hearts pumping again. This seems to imply that the brain is more important than the heart in thinking about moral status.

3. Brain Development, Pain, and Psychological Capacity Another possible stage at which a fetus might attain significant moral status is the point at which the brain is sufficiently developed. The brain seems to be an important feature of the human body that is the key to **sentience**, which we might define here as the ability to feel pain and pleasure and to be aware of your surroundings. The human brain is also the locus of consciousness, language, and communication, and it is these capacities of our brains that make us different from other animals. Sentience is often viewed as a morally significant place to draw a line. And the "higher" psychological capacities of consciousness seem to give human beings their unique status and value. Moreover, we now use the cessation of brain function (not heart function) as the determinant of death—a point that is important in thinking about euthanasia and end-of-life decisions. Why should we not use the beginning of brain function as the beginning of an individual's life? But as in the case of the heart, there is an open question about what we mean by brain development. And we might reasonably ask how much and what kind of brain activity matters. We can detect some neurological activity between the sixth and eighth weeks of fetal development, which makes that point the significant time period for this argument.

Of course, brain activity develops gradually, and at eight weeks neurological structures and activities are quite different from those of an adult human being. The difficulty here is that we cannot identify any single point during fetal development that presents an entirely unique or qualitative change in brain activity. And yet we might be satisfied with an approximation, rather than a determinate line. Other questions about the type of brain function also might be raised. At six to eight weeks, the brain is quite simple; only much later do those parts develop that are the basis of conscious function. Early in pregnancy, the brain is arguably not significantly different from other animal brains in structure or function. And while there is controversy about when exactly pain experience is possible, most experts maintain that neuronal development is not advanced enough to speak of the fetus as feeling pain until sometime beyond twenty weeks of development.[17] In a statement submitted to the U.S. Supreme Court during the *Dobbs* trial, the American College of Obstetricians and Gynecologists (along with a number of other medical organizations) stated, "Every major medical organization that has examined the issue of fetal pain and peer-reviewed studies on the matter have consistently reached the conclusion that pre-viability abortion does not result in fetal pain perception."[18]

4. Quickening A different approach is focused less on the fetus than on the mother's experience of the fetus. This is the idea of quickening, which is said to occur when the pregnant woman can feel the fetus move in the womb. This movement is thought to have some moral significance. It tends to occur at approximately the fourth month of fetal development, although different pregnant people experience fetal movement in different ways. In prescientific eras, people believed there was no fetal movement before this time—and if that were so, it would constitute a persuasive reason to consider this stage as crucial. While contemporary science can detect movement before this stage, one might still focus on quickening as the start of self-initiated movement in the fetus, arising from a new level of brain development. This would constitute a better reason for identifying quickening as the beginning of a new moral status or right to life because it would be a sign that the fetus is now moving about on its own. For much of Western history, civil and religious authorities prohibited abortion only after this stage.

Critics of this position may make the same argument about quickening as was made with regard to brain development, namely, that there is no dramatic moment in the development of the fetus at which it is suddenly able to move. Moreover, they might also point out that other animals and even plants move on their own, and this does not give them special moral status or a right to life. Why might someone think that movement is a sign of personhood? And what about adult humans who are incapable of movement due to paralysis—how would the focus on quickening inform our thinking about those human bodies?

5. Viability Viability is the ability of the fetus to live outside of the womb. With current medical technology, viability is possible at approximately the twenty-fourth week of fetal development. At this stage, the fetal organs and organ systems are sufficiently developed that the fetus may have the capacity to function on its own. The last of these systems to be functionally complete is the respiratory system, which often causes fatal problems for fetuses delivered before six months. During previous stages of fetal development, the fetus "breathes" amniotic fluid. Before twenty-three or twenty-four weeks of gestation, "capillaries have not yet moved close enough to the air sacs to carry gases to and from the lung."[19] A lubricant, called surfactant, can be administered to assist the lungs' capacity to breathe air, but even then, the chance of survival is slim.

One practical problem with using viability as a moral criterion is its variability. When *Roe v. Wade* took effect, the point of viability for a premature infant was considered to be approximately twenty-six weeks; the estimation has since been shortened by a couple of weeks thanks to advances in medical technology. At twenty-three or twenty-four weeks, a "micropreemie" weighs slightly less than a pound. Its viability is also a function of birth weight. This helps explain why the mother's socioeconomic status and overall health may affect fetal viability and premature birth: low birth weight may be correlated with poor maternal nutrition and with low socioeconomic circumstances.[20]

Why is the stage of viability singled out as the one at which the fetus may take on a new moral status? Some answer that it is the potential for life *independent* of the mother that forms the basis of the new status. However, if the fetus were delivered at this stage and left on its own, no infant would be able to survive. Perhaps the notion of separate existence is a better basis for viability as a moral criterion. The idea would be that the fetus is more clearly distinct from the mother at this point in pregnancy. Or perhaps the notion of *completeness* is what is intended—since the capacity for viable existence seems to indicate that the process of gestation and fetal development is essentially complete. Although the fetus is not fully formed at viability because much development takes place after birth, the argument might be made that the viable fetus is sufficiently complete, enabling us to think of it as an entirely new being.

Critics of the viability criterion may point again to the gradual nature of development and the seeming arbitrariness of picking out one stage of completeness as crucially different from the others. They also can point out that even if it were delivered at the point of viability, the fetus would still be dependent on others (and on an array of sophisticated medical technologies) for its survival. They can also question the notion of making moral status a function of independence. We are all dependent on one another, and those who are more independent (e.g., because they can live apart from others) have no greater value than those who are more dependent. Even someone dependent on medical machines is not, for this reason, less human, they might argue. Furthermore, a viable unborn fetus is still, in fact, dependent on its mother and does not have an existence separate from her. Birth, on these terms, would be a better stage to pick than viability, these critics might argue, if it is separateness and independence that are crucial.

Each point in fetal development may provide a reasonable basis for concluding something about the moral status of the fetus. However, as we can clearly see, none are problem free. In any case, the whole idea of grounding moral status and rights on the possession of certain characteristics also may be called into question.

6. Potentiality A final topic should be put on the table as we consider when and how the fetus gains moral status, which is the issue of potentiality. Opponents of abortion may point out that the ontological question of what the fetus *actually is* at a certain point of development is less important than the question of what the fetus *has the potential to become. Potentiality* literally means "power." Those who think potentiality matters may suggest that all beings that have the power to develop certain key characteristics have full moral worth. Thus, if a particular fetus had the potential for developing the requisite mental capacities, it would have full moral status. However, any fetus or other human being that does not have this potential (anencephalic infants or those in a permanent vegetative state, for example) does not have this status.

Some critics of abortion argue that abortion is wrong because it prevents the fetus from actualizing its potential. One version of this argument has been articulated by the philosopher Don Marquis (whose argument is included in the primary source readings at the end of this chapter). Marquis argues that it is seriously wrong to kill children and infants because we presume that children and infants have "futures of value."[21] According to Marquis, abortion is wrong for a similar reason, which is that it deprives the fetus from obtaining the future good it would have if it were left alone and allowed to be born. Marquis concludes, "The future of a standard fetus includes a set of experiences, projects, activities, and such which are identical with the futures of adult human beings and are identical with the futures of young children."[22] To kill the fetus is to deprive the fetus of those goods that it potentially could have enjoyed.

Yet how important is potentiality and what, in fact, is it? If a fetus is aborted and it is unaware that it even had the potential to develop into a person with a future of value, how has it been deprived of anything? Is it possible to deprive you of something if you are not aware or conscious of that deprivation? Potentiality appears to be vague and undefined. Suppose that one had the potential to become a famous musical star or hold high political office. Would one then deserve the same respect and powers of an actual musician or legislator?

And while those who focus on potentiality often extend their argument back to the point of conception (since a fertilized ovum has the potential to become a person), a question quickly arises regarding contraception. Does the focus on potentiality make contraception wrong since contraception prevents the potentiality contained in the sperm and egg from actualizing itself?

Marquis responds to this question by maintaining that there is a qualitative difference between contraception and abortion. Prior to fertilization, there is no actual thing—only a net of probabilities. We don't know, for example, which of the millions of sperm will fertilize the egg. And so, no definite subject is deprived of its potentiality through contraception. But, according to Marquis, once the fetus is developing in the womb, there is a definite set of potentialities that now are worthy of moral consideration.

The opposite of potentiality is actuality. Some may deny that potentiality is morally significant. We don't treat an acorn as a tree, even though the acorn has the potential to become a tree. For those who deny the importance of potentiality, only the actual possession of the requisite characteristics is sufficient for full moral status. Of course, there is still an open question about which characteristics or capacities count: for example, heartbeat, brain activity, independent existence, and so on. And it is worth noting that if focus on the actuality of certain rather high-level capacities (self-awareness or reasoning ability) is our standard of moral status, then newborns probably would not be included; and we may also rule out adults with brain damage. The claim that even newborns lack the high-level capacities relevant to full moral status has been defended in an argument made by philosopher Mary Anne Warren.[23] According to this view, although the fetus—and even newborn infants and extremely young children—are human beings biologically speaking, they are not yet actual persons or beings with the requisite moral status. They lack key psychological capacities and are not yet fully members of the moral community. There may be good reasons to treat them well and with respect, but it is not because they are persons with rights. And Warren argues, the rights of actual persons clearly outweigh the rights of potential persons. Warren says, "But even if a potential person does have some prima facie right to life, such a right could not possibly outweigh the right of a woman to obtain an abortion, since the rights of any actual person invariably outweigh those of any potential person, whenever the two conflict."[24] Warren's account of potentiality and personality also has implications for discussion of end-of-life issues, since in her view, if a person loses key mental capacities—in her words, if their "consciousness has been permanently obliterated"—they may lose their status as persons (we include an excerpt from Warren in the readings for this chapter).

Moral Approaches to Euthanasia

11.3 Evaluate the application of moral theories to different kinds of euthanasia.

Euthanasia literally means "good death" (the Greek *eu-* means "good"; the Greek *thanatos* means "death"). The moral question of euthanasia is whether there are circumstances in which death would be good. Typically, this question arises at the end of life, when people are suffering and desire "death with dignity," as the saying goes, as a way of avoiding continued suffering and indignity. One way to get a handle on what to think about the morality of euthanasia is to look at its various types. There are different forms of euthanasia. One distinction is between active and passive euthanasia. Active euthanasia involves actively doing something to end a person's life. Passive euthanasia occurs when we remove life support and allow the person to die. Another set of important distinctions differentiates voluntary, involuntary, and nonvoluntary euthanasia. The moral

Table 11-2 Types of Euthanasia

Passive euthanasia: Stopping (or not starting) some treatment, which allows the person to die. The person's condition causes their death.

Active euthanasia: Doing something such as administering a lethal drug or using other means that cause the person's death.

Voluntary euthanasia: Causing death with the patient's consent, knowingly and freely given.

Involuntary euthanasia: Causing death in violation of the patient's consent.

Nonvoluntary euthanasia: Causing the death of a patient who is unable to consent.

Physician-assisted suicide: Suicide that results from a physician's prescription of lethal medication.

discussion of euthanasia typically focuses on the idea of autonomous consent. As we've already seen, this is an important idea in medical ethics (see Chapter 10) and in the very idea of a "pro-choice" approach to the issues we are discussing here. We use the term "voluntary euthanasia" to indicate cases in which individuals voluntarily consent to a procedure that ends their life. Involuntary euthanasia would be euthanasia that occurs against the person's will; and nonvoluntary euthanasia occurs when we don't know what the person's wishes are. Physician-assisted suicide is yet a different kind of thing. It occurs when a physician prescribes a lethal medication but the patient takes it on their own.

Utilitarian and Consequentialist Approaches to Euthanasia

Consequentialists are often concerned with consent. Allowing people to choose how they die would likely have some beneficial consequences. For example, when people know that they will be allowed to make decisions about their own lives and not be forced into things against their will, they may gain a certain peace of mind, a sense of dignity, and feeling of autonomy and control. Moreover, those dying may be the best people to make good decisions about things that primarily affect them. These are good consequentialist reasons to respect a person's wishes in euthanasia cases. And almost everyone will agree that involuntary euthanasia (killing someone against their will) is wrong.

Of course, it is not only the person who is dying who is affected by these decisions. Thus, it can be argued that the effects on others—on their feelings, for example—are also relevant. Moreover, individual decisions are not always wise and do not always work for the greatest benefit of the person making them, or for that of others. For example, critics of euthanasia worry that people who are ill or disabled might refuse certain lifesaving treatments because they lack money, adequate palliative care, or because they do not know about services and supports available to them. From that standpoint, it would be more important to provide pain management, monetary support, and other social support for people who are suffering and dying. It is easy to imagine that those supports can also help the friends and loved ones of those who are suffering.

Rule utilitarians are also concerned with the usefulness of general social policies and procedures. Would a policy that universally follows individual requests about dying be most likely to maximize happiness? Or would a policy that gives no special weight to individual desires, but that directs us to do whatever some panel of medical experts decides, be more likely to have the best outcome? Or would some moderate policy be best, such as one that gives special but not absolute weight to what a person wants? An example of such a policy might place a substantial burden of proof on proposals that would deny a dying person's wishes. It is also worth noting that in discussions of end-of-life care there are other social pressures that may influence utilitarian considerations, including the profit motive in insurance and health care.

Non-Consequentialist Considerations regarding Euthanasia

To appeal to the value of personal autonomy in euthanasia decisions is to appeal to a non-consequentialist concern. The idea is that autonomy is a good in itself and therefore carries heavy moral weight. We like to think of ourselves, at least ideally, as masters of our own fate. According to Kant, autonomy makes morality possible. His famous phrase "ought implies can" indicates that if and only if we can act (or are free and able to act) in certain ways can we be commanded to do so. According to a Kantian deontological position, persons are unique in being able to choose freely, and this capacity for choice ought to be respected.

However, in many euthanasia cases, a person's mental competence and thus autonomy may be compromised. In some sad cases, the person is unconscious and unable to communicate consent (or lack of consent). When that happens in euthanasia discussions, we say that the case is "nonvoluntary": it is not necessarily against the person's wishes, but nor is there explicit consent. Apart from unconsciousness, autonomy and rationality can be undermined by fear, lack of understanding, dependency, or hopelessness. Illness and dependency can make a person more subject to undue influence or coercion. Moreover, patients with terminal illnesses can become depressed and despondent. One study of terminally ill patients who considered suicide concluded,

"Depression and hopelessness are the strongest predictors of desire for hastened death."[25] It might make sense that people with terminal illness would be depressed and feel hopeless. But it might also be that it is possible to treat the depression along with pain in order to provide patients with more autonomy as they confront the end of life.

While respect for autonomy may provide us with a justification for voluntary euthanasia or physician-assisted suicide, it is important to point out that Kant actually thought suicide was wrong. Kant held that suicide violated the categorical imperative, since the maxim of suicide was not universalizable. If the maxim of suicide were universalized, we'd end up saying that everyone should kill themselves, which Kant rejects as an impossible law of nature. Furthermore, if one kills oneself out of a self-interested motive (say to avoid misfortune), then there is a contradiction. Self-interest—what Kant calls self-love—contradicts itself when it leads to the killing of the self. Kant also held that suicide was disrespectful of personhood, in violation of the second form of the categorical imperative (as discussed in Chapter 6). The problem is that if a person destroys themself in order to escape painful circumstances, they are abusing their own life as a means to the end of escaping those circumstances.

Western religious traditions also tend to condemn suicide on similar non-consequentialist grounds. This is a central part of Catholic pro-life teaching, which is opposed to suicide, euthanasia, and abortion. From this standpoint, suicide is wrong because it is anti-life and violates the dignity and worth of the human person. Pope John Paul II claims, for example, that suicide is immoral because it is a "rejection of God's absolute sovereignty over life and death."[26]

As we mentioned above, the Catholic teaching about this can be understood in relation to the natural law. But there may be a different understanding of natural law that emphasizes autonomy and the importance of living with dignity and that is not opposed to suicide. This idea can be found in ancient Stoicism. The ancient Stoics were interested in living in accord with nature. They held that it is natural and good for human beings to be free, rational, and dignified. When conditions no longer permit us to fulfill our human nature in this manner, then suicide might be permitted. Seneca, a Roman philosopher, put it this way: "Mere living is not a good, but living well. Accordingly, the wise man will live as long as he ought, not as long as he can."[27] From this point of view what matters is the quality of one's life—and not the quantity of one's years.

Criteria for Death

Related to the discussion of the question of the ontological and moral status of the fetus is a question about the ontological and moral status of human beings who are dying or have suffered irreversible damage to their brains. This kind of question has appeared in controversial cases. Consider the case of Terri Schiavo, a woman with severe brain damage who was allowed to die in 2005 after more than a decade of being kept alive by a feeding tube. Schiavo remained in a **persistent vegetative state** (**PVS**) for fifteen years. A persistent vegetative state is often defined as one of "unconscious wakefulness" that lasts for more than a few weeks. A person in this state has lost all cerebral cortex function but retains a basic level of brain stem function. In contrast, someone who is not totally brain dead but who is in a coma is unconscious but "asleep." Their brain stem functions poorly, and thus the person does not live as long as someone in a persistent vegetative state.[28] Schiavo's case was contentious because of the difficulty in determining what was in her best interests and what she would have wanted for herself. Her parents disagreed with her husband about what she would have wanted. Eventually after a long legal battle, Terri Schiavo's feeding tube was removed and she was allowed to die on March 31, 2005, at age forty-one. An autopsy later revealed that her brain had shrunk to half its normal size, and thus that she had not been conscious or aware. Some had claimed over the years that Schiavo seemed to follow their motions and respond to their voices. However, we know from her autopsy as well as earlier brain scans that she had no conscious function and that these were autonomic or reflexive responses. Even though her body might have continued its basic functions for decades, the medical evidence strongly suggests that Schiavo's consciousness permanently ceased in 1990.

A similar case occurred more recently. Jahi McMath was a child who suffered severe brain damage after complications from a routine tonsillectomy in December 2013.[29] The hospital, in Oakland, California, declared that she was dead, even though her body was being kept alive on life support. The state of California issued a death certificate. But her family refused to accept that she was dead. They took her body to New Jersey, where she remained on life support for several years. During that time, her body continued to grow and develop—including, according to some reports, the onset of puberty. Some claimed that this indicated that Jahi was not dead. Eventually, Jahi died in 2018. Or was she already dead? This case raises significant issues about whether medical diagnoses can be mistaken and about what we take to be the criteria of death. The McMath case also raises issues of race, class, and religion. Jahi was Black and her family was deeply religious. They maintained that the hospital did not treat them fairly.

Of course, we need not believe that an individual is dead in order to think it justifiable to disconnect a respirator and let them die. In fact, only if someone is not dead can we then sensibly ask whether we may *let that person die*. But how do we know if someone is alive or dead?

Throughout history, people have used various means to determine whether a human being is dead, and those means were a function of what they believed to be essential aspects of life. For example, if spirit was thought of as essential and was equated with a kind of thin air or breath, then the presence or absence of this "life breath" would indicate whether a person was living. When heart function was regarded as the key element of life, and the heart was thought to be like a furnace, then people would feel the body to see if it was warm in order to know whether the person was still living. Even today, with our better understanding of the function of the heart, other organs, and organ systems, we have great difficulty with this issue. One reason for this is that we now can use various machines to perform certain bodily functions, such as respiration and blood circulation. Sometimes this is a temporary measure, such as during a surgery. However, in other cases, the person may have lost significant brain function. In this latter sort of case, it is important to know whether the person is to be considered alive or dead.

Determining a precise condition and test for death became even more problematic in the past half-century with the advent of heart transplants. Surgeons could not take a heart for transplant from someone who was considered living, only from someone who had been declared dead. Was an individual whose heart function was being artificially maintained but who had no brain function considered living or dead? As transplantation science and life-support technologies were developing in the 1960s and 1970s, some courts had difficulty in figuring out how to apply brain death criteria. In some cases, defendants who were accused of murder attempted to argue that since the victim's heart was still beating after an initial assault, the assailant did not actually kill the victim—but that a subsequent transplant procedure or removal from life-support did. Since the 1980s, the courts have clarified that brain death is the appropriate criteria for use in such cases.[30]

In 1968, an ad hoc committee of the Harvard Medical School was set up to establish criteria for determining when a person should be declared dead. This committee determined that someone should be considered dead if they have permanently lost all detectable brain function. This meant that if there was some nonconscious brain function, for example, or if the condition was temporary, then the individual would not be considered dead. Thus, various tests of reflexes and responsiveness were required to determine whether an individual had sustained a permanent and total loss of all brain function.[31] This condition is now known as **whole brain death** and is the primary criterion used for the legal determination of death. This is true even when other secondary criteria or tests, such as loss of pulse, are used.

Whole brain death is distinguished from other conditions such as persistent vegetative states. In PVS, the individual has lost all cerebral cortex function but has retained some good brain stem function. Many nonconscious functions that are based in that area of the brain—respiratory and heart rate, facial reflexes and muscle control, and gag reflex and swallowing abilities—continue. Yet the individual in a permanent or persistent vegetative state has lost all conscious function. One reason for this condition is that the rate of oxygen used by the cerebral cortex is much higher than that of the brain stem, so these cells die much more quickly if deprived of oxygen for some time. The result is that the individual in this state will never regain consciousness but can often breathe naturally and needs no artificial aid to maintain circulation. Such an individual does not feel pain because they cannot interpret it as such. Because the gag reflex may continue, individuals in this condition can clear their airways and thus may live for many years. They go through wake and sleep cycles in which they have their eyes open and then closed.

If we use whole brain death criteria to determine whether someone is dead, then neither a person in a persistent vegetative state nor a person in a coma is dead. In these cases, we might ask whether we should let such persons die (which would be passive euthanasia) or actively end their lives (which would be active euthanasia). On the other hand, if someone is dead by whole brain death criteria, then disconnecting equipment may not really even be a kind of killing. Would it make sense to say that we killed someone or let someone die who is already dead?

As we conclude this section, it is worth underlining how the ontological and moral questions involved in euthanasia and abortion connect. Some will argue that all life is good and that so long as a body is alive, it is worthy of respect. Such a comprehensive pro-life view may point back to the moment of conception or the presence of something like fetal heartbeat and may connect this all the way to a claim about the dignity and worth of bodies on life support. But others may argue that the most important feature of our humanity is consciousness and so ground their claims about personhood in the brain and in cognitive function. From this standpoint, fetuses are not yet persons, since they lack developed brains and advanced cognitive functions; and from the same vantage point, it is possible to argue that when the brain ceases to function, personhood also ceases.

Current Issues

11.4   Explain social justice and feminist concerns that arise in thinking about abortion and euthanasia.

Feminism and Abortion

Discussions of abortion are obviously connected with discussions of women's rights. Feminists have typically supported a woman's legal right to abortion. One important part of this argument has to do with the long history of the subjugation of women, including their sexual and reproductive lives. Women's rights advocates insist that women should have the right to choose abortion as part of a comprehensive right to control reproduction and sexuality. Prior to the *Roe v. Wade* decision in the United States, women lacked this legal and social power of autonomy and reproductive control—at least in some American states. We might also note that it is only about a hundred years since women were granted the right to vote (with the ratification of the Nineteenth Amendment in 1920). Women have also been empowered, as a result of the women's rights movement and the work of feminists, to pursue careers and education, and to own property. In prior centuries in the United States, women were also viewed as always sexually and reproductively available to their husbands. For example, as we discuss in Chapter 15, the concept of marital rape did not exist within the previous patriarchal culture the United States. It was only in the 1990s that all U.S. states finally recognized that spousal rape exists.[32] And more generally, women have been subject to abuse and sexual violence at the hands of men. With that history

in mind, it is easy to understand why feminists maintain that the right to abortion is essential. The phrase "my body, my choice" is one way of putting this idea. Notice how this phrase is connected to our evolving understanding of marriage, sexuality, and reproduction. Among the concerns of feminists is the problem of sexual violence, including rape. And indeed, rape is often discussed in connection with abortion. We previously mentioned Judith Jarvis Thomson's influential article about abortion—and how her "violinist analogy" can be understood as a case of rape. One basic argument in defense of abortion rights is that if a woman does not consent to be pregnant, she should have the right to terminate the pregnancy. As we mentioned earlier in this chapter, the terminology employed here can be subject to critique. We should note that rape is not only a concern for women; and we should also point out that violence against trans persons remains a problem and that trans men (biological women who identify as men) can become pregnant. We discuss trans issues in more detail in Chapter 15. The choice of language here, which emphasizes *women's rights*, is intended to highlight the relationship between abortion and feminism.

▶ Knowledge Check   Answers appear at the end of the chapter.

1. Which of the following is true?

   a. The pro-choice point of view is pro-abortion. It is interested in actively encouraging women to have abortion.

   b. The pro-choice point of view is in favor of voluntary euthanasia. It permits euthanasia if people consent.

   c. The pro-life point of view is in favor of involuntary euthanasia. It wants to end the suffering of people with terrible illnesses.

   d. The pro-life point of view is anti-viability. It aims to make sure that only wanted children are born.

2. Which of the following offers a pro-choice argument?

   a. J. Gay Williams

   b. Don Marquis

   c. Pope John Paul II

   d. Judith Jarvis Thomson

3. Which form of euthanasia occurs when a person asks for the removal of life support?

   a. Active voluntary euthanasia

   b. Passive voluntary euthanasia

   c. Active nonvoluntary euthanasia

   d. Passive involuntary euthanasia

4. In determining whether a fetus is a person and whether a brain-dead adult is a person, what kind of question are we considering?

   a. An empirical question

   b. A utilitarian question

   c. An ontological question

   d. A consequentialist question

Steve Pyke/Premium Archive/Getty Images

Figure 11-2 Judith Jarvis Thomson.

As American states continue to restrict abortion access, the question of a rape exception to prohibitions of abortion has arisen. Some abortion restrictions provide for exceptions in the case of rape, incest, or when pregnancy can harm the health or threaten the life of the mother. But some anti-abortion legislators have gone so far as to argue that there ought not be an exception in the case of rape, incest, or even health threats. As Oklahoma was debating changes in their abortion laws, a state representative, said, "It is not the baby's fault the circumstances of their conception, if it was something as horrible as that. The baby has the same right to life that you and I have." He continued, "Now, rape is a horrible, horrible, horrible crime and somebody needs to be punished for that. But it shouldn't be the baby. It should be the rapist who gets punished for it."[33]

A notorious case occurred in the summer of 2022, as states were responding to the changed legal framework introduced by the *Dobbs* decision. A 10-year-old girl was raped in Ohio and became pregnant as a result. But Ohio had passed a law that prohibited abortion based on fetal heartbeat. The Ohio law allowed for exception in the case of health danger to the pregnant girl, but it did not include an exception for abortion resulting from rape.[34] The girl was forced to travel to neighboring Indiana to obtain an abortion. Pro-choice advocates were outraged by this example. In the summer of 2022, as this case

was being widely discussed, President Joe Biden said it was difficult to accept that a 10-year-old girl should be "forced to give birth to a rapist's child." He continued, "I can't think of anything much more extreme."[35] Judith Jarvis Thomson appears to have foreseen this kind of case. In her article "A Defense of Abortion," she wrote, "a sick and desperately frightened fourteen-year-old schoolgirl, pregnant due to rape, may of course choose abortion, and that any law which rules this out is an insane law."[36]

This does not mean that all feminists are happy with the rationale that was provided in *Roe v. Wade*.[37] For example, some worry that the "right to privacy" could be interpreted in ways that are detrimental to women. If this right is taken to imply that everything done in the privacy of one's home is out of the law's reach, it might suggest that the subordination or abuse of people, including children within the home, is merely "domestic" and not a matter of public concern.

Some feminists also have misgivings about denying the moral status of the fetus, viewing the focus on moral status and individual rights as the product of a male-dominant worldview. Such a worldview is taken to approach individuals as distinct atomistic beings who are separated from one another and whose conflicts are best described as conflicts of rights. Feminists such as Catharine A. MacKinnon point out that, from the standpoint of women, things may be more complicated:

> So long as it gestates in utero, the fetus is defined by its relation to the pregnant woman. More than a body part but less than a person, where it is, is largely what it is. From the standpoint of the pregnant woman, it is both me and not me. It "is" the pregnant woman in the sense that it is in her and of her and is hers more than anyone's. It "is not" her in the sense that she is not all that is there. In a legal system that views the individual as a unitary self, and that self as a bundle of rights, it is no wonder that the pregnant woman has eluded legal grasp, and her fetus with her.[38]

This approach recognizes that abortion is morally problematic precisely because of the ontological and moral question of motherhood—which is a circumstance in which one being gives birth to another. Of course, it is also possible to be a mother without giving birth, which is what happens in the case of adoption. The very idea of "mothering" is a complex cultural and historical idea.

But with regard to abortion discussions, those cultural connotations are less significant than the biological process of gestating and birthing.

As we mentioned previously, the question of motherhood has itself been under interrogation by feminists and gender theorists, some of whom have argued that motherhood ought to be divorced from any essentializing idea of femininity. There are transgender "mothers," and some have begun speaking of "pregnant persons" rather than "pregnant women." It is not surprising that this linguistic shift has prompted outrage and backlash from conservatives who insist on more traditional gender norms. But it is also possible that feminists might insist that motherhood, pregnancy, and abortion are specifically women's issues, based on the history of the oppression of women and the ongoing need for a women's liberation movement.

Of course, different women experience pregnancy and the end of pregnancy in different ways. For many women, the loss of an early form of human life is a significant one, which is indicated by the seriousness with which most people treat miscarriages. However, this sense of loss does not necessarily imply that the fetus has full moral status and rights. Bertha Alvarez Manninen explains that one can support women who choose to have an abortion without completely denying the emotional impact of miscarriage and abortion. She argues, as a pro-choice advocate, that it may be callous to simply dismiss questions about the moral status of the fetus and the importance of pregnancy: "When pro-choice supporters dismiss fetal life as being no more valuable than a 'clump of cells,' we do a disservice to the many women who obtain abortions but who, nevertheless, feel quite strongly that there is a moral dimension to their action that they wish to openly discuss."[39] Manninen's approach is open to the possibility of a more diverse and inclusive conversation about abortion within feminism (we have an excerpt from her at the end of the chapter). She is also interested in opening the conversation to a broader focus on how social support for women can help change the conversation about abortion. This includes access to contraception, as well as support for poor and working mothers.

A related concern along these lines is associated with the work of philosopher Rosalind Hursthouse, who uses virtue ethics to consider the topic of abortion.

Hursthouse is critical of those who have abortions for frivolous or trivial reasons, but she argues that there may be a number of virtuous reasons that a woman could choose to have an abortion.[40] One reason might be that the mother is concerned for the well-being of her other children when an unexpected pregnancy occurs. Or perhaps a mother wants to prevent possible suffering for a fetus that would have a severe disability. To choose abortion, from this standpoint, does not mean that a woman is not a virtuous mother—rather, the choice may be based on certain maternal virtues, such as care for her existing children or the desire to prevent a disabled fetus from suffering.

This discussion of virtue points toward other considerations about what matters most in thinking about the morality of abortion. Hursthouse asks us to consider whether an abortion occurs as a result of a serious or a frivolous choice. As Hursthouse argues, "some women who choose abortion rather than have their first child, and some men who encourage their partners to choose abortion, are not avoiding parenthood for the sake of other worthwhile pursuits, but for the worthless one of 'having a good time.'"[41] Thomson made a similar point in her famous "Defense of Abortion" essay, where she speaks about "indecent" abortions. She argued that "It would be indecent in the woman to request an abortion, and indecent in a doctor to perform it, if she is in her seventh month, and wants the abortion to avoid the nuisance of postponing a trip abroad."[42] Thomson makes this remark in an article defending a woman's right to choose. But she is directing our attention beyond the question of a right to choose toward the question of what counts as a good (or virtuous) reason for having an abortion. What do you think: Could there be better or worse reasons for abortion within the context of an overall theory that permits pregnant people the right to choose?

Along these lines, some argue that abortion should not be used as birth control. But such a claim holds weight only if we believe that there is something wrong with abortion to begin with, perhaps because of a claim about the moral status of the fetus. Finally, remember that not everything that we consider immoral can (or should) be made illegal. Thus, even if abortion were, in some cases, thought to be immoral, one would need to give further reasons about the purpose of law to conclude that it also ought to be illegal. At the same time, we must ask if the only reason to make something illegal is if it is immoral. There may be cases when we want to permit people the liberty to choose for themselves about morally controversial issues. And from the point of view of feminism, it is important to recall that for most of recorded history, women were not legally permitted to choose for themselves about a number of things, including abortion. This remains true in some parts of the globe. And with the demise of *Roe v. Wade*, after *Dobbs*, feminists may worry that women's rights are being taken away in the United States.

Social Justice Concerns with Euthanasia and Abortion

It seems fairly obvious why feminists are concerned that prohibitions on abortion prevent people from exercising bodily control and autonomy. There are different but related social justice concerns that arise in discussions of euthanasia and assisted suicide. Among these is the risk that vulnerable people may be coerced into suicide or consenting to euthanasia. This has a gender component insofar as women may feel more social pressure when confronted with decisions about the end of their own lives. Moreover, elderly women often have fewer resources as a result of social inequality and gendered pay disparities. There is some data to support the worry that women may be more willing to end their lives so that they would not "be a burden" on their families.[43]

This kind of concern—about structures of oppression and inequality—is also connected to cultural, psychological, and other circumstances connected to race, economics, and other forms of inequality and injustice. People who live in poverty, for example, may find themselves unable to pay for health care at the end of life and so may seek death for reasons that reflect social inequalities. It is important to remember the problem of eugenic policies that could be connected to discussions of euthanasia (and reproduction, including abortion). Poor women, women of color, and women with cognitive disabilities have, in the past, been forcibly sterilized. And in the egregious example of the death camps of Nazi Germany, undesirable people—Jews, Gypsies, and people with disabilities—were killed. The Nazi death camps began as

"mercy killings" focused on people with disabilities (the German term was *Gnadentod*).[44] With this history in mind, it is worth considering how larger social and political factors can lead to unjust outcomes and atrocities.

Of particular concern in contemporary discussions of euthanasia is the perspective of people with disabilities. Activists working on behalf of people with disabilities have often warned against the idea of euthanasia. The worry from this standpoint is that society may make decisions about quality of life and living with dignity that are biased against the lives of people who are disabled. And especially in the case of people with cognitive impairment, the question of consent becomes problematic.

One example of this kind of concern involves a controversial argument made by utilitarian philosopher Peter Singer. Utilitarians are concerned with maximizing quality of life and eliminating suffering. They are also concerned with questions of expense and, as we've mentioned before, cost-benefit calculation. Following this line of reasoning, Singer has argued that it is possible to imagine euthanizing a "disabled infant" and "replacing" it with another, healthy baby in a subsequent pregnancy in order to achieve a net outcome of happiness. Singer notes that in places with permissive abortion laws, women are allowed to abort disabled fetuses, and he sees very little difference between abortion and euthanasia for infants. Singer argues that "killing a disabled infant is not morally equivalent to killing a person. Very often it is not wrong at all."[45] One of Singer's points is that severely disabled infants lack the sort of mental capacity that would give them moral status as "persons" who have a right to life.

Singer is not advocating an active euthanasia campaign directed against people with disabilities. He is arguing that in some tragic circumstances, parents may be justified in choosing euthanasia for an infant born with profound disability. But Singer's approach has prompted criticism and protest.[46] Disability rights advocates have been especially critical of him. Harriet McBryde Johnson argued that Singer was advocating genocide against people with disabilities. She explained that the problem is Singer's "unexamined assumption that disabled people are inherently 'worse off,' that we 'suffer,' that we have lesser 'prospects of a happy life.' Because of this all-too-common prejudice, and his rare courage in taking it to its logical conclusion, catastrophe looms."[47]

One significant problem here is whether we can accurately predict or judge the quality of an individual's life. Several authors have pointed out that it is difficult for nondisabled people to judge the quality of life of people with cognitive or physical impairments. Those in the disability rights movement also tend to argue, as Tom Shakespeare does, that judgments about quality of life depend on social context; in nurturing societies, with ample resources to support people with different abilities, some "impairments" may not be "disabling."[48] Shakespeare emphasizes that the primary focus should be on providing adequate health care, and not so much on the question of euthanasia.

Activists working with a network called "Not Dead Yet" have been making similar arguments and have lobbied against euthanasia for many years. One of the members of that network, John Kelly, published an op-ed in the summer of 2022 as legislators in Massachusetts were considering assisted-suicide legislation. Kelly argued that the problem of suffering is not remedied by killing people but by responding to the "existential distress" experienced by those who are disabled, dying, and suffering. Kelly, who is himself paralyzed below the shoulders, argued:

> The answer is to address people's real needs. That means a fully funded Medicare home care benefit to reduce burden and keep people out of nursing homes. It means more and better palliative care. . . . The answer is not medically assisted suicide. We disabled people demand full civil and human rights, equal protection under the law, equal suicide prevention, and more respect throughout society.[49]

A similar set of concerns may also apply in thinking about the morality of abortion. It is worth asking how abortion decisions are influenced by larger social circumstances including poverty, race, and disability. And it is worth considering what kinds of social supports could be put into place that would help vulnerable people.

In this regard, we might also want to consider the issue of abortion in the case of disabled fetuses, the issue of sex-selective abortion, and the role of poverty and race in abortion decisions. According to the Guttmacher Institute, Black women and Hispanic women are more likely than White women to have an abortion.[50] And, based on data from 2014, 75 percent of abortions were performed on women in the lowest socioeconomic bracket.[51] As abortion law changed in 2022, a number of commentators pointed out that lack of access to abortion will be felt most acutely by poor women and women of color.[52] Pro-choice advocates interpret this as another reason to support abortion rights, with lack of access to abortion viewed as disempowering poor women and women of color. But some pro-life advocates have argued that this kind of data shows that there is a racist result of a permissive abortion regime when Black fetuses are aborted (some even call this a kind of genocide against Black people).[53] In response to that argument, advocates of abortion access argue that the right to abortion empowers Black women, who ought to be trusted with the personal choice of when and whether they want to be pregnant.

A further concern is the issue of sex-selective abortion and abortion used in the case of disabled fetuses. Sex-selective abortion typically means an abortion decision guided by the desire for a male child. Some critics of this practice go so far as to use the word "femicide" to describe it.[54] Critics point out that in some countries, sex-selective abortions have led to gender disparities; China and India have often been identified in the media as places where this occurs. According to a study published in 2009, the ratio of boys to girls in China was 120 to 100. Among families' second births—which were often permitted only if the first child was a girl—the ratio at one point was 143 to 100.[55] Similar disparities have occurred in India, where the ratio of boys to girls in 2012 was reportedly 1,000 to 914.[56] And some reports indicate that immigrant communities in Europe and the United Kingdom also practice **sex-selective abortion**.[57] This practice is illegal in some countries. There is currently no such restriction on a national level in the United States, although American lawmakers have considered bills that would ban the practice (e.g., the Prenatal Nondiscrimination Act).[58] The Guttmacher Institute reports that as of 2022, eleven states ban sex-selective abortion, four states prohibit abortions for reasons of race, and six states prohibit abortions in case of fetal genetic abnormality (such as Down syndrome).[59]

In discussing this last set of issues, it is important to be cautious about generalizing about cultural preferences and individual choices with regard to abortion. To what extent does a discussion of sex-selective abortion in

Asian cultures represent a kind of racism or cultural bias: are Americans who criticize this practice able to judge impartially and without cultural bias? And from a pro-choice point of view, why should a pregnant person's reasons matter with regard to abortion? If the choice of ending a pregnancy is morally permitted, it should not matter whether the choice is made for reasons of sex selection or to eliminate a disabled fetus. Of course, opponents of abortion argue that the abortion choice is always wrong. But it is worth considering whether the choices of individuals can have significant impacts on the general population, including a kind of eugenic outcome that ends up eliminating certain kinds of people.

Abortion and the Legal Right to Privacy

11.5 Summarize the legal dispute in the United States about the right to privacy.

One of the difficult questions in the conversation about abortion and euthanasia is about the very nature of autonomy and the right to choose. Do we really have the right to choose how we live, die, and give birth? Is the right to choose a fundamental or basic human right? And how is that grounded in the law?

In thinking about that last question, let's briefly consider the legal history of abortion in the United States. As you know from the previous chapter and from the opening vignette of this chapter, the legal status of abortion in the United States changed dramatically in the summer of 2022, as the Supreme Court issued its *Dobbs v. Jackson* decision, which overturned *Roe v. Wade*, the fifty-year-old precedent that had made abortion legal in the United States. Roe v. Wade and subsequent decisions were connected to an evolving legal principle that held there was a "right to privacy" that allowed for individual choice when it came to abortion, passive euthanasia, and assisted suicide. This legal history includes cases focused on abortion such as *Casey v. Planned Parenthood* (1992) as well as cases focused on euthanasia, assisted suicide, and the so-called "right to die" as discussed in cases such as *Cruzan v. Missouri Department of Health* (1990) and *Washington v. Glucksberg* (1997).

One of the focal points of these cases is an ongoing debate about autonomy and its limits. This includes a contentious debate about the very idea of a right to privacy. Among the most important legal questions raised in the debate about *Roe v. Wade* and these other cases was whether there was indeed a constitutional right to privacy that guaranteed the right to have an abortion or the right to assisted suicide. In *Roe* and *Casey*, the Court had grounded the right to privacy in a variety of amendments to the Constitution including the First, Fourth, Fifth, Ninth, and Fourteenth Amendments. *Roe v. Wade* described the right to privacy as involving "personal marital, familial, and sexual privacy said to be protected by the Bill of Rights or its penumbras."[60] This language—of a penumbra of rights—was often a focal point of criticism of the *Roe* decision. A significant legal question is whether rights must be explicitly stated and enumerated or whether there are implicit rights to be found in connection with other explicit rights. The idea of a penumbra of rights is connected to the latter point (a *penumbra* is a shadow—the metaphor suggests that some of the enumerated rights of the Constitution cast a shadow on other topics). This idea showed up in an earlier case, *Griswold v. Connecticut* (1965), where the Court ruled that married couples had the right to buy and use contraception. In that case, the Court explained, "The First Amendment has a penumbra where privacy is protected from governmental intrusion."[61] But in the 2022 *Dobbs* decision, the Court rejected the idea of a penumbra of rights, describing it in a footnote as a "facial absurdity."

Figure 11-3 U.S. Supreme Court.

Stephen Finn/Shutterstock

In overturning fifty years of constitutional precedent regarding the right to privacy, the Court has opened the door to a reassessment of a number of topics. In connection with the *Griswold* case, the *Dobbs* decision may even call into question the right to use contraception. And some critics have warned that if the right to privacy is called into question, cases involving homosexuality (such as *Lawrence v. Texas* from 2003) and the right to same-sex marriage (*Obergefell v. Hodges* from 2015) may be subject to revision. It remains to be seen what happens next. (We discuss Obergefell and same-sex marriage in much more detail in Chapter 15.)

The question of a right to privacy is not only a question for constitutional law, it is also a moral question. Is there such a moral right to privacy—even if the Court suggests that there is no explicit legal right to privacy? It is worth noting that much of the language used to describe the right to privacy in the legal discussion of the topic points toward deeper moral concerns. After *Roe v. Wade*, the Court continued to refine and clarify the basic idea of a right to privacy. The *Casey* decision articulated a basic account of individual liberty, autonomy, and conscience. The Court wrote:

> These matters, involving the most intimate and personal choices a person may make in a lifetime, choices central to personal dignity and autonomy, are central to the liberty protected by the Fourteenth Amendment. At the heart of liberty is the right to define one's own concept of existence, of meaning, of the universe, and of the mystery of human life.[62]

This way of putting things is clearly connected to deep philosophical and ethical claims about human dignity, autonomy, and freedom. The so-called right to privacy was connected to the idea that the state should grant individuals extensive freedom to make decisions about how we want to live, give birth, and die. In subsequent decisions, this kind of reasoning was extended in various ways including the right to same-sex marriage (as in *Obergefell v. Hodges*).

The Court's 2022 *Dobbs* decision made a different kind of argument (we include some excerpts in the primary source readings). The Court maintains that the Constitution does not include the kind of right to privacy that those previous cases said it did. And the Court suggested in *Dobbs* that in putting too much emphasis on individual liberty, autonomy, and privacy, there was the risk of moral mayhem. The Court explained in *Dobbs*:

> The Court concludes the right to obtain an abortion cannot be justified as a component of such a right. Attempts to justify abortion through appeals to a broader right to autonomy and to define one's "concept of existence" prove too much [quoting *Casey*]. Those criteria, at a high level of generality, could license fundamental rights to illicit drug use, prostitution, and the like.[63]

It is easy to see that the legal question of a right to privacy connects to other concrete moral questions and to the general moral question of the value of liberty, autonomy, and toleration.

A basic libertarian approach to this issue might embrace a broad understanding of the right to privacy and advocate liberty across the board. In response to the Court's worry, as expressed above, about liberty creating licentiousness, a libertarian might simply say, "So what?" Committed libertarians might be willing to advocate for the right to choose abortion, the right to obtain assisted-suicide medication, the right to marry and have sex with whomever you want, and maybe even the right to use drugs, engage in prostitution, and so on. One version of libertarianism could be derived from an approach to morality that emphasizes natural rights, based on the idea that we have a basic right to life, liberty, and the pursuit of happiness. As long as we are not harming others, the libertarian argues, we should be left alone to do what we please. (We discuss economic libertarianism in more detail in Chapter 14.)

Utilitarians may support such a libertarian viewpoint, holding that extensive liberty can tend to help us maximize happiness and social good. As we mentioned in our discussion of John Stuart Mill in Chapter 5, Mill also advocated for extensive liberty since he thought that liberty was a central part of happiness. But utilitarians also ask about the costs and benefits of extensive liberty. They may worry, for example, about public health issues and the need to prevent disease. They also are concerned with the social costs and implications of policies that permit abortion, euthanasia, or assisted suicide. There are empirical issue to consider here, as well as social justice concerns. Will there be adverse impacts on certain populations if abortion or euthanasia is widespread, such as on people with disabilities? What kind of impact will the profit motive of insurance companies have on our choices? Utilitarians may also be interested in such abstract considerations as the eugenic implications of abortion and euthanasia. But of primary importance for a utilitarian approach is the happiness of those who choose to have abortions or who seek assistance in dying. This kind of happiness may also be connected to the importance of liberty in making those kinds of choices.

On the other hand, there are those who focus on the moral constraints that ought to limit liberty. The author of the *Dobbs* decision, Samuel Alito, appealed to the concept of "ordered liberty" to make this point. The *Dobbs* decision explains,

> While individuals are certainly free to think and to say what they wish about "existence," "meaning," the "universe," and "the mystery of human life," they are not always free to act in accordance with those thoughts. License to act on the basis of such beliefs may correspond to one of the many understandings of "liberty," but it is certainly not "ordered liberty."[64]

Alito is worried here about the idea that liberty without order or structure can become licentious. He further suggests that we need to consult history and tradition in order to figure out the proper moral limits of liberty. He says, "guided by the history and tradition that map the essential components of our Nation's concept of ordered liberty, we must ask what the Fourteenth Amendment means by the term 'liberty.'"[65] He concludes that in the history and tradition of the United States (and more broadly the "common law" tradition in the Anglo-American world), ordered liberty did not include the right to an abortion.

This appeal to tradition is connected to a theory of constitutional interpretation known as "originalism." Originalism focuses on the norms and values of the time the Constitution was written and ratified (i.e., the original meaning of the text). One worry with regard to originalism is that it opens up the problem of historical and

even cultural relativism. Why does the original context matter more than our evolved understanding of these issues? How do we evaluate contemporary concerns in light of historical values? And if the tradition (or some other tradition) did include the right to an abortion, would that make it acceptable under the law?

It is worth noting that abortion was not always prohibited or condemned by many of the authorities that are now most emphatically opposed to it, including the Roman Catholic Church. Following the teachings of Augustine and Aquinas, the Church held that the fetus was not human until sometime after conception when the matter was suitable for the reception of a human soul.[66] For example, the Church fathers held that the soul did not enter the fetus until forty days of gestation for males and eighty or ninety days for females, a calculation that they based on ideas found in Aristotle and in the Bible—a point that was noted in a footnote to the *Roe v. Wade* decision.[67] It was not until 1869 that Pope Pius IX decreed that the embryo's soul was present from conception, declaring abortion to be a sin.[68] Indeed, for much of Western history and in British common law, abortion before quickening was legal and not considered immoral.[69] Quickening is said to occur when the mother feels the fetus move in the womb—and it was historically taken to mean that the soul was present in the fetus. Nor was abortion always illegal in the United States before the 1970s. As noted in the *Roe v. Wade* opinion, "At the time of the adoption of our Constitution, and throughout the major portion of the 19th century, abortion was viewed with less disfavor than under most American statutes currently in effect."[70] But in the more recent *Dobbs* decision, a different account of this history was provided. The *Dobbs* decision argued that "*Roe* either ignored or misstated this history."[71] According to *Dobbs*, in the common law tradition, abortion had always been considered immoral and was illegal.

This debate reminds us that history can be interpreted in various ways, which poses a challenge for the idea of originalism (and for other arguments based in claims about history). And indeed, professional historians weighed in on the question in an amicus filing submitted to the U.S. Supreme Court in the *Dobbs* case. These historians concluded that history shows that in the past, the idea of abortion did not apply in the case of early pregnancy:

> The common law did not regulate abortion in early pregnancy. Indeed, the common law did not even recognize abortion as occurring at that stage. That is because the common law did not legally acknowledge a fetus as existing separately from a pregnant woman until the woman felt fetal movement, called "quickening," which could occur as late as the 25th week of pregnancy. This was a subjective standard decided by the pregnant woman alone and was not considered accurately ascertainable by other means.[72]

It is easy to see here that historical arguments require substantial interpretation. And for philosophers, these historical and legal arguments do not prove much in terms of the rightness or wrongness of a topic like abortion. Would it make a difference, for example, if there were different, more permissive legal traditions—including the tradition that developed through and after *Roe v. Wade*? And finally, we ought to ask whether it matters to the *morality* of abortion or euthanasia whether or not there is an *explicit legal right to privacy* found within the Constitution?

Assisted Suicide and Euthanasia in Current Practice

In 2015, California legalized physician-assisted suicide, joining a handful of other states where physicians are permitted to prescribe lethal medication for terminally ill patients. As mentioned earlier, this law avoids the word "suicide," preferring to speak of an "end of life option." In 2016, as the California law took effect, Canada also legalized assisted suicide. The model for most of this legislation is the physician-assisted suicide law in Oregon (where it is called the Death with Dignity Act), which holds that a doctor may prescribe lethal medication to a patient who has fewer than six months to live, according to the judgment of two independent doctors. The patient must be competent; must have a clear and continuing request, made orally and in writing; and must be able to take the drug without assistance. In the United States, physician-assisted suicide legislation has been subject to referenda and has been litigated in the courts. The practice was not legal in the United

States a generation ago, but it is slowly becoming accepted. In some countries, active euthanasia—where instead of simply prescribing lethal medication, the doctor administers the lethal injection—is now legal in a number of countries including the Netherlands, Belgium, and Luxembourg. Active euthanasia is not legal in the United States.

Since the state of Oregon legalized physician-assisted suicide, the state has kept detailed records. According to the state of Oregon, a slowly growing number of patients in Oregon obtain lethal prescriptions and take them. According to data published in February 2022, in the past two decades that assisted suicide has been legal in Oregon, 3,280 people have obtained lethal prescriptions and 2,159 patients have died as a result of these prescriptions.[73] In 2021, there were 383 prescription recipients, resulting in 238 deaths. Of those who completed suicide, the majority were over sixty-five, with a median age of seventy-five. The vast majority were White (95 percent), and most were college educated.

In the Netherlands, euthanasia has been legal since 2002, when the Termination of Life on Request and Assisted Suicide (Review Procedures) Act took effect. The law in the Netherlands stipulates that physicians must exercise "due care" in assisting in suicide or when terminating life on request. According to the law, due care means that the physician

- holds the conviction that the request by the patient was voluntary and well considered.
- holds the conviction that the patient's suffering was lasting and unbearable.
- has informed the patient about the situation and about its prospects.
- holds the conviction, along with the patient, that there was no other reasonable solution for the situation.
- has consulted at least one other, independent physician who has seen the patient and has given his or her written opinion on the requirements of due care.
- has terminated a life or assisted in a suicide with due care.[74]

Originally, the law was only supposed to apply to adults. But euthanasia for children over twelve was eventually allowed. Government officials in the Netherlands have been debating whether to allow it for children younger than twelve.[75] The practice of consensual child euthanasia has been legal in Belgium since 2014.[76] Some doctors have argued for years in favor of allowing euthanasia for children and infants when they suffer from "unbearable and hopeless pain" and when their parents agree in consultation with doctors.[77] The cases involved in these kinds of decisions are heartbreaking. Consider the case of an infant, Sanne, who was born with a severe form of Hallopeau-Siemens syndrome.[78] The disease caused the infant's skin to blister and peel, leaving painful scar tissue in its place. The prognosis was for a life of suffering until the child would eventually die of skin cancer before reaching her teenage years. The hospital refused to allow the infant to be euthanized, and Sanne eventually died of pneumonia. In such a case, would it be more humane to actively end the infant's life? In Belgium and the Netherlands, they are allowing for patients and parents to consent to euthanasia. A protocol has been proposed for dealing with infant euthanasia, the Groningen Protocol.

Although infant euthanasia remains rare in most places and is still a legal gray area in the Netherlands, adult euthanasia is regulated, and detailed records of the practice exist. The Dutch government was notified that in 2019, 6,361 people were actively euthanized, this included 245 cases of assisted suicide and another twenty-four cases involving a combination of assisted suicide and active euthanasia.[79] Most of these cases (4,100) involved patients with cancer, while 162 were for patients with dementia and sixty-eight were for patients with psychiatric disorders. The issue of euthanasia for dementia and psychiatric disorders is especially controversial, as the mental competency of those requesting death is up for debate. Is mental illness a sufficient cause for suicide or a euthanasia request?

Other questions arise with regard to this kind of data. Are these numbers small or large in comparison with the general population? In the 2019 report, the Dutch authorities explain that euthanasia deaths were 4.2 percent of the total number of people who died in the Netherlands (the total number was 151,793).[80] In Oregon, a similar question can be asked. And the Oregon report states, "During 2021, DWDA deaths accounted for an estimated 0.59 percent of total deaths in Oregon" (the total number of deaths was reported as 40,226).[81]

One interpretation of these numbers argues that small numbers of people will avail themselves of euthanasia or assisted suicide. But advocates argue that for that small number of people who do use these procedures, the result is beneficial and empowering, as these patients take control of their own dying. On the other hand, opponents of the policy point to the steady (if slow) growth of the numbers of euthanasia and assisted suicide over time. The critic may suggest that there is a slippery slope here and that people will begin using this option in larger numbers as it becomes normalized. Of course, those who support the right to die with dignity could respond to this worry by maintaining that more widespread use of euthanasia can be a good thing, so long as the choice remains autonomous. And in response, the anti-euthanasia argument will maintain that rather than encouraging the choice of death, we should insist on better health care, including better pain management and palliative care. But defenders of the right to die with dignity will argue that even with better health care and social supports, there do seem to be truly hopeless cases in which a quick and painless death would be preferable to prolonged suffering.

Palliative Sedation, Emergency Abortion, and Double Effect Reasoning

11.6 Analyze how double effect reasoning might apply in thinking about euthanasia and abortion.

Discussions of abortion and euthanasia are not merely abstract moral questions. Health care professionals are confronted with concrete cases in which dying patients suffer and in which people may need abortion as part of a medical emergency. These are difficult cases, made more difficult by changing legal and political circumstances. In the changing legal landscape, medical professionals will be confronted with difficult choices.

Consider the issue known as **terminal sedation** or **palliative sedation**. This is different from overtly active euthanasia. What we are talking about here involves giving significant amounts of pain medication to gravely ill and dying patients. In some cases, the amount of pain medication given can also be a contributing factor in bringing about death. To call this "terminal sedation" implies that the use of sedation aims at the termination of life; to call it "palliative sedation" implies that the sedation is intended as palliative (relieving or soothing) care. Palliative sedation can also hasten death when it is combined with other practices, such as cutting off food and water or withdrawing other medications. Various forms of palliative care, pain management, and passive euthanasia are now standard practices in hospice care (a *hospice* is a nursing facility that provides care for the dying). However, the intentional use of pain medication to end life remains controversial.[82] One notorious case involved the possibility that terminal sedation was used to end the lives of patients in the aftermath of Hurricane Katrina in New Orleans.[83] The disaster cut off power and water to health care facilities, and health care providers were confronted with the challenge of caring for sick and dying patients while awaiting rescue. One doctor involved in the Katrina case, Dr. Anna Pou, said, "I do not believe in euthanasia. I don't think it's anyone's decision to make when a patient dies. However, what I do believe in is comfort care, and that means that we ensure that they do not suffer pain."[84] Charges against her were brought before a grand jury, but Dr. Pou was not indicted.

Physicians are sometimes hesitant to administer sufficient pain medication to severely ill patients because they fear that the medication will actually cause their deaths. They fear that this would be considered comparable to mercy killing (or active euthanasia), which is illegal. (The fact that they might cause addiction in their patients is another reason why some doctors hesitate to give narcotics for pain relief. This seems hardly a reasonable objection, especially if the patient is dying!) The **doctrine of double effect** may help justify physicians' decision to increase palliative care in cases such as this. According to this idea, it is acceptable to do something morally permissible for the purpose of achieving some good, while knowing that it also may have a bad secondary effect.

Figure 11-6 may be used to help understand the essence of this principle. It shows a morally permissible act with two effects: one intended main effect and one unintended side effect.

According to the principle of double effect, it may be morally permissible to administer a drug with the intention of relieving pain (a good effect), even though we know or foresee that our action also may have a bad effect (weakening the person and risking death). Certain conditions must be met, however, for this to be permissible. First, the act itself must be morally permissible. One cannot do something that is wrong to bring about a good end. Second, the person who acts must intend to bring about the good end rather than the harmful result. Third, the good results must outweigh the bad ones.

The idea behind the double effect principle in the case of terminal sedation is that there is a moral difference between intending to kill someone and intending to relieve pain. There is also a moral difference between intending that someone die by means of one's actions (giving a drug overdose) and foreseeing that they will die because of one's actions (giving medication to relieve pain). Active euthanasia occurs when one intentionally administers a drug with the purposeful intention of bringing about a person's death. But when one's purpose or intention is pain mitigation, this may not count as active euthanasia, even if the one administering the pain medication understands that death may result.

In the excerpt from James Rachels included below, a related concern is raised about intention versus consequences. Rachels suggests that intentions are important and that we don't merely judge an act based on consequences and actions. Consider the difference between someone who passively watches another die because of some mean-spirited or selfish intention (say, as in Rachels's example that they hope to inherit some money) and someone who allows another to die because of a benevolent desire to help that person die with dignity. The consequences matter but also the

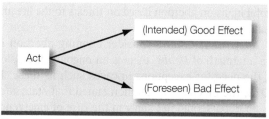

Figure 11-4 The doctrine of double effect.

intention with which one acts (or does not act, as the case may be).

The principle of double effect continues to be an object of debate as a basic principle of moral reasoning.[85] Consequentialists and utilitarians are not primarily concerned with intentions but with the outcome of actions. And there are significant questions about whether and to what extent we can assess people's intentions, including our own. How sure are you about what you actually intend when confronted with complex cases and difficult choices? In real-world medical situations—and especially in emergencies—it may be difficult to assess people's intentions. People may also have mixed or hidden motives for their actions. Nevertheless, trying to satisfy the principle of double effect can be useful for doctors, allowing them to give their patients sufficient pain medication without fear of being prosecuted for homicide. It is worth underlining here that patient consent ought to be a key part of any conversation about these kinds of issues. But there is a significant question in discussions of emergency cases about whether unconscious patients and loved ones, who are unavailable or inaccessible because of the emergency, could even be asked to consent. Nonetheless, killing patients against their wishes would be involuntary euthanasia—and wrong according to a moral framework that is focused on autonomy.

As we conclude this section, let's note that the doctrine of double effect may also be applied in thinking about abortion. In a case in which a pregnancy may be life-threatening or cause adverse health outcomes for the pregnant person, the doctrine of double effect could be employed to allow for an abortion. Obviously, this kind of case—in which abortion is used to save a person's health or life—would only be morally problematic for those who are opposed to abortion. But even for pro-life advocates, it is possible to imagine an exception to prohibitions on abortion based on threats to the life and health of the mother.

As American states consider banning abortion in the aftermath of *Dobbs*, there is an ongoing discussion of the need for exceptions in cases such as these. In 2022, the Biden administration stated that state bans on abortion should not apply in the case of emergency treatment for pregnant women. The U.S. Secretary of Health and Human Services, Xavier Becerra, stated, "no

matter where you live, women have the right to emergency care—including abortion care."[86] In response, the state of Texas sued the Biden administration, stating in their lawsuit, "President Biden is flagrantly disregarding the legislative and democratic process—and flouting the Supreme Court's ruling before the ink is dry—by having his appointed bureaucrats mandate that hospitals and emergency medicine physicians must perform abortions."[87]

This dispute shows us that as abortion law is changing in the United States in the post-*Dobbs* era, we may need to consider whether and how double effect reasoning might be applied. Adam Omelianchuk, a bioethicist working at Baylor University in Texas, argued that in the aftermath of *Dobbs*, double effect reasoning could be employed to "help enable clinicians legally provide appropriate medical care to at least some of their pregnant patients who are experiencing a medical emergency.[88] Notice that he articulates this as a *legal matter*. The legal situation creates a moral quandary for health care providers confronted with the question of whether abortion could be justified in the case of medical emergency, in a jurisdiction in which abortion is illegal: Should they violate the law in order to provide necessary care? What would a health care provider do if presented with an emergency such as this in a state where abortion is not legal? There are moral (and legal) risks for health care professionals in this context. The suggestion made by Omelianchuk is that the doctrine of double effect could provide some guidance for medical professionals when confronted with the need to act, especially in an emergency.

The basic application of double effect reasoning would be that a justifiable action—saving a pregnant person's life or, more broadly, caring for their long-term health—could be permitted even if we foresee that the fetus will be killed as an unintended result. In such a case, the intention of the act would be narrowly focused on the permissible action of saving the pregnant person. But some abortion opponents reject this application of the doctrine of double effect, claiming that if the abortion is the primary means to obtain the end of helping the mother, this is not really a legitimate case of double effect reasoning. That would be so because the double effect idea should not be used to justify the use of an immoral means for producing a good outcome. Philosophers have debated this question for decades. This debate reminds us that there are various ways that actions, intentions, and moral permission can play out in different cases. Philippa Foot, in an influential essay on double effect and abortion from the 1960s, pointed out that there are several versions of this kind of case.[89] Consider the difference between a case in which both mother and fetus will die unless an abortion is performed and another case in which the fetus might survive even if the mother dies. Foot suggests that moral judgment should attend to these complexities. But she states, "in general we do not think that we can kill one innocent person to rescue another."[90] Her assumption in making that claim is that abortion kills an innocent person. And of course, it is worth restating that this apparent conflict only exists if one assumes that the fetus is an "innocent person,"

which is a claim that is not accepted by some on the pro-choice side of the argument. As mentioned, this kind of case—life- and health-threatening pregnancy—comes up often as a reason to provide exceptions to prohibitions against abortion. Some pro-life advocates dismiss the concern about life- and health-threatening pregnancy by claiming that these kinds of cases are rare and by avoiding the use of the word "abortion" to describe procedures that result in the death of a fetus in order to save the mother: one pro-life group of physician calls such a procedure a medically necessary "separation" of mother and fetus.[91] On the other side of the debate, pro-choice advocates will see this discussion as an obvious reason why abortion should be legal, claiming that a pregnant person should have the legal right to choose abortion if pregnancy will have adverse impacts on their life or health.

Chapter Summary

11.1 How can we explain the conflict between pro-life and pro-choice points of view?

Pro-life arguments typically focus on the ontological claim that a fetus is a person deserving of respect. Often this is connected to other pro-life claims and a framework known as a "consistent ethic of life," which is opposed to euthanasia and other forms of killing, along with abortion. Pro-choice is focused on autonomy and consent. The pro-choice argument emphasizes a person's right to choose to have an abortion. This is not "pro-abortion" but rather focused on the right to choose. With regard to euthanasia, pro-choice thinking will focus on the importance of consent, as in the case of voluntary euthanasia. But a pro-life response to voluntary euthanasia may argue that death is bad and that it is wrong to consent to be killed (or to kill yourself). Pro-choice arguments may suggest that life is not always good and that in some cases it can be rational to autonomously choose death whether by euthanasia or by assisted suicide.

11.2 How can we evaluate moral and ontological issues involved in thinking about abortion?

Some arguments about abortion are not primarily concerned with the moral status of the fetus. Some

utilitarians may approach abortion in this way, focused on the question of creating the greatest happiness of all those involved in an abortion decision. A different approach could assume for the sake of argument that a fetus is a person and ask what should happen, in case of a conflicts of rights, as when the mother's right to choose conflicts with a fetus's right to life. A different focal point of arguments about abortion will be concerned with the question of what a fetus is and when it attains a certain kind of moral status (and thus offer an answer to the question of whether and when a fetus is a person with rights). Various criteria or stages were discussed involving a possible answer to the ontological question: conception, fetal heartbeat, brain development, quickening, and viability, along with the related question of potentiality. In order to evaluate these issues, we would need to defend a basic standpoint in moral theory (utilitarianism, rights-based arguments, etc.). We would also need to decide which criteria for personhood is the right one.

11.3 How can we evaluate and apply moral theories to different kinds of euthanasia?

The different kinds of euthanasia discussed fall into two broad categories. First, there are issues involving consent: voluntary, involuntary, and nonvoluntary euthanasia. Second, there are issues involving a distinction between doing and allowing: this is the focus of the distinction between active and passive euthanasia. Physician-assisted suicide is another topic that is closely related. In order to evaluate the morality of euthanasia, we would need to decide how important consent is and whether there is a morally significant difference between doing and allowing. Utilitarians are typically focused on outcomes and not on the difference between doing and allowing. Utilitarians are concerned with ameliorating suffering and may also consider social costs and benefits. Typically, they are also interested in liberty and consent. The distinction between doing and allowing may be of concern for deontological and non-consequentialist approaches to moral theory, which ask the very basic question of whether killing (including suicide) can ever be justified. Non-consequentialists may also be concerned with the motive and intentions of agents, warning that there can be cases in which euthanasia is employed with morally corrupt motives.

11.4 How can we explain social justice and feminist concerns that arise in thinking about abortion and euthanasia?

Abortion is a feminist concern, since at issue is the question of a woman's right to consent to pregnancy and the related right to terminate an unwanted pregnancy. The pro-choice approach to abortion rights is often connected to other issues involving women's rights including the right of a woman to consent to sexual relations and to pregnancy. Conversations about abortion and euthanasia also connect to discussions of how these practices impact vulnerable populations and how they can either harm or empower vulnerable members of society. One significant concern has been articulated by disability rights advocates who worry that abortion and euthanasia can be turned against people with disabilities and may have eugenic outcomes. From the social justice vantage point, people have also raised concerns about racial disparities in abortion access, the problem of sex-selective abortion, and impacts on people with disabilities. One important question in all of this is what society is doing to protect vulnerable people who may be harmed by euthanasia and who may be coerced in their decision-making. A similar question is also asked with regard to feminist concerns about abortion, which is about how women are harmed when they are denied access to abortion.

11.5 What is a summary of the legal dispute in the United States about the right to privacy?

The U.S. Supreme Court decision *Dobbs v. Jackson* (2022) overturned *Roe v. Wade*, the case that established the right to abortion in 1971. This decision did not ban abortion in the entire United States, but it did allow for a number of American states to pass laws against abortion. The *Dobbs* decision claimed that one significant flaw in *Roe* was the idea of a right to privacy. The *Dobbs* decision maintained that the Constitution did not contain any explicit right to privacy, while the *Roe* decision had maintained that the right to privacy could be found within a "penumbra" of rights that was created by other explicitly stated rights in the Constitution and its amendments. Another important issue was a dispute about history: *Dobbs* claimed that abortion was typically viewed as immoral and outlawed, but *Roe* and a prominent group of American historians argued that this was not true and that early abortion was not viewed as immoral. *Dobbs* was viewed as a triumph for the pro-life side of the argument. And after *Dobbs*, pro-choice advocates have warned that other rights might be vulnerable to reassessment, including ways in which the right to privacy connects to euthanasia, sexuality, and marriage.

11.6 How can double effect reasoning be applied in thinking about euthanasia and abortion?

The doctrine of double effect can be used to justify euthanasia or abortion if the primary intention of the agent (i.e., doctor or nurse) is to help the patient and the act done is morally permissible. At the end of life, this might include terminal sedation in which a lethal dose of pain medication is administered, even though the physician knows that death might occur. In that case, death is a foreseen but unintended secondary effect of the primary intention, which was to alleviate pain. With regard to abortion, a similar argument could be made with regard to pregnancies that are terminated in cases in which the mother's life or health is in danger. Not everyone agrees that the doctrine of double effect makes sense in moral reasoning. Nor does everyone agree that the idea can be applied in the case of abortion. At issue here are questions about the scope of our intention and about whether the first action is a legitimately intended action or whether it is an immoral means to some other end. Critics also raise the question of whether we know our intentions or if our intentions are pure.

11.7 How might you defend a thesis with regard to abortion and euthanasia?

In order to defend a thesis about abortion and euthanasia, you would need to think about the ontological question of what a fetus is, and what a brain-dead human being is. This requires you to think about the nature of personhood and what kind of criteria should be used to determine if a being is a person. With regard to abortion, this also includes making a judgment about development and potentiality. You would also need to consider the kind of moral theory you would apply in thinking about these issues: utilitarian, natural law, rights-based, or deontological theories. And you would need to decide how important liberty and the right to privacy are in your thinking about social issues, morality, and the law. Any thesis about these topics must be sensitive to the complexities of how, when, and why these actions are being considered. This would involve thinking about whether there is a difference between early abortion and later abortion and whether there are morally relevant differences between active and passive euthanasia, and/or physician-assisted suicide. In some cases, one might advocate a systematic and comprehensive pro-life or pro-choice point of view. But each topic is unique and involves a number of subsidiary concerns, so any comprehensive account might need to think about exceptions and complications.

Primary Source Readings

In the readings in this chapter, we begin with a short excerpt from Judith Jarvis Thomson's influential article published in 1971, before the U.S. Supreme Court guaranteed abortion rights across the United States. Thomson's basic argument is in defense of abortion rights for women, even if we grant that a fetus is a person. Her argument is outlined above. The next essay is from Mary Anne Warren, who provides a discussion of criteria for personhood. Her conclusion based on her criteria is that a fetus is not a person and thus that abortion can be justified. This set of criteria can also be applied to end-of-life questions about adults with brain damage. Following that is an excerpt from an article by Bertha Alvarez Manninen that looks at abortion from the vantage point of care ethics, virtue ethics, and from a psychological perspective. In this excerpt, she points to the need to think about preventing unwanted pregnancy and to a pro-choice point of view that does not completely ignore the fetus. Next is an excerpt from an article by Don Marquis, who provides an argument against abortion that focuses on the potential of the fetus to experience significant goods in its future. After those excerpts, we have excerpts from two influential articles about euthanasia. J. Gay-Williams discusses the natural instinct to live, while also considering some arguments against euthanasia and the problem of a slippery slope. James Rachels asks us to consider whether there is a moral difference between passive and active euthanasia and the importance of motive and intention. We then have an excerpt from an amicus brief written by a group of prominent philosophers, which connects concern for autonomy and choice to discussions of assisted suicide and abortion. Finally, we include an excerpt from the U.S. Supreme Court's *Dobbs v. Jackson* decision (2022), in which the Court argues that "ordered liberty" does not include the right to abortion while suggesting that states should be empowered to restrict abortion as they see fit.

Reading 11-1   A Defense of Abortion | Judith Jarvis Thomson

Study Questions

As you read the excerpt, please consider the following questions:

1. Why does Thomson suggest that abortion is not murder?

2. Why does Thomson say that "a sick and desperately frightened fourteen-year-old schoolgirl, pregnant due to rape, may of course choose abortion"?

3. What is the moral difference between a woman's right to end her pregnancy and a woman's desire to secure the death of her fetus?

If directly killing an innocent person is murder, and thus is impermissible, then the mother's directly killing the innocent person inside her is murder, and thus is impermissible. But it cannot seriously be thought to be murder if the mother performs an abortion on herself to save her life. It cannot seriously be said that she *must* refrain, that she *must* sit passively by and wait for her death....

Nobody is morally *required* to make large sacrifices, of health, of all other interests and concerns, of all other duties and commitments, for nine years, or even for nine months, in order to keep another person alive....

If a set of parents do not try to prevent pregnancy, do not obtain an abortion, but rather take it home with them, then they have assumed responsibility for it, they have given it rights, and they cannot *now* withdraw support from it at the cost of its life because they now find it difficult to go on providing for it. But if they have taken all reasonable precautions against having a child, they do not simply by virtue of their biological relationship to the child who comes into existence have a special responsibility for it. They may wish to assume responsibility for it, or they may not wish to. And I am suggesting that if assuming responsibility for it would require large sacrifices, then they may refuse.... While I do argue that abortion is not impermissible, I do not argue that it is always permissible. There may well be cases in which carrying the child to term required only Minimally Decent Samaritanism of the mother, and this is a standard we must not fall below. I am inclined to think it a merit of my account precisely that it does *not* give a general yes or a general no. It allows for and supports our sense that, for example, a sick and desperately frightened fourteen-year-old schoolgirl, pregnant due to rape, may *of course* choose abortion, and that any law which rules this out is an insane law. And it also allows for and supports our sense that in other cases resort to abortion is even positively indecent. It would be indecent in the woman to request an abortion, and indecent in a doctor to perform it, if she is in her seventh month, and wants the abortion just to avoid the nuisance of postponing a trip abroad....

Secondly, while I am arguing for the permissibility of abortion in some cases, I am not arguing for the right to secure the death of the unborn child. It is easy to confuse these two things in that up to a certain point in the life of the fetus it is not able to survive outside the mother's body; hence removing it from her body guarantees its death. But they are importantly different....

Judith Jarvis Thomson, "A Defense of Abortion." *Philosophy & Public Affairs* 1:1 (Fall 1971), pp. 47–66.

Reading 11-2   On the Moral and Legal Status of Abortion | Mary Anne Warren

Study Questions

As you read the excerpt, please consider the following questions:

1. How can we summarize Warren's basic argument in defense of abortion?
2. What does Warren mean when she says that the traits she lists as part of personhood are not connected to "genetic humanity"?
3. How might Warren's view be connected to questions about personhood at the end of life?

I suggest that the traits which are most central to the concept of personhood, or humanity in the moral sense, are, very roughly, the following:

- Consciousness (of objects and events external and/or internal to the being), and in particular the capacity to feel pain;
- Reasoning (the developed capacity to solve new and relatively complex problems);
- Self-motivated activity (activity which is relatively independent of either genetic or direct external control);
- The capacity to communicate, by whatever means, messages of an indefinite variety of types, that is, not just with an indefinite number of possible contents, but on indefinitely many possible topics;
- The presence of self-concepts, and self-awareness, either individual or racial, or both.

... All we need to claim, to demonstrate that a fetus is not a person, is that any being which satisfies none of (1)–(5) is certainly not a person. I consider this claim to be so obvious that I think anyone who denied it, and claimed that a being which satisfied none of (1)–(5) was a person all the same, would thereby demonstrate that he had no notion at all of what a person is—perhaps because he had confused the concept of a person with that of genetic humanity....

Now if (1)–(5) are indeed the primary criteria of personhood, then it is clear that genetic humanity is neither necessary nor sufficient for establishing that an entity is a person. Some human beings are not people, and there may well be people who are not human beings. A man or woman whose consciousness has been permanently obliterated but who remains alive is a human being which is no longer a person; defective human beings, with no appreciable mental capacity, are not and presumably never will be people; and a fetus is a human being which is not yet a person, and which therefore cannot coherently be said to have full moral rights....

Thus, neither a fetus's resemblance to a person, nor its potential for becoming a person provides any basis whatever for the claim that it has any significant right to life. Consequently, a woman's right to protect her health, happiness, freedom, and even her life, by terminating an unwanted pregnancy, will always override whatever right to life it may be appropriate to ascribe to a fetus, even a fully developed one....

And thus, in the absence of any overwhelming social need for every possible child, the laws which restrict the right to obtain an abortion, or limit the period of pregnancy during which an abortion may be performed, are a wholly unjustified violation of a woman's most basic moral and constitutional rights.

Mary Anne Warren, "On the Moral and Legal Status of Abortion." *The Monist* 57:1 (January 1973), pp. 43–61.

Reading 11-3   The Value of Choice and the Choice to Value | Bertha Alvarez Manninen

Study Questions

As you read the excerpt, please consider the following questions:

1. Why does Manninen suggests that pro-choice is not pro-abortion, and how is that claim connected to her goal of making abortion less frequent?

2. What are the two strategies suggested by Manninen for reducing abortion rates, and how do those concerns relate to larger feminist and social justice concerns?

3. What does Manninen mean when she suggests that pro-choice advocates should avoid "erasing" the fetus from moral consideration?

Although prochoice advocates need to continue fighting for a woman's right to safe and legal abortion, they should also make it an important part of prochoice advocacy that abortion is a right that is exercised with less frequency. Adopting this secondary goal helps to draw a distinction between being "prochoice" and being "proabortion"; a distinction that is often collapsed. The term "proabortion" denotes someone who encourages abortion, who celebrates abortion, who desires to see women choose abortion over other options. I know of no prochoice advocate who meets this definition.

There are, essentially, two ways to reduce abortion rates: one, via the prevention of unplanned pregnancies, and two, via changing certain aspects of society so that women aren't coerced into choosing abortion because they fear having a child will force them to compromise other worthwhile goals. Achieving the first goal is rather straightforward—various studies have confirmed that an essential component to reducing unplanned pregnancies is to increase access to effective contraception, in addition to comprehensive sex education that ensures its correct and consistent use.... The second part of the abortion-reducing equation is more difficult to achieve. The reality facing single young women if they decide to bring an unplanned pregnancy to term is stark enough to understand why so many decide to abort....

There is evidence that providing assistance in the form of financial help, childcare services, and medical services results in decreased abortion rates.... In addition to providing postnatal medical support, which eases the economic hardship that comes with raising a child, easy access to medical care means easy access to effective contraception, which, in turn, reduces the need to seek abortions in the first place....

Of course, this will not eliminate abortions—contraception will occasionally fail, even with perfect use, and some women simply do not want to be mothers, neither at the time of their unplanned pregnancy nor ever. Moreover, as long as sexual violence exists against women, abortion access is needed for the women who cannot bring themselves to gestate after being victimized....

We do not have to completely erase the fetus from moral consideration in order to defend abortion rights. The stereotype that prochoice advocacy inevitably entails the dehumanization of the fetus does not advance the prochoice position in the eyes of American society. Prochoice advocates must do more to combat this stereotype, and we must do more to broaden our arguments in favor of abortion rights in a way that is open to respecting fetal life. Given the constant onslaught of restrictive abortion laws, prochoice advocacy cannot afford to be reduced or erased from public discourse. Fetal life matters to many women, including women who abort and who defend the right to abortion....

To trivialize fetal life is to dismiss the phenomenology of pregnancy and abortions for many women. It is to be dismissive not just of nascent human life, but of the very women whose rights we fight so vehemently to defend and whose support we may stand to lose.

Bertha Alvarez Manninen, "The Value of Choice and the Choice to Value." *Hypatia,* 28:3 (2013), pp. 663–83.

Reading 11-4   Why Abortion Is Immoral | Don Marquis

Study Questions

As you read the excerpt, please consider the following questions:

1. What is it that makes killing a person wrong according to Marquis?
2. Why does Marquis believe that this also makes killing a fetus wrong?
3. Why does Marquis suggest that abortion is not necessarily wrong in all circumstance and that euthanasia could be justified?

The loss of one's life deprives one of all the experiences, activities, projects, and enjoyments that would otherwise have constituted one's future. Therefore, killing someone is wrong, primarily because the killing inflicts (one of) the greatest possible losses on the victim. To describe this as the loss of life can be misleading, however. The change in my biological state does not by itself make killing me wrong. The effect of the loss of my biological life is the loss to me of all those activities, projects, experiences, and enjoyments which would otherwise have constituted my future personal life. These activities, projects, experiences, and enjoyments are either valuable for their own sakes or are means to something else that is valuable for its own sake. Some parts of my future are not valued by me now, but will come to be valued by me as I grow older and as my values and capacities change. When I am killed, I am deprived both of what I now value which would have been part of my future personal life, but also what I would come to value. Therefore, when I die, I am deprived of all of the value of my future. Inflicting this loss on me is ultimately what makes killing me wrong....

... The claim that the loss of one's future is the wrong-making feature of one's being killed does not entail . . . that active euthanasia is wrong. Persons who are severely and incurably ill, who face a future of pain and despair, and who wish to die will not have suffered a loss if they are killed. It is, strictly speaking, the value of a human's future which makes killing wrong in this theory. This being so, killing does not necessarily wrong some persons who are sick and dying. Of course, there may be other reasons for a prohibition of active euthanasia, but that is another matter.

... The claim that the primary wrong-making feature of a killing is the loss to the victim of the value of its future has obvious consequences for the ethics of abortion. The future of a standard fetus includes a set of experiences, projects, activities, and such which are identical with the futures of adult human beings and are identical with the futures of young children. Since the reason that is sufficient to explain why it is wrong to kill human beings after the time of birth is a reason that also applies to fetuses, it follows that abortion is prima facie seriously morally wrong.

... Of course, this value of a future-like-ours argument, if sound, shows only that abortion is prima facie wrong, not that it is wrong in any and all circumstances. Since the loss of the future to a standard fetus, if killed, is, however, at least as great a loss as the loss of the future to a standard adult human being who is killed, abortion, like ordinary killing, could be justified only by the most compelling reasons.

Don Marquis, "Why Abortion Is Immoral." *The Journal of Philosophy* 86:4 (April 1989), pp. 183–95, 200–202.

Reading 11-5   The Wrongfulness of Euthanasia | J. Gay-Williams

Study Questions

As you read the excerpt, please consider the following questions:

1. Why does Gay-Williams believe that euthanasia acts against our nature?

2. Why does Gay-Williams think that euthanasia could undermine hope?

3. How could euthanasia have a corrupting influence and lead to a "slippery slope"?

Every human being has a natural inclination to continue living. Our reflexes and responses fit us to fight attackers, flee wild animals, and dodge out of the way of trucks. In our daily lives we exercise the caution and care necessary to protect ourselves. Our bodies are similarly structured for survival right down to the molecular level.... Euthanasia does violence to this natural goal of survival. It is literally acting against nature because all the processes of nature are bent toward the end of bodily survival....

Contemporary medicine has high standards of excellence and a proven record of accomplishment, but it does not possess perfect and complete knowledge. A mistaken diagnosis is possible, and so is a mistaken prognosis. Consequently, we may believe that we are dying of a disease when, as a matter of fact, we may not be. We may think that we have no hope of recovery when, as a matter of fact, our chances are quite good. In such circumstances, if euthanasia were permitted, we would die needlessly. Death is final and the chance of error too great to approve the practice of euthanasia.

Also, there is always the possibility that an experimental procedure or a hitherto untried technique will pull us through. We should at least keep this option open, but euthanasia closes it off. Furthermore, spontaneous remission does occur in many cases. For no apparent reason, a patient simply recovers when those all around him, including his physicians, expected him to die. Euthanasia would just guarantee their expectations and leave no room for the "miraculous" recoveries that frequently occur.

Finally, knowing that we can take our life at any time (or ask another to take it) might well incline us to give up too easily....

Doctors and nurses are, for the most part, totally committed to saving lives. A life lost is, for them, almost a personal failure, an insult to their skills and knowledge. Euthanasia as a practice might well alter this. It could have a corrupting influence so that in any case that is severe doctors and nurses might not try hard enough to save the patient. They might decide that the patient would simply be "better off dead" and take the steps necessary to make that come about....

Finally, euthanasia as a policy is a slippery slope. A person apparently hopelessly ill may be allowed to take his own life. Then he may be permitted to deputize others to do it for him should he no longer be able to act. The judgment of others then becomes the ruling factor. Already at this point euthanasia is not personal and voluntary, for others are acting "on behalf of" the patient as they see fit.... It is only a short step, then, from voluntary euthanasia (self-inflicted or authorized), to directed euthanasia administered to a patient who has given no authorization, to involuntary euthanasia conducted as part of a social policy.

J. Gay-Williams, "The Wrongfulness of Euthanasia," from *Intervention and Reflection: Basic Issues in Medical Ethics*, 7th ed. (Belmont, CA: Thomson/Wadsworth, 2004).

Reading 11-6   Active and Passive Euthanasia | James Rachels

Study Questions

As you read the excerpt, please consider the following questions:

1. Why does Rachels believe that letting a person die is sometimes worse than bringing about the person's death, such as through a lethal injection?

2. What is the example of Smith and Jones and their cousin supposed to show?

3. Why is the claim "I didn't do anything" not an adequate moral defense, according to Rachels?

If one simply withholds treatment, it may take the patient longer to die, and so he may suffer more than he would if more direct action were taken and a lethal injection given. This fact provides strong reason for thinking that, once the initial decision not to prolong his agony has been made, active euthanasia is actually preferable to passive euthanasia, rather than the reverse. To say otherwise is to endorse the option that leads to more suffering rather than less, and is contrary to the humanitarian impulse that prompts the decision not to prolong his life in the first place. . . .

One reason why so many people think that there is an important moral difference between active and passive euthanasia is that they think killing someone is morally worse than letting someone die. But is it? Is killing, in itself, worse than letting die? . . .

Let us consider this pair of cases:

In the first, Smith stands to gain a large inheritance if anything should happen to his six-year-old cousin. One evening while the child is taking his bath, Smith sneaks into the bathroom and drowns the child, and then arranges things so that it will look like an accident.

In the second, Jones also stands to gain if anything should happen to his six-year-old cousin. Like Smith, Jones sneaks in planning to drown the child in his bath. However, just as he enters the bathroom Jones sees the child slip and hit his head, and fall face down in the water. Jones is delighted; he stands by, ready to push the child's head back under if it is necessary, but it is not necessary. With only a little thrashing about, the child drowns all by himself, "accidentally," as Jones watches and does nothing.

Now Smith killed the child, whereas Jones "merely" let the child die. That is the only difference between them. Did either man behave better, from a moral point of view? . . .

It may be inferred from Smith's conduct that he is a bad man, although that judgment may be withdrawn or modified if certain further facts are learned about him—for example, that he is mentally deranged. But would not the very same thing be inferred about Jones from his conduct? And would not the same further considerations also be relevant to any modification of this judgment? Moreover, suppose Jones pleaded, in his own defense, "After all, I didn't do anything except stand there and watch the child drown. I didn't kill him; I only let him die." Again, if letting die were in itself less bad than killing, this defense should have at least some weight. But it does not. Such a "defense" can only be regarded as a grotesque perversion of moral reasoning. Morally speaking, it is no defense at all.

James Rachels, "Active and Passive Euthanasia." *The New England Journal of Medicine* 292:2, (January 9, 1975).

Reading 11-7   The Philosophers' Brief | Ronald Dworkin, Thomas Nagel, Robert Nozick, John Rawls, Judith Jarvis Thomson, and T. M. Scanlon

Study Questions

As you read the excerpt, please consider the following questions:

1. Why do these philosophers focus on the importance of "religious or ethical convictions" about the meaning of life?

2. What is the connection that is made here between thinking about abortion and thinking about end-of-life issues?

3. Why does this text emphasize the fact that a decision about suicide need not be considered irrational or foolish?

[The cases under consideration] do not invite or require the Court to make moral, ethical, or religious judgments about how people should approach or confront their death or about when it is ethically appropriate to hasten one's own death or to ask others for help in doing so. On the contrary, they ask the Court to recognize that individuals have a constitutionally protected interest in making those grave judgments for themselves, free from the imposition of any religious or philosophical orthodoxy by court or legislature. States have a con-stitutionally legitimate interest in protecting individuals from irrational, ill-informed, pressured, or unstable deci-sions to hasten their own death. To that end, states may regulate and limit the assistance that doctors may give individuals who express a wish to die. But states may not deny people in the position of the patient-plaintiff's in these cases the opportunity to demonstrate, through whatever reasonable procedures the state might institute—even procedures that err on the side of caution—that their decision to die is indeed informed, stable, and fully free. Denying that opportunity to terminally ill patients who are in agonizing pain or otherwise doomed to an existence they regard as intolerable could only be justified on the basis of a religious or ethical conviction about the value or meaning of life itself. Our Constitu-tion forbids government to impose such convictions on its citizens. . . .

Certain decisions are momentous in their impact on the character of a person's life—decisions about reli-gious faith, political and moral allegiance, marriage, procreation, and death, for example. Such deeply per-sonal decisions pose controversial questions about how and why human life has value. In a free society, individuals must be allowed to make those decisions for themselves, out of their own faith, conscience, and convictions. . . .

Like a woman's decision whether to have an abor-tion, a decision to die involves one's very "destiny" and inevitably will be "shaped to a large extent on [one's] own conception of [one's] spiritual imperatives and [one's] place in society." Just as a blanket prohibition on abortion would involve the improper imposition of one conception of the meaning and value of human exis-tence on all individuals, so too would a blanket prohibi-tion on assisted suicide. . . .

Some individuals, whose decisions for suicide plainly cannot be dismissed as irrational or foolish or prema-ture, must be accorded a reasonable opportunity to show that their decision for death is informed and free. It is not necessary to decide precisely which patients are entitled to that opportunity. If . . . this Court [denies the right assisted suicide], its decision could only be justi-fied by the momentous proposition—a proposition flatly in conflict with the spirit and letter of the Court's past decisions—that an American citizen does not, after all, have the right, even in principle, to live and die in the light of his own religious and ethical beliefs, his own convictions about why his life is valuable and where its value lies.

Ronald Dworkin et al., "Assisted Suicide: The Philosophers' Brief." *New York Review of Books*, March 27, 1997.

** Explanatory Note: A group of prominent philosophers wrote an amicus brief to the U.S. Supreme Court as it considered two cases regarding assisted suicide.

Reading 11-8   U.S. Supreme Court Decision June 24, 2022 | Dobbs v. Jackson

Study Questions

As you read the excerpt, please consider the following questions:

1. How does the Court, in overturning *Roe v. Wade*, return the decision to the states?

2. What is the basic argument made here against the kinds of liberty that were argued for in *Roe* and *Casey*?

3. What does the Court imply about abortion restrictions at the state level?

The Court finds that the right to abortion is not deeply rooted in the Nation's history and tradition. The underlying theory on which Casey rested—that the Fourteenth Amendment's Due Process Clause provides substantive, as well as procedural, protection for "liberty"—has long been controversial. . . .

Abortion presents a profound moral question. The Constitution does not prohibit the citizens of each State from regulating or prohibiting abortion. Roe and Casey arrogated that authority. The Court overrules those decisions and returns that authority to the people and their elected representatives. . . .

The Court considers whether a right to obtain an abortion is part of a broader entrenched right that is supported by other precedents. The Court concludes the right to obtain an abortion cannot be justified as a component of such a right. Attempts to justify abortion through appeals to a broader right to autonomy and to define one's "concept of existence" prove too much [quoting *Casey*]. Those criteria, at a high level of generality, could license fundamental rights to illicit drug use, prostitution, and the like. . . .

Instead of seriously pressing the argument that the abortion right itself has deep roots, supporters of Roe and Casey contend that the abortion right is an integral part of a broader entrenched right. Roe termed this a right to privacy, and Casey described it as the freedom to make "intimate and personal choices" that are "central to personal dignity and autonomy." Casey elaborated: "At the heart of liberty is the right to define one's own concept of existence, of meaning, of the universe, and of the mystery of human life." The Court did not claim that this broadly framed right is absolute, and no such claim would be plausible. While individuals are certainly free to think and to say what they wish about "existence," "meaning," the "universe," and "the mystery of human life," they are not always free to act in accordance with those thoughts. License to act on the basis of such beliefs may correspond to one of the many understandings of "liberty," but it is certainly not "ordered liberty." Ordered liberty sets limits and defines the boundary between competing interests. Roe and Casey each struck a particular balance between the interests of a woman who wants an abortion and the interests of what they termed "potential life." But the people of the various States may evaluate those interests differently. In some States, voters may believe that the abortion right should be even more extensive than the right that Roe and Casey recognized. Voters in other States may wish to impose tight restrictions based on their belief that abortion destroys an "unborn human being." Our Nation's historical understanding of ordered liberty does not prevent the people's elected representatives from deciding how abortion should be regulated.

United States Supreme Court, *Dobbs v. Jackson*, 597 U.S.___ (2022).

Review Exercises

1. Outline the difference between pro-choice and pro-life arguments regarding euthanasia and abortion.

2. Evaluate the importance of consent and privacy in thinking about these issues.

3. Evaluate utilitarian arguments for and against abortion/euthanasia.

4. Describe how Thomson uses the violinist analogy to make an argument about the moral permissibility of abortion. What kinds of cases might this apply to?

5. Evaluate various criteria for personhood and how they apply to abortion and to euthanasia.

6. How important is potentiality for thinking about abortion—and euthanasia?

7. What is the difference between active and passive euthanasia? Is physician-assisted suicide more like active or passive euthanasia? How so?

8. What kinds of arguments can be used for and against active and passive euthanasia?

9. Explain how feminist and social justice concerns arise in thinking about abortion and euthanasia.

10. Do you think that the doctrine of double effect can be used to justify abortion or euthanasia? Explain why or why not in each case.

Discussion Cases

1. Abortion for Sex Selection. Naomi and June meet in the waiting room of a clinic. Each is there for an amniocentesis that will be used to determine the sex of her fetus. June reveals that she wants to know the sex because her husband and his family really want a boy. Because they plan to have only one child, they plan to end this pregnancy if it is a girl and try again. Naomi's reason is different. She is a genetic carrier of a particular kind of muscular dystrophy. Duchenne muscular dystrophy is a sex-linked disease that is inherited through the mother. Only males develop the disease, and each male child has a 50 percent chance of having it. The disease causes muscle weakness and often some mental retardation. It also causes death through respiratory failure, usually in early adulthood. Naomi does not want to risk having such a child. Thus, if the prenatal diagnosis reveals that her fetus is male, she plans to end this pregnancy.

Is Naomi justified in her plan to abort a male fetus? Is June justified? Should there be laws regulating sex-selective abortion?

2. Father's Rights? Omar and Rheanna have been planning to have a child. However, their relationship has been tumultuous, and they have decided to break up. After the breakup, Rheanna discovers she is pregnant. She decides that she does not want to raise a child alone and does not want to raise Omar's child. However, Omar has long wanted a child, and he argues that the developing fetus is partly his own because he has provided half of its genetic makeup. He does not want Rheanna to end the pregnancy. He wants to keep and raise the child.

Do you think that Omar has any moral rights in this case, or should the decision be strictly Rheanna's? Why or why not?

3. Conscientious Nurses. Guadalupe and Anthony are nursing students who are taking an applied ethics course. In an online discussion forum for the class, they are discussing euthanasia and abortion. They disagree about what they might do if asked to participate in practices they morally disagree with. Anthony is staunchly pro-life. He disagrees with both abortion and euthanasia. He writes in one post: "I don't think I would ever take a job at a hospital that provided abortion or assisted-suicide medication. And if I did work there, I would not participate in those kinds of things." Guadalupe responds, "But your job as a nurse is to provide care for patients according to what they consent to. And if the standard of care calls for abortion or some kind of euthanasia, and the patient consents, then it's your duty to provide that care." Anthony responds, "I just couldn't participate. It's wrong." Guadalupe responds, "Then maybe you shouldn't become a nurse."

Who do you agree with here? What if the situation were somewhat reversed and Guadalupe found herself working in a state that banned abortion or euthanasia. Would she be justified in breaking the law in order to provide care for patients who requested it?

4. Respirator Removal. Marcus is an active person. He is a lawyer by profession. When he was forty-four years old, a routine physical revealed that he had a tumor on his right lung. After surgery to remove that lung, he returned to a normal life. However, four years later, a cancerous tumor is found in his other lung. He knows he has only months to live. Then comes the last hospitalization. He is on a respirator. It is extremely uncomfortable for him, and he is frustrated by not being able to talk because of the tubes. After some thought, he decides that he does not want to live out his last few weeks like this and asks to have the respirator removed. Because he is no longer able to breathe on his own, he knows this means he will die shortly after it is removed.

Do Marcus or the doctors who remove the respirator and then watch Marcus die as a result do anything wrong? Why or why not? If Marcus begins to suffer, after the respirator is removed, would the doctor be justified in administering a lethal dose of medication to end his pain?

5. Teen Euthanasia. Thirteen-year-old Samantha is in the last stages of cancer. She says she doesn't want any further treatment because she thinks that it is not going to make her well. Her parents want the doctors to try a new experimental therapy for which there is some hope. If they cannot convince Samantha to undergo this experimental procedure, should the doctors sedate Samantha and go ahead with it anyway, or should they do what she asks and let her die? Do you think that the doctors should be allowed to end her life with a fatal dose of a drug if that is what she wishes, even though her parents object and they are still her legal guardians?

6. Baby John Doe. Sarah and Esteban's baby boy was born with a defect called spina bifida, which involves an opening in the spine. In his case, it is of the more severe kind in which the spinal cord also protrudes through the hole. The opening is moderately high in the spine, and thus they are told that his neurological control below that level will be affected. He will have no bowel and bladder control and will not be able to walk unassisted. The cerebral spinal fluid has already started to back up into the cavity surrounding his brain, and his head is swelling. Doctors advise that they could have a shunt put in place to drain this fluid and prevent pressure on the brain. They could also have the spinal opening repaired. If they do not do so, however, the baby will probably die from an infection. Sarah and Esteban are afraid of raising such a child and worry that he would have an extremely difficult life. In a few cases, however, children with this anomaly who do not have the surgery do not die, and then they are worse off than if the operation were performed. What should this couple do? Why?

Knowledge Check Answer Key

1. **b.** Pro-choice is in favor of euthanasia if people consent.
2. **d.** Judith Jarvis Thomson offers a pro-choice argument.
3. **b.** Voluntary passive euthanasia occurs when a person asks for the removal of life support.
4. **c.** Determining whether a fetus is a person and whether a brain-dead adult is a person are examples of an ontological question.

12 Biotechnology and Bioengineering

Learning Outcomes

After reading this chapter, you should be able to:

12.1 Explain how the difference between a therapy and an enhancement can be used to asses different examples of biotechnology and bioengineering.

12.2 Describe the conflict between bio-conservatism and transhumanism.

12.3 Critically evaluate ethical problems involving performance-enhancing drugs.

12.4 Describe ethical controversies involved in reproductive technologies.

12.5 Evaluate stem cell research, cloning, and genetic engineering in humans.

12.6 Analyze controversies regarding genetically modified organisms.

12.7 Defend a thesis about biotechnology and bioengineering.

Genetic Engineering

In 2018, a Chinese scientist, He Jiankui, surprised the world by announcing that his lab had used a biotechnology known as CRISPR to edit the genes of human embryos. CRISPR stands for "clustered regularly interspaced short palindromic repeats." It is a biochemical tool that can be used to cut out sections of DNA and insert new genetic code. This is known as "gene editing." Biomedical researchers are able to use this technology to delete and insert bits of genetic code

iStock.photo/vchal

in human beings. The scientist, He, intended to provide these human babies with resistance to the HIV virus. Three children were born with edited genes. Bioethicists widely condemned the experiment. Some worried about the advent of a new age of "designer babies." But He explained he was not focused on creating perfect children. In fact, he explained that if we can prevent diseases using genetic engineering, it would be "inhuman" not to do so.[1] In many countries, this kind of use of CRISPR is banned. Eventually, the scientist was jailed. He was released from prison in 2022.

There were several concerns about the use of CRISPR in this case. One worry was the effect of the procedure on the infants themselves. A significant concern is that in targeting one set of genes for editing, there could be mistakes or unintended effects. Some suggested that this genetic intervention may have an impact on the development of the brains of these infants after birth.[2] A further worry is what might happen when the infants grow up and reproduce. Would the changes in their genomes be passed on to other generations? And of course, these infants did not consent to the procedure, which is a concern if we think that autonomy and informed consent are important values.

What Do You think?

1. Is there a good reason to ban the use of gene editing on humans?

2. Is there a moral difference between using gene editing to eliminate genetic diseases and using it to create enhancements and "designer babies"?

3. Does it matter that this experiment and procedure were used on human embryos without their consent?

4. Are you worried about the impact this technology might have on the gene pool and on future generations?

Introduction

12.1 Explain how the difference between a therapy and an enhancement can be used to assess different examples of biotechnology and bioengineering.

Scientists are working on a range of technologies that aim to improve the lives of people with disabilities. For example, they are developing artificial eyes and other devices that allow blind people to see, including so-called bionic eyes, retinal implants, and cameras that bypass the eye and interface directly with the brain's visual cortex.[3] It is also possible to help deaf people respond to sound by using a "cochlear implant," an electronic device that bypasses the ear and connects directly to the auditory nerve.[4] Other surgeries and interventions allow us to radically alter our bodies, including sex reassignment surgery, leg-lengthening surgeries, and so on. In the future, regenerative medicine and genetic interventions may be able to extend our life spans, screen out deadly genetic mutations, or allow us to grow replacement organs. Performance- and mood-enhancing drugs may make us stronger, improve memory and concentration, and help us achieve better emotional health. Other biotechnologies may make it possible to extend our physical capacities—to walk, run, or swim—as the human body has never done before.

While many emerging biotechnologies have obvious therapeutic applications that will benefit people with diseases and disabilities, some worry that these technologies will be abused in ways that are unethical. Others argue that a new form of humanity is looming on the horizon—one that is genetically, chemically, and mechanically enhanced. Some view the "transhuman" or "posthuman" future as a positive development; others worry that we are not wise or virtuous enough to properly handle these new technologies.

Biotechnology can be broadly defined as the manipulation of biological systems and organisms through technological means. Biotechnology includes performance-enhancing drugs, stem cell research, genetic engineering, cloning, and genetic screening. These technologies can be applied in human reproduction to select or even engineer desired offspring. They can also be applied to animals, in scientific breeding practices to increase meat production. And plants grown for food can be genetically modified in ways that improve crop yields. **Bioengineering** applies biological science to design machines and alter biological systems for a range of purposes, including the use of machines to supplement or enhance biological organisms, as in the case of the brain–computer interface discussed previously.

Some biotechnologies produce amazing therapeutic effects. For example, we have found ways to give paralyzed people the ability to feed themselves through the use of brain–computer interface connected to a robotic arm. And regenerative medicine has proven to be useful in regrowing tissues and organs. One inspiring example involves the use of stem cells to repair spinal cord damage.[5] This would be a welcome therapy for an injury that can result in paralysis. A **therapy** is an intervention that helps restore normal function to an organism that is suffering from an impairment due to disease or injury. But other technologies may be viewed as enhancements. An **enhancement** is the result of a technology that provides better than merely normal function. One of the ethical questions to be discussed here is whether anything is wrong with enhancements. While we might accept such uses of technology out of respect for individuals' rights to control their own bodies, some biotech enhancements appear to raise serious ethical questions about what is "natural" and about the value and nature of human life. There will also be concerns about enhancements that may give some people fair, or unfair, advantages over others.

Moral Approaches to Biotechnology

12.2 Describe the conflict between bio-conservatism and transhumanism.

A variety of ethical issues arise in thinking about biotechnology and bioengineering. We can begin to analyze these issues by referring back to some of the basic principles of bioethics, as discussed in Chapter 10: beneficence, autonomy, and nonmaleficence. It seems obvious that our biotechnological innovations ought to be beneficent: they ought to produce good outcomes. This helps us understand what counts as a therapy: therapies are supposed to produce some good. Autonomy also ought to be respected. Again, it would be wrong to kidnap someone and force them to be surgically enhanced. But things may begin to get confusing when thinking about how autonomy applies to reproductive technologies. Does it even make sense to think about "consent" when considering a genetic intervention done on an embryo? Obviously, it would be wrong to steal embryos or coerce women into donating their ova for medical experiments. But does a consideration of autonomy also include the "choices" of future generations?

And what if a person wants to explore a risky enhancement and freely consents to the procedure? There is also a significant tension between valuing our liberty to pursue biotechnologies for their immediate utility, on the one hand, and concerns over the potential negative impacts of such technologies in the long run on the other hand. Some consequentialists argue in favor of the benefits of these technological innovations. Others urge caution, appealing to a **precautionary principle**, which holds that we ought to avoid risks and harms when exploring new technologies. The precautionary principle can be understood in connection with the idea of nonmaleficence—the idea of "doing no harm." One strict version of the precautionary principle holds that we should not use a new procedure until it is proven that there are no risks. But if we are too risk-averse, we may miss out on potential benefits.

There are also tensions between those who defend the liberty of individuals to modify their own biology and those who are critical of misapplications of liberty, including the risk of "playing God" with our bodies and our biology. Those who approach ethics from the standpoint of natural law may think that there is something wrong with "playing God" and tampering with nature. This view, that it is generally wrong to mess with Mother Nature, can be described as **bio-conservatism**. Bio-conservatives generally want to leave biology and human nature alone, claiming both that we are not wise enough to play God and that there is something important about the natural order of things.

This idea—playing God—is of course a metaphor. But it brings to mind some versions of natural law ethics, which claim that there is an order and structure woven into the natural world that ought to be respected. To "play God" in this sense is to turn away from the natural law. Other related metaphors appear in the debate about biotechnology. Leon Kass, an author included in our primary source readings, has warned that those who are seeking enhancements are making a "Faustian bargain," which is another way of saying that they are making a deal with the devil.[6] The story of Faust is of a scientist who sold his soul in exchange for knowledge and power. Another metaphor is used by Michael Sandel, who suggested that the advocates of advanced biotechnology were behaving like Prometheus, the Titan of

Greek mythology who stole fire from the gods and gave it humanity. Prometheus was punished by the gods for providing this basic technology to humankind. Speaking of genetic engineering and enhancement, Sandel warned of a "Promethean aspiration to remake nature, including human nature, to serve our purposes and satisfy our desires."[7] Sandel warns that there is something dangerous about the human desire to have godlike mastery of nature, our bodies, and life itself.

Defenders of biotechnology argue that this concern is overblown and mistaken. Vigorous proponents of biotechnology can be described as espousing a kind of "**transhumanism**." Transhumanists embrace biotechnology and the effort to use technology to transform human life and experience. Transhumanism can be understood as including a critique of the natural law orientation of bio-conservatism. On the one hand, Guy Kahane has argued in response to Sandel, that the worry about playing God assumes that there is a God and a hierarchy that limits our powers and capacities.[8] It makes no sense to worry about overturning the supposed hierarchy of the universe if there is no such hierarchy. Such an idea can be understood as a critique of natural law ethics. Indeed, proponents of advanced biotechnology may argue, as Nick Bostrom does, that nature is not as good as we think it is. Nature gives us disease, disability, and death. Bostrom says, appealing to another metaphor, "If Mother Nature had been a real parent, she would have been in jail for child abuse and murder."[9] From his standpoint, we ought to use ingenuity and reason to improve on nature by curing diseases, creating technologies that provide therapies for disabilities, and so on.

Bostrom's approach is a kind of consequentialism. He supports biotechnologies that produce good consequences. One sort of consequence that is of interest here is the use of technology for the well-being of individual people. This may include both therapies and enhancements. Therapeutic interventions that return injured or sick people to normal function are obviously beneficent. But enhancements can also be justified in this way, as well, as being of benefit. Bostrom also claims on libertarian grounds that people should be allowed to access technologies, so long as autonomy is respected and those technologies are freely consented to.

But there is an added wrinkle in thinking about biotechnology that is connected to utilitarianism. You will recall that utilitarians are focused on producing the greatest happiness for the greatest number of people. But what if in pursuit of maximizing good outcomes in this way, we end up tolerating some harms to people in a kind of "trolley problem" scenario (as discussed in Chapter 5)? Once we start editing genes to eliminate diseases, might we also entertain the idea of forcing people who carry those diseases to edit their genes or avoid reproducing? From a utilitarian standpoint, it might make sense to promote a vigorous regime of genetic improvement. There is a risk here of a pernicious kind of eugenics. **Eugenics** is the science of improving the genetic components of a species. Livestock breeders have worked for centuries to create such genetic changes in animals. But eugenic practices become problematic when attempted with human beings, especially given the history of human eugenics efforts, which include forced sterilizations and abortions and other practices that violated people's liberty in the name of producing good offspring. There is a long history of eugenic projects, going back to Plato's plan for breeding good citizens in the *Republic*. Eugenic laws were enforced in the United States in the early part of the twentieth century, including the forced sterilization of thousands of people deemed "mentally defective." Nazi Germany took eugenic projects to another level of cruelty. The immoral effort to "purify" the Aryan race involved the killing of more than two hundred thousand people—many of them children—who were deemed disabled, degenerate, homosexual, or insane by Nazi doctors and therefore "unworthy of life."[10] Hundreds of thousands more were sterilized against their will. And eventually millions of people who were deemed "unworthy" were slaughtered in the Holocaust.

This is not to say that utilitarians support proactive and coercive eugenic policies. Most typically would not, aware of the dangers and unhappiness produced by such coercive policies. But there is an open question about how utilitarian reasoning might apply in thinking about biotechnology and bioengineering. If autonomy is a primary value, it may limit any grand utilitarian bioengineering project. But if autonomy is minimized, it is possible to imagine a situation in which society might encourage or even require people to participate in schemes to enhance humanity. Susan B. Levin imagines that a coercive utilitarian imperative to use biotechnology could emerge. She argues that transhumanists often argue for the widespread use of enhancements as a matter of public health and welfare, based on utilitarian concerns. She warns, "That state enforcement is a desired or logical outcome of the moral imperative to enhance is evident in the writings of transhumanists themselves."[11] In support of that claim she cites the work of Julian Savulescu and Gary Kahane, who argue in favor of a doctrine of "procreative beneficence," which is the idea that parents ought to use genetic interventions to ensure that their offspring are healthy and able-bodied.[12]

Savulescu and Kahane defend the notion of procreative beneficence by noting that parents already can choose whether and when to have children. If this is true, then parents ought to choose wisely and well, which means that if genetic engineering and screening options are available, they should use these technologies to "create children with the best chance of life." This would be good for the resulting child (and hence a kind of beneficence); it could also be justified on utilitarian grounds as promoting general welfare. But critics will point out that this seems to be a kind of eugenic imperative. This may not rise to the level of a coercive regime that requires parents to optimize their reproductive capacity. And Savulescu and Kahane do emphasize the importance of autonomy in their argument, both the autonomy of parents and the autonomy of the children who are selected for. This last point may seem odd, since if the parents select which children are born, this may seem to deny those children the "right to an open future," as some critics say. But Savulescu and Kahane suggest that a child with diminished capacities may be less autonomous than one who is born with more optimal capacities. As they explain, "it is likely that children with greater talents and health will have more options open to them."[13]

A moment's reflection shows that there are some "able-ist" assumptions built into this idea. Critics from a disability rights perspective may contend that Savulescu and Kahane fail to appreciate that the lives of people with disabilities can be rewarding and autonomous. Those critics may also point out that autonomy is not the only good in life. One line of criticism might come from an approach to morality, familiar from care ethics, that emphasizes that relations of care and dependence can be important and enriching. One author who articulates this idea is Rosemarie Garland-Thomson, a prominent voice in disabilities studies. She explained, "I would argue that disability is perhaps the essential characteristic of being human. The body is dynamic, constantly interactive with history and environment. We evolve into disability. Our bodies need care; we all need assistance to live."[14] Garland-Thomson has also offered a critique of the eugenic implications of emerging biotechnologies, including CRISPR. She calls this a kind of "velvet eugenics."[15] This would not be the kind of eugenics that is enforced by oppressive governments. Rather it would be a soft and cloying kind of eugenics that emerges from a world in which the focus on autonomy and beneficence subtly eliminates persons with disabilities. We have an excerpt from Garland-Thomson in the primary source readings for this chapter.

A related concern is the idea of protecting human dignity. This is a non-consequentialist concern that can be understood in relation with Kantian deontology. You'll recall from our discussion in Chapter 6 that Kant says that rational beings are "ends-in-themselves" who deserve to be respected. In the second formulation of his categorical imperative, Kant says that you should "always treat humanity, whether in your own person or that of another, never simply as a means but always at the same time as an end." If transhumanists are challenging the very idea of what it means to be human, then this may violate the Kantian imperative to respect humanity. A Kantian critique of transhumanism has been articulated by Francis Fukuyama, who claims that Kantian "autonomy" is deeper and more complex than the mere freedom to choose.[16] He points out that the Kantian idea of dignity is connected to the idea that moral principles are transcendent sources of moral authority not subject to the whims of the moment. In Kantian terms, the idea is that our dignity is found in obedience to the moral law and in respecting ourselves as having dignity and worth. From this perspective, it would be wrong to treat your body as a commodity to be altered and improved; and it would be wrong to view your genes as a programing code that can be altered in the way that a computer program could be altered. This idea of dignity can also be grounded in a natural law theory of ethics, which might hold that our bodies and our genetic endowment have a kind of "sacred" value, which ought not be tampered with.

Transhumanists such as Bostrom have responded to this worry about respecting dignity by asserting that they are not interested in disrespecting humanity. Rather, from Bostrom's perspective, transhumanism involves expanding our idea of what counts as human and what is worthy of respect. In this regard, transhumanism aims to expand the range of beings who are thought to have dignity. Bostrom calls this "post-human dignity," pointing to an idea of dignity that extends beyond prior conceptions of humanity. Bostrom explains, "By defending post-human dignity we promote a more inclusive and humane ethics, one that will embrace future technologically modified people as well as humans of the contemporary kind."[17] This last phrase, "humans of the contemporary kind," can be understood in connection with the general idea that human beings have evolved and that they continue to evolve. For the transhumanist, this evolution and continued evolution have involved the conscious choices of human beings to alter our environment and our biology. It is worth noting that by embracing change in this way, transhumanists argue against those who are wedded to a conception of humanity that is old-fashioned or traditional and that does not permit or encourage change. We could imagine that transhumanists would also embrace changed notions of sex and gender as one example of the kinds of changes that could be encouraged. And in this regard, the conversation about gender transition and transgender persons could be part of the conversation about biotechnology and transhumanism. Gender is one of the aspects of our bodies and social identities that could be transformed through the application of technology.

Of course, bio-conservatives are often critical of such things. One concern is that new technologies will diminish human dignity by turning human beings into products that are created and engineered. This kind of worry is especially pertinent in connection with the idea of reproduction. Are children a gift of nature to be enjoyed as they are? Or are they objects to be engineered through the application of biotechnology? We might ask a similar question about the human genome and about our own bodies. To what extent are our genes and our bodies a gift of nature that ought to be accepted and appreciated? And to what extent are our genes and our bodies simply objects that can be manipulated for our own enjoyment and benefit?

One part of the bio-conservative argument, associated with the work of bioethicist Leon Kass, claims that there is a kind of wisdom in our "repugnance" for certain forms of bioengineering, such as cloning. When a new technology makes us cringe and say "yuck," we may be tapping into a deeper insight about human nature. Human reproductive cloning can elicit this kind of response. If an adult man were cloned, would his clone be his brother or his son? On the one hand, the clone is the man's identical twin. On the other hand, the clone would need to be born as an infant and nurtured as a child—and if the man did this with his clone, wouldn't his clone be a kind of son to him? If this leaves you scratching your head and feeling uncomfortable, that's the experience of repugnance that Kass is pointing to. He suggests, in thinking about cloning, that the feeling of repugnance may be "the emotional expression of deep wisdom."[18] Among the examples he gives in support of this idea is the feeling of revulsion we experience at thinking about eating human flesh or engaging in incest.

Of course, others will reject the idea that repugnance should guide moral judgment. The ethical theory known as "emotivism" may suggest that moral judgments are basically expressions of emotion. But critics of emotivism urge us to seek a different and more stable or objective source of morality. One problem with the repugnance argument is that repugnance is often little more than taste and inclination without any deeper moral basis. Indeed, it seems true that what one generation finds disgusting is easily accepted by the next generation, as people get used to new norms and new ideas about what is natural and possible. This is also true across cultures, as relativists will point out. It is easy to imagine how this idea might apply to our thinking about sex and gender. At one point in Western culture, women were seen as inferior, interracial relationships were viewed with disgust, and homosexuality was condemned as "sick." The cultural norms that fueled emotional responses in those cases have changed to some extent. That change was the result of moral argument and ongoing struggles for civil rights and equality. The problem with emotivism and the repugnance argument is that emotional reactions appear to shift in response to changing social conditions and cultural norms. And sometimes people who were repulsed at things they are not familiar with change their minds after they learn more and become more familiar with the thing that initially revolted them. What does all of this tell us about the moral status of emotional reactions? Should repugnance be considered as we make moral judgments?

Let's consider how emotional responses have shifted with regard to a biotechnology such as organ transplantation. At one point, organ transplantation—taking an organ from a dead body and implanting it into a living body—was thought to be a weird and repugnant idea. But this can be a life-saving procedure. And people are generally no longer appalled at the idea. Transhumanists view these cases as examples of the way that progress is made: strange technologies and procedures become familiar as they prove to be useful. And so long as there is consent, benefit, and awareness of the need for precaution, these processes are justifiable—even if they go beyond therapy and create enhancements. Bio-conservatives are less confident about the benefits and much more worried about the creation of strange new and enhanced bodies. But this does not mean that they are opposed to therapies including ordinary surgeries, vaccinations, and so on. Kass himself has admitted that organ donation is a useful life-saving therapy, even though he says that he is "disinclined to be an organ donor."[19] The dividing line between these two approaches is often a matter of degree and connects to the difficult question of how we draw a line that distinguishes therapy from enhancement.

There are other relevant moral questions about biotechnology and bioengineering. The question of utilitarian justifications for widespread and proactive application of biotechnologies connects to the question of distributive justice and concerns for social justice in thinking about biotech. One significant question is who will have access to these technologies. Will they be distributed fairly and equally to those who need them? Or will the free market distribute them in a way that reflects social inequities? Medical procedures are expensive, including artificial reproduction techniques, genetic interventions, drugs, and surgeries. In all likelihood, wealthy people will benefit from biotechnologies, while poor people will not be able to afford them. In some cases, there may be good social reasons to make biotech widely available. The case of the COVID-19 vaccine is an obvious example. In pursuit of general immunity to a contagious disease, it makes sense to provide this biotechnology widely and to all who want it. But for more advanced biotechnologies and enhancements, there will be market forces at work and cost will be an impediment for widespread access. One worry is that this sort of economic divide will exacerbate a social divide that already exists. We know that poor people generally end up with worse health outcomes than wealthy people. If biotechnologies can be used to enhance performance, to increase life-span, and to produce disease-free "optimal" children, it will be likely that wealthy individuals and communities will benefit, while poor people and communities will continue to suffer. Along these lines, Kass has argued that it might be better to invest social resources in alleviating afflictions that are more widespread than to focus on creating boutique medical enhancements for wealthy consumers. He suggests that it would be more useful to focus on preventing malaria and malnutrition than on creating ways to enhance the lives of rich people. Transhumanists may respond by noting that technological innovations often begin with the wealthy and quickly expand to help poor people as well. When computers were first invented, they were very expensive and were viewed as a luxury item. But as production became more widespread and technological prowess increased, the price came down and the technology become more widely available. A similar trajectory may occur with biotechnologies. And in the background of this discussion, it is worth revisiting the question of the right to health care, which we discussed in Chapter 10. If a biotechnology is beneficial, shouldn't it be available to everyone who needs it?

As we've seen here, it is useful to organize ethical judgments about biotechnologies along a continuum from progressive to conservative. Progressives put great hope in the advantages of biotechnology, with some imagining embracing technologies that enhance human life, while imagining a radically altered transformation that could result in a transhuman or posthuman future. Bio-conservatives are not so sanguine about the promise of biotechnological enhancement, even though they would likely admit that therapeutic applications of biotechnology are beneficial. In the middle, there is a moderate approach that weaves a path between the two extremes. Note that in the table summarizing these ideas, we include the perspective associated with care ethics and expressed by Garland-Thomson in the "bio-conservative" side of things. This may not be an exact fit, since feminist care ethics is often critical of conservatism. But feminist care ethics shares common ground with bio-conservativism insofar as it is reluctant to embrace the eugenic implications of the pro-biotechnology, transhumanist theorists.

Table 12-1 provides an outline of moral approaches to biotechnology.

Table 12-1 Outline of Moral Approaches to Biotechnology

	Progressive or Transhumanist	Moderate	Bio-Conservative
Thesis	Embrace and explore the advantages of biotechnologies	Biotechnologies are neither all good nor all bad	Need for careful reflection about biotechnology (and prohibition in some cases)
Corollaries and Implications	Pro-enhancement; natural systems can be improved through human intervention; negative consequences outweighed by benefits/advantages; there are no inherent moral limits to human freedom to innovate through biotechnology; aspiration to transcend current limits	Balancing need for therapy with desire for enhancement; precautionary principle employed to counsel prudence with regard to harms and benefits biotech innovation; respect for autonomy and innovation balanced with recognition of stability of social and natural systems	Anti-enhancement (although not necessarily opposed to therapeutic interventions); strict risk-averse application of precautionary principle; fear of "playing God" and eugenics; need to respect the inherent dignity of natural processes including aging, disability, and death; need to care for those who are disabled
Connections with Moral Theory	Optimistic consequentialism; respect for liberty	Moderate consequentialism balanced with respect for autonomy/dignity	Natural law; concerns for human dignity; care ethics emphasis on caring for those with disabilities
Relevant Authors/Examples	Bostrom; Savulescu and Kahane		Kass; Garland-Thomson

Current Issues

Now that we have considered an overview of moral approaches to biotechnology and bioengineering, let's turn to a concrete examination of particular topics. Each of the topics to be discussed is complex, involving biological processes and evolving technological adaptations. The details are important. But this is an ethics textbook and not a technical manual. So, we will aim for a general level of understanding of each case and then focus our attention on the moral questions and disputes that arise in thinking about these cases.

Mind-Computer Interfaces

Jan Scheuermann suffered from a degenerative brain disease that has left her paralyzed from the neck down. In 2012, however, a revolutionary new technology allowed her to use a robotic arm to feed herself for the first time in years. By implanting special electrodes in Scheuermann's brain, her doctors were able to create a "brain–computer interface" and connect it to the robotic arm. With practice, Scheuermann learned to control the arm using only her thoughts. This technological feat might sound like science fiction, but it is part of a set of rapidly advancing technologies produced by engineers and doctors who are finding ways to cure disease and improve human capacities. Scheuermann's skill at working with the brain–computer interface improved so much that by 2015, she was able to control a flight simulator through this neurosignaling technique.[20] Scientists have been able to expand the use of brain–computer interfaces in amazing ways. Robotic exoskeletons— devices that allow paralyzed people to stand and walk— have been controlled through mind–machine interfaces. In 2014, Juliano Pinto, a paraplegic, controlled a robotic exoskeleton and kicked a soccer ball at the opening of the World Cup in Brazil.[21]

▶ **Knowledge Check**   Answers appear at the end of the chapter.

1. Which of the following is best understood as an enhancement (and not a therapy)?

  a. A surgical operation to implant a bionic eye in someone with "normal" vision.

  b. A surgery that connects a cochlear implant to the auditory nerve of someone who is deaf.

  c. The use of antidepressant drugs to treat people with clinically diagnosed depression.

  d. Reproductive technologies that allow infertile heterosexual couples to have children.

2. Which of the following best explains the precautionary principle?

  a. The precautionary principle is about economic planning. It tells us to plan ahead and save for the future.

  b. The precautionary principle is a principle of justice. It encourages us to focus on punishment for wrongdoing.

  c. The precautionary principle is related to non-maleficence. It aims to avoid causing harm.

  d. The precautionary principle is focused on autonomy. It requires that we never violate people's autonomy.

3. What do transhumanists tend to believe?

  a. That religion ought to guide our thinking about biotechnology.

  b. That it is wrong to use therapies that help people with disabilities.

  c. That technology is a gift from the gods.

  d. That nature can and should be improved.

4. How might a concern for justice influence thinking about biotechnology?

  a. Justice would tell us to avoid harmful technologies.

  b. Justice would encourage us to focus on fairness and equality.

  c. Justice would support the idea of respecting nature and avoiding enhancement.

  d. Justice would require that enhancements be made in pursuit of human excellence.

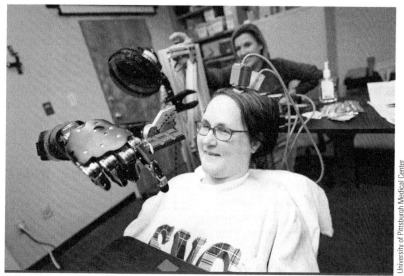

Figure 12-1 Jan Scheuermann feeds herself using a robotic arm attached to a brain–computer interface.

This technology has advanced quickly. One obvious example of this kind of technology is cochlear implants. These small devices can directly stimulate the auditory nerve and allow people who were profoundly deaf to "hear." This is not ordinary hearing. Rather, it is signal transmitted to the brain, which allows deaf people to respond to sound. Cochlear implants are gaining widespread use: as of 2019, over 730,000 of these devices have been deployed worldwide.[22] A similar technology fix may be developed for blindness: retinal implants, which stimulate the optical nerves.

Other technologies have been developed. It is now possible to wire one brain to another to create "brain-to-brain communication." For instance, a volunteer used his thoughts to trigger a muscle movement in the finger of another volunteer and played a video game using the other person's fingers.[23] In another experiment, one rat controlled the actions of another rat by way of implants connecting the two animals' brains.[24] Harvard researchers have connected human brain waves—detected by electrodes placed on the human's skull—to the nerves of a rat so that the human subject is able to make the rat's tail move by thought power.[25] While such experiments raise concerns from the standpoint of animal ethics,

they also suggest other moral issues. What if biotechnology and bioengineering could be used in ways that provide control over other human beings? Some oppose human cloning with that worry in mind; the idea of engineering or creating human beings for the purpose of organ harvesting or other usages is morally repugnant. We might worry about so-called mind-hacking on similar grounds: there is something morally repellent about reading the thoughts of another person or manipulating their thoughts. And yet there are obvious therapeutic benefits to mind–computer interfacing: paralyzed or brain-damaged people could communicate and interact in new ways.

An inspiring example of this kind of therapy was publicized in 2022, when scientists reported that a brain implant had been used by a patient with amyotrophic lateral sclerosis (ALS). As ALS progresses, patients lose control of the muscles and communication can become impossible. Eventually, an ALS patient may only be able to communicate through a machine that can track subtle eye movements. And in the worst cases, the patient ends up "locked in." But a new technological breakthrough involves brain implants that can detect neurological activity and translate it to communication.[26]

The distinction between therapy and enhancement is a useful guide in thinking about the moral questions involved in these kinds of technologies. The examples discussed briefly here are therapeutic. They help people who are paralyzed or locked in or who are deaf or blind. There are worries that these technologies can be abused. But this is true with any technology. Automobiles are useful, but they can also be used to run people down. It is the usage that ought to be the focal point of moral judgment, not the technology itself. And yet there are worries about the possibility of changing human nature, as we explore brain-machine interfaces. We might imagine that in the future, it will be possible to implant microchips in our brains for therapeutic purposes. And if that's possible, why not also use them to enhance our memories or processing capacity? But at what point do we become "cyborgs," beings that are a mix of human and machine? Bio-conservatives might worry about human beings altering their bodies with implants, magnetic devices, prostheses, and computer chips, claiming that this is not natural. But transhumanists might be excited to embrace a cyborg future. Indeed, one recent book by Stefan Lorenz Sorgner suggests that "we have always been cyborgs." One point to be made here is that human beings have always used artifice and technology to enhance our bodies.[27] We use jewelry and tattoos, glasses and smartphones. Why not also implants? It is difficult to draw a line between what is natural and what is not when it comes to the distinction between therapy and enhancement.

Athletic and Cognitive Enhancement

12.3 Critically evaluate ethical problems involving performance-enhancing drugs.

Another issue worth considering here is the use of drugs and other technologies to enhance performance. Steroid use by athletes who want to bulk up muscle and build strength is an enhancement rather than a therapy. There have been a number of controversies regarding the use of performance-enhancing substances by top athletes, such as baseball superstar Barry Bonds, Olympic sprinter Marion Jones, and tennis star Maria Sharapova. In 2013, cyclist Lance Armstrong admitted that he had used performance enhancements, including blood doping (a procedure that artificially increases the number of red blood cells in the body), in his seven triumphs in the Tour de France. Entire teams and nations have been implicated in these kinds of doping and cheating scandals. In 2019, Russia was banned from the Olympics and other international competition because of the systematic use of performance-enhancing drugs.

Most athletic organizations view performance enhancements as immoral, undermining fair play and allowing some athletes with sufficient money and connections to buy their victories. There are also questions about consent, autonomy, and coercion. Do athletes—especially young superstars and other youth—really understand the drugs they are taking or being asked to take? When Russian figure skater Kamila Valieva tested positive for banned substances during the 2022 Winter Olympics, significant questions were raised about this issue. Valieva was 15 years old. She was coached and trained by an entourage of adults. One concern of the International

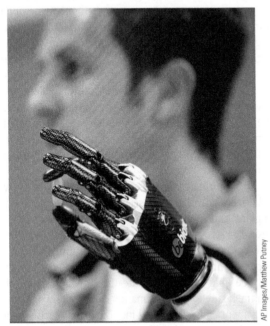

Figure 12-2 Biotechnology creates amazing new opportunities and unprecedented ethical challenges.

AP Images/Matthew Putney

Olympic Committee as it deliberated this case was the degree to which a minor child was responsible for taking a performance-enhancing drug. In response, the International Skating Union announced that it was raising the age at which minors could compete at the highest levels from 15 to 17 years of age.[28]

Another issue involves the question of a level playing field when it comes to biotechnologies and sports. Consider the case of disabled athletes who run on artificial legs—carbon-fiber blades. Should those athletes be allowed to compete against non-impaired athletes? One case involved Oscar Pistorius, who became famous as a "blade runner" and who was later implicated in the shooting death of his girlfriend. Pistorius wanted to compete in the Olympic games—not the Paralympics but the main event. After some controversy, the International Olympic Committee permitted Pistorius to run the 400-meter race in the 2012 London Olympics. Critics complained that Pistorius's prosthetic legs gave him an unfair advantage. *Scientific American* examined the issue and concluded that Pistorius used less energy due to the elastic action of the blades.[29] His lower "legs" are lighter than those of other runners, and they do not tire. On the other hand, Pistorius must compensate for the light springiness of

his blades by bearing down on his prostheses in a way that no other runner must do. In 2016, the issue of blade-wearing athletes was focused on Markus Rehm, who is called "the blade jumper." One of Rehm's legs was amputated, and he competes in the long jump by leaping off a blade. Rehm's jumps have reached 8.62 meters, a distance that would have won a gold medal in the Olympics. He wanted to compete in the Rio Olympics (2016) and the Tokyo Olympics (2020) but was prevented from doing so in each case because the authorities at the international Court of Arbitration for Sport were not convinced that his blade did not provide an unfair advantage.[30] The question of whether Pistorius or Rehm obtains an *unfair* advantage is not easy to answer. The distinction between therapy and enhancement is vague. Are these blades a therapeutic treatment, or do they enhance abilities in unfair ways?

There is no denying that therapeutic technologies can be used or abused in ways that enhance performance. One controversial development is in the field of so-called cognitive enhancements or smart drugs. Drugs such as Ritalin and Adderall, which are prescribed for diseases such as ADHD, can be used by healthy people in ways that may improve performance at school and at work. It is illegal to use these drugs to enhance performance in

Figure 12-3 Markus Rehm is a champion long jumper.

Naomi Baker/Getty Images

this way, and critics warn that such nontherapeutic use is addictive and dangerous. At least one suicide has been connected with abuse of Adderall.[31] But defenders argue that these drugs can provide an advantage in highly competitive fields, such as academia and business. Others argue that smart drugs are less like steroids than they are like caffeine or nicotine. In any case, there is no clear proof that such drugs actually work to consistently improve cognitive performance. "As useful as they may be during the occasional deadline crunch, no study has linked Ritalin or Adderall use in people without ADHD to sustained increases in things like grades or performance reviews."[32]

Nevertheless, other non-pharmaceutical technologies have been developed that purport to stimulate cognitive ability. One such technology is *transcranial direct-current stimulation*—the application of electric current to the brain. This technology has therapeutic applications, for example, treating depression or helping cognitive recovery after a stroke. But electric stimulation of the brain may also be used to enhance the cognitive abilities of healthy individuals. Some studies suggest that transcranial stimulation can aid memory and learning, producing, for example, a greater capacity to learn a new language or mathematical skill.[33] But of course there are dangers, especially as "do-it-yourself" brain hackers apply electrical currents to their own scalps. Scientists involved in this research published an open letter warning about these risks including unknown long-term effects of the procedure. They claimed that they had an ethical obligation to warn do-it-yourself brain hackers about the dangers.[34] If those dangers could be avoided, it is worth considering whether it would be ethical to use such a technology to enhance your ability to learn new information.

Some may defend cognitive and athletic enhancements by focusing on liberty. Libertarian defenders of biotechnology argue that individuals have a right to do whatever they want to their own bodies, including a right to enhance their performance, and a right to find ways to profit and benefit from technology so long as they do not hurt other people. Therapeutic technologies can be defended in terms of their immediate positive impact on impaired and disabled people. Those who want to use these technologies beyond mere therapy

argue that the benefits are obvious and that individuals should be free to take the risks that might be associated with the use of performance-enhancing drugs. Arguments along these lines might parallel ethical considerations regarding the use of other drugs, such as marijuana or nicotine. Defenders argue that so long as no one else is harmed, individuals should be allowed to choose to use these substances because of a basic right to do what one wants with one's own body.

On the other hand, critics argue that the benefits are not obvious. Steroid use by athletes has been proved to produce long-term negative health effects. Athletes may need to be protected from competitive or organizational pressures to alter their bodies in ways that are not healthy. Indeed, the international agreements that prohibit the use of performance enhancements in sport are partly intended to benefit the athletes themselves. If steroid use were allowed, for example, there is a worry that there would be an "arms race" among athletes, which might increase performance but would result in serious health problems. This might also be a special concern in cases involving minors who may be seduced or coerced into the use of performance enhancements. Critics of performance enhancements will also argue that these drugs and technologies create unfairness, as those who are willing to use these drugs (or those who can afford them) will have an unfair advantage over those who restrict themselves to developing their own natural talents and abilities. There is a worry, for example, that affluent students will benefit from smart drugs, giving them an unfair advantage over students without financial resources. Furthermore, critics argue that we may not yet understand the potential long-term impacts of these biotechnologies. The use of performance enhancements may create future impacts that we might come to regret.

Reproductive Technologies

12.4 Describe ethical controversies involved in reproductive technologies.

Among the technologies that we ought to think carefully about are reproductive technologies. Most prominent and familiar is the idea of in vitro fertilization (IVF).

The term "in vitro" means in glass; in vitro fertilization refers to the process by which a woman's egg (the ovum) is fertilized by introducing sperm in a "glass" container—a Petri dish or test tube. This is why such a process is sometimes described as making "test tube" babies. This process was first used on humans in 1978, and at the time was experimental and controversial. But IVF procedures have subsequently proved to be a useful therapy. Among those who can benefit from the procedure are same-sex couples and any individual or couple who cannot conceive through intercourse, or "naturally" as it is sometimes called.

Notice that the word "naturally" here can be understood to involve normative content. People who argue from the vantage point of natural law may argue against the moral permissibility of IVF. Often this kind of argument is connected to a set of related moral claims about sex, reproduction, and even abortion. Not only is the process of IVF "unnatural," but it also typically involves the creation of extra human embryos. The process often involves harvesting more than one ovum from the ovaries of the woman. After fertilization in vitro, there may be more than one attempt to implant an embryo into the woman's uterus. From a perspective that thinks that human life begins at conception, these "surplus embryos" present a moral problem. Can they simply be disposed of? Or are they potential persons? Many couples who have used IVF keep their "spare embryos" frozen in storage, in case they need them in the future. A report from 2016 stated that there were over one million embryos in frozen storage in the United States.[35] That kind of problem may be used to argue, from a natural law standpoint, that this shows us why we should not be engaging in this kind of "unnatural" reproductive activity.

On the other hand, there are obvious therapeutic benefits of IVF for those who cannot conceive naturally. And so long as the interested parties consent and they are happy with the outcome, then this kind of procedure can be supported as both beneficent and respectful of autonomy. But how far should we push the envelope when it comes to human reproduction? We'll talk further in a moment about human cloning, which remains a mostly taboo topic. And there are other controversial reproductive procedures made possible by advances in biotechnology. One example is the issue of surrogacy. Surrogate mothers can gestate a human fetus and give birth to a child. Typically, this involves IVF, which produces embryos that are then implanted into the surrogate's uterus. This can be viewed as a therapy that is useful when a woman is unable to carry and birth a child. And again, those who emphasize beneficence and autonomy argue that so long as all parties consent and are happy with the outcome, then this is a useful and ethically permissible therapy. But others may object that this introduces confusion into the idea of who is actually the mother of a child. Is motherhood defined in terms of the egg donor, the person who births the child, or something else? To make this even more complicated, there have been cases in which there are disagreements among these parties. Consider the case of Stephanie Levesque.[36] Levesque had acted as a surrogate more than once. But in one case, the fetus she was carrying was detected as having a birth defect. The biological parents wanted her to have an abortion and end the pregnancy. She refused and carried the baby to term. This kind of case opens up some complicated ethical (and legal) questions. Related questions arise with regard to the potential exploitation of poor women who offer themselves as surrogates. At one point, women in Europe and the developed world would hire women in India to act as surrogates because they were willing to carry and deliver a baby for a lower price. But India has recently tightened the rules regarding surrogacy in an effort to protect Indian women from exploitation.[37]

At the same time, medical science has been able to extend women's fertility, which makes it possible for older women to conceive and carry babies. This has allowed some interesting and creative uses of IVF. In 2019, it was widely reported that a grandmother gave birth to her own granddaughter.[38] The grandmother was Cecile Eledge. Her son, Matthew Eledge, and his husband, Elliot Dougherty wanted to have a child. Matthew donated sperm and Elliot's sister donated eggs. The embryo produced was implanted into Matthew's mother's uterus. At the time, Cecile was 59 years old. From a libertarian and utilitarian perspective, this example can easily be justified. All parties consented and they were all happy when a healthy baby was born. But from a more traditional, natural law standpoint there may be worries. A bio-conservative might argue that this kind of example is mixing the natural process of reproduction up too much. Other examples of new and unprecedented kinds of reproduction are occurring. Scientists are now able to create a human embryo from three different "parents," by combining mitochondrial DNA from one ovum with regular DNA from another ovum along with sperm.[39] These technologies have potential therapeutic benefits. The three-parent process would provide a remedy for diseases connected to mitochondrial DNA. This technology may produce good consequences, which utilitarians would applaud; or they may be decried as a violation of ethical ideas associated with the natural law tradition, which are damaging to human dignity. In a three-parent combination or in other situations involving surrogates or IVF, would it make sense to use terms such as "mother" or "father"? Do these terms designate "natural" biological relationships? Or are they culturally relative terms?

Regenerative Medicine and Stem Cell Technology

12.5 Evaluate stem cell research, cloning, and genetic engineering in humans.

An important current issue in bioethics is stem cell technology. Stem cells are found in bone marrow and in other parts of the body. These cells are of interest for biomedical research because they have not yet developed into specific skin, muscle, or other types of body cells and tissues.

At one point, this technology was especially controversial because of its connection to debates about abortion. Stem cell research was once focused on embryonic stem cells, which are stem cells taken from fertilized eggs (which come from IVF procedures). Embryonic stem cells are useful because they are "pluripotent," which means that they are not yet specialized and so have the potential to develop into different kinds of tissues: nerve, muscle, bone, and so on. These cells could be used to regenerate damaged tissues or even to grow replacement tissues, organs, and body parts. But if a human embryo is used in this way, opponents of abortion may raise an

objection. This kind of objection led to severe restrictions on the use of human embryonic stem cells in the United States. In 2001, President George W. Bush introduced a ban on federally funded research using stem cells from new embryos, stating that, "[l]ike a snowflake, each of these embryos is unique, with the unique genetic potential of an individual human being."[40] In 2009, President Barack Obama expanded the number of stem cell lines available for use and allowed federal grant money to be used for research on these lines. These stem cell lines are to be derived from excess embryos created in fertility clinics and donated for research purposes with the consent of the donor. (If not used in this way, these excess embryos would be thrown away.) But the controversy continues.

One response to that contentious issue is to focus on other kinds of stem cells. Adult stem cells exist in bone marrow and purportedly in other parts of the body such as the brain, skin, fat, and muscle. The therapeutic use of these cells seems to work in some situations. Adult stem cells have been used to grow different types of cells, including heart cells, which could be useful for treating heart disease.[41] However, adult stem cells may be limited in their ability to develop into tissues. They may only be *multipotent* rather than pluripotent.

In 2006, a Japanese team led by Shinya Yamanaka figured out how to create stem cells without using embryos. In 2012, the Nobel Prize for Medicine was given to Yamanaka and John Gurdon for demonstrating how mature cells could be "reprogrammed" into an immature state capable of growing into various kinds of tissue—a capacity that resembles the pluripotency of embryonic stem cells.[42] Scientists are now able to transform ordinary somatic cells into stem cells (these are called "induced pluripotent stem cells" as opposed to embryonic stem cells).[43] These induced pluripotent stem cells have allowed this research and the therapies emerging from it to proceed without worrying about the connection with abortion. This is not to say that the use of embryonic stem cells has come to an end. There may still be a place for the use of embryonic stem cells—and this use will remain problematic for those who are concerned about abortion. But as the science of using induced pluripotent stem cells advances, many of those controversies may be avoided.

Stem cell research is part of the field of *regenerative medicine*. One long-term goal of such research is to produce new cells, tissues, and organs that can be used to treat disease or injury. Certain stem cell therapies have been around for some time. One example is transplanting bone marrow stem cells to treat certain forms of leukemia. Another more recent example is the extraction from cadavers of certain parts of the human pancreas for an experimental treatment of diabetes.[44]

But new therapies are emerging. In 2012, scientists were able to find a way to grow a replacement windpipe for a patient with a tracheal tumor. They induced stem cells from the patient's own bone marrow to grow on an artificial windpipe scaffolding, which ensured that the plastic scaffolding would not be rejected by the body's immune response. The stem cells went on to develop into the kind of tissue that is found in normal windpipes. The patient recovered with the plastic scaffolding in place, the stem cells developing into the appropriate form of tissue.[45] A similar procedure has been employed to grow a replacement windpipe for a 2-year-old girl born without a windpipe—the youngest person ever to undergo the procedure and the first in the United States.[46] Unfortunately, the child died of complications in July 2013.[47] More recently, scientists have been able to grow "organoids" from stem cells—tissues for rudimentary organs such as intestines and kidneys.[48] And scientists are working on a process involving stem cells that would grow new livers for people with end-stage liver disease.[49] One exciting development in this field is the use of stem cell therapy to treat spinal cord injuries.[50] Another therapy could use stem cells to help stroke victims recover.[51]

As mentioned, stem cell technologies were once controversial because they were linked to the question of abortion. This continues to be a concern for some people and in cases in which embryonic stem cells are still used. But there are other ethical concerns. One involves safety. Stem cells are powerful. And while they may be used to grow organs or replacement tissues, this growth could also cause tumors or other unintended side effects. At the same time, people are excited about the prospect of new therapies. But the precautionary principle might cause us to be patient and wary of the promise of miracle cures. The medical world and regulatory agencies are in the process of weighing harms and benefits, and the U.S. Food and Drug Administration advises a slow and cautious approach.[52]

Another concern is what the possibility of regenerative medicine might mean for our conception of ourselves. Leon Kass warned against the idea that we might engineer "ageless bodies." He explained that although it is understandable that we would cheer on the scientists who are working in the field of regenerative medicine, we might lose something important if we came to see our bodies as having replaceable (or re-growable) parts. Kass worries that the technology of regenerative medicine might change our conception of life, aging, disability, and death. He asks in the essay we've included in the primary source readings for this chapter, what if everyone "lived life to the hilt," assuming that our parts were replaceable.[53] He suggests that it might be better to admit that there is a "shape to life" and the life-course. Bodies decay with age and eventually die. If we viewed our bodies as potentially ageless, that might have a profound impact on our understanding of human life.

In response, it is worth returning to the conceptual distinction between a therapy and an enhancement. It would obviously be therapeutic to use stem cell technologies to treat a spinal cord injury in a younger person or a stroke in a person of middle age. The purpose would be to help that person regain normal function. But would it also be therapeutic to use these techniques on older people? Or would that count as an enhancement? The difficulty here is drawing a line between therapy and enhancement in such a case that is not ageist (as we discussed in Chapter 10 in connection with the problem of rationing health care according to age). In response to this kind of problem, a more progressive view of regenerative medicine might embrace these technologies, so long as they were beneficial and consented to. And it is possible that an advocate of transhumanism might suggest that it would be wonderful if we could enhance our lives by extending our life spans and bring greater vigor to old age by using regenerative medicine. One significant question here is whether aging is a "disease" that ought to be treated therapeutically or whether it is something natural.

Another significant concern of stem cell research is the possible creation of *chimeras*, or new creatures that cross species borders. The National Academy of Sciences guidelines prohibit research in which human embryonic stem cells "are introduced into nonhuman primate blastocysts or in which any embryonic stem cells are introduced into human blastocysts." Furthermore, the guidelines maintain, "no animal into which human embryonic stem cells have been introduced such that they could contribute to the germ line should be allowed to breed."[54]

The possibility of creating and breeding partially human or cross-species genetic mutants raises a number of serious ethical worries about how such creatures might be treated, about just *how* human such beings would need to be to deserve human rights and personhood, and, more generally, what it means for scientists to "play God" and create unprecedented new life forms. Such moral questions are not merely speculative or limited to the realm of science fiction. Some medical therapies already do include tissues and genes taken from animals. For example, pig heart valves that contain some human cells have been used to treat human patients with cardiac diseases. While recommending that these therapies and research programs be allowed, the NAS also recommended that: (1) chimeric animals not be allowed to mate because if human cells invaded the sperm and eggs of an animal host, it could lead to the remote possibility of a being with human DNA being conceived in a nonhuman host; (2) human stem cells not be allowed to become part or all of an animal's brain and not be injected into other primates because this could have the possible result of a human mind trapped in a nonhuman body; (3) embryos used in stem cell research should not be allowed to develop for more than fourteen days; and (4) women who donate eggs not be paid in order to avoid financial inducement.[55]

Cloning

A separate but related issue is cloning. In 2014, scientists successfully created human embryo clones from adult human cells.[56] The purpose of this research is ultimately aimed at creating embryonic stem cells from these clones that could be used in regenerative medicine. The idea is basically that through a process described as "**therapeutic cloning**," we might use our own cells to grow replacement body parts. This process would help to avoid "organ rejection," which can happen when a transplanted organ is not a genetic match. Notice that this conception of cloning is different from what is called "**reproductive cloning**." There are significant questions about the morality of producing human babies through cloning technology. But the ethical questions are complicated, even at the stage of embryonic clones. Is a cloned human embryo a person? How does our thinking about cloned embryos connect with our thinking about other embryos created by natural reproductive techniques?

A clone is a genetically identical copy, produced asexually from a single living being. Since the birth of Dolly the sheep at the Roslin Institute near Edinburgh, Scotland, in March 1996, people have wondered whether it also would be possible to produce humans by cloning. Dolly was a clone or generic copy of a 6-year-old ewe. She was created by inserting the nucleus of a cell from the udder of this ewe into a sheep egg from which the nucleus had been removed. After being stimulated to grow, the egg was implanted into the uterus of another sheep, from which Dolly was born. Dolly was produced from a somatic cell of an adult sheep with already-determined characteristics. Because the cells of an adult are already differentiated—that is, they have taken on specialized roles—scientists had previously assumed that cloning from such cells would not be possible. After Dolly, it was clear that it was possible to produce an identical, although younger, twin of an already existing mammal. Cloning can involve *somatic cell nuclear transfer* (SCNT), which transfers the nucleus of a somatic or bodily cell into an egg whose own nucleus has been removed. Cloning can also be done through *fission*, or cutting, of an early embryo. Through this method it may be possible to make identical twins or triplets from one embryo. A new technique has been described as *parthenogenesis* (a word of Greek origin which means "virgin birth"). This technique used CRISPR technology on unfertilized mouse ova, which were then induced into developing into mouse pups without the use of sperm.[57]

In recent decades, many higher mammals have been produced through cloning, including cows, sheep, goats, mice, pigs, rabbits, and a cat named "CC" for "carbon copy" or "copy cat." CC was produced in a project funded by an Arizona millionaire, John Sperling. The company that he and his team of scientists established, Genetic Savings and Clone, was based in Sausalito, California, and Texas A&M University at College Station, Texas.[58] In 2004, it charged $50,000 for a cloned cat and $295 to $1,395 to store genetic material from a cat. Two kittens, Tabouli and Baba Ganoush, who were cloned from the same female Bengal tiger cat, were displayed at the annual cat show at Madison Square Garden in October 2004. According to the owners, the kittens have personality similarities as well as differences.[59] Genetic Savings and Clone shut down in 2006.[60] However, Sperling established a new company, BioArts, in 2007. He cloned a dead pet dog, producing three puppies born in February 2008. Sperling said that "cloning techniques had become more efficient over the years" such that "1 percent to 4 percent of embryo transfers now result in a puppy."[61] Cloned animals have themselves produced subsequent offspring that were not cloned. Dolly had six seemingly normal lambs. Unfortunately, animal cloning has not always been efficient or safe. In the case of Dolly, for example, 277 eggs were used but only one lamb was produced. Moreover, cloned animals also have exhibited various abnormalities. In February 2003, Dolly was euthanized because she had developed an infectious and terminal lung disease.

Some cloning proponents argue that cloning animals might help farmers to more efficiently produce livestock herds. Others argue that cloning could provide a way to save endangered species. Critics argue against animal cloning by appealing to beliefs about animal welfare and animal rights (see Chapter 20). These critics argue that animal clones have high rates of abnormalities and that the risk of animal suffering and illness outweighs potential benefits.[62]

Given the controversy surrounding animal cloning, it is not surprising that human cloning is subject to even more scrutiny. However, proponents of human cloning point to potential benefits for both therapeutic and reproductive goals. As we've indicated, therapeutic cloning is cloning for medical purposes. One therapeutic use of cloning might be in conjunction with stem cell therapy, to help avoid the immunological rejection by a patient's body of "foreign" tissues or organs grown from stem cells. In this type of cloning, the nucleus of a somatic or bodily cell from the patient, such as a skin cell, would be inserted into an unfertilized egg that had its own nucleus removed. The egg would then be stimulated to develop into an embryo. The stem cells in this blastocyst would be genetically identical with the patient, and tissue grown from them might not then be rejected by the patient's immune system as foreign. The ethical issues raised by this type of cloning mirror those of embryonic stem cell research, especially the moral question of the status of the human embryo.

As opposed to therapeutic cloning, reproductive cloning aims to produce a new human being who would be the genetic twin of the person whose cell was used in the process. Reproductive cloning is one of several reproductive technologies developed in recent decades. Among these are artificial insemination, in vitro fertilization, donated and frozen embryos and eggs, and the use of surrogates. Although these other methods of reproduction have been accepted, there is almost universal objection to reproductive cloning, even among those jurisdictions that allow and support stem cell research or therapeutic cloning. Despite legal obstacles, some scientists continue to push the envelope with regard to cloning, as in the case of mouse parthenogenesis. Meanwhile, one of the leading scientists in the field, John Gurdon, a cowinner of the Nobel Prize for medicine, has predicted that we will be able to safely clone human beings within fifty years.[63] Gurdon suggests that one reason to develop such techniques would be so that parents of children who die could replace their lost child with a copy. Gurdon further suggests that just as the public has gotten used to in vitro fertilization, the public will eventually come to accept the practice of reproductive cloning. People are already able to clone beloved pets. It is worth wondering whether a parent would also want to "replace" a beloved child.

Others worry that such concepts of "replacing" individuals through cloning could lead to a devaluation of human life and a mechanistic "mass production" of babies. They point to the growing acceptance of paying surrogates to bear children and argue that we are already commercializing reproduction, allowing (often wealthy and Western) couples to "rent" the wombs of women (often poor and in the developing world). When combined with cloning, such practices might seem to spring from the dystopia of Aldous Huxley's novel *Brave New World*, in which the production of children was outsourced and managed for sinister eugenic purposes. Huxley's novel is often invoked as a cautionary tale about the totalitarian dangers of cloning and technologized reproduction.

In evaluating human reproductive cloning, various moral theories approach the topic in different ways. A theory that emphasizes respect for human dignity might argue that a cloned child may have less than full human value. Some speak of the "right to an open future" in this regard and worry that a cloned human may have a strange understanding of their own existence if they understood that they were produced to "replace" a former person. And authors like Kass have suggested that a sense of repugnance with regard to cloning provides a clue to its immorality. Utilitarians would wonder whether the process is safe and if it results in happiness. The fact of defects and deformities that have occurred in cloned animals is a concern. But if the technology were perfected, then perhaps a utilitarian might approve of the process.

One classic objection to human cloning is that it amounts to "playing God." The idea is that only God can and should create a human life. Those who hold this view might use religious reasons and sources to support it, but although this looks like a religious position, it is not necessarily so. For example, it might simply suggest that the coming to be of a new person is a *creation*, rather than a making or production. According to this view, the creation of a human is the bringing into being of an individual, a mysterious thing and something that we should regard with awe. When we take on the role of *producing* a human being, as in cloning, we become makers or manipulators of a product that we control and over which we have some kind of power. Another version of this objection stresses the significance of nature and the natural. In producing a human being through cloning, we go against human nature.

For example, in humans, as in all higher animals, reproduction is sexual. Cloning, by contrast, is asexual reproduction, and thus may be seen to go beyond the "natural" boundaries of human biology. Kass is one of the strongest proponents of the view that in cloning someone, we would wrongly seek to escape the bounds and dictates of our sexual nature. According to another related criticism, attempting to clone a human being demonstrates *hubris*, an arrogant assumption that we are wise enough to know and handle its potential consequences. Tampering with a process as fundamental as human reproduction should only be undertaken with the utmost caution, this argument claims. Above all, we should avoid doing what unknowingly may turn out to be seriously harmful for the individuals produced as well as for future generations.

Those who defend human cloning respond to this sort of objection by asking how cloning is any different from other ways we interfere with or change nature in accepted medical practices such as in vitro fertilization, for example. Others argue from a religious perspective that God gave us brains to use, and that we honor God in using them, especially for the benefit of humans and society. Cloning advocates also point out that in using technology to assist reproduction, we do not necessarily lose our awe at the arrival of a new being, albeit one who comes into being with our help.

A second objection to the very idea of cloning a human being is that the person cloned would not be a *unique individual*. They would be the genetic copy of the person from whom the somatic cell was transferred, the equivalent of an identical twin of this person, although years younger. Moreover, because our dignity and worth are attached to our uniqueness as individuals, this objection suggests that cloned individuals would lose the unique value we believe persons have. We might find that the difficulties that clones have in maintaining their individuality would be a more confusing and troubling version of the difficulties that identical twins sometimes face. For example, often identical twins are expected to act alike. The implication is that they do not have the freedom or ability to develop their own individual personalities. A related objection is that a cloned human being would not have a soul, or that they would be a hollow shell of a person. The idea is that if we take on the role of producing a human being through cloning, we prevent God or nature from giving it the spiritual component that makes it more than a material body.

One response to this objection points out how different the cloned individual would be from the original individual. Identical twins are more like each other than a clone would be to the one cloned. This is because twins develop together in the same womb in addition to sharing the same genetic code. Clones would develop in different uteruses and would have different mitochondria—the genes in the cytoplasm surrounding the renucleated cell that play a role in development. They would also likely grow up in very different circumstances and environments. Developmental studies of plants and animals give dramatic evidence of how great a difference the environment makes. The genotype (the genetic code) does not fully determine the phenotype (the genes' actual physical manifestations). CC, the cloned cat mentioned previously, does not quite look like its genetic donor, Rainbow. They have different coat patterns because genes are not the only things that control coat color. They exhibit other differences. "Rainbow is reserved. CC is curious and playful. Rainbow is chunky. CC is sleek."[64] Although genes do matter, and thus there would be similarities between a human clone and the person who was cloned, they would not be identical. On the matter of soul, cloning defenders ask why could God not give each person, identical twin or clone, an individual soul; any living human being, cloned or not, would be a distinct being and so could have a human psyche or soul, they suggest.

Another objection to human cloning is that while any person born today has a *right to an open future*, a cloned human being would not. They would be expected to be like the originating person and thus would not be free to develop as they chose. The genetic donor (or their life story) would be there as the model of what they would be expected to become. Even if people tried not to have such expectations for the one cloned, they would be hard-pressed not to do so. Critics of this argument point out that while there might indeed be certain expectations for a clone, this undue influence is a possibility in the case of all parents and children, and thus a possibility that is not limited to clones. Parents select their children's schools and other formative experiences and promote certain activities, perspectives, and tastes. Thus, any child, cloned or sexually reproduced, would seem to run the risk of being unduly influenced by those who raise them or contribute to their genetic makeup.

Related to the previous objection to cloning is one that holds that cloned children or adults would tend to be *exploited*. If one looks at many of the potential motivations for cloning a person, the objection goes, they indicate that cloning would often be undertaken for the sake of others, rather than for the sake of the new cloned person. For example, the cloned child could be viewed as a potential organ or blood donor—a so-called "savior sibling"—or to "replace" a child who has died. A more far-fetched scenario might include making clones who were specifically produced for doing menial work or fighting wars. We might want to clone certain valued individuals, such as stars of the screen or athletics. In all of these cases, the clones would neither be valued for their own selves nor respected as unique persons. They would be valued for what they can bring to others. Kant is cited as the source of the moral principle that persons ought not simply be used but ought to be treated as ends in themselves, and such practices would seem to be condemned by Kantian ethics.

Critics of these objections could agree with Kant but still disagree that a cloned human being would be more likely than anyone else to be used by others rather than valued as an individual. Just because a child was conceived to provide bone marrow for a sick sibling would not prevent them from also being loved for their own sake. Furthermore, the idea that we would create and confine a group of human beings while training them to be workers or soldiers must presuppose that we abandon a host of legal protections against such treatment of children or other individuals. Equally far-fetched, these critics say, is the notion of a eugenic "brave new world" in which children are produced only through cloning.

Some people believe that if human cloning were widely practiced, it would only add to the *confusion within families* that is already generated by the use of other reproductive technologies. When donated eggs and surrogates are used, the genetic parents are different from the gestational parents and the rearing parents, and conflicts have arisen regarding who the "real" parents are. Cloning, objectors contend, would create even more of a problem, adding to this confusion the blurring of lines between generations. The birth mother's child could be her twin or a twin of the father or someone else. What would happen to the traditional relationships with the members of the other side of the family, grandparents, aunts, and uncles? And what would be the relationship of a husband to a child who is the twin of his wife or of a wife to a child who is the twin of her husband?

Critics of these arguments respond that although there is a traditional type of family that, in fact, varies from culture to culture, today there are also many different kinds of nontraditional families. Among these are single-parent families, adopted families, blended families, and same-sex-parent families. It is not the type of family that makes for a good, loving household, they argue, but the amount of love and care that exists in one.

A final objection to human cloning returns us to Kass's claim about the "wisdom of repugnance." Sometimes we have a *gut reaction* to something we regard as abhorrent, and we are offended by the very thought of it. We cannot always give reasons for this reaction, yet we instinctively feel that what we abhor is wrong. Many people react to human cloning in this way. The idea of someone making a copy of themselves or many copies of a celebrity is simply bizarre, revolting, and repugnant, and these emotional reactions tell us there is something quite wrong with it, even if we cannot explain.

Any adequate response to this argument would entail an analysis of how ethical reasoning works when it works well. Emotional reactions or moral intuitions may indeed play a role in moral reasoning. However, most philosophers would agree that adequate moral reasoning should not rely on intuition or emotion alone. Reflections about why one might rightly have such gut reactions are in order. People have been known to have negative gut reactions to things that, in fact, are no longer regarded as wrong—interracial marriage, for example. It is incumbent on those who assert that something is wrong, most

philosophers believe, that they provide rational arguments and well-supported reasons to justify these beliefs and emotional reactions.

Genetic Engineering, Genetic Screening, and Gene Therapy

These moral questions about cloning may also apply to questions arising with regard to genetic engineering and genetic screening, as well as with regard to the related issue of gene therapy. As discussed previously in this chapter, developments in modern genetics can create significant new ethical problems. With the development of CRISPR technology, it is possible edit human genes. Even before CRISPR came along, it was possible to screen embryos. And our growing knowledge of genetics is opening the door to genetic therapies.

Let's define each of these terms. *Genetic screening* occurs when human embryos are sorted and selected in an in vitro reproduction process. Embryos with genetic diseases may be disposed of. It might also be possible to select embryos with positive genetic attributes. Genetic screening does not actively alter the genome. *Genetic engineering* (or *genetic modification*) focuses on manipulating, changing, or modifying genes found in DNA. Sometimes people use the term genetic engineering to imply that there is some new genetic information introduced, which would be an enhancement. A genetic modification that is not an enhancement would be therapeutic, that is, "gene therapy," intended to fix a disease

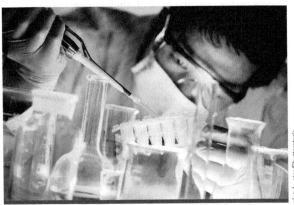

Figure 12-4 Genetic engineering creates new ethical challenges.

fotohunter/Shutterstock

and not to enhance. In a general sense, however, genetic engineering includes both therapies and enhancements. When genetic therapies are employed in the cells and body of a living person, this is referred to as *somatic gene therapy*. These therapies do not extend to changes made in reproductive cells, that is, sperm and egg. As such, the changes made are not inherited by the next generation. Therapies that involve interventions that can be passed on to future generations are referred to as *germ line* interventions.

As mentioned before, there is a risk of eugenics in all of this, especially in germ line interventions, which can be inherited. The controversial history of the eugenics movement mentioned previously is an important concern. For the most part, contemporary societies view eugenics as fundamentally immoral. But this sense is based on the worry that coercion would be involved. Contemporary genetic research may open the door to a different form of eugenic outcome, with parents selecting the genes of their children. We mentioned before the idea of "reproductive beneficence" that would optimize the genetic endowment of offspring. Consider what decisions you might make if it were possible for you to engineer a "designer baby" or to screen out an embryo with an unwanted genetic mutation—and how those decisions relate to your ideas about the value of natural reproduction, your view of disability, and your ideas about harms and benefits.

One technique involved in this process is known as *preimplantation genetic screening*, by which embryos with harmful or perhaps even simply unwanted genetic mutations can be selected out during the in vitro fertilization process. This seems like a prudent step to take in cases where the risk of genetic diseases, such as Huntington's disease, could be eliminated through a preimplantation genetic test. But consider the controversy surrounding a Maryland couple—both born deaf—who opted to increase the likelihood that their child would also be born deaf. This same-sex couple sought out a sperm donor with hereditary deafness out of a conviction that deafness is not a disability and that they wanted to share deaf culture with their children. "A hearing baby would be a blessing," one of the mothers said. "A deaf baby would be a special blessing."[65] After one of the women did, in fact, give birth to a deaf baby, some critics argued that the selection of a deaf donor was an abuse of genetic screening practices. But one of the mothers argued in reply that if Black parents were able to choose Black sperm donors, a deaf mother should be allowed to choose a deaf sperm donor.[66]

Many of the ethical controversies surrounding genetic engineering and screening have been intensified by the great progress scientists have made in recent decades in understanding the human genetic structure. The Human Genome Project, an effort to map the entire human genome, was completed in the summer of 2000 and its results first published in early 2001. The project found that humans have approximately twenty thousand genes—roughly the same number as most other animals—and helped scientists determine that "we have only 300 unique genes in the human [genome] that are not in the mouse."[67] However, although humans have approximately the same number of genes as a spotted green puffer fish, it is surmised that human capacity comes from "a small set of regulatory genes that control the activity of all the other genes." These would be different in the puffer fish.[68]

Two entities competed in the race to map the entire human genome. One was a public consortium of university centers in the United States, Great Britain, and Japan. It made its findings publicly available and used the genome from a mosaic of different individuals. The other research was done by Celera Genomics, a private company run by Dr. Craig Venter. It used a "shotgun" strategy, with genetic source material from Venter and four others. Celera performed an analysis of the DNA—identifying where the genes lay in the entire DNA sequence—and in 2007 Venter published his entire genetic sequence.[69] Although initially having one's complete genome sequenced was quite expensive, the cost has come down. And a few companies, such as 23andMe, have brought genetic screening to the mass market. These companies can also tell you something about your ancestry.

One ethical problem created by mass-market genetic testing is what do we do with knowledge about our genetic predisposition. If you knew you had a genetic tendency toward a disease, would you be obligated to share that knowledge with your siblings (who share some of your genetic endowment)? Or with your children? And if "knowledge is power," as they say, what about insurance companies and employers? Would an insurance company or an employer have a right to know the results of your genetic tests? Or is your genetic information private?

Since the initial mapping of the human genome, various scientific projects have attempted to determine the precise role that hereditary elements, including the genes, play in human development, health, personality, and other characteristics. In this effort, one focus has been on individual differences. The human genome, "a string of 3 billion chemical letters that spell out every inherited trait," is almost identical in all humans—99.99 percent. But some differences, so-called genetic misspellings that are referred to as *single nucleotide polymorphisms* (SNPs or "snips"), can be used to identify genetic diseases. The SNPs give base variations that contribute to individual differences in appearance and health, among other things. Scientists look for differences, for example, by taking DNA samples of five hundred people with diabetes and a similar number from people without the disease and then look for contrasting DNA patterns.[70] SNPs also influence how people react differently to medications. Some people can eat high-calorie and high-fat foods and still not put on weight, while others are just the opposite. Some have a high risk of heart disease, whereas others do not. With genetic discoveries based on the Human Genome Project and more recent efforts, one hope is that diets can be tailored to individual human genetic makeups.

Since the early 2000s, an international consortium of scientists has been working on the "hapmap" project, a $100 million endeavor "to hasten discovery of the variant genes thought to underlie common human diseases like diabetes, asthma, and cancer."[71] Scientists have used the Human Genome Project map as a master reference and compare individual genomes to it. Some diseases are caused by single genes, such as that producing cystic fibrosis, but others are thought to be caused by several genes acting together.

Other efforts are directed to finding genes that relate to certain beneficial human traits. For example, some scientists are working on locating what they call the "skinny gene." One candidate for this gene is found in mutations of anaplastic lymphoma kinase (ALK).

Some mutations of this gene are correlated with some cancers. But another mutation may be linked to thinness.[72] It is easy to imagine a therapeutic intervention designed to fight obesity by focusing on ALK. It is also possible to imagine genetic manipulation of embryos that are intended to somehow prevent obesity, or some screening process that would select for thin children.

Our growing knowledge of the human genome may lead to powerful new medical treatments but also raise new ethical questions. Consider, for example, gene therapies that could impact the growth of muscle. Myostatin is a hormone that curbs the growth of muscles. Gene therapies might be able to block myostatin, which could promote muscle growth. As a therapy this could be useful for treating muscular dystrophy or frailty in older persons. Myostatin mutations are already responsible for the development of a breed of cattle called the Belgian Blue that has huge muscles and very little fat. And some human beings have a myostatin mutation, which promotes muscle growth—a natural abnormality that has helped produce exceptional athletes, including a gold medalist in cross-country skiing.[73] While myostatin treatments could save lives, there is also concern that athletes and other healthy individuals might purchase them to gain an advantage in competition or for cosmetic purposes. Such genetic enhancements might not leave traces in urine or blood the way that other performance-enhancing drugs do. However, in recent years, the World Anti-Doping Agency has begun to develop new blood tests to detect so-called gene doping, including other genetic enhancements that allow the human body to produce extra red blood cells.[74]

Ethical issues have also arisen over new genetic screening procedures made possible by the genome map. While such screenings may benefit health, insurers and prospective employers might also use genetic screening to their own advantage but not necessarily to the advantage of the person being screened. Although the procedures may be new, the ethical issues are similar to those raised by other types of screening, including drug screening. While we may agree that athletes and airline pilots should have their blood and urine screened for the use of performance enhancements and recreational drugs, do we also agree that students or retail employees should be subject to similar screenings?

Related to this is the question of whether insurance companies or employers should be able to obtain information about an individual's genetic code. In 2013, scientists published the results of a study that showed that it was finally possible to identify individuals based on an analysis of genetic codes in comparison with publicly available databases containing the genetic information of individuals whose genes have been sequenced.[75] This technology could be useful for tracing out genealogies. But it could also raise privacy concerns, for example, among people who fear being stigmatized because of a genetic abnormality or disease.

Finally, there is also an ethical question here about whether individuals themselves would want to know about their own genetic predisposition. Would you want to know if you had some genetic mutation that was likely to cause a terrible disease? On the one hand, you might think that you could take preventive measures if you know you had a genetic risk factor. On the other hand, such knowledge could produce despair. A similar question arises when thinking about reproducing. If you knew you carried a genetic disease, would you think twice about having children? Some bio-conservatives might warn that these kinds of questions show us the dangers of our new knowledge and power over our genes. Maybe this kind of knowledge and power is too much for us to deal with. In response, the progressives argue that there is potential for great good from our increase in knowledge and power. From a utilitarian perspective, we can take steps to eliminate diseases. And we can fight diseases with gene therapies and exercise "procreative beneficence" with regard to our own offspring.

Genetically Modified Plants and Animals

12.6 Analyze controversies regarding genetically modified organisms.

Our genetic knowledge has applications beyond the human species. During the past few decades, a lively debate has sprung up in the United States and beyond about **genetically modified organisms**, or GMOs.

While, strictly speaking, humans have been modifying the genes of plants and animals for centuries—through such practices as plant hybridization and selective animal breeding—GMOs are created through new biotechnologies such as gene splicing, radiation, or specialized chemicals. These technologies often change the genetics of plants and animals that humans grow for food, in an attempt to make them hardier, larger, more flavorful, or more resistant to drought or freezing temperatures. Although some of these traits could be established through traditional breeding methods, some could not, and a highly profitable new industry now revolves around creating (and usually patenting) these new forms of life.

Critics of GMOs argue that they open a "Pandora's box" of potential risks to ecosystems and to human health. (In Greek mythology, Pandora's seemingly minor act of opening a beautiful box releases a host of evils into the world.) In 2004, the National Academy of Sciences (NAS) determined that "genetically engineered crops do not pose health risks that cannot also arise from crops created by other techniques, including conventional breeding."[76] It is not the method of production that should be of concern, the NAS argued, but the resulting product. Nevertheless, there is much that the general public does not understand about so-called genetically modified food.

Strictly speaking, genetic engineering involves inserting a specific gene from one organism into another in order to produce a desired trait. In a broader sense,

Figure 12-5 What ethical issues are created by genetically modified organisms?

Carlos Amarillo/Shutterstock

"nearly every food we eat has been genetically modified" as crops and domesticated animals have been bred by humans for centuries.[77] Cross-breeding crops "involves the mixing of thousands of genes, most unknown," and trying to select desirable mutations.[78] In the case of some contemporary GMOs, such mutations are now often caused by "bombarding seeds with chemicals or radiation" and seeing what comes of it. For example, lettuce, beans, and grapefruit have been so modified.[79]

An increasing number of crops have been genetically modified in recent decades, especially staple crops such as soy and corn. According to the Non-GMO Project, "The USDA estimates that up to 80 percent of groceries in North America contain GMOs and GMO derivatives, which reflects the fact that more than 90 percent of our farmland is planted in GMO commodity crops."[80] The Non-GMO Project has spearheaded a campaign to certify foods that do not contain GMOs. And in the United States, legislation requiring GMO labeling is connected to a law known as the National Bioengineered Food Disclosure Standard, which required that labeling appear by 2022. In 2013, the grocery chain Whole Foods announced that it would label products that contain GMOs in its stores, and it continues to focus on labeling GMOs in foods it sells.[81] While some are pushing back against GMOs, mainstream science tends to hold that these products are beneficial or at least not harmful. GMO crops are easier and cheaper to grow and can provide more food from less land. They may be engineered to survive the use of herbicides and insecticides or to be more resistant to pests. Critics argue, however, that herbicide- and pesticide-resistant crops will lead to more toxic chemicals in agriculture, which may have long-term negative impacts on the environment and human health. One article claims that the use of genetically modified crops has unleashed a "gusher" of pesticides.[82] But proponents of GMOs explain things differently. One technique has inserted *Bacillus thuringiensis* (B.t.) genes into corn, which enables it to resist a devastating pest called the corn borer. With this mutation, the use of environmentally damaging herbicides intended to combat the corn borer can then be reduced.

Other benefits of GMOs include the possibility of engineering crops so that they contain more nutritional value.

New strains of rice have been developed specifically to combat famine and to reduce a vitamin A deficiency that commonly causes blindness and other infections among the world's poorest children. Plans for GMOs include "edible vaccines" in fruits and vegetables that would make them more easily available to people than injectable ones.[83] Perhaps most significant for global public health, genetically modified foods offer a chance to "produce more food on less land—using less water, fewer chemicals, and less money."[84] And opposition to GMOs in the wealthy West may have negative consequences for developing countries where famine and malnutrition are serious problems. For example, opposition to genetically modified food led Uganda to prohibit efforts to develop a fungus-resistant banana, even though fungus has seriously damaged its banana crop, one of its most important.[85]

At the same time, protests against genetically modified foods have increased, especially in Europe and Japan, but also in the United States. The European Union (EU) had very strict regulations against GMOs. But as Europe is responding to the adverse agricultural impacts of climate change and drought, European nations are reconsidering their opposition to GMOs. At the same time, the technology employed to modify food crops is evolving (i.e., as CRISPR and other techniques have developed). As a result, it was reported in the fall of 2022 that the EU may revisit its ban on GMOs.[86] The problem of climate change and drought are severe. And as the human population continues to grow, we may need to quickly find ways to develop crops that can feed that population on a hot, crowded, and dry planet.

One significant concern that critics have with regard to GMOs is food allergies that could result from products containing new genetic information.[87] Although some of the criticism may be based on ungrounded fears about new technologies, some GMO-related hazards may be real. There is some evidence, for example, that crops genetically modified for antibiotic resistance may transfer that resistance to humans who eat them, raising serious health concerns.[88] There is also evidence that herbicide-resistant crops may help create "super-weeds" that require ever more toxic chemicals to try to control them. Neighboring non-GMO crops may become contaminated by GMO crops, which has, ironically, allowed giant GMO producers such as Monsanto to sue farmers for patent infringement when pollen from GMO crops blows onto their land. It may well be possible to reduce some of these risks, for example, by creating sterile plants that do not produce pollen. But clearly, we are still learning about GMOs. So far, many of the dangers that people associate with GMOs have not materialized, but this does not prove their safety for humans and the environment.

Again, we might apply moral theories in various ways here. Certainly, the precautionary principle would encourage us to make sure that the food we are consuming is safe and nutritious. But utilitarian concerns for food safety in a world with increasing demand for food and a changing climate might encourage us to be proactive in using GMOs. As we saw in this section, GMO foods could improve human nutrition. But we might also worry that genetic mutations may have unintended side effects that are yet to be discovered. Critics of GMOs may also argue that we ought to avoid modifying crops that can "infect" the natural world and destroy complex ecosystems. Some critics are also distrustful of the big corporations that own seeds and control agriculture. On the other hand, as the demand for food increases, GMOs may be part of the solution to hunger and malnutrition.

In general, the ethical debate over genetically modified food and crops has involved a consequentialist analysis of costs and benefits. Cost–benefit analysis first involves estimating risks and potential benefits—an empirical matter—and then a comparative evaluation in which one tries to analyze and weigh the various values involved. Longer and healthier lives for more people clearly belong on the positive side, and risks to longevity and health belong on the negative side, but we must also try to determine the relative value of life, health, well-being, and so on. There is also the problem of how to count speculative and unknown risks. If we are risk-averse and come down on the side of conservatism, we may avoid unknown risks but also eliminate possible benefits, including saving lives.

Such problems are particularly vexing when it comes to GMOs, which appear to have striking potential benefits but also risks. GMOs may promote economic efficiency, as animals are modified to produce more meat or meat with less fat or to have better resistance to disease. Still, GMOs may also pose risks. For example, some critics worry that farm-raised and genetically altered salmon, if released into the wild, might harm other species of fish.[89] Weighing potential benefits and risks of GMOs will likely be an ongoing process in the decades to come—one that may reach different conclusions about different techniques of modifying organisms along the way.

A different ethical debate over GMOs involves the idea that humans should not modify or interfere with the fundamental design of nature. Shouldn't the world of plant and animal species as we find them inspire our respect and awe and place some limits on our efforts to manipulate or change them? One problem with this line of criticism is that it is difficult to distinguish good forms of manipulating nature from unacceptable ones. Some critics of GMOs argue that we ought to leave species as we find them, and that it is the cross-species transfers of genetic material involved in some GMOs that make them unacceptable. One problem with this objection is that similar transfers have occurred in nature—from basic plant genetics to the long-term patterns of evolution.

In addition, the "yuck" objection introduced earlier is sometimes also raised in this context. Consider *xenotransplantation*, which would occur when animal parts are transplanted into human bodies ("xeno-" means foreign; this would be a "foreign" transplant). Scientists have been perfecting the use of pig organs for transplantation into humans. Recently, there have been successful transplants involving putting pig hearts and pig kidneys into human bodies.[90] But for this to work, it requires a genetically modified pig, engineered in order to avoid the immune response. One future project involves the use of genetically engineered pig blood in human blood transfusions.[91] The use of animal blood in the human body can cause immune rejection. But if pigs were genetically modified and their blood could be used in this way, we would solve the problem of blood shortages. Of course, the idea of having genetically modified pig blood in your own body might provoke a kind of repugnance. As with similar objections to human cloning, however, we must question whether such reactions are, by virtue of their intuitive force alone, legitimate moral insights. Even more important, in the case of genetically modified animals, is the question of their ethical or humane treatment and potential violations of their dignity or rights. This may involve not only the engineering of such animals but also their suffering and death as in the case of pigs whose organs would be transplanted. Animal welfare and rights arguments (as discussed in Chapter 17) should be considered with regard to such cases.

As we have seen in this chapter, biotechnology and bioengineering raise a host of ethical issues—something that should probably come as no surprise. With every new scientific advance and development come new ethical problems, for new questions arise about what we ought and ought not to do. To judge

well with regard to these issues, we need to understand the facts, including facts about possible benefits and adverse consequences. We also need to clarify our values about issues such as autonomy, liberty, and privacy. And we need to consider whether there is anything wrong with "playing God" and using technology to alter natural beings, including ourselves. Bio-conservatives will emphasize caution and modesty when it comes to exploring and utilizing these new technologies. But transhumanists and others will emphasize the potential benefits that could be created when human ingenuity is used to engineer and transform our bodies and the world of living things.

Chapter Summary

12.1 How can we explain the difference between a therapy and an enhancement and use it to assess different examples of biotechnology and bioengineering?

Therapies return people to normal function, while enhancements go beyond normal function. In some cases, there are very clear therapeutic uses of a biotechnology. A cochlear implant can help deaf people respond to sound, for example, and is clearly therapeutic. But many biotechnologies can be used in both ways, either as a therapy or as an enhancement. For example, genetic engineering could be used to eliminate diseases, but it could also be used to create enhancements. In thinking about biotechnology, it is useful to ask whether the usage is therapeutic or for enhancement purposes. Some moral approaches only approve of therapeutic technologies, while others may be open to the idea of enhancement.

12.2 How can we describe the conflict between bio-conservatism and transhumanism?

Bio-conservatives tend to oppose enhancement, while transhumanists tend to embrace it. Bio-conservatives typically focus on non-consequentialist concerns such as respect for dignity and avoiding "playing God" and changing nature. They may also be sympathetic to the natural law tradition. Transhumanists are often more

focused on consequentialism, imagining that biotechnology can produce good outcomes for people. Bio-conservatives will likely accept therapeutic biotechnologies that return people to normal function. Transhumanists embrace therapies. But they are also interested in going beyond normal function. Each will be sympathetic to the precautionary principle. But bio-conservatives are usually much more cautious, while transhumanists are more willing to take risks in pursuit of benefits of technological innovation.

12.3 How can we critically evaluate ethical problems involving performance-enhancing drugs?

Performance-enhancing drugs such as steroids can be used by athletes to enhance their athletic ability. There are also enhancements that may increase cognitive and academic performances. Transhumanists will not be opposed to such technologies, so long as there is consent and benefit (and minimal risk of harm). But in cases involving minors or when there is the possibility of coercion, there will likely be limits. Bio-conservatives are even more cautious, suggesting that using a chemical to manufacture a shortcut to superior performance is like cheating. Another important concern is fairness and justice—both in terms of fair competition and in terms of who has access to this technology.

12.4 How can we describe ethical controversies involved in reproductive technologies?

In vitro fertilization (IVF) techniques allow for reproduction by infertile heterosexual couples, by LGBTQ+ people, and others who cannot reproduce through sexual intercourse, including singe parents. Natural law tradition often warns against these technologies, suggesting that it is "unnatural." One problem from this perspective is the creation of spare embryos, which must be disposed of or kept frozen. Some conservatives argue that these spare embryos are persons. On the other hand, a more progressive approach would suggest that there are obvious therapeutic benefits of IVF, as a treatment for infertility. And so long as there is consent, a progressive would embrace these technologies. Reproductive technologies can also include surrogacy, which introduces a third party into the reproductive process and can create potential conflicts of interest.

12.5 How can we evaluate stem cell research, cloning, and genetic engineering in humans?

IVF processes make stem cell research possible by creating human embryos, which contain cells that are pluripotent. These cells can be used in regenerative medicine to regrow damaged tissues. IVF technologies also allow for the possibility of cloning and genetic engineering. These technologies depend on access to ova and embryos outside of the uterus. Questions arise with regard to embryonic stem cell research in connection with abortion: if embryos are persons, then using them is akin to abortion. But new technology that is able to create induced pluripotent stem cells (from somatic cells) may solve that problem, since embryos would no longer be employed. With regard to cloning and genetic engineering, there are ethical concerns regarding human interventions that tamper with the natural process of procreation. Conservatives tend to argue against such processes on natural law grounds. But there could be therapeutic usages of these technologies—as in using genetic engineering, screening, or gene editing to eliminate diseases. Progressives and transhumanists tend to embrace

genetic engineering, although there is a fairly significant hurdle in terms of the precautionary principle, since germ line interventions can be based down to future generations. There are also questions here about respecting "nature" and the right of offspring to have an "open future." Conservatives also suggest that these processes create a sense of repugnance, which may be an indication of wrongness. Progressives suggest that repugnance is not a useful moral judgment and that we will learn to appreciate these technologies as we become familiar with them.

12.6 How can we analyze controversies regarding genetically modified organisms?

The term "genetically modified organisms" (GMOs) is typically focused on genetic engineering of non-human beings, that is, plants and animals. There are some benefits to the use of GMOs: crop yields can increase and food production can respond to environmental changes including climate change and drought. Crops can also be engineered to increase nutritional value. But critics argue that there is something unnatural about this. And they warn against unanticipated negative side effects—both on human health and on the ecosystem. We mentioned the creation of genetically engineered pigs and other animals that could be used in xenotransplantation. This has a therapeutic benefit, but it may also elicit a sense of repugnance.

12.7 How might a student defend a thesis about biotechnology and bioengineering?

In order to defend a thesis about biotechnology and bioengineering, a student would need to understand the details of a specific technology, including its proposed benefits, the importance of consent, and risks of harm. The student would also need to decide what they think about the distinction between therapy and enhancement: whether enhancements are permissible and whether a proposed technology is being used as a therapy or as an enhancement. Students can employ moral theories such as utilitarianism, natural law, or Kantian deontology to decide where they stand in the dispute between bio-conservativism and progressive transhumanism. They will need to decide how seriously they take the precautionary principle, what they think about questions involving justice in the distribution of these technologies, and whether they are worried about tampering with the basic structure of life.

Primary Source Readings

The readings for this chapter begin with "The Transhumanist Declaration," a manifesto drafted by a number of authors including Nick Bostrom, a futuristically oriented bioethicist and director of the Future of Humanity Institute at Oxford University. The next reading is an excerpt by the bioethicist Leon Kass reflects on the question of new technologies. Kass is a prominent geneticist and physician who once served as the chairman of the President's Council on Bioethics under President George W. Bush. Kass is deeply concerned about the way that technologies are impacting our understanding of human nature and human values; he argues for greater humility with respect to our "given" biological life and respect for our intuitive repugnance at altering it. As a response to Kass, we have a short excerpt from an article by Nick Bostrom, which defends the idea of transhumanism and advocates using technology to improve human nature. Our final excerpt is from disability-rights theorist Rosemarie Garland-Thomson. Garland-Thomson warns against a kind of "velvet eugenics" that she fears will develop as CRISPR technology makes it easier to edit out disability and disease.

Reading 12-1   Transhumanist Declaration | Various Authors

Study Questions

1. What sorts of problems does this declaration imagine being solved through science and technology?
2. Is this manifesto hopeful or fearful about the use of technology in the future?
3. How does the manifesto appeal to ideas about autonomy, individual rights, and freedom of choice?

Humanity stands to be profoundly affected by science and technology in the future. We envision the possibility of broadening human potential by overcoming aging, cognitive shortcomings, involuntary suffering, and our confinement to planet Earth.

We believe that humanity's potential is still mostly unrealized. There are possible scenarios that lead to wonderful and exceedingly worthwhile enhanced human conditions.

We recognize that humanity faces serious risks, especially from the misuse of new technologies. There are possible realistic scenarios that lead to the loss of most, or even all, of what we hold valuable. Some of these scenarios are drastic, others are subtle. Although all progress is change, not all change is progress.

Research effort needs to be invested into understanding these prospects. We need to carefully deliberate how best to reduce risks and expedite beneficial applications. We also need forums where people can constructively discuss what should be done, and a social order where responsible decisions can be implemented.

Reduction of existential risks, and development of means for the preservation of life and health, the alleviation of grave suffering, and the improvement of human foresight and wisdom should be pursued as urgent priorities, and heavily funded.

Policy making ought to be guided by responsible and inclusive moral vision, taking seriously both opportunities and risks, respecting autonomy and individual rights, and showing solidarity with and concern for the interests and dignity of all people around the globe. We must also consider our moral responsibilities towards generations that will exist in the future.

We advocate the well-being of all sentience, including humans, non-human animals, and any future artificial intellects, modified life forms, or other intelligences to which technological and scientific advance may give rise.

We favour allowing individuals wide personal choice over how they enable their lives. This includes use of techniques that may be developed to assist memory, concentration, and mental energy; life extension therapies; reproductive choice technologies; cryonics procedures; and many other possible human modification and enhancement technologies.

_____

https://www.humanityplus.org/the-transhumanist-declaration

Reading 12-2   Ageless Bodies, Happy Souls | Leon R. Kass

Study Questions

1. How does Kass explain the repugnance and disquiet of using biotechnology to improve human nature?

2. What does Kass mean by "modesty born of gratitude" for the "givenness" of life?

3. What kinds of goods does Kass seem to think are linked to acceptance of the aging body?

What is disquieting about our attempts to improve upon human nature, or even our own particular instance of it? It is difficult to put this disquiet into words. We are in an area where initial repugnances are hard to translate into sound moral arguments...

A common man-on-the-street reaction to these prospects is the complaint of "men playing God." An educated fellow who knows Greek tragedy complains rather of hubris. Sometimes the charge means the sheer prideful presumption of trying to alter what God has ordained or nature has produced, or what should, for whatever reason, not be fiddled with. Sometimes the charge means not so much usurping God-like powers, but doing so in the absence of God-like knowledge: the mere playing at being God, the hubris of acting with insufficient wisdom....

... Modesty born of gratitude for the world's "givenness" may enable us to recognize that not everything in the world is open to any use we may desire or devise...

Only if there is something precious in the given... does what is given serve as a source of restraint against efforts that would degrade it. When it comes to human biotechnical engineering, only if there is something inherently good or dignified about, say, natural procreation, human finitude, the human life cycle (with its rhythm of rise and fall), and human erotic longing and striving... only then can we begin to see why those aspects of our nature need to be defended....

A flourishing human life is not a life lived with an ageless body or untroubled soul, but rather a life lived in rhythmed time, mindful of time's limits, appreciative of each season and filled first of all with those intimate human relations that are ours only because we are born, age, replace ourselves, decline, and die— and know it. It is a life of aspiration, made possible by and born of experienced lack, of the disproportion between the transcendent longings of the soul and the limited capacities of our bodies and minds. It is a life that stretches towards some fulfillment to which our natural human soul has been oriented, and, unless we extirpate the source, will always be oriented. It is a life not of better genes and enhancing chemicals but of love and friendship, song and dance, speech and deed, working and learning, revering and worshipping. The pursuit of an ageless body is finally a distraction and a deformation. The pursuit of an untroubled and self-satisfied soul is deadly to desire. Finitude recognized spurs aspiration. Fine aspiration acted upon is itself the core of happiness. Not the agelessness of the body, nor the contentment of the soul, nor even the list of external achievement and accomplishments of life, but the engaged and energetic being-at-work of what Nature uniquely gave to us is what we need to treasure and defend. All other perfection is at best a passing illusion, at worst a Faustian bargain that will cost us our full and flourishing humanity.

Leon Kass, "Ageless Bodies, Happy Souls." *The New Atlantis* 1 (Spring 2003).

Reading 12-3   In Defense of Posthuman Dignity | Nick Bostrom

Study Questions

1. How does Bostrom explain the transhumanist view of morphological freedom and reproductive freedom?

2. Explain why Bostrom says that "nature's gifts are sometimes poisoned" and how this relates to the goals of transhumanism.

3. To what extent is Bostrom right that we would appear as "posthuman" to our hunter–gatherer ancestors?

Transhumanism. . . . can be viewed as an outgrowth of secular humanism and the Enlightenment. It holds that current human nature is improvable through the use of applied science and other rational methods, which may make it possible to increase human health-span, extend our intellectual and physical capacities, and give us increased control over our own mental states and moods. . . .

Transhumanists promote the view that human enhancement technologies should be made widely available, and that individuals should have broad discretion over which of these technologies to apply to themselves (morphological freedom), and that parents should normally get to decide which reproductive technologies to use when having children (reproductive freedom). Transhumanists believe that, while there are hazards that need to be identified and avoided, human enhancement technologies will offer enormous potential for deeply valuable and humanly beneficial uses. Ultimately, it is possible that such enhancements may make us, or our descendants, "posthuman," beings who may have indefinite health-spans, much greater intellectual faculties than any current human being— and perhaps entirely new sensibilities or modalities— as well as the ability to control their own emotions. The wisest approach vis-à-vis these prospects, argue transhumanists, is to embrace technological progress, while strongly defending human rights and individual choice, and taking action specifically against concrete threats, such as military or terrorist abuse of bioweapons, and against unwanted environmental or social side-effects. . . .

Nature's gifts are sometimes poisoned and should not always be accepted. Cancer, malaria, dementia, aging, starvation, unnecessary suffering, and cognitive shortcomings are all among the presents that we would wisely refuse. Our own species-specified natures are a rich source of much of the thoroughly unrespectable and unacceptable—susceptibility for disease, murder, rape, genocide, cheating, torture, racism. . . . Rather than deferring to the natural order, transhumanists maintain that we can legitimately reform ourselves and our natures in accordance with humane values and personal aspirations. . . .

If the alternative to parental choice in determining the basic capacities of new people is entrusting the child's welfare to nature, that is blind chance, then the decision should be easy. Had Mother Nature been a real parent, she would have been in jail for child abuse and murder. . . .

In the eyes of a hunter-gatherer, we might already appear "posthuman." Yet these radical extensions of human capabilities—some of them biological, others external—have not divested us of moral status or dehumanized us in the sense of making us generally unworthy and base. Similarly, should we or our descendants one day succeed in becoming what relative to current standards we may refer to as posthuman, this need not entail a loss of dignity either.

From the transhumanist standpoint, there is no need to behave as if there were a deep moral difference between technological and other means of enhancing human lives. By defending posthuman dignity we promote a more inclusive and humane ethics, one that will embrace future technologically modified people as well as humans of the contemporary kind.

Nick Bostrom, "In Defense of Posthuman Dignity." *Bioethics* 19: 3 (2005).

Reading 12-4   CRISPR and Velvet Eugenics | Rosemarie Garland-Thomson

Study Questions

1. What does Garland-Thomson mean by "velvet eugenics," and how does she think this might happen?
2. What does Garland-Thomson have in mind with regard to "humane technologies" that honor and accommodate "human biodiversity"?
3. How might Garland-Thomson envision the use of biotechnology to sustain human variation?

Much current reproductive technology, including gene editing, carries out a new eugenics in the name of health and reproductive liberty. The other side of the debate supports the free development and use of these reproductive technologies not only in the interest of liberty, but also in the name of a parental and medical obligation to fulfill the best interests of future children. Those who oppose genetic editing as a new eugenics are of the existential bent that I describe here, and which I hold myself. . . .

Commercialized medical technology development produces a culture of reprogenetics that carries out what I call a "velvet eugenics"—one that standardizes human variation in the interest of individual, market-driven liberty at the expense of social justice and the robust diversity and inclusion upon which modern egalitarian social orders depend. . . .

Eugenic technologies assure that the existence of all future persons is conditional. In contrast, humane technologies honor and accommodate the widest range of human variation. That means designing and building a world shaped to fit human variation and individual distinctiveness, rather than attempting to shape bodies to fit into the extant world. . . . It also means developing an attitude of humility toward human biodiversity when imagining another's life and how any of us live. This requires resisting a notion of technological progress that continually categorizes human diversity in terms of new disease to be identified and eliminated. Such an enterprise regularizes human minds and bodies according to concepts of advantage or disadvantage, a narrow version of health, a commercially incentivized growth industry of pathological diagnosis, or a notion of individual liberty at the expense of the common good. Humane technologies, in contrast, support the existence of present and future persons in our human distinctiveness.

Humane technologies, then, create an environment in which people grow into themselves. For humans to thrive, we need to be ensconced in an environment that sustains the particular form, function, and needs of our bodies. We should devote technology to the humane goal of providing every human being with a genuinely open future to grow into a distinct and particular individual, rather than making them as we think they should be. Providing this open future does not preclude appropriate interventions—sometimes medical, sometimes social—that ameliorate pain and suffering, promote human functioning and flourishing, or provide technologies that bridge flesh and world. Rather than researching and developing commercial

medical technology to reduce human variation, we should invest more resources in sustaining human variation. Resource allocation should develop and support environments and technologies through which human distinctiveness can flourish. Within a humane technologies framework, liberty can be understood as the freedom to grow from our distinctive individuality, not according to conceptions of health, normalcy, advantage, preferences, or future concepts of life quality imposed through parental will or medical authority and justified as the best interests of the child. Humane technologies accommodate rather than eliminate human diversity.

Rosemarie Garland-Thomson, "How We Got to CRISPR: The Dilemma of Being Human." *Perspectives in Biology and Medicine* 63: 1 (Winter 2020), pp. 28–43.

Review Exercises

1. What is the basic difference between a therapy and an enhancement? Explain by using an example.

2. How do bioengineering and biotechnology provide opportunities for people with disabilities? How might these techniques point toward a posthuman future?

3. How does your thinking about animal ethics, the ethics of abortion, and even sexual ethics connect with your thinking about the ethics of biotechnologies? What concepts overlap among these issues?

4. Summarize the arguments for and against cloning and other reproductive technologies based on the idea that it would be "playing God" and would undermine human dignity.

5. Summarize the idea that cloning and/or genetic engineering might pose a threat to the clone's individuality and the right to an open future. Does this worry you?

6. Evaluate the arguments regarding human cloning related to exploitation, confusion of families, and the "yuck" factor of the repugnance argument.

7. Evaluate arguments for and against genetic screening and genetic engineering of offspring.

8. What are the ethical arguments pro and con with regard to the production and use of genetically modified plants and crops?

9. Discuss the worry about "velvet eugenics" and the idea of "procreative beneficence."

10. What concerns might we have about biotechnologies from the standpoint of justice, fairness, and equality?

Discussion Cases

1. Human Cloning. Victor and Jenny have one son, Alan, who was hit by a car at age four and then lapsed into a coma. The prognosis is bleak for Alan, but Jenny cannot bear to see him die, and so they have kept him on life support. Victor has heard that scientists working at a secret lab have been successfully cloning human beings. Victor suggests that they contact the scientists to see if they can clone Alan—using Alan's DNA to grow a new baby, which would be a genetic copy of him. Jenny is appalled at this idea. "But it wouldn't be Alan. It would be a totally different person." But Victor suggests that the clone would be very similar. "The new baby would be created to honor Alan. Of course, it wouldn't literally be *him*. But we could honor Alan's memory and keep Alan's unique genetic gifts alive by cloning him."

What do you think? To what extent would a clone be the same person as the original? Would it be unethical to clone Alan? Why or why not?

2. Smart Drugs. Ramsey has obtained a "smart drug" from someone else in the dorms. He's heard that it may be possible to increase cognitive ability through the use of this drug and hopes it will help him on his upcoming finals. He knows it is illegal to use the drug in this way. But he does not believe that it would be unethical. "I think they ought to legalize marijuana too," he says to his roommate, Marc. "That's not the same, man," Marc replies. "Marijuana is just for fun. You're talking about using a drug to get an edge over other people on tests and in studying. That's just not fair. It's cheating." Ramsey rolls his eyes. "That's ridiculous. It's not really cheating," he says. "The drug won't make me smart. I still have to study. The drug will just make me more effective at studying. It's like coffee but stronger. Besides, the guy I got the drugs from has a prescription for them because he's got ADHD. If he gets to use the drugs to improve his performance, why can't I?"

Who do you agree with here: Ramsey or Marc? Is it "cheating" to use a "smart drug"? Explain your answer using concepts discussed in the chapter.

3. Designer Babies. Steven and Marisol are a young married couple who are concerned about passing genetic diseases on to their children. Members of Steven's family have been diagnosed with Huntington's disease, an incurable genetic disorder that causes cognitive problems, difficulties with movement that ultimately require full-time nursing care, and reduced life expectancy. Members of Marisol's family have tested positive for a mutation of the BRCA genes that are strongly associated with breast and ovarian cancer. At a family reunion, they are discussing their decision to use in vitro fertilization and preimplantation genetic screening of embryos. Steven's cousin, Valerie, is appalled. She is opposed to the idea of in vitro fertilization and to the entire idea of genetic screening. Valerie says, "You can't just choose the babies you want to have. God will only give you the challenges that He knows you can handle. And if a child is born with a disease, your job is to love that child, no matter what." Steven is speechless. But Marisol is not. "But if we can guarantee that our child is healthy and will live a happy life, shouldn't we do that? We don't want to raise a child who is doomed to genetic diseases." Valerie shakes her head. "There is no way to know," she says. "Kids get sick and die. Some who have diseases get better. You can't control everything. And besides, that test-tube baby stuff is really expensive. How can you afford it?" Now Steven replies, "We want to invest in this procedure now because it might save money in the long run. I've seen how much Huntington's costs a family—so have you. I'd rather pay to prevent it now than have to deal with the costs later." Valerie responds, "That sounds really rude. It sounds like you resent people who get sick and need your help. The whole thing is very selfish."

Whom do you agree with here: Steven and Marisol or Steven's cousin, Valerie? Is it wrong to want to prevent genetic disease? Is it a wise investment? Is it selfish to want to control your child's genes? Explain your answer.

Knowledge Check Answer Key

1. **a.** Surgery to implant a bionic eye in a patient with normal vision is best understood as an enhancement.

2. **c.** The precautionary principle is related to nonmaleficence, that is, avoiding causing harm.

3. **d.** Transhumanists tend to believe that nature can and should be improved.

4. **b.** Justice focuses on fairness and equality.

13 Equality and Discrimination

Learning Outcomes

After reading this chapter, you should be able to:

13.1 Describe the principle of equality and apply it to the concerns of social justice.

13.2 Explain concepts found in critical philosophical accounts of race and racism.

13.3 Apply the concept of intersectionality to discussions of inequality.

13.4 Evaluate arguments in defense of affirmative action and reparations.

13.5 Defend a thesis about the ethics of racial profiling, affirmative action, and reparations.

Black Lives Matter

In 2013, a movement known as "Black Lives Matter" appeared as a response to a series of killings in which unarmed Black men were shot by police or died while in police custody. The killing of George Floyd in 2020 provides an important recent example of the problem. A police officer, Derek Chauvin, knelt on Floyd's neck for nearly ten minutes. Floyd passed out and died, while other officers stood nearby and onlookers watched. One bystander, a teenager named Darnella Frazier, took a video on her phone. That video and other evidence led a jury to convict Derek Chauvin of murdering George Floyd.

The George Floyd killing prompted a series of social protests loosely organized under the banner of Black Lives Matter, which directed the world's attention to the problem of police brutality and more generally to the problem of racial inequality and the need for social justice. Some argue that cases like this shows us that racism and violations of civil rights are serious and ongoing problems. Others argue that the fact that Chauvin was convicted of murder and of violations of George Floyd's civil rights shows that we are making progress in comparison to previous centuries when Jim Crow laws and lynching were common. But even those who think we have made progress will likely agree that there is more progress to be made with regard to race relations and social justice. Among the policies and proposals that have been suggested along these lines are affirmative action programs, racially targeted reparations projects, eliminating racial profiling, and ongoing work to dismantle structural racism. Of course, each of these proposals prompts political backlash and ethical and legal questions.

What Do You Think?

1. How concerned are you about racism, inequality, and social justice in the world today?

2. What is the role of individual citizens—like Darnella Frazier—in responding to violations of civil rights and other inequalities?

3. Should there be reparations for past discrimination or affirmative action for members of certain racial groups?

4. Are there other ways you could imagine for society to address racism, discrimination, and inequality?

Introduction

In this chapter and those that follow in this section of the book, we will consider ethical issues that can be grouped under the general idea of "social justice." Social justice has been defined and explained in various ways, but a very basic and general idea of justice emphasizes treating things fairly or equitably. A definition of justice that goes back to Aristotle holds that justice requires that similar things should be treated similarly. Thus, for example, similar grades should be given to students who perform at similar levels. It would be unfair or unjust to give students different grades for the same level of performance.

The idea of social justice takes that basic idea of justice and applies it to the social world. Unlike the concept of criminal justice, which is about how we should punish crime, social justice is not necessarily concerned with punishment. And unlike justice as a virtue of individuals or a characteristic of individual behavior, social justice is focused on broad social issues involving distributions of goods across large numbers of people.

Of significant concern for social justice then are inequalities and injustices that occur in society. In this chapter, we'll focus on injustices involving race and related topics. In the next chapter, we will focus on economic inequalities. In the chapter after that, we'll consider issues arising from globalization and the challenge of global justice. Finally, we'll conclude this section of the text with a chapter on sexual morality including the question of who has a right to marry. These topics could be organized and addressed in different ways. Sexual morality also includes questions about whether certain sexual acts are right or wrong. The issues of racial and economic justice overlap with moral questions about the criminal justice system. And questions of global justice may have something to do with war and peace. We'll make these connections as we proceed. But the prevailing question in each of the four chapters in this section of the book is about social injustices and inequalities. We might also note that health care ethics includes questions about social justice in health care distributions and that there are important social justice questions in environmental ethics (often called "environmental justice").

Moral Approaches and Conceptual Issues

As you might suspect, people disagree about what counts as social justice and what social justice requires. This typically involves either a disagreement about basic normative theory or a disagreement about the facts of the case. On the one hand, in terms of disagreements about normative theory, it is worth noting that utilitarian accounts of social justice may have a different focus than approaches to social justice that emphasize basic human rights or natural law. And even within a given theoretical approach, there may be disagreements. Utilitarians will have to consider, for example, whether some inequalities could be permitted if they help promote the greatest happiness for the greatest number of people. Others will maintain that basic human rights and dignity must be respected. There is also, on the other hand, disagreement about facts. This kind of disagreement may be about the empirical facts that are being used to describe certain kinds of injustice; it may also be about the efficacy of proposed remedies for social injustice.

For example, disagreements about affirmative action may be about factual matters, such as the causes of inequality or the results of affirmative action programs. But disputes about affirmative action also include theoretical disagreements about the importance of rights, respect, equal treatment, and the degree to which the social consequences of these programs matter. In 2022, as this book was being revised, the U.S. Supreme Court revisited the argument about affirmative action in university admissions in a pair of cases involving Harvard University and the University of North Carolina. Opponents of the admissions policies used in these universities argued in the Court that these policies gave unfair preference to members of certain racial groups. They further argued that "racial classifications are wrong" and that employing them in the admissions process produces bad consequences (such as people lying about or concealing their racial identities).[1] But defenders of using race as part of the admissions process argued that "diversity is our nation's greatest source of strength."[2] The University of North Carolina argued that through its admissions process it was "assembling a student body that is diverse along the many dimensions that matter in American life, including race, but also social class, geography, military status, intellectual views, and much more."[3] They argued that building a diverse student body was good for students, since it helps to "equip students with the tools needed to function effectively as citizens and leaders in our complex and increasingly diverse society." Notice that here we have a number of different claims and arguments—about factual matters and moral values. What do you think? Can affirmative action in college admissions be justified? Is it useful? Is it fair?

This topic is contentious, as is the issue of police brutality and racism with which we began. Questions about discrimination and inequality often prompt emotional responses. This chapter will examine these issues, with the goal of promoting critical thinking. We will not be able to explore all of the possibilities here that involve disputes about normative theories and factual disagreements. But it is worth keeping in mind a few basic ideas. Utilitarianism provides a notion of social justice that develops from the basic idea that each person should count equally in the utilitarian calculation. A Kantian approach to social justice would focus on universalizable rules and respect for the autonomy of person. Natural law traditions will understand social justice in terms of the natural structure and order of society that is discernable through reason. We could also develop accounts of social justice based on an emphasis on human rights, respect for the dignity of person, and the idea of giving people what they deserve. We might also understand social justice as a goal of the basic social contract. In the next chapter, we will explore a few other options including ideas found in John Rawls's account of distributive justice, libertarianism, socialism, and communitarianism. For present purposes, suffice it to say that there are various ways of grounding the idea of social justice.

Despite this diversity of moral approaches to the topic, equality is a crucial idea for any account of social justice. Racism, sexism, and other forms of discrimination are unfair and unjust because they result in unequal treatment. The racist, sexist, or homophobic individual treats people of a particular race, gender, or sexual orientation unfairly because of a specific facet of their identity. Yet the apparent unfairness of racism or sexism still needs to be explained. Different treatment is not always unfair. Suppose that our views about members of a group are not based on prejudice, but on an objective factual assessment of that group.

For example, if men differ from women in significant ways, is this not a sufficient reason to treat them differently? What if there were some quantifiable differences between men and women in terms of strength or aggression? Would that justify a ban on women serving in leadership roles in the military, or would it justify preventing women from serving in combat? It is, of course, an open question as to whether there actually are general differences between men and women with regard to strength or aggression, and whether those generalizations are relevant to different treatment. And the history of discrimination against women has included supposedly "factual" generalizations that were used to justify discrimination and that were based on a biased assessment of the "facts." In the case of women in combat, the United States changed its policies in 2015, allowing women to serve in combat. But some military leaders have argued that this should only occur if female soldiers can pass the same physical fitness testing as male soldiers.

As Kristen Griest, one of the first women to graduate from the U.S. Army Ranger School, argued, there are "objective physical standards to which all soldiers should be held, regardless of gender."[4] It is not the gender of the person that matters in this regard but their physical ability. And it would be unfair to discriminate against a person who has that ability based solely on gender.

But some objective generalizations are useful. Consider a different example. If members of a certain racial group tend to suffer from a certain disease more than members of other groups (as in the case of African Americans and sickle cell anemia), does that give us a reason to treat members of the former group differently (say in focusing efforts at treating sickle cell anemia on them)? Would it be "racist" to focus sickle cell anemia treatments on members of that group? Part of what matters here is the intention and purported benefit of forms of differential treatment.

A further significant question arises in trying to remedy past injustices. Is it fair and just to offer reparations to those who have been unjustly discriminated against in the past or to create affirmative action programs that try to remedy past inequities? Is it "racist" to notice that there are racially differential outcomes in the world or to point out that some racial groups have been discriminated against in the past? Or should we strive to be "color-blind" or "not see race" despite the fact that racial disparities exist? As you can see, these questions are complicated and potentially contentious. And one difficulty is that there is a legacy of unequal treatment that we are still coming to terms with in the United States and elsewhere.

The Principle of Equality

13.1 Describe the principle of equality, and apply it to the concerns of social justice.

Now let's consider a basic moral principle that can be used to help us think about these issues. The **principle of equality** is the idea that we should treat equal things in equal ways and that we may treat different things in unequal ways. In analyzing this principle, we will be able to clarify whether or why discrimination

(including racism, homophobia, sexism, and the like) is morally objectionable. The principle of equality can be formulated in various ways. Consider the following formulation:

> It is unjust to treat people differently in ways that deny to some of them significant social benefits unless we can show that there is a difference between them that is relevant to the differential treatment.

To better understand the meaning of this principle, we can break it down into several related concerns.

Non-Bias

The principle of equality is a principle of justice. It tells us that certain actions or practices that treat people unequally are unjust. Consider the symbolic representations of justice that are found in statues on public buildings. For example, the statue of Lady Justice stands outside the U.S. Supreme Court building in Washington, D.C., where she is depicted as blindfolded and holding a scale in one hand. The idea here is that justice is blind—in other words, it is not biased. It does not favor one person over another on the basis of any identity or characteristic. The same laws are supposed to apply to all, without bias.

Proportionality and Equity

Sticking with our example of the statue of justice holding the scale, it is clear that the scale symbolizes the way that justice balances things out. This may involve strict (or formal) equality—as when each student in a class is given the same number of minutes to complete an assignment. But it can also involve balancing things out proportionally. The idea of proportionality may allow us to distribute things in different amounts to people depending on what they need or deserve in light of some relevant difference. Thus, people may end up with different amounts of goods in proportion to some relevant difference (or we might also say depending on or in relation to some difference). And so, for example, a student with a documented disability may need more time on an exam to have a fair chance. In some cases, the term "equity" is used to describe this—and the term is used in contrast to strict or formal equality. You may have seen examples of this on bumper stickers or in posters. One familiar image shows people of different heights trying to see over a fence. If we give each one of them a similarly sized box to stand on, we have not really made things "equal"—since the shorter person may still not be able to see over the fence and since a taller person standing on a box may have an even better vantage point. To make things equitable, we might in fact have to give them differently sized boxes to stand on, with that difference determined in proportion to their height. That way, even though each person does not get the same exact box, everyone can see clearly. At any rate, the principle of equality requires that there should be valid moral reasons for differential treatment.

Social Benefits and Harms

We are not required to justify treating people differently from others in every case. For example, I may give personal favors to my friends or family and not to others without having to give a reason. However, sometimes social policies and practices treat people differently in ways that harm some and benefit others. This harm can be obvious or it can be subtle. In addition, there is a difference between *primary* discrimination and *secondary* discrimination.[5] In primary discrimination, a person is singled out and directly penalized simply because they are a member of a particular group, as when they are denied school admissions or promotions because of this characteristic of identity. In secondary discrimination, criteria for benefit or harm are used that do not directly apply to members of particular groups and only indirectly affect them. Thus, the policy "last hired, first fired" is often likely to have a discriminatory effect. Such a policy may seem harmless but can actually have a harmful effect on certain groups—particularly if these groups, such as women or Black people, have traditionally been excluded from a particular profession. The principle of equality directs us to consider the ways that social benefits and harms are distributed.

Proof and Reality of Difference

The principle of equality states that we must show or prove that certain differences exist if we are to justify treating people differently. The principle can be stronger or weaker depending on the kind of proof of differences required by it. It is not acceptable to treat people differently on the basis of differences that we only think or suspect exist. Consider the example of women in combat that we discussed above. It is not justifiable to discriminate against women in the armed forces based on some stereotype about gender roles. The principle of equality requires that we show or prove that measurable or quantifiable differences exist between the people whom we would treat differently. We might say that any supposedly relevant difference ought to be based on a matter of fact and not mere opinion. We would need unbiased empirical studies that show that there is a difference that merits differential treatment. As Kristen Griest suggested (as quoted previously), there are objective physical tests required of those who serve in combat (such as lifting, running, etc.). But is everything as objective as that? Could there be cases in which we would want to be sensitive to individual differences, since not every individual fits the norm? In the case of extra time for testing, it might make sense to accommodate different kinds of abilities. But would we also want to make those kinds of accommodations in the case of those serving in combat?

Empirical studies that examine supposed differences between males and females may also end up with results that are biased by the fact that they look at males and females after they have been socialized. In a culture that socializes girls and boys differently, it would not be surprising to find gender differences. Suppose that a study found that little girls play with dolls in nurturing games while boys play with guns in games that are aggressive. Would this necessarily mean that some *innate* difference causes this? If there were an innate difference, this might be relevant to how we would structure education or some other aspects of society. We might prefer women for the job of nurse or teacher, while preferring men for the job of police officer or soldier. However, if we cannot prove that these or any such characteristics come from nature rather than nurture, we should be more careful about differential treatment. We should consider whether our social institutions perpetuate socially induced differences. And we might also consider whether a changed social system—say, one in which girls are encouraged to play with guns and expected to serve in combat—might change the nature of our empirical observations.

Relevant Differences

The principle of equality requires more than proving that innate or real differences exist between groups of people before we are justified in treating them differently. It also requires that the differences be relevant. For example, if it could be shown that women are by nature better at bricklaying than men, this would be a "real" difference between them. Although we might then be justified in preferring women for bricklaying jobs, we would not be justified in using this difference to prefer women for the job of airline pilot. On the other hand, if men and women think differently and if certain jobs require these particular thinking skills, then according to the principle of equality we may well prefer those individuals with these skills for the jobs. We might also prefer different people for bona fide reasons, such as hiring men to model male swimsuits and women to model female swimsuits. What counts as a bona fide reason will depend on the context. And this context is culturally dependent. The question of what is considered a male swimsuit or a female swimsuit is really a cultural matter.

The relevance of a talent, characteristic, or skill to a job is not an easy matter to determine. For example, is upper-body strength an essential skill for the job of firefighter or police officer? In answering this question, it would be useful to determine what kinds of things firefighters usually have to do, what their equipment is like, and so forth. Similarly, with the job of police officer, we might ask how much physical strength is required and how important are other physical or psychological skills or traits. Or to consider another sort of example, we might ask whether identifying as Black, Asian, or female is an essential qualification for a position as university teacher of courses in Black Studies, Asian Studies, or Women's Studies? It may not be an essential qualification, but some people argue that one's identity does help qualify a person for such a position because they are more likely to understand the issues and problems with which such courses deal. Nevertheless, this view has not gone unchallenged.

In addition to determining which characteristics or skills are relevant to a particular position, we must be able to assess adequately whether particular persons possess these characteristics or skills. Designing such assessments presents a difficulty, as prejudice may play a role in designing or evaluating them. For instance, how do we know whether someone works well with people or has sufficient knowledge of the issues that ought to be treated in a Women's Studies course? This raises a broader issue. Should we always test or judge people as individuals, or is it ever permissible to judge an individual as a member of a particular group?

Identity and Individuality

One significant problem for the principle of equality stems from the fact that those group differences that are both real and relevant to differential treatment are often, if not always, *average* differences. In other words, a characteristic may be typical of a group of people, but it may not belong to every member of the group. Consider height. Men are typically taller than women. Nevertheless, some women are taller than some men. Or consider mental acuity in relation to age. Some older adults experience memory loss, suffer hearing loss and vision impairment, and may lose the sharpness and focus they had when younger. But this does not mean that all older adults are less adept than younger people in their thinking. Thus, it would seem that we ought to consider what characteristics an individual has rather than what is typical of the group to which they belong. This would only seem to be fair or just. But social life does occasionally require that we deal with individuals as members of groups, especially when making policies from a utilitarian perspective that aims to produce the greatest happiness for the greatest number of people. Critics will object, however, that individuals, rather than groups, ought to be the focal point of moral concern. Such an objection might be a Kantian one that holds that we should respect persons as ends in themselves and that to consider individuals merely as members of a group is an affront to their dignity.

Are we ever justified in treating someone differently because of their membership in a particular demographic and because of that group's typical characteristics—even if a particular person does not possess them? We do this in some cases and presumably think it is just. Consider our treatment of people as members of an age group, say, for purposes of driving or voting. But some individuals who are fourteen or fifteen may be better drivers or more responsible voters than some individuals who are over eighteen. Yet in this case we make rules on the basis of a group characteristic, rather than individual ability.

Social policies about voting and driving are based on generalizations about age cohorts. Those who agree to the policies resulting from these generalizations most likely do so for utilitarian reasons; these policies tend to produce good outcomes for most of us. If a fourteen-year-old is well qualified to drive, they only have to wait a year or two, depending on the laws in their state. This causes no great harm to them. Nor is any judgment made about their natural abilities. And eventually the young person can take a test and get a driver's license. Furthermore, suppose that we tried to judge people as individuals for the purposes of voting. We would need to develop a test of "intelligent voting ability" or something like that. Can you imagine what political and social dynamite this testing would be? The cost to our democracy of instituting such a policy would be too great, whereas the cost to the individual of being judged as a member of an age group and having to wait a couple of years to vote is comparatively small. Thus, this practice does not seem unduly unfair.

However, in other cases, differential treatment seems manifestly unfair. Those who are denied consideration because of some difference in race, gender, age, or ability would rightly complain that it was unfair to deny them a chance at a position for which they were qualified. And denying opportunities to people because of such generalizations may also come at great social cost to society, if qualified persons who might make useful consideration are not given opportunities—and if this differential treatment contributes to ongoing social divisions and to the continuation of racism, sexism, ageism, and other forms of unjust exclusion.

Again, consider the case of women serving in combat roles in the American military. In 2015, the U.S. military lifted its ban on women in combat. Prior to this decision, the military careers of women were limited because of a "brass ceiling": high-level military jobs tend to go to soldiers with combat experience. Proponents of combat roles for women argue that now individual women will have the opportunity to be judged on merit and ability, and not merely on their membership in a group. And it might be that female fighters and leaders in the military and in combat will bring different skills and insights to their role that would be lost if they were prevented from serving. As former army captain Tanya L. Domi concluded as women were finally given the opportunity to serve in combat, "With this momentous shift, America once again reaffirms its core values of equality and respect—values predicated on a person's capabilities and demonstrated competence, not an immutable characteristic like gender. This is good for our military, and our country too."[6]

Racism and Unjustified Discrimination

13.2 Explain concepts found in critical philosophical accounts of race and racism.

In addition to the principle of equality, another important component of social justice is the ideal of non-discrimination. Now, not all discrimination is bad or immoral. Rather, the moral problem is the issue of unjustified discrimination. A very basic definition of discrimination tells us that to discriminate is to distinguish between things, usually in ways that imply a judgment about what is better or worse. We say, for example, that someone has discriminating taste, which implies that they make good judgments about what is good or bad (say, with regard to food, wines, art, or music). As we shall see in the chapter on war and peace (Chapter 18), discrimination is viewed as a good thing in the ethics of war; the just war theory encourages soldiers and armies to discriminate between those who can legitimately be killed (combatants) and those who ought not be deliberately targeted or killed (noncombatants). But in this chapter, we are primarily concerned with *unjust* discrimination. In this negative sense, discrimination is unjustified differential treatment, especially on the basis of characteristics such as race, ethnicity, gender, sexual orientation, religion, age, or ability. Unjustified discrimination is wrong based on the principle of equality, since it treats people who ought to be treated equally in ways that are not equitable, fair, or just.

The goal of eliminating unjustified discrimination is an established policy of the American legal system, with a variety of civil rights laws focused on preventing and finding remedies for it. The Civil Rights Act of

1964 explicitly states that its goal is to "provide relief from discrimination" and to "prevent discrimination" in public and federally funded programs and institutions.[7] This idea has led to the development of explicit equal opportunity clauses that appear in policy statements and contracts for a variety of institutions. The Equal Employment Opportunity Commission (EEOC) explains its mission as follows: "The EEOC's core mission is to prevent and remedy discrimination in America's workplaces and advance equal employment opportunity for all." And it explains its own antidiscrimination policy as follows:

> EEOC employees and applicants for employment are covered by federal laws and Presidential Executive Orders designed to safeguard federal employees and job applicants from discrimination on the basis of race, color, religion, sex (including pregnancy, gender identity, and sexual orientation), parental status, national origin, age, disability, genetic information (including family medical history), political affiliation, military service, or other non-merit based factors.[8]

This exemplary statement of nondiscrimination provides an extensive list of factors that should *not* be considered as relevant to employment. Indeed, as the statement's conclusion implies, the only relevant consideration should be "merit." Most workplaces in the United States have a similar statement of nondiscrimination and are supposed to adhere to this kind of policy in their hiring, promotion, and other practices.

Racial Discrimination

While each of the potentially discriminatory factors listed in the EEOC statement is worthy of further consideration—involving unjustified discrimination based on disability, age, national origin, political affiliation, and so on—in this section, we'll look more closely at the issue of *racial* discrimination and racism as a paradigmatic example of the problem of unjustified discrimination. At issue in thinking about racial discrimination is the very question of what constitutes race, as well as the role that racial discrimination has played in the past and the role it continues to play in the contemporary world. Racial discrimination occurs when there is unjustified differential treatment given to someone based on their racial identity (or perceived racial identity). It is easy to see that unjustified differential treatment based on race is a violation of the principle of equality. However, things get complicated when we think about possible remedies for past racial injustice—such as affirmative action or reparations. Would it be just to give preference to members of groups that were previously discriminated against or to provide grants, loans, or other payments to communities that have been harmed by past racism? Some claim that affirmative action programs are another form of unjustified discrimination—sometimes called by its critics "reverse discrimination" and even "reverse racism." But defenders of such programs claim that it is justified as a way of promoting equity and that reparations can be justified as a way of honoring victims and supporting communities that have been damaged by racism.

Race, Racialism, and Critical Philosophies of Race

One significant philosophical problem in discussions of racial discrimination is the very idea of race, a category that attempts to identify similarities among diverse individuals. Some may deny that race and racial differences matter, arguing that supposed racial differences are merely skin-deep and that we should look beyond race to a sort of "color-blind" equality of persons. Others will argue that in today's world, race still remains a powerful concept with deep historical roots that helps to explain ongoing inequality and discrimination. One issue that arises in thinking critically about race connects us back to the question of group membership discussed previously. Racial stereotypes—whether positive or negative—are based on generalizations about groups. These generalizations treat different people in groups as if they were all alike. But as we've noted previously, individuals do not fit neatly into such categories. How can biracial or multiracial people be identified, for example, in a system of fixed categories? An uncritical use of racial categories may involve a reductive approach to identity that keeps individuals confined within categories that ignore a deeper kind of diversity—and that may impose categories on people that they did not choose for themselves and that they do not identify with. When this kind of categorization is based on negative stereotypes about members of that group that are used to justify practices that are oppressive of those people, this is racism.

Philosophers and other scholars ask critical questions about race and racism. One question to be asked is whether race is something real—a fact of biology, for example—or whether race is a social construction. In asking this question, we are considering the ontological status of race—that is, we are asking a question about the being and existence of race. This question is important as we go on to think about the moral, social, and political implications of race and racism.

In asking these sorts of questions, we are engaged in an effort that has come to be known as the "critical philosophy of race."[9] In the background of this broad philosophical inquiry into race and racism is a movement and approach known as "critical race theory." Critical race theory was originally focused on a critique of the way race, racism, and racial privilege were manifest in the legal system in the United States. But the idea has been pushed much farther. The philosopher Cornel West has explained that critical race theory is a "comprehensive movement in thought and life" that "compels us to confront critically the most explosive issue in American civilization: the historical centrality and complicity of law in upholding white supremacy (and concomitant hierarchies of gender, class, and sexual orientation)."[10]

This focus on the critique of white supremacy in law and culture has led critics to single out critical race theory (sometimes abbreviated as CRT) in recent years. The idea of critical race theory has come under fire recently in well-publicized public forums in which conservative thinkers in the United States have claimed that it teaches a one-sided and negative view of American history and that it suggests that all white people are racist. As a result, a number of American states have banned its teaching.[11] One of the leaders in this effort was the state of Florida. In 2022, the state banned the teaching of critical race theory. The governor of Florida, Ron DeSantis explained this by saying, "No one should be instructed to feel as if they are not equal or shamed because of their race. In Florida, we will not let the far-left woke agenda take over our schools and workplaces. There is no place for indoctrination or discrimination in Florida."[12] The state's lieutenant governor Jeanette

Nuñez further explained, "By signing this legislation, which is the first in the nation to end corporate wokeness and Critical Race Theory in our schools, we are prioritizing education not indoctrination."[13] This effort to ban critical race theory raises a number of interesting ethical questions relating to the role of public education in teaching about and responding to racism.

And, of course, in the background is the question of white supremacy in American history. This question has been a focal point of significant public debate, stimulated in part by the publication in 2019 of the *1619 Project*, a journalistic project and book by Nikole Hannah-Jones, which claimed that the history of slavery was central to the founding and subsequent history of the United States.[14] In response, conservatives in the United States offered a different account of history that was published as the *1776 Project* by a commission appointed by the then-President Donald Trump.[15] As one might imagine, these rival versions of American history provoked controversy and conversation.

It is clear that question of race and racism continue to be on people's minds. And despite the social and political pushback against critical race theory, the critical scholarship regarding race and racism continues to develop. The literature in the critical philosophy of race asks significant questions about human identity, the nature of human groups, our tendency to deal in stereotypes, remedies to oppression and injustice, and the past and ongoing legacy of racism. It also reminds us of the importance of the principle of equality and the related critique of unjustified discrimination. We cannot consider all of these issues here; instead, we will touch briefly on a few.

Let's consider the ontological status of race. Racial differences have often been held to be natural biological differences. Racial distinctions have been drawn based on such factors as appearance, blood (as in the idea of a "blood quantum" or proportion of one's "blood" inherited from ancestors of a given race), geographic location, and DNA and gene frequency. However, it is difficult to clearly define the sorts of biological differences that might create racial identity. It is also difficult to narrow down the number of races of human beings. Depending on which characteristics and criteria are employed, anthropologists have classified the human species into different races. But there is no agreement about the number of races or what criteria should be used to distinguish one race from another. Thus, any strictly biological definition of race is seriously flawed, leading some to claim that the idea of race is arbitrary and subjective.[16] One problem is that human populations have rarely been isolated in ways that would limit genetic intermingling. Indeed, even if we were able to isolate populations in this way, there would be substantial overlap among the supposedly different races, and individuals within a given racial or ethnic group show substantial genetic variation. Another problem with genetic accounts of race is that human populations across the globe do not vary that much from one another genetically. As one study from thirty years ago concludes, "the major stereotypes, all based on skin color, hair color and form, and facial traits, reflect superficial differences that are not confirmed by deeper analysis with more reliable genetic traits and whose origin dates from recent evolution mostly under the effect of climate and perhaps sexual selection."[17] The consensus of more recent work on the topic is that race is not a biological category—but rather a social construct. In 2021, an article in the journal *Science* explained, "Human geneticists have mostly abandoned the word 'race' when describing populations in their papers. . . . That's in line with the current scientific understanding that race is a social construct."[18] The point is that race is a category that was made up for social purposes and that it tracks very minor genetic or biological differences.

While we should be wary of reductive biological accounts of racial differences—especially those racial categories that are used to unjustly discriminate—we might want to consider a genetic basis of something like "race" for benign purposes. In thinking about this, we might want to follow the lead of those human geneticists mentioned here and be more precise in our language by focusing on genetic heritage or ancestry and yet the term "race" continues to be employed in popular and scholarly discussions. And population-specific genetic variations, ancestry, and "race" are worth considering in relation to questions about human health. Different ethnic and racial groups may have different susceptibilities to disease, for example. Thus, it is important to understand how medical treatments affect

different genetically related groups. It would be beneficial to understand how these differences affect susceptibility to diseases such as sickle cell anemia, diabetes, and hypertension. It would be useful to determine why certain groups suffer differential rates of high blood pressure and heart attacks, for example, by finding genetic variants or mutations that may be involved in these conditions. Such information might help scientists design drugs or treatments for people in these groups.

Nevertheless, the conceptual and scientific basis for race remains highly contested. Philosophers have been discussing this question for many years. At the end of the nineteenth century, W. E. B. Du Bois articulated an understanding of race as a social, historical, and spiritual entity—one that had as much to do with language and traditions as it did with biology.[19] More recently, Kwame Anthony Appiah has argued that the idea of firm and essential differences among the races is false. (See the excerpt from Appiah at the end of this chapter.) Appiah uses the term "racialism" to describe the problematic notion that there are firm distinctions among races and that these distinctions point toward some substantive difference among people. As Appiah explains, racialism attempted to identify characteristics of people that went deeper than "the visible morphological characteristics—skin color, hair type, facial features—on the basis of which we make our informal classifications."[20] Appiah argues that the superficial characteristics that people use to distinguish among the races are not tied to a deeper essential difference. Another problem for racialist views is that there is a long history of people marrying, having children, and raising families across so-called racial divides. In many cases, it is difficult for people to decide how they might identify themselves based on antiquated racial categories. Critics of racialism generally agree that race is a social construct, made up for social purposes, which are not clearly grounded in hard and fast natural distinctions. Not everyone agrees with Appiah's deflationary analysis of the concept of race. For example, Lucius Outlaw Jr. argues that race is not merely a social construction. Outlaw points out that genetic differences exist that help explain morphological differences, and that these differences are actually created in part by cultural practices (such as marriage and reproduction practices, which have often been racially exclusive).

Building on his interpretation of the work of W. E. B. Du Bois, Outlaw argues that the existence of cultural, historical, and biological groupings should not be denied or neglected.[21] Indeed, from this point of view, oppressed racial groups may benefit from affirming their own racial identity, which may help solidify social power in the struggle for equal treatment. From this standpoint, to deny the importance of race is to ignore the reality of struggles for equality in the world. Outlaw suggests that race "continues to be a major fulcrum of struggles over the distribution and exercise of power."[22]

Whether we think that race should be deconstructed and discarded as a mere social construct without any basis in biology or whether we think that race remains an important and useful concept, the ethical question is whether racial categories are used to make *unjust* discriminatory judgments, which are typically described as racist.

Racism Now we are ready to discuss racism. **Racism** makes race a significant factor in the unjust treatment of people. It distinguishes between groups of people in ways that lead to the creation of unequal, oppressive, or hierarchical social conditions. Racism can be overtly written into laws and social codes such as in systems of legal racial apartheid. Or it can occur in more subtle systems of social organization that produce disparate social opportunities and outcomes for different racial groups in cases that are described as embodying **structural racism** (to be discussed further in a moment).

Racism has psychological implications for those who are on both the top and the bottom of racially structured social systems. Ibram X. Kendi, a Black American, explained this as follows in his account of the way that anti-Black racism in the United States influenced him.

> Racist ideas make people of color think less of themselves, which makes them more vulnerable to racist ideas. Racist ideas make White people think more of themselves, which further attracts them to racist ideas.[23]

Racism involves not only making distinctions and grouping people, but also denigration and unjustified discrimination. It violates the principle of equality insofar as it results in unequal treatment. It involves the false belief that all persons of a certain race are inferior or superior to persons of other races in some way. Racism appears to be unjust to individuals not just because such generalizations are false, but also because individuals do not choose their own racial identity. Rather, in a racist society, individuals are oppressed and identified within a system of categorization that they did not choose. Similarly, racist individuals or racial supremacists who celebrate their own race take credit for something over which they have no control.

This explains how we might appeal to Kantian moral language to argue against racism (despite the fact that Kant himself was racist, as we discussed in Chapter 6). Racism is wrong from a Kantian perspective because it violates the autonomy of persons, failing to respect

Figure 13-1 W.E.B. Du Bois (1868–1963) is a founding figure in the philosophy of race.

John Deakin/Picture Post/Hulton Archive /Getty Images

them as ends in themselves. Notice that this argument against racism is somewhat different from a utilitarian argument against racism. The utilitarian argument against racism would point out that racism produces harm and unhappiness. We might also note that the natural law theory may offer a different argument about the wrongness of racism, based on a claim about the inherent dignity of all human persons. A similar claim may be made from the standpoint of a theory of human rights, which would claim that racism violates the inherent right of all people to be treated as full members of the human family.

Let's return to the issue of unjustified discrimination. As we noted previously, not all discrimination is wrong. There is nothing inherently wrong with noting our physical differences. In the abstract, it would seem that believing that someone is shorter than another or stronger is not necessarily objectionable, especially if the belief is true. However, what makes racism wrong is that it involves making false judgments about people and their worth. It also involves power and oppression: those false generalizations and judgments are used to subordinate some people and empower others. By noting the unjustified nature of the discrimination that happens in racism, we can distinguish racism from other cases in which noting racial differences is justifiable and benevolent. The example we discussed before about racial differences in health care and public health outcomes provides an example. It is not racist to note that there are disparities in health outcomes among racial groups or that members of some racial groups are more likely to be harmed by certain diseases. Noting these kinds of facts would be racist if we drew from these facts the conclusion that members of that racial group were therefore inferior or deserved to be oppressed. But it is not racist to note these facts, if by noting them good outcomes are produced.

This brings us to the question of whether talking about racism is itself racist. There are some who argue that by continuing to focus on racial differences, we continue to operate in a racially segregated world and thereby contribute to ongoing racism. From this point of view, the claim is made that it would be better "not to see color" or to be "color-blind." Sometimes this idea is taken a step further by those who claim that it

is racist to continue to talk about racism. In response to this kind of claim, Ibram X. Kendi has argued that the opposite of racism is not simply ignoring racism. Rather, he maintains that the opposite of racism is "anti-racism." In other words, Kendi suggests that it is not racist to note that there are differential racial outcomes in society or that there are racists in the world. Rather than ignoring racism, by naming it and opposing it, we become anti-racists. (A short excerpt from Kendi is included among the primary source readings for this chapter.)

Structural Racism and Implicit Bias Racism is usually thought of in terms of the attitudes and behaviors of individuals. However, racism and other forms of oppression also occur at the level of institutions and social structures.[24] **Structural** or **institutional racism** occurs when social structures and institutions are set up in ways that are oppressive or produce unfair and unequal outcomes. It may be more difficult to see institutional or structural oppression if we uncritically take social structures for granted. Moreover, nonbiased individuals may be working within a system that produces racially biased outcomes. These individuals may not be racist themselves—even if the system or institution produces undeserved unequal outcomes.

Consider this issue in the context of education. Education is often thought of as the great equalizer and a path for upward mobility. However, educational outcomes are often strikingly unequal in the United States. Poor urban schools in predominantly non-White neighborhoods typically have lower standardized test scores and lower graduation rates than affluent, largely White schools in the suburbs. The problem is not typically that teachers or administrators are racist. Rather, the problem may be that present (and past) institutions have been set up in ways that reinforce disparate outcomes.

Consider one example that may be familiar to American college students, regarding the issue of standardized tests such as the SAT and the ACT. These tests were once widely used as important components of a college application. But the tests have often been criticized as making manifest the problem of structural racism. A significant problem is that Black and Latinx or

Hispanic students generally score lower on these tests than White or Asian students. For example, in 2021, the average scores on the SAT, broken down by demographic category, were as follows.[25]

> White: 562 (verbal); 550 (math); 1112 (total)
> Black: 477 (verbal); 457 (math); 934 (total)
> Hispanic: 490 (verbal); 477 (math); 967 (total)
> Asian: 597 (verbal); 642 (math); 1239 (total)

This kind of racial disparity in the test is typical of an ongoing pattern and has long been noted as an area of concern. The authors of a recent Brookings Institution report on this issue conclude, "Black and Hispanic or Latino students routinely score lower on the math section of the SAT—a likely result of generations of exclusionary housing, education, and economic policy—which too often means that, rather than reducing existing race gaps, using the test in college admissions reinforces them."[26] That interpretation of the data points to the idea of structural racism. The idea is that Black and Hispanic students tend to come from school districts and social circumstances that make academic achievement (as measured by the SAT) more difficult. To see that this is a matter of structural racism, note that the authors of the SAT and the educational establishment that supports it are not overtly racist and do not intend that the test should have these racially disparate outcomes. But those disparities exist and are reflected in the test scores. Furthermore, there is a concern about a vicious cycle here. Low test scores may impair future earnings and educational opportunities for Black and Latinx people, as their lower scores prevent them from attending more selective universities and gaining advantages that may be passed on to their children. A test that reflects racial disparities may end up unintentionally contributing to those disparities.

Critics of the SAT and other standardized tests have argued that these tests are culturally biased. For example, the verbal portion of the test may rely on references and associations tied to a particular class or cultural background. Children from middle- and high-income families with access to well-funded schools will have an advantage over other children. To see that economics matter, bear in mind that children of affluent parents can afford to take expensive SAT preparation courses. This has led one critic to claim, "The SAT is increasingly a wealth test, and it provides the highest scores for those who have the most opportunity in society."[27] This is not necessarily the fault of any of the parents or children involved. Rather, it is a feature of the structure of institutions that results in unequal outcomes.

Those who seek to remedy institutional and structural disparities remind us that these institutions could be organized differently. We could devote greater funds to schools in neighborhoods that serve Black and Hispanic students so that children will have more opportunities to succeed later in life. Or colleges and universities could offer greater financial aid and other forms of assistance to students from low socioeconomic backgrounds. Further, we could encourage schools or employers to take positive steps ("affirmative action") to recruit and train applicants from diverse racial, ethnic, and socioeconomic backgrounds. In recent years, as a result of the critique of structural racism in testing, a significant change has occurred. Many elite schools have eliminated their use of these kinds of exams. As of 2022, the SAT is no longer used in admissions to public universities in the state of California.[28]

As we conclude this discussion of structural racism as it appears in academic settings, it is worth noting that not all racial and ethnic minority groups are underrepresented and disadvantaged. As the data cited above indicate, Asian students perform better on the SAT than do Black, Hispanic, or White students. This kind of data can be used to support the idea of Asian Americans as a "model minority," that is, a high-achieving and well-adjusted racial minority. And in discussions about racial quotas and access to educational opportunities, there has been some pushback from Asian communities who worry that they would be disadvantaged by a policy that attempted to equalize university admissions, since high-scoring Asian students may be overrepresented in the demographic distribution of university students. This issue was a focal point of the 2022 Supreme Court case we discussed previously, in which those arguing against the admissions policies at Harvard and other schools claimed that affirmative action programs discriminated against Asian American students.[29] This issue is complicated by the fact that the very category

"Asian American" is an oversimplification that obscures significant difference among communities. The category encompasses Japanese Americans, Chinese Americans, Indian Americans, Pakistani Americans, as well as immigrants and descendants of immigrants from Southeast Asia (Laos, Thailand, Vietnam), the Philippines, Indonesia, and so on. (A broader category has evolved to include Asian American and Pacific Islanders, which is abbreviated as AAPI.) These diverse people have different cultural practices, immigration histories, and community identities. This is one of the reasons that scholars have often questioned the idea of the Asian "model minority myth."[30] And indeed, it is possible that the model minority myth is itself racist—insofar as it lumps many different people together into one category that ignores the differences and individuality of those who are categorized in this way.

Another potential source of structural racism may be racial stereotyping that occurs in the media. To illustrate another issue that impacts the Asian American community, we might note that while Asian Americans are sometimes viewed as a "model minority," there are also stereotyping and unflattering representations of Asians and Asian Americans in television and in films. It is worth asking ourselves what kinds of stereotypes and caricatures we see in the media about racial groups—and what kind of impact those stereotypes have on society as a whole. How does what you are seeing in the media reinforce racism? What would things look like in the media if we were more actively attempting to end racism? Of significant concern are negative stereotypes involving Black people. A 2008 analysis by Travis Dixon, an expert on stereotypes in the media, concludes, "African Americans typically occupy roles as poor people, loud politicians, and criminals on network news."[31] There is evidence that these stereotypical depictions can negatively impact people's judgments about individual African Americans. Dixon conducted a related study in which he examined how attitudes about crime and race correspond to media viewing habits. He concludes that "exposure to Blacks' overrepresentation as criminals on local news programming was positively related to the perception of Blacks as violent."[32] This kind of research—and numerous other examples—supports the idea of **implicit bias**. People who do not directly admit to having racist

attitudes may still have biased attitudes toward members of different racial groups (as well as bias toward gender identity, sexual orientation, religion, disability, etc.). It is not that those of us who are implicitly biased (and there is a good chance that we all harbor implicit biases) are lying or denying our biases and prejudices. Rather, the biases are often unconscious, and well-meaning individuals may not be aware of their own racial (and other) biases.

Critics of structural racism argue that things could be different; news organizations could de-emphasize race in their coverage of crime stories and focus instead on economic issues, for example. And the more we are aware of our implicit biases, the better we will be able at correcting for biased and prejudicial outcomes. Those who are concerned with structural racism will argue that structural and institutional changes must be made to remedy the unequal outcomes that occur in society. It is not enough for individuals to overcome racist attitudes; the institutions must be changed and proactive remedies must be employed to respond to racially disparate outcomes. One example of this is affirmative action, which we discuss in more detail below.

Intersectionality and Other Forms of Discrimination

13.3 Apply the concept of intersectionality to discussions of inequality.

As we noted in the previous section, there are different types of racism that manifest themselves in different ways in different contexts. AAPI people may experience discrimination that is different from what is experienced by Blacks, Latinx, and Native American individuals. And even within these groups, there will be differences. In order to account for these differences, let's introduce another concept that is important in thinking about inequalities and discrimination—the notion of **intersectionality**. Intersectionality is the idea that discrimination occurs in different ways depending on the intersection of identities that make up the life of real people.

We have considered racism as one example of unjustified discrimination. Similar issues come up in consideration of other forms of discrimination. Consider gender discrimination, which we discussed in more detail in Chapter 9. At the end of that chapter, we noted that some philosophers, such as Judith Butler, argue that gender is a social construction—an argument that can be seen as similar to Appiah's claim that race is a social construction. Feminists also speak of structural or institutional gender discrimination, which occurs when institutions are set up in ways that privilege men and unjustifiably harm women. For example, while the average income of women compared to that of men has improved over the years, in 2022 women on average still only earned 83 percent of what men earned.[33]

This gender wage gap also has a racial element, with Hispanic and Black women earning the least. One analysis from 2022 concluded, "American Indian and Native Alaskan women and Hispanic women are more likely to occupy lower paying jobs. Black women are most likely to be paid less despite having the same level of experience and other compensable factors as white men doing the same job."[34]

Intersectionality obviously includes the intersection of race and gender that we've mentioned here. It might also include the intersection of sexual orientation, religion, ability, age, geography, and so on. Kimberlé Crenshaw is credited with introducing the term "intersectionality." Crenshaw is a feminist legal theorist who has also contributed to discussions of critical race theory. She has defined intersectionality as an attempt to link "multiple systems of subordination," which can also be called "compound discrimination, multiple burdens, or double or triple discrimination."[35] She further explains:

> Intersectionality is a conceptualization of the problem that attempts to capture both the structural and dynamic consequences of the interaction between two or more axes of subordination. It specifically addresses the manner in which racism, patriarchy, class oppression and other discriminatory systems create background inequalities that structure the relative positions of women, races, ethnicities, classes—and the like.[36]

The lens of intersectionality allows us to see and consider these various and overlapping ways in which unjustified discrimination occur. When combined with the idea of structural racism, this provides a powerful tool for understanding inequality. It is easy to understand how a structural or institutional analysis, informed by intersectionality, can be used to explain the gender and racial wage gap. Those who do so-called women's work—traditionally, teaching, nursing, food service, and so on—have historically been underpaid. And when women are encouraged by society to take those kinds of typically lower-paying jobs, they end up making less money. The same kinds of historically unfair conditions exist for women of color. And when race and gender intersect, there can be multiple layers of discrimination and inequality.

This discussion of intersectionality invites us to consider the ways that various forms of discrimination occur and overlap. Forty-three million Americans have one or more physical or mental disabilities. Substantial legal efforts have been made to remove barriers and expand opportunities for such individuals, most notably the Americans with Disabilities Act (ADA) of 1990. But individuals with disabilities are still disadvantaged in many areas. Although fewer people with disabilities are confined to their homes or institutionalized, stereotypes and stigma remain. And social institutions are sometimes set up in ways that create structural and institutional impediments for those with both physical and intellectual disabilities. For example, many private businesses still provide no alternatives to steps and staircases for customers in wheelchairs. The architects and planners who designed buildings with such features were not necessarily actively discriminating against people with disabilities, but they did not consider how their designs caused systematic hardship. The ADA requires that new construction and remodeling include ramps, if necessary, to give people with physical disabilities greater access.

Age can also be grounds for unjust discrimination and stereotyping. Older workers are subjected to arbitrary age limits in employment, as, for example, when age alone, rather than judgments of individual job performance, is used to dismiss someone. Discrimination also occurs against lesbian, gay, bisexual, and transgender people (LGBTQ), a topic we discussed in Chapter 12. Religious minorities can also be discriminated against, which includes among other problems anti-Semitism, Islamophobia, anti-Mormon sentiment, and other forms of religious bigotry. Poor people can suffer discrimination, and so on. With the lens of intersectionality, we can see that there may be relevant differences in thinking about how discrimination and structural inequalities are experienced by different people. Intersectionality also directs attention toward the oppression and disadvantage experienced by those whose identities intersect with more than one marginalized group.

Applying the Principle of Equality

In concluding this section, let's return to the principle of equality, which provides us with the primary argument against racism and other forms of discrimination. The ideal of equal treatment and equal respect for all people regardless of race, ethnicity, sex, sexual orientation, national origin, and religion is an important goal, one that contemporary societies are still working to achieve. As we've seen in this section, there are complex conceptual issues that need to be considered in thinking about how we might apply the principle of equality in the real world. It is one thing to say that racism is wrong and that people should be treated fairly and equitably. But what might that look like in a world in which there are disputes about the meaning, reality, and implications of racism and other forms of discrimination? What might the principle of equality tell us about concrete proposals for social justice in a world in which there are intersectional identities? How does that principle help to resolve disputes about race and racism? And what kinds of remedies might be justified in a world in which structures and institutions create racially disparate outcomes? In the next section we will consider some examples with regard to preferential treatment programs, reparations, racial profiling, and hate crimes.

▶ Knowledge Check   Answers appear at the end of the chapter.

1. How is the principle of equality related to the idea of social justice?
   a. Justice requires that we punish crimes and reward good deeds. The principle of equality creates a scheme of justified social punishment.
   b. Justice encourages us to treat similar things in similar ways. The principle of equality helps us make sure social goods are fairly distributed.
   c. Justice is whatever is legally required by the social system. The principle of equality aims to make sure that all people in society obey the law equally.
   d. Justice is a relative concept, defined in different ways by different societies. The principle of equality is a kind of relativism that demands that we treat all social systems and theories of justice equally.

2. Which of the following is *false* with regard to race and racism?
   a. Race is viewed by most contemporary scholars as a social construction.
   b. Racism occurs when negative stereotypes about racial groups are used to create unjust social systems.
   c. There can be benign reasons for acknowledging racial differences and disparities in health care, education, and other fields.
   d. Anti-racists do not believe that race or racism exists and advocate instead for a color-blind view of the world.

3. What would we call it when there are significant racial disparities that are reflected in and produced by social systems?
   a. Racialism
   b. Structural racism
   c. Implicit bias
   d. Dynamic inequality

4. Which concept applies when we take note of the fact that older Black women earn less money than young White women, older White men, or young Asian men?
   a. Affirmative action
   b. Implicit bias
   c. Intersectionality
   d. Institutional neglect

Current Issues

Police Brutality and Black Lives Matter

In 2013, a movement known as "Black Lives Matter" appeared as a response to a series of killings in which unarmed Black men were shot by police or died while in police custody. The killing of George Floyd in 2020 provides an important recent example. But before George Floyd was murdered, there were a number of similar high-profile cases: Oscar Grant in Oakland, California (2009); Michael Brown in Ferguson, Missouri (2014); Eric Garner in New York (2014); Tamir Rice— a 12-year-old—in Cleveland, Ohio (2014); Freddie Gray in Baltimore, Maryland (2015); Philando Castile in Minneapolis, Minnesota (2016); Alton Sterling in Baton Rouge, Louisiana (2016). And there have been other, more recent examples. In the summer of 2022, Jayland Walker, an unarmed Black man, was shot more than sixty times by police in Akron, Ohio.[37] We might also include the case of Trayvon Martin, an unarmed 17-year-old who was shot by George Zimmerman in 2012 in Florida, although this case was not a case of police brutality: Zimmerman was a "neighborhood watch" coordinator, not a police officer. In a number of cases, the killers were acquitted—as happened with Zimmerman, who claimed that he killed Martin in self-defense. As a response to the Trayvon Martin killing and other acts of police brutality, in 2013, three activists—Alicia Garza, Patrisse Cullors, and Opal Tometi—responded to public outrage by creating a hashtag, #BlackLivesMatter, that gave birth to a movement. This idea has evolved into a global movement to oppose police brutality and in general to advocate for the civil rights of Black people.

In response to these killings and others, massive protests and civil unrest have broken out in a number of American cities during the past decade. These protests were particularly confrontational in the aftermath of the killing of George Floyd, as anger and anxiety about COVID-19 lockdown combined with social justice outrage to produce a particularly volatile situation. In some cities, such as Portland, Oregon, the protests lasted for months. One highly publicized moment occurred in Washington, D.C., when officials used tear gas to disrupt and disperse protestors who had gathered at the White House to demonstrate against the killing of Floyd. Former President Trump walked from the White House to St. John's Episcopal Church in a symbolic act. Trump had called for "law and order" in response to the nationwide protests, calling those who were protesting "thugs" and expressing support for police forces.[38] The president had also referred to the Black Lives Matter movement as a "symbol of hate" in arguing against New York City's plan to paint a mural stating "Black Lives Matter" on Fifth Avenue in front of Trump Tower.[39] This is a reminder of the fact that not everyone supports the idea of the Black Lives Matter movement and the protests that have erupted after police killings of Black people. Trump seemed especially concerned about animosity directed toward the police. Police officers have been ambushed and shot by individuals who claimed outrage over police brutality. Three police officers were killed in Baton Rouge in 2016. Five cops were killed in a related attack in Dallas in 2016. We will discuss political violence in Chapter 18 and criminal justice issues in Chapter 17. But we might note here that no theory of morality that we are discussing in this book would provide justification for police brutality or for attacks on police. Indeed, the general problem of racism in policing is a structural or institutional problem that requires comprehensive critique of the system of criminal justice. This includes using the system of criminal justice to prosecute officers who engage in police brutality.

Of course, the outrage that has driven Black Lives Matter protests was linked to the sense that those involved in these killings were not properly punished. The case of Trayvon Martin and George Zimmerman is often cited in this regard. In other cases, the police officers involved have often been acquitted, although this is not always true. The police officer who killed George Floyd, Derek Chauvin, was convicted of murder and sentenced to prison. Other officers involved in the George Floyd case, J. Alexander Kueng, Tou Thao, and Thomas Lane, were also convicted of various crimes involving violations of George Floyd's civil rights.[40] A related conviction occurred in the killing of Ahmaud Arbery, a Black man who was chased down and murdered in Georgia in 2020. His killers were three White men—who were convicted of murder in 2021.

Police brutality is a subject of concern, which might properly be addressed in a chapter on criminal justice and punishment (see Chapter 17). In that chapter, we also discuss issues involving racial disparities in sentencing and in incarceration rates, which are issues that can also be analyzed in terms of structural racism. But here, let's consider police brutality in connection with the problem of violations of civil rights. The police are supposed to protect and serve, as the saying goes—and this is supposed to be a matter of equal protection for everyone, without bias. Unjustified police violence is obviously wrong, no matter who it is directed toward. But police brutality connects with issues of social justice when those on the receiving end of police brutality are Black people and members of other marginalized communities whose civil rights have been historically violated by the criminal justice system. And as critics have pointed out, this is a problem that is connected to systematic racism and implicit bias, as the police tend to harbor prejudices about Black people and to use more forceful tactics against Black people, as we discuss in a moment in relation to racial profiling.

Some have responded to the Black Lives Matter movement by arguing that "All Lives Matter" (a motto some counterprotesters have used when they have spoken up in defense of law enforcement). Other counterprotesters have claimed that "Blue Lives Matter," establishing their solidarity with the police. There is no doubt that the Black Lives Matter activists believe that all lives matter, but those activists maintain that our society perpetuates racist discrimination in which the lives of Black people matter less than the lives of others. And these activists will point to institutional and systemic structures that create a world of unequal outcomes, including problems such as implicit bias (which causes people—the police included—to respond negatively to Black individuals or associate them with crime) and **racial profiling** (through which police engage in tactics that target people based on racial identity). Defenders of police action claim that the police must do a difficult and dangerous job and that most officers of the law are not racist. Critics argue that structural racism plagues the criminal justice system and informs police tactics that inflict disproportional harm on Black people.

Of course, those critics are appealing to something like the principle of equality, which holds that it is wrong for police to engage in biased policing and that there is something morally wrong with the unequal outcomes they are criticizing. It might be that the principle of equality also guides the thinking of those who are critical of the Black Lives Matter movement. It is likely that those who "support the blue," as the saying goes, believe that police are in fact guided by the principle of equality insofar as police are required by law to defend the law and to uphold the civil rights of people. Perhaps common ground can be found in some basic agreement about the importance of equality, fairness, and justice in policing and in response to police brutality.

But this may take some work. Consider the case of Breonna Taylor in Louisville, Kentucky. In 2020, Taylor, a Black woman, was shot in her apartment by three police officers who were part of a team that burst into the apartment in search of a drug dealing operation. Taylor was not a drug dealer. After an investigation, one officer, Brett Hankison, was put on trial. He was found not guilty in 2022. This verdict outraged those who saw this as yet another case of a White police officer getting away with murder. But by the summer of 2022, Hankison and the other three officers were accused of civil rights violations by Federal authorities. These separate charges indicate how legal authorities might deal with issues of police brutality. First there may be an investigation into the act by local authorities. This might be followed up by investigations by federal authorities regarding civil rights violations. Something similar

Figure 13-2 The Black Lives Matter movement began in 2013 as a protest against anti-Black racism.

Joseph Sohm/Shutterstock

happened in the case of Derek Chauvin. He was convicted by state authorities of murdering George Floyd. He later pleaded guilty to the federal crime of violating Floyd's civil rights.

Civil Rights

Civil rights laws enacted in the United States and other Western countries have proved to be powerful tools for reducing racial injustice and promoting equal treatment of citizens. When we speak of *civil rights*, we are referring primarily to rights that are granted by the government—they are rights of civil or political society, so-called rights of citizenship. Civil rights can be contrasted with the idea of natural rights or human rights, which we discussed in Chapter 7. Some may think these rights are synonymous. To understand the difference between civil rights and human rights, you might consider whether citizens should have different rights than noncitizens. Most civil societies do recognize a difference between the rights of citizens and the natural rights possessed by noncitizens. Civil rights are sometimes thought of as applications of or means for the protection of more basic human rights. As Thomas Paine explained, "every civil right grows out of a natural right; or in other words, is a natural right exchanged."[41] Thus, the right to vote may be understood as the result of certain democratic social and political arrangements. Such a right is ultimately based on some other claim about natural rights, such as the right to liberty or self-governance. In the United States, civil rights are thought to rest on constitutional bases, such as the rights enumerated in the Bill of Rights (the first ten amendments to the Constitution, which were ratified in 1791).

From the founding of the United States onward, there were deep and often violent conflicts about which members of society should be granted civil rights—most notably with regard to the issue of slavery. Enslaved Africans had become an integral part of the American colonies' culture and economy long before the nation's independence from Britain. By the time the founding documents were written, slavery was so ingrained in America, particularly in the South, that its presence was officially affirmed in Article I of the Constitution. (Enslaved people were to be counted as three-fifths of a person for purposes of taxation and representation.) Thus, from the start, America's concept of civil rights for all "men" explicitly excluded several categories of people living in America (women were also excluded from many of these civil rights, including the right to vote).

In the nineteenth century, grassroots movements to abolish slavery developed in America, particularly among Northern religious constituencies. As the abolitionist movement gained political traction, a stark regional conflict arose between North and South, a struggle that culminated in the Civil War. In 1868, after the Civil War ended slavery in the United States, the Fourteenth Amendment to the Constitution was ratified. This amendment declares that no state may "deny to any person within its jurisdiction the equal protection of the law." The Fourteenth Amendment guaranteed full citizenship rights to adult males who were born or naturalized in the United States. (It was not until 1920 that women secured voting rights, with the ratification of the Nineteenth Amendment.) Although the Fourteenth Amendment established formal equality for males, the United States remained racially segregated after its passage due to a combination of laws known as "Jim Crow." The Jim Crow system in the American South included laws that restricted voting rights and others that kept Black people segregated from White people. A challenge to Jim Crow was mounted by Homer Plessy, a Black man who sat in a White-only railroad car. After he was arrested, he sued in a case that made it to the U.S. Supreme Court. The Court ruled in *Plessy v. Ferguson* (1896) that it was acceptable for states to create a segregated system based on the idea of "separate but equal." But the "equality" affirmed by this ruling was in name only; accommodations and services for Black Americans were invariably below the quality of those provided for White Americans. This legal system of segregation and discrimination continued largely unchallenged until the U.S. Supreme Court ruling *Brown v. Board of Education* (1954) overturned the idea that "separate but equal" schooling was justifiable. In 1955, Rosa Parks challenged the segregated bus system in Montgomery, Alabama, by sitting in a bus seat reserved for Whites. This prompted a bus boycott in Montgomery led by a young Baptist minister named Martin Luther King Jr.

The 1960s ushered in a host of significant civil rights legislation. In an executive order in 1961, President John F. Kennedy instituted affirmative action in government hiring and in governmental contracts with the goal of encouraging "by positive measures" equal opportunity for all qualified persons.[42] These new hiring procedures increased the number of African Americans in the employ of the federal government.[43] In 1965, President Lyndon B. Johnson issued enforcement procedures such as goals and timetables for hiring women and underrepresented people. The Equal Pay Act of 1963 required that male and female employees receive equal pay for substantially equal work. The landmark Civil Rights Act of 1964 prohibited a range of discriminatory practices by private employers, employment agencies, and unions; it also prohibited, among other things, discriminatory voter registration requirements. In 1965, the Voting Rights Act prohibited states from creating restrictions on voting that would "abridge the right of any citizen to vote based on race or color."

While the 1960s saw a broad expansion of civil rights protections, more recent decades have witnessed a narrowing of their scope and legal foundations. Take, for instance, affirmative action laws. In the 1978 *Bakke v. U.C. Davis Medical School* decision, the Supreme Court forbade the use of racial quotas in school admissions but allowed some consideration of race in admissions decisions. This decision was challenged by the 1995 decision *Adarand v. Pena*, which held that any race-conscious federal program must serve a "compelling state interest" and must be "narrowly tailored" to achieve its goal. However, in 2003, a less rigid standard for acceptance of a race-conscious program was used by the Court in its decision regarding the affirmative action practices of the University of Michigan. In *Grutter v. Bollinger*, the Court upheld the university's law school policy, which considers an applicant's race as one factor among others such as test scores, talent, and grade-point average in admissions. The Court rejected the undergraduate school's more mechanical practice of automatically giving extra points to applicants with specific racial backgrounds. The Court also gave added support to earlier rulings that there was a "compelling state interest" in racial diversity in education.[44] In an affirmative action case involving an employer, the 1979 *Weber v. Kaiser Aluminum* decision, the Court permitted a company to remedy its past discriminatory practices by using race as a criterion for admission to special training programs. These programs were aimed at ensuring that a percentage of Black persons equal to that in the local labor force could rise to managerial positions in the company.

In the 1990s, two significant pieces of civil rights legislation were passed: the Americans with Disabilities Act of 1990, which prohibited discrimination based on disability and was discussed previously, and the Civil Rights Act of 1991. The latter required that businesses using employment practices with a discriminatory impact (even if unintentional) must show that the practices are business necessities; otherwise, these businesses must reform their practices to eliminate this impact.[45] Hiring quotas were forbidden except when required by court order for rectifying wrongful past or present discrimination. Sexual harassment was also noted as a form of discrimination.

Many of the most recent advances in civil rights law have involved issues of sex, gender, and sexual harassment. Today, two forms of sexual harassment are generally recognized. One promises employment rewards for sexual favors, and the other creates a "hostile work environment." Sexual harassment also includes harassment based on sexual orientation or gender identity; discrimination based on these categories is also illegal in some, but not all, areas in the United States. A case decided by the Equal Employment Opportunity Commission in 2012 (*Macy v. Department of Justice*) established that Title VII of the Civil Rights Act of 1964 extends to protect transgendered persons against discrimination.[46] Other recent developments include the passage in 2009 of the Lilly Ledbetter Fair Pay Act, which guarantees an employee's right to fair compensation without discrimination.[47] The law is named after a supervisor at a Goodyear tire plant who experienced systematic pay discrimination based on gender for nearly two decades.

These are just a few of the highlights of the past 150 years of civil rights laws. And the law continues to evolve. It is possible that the Supreme Court may revisit some of the rulings mentioned above. For example, the decision in *Grutter v. Bollinger* has come up as an issue in a 2022 case involving university admission. A more thorough discussion might involve laws and court decisions that concern housing, lending, and the busing of school students, as well as laws that have been designed to prevent discrimination on the basis of religion, age, and other characteristics.

Profiling

One basic issue that arises in the context of civil rights law is the problem of profiling, which returns us to the question of law enforcement. Profiling happens when law enforcement agencies treat individuals as suspects simply because of their race, ethnicity, religion, or other traits.

Profiling has sometimes been endorsed by law enforcement agencies as a useful tool for identifying criminals. One example of this is so-called stop-and-frisk policing, in which police stop individuals and search for contraband or illegal activity. Although not obviously a form of racial profiling, it turns out that stop and frisk policing is often differentially applied. Critics complain that profiling leads to unjustified harassment. For example, African Americans have for decades reported being stopped by traffic police simply because they were Black—for the supposed crime of "driving while Black."[48] One analysis offered this data from traffic stops in Missouri in 2007:

> Blacks were 78 percent more likely than Whites to be searched. Hispanics were 118 percent more likely than whites to be searched. Compared to searches of White drivers, contraband was found 25 percent less often among Black drivers and 38 percent less often among Hispanic drivers.[49]

Police stopped Black and Hispanic drivers more often but found contraband at a lower rate among these drivers. This makes one wonder whether profiling of this sort is really effective, since it does not seem to serve the purpose of finding contraband.

Profiling is often connected to drug enforcement practices, such as the federal Drug Enforcement Administration's Operation Pipeline drug interdiction project. According to critics, in the 1980s and 1990s, police agencies involved in Operation Pipeline used racial profiling in their effort to stop drug traffickers on the highways.[50] U.S. courts have tended to rule that racial profiling is illegal—under the Constitution's Fourth Amendment protection against unreasonable searches and seizures and the Fourteenth Amendment requirement of equal protection under the law. But the practice continues. In 2010, the ACLU and the NAACP filed a lawsuit against the state of Maryland, alleging that the state police practiced racial profiling and demanding that the state turn over internal documents—a request that was affirmed by the Maryland Supreme Court in 2013. Similar issues have arisen in New York City, where a widespread policy of stop-and-frisk policing was criticized as relying heavily on racial profiling. According to ABC News in 2013, "While [B]lack and Hispanic residents make up only 23 percent and 29 percent of the city's population respectively, 84 percent of recorded stops are young men of color and only around 6 percent of stops lead to an arrest."[51] In 2013, a federal court ruled that the stop and frisk policy of New York had violated people's civil rights. When a new mayor Bill de Blasio, was elected in 2014, he ended the procedure. But the problem persists of racially differential policing. *The New York Times* reported the following in 2020: "Black teenagers, 16 and 17 years old, were nine times more likely to encounter police enforcement in 2018 than their White counterparts. That same year, Black people 18 to 20 years old were nearly eight times more likely to be stopped or arrested than Whites of the same age." And: "Black New Yorkers were still arrested and stopped at nearly twice the rate of the average city resident."[52] While stop-and-frisk policing was no longer official policy, there was still more substantial police presence in Black neighborhoods, which critics complain is still a kind of racial profiling.

Other recent events have raised concerns about profiling. In 2010, the governor of Arizona, Jan Brewer, signed into law Senate Bill 1070, which gave local police extensive power to enforce federal immigration law. The law was known as the "show me your papers" law. It intended to discourage illegal immigration, and its stated goal was to "discourage and deter the unlawful entry and presence of aliens and economic activity by persons unlawfully present in the United States."[53] The law authorized local police officers to stop people if they have a "reasonable suspicion" of their being unauthorized immigrants.[54] Police could demand that they show proof of citizenship without there being any indication of criminal activity. Other states, such as Alabama, Georgia, Indiana, South Carolina, and Utah, have modeled immigrations laws on the Arizona law. However, the Arizona law was soon legally contested, and parts of it were overturned by the U.S. Supreme Court in 2012. Nevertheless, the Court allowed law enforcement to act on "reasonable suspicion" that a person is an unauthorized immigrant, a standard that critics say encourages profiling and discrimination. They argue that racial and ethnic characteristics are the only possible basis for a "reasonable suspicion" that a person is in the United States illegally. Some immigration advocates call such legal measures "Juan Crow" laws—recalling the Jim Crow laws of the twentieth century, which discriminated against African Americans.[55] They cite cases of harassment and wrongful detention such as that of Antonio Montejano. In 2011, Montejano was stopped by the police on suspicion of shoplifting a $10 bottle of perfume. The shoplifting charge was dropped, but the police suspected him of being an illegal immigrant and held him on those grounds. He was incarcerated for four nights, until authorities confirmed that Montejano was in fact a U.S. citizen. Apparently, Montejano had triggered a positive identification in Homeland Security databases because he had been mistakenly deported in 1996. Montejano argued that he had been singled out for such treatment because "I look Mexican, 100 percent."[56] In 2022, there are still issues regarding racial profiling at the border. Apparently, profiling is still used by immigration and customs agents. This has led some scholars and activists to renew the call to ban profiling at the border.[57]

A different type of profiling involves suspicions based on a person's religion. Since the September 11 terrorist attacks, there have been a number of cases in which American Muslims have been harassed and profiled. For example, consider the 2006 case of six imams (Muslim religious leaders) detained at the Minneapolis–Saint Paul airport while trying to return from an Islamic conference. Several passengers and a gate agent complained that the imams' behavior was suspicious. They said the imams had knelt and prayed loudly at the boarding gate and made anti-American comments. When the imams boarded their U.S. Airways flight, they sat in different places throughout the plane, and a couple of them asked for seat belt extenders with heavy buckles on the ends. In response to the reports of fellow passengers, security personnel asked the six imams to leave the plane before takeoff. When they refused, the police were called, and they were handcuffed and taken off the plane. After hours of questioning, they were allowed to take another flight.[58] The imams later said they had not acted suspiciously or even prayed loudly and that their only "crime" was being identifiable as Muslims. They sued the airline, the police authorities, and the passengers who had reported them to authorities, claiming that they had been discriminated against. Their lawsuit was settled in 2009 for an undisclosed amount. A similar case occurred in 2009 when a Muslim family from Alexandria, Virginia, was ordered off an AirTran flight and detained after other passengers overheard them discussing the safest place to sit on a plane. Despite the absence of evidence that the family meant any harm, the airline refused to let them purchase new tickets. After the story became public, AirTran apologized and offered to refund the family for the price of their replacement tickets on another airline.[59]

While many people condemn such incidents as unjustified discrimination, author Sam Harris has argued that security officials should use profiling at airports. He contends that it is a waste of security resources to try to be fair and randomly screen people, including elderly women in wheelchairs, who pose no threat. Harris calls the effort to avoid profiling "the tyranny of fairness," writing, "Some semblance of fairness makes sense and, needless to say, everyone's bags should be screened, if only because it is possible to put a bomb in someone else's luggage. But the TSA has a finite amount of attention: Every moment spent frisking the Mormon Tabernacle Choir subtracts from the scrutiny paid to more likely threats."[60] Arguments of this sort are often subject to criticism from civil rights advocates. Not only does profiling unfairly generalize about group members, but it also can have negative consequences, generate resentment, and provoke backlash. And most basically, racial profiling appears to be a civil rights violation.

One of the problems of profiling is that it tends to focus on obvious and overt signs of racial, ethnic, or religious belonging and then involves sweeping generalizations about the behaviors of individuals who appear to fit those categories. Whether a policy counts as profiling and whether it always implies discrimination are a matter of some debate. For example, when decisions to stop motorists are made primarily or solely on the basis of race, this is surely discriminatory. However, in other cases in which race is just one of many factors in selecting targets of investigation, the question of discrimination is not so clear. This is the difference between "hard" and "soft" profiling. In the former case, race is the only factor used to single out someone, whereas in the latter it is just one of many factors. An example of the latter might be "questioning or detaining a person because of the confluence of a variety of factors—age (young), dress (hooded sweatshirt, baggy pants, etc.), time (late evening), geography (the person is walking through the "wrong" neighborhood)—that include race (Black)."[61] Sometimes it may be hard to tell what kind of profiling an example involves. Consider a New Jersey highway patrolman who pulls over a Black driver in a Nissan Pathfinder because the police have intelligence that Jamaican drug rings favor this car as a means for their marijuana trade in the Northeast.[62] Is this an example of unjust discrimination or a reasonable procedure?

Hate Crimes

A more obvious expression of discrimination and bias can be found in hate crimes, which are defined as crimes accompanied or motivated by bias. The killing of Ahmaud Arbery, which we mentioned previously, was considered to be a hate crime. In the federal hate crimes trial, the government accused the murderers of having publicly expressed racist ideas, while arguing that it was those racist ideas that led them to chase Ahmaud Arbery down and kill him.[63] After the murderers were convicted of hate crimes, the attorney general of the United States, Merrick Garland, issued a statement regarding the case. He said, "No one in this country should have to fear the threat of hate fueled violence. No one should fear being attacked or threatened because of what they look like, where they are from, whom they love, or how they worship."[64]

We could add a long list of examples of atrocities that have been classified and tried as hate crimes. But let's consider how this idea has come to be defined in federal law. The FBI defines a hate crime as a "criminal offense against a person or property motivated in whole or in part by an offender's bias against a race, religion, disability, sexual orientation, ethnicity, gender, or gender identity."[65] This does not mean that it is a crime to hate people. Hate crimes are criminal acts accompanied by hate; they occur when the hateful bias motivates some criminal act. The legal focus on crimes that are motivated by hateful bias became an issue in the 1980s, as Washington and Oregon passed legislation identifying this category of crime.[66] By 2009, the U.S. Congress passed the Matthew Shepard and James Byrd Jr. Hate Crimes Prevention Act. The two individuals named in this legislation were murdered by offenders who targeted them because of bias. Matthew Shepard was brutally beaten, tied to a fence, and left to die in 1998 in Laramie, Wyoming, where he was a university student. Shepard's assailants targeted him because he was gay. However, Wyoming did not have a hate crime law at the time. James Byrd Jr. was a Black man who was murdered in 1998 in Jasper, Texas, by three White men who beat him, urinated on him, tied a chain around his legs, and dragged him behind their truck until his arm and head were severed when his body hit a culvert. The murderers were White supremacists. Byrd's murder prompted the Texas legislature to pass hate crime legislation in 2001.

As a result of the federal Hate Crime Statistics Act of 1990, the Department of Justice keeps extensive data on hate crimes.[67] The most recent data available (from 2019) indicates that more than 7,300 hate crimes were reported in 2019, involving more than 8,500 victims.[68] Of those crimes,

- 55.8 percent were motivated by a race/ethnicity/ancestry bias.
- 21.4 percent were prompted by religious bias.
- 16.8 percent resulted from sexual-orientation bias.
- 2.8 percent were motivated by gender-identity bias.
- 2.2 percent were prompted by disability bias.
- 1 percent were motivated by gender bias.

While hate crimes occur in a variety of ways, they often focus on humiliating the victim. Consider, for example, a hate crime that occurred in Ohio in 2011 among the Amish. Some Amish men attacked other Amish people, holding them down and cutting off the women's hair and the men's beards. The beards and hair were a symbol of faith. The crime was motivated by religious reasons. And so it was prosecuted as a hate crime.[69]

Just as there are special, more severe penalties for killing police officers, federal and state laws sometimes impose more severe penalties for crimes motivated by hatred. Critics of these policies respond that to do this is to punish people for the views they hold, and that no matter how objectionable hate crimes might be, such laws constitute a violation of free speech. The FBI makes it clear, however, that its hate crime prosecutions are focused on crimes such as murders, arsons, and assaults that are *accompanied by* bias—and not in prosecuting bias itself, which is protected by the First Amendment. As we have seen in other chapters, equality and nondiscrimination are ethical values that must be balanced against other values, such as the free speech and privacy rights of individuals.

Affirmative Action and Reparations

13.4 Evaluate arguments in defense of affirmative action and reparations.

One recurrent question in discussions of equality and discrimination is whether it is ever justified to treat people in unequal ways as a remedy for past discrimination. This question is most frequently raised with regard to programs of affirmative action and preferential treatment. This may also include proposals for reparations. Affirmative action plans try to take active ("affirmative") steps to remedy past inequality. One way to do this is to give preferential consideration or treatment to members of groups that have been discriminated against in the past. Another model is to provide payments and other forms of economic and social aid to those who have been victimized in the past.

Affirmative action comes in many forms. The idea suggested by the term is that to remedy certain injustices, we need to do more than follow the negative requirement "Don't discriminate" or "Stop discriminating." The basic argument given for doing something

more is usually that merely ceasing discrimination will not or has not worked. Psychological reasons may be cited, for example, that discrimination and prejudice are so ingrained in people that they cannot help discriminating and do not even recognize when they are being discriminatory or prejudiced. To illustrate this dynamic, the philosopher Robert Fullinwider asks us to imagine that we have been transported to a land of giants, where everything is made for folks their size. They might fail to see why smaller people like us might have difficulties, assuming instead that we are just inferior or incompetent.[70] Social and political reasons for affirmative action can also be given, such as evidence of structural or institutional racism (as we discussed previously). The only way to change things, the argument goes, is to do something more positive, which would change established patterns of discrimination.

But what are we to do? There are many possibilities. One is to make a greater positive effort to find qualified persons from underrepresented groups. Thus, in hiring, a company might place ads in newspapers or on websites that are read by people from underrepresented communities. In college admissions, counselors might recruit more actively among marginalized and underrepresented groups. Once the pool is enlarged, then all in the pool are judged by the same criteria, and no special preferences are given on the basis of race or sex.

Other versions of affirmative action involve what have come to be known as *preferences*. In this approach, preference is given to members of underrepresented groups who are as well qualified as other candidates—their membership in a marginalized group simply gives them an edge. Preference also may be given to underrepresented group members who are somewhat less well qualified than other applicants. In either case, it is clear that determining equality of qualifications is itself a problem. One reason for this is that applicants are usually better qualified for some aspects of a given position and less well qualified for others. Another is the difficulty of deciding just what qualifications are necessary or important for a given position. Although those who support and those who oppose preferences often imply that determining requirements for a position is easy, it is not all that simple.

Other forms of affirmative action also exist. For example, companies or institutions may establish goals and quotas to be achieved for increasing representation among those who are marginalized. *Goals* are usually thought of as ideals that we aim for but that we are not absolutely required to reach. Goals can be formulated in terms of percentages or numbers. *Quotas*, in contrast, are usually fixed percentages or numbers that an institution intends to actually reach. Thus, a university or professional school might set aside a fixed number of slots for its incoming first-year class for certain minority group members. The institution would fill these positions even if this meant admitting people with lesser overall scores or points in the assessment system.

In past decades, an effort was made to increase the numbers of those from underrepresented groups on college campuses. These efforts have prompted a backlash against race-based admissions processes. In its 1996 decision in *Hopwood v. Texas*, a three-judge panel of the U.S. Court of Appeals for the Fifth Circuit struck down an affirmative action program at the University of Texas law school. This program had accepted lower scores on the Law School Admission Test (LSAT) for Black and Hispanic applicants. In a parallel development, Proposition 209 in California outlawed racial preferences in the public sector, and in 1995, the board of regents of the University of California (UC) system voted to ban race considerations in admissions. As we saw previously, the U.S. Supreme Court upheld the University of Michigan's graduate admissions program, in which race was one of several factors, but found unconstitutional the university's undergraduate admissions program, which gave a fixed number of additional points to minority applicants.

The *Hopwood* decision and others like it had negative impacts on the enrollment of non-White students in colleges and universities. In Texas, Black college enrollment fell by 28 percent in the two years following *Hopwood*.[71] In California, between 1995 (when Prop. 209 passed) and 1998, enrollments at UC Berkeley and UCLA of non-White students dropped by more than 50 percent. According to one report from 2012, the numbers of "African American, Latino and American Indian" students were low and failed to reflect California's rapidly changing demography.[72] A more recent analysis (from 2020) concluded that the policy from twenty years ago "has harmed Black and Hispanic students, decreasing their number in the University of California system while reducing their odds of finishing college, going to graduate school and earning a high salary."[73]

As the law was being revised, universities were still concerned to find ways to increase racially and ethnically diverse enrollments. Revised policies emphasized the importance of *diversity* as an educational value and avoided making claims about the need for affirmative action as a remedy for past injustice. Some states have attempted to find other ways to help generate a diverse student body. In Texas, the legislature guaranteed a place in Texas's public universities to the top 10 percent of graduates from Texas high schools. The idea of this approach was to ensure that students from high schools that primarily serve students of color had a better chance at college admissions.

Most recently, the Supreme Court considered affirmative action in *Fisher v. University of Texas at Austin*, in which the plaintiff challenged the University of Texas's affirmative action policy. The plaintiff claimed that the state had achieved a sufficient level of diversity in the university and thus that the university no longer had a need to give extra consideration to applicants based on race. It is a factual question as to whether affirmative action has been effective or not. The moral question of whether affirmative action is justified is another matter. At any rate, the Supreme Court's decision in *Fisher* was not decisive. A final ruling was made in June 2016, when the Court affirmed race-based admissions that aim to recruit a diverse student body. But there are ongoing legal challenges to affirmative action programs. In 2022, as we discussed previously, the U.S. Supreme Court heard arguments in two related cases, brought by Students for Fair Admissions, that asked the Court to revisit its 2003 *Grutter v. Bollinger* decision. That organization, Students for Fair Admissions, maintains that "racial classifications and preferences in college admissions are unfair, unnecessary, and unconstitutional."[74] They do not think that it is fair or necessary to consider race and ethnicity as factors in university admissions.

While people have been debating affirmative action programs, others have been discussing the question of reparations for members of groups that have been adversely impacted by racism. A model for this is provided by the U.S. government's payment of reparations to Japanese Americans who were victims of the internment policy of the American government during World War II. People of Japanese heritage were dispossessed and imprisoned in internment camps during the war. The Civil Liberties Act of 1988 offered a formal apology to the victims of the Japanese internment, while also providing $20,000 in reparations to each of those victims. President Reagan said, as he signed that law:

> The legislation that I am about to sign provides for a restitution payment to each of the 60,000 surviving Japanese-Americans of the 120,000 who were relocated or detained. Yet no payment can make up for those lost years. So, what is most important in this bill has less to do with property than with honor. For here we admit a wrong; here we reaffirm our commitment as a nation to equal justice under the law.[75]

With this example in mind, we might consider whether other groups that have been oppressed and whose rights have been violated might also be offered reparations. And indeed, arguments in favor of reparations have been made with regard to the Black community, Native Americans, and others. The issue was studied by a legislative committee in California in 2022, which issued a report in June 2022 that proposed a number of remedies and reparations for past racial injustice. The harms that might be addressed by a reparations policy could include the harm caused by slavery, redlining, mass incarceration, police brutality, and the wage gap. In addition to cash payments, a reparations policy could include grants, tuition help, low-interest loans, funding for public health and mental health efforts in Black communities, support for Black-owned business, and other proposals. Some of these proposed reparations projects may overlap with affirmative action programs. But reparations could also specifically target remaining inequalities and injustices through direct payments, grants, and so on.

The idea of reparations prompts interesting ethical questions. Defenders of the idea will claim that it is justified as a way of remediating harm and providing a sense of closure and accountability. They may also argue on utilitarian grounds that in the long run, everyone will be better off if we could find ways to improve conditions for members of racial and ethnic minority groups who continue to face inequalities of wages, wealth, health, education, and opportunity. But critics of these proposals will argue that the present generation of taxpayers should not be asked to bear the burden of paying for the injustices of past generations. These critics may also point out that the historical situation is more complicated than a policy of reparations can address.

For example, it is worth considering which members of which communities would be entitled to reparations. Not all Black Americans are descended from former slaves. Some have migrated here in the century and a half after slavery was abolished. Would there be some requirement that reparations be targeted toward those who are in fact descendants of slaves—or whose families were otherwise deliberately harmed, say by suffering from redlining or Jim Crow policies? One of the leaders of the reparations effort in California, Shirley Weber, suggested that reparations should be narrowly targeted to descendants of slaves.[76] Weber is a Black woman who was California's secretary of state in 2022. Her great-grandfather was born into slavery. She pointed out that there is a difference between her family's experience and the experience of someone like Barack Obama, whose mother was White and father was Kenyan.

The question of reparations is not only a concern for Black people who are descendants of slaves. In 2019, the governor of California, Gavin Newsom, established a Truth and Healing Council that would consider reparations for the Native tribes of California. The Truth and Healing Council explains that it "bears witness to, records, examines existing documentation of, and receives California Native American narratives regarding the historical relationship between the State of California and California Native Americans in order to clarify the historical record of such relationship in the spirit of truth and healing."[77] The idea of truth and healing is part of the project of reparations. The point is not only to distribute funds to those communities that have been harmed, but also to publicly admit those harms and "bear witness" to the truth, as the Council puts it here. But public admissions of harm are sometimes viewed as insufficient. When Pope Francis visited Canada in the summer of 2022, he offered an apology on behalf of the Catholic Church to the Indigenous people of Canada, who suffered abuse in Canada's church-run residential schools. But some Canadian officials and tribal members suggested that an apology was not enough and that the Catholic church needed to do more.[78] A model of a more robust response can be found in Canada's official policy of reparations: admitting its past wrongdoing in facilitating atrocities against native people and pledging $30 billion to compensate Indigenous people who suffered abuse in Canadian residential schools.[79]

In any discussion of affirmative action and reparations, it is important to specify exactly what kind of practice one favors or opposes. There are different ways that affirmative actions and reparations policies can be configured. The details matter. But let us now examine the general ethical arguments for and against these various types of programs. As in other chapters, these arguments can be divided into consequentialist and non-consequentialist approaches.

Consequentialist Considerations

Consequentialist arguments can be made both for and against various affirmative action and reparation programs. These arguments are broadly utilitarian in nature. The question is whether such programs do more good than harm or more harm than good.

People who argue in favor of these programs urge the following sorts of considerations. The utilitarian argument in favor of these programs claims that ultimately such programs benefit everyone, even though they are targeted toward helping those who come from historically disadvantaged groups. We live in a multiracial society and benefit from mutual respect and harmony. We all bring diverse backgrounds to our employment and educational institutions, and we all benefit from the contributions of people who have a variety of diverse perspectives. Our law schools should reflect the full diversity of our society to help ensure that all people have access to adequate representation and protection under the law. Others argue that

affirmative action and reparations are one way to break the vicious cycle of discrimination and inequality. Past discrimination has put women and members of some racial and ethnic groups at a continuing disadvantage. Unless something is done, they will never be able to compete on an equal basis. Low family income leads to poorer education for children, which leads to lower-paying jobs, which leads to low family income, and so on. Children need role models to look up to. They need to know that certain types of achievement and participation are possible for them. Otherwise, they will lack hope and opportunities to pursue success. Without affirmative action programs, supporters argue, things are not likely to change. Discrimination and its long-term effects are so entrenched that positive measures are needed to overcome them, including perhaps outright reparations for those who lack wealth and power and whose disadvantage is the result of previous discrimination.

Those who argue against affirmative action on consequentialist grounds usually maintain that the programs do not work or that they do more harm than good. They cite statistics to show that these programs have benefited middle-class African Americans, for example, but not the lower class. As Stephen Carter argues, "The most disadvantaged black people are not in a position to benefit from preferential admission."[80] Critics such as Carter suggest that unless affirmative action admissions programs are accompanied by other aid, both financial and tutorial, they are often useless or wasted. Some critics point out that lawsuits filed under the 1964 Civil Rights Act have done more than affirmative action to increase the percentage of Black employees in various white-collar positions.[81] Other consequentialist critics argue that there is a stigma attached to those who have been admitted or hired through affirmative action programs and that this can be debilitating for those so chosen. Some Black neoconservatives even argue that quotas and racially weighted tests "have psychologically handicapped blacks by making them dependent on racial-preference programs rather than their own hard work."[82] A similar argument could be made against reparations, which is that it may be viewed as a kind of handout that increases dependence and undermines initiative.

Table 13-1 Outline of Moral Approaches to Affirmative Action and Reparations

	Strong Affirmative Action and Reparations	Moderate Affirmative Action	Opposed to Affirmative Action
Thesis	Positive steps should be taken to remedy past discrimination including reparations and affirmative action policies.	Some affirmative action and reparations can be justified.	Affirmative action and reparations projects are wrong.
Corollaries and Implications	Past inequalities will only be overcome when disadvantaged groups are given extra advantages, including possibly fulfilling *quotas and providing reparations for past injustices and inequalities.*	Need to balance merit, equality, and redress for disadvantage; diversity is viewed as an asset worthy of preference and special consideration; some reparations could be helpful in cases of obvious inequality and disadvantage.	Nondiscrimination is enough; reparations would ask the present generation to pay for past injustices and is unfair; affirmative action causes more unequal treatment and is a kind of *reverse discrimination.*
Connections with Moral Theory	*Compensatory justice* requires redress for past injustice; consequentialist considerations aim to remedy lack of opportunity for members of historically disadvantaged groups; *restorative justice* helps reconcile victims and oppressors.	Respect for individual merit is balanced with social value of diversity; consequentialist concern for fixing past injustice and establishing more equitable social outcomes.	*Merit* as the primary consideration is based on respect for individual achievement; consequentialist concern that affirmative action increases racial tension and causes disrespectful *tokenism.*

Those who oppose affirmative action programs also cite the increased racial tension that they believe results from these programs—in effect, a White male backlash against women and members of non-White groups. Some of the same writers who support affirmative action for underrepresented racial groups and women have also made a case for giving special attention to economically disadvantaged students in college and university admissions.[83] They point out that elite universities have only a minuscule percentage of admissions from lower-income families, even when they have racially and ethnically diverse enrollments. These thinkers argue that such class-based affirmative action not only is justified for reasons of fairness but also serves the purpose of increasing class diversity.

The key to evaluating these consequentialist arguments both for and against affirmative action is to examine the validity of their assessments and predictions. What, in fact, have affirmative action programs achieved? Have they achieved little because they benefit those who least need it and might have succeeded without them, or have they actually brought more disadvantaged students into the system and employees into better and higher-paying jobs, thus helping break a vicious cycle? Have affirmative action programs benefited society by increasing diversity in the workforce and in various communities, or have they led only to increased racial tensions? And what about efforts at reparations—have they produced positive results by helping to level the playing field and by compensating people for past harm? These are difficult matters to assess. Here is another place where ethical judgments depend on empirical information drawn from the various sciences or other disciplines. The consequentialist argument for affirmative action programs will succeed if it can be shown that there is no better way to achieve the good the programs are designed to achieve and that the good done by these affirmative action programs and reparations projects outweighs any harm they cause. The consequentialist argument against affirmative action programs and reparations will succeed if it can be shown that there are better ways to achieve the same good ends or that the harm they create outweighs the good they help achieve.

Non-consequentialist Considerations

Not all arguments about affirmative action programs and reparations are based on appeals to consequences. Some arguments appeal to deontological considerations. The statement from Ronald Reagan that we quoted previously points in this direction. He spoke of restoring "honor" for the Japanese Americans who were interned. This is not simply a matter of economics; rather, it is a matter of dignity and respect. Reparation schemes can be understood in connection to the idea of *restorative justice* (an issue we discuss further in Chapter 17). One concern for restorative justice projects is restoring broken communities by acknowledging the experience of victims. Part of this effort includes reconciling victims and perpetrators around the shared truth of past injustice. Perhaps a plan for reparations could work in this way and be justified in connection to claims about human rights and respect for the dignity of persons. Related to this in the discussion of affirmative action programs is the claim that they provide *compensatory justice*, a way of compensating for past wrongs done to members of certain groups. People have been harmed and wronged by past unjust discrimination, and we now need to make up for that by benefiting them, by giving them preferential treatment. However, it can be difficult to assess how preferential treatment can right a past wrong. We may think of it

as undoing the past harm done. But it may be quite difficult to undo the harm of generational trauma and the long legacy of racism. One interpretation of compensation focuses simply on producing good consequences or eliminating bad ones. It is a matter of trying to change the results of past wrongs. But in a non-consequentialist sense, we might think about a different sense of righting a wrong—a sense of justice being done in itself, whether or not it makes any difference in the outcome. This could also be understood as a matter of human rights that would appeal to the basic idea that victims of past harm have a right to have those wrongs admitted and repaired.

Some non-consequentialist critics also argue against affirmative action by claiming that such programs are unfair or unjust. The argument against affirmative action might appeal to the principle of equality, contending that race, sex, or any other category is an irrelevant characteristic that should not be singled out and recognized by government policy, even if that policy is an attempt to rectify past injustice. Just as it was wrong in the past to use these characteristics to deny people equal chances, so it is also wrong in the present, even if it is used this time to their advantage. Race should simply not count in treating people differently, they argue, perhaps thinking that the law ought to be color-blind. But of course, as we discussed with reference to Kendi's idea of anti-racism, proponents of racial preferences and other policies may argue that the world is not color-blind and that we need to "see color" and provide race-based preferences as a way of compensating for the past injustices and as a way of fighting against the racism that still exists in the world.

A further argument by the critic of these policies may suggest that preferences for some also mean denial of benefits to others. For this reason, preferential treatment programs have been labeled by critics as *reverse discrimination*. Moreover, opponents of affirmative action criticize the use of compensatory justice arguments. In a valid application of compensatory justice, they argue, only those who have been directly wronged should be compensated, and only those directly responsible for the wrong should be made to pay. With this in mind, a critic of reparations or affirmative action would object to programs that compensate individuals based on group membership and without establishing whether those individuals themselves have been directly harmed by past discriminatory practices.

Consider the case of a group of White firefighters in New Haven, Connecticut, that went to the U.S. Supreme Court in 2009. That city administered a test to its firefighters to determine who would be promoted. When no Black firefighters passed the test, the city simply dropped all of the results. Those White firefighters who had passed the test complained of reverse discrimination. By a 5–4 ruling, the Court agreed with them.[84]

The arguments for affirmative action based on considerations of justice will succeed only if those persons who make them also can make a case for the justice of the programs. They must show that such programs do in fact compensate those who have been wronged, even if they have been affected by discrimination in ways that are not immediately obvious. Supporters may also argue that those who lose out as a result of preferences are not badly harmed—they have other opportunities and are not demeaned by their loss. And though they have not intentionally wronged anyone, they have likely benefited from structures of discrimination.

Those who oppose affirmative action based on considerations of justice will succeed if they can effectively apply the principle of equality to their arguments. They may argue, for example, that affirmative action singles out some groups for special treatment in a way that is inconsistent with the idea of equality. But if they rely primarily on the harms done by continuing to use race or sex as grounds for differential treatment, they will be appealing to a consequentialist consideration and must be judged on that basis.

This chapter has dealt with a range of issues collected together under the general rubric of equality and discrimination. This includes racial profiling, racism, hate crimes, reparations, and affirmative action. The guiding principle is that we should treat people fairly and equally. While there is disagreement about how the principle of equality applies in these cases and about its moral basis, there is widespread agreement that equality matters.

Chapter Summary

13.1 How can we describe the principle of equality and apply it to the concerns of social justice?

The principle of equality states that we ought to treat people equally. It is not fair to treat people differently unless there is some valid reason for that different treatment. This is a basic principle of justice, related to Aristotle's idea that similar things should be treated in similar ways. This principle can be supported from a non-consequentialist perspective that emphasizes the importance of human rights or Kantian respect for dignity. It can also be supported from a consequentialist or utilitarian concern for happiness and social harmony. The concerns of social justice are focused on applying this principle to social issues such as racism and other forms of oppression. The concept can also be applied to economic issues and to other issues involving distributions of social goods. The principle of equality tells us to distribute social goods fairly and equally, unless there is some relevant reason for an unequal distribution.

13.2 What are the key concepts of critical philosophical accounts of race and racism?

Critical philosophy of race asks about the ontological status of race while also providing a critical ethical analysis of racism. Most scholars agree that race is a social construction, which means that it is not an idea that can be defined in strictly biologically terms. Nonetheless, it is an important factor in social organizations that are oppressive and hierarchical. Philosophical accounts of race also include discussions of structural and institutional racism—which is a way of describing racially oppressive outcomes of social structures and organizations. A significant question is whether, in opposing racism, we ought to view the world in color-blind terms or whether in opposing racism, it is preferable to be explicitly anti-racist.

13.3 How can we apply the concept of intersectionality to discussions of inequality?

Intersectionality is a concept that reminds us to consider the complex and intersecting identities of people. In discussions of inequality and discrimination, an intersectional lens directs our attention to the various ways that racism, sexism, and other forms of oppression can be manifest in complex ways. This concept was developed by scholars such as Kimberlé Crenshaw, working in the field of critical race theory and its intersection with feminism. This concept is useful insofar as it reminds us to attend to these sorts of differences and the diverse ways that discrimination might appear. It also reminds us to attend to this kind of complexity in imagining remedies.

13.4 How can we evaluate arguments in defense of affirmative action and reparations?

Affirmative action programs take action to remedy past discrimination and racially disparate outcomes. This might include preferences for previously excluded people or even quotas. This means that there may be differential treatment based on race—in hiring, in college admissions, or in some other ways that social goods are distributed. Critics of such programs argue that this is a form of reverse discrimination that is posed against those who were previously privileged. Such critics may emphasize a color-blind approach to social distributions. Those arguments could be based on utilitarian claims or on claims about the equality and dignity of persons in a color-blind society. But proponents of these programs argue that some positive steps need to be done to remedy past discrimination, perhaps contending that we need programs that are proactively anti-racist. On utilitarian grounds, these programs may be defended as promoting greater equality and greater happiness. From a non-consequentialist standpoint, affirmative action programs can be supported as promoting conditions that allow for dignity and respect. Proposals for reparations can be supported or criticized based on similar arguments. A significant concern for such proposals is who gets counted and included in a program of affirmative action or reparation.

13.5 How could one defend a thesis about the ethics of racial profiling, affirmative action, and reparations?

Social justice proposals typically depend on some application of the principle of equality. Proposals to remedy inequalities begin from a critique of unjustified unequal treatment and unjustified discrimination. Inequalities continue to exist in social settings. This includes concerns about police brutality. The critique of police brutality may be connected to the issue of racial profiling. Racial profiling is involved in police tactics that focus on race. Often these programs depend on racist assumptions. But defenders of those programs argue that it can be effective to focus on racial assumptions (as well as age, gender, and other assumptions) in fighting crime. There are open questions here about how effective this is—and whether even if effective, racial profiling is fair, just, or equitable. Arguments can be mounted on either side of this issue depending on whether one adopts a consequentialist or non-consequentialist normative theory. The arguments in defense of (or against) racial profiling are similar to arguments in favor of (or against) affirmative action and reparations. A significant question to be addressed in any argument about these issues is the degree to which race and racism are significant factors in society.

Primary Source Readings

In the first reading for this chapter, we have an excerpt from Iris Marion Young's "Five Faces of Oppression." Young's essay has been influential in helping to explain the idea of *institutional* or *structural oppression*. In the second excerpt, Kwame Anthony Appiah discusses *racialism* and *racism*. He argues that there are good reasons to be suspicious of what he calls *racialist* reasoning, which holds that racial difference are biologically grounded, and the *racist* ideas that often follow from it. He applies Kantian insights and argues that racism is wrong because it violates the ideal of universality. We then have an excerpt from Ibram X. Kendi's discussion of racism, the problem of neutrality, and the importance of being anti-racist. In the final reading of the chapter, we offer an excerpt from Naomi Zack's book *White Privilege and Black Rights*. Zack outlines some of the problems that have given rise to the Black Lives Matter movement, while arguing that, at bottom, unequal treatment is a human rights violation.

Reading 13-1   Five Faces of Oppression | IRIS Marion Young

Study Questions

As you read the excerpt, please consider the following questions:

1. How does Young suggest that the idea of oppression has evolved?
2. How can oppression be unconscious, structural, and systematic, according to Young?
3. Why does Young's account still leave us with the idea of a privileged group who benefits from oppression?

One reason that many people would not use the term oppression to describe injustice in our society is that they do not understand the term in the same way as do new social movements. In its traditional usage, oppression means the exercise of tyranny by a ruling group. Thus many Americans would agree with radicals in applying the term oppression to the situation of Black South Africans under apartheid. Oppression also traditionally carries a strong connotation of conquest and colonial domination. . . .

In dominant political discourse it is not legitimate to use the term oppression to describe our society, because oppression is the evil perpetrated by the Others.

New left social movements of the 1960s and 1970s, however, shifted the meaning of the concept of oppression. In its new usage oppression designates the disadvantage and injustice some people suffer not because a tyrannical power coerces them, but because of the everyday practices of a well-intentioned liberal society. In this new left usage, the tyranny of a ruling group over another as in South Africa, must certainly be called oppressive. But oppression also refers to systemic constraints on groups that are not necessarily the result of the intentions of a tyrant. Oppression in this sense is structural, rather than the result of a few people's choices or policies. Its causes are embedded in unquestioned norms, habits, and symbols, in the assumptions underlying institutional rules and the collective consequences of following those rules. . . . In this extended structural sense oppression refers to the vast and deep injustices some groups suffer as a consequence of often unconscious assumptions and reactions of well-meaning people in ordinary interactions, media and cultural stereotypes, and structural features of bureaucratic hierarchies and market mechanisms—in short, the normal processes of everyday life. We cannot eliminate this structural oppression by getting rid of the rulers or making some new laws, because oppressions are systematically reproduced in major economic, political, and cultural institutions.

The systemic character of oppression implies that an oppressed group need not have a correlate oppressing group. While structural oppression involves relations among groups, these relations do not always fit the paradigm of conscious and intentional oppression of one group by another. . . .

The conscious actions of many individuals daily contribute to maintaining and reproducing oppression, but those people are usually simply doing their jobs or living their lives, and do not understand themselves as agents of oppression.

I do not mean to suggest that within a system of oppression individual persons do not intentionally harm others in oppressed groups. The raped woman, the beaten Black youth, the locked-out worker, the gay man harassed on the street are victims of intentional actions by identifiable agents. I also do not mean to deny that specific groups are beneficiaries of the oppression of other groups, and thus have an interest in their continued oppression. Indeed, for every oppressed group there is a group that is privileged in relation to that group.

Iris Marion Young, *Justice and the Politics of Difference* (Princeton, NJ: Princeton University Press, 1990), pp. 40–42.

Reading 13-2   Racisms | Kwame Anthony Appiah

Study Questions

As you read the excerpt, please consider the following questions:

1. What does Appiah mean when he says that racists have a cognitive incapacity?

2. According to Appiah, why is racism based on false or mistaken racialist ideas?

3. How does Appiah employ Kantian moral ideas in his critique of racism?

Racialism is not, in itself, a doctrine that must be dangerous, even if the racial essence is thought to entail moral and intellectual dispositions. Provided positive moral qualities are distributed across the races, each can be respected, can have its "separate but equal" place.... I believe—and I have argued elsewhere—that racialism is false; but by itself, it seems to be a cognitive rather than a moral problem....

Racialism is, however, a presupposition of other doctrines that have been called "racism," and these other doctrines have been, in the last few centuries, the basis of a great deal of human suffering and the source of a great deal of moral error.

One such doctrine we might call "extrinsic racism": extrinsic racists make moral distinctions between members of different races because they believe that the racial essence entails certain morally relevant qualities. The basis for the extrinsic racists' discrimination between people is their belief that members of different races differ in respects that *warrant* the differential treatment, respects—such as honesty or courage or intelligence—that are uncontroversially held (at least in most contemporary cultures) to be acceptable as a basis for treating people differently. Evidence that there are no such differences in morally relevant characteristics—that Negroes do not necessarily lack intellectual capacities, that Jews are not especially avaricious—should thus lead people out of their racism if it is purely extrinsic. As we know, such evidence often fails to change an extrinsic racist's attitudes substantially ... if the racist is sincere—what we have is no longer a false doctrine but a cognitive incapacity....

This cognitive incapacity is not, of course, a rare one. Many of us are unable to give up beliefs that play a part in justifying the special advantages we gain (or hope to gain) from our positions in the social order—in particular, beliefs about the positive characters of the class of people who share that position. Many people who express extrinsic racist beliefs—many white South Africans, for example—are beneficiaries of social orders that deliver advantages to them by virtue of their "race," so that their disinclination to accept evidence that would deprive them of a justification for those advantages is just an instance of this general phenomenon....

But even if racialism were true, both forms of theoretical racism would be incorrect. Extrinsic racism is false because the genes that account for the gross morphological differences that underlie our standard racial categories are not linked to those genes that determine, to whatever degree such matters are determined genetically, our moral and intellectual characters. Intrinsic racism is mistaken because it breaches the Kantian imperative to make moral distinctions only on morally relevant grounds—granted that there is no reason to believe that race, *in se*, is morally relevant, and also no reason to suppose that races are like families in providing a sphere of ethical life that legitimately escapes the demands of a universalizing morality.

Kwame Anthony Appiah, "Racisms," in *Anatomy of Racism*, ed. David Goldberg (Minneapolis: University of Minnesota Press, 1990).

Reading 13-3   How to Be an Anti-Racist | Ibram X. Kendi

Study Questions

As you read the excerpt, please consider the following questions:

1. What does Kendi mean by suggesting that anti-racism is the opposite of racism?
2. According to Kendi, how might we work against racism?
3. What does Kendi mean when he suggests that the idea of color-blindness can be linked to White supremacy?

What's the problem with being "not racist"? It is a claim that signifies neutrality: "I am not a racist, but neither am I aggressively against racism." But there is no neutrality in the racism struggle. The opposite of "racist" isn't "not racist." It is "antiracist." What's the difference?

One endorses either the idea of a racial hierarchy as a racist, or racial equality as an antiracist. One either believes problems are rooted in groups of people, as a racist, or locates the roots of problems in power and policies, as an antiracist. One either allows racial inequities to persevere, as a racist, or confronts racial inequities, as an antiracist.

There is no in-between safe space of "not racist." The claim of "not racist" neutrality is a mask for racism. This may seem harsh, but it's important at the outset that we apply one of the core principles of antiracism, which is to return the word "racist" itself back to its proper usage. "Racist" is not . . . a pejorative. It is not the worst word in the English language; it is not the equivalent of a slur. It is descriptive, and the only way to undo racism is to consistently identify and describe it—and then dismantle it. The attempt to turn this usefully descriptive term into an almost unusable slur is, of course, designed to do the opposite: to freeze us into inaction.

The common idea of claiming "color blindness" is akin to the notion of being "not racist"—as with the "not racist," the color-blind individual, by ostensibly failing to see race, fails to see racism and falls into racist passivity.

The language of color blindness—like the language of "not racist"—is a mask to hide racism. "Our Constitution is color-blind," U.S. Supreme Court Justice John Harlan proclaimed in his dissent to Plessy v. Ferguson, the case that legalized Jim Crow segregation in 1896. "The white race deems itself to be the dominant race in this country," Justice Harlan went on. "I doubt not, it will continue to be for all time, if it remains true to its great heritage." A color-blind Constitution for a White-supremacist America.

The good news is that racist and antiracist are not fixed identities. We can be a racist one minute and an antiracist the next. What we say about race, what we do about race, in each moment, determines what—not who—we are.

I used to be racist most of the time. I am changing. I am no longer identifying with racists by claiming to be "not racist." I am no longer speaking through the mask of racial neutrality. I am no longer manipulated by racists ideas to see racial groups as problems. . . .

I've come to see that the movement from racist to antiracist is always ongoing—it requires understanding and snubbing racism based on biology, ethnicity, body, culture, behavior, color, space, and class. And beyond that, it means standing ready to fight at racism's intersections with other bigotries.

Ibram X. Kendi, *How to Be an Anti-Racist* (New York: Penguin Random House, 2019).

Reading 13-4   White Privilege, Black Rights | Naomi Zack

Study Questions

As you read the excerpt, please consider the following questions:

1. How does Zack contrast the problems of implicit racism and more overt violations of human rights?

2. How does Zack explain the need for criticism of police violence directed against young Black men?

3. What does Zack mean when she suggests that the issue of unpunished killings of Black youth is a symbol of overall social injustice?

Trayvon Martin, Michael Brown, Eric Gamer, Tamir Rice, and many others. *"Hands up, don't shoot, Black Lives Matter, I can't breathe, I can't breathe, I can't breathe...I can't breathe."* If you work in philosophy of race and are black or have black ancestry—I am multiracial—and if your personal sensitivity is greater than that of a plant, then the past two years have been painful and shameful to live through. There seems to be something drastically wrong about a justice system that allows police to kill unarmed young black men with impunity, with American elites of all races, who feel sorry for the misfortunes of our already disadvantaged but cannot do anything to help them, with academic whites who have created a discourse about their privilege, and with all those who are apathetic in the face of black tragedy in our time. I wrote this book quickly and with a sense of urgency, in November and December 2014, while interrupting work on a longer and more theoretical project (*Applicative Justice: A Pragmatic Theory for Correcting Injustice*) that will eventually provide more comprehensive underpinnings for this work. In other words, I had to stop philosophizing for a minute, to think about reality.

This book focuses on one specific problem: police killings of unarmed young black men that are not legally punished. The writing also had two specific promptings. First I was inspired by responses to my November 5, 2014 *NY Times* Stone interview by George Yancy, "What 'White Privilege' Really Means."[1] The liveliest hostile reader commentary (and maybe, also, 1274 "likes" on the *NY Times* Facebook page for November 6[2]) focused on this: *"Not fearing that the police will kill your child for no reason isn't a privilege. It's a right."*

My second inspiration was the heated argument between former New York City Mayor Rudolf Giuliani and Georgetown University Professor Michael Eric Dyson on *Meet the Press* on November 24, 2014. The moderator introduced the claim that white police officers do not racially reflect the population of black communities. Giuliani said it was more important to talk about the fact that 93 percent of blacks who are killed, are killed by other blacks. Dyson said that black-on-black crime was a "false equivalency" to white police officers shooting blacks, because blacks were punished for killing other blacks and white police officers were not. Giuliani said, "White police officers wouldn't be there if you weren't killing each other 70 percent of the time." Dyson replied that Giuliani had a white supremacist mindset.[3]

The same 93 percent figure was trotted out in comments (mostly from Internet "trolls") about what I said in the *NY Times* interview. It is completely irrelevant to the discussion of racial profiling and the impunity enjoyed by white police officers who kill blacks in "stop and frisks" or while attempting to perform stop and frisks.[4] The reason acquittals and failures to indict ignite such strong public protest is that the police are presumed to *protect* members of the communities in which they serve. These ruptures between police and communities undermine trust in government, as well as the constitutional legitimacy of government as represented by such police action and its prosecutorial and juridical blessings. Distrust of government is an unfortunate trend now shared by both extremes of the political spectrum. Tea Party Republicans distrust government because they fear it gives too much to the undeserving.

Radicals to the left distrust government because they view it as crushing, when it is not ignoring, the rights of the disadvantaged, especially poor nonwhites, and especially poor blacks. Indeed, a strong case can be made for negative *black male exceptionalism*, not only throughout U.S. history, but in present conditions of police racial profiling and homicide.[5]

Moreover, to bring up the 93 percent statistic when the subject is white police officer homicide following racial profiling is a distraction back to the mode of discourse preferred by those who insist that American society is not racist against blacks. That mode of discourse seeks to find ways to blame victims and hold them responsible for their own misfortune and disadvantage. The reasoning that could be implicit in Giuliani's remarks is that if blacks can be blamed for most of the death rate of young black males, then homicides against blacks committed by white police officers are less blameworthy, by comparison. However, blame is a moral assessment that is not a matter of numbers alone. American citizens have constitutional rights that are at stake in these cases of police homicide. The Fourth Amendment is supposed to protect against arbitrary searches and seizures. The Fourteenth Amendment is supposed to guarantee equal protection under the law and in actions of government officials. Police racial profiling violates both amendments, first by arbitrary stops and searches, and second by disproportionate use of those methods against blacks. The police have a special duty, stated in their oaths, to "uphold the Constitution." That is the issue missed by Giuliani and many others.

Contemporary academic discussion of social justice has now shifted to the discourse of white privilege. I think this is a mistake, insofar as privileges are extra perks and more is at stake in recent police killings of unarmed black men than denial of perks. I hope we have not sunk so low in American society that plain, simple justice according to the Constitution must be regarded as a perk. Police killings that rest in impunity when grand juries do not indict and trial juries do not convict violate ultimate, nonnegotiable rights.

About two-thirds through the writing of this manuscript, on December 17, 2014, I attended a very timely event at the University of Oregon. Yvette M. Alex-Assensoh, Vice President for Equity and Inclusion, organized "'I Can't Breathe': A Conversation Starter about Racism, Justice, and Love." A diverse group of administrators, staff, faculty, students, community representatives, faith-based representatives, campus police, and city police assembled to discuss the effects on their lives of the recent killings that have not been followed by jury convictions or grand jury indictments, and how a university community might respond.

We sat at round tables of six or eight people, beginning with one-on-one discussions, expanding to full table discussions, and then summarizing to the rest of room. At my table, a young woman of color commented on responses to recent police killings on social media. She reflected that those who were nonwhite among her friends and relations showed engaged responses on their Facebook pages, while her white friends and relations seemed unaware of these events and posted nothing about them. A young white woman at the table talked about the silence on our campus about these incidents. African Americans are underrepresented at all levels at the University of Oregon, perhaps reflecting the racial demographics of Oregon itself, which in 2013 had only 2 percent blacks in its population, compared to 13.2 percent for the United States overall.[6] (Oregon's racial statistics may be related to a nineteenth-century history of the exclusion of blacks by law, and race-restrictive real estate covenants, which were not fully corrected until 1968.[7])

I was led to wonder if reactions to public trauma depend on the race of those observing and responding. Have we re-inscribed old-fashioned segregation into social media, so that blacks care when terrible things happen to black youth, but whites are unmoved? Is our collective sense of justice dead? I hope not. The great masses of people of all races and ethnicities go about their daily lives, working, socializing, falling in love, ending romantic relationships, raising families, getting sick, and worrying about money. In all of this, most are fully enmeshed in what D. H. Lawrence called the lesser day of ordinary life that can crack "like some great blue bubble" so that we seem to see "through the fissures the deeper blue of that other

Greater Day where [moves] the other sun shaking its dark blue wings."[8]

The Greater Day for race in our time is not a matter of what race a person is, but a matter of justice for persons of all races. Justice is not based on common early homo sapiens African ancestry, an immigrant melting pot, or equal opportunities for material success. Justice is a matter of human rights and human dignity. Fortunately, we have a Constitution that names and supports protection for such rights. But unfortunately, that constitution has been interpreted by U.S. Supreme Court judges in ways that ignore both individual and institutional racism. Failure to recognize and support constitutional rights is unjust. People can come together in response to injustice and share the simple, common aspiration that those who are innocent will be left alone by the government as represented by the police and those who are guilty, including the police, will be punished. That aspiration is an attainable goal which we can reach by understanding the nature of the injustices now committed. The focus of this book is very narrow—How do the injustices of the police killing of innocent young African American men work? Why are such homicides not punished? What can be done about this?

In *The Souls of Black Folk*, W. E. B. Du Bois predicted in 1903 that "The problem of the twentieth century is the problem of the color-line—the relation of the darker to the lighter races of men in Asia and Africa, in America and the islands of the sea."[9] More than a century later, it is evident that the color line has blurred in a number of ways: the U.S. Civil Rights Movement has yielded formal equality; the "darker races of men in Asia and Africa . . . and in the islands of the sea" are viewed not in racial terms but in terms of economic development and military capability and threat (which may be as bad, but it is something different); it is well understood by intellectuals in the humanities that much of older definitions of race were based on myths and stereotypes; there is a consensus in the physical biological sciences that racial kinds are not real natural kinds, independently of social divisions: that are projected onto genetic and phenotypical taxonomies;[10] in the United States, where race was most drastically a matter of black and white, multiracial individuals are accorded some recognition

and Latino/Hispanics, while officially an ethnicity, nonetheless are regarded as racially nonwhite, for the most part.

However, it is important to return to the black-white dichotomy in these early decades of the twenty-first century, not as a matter of racial identities, but as a matter of justice. Justice, or good enough approximations to justice, exists for white Americans, but not in the same ways for the rest. The starkest examples of injustice are evident in how black Americans are treated by the police. Yes, there is overt and implicit racism and bias, and yes, there are institutional structures, including the U.S. prison system, which make black Americans, especially young males, especially vulnerable. But the crucial issue at stake is application of the forms of justice that are stated in U.S. Constitutional Amendments and the Civil Rights legislation of the 1960s, to black Americans. To do that will require beginning with contemporary instances of race-based injustice that have fallen through the cracks in U.S. Supreme Court opinions since 1968 and revisiting some of those opinions. This will be a long-term legal project. First, it is necessary to understand how the legal system now works unjustly and how a number of progressive academics, who should know better, have been politically anesthetizing themselves.

Overall, the present situation in New York City and beyond does not support optimism about an end to police racial profiling and homicide following stops and frisks, or their attempts. There are unlikely to be fast dramatic solutions to the underlying legal and social problems that have erupted into the recent events that prompted this book. Nevertheless, hope is a healthy attitude and violent response is not an option. No reasonable or sane voices in this ongoing crisis want more violence and that does speak positively to future solutions.

Recent U.S. Supreme Court opinions do not explicitly take racial bias into account, as the mental and emotional content of what may motivate individual police action. The Court's objective standards for what "a reasonable police officer" decides to do in what is perceived to be a dangerous situation, would inevitably defer to broad beliefs and attitudes within existing police culture. Policies of racial profiling that are based on racial proportions in the prison population, rather than crime rates in areas being patrolled, have not been thoroughly challenged in the courts. American police officers remain within their legal rights to both practice racial profiling and shoot to kill while attempting stops and frisks, in the absence of probable cause. Indictments and guilty verdicts for police homicide of unarmed suspects are constrained by very broad police discretion and criminal laws that were designed for civilians and are preempted by that discretion. Definitive legal solutions to these problems are in need of new, brilliant, and dedicated lawyering, which will take years to succeed, and more years to effectively apply.

Applicative justice requires that the legal treatment of American blacks be brought on a par with that of American whites, beyond written law, into real life practice. Simply reiterating how whites are "privileged" is not an effective response on the part of concerned academics, because it merely reinscribes their white privileges into new white identities. Perceptions of current injustice rest on basic human rights that people value intuitively and call for in anguished protests and demonstrations, but without understanding how the American legal system fails to protect the rights of black Americans. It may be possible to improve the situation by correcting specific comparative injustices, before the relevant interpretations of constitutional law change, or even if they never do change. Institutional and government practices go far beyond what is formally written, into real life. Such practices can mirror formal law, be less just than it describes, or more just.

Many responsible and compassionate leaders and officials feel that they should do something, offer some reassurance to the disillusioned, some balm to the bereaved. When part of the population perceives injustice in specific harm or death to some of its members, it is essential that responsible leadership in all areas of public life offer consolation. Present blame, violent reaction, and protests and demonstrations have bypassed or denied the need for what should be a period of official nationwide (if not formally "national") mourning. The killing of innocent young people—Tamir Rice was a twelve-year-old child!—by government officials is a national concern, even if it is not acknowledged. It is a national concern because whites and nonwhites together make up the nation in which such events now occur and they draw their individual and collective identities from being members of that nation. Such sudden and unjust loss of life should be publically shared, during time respectfully set aside for sadness. It calls not only for black armbands, but for public memorials, communal prayer or meditation, and designated *silence*. Reactions of this nature should be immediate, but it is just as important that permanent public memorials be planned in honor of those killed, so that people do not forget wrongful deaths.[3]

After sadness and silence, immediate practical remedies should be designed for institutional and social change out of concern for the well-being of over 90 percent of the black population who are not criminals. Racial profiling or fear and suspicion is not primarily a moral matter for whites in terms of their moral virtues or vices, but an offense to blacks, as individual human beings. As Judge Shira Scheindlin stated, "No one should live in fear of being stopped whenever he leaves his home to go about the activities of daily life." So long as police racial profiling continues, concerned educators and other leaders of societal institutions can continue to host conversations for those who are not directly affected by it, to consider what it is like to live in such fear, for one's children and grandchildren, as well as oneself.[4]

Americans are not about to abandon their ideals concerning the police. Police officers, like military personnel, remain enshrined as sources of protection, heroism, and the kind of discipline that administers public order. It is not accidental that Wikipedia prefaces its 2014 alphabetical list of over five hundred police shows with, "Dramas involving police procedural work, and private detectives, secret agents, and the justice system have been a mainstay of broadcast television since the early days of broadcasting."[5] As popular entertainment, police television shows, movies, and fiction are usually morality plays, narratives of good triumphing over bad. People watch them as food for moral aspirations and the expression of shared intuitions about justice and glory. No matter how long it will take to bring the treatment by police of innocent young blacks on a par with their treatment of innocent young whites, no matter how difficult and bitter that struggle may be, police officers, like military personnel, will remain enshrined as sources of protection, heroism, and the kind of discipline that administers public order. But that doesn't mean they should not be recognized to have the same frailties of others, in beliefs and motivations that derive from anti-black cultural norms and myths, or that there are not ways in which they can become better, in how they regard and treat people of color, in their roles as first responders.

Not only are police officers first responders to crime, but they represent the entire legal and criminal justice system to members of the public in public places. For society to be orderly, it is essential that members of the public, especially young people, and especially young people who are not white, have good reason to believe that police officers will deal with them fairly. To criticize police practices is not the same thing as saying that all American police officers are bad people. In a democratic society, it must be possible for everyone in a position of power to accept criticism and be open to the possibility of change. Local police departments often create the impression of not distinguishing between being blameworthy and accepting responsibility. Blame is accusatory and may be avoided as dishonorable, whereas the acceptance of responsibility allows for future growth and honor. By the same token, just as it is not necessary "to burn the whole house down in order to get rid of the mice," neither is it necessary to rebuild the entire house in order to refurbish a damaged part. What many critics may correctly perceive as society-wide and historically deep antiblack racism in the United States does not have to be thoroughly corrected before the immediate issue of police killings of unarmed young black men can be addressed. The immaturity of some armed young police officers and their lack of experience in interacting with members of the communities they serve can be addressed by police administrators and supervisors, who have as much at stake in the public's trust of them as the public does. The American police, as a professional community, appear to know this. Not one of the officers responsible for the death of innocent victims in the high profile cases has been lauded or honored by his peers. Most have resigned or been dismissed and that

is an indication of responsiveness within police ranks, even if it is not part of their culture to readily and publicly admit wrongdoing.

The way that the Broken Window Policy has been implemented in major U.S. cities has failed to serve many members of communities it was deigned to support, as totalities. Former New York City mayor Giuliani has reportedly brought attention to the fact that 93 percent of black homicide victims are killed by other blacks. While that fact is irrelevant to the issue of recent killings of unarmed young black men by young white police officers performing or attempting to perform stop and frisks, it is a major social problem. To the extent that it is a responsibility of the police to address, and it is insofar as their charge is to detect and prevent serious crime, it should be remembered and emphasized that stop and frisk policies were originally designed to be part of a much wider program that included *community policing*. The core idea in community policing is that members of police departments interact with members of high-crime communities, to build community and prevent crime.[6] The importance of that idea lies in its ability to diffuse perceptions on the part of the public within and from these communities that the police are pitted against them as an occupying force. By the same token, attitudes on the part of the police that the prevention and detection of crime always or usually requires direct combat with criminals and suspects require reexamination.

As offensive as stop and frisk policies are to those caught in their nets, the numbers of deadly escalations of attempts to stop and frisk can be considered against bigger numbers. As noted earlier, from 2002–2012, over 4.4 million stops and frisks were performed in New York City. At a rate of about 50 percent black suspects, this would amount to 220,000 stops of black suspects a year. Compared to nationwide estimates of 136–200 killings of blacks by police on a yearly basis, the odds of death for a black person from a police stop and frisk based on the New York City statistics would be at most near 1 in 1,000 each year. The odds are likely better on a national level, because New York City has a disproportionately large black population. Still, the odds of a black person being killed by a police officer are significantly higher than the likelihood of being killed in a car crash, which is 1 in 6,500 a year.[7]

Communities of color react to killings of unarmed young black men, symbolically and iconographically, as they should, because even one unjust race-related event creates an atmosphere of race-related injustice. Each unpunished killing is treated as a symbol of overall social injustice to whole communities of people of color. Attempts to suppress nonviolent expressions of outrage are disturbing insofar as they fail to respect human sensibilities and encroach on First Amendment rights. But on the other side, American police have been behaving within the law concerning stop and frisk polices and the use of deadly force. If judges and legislatures change the law, there is every reason to believe that American police will behave in accordance with new regulations, policies, and laws. Until then, because police officers have such important roles in American society and culture, their full understanding of black innocence, black crime, and black poverty is a worthy goal for all concerned individuals and groups.[8]

Ian Ayres and Daniel Markovits suggested in a December 25, 2014, opinion piece in the *Washington Post* that before racially profiled encounters with police can escalate into homicide, in the absence of probable cause for a serious crime, there ought to be rules of engagement for police encounters. Ayres and Markovits propose that officers issue warnings to stop, and then secure warrants for arrests if they are not obeyed. Such measures would check the present situation, where police homicides for attempted stops regarding minor misdemeanors can result in far more drastic punishment than convictions for minor crimes would.[9]

What about the responses of prosecutors, juries, and grand juries to cases of police homicide involving unarmed black victims? Joshua Deahl, writing for

Bloomberg View, cites the Cato Institute's National Police Misconduct Reporting Project's documentation of 4,861 unique reports of misconduct in 2010, including 127 fatalities. In almost all U.S. jurisdictions, police and prosecutors are on the same legal team in their jurisdictions. Deahl reasons that federal prosecution is not a solution because it would require difficult-to-apply charges of civil rights violations based on victims' race or ethnicity. To achieve some distance from the police-prosecutor team loyalty, Deahl proposes permanent special prosecutors, who would be less costly to maintain than ad hoc special prosecutors.[10]

An especially poignant case of police homicide by a white officer against a black suspect involved Jonathan Ferrell, twenty-four, a former Florida A&M football player, who sought help after a car crash. He knocked on the door of the home of a woman who was alone with her infant child and she called 911. When police arrived, Ferrell approached them and was first tasered and then shot dead by Officer Randall Kerrick, age twenty-seven. The Charlotte-Mecklenburg Police Department called the shooting unlawful, but a first grand jury did not indict. A week later, a second grand jury, from which the district attorney had recused himself, did indict Kerrick for voluntary manslaughter.[11]

Cultures change in small unnoticed ways over varied periods of time and then they can change overnight. Violence will not improve the present situation. Apathy and civic incivility add to personal stress and tensions based on racial identities. Peaceful protest and assembly is still protected under the First Amendment. Living with this crisis requires concern, restraint, civility, and moral appeal to basic human rights that fall through the cracks of present U.S. law.

Naomi Zack, *White Privilege and Black Rights: The Injustice of U.S. Police Racial Profiling and Homicide* (Lanham, MD: Rowman and Littlefield, 2015).

Notes

1. George Yancy and Naomi Zack, "What 'White Privilege' Really Means." The Stone, Opinionator, *NY Times*, November 5, 2014, Http://opinionator.blogs.nytimes.com/2014/11/05/what-white-privilege-really-means/#more-154773

2. George Yancy and Naomi Zack, "What 'White Privilege' Really Means." The Stone, Opinionator, November 5, 2014, *The New York Times*, Posts, November 6, 2014, Facebook, https://www.facebook.com/nytimes/posts/10150482504744999

3. "Giuliani and Dyson Argue over Violence in Black Communities," *Meet the Press*, NBC, Nov. 24, 2014. http://www.nbcnews.com/storyline/michael-brown-shooting/giuliani-dyson-argue-over-violence-black-communities-n254431. For a transcript see, http://www.realclearpolitics.com/video/2014/1l/23/fireworks_giuliani_vs_michael_eric_dyson_white_police_officers_wont_be_there_if_you_werent_killing_each_other_70_of_the_time.html

4. For discussion of the importance of how early on in a chain of criminal justice such homicides have occurred, and a specific suggestion to correct that with a change in police procedure, see: Ian Ayres and Daniel Markovits, "Ending Excessive Police Force Starts with New Rules of Engagement," *The Washington Post*, December 25, 2014, http://www.washingtonpost.com/opinions/ending-excessive-police-force-starts-with-new-rules-of-engagement/2014/12/25/7fa379c0-8ale-lle4-a085-34e9b9f09a58_story.html

5. Thanks to Yvette Alex-Assensoh for making this point after reading the manuscript.

6. Oregon, State and County Quickfacts, U.S. Census, http://quickfacts.census.gov/qfd/states/41000.html

7. See: Blackpast.Org. "The Black Laws of Oregon, 1844–1857," http://www.blackpast.org/perspectives/black-laws-oregon -1844-1857 "NAREB (National Association of Real Estate Brokers) Code of Ethics, "The Oregon History Project," http://www.ohs.org/education/oregonhistory/historical_records/dspDocument.cfm?doc_ID=C62459FE-B688-7AC7-1F037E830F143F40

8. The distinction between the lesser day of ordinary life and the Greater Day goes back to Ovid's *Fasti*, through the medieval *Book of Days* and the nineteenth century version by Robert Chambers. The passage is from Lawrence's, "The Flying Fish." See: Keith Sagar, *The Art of D.H. Lawrence*, New York, NY: Cambridge University Press, 1996, pp. 205–230, quote from p. 206.

9. W. E. B. Du Bois, *The Souls of Black Folk*, New York, NY: New American Library, 1903, p. 19.

10. On the lack of independent scientific foundation for social racial categories, see: Albert Atkin, *The Philosophy of Race*, Oxford, UK: Acumen, 2012; Nina G. Jablonski, *Living Color: The Biological and Social Meaning of Skin Color*, Oakland, CA: University of California Press, 2012. John Relethford, *The Human Species: An Introduction to Biological Anthropology*, McGraw Hill, 2009–2012; Naomi Zack, *Philosophy of Science and Race*, New York, NY: Routledge, 2002.

Conclusion*

3. On the subject of the importance of public memorials and collective remembering for harms done to African Americans, see Al Frankowski, *Post-Racial Violence, Mourning, and the Limits of Memorialization*, Lanham, MD: Lexington Books, forthcoming.

4. Marc Santora, "Mayor de Blasio Calls for Suspension of Protests." *NY Times*, December 22, 2014. http://www.nytimes.com/2014/12/23/nyregion/mayor-bill-de-blasio-nypd-officers-shooting.html; Patrick Lynch's vulgar political rhetoric is directly quoted in Tina Moore, Rocco Parascandola, and Thomas Tracy, "Patrolmen's Benevolent Association President Patrick Lynch Blasts de Blasio, Says He Is 'Running a F—ing Revolution.'" *New York Daily News*, December 18, 2014. http://www.nydailynews.com/news/politics/pba-president-blasts-de-blasio-ruris-revolution-article-1.2050551; for argument about the harms of racial profiling, see Annabelle Lever, "Why Racial Profiling Is Hard to Justify: A Response to Risse and Zeckhauser." *Philosophy and Public Affairs* 33: 1 (2005), pp. 94–110.

5. "List of Police Television Drama," *Wikipedia*. http://en.wikipedia.org/wiki/List_of_police_television_dramas

6. Carlos Fields, "Award-Winning Community Policing Strategies, 1999–2006, A Report for the International Association of Chiefs of Police." Community Policing Committee, U.S. Department of Justice, COPS Office Community Policing, http://ric-zai-inc.com/Pubhcations/cops-w0451-pub.pdf

7. Ronald Bailey, "Don't Be Terrorized." *Reason.Com*, August 11, 2006. http://reason.com/archives/2006/08/11/dont-be-terrorized

8. Thanks to Kwandwo Assensoh for stressing this point in relation to general ways in which those who are motivated by ideologies may not fully understand their own actions.

9. Ian Ayres and Daniel Markovits, "Ending Excessive Police Force Starts with New Rules of Engagement." *Washington Post*, December 25, 2014, http://www.washingtonpost.com/opinions/ending-excessive-police-force-starts-with-new-rules-of-engagement/2014/12/25/7fa379c0-8ale-lle4-a085-34e9b9f09a58_story.html

---

* The note numbers correspond to the original excerpt.

10. Joshua Daehl, "Police Killings Call for New Kind of Prosecutor." *Bloomberg View*, December 4, 2014. http://www.bloombergview.com/articles/2014-12-04 /police-killings-call-for-new-kind-of-prosecutor

11. "Jonathan Ferrell Killed: Man Shot in North Carolina Was a Former FAMU Football Player." AP, November 13, 2013.

Huffington Post, Crime, http://www.huffingtonpost .com/2013/09/15/jonathanferrell-killed_n_3931282. html; Eliott C. McLaughlin, "2nd Grand Jury Indicts Officer in Shooting of Ex-FAMU Football Player." *CNN*, January 28, 2014. http://www.cnn.com/2014/01/27/us /north-carolina-police-shooting/

Review Exercises

1. Should differences in race, gender, or other identity categories ever be relevant to making decisions about qualified candidates for jobs or educational opportunities? Support your answer with reference to the principle of equality.

2. Evaluate the idea that race is a social construction. What implications follow from that idea in thinking about racism?

3. How does the idea of intersectionality affect conversations about race and racism?

4. Evaluate the ethics of racial profiling and hate crime legislation. Are these useful legal tools?

5. What is "affirmative action," and why does it have this name? Why might critics argue that it is reverse discrimination? And how might a defender of affirmative action reply?

6. Summarize the history of civil rights law, including recent affirmative action decisions. Have we made progress in actualizing the principle of equality in the law? Why or why not?

7. Summarize arguments for and against reparations.

Discussion Cases

1. Reparations. As mentioned in this chapter, there have been various proposals for reparations for past discrimination and injustice, including proposals for reparations for the descendants of formerly enslaved people and for members of Native American tribes. Let's listen in on an imagined conversation between Winona and Ron. Winona argues that what Native Americans deserve is land. "The land was stolen from the tribes," she says. "And the only way to pay for that crime," she continues, "is for land to be returned to the tribes." Ron disagrees. He says, "It's false that the land was stolen. There were treaties and negotiations." Winona shakes her head in disagreement and frowns. "Those treaties were not fair and the natives were usually dispossessed without mercy," she says. "Well anyway," Ron continues, "Even if some land was 'stolen,' there's no way we can give it back." Winona responds, "But Ron, justice requires eye-for-eye. If something is stolen, you have to give it back." Ron says, "But who do we give it back to? And what do we do about people who are living on the land today? Why should our generation be on the hook for something that happened hundreds of years ago?" "Yes, it's a complicated question. I'm not sure what reparations would look like exactly," Winona says. "But before we figure out those details, we need to agree that justice requires reparations. And I'm convinced that the only way to move forward is to account for past injustice."

Who do you agree with in this discussion, Ron or Winona? What proposals for reparations make sense to you, if any? Would the conversation be different with regard to other forms of reparations—say for the descendants of formerly enslaved people?

2. Campus Diversity. During the past couple of decades, colleges and universities have tried to increase their numbers of non-White students by various forms of affirmative action. Some students criticize this as unfair, claiming that it is reverse discrimination to accept students with lower SAT and other scores in an affirmative action program. A different type of problem has recently surfaced. Because Asian Americans often have higher test scores, they are represented on some campuses in numbers greater than their percentage of the population. Some campuses have considered restricting the percentage of Asian and Asian American students they will accept even when their scores are higher than others. At the same time, university campuses across the country are eliminating the use of SAT tests entirely because there appears to be racial bias in these tests and because Black and Hispanic students have lower average test scores than White and Asian students.

Do you think that diversity ought to be a goal of campus admissions? Or do you believe that only academic qualifications ought to count? Do you think limiting the university enrollment of overrepresented groups (such as Asian, Asian American, and White students) based on their percentage of the overall population would be justified? And should universities eliminate these tests entirely? Why or why not?

3. Profiling. Daniel and Ezra were both recently stopped and frisked by the police while walking down the street in New York City. Daniel is African American. Ezra is an immigrant from Israel. Daniel feels that stop-and-frisk policing is blatantly racist. "The cops just target people of color, looking for an excuse to hassle us," he says. "I've got no reason to fear the police. I've done nothing wrong. But it makes me mad." Ezra is a bit more sympathetic to stop-and-frisk policing. In Israel, people's bags are searched when they go to the corner store—especially when there are worries about terrorist attacks. Ezra says, "I'm not worried about it. The cops know something about who is likely to commit a crime. They're not searching old ladies. That would be a waste of time. There are bad guys out there. And I want the cops to catch them. If I fit the profile somewhat, it's worth the hassle. It actually makes me feel safer to know that they are targeting their searches." Daniel replies, "Yeah, but this is America, not the Middle East!"

Is it racist and discriminatory to target certain people for searches? Would it make you feel safer to know that the police were targeting people in this way? Should equal treatment be sacrificed in the name of public safety?

Knowledge Check Answer Key

1. **b.** Justice encourages us to treat similar things in similar ways. The principle of equality helps us make sure social goods are fairly distributed.

2. **d.** It is false that: "Anti-racists do not believe that race or racism exists and advocate instead for a color-blind view of the world."

3. **b.** Structural racism is the term for significant racial disparities that are reflected in and produced by social systems.

4. **c.** Intersectionality allows us to see and consider the various ways in which unjustified discrimination occurs. For example, the gender wage gap is a reality that reflects the effects of intersecting racial, ethnic, and gender biases, resulting in unequal pay, particularly for women of color.

14 Economic Justice

Learning Outcomes

After reading this chapter, you should be able to:

14.1 Explain the concepts of social justice and economic justice from utilitarian, natural law, and deontological points of view.

14.2 Describe the difference between procedural and end-state ideas about justice.

14.3 Explain differences between libertarianism, socialism, and modern liberalism.

14.4 Recount John Rawls's theory of justice and the communitarian critique of his theory.

14.5 Analyze some proposals for responding to economic inequality.

14.6 Defend a thesis about economic justice.

Loan Forgiveness

In the summer of 2022, President Joe Biden signed an executive order that offered loan forgiveness to millions of student loan borrowers. The Biden plan provided $10,000 in loan forgiveness to most borrowers. Proponents of the plan argued that canceling student loan debt would help those who were burdened with loans and struggling to make ends meet. They argued that student loan debt was contributing to growing inequality, as low-income and working-class students were often saddled with debt that prevented them from getting ahead economically. The proponents of the idea also noted race as a factor in economic inequality and suggested that loan forgiveness would help to eliminate the racial wealth gap. And indeed, some proponents of loan forgiveness criticized the Biden plan for being too small. Critics from the NAACP suggested that the $10,000 loan forgiveness was like "pouring a bucket of ice water on a forest fire," noting that Black Americans have much higher levels of student loan indebtedness.[1]

JGI/Blend Images/Thinkstock

But critics of the loan forgiveness plan argued that the plan would contribute to inflation (which was already quite significant in 2022), that it would not help the working poor who did not attend college, and that the funds would mostly go to college-educated people who already have an economic advantage over non-college-educated folks. Senate minority leader Mitch McConnell (R-KY) said, "Democrats' student loan socialism is a slap in the face to working Americans who sacrificed to pay their debt or made different career choices to avoid debt."[2]

What Do You Think?

1. Can the idea of forgiving some student loan debt be justified?

2. What do you think about the two critiques of the Biden plan: from the NAACP and from Mitch McConnell?

3. How important is a college education in economic terms, and is it worth the cost?

4. Can you imagine any other solutions to the problem of economic inequality and the racial wealth gap?

Introduction

14.1 Explain the concepts of social justice and economic justice from utilitarian, natural law, and deontological points of view.

In the previous chapter, we discussed social justice with a focus on equality and discrimination and the question of race. In the current chapter, we continue our discussion of social justice by focusing on economic issues. As you see in the opening vignette, questions about economic inequality are connected to questions about race and racial disparities. As you think about economic issues in this chapter, bear in mind the notion of "intersectionality" that we discussed in the prior chapter: inequality, discrimination, and proposals for social justice involve many intersecting factors including race, gender, and economics.

The question of economic justice asks us to consider inequalities that are reflected in and created by the economic system. This has long been a concern for philosophers. Among the most famous philosophical proposals regarding economics is Plato's. Plato offered a bold proposal in his *Republic* suggesting that among the guardians of society, there should be a kind of communism that went so far as to prohibit private property for the guardian class. He also suggested that these guardians should share their spouses and children in common. Plato even suggested that women would be treated as equals among the guardians. He offered this arrangement as an ideal for the ruling class, with the idea that private property, greed, and family loyalties were often divisive and could distract the rulers from caring for society as a whole. In a book on

the history of philosophy, we might spend more time reflecting on Plato's *Republic* and consider whether he was seriously proposing this kind of communism. In what follows here, we are going to concentrate on more modern proposals for thinking about economic justice, with a special focus on the thinking of Western philosophers during the past half-century. The conversation about economic justice in this modern tradition typically focuses on arguments about key concepts such as socialism, liberalism, capitalism, and libertarianism. These terms will be defined in what follows. And as you'll see here, philosophical accounts of these ideas are often more subtle and more complex than the use of these concepts in popular political discourse.

One important feature of the philosophical debate about economic justice is a fundamental dispute between those who focus on the fairness of social institutions in terms of their outcomes and those who advocate the importance of individual choice and the free market. The first concern—for the impact that social arrangements have on people—is related to the concerns of **social justice** that we discussed in the previous chapter (and that can be distinguished, for example, from criminal justice). The second concern—which focuses on the choices of individuals—can lead to an emphasis on individual wealth creation and individual charity. As we'll discuss in this chapter, there is usually thought to be a difference between social justice and charity: social justice usually includes some claim about obligation or necessity, while charity is more of a gift or a choice.

The idea of social justice has roots in the natural law tradition and in religious approaches to ethics. As we saw in Chapter 7, the Western philosophical tradition traces the natural law idea through the work of Thomas Aquinas and the developed Catholic tradition. Thomas Massaro, a Jesuit scholar of social justice, explains that the notion of social justice boils down to "the goal of achieving a right ordering of society. A just social order is one that ensures that all people have fair and equitable opportunities to live decent lives free of inordinate burdens and deprivation."[3] We saw in the previous chapter how this kind of concern would apply in thinking about racism and other forms of discrimination. But the social justice ideal has also been applied to the economy more generally. Such an application has been advocated by the Roman Catholic Pope Francis, an outspoken critic of consumer society and unbridled capitalism that neglects people in need. In a text that he wrote during the COVID-19 pandemic, *Fratelli Tutti* (which can be translated as "All Are Brothers"), he said, "Once this health crisis passes, our worst response would be to plunge even more deeply into feverish consumerism and new forms of egotistic self-preservation."[4] He explained further, using religious language:

> In God's plan, each individual is called to promote his or her own development, and this includes finding the best economic and technological means of multiplying goods and increasing wealth. Business abilities, which are a gift from God, should always be clearly directed to the development of others and to eliminating poverty, especially through the creation of diversified work opportunities. The right to private property is always accompanied by the primary and prior principle of the subordination of all private property to the universal destination of the earth's goods, and thus the right of all to their use."[5]

This account reflects a Christian social justice idea that can be connected to the natural law theory of ethics. (We have an excerpt from Pope Francis at the end of this chapter.) It is worth underlining the pontiff's suggestion that the right to private property is not absolute and that the goal of eliminating poverty is more important than the desire of individuals to amass wealth.

Similar ideas can be found in other religious traditions. The concept of *zakat*, often translated as *almsgiving*, is one of the five pillars of Islam: this typically includes a mandatory contribution of individual wealth to the common good, with a special focus on aid to the people in greatest need. Sohail Hashmi explains: "Apart from voluntary efforts to relieve poverty, the Islamic tradition contains an array of obligatory measures as well. Distributive justice in Islam is not simply a recommendation; it is a requirement of faith."[6]

Of course, this book is not about religious ethics. So our focus here will be on secular thinking about social justice, economic justice, and distributive justice as articulated within the Western philosophical tradition. Social justice is generally focused on distributions of goods among people in society, with an emphasis on minimizing inequalities across social classes. This idea can easily be grounded in utilitarianism. For example, John Stuart Mill was particularly interested in the question of economic justice. Mill thought that the vast majority of workers were "slaves to toil in which they have no interest, and therefore feel no interest— drudging from early morning till late at night for bare necessaries, and with all the intellectual and moral deficiencies which that implies."[7] As a utilitarian, Mill was interested in finding ways to alleviate drudgery and poverty while producing the greatest happiness for the greatest number. With this in mind, it is not surprising that he was opposed to slavery (we discussed this as well in Chapter 5). Not only did Mill reject the notion that White people should have despotic power over Black people, but he also rejected the idea that individuals should be reduced to mere working machines. He saw no value in "work for work's sake," and he thought that human happiness required leisure. Mill concluded, "To reduce very greatly the quantity of work required to carry on existence, is as needful as to distribute it more equally."[8] He also thought that the economy was unjust insofar as it did not connect hard work with profit. From Mill's perspective, the problem is that the rich are born into wealth and leisure, while the poor are born into a life of poverty and hard work. This runs counter to the idea that there should be a connection between success and merit. As Mill explains with reference to the gross inequalities of the nineteenth century, "The very idea of distributive justice, or of any proportionality between success and merit, or between success and exertion, is in the present state of society so manifestly chimerical as to be relegated to the regions of romance."[9] Mill means that there is no justice in an economy in which those who work hard remain poor, while the rich don't work. Mill wanted to find a way to help poor people without making them dependent on that help. As he explained it, the goal is to "give the greatest amount of needful help, with the smallest encouragement to undue reliance on it."[10] From the utilitarian standpoint, the challenge is to figure out how best to regulate the economy in a way that produces encouragement for hard work while also preventing impoverished, unemployed, and working poor people from falling through the cracks.

Concern for social justice is sometimes connected with claims about the value of equality itself, as well as that of human rights, human dignity, and solidarity among people. There are disagreements about the exact definition of these terms, even among those who are concerned with social justice. For example, equality may be defined as *substantive equality*, meaning that individuals should have exactly the same access to and amount of substantive goods. Or equality can be defined as *equality of opportunity*, meaning that individuals should have an equal chance to obtain goods. In either case, the pursuit of equality can lead to a conflict with other values, such as liberty. For example, to ensure equality, we may have to violate the liberty of those who possess certain goods so that we might redistribute those goods among others (as we do to some extent in a system of taxation that redistributes private property for social welfare purposes). Some conceptions of justice do emphasize liberty as the central value, as Mill himself did in his work *On Liberty*. The trick, for a utilitarian like Mill, is to find a way to balance liberty and the need for distributive or social justice.

The deontological theory of Immanuel Kant provides another source for thinking about human dignity and respect for autonomy and human dignity. Kant is opposed to using individuals as a means to an end, and some would argue that to take a part of someone's income through taxation and redistribute it to others is a form of using that person as a means. But Kant also thought that charity and beneficence were important

values. In the *Foundations of the Metaphysics of Morals* (excerpted in Chapter 6), Kant indicates that those who refuse to help people in need may end up contradicting themselves, since they would expect others to help them if they were in need. In his *Lectures on Ethics*, Kant indicates that one reason to give to people in need is out of a sense that the social structure is unjust:

> In giving to an unfortunate man we do not give him a gratuity but only help to return to him that of which the general injustice of our system has deprived him. For if none of us drew to himself a greater share of the world's wealth than his neighbor, there would be no rich and no poor. Even charity therefore is an act of duty imposed upon us by the rights of others and the debt we owe to them.[11]

Notice that Kant emphasizes here that the existence of inequality (when some take a greater share of the world's wealth than others) leads to the conclusion that "charity" is required by duty and the debt we owe to others who have less than we do. We put this in scare quotes here because, as we'll see in a moment, there is something counterintuitive about claiming that charity (which is typically understood as a gift) is required by duty. At any rate, given what Kant says here about the need to help the unfortunate, it is not surprising then that he supports the right of the state to tax the wealthy and redistribute those funds to support people in need. Kant says that since there are some members of society who are not able to support themselves, "the government is authorized to constrain the wealthy to provide the means of sustenance to those who are unable to provide for their most necessary natural needs."[12] He further explains, "The wealthy have acquired an obligation to the commonwealth, since they owe their existence to an act of submitting to its protection and care, which they need in order to live; on this obligation the state now bases its right to contribute what is theirs to maintaining their fellow citizens."[13] This might mean that Kant is imagining some kind of socialism (as some scholars contend), or it might mean that he is merely in favor of some kind of welfare system within a capitalist economy.[14] But however we interpret this, it seems clear that Kant thinks that governments are entitled to tax wealthy people to support those in need.

Let's return now to the worry expressed above in Kantian language, which is that taxing people seems to use the labor of those who are taxed as a means to satisfy other people's needs. Some critics of taxation go so far as to claim this is a kind of "slavery of the talented" or "exploitation of the hard working."[15] This kind of objection to redistributions of income and wealth is typically made from a **libertarian** point of view that emphasizes liberty in contrast with equality. Libertarian accounts of justice are often grounded in a natural law approach to ethics with roots in the work of John Locke (excerpted in Chapter 7). Locke's emphasis on a natural right to property is a fundamental starting point for those who defend a free market economy. Other philosophers who focus on liberty connect their ideas to those of Ayn Rand (mentioned in our discussion of egoism in Chapter 4—see the excerpt at the end of this chapter). Tibor Machan, a libertarian author who builds on Rand's ideas, stresses that individual human beings "possess free will and need to guide their own lives to achieve excellence or to flourish."[16] Machan contrasts his theory of justice with other views of justice that require fairness, order, harmony, or social welfare. From Machan's libertarian point of view, the economy should be left alone so that individuals are free to create, trade, and earn whatever nature and the market allow them to. From this standpoint, charity is acceptable—but as the free choice of an individual to help others in need and not as an obligation of justice.

We can see here that we should distinguish justice from certain other moral notions. For example, justice is not the same as charity. It is one thing to say that a community, like a family, should help members when they are in need, out of concern for their welfare. But is helping people in need ever a matter of justice? If we say that it is, we imply that it is not morally optional. Justice is often defined as giving people what is rightly due. Charity gives above and beyond the requirements of justice. Ethicists use the term **supererogatory** to describe actions that go above and beyond the call of duty. The word *supererogatory* comes from Latin roots, meaning "paying more than is due" or "payment in addition." There is nothing unjust about giving charity. But we usually think that charity is not required by justice, it is supererogatory. Furthermore, justice is not the only relevant moral issue in economic matters. Efficiency and liberty are also moral values that play a role in discussions on ethics and economics. When we say that a particular economic system is *efficient*, we generally mean that it produces a maximum amount of desired goods and services, or the most value for the least cost. Thus, some people say that a pure free market economy is a good economic system, based on the claim that it is the most efficient, the one best able to create wealth. But it is quite another question whether such a system is also a *just* system or if it enhances liberty. If we could have the most efficient and perhaps even the most just economic system in the world, would it be worth it if we were not also free to make our own decisions about many things, including how to earn a living?

Distributive Justice

14.2 Describe the difference between procedural and end-state ideas about justice.

Sorting out the relationship among these values is one of the primary goals of philosophical reflection on distributive justice. A significant concern is how the benefits and burdens of society are allocated—for example, who and how many people have what percentage of the goods or wealth in a society. Thus, suppose that in some society, 5 percent of the people possessed 90 percent of the wealth, and the other 95 percent of the people possessed only 10 percent of the wealth. Asking whether this arrangement would be just raises a question of distributive justice. Now, how would we go about answering this question? It does seem that this particular distribution of wealth is quite unbalanced. But must a distribution be equal for it to be just? To answer this question, we can examine two quite different ways of approaching distributive justice. One is what we can call a *process view*, and the other is an *end-state view*.

Process Distributive Justice

According to some philosophers, any economic distribution (or any system that allows a particular economic distribution) is just if the process by which it comes about is itself just. Some call this **procedural justice**. For example, if the wealthiest 5 percent of the people got their 90 percent of the wealth fairly—they competed for jobs, they were honest, they did not take what was not theirs—then what they earned would be rightly theirs. In contrast, if wealthy individuals obtained their wealth through force or fraud, then their having such wealth would be unfair because they took it unfairly. Indeed, we might suspect that because talent is more evenly distributed, there is something suspicious about this uneven distribution of wealth. But there would be nothing unfair or unjust about the uneven distribution in itself. Some people are wealthy because of good luck and inheritance, and others are poor because of bad economic luck. However, in this view, those with money they get through luck or inheritance are not being unjust in keeping it even when others are poor. (See the reading selection by Robert Nozick, which appears at the end of this chapter, for an example of elements of this view.)

End-State Distributive Justice

Other philosophers believe that the process by which people attain wealth is not the only consideration relevant to determining the justice of an economic distribution. They believe that we also should look at the way things turn out, the end state, or the resulting distribution of wealth in a society, and ask about its fairness. Suppose that through inheritance, a small minority of lucky people came to possess 95 percent of society's wealth. Would it be fair for them to have so much wealth when others in the society are extremely poor? How would we usually judge whether such an arrangement is fair? We would look to see if there is some good reason why the wealthy are wealthy. Did they work hard for it? Did they make important social contributions? These might be nonarbitrary or good

reasons for wealthy people to possess their wealth rightly or justly. However, if they are wealthy while others are poor because they, unlike the others, were born of a certain favored race, sex, eye color, or height, we might be inclined to say that it is not fair for them to have more. What reasons, then, justify differences in wealth?

Several different views exist on this issue. Radical egalitarians deny that there is any good reason why some people should possess greater wealth than others. Their reasons for this view vary. They might stress that human beings are essentially alike as human and that this is more important than any differentiating factors about them, including their talents and what they do with them. They might argue that society is an agreement for the mutual advancement of all and should treat each of its members as free and equal citizens. Or they might use religious or semireligious reasons, such as the idea that the Earth is given to all of us equally, and thus, we each have an equal right to the goods derived from it. However, even egalitarians must decide what it is that they believe should be equal. For example, should there be equality of wealth and income or equality of satisfaction or welfare? These are not the same. Some people have little wealth or income but nevertheless are quite satisfied, while others who have great wealth or income are quite dissatisfied.

On the other hand, at least some basic differences between people should factor into what distribution of goods is thought to be just. For example, some people simply have different needs than others. People are not identical physically, and some of us need more food and different kinds of health care than others. Karl Marx's phrase "To each according to his need" captures something of this variant of egalitarianism.[17] Nevertheless, it is puzzling why only this particular differentiating factor—need—should justify differences in wealth. In fact, we generally would tend to pick out others as well—differences in merit, achievement, effort, or contribution.

Suppose, for example, that someone uses their talent and education, training and skill, to produce something useful—whether an athlete, an inventor, or an artist. If people value what that person creates, don't they deserve to earn a profit? Wouldn't they *merit*, or have a

Library of Congress, Prints & Photographs Division, Reproduction number LC-US262-16530 (b&w film copy neg.)

Figure 14-1 Karl Marx (1818–1883) was a critic of capitalism.

right to, this money? Wouldn't it be fair that the athlete, inventor, or artist makes a profit, even if others do not earn as much? It would seem so. But is this because the artist, athlete, or inventor has an innate or *native talent* that others do not have? But talent is a matter of luck. The athlete, artist, or inventor is lucky to have that talent, while others are not so lucky. But this seems morally arbitrary.

But perhaps the wealth of the artist, inventor, or athlete stems not only from their talent, but also from the way they used and developed it. They put a great deal of *effort* into cultivating their talent. Would this be a good reason to say that they deserved the wealth that they earned from it? This might seem reasonable if we did not also know that motivation and work ethic might also have been, in some ways, gifts of circumstance, opportunity, and social support. Furthermore, effort alone would not seem to be a good reason for monetary reward, or else a farmer, plumber, or auto mechanic who works long hours in dirty, hot, or difficult conditions could have a claim to making more money than an engineer who sits comfortably working at a computer screen. Similarly, a student would not be justified in demanding an A simply because they spent

a lot of time and effort studying for a test—when their performance actually merited a B.

Finally, perhaps the artist, inventor, or athlete deserves to earn wealth because of the nature of their *contribution*, because what they produce is valuable to people. Again, this argument seems at first reasonable, and yet, there are also fairness problems here. Suppose an inventor or artist produces something that is potentially valuable—but that the market shifts or that someone else has created a similar product. Then this happenstance would also lessen the value of the product and its monetary reward. Isn't this also a matter of luck? And is it fair? Furthermore, it is often difficult to know how to value particular contributions to a jointly produced product or result. How do we measure and compare the value of the contributions of the person with the idea, the investors, the product developers, and so forth, so that we can know what portion of the profits are rightly due to them? Marxists are well known for their claim that the people who own the factories or have put up the money for a venture profit from the workers' labor unfairly or out of proportion to their own contributions.

This mention of Marx and Marxism reminds us that there is no consensus about what counts as a fair distribution of wealth. Revolutions and wars have been fought in the name of various ideas of economic justice.

Equal Opportunity

Another viewpoint on distributive justice does not fit easily into either the process or end-state category. In this view, the key to whether an unequal distribution of wealth in a society is just is whether people have a fair chance to attain positions of greater income or wealth. That is, equality of wealth is not required, only equal opportunity to attain it. (We discussed equal opportunity in connection to civil rights and nondiscrimination in Chapter 13.) We might see the notion of equal opportunity as symbolized by the Statue of Liberty in New York Harbor. The statue sits on Liberty Island, where, historically, new immigrants to the United States were processed. It represents the idea that in the United States, all people have a chance to make a good life for themselves provided they work hard. But just what is involved in the notion of equal opportunity, and is it a realizable goal or ideal? Literally, it involves both opportunities and some sort of equality of chances to attain them. An *opportunity* is a chance to attain some benefit or goods. People have equal chances to attain these goods, first of all, when there are no barriers to prevent them from doing so. Opportunities can still be said to be equal if barriers exist, as long as they affect everyone equally. Clearly, if racism, sexism, or other forms of prejudice prevent some people from having the same chances as others to attain valued goals or positions in a society, then there is not equal opportunity. For example, if women have twice the family responsibilities as men, do they really have an equal opportunity to compete professionally? Our discussion of the gender pay gap previously shows how opportunities that are supposed to be equal by law or policy may, in fact, be rendered unequal by social practices.

According to James Fishkin, an expert on political theory, if there is equal opportunity in my society, "I should not be able to enter a hospital ward of healthy newborn babies and, on the basis of class, race, sex, or other arbitrary native characteristics, predict the eventual positions in society of those children."[18] However, knowing what we do about families, education, and the real-life prospects of children, we know how difficult this ideal would be to realize. In reality, children do not start life with equal chances. High-income families are able to give many educational, motivational, and experiential benefits to their children but families with lower incomes cannot, and this makes their opportunities effectively unequal. Schooling greatly affects equal opportunity, and money spent for a school—teachers, facilities, and books—can make a big difference in the kind of education provided. However, funding per pupil on schooling in the United States varies considerably according to locale. And affluent parents can supplement public schooling with private tutors, educational summer camps, music lessons, specialized athletic coaching, and other educational opportunities. Is it fair that some kids have these opportunities while others do not?

One version of equal opportunity is the *starting-gate theory*, which assumes that if people had equal starts in life, they would have equal chances. The philosopher Bernard Williams provides a famous example of this theory. In his imaginary society, a class of skillful warriors has for generations held all of the highest positions and passed them on to their offspring. At some point, the warriors decide to let all people compete for membership in their class. The children of the warrior class are much stronger and better nourished than the other children, who, not surprisingly, fail to gain entrance to the warrior class. Would these other children have had effective equality of opportunity to gain entrance to the warrior class and its benefits? Even if the competition was formally fair, the outside children were at an extreme disadvantage and had no real chance of winning. But how could initial starting points then be equalized? Perhaps by providing special aids or help to the other children to prepare them for the competition. Applying this example to our real-world situation would mean that a society should give special aid to the children of disadvantaged families if it wants to ensure equal opportunity.[19] According to Fishkin, however, to do this effectively would require serious infringements on family autonomy. For it would mean not only helping disadvantaged children, but also preventing wealthier parents from giving special advantages to their children. Moreover, people have different natural talents and abilities, and those who have abilities that are more socially valued will likely have greater opportunities. Does this mean, then, that the idea of equal opportunity is unrealizable? It may only mean that our efforts to increase equality of opportunity must be balanced with the pursuit of other values, such as family autonomy and efficiency.

Still, some philosophers have other questions about the ideal of equal opportunity. They argue that the whole emphasis on equality is misplaced and distracts us from what is really important. The philosopher Harry Frankfurt claims that rather than focusing on the fact that some have more than others, it would be better to focus on whether people have enough. We care not that one billionaire makes a few million more than another, but rather, that everyone should have sufficient means to pursue their aspirations. Frankfurt calls his position the "doctrine of sufficiency," in contrast to theories that make equality, in itself, the primary goal.[20]

Although the doctrine of equal opportunity is appealing because it implies equal rewards for equal performance and doors open to all, some thinkers object to the notion of meritocracy on which it is based. According to John Schaar, the equal opportunity ideal is based on notions of a natural aristocracy.[21] Those of us who do not have the natural talent of an Einstein, a Serena Williams, or a Beyoncé will not have the same chances to succeed and prosper as those who do have such talents. We can enter the race, but we delude ourselves if we think that we have a real chance to win it. Schaar believes that stress on equal opportunity thus contributes to the gap between rich and poor. He also argues that emphasis on equal opportunity threatens the foundations of equality and democracy. Based, as it is, on the notion of a marketplace in which we, as atomic individuals, compete against our fellows, it threatens human solidarity. It does so even more if it is accompanied by a tendency to think that those who win are in some way more valuable as persons.[22]

Other philosophers argue that justice demands that people should not be penalized for things over which they have no control. Thus, it would seem unjust or unfair for people to suffer who, through no fault of their own, cannot compete or cannot compete well in the market, for example, people with physical or mental illness, or individuals with physical or mental disabilities.[23] Here we return to the idea that matters of luck may be seen as morally arbitrary and should not be reflected in a just distribution of society's benefits and burdens.

Political and Economic Theories

14.3 Explain differences between libertarianism, socialism, and modern liberalism.

In discussions of economic justice, people often make use of specific economic and political terms and theories—including *libertarianism, capitalism, socialism, liberalism,* and *communitarianism.* To more fully understand the central issues of economic justice, it will be helpful to take a closer look at these terms and theories, to distinguish them from each other and to determine how each relates to different conceptions of justice. Some of the theories—capitalism and socialism, for example—can be differentiated from one another not only by basic definitions, but also by the different emphases they place on the values of liberty, efficiency, and justice. They are further differentiated by how they

favor or disfavor process or end-state views of distributive justice. A brief discussion of each will help elucidate these values and views of distributive justice.

Libertarianism

Libertarianism is a political theory about both the role of government and the importance of liberty in human life. Libertarians such as Tibor Machan and Ayn Rand (see Chapter 4) believe that we are free when we are not constrained or restrained by other people. Sometimes, this type of liberty is referred to as a basic right to noninterference. Thus, if you stand in the doorway and block my exit, you are violating my liberty to go where I wish. However, if I fall and break my leg and am unable to leave, my liberty rights are violated by no one. The doorway is open and unblocked, and I am free to go out. I cannot go out simply because of my injury.

According to libertarianism, government has a minimal function that is primarily administrative. It should provide an orderly civic space in which people can go about their business. It does have an obligation to ensure that people's liberty rights are not violated, that people do not block doorways (or freeways, for that matter). However, government has no obligation to see that my broken leg is repaired so that I can walk where I please. In particular, it has no business taxing you to pay for my leg repair or any other good that I (or you) might like to have or even need. Such needs can be addressed by charities, but they are not matters of social justice or obligation.

Libertarians would be more likely to support a process view of distributive justice than an end-state view. Any economic arrangement would be just so long as it resulted from a fair process of competition, and so long as people did not take what is not theirs or get their wealth by fraudulent or coercive means. However, libertarians do not believe that governments should be concerned with end-state considerations. They should not try to even out any imbalance between rich and poor that might result from a fair process. They should not be involved in any redistribution of wealth. This includes potential redistributions from social insurance arrangements such as Social Security, Medicare, and Medicaid.

The reading at the end of this chapter by Robert Nozick illustrates many aspects of the libertarian theory. For example, he argues that people ought to be free to exchange or transfer to others what they have acquired by just means. Nozick's theory of justice is not focused on end states. He refers to end-state concerns as "patterned" or "current time-slice principles of justice." For Nozick, the goal should not be to establish a pattern of distribution, since that pattern would hold good only for a limited slice of time. If individuals were free to trade and create, the pattern would be disrupted. To ensure that the distributive pattern would continue to hold, the state would have to employ coercive measures to enforce the ideal pattern. Those coercive measures would violate the liberty of individuals to create, to trade, and to acquire surpluses that create inequalities. Following other libertarians, Nozick thinks of taxation of earnings to achieve even desirable public goods as "on a par with forced labor."[24] You can reflect further on these views as you study this selection.

Ultimately, libertarianism is a theory about the importance of liberty, of rights to noninterference by others, and of the proper role of government. Libertarians also have generally supported capitalist free market economies, so brief comments about this type of economic system and its supporting values are appropriate here.

Capitalism

Capitalism is an economic system in which individuals or business corporations (not the government or community) own and control much or most of the country's capital. *Capital* is the wealth or raw materials, factories, and other means that are used to produce more wealth. Capitalism is also usually associated with a free-enterprise system, an economic system that allows people freedom to set prices and determine production, and to make their own choices about how to earn and spend their incomes. A more extreme version of free enterprise is often called a **laissez-faire** economic system. *Laissez-faire* means "leave alone" or "let be"; in laissez-faire capitalism, the government is supposed to leave the economy and markets alone, without regulation or other interference. It generally assumes that people are motivated by profit and engage in competition, and that value is a function of supply and demand. Proponents of laissez-faire capitalism take a range of positions—with some

arguing that the government should keep its hands entirely off the economy and others accepting various minimal forms of governmental regulation.

Certain philosophical values and beliefs also undergird capitalism. Among these can be a libertarian philosophy that stresses the importance of liberty and limited government. Certain beliefs about the nature of human motivation also are often implicit, for example, that people are motivated by rational self-interest. Some people argue that capitalism and a free market economy constitute the best economic system because it is the most efficient one, producing greater wealth for more people than any other system. People produce more and better, they say, when there is something in it for them or their families, or when what they are working for is their own profit. Moreover, producers will usually make only what consumers want, and they know what consumers want by what they are willing to buy. So if people make mousetraps and mind-reading computers that consumers want, they will be rewarded by people buying their products. Exemplifying this outlook is economist Milton Friedman, who maintained that the one and only "social responsibility" of a business is "to use its resources and engage in activities designed to increase profits."[25] Friedman warned that it was "subversive" to claim that corporations have any other form of responsibility than profit-making. "Few trends could so thoroughly undermine the very foundations of our free society as the acceptance by corporate officials of a social responsibility other than to make as much money for their stockholders as possible."[26] Libertarians and other supporters of capitalism stress process views of justice. They generally agree that people deserve what they earn through natural talent and hard work.

Socialism

Socialism is an economic system, a political movement, and a social theory. Socialists tend to hold that the economy should be deliberately structured so that the results benefit most people. This way of describing socialism suggests its overlap with utilitarianism. Indeed, it is not surprising that John Stuart Mill was sympathetic to socialism (as might be inferred from some of his comments discussed previously).[27] In contemporary societies, socialism often involves some degree of public management and ownership of goods and services such as education, health care, utilities, or (more rarely) industry and natural resources.

Communism, which can be considered an extreme version of socialism, calls for public ownership of all means of production, radical equality, and the abolition of social classes. Communism is most closely associated with the ideas of the philosopher Karl Marx, who called for a revolution of the working class (what he called *the proletariat*) against the ruling upper class of capitalists (what he called *the bourgeoisie*). But there are degrees of socialism. Not all socialists are Marxists or communists. And there are various forms of socialist political philosophy including democratic socialism and social democracy. These terms have been associated with positions taken by American politicians such as Bernie Sanders and Alexandria Ocasio-Cortez.

Socialists generally criticize capitalism for its unpredictable business cycles, which often produce unemployment and poverty. They argue that it inevitably generates conflicts between workers and the owners of the means of production. Rather than allow the few to profit, often at the expense of the many, socialism holds that the government should engage in planning and adjust production to the needs of all of the people. Justice is stressed over efficiency, but central planning is thought to contribute to efficiency as well as justice. Generally, socialism is concerned with end-state justice and is egalitarian in orientation, while making allowances for obvious differences among people in terms of their different needs. Socialism can also be seen to emphasize the value of a certain form of liberty. But in contrast to libertarianism, socialism holds that it is not just external constraints, such as laws, that can limit people's liberty. Socialists tend to think that liberty actually requires freedom from such "internal" constraints as lack of food, education, or health care. Socialists believe that the government has an obligation to address these needs.

As with all labels, the term socialism simplifies. Thus, there are also different kinds or levels of socialism. Some are highly centralized and rely on a command economy, where the state determines prices and wages. Others stress the need for the government to cushion the economy in times of recession, for example, by manipulating interest rates and monetary policy. Most contemporary societies are, in fact, hybrids of socialism and capitalism. For example, in the United States, most K–12 education is socialized, along with police and fire services and such programs as Medicare and Social Security. In various European countries, such services as health insurance, health care, and higher education may be publicly managed or provided.

One key distinction between a libertarian and a socialist conception of justice is that the former recognizes only negative rights and the latter stresses positive rights. **Negative rights** are rights not to be harmed in some way. Because libertarians take liberty as a primary value, they stress the negative right of people not to have their liberty restricted by others. These are rights of noninterference. In the economic arena, libertarians support economic liberties that create wealth, and they believe that people should be able to dispose of their wealth as they choose. For the libertarian, the government's role is to protect negative rights, not positive rights. Contrary to this view, socialists believe that the government should not only protect people's negative rights not to be interfered with, but also attend to their positive rights to basic necessities. Consequently, a right to life must not only involve a right not to be killed, but also a right to what is necessary to live, namely, food, clothing, and shelter. **Positive rights** to be helped or benefited are sometimes called "welfare rights." Those who favor such a concept of rights may ask what a right to life would amount to if one did not have the means to live. Positive economic rights are often defined as rights to basic economic subsistence. Those who favor positive rights would allow for a variety of ways to provide for them, from direct public grants to incentives of various sorts. Socialists generally place more emphasis on positive rights—including, for example, the right to a basic income or the right to work, while libertarians focus more on negative rights.

None of these systems is problem free. Socialism, at least in recent times, often has not lived up to the ideals of its supporters. Central planning systems have often failed as societies become more complex and participate in international economic systems. Communist societies have tended to become authoritarian, in part, because it is difficult to get universal voluntary consent to centrally controlled plans for production and other policies. Basic necessities may be provided for all, but their quality has often turned out to be low.

Capitalism and a free market economy also are open to moral criticism. Many people, through no fault of their own, cannot or do not compete well and fall through the cracks. Unemployment is a natural part of the system, but it is also debilitating for the unemployed worker. When unemployment is high and labor markets are tight, as they have been in recent years, employers can make ever-increasing demands on their employees, knowing that they can always be replaced by someone who will be grateful for a job. While this means that recessions and high unemployment help to increase productivity, the cost of increased productivity is felt in the lives of laborers. As productivity increases, those at the top profit, while those at the bottom may suffer. From a social justice standpoint, what matters most is the dignity and well-being of working people, not the profits of those at the top of the corporate ladder.

Libertarianism has been criticized for failing to notice that society provides the means by which individuals seek their own good, for example, by means of transportation and communication. It often fails to notice that state action is needed to protect liberty rights and rights to security, property, and litigation. It has also been criticized for rejecting popular social welfare programs such as publicly funded compulsory primary education.[28] Libertarians have been accused of ignoring the effects that individuals' initial life circumstances have on their fair chances to compete for society's goods.

Let us consider whether a hybrid political and economic system might be better, one that combines aspects of libertarianism, capitalism, and socialism. The most accurate term for such a system is *modern liberalism,* even though the term *liberalism* has meant many things to many people. One reason for using this name is that it is typically applied to the views of one philosopher whose work exemplified it and whose philosophy we shall also discuss here: John Rawls, whose theory of justice we will discuss in more detail in what follows.

Table 14-1   Outline of Moral Approaches to Theories of Economic Justice

	Socialism	Liberalism	Libertarianism
Thesis	Equality is a primary value.	Liberty and equality are values that ought to be balanced.	Liberty is a primary value.
Corollaries and Implications	Economic inequality should be moderated through centralized redistributions of wealth.	Two principles of justice aim to balance liberty and equality, with the state playing a role in distributive justice.	Capitalist property relations and market exchanges produce innovation and wealth; liberty upsets patterned distributions.
Connections with Moral Theory	Utilitarian concern for greatest happiness for the greatest number; natural law concern for social justice; focus on "positive" rights	Ideal social contract under a veil of ignorance, based on intuitions about fairness; utilitarian concern for balancing liberty with welfare	Autonomy is a key value, including respect for property rights, which is considered a "negative" right.
Relevant Authors/ Examples	John Stuart Mill; Pope Francis	John Rawls	Robert Nozick; Ayn Rand

Modern Liberalism

But before turning to Rawls's theory of justice in more detail, let's provide an overview of modern liberal political and economic theory. Suppose we were to attempt to combine the positive elements of libertarianism, capitalism, and socialism. What would we pull from each? Liberty, or the ability to be free from unjust constraint by others, the primary value stressed by libertarianism, would be one value to preserve. However, we may want to support a fuller notion of liberty that also recognizes the power of internal constraints. We also might want to recognize both positive and negative rights and hold

that government ought to play some role in supporting the former as well as the latter. Stress on this combination of elements characterizes modern liberalism.

In a draft version of the American Declaration of Independence, Thomas Jefferson wrote of the inalienable rights to life, liberty, and happiness, and concluded that "in order to *secure these ends* governments are instituted among men." In Jefferson's final draft, the phrase is "in order to *secure these rights* governments are instituted among men."[29] In some ways, these two accounts of the purpose of government parallel the two major approaches to determining when a distribution of wealth is just: the

---

▶ **Knowledge Check**   Answers appear at the end of the chapter.

1. Which of the following would a utilitarian like John Stuart Mill agree with?

   a. Poor people deserve to be poor because they are not willing to work.

   b. The proletariat should rise up in a revolution against the bourgeoisie.

   c. It would be better for everyone if poverty, drudgery, and extreme inequality were eliminated.

   d. The idea of private property ought to be eliminated because it is a violation of the natural law.

2. Which of the following ideas claims that charity is not a duty, but something extra?

   a. The idea that charity is supererogatory

   b. The idea that charity is deontological

   c. The idea that charity is socialism

   d. The idea that charity is Marxist

3. What is procedural justice?

   a. The idea that we should try to create a fixed pattern of distributions that results in substantive equality

   b. The idea that some inequalities can be justified so long as the processes that result in those inequalities are fair

   c. The idea that we need to take our time in processing our thinking about justice

   d. The idea that since inequalities in wealth are immoral, we need a process of taxation to eliminate wealth

4. Which of the following best explains the difference between laissez-faire capitalism and socialism?

   a. Laissez-faire capitalism encourages the ruling class to be lazy and inefficient, while socialism forces people to work.

   b. Laissez-faire capitalism emphasizes the importance of equality, while socialism focuses more on the importance of liberty and individual merit.

   c. Laissez-faire capitalism is a kind of utilitarian theory that aims to abolish private property, while socialism aims to encourage private wealth creation.

   d. Laissez-faire capitalism wants the government to leave the economy alone, while socialism encourages government regulation and control of the economy.

end-state view with its stress on positive rights ("to secure these ends") and the process view with its stress on negative rights of noninterference ("to secure these rights"). Liberalism features a mixture of these two conceptions of rights.

Modern liberalism also generally seeks to promote an economic system that is efficient as well as just. Thus, it usually allows capitalist incentives and inequalities of wealth. However, since it values positive as well as negative rights, modern liberalism is also concerned about the least advantaged members of the society. In this view, companies and corporations are generally regarded as guests in society, because government allows their creation and protects them from certain liabilities, with the understanding that they will contribute to the good of all. Accordingly, they are thought to owe something in return to the community—as a matter of justice—and have responsibilities beyond their own best interest. Modern liberalism also points out that the economic productivity and efficiency of a society depend on human development and communication and transportation systems. Thus, public investment in education, health, roads, technology, and research and development provides a crucial foundation for the private economy.[30] Of course, the modern liberal idea has been fleshed out in various ways in concrete situations. But the basic idea is that we need to work to find a balance between liberty and equality.

John Rawls's Theory of Justice

14.4 Recount John Rawls's theory of justice and the communitarian critique of his theory.

During the past half-century, philosophers who think about distributive justice have typically focused their reflections on the work of John Rawls, whose theory of justice embodies the basic idea of a modern liberal approach. In this section, we'll consider Rawls's theory in some detail, while also considering a response to this theory known as communitarianism. In the next section, we'll look more carefully at a few current issues in economic justice.

The most widely discussed work of political philosophy of the past five decades is John Rawls's 1971 book

Figure 14-2 John Rawls (1921–2002) offered a theory of "justice as fairness."

A Theory of Justice, which lays out a moral justification for a modern liberal state.[31] According to Rawls, justice is the first virtue of social institutions, just as truth is the first virtue of scientific systems. It is most important for scientific systems to be true or well supported. They may be elegant or interesting or in line with our other beliefs, but that is not the primary requirement for their acceptance. Something similar would be the case for social and economic institutions with regard to justice. We would want them to be efficient, but what is the point of efficiency if the overall society is unjust? Among the fundamental questions Rawls raises are: What is justice, and how do we know whether an economic system is just? Rawls sought to develop a set of principles or guidelines that we could apply to our institutions, enabling us to judge whether they are just or unjust. To do so, he uses a famous thought experiment, which he calls the *original position,* designed to produce basic principles of justice.

Rawls asks us to consider what rational individuals would agree on if they came together to form a society for their mutual benefit. He argues that the principles these rational individuals would select to guide their society can be taken as basic principles of justice, provided that the decision procedure was genuinely fair. In other words, we must first ensure that these individuals are so situated that they can choose fairly. We can then ask what principles of justice they would be likely to accept.

But what makes a choice or a choice situation fair, and what would make it unfair? One obvious answer is that a fair decision should be free from *bias*; it should prevent individuals from being able to "rig the system" in their favor or "stack the deck" to benefit people like them. The way to avoid bias is for people to ignore or forget their own particular situation so that their judgments might be free from bias. To eliminate such bias, then, Rawls argues that people in the original position must not be able to know biasing information about themselves. They must not know their age, sex, race, talents, education, social and economic status, religion, political views, and so on. A truly fair choice can thus be made only from behind what he calls a *veil of ignorance*.

With this basic requirement of fairness established, we can then try to determine what principles of justice our would-be citizens might select. Rawls takes pains to emphasize that we need not think of these people as altruistic or selfless. Indeed, they are assumed to want what most people want of the basic goods of life. And they want the means to be able to pursue their own conceptions of a good life (whatever those may be), free from unnecessary interference. Based on these simple motives, and assuming that our citizens make a rational choice (rather than one made out of spite or envy), what basic principles would they select? Rawls argues that we can determine that they would choose two fundamental principles in particular. The first has to do with their political liberties, and the second concerns economic arrangements:

1. Each person is to have an equal right to the most extensive total system of equal basic liberties compatible with a similar system of liberty for all.
2. Social and economic inequalities are to be arranged so that they are:
   a. to the greatest benefit of the least advantaged... , and
   b. attached to offices and positions open to all under conditions of fair equality of opportunity.[32]

Much of *A Theory of Justice* is devoted to explaining why individuals would in fact choose these two principles for their society if they didn't know their identities or position in that society. But the basic reasoning for each principle is fairly simple. Rawls believes that such individuals, seeking liberty to pursue their own conceptions of the good life (but not knowing what they are), would require that there be *equality of liberties*—that is, they would not be willing to be the people who had less freedom than others. They would want as much say about matters in their society that affect them as any other people, no matter what their personal characteristics or conceptions of life happen to be. This reflects the importance of liberty to all people as people, no matter who they are.

When it comes to society's goods, however, Rawls argues that the would-be citizens would accept a society with *unequal shares* of wealth and other goods, provided certain conditions were met. They would accept that some would be richer and some poorer, provided that those who are poorer would be better off than they otherwise would be if everyone had equal amounts of wealth. Since each individual could turn out to be the poorest member of the society, this principle makes sense as a kind of insurance against the worst outcome.

You can test yourself to see if your choices coincide with Rawls's claim for the acceptance of unequal shares. Table 14-2 shows the average yearly income at three different wealth levels (high, medium, and low) in three societies (A, B, and C). Assume that you have no information about which income group you will end up in, or about your relative odds of ending up in one rather than another. Under these circumstances, to which society would you want to belong?

If you chose Society A—perhaps because you think it would be great to earn $200,000 a year—then you are

Table 14-2   Applying Rawls's Theory

Wealth Levels	Society A	Society B	Society C
High income	$200,000	$70,000	$20,000
Medium income	$70,000	$40,000	$20,000
Low income	$15,000	$30,000	$20,000

taking an irrational risk, according to Rawls. For you do not know (under the veil of ignorance) what your chances are of being in any of the three positions in the society. For example, you do not know whether your chances of being in the highest-income group are near zero or whether your chances of being in the lowest-income group are greater than 50 percent. Your best bet, when you do not know what your chances are, is to choose Society B. In this society, no matter what group you are in, you will do better than you would in any position in completely egalitarian Society C. And even if you were in the lowest-income group in Society B, you would be better off than you would be in the lowest groups of either A or C. Choosing Society B for these reasons is often called a *maximin* strategy; in choosing under conditions of uncertainty, you select that option with the best worst or minimum position.

The maximin approach has clear relevance to Rawls's principles of justice and his argument that they would be selected in the original position. Remember that to avoid bias, people in the original position must choose principles for their society in ignorance of the basic facts about who they are. They do not know the economic or social position they will occupy—and they know that they might end up in the group that is worst off. Thus, Rawls argues that rational self-interest will demand that they look out for the bottom position in society. If economic inequalities (some people being richer than others) would produce a better situation for the worst off than equal shares would, it should be selected. For it ensures the best possible life for the individuals in the lowest group (which could be them). This is the rationale for the first part of Rawls's second principle of justice, which says that economic inequalities should be arranged to the benefit of people with the least advantage.

Rawls also provides a corollary argument for his maximin principle, one that does not depend on the idea of the original position. Here he examines "accidents of natural and social circumstance," the random facts of where one is born and what capacities one is born with— which he says are neither just nor unjust, but *morally arbitrary*. If some are born into unfortunate circumstances, it is through no fault of their own but merely because of the arbitrary circumstances of their birth.

Similarly, "No one deserves his greater natural capacity nor merits a more favorable starting place in society."[33] While society cannot eliminate these different starting places, a just society should not blindly accept such morally arbitrary facts—as does the warrior aristocracy imagined by Bernard Williams described previously. Rawls maintains that in a just society, those who have been favored by nature may be permitted to gain from their good fortune "only on terms that improve the situation of those who have lost out."[34] Again, the idea is that economic inequalities can be allowed by justice, but only if these inequalities work to the benefit of society's least advantaged members.

The second part of Rawls's second principle concerns equal opportunity. If inequality of income and wealth are to be considered just, society's institutions must provide an equal opportunity for those with the relevant interests, talents, and ambition to attain positions of wealth, power, and prestige. For Rawls, social class distinctions should not prevent social mobility. As he explains, the point is not merely to guarantee *formal* equality and nondiscrimination, but to guarantee that everyone should have a fair chance at gaining access to social goods. "The expectations of those with the same abilities and aspirations should not be affected by their social class."[35] Rawls's primary concern is to limit the impact of social class. But the idea of fair equality of opportunity can also apply to racial and gender disparities (such as we discussed in Chapter 13).

Rawls's two principles would most likely be accepted by people who are brought up in modern democratic and liberal societies. But modern democratic societies are also pluralistic—that is, their people will have many different and irreconcilable sets of moral and religious beliefs. Rawls admits that pluralism is a problem in his later works.[36] He acknowledges that in modern societies, people have sharply different moral and religious views; there is irremediable and irreducible pluralism. Thus, the only way that citizens can agree is by thinking of themselves as persons who want whatever persons in general would want and who do not bias the rules of society in their own favor based on their particular characteristics. But such an approach may not satisfy all those with diverse points of view on culture, religion, economics, and justice; for example, libertarians and communists may not agree with the procedures Rawls uses to derive his basic principles of justice. This substantial problem points back toward the issues of pluralism and relativism, which we discussed in Chapters 2 and 3.

Communitarian Response to Rawls

The issue of pluralism reminds us that there are other possible views of economic justice. Some might defend traditional class structures based on religious or cultural claims about caste. Others might argue in favor of radical egalitarianism that requires a kind of communal pooling of assets. And others may maintain, as egoists do, that in the dog-eat-dog world of economics, it is every person for themselves.

While Rawls's version of economic liberalism is based on the notion of rational beings applying a maximin strategy to the problem of economic justice, not everyone agrees with this strategy. One line of substantial criticism of Rawls's notion of rationality and his vision of economic justice has been offered by communitarian philosophers. Communitarians generally reject Rawls's idea that justice should be understood as a maximin strategy developed from within the original position. They also think that liberals like Rawls smuggle in claims about rationality and about social justice when they make claims about how rational persons would think about justice. Some communitarian writers object to what they believe are the individualistic elements in Rawls's theory. For example, Rawls asks us to imagine thinking about social justice as individuals under a veil of ignorance, rather than as members of families, who have substantial obligations to the welfare of our family members.

Communitarians, in general, tend to believe that people are by nature social and naturally belong to communities. They often invoke Aristotle and Aquinas as sources, who each claimed that human beings are naturally social beings. Communitarians do not generally accept the idea that individuals are rational choosers who could consistently apply the maximin theory of rationality that Rawls advocates. They stress the importance of belonging to families, cities, nations, religious communities, neighborhood associations, political parties, and groups supporting particular causes. The communitarian view of social justice may depend on the views of the groups to which they belong, as a matter of tradition and culture. But, in general, communitarian ideas emphasize concrete social relations instead of abstract principles of distributive justice. One explanation can be found in the "Responsive Communitarian Platform," which asserts, "At the heart of the communitarian understanding of social justice is the idea of reciprocity: each member of the community owes something to all the rest and the community owes something to each of its members. Justice requires responsible individuals in a responsive community."[37]

There is some connection between communitarian ideas of social justice and the ideas of care ethics (as discussed in previous chapters). But the communitarian approach is more focused on economic issues, including the problem of economic inequality. Amitai Etzioni, one of the authors of the aforementioned "Responsive Communitarian Platform" and an important proponent of communitarianism, explains that inequality creates a serious social problem. "If some members of a community are increasingly distanced from the standard of living of most other members, they will lose contact with the rest of the community. The more those in charge of private and public institutions lead lives of hyperaffluence... the less in touch they are with other community members."[38]

Rawls might permit economic inequalities so long as they benefit people with the least socioeconomic advantage and so long as there is fair opportunity for advancement. Nozick and the libertarians would not see economic inequality as a problem, so long as it results from a free marketplace in which individual talent and ambition were rewarded. But the communitarian critique worries that the fabric of community becomes frayed when there is too much inequality. A version of communitarianism can be derived from Catholic social justice teachings, which view economics as "the art of achieving a fitting management of our common home," as the Roman Catholic Pope Francis has explained (in the excerpt at the end of this chapter).

A problem for communitarianism is that it can sometimes seem to resemble a kind of cultural relativism that claims the values of any community are as good as the values of any other. Some communitarian authors do appear to affirm a version of cultural relativism. However, Etzioni focuses on basic features of human communities and human functions, such as the need for solidarity and a sense of connection within a community. The idea of basic human function is also central to the work of Amartya Sen, a Nobel Prize-winning economist. Sen rejects relativism, but he is also critical of Rawls's abstract approach to distributive justice. Sen's idea is that concerns about economic equality should focus on human functions and capabilities—what people can actually do with their resources—and not merely on the abstract idea of income equality.[39] (Sen's account is connected with Martha Nussbaum's ideas about human capabilities as discussed in Chapter 3.) The point of this sort of criticism is that there are a variety of concerns that we ought to attend to when thinking about equality including family structure, age, ability (or disability), gender roles, cultural practices, traditions, and so on. A concern for equality requires us to account for the complexity of human life in all of its richness.

Current Issues

14.5 Analyze some proposals for responding to economic inequality.

Now that we've discussed major economic and political theories, including Rawls's theory of distributive justice and the communitarian response, let's apply what we've learned to a few examples. As we've discussed implicitly in the previous sections of this chapter, one of the basic assumptions of the modern liberal approach to inequality is that taxation of some sort can be justified. If inequalities of income and wealth are going to be remedied in some way, a system of taxation will provide the social resources that are to be redistributed. As we saw previously, some libertarians suggest that taxation is a kind of theft—Nozick called it "forced labor." So in the background of the discussions that follow is the question of whether any taxation and redistribution is justifiable. But assuming that taxation can be justified in some way, concrete questions emerge about how much inequality is too much and about various proposals for social justice redistributions. We'll begin by considering wage and wealth gaps.

Wage and Wealth Gaps

In the United States, in 2020 (the last year for which data was available), 37.2 million people—over 11 percent of the population—lived in poverty. For children under age eighteen, the poverty rate was higher: 16.1 percent of children live in poverty.[40] In 2020, the poverty rate went up after several prior years of improvement. The census's poverty threshold varies according to family size. But, for example, in 2020, the poverty threshold for a family of five was set at an income below $31,417 per year.[41] As a point of comparison, note that the median household income in the United States in 2020 was $67,521.[42]

In this chapter, we are discussing both wealth and wages (or income), and disparities of each. Wealth is basically understood in terms of what you own, which includes your bank account, investments, and property. A related concept is "net worth," which is the result of subtracting your debts from what you own. Income, on the other hand, is what you earn on a monthly or yearly basis. Income is usually the result of wages. It can also be the result of interest or dividends on savings and investments. As we discuss wealth and wage gaps, it is worth noting that there is some truth to the old adage that "the rich get richer." One reason for this is that wealthy people earn interest and dividends on their investments, which can be reinvested and which grow through the process of compound interest. On the other hand, poor people who lack wealth can find themselves in a "poverty trap" or a "cycle of poverty." This occurs, for example, when debt accumulates and individuals or families are unable to pay off their debts and cannot begin accumulating wealth.

At the bottom of the wealth and income pyramid are people who are homeless. The numbers of people experiencing homelessness vary from year to year. But in 2020, the U.S. Department of Housing and Urban Development estimated that more than 580,000 people were homeless in the United States.[43] This number includes approximately 226,000 "unsheltered homeless" people (i.e., people who were not housed in homeless shelters). Meanwhile, the wealthiest people in the world are worth hundreds of billions of dollars. In 2022, the wealthiest people in the United States included Elon

Figure 14-3 Is it fair that some experience homelessness while others earn billions?

Andrey_Popov/Shutterstock.com

Musk (net worth estimated at $219 billion), Jeff Bezos ($171 billion), Bill Gates ($129 billion), and Warren Buffett ($118 billion).[44]

These statistics point toward the problem of income and wealth inequality. In March 2007, Alan Greenspan, the former chairman of the Federal Reserve, noted, "Income inequality is where the capitalist system is most vulnerable. You can't have the capitalist system if an increasing number of people think it is unjust."[45] Greenspan made those remarks just as the global economy was afflicted by a financial crisis that stemmed, in part, from the bursting of a speculative housing bubble. People lost their homes. The banking and financial sector experienced a massive shock. Many wondered about the causes of this catastrophe. Some blamed banks for making bad loans. Others blamed the financial industry for creating exotic financial instruments, which allowed some investors to profit at the expense of homeowners and others. And some blamed unscrupulous financiers such as Bernie Madoff, who ran an elaborate Ponzi scheme—a pyramid scheme that takes money from new investors and uses it to pay previous investors in an ever-growing cycle of debt. Eventually, the crisis caused several important financial firms to collapse. Lehman Brothers—the fourth-largest investment bank in the country—declared bankruptcy. The U.S. government stepped in and bailed out several other large banking and financial concerns, insurance companies, and auto manufacturers. The world economy eventually revived itself and growth returned. But then in 2020, the COVID-19 pandemic caused the global economy to shut down. People lost their jobs. And the government stepped in with bailouts for businesses and individuals. The remedies for the economic disruption caused by COVID-19 included a moratorium on evictions and on student loan repayment (which we discuss further below). Throughout the booms and busts of the economy, people continue to wonder whether the system is working fairly and justly.

Wage and wealth gaps point toward significant questions about fairness and social justice. From a standpoint that emphasizes equality and fairness, something seems wrong with a system that includes the startling levels of inequality that we see today. We already mentioned the difference between the vast wealth of people like Elon Musk and the meager means of folks struggling in poverty. But it is also worth noting that as working-class people struggle to make ends meet during economic downturns, people with wealth continue to amass more wealth. One report from 2021 explains that "the richest Americans became 40% richer during the pandemic."[46] This can be explained by noting that billionaires make their money off assets and investment—they do not earn a wage but rather earn interest and appreciation on stocks, real estate, and other investments. The levels of wealth of the billionaire club are difficult to imagine. One report based on 2020 data concluded, "Three U.S. billionaires—Jeff Bezos, Bill Gates, and Warren Buffett—continue to own as much wealth as the bottom half of all U.S. households combined. The 400 richest Americans on the Forbes 400 list own as much wealth as America's bottom 64 percent, nearly two-thirds of the nation's households, combined."[47] That report also maintains that 78 percent of households are living "paycheck to paycheck," while 20 percent of Americans have zero or negative net worth (meaning they owe more money than they have). Another measure of economic disparity is the difference between the amount of money the average worker makes and the compensation of corporate CEOs.

CEO compensation continues to rise. *Forbes* reports that CEOs at S&P 500 companies earn more than 324 times more than what their median workers earn.[48] *Forbes* reports that the total compensation in 2021 of one CEO, Andy Jassy of Amazon, was $212.7 million, which was 6,474 times more than Amazon's median worker. (If you do the math, that means that Amazon's median worker wage is about $33,000.)

These disparities in wealth might not matter all that much if it were possible for each of us to do better through hard work and natural talent. Modern social life is no longer bound by traditional class distinctions, and there are no legal barriers to social and economic advancement. However, in reality, social mobility is not easy as one might think. One analysis of mobility in the United States from 2013 concludes that "overall, children born into the bottom quintile are more likely to stay there. Similarly, those born into the top income quintile are relatively likely to remain in the top."[49] This kind of finding has been confirmed more recently. A study published in 2021 concluded, "The United States has less economic mobility than other industrialized countries. Researchers have commented on the 'stickiness' at the bottom and top of the U.S. income distribution. In particular, those growing up in the bottom 20 percent of the U.S. income distribution have a much harder time pulling themselves upward than their counterparts in other countries."[50]

Other facts help describe economic inequality. The wealth and wage gaps are also linked to substantial differences among racial groups. The U.S. Census reports that 8.2 percent of non-Hispanic White people were in poverty in 2020, while Hispanic people had a poverty rate of 17 percent and Black people had the highest poverty rate at 19.5 percent.[51] That means that nearly one in five Black persons is living in poverty. The Federal Reserve notes, "In the United States, the average Black and Hispanic or Latino households earn about half as much as the average White household and own only about 15 to 20 percent as much net wealth."[52] This kind of disparity has been used in support of arguments about reparations (a topic we also discussed in Chapter 13). William A. Darity and A. Kirsten Mullen estimate in their book *From Here to Equality* that what they call "the black-white wealth gap" is $840,900 per household;

this is a "black-white disparity" of roughly $350,000 per individual.[53] They point out that one-quarter of all White households have a net worth in excess of $1 million, while only 4 percent of Black households have that level of net worth. With those disparities in mind, Darity and Mullen calculate the amount of reparations that should be provided to descendants of slaves at $14 trillion.

There are also disparities connected to gender. As we noted in Chapter 13, in 2022, women only earned 83 percent of what men earned.[54] There have been improvements in women's income in the past several decades. But inequalities remain. Some have pointed out that the gender income gap may be, in part, a result of the fact that more women leave work to care for children and elderly parents, and they are more likely to work part-time. It should be noted, though, that women experience a variety of social and economic pressures that men do not—including the gender pay gap—that may push them to put caregiving ahead of their careers.

One explanation of general income inequality is that it reflects differences in employees' value to their employers. In this theory, if a person takes time off to raise a family, they will earn less as a result of missing out on training and experience that would have occurred during the absence. But does a similar argument work to explain the gross disparities in income between CEOs and average workers? Are CEOs justified in earning hundreds of times more than the average worker? One justification of those sorts of disparities focuses on the skills, intelligence, effort, and experience of CEOs and other top earners. Maybe the CEO is simply a better worker than the average employee. But does that kind of justification really work to explain such large disparities—and the racial and gender inequalities involved here?

And now let's consider how we might apply the various theories discussed previously in this chapter to the issue of wage and wealth gaps. Free market capitalism may see these inequalities as the inevitable outcome of the market. The default assumption of the free market is that the market should determine compensation—people should be free to negotiate and earn whatever the market will pay them. And people and companies should be free to amass wealth, which can then be used to invest in new businesses, technologies, and innovations. Socialists will, of course, be concerned to foster or create a more equitable distribution, worrying that there is something unfair or unjust about the gaps and inequalities we have discussed here. As we've mentioned, there are various versions of socialism. Some may be interested in creating a kind of social and economic equality that would seriously reduce the wealth of those at the top of the scale and redistribute it to those at the bottom. And somewhere between socialist equality and capitalist freedom we find modern liberalism of the sort associated with John Rawls. Recall that Rawls was in favor of basic liberty but that he also suggested that inequalities can be permitted only if they are to the advantage of those people who earn the least amount of money (this is the gist of his second principle of justice). The Rawlsian theory would appear to permit growing inequality and the massive wealth of people like Elon Musk and Jeff Bezos, if it turns out that people at the bottom of the income ladder are doing better. But as we've seen, there is remaining poverty for many people—and a lack of upward social mobility. Some modern liberals may think that Rawlsian principles could be used to justify higher taxes on the rich that could be used to redistribute wealth to the poor. These tax dollars could be used to help lift people out of poverty—and perhaps to fund a reparations project. Rawls indicates this in speaking of what he calls a "principle of redress." He says, "undeserved inequalities call for redress; and since inequalities of birth and natural endowment are undeserved, these inequalities are to be somehow compensated for. Thus the principle holds that in order to treat all persons equally, to provide genuine equality of opportunity, society must give more attention to those with fewer native assets and to those born into the less favorable social positions."[55] But the question of how much to tax and redistribute is not answered in any concrete way by an approach inspired by Rawls. And his account may in fact permit substantial inequality to persist.

Minimum Wage and Living Wage

And indeed, that seems to be the situation in the United States today, a modern liberal society in which there is substantial inequality. But a critic might point in another direction, toward the sorts of burdens faced by people whose income places them at the bottom of the economic pyramid. This might return us to the vantage point of socialism and to the idea that what's at issue is not fair procedures such as those imagined by Rawls but rather something more substantial. This is also the idea found in those approaches to social justice associated with the natural law tradition and some religious faiths.

From this vantage point, we might ask whether there is a decent minimum wage and a minimum amount of money that people need in order to support themselves. We might also ask whether it is fair that poor and unemployed people have reduced opportunities and decreased life prospects. One problem for unemployed people is that even if they are willing to work, they often cannot find jobs that suit their skills and interests. There are also challenges in finding transportation or childcare for people searching for work—especially if the jobs that are available do not pay well enough to support childcare or transportation costs.

One solution to the problem of unemployment is some kind of unemployment insurance. Other solutions to the challenges created by the labor market include job training and other kinds of assistance. A more socialist approach may draw on the motto "a job for every worker and a worker for every job," and suggest that the state should work to guarantee something like "full employment." This might include a kind of "positive right" to work. Some go so far as to call for a universal basic income.

The idea of full employment may be a concern of theories of distributive justice. Rawls suggested something like this in his *Theory of Justice*, where he discussed the idea that government might try "to bring about reasonably full employment in the sense that those who want work can find it."[56] Whether "reasonable full employment" means that the government should actively create jobs or serve as an employer of last resort is an important question. Libertarians generally want the government to stay out of the labor market. But Rawlsian liberalism might justify the need for government efforts at job creation by appealing to the idea that work is a basic good that should be part of the government's approach to distributive justice. Rawls pointed in this direction in his later book *Political*

Liberalism, where he explained the importance of "meaningful work and occupation."[57] This reminds us that work is not only a method of making money and supporting oneself but also a source of meaning. As we think about minimum wage and living wage regulations, we might also think about working conditions and the basic need for decent and respectful work.

In addition to unemployment insurance, some have argued that there ought to be a system of "universal basic income." This idea was proposed recently by Andrew Yang, a candidate for president in 2020. Yang argued in favor of a universal basic income for all American adults of $1,000 per month.[58] But on the other side of this argument, the defenders of the free market argue that the labor market must be left alone so that inefficient workers are forced to become more efficient, productivity can go up, and progress can be made. And proponents of the free market often worry that the idea of a universal basic income would lead people to become lazy and dependent on government handouts.

Leaving these matters aside, a further problem exists for working poor people, which is that even though they do work, they cannot earn a decent living. One factor to consider is the difference between the minimum wage and a living wage. The **minimum wage** is the minimum hourly wage an employer can pay its employees, a standard that is set by federal and state governments. In the United States, in 2022, the federal minimum wage was set at $7.25 per hour, which is where it has been since 2009. (In some states, it is higher. For example, in 2022, the minimum wage was $14.00 per hour in California, $14.25 per hour in Massachusetts, and $13.00 in New Jersey, while in some states—Wisconsin and Texas, for example—it is set at the federal level of $7.25.)[59]

Disputes about the idea of a minimum wage will echo disputes about unemployment compensation and wealth and wage disparities. Free market capitalists may want to let the market determine wages. Rawlsian liberals will be more sympathetic to the idea of providing a floor for people at the bottom of the income ladder. And some socialists may be interested in more radical proposals to create greater equality in wages. Some even go so far as to suggest a "maximum wage" or an "income ceiling." President Franklin Roosevelt proposed something like that in 1942 when he said,

"No American citizen ought to have a net income, after he has paid his taxes, of more than $25,000 a year."[60] In today's dollars that would be about $440,000.

In contrast with a minimum wage, a **living wage** is calculated based on the cost of living in a given region, factoring in things like rent, food, transportation, and childcare. Living wage calculations vary from place to place. In New York City, in 2022, the living wage is calculated at $22.71 an hour for a single adult and $42.91 an hour for an adult with one child. In Los Angeles, California, the living wage is $21.62 an hour for a single adult and $44.19 an hour for an adult with one child. In a small town like Green Bay, Wisconsin, the living wage is $15.92 an hour for a single adult and $31.84 an hour for an adult with one child.[61] In each of these cases, the living wage is above the federal minimum wage. And in each of these places, a working mother with one child would be unable to provide for herself and her child by working at a minimum wage job. This helps explain why 16 percent of children were living in poverty in 2021.[62] The question of fairness and justice arises here again: Is it fair to impoverished children that, through no fault of their own, they grow up in poverty?

Proponents of raising the minimum wage and advocates of a living wage argue that by raising wages at the low end of the income scale, many people—including children—can be lifted out of poverty. This approach seems to make good sense from a Rawlsian standpoint. But the idea of raising the minimum wage is rejected by defenders of the free market. One argument cited against the minimum wage is connected to the risk of inflation. As wages go up, so too must the costs of products and services that are produced by minimum wage workers. Or so the argument goes. But proponents of minimum and living wage proposals argue that the problem is inequalities within the corporate system. When the CEO earns hundreds of times more than the ordinary worker, perhaps the minimum wage could be raised not by raising prices but by paying the CEO less.

Poverty, Education, and Health Care
There are complexities of supply and demand and economic systems that will need to be worked out in detail in order to determine what might work or won't work

in terms of the minimum wage and a living wage. But now let's ask a more fundamental question of social justice. Why does poverty matter? One argument about the need for a more equitable distribution of income and wealth focuses on a basic claim about human dignity. The claim is made that when people can barely survive, even when they work for a living, they are not living a decent human life. And when people are forced to borrow to pay for basic needs, they can feel like slaves to their debt. Although modern workers are not slaves, there is indignity and exploitation that occurs when work is not respected or adequately rewarded. We mentioned this previously with regard to Rawls's notion of meaningful work. A further problem is that when people cannot get ahead or get out of debt no matter how hard they work, this may feel like a form of debt servitude—and is related to the problem of the "poverty trap," which we discussed previously.

There is a basic indignity in being exploited or unable to support oneself. Some go so far as to claim that extreme poverty is a human rights violation that is a fundamental assault on human dignity. The United Nations High Commission on Human Rights explains:

> Besides deprivation of economic or material resources, poverty is also a violation of human dignity. No social phenomenon is as comprehensive in its assault on human rights as poverty. Poverty erodes economic and social rights such as the right to health, adequate housing, food and safe water, and the right to education. The same is true of civil and political rights, such as the right to a fair trial, political participation and security of the person.[63]

The UN High Commission suggests here that poverty makes it difficult to actualize other rights—including economic, social, and political rights. Aside from basic claims about human dignity, the problem of poverty is often understood in consequentialist terms. Poverty and income disparities lead to disparate outcomes in terms of life prospects. People in poverty suffer from a variety of problems, many of which also impact society as a whole. One significant problem is the educational achievement gap between children from different socio-economic backgrounds. Children from poor families do worse in school. In the previous chapter, we discussed racial disparities in academic achievement. A similar gap shows up in terms of college completion—fewer children from low-income families complete college. This has a lifelong impact, as college completion is correlated with better prospects for future income.[64] And—in light of the issue of student loan debt that we raised at the outset of this chapter—more people are building up more debt as college becomes more expensive.

Income inequities are also matched by inequities in health care. Although genes and lifestyle certainly play roles in a person's health, poverty does as well. Obesity, diabetes, and heart disease are statistically more prevalent for people who live in poverty. Low-income families also tend to be uninsured and to defer preventive medical and dental care. Children in low-income families are more prone to asthma, lead poisoning, anemia, and other ailments that create cognitive and behavioral problems. They are more likely to live in neighborhoods that are unsafe.

One report published in 2020 by Healthypeople.gov concludes:

> Residents of impoverished neighborhoods or communities are at increased risk for mental illness, chronic disease, higher mortality, and lower life expectancy. Some population groups living in poverty may have more adverse health outcomes than others. For example, the risk for chronic conditions such as heart disease, diabetes, and obesity is higher among those with the lowest income and education levels. In addition, older adults who are poor experience higher rates of disability and mortality. Finally, people with disabilities are more vulnerable to the effects of poverty than other groups.[65]

Such health disparities between wealthy and poor people are even starker outside the developed world (we will look at the issue of global poverty in more detail in a subsequent chapter—and we address issues of health care justice in Chapter 10).

One pressing issue in the United States is the high cost of health care and health insurance. A family's savings can be wiped out by a major health problem if the family lacks health insurance. One study from Harvard from a decade ago found that seven hundred thousand Americans go bankrupt every year due to medical bills. (Medical bankruptcy is unheard of in almost all other developed nations.)[66] One of the goals of the Affordable Care Act, passed in 2010, was to expand health insurance coverage to many of the tens of millions of uninsured, mostly low-income Americans. One of the mechanisms to accomplish this is to expand Medicaid to allow the working poor to obtain coverage through the program. The Affordable Care Act includes coverage for preventive care for conditions such as blood pressure, diabetes, and cholesterol tests. It also covers prenatal care and well visits and checkups for children. And it covers routine health care for women, including mammograms. Another of the goals of the Affordable Care Act was to address health care inequities related to income level and employment—those in lower-income jobs tend to lack health care benefits while people in high-paying jobs tend to be offered generous health care benefits. But despite these provisions, medical bankruptcy continues to be a problem, and people often incur huge costs from medical emergencies.[67]

Defenders of the Affordable Care Act argue that it provides access to the basic good of health care. But opponents of the act criticize it as "socialized medicine." They argue that the government should not heavily regulate, much less provide, health insurance because this interferes with the free market. According to the conservative Heritage Foundation, which opposes the Affordable Care Act and is calling for its repeal, the solution is "market-based health care that gives people better choices and allows them to take account of the price and value of health care."[68]

This free market capitalist approach is premised on the idea that government should stay out of the health care business, allowing individuals to make their own choices about insurance coverage. From this perspective, health care, like other businesses, should be left alone so that free markets might work to regulate prices and basic services. In this view, health care is a commodity, like others, to be bought and sold in an open market, where the laws of supply and demand would operate freely. Some people may end up with bad outcomes in such a system—losing their savings to pay for health care or being denied health care—but this is part of the risk of a free market society. Some

conservatives even suggest that emergency medical care (currently guaranteed by law in the United States, regardless of one's ability to pay) should also be subject to market forces, allowing hospitals to turn away indigent or uninsured dying patients.

The idea is that the market will provide the best outcome for the greater number of people. Some conservatives have also worried that government regulation of health care may result in "rationing," with the government denying coverage for certain expensive treatments. But liberals reply that the market also "rations" health care in other ways, namely, by price and ability to pay.[69] Furthermore, liberals argue that health care is a basic right that should be guaranteed by the government and not be subject to market forces. From this perspective, health care is not simply a commodity to be bought and sold; rather, justice requires that individuals be provided with basic health care—even if they cannot afford it. While other nations do stipulate that health care is a basic right, in the United States, there is no civil right to health care (see Chapter 13 for a discussion of civil rights).[70] The Constitution does not guarantee a right to health care. However, some argue that there is a basic human right to health care, as well as a right to a living wage, a right to education, and so on.

Loan Forgiveness, Eviction Moratoriums, and Other Remedies

We've seen that there are a variety of reasons to be concerned about economic inequality and the adverse effects of poverty. And so now let's return to the question of loan forgiveness with which we began this chapter and consider ethical arguments involved in this idea. As we saw earlier, some proposals to remedy economic inequality involve regulating what people are paid—as in the case of minimum wage and living wage policies. A different proposal would focus on helping people get out of debt. During the last several decades, levels of individual debt have grown. This is the result of the growth of credit cards and other forms of consumer loans including automotive loans, home equity loans, and mortgages. The good news about debt is that it allows people to access funds to make major purchases, which in turn fuels our consumer society. It is possible to finance most purchases by taking on debt. This includes forms of debt that are often not noticed by consumers—such as the way that smartphones are financed by folding the cost of the phone into monthly payments that include Internet and Wi-Fi connectivity. The bad news about debt is that it prevents consumers from generating wealth. This is especially a problem for those who are not able to pay off their loans in a timely manner and who then fall further into debt as late fees and interest charges add up.

Among the significant sources of debt for Americans is student loan debt. According to an analysis from 2021, Americans owed about $14.56 trillion on outstanding debts. By far the biggest percentage of debt is homeowner mortgages, which is 69 percent of debt. Student loans are the next biggest percentage of the debt pie, at 11 percent. And 9 percent of American debt is from auto loans. Credit cards (5 percent) and other loans (6 percent) make up the rest.[71] This particular data set did not include medical debt. But an analysis from the Kaiser Family Foundation reported in 2022 that 9 percent of adults have some form of outstanding medical debt, for a total of about $195 billion. That's much smaller than the estimated amount of student loan debt, which is about $1.7 trillion.[72]

This huge amount of student loan debt resulted from a combination of factors. University tuition has become more expensive, along with room and board. At the same time, states have cut back on the subsidies they used to provide to help students pay for college. Furthermore, there has been a social push to get more people to attend college and complete a university degree. Of course, in our social and economic system, a college degree leads to increased wages and lifetime earning potential. It is no wonder that young people and poor people are willing to take on student loan debt, as a way of financing "the American dream," of a college degree that leads to a high-paying and stable career.

Unfortunately, as the costs have gone up, students (and their families) have taken on more and more debt. When the global economy came to a standstill during the COVID-19 pandemic, a number of policies were enacted that were intended to help people survive the economic downturn. One of these policies was a moratorium on eviction and foreclosure, which meant that landlords and mortgage holders could not evict people for not paying their rent or their mortgage. This was intended to help keep a roof over the heads of people who were out of work because of the COVID-19 shutdown. While this may seem like a useful proposal inspired by the idea of social justice, there were protests against this from landlords and banks. One rationale behind those who argued against these eviction moratoriums was that the landlords still had bills to pay including property taxes, maintenance, and mortgages. Those who argued against these moratoriums sometimes used the word "socialism" to decry these policies.

This brings us back to the debate about student loan forgiveness. As we saw in the opening vignette, Senator Mitch McConnell (among others) said that the policy of loan forgiveness was a socialist plan proposed by Democrats. Among conservative Republicans, the term socialism is meant as a pejorative that is used to condemn "government handouts." Leaving the political rhetoric aside, there were two significant moral arguments against the student loan forgiveness plan. The first is a non-consequentialist argument that holds that loan forgiveness is not fair to students who went to college without taking out student loans or to students who paid their loans off. The loan forgiveness plan appears to fail to respect or reward the responsible choices of those individuals, who will not benefit from the loan forgiveness program. The argument can be extended to include the claim that money provided by taxpayers who paid off their loans will be "redistributed" to taxpayers who did not. It is important to notice that this kind of argument focuses on the merit and desert of individuals, holding that the law ought to respect the responsible choices of those who "did the right thing," as was often said in this debate, and who took responsibility for paying for their education without asking for a "handout." A different kind of argument was made by those who claimed that student loan forgiveness would increase inflation. The basic idea of this kind of argument is utilitarian. It holds that government bailouts, by increasing the supply of money that can be spent in the economy, can end up causing an increase in prices. And these increased prices affect everyone, including those who do not benefit from loan forgiveness.

On the other hand, the argument in favor of this policy is often less focused on that kind of individualistic moral judgment that focuses on merit and desert. Rather, the argument in favor of loan forgiveness tends to focus on the suffering of those who are in debt. The loan forgiveness program is intended as a way of helping those individuals to get out of debt and begin to accumulate wealth. This kind of argument was also combined in the debate about loan forgiveness with a claim about racial justice, since loan forgiveness would help Black people, who tend to have a higher level of debt in comparison with their wealth. There is also a utilitarian argument that could be made in favor of loan forgiveness, which is that when more people have less debt it is good for the overall economy, despite the risk of inflation.

So what might Rawls say about the loan bailout plan? Well, he might be in favor of it, if it were the kind of policy that actually helped people at the bottom of the income ladder. Recall that he encourages us to imagine distributions of wealth that allow for inequality but that are beneficial to individuals with low socioeconomic standing. But as we imagine applying this idea to the student loan forgiveness proposal, we might note that in helping those with student loans, we are not specifically targeting people in the lowest income bracket. Indeed, people who use student loans to go to college are doing so, at least in part, to increase the likelihood that they will earn more money as a result of earning a college degree. Some critics of the loan forgiveness plan argued that it was a bailout to the affluent that did nothing to help most people who live in poverty.

With that on the table, we might also consider whether some other forms of loan forgiveness might in fact make better sense from the standpoint of social justice—for example, providing people with a way to get out from under huge medical debt. Indeed, it is easy to imagine an argument about the need to help people suffering under medical debt from a social justice perspective, since those who find themselves so indebted are likely suffering from adverse health conditions to begin with—and burdened with afflictions that may require special assistance. Of course, the idea of canceling medical debt is not currently on the table. Socialists would likely be in favor of it, especially if it were targeted at those who are most in need. But defenders of the free market might be opposed to the idea, making arguments of the sort we considered about the need for the market to be left alone to do its work of distributing goods and services according to principles of supply and demand.

This chapter has considered the complicated issues of economic justice and social justice, while also touching on some issues in social and political philosophy. One basic question of this chapter is whether one should egoistically pursue one's own self-interest and maximize profit or whether there are ethical constraints to profit, such as a worry about inequality or equality of opportunity. There is much more to be said about the limits of political power and the proper relation between the state and the economy. To better evaluate the theories we've examined here, we would also need further empirical study of the efficiency of various forms of economic organization. And there are vexing psychological and sociological problems that remain to be considered, such as how best to help those in poverty and unemployed individuals without disempowering or denigrating them. These issues remind us that questions of justice also need to be informed by practical information from empirical fields of study.

Chapter Summary

14.1 How can we understand the concepts of social justice and economic justice from utilitarian, natural law, and deontological points of view?
The natural law tradition encourages creating a just and equitable distribution of social goods in an ordered society in which people are able to live decent and dignified lives. The natural law approach tends to be critical of consumerism and unbridled capitalism. Utilitarian theories are also critical of distributions of economic goods that produce poverty and unhappiness. Utilitarianism may seem to be sympathetic with socialism, although utilitarians like Mill also emphasize the importance of liberty. Deontological ethics, as associated with Kant, is typically

concerned with helping people in need—and Kant supports the idea of taxing wealthy people in order to help those who live in poverty. For Kant, this is a matter of justice and not merely a gift of charity.

14.2 How would you describe the difference between procedural and end-state ideas about justice?
Procedural justice focuses on the fairness of processes that are employed in social systems and distributions of goods. If the procedures are fair (equitable or just), inequalities of outcome are permitted according to the idea of procedural justice. From this point of view, so long as there are equal opportunities, unequal outcomes may be acceptable. In opposition to this, theories of justice that are focused on "end states" are interested in creating patterns of distributions, typically focused on substantive equality. When those patterns or ideal distributions become disrupted, the end-state view may encourage interventions in the economy and redistributions of wealth in order to create the ideal end state.

14.3 What are the key differences between libertarianism, socialism, and modern liberalism?
Libertarianism emphasizes leaving individuals alone to create and innovate, and to generate profit and wealth. This view is linked to laissez-faire capitalism. Libertarianism is less concerned about equality than with respecting the rights of private property owners. Socialism is much more concerned with equality. There are varieties of socialism, but generally socialists believe that the state should intervene in the economy in order to eliminate inequalities. Modern liberalism is a hybrid theory that respects liberty while also seeking to moderate inequality. Typically, modern liberalism uses forms of taxation to redistribute wealth and income.

14.4 What is John Rawls's theory of justice, and what is the communitarian critique of his theory?
John Rawls's theory of justice includes two basic principles: a concern for liberty and the idea that inequalities should benefit people in the lowest income brackets. Rawls argues for these two principles by making use of an idealized version of the social contract in which we imagine a theory of justice from behind a veil of ignorance in which we appeal to kind of "maximin" rationality. Critics of Rawls's theory include libertarians who emphasize liberty in a way that Rawls does not. Other criticism of Rawls comes from communitarianism. Communitarians reject the individualistic assumptions of the Rawlsian approach. The communitarian critique tends to emphasize the importance of familial and social relationships of reciprocity, as found within traditional cultures.

14.5 What are some proposals for responding to economic inequality, and how can we analyze them?
In this chapter, we have talked about charity, taxation, reparations, minimum wages, living wages, education, health care, and loan forgiveness among other proposals for responding to economic inequality. Those proposals depend on concrete details involving wealth and income disparities, as well as discussions of the causes and adverse impacts of poverty and inequality. Generally, proponents of natural law advocate for proactive policies that help people who live in poverty or are disadvantaged. We saw that utilitarians and Kantians also think we ought to help people in need. Socialists suggest that these kinds of policies may require substantial interventions in the economy by the government. Modern liberals such as Rawls may support forms of taxation and redistribution that aim to help people living in poverty. But Rawlsians also want to ensure that liberty is protected. Libertarians such as Nozick or Machan warn that proposals that raise taxes may end up violating liberty. There are also economic concerns with regard to plans to redistribute wealth, including the worry that government interventions such as raising the minimum wage may contribute to inflation.

14.6 How can we defend a thesis about economic justice?
In this chapter, we have discussed various approaches to thinking about economic justice and social justice. In order to defend a thesis about this topic, students will need to identify and defend a normative moral theory—natural law, utilitarianism, Kantian deontology—along with a theory about the relationship

between the government and the economy—socialism, libertarian or laissez-faire capitalism, or modern liberalism. With this theoretical framework in place, students will then need to consider concrete details about inequality and economic arrangements. We discussed various proposals for redistributions and remedies for inequality. A thesis about economic justice should consider the details of these kinds of proposals while evaluating these proposals from the vantage point of a moral and political theory.

Primary Source Readings

The readings in this chapter are selections from John Rawls's *A Theory of Justice* and Robert Nozick's *Anarchy, State, and Utopia.* Rawls is a proponent of modern liberalism, while Nozick's entitlement theory of justice is most closely related to libertarian theory. Rawls was one of the most prominent moral and political philosophers of the twentieth century, and Nozick was an influential colleague of Rawls at Harvard. *Anarchy, State, and Utopia*, first published in 1974, is in part a response to Rawls's *A Theory of Justice*, which was first published in 1971. The other two readings are from Ayn Rand—whose defense of egoism and capitalism was explained in this chapter (and in Chapter 4)—and from the Roman Catholic Pope Francis— whose critique of global capitalism, *Evangelii Gaudium* (translated as "The Joy of the Gospel"), was published in 2013.

Reading 14-1   Justice as Fairness | John Rawls

Study Questions

As you read the excerpt, please consider the following questions:

1. Why does Rawls think it is useful to imagine justice from behind a "veil of ignorance"?

2. What are the two basic principles of justice that Rawls describes—and how or why would they be chosen under the veil of ignorance?

3. How and why is equality a significant concern for Rawls?

In justice as fairness the original position of equality corresponds to the state of nature in the traditional theory of the social contract. This original position is not, of course, thought of as an actual historical state of affairs, much less as a primitive condition of culture. It is understood as a purely hypothetical situation characterized so as to lead to a certain conception of justice. Among the essential features of this situation is that no one knows his place in society, his class position or social status, nor does anyone know his fortune in the distribution of natural assets and abilities, his intelligence, strength, and the like. I shall even assume that the parties do not know their conceptions of the good or their special psychological propensities. The principles of justice are chosen behind a veil of ignorance. This ensures that no one is advantaged or disadvantaged in the choice of principles by the outcome of natural chance or the contingency of social circumstances. Since all are similarly situated and no one is able to design principles to favor his particular condition, the principles of justice are the result of a fair agreement or bargain. For given the circumstances of the original position, the symmetry of everyone's relations to each other, this initial situation is fair between individuals as moral persons....

The persons in the initial situation would choose two rather different principles: the first requires equality in the assignment of basic rights and duties, while the second holds that social and economic inequalities, for example inequalities of wealth and authority, are just only if they result in compensating benefits for everyone, and in particular for the least advantaged members of society. These principles rule out justifying institutions on the grounds that the hardships of some are offset by a greater good in the aggregate. It may be expedient but it is not just that some should have less in order that others may prosper. But there is no injustice in the greater benefits earned by a few provided that the situation of persons not so fortunate is thereby improved....

I shall now state in a provisional form the two principles of justice that I believe would be chosen in the original position....

> First: each person is to have an equal right to the most extensive basic liberty compatible with a similar liberty for others.
>
> Second: social and economic inequalities are to be arranged so that they are both: (a) reasonably expected to be to everyone's advantage, and (b) attached to positions and offices open to all....

The two principles...are a special case of a more general conception of justice that can be expressed as follows:

> All social values—liberty and opportunity, income and wealth, and the bases of self-respect—are to be distributed equally unless an unequal distribution of any, or all, of these values is to everyone's advantage.

John Rawls, *A Theory of Justice* (Cambridge, MA: Belknap Press of Harvard, 1971, 1999).

Reading 14-2   Distributive Justice | Robert Nozick

Study Questions

As you read the excerpt, please consider the following questions:

1. According to Nozick, why can the term *distributive justice* be misleading? Why is the focus on "distribution" misleading?

2. How is Nozick's focus on entitlement different from the focus on "patterns" of distribution?

3. How do patterned systems of distributive justice lead to "continuous interference" in the life and liberty of people?

We are not in the position of children who have been given portions of pie by someone who now makes last minute adjustments to rectify careless cutting. There is no *central* distribution, no person or group entitled to control all the resources, jointly deciding how they are to be doled out. What each person gets, he gets from others who give to him in exchange for something, or as a gift. In a free society, diverse persons control different resources, and new holdings arise out of the voluntary exchanges and actions of persons. There is no more a distributing or distribution of shares than there is a distributing of mates in a society in which persons choose whom they shall marry. The total result is the product of many individual decisions which the different individuals involved are entitled to make....

The general outlines of the theory of justice in holdings are that the holdings of a person are just if he is entitled to them by the principles of justice in acquisition and transfer, or by the principle of rectification of injustice (as specified by the first two principles). If each person's holdings are just, then the total set (distribution) of holdings is just. . . .

Almost every suggested principle of distributive justice is patterned; to each according to his moral merit, or needs, or marginal product, or how hard he tries, or the weighted sum of the foregoing, and so on. The principle of entitlement we have sketched is *not* patterned. There is no one natural dimension or weighted sum or combination of a small number of natural dimensions that yields the distributions generated in accordance with the principle of entitlement. The set of holdings that results when some persons receive their marginal products, others win at gambling, others receive a share of their mate's income, others receive gifts from foundations, others receive interest on loans, others receive gifts from admirers, others receive returns on investment, others make for themselves much of what they have, others find things, and so on, will not be patterned. . . .

No end-state principle or distributional patterned principle of justice can be continuously realized without continuous interference with people's lives. Any favored pattern would be transformed into one unfavored by the principle, by people choosing to act in various ways; for example, by people exchanging goods and services with other people, or giving things to other people, things the transferrers are entitled to under the favored distributional pattern. To maintain a pattern one must either continually interfere to stop people from transferring resources as they wish to, or continually (or periodically) interfere to take from some persons resources that others for some reason chose to transfer to them.

Robert Nozick, "Distributive Justice," in *Anarchy, State, and Utopia* (New York: Basic Books, 1977), pp. 149–157, 161–163, 167–169.

Reading 14-3 Capitalism: The Unknown Ideal | Ayn Rand

Study Questions

As you read the excerpt, please consider the following questions:

1. What is the virtue of capitalism, as Rand describes it?

2. What is Rand's opinion of sacrifices made for the common good?

3. What is the basic right on which capitalism and its success are grounded, according to Rand?

The magnificent progress achieved by capitalism in a brief span of time, the spectacular improvement in the conditions of man's existence on earth, is a matter of historical record. It is not to be hidden, evaded, or explained away by all the propaganda of capitalism's enemies. But what needs special emphasis is the fact that this progress was achieved by non-sacrificial means.

Progress cannot be achieved by forced privations, by squeezing a "social surplus" out of starving victims. Progress can come only out of individual surplus, i.e., from the work, the energy, the creative over-abundance of those men whose ability produces more than their personal consumption requires, those who are intellectually and financially able to seek the new, to improve on the known, to move forward. In a capitalist society, where such men are free to function and to take their own risks, progress is not a matter of sacrificing to some distant future, it is part of the living present, it is the normal and natural, it is achieved as and while men live—and enjoy—their lives.

. . . .

America's abundance was not created by public sacrifices to "the common good," but by the productive genius of free men who pursued their own personal interests and the making of their own private fortunes. They did not starve the people to pay for America's industrialization. They gave the people better jobs, higher wages, and cheaper goods with every new machine they invented, with every scientific discovery or technological advance—and thus the whole country was moving forward and profiting, not suffering, every step of the way.

Do not, however, make the error of reversing cause and effect: the good of the country was made possible precisely by the fact that it was not forced on anyone as a moral goal or duty; it was merely an effect; the cause was a man's right to pursue his own good. It is this right—not its consequences—that represents the moral justification of capitalism.

. . . .

While altruism seeks to rob intelligence of its rewards, by asserting that the moral duty of the competent is to serve the incompetent and sacrifice themselves to anyone's need—the tribal premise goes a step further: it denies the existence of intelligence and of its role in the production of wealth.

It is morally obscene to regard wealth as an anonymous, tribal product and to talk about "redistributing" it. The view that wealth is the result of some undifferentiated, collective process, that we all did something and it's impossible to tell who did what, therefore some sort of equalitarian "distribution" is necessary—might have been appropriate in a primordial jungle with a savage horde moving boulders by crude physical labor (though even there someone had to initiate and organize the moving). To hold that view in an industrial society—where individual achievements are a matter of public record—is so crass an evasion that even to give it the benefit of the doubt is an obscenity.

Ayn Rand, *Capitalism: The Unknown Ideal* (New York: Signet, 1967), pp. 21–23.

Reading 14-4   Evangelii Gaudium | Pope Francis

Study Questions

As you read the excerpt, please consider the following questions:

1. How and why does Pope Francis criticize the economy of "exclusion and inequality"?
2. What is Pope Francis's opinion of consumerism and our obsession with money?
3. What would an ethical economy and ethical business look like, from Francis's perspective?

Just as the commandment "Thou shalt not kill" sets a clear limit in order to safeguard the value of human life, today we also have to say "thou shalt not" to an economy of exclusion and inequality. Such an economy kills. How can it be that it is not a news item when an elderly homeless person dies of exposure, but it is news when the stock market loses two points? This is a case of exclusion. Can we continue to stand by when food is thrown away while people are starving? ... Today everything comes under the laws of competition and the survival of the fittest, where the powerful feed upon the powerless. As a consequence, masses of people find themselves excluded and marginalized: without work, without possibilities, without any means of escape.

Human beings are themselves considered consumer goods to be used and then discarded. We have created a "throw away" culture which is now spreading. It is no longer simply about exploitation and oppression, but something new. Exclusion ultimately has to do with what it means to be a part of the society in which we live; those excluded are no longer society's underside or its fringes or its disenfranchised—they are no longer even a part of it. The excluded are not the "exploited" but the outcast, the "leftovers."

In this context, some people continue to defend trickle-down theories which assume that economic growth, encouraged by a free market, will inevitably succeed in bringing about greater justice and inclusiveness in the world. This opinion, which has never been confirmed by the facts, expresses a crude and naïve trust in the goodness of those wielding economic power and in the sacralized workings of the prevailing economic system. Meanwhile, the excluded are still

waiting. ... Almost without being aware of it, we end up being incapable of feeling compassion at the outcry of the poor, weeping for other people's pain, and feeling a need to help them, as though all this were someone else's responsibility and not our own. The culture of prosperity deadens us; we are thrilled if the market offers us something new to purchase. In the meantime, all those lives stunted for lack of opportunity seem a mere spectacle; they fail to move us. ...

We have created new idols. The worship of the ancient golden calf ... has returned in a new and ruthless guise in the idolatry of money and the dictatorship of an impersonal economy lacking a truly human purpose. ...

The dignity of each human person and the pursuit of the common good are concerns which ought to shape all economic policies. ... Business is a vocation, and a noble vocation, provided that those engaged in it see themselves challenged by a greater meaning in life; this will enable them truly to serve the common good by striving to increase the goods of this world and to make them more accessible to all.

---

http://w2.vatican.va/content/francesco/en/apost_exhortations /documents/papa-francesco_esortazione-ap_20131124_evangelii -gaudium.html

Review Exercises

1. Consider the sorts of economic inequalities discussed in this chapter; are they justifiable?

2. What is the difference between a process view of distributive justice and an end-state view?

3. What is the meaning of *equal opportunity*? What criterion does James Fishkin use for judging whether it exists? What is Bernard Williams's "starting-gate theory" of equal opportunity?

4. Describe some problems raised by philosophers Frankfurt and Schaar regarding equal opportunity.

5. What do libertarians think about liberty, equality, taxation, and the role of government—and about positive and negative rights?

6. What do socialists tend to think about liberty, equality, taxation, and the role of government—and about positive and negative rights?

7. What is Rawls's *original position,* and what role does it play in his derivation of principles of justice?

8. What is Rawls's "maximin" principle, and how is it related to his second principle of justice?

9. How does communitarianism differ from liberalism?

10. Explain how loan forgiveness, minimum wage laws, and other proposals can be justified.

Discussion Cases

1. Homelessness. Joe was laid off two years ago from the auto repair company where he had worked for fifteen years. For the first year, he tried to get another job. He read the want ads and left applications at local employment agencies. After that, he gave up. He had little savings and soon had no money for rent. He has experienced homelessness now for a year. He will not live in the shelters because they are crowded, noisy, and unsafe. As time goes by, he has less and less chance of getting back to where he was before. When he can, he drinks to forget the past and escape from the present. Other people he meets on the streets are sometimes developmentally disabled or suffer from mental illness. He realizes that the city offers some things to try to help people like him, but there is little money and the number of people without permanent shelter seem to be growing. Does society have any responsibility to do anything for people like Joe? Why or why not? What ethical principles might be relevant to this situation?

2. Rights to Keep What One Earns. In the breakroom at work, a few colleagues are talking over lunch about the taxes that are deducted from their paychecks. Some complain that the harder they work, the less they are making. Others are upset because their taxes are going to pay for things they do not believe the government should support with their tax dollars—the arts, for example. "Why should we support museums or arts programs in public schools when we don't use these services?" they ask. They argue these should be matters for charity. They also complain that they work hard but that their income is being used to take care of others who could work but do not.

Are they right? Why or why not?

3. Inequality. Stephanie and Peyton are working the midnight shift at a fast-food restaurant, where they make slightly above the national minimum wage. Business is slow, and they begin discussing income inequality after a Mercedes SUV full of college-aged kids comes through the drive-thru for burgers and shakes. Stephanie believes that the growing disparity between rich and poor people is wrong: "It's just not fair that people like us are poor and often out of work, while millionaires and their kids are living large." Peyton is not so sure. "Well, millionaires work hard for their money. They deserve to enjoy the fruit of their labors." Stephanie says, "But we work hard too. I could work forever at this minimum wage job and never get ahead. Most rich people start out with an advantage, go to a good college, and then get richer. And that's not fair." Peyton responds, "It may not be fair, but capitalism is the only system that works, and everyone deserves a chance to get rich. Would you prefer a communist system where nobody has that chance?" Stephanie shrugs. "Maybe not communism," she replies. "But I say we should tax the rich more heavily and use that money to reduce the burden on poor and unemployed people." Peyton shakes his head. "Do that and you'll ruin our country."

Whose side are you on? Do you agree with Stephanie or with Peyton? Is there a third alternative? Explain your answer with specific concepts discussed in this chapter.

Knowledge Check Answer Key

1. **c.** A utilitarian, like John Stuart Mill, would agree that it would be better for everyone if poverty, drudgery, and extreme inequality were eliminated.

2. **a.** The idea that charity is supererogatory claims that charity is not a duty, but something extra.

3. **b.** Procedural justice is the idea that some inequalities can be justified so long as the processes that result in those inequalities are fair.

4. **d.** Laissez-faire capitalism wants the government to leave the economy alone, while socialism encourages government regulation and control of the economy.

15 Global Justice and Globalization

Learning Outcomes

After reading this chapter, you should be able to:

15.1 Describe some of the challenges of globalization and global justice.

15.2 Analyze arguments and proposals for alleviating global poverty.

15.3 Apply concepts such as utilitarianism, justice, and rights to global issues.

15.4 Evaluate arguments about decolonization and the inclusion of Indigenous voices.

15.5 Evaluate supposed clashes of civilizations and the challenge of unequal development.

15.6 Explain the critical perspective of anti-globalization.

15.7 Analyze the ideas of ethical consumerism, fair trade, and other individualistic approaches to global justice.

15.8 Defend a thesis about proposals for dealing with global poverty, immigration, and other global justice issues.

Global Poverty

The world community has worked for decades to reduce poverty across the globe. In the 1970s, the international community established a target of 0.7 percent of gross national income as a guide for rich countries in providing foreign aid.[1] Very few nations give 0.7 percent. A few have exceeded that amount: Norway, Sweden, Luxembourg, Denmark, and the United Kingdom.[2] But the United States ranks near the bottom of economically advanced countries, giving about 0.2 percent. Of course, the U.S. economy is huge. So, in

hikrcn/Shutterstock.com

raw numbers, the United States gives a substantial amount: about $42 billion in 2021.[3] As donor nations worked on the project of alleviating global poverty, progress was made through the early part of the twenty-first century. Unfortunately, the COVID-19 pandemic, the war in Ukraine, and economic crises and inflation have caused global poverty rates to increase again. The global community had once imagined eliminating "extreme poverty" by 2030 (defined today as living on less than $2.15 per day). Unfortunately, that goal seems out of reach. In 2022, the World Bank predicted that by 2030 there will be nearly six hundred million people living in extreme poverty— around 7 percent of the global population. In addition to extreme poverty, the global population includes more than three billion impoverished people who live on less than $6.85 per day.[4] Meanwhile, vast wealth is amassed by a few, and people in affluent nations enjoy high standards of living.

That level of global inequality and the abject suffering of the poorest people on earth combine to create a situation that appears both unjust and unstable. Of course, one could argue that so long as they did not steal their money, the billionaires of the earth have a right to their wealth. One could also argue that rich countries ought to take care of the suffering within their own borders first—and that they have no moral obligation to help people who suffer abroad. But proponents of global justice argue that social justice concerns apply globally and that affluent nations have an obligation to help starving and impoverished people across the globe. Of course, it remains an open question as to what exactly ought to be done to help end global poverty.

What Do You Think?

1. Do high-income countries have an obligation to help low-income countries?
2. How much should you (or your country) give?
3. Do you want your tax dollars going to help strangers in foreign lands?
4. Is charity sufficient or do we need an account of global justice that requires aid?

Introduction

15.1 Describe some of the challenges of globalization and global justice.

In recent years, it has become obvious that the globe is increasingly integrated. The COVID-19 pandemic started in Asia and quickly spread across the world. And as hurricanes, typhoons, floods, droughts, and wars rage across the planet, refugees flee their homes in search of security. European countries have struggled to respond as immigrants and refugees from Africa, the Middle East, and Eastern Europe have fled their homelands. In the United States, there is an ongoing political struggle to respond to immigrants and refugees who cross the American border in search of work, safety, and opportunity. Climate change and other global environmental problems threaten all of us. But environmental disasters have the most serious impact on people in poor countries, where infrastructure is lacking. Modern media and the Internet mean that everyone on earth can witness earthquakes, famines, terrorist attacks, and political violence anywhere they unfold. And our integrated global economy means that a downturn in markets in one part of the world can have an impact on prices in faraway lands. Oil, electronics, books, films, music, airplanes, and people flow across borders in ways previously unimaginable. All of this is part of a process known as **globalization**. Globalization is facilitated by modern systems of trade, technology, and transportation, which create a global circulation of ideas, people, goods, and capital.

An old story holds that a butterfly flapping its wings in one part of the world may be a contributing cause to a hurricane in another part of the world. Some warn that this so-called butterfly effect becomes dangerous in a world that is not prepared to respond to the interconnected systems of our global era. The authors of *The Butterfly Defect* argue that the ethical justification of globalization rests on its promise to improve living conditions and life prospects for people around the world—but also that this justification is undermined when globalization does not deliver on this promise.[5] This basic justification of globalization appeals to consequentialism: globalization is thought to be good if it produces good outcomes. A different question focuses on rights and obligations. Do we have obligations to care for others across the globe—those who live in

palash khan/Alamy Stock Photo

Figure 15-1 Globalization creates moral questions about global justice, including decent working conditions for people across the globe.

poverty, for example? And how ought we to respond to the challenges produced by global integration, including the demand to admit refugees and the need to respect the rights of Indigenous cultures? There are a variety of connected issues to be discussed here. We cannot focus on all of them. Instead, we will focus on a few issues, reminding ourselves that similar issues—economic opportunity, social justice, respect for rights, and the challenge of cultural relativism—have been addressed in other chapters.

One significant question in thinking about globalization and global justice is the degree to which people in the developed world should be concerned about inequality, poverty, and suffering in other parts of the globe. Not everyone agrees we should go out of our way to help others. And many will argue that it is perfectly fine to maximize one's own self-interest, or to refuse to donate to charities that send aid abroad. For many, it just does not seem rational to pay more for fair trade coffee or to buy sneakers or T-shirts that

are produced without sweatshop labor when cheaper products can be found. Why should North Americans be concerned with the deaths of garment workers in distant countries? Why should Europeans care whether foreign workers earn a living wage? And what obligation do people in the developed world have when confronted with the suffering of people in far-flung places whose lives are threatened by famines, earthquakes, and storms? Those questions are part of a larger question about the sorts of obligations human beings have toward those who suffer and die anywhere. But geographic distance makes this question complicated. So, too, are there important questions about the effectiveness of global aid and about the history of colonialism and imperialism. These sorts of ethical questions arise in the context of thinking about globalization; they are the concerns of global justice.

Globalization is the process through which the world's business, cultural, and political systems are becoming more integrated. Globalization can be defined as a historical process that includes the growing interconnection of local and national economies from all corners of the world, which occurs as capital, goods, services, labor, technology, ideas, and expertise move across international borders. Globalization is a fact; the world is increasingly integrated. Global justice is focused on the moral question of the underlying fairness and justice of the current globalized situation. While this involves international affairs, the primary focus of global justice is not relationships among nation-states. Rather, global justice takes into account the rights, needs, and interests of individuals and local communities within the international system, which may include a critical perspective on the ways that nation-states and international organizations fail to adequately address those rights, needs, and interests. Proponents of global justice are focused broadly on the question of what sort of concern we ought to have for all human beings, regardless of national status or citizenship. In this sense, global justice is *cosmopolitan*—directed toward the universal concerns of all citizens of the world. We discussed cosmopolitan concerns in Chapter 2, where we dealt with the problem of relativism and religious difference. Those issues remain in the background of the consideration of global justice. Is there a moral framework that can encompass the entire globe, despite global diversity? Or is the world fragmented into rival nations, economies, and civilizations that each ought to fend for themselves? What sorts of obligations do individuals have toward each other in the context of a world that is controlled by national governments, international treaties, nongovernmental organizations, and multinational corporations? And how can those in the developed world help people in need in the developing world without imposing values on them, interfering with local traditions, and harming Indigenous cultures?

One of the primary concerns of global justice is poverty and gross inequalities across the globe. This topic is connected to our discussion of economic justice and inequality in Chapter 14. But the issue of global economic inequality is complicated by two key issues. First, there is a question of how proposals to remedy poverty and inequality might operate in a world of sovereign nation-states. Within nations, there are often social welfare programs, systems of taxation, and proposals for distributive justice. But similar programs at the global level will run up against the fact that sovereign states are currently understood as the primary entities that are empowered to employ those kinds of programs and policies. In this regard, global justice programs may be linked to charities and nongovernmental organizations. But global organizations like the United Nations lack enforcement mechanisms. These international and nongovernmental entities depend more on goodwill and moral persuasion than on some set of legally binding duties enforced by state power. Second, there is the fact that many current inequities can be traced to past colonial and imperial injustices. Some nations have built up their present economic power by exploiting other nations. Perhaps some system of international reparations or compensation is in order that is similar to the issue of reparations we discussed in Chapter 13. In the international arena, this may include a system of international debt forgiveness, especially if the national debt of impoverished countries is the result of prior exploitation of those countries. But without an international enforcement mechanism such proposals will again depend on goodwill and moral persuasion. A further problem is the presence of national and cultural differences. This includes diversity of aims and values

among local governments of various types, religious organizations that cross borders, and other groups that operate as intermediaries between individual citizens and the demands of global justice.

We are primarily concerned here with moral arguments and how they apply to questions of global justice. This will also require us to consider which theory of economics and politics makes sense in thinking about global justice. But the fact of global diversity and the history of colonialism make this project complicated. We will need to think about how moral arguments about global justice and policies and proposals should be applied in a world of vast cultural differences and without reimposing colonial hierarchies. Clearly, there are difficult questions to be addressed here.

Moral Approaches to Global Justice and Global Poverty

15.2 Analyze arguments and proposals for alleviating global poverty.

Global justice includes a variety of complex topics: global poverty, inequities involving gender and sexuality, questions about immigration and refugees, racism and ethnocentrism, and issues involving global resource allocation and preservation, as well as environmental issues involving climate change and endangered species. Global justice also includes questions about how best to provide aid in disasters, how to stimulate economic development, and how to prevent war and terrorism. Some of these issues are discussed in other chapters. So we will focus here primarily on global poverty, while also considering some of these other topics, albeit in less detail.

In 2013, the president of the World Bank, Jim Yong Kim, announced the goal of eliminating extreme poverty across the globe by the year 2030. As we noted in the opening vignette, some progress was made. But the COVID-19 pandemic and other crises has meant that it is unlikely to attain that goal by 2030. Kim linked the moral goal of eliminating global poverty to the goal of sustainable development for all peoples: "Assuring that growth is inclusive is both a moral imperative and a crucial condition for sustained economic development."[6] Kim suggested that sustainable development for everyone requires us to address global poverty and inequality—and that it is beneficial for those in affluent nations when those in the developing world are also doing better. One obvious way to ground global justice is to appeal to self-interest in this way. It is good for wealthy nations when poorer nations thrive, since this is the key to a sustainable global economic system—and since it builds resilience, stability, and self-sufficiency in developing nations. And when inequalities grow and poorer nations suffer, the entire global system is threatened by resentment and distrust. U.N. secretary general António Guterres made this point in November 2022, in an essay that was published in commemoration of the date the global population surpassed eight billion people. Guterres said, "Unless we bridge the yawning chasm between the global haves and have-nots, we are setting ourselves up for an 8-billion-strong world filled with tensions and mistrust, crisis and conflict." He continued:

> The facts speak for themselves. A handful of billionaires control as much wealth as the poorest half of the world. The top one percent globally pocket one fifth of the world's income, while people in the richest countries can expect to live up to 30 years longer than those in the poorest. As the world has grown richer and healthier in recent decades, these inequalities have grown too.... Anger and resentment against developed countries are reaching breaking points.[7]

Beyond resentment and self-interest, there are other moral concerns. Some theories of social justice maintain that there is a "moral imperative" (to use Kim's language quoted above) to alleviate poverty. This imperative could come from a natural law account of justice. It could also be grounded in a Kantian claim about the importance of respect for the dignity of persons. If there is a moral duty to help people in poverty, it would be wrong not to help them. And this sense of moral duty holds regardless of geographic location or political borders. A universal sense of moral obligation holds that there is no significant moral difference between the obligation to help poor people living down the street or across the world. Of course, there are practical problems about how

such assistance is to be allocated and administered. But the moral imperative remains the same if we understand the obligation to help people in poverty as a universal moral duty. Moreover, if it is wrong not to help people in poverty, one might wonder whether we should feel guilty if we do not help them. With billions of people living on a few dollars per day, should you feel guilty if you are enjoying a $5 caffe latte or ice cream treat? For the price of one of those luxuries, you could be helping children who might die from poverty. If you don't feel guilty when you enjoy your tasty treat, is there something morally wrong with you?

A critic may reply that the fact that some people do not feel guilty about their indulgences and luxuries is a sign that there is no moral obligation to care about the suffering of distant people. Of course, it might be that feelings are poor guides for morality and that we really should feel guilty. Emotivists may argue that feelings matter. But the mainstream moral theories we've discussed in the book tend to look for something more than emotion. A further argument is needed—and perhaps moral arguments can educate our feelings. A critic of the idea that we ought to help the global poor might provide a deeper argument by claiming that our individual choices can have little effect on something as complex as the global economy. There is no guarantee that by donating to charity instead of enjoying a luxury good, you will actually help anyone. And besides, the critic may continue, the old saying holds that if you give a person a fish, you only feed them for a day, but when you give a person a fishing pole, you feed them for a lifetime. Following that line of reasoning, the critic may argue that giving to people only makes them dependent on handouts. It is better, from this perspective, to buy commodities produced by people who live and work in poverty than to give money to them directly, since trading on the market is the key to long-term economic well-being. And perhaps by drinking that latte, you are supporting coffee growers and the economy in Guatemala or some other coffee-growing land.

Another criticism of the idea of donating to people in need focuses on the nature of obligation and duty. Many feel that although it would be nice to help poor people, charity is *supererogatory*—something that goes above and beyond what is required. From this standpoint, aid to people in need is not required. Furthermore, some may argue, charity should begin at home, as the saying goes. In this view, we have obligations to care for our close relations, our friends, and our co-citizens, and those obligations are more important than any charitable obligation we might have to suffering foreigners. These critics may also argue that global poverty is simply not our fault. Guilt and responsibility are appropriate if you have done something wrong. But there is nothing wrong with buying a latte or a pair of sneakers, and your consumer choices do not actively harm people who live in poverty. In fact, some may argue, by buying sneakers produced in sweatshops in Cambodia, you are helping the Cambodians who produce them by purchasing their products. Without the purchases of consumers in affluent countries, those workers might have no jobs at all.

One response to that argument has been given by the philosopher Thomas Pogge, an important proponent of the idea of global justice. Pogge argues that the international system violates the rights of the world's poor people. He claims that the international system is rigged against people who are poor—as large corporations and conditions created by historical injustices contribute to the continuing plight of the disadvantaged. Pogge acknowledges that there is a difference between failing to save people and actively killing them. But he claims that we are not merely failing to save people in poverty but are actively perpetuating their predicament because historical and international structures create a "massive headwind" that poor people cannot overcome. He concludes that affluent nations and citizens of affluent nations owe compensation to people in poverty.[8] He has proposed, for example, a "global resource dividend" as one aspect of a global scheme for compensating people living in poverty. This is a sort of tax on resources that would be used to help alleviate global poverty. One example he proposed was a surcharge on oil. This would raise the price of oil, but the revenue generated by adding a few cents to a gallon of gas would create sufficient funding to eradicate world hunger within a few years.[9] Practical and political details remain to be worked out for such a proposal. For example, how do we institute and collect such resource dividends? But the practical concerns do not change the nature of Pogge's

moral claim—that we owe compensation to people in poverty and that we ought to find ways to help alleviate world hunger.

The idea of compensation can be linked to the idea of reparations. Compensation implies that there should be some adjustment to rectify current inequalities. In addition to Pogge's idea of a resource dividend, other proposals include debt forgiveness for impoverished countries, who have accrued debt as a result of the work of international development agencies such as the World Bank. Furthermore, those who argue in favor of global justice reparations often dig deeper into the past, claiming that current inequalities are the result of centuries of colonial exploitation that have resulted in a world in which former colonizing powers are rich, while many former colonies remain impoverished. Much more could be said about the question of how wealth, culture, knowledge, and power are organized around the globe (we return to this below in discussing cultural diversity). But we are focused here on the question of reparations. In contemporary discussion of global justice, authors such as Kok-Chor Tan have considered this question. Tan explains that this is complicated by the fact that reparations for slavery, for the expropriation of land, and for past colonial exploitation involves an "intergenerational dimension." Tan asks, "Can the sins of previous generations be visited upon the present?"[10] In asking that question, Tan is specifically focused on the question of climate change. He is wondering whether the present generation living in a high carbon-emitting economy like Britain owe reparations to those in India or China for the harms of climate change, which are the result of the choices of past generations. A number of philosophical problems emerge from this kind of question and for the idea of reparations for colonialism. Those who committed the original "sins" of colonialism are no longer alive, nor are their original victims alive. Defenders of the idea of reparations argue that if present inequalities depend on past injustice, some reparations are still merited. However, we might ask who are the "agents" and "recipients" of reparations? One of the goals of global justice is to help individuals in need, but the idea of reparations focuses on groups or "collectives"—and those collectives are complex. Consider, for example, what the present generation of British people might owe to people in India in terms of reparations for colonial exploitation in prior centuries. One difficulty is that "the British" currently include the children and grandchildren of people who emigrated to Britain from South Asia. And if aid is directed toward "India," how would that aid be targeted to help people in need—given the fact that there are also billionaires in India?

Global Utilitarianism and Other Moral Theories

15.3 Apply concepts such as utilitarianism, justice, and rights to global issues.

The ideas of reparation, compensation, and debt forgiveness open an interesting set of questions about who is responsible for providing aid and how that aid might be directed or coordinated. But a different approach to global justice sets those questions aside to focus on the concrete needs of people. This approach is found in the work of utilitarian philosopher Peter Singer, an author whom we discuss in other chapters (we will consider his views on animal welfare, e.g., in Chapter 20). Singer maintains that if people are starving or in need, we ought to help them. His basic argument does not depend on claims about past injustices or the need for compensation. Rather, he is focused, as a utilitarian, on the question of promoting good outcomes and optimizing costs and benefits. Utilitarianism basically holds that we ought to promote the greatest happiness for the greatest number of people. Some forms of utilitarianism will stop their calculation of utilities at the border and focus only on how to promote the greatest happiness for members of nation-states. But Singer offers a universal application of the utilitarian calculation that extends beyond borders toward a global consideration of how the principle of utility applies in a world of abject poverty and unequal distributions of wealth. His basic argument is that if we—those living in affluent nations—can alleviate significant suffering at very little cost, that's what we should do. This leads him to maintain that giving to victims of famines is not merely *charity* (i.e., something good but optional). Rather, the utilitarian calculation tells us what we ought to do, as a duty. Singer stipulates that "if it is in our power to prevent something very bad from happening, without thereby sacrificing anything morally significant, we ought, morally, to do it." He uses an analogy of saving a child from drowning in a mud puddle to make his point: "If I am walking past a shallow pond and see a child drowning in it, I ought to wade in and pull the child out. This will mean getting my clothes muddy, but this is insignificant, while the death of the child would presumably be a very bad thing."[11] Singer maintains that proximity does not matter—if the dying child is far away or nearby, we still have the same obligation. And he denies that our individual responsibility can be diffused by the fact that there are lots of others who could also help; each should help, whether there are others who could help or not. Singer believes that we have an obligation to help those less well off than ourselves up to the point that helping them would leave us less well off than they are. He explains that we ought to give to charity up to the point of "marginal utility," that is up to the point at which giving causes us to suffer significantly: the point at which we ought to stop giving is when our charitable donations leave us in as impoverished a state as those we are trying to help.

Singer's idea is demanding when presented in this abstract way. But he notes that in reality, if everyone donated a little, there would be no need for anyone to give very much. Nonetheless, his argument implies that you must justify spending money on yourself or your family or friends when you could be giving to charity. Whether you are justified in doing so, in this view, depends on whether anything you do for yourself or your friends and family is of comparable moral importance to saving the lives of others who are starving and lacking in basic necessities. As you'll see in the excerpt from Singer's book *The Life You Can Save* at the end of this chapter, he asks you to consider whether you can justify spending money on a soft drink or bottled water when the money spent on those luxuries could be used to help people who are dying from easily prevented diseases.

Singer's arguments have resonated with a number of people. Michael Schur, the creator of the TV show *The Good Place*, wrote a foreword to the 2019 edition of *The Life You Can Save*. He explains Singer's utilitarian point of view in simple terms:

At its core, Singer's book asks us to consider a very simple truth: a life is a life, no matter where that life lives. A human being over there is no less valuable than a human being over here. It then asks us, given that simple transitive property of inherent human value, to consider treating that life over there with the same care and attention we give to lives over here.[12]

Singer's work has had influence on the way some people live. The *Washington Post* reported a decade ago on a number of people who have pursued big salaries on Wall Street and in other ventures with the goal of earning lots of money precisely so they can give much of it away to help people in poverty. The phenomenon has been described as "earning to give." Several of the individuals who are "earning to give" explain that they were motivated by Singer's concerns.[13] Singer's idea has helped to inspire a movement known as "effective altruism," where the goal is to do as much good for others as possible. And while he admits that earning to give is "not for everyone," he also notes that some people "seem to enjoy earning money and thrive on the extra motivation provided by giving a large slice of it to good causes."[14]

Among the difficult question of effective altruism is whether it makes more sense to focus your philanthropy on local organizations or on alleviating poverty in the poorest parts of the world. Singer suggests that the abject poverty of the developing world should be our primary concern. He explains in his book *The Most Good You Can Do*:

I have no doubt that being poor in a rich nation makes life extremely difficult and often degrading. My point is only that there is a wide gulf between being poor in the United States and being in extreme poverty as defined by the World Bank. For effective altruists, the most important consequence of this gulf is that their dollars go much further when used to aid those outside the affluent nations.[15]

Of the opposite point of view is Garrett Hardin (whose work is excerpted below), who believes that we have no obligation to give to people in poverty because to do so will do no good.[16] We discuss Hardin (in Chapter 19) with regard to the problem of the tragedy of the commons—the problem that arises when everyone pursues their own self-interest without regard for common environmental goods. Hardin's thinking is linked to a related worry about growing populations and lack of adequate resources to feed everyone. He maintains that the nations of the world are struggling for existence as if each nation is an individual lifeboat on a stormy sea. Each of these lifeboats has a limited carrying capacity and is subject to environmental threats, which means that the members of each lifeboat have to look out for themselves by building up reserves and avoiding overuse of their own resources. Hardin further suggests that famine relief only postpones the inevitability of death and suffering when there is not enough food to go around. According to Hardin, this is because overpopulation produced by famine relief will lead to more famine and even worse death in the future. From his perspective, there is a natural process of boom and bust, binge and purge that follows along lines outlined by Thomas Malthus, the eighteenth-century author and economist. Malthus predicted that populations grow until they outstrip their resources, after which they die back. Hardin maintains—as Malthus did—that it is wrong to help starving people because such help only causes them to live longer and reproduce, which will produce more mouths to feed and more suffering and a worse population crash in the future.

Whether Hardin's Malthusian predictions are correct is an empirical matter. These predictions would need to be verified or supported by observation and historical evidence. And many factors must be considered. For example, will all forms of famine relief, especially when combined with other aid, necessarily do more harm than good as Hardin predicts? Is it possible to provide assistance to the impoverished while also encouraging birth control, responsible farming practices, liberation for women, and sustainable industrial development—all of which would prevent overpopulation and subsequent dieback?

Answering such questions is difficult because it requires knowledge of the effects of aid in many different environmental, cultural, and political circumstances. It is worthwhile reflecting, however, on the consequentialist nature of these arguments. The primary focus of most discussions of global poverty is a sort of global utilitarianism, which is concerned with the suffering of mass numbers of the global poor. For utilitarians a primary concern is what works. Hardin's views might also be considered as a kind of utilitarianism—but a utilitarianism that is focused on the happiness of those within nation-states and which claims that famine relief and international aid will not be effective.

A different sort of concern can be grounded in the natural law tradition associated with the Catholic Church. Thirteenth-century theologian Thomas Aquinas suggested, for example, that when people are in severe need, they have a natural right to be fed and that it is immoral for those with a superabundance of food to withhold assistance to the needy: "Whatever certain people have in superabundance is due, by natural law, to the purpose of succoring the poor." Aquinas quotes St. Ambrose, who says of rich people who hoard their wealth: "It is the hungry man's bread that you withhold."[17] Claims about the need to alleviate poverty can also be derived from other non-consequentialist arguments that rely on notions of justice and fairness. One might argue, for example, that starving people have a right to food and that global inequalities are unfair or unjust. Objections to these sorts of arguments may appeal to other non-consequentialist concerns such as concern for property rights. My right to my own property, for example, might trump another person's entitlement to be helped. Other non-consequentialist considerations may involve claims about the importance of proximity and relatedness. For example, I may have stronger obligations to my own kin or to members of my own country than I do to distant strangers. It is worth asking yourself about this matter: Do you think you have the same obligation to help distant strangers as you do to help your family or friends?

Now let's consider a few other basic ethical ideas that could be appealed to in thinking about global poverty and global justice.

Self-Interest

We mentioned self-interest briefly already. The basic argument is that the self-interest of affluent nations may lead them to work to lessen the gap between rich and poor nations and alleviate the conditions of human suffering. There are positive goods to be enjoyed by affluent nations when poorer nations thrive. In terms of trade, poorer nations can contribute to the economic well-being of affluent nations by purchasing goods from them. As discussed above, resentment and distrust are disruptive forces, and it may be in the interest of affluent nations to take steps to reduce those forces. Equitable development may help to the challenge of migration. When poorer nations thrive, there may be fewer desperate people seeking to escape poverty by moving to more affluent parts of the world. Furthermore, the problem of terrorism based on anger and resentment might be reduced if we could reduce poverty and suffering abroad. Some critics argue that it is not poverty that breeds terrorism but "feelings of indignity and frustration."[18] At any rate, poverty is destabilizing and inequality breeds resentment. In the long run, other people's poverty can have negative consequences for our own self-interested concerns.

In terms of self-interest, we may also be concerned about the impact of global poverty on the environment and with regard to other social issues that affect us. Global poverty causes stress on the environment. Poor people in the Amazon region, for example, cut down trees to make farms and charcoal to sell. Impoverished people burning wood for cooking and warmth produce pollution that contributes to climate change. Because we are all affected by damage to the environment, it is in our best interest to find ways to eliminate the poverty that leads to some of this damage. Furthermore, new infectious diseases may break out in impoverished areas, which can then spread across the globe. The lack of health care infrastructure in poorer nations is thus a concern for everyone.

Justice

Apart from self-interest, there may be requirements of justice that tell us we ought to care for people in poverty. We discussed this already. Here let's dig a bit deeper into the complexity of thinking about justice. We might begin by reminding ourselves that justice is not charity. It may well be that *charity* or altruistic concern for the plight of others ought to play a role in how we relate to distant peoples. Charity is certainly an ethically important notion, but a more difficult consideration is whether we have any obligation or duty to help those in need in faraway places. Charity, in some sense, is optional. But if we are obligated to help others, this is not an optional matter. Are we under any obligation to help those faraway persons in need, and why or why not? Recall from Chapter 14 that considerations of justice play a role in evaluating the distribution of goods. In that chapter, we discussed this in relation to such a distribution within a society. However, it can also be used to evaluate the distribution of goods in the human community as a whole. We can then ask whether a particular distribution of goods worldwide is just. As noted in Chapter 14, there are differences of opinion as to how we ought to determine this.

One idea of justice is the *process view*, according to which any distribution can be said to be just if the process by which it comes to be is just. In other words, if there was no theft or fraud or other immoral activity that led to the way things have turned out, the resulting arrangement is just. In applying this at the global level, we can ask whether the rich nations are rich at least partly because of wrongful past actions, such as colonialism, the slave trade, or other forms of exploitation. If affluent nations caused poverty in poor nations through colonial exploitation, the affluent countries might owe some sort of reparation to poor nations. But a critic may respond by saying that even if past exploitation was wrong, at some point history is over and we have to move forward.

Another idea of justice is called *end-state justice*. According to this view, the end state, or how things have turned out, is also relevant. Egalitarians argue that the gap between rich and poor is something wrong in itself because we are all members of the same human family and share the same planet. On the one hand, some argue that it is morally permissible for some people to have more than others if the difference is a function of something like the greater effort or contributions of the affluent. From this perspective, those who work harder and who are thrifty are entitled to what they have. They sacrificed and saved while others did not. On the other hand, if the wealth of some and the poverty of others result instead from luck and fortune (or exploitation of people), it does not seem fair that the lucky have so much and the unlucky so little. Is it not luck that one nation has oil and another does not? But the primary concern for the defenders of end-state

justice is the actual distribution of things; if it is too unequal, it is wrong.

Justice is also a matter of *fairness*. People in affluent nations consume a much larger proportion of goods and resources than people in less affluent nations. The ecological footprint of affluent nations is also larger than that of underdeveloped countries. People in affluent countries consume more, use more resources, and produce more pollution. We could ask whether this is a fair distribution. How would we determine an equal or fair share of resource use or pollution production, while also taking into account global diversity? Do people in very hot or very cold climates deserve more or less energy usage? Are people in cities entitled to more or less pollution than people who live in rural or wilderness areas? To address this issue more fully would require complex analysis of the idea of fair shares of world resources.

In Chapter 14, we discussed the idea of justice as fairness, which is associated with the ideas of John Rawls. Rawls's account is primarily focused on distributive justice within the domestic arena. Late in his career, he extended his considerations toward global issues in a book called *The Law of Peoples*.[19] In that text, Rawls outlined a way of approaching what we might call *international distributive justice*—the question of how we ought to distribute goods among nations. One important point to note here is that when we focus on the issue as one of "international" concern, we assume a framework based on agreements among nations. In other words, from this point of view the concerns of global justice are mediated by the nations of the world. While someone like Peter Singer may direct our attention to the question of what affluent individuals ought to do about starving others, a liberal internationalist approach is focused more on the question of what nations (or as Rawls calls them, "peoples") owe one another. Applying this framework, Rawls concludes, among other things: "peoples have a duty to assist other peoples living under unfavorable conditions that prevent their having a just or decent political and social regime."[20] We should note that Rawls's account seems to agree with the mainstream approach of institutions such as the World Bank, which want to approach the alleviation of global poverty within the framework of existing international institutions and nation-states.

Rights

Most Western governments and international organizations agree that political freedoms, civil rights, and labor standards are not separable from economic progress. They stress that prohibitions on child labor, enforcement of women's rights, prevention of deforestation and pollution, and the enhancement of intellectual property rights, freedom of the press, and other civil liberties must be central to economic development. As the global economy is becoming more integrated, many would argue that this integration must be based on ideas about human rights, which are supposedly universally valid and applicable.

The idea of human rights is complex. There are positive rights—to welfare—and negative rights—to liberty and property (as discussed in Chapter 14). Some proponents of global justice argue that every person has a positive right to subsistence—a basic right to clean water, basic food, and freedom from want. It is not enough, from this perspective, to avoid harming others or exploiting them. Rather, such a positive right to subsistence implies a positive obligation on the part of those who have surplus wealth. Others maintain that the negative rights to liberty and property are primary. From this perspective, we only have an obligation not to exploit others, steal their property, or enslave them.

Table 15-1   Outline of Moral Approaches to Global Justice and Global Poverty

	Universal Global Justice	Moderate Internationalism	Self-Interested Nationalism
Thesis	The demands of global justice are primary and universal.	Respect international agreements and pursue international justice as fairness.	National interest and self-interest are primary.
Corollaries and Implications	There are universal obligations to the global poor including refugees; avoid exploitative international economic arrangements; engage in fair trade and pursue ethical consumption; former colonial powers and affluent nations may owe compensation and reparations to impoverished people	Globalization ought to produce benefits for all parties, but national self-determination remains important; goal of international agreements to help people in poverty combined with aspects of capitalist globalization including free markets and political liberalization	Primary obligation is to national interest and obligations toward future generations and conationals; charity toward global poor creates dependence and population pressures that exacerbate problems; developed nations do *not* owe compensation or reparation to the poor
Connections with Moral Theory	*Utilitarian* concern for *global application* of the idea of greatest happiness for the greatest number; prior violations of the *rights* of the global poor require reparation and compensation; *positive right* to subsistence	*Utilitarian* concern to balance national productivity and profit with global concern; *right* of nations to their own product balanced with the need to help people in poverty within *modern liberal* economic and political theory	*Egoism*; at the national level, *utilitarianism* focused *domestically*; *libertarian* economic theory views global economy as a struggle limited only by *negative rights*
Relevant Authors/ Institutions	Singer, Pogge	The World Bank, Rawls	Malthus, Hardin

Decolonization and Inclusion

15.4 Evaluate arguments about decolonization and the inclusion of Indigenous voices.

As we conclude this discussion of moral approaches to global justice and global poverty, it is important to note that some scholars and activists worry that this discussion is one-sided. Some critics contend that this discussion fails to include the concerns of those who are being aided, and also that the global justice conversation reiterates old colonial hierarchies. Some critics have characterized this as "White saviorism," suggesting that the narrative of global justice reinforces the idea that the Global North must come to the rescue of the Global South. This criticism links this approach with the old theory of the "White man's burden," the idea that European nations had an obligation to save the rest of the world from "darkness" and lift colonized people into modernity and civilization. Among the criticisms that are made from this perspective is of eco-tourism and missionary trips in which affluent folks swoop in for a holiday spent helping "the natives." This concern was explained ten years ago by Teju Cole, a Nigerian American author, who pointed out in an influential article that if Americans really wanted to help Africans, they ought to reevaluate American foreign policy, which props up corrupt governments and extracts resources. Cole said, "The White Savior Industrial Complex is a valve for releasing the unbearable pressures that build in a system built on pillage."[21] His point is that donations to charity may make people who live in wealthy countries feel better but that there is a system in place that continues to benefit wealthy people while contributing to the oppression of poor and marginalized people.

Furthermore, critics also argue that discussion of global justice too often occurs as a closed conversation among Western academics and policy-makers, which fails to attend to other worldviews and ideas about justice. One version of this critique contends that even after former colonies were liberated, the former colonizers continue to dominate the global conversation in a kind of neocolonialism. As a result, formerly colonized people continue to employ ideas and methodologies adopted from those colonial powers. Further liberation from Eurocentric thinking is required from this point of view, work that is referred to as "decolonization." This critique can be traced to the work of Frantz Fanon (who will be discussed subsequently), as well as Edward Said, Gayatri Chakravorty Spivak, and Kwasi Wiredu. One important idea connected with this project (sometimes referred to as "postcolonialism") is that knowledge and identity claims have been constructed by colonial powers at the expense of those who were colonized. Edward Said, for example, explained how "the Orient" was categorized and studied as an exotic "other" to European culture—and that this was connected to the history of colonial exploitation of Asia and the Middle East.[22] Kwasi Wiredu suggested something similar with regard to Africa and the need for "conceptual decolonization" in African thought. He called for African philosophy to free itself of European modes of thought and expression, encouraging "African philosophers to try to think philosophically in their own vernaculars."[23]

Postcolonial theory offers a critique of what we might call "cultural imperialism." Cultural imperialism occurs when one dominant set of ideas or a singular way of thinking is imposed on others. Critics suggest that the Western-dominated academic and political discourse of global justice needs to include other voices. From this standpoint, an important concern for global justice would be to listen to the needs, ideas, and cultural norms of "the other," that is, historically marginalized peoples and communities. This includes especially responding to the concerns and needs of Indigenous peoples. One important example of this approach can be found in the work of Martha Nussbaum and Amartya Sen and their idea of a "capabilities approach" (as we discussed in more detail in Chapter 3), which is focused on helping people to actualize their basic human capabilities. Nussbaum and Sen appear to understand the importance of responding to the needs of local and Indigenous people in thinking about how human capabilities might be actualized globally. But Krushil Watene, a Māori philosopher working in New Zealand, has recently pointed out that despite the usefulness of the capabilities approach, the prevailing conversation about global justice has failed to consider and include the wisdom of Indigenous philosophies. She explains:

Global justice theorizing will be at its strongest when it includes the voices of all of the communities that make up our global landscapes. This level of inclusion requires that justice theorizing is able to make room for indigenous philosophies to be articulated in ways appropriate to those communities.[24]

We have a short excerpt from Watene among the primary source readings for this chapter. Her call for the inclusion of Indigenous voices echoes calls among activists to provide a place at the global table for representatives of Indigenous cultures as the global community attempts to respond to past injustices and current crises. A related point has been made by philosopher Eddy Souffrant, who has articulated a critique of contemporary global justice theory and practice from a standpoint that encourages us to listen more carefully to the voices of those who have been marginalized. Souffrant also suggests that global justice solutions should not simply rely on traditional forms of global capitalism. Rather, he says, "a global and moral capitalism cannot be enforced through forces outside of local traditions. It must adapt to the local traditions or better yet, in order to be successful, global capitalism must be créolized by

▶ Knowledge Check   Answers appear at the end of the chapter.

1. Which of the following best describes the idea of "globalization"?

   a. Globalization is the name for a movement in geography that sees the earth as a sphere.

   b. Globalization is an idea that is focused on the moral ideal of providing reparations for past injustice.

   c. Globalization names a process by which the world is connected by trade, transportation, and technology.

   d. Globalization is a term that identifies the need to defend the earth against technologies that exploit its resources.

2. Which of the following best describes Peter Singer's approach?

   a. Singer is a Malthusian.

   b. Singer is a consequentialist.

   c. Singer is focused on human rights.

   d. Singer is interested in religiously oriented arguments.

3. How can we best describe the difference between charity and justice?

   a. Charity views helping people in poverty as something supererogatory, while justice requires poverty alleviation as a duty.

   b. Justice focuses on good outcomes and consequences, while charity focuses on basic rights.

   c. Charity is primarily concerned with negative rights, while justice is focused on positive rights.

   d. Justice is a supererogatory requirement involving taxation, while charity is a duty of all people that happens before taxation.

4. What is meant by decolonization in thought, culture, and philosophy?

   a. Decolonization is the idea that justice requires national boundaries to be erased.

   b. Decolonization aims to liberate formerly colonized cultures from the norms and thought process of the colonizers.

   c. Decolonization aims to invert political power so that the former colonies achieve mastery of the earth.

   d. Decolonization is the idea that people in the developing world still need to discover the wisdom of European culture.

local traditions."[25] The idea of *creolization* points to a process through which cultures intermingle, which produces something new and different. Souffrant suggests that "moral capitalism would include the neglected and alienated."[26] The point is that the theory and practice of global justice must do a better job of including those who have been marginalized—and that when this happens a new and different idea of global justice may appear.

In response to this kind of critique, the theorists we discussed might point out that the primary goal of global justice is to help those who need help. As mentioned previously, consequentialist or utilitarian moral reasoning provides one of the primary moral motivations for this idea. With this in mind, consider how Peter Singer responded to the "White savior" critique in a 2019 essay. In that year, a British charity called Comic Relief had raised $83.5 million for people in need. But a British Member of Parliament, David Lammy, claimed that there was something odd about White British comedians helping Black people in Africa—and posting pictures of themselves with Black children. Lammy criticized the practice as "poverty porn" and said, "The world does not need any more white saviours."[27] In response to this controversy, Peter Singer argued that race and nationality are irrelevant to the project of saving people in need. He concluded, "very few people in need care about the color of the skin of the people who direct the organizations helping them, or whether they live in Africa. If the goal is to help those living in extreme poverty, we need all the saviors we can find."[28] What do you think: is there a White savior problem with regard to global justice? And how important is decolonization and the problem of marginalization of Indigenous voices in the conversation about global justice?

Current Issues

The conversation about global justice is complicated by the fact that people approach the topic using different moral theories and by the fact of global diversity and inequality. In the first half of this chapter, we discussed moral concepts and conflicts that can guide our thinking about global justice, especially as it applies to thinking about global poverty. We extend this conversation further here and consider details and current issues. As mentioned previously, some global justice issues show up in other chapters of this book—concerning war, climate change, or health care, for example. In what follows we will discuss some of the processes involved in globalization (including critiques of those processes), concrete details about inequality and poverty including some of its causes, and some proposed solutions including international accords, fair trade, and international aid.

Globalization and Its Critics

15.5 Evaluate supposed clashes of civilizations and the challenge of unequal development.

To think about global justice, it is useful to understand the causes and effects of globalization. One key causal factor in globalization is the development of technologies that improve economic efficiency and allow for broader economic and cultural influence. According to the journalist and scholar Robert Wright, "globalization dates back to prehistory, when the technologically driven expansion of commerce began."[29] Technological innovations—from roads and boats to writing, airline travel, and the Internet—allow for commercial and cultural interchanges among formerly isolated peoples. The journalist Thomas Friedman described globalization as a process that has made the world "flat."[30] People around the world are now connected in ways unimaginable a generation or two ago, and the playing field in which the world's peoples operate is now more even—provided that they have access to the Internet. This increases opportunities for collaboration and development. It also changes the nature of the economy.

According to Jan Scholte, a leading expert on globalization, there are at least five different interpretations of globalization, some of which are overlapping: internationalization, liberalization, universalization, modernization or Westernization, and deterritorialization or respatialization.[31] *Internationalization* refers to "cross-border relations between countries." Among these are trade, finance, and communication, which create international interdependence among nations and peoples. *Liberalization* focuses on the free and "open, borderless world economy." Trade and foreign exchange, as well as travel barriers, are abolished or reduced, making it possible to participate in the world as a whole. *Universalization* refers to the various ways in which a synthesis of cultures has taken place. This covers such things as having a common calendar, shared communication technologies, and similar methods of manufacturing, farming, and means of transportation. *Modernization* refers to the ways "the social structures of modernity"—capitalism, science, movies, music, and so forth—have spread throughout the world. (Sometimes this is also called *Westernization*, meaning a process by which the globe has adopted Western norms and standards, i.e., the norms and standards of European and American culture, economics, and politics.) Among the characteristics of modernity is an emphasis on scientific rational thought in combination with technological innovation—as well as a move toward secular institutions that are independent of traditional religious organization. *Deterritorialization* or *respatialization* refers to the fact that in the globalized world "social space is no longer wholly mapped in terms of territorial places . . . and borders."[32] Thus corporations as well as nongovernmental organizations transcend local geographic constraints.

Sometimes the processes of globalization have increased people's understanding and sympathy for other peoples, while fostering tolerance, respect, and concern for human equality. The economic integration of isolated communities often brings with it greater peace as people of different races and cultures trade and rub shoulders with one another. But this globalizing process can also be the basis of resentment and antipathy. One source of complaint is the way that globalization affects local economies. Another complaint involves the problem of cultural diversity and the threat that globalization poses for local communities and Indigenous cultures.

Supporters of globalization argue that it increases productivity, profit, and innovation. But others complain that this produces certain costs that may not be outweighed by such benefits. *Outsourcing* is one example. Outsourcing occurs when part of a process—say, tax preparation or customer service information—is contracted out to workers in other countries where labor costs are cheaper. A related issue is *offshoring*.

This differs from outsourcing in that rather than taking some specific function and hiring it out, entire factories or operational units are moved to cheaper offshore locations. Outsourcing and offshoring may help to produce profit and lower the price of commodities, but they also undermine opportunities in countries that lose jobs to cheaper countries. Furthermore, if jobs are allowed to go where the lowest-priced workers are located, this produces a "rush to the bottom" in which labor, safety, and environmental standards are constantly undermined. Defenders of these practices argue that in the long run globalization is good for everyone as products become cheaper, capital flows toward labor markets, and jobs and wealth are created.

Globalization will be evaluated in different ways by those who think in different ways about economic and political issues. Proponents of free-market capitalism see globalization as a further stage of economic development as markets go global and capital, labor, and commodities are free to flow around the world. Others worry that the development of global capitalism will come at the expense of social welfare and the interests of the global poor and working classes. Some praise the development of cosmopolitan social concern and international laws that regulate wars, environmental impacts, and economic development. Others rue the demise of state sovereignty and the autonomy of the more traditional nation-state. Another critical perspective is more concerned that the development of global culture poses a threat to traditional familial, cultural, and religious values.

This last issue points toward cultural problems created by modernization, Westernization, and secularization. Some have argued that there is a clash of civilizations in the world today—most notably between secular Westernized democracies and more conservative, traditional, and less democratic societies.[33] Those who focus on such civilizational conflict may argue that there are deep cultural and historical values found in various "civilizations" that reflect divergent ideas about the public role of religion, the importance of democracy, and the value of modernity. From this perspective, the process of globalization will be fraught with conflict, instead of being a process of harmonious integration and global development.

One supposed civilizational fissure is that between Western and Asian values. For many years, there has been a discussion of whether and how "Asian values" conflict with the values of Western liberal democracy and capitalism. This idea was propounded by a number of Asian leaders. For example, in the 1990s, Lee Kuan Yew, the former prime minister of Singapore, maintained that Asian values were founded on a communitarian approach that could be traced back to Confucian ethics. (See the discussion of communitarianism in Chapter 14.) He held that there was a social pyramid with a good leader at the top, good executives in the middle, and civic-minded masses at the bottom.[34] From this standpoint, the welfare of society and economic development ought to come first before political rights, and human rights may temporarily be put on hold for the sake of economic growth. As one saying puts it, it would be better to give starving people food than to provide them with a forum in which to speak their minds. This kind of conflict has been manifest in a number of cases involving conflicts about human rights in Asia. One very prominent example involves the city of Hong Kong, which was once a British colony. In the 1990s, Hong Kong became reunited to mainland China under a "one country, two systems" policy. But the people of Hong Kong tended to be more Western and democratic than in China. Resistance and protest developed in Hong Kong. And Western nations rallied to support the protesters in Hong Kong in the name of human rights and democracy, while China cracked down on the protest movement. In 2019, for example, the United States passed the "Hong Kong Human Rights and Democracy Act," which aimed to "support the democratic aspirations of the people of Hong Kong."[35] This example shows us a conflict of values, while also demonstrating that so-called Asian values are not monolithic.

One worry in this conversation is that when Asian leaders appeal to Asian values, they are attempting to protect their authoritarian regimes from external critique. Are the communitarian values associated with "Confucian cultures" organic and essential to Asian nations, or are they appealed to as an ideological defense against critique from the outside? From the standpoint of global justice, which appeals to universal human rights, this sort of relativism appeals to culturally

specific value systems should not be used as a justification for the continued exploitation of oppressed groups within countries that are reluctant to democratize and modernize. Proponents of global justice worry that criticism of Western, democratic values may be used to serve the ideological purposes of authoritarianism. And yet there may be good reasons for Western powers to be cautious about imposing modern liberal values on Confucian societies. One of these reasons is the problematic history of prior colonialism.

Another concern is the idea of Asian values is so broad and obscure as to be meaningless. The economist Amartya Sen concludes, for example, that we must recognize diversity within different cultures and that we should avoid simplifying concepts such as "Western civilization," "African cultures," or "Asian values." He concludes, "the grand dichotomy between Asian values and European values adds little to our understanding, and much to the confounding of the normative basis of freedom and democracy."[36] There are liberal-democratic and capitalist elements in Asian cultures just as there are anti-liberal and authoritarian strands in Western cultures. The conflict between Hong Kong and China provides a useful example.

Another line of supposed civilizational conflict is that between the Arab/Muslim world and the European/Christian world. Some claim that "Islamic values" do not fit within the increasingly globalized and Westernized economic system.[37] This conflict of values has been at the root of issues involving fears of terrorism and the challenge of responding to immigrants and refugees from North Africa and the Middle East who are seeking to move to Europe and North America. Those refugees are fleeing authoritarian regimes, war, poverty, and food insecurity. Some of this was exacerbated by political instability and authoritarian responses to the "Arab Spring" (short-lived revolutions across the Arab world in 2011). Ongoing turmoil in the Arab world has resulted in violence, unrest, and civil war that exacerbate poverty and inequality. This has included a civil war in Syria, a war between Saudi Arabia and Yemen, and the development of entities like the Islamic State in Syria and Iraq (known as ISIS or ISIL). Political turmoil has led to unemployment, food insecurity, and a growing refugee crisis. Political instability makes it difficult to develop natural resources, create educational opportunities, and build businesses. Prior to the COVID-19 pandemic, there was a continuous flow of refugees attempting to leave the Middle East and North Africa heading for European countries. While some refugees were admitted, in other cases they confronted closed borders and have been turned back. Some drowned in boats used to cross the sea; others remain in refugee camps. While some European countries have welcomed limited numbers of refugees from Syria and the Middle East, in some cases, refugees have faced discrimination. Countries in the Middle East and North Africa have lagged behind on key indicators of development, such as poverty rates and literacy. There had been some improvement prior to the COVID-19 pandemic. But the pandemic made development more complicated—and more work remains to be done. Consider literacy rates, for example. A 2022 UN report on development in the Arab world (which includes a range of countries such as Algeria, Lebanon, Morocco, Saudi Arabia, Syria, Somalia, and Yemen) states:

> The adult literacy rate in the region rose from 65.3 percent in 2000 to 75.1 percent in 2019, while the youth literacy rate rose from 82.1 percent to 86.2 percent. Despite this progress, adult and youth literacy rates lagged behind the world averages of 86.5 percent and 91.7 percent.[38]

Another indicator of development is women's rights and equality. There has been some progress in this regard with regard to the Arab world but countries in the Middle East and North Africa still lag behind with regard to women's issues. A 2021 report from the World Economic Forum (WEC) stated this bluntly: "the Middle East and North Africa region has the largest gender gap (about 40%) yet to be closed. The progress is slow, and it will take 142.4 years to close the gender gap."[39] The WEC measures the gender gap with regard to four broad categories: economic participation and opportunity, educational attainment, health and survival, and political empowerment. To support its conclusions, it notes among other things that women in countries in the Middle East and North Africa tend to be excluded from positions of power in the economy and in political life.

This discussion directs our attention back to the issue of cultural relativism and the difficulty of thinking about global ethics, which we discussed in Chapters 2 and 3. Are we employing Eurocentric values when thinking about development issues—and about questions such as literacy and women's rights? Is it possible to focus on helping impoverished people and political refugees while also respecting cultural practices that may be contributing to poverty and instability? And how can we encourage and support Indigenous cultural values that can help deal with these problems? Muslims practice *zakat*, or almsgiving, for example. How can aid to people in poverty be coordinated with traditional religious practices such as this? A further problem involves cultural and political conflicts of the past. Will predominantly Muslim countries welcome aid that comes from the United States, when, in the past, this aid has been used to prop up unpopular governments—in Egypt and elsewhere—or when the United States has engaged in military interventions in Muslim countries (in Iraq, for example)?

This kind of problem came to the fore in 2022, when a global meeting focused on climate change (COP 27) met in Egypt and as the soccer World Cup was taking place in Qatar. Activists used the COP 27 meeting in Egypt as an opportunity to point out that Egypt had a number of political prisoners in custody, including some who were on hunger strikes.[40] Does it make sense to hold a global meeting in Egypt given this political circumstance? Perhaps this is a way of publicizing atrocities and putting pressure on oppressive governments? Or maybe the global community should marginalize such regimes? A similar issue arose in relation to the FIFA soccer World Cup. That global tournament was held in 2022 in Qatar, a nation accused of abusing its migrant labor force and disregarding basic freedoms and civil liberties.[41] Should the World Cup be held in such a place with the hope of engaging and modernizing the regime? Or would it be better to marginalize and avoid a place such as Qatar? We might also ask how the forces of global capitalism—including oil companies, professional sports leagues, and other corporations—help or hinder development.

In the background of these questions is the problematic fact of prior colonialism and imperialism.

A number of political and historical problems haunt aid efforts, with former colonial powers in the developed world dealing with residual political issues as they also try to fulfill obligations to assist. Do the British have more of an obligation to help in Hong Kong or India? Do the French have more of an obligation to help in North Africa because of their past colonial relations? And how will assistance be perceived by former colonies? We might also wonder about the United States and its responsibility to help impoverished nations in the Western Hemisphere such as Haiti, Cuba, Guatemala, and other countries that were on the receiving end of prior "Yankee imperialism." And we should consider whether there are special relationships or treaties in place that create specific obligations, as in the American relationship with Puerto Rico.

Western values play a dominant role in global culture, and the United States is among the most powerful cultural and economic forces on earth. Western-style clothing, advertising, and products are becoming more and more pervasive. Coca-Cola, McDonald's, American pop music, and American computer and Internet technologies seem to be everywhere. Do people around the world admire or want U.S. goods? Or are these goods somehow foisted on them by American corporations?

There is also cultural backlash against the values of Western consumerism and individualism. These values are viewed with antipathy and resentment by some people who hold other, traditional cultural or religious values. For example, some traditional cultures reject the Western world's lack of modesty in dress for women and in graphic and sexualized forms of popular entertainment and music. Or consider the problem of alcohol sales during the FIFA World Cup in Qatar. As a Muslim country, Qatar prohibits alcohol. But global soccer culture involves beer, and one of the major sponsors of the World Cup is Budweiser.[42] Clearly, there are remaining conflicts of values in the move toward globalization that will not be resolved in the near future. And perhaps there are legitimate criticisms to be made of some elements of Western societies. On the other hand, we may want to argue that other elements of modern culture ought to become universally accepted. Take, for example, the rights of women or the rights of LGBTQ people. Should modern notions of individual rights and freedoms and equality for women and LGBTQ persons become the international norm? And how should development aid or global projects be directed toward countries that retain cultural and religious practices that subordinate women or oppress gay, lesbian, and trans persons? Consider again, the case of the World Cup in Qatar. Homosexuality is illegal in Qatar. Does it make sense for European and American teams and fans who support LGBTQ rights to travel to or play in Qatar? The more general question is whether it is colonialist or Eurocentric to want to encourage development toward a more secular and liberal social and political system that respects human rights including the rights of women or LGBTQ persons.

The larger question here is whether we can actually judge the practices of another culture. Are one culture's values as good as any other? This is the issue of ethical relativism discussed in Chapters 2 and 3. This issue remains significant in a world that is, in ever-increasing ways, becoming one.

Let's conclude this section by mentioning the conflict between modernization and globalization and traditional religion. The modernized world is a secular one, which keeps traditional religious values distinct from the public values of the political sphere. While religions have "gone global" during the past millennia—spreading around the globe through conquest and missionary work—economic and political globalization poses a threat for traditional religion. The modern Western nation-state is grounded in basic claims about human rights including the right of freedom of religion. And the modern economy is a 24/7 activity oriented toward progress and development, ignoring the ritual time frames and Sabbath days of rest in traditional religions.

Some critics of globalization, modernization, and secularization argue that all of this is heading in the wrong direction. Some want to return to tradition—as religious fundamentalists do—withdrawing from the global economy and finding a separate peace apart from the secular, modern world. Other fundamentalists may take up arms against the global system—as religiously motivated terrorists do. Others want to find ways to humanize and universalize traditional religious values. And others will insist that the way forward must be to find universal human values that can transcend cultural and religious differences and that can be used to deal with the difficult challenges of the future, such as those we have discussed in this book.

Global Inequality and Poverty, and Its Causes

At the heart of many arguments about the need to help those who live in extreme poverty around the globe is the claim that gross inequalities across the globe are fundamentally unjust. A related claim is that there is an obvious moral demand for affluent people to respond to the abject suffering of those who live in poverty. Singer, Pogge, and others argue that the wealth of rich nations (and the affluent citizens of those nations) should be used to alleviate major suffering for a minor cost—an empirical claim that should prompt us to examine the severity of global inequality.

As we mentioned previously, the global community has been working to alleviate poverty, especially extreme poverty. In 2022, the World Bank estimated that extreme poverty occurs when people earn less than $2.15 per day (a figure that they updated to keep up with inflation).[43] As we mentioned in the opening vignette of this chapter, in 2022, the World Bank predicted that by 2030 there will be nearly six hundred million people living in extreme poverty—around 7 percent of the global population.[44] This low wage level includes the working poor. Consider, for example, that workers in Bangladeshi garment factories earn a minimum wage of 5,300 taka per month, which is about $50—or less than $2.00 per day.[45] These factories produce clothing worn by Europeans and Americans. Bangladeshi garment factories have, in the past, collapsed or caught fire, killing hundreds.[46] This means that if an American donated a couple of dollars per day (or paid more for their clothes), they could double the income of someone who is making their clothes and who works in precarious conditions.

Extreme poverty is "poverty that kills." According to one account, from Jeffrey D. Sachs, people in extreme poverty are "chronically hungry, unable to get health care, lack safe drinking water and sanitation, cannot afford education for their children, and perhaps lack rudimentary shelter...and clothing."[47] Children of the global poor are particularly vulnerable, dying from various causes including easily preventable diseases and illnesses.[48] For example, hundreds of millions of people come down with malaria every year and hundreds of thousands die. In 2020, there were an estimated 241 million malaria cases worldwide, including and 627,000 malaria deaths.[49] People living in the poorest countries, particularly children, are especially vulnerable to malaria, which can be easily prevented by the use of mosquito nets and other prophylactic measures. There has been an improvement over past mortality rates as a result of an active campaign to prevent and treat malaria. Nonetheless, the disease still preys on people who are poor.

Poverty in the developing world undermines opportunities. It is connected to a variety of issues including the oppression of women, illiteracy, governmental corruption, and so on. There are vast inequalities across the globe. One obvious measure of inequality is found in mortality rates and life expectancy. Life expectancy in rich countries is substantially higher than in poor countries. In 2022, life expectancy in Japan, Switzerland, Germany, Norway, Canada, and the United Kingdom was above eighty years. In the United States, life expectancy is seventy-nine years; it is seventy-five years in Mexico. But in Kenya, life expectancy is sixty-seven years; it is seventy-four years in Bangladesh and seventy-one years in Cambodia. The country of Chad has the second lowest life expectancy, fifty-five years, while the lowest life expectancy was in the Central African Republic, at fifty-four years.[50] Those who argue that we ought to take action to alleviate global poverty point out the injustice of these sorts of inequalities. Is it fair that Americans and Europeans live long and live well while others suffer and die young?

Another measure of inequality is in economic terms. According to the World Bank, the United States is the world's richest country in terms of gross domestic product (GDP). The GDP in the United States in 2021 was over $23 trillion, compared, for example, to Kenya, with a GDP of $110 billion or with some smaller nations such as the Marshall Islands, with a GDP of around $250 million.[51] A more precise measure of inequality is to compare per capita GDP, which divides the gross domestic product of a nation by its population. Using that measure, Burundi had the lowest per capita GDP in 2021, at $237. By comparison, Kenya's per capita GDP in 2014 was $2,007, Chad's was $69 and the Central

African Republic was $512. The per capita GDP for Bangladesh was $2,503, while in the United States, per capita GDP was $69,288 and Canada's was $52,051.[52] The per capita GDP in the United States was lower than that of a number of other countries, including Ireland, Switzerland, Norway, and Singapore.

The causes of extreme poverty and lack of development in a nation are many and complicated. Among them are geographic isolation, epidemic disease, drought and other natural disasters, lack of clean water, poor soil, poor physical infrastructure, lack of education and a decent health care system, civil war and corruption, and the colonial and trade practices of Western nations.

Some blame colonialism and its aftermath as the cause of inequality and ongoing poverty in many of the world's poorest countries. Among those who hold this to be the case is Frantz Fanon, a North African intellectual who was born in the Caribbean. Fanon's work *The Wretched of the Earth* is a seminal text in postcolonial studies.[53] Fanon's idea is that the Western nations stole the riches of their colonies, thus enhancing their own wealth while depressing the wealth of the colonies. According to Fanon, "European opulence is literally scandalous, for it has been founded on slavery, it has been nourished with the blood of slaves and it comes directly from the soil and from the subsoil of that underdeveloped world. The well-being and the progress of Europe have been built up with the sweat and the dead bodies of Negroes, Arabs, Indians, and the yellow races."[54] From this standpoint, the poverty of much of the world is due to a long history of European intervention, colonial domination, slavery, and theft. Moreover, the argument continues, deprivation in what Fanon calls the "third" or underdeveloped world can be attributed to continued exploitation of people who are poor by people who are wealthy. Even though outright colonialism ended in the twentieth century, as former colonies gained their independence, Fanon argues that the institutions, corporate structures, military treaties, and trade relations left behind continue to favor the First World to the detriment of the Third World.

One response to this sort of argument is to claim that colonialism was not the evil it is made out to be. Dinesh D'Souza—an Indian-born American intellectual—has argued, for example, that "colonialism has gotten a bad name in recent decades."[55] D'Souza is a controversial conservative author who promoted conspiracy theories about Donald Trump's loss of the 2020 Presidential election (Trump pardoned him for campaign finance crimes in 2018). D'Souza maintains that in some ways colonialism may have been good for the colonized countries. In a book in which he accused then-President Obama of being a proponent of Fanon-style anti-colonialism, D'Souza concludes,

> When the British came to India and Kenya, they came for selfish reasons: they came to rule and to benefit from that rule. Nevertheless, in order to rule effectively the British introduced Western ideas and Western institutions to the subject peoples. Eventually those people used British ideas of self-determination and freedom to combat British rule. As a native-born Indian, I have to say that even our freedom was a consequence of what we learned from our Western captors.[56]

D'Souza has also pointed out that Western colonialism is only part of a much larger history that includes a long litany of colonial interventions, including colonizing by the Egyptians, the Persians, and so on. D'Souza concludes that to blame European colonialists for stealing and exploitation in the Third World is to "relieve the Third World of blame for its wretchedness."[57] From his perspective, the corruption, injustice, and poverty found in the Third World are not the result of European exploitation but of insufficient Westernization. D'Souza argues that the solution is further expansion of Western European ideas about human rights, technology, and free markets. But those who follow Fanon argue that the solution is further decolonization (as we discussed previously)—and possibly also reparations and compensation for past exploitation.

Another cause of global inequalities may be protectionism including farm subsidies and barriers to trade. Subsidies for the farms of Western countries have been blamed by some critics for the poverty in developing countries. In the United States, these subsidies originally were intended to help farmers hurt by the Great Depression. But they have been maintained and expanded. Between 1995 and 2020, farmers in the United States received $425 billion in subsidies—both by direct payments and through crop insurance.[58] In other countries, subsidies are given to small specialty farms, for example, those in the grape-growing or cheese-producing regions of France. Such distortions of the international agriculture market can make it extremely difficult for poor farmers in Mexico or in sub-Saharan Africa to compete. Moreover, in some cases (especially in the United States) such subsidies go to large industrialized farms that then produce huge crop surpluses for cheap export—undercutting the sale of local agricultural products in the developing world. Substantial evidence suggests that reducing subsidies and removing trade barriers would help end poverty. Ten years ago, economist Gary S. Fields points out, "Agricultural subsidies by the United States, Europe, and Japan total $350 billion a year—seven times the foreign aid provided by all developed countries." He concluded that ending farm subsidies could lift 140 million people out of poverty.[59] Other people argue, however, that there is no guarantee that eliminating these subsidies would help poor farmers. Moreover, perhaps all nations should have a right to protect and support their own farmers, whatever the consequences abroad.

One of the issues with regard to subsidies is fairness. The International Monetary Fund and the World Bank often ask developing countries that receive loans and other aid to eliminate subsidies for their exports. However, developed countries such as the United States continue to subsidize their own agricultural products. As a result, foreign farmers frequently cannot compete on the global market with products grown on U.S. farms. At the same time, U.S. producers lobby against trade barriers enacted by foreign countries, which prevent Americans from selling U.S. products in foreign markets. It makes sense for nations to want to protect their own farmers and producers. And it also makes sense that farmers and producers would want to have access to markets abroad. The reality of globalized business is complicated, and there is a constant struggle to maximize profit and minimize risk. All of this results in unequal outcomes across the globe. Consider the North American Free Trade Agreement (NAFTA), which linked Canada, Mexico, and the United States in a Free Trade Zone between 1994 and 2020, when NAFTA was replaced by the United States–Mexico–Canada Agreement (USMCA).[60] As a result of the NAFTA agreement, Mexico was flooded with cheap corn and corn products from the United States,

such as animal feed. (Corn is one of the most heavily subsidized crops in the United States.) This had a devastating impact on small Mexican farmers. According to one estimate, nearly two million farm jobs were lost in Mexico as a result. Many of these small farmers abandoned their fields and headed north to work as illegal laborers in the United States. The general cross-border economy is doing well. But the chief beneficiaries of NAFTA and other trade agreements were big companies, while the small operations have been hurt.[61] The moral ideal of fair competition is certainly relevant in such discussions. Just how to make competition fair is, however, a matter for debate.

Globalizing Institutions and Anti-Globalization Movements

15.6 Explain the critical perspective of anti-globalization.

Debate also continues about the role played by international financial institutions. The International Monetary Fund (IMF) and World Bank were both established in 1944 to preserve international financial stability. A newer international organization is the World Trade Organization (WTO), formed in the 1990s. And there are other organizations such as the G7 ("group of seven"), which represents the interests of seven of the world's largest economies, accounting for more than half of global GDP. The group of seven countries are the leading industrial nations of the world: Canada, France, Germany, Italy, Japan, the United Kingdom, and the United States. (The G7 expanded to include Russia at one point, becoming the G8, but Russia was suspended from the organization in 2014.)[62] The G20 includes twenty finance ministers and central bank governors and represents the financial interest of nations that account for about 80 percent of world trade. In recent years, there have been massive protests at meetings of these organizations and others like them. Pro-labor and environmental groups have protested against economic globalization at meetings of the WTO, the G7/8, the G20, the IMF, and the World Bank. These anti-globalization protests culminated in police crackdowns, mass arrests, vandalism, and street fighting in Seattle,

Washington, in 1999; in Genoa, Italy, in 2001; and in Geneva in 2009. In Toronto, in 2010, more than 1,100 people were arrested in anti-G20 protests. [63] The anti-globalization protesters have a variety of specific concerns, but among them is a feeling that economic decisions are being made by bureaucrats and bankers without concern for the interests of working people. One concern is that the globalizing institutions of international finance have caused the developing world to fall into debt that serves the interests of those in the developed world. Furthermore, the critics contend that these institutions have failed to address the indebtedness of nations in the developing world. Thus, one proposal for remediation is debt relief. But a further problem is lack of adequate representation in decision-making for those in the developing world. Thus, Canadian journalist and author Naomi Klein has explained the anti-globalization movement as developing out of a perceived "crisis of democracy." [64] Critics of the economic institutions of globalization insist that they are not opposed to international integration and cooperation. Rather, they say they are opposed to that type of globalization that is more concerned about the rights of investors than the rights of workers. Noam Chomsky, a well-known critic of globalization and of American foreign policy, argues, "the term 'globalization' has been appropriated by the powerful to refer to a specific form of international economic integration, one based on investors rights, with the interests of people incidental." [65] The alternative would be a form of economic integration that was more concerned with human development and the concerns of ordinary people than with the bottom line of banks and corporations.

In response, defenders of the international finance and business system argue that investing in and supporting the current economic system is the best (and possibly only) way to help poor people around the world—by using banks and other global economic infrastructure to invest in opportunities for impoverished people. We've already seen that the World Bank is concerned with poverty reduction across the globe. And international agreements (such as the 0.7 percent aid target) are aimed at reducing poverty by increasing foreign aid.

However, some criticize the methods employed by international institutions such as the World Bank, IMF, and WTO. According to Joseph Stiglitz, a Nobel Prize–winning economist, the key to problems in developing nations has been these international financial institutions' ideological support of strict capitalism. He argues that free markets and global competition are not the solution to all problems. And he worries about the lack of representation of poorer countries: "these institutions are not representative of the nations they serve." [66] Some IMF and World Bank policies, for example, have harmed rather than helped the development of poorer countries. High interest rates harmed fledgling companies, trade liberalization policies made poorer countries unable to compete, and liberalization of capital markets enabled larger foreign banks to drive local banks out of business. Privatization of government-owned enterprises without adequate local regulation also contributed to the increasingly desperate situation of some developing countries. According to Stiglitz, these international financial institutions have ignored some of the consequences of their policies because of their belief in unfettered capitalism. He writes:

> Stabilization is on the agenda; job creation is off. Taxation, and its adverse effects, are on the agenda; land reform is off. There is money to bail out banks but not to pay for improved education and health services, let alone to bail out workers who are thrown out of their jobs as a result of the IMF's macroeconomic mismanagement. [67]

In response to Stiglitz and others, defenders of the international economic system have argued that these worries are overblown and based on a limited analysis that does not take economic realities into account. Moreover, defenders of economic globalization argue that the critics of globalization have actually made things worse by encouraging developing countries to feel that they are being taken advantage of and that the global institutions that are their best hope for development are hypocritical and mercenary. The economist Jagdish Bhagwati has argued, for example, that globalization actually does have a human face. He contends that economic globalization—by promoting competition in wages across international borders—has benefited women by equalizing gender-based wage disparities, which were more typical of countries where the wage gap was protected against global competition. [68] To assess these arguments would require a much deeper examination of economic issues.

For many years, the anti-globalization movement was associated with the political Left and connected with labor unions, socialism, and even anarchism. But a different strain of anti-globalization sentiment has emerged on the political Right with the rise of new forms of nationalism and ethnocentric and racist ideologies.[69] In the United States, Donald Trump has advocated for "America First" policies (connected with his slogan "Make America Great Again"). Trump was often opposed to open markets, free trade zones, and international agreements (such as those regulating climate change). Further to the Right are racist and anti-Semitic organizations and individuals who see globalization as an attempt to "replace" White populations with "others." In European countries, neo-Nazi parties and other nationalist movements have grown in strength recently. These movements often focus their energy against immigrants and in defense of a vision of European culture that has roots in White supremacy and Western Christianity.

A further criticism should be mentioned here, which is the concern for corruption and self-interest. Just as the left-wing anti-globalization movement suspects that the global financial sector is interested only in profit, a similar suspicion is held more generally by those who worry that local governments and aid organizations are corrupt. Not all financial aid given to poor countries actually gets directly to the people. Much of it, for example, covers consultants, administrative costs, and debt relief. Furthermore, aid dollars are used to purchase supplies and expertise that are manufactured in the developed world. Journalist Loretta Napoleoni argues that "foreign aid is mostly beneficial to those who give it" because aid creates a market for Western products.[70] One of the difficult practical challenges to be confronted is how we can best provide aid in a global economy that includes corrupt local politicians as well as international corporations and banks that are seeking to make a profit.

Poor countries suffer from serious political problems: continuing civil wars and corrupt and unstable governments. Corruption and mismanagement have contributed not only to the poverty of the people but also to the hesitancy of wealthy countries to give aid. Any solution to the issue of global poverty will have to deal with a variety of issues: the problem of local corruption, the challenge of making sure that aid is effective, and the concern that large multinational banking and corporate concerns are seeking profit. But it is important to note that none of these empirical matters changes the moral question of whether we ought to be concerned about the suffering of others in foreign countries.

Institutional Solutions

The issues discussed in this chapter are complex. It will be difficult to solve problems like global poverty, inequality, and lack of development while also imagining effective responses for the ongoing cultural, political, and economic conflicts that are part of the era of globalization. Nonetheless, some thinkers argue that there are some fairly obvious solutions to the most pressing issues, such as poverty. We saw that Thomas Pogge proposed a resource tax and that Peter Singer argued that we have a duty to donate to charity.[71] Development economist Jeffrey Sachs contends that we should focus on five "development interventions": (1) boosting agriculture, with improvements in fertilizers and seeds; (2) improving basic health, in particular through bed nets and medicines for malaria and treatments for AIDS; (3) investing in education, including meals for primary school children; (4) providing power, transportation, and communications technologies; and (5) providing clean water and sanitation.[72] Others argue that changing intellectual property laws and freeing up patents would help to make new technologies—such as better seeds for growing crops or beneficial medicines—available to poor people who could use them.[73] Some suggest that money is the most basic solution and that rich nations should live up to a widely accepted standard of donating 0.7 percent of their gross national product (GNP) to foreign aid.

The rich nations of the world do allocate some of their budgets to the alleviation of global poverty and inequality. Most affluent nations acknowledge that there is some need to help people in poverty, either because they see a moral imperative to help or they believe that helping is in everyone's interest, since poverty and inequality are destabilizing forces in the global economy. International agreements have established a goal for rich countries to donate 0.7 percent of their GNP to alleviate poverty. (GNP is calculated in ways that are similar to GDP, or gross domestic product.) This international effort has been established in a variety of treaties in recent decades including the UN Millennium Development Project and the Monterrey (Mexico) Conference on Financing for Development and a subsequent agreement in Johannesburg, South Africa.[74] One of the difficulties in discussing foreign aid is that many Americans think the United States gives much more in aid. A poll in 2014 reported that the average American thinks that around 25 percent of the federal budget goes to foreign aid.[75] When asked what they considered the appropriate amount of foreign aid to be, the typical response was about 10 percent of the budget—which is actually ten times the amount of aid allocated in the federal budget.[76] Only 1 percent of the U.S. budget goes to foreign aid. Out of a$4 trillion budget that is a significant amount.[77] But even at 1 percent of the federal budget, the United States falls short of the 0.7 percent of GNP target set by the United Nations. A recent (2021) analysis of U.S. aid donations reports that the U.S. is the largest donor country: "Official development assistance (ODA) at $42.3 billion in 2021." But that report concludes, "relative to economic size," the aid budget of the United States is "low," at "0.18% of gross national income," which puts the United States twenty-third out of the twenty-nine donor countries.[78] If we use the number of U.S. GDP mentioned above as a basis ($23 trillion), this would mean that if the United States donated 0.7 percent, it should donate around $160 billion. A different way of looking at these targets would focus on what the 0.7 percent target would mean for every $100 of GNP, which would be 70 cents. If the United States hit the 0.7 percent target and donated 70 cents for every $100 of GNP, its aid budget would increase from its current $42 billion to around $160 billion. That extra $118 billion could go a long way toward solving the problem of global poverty and other global justice problems.

Some rich nations have made an effort to reach the target of donating 0.7 percent, with European nations in the lead. A 2019 report shows that Luxembourg, Norway, Sweden, and Denmark are the most generous nations, typically exceeding that amount.[79] The United Kingdom has made an effort as well, passing a law in 2015 making a commitment to the 0.7 percent target, which made it the first G7 country to make such a commitment.[80]

Individual Solutions and the Challenge of Immigration

15.7 Analyze the ideas of ethical consumerism, fair trade, and other individualistic approaches to global justice.

The question of international aid is about what countries do. But there are also solutions to the challenges of global justice that involve nongovernmental organizations—and individual choices. Among the most obvious points to be made here is that there are private charities and religious charities that provide assistance to those in need. Peter Singer's "effective altruism" movement, discussed previously, includes the work of these kinds of agencies and organizations. Among the things an individual can do to help promote global justice is to donate to those organizations. There are complications to be considered in evaluating a charitable organization involving questions about administrative costs and the effectiveness of a charity in actually helping those in need. Among the more famous organizations doing this kind of work are Oxfam, the Red Cross, UNICEF, Save the Children, and others, who raise substantial amounts of money for disaster relief and direct aid. There are a number of websites that can help you figure out who to donate to if that's something that interests you after reading this chapter.

Beyond the obvious focal point of big charities, there are also international labor organizations and other groups and ideas aiming to help promote global justice.

Consider, for example, the question of where our food and clothing come from. There is a good chance that at least some of the food you ate for breakfast today was either produced in a foreign country or processed by a workforce of immigrant labor. The same is true for the clothes on your back. Take a look at the labels on your clothing and other consumer goods: chances are that your clothes, electronics, furniture, and toys are

ranpletr/E+/Getty Images

Figure 15-2 Fair trade aims to support producers without exploiting them.

produced in places such as China, Sri Lanka, or Bangladesh. One reason for this is that it is cheaper to manufacture goods in these places. But cheap manufacturing is not without social costs and ethical challenges. In 2013, a garment factory in Bangladesh collapsed, killing more than 1,120 workers. The previous year, a fire at another Bangladeshi garment factory resulted in more than a hundred deaths. In 2013, a shoe factory caved in on workers in Cambodia, killing two and injuring dozens of others.[81] In 2011, two explosions at plants manufacturing iPads in China killed four workers, injured seventy-seven others, and raised serious questions about safety conditions throughout Apple's supply chain.[82] These industrial disasters prompted calls for more equitable and just treatment of workers across the globe. In response to these tragedies, labor unions, manufacturers, and activists created an International Accord on Health and Safety in the Textile and Garment Industry that came into effect in 2021.[83] Such international agreements are tricky, however, since there is no international police agency that can enforce them. Nonetheless, consumer choice, labor agreements, and public perception can work as enforcement mechanisms. And such policies are only effective among countries (and corporations) that participate in them. In November 2022, the "Clean Clothes Campaign" called for the international textile accord to be extended to include

Pakistan, which has also suffered from mass deaths resulting from fires in textile factories.[84] Some of the impetus for the Clean Clothes Campaign had to do with consumers pushing back against corporations that were employing sweatshop labor. One way you can contribute to global justice is to avoid purchasing products that are produced in exploitative ways.

This can be effective. About ten years ago, the Walt Disney Company announced that it was going to stop producing Disney brand products in developing countries that have lax labor standards and poor regulation, including Bangladesh, Pakistan, Belarus, Ecuador, and Venezuela.[85] Some viewed this as a good move on the part of Disney, motivated by a sense of moral responsibility. But critics worry that if big corporations pull out of the developing world, it will cause unemployment and create negative outcomes for the workers there. Some brands and retail chains are working with local labor and business leaders in the developing world to forge agreements on fire codes and other safety codes for the factories they do business with.

Of course, if working conditions in the developing world are improved, consumer prices in the developed world may rise. While rising prices of consumer goods would create hardship for many, some consumers may not mind paying more for products that are produced and traded in nonexploitative markets. Indeed, some people conscientiously choose to pay more for clothing and other products that are not produced in sweatshops, pursuing a path called, variously, *ethical consumption, ethical consumerism,* or *shopping with conscience.* This approach to consumption aims to channel consumer choices in morally responsible and sustainable directions. Would you be willing to pay more for a product to ensure that it is not produced in a sweatshop or by other exploitative labor practices?

One concept associated with the idea of ethical consumerism is the idea of *fair trade practices.* Fair trade aims to help disadvantaged people in the developing world by buying goods that are produced in beneficial and nonexploitative conditions.[86] You may have seen fair trade items advertised in stores or on websites. Fair trade coffee, for example, is typically certified by one of several nonprofit organizations (such as Fair Trade USA) to be grown and harvested by workers who are able to earn a living wage under safe working conditions. (See the discussion of living wage in Chapter 14.) But some critics worry that the fair trade label simply makes consumers feel good while being used as a marketing ploy by big corporations.[87] Similar worries have been voiced about contributions to aid organizations. How can we be sure that those we intend to help actually receive the help we intend to give? There is an important practical question here, one that does not, however, change the moral question of whether we should help others in need—especially very poor people in other parts of the globe.

As we conclude this chapter, let's note that a significant area of concern is how nations respond to the challenge of immigration. As the global population passes eight billion, more people are on the move. This includes refugees seeking to escape war and insecurity and others simply seeking better opportunities. Affluent nations have struggled to find ways to manage influxes of immigrants and refugees. One set of issues to consider here are the domestic policies of the affluent countries. Another concern is whether and how the global system might be changed so that immigrants and refugees are not pushed out of their homelands or pulled into other lands. The push and pull of immigration involves poor conditions in one country and better conditions elsewhere. One solution to this challenge is to work to equalize those global inequalities that constitute those push and pull factors. And this might require us to rethink much of what we take for granted in terms of justice, sovereignty, and economics. Philosopher José Jorge Mendoza has argued that the issue of immigration "exposes the limits of our current conceptions of justice and in doing so challenges us to rethink them."[88] Mendoza suggests that in thinking about immigration, we need to consider past colonial injustices, the current needs of immigrants, and how we might reimagine a future in which those push and pull factors are radically altered. (We have an excerpt from Mendoza's work in the primary sources of this chapter.)

Most of this work would involve changes in the political policies of nations and in the structures of the global economy. But individuals can also find ways to help immigrants and refugees, for example, by donating to organizations that help to support refugees or help to relocate and welcome immigrants. Of course,

as we've noted, there are complicated moral questions about immigration and refugee resettlement. Some argue for closed borders, thinking perhaps that Hardin was right to describe nation-states as lifeboats with limited carrying capacities. But others may believe that rich nations should welcome immigrants and that compassion requires us to help refugees. Governmental agencies and nongovernmental organizations are engaged in working with refugees and trying to figure out how best to regulate immigration. But local communities can play a role.

Consider a couple of examples that show us the complexity of the challenge of immigration and refugee resettlement. As the Russian invasion of Ukraine was unfolding in 2022, European nations opened their arms to Ukrainian refugees. Train stations and airports in European cities flew Ukrainian flags and had signs in Ukrainian language offering assistance. This was an inspiring example of how cities, municipalities, and local organizations can do work that contributes to the project of global justice. Of course, one might argue that those same European cities and nations were less welcoming in the past of refugees coming from Africa or the Middle East.[89] A similar dynamic has played out in the United States, where some advocate closed borders and building a wall to keep immigrants out, while others argue that the United States ought to welcome immigrants and refugees. This has resulted in dramatic scenes in recent years, with immigrant children from Latin American being separated from their parents at the U.S. border and with U.S. immigration officials rounding up Haitian immigrants and forcibly returning them to Haiti—a country plagued by natural and political disasters.

The debate about immigration involves complicated questions about national identity, human rights, as well as complex considerations about global economics and national sovereignty. The immigration debate is also connected to the issue of global poverty and issues involving human rights violations in the home countries of those fleeing oppression. As the global population grows past eight billion—and as climate change, pandemics, and economic crises occur—the nations of the globe will need to continue thinking about how best to respond to the challenge of global justice we've discussed here.

Chapter Summary

15.1 What are some of some of the challenges of globalization and global justice?

Globalization is a historical process creating global interconnection involving trade, transportation, and technology. Challenges include issues related to poverty in the developing world, inequality, immigration, and compensation and reparation in response to these problems. Global justice asks ethical questions about how the global community ought to respond to global challenges. This is focused not only on questions of how nation-states ought to interact but also on the kinds of obligations and responsibilities that we have for people who are suffering beyond our borders.

15.2 How might we analyze arguments and proposals for alleviating global poverty?

Different moral theories can be applied in different ways to the challenge of global poverty. This includes concern for those living in extreme poverty, which is currently defined by the international experts as those earning less than $2.15 per day. This is "poverty that kills." And in the developing world, there are limitations on infrastructure that make poverty more deadly than in more affluent nations. Proposals for alleviating poverty include claims about the need for compensation (a "resource dividend," for example) and reparations for prior colonialism. This might also include charity and aid given either by individuals or by states. Among the main proposals discussed here is that affluent nations should contribute 0.7 percent of GNP as aid to poorer nations.

15.3 How can we apply concepts such as utilitarianism, justice, and rights to global issues?

Peter Singer is a well-known utilitarian who argues that the affluent have an obligation or duty to give significant aid to those who are suffering. That obligation is not dependent on proximity, which means that each of us has a duty to give. On the other hand, someone like Garrett Hardin suggests that utilitarian concern stops at the border and that we only have obligations to those within our nation (using an analogy that views nation-states as lifeboats with limited carrying capacities). Other approaches to global justice focus on human rights claims or may appeal to a natural law account of the need for charity. One issue to be considered is whether aid to the suffering is supererogatory charity or whether aid is a duty of justice. Theories of justice can be applied to these issues in various ways, depending on whether the focal point is a fair set of procedures (the process view) or some equitable end-state of global distributive justice.

15.4 How might you evaluate arguments about decolonization and the inclusion of Indigenous voices?

Some argue that affluent nations that gained their wealth through prior colonial exploitation owe reparations or compensation to poorer nations. Furthermore, some authors and activists advocate a kind of "postcolonial" theory that calls for the decolonization of the ideas, economies, and identities of non-Western cultures. The call for decolonization includes a critique of dominant Eurocentric ideas about justice as well as a call for the inclusion of Indigenous voices. To evaluate this argument, you would have to evaluate the relative importance of a utilitarian concern to alleviate suffering (such as we find in Singer's work) in comparison with the worry that global aid reinforces colonial hierarchies. Such an evaluation would also have to decide whether there is such a thing as "global justice" that can be understood in terms of universal concepts of rights, equality, and justice—or whether non-Western and Indigenous thought offers a rival approach that cannot be reduced to the terms of Western philosophy. It might also be that there is a process that Eddy Souffrant describes as "creolization," in which European philosophies will mix and learn from Indigenous cultures, and vice versa.

15.5 How can you evaluate supposed clashes of civilizations and the challenge of unequal development?

Globalization is a process that creates interactions between cultures and so-called civilizations. This process involves modernization and what some call Westernization. If this process involves the spread of Western values, there may be a clash between Western values and other values. Two supposed clashes were described here: that between Western values and Asian values, and that with Western and Islamic values.

These clashes involve conflicting ways of understanding identity, politics, and the economy. To evaluate this, we would have to decide if there really is such a clash. One worry is that such generalizations about civilizations and cultures fail to account for the diversity found within different parts of the globe. Some argue that the defenders of Asian values, for example, are merely using the clash of values as a way to avoid a more general critique of authoritarianism (in China and Hong Kong, for example). We would also have to decide what we think are likely causes (and solutions) to unequal development. Nations in the Middle East and North Africa lag behind European nations in terms of development. Is this a matter of culture (involving, e.g., a lack of rights for women and for LGBTQ people)? Or is there some other causal story—perhaps involving prior colonial exploitation? And what remedies might be employed? An evaluation of this kind of problem would also have to ask whether former colonial powers have specific responsibilities for development in their former colonies.

15.6 How might you explain the critical perspective of anti-globalization?

Globalizing institutions such as the World Bank and International Monetary Fund have been criticized for failing to include voices from the developing world and for creating a system of inequality and indebtedness. On the Left, critics claim that these institutions are not democratic and do not serve the interests of people in the developing world, especially Indigenous people, laborers, and people who live in poverty. On the Right, the critique of globalization includes ethnocentric and even racist ideas that are opposed to immigration and integration of the global economy at the expense of citizens and ethnic groups in the developed world.

15.7 How can you analyze the ideas of ethical consumerism, fair trade, and other individualistic solutions to global problems?

One suggestion for solutions to global problems encourages individuals to take action. Peter Singer's theory of effective altruism is one of these ideas. Singer suggests that individuals have an obligation to give to charities. Related ideas include shopping with conscience and purchasing fair trade items. The idea here is that individual consumers can make choices that support working people in other parts of the world while avoiding products made in sweatshops or other exploitative and unsafe conditions. In thinking about this kind of approach, one would need to consider whether individual choices can actually be effective or whether the problems of global justice involve much larger forces and require institutional responses.

15.8 How could someone defend a thesis about proposals for dealing with global poverty, immigration, and other global justice issues?

The issues discussed here are challenging and complex, involving large historical forces (colonialism) and international institutions such as the IMF and World Bank. To defend a thesis about these issues, one would need to decide what wealthy people owe (if anything) to poorer people. One would also need to consider whether former colonizing powers owe obligations of reparations to those who were previously exploited. Another difficult question involves issues related to "the clash of civilizations" and the challenge of Eurocentrism, cultural diversity, and decolonization. Finally, to defend a thesis about these issues, a student will need to decide which moral theory is to be applied—and how. Peter Singer's utilitarian approach is one important focal point that claims we have an obligation to help others without regard for proximity. There is also the question of self-interest (of individuals and of nation-states). To defend a thesis about these issues, one would need to decide whether individuals or states have obligations of altruistic concern or whether the world is as Hardin described it, as lifeboats that should focus only on taking care of themselves. One would need to consider ideas and proposals that are found in thinking about rights, justice, and the concerns of natural law, as well as ideas that can be found in Indigenous cultures and traditions. Finally, a thesis about global justice also needs some analysis of concrete proposals such as the idea that affluent nations should give 0.7 percent of the income to aid.

Primary Source Readings

In the readings in this chapter, we first have an excerpt from a text by utilitarian philosopher Peter Singer, who asks us to consider whether it is ethical to enjoy luxury goods when others are suffering in poverty. Then we have an excerpt from Garrett Hardin's argument about lifeboat ethics, which makes a different argument—against the idea of helping people who live in poverty. After those two articles, we have an excerpt from Krushil Watene, a scholar from New Zealand with expertise in Māori philosophy and Indigenous thought. Our primary source readings conclude with an excerpt from José Jorge Mendoza, a philosophy professor at the University of Washington and an expert on Latin American philosophy.

Reading 15-1   The Life You Can Save | Peter Singer

Study Questions

As you read the excerpt, please consider the following questions:

1. How does Singer differentiate between luxury goods and the basic needs of poor children?

2. What does Singer mean when he suggests that poverty is a "moral stain" on a world as rich as ours.

3. Explain how Singer relates your concern for your family to a more global concern for strangers.

Do you have a bottle of water or a can of soda on the table beside you as you read this book? If you are paying for something to drink when safe drinking water comes out of the tap, you have money to spend on things you don't really need. Around the world, over 700 million people struggle to live each day on less than you paid for that drink. Because they can't afford even the most basic health care for their families, their children may die from simple, easily treatable diseases like diarrhea. You can help them, and you don't have to risk getting hit by an oncoming train to do it. . . .

We live in a unique moment. The proportion of people unable to meet their basic physical needs is smaller today than it has been at any time in recent history, and perhaps at any time since humans first came into existence. At the same time, when we take a long-term perspective that looks beyond the fluctuations of the economic cycle, the proportion of people with far more than they need is also unprecedented. Most importantly, rich and poor are now linked in ways they never were before. Moving images, in real time, of people on the edge of survival are beamed onto our mobile devices. Not only do we know a lot about the desperately poor, but we also have much more to offer them in terms of better health care, improved seeds and agricultural techniques, and new technologies for generating electricity.

We can't become complacent: 5.4 million children under five dying every year, with over half of those deaths due to conditions that could be prevented or treated with access to simple, affordable interventions, is an immense tragedy, not to mention a moral stain on a world as rich as ours. . . .

It may not be possible to consider ourselves to be living a morally good life unless we give a great deal more than most of us would think is realistic to expect human beings to give. This may sound absurd, and yet the argument for it is remarkably simple. It goes back to that bottle of water, to the money we spend on things that aren't really necessary. If it is so easy to help people who are in desperate need through no fault of their own, and yet we fail to do so, aren't we doing something wrong? . . .

Think about someone you love, and then ask yourself how much you would give to prevent that person from dying of malaria, or to enable that person to be treated for a childbirth injury that made her a social outcast, or to have their sight restored if they should become blind? Then ask yourself how much you are doing to help people living in poverty who lack the means to do just those things for themselves and their families.

Peter Singer, Preface to *The Life You Can Save: How to Do Your Part to End World Poverty*, 10th anniversary ed. (Bainbridge Island, WA: The Life You Can Save, 2019). For more information: https://www.thelifeyoucansave.org/the-book/

Reading 15-2   Living on a Lifeboat | Garrett Hardin

Study Questions

As you read the excerpt, please consider the following questions:

1. How is Hardin's lifeboat metaphor supposed to apply to thinking about immigration and global justice?
2. What is the problem that Hardin sees for the Christian solution?
3. What does Hardin suggest about guilt that might result from an "unjust" solution?

Metaphorically, each rich nation amounts to a lifeboat full of comparatively rich people. The poor of the world are in other, much more crowded lifeboats. Continuously, so to speak, the poor fall out of their lifeboats and swim for a while in the water outside, hoping to be admitted to a rich lifeboat....

We must acknowledge that each lifeboat is effectively limited in capacity. The land of every nation has a limited carrying capacity.... Let us look at only one lifeboat—ours. The ethical problem is the same for all, and is as follows. Here we sit, say 50 people in a lifeboat. To be generous, let us assume our boat has a capacity of 10 more, making 60. (This, however, is to violate the engineering principle of the "safety factor." A new plant disease or a bad change in the weather may decimate our population if we don't preserve some excess capacity as a safety factor.)

The 50 of us in the lifeboat see 100 others swimming in the water outside, asking for admission to the boat, or for handouts. How shall we respond to their calls? There are several possibilities.

One. We may be tempted to try to live by the Christian ideal of being "our brother's keeper," or by the Marxian ideal of "from each according to his abilities, to each according to his needs." Since the needs of all are the same, we take all the needy into our boat, making a total of 150 in a boat with a capacity of 60. The boat is swamped, and everyone drowns. Complete justice, complete catastrophe.

Two. Since the boat has an unused excess capacity of 10, we admit just 10 more to it. This has the disadvantage of getting rid of the safety factor, for which action we will sooner or later pay dearly. Moreover, *which* 10 do we let in? "First come, first served?" The best 10? The neediest 10? How do we *discriminate*? And what do we say to the 90 who are excluded?

Three. Admit no more to the boat and preserve the small safety factor. Survival of the people in the lifeboat is then possible (though we shall have to be on our guard against boarding parties).

The last solution is abhorrent to many people. It is unjust, they say. Let us grant that it is.

"I feel guilty about my good luck," say some. The reply to this is simple: *Get out and yield your place to others.* Such a selfless action might satisfy the conscience of those who are addicted to guilt but it would not change the ethics of the lifeboat. The needy person to whom a guilt-addict yields his place will not himself feel guilty about his sudden good luck. (If he did he would not climb aboard.) The net result of conscience-stricken people relinquishing their unjustly held

positions is the elimination of their kind of conscience from the lifeboat.

Garrett Hardin, "Living on a Lifeboat." *BioScience* 24:10 (October 1974), pp. 561–68.

Reading 15-3 Transforming Global Justice Theorizing | Krushil Watene

Study Questions

As you read the excerpt, please consider the following questions:

1. Why does Watene argue for the inclusion of Indigenous philosophies in conversations about global justice?

2. What are some of the sources of Indigenous philosophy, knowledge, and worldviews?

3. What does Watane suggest is problematic about the approach to global justice associated with "mainstream" political and philosophical thought?

The ideas inherent in colonization silenced, oppressed, and marginalized indigenous ways of knowing, being, and doing. Continuing struggles for recognition, rectification, and for self-determination by indigenous communities around the world serve to illustrate the extent of this continuing oppression and domination. Unsurprisingly, indigenous activists and scholars have written widely on the structures of colonial oppression—including the extent of colonizing processes even within systems designed to mitigate them today. Central to this scholarship and activism are projects concerned with transforming (social, political, economic) institutions in ways that nourish and privilege indigenous philosophies. The pursuit and realization of indigenous peoples' self-determination is, thus, intimately bound up with the revitalization of indigenous philosophies. The capabilities of indigenous peoples to be able to define who they are and to pursue and realize lives they value relies on the extent to which indigenous communities are able to articulate and appropriately apply and reapply their concepts and values to their lives and futures.

Indigenous philosophies are diverse bodies of knowledge within which indigenous worlds were framed prior to European colonization, and which have come to also include deep knowledge of the (ongoing) experiences of colonization. These philosophies chart ideas about time and space, reality, being, knowledge, beauty, well-being, right and wrong, and justice (among many other things). The philosophies have travelled across geographical spaces, and are woven through multiple generations of lived experiences within diverse (social, political, cultural, economic and natural) environments. Indigenous philosophies find expression in oral histories, narratives, ceremonies, social and political organizations, the natural environment, astronomy, and in art forms such as weaving, carving, architecture, music, and dance.

Despite moves to globalize justice theorizing from within mainstream political philosophy itself, very few attempts to open up justice theorizing to a wider range of philosophical perspectives have been made. The "global" in global justice has primarily concerned extending the scope within which existing ideas about justice apply, rather than with widening the scope of perspectives from which ideas and principles of justice can be drawn. As such, indigenous philosophies ... remain largely absent from justice theorizing. The result is that indigenous peoples occupy a silent space in mainstream justice theorizing. Not only is this a space in which indigenous peoples remain unable to define who they are and want to be, but it is also a space in which indigenous peoples are denied an active role....

A commitment to conceptions and principles of social and global justice must resonate with the concepts and values of the communities that make up our social and global landscapes. What is more, we know that many of our challenges are global, and that we need global conversations and solutions to move forward. A commitment to including indigenous peoples in global justice requires a commitment to the philosophies of indigenous peoples so fundamental to the pursuit and realization of self-determination. A commitment to global justice requires that we create space for what indigenous peoples (indeed all local communities) themselves have to say about justice.

Krushil Watene, "Transforming Global Justice Theorizing" in *Oxford Handbook of Global Justice*, ed. Thom Brooks (Oxford, UK: Oxford University Press, 2020).

Reading 15-4 Moral and Political Philosophy of Immigration | Jose Jorge Mendoza

Study Questions

As you read the excerpt, please consider the following questions:

1. Why does Mendoza suggest that in thinking about immigration we need to consider free trade agreements and the legacy of colonialism?

2. What is Mendoza's view of current immigration policies and the "normalization" process?

3. What kinds of proposals does Mendoza suggest might be useful in order to "curb" mass immigration in the future?

Immigration (and especially undocumented immigration) cannot be understood without seeing it as part of a historical process—in our particular case an exploitive economic process—that continues into the present. Theorists and activists ... have persuasively argued, for example, that the free-trade agreements initiated by (and that have largely benefited) countries like the U.S. are also primary contributors of the push and pull factors that are bringing Latin American immigrants to the U.S. and in greater numbers than current U.S. immigration policy allows. To put this even more simply, a framework for just immigration reform is impossible without adequately taking into account historical legacies like colonialism and other similar relationships that have solidified the constant exchange of people....

A second area of general concern is the present. This area of attention focuses on the fate of noncitizen residents, both documented and undocumented. With regard to this area of general concern, it would be necessary to develop a method to normalize the status of undocumented immigrants, clear the backlogs for family reunification—especially immediate family members such as children, parents, and spouses—fix current guest-worker programs and end the practice of "deportable offenses" in criminal law (e.g., crimmigration). A pathway to normalization is necessary for any just immigration reform. This is because it is not feasible, and maybe even immoral, to believe that millions of people can simply be rounded up and deported. A process of normalization does not need to be unconditional. It can have various stipulations attached to it (e.g., years of residence, good standing during those years, fines, etc.), but a clear and reasonable normalization process is essential....

The third area of general concern is the future. If the ultimate goal is to bring unauthorized immigration to an end and also to help immigrants who are admitted better acclimate to and feel as though they are part of their new communities, then the roots of displacement and xenophobia must be addressed. To address this last area, I argue that there is going to have to be a concerted effort by international entities like the IMF and the World Bank to both forgive the debt of poor countries and end structural adjustment programs (and any other variants of these sorts of programs), which in many cases have been part of the original loan agreements that have resulted in the loss of social safety nets in immigrant-sending countries. In places where these economic programs have failed, sustainable economic plans need to be put in place that will help many of these countries build up their own economies.... The way to end economic displacement, which more accurately describes the condition of most undocumented immigrants today, is to create an environment in which people do not need to leave their home countries in order to have a minimally decent life. Creating this sort of environment requires that the international community be proactive, rather than reactive, in helping to curb future mass migration.

José Jorge Mendoza, *The Moral and Political Philosophy of Immigration: Liberty, Security, and Equality* (Lanham, MD: Lexington Books, 2016).

Review Exercises

1. What is extreme poverty and how does it connect to the moral question of global justice?

2. What self-interested reasons can be given for doing something to remedy the situation of poor countries?

3. Contrast Singer's and Hardin's views on how we ought to deal with poverty and famine.

4. What is justice and what role does it play in determining what ought to be done about global poverty?

5. Explain how the history of colonialism might be connected to current inequalities—and what should be done about that.

6. What is meant by "decolonization" in the context of postcolonial theorizing?

7. Why is cultural relativism a concern when thinking about global justice?

8. Why might we think that we have an obligation to be concerned with the suffering of those in distant lands? Explain one criticism of this idea.

9. Summarize the difference between globalization and global justice.

10. What are some moral issues to consider with regard to immigration and global justice?

Discussion Cases

1. Ethical Consumption. Chris is an advocate of ethical consumption. He tries to buy only fair trade products, and he is willing to pay more for an item when he is certain it is produced without exploitation. This means that he often pays 10 to 25 percent more for certain products. His father thinks this is a bad idea. He tells Chris, "You could buy cheaper stuff and with the money you save, you could save for your own future and retirement. Heck, you could even give that money to the poor." Chris is not concerned with his retirement fund. But he is concerned about alleviating poverty. He's puzzled by his father's response.

Should Chris try to find the cheapest products and save money, which he would then donate to charity? Or should he continue to seek out fair trade items, which would leave him with less to donate to charity? What is the solution to this problem? Explain your thinking.

2. Which Poverty Matters? Maria is a successful businessperson who has become convinced that she ought to give a substantial amount of her earnings to help those in extreme poverty in the developing world. Her brother, Thomas, a local college student, is not persuaded that such donations are a good idea. "It just makes people ask for more handouts later," he says. "And besides," he adds, "there are a lot of poor people here in our city: homeless people living on the streets. And I'm not doing too well myself. You ought to give me some of your charity so I can pay for college. I'm going to be swamped with student loan debt."

How should Maria reply? Does she have an obligation to help her brother pay for school, to help homeless people in her city, or to help those in poverty in other countries? Should her proximity or relationship to these various people make a difference here? Or is Thomas right that handouts don't help?

3. Global Culture. Moua and Tyler are arguing about the effects of globalization as a form of modernization or Westernization of the world. Moua points out all of globalization's crass and commercialized aspects—the same McDonald's, consumer electronics, and pop culture icons all over the world—and the negative impact that Western culture has on local and Indigenous cultures. Tyler argues that Western personal and political freedoms ought to be made universal and that a more homogenous culture is a small price to pay for democracy and the liberation of women and minority groups.

With whom do you agree, Moua or Tyler? Can economic and political modernization be divorced from cultural globalization?

4. Colonialism and Globalization. Robert is excited about the recent focus on global justice within institutions such as the United Nations and the World Bank. His family emigrated from Africa to the United States to escape the poverty and political instability of his home country. He thinks these new initiatives will be helpful to those they left behind. But his brother, Daniel, is not convinced. Daniel complains, "Nobody helps without asking for something. Most of those international organizations serve the interests of the countries who caused our unhappiness to begin with. The rich countries are always taking advantage of the poor. They enslaved and marginalized lots of us and exploited our countries' resources. Then they left us with a mess." Robert disagrees. "I don't know why you blame others for the poverty back home. Anyway, I'm glad that the rich countries are finally helping. Our people need any help they can get." Daniel responds, "They owe us for what they did to us. But I still don't trust them."

What do you think? Do rich countries owe something to poor countries? Do rich countries offer their help without strings attached? Or is Daniel right to be cynical?

Knowledge Check Answer Key

1. **c.** Globalization is a process by which the world is connected by trade, transportation, and technology.

2. **b.** Singer is a consequentialist.

3. **a.** Charity views helping people in poverty as something supererogatory, while justice requires poverty alleviation as a duty.

4. **b.** Decolonization aims to liberate formerly colonized cultures from the norms and thought process of the colonizers.

16 Sexual Morality

Learning Outcomes

After reading this chapter, you should be able to:

16.1 Describe basic philosophical views of sex including hedonism and the ideal of "platonic love."

16.2 Apply normative theories to sex and sexuality.

16.3 Explain the argument against sexual coercion and violence, as well as the importance of affirmative consent.

16.4 Evaluate moral and legal arguments about marriage equality.

16.5 Evaluate issues involving trans and gender nonconforming people.

16.6 Evaluate arguments about sexually transmitted diseases, sex education, and sex work.

16.7 Defend a thesis about sexual morality.

Ethical Pornography?

Everyone knows that pornography is widely available on the Internet. Some studies suggest that over 80 percent of people have viewed pornography.[1] Critics argue that pornography creates unhealthy sexual habits and unrealistic expectations about sex. Feminist critics will add that pornography tends to promote degrading images of women that contribute to the general objectification and subordination of women. Critics contend that there is the risk of addiction to pornography and that violent pornography can contribute to sexual

Eyecandy Images/Thinkstock

violence in the real world. These critics are also concerned about the problem of coercion, sex trafficking, and lack of consent in the pornography industry. Some worry, additionally, that the very idea of pornography, as a way of obtaining sexual pleasure without intimacy or social connection, is based on a fundamental misunderstanding and abuse of human sexuality.

In response, some have argued about the need for "ethical pornography." While this may seem to be an oxymoron to those who are opposed to pornography on principle, the proponents of ethical porn argue that instead of banning it, there should be a way to provide consumers of porn with content that is healthy and not exploitative. Ethical pornography would have to make sure that the performers are not coerced, that they are fairly compensated, and that they are free of sexually transmitted diseases. Ethical pornography would avoid violent and racist imagery, while demonstrating to its viewers the use of condoms and other practices of good sexual hygiene. Ethical porn would also display "normal bodies," instead of promoting unrealistic body images. And ethical porn might be used in ways that promote intimacy instead of isolation. But the critics of porn suggest that given the nature of most pornography, it is unlikely that the idea of ethical porn will catch on.[2]

What Do You Think?

1. Is there anything wrong with pornography in general?
2. Are you concerned about problems like sex trafficking, coercion, and images of violence and degradation in pornography?
3. Is the concept of "ethical pornography" a good or useful idea?
4. Do you think there could in fact be "ethical porn"?

Introduction

16.1 Describe basic philosophical views of sex including hedonism and the ideal of platonic love.

In this chapter, we will discuss sexual morality. This is a broad topic that includes questions about sex work, such as pornography and prostitution, as well as a discussion of the broad range of human sexual practices and identities including marriage and other social norms that are used to regulate sex and sexuality. It is worth noting, as we begin, that these things often carry with them implicit moral judgments. For example, do we call people who sell their bodies for sex "prostitutes" or "sex workers" (or do we use other, more pejorative terms)? The word "prostitute" already includes a kind of negative judgment in our world, which is why some people who engage in this business prefer the more neutral word "sex worker" (which might also include strippers, dancers, etc.). A similar set of moral connotations are found in thinking about the terms and terminology we use to describe certain sex acts, sexual identities, and sexual behavior. One goal of this chapter is to think critically and to be more careful in our judgments about these topics.

This chapter is included in the larger subsection of the book that is focused on social justice. So, in addition to thinking about sex from a broadly moral point of view, we will also focus on questions of equality and human rights. This focus has been an important part of the so-called "sexual revolution" or sexual liberation movement that has occurred in Western nations during the past few generations. This shift in norms occurred as movements for civil rights and women's liberation were also changing social values during the past fifty to one hundred years. The sexual "revolution" has involved changing views of the meaning and value of sex, marriage, and intimacy. As an example of evolving social justice claims about sex, we might consider the issue of interracial dating and marriage. Furthermore, we ought to consider the liberation and inclusion of LGBTQ+ people (this acronym stands for "lesbian, gay, bisexual, trans, and queer," with the plus sign indicating the inclusion of other sexual and gender identities). These two issues were linked in the Respect for Marriage Act, which was signed into law in the United States at the end of 2022.[3] That law states that interracial and same-sex couples have the right to marry.

The inclusion of LGBTQ+ people indicates an expansive way of understanding sexual and gender identities that runs counter to the more traditional conception of sex and gender that is associated with the natural law tradition. That tradition generally maintains that there are two genders (male and female) and that heterosexual relationships are natural or normal and should properly occur within marriage. As we'll see in this chapter, the traditional natural law assumptions about sex, gender, and marriage are a matter of dispute and have been criticized both by theorists of sex and gender and by libertarians and utilitarian moral theorists who maintain that consent and pleasure are the proper focus of moral judgments about sex. The traditional natural law view is "hetero-normative" and "cis-normative," which means that it assumes that heterosexual sex between cisgender couples is the presumed norm. Cisgender is a term used to describe a person whose gender identity corresponds with the sex assigned at birth. Transgender is a gender identity that does not correspond in this way to sex at birth. We will discuss these issues of identity in further detail later in the chapter. But note here that when we discuss "traditional" notions of sex, gender, and sexual morality in this chapter, we are focusing on the idea that sex should only occur within heterosexual marriages. The sexual revolution of the past several decades challenged that traditional way of thinking about sex, gender, and sexuality. It involved a substantial change in the way society viewed sex and sexuality that has typically included more widespread acceptance of sex outside of marriage. This also includes a more permissive attitude toward pornography, a recognition of diverse forms of sexual experience and expression, and a more tolerant view toward divorce and cohabitation. This has also included growing acceptance of LGBTQ+ identities and the legalization of same-sex marriage, as well as a shift away from a binary understanding of sexuality and gender. The idea behind the sexual revolution was that sexual repression and traditional conceptions of sex and sexuality were detrimental to human happiness and that they violated the spirit of liberty and equality. In some cases, this led people to encourage "free love," which often meant sexual promiscuity and episodic sexual encounters (i.e., "casual sex") that were unconstrained by traditional views of sex, love, and marriage. Of course, not everyone is happy about these shifting attitudes. Defenders of the natural law tradition and adherents of conservative religious traditions have not welcomed the changes wrought by the sexual revolution, encouraging us to remain wedded to a view of sex that connects it to traditional, heterosexual marriage. And utilitarians, Kantians, and other moral theorists will warn us about the risk of sexual disease and exploitation, while emphasizing the need for caring, healthy, and consensual sex.

The idea that sexual expression and pleasure should be "liberated" has sometimes been connected to a kind of hedonism and even libertinism. In its most basic form, **hedonism** is the idea that pleasure is the highest good (the Greek for pleasure is *hēdonē*). But hedonism is not necessarily a kind of **libertinism**. The term "libertine" has been used to describe those who reject all sexual constraints and who view themselves as free to pursue sexual pleasure wherever they find it. A libertine would be someone like Don Juan, the dramatic character who had a long list of his sexual conquests. That list was made famous in Mozart's opera *Don Giovanni*, where Don Giovanni (which is the Italian name for Don Juan) brags of his sexual exploits. Another famous (or notorious) libertine was the Marquis de Sade—an author whose name provides the root of the idea of "sadism," which means obtaining sexual pleasure by causing others pain. As opposed to these extremes, a more restrained form of philosophical hedonism would emphasize the need to moderate and control sexual desire in order to maximize sexual happiness.

Some trace hedonism back to the thinking of the ancient followers of Epicurus, whose school did in fact focus on the importance of pleasure. But while Epicurus is sometimes caricatured as a wild hedonist, he was not a proponent of unbridled sexual license or of sexual promiscuity. Instead, his school emphasized the importance of organizing, regulating, and controlling pleasure. The basic idea is that we need to be smart about which pleasures we pursue and pursue them with moderation. And like most philosophers of the ancient world, Epicurus thought that sex was a kind of lower, animalistic pleasure that was less important than the higher pleasures of the mind.

A different approach, which is critical of hedonism, argues more explicitly that sex and human sexuality are dangerous impulses that ought to be strictly regulated and controlled. We might call this a kind of **asceticism**. Asceticism is broadly associated with a kind of disciplined self-denial and a worldview that sees pleasure as a seductive distraction from what is truly good. (The Greek root of the term, *askesis* means discipline or control.) In some cases, asceticism goes so far as to call for the renunciation of sex and encourage abstinence or celibacy. One need not go that far in the direction of asceticism, however, to encounter another critique of hedonism and the sexual revolution. Abstinence seems to require too much of a sacrifice in terms of pleasure, but we might also think that there can be such a thing as too much sex (or sex with too many different people). Perhaps the problem is promiscuity and the solution is something like sexual moderation, monogamy, or at least so-called "serial monogamy" (i.e., sticking with one sexual partner at a time). Of course, from the standpoint of traditional view of marriage, serial monogamy is not sufficient. The focal point of that traditional view is a single and lifelong commitment to one other person, within a heterosexual relationship. This idea has been defended by those who affirm a natural law approach to morality in general. This approach maintains that sex can be a source of pleasure but that it ought only to occur within heterosexual marriage and that it ought to be done for the purposes of reproduction and promoting love and intimacy. It is also worth noting that feminists and other social critics have offered a critique of unbridled sexual expression when it comes at the expense of women and contributes to sexual harassment and sexual violence. Promiscuity might be criticized from this standpoint, especially if it involves exploitation of women and a gendered double standard in which men are praised for their sexual conquests, while women are "slut-shamed" for promiscuous behavior.

One need not embrace the traditional natural law view of sex, sexuality, and marriage to worry that there may be something wrong with a sexual liberation movement that embraces libertine behavior at the expense of love, respect, and human decency. Louise Perry published a book in 2022 with the provocative title, *The Case against the Sexual Revolution*. She argued:

> We should treat our sexual partners with dignity. We should not regard other people as merely body parts to be enjoyed. We should aspire to love and mutuality in all of our sexual relationships, regardless of whether they are gay or straight. We should prioritize virtue over desire. We should not assume that any given feeling we discover in our hearts (or our loins) ought to be acted upon.[4]

Among the most important points to be made in connection with Perry's idea of treating our sexual partners with dignity is the fact that rape is among the most obvious concerns of sexual morality. Rape is sexual violence; it is sexual activity that violates autonomy and causes harm—and that's why it is wrong. The normative theories we are discussing in this book all agree about the wrongness of rape. But where they disagree is about questions regarding issues such as sex work (pornography and prostitution), same-sex marriage, and related topics. There is also a remaining and substantial disagreement between natural law theories and other theories of ethics with regard to policies, laws, and norms that acknowledge and protect sexual orientation and gender identification that is considered to be outside of normative heterosexual binaries.

What Is Sex?

Discussions of sexual morality will benefit from a careful analysis of sex and sexuality. Just what are we talking about when we speak of sexual pleasure, sexual desire, or sexual activity? Consider the meaning of the qualifier *sexual*. Suppose we said that behavior is sexual when it involves "pleasurable bodily contact with another." Will this do? This definition is quite broad. It could include passionate caresses and kisses as well as massage and dance. And somewhere on a continuum that includes hand-holding and intimate touch, we find sexual intercourse and other acts that result in orgasm. But is orgasm the only thing that counts as sex or sexual? And does it matter how an orgasm is achieved if all we are focused on is a spasm of muscles and a jolt of pleasure? Furthermore, a definition of sex that focuses on bodily contact would not include activity that does not involve touching another individual, such as masturbation or looking at pornography. It would also exclude erotic dancing, phone sex, and "sexting" because these activities do not involve physical contact with another. So the definition seems to be too narrow.

However, this definition is also too broad. It covers too much. Not all kisses or caresses are sexual, even though they are physical and can be pleasurable. And the contact sport of football is supposedly pleasurable for those who play it, but presumably not in a sexual way. It seems reasonable to think of sexual pleasure as pleasure that involves our so-called erogenous zones—those areas of the body that are sexually sensitive.

Could we then say that sexuality is necessarily bodily in nature? To answer this question, try the following thought experiment. Suppose we did not have bodies—in other words, suppose we were ghosts or spirits of some sort. Would we then be sexual beings? Could we experience sexual desire, for example? If we did, it would surely be different from that which we now experience. Moreover, it is not just that our own bodily existence seems required for us to experience sexual desire, but sexual desire for another would seem most properly to be for the embodied other. It cannot be simply the body of another that is desirable—or dead bodies generally would be sexually stimulating. It is an embodied person who is the "normal" object of sexual desire. This is not to say that bodily touching is necessary, as is clear from the fact that dancing can be sexy and phone sex can be heated. Finally, if the body and achieving orgasm are so important for sexuality, we may also wonder whether there are any significant differences between male and female sexuality in addition to, and based on, genital and reproductive differences. Finally, it is important to note that the reality of homosexual, bisexual, and transgender experience may cause us to question whether there is any substantial difference between male and female sexuality and experience—or whether there is a continuum of identity and experience that is not easily conceptualized in such a binary conceptual scheme.

According to Raja Halwani, a philosophical expert on sex and love, sexual desire and activity are valuable for at least four reasons.[5] First, sexual pleasure itself is "incredibly powerful." Second, sex creates physical intimacy. Third, sex may involve procreation. And fourth, sex is a useful form of "recreation." Halwani notes that sexual desire can be morally problematic when it reduces another person to their body and objectifies them. Sex also produces vulnerability and can leave us feeling exposed. Sexual desire can even be "oppressive"—distracting, overpowering, and even self-degrading. And yet Halwani also notes that when "moral considerations" intrude into sexual life, this can "dampen sexual pleasure."

On the other hand, philosophers have warned that sex should be connected to love, which can improve and even complete sex. This idea can be traced back to Plato. Plato discussed love in a number of places in his dialogues. The most famous of these is his *Symposium*, where he argues in defense of an idea that we know today as "platonic love." Platonic love is not sexual. In ordinary English, when we say that a relationship is "platonic," we mean that it does not involve sex. The root of this notion is found in *Symposium*, where Socrates (the main character in the dialogue) argues that love transcends sex. Sexual relationships are focused on bodies and experiences that are less elevated than the life of the mind. Socrates suggests that the best relationships—what we might call ethical or philosophical friendships—transcend the body and aim toward higher values than mere sex.

And yet many people refer to sexual intercourse as *making love*. So there is clearly a connection between sex and love. Some people argue that sexual intercourse should be accompanied by or be an expression of love, while others do not believe that this is necessary. If you want to generate an interesting discussion, you might ask your friends what they think about sex without love—is that a good thing or not? It is also, of course, possible to have love without sex. We love our relatives and friends. But that kind of love is "platonic" and not sexual. To genuinely love someone in this way is to be actively directed to that person's good. We want the best for them. In his essay on friendship in *The Nicomachean Ethics*, Aristotle wrote that true friendship is different from that which is based on the usefulness of the friend or the pleasure one obtains from being with the friend. The true friend cares about their friend for the friend's own sake. According to Aristotle, "Those who wish well to their friends for their sake are most truly friends."[6] This kind of friendship is less common, he believed, though more lasting.

For Plato, Aristotle, and the Greeks of his time, true friendship was more or less reserved for men (although Socrates hints that he learned quite a bit about love from a female friend named Diotima). In the patriarchal culture of ancient Athens, women were typically viewed as inferior beings and the higher goods of life were reserved for freemen (you might want to review, at this point, our discussion of what Aristotle said about women and slavery in Chapter 8). It is also worth noting that ancient Greek men also occasionally had sex with other men and some older men had sex with younger boys. The presence of same-sex attraction in the ancient world helps us understand one of the memorable scenes in Plato's *Symposium*, where one of the characters offers a mythological account of three kinds of sexual attraction. The character who offers this story is Aristophanes, the Greek comic poet. Aristophanes suggest that the gods originally created three types of human being and three genders: the male, the female, and the androgynous ("androgynous" means both male and female). But, so the story goes, Zeus wanted to make life difficult for these humans. So, he cut them in half. And then the humans went through their lives searching for their other half. Aristophanes thus explains three kinds of sexual desire: male–male, female–female, and male–female. Furthermore, this comedic myth helps to explain the nature of love and desire. We are looking for our other half, someone with whom we can unite and find wholeness.

As mentioned, the Greeks thought the highest form of love was that between men, with Plato insisting that this was nonsexual love. We could describe this as a patriarchal or male-dominant point of view. Women and their sexuality were not the primary subject of philosophical concern for the ancients of the Western tradition. A patriarchal point of view was common in the ancient world. In the Biblical tradition, the ancient creation myth of the book of Genesis explains that God made Adam in his image, while the woman (Eve) was created to help Adam. In the Garden of Eden, where the first couple lived, there was most likely no sexual relationship between Adam and Eve. Rather, in one traditional interpretation of this myth, it was not until sin entered into the world (with Eve disobeying God and eating "the forbidden fruit") that sex, lust, and reproduction began to occur. Some versions of Christianity thus speak of original sin and connect it with sexuality, while also blaming the sin of lust on Eve and on women more generally. Of course, not all Christians share this opinion. And this patriarchal point of view is not unique to Christianity.

One alternative to patriarchal tradition is offered by a feminist ethics of care (which we discussed in Chapter 9). Feminism generally aims to criticize patriarchal systems of belief that blame women for sin, denigrate women, or that ignore the experience of women. From this standpoint, sexual relationships that are not equal are wrong, as are sexual relationships that are built on hierarchy and domination. In addition, care ethics seeks to remind us of the importance of relationality and the altruistic, other-oriented focus of care. From the vantage point of care ethics, sexual activities ought to focus on building, nurturing, and supporting relationships. The gender identity or sexual orientation of the partners is irrelevant from this point of view, so long as care is involved. And it should be obvious that from this point of view, coercive and exploitative sexual relations are wrong.

Relevant Factual Matters

In addition to conceptual clarification, certain factual matters may also be relevant to what we say about matters of sexual morality. For example, would it not be morally significant to know the effects of celibacy or of restraining sexual urges? It is well known that Freud thought that if we repressed our sexual desires, we would become neurotic—or if we repressed our sexual urges but "sublimated" them appropriately, we could transform sexual energy (called "libido") into something else, such as artistic creation. Art, Freud argues, provides an emotionally expressive outlet for repressed sexual feelings. Freudian theory about both sexual repression and the basis of art still has supporters—for example, Camille Paglia is a social critic and theorist of sexuality who credits Freud with inventing "modern sex analysis."[7] It also has not gone unchallenged. And Freud's theory of sexuality has been subject to criticism for decades by those who argue that his theory is both

Aedificavit Dominus Deus costam quam tulerat de Adam in mulierem.

Figure 16-1 An artistic rendering of the creation of Eve.

Library of Congress, Prints & Photographs Division, Reproduction number LC-DIG-ppmsca-40197 (digital file from original item)

male-oriented and out of touch with regard to the way that sexual practice and our understanding of sexuality have changed in the past hundred years. And yet Freud is also viewed as a source of the "sexual revolution," since he made sexuality and sexual repression a focal point of his theory.

At any rate, there are more obviously factual matters involved in thinking about sexual morality. Knowing what the likely effects of sexual promiscuity would be, both psychologically and physically, is important for thinking about sexual morality. Factual matters such as the likelihood of contracting a disease, such as AIDS, would be important for what we say about the moral character of some sexual encounters. It is also important to understand how contraception works and the possibility of pregnancy resulting from sexual intercourse. Our conclusions about many factual or empirical matters would seem to influence greatly what we say about sexual morality—that is, the morality of sex, just like the morality of other human activities, is at least sometimes determined by the benefits and harms that result from it. And these benefits and harms are determined by the way the world works.

It is also helpful to think about the various ways that sex, gender, and sexuality have manifested themselves throughout history. We mentioned previously that the ancient Greeks engaged in same-sex relationships. This is a reminder of the fact that homosexuality is not an invention of the modern world. Something similar holds true for transgender persons and those who do not conform to traditional binary norms of sex and gender. In India, to cite one example, people described as *hijra* make up a so-called "third gender."[8] The British rulers of India tried to eliminate this possibility by arresting *hijras*. But India, Nepal, and Bangladesh have come to recognize the rights of people to choose their gender. The Supreme Court of India issued a ruling in 2014 saying, "It is the right of every human being to choose their gender."[9] Moreover, modern science and medicine has long recognized the reality of "intersex" people, who are biologically and genetically nonbinary. These are people who have genes and body parts that do not conform to the binary distinction between male and female. Different cultures in history have also deliberately created eunuchs, men who were castrated as boys (and sometimes as adults). European cultures removed the testes in some cases to produce so-called "castrati"—prepubescent boys who were castrated in order to prevent the appearance of secondary sex characteristics: the castrati were castrated in order to preserve a high-pitched and boyish singing voice. This procedure was banned in the nineteenth century.

But cultural traditions continue to engage surgeries and procedures on the genitalia of children and infants. Here we might consider male circumcisions, in which the foreskin of the penis is removed. Some claim that this is useful for hygiene, but critics maintain that it is both unnecessary and that it may cause a decrease in sexual pleasure. Female "circumcision" has been especially controversial. Sometimes this is called by the neutral-sounding name "female genital cutting." But the critics describe it as "female genital mutilation" (FGM), which is a term that has been widely employed in the human rights community critical of the practice. According to a World Health Organization report updated in January 2022:

> FGM is mostly carried out on young girls between infancy and adolescence, and occasionally on adult women. According to available data from 30 countries where FGM is practiced in the Western, Eastern, and North-Eastern regions of Africa, and some countries in the Middle East and Asia, more than 200 million girls and women alive today have been subjected to the practice with more than 3 million girls estimated to be at risk of FGM annually.[10]

FGM can involve different degrees of severity—from excision of the skin surrounding the clitoris, to removal of all or part of the clitoris and some of the surrounding tissues, to stitching the labia together so that only a small opening remains. Among the cultural and parental reasons given for these practices are to enable families to exercise control over reproduction, to keep women virgins until marriage, and to reduce or eliminate female sexual pleasure.[11] The procedure is usually done without a local anesthetic and often performed with unclean and crude instruments. If the labia have been stitched together, a reverse cutting is frequently necessary before intercourse can take place—this subsequent procedure can also be quite painful. In addition, FGM can cause problems in childbirth.[12] In fact, the more extensive forms of this procedure raise "by more than 50 percent the likelihood that the woman or her baby will die."[13] The World Health Organization explains, "the FGM procedure that seals or narrows a vaginal opening needs to be cut open later to allow for sexual intercourse and childbirth. Sometimes it is stitched again several times, including after childbirth, hence the woman goes through repeated opening and closing procedures, further increasing both immediate and long-term risks."[14] Critics have sought to ban the procedure, but there is a risk in this conversation of imposing a Eurocentric standard on cultures that do it.

Ethical disputes about altering the genitals include disagreements about gender-reassignment procedures. These days it is possible to use modern medical technology to change gender, including both surgeries and hormones. Our society is currently debating a number of issues related to the rights of trans persons, including the question of whether irreversible gender-reassignment procedures are justifiable when done on children. One important part of these debates involves how to regard people whose gender identity does not conform to societal norms governing gender. Some defenders of traditional cisgender norms assume that this is a new or modern issue. But people who do not conform with society's gender norms have always existed. What's new are changing social norms regarding nonbinary and trans persons. Innovations in modern medical technology also allow for safe procedures for those who elect to alter their bodies. We'll discuss issues involving trans persons in more detail later in the chapter.

It is also worth noting that marriage and love have also been defined in different ways in different cultures and at different times. The "nuclear" family that is familiar in the Western world (based on monogamous heterosexual marriage) is only one possibility. For example, the Mormons in the United States (adherents of the Church of Jesus Christ of Latter-Day Saints, i.e., LDS) at one point allowed for polygamy (one man and more than one wife). The mainstream LDS Church prohibited polygamy at the end the nineteenth century. But some minor Mormon sects continue the practice. And in Tibet, fraternal polyandry occurs: a marital relation in which two or more brothers marry one woman, sharing her sexually as well as sharing the responsibility of acting as father to the resulting children.[15] These facts remind us that human marital customs and sexual relations are variable.

Sexual Morality and Ethical Theories

16.2 Apply normative theories to sex and sexuality.

Factual matters are especially relevant if we are judging the morality of actions on the basis of their consequences. Thus, we would be concerned, from a consequentialist point of view, with questions about happiness and the possible outcomes of various sexual practices and marital arrangements. If, instead, we adopt a non-consequentialist moral theory such as Kant's, our concerns will not be about the consequences of sexual behavior but about whether we are cherishing or using people, for example, or being fair or unfair. If we adopt a natural law position, our concerns will again be significantly different, or at least based on different reasons. We will want to know whether certain sexual behavior fits or is befitting of human nature. We could also focus on virtues, including the virtue of care. We might ask, for example, whether certain sexual practices exhibit temperance, modesty, loyalty, or love—and whether other practices encourage immoderate behavior or the vice of unbridled sexual desire that is called "lust."

In fact, the moral theory that we hold will even determine how we pose the moral questions about sex. For example, if we are guided by a consequentialist moral theory such as utilitarianism, we will be likely to pose moral questions in terms of good or bad, better or worse outcomes of sexual behavior. If we are governed by deontological principles, our questions will more likely be in terms of right or wrong, justifiable or unjustifiable sexual behavior. If we judge from a natural law basis, we will want to know whether a particular sexual behavior is natural or unnatural, proper or improper, or even "perverted." And the virtue ethics approach will use words like "modesty" of "fidelity" that may have little resonance for those who are only concerned with pleasure. Let us consider each of these ways of posing moral questions about sexual matters and see some of the probable considerations appropriate to each type of reasoning.

Consequentialist or Utilitarian Considerations

If we were to take a consequentialist point of view—say, that of an act utilitarian—we would judge our actions or make our decisions about how to behave sexually one case at a time. In each case, we would consider our alternatives and their likely consequences for all who would be affected by them. In each case, we would consider who would benefit or suffer, as well as the type of benefit or suffering. In sexual relations, we would probably want to consider physical, psychological, and social consequences. Considerations such as these are necessary for arguments that are consequentialist in nature. According to this perspective, the sexual practice or relation that has better consequences than other possibilities is the preferred one. Any practice in which the bad consequences outweigh the good consequences would be morally problematic.

Among the negative consequences to be avoided are physical harms, including sexually transmitted diseases. Psychic harms are no less real. There is the shame caused by sexual rejection or sexual exploitation. And of course, the harm and trauma of rape is among the worst possible outcomes of sexual behavior. Also to be considered are possible feelings of disappointment and foolishness for having false hopes or of being deceived or used. Pregnancy, although regarded in some circumstances as a good or a benefit, may in other circumstances be unwanted and involve significant suffering. Some people might include as a negative consequence the effects on the family of certain sexual practices. Incest could create harms and dysfunction within the family. And adultery is generally seen to undermine marriages, although some couples in "open marriages" (with a mutual agreement to have sexual partners outside of the marriage) would disagree. Opponents of same-sex marriage go further, arguing that it undermines the institution of marriage. By contrast, defenders of same-sex marriage maintain that there is no evidence that it would have any impact whatsoever on "straight" marriages. And same-sex couples claim the right to marry in order to strengthen and benefit their families, including especially their children. In consequentialist reasoning, all of the consequences count, and short-term benefit or pleasure may be outweighed by long-term suffering or pain.

One might object to a utilitarian approach to sexual morality by claiming that utilitarianism makes it possible that the pain caused to one person can be outweighed by the pleasure given to another or others. Would it be possible for a utilitarian to support the degradation of a few sex workers and pornographic actors if that results in substantial pleasure for lots of other people? In response,

act utilitarians might suggest that we ought to develop our utilitarian calculation based on general rules, such as a general rule that says that sexual exploitation is wrong because it produces unhappiness. As we'll see, John Stuart Mill made this kind of utilitarian argument against prostitution, holding that it was generally degrading—both to the prostitutes and to their customers. And as we'll also see, Jeremy Bentham argued on utilitarian grounds toward an opposite conclusion: he held that if prostitution were well regulated, it could produce profit and pleasure without too many ill effects.

It is fairly obvious that consequentialists will be interested maximizing sexual pleasure and the happiness of intimate relations. There are number of positive consequences or benefits that may come from sexual relations or activity. First of all, there is sexual pleasure itself. Furthermore, we may benefit both physically and psychologically from having this outlet for sexual urges and desires. It is relaxing. It enables us to appreciate other sensual things and to be more passionate and perhaps even more compassionate. It may enhance our perceptions of the world. For many people, intimate sexual relations can improve mood and self-esteem. And sexual relations can improve personal relations by breaking down barriers and bringing people together in shared intimacy. However, many would argue that this is likely to be so only where a good relationship already exists between the persons involved.

What about sex in the context of marriage and children? The future happiness or unhappiness of potential children must play a role in consequentialist considerations. The increased availability of contraception now makes it easier to control these consequences, so offspring that result from sexual relations are presumably (but not necessarily) more likely to be wanted and well cared for. Abortion and its consequences also may play a role in determining whether a particular sexual relation is good from this perspective.

Finally, consequentialist thinking has room for judging not only what is good and bad, or better and worse, but also what is best and worst. On utilitarian grounds, the most pleasurable and most productive of overall happiness is the best. If one cannot have the ideal best, however, one should choose the best that is available, provided that this choice does not negatively affect one's ability to have the best or cause problems in other aspects of one's life. It is consistent with a consequentialist perspective to judge sexual behavior not in terms of what we must avoid, but in terms of what we should hope and aim for as the best. Nevertheless, in classical utilitarianism, the ideal is always to be thought of in terms of happiness or pleasure.

It is important to note, in this regard, that although the utilitarian philosopher John Stuart Mill was a proponent of liberty, he was also a defender of sexual equality. This helps explain why Mill was opposed to prostitution:

> Of all modes of sexual indulgence, consistent with the personal freedom and safety of women, I regard prostitution as the very worst; not only on account of the wretched women whose whole existence it sacrifices, but because no other is anything like so corrupting to the men. In no other is there the same total absence of even a temporary gleam of affection and tenderness; in no other is the woman to the man so completely a mere thing used simply as a means, for a purpose which to herself must be disgusting.[16]

Mill's point is that appropriate sexual relations should be mutual and equal. To use another as a means for sexual gratification may produce pleasure. But from a utilitarian perspective, this produces more unhappiness on balance, since it corrupts the men involved and degrades the women.

A rival utilitarian argument was made by Jeremy Bentham. Bentham held that although prostitution was shameful, it was better to legalize it than to make it illegal. Bentham thought that illegal prostitution increased the corrupting effect of prostitution on the prostitute, driving them to excessive use of "intoxicating liquors, that they may find in them a momentary oblivion of their misery," which also renders them "insensible to the restraint of shame."[17] A utilitarian might argue in a similar way that if sex work were legalized and regulated, it might provide happiness for all people involved. The customers would obtain sexual pleasure, the prostitutes would be able to capitalize on the transaction, state regulation would ensure healthy and safe sex, and the state could tax the transaction. But opponents of this idea, such as Carole Pateman, argue that there is something wrong with the idea that men could pay to use women's bodies in this way.[18] Pateman's feminist argument against prostitution is linked to a general critique of the way that men dominate women and the way that masculine sexuality is, from her perspective, overly focused on gaining access to and control of female bodies. We have an excerpt from Pateman at the end of this chapter. We also have an excerpt from Jessica Flanigan, who argues from a human rights perspective that sex work should be decriminalized. Flanigan claims that sex workers have a right to make a living—and to have sex with whomever they choose.

Non-consequentialist or Deontological Considerations

The claim that it is simply wrong to pay to use another person's body for sexual pleasure is a deontological one. So too is the claim made by Flanigan that people have a right to engage in sex (and sell it if that's what they freely choose to do). Discussions of what is corrupting and degrading also point toward non-consequentialist concerns. Non-consequentialist moral theories, such as that of Kant, would direct us to judge sexual actions, as well as other actions, quite differently from consequentialist theories. Although the Golden Rule is not strictly the same thing as the categorical imperative, there are similarities between these two moral principles. According to both, as a person in a sexual relation, I should do only what would seem acceptable no matter whose shoes I were in or from whose perspective I judged. In the case of a couple, each person should consider what the sexual relation would look like from the other's point of view, and each should proceed only if a contemplated action or relation is also acceptable from that other viewpoint. This looks like a position regarding sexual relations according to which anything is permissible sexually as long as it is agreed to by the participants.

In one interpretation of Kantian sexual ethics—which focuses on respect for persons—consent and autonomy are the key factors to be considered. However, it is important to note that Kant's own views of sexual ethics are not exclusively focused on consent. Instead, he brings in considerations of the function and natural purpose of sex. In fact, he views the purpose of sexuality as the preservation of the species and condemns homosexuality, masturbation, and sex with animals on these grounds.[19]

Notice that there is an interesting question about the limits of consent as a focal point with regard to something like masturbation. Indeed, one might argue that masturbation is the only obviously consensual sexual practice—since it is something one does to oneself. And yet authors like Kant argue that what he calls "self-defilement" is one of the worst things a human being can do—a vice so appalling that it is even shameful to speak of. In Kant's view, masturbation degrades one's own humanity, focusing only on the satisfaction of an "animal impulse." Kant suggests we have a duty of "chastity" that is a duty to ourselves, that is, a duty not to "abuse" our sexual organs in such a "loathsome" fashion.[20] Kant's theory of sexuality appears to be connected here with a natural law argument. From his standpoint, the purpose or function of sex is reproduction—not mere sexual pleasure. This claim is what leads Kant to argue that sex with animals and sex between members of the same sex are both also immoral because they are "unnatural."[21] As should be obvious, to equate homosexuality with bestiality is offensive to members of the LGBTQ+ community and their allies. With this critical point in mind, we might also connect Kant's disparaging and derogatory view of homosexuality with his similarly negative views of women and non-White people (as we discussed in Chapter 6).

We will turn to the natural law argument further in the next section. But let's first further examine the Kantian emphasis on consent and respect for autonomy. The primary concern would be whether mutual consent to any given sexual act is real. For example, we would want to know whether the participants are fully informed and aware of what is involved. Lying would certainly be morally objectionable. So also would other forms of deceit and failure to inform. Not telling someone that one is married or that one has a communicable disease could also be forms of objectionable deceit, in particular when this information, if known, would make a difference to the other person's willingness to participate.

In addition, any sexual relation would have to be freely entered into. Any form of coercion would be morally objectionable on Kantian grounds. This is one of the strongest reasons for prohibiting sex with children, namely, that they cannot fully consent to it. They have

neither the experience nor understanding of it, and they are not independent enough to resist pressure or coercion. As with deceit, what counts as coercion is not always easy to say, both in general and in any concrete case. Certainly, physically forcing a person to engage in sexual intercourse against their will is coercion. That is what we call rape. Kant called rape a "crime against humanity."[22] He maintained that it ought to be punished by castration.

The Kantian argument against rape tends to view it as an assault on a person's dignity and autonomy. However, some forms of "persuasion" may also be coercive. Threats to do what is harmful are coercive. For example, threatening to demote an employee or deny a person a promotion if they do not engage in a sexual relation can be coercive. But subtler forms of coercion also exist, including implied threats to withhold one's affection from the other or to break off a relationship. Some offers or bribes are obviously coercive. Saying to a homeless person, a political refugee, or undocumented immigrant, "I know that you are in need, but I will help you if you have sex with me or if you prostitute yourself for me" is surely coercive. This would be wrong from the Kantian standpoint.

Furthermore, good sexual relations should involve more than avoiding coercion and disrespect. Onora O'Neill has argued that a Kantian theory of sexual ethics should not only be about avoiding coercion but also about cultivating love and benevolence. She quotes Kant as saying that respect keeps people apart (by preventing them from violating each other's rights) but love brings people together in mutual concern for one another's happiness. Using Kantian language, she explains: "If we are to treat others with whom we are intimate with love as well as respect, we must both see and (to some extent) support their ends."[23] In other words, love and respect come together when we support the other person's dignity, autonomy, happiness, and well-being.

Natural Law Considerations

Natural law theories (as described in Chapter 7) hold that morality is grounded in human nature. That is good which furthers human nature or is fitting for it, and that is bad or morally objectionable which frustrates or violates or is inconsistent with human nature. How would such a theory be used to make moral judgments about sexual behavior? Obviously, the key is the description of human nature.

In any use of human nature as a basis for determining what is good, a key issue will be describing that nature. To see how crucial this is, suppose that we examine a version of natural law theory that stresses the biological aspects of human nature. How would this require us to think about sexual morality? It would probably require us to note that an essential aspect of human nature is the orientation of the genital and reproductive system toward reproducing young. The very "nature" of heterosexual sexual intercourse (unless changed by accident or human intervention by sterilization or contraception) is to release male sperm into a female vagina and uterus. The sperm naturally tend to seek and penetrate an egg, fertilizing it and forming with the egg the beginning of a fetus, which develops naturally into a young member of the species. In this version of natural law theory, that which interferes with or seeks deliberately to frustrate this natural purpose of sexual intercourse as oriented toward reproduction would be morally objectionable. Thus, contraception, masturbation, and homosexual relations would be contrary to nature. Further arguments would be needed for natural law theories that claim that sexual relations should take place only in marriage. These arguments would possibly have to do with an account of how sex is related to love and commitment, as well as with an account of the importance of the biological relation of the child to the parents, and with the necessary or best setting for raising children.

Given this description of the natural purpose of sexuality, natural law theory often argues against same-sex and other nonreproductive forms of sexual experience. From this standpoint, masturbation, or any kind of sex that does not involve a penis penetrating a vagina, would be wrong. This point of view has often been defended from conservative religious points of view. But there are natural law theorists, such as John Finnis, who have articulated a natural law account of sexual ethics from a standpoint that does not invoke religion. Finnis argues against any "nonmarital" sexual activity, claiming that acts such as oral sex, masturbation, anal sex, and homosexuality in general are wrong. Finnis writes:

> Genital intercourse between spouses enables them to actualise and experience (and in that sense express) their marriage itself, as a single reality with two blessings (children and mutual affection). Non-marital intercourse, especially *but not only* homosexual, has no such point and therefore is unacceptable.[24]

Finnis's account represents a conservative and traditional view of sexual ethics. (We have an excerpt from Finnis in the primary source readings for this chapter.) This kind of conclusion has led some critics to argue that there is something wrong with the notion of what counts as "natural" and with natural law ethics in general. John Corvino has argued that what he calls "the new natural law theory" is confused in its claims about what is natural, normal, good or bad—and that often the account of what is "natural" in terms of sexuality merely expresses an author's prejudiced opinion about what they think is normal. (We have an excerpt from Corvino in this chapter, as well.)

We could also envision other nature-focused arguments about sexual morality that are based on somewhat different notions of human nature. For example, we could argue that the natural purpose of sexual relations is pleasure because nature has so constructed the nerve components of the genital system. Furthermore, the intimacy and naturally uniting aspect of sexual intercourse may provide a basis for arguing that this is its natural tendency—to unite people, to express their unity, or to bring them closer together. This account of the function of sex would not necessarily rule out same-sex intimacy or any other form of sexual experience that is not explicitly heterosexual.

To believe that there is such a thing as "natural" sexual behavior that is consistent with human nature also implies that there can be sexual behavior that is inconsistent with human nature or unnatural. Sometimes the term *perverted* has been used synonymously with *unnatural*. Thus, in the context of a discussion or analysis of natural law views about sexual morality, we also can consider the question of whether there is such a thing as sexual perversion. This is not to say that notions of sexual perversion are limited to natural law theory, however. *Perversion* literally means "turned against" or "away from" something—usually away from some norm. Perverted sexual behavior would, then, be sexual behavior that departs from some norm for such behavior. "That's not normal," we say. By norm, here, we mean not just the usual type of behavior, for this depends on what people do. Rather, by norm or normal, we mean what coincides with a moral standard.

To consider whether there is a natural type of sexual behavior or desire, we might compare it with another appetite, namely, the appetite of hunger, whose natural object we might say is food. If a person were to eat pictures of food instead of food, this would generally be considered abnormal. Would we also say that a person who was satisfied with pictures of a sexually attractive person and used them as a substitute for a real person was in some sense abnormal or acting abnormally? This depends on whether there is such a thing as a normal

sex drive and what its natural object would be. People have used the notion of normal sex drive and desire to say that things such as shoe fetishism (being sexually excited by shoes) and desire for sex with animals or dead bodies are abnormal. One suggestion is that the object of normal sexual desire is another individual, and the desire is not just for the other but for the other's mutual and embodied response.

These notions of perverted versus normal sexual desire and behavior can belong in some loose way to a tradition that considers human nature as a moral norm. Like the utilitarian and Kantian moral traditions, natural law theory has its own way of judging sexual and other types of behavior. These three ways of judging sexual behavior are not necessarily incompatible with one another, however. We might find that some forms of sexual behavior are not only ill-fitted for human nature, but also involve using

Table 16-1   Outline of Moral Approaches to Sexual Relations

	Liberal	Moderate	Conservative
Thesis	Sexual relations ought to be free and open.	There are reasons to limit and regulate sexual behavior.	Sexual relations ought to be subject to strict regulation.
Corollaries and Implications	Marriage equality should be affirmed, allowing LGBTQ+ persons to marry; pornography, prostitution, and freely adopted sexual identity should be permitted—with limits based on consent.	Sexual relations and identities should be limited by social concerns, including regulating disease, protecting the rights of women, minimizing unwanted pregnancy, and other issues involving human rights, health, and dignity.	Sexual relations ought to conform to traditional heterosexual norms, including limiting sexual relations within traditional marriages; opposition to same-sex marriage.
Connections with Moral Theory	Libertarian freedom based on respect for autonomy; consequentialist focus on producing happiness for people to explore sexual experience and sexual identities.	Respect for individual liberty balanced with need to minimize harms; utilitarian and feminist concern for the well-being of women and others who may be exploited.	Natural law basis for cisgender identities and heterosexual norms; consequentialist focus on maintaining social stability and traditional values.
Relevant Authors	John Corvino; Jessica Flanigan	Jeremy Bentham; John Stuart Mill; Carol Pateman	John Finnis; Immanuel Kant

another as a thing rather than a person, and that such behavior also has bad consequences. Or we may find that what is most fitting for human nature is also what has the best consequences and treats persons with the respect that is due to them. The more difficult cases will be those in which no harm comes to persons from a sexual relation, but they have nevertheless been used. No less difficult will be cases in which informed consent is present, but it is for activities that seem ill-fitted for human nature or do not promise happiness, pleasure, or other benefits.

Feminism, Virtue, and Care

As we conclude our discussion of basic approaches to sexual morality, let's return to a set of concerns we began with: questions about the status of women and questions about key virtues in sexual life. We have discussed these issues previously in passing, so let's briefly bring them together. A feminist approach would be concerned with thinking about ways in which sexual morality empowers or disempowers women. Carole Pateman, whom we discussed previously, suggested that prostitution was wrong because it implies that it is morally acceptable for women's bodies to be bought and sold. That's a feminist argument. Pateman's thinking has been criticized by more contemporary feminists who suggest that prostitution could be empowering if women are protected from violence and earn money doing it. Among those making that kind of argument is Jessica Flanigan, who contends that when sex work is criminalized, it disempowers some women—namely the sex workers themselves, who are prevented from making a living.[25] In the most recent (2018) edition of her book *The Sexual Contract*, Pateman explains that she was surprised that some feminists were critical of her critique of prostitution, especially in light of the growing sex industry.[26] This dispute between Pateman and her critics reminds us that there are disagreements even among those who adhere to some general theory such as feminism.

Now let's turn to virtue ethics and the ethics of care. From the vantage point of virtue ethics, the key question is which virtues matter and how they ought to apply in sexual relationships. One traditional set of virtues emphasizes ideas such as fidelity, loyalty, honesty, temperance, and love. These virtues may tend to point toward the importance

Figure 16-2 Carole Pateman (b. 1940) is a feminist critic of pornography.

Mark Hawkins / Alamy Stock Photo

of careful, honest, and restrained sexual behavior. Such virtues could be found in heterosexual, homosexual, or other relations that do not fall neatly into traditional sex and gender norms. So virtue ethics may result in a more inclusive approach than natural law. But this set of virtues would still be critical of promiscuity and, most likely, of prostitution. Could one be temperate and loving while engaged in sex work or while participating in promiscuous sex? But it remains an open question whether fidelity, for example, requires marriage or something less stringent like "exclusivity" or serial monogamy. As you consider this, you might want to ask yourself whether you think that fidelity is an important virtue—and whether it require something like marriage (for heterosexual and for nonheterosexual relationships)?

Finally, let's return to the importance of care. Sexual relations are intimate. And this intimacy often leaves us vulnerable and exposed. For that reason, care ethics is a useful frame of reference. Care ethicists tell us that we ought to be focused on creating nurturing relationships and that we should be especially concerned with protecting those who are vulnerable. Again, care should be the basis of any kind of sexual relationship. And, as in the case of virtue ethics, care ethics would likely also be critical of promiscuity and prostitution. Obviously, the ethics of care would advocate for the importance of autonomy and consent. Care would also focus on producing pleasure, happiness, and other good outcomes, while avoiding bad consequences (such as disease transmission).

Care ethics would also caution us against exploitation, coercion, and manipulation of those with whom we share intimacy, while generally encouraging us to respond with compassion and empathy to the needs of those with whom we share our vulnerability.

Current Issues

There are a number of issues related to sexual morality that are on the table for consideration in the contemporary world. Some of these issues may overlap with considerations found in other chapters. Sexual relations produce offspring, which may point to discussions of contraception and abortion (as we discuss in Chapter 11), as well as discussions of the use of biotechnologies including in vitro fertilization and genetic testing (as discussed in Chapter 12). Questions about sexuality are connected to issues related to gender identity, women's rights, and male dominance (as discussed in Chapter 9). A thorough examination of sexual morality would include considerations of a range of issues including honor crimes, genital mutilation, sex trafficking, prostitution, pornography, polygamy, and so on. Here we will focus only on a couple of those topics.

▶ **Knowledge Check**   Answers appear at the end of the chapter.

1. Which best explains the difference between hedonism and asceticism?

   a. Hedonism encourages abstinence, while asceticism encourages free love.

   b. Hedonism encourages platonic love, while asceticism encourages marriage.

   c. Hedonism encourages the healthy pursuit of pleasure, while asceticism encourages us to overcome the pursuit of pleasure.

   d. Hedonism encourages traditional love and marriage, while asceticism encourages sexual revolution and free love.

2. What is meant by nonbinary in discussions of sex and gender?

   a. Nonbinary implies that there are more than two options when it comes to gender.

   b. Nonbinary means that we should refuse to judge other people's choices about gender or sexuality.

   c. Nonbinary directs our attention to the idea of sex without love, as in the idea of nonbinding sexual relations.

   d. Nonbinary means that there is only one answer to the way that sex and gender ought to be understood.

3. Which of the following is false?

   a. Plato and Aristophanes understood that same-sex attraction exists.

   b. Kant thought masturbation and homosexuality were wrong.

   c. Mill was opposed to prostitution.

   d. Human beings have never cut or mutilated children's genitals.

4. How do care ethics and virtue ethics approach sexual morality?

   a. These theories focus on the harms and benefits of sexual relations, including pleasure and pain.

   b. These theories emphasize ideas like loyalty, fidelity, compassion, and empathy in thinking about sexual relations.

   c. These theories focus on autonomy and consent, permitting any form of sexual relationship that is not coercive.

   d. These theories focus on overcoming sexual desire in order to put the mind in touch with higher things.

Rape, Sexual Harassment, and Affirmative Consent

16.3 Explain the argument against sexual coercion and violence, as well as the importance of affirmative consent.

In the last few years, a number of women have spoken out against sexual harassment and violence, and a number of prominent men have been accused of sexual harassment and even rape as part of a cultural reckoning known as the "#MeToo" movement. Over 250 celebrities, CEOs, politicians, and other prominent men were accused between 2017 and 2021.[27] These accusations involved prominent men such as U.S. senator Al Franken, Hollywood producer Harvey Weinstein, TV personalities Bill O'Reilly and Matt Lauer, and former president Donald Trump. As a result, many of these men lost their jobs or were put on trial. Senator Franken resigned, as did Bill O'Reilly, while Matt Lauer was fired. Harvey Weinstein was put on trial in New York and in Los Angeles and was found guilty of rape in both cases.[28] The accusations against Donald Trump involved both the notorious *Access Hollywood* tape, where he said, "When you're a star, they let you do it. You can do anything. Grab 'em by the pussy. You can do anything."[29] Trump's campaign paid off porn star Stormy Daniels, and there is ongoing litigation involving the former president and other accusations of sexual assault and harassment. The name of this movement, #MeToo, came from the way that when women (and to a lesser degree men) spoke out about sexual harassment, other women came forward and said, "that happened to me too."

Feminists will see this litany of harassment as a symptom of the continued problem of male dominance and patriarchy. Men feel as if they are somehow empowered to grab and grope women. They use their power to exploit women sexually. And they engage in quid pro quo sexual exchanges, promising jobs or power in return for sexual favors. It should be stated that not all men behave this way. But the #MeToo movement is a reminder that women still suffer from sexual harassment, sexual violence, and unfair and unequal working and social conditions. The *New York Times* reported in 2018 that sexual harassment and exploitation are not uncommon. They explain:

> Many encounter sexual harassment from a young age. More than half of the women and just under half the men surveyed said they had experienced some form of harassment or assault by the age of 17.... Quid pro quo sexual harassment—being pressed by someone to offer sex in return for something—was reported by 13 percent of the women and 5 percent of the men in the survey.[30]

Other studies support this kind of finding. According to the U.S. Centers for Disease Control, sexual violence is common. They report the following.[31]

- Over half of women and almost one in three men have experienced sexual violence involving physical contact during their lifetimes.
- One in four women and about one in twenty-six men have experienced completed or attempted rape.
- One in three women and about one in nine men experienced sexual harassment in a public place.
- More than four in five female rape survivors reported that they were first raped before age twenty-five and almost half were first raped as a minor.

It is important to note that no legitimate moral theory would justify or condone rape or harassment. Such actions are violations of autonomy, disrespectful of personal dignity and human rights, and cause suffering.

As a result of ongoing discussion and critique of sexual violence, sexual harassment, and rape, cultural norms governing sexual behavior have continued to evolve. At one point, rape was rationalized as being the result of uncontrollable male lust. But starting in the 1970s, feminists such as Susan Brownmiller began pushing society to recognize that rape is "not a crime of irrational, impulsive, uncontrollable lust, but is a deliberate, hostile, violent act of degradation and possession on the part of a would-be conqueror."[32] While it is important to recognize that rape is a crime of violence and domination, it also has an unmistakably sexual element. Reliable statistics on the incidence of rape are difficult to establish. One reason is underreporting. Another reason is the incidence of acquaintance rape. Two-thirds of rapes are committed by someone known to the victim.[33] One form of this is so-called "date rape," a type of sexual assault that is particularly prevalent among young adults of college age. While there are problems in how data on rape and sexual assault are collected, one estimate, from the Rape, Abuse & Incest National Network, is that every sixty-eight seconds someone in the United States is sexually assaulted; that's nearly one person every minute.[34]

Rape is clearly wrong according to many different ethical standards. But in many parts of the world, women are still blamed (to varying degrees) for being victims of rape. As we mentioned in our discussion of honor crimes in Chapter 9, in some cultures, rape victims are forced to marry their rapists or are even killed by family members for bringing shame on the family. A report from 2021 indicated that in twenty countries, including Russia, Thailand, and Venezuela, a rapist can escape punishment by marrying his victim.[35]

Rape can also happen within the family. In most cases, incest is a form of rape because it involves minors who cannot consent to sexual acts. And since the 1970s, European countries and individual states in the United States have recognized that women can be raped by their husbands. It wasn't until 1993, however, that all states in the United States criminalized spousal rape.[36] And today, married women in other parts of the world are still not protected by marital rape laws. In India, in 2022, a Supreme Court ruling acknowledged the existence of marital rape in a case involving abortion access for a married woman.[37] However, there is no criminal penalty for marital rape in thirty or more countries, including Saudi Arabia, Iran, Iraq, and China.[38]

The idea that rape could occur within marriage is based on the claim that consent is required for sexual relations—and that marriage does not give a husband the right to use his wife's body for sex without her consent. A growing recognition of the importance of consent has led to the doctrine of "affirmative consent" as a guide for sexual relations and intimate contact. In California, for example, in 2014, a law was passed that requires "affirmative consent" for sexual relations. One intent of the so-called "yes means yes" law was to rule out sexual relations that happened, for example, when someone is intoxicated or under the influence of drugs or otherwise unable to consent due to mental ability or age. Proponents of this kind of legislation worry that in some cases "no means no" was not enough. And behind this was a concern about an epidemic in sexual assaults and rapes on college campuses. According to one estimate,

based on 2020 data, more than one-fourth (26 percent) of college women will experience rape or sexual assault involving "physical force, violence, or incapacitation."[39] In response, most universities require students (and faculty and staff) to be educated and trained on avoiding and preventing sexual assault and sexual harassment. The affirmative consent standard of "yes means yes" rules out indifference, ignorance, and mixed feelings. If someone doesn't say no, that's not enough; consensual sex requires a positive affirmation. You must ask your partner for a "yes" before touching or proceeding with sexual contact or activity. And if consent is withdrawn, you must cease that sexual activity.

Marriage Equality

16.4 Evaluate moral and legal arguments about marriage equality.

In 2015, the U.S. Supreme Court ruled that same-sex marriages must be legally recognized in all states. The Court concluded in its landmark *Obergefell v. Hodges* decision, "same-sex couples may exercise the fundamental right to marry in all States...there is no lawful basis for a State to refuse to recognize a lawful same-sex marriage performed in another State on the ground of its same-sex character."[40] This decision concluded a decades-long debate that had raged across the country regarding the legality of marriages involving gay, lesbian, bisexual, or trans people. Preceding this was another long struggle for "gay liberation" or what we might call more broadly, the LGBTQ+ civil rights movement, that extended back, at least, to the Stonewall Riots or Stonewall Uprising of 1969 (these were protests that broke out after police raided a gay bar, the Stonewall Inn, in New York). For many, *Obergefell* marked the culmination of fifty years of struggle for equality for LGBTQ+ people. Indeed, the terminology used to describe things after the *Obergefell* decision has shifted. It is used to be common to speak of "gay marriage" or "same-sex marriage" (in previous editions of this book, we used this terminology). But once LGBTQ+ couples are legally permitted to marry, it may be appropriate to drop the qualification "same-sex" and simply speak of "marriage equality" or maybe diverse or inclusive marriages. And in some parts of the country, it is now common to hear a man speak of his husband or a woman to speak of her wife. This kind of language would be very surprising to Americans of previous generations, who were used to the traditional idea that marriage was exclusively for a "husband and wife" couple.

The moral and legal question remains on the table for some who disagree both with the idea of marriage equality and, more generally with the morality of homosexual relations. Soon after the *Obergefell* decision was reached, for example, a county clerk in Kentucky, Kim Davis, refused to issue marriage licenses for same-sex unions. She stated, "To issue a marriage license which conflicts with God's definition of marriage, with my name affixed to the certificate, would violate my conscience."[41] Davis was jailed as a result of her refusal. For some, Davis was a hero. For others, her moral and religious objection to same-sex marriage is old-fashioned and intolerant.

And although *Obergefell* seemed to settle the legal questions, as we mentioned in our discussion of the Supreme Court's *Dobbs v. Jackson* decision (of 2022), which overturned *Roe v. Wade*, this case may have implications for *Obergefell* and for other Court decisions involving sex and marriage. Justice Clarence Thomas said, in his concurring opinion in *Dobbs*, "in future cases, we should reconsider all of this Court's substantive due process precedents, including Griswold, Lawrence, and Obergefell."[42] The *Griswold* case, which Justice Thomas mentions here, involves the right to contraception. The *Lawrence* case overturned anti-sodomy laws. And as we're discussing here, *Obergefell* made same-sex marriage legal. Justice Thomas suggests that all of these decisions may need to be revisited.

The issue of marriage equality is a matter of civil rights. It fits with topics we discussed in Chapter 13 in our consideration of equality and discrimination. In this regard, the discussion of marriage equality might also include a discussion of interracial marriage, which was made legal in the United States in 1967 with the case of *Loving v. Virginia*. In some communities, interracial dating, sex, and marriage may still be seen as controversial. But they are not nearly as controversial today as they were a couple of generations ago. At any rate, in response to the uncertainty in the law produced by the *Dobbs* decision, the U.S. Congress passed a law in 2022, The Respect for Marriage Act, which legally protects both same-sex and interracial marriages. When President Joe Biden signed the law, he said:

> Marriage is a simple proposition: Who do you love, and will you be loyal with that person you love? It's not more complicated than that. And the law recognizes that everyone should have the right to answer those questions for themselves without the government's interference. It also secures the federal rights, protections that come with marriage.... For most of our nation's history, we denied interracial couples and same-sex couples these protections. We failed. We failed to treat them with an equal dignity and respect. And now, the law requires that interracial marriages and same-sex marriage must be recognized as legal in every state in the nation.[43]

Underlying many of the arguments against marriage equality is a moral claim about the proper form of sexual relationships. As we mentioned, the Supreme Court's decision in *Lawrence v. Texas* (decided in 2003) declared that laws against sodomy are unconstitutional. *Sodomy* is usually taken to include any form of sex that does not involve vaginal penetration by a penis. This word has typically been used to condemn homosexual relations. But it could also include oral and anal sex between heterosexual couples. The late Supreme Court justice Antonin Scalia, who died in 2016, explained the thinking of those who are opposed to homosexuality in his dissent in the *Lawrence v. Texas* decision. He accused the Court of signing on to the "homosexual agenda" and lamented the fact that the Court was seeking to eliminate "the moral opprobrium that has traditionally attached to homosexual conduct." He continued: "Many Americans do not want persons who openly engage in homosexual conduct as partners in their business, as scoutmasters for their children, as teachers in their children's schools, or as boarders in their home. They view this as protecting themselves and their families from a lifestyle that they believe to be immoral and destructive."[44] Scalia's claim that homosexuality is "immoral" and "destructive" points beyond the question of civil rights toward a deeper moral analysis of sexual morality.

The evolution of Americans' perspectives on same-sex marriage has ranged across several decades. The federal Defense of Marriage Act was passed in 1996 and signed into law by President Bill Clinton—and at the time the then senator Joe Biden voted in favor of it. That act was intended to "define and protect the institution of marriage" and defined marriage as follows: "The word 'marriage' means only a legal union between one man and one woman as husband and wife, and the word 'spouse' refers only to a person of the opposite sex who is a husband or a wife."[45] The law stipulated that states do not have to recognize marriages between same-sex couples or provide these couples with the federal benefits accorded to couples in heterosexual marriages. There were many benefits that did not extend to same-sex partners, including eligibility to file joint income taxes, to inherit Social Security benefits, and to defer estate taxes by passing property on to surviving spouses.[46] In June 2013, the Supreme Court ruled, in *United States v. Windsor*, that part of the Defense of Marriage Act was unconstitutional. The Court concluded, "DOMA instructs all federal officials, and indeed all persons with whom same-sex couples interact, including their own children, that their marriage is less worthy than the marriages of others." The Court ruled that by "treating those persons as living in marriages less respected than others," the law violated citizens' due process rights.[47] During the course of the past two decades, same-sex couples have gradually been granted legal rights and equal opportunities, culminating in the *Obergefell* decision of 2015 and the Respect for Marriage Act of 2022, which as we noted was signed into law by President Joe Biden—whose thinking about sex and marriage evolved from his earlier support of the Defense of Marriage Act. Other changes in terms of protections for LGBTQ+ people have occurred in recent decades. In 2011, for example, homosexual people were allowed to openly serve in the military; in 2013, the Pentagon extended medical and other benefits to the partners of gay soldiers.[48]

While the United States has been debating the issue, other countries have also legalized same-sex marriage. According to research published in 2019, some thirty countries permit same-sex marriage, primarily in Western Europe and the Americas.[49] While the legal tide appears to be rapidly turning in favor of same-sex marriage in some parts of the world, homosexuality and legal recognition of marriage equality are fiercely contested in other parts of the world. In sixty-nine countries (mostly in Africa and the Middle East), homosexuality is illegal.[50] In some countries, including in Iran, Saudi Arabia, Somalia, and Yemen, homosexuality is punishable by death.[51] And violence against LGBTQ+ people continues to be a problem. In June 2016, a mass murderer opened fire in a gay nightclub in Orlando, Florida, killing forty-nine people in the worst atrocity committed against the LGBTQ+ community in the history of the United States. While some may think that discussions of sexual ethics are of minor importance since sex is a private matter, the fact that some people are liable to be killed because of their sexual orientation indicates the importance of the discussion and the depth of the dispute about sexual ethics.

When making moral judgments about homosexuality and marriage equality, the same considerations can be used as for sexual morality generally: consequentialist and non-consequentialist considerations, as well as naturalness. Some issues are conceptual, such as what is meant by *homosexual* as opposed to *heterosexual* and *bisexual*. And there is a deep and contested empirical question of whether one's gender or sexual identity is a naturally given fact of life or whether it is a matter of individual choice. Some opponents of same-sex marriage claim that sexuality is a matter of choice and that individuals simply ought to choose traditional heterosexual relationships. In opposition to this, some proponents of same-sex marriage contend that individuals should be free to choose to marry whomever they want. Other defenders of same-sex marriage argue that since sexual attraction is not a matter of choice but, rather, a natural disposition over which individuals have no control, people of all sexual orientations should be free to engage in relationships that are natural and rewarding for them.

From a consequentialist point of view, there is nothing in the nature of sex itself that requires that it be heterosexual or for reproductive purposes. In this view, the sexual activity that produces the most happiness for the people involved is the best, regardless of the gender of the parties involved and whether or not they intend to produce children. Some have argued against same-sex marriage and homosexuality in general on the grounds that such relationships and sexual behavior produce more bad consequences than good ones—that they undermine the traditional family, decouple marriage from reproduction, and deprive children of a stable family environment. As with many other controversial topics, the empirical evidence supporting such consequentialist claims is disputed. One widely discussed recent study by sociologist Mark Regnerus has been cited by conservatives who claim that it shows that children raised by same-sex couples fare poorly.[52] This study was cited by the U.S. Conference of Catholic Bishops in its *amicus* brief filed in the *Hollingsworth v. Perry* case, which legalized same-sex marriage in California in 2013. The bishops appealed to the Regnerus study in arguing that heterosexual marriages created the "optimal environment" for raising children.[53] On the other side, sociologists have criticized the Regnerus study's conclusions as well as its source of funding (the study was supported by funding from conservative, "family values" sources).[54] The American Sociological Association concluded, in its *amicus* brief for the *Hollingsworth v. Perry* case, that the "scholarly consensus is clear: children of same-sex parents fare just as well as children of opposite-sex parents."[55]

Another sort of argument made in defense of traditional marriage focuses on the gradual decline of heterosexual marriage in general. More people are remaining single or cohabiting without marrying.[56] Married couples also end up divorcing. Marriage is typically viewed as an important social institution, but fewer people seem interested in it. So one traditionalist argument would claim that society should work to protect and support traditional marriage. But while it is true that traditional heterosexual marriage has declined as a social value—with more divorce and more people cohabitating outside of marriage—there is no evidence that same-sex marriage is the cause of these phenomena. Rather, the general decline in marriage is better described in terms of a variety of causal factors, including the decline of religious traditionalism, changing sexual mores, the liberation of women, and larger economic forces.[57] Moreover, if marriage is a social good, it might make sense to support marriage equality and allow more couples to get married. Of course, the traditionalists argue that same-sex marriages lack the capacity to produce children through natural reproductive means. But adoption and in vitro fertilization and surrogacy are possibilities these days for LGBTQ+ people. Proponents of marriage equality have also pointed out that if the true moral purpose of marriage is reproduction, we should ban infertile heterosexual couples from marrying, as well as older couples and couples who desire to remain childless.

Consequentialists focus on the happiness and well-being of LGBTQ+ people—and their children and families. In the old days, LGBTQ+ people were ostracized,

Figure 16-3 Same-sex marriage was made legal in the United States in 2015 by the Supreme Court's *Obergefell v. Hodges* decision.

Rob Melnychuk/Digital Vision/Getty Images

pathologized, and even institutionalized. The gay liberation movement argued that the problem was not a person's sexual orientation but rather, the social response to that identity. The social context makes a difference to consequentialist viewpoints on homosexuality and marriage equality. Social acceptability or stigma will make a difference in whether people can be happy in certain kinds of relationships. Greater social acceptance of diverse sexual identities—along with expanded marriage equality—will likely produce more happiness for LGBTQ+ folks. Moreover, when there is legalized marital equality, the full benefits of marriage would be extended to LGBTQ+ people and their families, including benefits for married couples that are obtained through tax policy, insurance coverage, and inheritance law.

Non-consequentialist considerations also apply to discussions about homosexuality and marriage equality. One of the most common non-consequentialist arguments against homosexual sex is that it is "unnatural" or that it goes against nature. We discussed this previously in connection with the views of Immanuel Kant and the dispute between John Corvino and John Finnis about the meaning of the world "natural" in discussions of sex. Many gay and lesbian people respond to such arguments by emphasizing that their same-sex attractions are profoundly "natural" and were present from childhood. They may also point to the occurrence of same-sex sexual behavior in the natural world.

According to traditional natural law theory, although we differ individually in many ways, people share a common human nature. I may have individual inclinations or things may be natural to me that are not natural to you, simply because of our differing talents, psychic traits, and other unique characteristics. Natural law theory tells us that certain things are right or wrong not because they further or frustrate our individual inclinations, but because they promote or work against our species' inclinations and aspects of our common human nature. Arguments about sexual orientation that appeal to traditional natural law theory may need to determine whether nonheterosexual sexual orientation is consistent with a common human nature.

Thus, the argument that gay men or lesbian women find relating sexually to members of their own sex "natural" to them as individuals may or may not work as part of a natural law argument that supports that behavior. However, if one takes a broader view of sexuality in its passionate, emotional, and social aspects, then one could make a reasonable argument based on natural law that homosexuality is but one expression of a broad range of human sexuality. Historically, natural law arguments have not gone this way. But this is not to say that such an argument could not be reasonably put forth.

Natural law arguments against homosexuality and same-sex marriage have often traditionally been grounded in religious viewpoints on sexuality and the sanctity of heterosexual marriage. For example, many Christian and Jewish people who denounce homosexuality do so on the basis of Old Testament Bible verses such as Deuteronomy 23:17–18, Leviticus 18:22, and Leviticus 20:13. The apostle Paul also condemns it in the New Testament: 1 Corinthians 6:9–10 and Timothy 1:9–10 and in Romans 1:26–27.[58] One problem for such scripturally based arguments is that these sacred texts are based on ancient social mores, which include values that we might find objectionable today such as the subordination of women. The Old Testament appears to permit polygamy. And the New Testament prohibits divorce. If we reject same-sex marriage on biblical grounds, should we also reject divorce and permit polygamy? Some religions (some forms of Islam, e.g., and Mormonism at one point in its history) do permit polygamous marriage, which is now illegal in the United States and other Western countries. An explicitly religious foundation for marriage also runs afoul of secular principles (as discussed in Chapter 2), which aim to keep the legal system neutral with regard to religion.

As noted earlier, arguments about homosexuality and same-sex marriage may be more properly framed as civil rights issues rather than moral issues per se. It may be helpful to put this issue in a larger context. For example, Black people in the United States were not allowed to marry until after the Civil War, and mixed-race couples could not do so everywhere in the United States until a Supreme Court decision in 1967. The movement for marriage equality may also be understood as benefiting interracial couples and members of other marginalized communities.

At one point, there was a suggestion that focused on "civil unions" as an alternative to marriage for LGBTQ+ people. Civil unions were supposed to be legally similar to marriages, insofar as they would allow for shared social benefits for partners in a civil union; but these would also be different since they were not considered full or "proper" marriages. Proponents of civil unions may have thought that this solved the question without extending the concept of marriage in a way that includes same-sex marriages. But the debate about marriage equality points beyond the legal issue of how domestic partners might share social benefits. The larger question is whether homosexual relationships deserve to be considered as the same kind of loving and sexual relationship as heterosexual relationships. The Defense of Marriage Act of 1996, which we mentioned earlier, was described in a report to Congress as focused on the *moral* question of homosexuality: "Civil laws that permit only heterosexual marriage reflect and honor a collective moral judgment about human sexuality. This judgment entails both moral disapproval of homosexuality and a moral conviction that heterosexuality better comports with traditional (especially Judeo-Christian) morality."[59] The 2013 Supreme Court ruling overturning the Defense of Marriage Act (*U.S. v. Windsor*) rejected this institutional expression of moral disapproval of homosexuality. And the *Obergefell* decision of 2015 took this a step further by acknowledging that past discrimination against homosexual couples was wrong and that same-sex couples have a right to marry. The Court stated: "The limitation of marriage to opposite-sex couples may long have seemed natural and just, but its inconsistency with the central meaning of the fundamental right to marry is now manifest."[60] (We have an excerpt from the *Obergefell* decision among the primary sources of this chapter.)

Let's note one other of the issues discussed in the debate about marriage equality—the challenge of polygamy and plural marriage. In a dissent to the *Obergefell* decision, Chief Justice John Roberts wrote the following:

> Although the majority randomly inserts the adjective "two" in various places, it offers no reason at all why the two-person element of the core definition of marriage may be preserved while the man-woman element may not. Indeed, from the standpoint of history and tradition, a leap from opposite-sex marriage to same-sex marriage is much greater than one from a two-person union to plural unions, which have deep roots in some cultures around the world.... It is striking how much of the majority's reasoning would apply with equal force to the claim of a fundamental right to plural marriage.[61]

Roberts raises this point as a warning, suggesting that in allowing same-sex marriage, the Court has opened the door to permitting plural marriage. He implies that this would be a bad thing. This may seem like a red herring. Most proponents of same-sex marriage are not also arguing in favor of plural marriage. John Corvino, a philosophical advocate for marriage equality, explains, "It does not follow that we will or should legalize polygamy.... Some marriage-equality advocates endorse polygamy, but most do not; some polygamy advocates endorse marriage equality, but most do not."[62] Corvino's point is that the issue of two-person same-sex marriage must be distinguished from the question of plural marriage. But one could imagine some defenders of marriage equality affirming the possibility of plural marriage. Some defenders of traditional marriage may want to argue that according to natural law, marriage is defined monogamously. But as Justice Roberts points out, plural marriage is not unusual in the history of the world, which implies that it might not be "unnatural." And as Corvino explains, "the majority of cultures in recorded history have preferred polygamy (and specifically, polygyny) to monogamy. It's not 'one man/one woman': it's one man, several women, and perhaps some concubines for good measure."[63] His point is that marriage has been defined in various ways in different places—and that there is nothing "natural" about it. If that's so, then we should probably focus our attention on autonomy, consent, and happiness. And so, a relevant set of moral questions could be asked about plural marriages: would they produce good outcomes and would they be based on consent and respect for autonomy?

Issues Involving Trans and Gender Nonconforming Persons

16.5 Evaluate issues involving trans and gender nonconforming people.

Another issue to consider is the matter of trans identity and equality and respect for trans persons. The term "trans" has often been understood in conjunction with some other notion such as "gender" or "sexual"—as in terms such as "transgender" or "transsexual." The prefix is meant to point to the idea of transcending or transitioning, and the idea of moving, changing, or going beyond. (We discussed something similar with regard to trans-humanism in Chapter 12.) And in a sense the idea of transgender points beyond traditional notions of gender as a natural binary biological difference. Some people who identify as trans may identify as either men or women—and so be considered as a trans man or a trans woman. But there are individuals who embrace a "nonbinary" identity. And so, the notion of trans can be used in a way that is not reduceable to the gender binary of male and female. As Talia Bettcher, a trans philosopher, has explained in discussing the idea of trans, which she renders as "trans*":

> Those who do not place themselves within the binary (e.g., genderqueer people) are effectively left out, despite the original intention behind transgender as an inclusive umbrella term. Since its introduction, unfortunately the term is also now frequently used as a prefix that occurs before woman or man (as in trans* man and trans* woman) in well-intentioned efforts at inclusivity. A problem, however, is that such a use may replicate the very problem that led to the introduction of trans* in the first place by generating the expectation that trans* people are either trans* men or trans* women and thereby eliding trans* identities that resist placement within a gender binary. Moreover, many trans people may not self-identify as trans* and so there is a problem of wrongfully imputing identities (and political agendas) that run contrary to self-identifications.[64]

Bettcher's account helps us understand the range of pronouns that people now employ in describing their gender identity. In addition to "he/him/his" and "she/her/hers," there are also "they/them/their" and "ze/zir/zie." This range of pronouns shows that gender identity is not reducible to the traditional binary distinction between male and female. Most college students in the United States are familiar with this, as it has become a commonplace on American university campuses to ask about gender identity and pronoun preference.

In articulating one's pronouns, a person acknowledges that gender identity is not always associated with one's sex at birth, and that gender identity is not reducible to a binary distinction between male and female. This may be confusing for people who are accustomed to looking at gender in binary terms. From a binary perspective, there are only two genders—and if choice is on the table at all, one should choose one of those genders. But trans theorizing asks us to consider the idea of a binary choice. Related to this are identities such as "gender-fluid" or "gender nonconforming." When people identify as gender-fluid, this means they do not identify with a single fixed gender; people who identify as gender nonconforming are those whose gender does not fit into a specific category. Sometimes the word "queer" is used in this regard. The Human Rights Campaign explains, "Queer is often used as a catch-all to include many people, including those who do not identify as exclusively straight and/or folks who have nonbinary or gender-expansive identities."[65] At one point the word queer was used as an insult. But folks in the LGBTQ+ community have reappropriated the term. As mentioned, the acronym LGBTQ+ stands for "lesbian, gay, bisexual, transgender, and queer." (Some add other letters and identities here including questioning, intersex, pansexual, asexual, etc.) Terms like trans and transgender can be understood in relation to the term "cisgender," which describes those whose gender identity aligns with the identity typically associated with the sex assigned to them at birth. Cisgender individuals feel at home in traditional gender identities and in the gender identity that is associated with their biological or anatomical sex organs. Transgender individuals often confront exclusion and marginalization due to the fact that they do not conform to the binary norms of the traditional understanding of gender. Discussions of the ethics of gender overlap somewhat with discussions of feminist concerns (as discussed in Chapter 9). The question of sex or gender-reassignment surgeries and other procedures also overlaps with issues in biotechnology and medical ethics (see Chapters 10 and 12).

One significant question here is the degree to which autonomy and respect for individual liberty with regard to sex and gender are to be respected and acknowledged. One very obvious libertarian argument is that people should be free to do what they want with their own bodies and identities. So long as no one else is harmed, gender fluidity is one possibility for free and autonomous adults. This issue becomes complicated when thinking about children. And even from a libertarian vantage point, one might wonder whether "irreversible" gender-oriented medical interventions are appropriate—say surgeries or hormonal treatments that could prevent a future change of heart in terms of gender. In this regard, the other concerns of bioethics might be appealed to: both the idea of providing beneficent care and the concern to "do no harm" (see Chapter 10). But apart from that, the libertarian argument would hold that individuals should be free to choose—and that other people should mind their own business.

Of course, not everyone agrees that we should be free to choose or change our gender. The anti-libertarian argument is typically offered by defenders of a natural law approach. This approach holds that we should conform to supposed natural gender roles and the sexual categories associated with the notion of "man and wife" in a traditional marriage. The natural law critics of trans theory might claim that there is no such thing as a choice of gender, understanding "gender" in a reductive way as anatomical and biological. Traditional natural law approaches typically claim that there are two genders. One version of that idea traces it back to the Biblical creation story we mentioned earlier, which holds that God created Adam and Eve along with the distinction between genders. A similar point is made without appealing to the Bible by claiming that sex and gender exist in nature for purposes of reproduction and that in nature there are only male or female genitals and reproductive organs. From a natural law standpoint, it makes no sense to suggest that there could be nonbinary gender. Nor do natural law theorists tend to support the idea of changing genders or gender fluidity. And natural law thinkers tend to suggest that gender and sex are naturally linked in a male–female dyad. One example of this comes from the Catholic Church. The Vatican's Congregation for Catholic Education published a guide for "gender theory" in 2019 with the title "Male and Female He Created Them." The document states that "sexual difference between male and female is constitutive of human identity" And it sees trans identity as an outgrowth of "postmodern culture" that has "moved away from nature" and affirmed a "confused concept of freedom."[66]

In response, however, trans theorists point out that human biology is not so clear-cut. We mentioned previously the fact of "intersex" people. Intersex people may have chromosomes that do not fit the typical XY (male) or XX (female) pattern, or there may be other nonbinary manifestations of sex organs and secondary sexual traits. It is estimated that 1–2 percent of people may have some kind of intersex condition.[67] This fact may make us wonder about the "natural" reality of a binary system of sex and gender. And, to return to the issue of irreversible medical procedures for children, it is worth noting that there is a complicated question in health care ethics about the kinds of choices that are made with regard to intersex infants. These surgeries have been criticized by human rights groups. At the same time, state laws that ban "irreversible gender reassignment" allow exceptions in the case of intersex infants.[68] If this seems confusing, that may be because the world is still working through contested cultural, moral, and legal questions with regard to sex and gender.

A trans theorists might also point out, in response to the natural law argument, that even in nature there are nonhuman animals that are gender-fluid. An often-cited example is the clownfish (familiar from the *Finding Nemo* film). Clownfish change genders according to status and structure within schools of fish. Furthermore, the trans argument holds, against the natural law approach, that human notions of sex and gender are cultural anyway and are not easily reducible to biology.

Another challenge for trans people has been the question of whether they should be included among the concerns of feminism. From the standpoint of a certain kind of feminism that is focused on the struggle for women's rights and equality, trans persons are not included in that struggle (we discuss feminism in more detail in Chapter 9). On this conception, feminists are focused on protecting the rights of women, criticizing patriarchy and sexual violence, and advocating for equality for women. But those making this kind of argument sometimes argue against the inclusion of trans women (biological men who have transitioned to become women) within the women's rights movement. Or they suggest that the struggle for women's rights and the struggle against misogyny and violence against women is significantly different from the struggle for trans rights and the struggle against transphobic violence.

For example, it is worth considering the status of trans women athletes from the vantage point of feminists who argue that women's sports ought to be for women, while appealing to remaining inequalities between male and female athletes. Should trans athletes such as Lia Thomas, who began her swimming career on the men's team at Penn State, be allowed to compete on the women's team? Thomas won an NCAA 500-meter championship swimming in the women's division. Martina Navratilova, the women's tennis champion, said that there should be an asterisk beside Thomas's name, since she was born a man and had an unfair advantage. Navratilova is involved in a working group that is trying to figure out rules that might apply to trans athletes.[69] Is it fair to allow trans women to compete against cisgender women? Or is it transphobic to exclude people like Lia Thomas?

Among the most famous people to raise questions about trans identity from a feminist point of view is J. K. Rowling, the author of the *Harry Potter* series. Rowling has stated:

> I want trans women to be safe. At the same time, I do not want to make natal girls and women less safe. When you throw open the doors of bathrooms and changing rooms to any man who believes or feels he's a woman—and, as I've said, gender confirmation certificates may now be granted without any need for surgery or hormones—then you open the door to any and all men who wish to come inside. That is the simple truth.[70]

In response, trans activists have accused Rowling of being transphobic and of failing to understand the struggles of trans people—and for suggesting that there is something dangerous about allowing trans women into female bathrooms. A pejorative term has been employed in this debate, TERF, which stands for "trans exclusionary radical feminist." Rowling was accused of being a TERF and for hating trans people and encouraging violence against them. She has argued in response that defending the rights of women does not mean that she wants to exclude trans people or that she is transphobic. Rather, she has said that her focus is on defending the rights of cis women and girls who are still treated unequally and threatened with sexual violence. The debate about Rowling's views of sex and gender have

led some to call for a boycott of her work. In response, Rowling has argued against bullying and cancel culture, while also arguing about the need for continued work on behalf of women and girls.

We mentioned here the problem of violence against trans people. From a consequentialist point of view, this would be among the most important issues to consider. Utilitarianism wants to promote flourishing and happiness—and violence, exclusion, and oppression are not part of flourishing. Violence against trans people is a significant problem that causes obvious unhappiness—and it continues, as chronicled by the Human Rights Campaign, who reports that 2021 was "The Deadliest Year on Record for Transgender and Non-Binary People."[71] Violence against trans people would also be viewed as a problem from a standpoint that emphasizes human rights and respect for persons. And it is a concern for civil rights and social justice. We mentioned previously that in India, choice of gender has been recognized as a basic right. In the United States, antidiscrimination law has gradually expanded to include the rights of trans people. In the case of *Bostock v. Clayton County* (2020), the U.S. Supreme Court held, for example, that it was illegal to fire a person simply because they are gay or transgender. But in a dissent to the case, Justice Samuel Alito worried that by extending the right of nondiscrimination to trans people, the Court was opening the door to a world in which "an unclothed person with the anatomy of a male" may be granted access to "a confined and sensitive

Figure 16-4 Lia Thomas is a trans athlete.

location such as a bathroom or locker room" and that this might "cause serious psychological harm" to the girls in the girl's locker room.[72] It is worth noting that Alito's worry here may be similar to the concern expressed by J. K. Rowling. In response, Loren Cannon, a trans philosopher, has argued that this kind of concern is connected to a generally unfounded fear of trans people and a tendency to scapegoat them. Cannon has argued that recent legislation aimed at protecting bathrooms and excluding trans people from sports and so on are part of a "backlash" and even "trans panic" that has resulted as society is coming to terms with new social norms and ways of thinking about sex and gender. Cannon focuses his account on a backlash to the *Obergefell* decision that normalized gay and lesbian relationships. And it worth noting that in the summer of 2015, as the Supreme Court was ruling on the *Obergefell* case, trans identity burst into public awareness as Caitlyn Jenner publicly announced that her transition from the male Bruce to the transgender woman Caitlyn was complete. Suddenly, a range of issues related to gender and sexual identity came into public focus. And soon after that, conservative states were considering "bathroom bills" that would sort bathrooms by anatomy rather than by gender identity. Conservative states also began working on legislation that would prevent trans athletes from competing in sporting events that did not fit their anatomical gender identity. In Cannon's view, the feared consequences that Justice Alito conjures up here are based on hyperbole and lack of understanding. Cannon concludes, "there is no justifiable reason that transgender, gender non-binary, or gender fluid persons should be barred from participation in society in all respects."[73]

STD's, Sex Ed, Sex Work, and Other Issues

16.6 Evaluate arguments about sexually transmitted diseases, sex education, and sex work.

Sexual activity is not risk free. One obvious possible consequence of heterosexual intercourse is pregnancy. There are also sexually transmitted diseases. In the United States, there are millions of cases of sexually transmitted diseases every year. And there is an increasing trend in recent years with regard to STDs. The CDC reports that cases of gonorrhea and syphilis have increased, even during the isolation of the COVID-19 pandemic.[74] And a new disease, monkeypox, has appeared on the scene recently that appears to be sexually transmitted. Deadly diseases like HIV and AIDS continue to afflict people—and continue to result in social stigma. More work still needs to be done to prevent sexually transmitted diseases, including commonsense use of condoms for protection. From a utilitarian standpoint, condom use seems like an obvious focal point, along with comprehensive sex education, that teaches people how to use condoms and avoid disease. Comprehensive education about birth control would also help to reduce unwanted pregnancy.

But some argue that condom use—and contraception in general—is immoral. For example, the Catholic Church has been opposed to condom use on moral grounds—and condemned by some for this. But in recent years, the Church has softened its position. In 2010, Pope Benedict XVI hinted that condom use might be a sort of lesser evil, since it would prevent sexually transmitted disease.[75] But the Catholic Church continues to encourage abstinence as the best way to avoid STDs and unwanted pregnancy. And there are some conservatives who are opposed to comprehensive sex education. This opposition may come from the fear that teaching young people about sex, contraception, and related issues may encourage them to experiment with sex and sexuality. But a more pragmatic and utilitarian approach would suggest that young people are going to engage in sexual activity anyway, and that it would be better to prepare them to do so safely.

In some states, like California, comprehensive sex education is required. A California law, the California Healthy Youth Act, requires education about contraception, LGBTQ sexuality, and abortion. According to a state website[76]:

All instruction and materials in grades K-12 must be inclusive of LGBTQ students. Instruction shall affirmatively recognize that people have different sexual orientations and, when discussing or providing examples of relationships and couples, must be inclusive of same-sex relationships. It must also teach students about gender, gender expression, gender identity, and explore the harm of negative gender stereotypes. This means that schools must teach about all sexual orientations and what being LGBTQ means.

The State of California further explains that sex education should include:

> Information about the effectiveness and safety of all federal FDA-approved contraceptive methods in preventing pregnancy (including emergency contraception); Information that abstinence is the only certain way to prevent unintended pregnancy and HIV and other STIs; Information about the value of delaying sexual activity must be included and must be accompanied by information about other methods for preventing pregnancy, HIV and STIs; Information about pregnancy, including 1) the importance of prenatal care; 2) all legally available pregnancy outcomes, including parenting, adoption, and abortion; and 3) California's newborn safe surrender law; and Information about sexual harassment, sexual assault, adolescent relationship abuse, intimate partner violence, and human trafficking.

Again, some conservative educators and parents may worry that there is something wrong about teaching young people about contraception and abortion. They may worry that this would encourage behavior they see as immoral. But again, from a utilitarian standpoint, this makes sense as a way to encourage responsible and healthy sexuality. What do you think? Did you receive comprehensive sexual education in your own upbringing? And is it a good idea?

It is fairly obvious that in the United States, sex education is a contested area. Some want to promote abstinence and discourage sexual activity among teenagers and outside of marriage. Others maintain that the key is to teach sexual health, including information about condoms—which prevent STDs—and other forms of birth control. Studies do not clearly indicate whether any single approach to sex education has any significant impact on the subsequent sexual behavior of students.[77] But some studies do indicate that comprehensive sex education may help reduce teen pregnancies without increasing levels of sexual intercourse or sexually transmitted disease.[78] Sexual education curricula pose ethical challenges. Proponents of comprehensive sex education want to empower students to make informed choices about sexuality without imposing moral values on students. But proponents of abstinence-only sex education

maintain that teenagers are too young to be engaging in sexual acts, which they believe should take place only within marriage. Defenders of abstinence-only sex education also worry that when sexual practices are discussed with children, it can stimulate unhealthy interest in having sex. Opponents of abstinence-only sex education complain that abstinence programs sneak religious ideas about marriage and sexuality into the classroom, while proponents of abstinence maintain that their primary concern is student health.

Sexually transmitted diseases raise a number of ethical issues. Lying or concealing one's STD status from sexual partners is generally considered to be a violation of moral standards, although ethicists disagree about when in a romantic relationship this information must be disclosed. One could also argue that risky sexual behavior is dangerous not only for the individuals involved but also for society. From a utilitarian perspective that is concerned with public health—including the costs of sexually transmitted diseases—it is important to work to reduce the incidence of such diseases. One conservative strategy is to minimize casual sexual encounters and encourage monogamous sex within the confines of marriage. A more liberal strategy is to find ways to increase usage of condoms, especially among sex workers and others who are at an increased risk of contracting and transmitting disease. One interesting related case is the effort to require adult film stars to use condoms. Proponents of such regulation argue that this models appropriate sexual behavior and prevents disease in an era when pornography is more readily available. Opponents argue that when adults engage in sexual activity in the pornography industry, it is up to them to make their own decisions about protection against disease.

This brings us to a discussion of pornography and back to the consideration of "ethical porn" with which we began this chapter. In the Internet age, pornography is easily found, even stumbled on. Defenders of pornography argue that it provides an outlet for sexual desire and a source of sexual stimulation that can enhance sexual relations, and that as long as it is consensual, there is no harm done. On the other hand, opponents of pornography argue that pornography represents a general loosening of sexual mores in our culture. Opponents also contend that pornography has a negative impact on gender relations because it tends to objectify women (see further discussion in Chapter 9). Opponents further argue that pornography can undermine healthy sexual relations, especially when men expect women to behave and respond as they do in pornography or when pornography helps create sex addiction and unhealthy attitudes toward sex. They also maintain that pornography is often produced as a result of coercion and sex trafficking, which is linked to illegal prostitution and rape.

The connection between pornography and prostitution is not incidental. In its etymological root, pornography is literally "pictures of prostitutes." And insofar as women (and men) make money off of sexually explicit pictures, they are in a sense "prostituting" themselves (i.e., selling their bodies for sexual pleasure). But let's pause here to problematize this way of describing things. The word "prostitute" carries with it a lot of moral baggage. And some women who provide sex for money have argued that it would be better to use the term "sex worker," which avoids moral judgment, while making it clear that this is "work." And in fact, sex workers (including strippers, dancers, and others) have occasionally argued for the need for fair compensation and decent working conditions. Furthermore, because this work is done primarily by women, there is the risk of exploitation as in other "women's work"—with sex workers being especially vulnerable to exploitation given the nature of the work they do. In some places, sex workers have united, formed unions, and lobbied for protections and fair pay.

This may be more complicated in the era of free Internet porn and apps like "OnlyFans" that blur the line. At any rate, our moral intuitions about pornography may overlap with our thoughts about prostitution. As noted earlier, there is a debate among utilitarians about the justification of sex work: Bentham thought prostitution should be legalized and regulated, while Mill thought it was wrong because it is degrading. We might extrapolate these arguments and apply them to pornography to come up with a utilitarian account: Mill would likely find it to be degrading, while Bentham may want to regulate it to make it safe. Carole Pateman and other feminists would likely argue that both porn and prostitution are wrong because they exploit women. But some may want to more carefully distinguish between pornography and prostitution. Are these really the same thing? Is there a difference between a completed sexual act involving real bodies and viewing such acts or bodies without touching them?

Furthermore, as we noted in the opening vignette of this chapter, some might suggest that there could be ethical pornography. That would be pornography that is consensual, respectful, and promotes "good sex" (as defined from within some moral theory about what counts as good sex, of course). It would involve consenting adults who are disease-free and also able to retract images of themselves if they change their minds. As we discussed briefly in the chapter opener, this might also include the use of condoms in pornography. It might involve pornography that avoids promoting unrealistic notions of body image. And it would not involve images of violence, rape, or degradation. Of course, as we mentioned, whether actual pornography lives up to that standard is an open and important question.

Other problems include child pornography, in which images of underage minors are exchanged; so-called "revenge porn," where people post pornographic images of former partners; and the problem of "sexting." Sexting involves trading explicit photos via email or through text messages. While sexting between consenting adults might seem to be morally unproblematic, sexting has become a problem in high schools. Minors who exchange sexually explicit pictures are engaging in the exchange of child pornography, according to the legal definition of the term. Although the legal system and disciplinary systems in the schools have tried to find a way to deal with high school sexting that does not result in labeling experimenting teens as child pornographers and sex offenders, this issue points to the problem of sexual morality and pornography in the era of smartphones and social media. Related to this is the emerging problem of "deep fake" porn, in which people's images are used against their will—and the related question of simulated child pornography. Does it matter if it is not real if the content is objectionable or exploitative?

Finally, another issue of profound moral concern is sex trafficking, which generally involves women and girls being coerced into the sex trade both in the United States and abroad (this can also happen with men and boys). Sex trafficking is a subset of human trafficking, which involves the transport and captivity of individuals across borders for a variety of illegal purposes, including for use as prostitutes or in pornography. The bleak and brutal reality of sex trafficking throws a moral wrench in the arguments of those who would defend prostitution or pornography as victimless crimes. It might be that some sex transactions are consensual and mutually beneficial both for the prostitute and for the customer. But in many cases, there is coercion and exploitation. One proposal to solve this problem is to legalize prostitution, as Bentham had argued, in order to encourage healthy and noncoercive sexual exchanges. In Nevada, some counties allow highly regulated brothels to operate legally. And in some countries, such as the Netherlands, prostitution is legal. In other countries, such as Thailand and Belgium, prostitution is nominally illegal, but in practice, it is tolerated. It remains an open question whether legal sex trades prevent or reduce sex crimes and abuse.

Sex trafficking clearly raises serious moral issues about human autonomy, agency, and rights to bodily integrity. Some ethicists argue that it is these ethical standards as well as concerns for social justice that should be the focus of what we call "sexual morality"—rather than any judgments we make about the sexual preferences and practices between consenting adults. Some people may even be inclined to say that an adult's private sexual behavior is not a moral matter at all, since it does not affect others—or only affects that adult's consenting sexual partners. But is sex really an entirely private matter and too personal and individual to be a focal point of moral concern and ethical judgment? To hold that it is not a moral matter, however, would seem to imply that our sexual lives are morally insignificant. It also ignores the fact that sex can spread disease and cause pregnancy—and that the sex industry makes billions of dollars selling its products. The opponents of sex education might suggest that sex education should be left to parents and kept within the privacy of family life. But sexually transmitted diseases, sex trafficking, and attitudes toward LGBTQ+ people have social impacts, and society may have an interest in making sure that people are educated about sex, gender, and sexuality.

Chapter Summary

16.1 How can we describe basic philosophical views of sex including hedonism and the ideal of "platonic love"?
Hedonists claim that pleasure is our primary focus. Some hedonists may advocate for free love and sexual libertinism of the sort associated with Don Juan and the Marquis de Sade. But a more moderate form of hedonism is found in the ancient Greek philosophy of Epicurus. The opposite of this might be a kind of asceticism that focuses on the denial of pleasure. In addition, there is a view of love associated with Plato's philosophy that looks beyond sex toward something higher. Platonic love is a kind of friendship that has transcended sex.

16.2 How can we apply different normative theories to sex and sexuality?
Key theories include Kantian, utilitarian, natural law and virtue ethics, as well as feminism and care ethics. Kantian theories might focus on consent and respect for autonomy. Utilitarians will focus on maximizing happiness. Natural law tends to focus on conservative or traditional marital sex, claiming that sex ought to be procreative and based on love. Virtue ethics and care ethics emphasize values like fidelity, honesty, and caring relations. And feminists focus our attention on the exploitation and objectification of women.

16.3 What is the argument against sexual coercion and violence, and what is the importance of affirmative consent?
Rape and sexual harassment are viewed as wrong by the moral theories we are discussing in this book. Kantian theory emphasizes respect for persons. Natural law focuses on human dignity. And utilitarianism focuses on happiness. Feminists focus on exploitation of women. Rape and sexual harassment are wrong in any of these theories. A growing movement known as #MeToo that promotes awareness of and fights to stop sexual harassment shows the importance of this topic. A new standard of sexual consent has evolved. No longer should we focus only on "no means no"; rather, the idea of affirmative consent means that each moment and movement in a sexual encounter requires partners to say "yes."

16.4 How can we analyze moral and legal arguments about marriage equality?

Marriage equality is about evolving legal and moral norms governing marriage, which includes the legalization of same-sex marriages. In the United States, the Supreme Court's *Obergefell v. Hodges* decision legalized same-sex marriages. The basic argument made is about liberty and rights—and the more general idea that LGBTQ+ persons should be treated equally and with respect. The legalization and normalization of same-sex marriages was opposed by natural law theorists like John Finnis, who is also opposed to the very idea of homosexual sex. The argument in favor of marriage equality was made by John Corvino and others who argue on utilitarian and libertarian grounds.

16.5 How can we evaluate issues involving trans and gender nonconforming people?

Transgender athletes and other concerns about trans people have been in the news. Philosophers who theorize about trans identity, trans experience, and the law, like Talia Bettcher and Loren Cannon, argue that trans people deserve respect and that the legal backlash against trans people is unjustified. Others, including feminists such as Martina Navratilova and J. K. Rowling, have been reluctant to welcome trans women into athletics and traditional female spaces. A further issue that arises from this perspective is the idea of gender fluidity and a critique of binary conception of sex and gender. Natural law tradition would affirm a binary conception of *sex* and gender, but trans theory may lead us to question that kind of approach.

16.6 How can we evaluate arguments about sexually transmitted diseases, sex education, and sex work?

Sexually transmitted diseases are dangerous and should be of concern for utilitarian theories about sex. One solution is comprehensive sex education that includes information about condom use as well as about the range of sexual experience. This idea is opposed by traditional and conservative religious thinkers, who want to encourage abstinence. Related to this is the question of ethical pornography. Natural law thinkers claim that pornography and masturbation are wrong. And feminists warn against abusive, objectifying, and degrading forms of pornography (and prostitution). But on utilitarian grounds, it might be appropriate to argue in favor and support of ethical porn that is not degrading or unhealthy—and that teaches good sexual hygiene.

16.7 How might a student defend a thesis about sexual morality?

To defend a thesis about sexual morality, a student might begin by deciding where they stand with regard to pleasure (i.e., what they think about hedonism versus asceticism). Then a thesis would have to consider which ethical theories (libertarianism, utilitarianism, or natural law) are going to be applied and how they are applied in specific cases. This is obviously complicated, as students will have to explain the theory as well as the details of issues involving the range of topics we have addressed here—from the legalization of prostitution to marriage equality, and including questions about sex, gender, and sexual orientation. Finally, a thesis about sexual morality should attend to the complexity of the topics involved here, including the diversity of human sexual experience.

Primary Source Readings

In this chapter's readings, the issue of sexual morality is discussed from a variety of perspectives. First, we have an excerpt from Carol Pateman, who makes a feminist argument against prostitution. Following that is an argument from Jessica Flanigan that argues in favor of decriminalizing sex work based on a claim about rights. Then we have an excerpt from the majority opinion of the U.S. Supreme Court's *Obergefell v. Hodges* decision, which legalized same-sex marriage in the United States. Following that is an essay by John Finnis, which presents an argument based in natural law tradition that homosexuality is wrong and that marriage is supposed to be heterosexual. Finally, we conclude with an excerpt from a book by John Corvino, which critically examines the claim that homosexuality is unnatural and the natural law arguments presented by theorists such as Finnis.

Reading 16-1   "What's Wrong with Prostitution" | Carole Pateman

Study Questions

As you read the excerpt, please consider the following questions:

1. Why does Pateman think that prostitution is sex without love (and why does that matter)?

2. What is Pateman's point in her comparison of sex and food?

3. Why does Pateman suggest that prostitution is part of an expression of contemporary masculine sexuality?

There is a universal, natural (masculine) impulse that, it is assumed, requires, and always will require, the outlet provided by prostitution. Now that arguments that extramarital sex is immoral have lost their social force, defenders of prostitution often present prostitution as one example of "sex without love," as an example of the satisfaction of natural appetites. The argument, however, is a *non sequitur*. Defenders of sex without love and advocates of what once was called free love, always supposed that the relationship was based on mutual sexual attraction between a man and woman and involved mutual physical satisfaction. Free love and prostitution are polls apart. Prostitution is the use of a woman's body by a man for his own satisfaction. There is no desire or satisfaction on the part of the prostitute. Prostitution is not mutual, pleasurable exchange of the use of bodies, but the unilateral use of a woman's body by a man in exchange for money. That the institution of prostitution can be presented as a natural extension of a human impulse, and that "sex without love" can be equated with the sale of women's bodies in the capitalist market, is possible only because an important question is begged: why do men demand that satisfaction of a natural appetite must take the form of public access to women's bodies in the capitalist market in exchange for money?

In arguments that prostitution is merely one expression of a natural appetite, the comparison is invariably made between prostitution and the provision of food. . . . Without a minimum of food (or water, or shelter) people die, but to my knowledge no one has ever died for want of an outlet for their sexual appetite. There is also one fundamental difference between the human need for food and the need for sex. Sustenance is sometimes unavailable but everyone has the means to satisfy sexual appetites to hand. There is no natural necessity to engage in sexual relations to assuage sexual pangs. . . .

The general display of women's bodies and sexual parts, either in representation or as live bodies, is central to the sex industry and continually reminds men—and women—that men exercise the law of male sex-right, that they have patriarchal right of access to women's bodies. . . . Satisfaction of a mere natural appetite does not require a man to have access to a woman's body.

[This] is part of the construction of what it means to be a man, part of the contemporary expression of masculine sexuality. The satisfaction of men's natural sexual urges must be achieved through access to a woman, even if her body is not directly used sexually. Whether or nor any man is able and willing to find release in other ways, he can exhibit his masculinity by contracting for use of a woman's body.

Carole Pateman, *The Sexual Contract*, 30th anniversary ed. (Cambridge, UK: Polity Press, 2018).

Reading 16-2 "Decriminalize Sex Work" | Jessica Flanigan

Study Questions

As you read the excerpt, please consider the following questions:

1. What does Flanigan think about health and safety issues?
2. What are the rights that are violated when sex work is criminalized, according to Flanigan?
3. How is Flanigan's argument connected to claims about interracial or same-sex relationships and premarital sex?

Sex work should be treated like other kinds of work, such as nursing, massage therapy, performance arts, and marriage counseling. Though the criminalization of paying for sex or selling sex may reduce the prevalence of sex work in a political community, this is not a legitimate goal for public policy because it is not wrong for people to pay for sex or to sell sexual services. Criminalization does not eliminate the sex industry and it does make it more dangerous for workers and their clients. Political communities should decriminalize sex work across-the-board because criminalization violates workers' and clients' rights, threatens sex workers' health and safety, and magnifies existing injustices associated with the carceral state.

Critics of decriminalization claim that decriminalizing sex work would endanger women, including female sex workers. The critics' concerns about decriminalization are not supported by the evidence....

The following arguments apply to adult, consensual sex work in the absence of coercion....

The criminalization of sex work violates the rights of sex workers and their clients. There are four ways that criminalization violates people's rights. First, a prohibitive approach to the sex industry violates people's rights to make intimate and personal decisions and rights to freedom of association in choosing their sexual partners. Second, prohibition violates sex workers right to freedom of expression. Third, prohibition violate sex workers' right to occupational freedom and freedom of contract. Fourth, the enforcement of policies that prohibit sex work is unjustified more generally because it is wrong for public officials to use threats of incarceration to prevent people from engaging in conduct that is not morally wrong.

Consider first the right to make intimate and personal decisions and the right to freedom of association. In general, people have the right to choose their sexual partners as long as their partner is willing and capable of giving valid consent. Laws that prohibit people in same-sex relationships from having sex violate their basic rights, as did laws prohibiting interracial relationships. Part of the justification for a right to form intimate partnerships derives from the values of privacy, sexual freedom, and bodily autonomy. It is important for people to have control not only over their ability to refuse sex, but also their ability to have sex with any other willing, adult partner they choose. This right to form intimate partnerships derives from the values of privacy, sexual freedom, and bodily autonomy. It is important for people to have control not only over their ability to refuse sex, but also their ability to have sex with any other willing, adult partner they choose. This right to form intimate partnerships is protected even in cases where people's relationships may be viewed as distasteful or imprudent. For example, some people object to premarital sex or promiscuity on religious grounds or on the grounds that marriages are stronger when people abstain from sex beforehand. But widespread objections to premarital sex and promiscuity would not justify legal interference with people's premarital relationships.

Jessica Flanigan, "The Case for Decriminalizing Sex Work" in *The Routledge Handbook of Philosophy of Sex and Sexuality*, eds. Lori Watson, Clare Chambers, and Brian D. Earp (New York: Routledge, 2022).

Reading 16-3 U.S. Supreme Court Decision June 26, 2015 | Obergefell v. Hodges

Study Questions

As you read the excerpt, please consider the following questions:

1. How does the Court situate homosexuality and same-sex marriage in the evolving sexual morality of the United States?

2. What basic rights are appealed to in the Court's decision?

3. What is the Court's view of the value of marriage to children and to the nation?

The history of marriage is one of both continuity and change. Changes, such as the decline of arranged marriages and the abandonment of the law of coverture, have worked deep transformations in the structure of marriage, affecting aspects of marriage once viewed as essential. These new insights have strengthened, not weakened, the institution. Changed understandings of marriage are characteristic of a Nation where new dimensions of freedom become apparent to new generations.

This dynamic can be seen in the Nation's experience with gay and lesbian rights. Well into the 20th century, many States condemned same-sex intimacy as immoral, and homosexuality was treated as an illness. Later in the century, cultural and political developments allowed same-sex couples to lead more open and public lives. Extensive public and private dialogue followed, along with shifts in public attitudes. Questions about the legal treatment of gays and lesbians soon reached the courts, where they could be discussed in the formal discourse of the law. . . .

The fundamental liberties protected by the Fourteenth Amendment's Due Process Clause extend to certain personal choices central to individual dignity and autonomy, including intimate choices defining personal identity and beliefs. . . . Courts must exercise reasoned judgment in identifying interests of the person so fundamental that the State must accord them its respect. History and tradition guide and discipline the inquiry but do not set its outer boundaries. When new insight reveals discord between the Constitution's central protections and a received legal stricture, a claim to liberty must be addressed.

Applying these tenets, the Court has long held the right to marry is protected by the Constitution. For example, *Loving* v. *Virginia* invalidated bans on interracial unions, and *Turner* v. *Safley* held that prisoners could not be denied the right to marry. . . .

Four principles and traditions demonstrate that the reasons marriage is fundamental under the Constitution apply with equal force to same-sex couples. The first premise of this Court's relevant precedents is that the right to personal choice regarding marriage is inherent in the concept of individual autonomy. This abiding connection between marriage and liberty is why *Loving* invalidated interracial marriage bans under the Due Process Clause. Decisions about marriage are among the most intimate that an individual can make. . . . This is true for all persons, whatever their sexual orientation.

A second principle in this Court's jurisprudence is that the right to marry is fundamental because it supports a two-person union unlike any other in its importance to the committed individuals. The intimate association protected by this right was central to *Griswold v. Connecticut*, which held the Constitution protects the right of married couples to use contraception. . . . Same-sex couples have the same right as opposite-sex couples to enjoy intimate association, a right extending beyond mere freedom from laws making same-sex intimacy a criminal offense.

A third basis for protecting the right to marry is that it safeguards children and families and thus draws meaning from related rights of childrearing, procreation, and education. Without the recognition, stability, and predictability marriage offers, children suffer the stigma of knowing their families are somehow lesser. They also suffer the significant material costs of being raised by unmarried parents, relegated to a more difficult and uncertain family life. The marriage laws at issue thus harm and humiliate the children of same-sex couples. This does not mean that the right to marry is less meaningful for those who do not or cannot have children. Precedent protects the right of a married couple not to procreate, so the right to marry cannot be conditioned on the capacity or commitment to procreate.

Finally, this Court's cases and the Nation's traditions make clear that marriage is a keystone of the Nation's social order. States have contributed to the fundamental character of marriage by placing it at the center of many facets of the legal and social order. There is no difference between same- and opposite-sex couples with respect to this principle, yet same-sex couples are denied the constellation of benefits that the States have linked to marriage and are consigned to an instability many opposite-sex couples would find intolerable. It is demeaning to lock same-sex couples out of a central institution of the Nation's society, for they too may aspire to the transcendent purposes of marriage. The limitation of marriage to opposite-sex couples may long

have seemed natural and just, but its inconsistency with the central meaning of the fundamental right to marry is now manifest....

The challenged laws burden the liberty of same-sex couples, and they abridge central precepts of equality. The marriage laws at issue are in essence unequal: Same-sex couples are denied benefits afforded opposite-sex couples and are barred from exercising a fundamental right. Especially against a long history of disapproval of their relationships, this denial works a grave and continuing harm, serving to disrespect and subordinate gays and lesbians.

Finally, the First Amendment ensures that religions, those who adhere to religious doctrines, and others have protection as they seek to teach the principles that are so fulfilling and so central to their lives and faiths.

United States Supreme Court, *Obergefell v. Hodges*, 576 U.S.___ (2015).

Reading 16-4 Law, Morality, and "Sexual Orientation" | John Finnis

Study Questions

As you read the excerpt, please consider the following questions:

1. Why does Finnis condemn all nonmarital intercourse, including homosexual relations?
2. What are the two purposes of marriage and marital sex, according to Finnis?
3. What does Finnis say about "non-traditional" sexual activities performed by heterosexual, married couples?

Genital intercourse between spouses enables them to actualise and experience (and in that sense express) their marriage itself, as a single reality with two blessings (children and mutual affection). Non-marital intercourse, especially *but not only* homosexual, has no such point and therefore is unacceptable....

The union of the reproductive organs of husband and wife really unites them biologically (and their biological reality is part of, not merely an instrument of, their *personal* reality); reproduction is *one* function and so, in respect of that function, the spouses are indeed one reality. So their union in a sexual act of the reproductive

kind (whether or not actually reproductive or even capable of resulting in generation in this instance) can *actualise* and allow them to *experience* their *real common good*. That common good is precisely *their marriage* with the two goods, parenthood and friendship, which are the parts of its wholeness as an intelligible common good even if, independently of what the spouses will, their capacity for biological parenthood will not be fulfilled by that act of genital union. But the common good of friends who are not and cannot be married (for example, man and man, man and boy, woman and woman) has nothing to do with their having children by each other, and their reproductive organs cannot make them a biological (and therefore personal) unit. So their sexual acts together cannot do what they may hope and imagine. Because their activation of one or even each of their reproductive organs cannot be an actualising and experiencing of the *marital* good—as marital intercourse (intercourse between spouses in a marital way) can, even between spouses who *happen* to be sterile—it can do no more than provide each partner with an individual gratification. For want of a *common good* that could be actualised and experienced *by and in this bodily union*, that conduct involves the partners in treating their bodies as instruments to be used in the service of their consciously experiencing selves; their choice to engage in such conduct thus disintegrates each of them precisely as acting persons....

The traditional sex ethic which, despite all backsliding, was fairly perspicuous to almost everyone until the acceptance by many people of divorce-for-remarriage and contraception began to obscure its coherence a few decades ago, is no more and no less than a drawing out of the implications of this same reasonable thought: the intending, giving, and/or receiving of pleasure in sex acts is reasonably respectful of and coherent with intelligible human goods *only* when those acts are fully expressive of and (so far as my willing goes) instantiations of the complex good of marriage. Acts of the kind that same-sex partners engage in (intended to culminate in orgasmic satisfaction by finger in vagina, penis in mouth, etc.) remain non-marital, and so unreasonable and wrong, when performed in like manner by a married couple.

John Finnis, "Law, Morality, and Sexual Orientation." *Notre Dame Law Review* 69 (1994), pp. 1049–76.

Reading 16-5 "It's Not Natural" | John Corvino

Study Questions

As you read the excerpt, please consider the following questions:

1. Why does Corvino think that "new natural law" (NNL) theorists have "mislocated" the moral value of sex?

2. What is Corvino's criticism of the term "unnatural"?

3. What is Corvino's view of noncoital sex in general?

Consider the goods people usually associate with sex. "Organic bodily union" is generally not on the list. Procreation sometimes is, but neither the sterile heterosexual couple nor the homosexual couple can achieve procreation. There are others, however: the expression of a certain kind of affection, the building of intimacy, and shared pleasure, to name a few. The NNL [New Natural Law] theorists must either deny that these are genuine goods or else deny that non-coital sex can achieve them. Such denials fly in the face of common sense....

Consider a man who enjoys performing cunnilingus with his wife to express affection and experience mutual pleasure. He need not be choosing such an activity as a counterfeit version of coitus. He might choose it, rather, in order to please his wife, a result that in turn pleases him. Such an act constitutes a genuine expression of affection, and it may facilitate each partner's emotional and physical well-being. It may be a special intimacy that they reserve only for each other, something that enhances the bond between them.... They are bodily persons expressing affection in a bodily way, and that real bodily experience, which they know to be intensely pleasurable, is what they choose.... They seek genuine personal interaction in the form of non-coital sex....

But what about various arousing activities that may, but need not, lead to male orgasm: kissing, stroking, licking, erotic massage, and so on? What about cuddling? In ordinary romantic life—for gays as well as straights—the line between the sexual and the nonsexual is typically not so sharp. There is no obvious point where one starts choosing gratification for its own sake, and it's hard to imagine that NNL would condemn *all* these activities unless they were followed by coitus. It would be interesting to see the NNL reasons—if there are any—for why gay *kissing* might be unnatural.

I conclude that the NNL theorists have mis-located the moral value of sex, and that even if there's something distinctively valuable about coitus (apart from its procreative potential), they have failed to show what it is, let alone that other forms of sex are positively bad. The very same things that make non-coital sex valuable for heterosexual partners—expression of affection, experience of mutual pleasure, physical and emotional well-being, and so on—make it valuable for same-sex couples as well....

It is worth adding that any view that rests the wrongness of homosexual conduct on the wrongness of masturbation ought to face a severe burden of persuasion.... Like Aquinas, the NNL theorists label masturbation, contraception, and non-coital heterosexual sex unnatural for the very same reasons that they label homosexual sex unnatural: the failure to achieve a reproductive-type union....

"Unnatural" according to this view is simply a term of abuse, a fancy word for "disgusting," a way to mask visceral reactions as well-considered moral judgments. We can do better.

John Corvino, *What's Wrong with Homosexuality?* (Oxford, UK: Oxford University Press, 2013), pp. 78–97.

Review Exercises

1. What is the best approach to take with regard to sex: a hedonistic approach or an ascetic approach?

2. What is "platonic friendship" or "platonic love," and how is that idea related to other ideas about sex and love?

3. What are some factual matters that would be relevant for consequentialist arguments regarding sexual behavior?

4. According to a Kantian type of morality, we ought to respect persons. What kinds of sexual actions would be morally objectionable from this standpoint?

5. What are the two proper functions of sex from the natural law standpoint, and how does this apply to specific examples?

6. What do you think about the debate between Carole Pateman and Jessica Flanigan regarding sex work?

7. To what extent does the idea of "affirmative consent" help respond to the problem of sexual harassment and rape?

8. How do arguments about homosexuality and marriage equality connect to claims about other issues involving sexual morality, equality, and social justice in general?

9. What kinds of ethical and social justice issues arise in thinking about trans people?

10. What kinds of argument are employed in discussions of whether sex work should be legal?

Discussion Cases

1. Date Rape. Early one Sunday morning, Dalia opens her dorm room door and finds her friend Amy standing there, her eyes red from crying. Inside Dalia's room, Amy begins talking about what happened to her the night before. She had been at a large party in another dorm, drinking and dancing with a group of friends, until the party started winding down around 2:00 a.m. Then a guy she'd been flirting with invited her back to his room down the hall from the party. She said goodbye to her friends and went with him. In his room, they had another drink and started making out. Amy tells Dalia that everything was fine until the guy pushed her down hard onto his bed and began pulling off her clothes. "It happened so fast," Amy said. "I was in shock and was scared because all of a sudden, he was acting so rough. I just sort of let it happen, but it was awful." Amy begins to cry. "Did you tell him to stop?" Dalia asks. "I didn't say anything,"

Amy says. "But inside, I was screaming 'no.' I just lay there completely still until it was over."

"Are you saying he raped you?" Dalia asks. "I don't know," Amy says. "Maybe."

Do you think what happened to Amy was rape? Why or why not? What do you think is required for true consent to a sexual encounter?

2. Slippery Slopes. Maria and Richard are arguing about recent changes in social norms. Maria says, "It's all too much, too fast. First, we legalized gay marriage. And now trans girls are playing boys' sports." Richard is gay. He responds, "That's ridiculous. All we're asking is that our relationships and identities be respected by society and the law." "But it really is a slippery slope," Maria says. "Next thing you know, we'll have polygamy and bestiality," she adds. Richard is getting angry. "Nobody is asking to legalize polygamy," he says, "or something as bizarre as bestiality." Maria replies, "I know the Mormon Church gave up polygamy. But there are still Mormons who live in polygamous families. And once you let people do whatever they want, that's exactly what they'll do." Richard pauses and takes a deep breath. "You are comparing apples and oranges," he says. "Same-sex marriage is not at all like polygamous marriage. You can legalize the one without legalizing the other. And trans people are people too. Your 'slippery slope' sounds like intolerance to me. Frankly, it's insulting." Maria responds, "I'm not trying to be offensive. But how can you draw a line once you let people do whatever they want?"

Is there a slippery slope here? Is it intolerant to worry about that? Is it possible to draw a clear line—and where do we draw that line?

3. Sex Work. David's friends are arranging his bachelor party. They are making plans to go as a group to Las Vegas for one last weekend "out with the boys." One of David's friends, Steven, suggests that they pool their money and treat David to a night in one of Nevada's legal brothels. Another friend, Antonio, is opposed to the idea. Antonio says that prostitution is wrong. Antonio thinks prostitution exploits women. Antonio also thinks that David's fiancée, Monica, would be hurt if she ever found out about it. But Steven argues that prostitution is legal in Nevada and the women make good money doing what they do. Steven also says that David has already told him that he wants to go to a strip club as part of the bachelor party. "There's not much difference between a strip club and a brothel," Steven says. Antonio responds, "But one is fantasy and the other is reality." Steven shakes his head. "It's all sex, man," he adds. Antonio thinks about that for a moment. Then he says, "You know, maybe we shouldn't go to the strip club either. Monica wouldn't like it." Steven replies, "Well, this is David's party. And it all depends on what we tell Monica. Remember, what happens in Vegas stays in Vegas!"

Whose side are you on? Is there something wrong with prostitution? Is there a difference between visiting a strip club and visiting a prostitute? Would it make a difference if David and his friends were honest with Monica about their plans?

Knowledge Check Answer Key

1. **c.** Hedonism encourages the healthy pursuit of pleasure, while asceticism encourages us to overcome the pursuit of pleasure.

2. **a.** Nonbinary implies that there are more than two options when it comes to gender.

3. **d.** It is false that "Human beings have never cut or mutilated children's genitals."

4. **b.** Care ethics and virtue ethics emphasize ideas like loyalty, fidelity, compassion, and empathy in thinking about sexual relations.

17 Punishment and the Death Penalty

Learning Outcomes

After reading this chapter, you should be able to:

17.1 Explain current trends in punishment and the death penalty.

17.2 Explain the deterrence theory of punishment.

17.3 Describe the idea of retributive justice.

17.4 Describe the idea of restorative justice.

17.5 Defend a thesis about sentencing reform and the problem of mass incarceration.

17.6 Evaluate racial disparities in the punishment system.

17.7 Evaluate moral arguments for and against the death penalty.

17.8 Defend your own ideas about punishment and the death penalty.

Decriminalization and Sentencing Reform

During the past several years, a number of states have legalized or decriminalized marijuana for adult recreational use. The drug remains illegal under federal law. The decriminalization of marijuana removes or reduces criminal sanctions. Complete legalization allows for the sale and consumption of marijuana by adults with regulations similar to those applied to alcohol and tobacco. Proponents of legalization have argued on libertarian grounds that adults have a right to use marijuana and other intoxicants. They have also argued on utilitarian grounds that marijuana enforcement is expensive and ineffective. And they have argued on social justice grounds that the criminalization of marijuana was part of a failed "war on drugs" that swelled prison populations and contributed to racial disparities in incarceration rates. On the other hand, defenders of criminalization argue that marijuana intoxication can cause automobile accidents and that marijuana is unhealthy. They also contend that marijuana use can lead people to try harder drugs. And some opponents of marijuana legalization have argued that new and potent types of marijuana can have dangerous effects on the mental health of users, including psychosis and paranoia that can contribute to violent behavior.

Proxima Studio/Shutterstock.com

The decriminalization of marijuana is linked to general movement toward sentencing reform. In 2018, former president Trump signed the First Step Act into law. This law attempted to respond to racial inequalities by, among other things, shortening sentences for nonviolent drug offenders. Trump said that this prison reform legislation would "reduce crime while giving our fellow citizens a chance at redemption."[1] At the time, the idea of criminal justice reform had bipartisan support. But as crime rates have slowly crept higher, some Americans began to question the wisdom of sentencing reform.

What Do You Think?

1. Should marijuana be legalized or decriminalized?

2. Should we be worried about high incarceration rates and racial disparities in incarceration?

3. Are you in favor of criminal justice reform that reduces incarceration rates?

4. What kinds of penalties should be used to prevent drug and alcohol abuse, addiction, and driving under the influence of drugs and alcohol?

Introduction

17.1 Explain current trends in punishment and the death penalty.

The public is concerned about crime and punishment. We want to feel safe and secure in our lives. But there are costs associated with the criminal justice system. And underlying any legal system of punishment there ought to be a moral theory of who we punish, how we punish, and why we punish.

One significant concern is violent crime. Every day, it seems, we hear stories of horrible violence. School shootings, kidnappings, rapes, and other violent crimes flood the headlines. In some cases, the perpetrators of mass atrocity wind up dead—either killing themselves or being killed by police. If mass murderers are captured alive, is it appropriate to sentence them to death? We tend to assume that police, in the heat of the moment, are entitled to kill dangerous criminals, without a trial, in order to protect themselves or the general public. But can that justification of lethal violence be extended to a justification of the death penalty, which is carried out after a legal trial and subsequent appeals long after the original crime occurred? Would the death penalty be justifiable in cases of mass murder or terrorism?

A number of American states have moved to abolish the death penalty, as have a growing number of nations. In 2018, Catholic opposition to the death penalty became part of the official catechism of the church, stating: "the death penalty is inadmissible because it is an attack on the inviolability and dignity of the person."[2] A similar claim has been made by the European Union, which stated its opposition to the death penalty in 2021 saying, "The death penalty is a cruel, inhuman and degrading punishment contrary to the right to life. Its abolition is essential to ensure respect for human dignity."[3] Amnesty International claims that there is a global trend toward death penalty abolition: only eighteen nations on earth executed someone during 2021.[4]

While horrific crimes can make us feel insecure, the good news is that crime, in general, is down in the United States. And while there was an uptick in crime in 2020 and 2021, crime rates—including murder rates—are still lower than they were in the 1990s. Some American cities still have significant crime problems, but nationwide, there has been a general downward trend in violent crime. There is also a trend toward less violent forms of punishment. The Supreme Court has restricted the use of the death penalty. For example, it has forbidden the practice when the convicted is "mentally retarded" (in the language of *Atkins v. Virginia* from 2002), although in reality some people with intellectual disabilities have been executed.[5] In the meantime, a number of states have abolished capital punishment altogether. As of 2022, twenty-three states have eliminated capital punishment, including Colorado, which abolished the death penalty in 2020, and Virginia, which abolished it in 2021. Three states—California, Oregon, and Pennsylvania—have moratoriums on the death penalty even though the punishment remains on the books.[6]

Recent history thus provides a fascinating story with regard to crime and punishment. Crime appears to have gone down over the past several decades, while the use of the death penalty has also declined. More recently, a movement toward criminal justice reform has been successful at reducing sentences for nonviolent criminals. But in recent years, there has been an uptick in crime. Some blame the increase in crime on sentencing reform, calling for stiffer sentences—and even calling for a return to the death penalty. But experts caution that there are no easy answers as to why there was this recent increase in crime. Among those calling for a return to the death penalty was former president Donald Trump. Despite his advocacy for sentencing reform for nonviolent offenders, Trump also called for more widespread use of the death penalty; and toward the end of his administration, the federal government was more active in executing people.[7] At the same time, polarizing political rhetoric in the United States involved calls on the left to "defund the police," which provoked a response on the right by those who claim that leftists wanted to abolish police entirely.

Such polarizing rhetoric is not helpful. There are complicated questions about why crime rates declined in past decades and equally complicated hypothetical suggestions about why crime rose again during the Trump years. Experts debate the reasons for all of this—and caution against jumping to simplistic conclusions.[8] Some worry that if we get soft on crime, crime rates will rise. They might argue that crime rates declined in past decades because so many people were in prison. And they may worry that sentencing reform movements and the use of alternatives to incarceration may put more criminals on the street, leading to higher future crime rates.[9] But the causal story here is complicated. Crime rates may have something to do with economics and opportunities. Perhaps the dislocations caused by COVID-19 had something to do with the recent uptick in crime. And even if the decrease in crime in prior decades had something to do with the massive prison system and the huge numbers of people that were incarcerated in the United States during that time, it is possible to ask whether there is a better way.

In addition to economics, there may be other causal factors that influence crime rates. Maybe crime has something to do with the epidemiology of drug addiction. Or decreasing crime rates may have to do with aggressive policing—for example, the use of "stop and frisk" techniques. On the other hand, it may have to do with more engaged community policing and grassroots neighborhood activism. Perhaps it has to do with the success of social welfare programs, which provide hope, opportunities, and alternatives to crime and violence. Steven Levitt and John Donohue have argued that the decline in crime may have something to do with the legalization of abortion, which prevents children born from unwanted pregnancies. They presented this argument two decades ago in 2001, and have recently updated their analysis and reaffirmed their conclusion with more recent data.[10] Another fascinating theory holds that the decrease in crime in the past decades may be a result of decreasing levels of lead in the atmosphere. According to this view, the lead produced by old-fashioned leaded gasoline—which causes neurological and behavioral problems—may have produced the rise in violence and deviance that peaked in the 1990s.[11]

Of course, each of these theories is subject to debate. But the debate is likely more complicated than we think as environmental, economic, cultural, and psychological factors will need to be considered in addition to a straightforward connection between crime and punishment.

Moral Approaches to Punishment

Those who focus on crime rates and incarceration rates are likely adopting a basic utilitarian approach to punishment. Utilitarians support punishment to the extent that it prevents or deters crime. Some utilitarians defend the death penalty, for example, by claiming that capital punishment has a strong deterrent effect. Others defend long prison sentences by arguing that this increases public safety by keeping criminals off the street. But utilitarian reasoning can reach different conclusions—if the death penalty does not deter crime, or if there are equally useful (and cheaper) alternatives to incarceration.

A different approach to punishment focuses on deontological or natural law claims about the demand for retributive justice and retaliation. Retributivism tends to hold that murderers simply deserve to be executed, and thieves and rapists deserve long prison sentences. The question of "desert" is quite different from the question of what works.

Moral questions abound with regard to punishment. How do we determine appropriate sentences for criminals, converting such disparate crimes as shoplifting, selling drugs, and murder into the common currency of months and years in prison? And while some argue against the death penalty in favor of life imprisonment without the possibility of parole, we may wonder whether it remains useful to keep seventy-year-olds in prison for crimes committed half a century ago. We might also wonder why taxpayer dollars should be used to keep people in prison, feeding and housing them for decades, while the victims of crime have to fend for themselves and pay their bills just like anyone else. Other moral questions might focus on the conditions in prison—for example, whether it is cruel to use solitary confinement in supermax facilities as a way to control the most dangerous and violent criminals. We might also be concerned about the impact of prison or the death penalty on the families and communities of those who are imprisoned or executed. We may be concerned, as well, with questions about racial inequalities in the criminal justice system. Further, we may consider whether there are ways to rehabilitate criminals and restore communities that are broken by crime.

Legal Punishment

To know what to think about the ethics of prison and the death penalty, we need to first examine some of the reasons that have been given for the practice of legal punishment. Our focus here is primarily on legal punishment. A child's parents can punish him with no TV for a week for a failing grade, and I can punish myself for a caloric indulgence by spending twice as much time at the gym—but these punishments are not legal. Legal punishment, in common with parental and self-punishment, is designed to "hurt"; if something is gladly accepted or enjoyed, it is not really punishment. The most visible form of legal criminal punishment is imprisonment. Other forms include fines and court-mandated community service.

However, legal punishment is distinct from other forms of punishment in several respects. Legal punishment must follow legal rules of some sort. It is authorized by a legal entity and follows a set of laws and procedures that establish who is to be punished, how, and by how much. Lynching is not a legal punishment since it is carried out by a mob and not by a constituted authority. Nor are individual acts of revenge acts of legal punishment. Furthermore, to be legally punished, a person must be convicted of a crime. Indeed, "pretrial detention"—which holds people in jail before being convicted by a court—is a problematic notion, since those who are incarcerated in this way are still formally "innocent" (in a system that assumes one is innocent until proven guilty). A further controversial issue involves detaining people in anticipation that they might commit a crime, what is called "preventive detention." Whatever we say about the justification of detaining people before they commit (or we think they will commit) a crime, it is not punishment. Punishment of any sort presumes someone has done something to merit the penalty. In the case of legal punishment, it is a penalty for doing what the law forbids. Criminal law, by its very nature, must have some sanction, some threat attached to breaking it, or else it loses its force. Without such force, it may be a request, but it is not law.

Thus, we can say that legal punishment is the state's infliction of harm or pain on those who break the law, according to a set of legally established rules. But is such a practice justified? What gives a society the right to inflict the pain of punishment on any of its members? In asking this, we are asking a moral and not just a legal question. Is legal punishment of any sort morally justifiable? If so, why?

Traditional approaches to the justification of punishment focus on **deterrence** and prevention, or the idea of **retributive justice** and just deserts. When we say a punishment *deters*, we mean that it prevents other crimes in the future. When we speak of *retribution*, we mean making wrongdoers somehow pay for the crimes they have committed. But it is important to note that an alternative to these approaches can be found in the ideas of rehabilitation, crime prevention, and restorative justice. These approaches aim to transform the social situation in ways that minimize the need for punishment.

While restorative justice is an important idea, it is not exactly "punishment," but rather an alternative to punishment. The traditional justifications for punishment focus either on utilitarian concerns about preventing and deterring crime, or on natural law or deontological ideas about the need for just retribution. We will turn to utilitarian arguments first.

The Deterrence Argument

17.2 Explain the deterrence theory of punishment.

One answer to the question of whether legal punishment is morally justifiable is, "Yes, if (and only if) the punishment could be fashioned to prevent or deter crime." The general idea involved in this first rationale for legal punishment is related to both the nature of law and its purpose. For a criminal law to be a law and not just a request, sanctions must be attached to it. It must have force behind it. Further, law has many possible purposes, and one purpose is to prevent people from harming others. Since our laws presumably are directed to achieving some good, penalties for breaking these laws should help ensure that the good intended by the laws will be achieved. Of course, not all laws are good laws. However, the idea is that we want not only to have good laws, but also to have them enforced in ways that make them effective.

The purpose of legal punishment, according to this reasoning, is to prevent people from breaking the law, deter them from doing so, or both. As such, this is a forward-looking, consequentialist rationale. In terms of prevention, crime is prevented when would-be or actual criminals are arrested and held somewhere so that they cannot do social damage. We also can prevent crime by other means such as increased street lighting, more police officers, and so on. In terms of deterrence, we deter crime by holding out a punishment as a threat, which persuades would-be criminals not to break the law. If a punishment works as a deterrent, it works in a particular way through the would-be lawbreaker's thinking and decision-making processes. One considers the possibility of being punished for doing some contemplated action and concludes that the gain achieved from the act is not worth the price to be paid, namely, the punishment. Then one acts accordingly.

If deterrence works as described above, we can readily identify certain circumstances in which it is not likely to succeed in preventing crime. For instance, deterrence is not likely to prevent crimes of passion, in which people are overcome by strong emotions. They are not in the mood to calculate the risks and benefits of what they're about to do and unlikely to stop themselves from continuing to act as they will. The threat of punishment is also not likely to work in cases in which people *do* calculate the risks and the benefits and decide the benefits are greater than the risks. These would be cases in which the risks of being caught and punished are perceived as small, and the reward or benefit is perceived as great. The benefit could be financial, status oriented, or even the reward of having done what one believed to be right as in acts of civil disobedience or in support of any cause, whether actually good or bad. Although punishment does not deter in some cases, in others, presumably, it does. A system of legal punishment is worthwhile if it works for the great majority, even if not for all, and if bad consequences do not outweigh good ones.

The deterrence rationale for legal punishment raises a more general issue about any utilitarian perspective on punishment, which relies on weighing costs and benefits. In this view, punishment is *externally related* to lawbreaking. In other words, it is not essential. If something else works better than punishment, then that other means ought to be used, either as a substitution for punishment or in addition to it. Some people argue that punishment itself does not work, but might only be effective when combined with rehabilitation, psychological counseling, and perhaps even job training or placement. However, if a punishment system is not working, then, in this view, it is not morally justifiable, for the whole idea is not to punish for punishment's sake but to achieve the goal of law enforcement. On utilitarian grounds, pain is never good in itself. Thus, if punishment involves suffering, it must be justified. The suffering must be outweighed by the good to be achieved by it.

One problem is that if deterrence is the sole ground of legal punishment, we might seem to be justified in using extreme measures to achieve the desired deterrent effect—if these measures work better than less extreme ones. Suppose a community has a particularly vexing problem with graffiti. To get rid of the problem, suppose the community decides to institute a program in which it randomly picks up members of particular gangs believed to be responsible for the graffiti and punishes them with floggings in the public square. Or suppose that cutting off their hands would work better! We would surely have serious moral objections to this program. One objection would be that these particular individuals may not have been responsible for the graffiti; they were just picked because of their gang affiliation. Another objection would be that the punishment seems out of proportion to the offense. However, on deterrence grounds, there would be nothing essentially wrong with such punishments. What is crucial for the deterrence argument is whether the punishment worked or worked better than alternative forms, not whether the individual is guilty or the punishment fits the crime.

Another version of the deterrence argument that we might evaluate has to do with how deterrence is supposed to work. According to this view, legal punishment is part of a system of social moral education. A society has a particular set of values, and one way to instill those values in its members from their youth is to establish punishments for those who undermine them. If private property is valued, society should punish those who damage or take others' property. These punishments would act as deterrents, helping individuals to internalize social values and giving them internal prohibitions against violating those values. Key to evaluating this view is determining whether punishment actually works in this fashion. What does punishment teach us? Does it help us internalize values, and does it motivate us? The way the system is administered also can send a message, and in some cases, it might be the wrong message. For example, if legal punishment is not applied fairly or equally, what might people learn?

The Retributivist Argument

17.3 Describe the idea of retributive justice.

The second primary rationale for legal punishment is retribution. In the retributivist view, legal punishment

is intended to make those who are responsible for a crime pay for it. As such, it is a backward-looking argument because it is based on past actions. This idea can be understood from a natural law or deontological perspective. The natural law approach maintains that it is only fair or right for a criminal to pay for what they have damaged, and as Locke suggests in his *Second Treatise on Government* (discussed in Chapter 7), there is a natural right to repayment. A retributivist might say that when someone harms another, it is only just or fair that they suffer similarly or proportionately to the harm or pain they caused the other person. Or we might say that a criminal deserves to suffer because they made a victim suffer; the punishment is deserved as fair recompense. In this view, punishment is *internally related* to the wrongful conduct. In a sense, the punishment "fits the crime." From the retributivist standpoint, one cannot say that if something else works better than punishment, then that is what ought to be done. The concern here is not what works but, rather, what is right. Indeed, retributivists might also maintain that punishment is required as a matter of duty; from a deontological standpoint, we ought to punish people who do wrong because they *deserve* to be punished. From this perspective, it would be wrong not to punish criminals, since failing to punish them would give them less than what they deserve.

This approach is based on a somewhat abstract notion of justice. We punish to right a wrong or restore some original state, or to reset the scales of justice. However, in many cases, we cannot really undo the suffering of the victim by making the perpetrator suffer. One can pay back stolen money or return stolen property. But even in these cases, there are other harms that cannot be undone, such as the victim's lost sense of privacy or security. Thus, the erasing, undoing, or righting of the wrong is of some other abstract or metaphysical type. It may be difficult to explain, but supporters of this rationale for punishment believe that we do have some intuitive sense of what we mean when we say "justice was done."

According to the retributivist view, payment must be made in some way that is equivalent to the crime or harm done. Philosophers distinguish two senses of equivalency: an *egalitarian* sense and a *proportional* sense. With egalitarian equivalency, one is required to pay back something identical or almost identical to what was taken. If you make someone suffer for two days, you should suffer for two days. It would also mean that if you caused someone's arm to be amputated, your arm should be cut off as well. This version of retributivism is often given the label *lex talionis*. Translated, it means the "law of the talon" (as among birds of prey). We also call egalitarian equivalency the "law of the jungle" or taking "an eye for an eye."

Proportional equivalency holds that what is required by punishment is not something more or less identical to the harm done or pain caused, but something proportional. In this version, we can think of harms or wrongs as matters of degree, namely, of bad, worse, and worst. Punishments are also scaled from the minimal to the most severe. In this view, punishment must be proportional to the degree of the seriousness of the crime.

Obviously, there are serious problems, both practical and moral, with the *lex talionis* version of the retributivist view. In some cases—for example, in the case of multiple murders—it is not possible to deliver something equal to the harm done, for one cannot kill the murderer more than once. Presumably, we would also have some moral problems with torturing a torturer or raping a rapist.

We should notice that the retributivist justification of legal punishment responds to two major problems with the deterrence argument, namely that deterrence-focused punishments need not punish actual criminals or be proportional to crimes. By contrast, if retributivist punishments are to be just, they must fit both the perpetrators and the crimes.

First, only those who are responsible for a crime should be punished: guilt must be proved, and we should not single out likely suspects or representatives of a group to make examples of them or use them to intimidate other group members, as in our graffiti example. It is also important that the punishment fit the person in terms of the degree of their responsibility. This requirement would address concerns we have about differentiating between criminals and their accomplices and also about the mental state of a criminal. Diminished mental capacity, mitigating circumstances, and duress—which lessen a person's responsibility—are significant elements of the U.S. criminal punishment system.

Second, it is essential in the retributivist view that the punishment fit the crime. Defacing property is not a major wrong or harm and thus should not be punished with amputation of the perpetrator's hand, however, well that might work to deter graffiti. Thus, this view requires that we have a sense of what is more or less serious among crimes and also among punishments so that they can be well matched.

It is because the punishment should fit the crime that many people argue against the so-called "three-strikes" laws for "persistent" or "habitual" offenders that several states have passed. These laws mandate life imprisonment for anyone with two previous convictions for serious crimes who is then found guilty of a third felony. In California in 2012, voters modified the state's three-strikes law. Opponents had noted that in some cases the third "strike" was merely petty theft—a felony charge for anyone who had already served a prison sentence for theft. A life sentence looks quite out of proportion to such infractions. On the other side, however, consequentialists might support three-strikes laws, arguing that it is better for all of us when people who have a history of lawbreaking are removed from society and prevented from continuing in such behavior.

As with the deterrence argument, one might raise objections against the retributivist argument. We have already referred to one: that punishing the perpetrator does not concretely undo the wrong done to the victim. Those who defend retributivism would have to explain in what sense the balance is restored or the wrong righted by punishment. However, the retributivist would not have any problem with those who point out that a particular form of punishment does not work. According to a retributivist, this is not the primary reason to punish. A perpetrator should be punished as a way of achieving satisfaction or restitution, even if it does the perpetrator or others no good.

A more common objection to the retributivist view is that it amounts to condoning revenge. To know whether or not this is true, we would have to clarify what we mean by *revenge*. Suppose we mean that particular people—say a victim or their family—will get a sense of satisfaction in seeing the wrongdoer punished.

This sense of satisfaction is merely contingent and psychological—a matter of feelings. We may not want a system of legal punishment to be used to satisfy merely personal feelings of vengeance or resentment. But the retributivist view is not about our feelings. Indeed, if we have a duty to punish on retributivist grounds, we ought to carry out the punishment, even if we do not feel inclined to do so (perhaps because we are squeamish about carrying out a particular punishment). Retributive justice requires that justice be done, whether or not people feel good about it. However, some may question whether any type of justice exists that is not a matter of providing emotional satisfaction to victims or others who are enraged by a wrong done to them.

Finally, we can wonder whether the retributivist view provides a good basis for a system of legal punishment. Is the primary purpose of such a system to see that justice is done? Do we not have a system of legal punishment to ensure social order and safety? If so, then it would seem that the deterrence argument is the best reason for having any system of legal punishment.

One solution to the problem of whether to use deterrence or retribution to justify legal punishment is to use both.[12] In designing such a hybrid system, we could retain consequentialist reasons for having a legal punishment system, and consider first what works best to deter and prevent crimes. However, we could also use retributivist standards to determine who is punished (only those who are guilty and only to the extent that they are guilty) and by how much (the punishment fitting the crime). In fashioning the punishment system, however, there may be times when we need to determine which rationale takes precedence. For example, in setting requirements for conviction of guilt, we may need to know how bad it is to punish an innocent person. We may decide to give precedence to the retributivist rationale and then make the requirements for conviction of guilt very strict, requiring unanimous jury verdicts and guilt beyond a reasonable doubt. In doing so, we also let some guilty people go free and thus run the risk of lessening the deterrent effect of the punishment system. Or we may decide to give precedence to the deterrence rationale. Thus, we may weaken the requirements for conviction so that we may catch and punish a greater number of guilty people. In doing so,

however, we run the risk of also punishing a greater number of innocent persons.

Punishment and Responsibility

A key element of our legal punishment system and practice is the link between punishment and responsibility. The retributivist believes responsibility is essential for punishment, and thus, it is unjust to punish those who are not responsible for a crime. This concept can also be supported on deterrence grounds; it probably would work better to punish only those who are responsible for crimes, since this focuses punishment in a way that encourages obedience to the law.

Our legal system allows for defenses that appeal to the question of responsibility. For example, under the defense of *duress*, we would probably say a person was not responsible if they were forced to commit a crime, either physically forced or under threat to life. One may have committed the crime, but that is not enough to prove responsibility. (We do not have a system of strict liability, in which the only issue is whether or not you actually did or caused something.)

One of the most problematic defenses in our criminal justice system may well be the insanity defense. It involves a plea and a finding of "not guilty by reason of insanity," or something similar such as "mental defect." Another verdict available in some jurisdictions is that the defendant is "guilty but mentally ill." The difference between these two ways of conceiving crime, guilt, and mental illness is significant. Is someone *guilty but mentally ill* or are they *not guilty* because of a mental illness? This points to a deep question about responsibility and guilt. We presume that people ought to know the difference between right and wrong in order to be held responsible for their actions, and that a responsible person has the capacity to control their own behavior. There have been a variety of standards for describing responsibility and guilt, and their connection with mental competence. One significant event in the evolution of these standards in the United States was the trial of John Hinckley Jr., who shot President Ronald Reagan and two other individuals in 1981. Hinckley was found not guilty by reason of insanity and confined to a hospital. Hinckley was released from further confinement and supervision in the summer of 2022. In response to the Hinckley case, there was a backlash against the insanity defense, with some states—Idaho, Montana, and Utah—abolishing it altogether. States that retain some version of the insanity defense have different standards for determining mental illness. One common standard has roots in nineteenth-century England, with the M'Naghten Rule (1843). According to this rule, people are not responsible for their actions if they did not know what they were doing or did not know that it was wrong. This is often referred to as the "right from wrong test." Since that time, other attempts have been made to list the conditions under which people should not be held responsible for their actions. One example is the "irresistible impulse test." The idea underlying this test for insanity is that sometimes persons are not able to control their conduct and thus act through no fault of their own. The moral question of responsibility and guilt rests on our capacity to understand right from wrong and the ability to control our own behavior.

Common criticisms of the insanity defense concern our ability to determine whether someone is mentally insane or incompetent. Can't someone feign this? How do psychiatrists or other experts determine whether a person knows what they are doing? Even if we could diagnose these conditions with absolute certainty, a more basic question would still remain, namely, would the conditions diminish or take away responsibility? If so, would punishment be appropriate? In the extreme case in which a person has a serious brain condition that prevents normal mental function, we assume that this would excuse them from full responsibility. However, this person may be dangerous, and this may be another reason to detain as well as treat them.

Some people have criticized the entire notion of mental illness, especially as it is used in criminal proceedings. For example, it may result in indeterminate sentences for minor crimes because one must remain in custody in a criminal mental institution until they are determined to be of sound mind. One longtime critic of the penal system, Thomas Szasz, holds that we have sometimes used the diagnosis of mental illness to categorize and stigmatize people who are simply different.[13] He finds this diagnosis often to be a dangerous form of social control. Another significant concern here is

indefinite civil commitment for sex offenders. In some states in the United States, sexual predators who continue to report having violent sexual thoughts can be detained indefinitely out of suspicion that they will commit a crime.[14] But does it make sense to confine people for their thoughts when they have not yet committed a crime?

Some of us tend to look at heinous crimes and say, "No sane person could have done that!" Or we might say that a certain crime was "sick." We use the horror of the crime, its serious wrongness, to conclude that the person committing it must have an acute and untreated mental illness. One problem with this conclusion is that it implies that the person is not responsible, since mental competence is a requirement for criminal liability. Are we then implying that people who do evil things are not responsible for what they do on account of mental illness? If so, perhaps they should not be punished. The connection between punishment and responsibility is not only central to our system of legal punishment, but it is also an important element of the morality of legal punishment.

Underlying this discussion of responsibility is a metaphysical account of free will. We hold people responsible for things that they freely choose to do. But, of course, there are deep questions here. Are we really free? Or are our actions determined by genetics, by social context, and by the laws of physics? If our actions are entirely determined, we are not entirely responsible for what we do (in the sense that we could not have done otherwise). If we are not free, it would seem that punishment as such (at least in the retributive sense of giving someone what was due to them) would never be appropriate. Our legal system normally assumes that we have free will and treats criminals accordingly. But social context and physiological factors can mitigate responsibility and guilt.

Restorative Justice

17.4 Describe the idea of restorative justice.

An alternative approach to punishment offers something that neither the deterrence nor the retributivist considers: the possibility of rehabilitation, reconciliation, and even forgiveness. Such an approach draws on the idea of **restorative justice**, which seeks to heal the wounds caused by crime while finding a way to allow criminals to take responsibility, make amends, and restore the community that they have broken. Proponents of restorative justice admit that it is not appropriate for all crimes, especially in situations where offenders are unable or unwilling to take responsibility or make amends. But proponents argue that restorative justice can produce better outcomes for both victims and offenders, while also reducing recidivism.[15] Interest has been growing in restorative justice programs as ways of dealing with bullying and other forms of misbehavior in schools. These programs have been developed for school systems in cities such as in Oakland, California, in which the goal is to build community and defuse conflict among students whose lives are impacted by violence.[16]

Restorative justice is typically part of a broader conception of social justice that aims to alter social conditions so that crime is prevented and its harms are minimized. The move toward restorative justice and away from prisons is often connected with religious groups that have a historical commitment to pacifism, such as the Quakers and the Mennonites.[17] Key values in this approach include mercy and forgiveness, as well as justice.[18] The idea has been defended by the U.S. Conference of Catholic Bishops, which maintains that the human dignity of crime victims and perpetrators should both be respected. The bishops note that "the status quo is not really working—victims are often ignored, offenders are often not rehabilitated, and many communities have lost their sense of security."[19] The bishops emphasize "responsibility, rehabilitation, and restoration." They conclude,

> We respect the humanity and promote the human dignity of both victims and offenders. We believe society must protect its citizens from violence and crime and hold accountable those who break the law. These same principles lead us to advocate for rehabilitation and treatment for offenders, for, like victims, their lives reflect that same dignity. Both victims and perpetrators of crime are children of God.[20]

This may make it seem that restorative justice is a religious idea. But there are also secular, nonreligious reasons to support the idea. Key values found in restorative justice, such as compassion and respect for the dignity of persons, can be grounded in a secular, nonreligious view of ethics. And if restorative justice and rehabilitation efforts work to reduce crime, satisfy victims, and bring criminals back into the community, utilitarians ought to support the idea. The model has been advocated by secular institutions such as the United Nations, which maintains that restorative justice is "a means to promote tolerance and inclusiveness, uncover truth, encourage the peaceful expression and resolution of conflict, build respect for diversity and promote responsible community practices."[21]

Restorative justice includes concrete practices of victim–offender mediation and other methods of conflict resolution. These practices are based on dialogue and community. In the background of this approach is an understanding of the importance of social context in thinking about crime. From this standpoint we might argue that instead of seeking retribution, we should work to change the social conditions that cause crime. From a consequentialist perspective, if drug-treatment programs or job-training programs in prison would help reduce crime, those programs would be morally recommended. From a non-consequentialist perspective, there might also be grounds for promoting such programs. One might want to consider whether persons ought to be given a second chance in light of the fact that, given certain circumstances, they might not have been fully responsible for their crimes. On the other hand, those who argue from a consequentialist perspective might point out that in certain kinds of cases—say, with sexual predators—there is not much likelihood of reform. Similarly, from a non-consequentialist perspective, some might argue that given the severity of certain crimes, persons deserve the strictest and most severe punishment, not a second chance.

The most famous example of restorative justice is the "truth and reconciliation" process that occurred in the 1990s in South Africa. South Africa had suffered for decades under the racist system of apartheid that bred violence and resentment. The truth and reconciliation process allowed offenders to apply for amnesty from prosecution in exchange for honest testimony and public scrutiny. In the six-year period during which the Truth and Reconciliation Committee did its work, twenty-two thousand victim statements were taken and seven thousand perpetrators applied for amnesty;

849 people were granted amnesty, while thousands of others were not.[22] The process was contentious, but it is generally regarded as a successful model. Archbishop Desmond Tutu explained in his foreword to the South African Truth and Reconciliation Committee report, "We believe, however, that there is another kind of justice—a restorative justice which is concerned not so much with punishment as with correcting imbalances, restoring broken relationships—with healing, harmony and reconciliation."[23] While rehabilitation and restorative justice sound like noble ideas, they appear to run counter to the demand for retributive justice. And from a utilitarian perspective, one might wonder whether those ideas are useful for deterring and preventing crime.

Current Issues

Now let's take what we've learned about deterrence, retribution, and restorative justice and apply it to some concrete issues. We'll discuss here prisons and incarceration rates, racial disparities in the justice system, and issues regarding the death penalty. There are a complicated set of facts and conflicting value judgments involved in thinking about these issues.

Prisons and Incarceration Rates

17.5 Defend a thesis about sentencing reform and the problem of mass incarceration.

In the past half-century, the incarceration rate in the United States has increased substantially. Many people are in jails, prisons, and under correctional supervision. According to the U.S. Bureau of Justice Statistics, at the end of 2020 (the most recent year for which complete data were available), there were over 5.5 million people under the supervision of adult correctional systems in the United States. According to the Bureau, "This was the first time since 1996 that the total correctional population dropped to less than

---

► **Knowledge Check** Answers appear at the end of the chapter.

1. Which of the following is false, concerning the death penalty?
   a. The European Union is opposed to it.
   b. The Catholic church is opposed to it.
   c. A number of American states have recently abolished it.
   d. It is not legal under the federal law of the United States.

2. What is the most basic concern of retributivist theories of punishment?
   a. Mercy
   b. Compassion
   c. Desert
   d. Rehabilitation

3. Which idea is most typically associated with utilitarian thinking about punishment?
   a. Deterrence
   b. Retaliation
   c. Revenge
   d. Forgiveness

4. Which of the following is true, with regard to restorative justice?
   a. It aims to restore the community by retaliating against the wrongdoer.
   b. It emphasizes healing a broken community by reconciling victims and offenders.
   c. It maintains that criminals are evil and can only be returned to the good by suffering pain and doing penance.
   d. It holds that crime can be prevented by promoting conformity and making people afraid of the law.

5.6 million."[24] This number included around 1.7 million who were incarcerated in state or federal prisons or in local jails and approximately 3.9 million under community supervision. The recent decline in the correctional population has been significant. Some of this had to do with the COVID-19 pandemic and changes in incarceration, policing, and court procedures in response to the pandemic. But there is no denying a significant decrease in the prison population. In 2011, the U.S. correctional population hit a high of almost seven million people.[25] The 2022 report (based on 2020 data) stated that "from 2010 to 2020, the correctional population decreased 22.4%."[26] The report also stated that "the incarceration rate dropped each year during the last decade, from 960 per 100,000 adult U.S. residents at year end 2010 to 660 per 100,000 at year end 2020."[27] Despite these trends, there is still a significant proportion of people incarcerated and under correctional supervision: in 2020, one in forty-seven adult U.S. residents were under some form of correctional supervision (including probation and alternatives to incarceration)—that is 2.1 percent of the population.[28] In raw numbers, as of 2021, the United States still has the world's largest prison population. Of the approximately eleven million people in prisons and jails around the world, a significant proportion of them are in American prisons and jails, and the United States has the highest number of prisoners per one hundred thousand of any country on earth.[29]

The problem of "mass incarceration" in the United States (i.e., the high numbers and rate of incarceration in the United States) remains a subject of concern. The problem of mass incarceration has led to calls for criminal justice reform, sentencing reform, and legalization or decriminalization of drugs like marijuana, as mentioned above.

We mentioned at the outset of this chapter that U.S. crime rates have declined since a high in the 1990s (with a recent uptick in the past couple of years). As we discussed above, it is difficult to establish any single reason why crime is down; one fact may be that more people are in prison. If deterrence is one of the primary purposes of punishment, we might conclude that the prison system is doing a good job. However, the U.S. incarceration system continues to generate serious charges of injustice and inefficiency, which led to the movement for sentencing reform. One concern is the cost and extent of the American prison system. Another worry is racial disparities in incarceration rates. Still others argue that rehabilitation or restorative justice could provide a more effective and humane alternative to prison. Some argue for further prison reform and for finding alternatives to incarceration. Others have strongly criticized what they call "the prison industrial complex" (which includes the so-called school-to-prison pipeline and the way that prison funding is tightly woven into state budgets). The most radical suggestions aim at **decarceration**, the idea of eliminating prison as a form of punishment (or at least radically reducing the use of prisons).

Even with criminal justice and sentencing reform, the number of people incarcerated in the United States dwarfs that of other countries. There are various reasons for the high rate of incarceration in the United States. The causes most often cited are mandatory sentences for drug crimes, an increase in the number of so-called three-strikes violations, and truth-in-sentencing laws that lessen the number of prisoners released early.[30] Also mentioned are democratically elected judges, as they may "yield to populist demands for tough justice."[31] There is also the issue of gun ownership and the easy availability of guns. Some claim that gun ownership could decrease crime by empowering citizens to defend themselves, while others argue that the high number of guns available in the United States exacerbates the problem of crime. While some see high incarceration rates as a justifiable response to the threat of violent crime, critics contend that the prison system reinforces a legacy of racial and class division in the United States. Moreover, a significant proportion of the prison population suffers from mental illness.[32] And during the COVID-19 pandemic, prisons were sites of mass contagion, leading some critics to argue that mass incarceration was a threat to public health.[33] There are also reports of violence within prison that includes gang-related violence, rape and sexual abuse, abuse and neglect by prison guards, and the risk of suicide and post-traumatic stress disorder.[34] There are also problems that arise from a growing population of elderly prisoners, the incarceration of children in adult facilities, and the use of solitary confinement.[35]

The average annual cost to incarcerate an inmate in a federal facility in the United States in 2019 (the most recent year for which data was available) was about $39,000.[36] But often the cost is higher in individual states. In Hawaii, for example, the 2019 cost was estimated at $72,000 per inmate.[37] Out of all states, California typically has the highest overall expenditure on prisons. For the 2021–22 reporting cycle, the California Legislative Analyst's Office estimates that it cost $106,000 per year to incarcerate a prisoner in California.[38] This high cost reflects increased cost for security and health that were caused by the COVID-19 pandemic. With a prison population of about 115,000, the total annual budget in California for prisons is more than $14 billion.[39] In California, the amount spent on prisons has often exceeded the amount it spent on higher education.[40] In 2018, the *San Francisco Chronicle* reported that "California spends 6 times more on prisoners than on students."[41] One explanation for this is that it takes more personnel to run a prison than it does to run a school. But this kind of disparity once prompted former governor Arnold Schwarzenegger to opine, "the priorities have become out of whack over the years. . . . What does it say about any state that focuses more on prison uniforms than on caps and gowns?"[42] The comparison serves as a reminder that budget priorities reflect ethical judgments. Are we spending too much on prisons? And is this spending working? Perhaps if crime is down, this kind of expenditure is worth it. But critics of prison expenditures may argue that it would make more sense to put state funds to work on preparing students for careers and providing them with opportunities that might keep them out of prison.

Racial Disparities in the Justice System

17.6 Evaluate racial disparities in the punishment system.

Other ethical concerns arise from the stark racial disparities in the criminal justice system. Black and Hispanic males are imprisoned at dramatically higher rates than White non-Hispanic males. According to the Bureau of Justice Statistics, in 2020, "2% of all black male U.S. residents" were serving time in state or federal prison.[43] And: "Black males were 5.7 times as likely to be imprisoned in 2020 as white males; black males ages 18 to 19 were 12.5 times as likely to be imprisoned as white males of the same age."[44] Similar disparities hold for Hispanic and American Indian/Alaskan Native males. The incarceration rates per one hundred thousand of the demographic cohort in 2020 were as follows: White male—332; Black male—1,890; Hispanic male—837; American Indian/Alaskan Native male—1,418.[45] Approximately 29 percent of the male prison population was White, about 34 percent was Black, 23 percent was Hispanic, and about 2 percent was American Indian/Alaskan Native.[46] Critics have argued that there is something wrong with a society that locks away so many people, many of them people of color, who are incarcerated at rates that are out of proportion to the racial and ethnic makeup of the general population.

A widely quoted statistic once held that one in three Black males will serve time in prison. That statistic was based on data from 2001. Prison rates have changed since then. A *Washington Post* report from 2015 suggested that the rate may have declined to one in four.[47] But whether it is 30 percent or 25 percent of Black men that have been incarcerated, these numbers are still significant. These kinds of racial disparities have led critics to focus on questions of **structural and institutional racism** that are linked to the general claim that the criminal justice system is racist. We discuss this issue further in Chapter 13. But note here that this claim does not mean that all the people working in the criminal justice system are explicitly and overtly racist. The idea of structural racism has been explained by way of a metaphorical birdcage by Michelle Alexander, a civil rights lawyer and law professor, in her influential book *The New Jim Crow*. Alexander borrows the birdcage metaphor from other scholars such as Iris Marion Young and Marylin Frye. She explains that the wires of the cage operate in a system that keeps the bird confined within the cage. Each of those wires may have its own logic. Each wire, when examined independently, need not be explicitly and overtly oppressive or racist. But the structural analysis is not about the individual wire—it is about the resulting system. Alexander explains:

> Not every aspect of a racial caste system needs to be developed for the specific purpose of controlling black people in order for it to operate (together with other laws, institutions, and practices) to trap them at the bottom of a racial hierarchy. In the system of mass incarceration, a wide variety of laws, institutions, and practices—ranging from racial profiling to biased sentencing policies, political disenfranchisement, and legalized employment discrimination—trap African Americans in a virtual (and literal) cage.[48]

Notice that Alexander offers some examples of aspects of the network of policies that produce the structural problem. One of these is racial profiling. **Racial profiling** occurs, for example, when law enforcement officers target certain people for surveillance and possible arrest primarily because of the racial group to which they belong (we discuss this further in Chapter 13). The structural combination of tactics, policies, and institutions—including racial profiling—creates a system that traps Black people in a cage and, in Alexander's words, "is structured to lock them into a subordinate position."[49]

Now, some may suggest in response that disparate incarceration rates must reflect the rates at which various groups of people commit crime. Some defend racial profiling in this way as well, contending that if members of a certain racial group tend to commit more crime, it makes sense to surveil and arrest them in larger numbers. In response, critics of racial profiling argue that it violates people's basic rights, that it unfairly criminalizes members of certain communities, that it alienates and antagonizes those communities, and that it is less effective than other forms of policing. As with other topics in this book, there are complicated legal and ethical questions about racial profiling.

There is also a complicated causal story involving a variety of factors that help explain racially disparate incarceration rates. One example may help to show part of the problem: the issue of plea bargaining. As you might know from watching crime shows and movies, a plea bargain occurs when someone agrees to plead guilty to a crime in exchange for some kind of leniency—and a lengthy and expensive jury trial is avoided. In the United States, most criminal cases are settled by way of plea bargains and without a trial—between 94 percent and 97 percent of cases.[50] One analysis of the way that plea bargaining works in the state of Wisconsin shows that White defendants are more likely to have charges dismissed or reduced from a felony to a misdemeanor than Black defendants.[51] And this process occurs without a trial—it is the result of prosecutors and judges, who come to their task with a variety of biases, which may include assumptions about how race is connected to "criminality" or the likelihood of recidivism.

Of course, the claim about racism in the criminal justice system is also connected to the problem of unarmed Black men who have been killed by police. A number of highly publicized incidents have occurred in the past decade. In 2014, the killing of Michael Brown in Ferguson, Missouri, prompted the formation of the Black Lives Matter movement. Similar killings by police have continued to occur, prompting protests in the streets and calls for reform. This has included the call to "defund" the police, which typically means that police budgets should be cut and that military weaponry should be taken away from police departments. But the killing of Black people by police continues, including much-publicized cases such as that of George Floyd, who was murdered when a police officer knelt on his neck in 2020, and Breonna Taylor, a Black woman who was shot by police who burst into her room in Louisville, Kentucky, in 2020. According to NBC News, "Black people, who account for 13 percent of the U.S. population, accounted for 27 percent of those fatally shot and killed by police in 2021, according to Mapping Police Violence, a non-profit group that tracks police shootings. That means Black people are twice as likely as white people to be shot and killed by police officers."[52] One explanation of this is that police—like the judges and prosecutors mentioned above—have an implicit bias that makes them think of Black men as criminals who pose a threat and respond violently.

Any discussion of racial disparities, structural racism, and implicit bias in the criminal justice system will likely open complicated and contentious questions. We should note again that claims about structural racism do not mean that police officers, prosecutors, and judges are full-fledged and unapologetic racists and White supremacists. Rather, the point is that each of the actors in the criminal justice system finds themselves in a world that is structured by preexisting racial stereotypes and racial disparities. In this regard, there is a kind of vicious circle in a system in which there are racial disparities in the criminal justice system. In such a system, it is more likely that police officers, prosecutors, and judges will unconsciously adopt a view that is biased by the racial disparities that already exist. And in such a system, it will be difficult to see these racial disparities as a problem if one assumes that the system of justice is in fact color-blind. There are complicated issues to be considered here that are linked to the history of racism in the United States including the long legacy of slavery, segregation, and Jim Crow. We cannot analyze all of the legal, historical, political, and psychological factors at play in this problem here.[53]

But the moral problem is obvious. Justice is supposed to be blind, which means impartial and unbiased. The deontological idea of retributive justice holds that criminals are supposed to be punished in proportion to what they deserve. But if this is not true—if racial disparities in the system mean that Black defendants are punished more harshly or more frequently than White defendants—then the system fails to be just. If we adopt a utilitarian approach to thinking about this issue, we will have to consider the social costs of these racial disparities in terms of social dislocation, anger, and despair caused by a system that contains these racial disparities. This also discloses an obvious social justice problem if we believe that equality matters—and that we ought to concern ourselves with the well-being of those who are oppressed, downtrodden, and who suffer injustice.

Let's consider one further point, which is how racial disparities in the criminal justice system create lasting negative impacts for the Black community. There are economic and political implications to the racial disparities in incarceration rates. For example, given that many states do not allow ex-felons to vote, this results in disenfranchisement. According to one estimate, and using conservative figures on voting, if ex-felons had been able to vote in the 2000 presidential election, Al Gore would have carried the state of Florida by thirty thousand

votes and, thus, would have won the Electoral College and the presidency.[54] Prison also tends to produce social stigma and disadvantage for ex-convicts and their families. Families lose income and opportunities to generate wealth due to incarceration. It is difficult for ex-cons to get jobs or gain positions of trust. And so on. Michelle Alexander suggests that these social costs have a racial complexion that has contributed to the creation of a new "Jim Crow" system. Alexander explains, "the criminalization and demonization of black men has turned the black community against itself, unraveling community and family relationships, decimating networks of support, and intensifying the shame and self-hate experienced by the current pariah caste."[55] (You can read an excerpt from Alexander's essay at the end of this chapter.)

Racial disparities in imprisonment are also linked to disparities in social class. Affluent people get better lawyers, while poor people are more likely to take a plea bargain, resulting in incarceration.[56] Some sociologists have noted that incarceration fosters social stratification, with imprisonment helping to define the experience of those in the so-called "underclass." Again, this can be understood in racial terms—but the adverse impact of incarceration afflicts White, Hispanic, Black, and Native American communities, albeit in disparate ways. Incarceration disrupts families. And it pushes convicts out of the labor market, depresses their wages, and undermines their long-term life prospects.[57] Although it is illegal to discriminate against ex-convicts, employers remain wary of hiring those with prison records.[58] From a perspective that

Figure 17-1 Michelle Alexander is a civil rights activist and author of *The New Jim Crow*.

takes equality and social justice concerns seriously (as discussed, e.g., in Chapter 13), racial disparities in incarceration are a cause for moral concern.

These sorts of issues have led some authors—such as Angela Davis, whom we will read at the end of this chapter—to argue that the current system of mass incarceration ought to be abolished. Davis is concerned with the way that racial, gender, and economic inequities structure the prison system. She suggests that the prison system ought to be replaced with a system that is focused on principles of reparation, restoration, and rehabilitation, rather than on principles of retributive justice. Called decarceration, this is obviously a controversial idea. Davis's proposals for prison reform and abolition include a call to decriminalize drug use and sex work. The movement to decriminalize or legalize marijuana—the case with which we began this chapter—has often been defended as a way to reduce prison populations and to help remedy racial disparities in prison.[59] Davis discusses this in her work, along with the need to decriminalize immigration and other proposals for reforming the use of prison as punishment.

The Death Penalty

17.7 Evaluate moral arguments for and against the death penalty.

One of the most contentious issues for any philosophical conception of legal punishment—whether focused on retribution, deterrence, or some other value—is capital punishment. While the vast majority of developed nations (the United States being a notable exception) have abolished the death penalty, this most extreme form of punishment raises profound moral questions about the nature of punishment itself. Retributivists might be seen to favor capital punishment for murderers as an application of *lex talionis*, but it is hard to see how the death of another person "makes up for" the loss of the victim. Consequentialists may argue that the death penalty deters people from committing murder, but scholars continue to debate the actual deterrent effect of the death penalty.

The outrage, harm, and injustice of murder seem to call for the harshest of punishments, which may be why murder remains one of the only crimes punishable by death (at least in some states within the United States). However, we should note that advocates of restorative justice are often opposed to the death penalty. The U.S. Conference of Catholic Bishops also rejects the death penalty as part of a broader theological and philosophical commitment to a "culture of life." But retributivist advocates of the death penalty argue that for murder, the only acceptable punishment is death. The murder victim cannot be restored to life, and it also seems unlikely that the murderer can make amends for their crime in the same way that a thief can. Moreover, for some unrepentant predatory criminals—such as those who continue to murder while in prison—execution may be viewed as the only solution. Although the death penalty was once widely used for a variety of crimes, most people now view it as an extraordinary sort of punishment that requires extra justification. Ethicist Lloyd Steffen argues on natural law grounds (in the excerpt included at the end of this chapter) that we ought to preserve life and not kill people, and that the state ordinarily ought not to kill its own citizens. Thus, he maintains that the death penalty requires special justification and that it may no longer be justifiable in contemporary social and political circumstances.

Legal Issues

As mentioned at the outset of this chapter, there is a global trend toward the abolition of the death penalty. According to Amnesty International, in 2021 only 579 people were executed in the eighteen nations that recorded executions.[60] This low number does not include executions in China, which are not publicly reported. Nonetheless, Amnesty maintains that China is "the world's lead executioner," estimating that its annual execution number is in the thousands.[61] After China, the largest numbers of executions in 2021 (according to official reports) occurred in Iran (314), Egypt (83), Saudi Arabia (65), Syria (24), Somalia (21), Iraq (17), Yemen (14), and the United States (11). (Amnesty International notes that the numbers may be higher in some countries that conceal or underreport executions—and that in addition to China there are likely significant numbers of unreported executions in North Korea and Vietnam.)

Capital punishment has a long history in the United States, but by the 1960s, a majority of Americans had come to oppose it.[62] In 1972, the U.S. Supreme Court case *Furman v. Georgia* ushered in a brief moratorium on the death penalty, as the Court found that its imposition had become too "arbitrary and capricious" and thus violated the Constitution's ban on cruel and unusual punishment. That ruling also invalidated the use of the death penalty as punishment for the crime of rape. By 1976, however, the country's mood had again begun to change, and states had established less arbitrary sentencing guidelines. That year, the high court ruled in *Gregg v. Georgia* that the death penalty does not violate the Eighth Amendment's ban on cruel and unusual punishment. The Court argued that the death penalty is justifiable on both retributivist and deterrence grounds, concluding that it could be "an expression of the community's belief that certain crimes are themselves so grievous an affront to humanity that the only adequate response may be the penalty of death."[63] The Court acknowledged that there was no conclusive empirical evidence about the deterrent effect of the death penalty but that it was reasonable to suspect that it might deter.

One interesting ruling returned to the question of whether the death penalty is cruel and unusual punishment. In 2014, federal judge Cormac Carney ruled that the death penalty in California was indeed cruel and unusual because it was so rarely applied. California has the nation's largest death row population (690 convicts on death row as of January 2022, but the last person California executed was Clarence Ray Allen, in 2006. One reason that California executes so few convicts is that there is ongoing resistance to the death penalty, including legal challenges and difficulty obtaining the drugs for lethal injection. Judge Carney argued that since California exercised the death penalty so infrequently, an execution would be the result of arbitrary factors; he concluded that arbitrary executions serve neither a retributive nor a deterrent purpose. Carney's decision was overturned by the Ninth Circuit Court of Appeals in 2015.[64] In 2016, Californians voted on two referendums and registered basic support for the death penalty. But in 2019, California's governor, Gavin Newsom, instituted a moratorium on it. And in 2022,

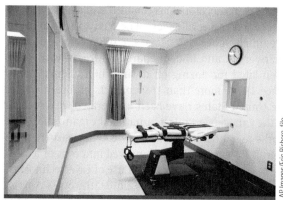

Figure 17-2 The lethal injection chamber at California's San Quentin Prison.

Newsom ordered the execution chamber at San Quentin to be dismantled while also transferring prisoners off of San Quentin's death row.[65]

As we mentioned at the outset of this chapter, American states are divided about the death penalty. Currently, twenty-six states and the District of Columbia do not have the death penalty. And the federal use of the death penalty has shifted depending on the political winds. Under former president Trump, there was an increase in federal executions; but under President Biden, there has been a moratorium on federal executions. As of mid-2022, there have been over 1,500 executions in the United States since the death penalty was reinstated in 1976.[66] The largest number of executions has occurred in Texas (with 74 executions as of mid-2022), Oklahoma (with 116), and Virginia (with 113), and Florida (with 99).[67] It is worth noting, given its place in this list, that the state of Virginia abolished the death penalty in 2021.

Exonerations

One issue of grave concern is whether the U.S. justice system can ensure that people are never wrongfully executed for crimes they did not commit. Indeed, many opponents of the death penalty believe the United States has already executed innocent people. How could this happen? Explanations range from the sinister to the banal: "revelations of withheld evidence, mistaken eyewitness identification, questionable forensic practices, prosecutorial misconduct, and simple error."[68] Defendants, especially those who have to rely on court-appointed public defenders, are often represented by overworked and underprepared lawyers—with some even cited for dozing off during their clients' trials. Since 1973, more than 189 convicts on death row in the United States have been exonerated.[69] According to the Innocence Project, a national organization that works to exonerate the wrongly convicted, there have been 375 people who were proved innocent of a variety of crimes since 1989 by the use of DNA technology, including twenty-one people on death row.[70] Among those exonerated, the average prison time served is fourteen years.[71]

Such revelations of innocence have raised doubts about the death penalty for some political leaders who once supported it. In January 2000, the governor of Illinois, George Ryan, ordered that all executions in his state be halted after Northwestern University journalism students reviewed cases and proved the innocence of several inmates, including one who was within forty-eight hours of his scheduled execution. "Until I can be sure with moral certainty," Ryan said, "that no innocent man or woman is facing a lethal injection, no one will meet that fate."[72] Because of these concerns and after a review of the cases, Ryan—in one of his last acts as governor in 2003—pardoned four inmates and commuted the death sentences of the remaining 167 on death row. Illinois officially abolished the death penalty in 2011.

Racial Bias and Fairness

Another issue that raises concerns about the death penalty is the evidence of racial bias in death penalty sentencing. A number or sources, including Amnesty International, have indicated that there is racial bias in the death penalty system.[73] The Death Penalty Information Center has collected a number of empirical studies that show racial bias in the death penalty in a number of states. For example, in many states, Black inmates are more likely to receive a death sentence than White inmates especially when the murder victim is White.[74]

Not surprisingly, then, there are significant racial disparities in the number of prisoners executed. Since 1976, the race of the executed is 56 percent White, 34 percent Black, 8 percent Hispanic, and 2 percent other; and 41 percent of the death row population is Black.[75] Compare this to the general population (based on 2021 data), in which Whites make up 75.8 percent of the population, Hispanics are 18.9 percent, and Blacks constitute only 13.6 percent.[76] Most problematic, perhaps, is the fact that cases resulting in death sentences for interracial murders are quite skewed. Twenty-one White inmates have been executed for murdering a Black victim, but 300 Black inmates have been executed for killing a White victim.[77] One issue of concern has to do with the racial makeup of juries in death penalty cases.[78] Consider the case of Johnny Lee Gates, a Black man who was convicted of murder and sentenced to death by an all-White jury in Georgia in 1976. He served twenty-six years on death row until he was judged to be intellectually disabled and resentenced to life imprisonment without the possibility of parole. In 2020, after DNA evidence was reexamined, Gates's murder conviction was overturned and he was released from prison. The judge in the case found that "evidence of systematic race discrimination during jury selection in this case is undeniable."[79] These kinds of racial disparities have been employed in abolitionist arguments by scholars and activists such as Angela Davis, who has contended that the racist application of the death penalty is part of an overall pattern of racism that extends back to slavery. For that reason, Davis has called for the abolition of the death penalty.[80]

Other issues related to the death penalty have recently gained public attention, for example, whether persons with intellectual disabilities or juveniles should be executed. In June 2002, in *Atkins v. Virginia*, the U.S. Supreme Court ruled that defendants with intellectual disabilities should not be subject to the death penalty. Obviously, one practical problem is how to determine when someone has an intellectual disability and to what degree that it could exempt that person from the death penalty. In Georgia, for example, the defense has to determine beyond a reasonable doubt that a convict has an intellectual disability. This standard is quite strict, requiring substantial proof of disability. Consider the case of Warren Lee Hill, a convicted Georgia murderer with an IQ of 70.

(Those with IQs below 70 are generally regarded as intellectually disabled.) Hill was scheduled to be executed in February 2013, but the execution was stayed hours before it was scheduled to allow courts to review the issue of his mental capacity. His execution was subject to ongoing legal challenges.[81] Hill's lawyers hoped that a 2014 Supreme Court ruling might save him. That decision, *Hall v. Florida*, ruled that IQ alone was not sufficient to prove intellectual disability. Unfortunately for Hill, the ruling did not change the outcome. Hill was executed by the state of Georgia in 2015. Related to the question of mental capacity is the issue of executing juveniles. In March 2005, the U.S. Supreme Court ruled (in *Roper v. Simmons*) that it was cruel and unusual punishment, forbidden by the Constitution, to execute those who were under age eighteen when they committed their crimes. (A growing body of biological and psychological evidence suggests that adolescents "lack mature judgment and a full appreciation of the consequences of their actions."[82]) Until this ruling, the United States had been the only remaining country in the world that executed juveniles, as Justice Kennedy explained in the Court's majority decision.

Racial disparities in executions, as well as executions of juveniles and individuals with intellectual disabilities, raise serious questions about the fairness of the death penalty and its application. These cases remind us that concepts such as criminal responsibility and appropriate punishment are complex and highly disputed issues, and are all the more so when the punishment being considered is death.

Costs

Death penalty cases are expensive, in terms of both court costs and prison costs. While costs vary from state to state, one analysis from the Death Penalty Information Center in 2009 concludes that "for a single trial, the state may pay $1 million more than for a non-death penalty trial. But only one in every three capital trials result in a death sentence, so the true cost of that death sentence is $3 million. Further down the road, only one in ten of the death sentences handed down may result in an execution. Hence the cost to the state to reach that one execution is $30 million."[83]

As noted in our discussion of prisons, costs vary from state to state, and California is one of the most expensive states to imprison people. This translates to a very expensive execution system in California. In a report from 2021, from a committee of the California state legislature, the death penalty costs the state about $150 million per year. As noted above, California has executed very few people since the death penalty was reinstated in the 1970s. The committee claims "California has executed 13 people at a cost of $4 billion."[84] And "it costs at least tens of millions of dollars more each year to house people on death row compared to a non-death row prison setting."[85] It is not surprising that the committee recommended repealing the death penalty and reducing the size of death row.

Opponents of the death penalty often cite the high cost as an argument against capital punishment. This is certainly a concern for utilitarians who are interested in cost–benefit analysis. Proponents of the death penalty will argue, however, that costs could be controlled by speeding up the trial and appeals process. But a central reason for the lengthy trials and appeals is to ensure that innocent people are not executed, which is a concern for those interested in the basic idea of retributive justice.

The controversies surrounding the death penalty point to deeper philosophical questions about its justification. Generally, the same two arguments regarding legal punishment—deterrence and retribution—are used in arguments about the death penalty. We will return now to these rationales and see what considerations would be relevant to arguments for and against the death penalty.

Deterrence Considerations

Utilitarian philosopher John Stuart Mill defended the death penalty by arguing that it was the least cruel punishment that works to deter murder.[86] Mill pointed out that there were punishments worse than death—torture, for example. However, Mill argued (see his speech at the end of this chapter) that people fear death, even though a quick and painless death is not nearly as bad as a life of torture. For a utilitarian such as Mill, the death penalty works to minimize pain (for the convict), while promoting the greatest happiness (by deterring murder).

But is the death penalty a deterrent? Does it prevent people from committing certain capital crimes? Consider first the issue of prevention. One would think that at least there is certainty here. If you execute someone, that person will not commit any future crime—including murders—because they will be dead. However, on a stricter interpretation of the term *prevent,* this may not necessarily be so.[87] When we execute a convicted murderer, do we really prevent that person from committing any further murders? The answer is "Maybe." If that person would have committed another murder, we have prevented them from doing so. If that person would not have committed another murder, we would not have prevented them from doing so. In general, by executing all convicted murderers we would, strictly speaking, have prevented some of them (those who would have killed again) but not others (those who would not have killed again) from doing so. How many murders would we have prevented? It is difficult to tell. Those who support the death penalty may insist that it will have been worth it, no matter how small the number of murders prevented, because the people executed are convicted murderers anyway.

By contrast, what do we make of arguments for the death penalty that claim it deters those who have not already committed murder? If the death penalty deters would-be murderers from committing their crimes, it is worth it, according to this rationale. Granted, it will not deter those who kill out of passion or those who determine the crime is worth the risk of punishment, but presumably it would deter others. How can we determine if the death penalty really is an effective deterrent? First, we can consider our intuitions about the value of our own lives—that we would not do what would result in our own death. Threats of being executed would deter us, and thus, we think, they also would deter others. More likely, however, reasons other than fear of the death penalty restrain most of us from committing murder.

We might also gauge the death penalty's deterrent effect by examining empirical evidence. For example, we could compare two jurisdictions, say, two states. One has the death penalty, and one does not. If we find that in the state with the death penalty there are fewer murders than in the state without the death penalty, can

we assume that the death penalty has made the difference and is thus a deterrent? Not necessarily. Perhaps it was something else about the state with the death penalty that accounted for the lesser incidence of murder. For example, the lower homicide rate could be the result of good economic conditions or a culture that has strong families or religious institutions. Something similar could be true of the state with a higher incidence of homicide. In this case, the cause could be high unemployment, high rates of drug and alcohol abuse, and other social problems. So, also, if there were a change in one jurisdiction from no death penalty to death penalty (or the opposite), and the statistics regarding homicides also changed, we might conclude that the causal factor was the change in the death penalty status. But again, this is not necessarily so. For example, the murder rate in Canada actually declined after that country abolished the death penalty in 1976.[88] Other studies have found no correlation between having, instituting, or abolishing the death penalty and the rate of homicide.[89] For example, statistics show that states without the death penalty and with similar demographic profiles do not differ in homicide rates from states with the death penalty. Moreover, since 1976, homicide rates in states that instituted the death penalty have not declined more than in states that did not institute the death penalty. And homicide rates in states with the death penalty have been found to be higher than in states without it.[90] But some studies still maintain that executions have a deterrent effect. A 2007 article in the *Wall Street Journal* claimed that "Capital Punishment Works." The authors charted execution rates and murder rates for the twenty-six-year period from 1979 through 2004. The data indicate that as execution rates increase, murder rates decline. They conclude, "each execution carried out is correlated with about 74 fewer murders the following year."[91] These results—and others like them from recent studies—have been criticized by economists and statisticians who maintain that any deterrent effect, if there is one, is "too fragile to be certain."[92] One problem is that there are very few executions and these occur in a few states. It is difficult to draw general conclusions about a causal relation between execution rates and murder rates from the sorts of correlations mentioned here. The National Academy of Sciences concluded in 2012, "research to date on the effect of capital punishment on homicide is not informative about whether capital punishment decreases, increases, or has no effect on homicide rates."[93]

To make a good argument for the death penalty on utilitarian grounds, a proponent would have to show that it works to deter crime. In addition, the proponent may have to show that the death penalty works better than alternatives—for example, life in prison without the possibility of parole or community-based crime prevention efforts. If we have the death penalty and it does not provide an effective deterrent, we will have executed people for no good purpose. If we do not have the death penalty and it would have been an effective deterrent, we risk the lives of innocent victims who otherwise would have been saved. Because this is the worse alternative, some argue, we ought to retain the death penalty. But because the deterrence argument broadly construed is a consequentialist argument, using it also should require thinking more generally of costs and benefits. Here, the higher cost of execution could be compared to the lower cost of life imprisonment.

Retributivist Considerations

Immanuel Kant defended the death penalty on retributivist grounds. He argues, "undeserved evil which any one commits on another, is to be regarded as perpetrated on himself."[94] This principle has obvious connections with Kant's idea that the categorical imperative requires that we view our maxims as universal moral laws (as discussed in Chapter 6). Kant advocates a type of retaliation, which demands like for like or life for life. He maintains that the death penalty is justified because it treats a murderer as a rational being, giving a person what they deserve according to this basic principle of retributive justice. Kant also maintains that we should respect the human dignity of a prisoner awaiting execution and not torture or abuse any individual.

As we have already noted, according to the retributivist argument for legal punishment, we ought to punish people to make them pay for the wrong or harm they have done. Those who argue for the death penalty on retributivist grounds must show that it is a fitting punishment and the only or most fitting punishment for certain crimes and criminals. This is not necessarily

an argument based on revenge—that the punishment of the wrongdoer gives others satisfaction. It appeals, rather, to a sense of justice and an abstract righting of wrongs done. Again, there are two different versions of the retributive principle: egalitarian (or *lex talionis*) and proportional. The egalitarian version says that the punishment should equal the crime. An argument for the death penalty would attempt to show that the only fitting punishment for someone who takes a life is that their own life be taken in return. In this view, the value of a life is not equivalent to anything else. Thus, even life in prison is not sufficient payment for taking a life, though it would also seem that the only crime deserving of the death penalty would be murder. Note that homicide is not the only crime for which we have assigned the death penalty. We have also done so for treason and, at times, for rape. Moreover, only some types of murder are thought by proponents of the death penalty to call for this form of punishment. And as noted in the critique of the *lex talionis* view previously, strict equality of punishment would be not only impractical in some cases but also morally problematic.

Perhaps a more acceptable argument could be made on grounds of proportionality. In this view, death is the only fitting punishment for certain crimes. These are worse than all others and should receive the worst or most severe punishment. Surely, some say, death is a worse punishment than life in prison. However, others argue that spending one's life in prison is worse. This form of the retributivist principle would not require that the worst crimes receive the worst possible punishment. It only requires that, of the range of acceptable punishments, the worst crimes receive the top punishment on the list. Death by prolonged torture might be the worst punishment, but we probably would not put that at the top of our list. So, also, the death penalty could be—but need not be—included on that list.

Using the retributivist rationale, one would need to determine the most serious crimes. Can these be specified and a good reason given as to why they are the worst crimes? Multiple murders would be worse than single ones, presumably. Murder with torture or of certain people also might be found to be among the worst crimes. What about treason? What about huge monetary swindles that cost thousands of people their life savings? We rate degrees of murder, distinguishing murder in the first degree from murder in the second degree. The first is worse because the person not only deliberately intended to kill the victim, but also did so out of malice. These crimes are distinguished from manslaughter (both voluntary and involuntary), which is also killing. Supposedly, the idea is that the kind of personal and moral involvement makes a difference. The more the person planned with intention and deliberateness, the more truly the person owned the act. The more malicious crime is also thought to be worse. Critics of the death penalty sometimes argue that such rational distinctions are perhaps impossible to make in practice. However, unless it is impossible in principle or by its very nature, supporters could continue to try to refine the current distinctions.

Mercy and Restorative Justice

Opponents of the death penalty often argue against it on deterrent grounds, maintaining that if it does not work to deter crime (or if some other punishment works better), it causes unnecessary and unjustifiable pain. For example, utilitarian philosopher Jeremy Bentham opposed the death penalty by arguing that life imprisonment would work better. Others argue against the death penalty while acknowledging the retributivist argument in favor of capital punishment. Philosopher Jeffrey Reiman maintains that the death penalty represents a sort of maximal amount of retribution that can be justified. We can execute a murderer, for example, but we cannot kill their family. Reiman further suggests that there are circumstances in which it is morally permissible to give criminals less than the maximum punishment, so long as we attend to the needs and interests of the victims of crime.[95] In other words, we could execute murderers, but there may be good reasons for not doing so. Among the reasons for not executing may be upholding other values, such as mercy.

Indeed, the relatively greater value of mercy is often a central claim for religious opponents of the death penalty. Such opposition to capital punishment is often connected with a broader commitment to nonviolence and pacifism (see Chapter 18), one that sees little purpose in responding to violence with violence. "An eye for an eye

leaves the whole world blind" is a sentiment that is frequently attributed to Mohandas Gandhi, and connected to his philosophy of nonviolence. Gandhi explained that prisons should be used as "reformatories" and not as "places of punishment."[96] He also rejected corporal and capital punishment as both too violent and too final. Gandhi said, "Once a man is killed, the punishment is beyond recall or reparation. God alone can take life, because He alone gives it."[97]. In the Christian tradition, the value of mercy is connected to other values such as forgiveness and compassion.[98] The Catholic Church is opposed to the death penalty on these grounds, holding that mercy is an important value and that the death penalty is simply not the best way for murder victims to find closure.[99]

The idea of finding closure is connected with arguments in favor of restorative justice. While it is certainly not possible to restore a murder victim to life, it may be possible to imagine responses to murder that do not involve the desire for retribution. Consider, for example, the response to a 2006 school shooting in an Amish community in Nickel Mines, Pennsylvania. (Ten Amish children were shot and five killed by a local milk truck driver who was not Amish.) The community gathered together after these murders and offered forgiveness to the murderer (who had committed suicide) and his family.[100] Afterward, the mother of the murderer recalled how the Amish community's forgiving attitude helped her heal and recover from the horror of knowing that her son was a mass murderer.[101] Another example comes from Tallahassee, Florida. Ann Grosmaire, a 19-year-old college student, was shot and killed by her boyfriend, Conor McBride, in 2010. Despite their grief and the horrific nature of the crime, the Grosmaire family reached out to Conor's family. Citing their Christian faith and a belief that Ann would want them to forgive Conor, the Grosmaires worked with the prosecutor to implement a version of restorative justice. A conference was held in which Conor confessed his crime to Ann's family, and Ann's family explained the depth of the loss that they had experienced. Conor was eventually sentenced to twenty years in prison. Kate Grosmaire, Ann's mother, later explained that forgiveness had a positive effect on her. "Forgiveness for me was self-preservation," she said. But she also noted that forgiveness is a difficult and ongoing process, "Forgiving Conor doesn't change the fact that Ann is not with us. My daughter was shot, and she died. I walk by her empty bedroom at least twice a day."[102] While proponents of restorative justice argue that the message of forgiveness and mercy provides an important addition to discussions of the death penalty, retributivists argue that mercy and forgiveness give people less than what they deserve.

Humane Executions

Other concerns with regard to the death penalty are often about the nature of political power. Should the state have the power to kill people? As mentioned previously, most Western nations no longer have a death penalty. One reason may be that liberal-democratic polities want to limit the power of the state. Others may argue, as Reiman suggests, that killing is uncivilized, brutalizing, degrading, barbarous, and dehumanizing. This sort of argument may be grounded in a kind of visceral repugnance about the act of killing. But it also appeals to the constitutional prohibition on cruel and unusual punishment. Is the death penalty inherently cruel or inhumane? Or is it possible to humanely execute criminals?

Contemporary methods of execution can sometimes appear to cause suffering. Depending on the form of execution, the person put to death may gasp for air, strain, or shake uncontrollably. With some methods, the eyes bulge, the blood vessels expand, and sometimes more than one try is needed to complete the job. In 1999, for example, 344-pound Allen Lee Davis was executed in Florida's electric chair. The execution caused blood to appear on Davis's face and shirt, which some believed demonstrated that he had suffered greatly.

Table 17-1 Outline of Moral Approaches to the Death Penalty

	Death Penalty Abolition	Moderate	Death Penalty Retention
Thesis	Abolish the death penalty.	Employ the death penalty for a limited number of crimes.	Keep the death penalty.
Corollaries and Implications	Replace the death penalty with life imprisonment	List of crimes deserving death might include special circumstances, mass/serial murder, treason, etc., with high burden of proof	Death penalty for ordinary murder and perhaps for other crimes
Connections with Moral Theory	Restorative justice, forgiveness, and mercy (natural law, care ethics, virtue ethics); consequentialist claim that the death penalty does not deter or that life imprisonment is a sufficient deterrent	Natural law and deontological justification of the death penalty moderated by mercy and desire to protect the innocent; consequentialist concern for costs of death penalty administration	Retributive justice (natural law, deontology) concern for retaliation or *lex talionis*; consequentialist focus on deterrence and prevention
Relevant authors/ examples	Lloyd Steffen (abolition in practice); Gandhi; Angela Davis	Lloyd Steffen (justification of the death penalty in exceptional circumstances)	John Stuart Mill; Immanuel Kant

Others said it was simply a nosebleed.[103] Nevertheless, in 2000, the Florida legislature voted to use lethal injections instead of the electric chair in future executions.

Just as the electric chair was thought to be more humane than earlier execution methods when Thomas Edison invented it in 1888, so now, death by lethal injection has generally taken the place of electrocution and other earlier methods. The last death by gas chamber was in 1999 in Arizona, and the last death by hanging was in 1996 in Delaware. In June 2010, Ronnie Lee Gardner was executed by firing squad in Utah, but this was at his own request. Though there has been a move toward lethal injections as other methods of execution have been criticized, one of the current debates regarding the death penalty is whether lethal injection, itself, is humane.

Three chemicals are used in a lethal injection, which is administered via an IV. First, an ultrashort-acting barbiturate, usually sodium thiopental, is given. This causes the inmate to become unconscious. Next, a muscle relaxant, either pancuronium bromide or a similar drug, is given to cause paralysis of the muscles, including those responsible for breathing. Finally, potassium chloride, which causes cardiac arrest, is given. If all goes as expected, the inmate loses consciousness and does not experience any pain as death takes place. The entire process can take as little as ten minutes or much longer. Some of the delay is caused by the difficulty the technicians sometimes have in finding an acceptable vein to use. For example, there have been cases of drug users whose veins were not in good condition or who had to help the technician find a good vein. It is also possible that the condemned person may remain conscious or partially conscious and experience acute pain or the feeling of suffocation but cannot communicate this because of the inability to move caused by the second chemical. Technicians can be more or less capable of giving the drugs correctly and in sufficient quantity. Doctors would be more capable but are prohibited by their code of ethics from taking part in executions in this way.[104] There have been at least forty-three cases of botched executions recorded since 1976. These include instances in which IVs were not administered properly,

prolonging the execution process; those in which the initial administration of gas or electricity failed to kill; and those in which the bodies of the condemned caught fire during electrocutions.[105] In recent years, several states suspended lethal injection out of a concern that the practice was not humane.[106] Meanwhile, American prisons have had difficulty obtaining lethal drugs since European manufacturers oppose their use in executions and have refused to sell them to American prisons.[107] Clearly, both opponents and supporters of the death penalty may find evidence for their positions in the various descriptions of lethal injection as a more or less humane method of execution.

The concern about lethal injection is related to a range of questions about the meaning of the death penalty and what it symbolizes. For example, some who favor more violent forms of execution argue that those who spill blood must have their own blood spilled. In this view, a firing squad may be more appropriate than lethal injection. Nevertheless, Americans tend to view beheading, such as happens in Saudi Arabia and elsewhere, as a barbaric way to execute a criminal. Consider, further, the question of whether a condemned prisoner should have the right to choose their own means of execution. Is it morally appropriate to give a criminal that choice? As noted, the Utah execution by firing squad in 2010 was selected by the condemned man himself. A further question in terms of the symbolic value of executions is whether they should be held in public or videotaped for purposes of information and instruction. We might consider the potential deterrent power of public executions. But we may also think that executions are no longer held in public for good reasons. Is it because we are ashamed of them? Do we think it is cruel or inhumane to display an executed person's body in public as a warning to others? Or are we simply trying to keep the proceedings dignified, while avoiding the use of the executed criminal's death as a "means" to the end of deterrence (in a way that Kant might find immoral)? When we ask questions such as these, our views on the death penalty and our reasons for supporting or opposing it will be put to the test, which is probably not a bad thing.

Chapter Summary

17.1 How can we explain current trends in punishment and the death penalty?

Crime rates have trended down in the past several decades, while incarcerations rates have gone up. This has led to more recent calls for sentencing reform, which may have led to a recent uptick in crime, although the causal story is complex. At the same time, there has been a widespread call for the abolition of the death penalty and a general move toward more humane forms of punishment.

17.2 How can we explain the deterrence theory of punishment?

The deterrence theory is based on the idea that punishment should primarily be used to deter people from committing crime. This is a consequentialist approach to punishment that seeks to reduce crime and support social order. A deterrence theory can also be used to support the death penalty, as in the case of utilitarian philosopher John Stuart Mill.

17.3 How can we describe the idea of retributive justice?

Retributive justice is focused on retaliation against those who have committed a crime and who deserve to be punished. It is typically grounded in natural law or in Kantian deontology and the basic idea of *lex talionis* (eye for eye). The theory relies on claims about accountability and free will.

17.4 How can we describe the idea of restorative justice?

Restorative justice is focused on restoring broken communities. It tends to focus on values such as compassion, forgiveness, and mercy. It does not allow criminals to "get away" with crime, since it emphasizes truth in addition to reconciliation. The idea can be supported by secular, utilitarian thinking—if it works.

17.5 How might we defend a thesis about sentencing reform and the problem of mass incarceration?

Mass incarceration may appear to be a problem if we think there is something wrong when large numbers of people are in prison (although if crime is down, perhaps the prison population is working to reduce crime). Critics of mass incarceration have often advocated for sentencing reform, including, for example, the decriminalization or legalization of drugs such as marijuana. This may be part of a larger effort that could be called decarceration. Retributivists may not support this idea if it means that criminals get away with crimes. Utilitarians may support the project if cost–benefit analysis shows that it is effective. Restorative justice advocates are often in favor of some form of sentencing reform, especially if it helps to rebuild and restore broken communities.

17.6 How can we evaluate racial disparities in the punishment system?

The prison system in the United States has disproportionate numbers of Black and Hispanic prisoners. While some may argue that there is nothing wrong with this if it reflects the rate at which members of these demographic groups commit crime, many scholars and organizations argue that these disparities represent structural or institutional racism. This idea is explained by Michelle Alexander as a problem that results from a variety of causal factors including racial profiling. Bias in the plea bargaining system may also account for the problem.

17.7 How can we evaluate moral arguments for and against the death penalty?

Retributivists will generally support the death penalty, appealing to something like the *lex talionis*, which states eye for eye and life for life. Deterrence theories support the death penalty if it works. But there is no conclusive evidence showing that the death penalty works to deter. And the costs of the death penalty are quite high. There is a global trend to abolish the death penalty, which is grounded in a basic claim about human dignity. And finally, defenders of restorative justice will be opposed to the death penalty.

17.8 How might you defend your own ideas about punishment and the death penalty?

To defend a thesis about punishment and the death penalty, you would first need to clarify which moral theory and theory of punishment you adopt: deterrence, retributivism, or restorative justice. You would then need to consider concrete questions about punishment systems, prisons, and the death penalty. These questions should include issues related to mass incarceration, crime rates, racial disparities, and the cost and effectiveness of prisons and the death penalty.

Primary Source Readings

As you can see from the discussions in this chapter, legal punishment and the death penalty are complex issues. The readings for this chapter will take us deeper into these issues. First, we'll read an excerpt from Michelle Alexander's critique of prisons, *The New Jim Crow*. Alexander's analysis of racial disparities in the system, which was first published in 2010, has been widely influential and often cited by proponents of prison reform, decarceration, and alternatives to incarceration. Next, we'll read an excerpt from the radical author, social theorist, and political activist Angela Y. Davis. Drawing on her critiques of racism, sexism, and economic inequality, Davis uses this essay to challenge the idea that prisons are necessary features of the social landscape. Her argument builds on the insights of the French philosopher and social theorist Michel Foucault, who viewed prisons as mechanisms of social and political control. Next, we'll read an excerpt from John Stuart Mill's 1868 defense of capital punishment, delivered when he was serving as a member of parliament. Mill's defense is based on utilitarian reasoning (see Chapter 5). The last selection is an excerpt from Lloyd Steffen, a religious studies scholar and university chaplain at Lehigh University. Drawing on natural law ethics, Steffen maintains that there is a common set of moral agreements that can allow us to reach consensus on issues such as the death penalty. His theory of just execution is derived from the idea of justified war (which we discuss in more detail in Chapter 18).

Reading 17-1 The New Jim Crow | Michelle Alexander

Study Questions

1. As you read the excerpt, please consider the following questions:
2. How does Alexander explain the discriminatory outcome of the criminal justice system?
3. Why does Alexander use the term "Jim Crow" to describe the result of the criminal justice system?
4. What is the significance of Alexander's use of the term "mass incarceration"?

America is still not an egalitarian democracy. The arguments and rationalizations that have been trotted out in support of racial exclusion and discrimination in its various forms have changed and evolved, but the outcome has remained largely the same. An extraordinary percentage of black men in the United States are legally barred from voting today, just as they have been throughout most of American history. They are also subject to legalized discrimination in employment, housing, education, public benefits, and jury service, just as their parents, grandparents, and great-grandparents once were.

What has changed since the collapse of Jim Crow has less to do with the basic structure of our society than with the language we use to justify it. In the era of colorblindness, it is no longer socially permissible to use race, explicitly, as a justification for discrimination, exclusion, and social contempt. So we don't. Rather than rely on race, we use our criminal justice system to label people of color "criminals" and then engage in all the practices we supposedly left behind. Today it is perfectly legal to discriminate against criminals in nearly all the ways that it was once legal to discriminate against African Americans. Once you're labeled a felon, the old forms of discrimination—employment discrimination, housing discrimination, denial of the right to vote, denial of educational opportunity, denial of food stamps and other public benefits, and exclusion from jury service—are suddenly legal. As a criminal, you have scarcely more rights, and arguably less respect, than a black man living in Alabama at the height of Jim Crow. We have not ended racial caste in America; we have merely redesigned it.

. . . .

When I began my work at the ACLU [American Civil Liberties Union], I assumed that the criminal justice system had problems of racial bias, much in the same way that all major institutions in our society are plagued with problems associated with conscious and unconscious bias. As a lawyer who had litigated numerous class-action employment-discrimination cases, I understood well the many ways in which racial stereotyping can permeate subjective decision-making processes at all levels of an organization, with devastating consequences. I was familiar with the challenges associated with reforming institutions in which racial stratification is thought to be normal—the natural consequence of differences in education, culture, motivation, and, some still believe, innate ability. While at the ACLU, I shifted my focus from employment discrimination to criminal justice reform and dedicated myself to the task of working with others to identify and eliminate racial bias whenever and wherever it reared its ugly head.

By the time I left the ACLU, I had come to suspect that I was wrong about the criminal justice system. It was not just another institution infected with racial bias but rather a different beast entirely. . . . I came to see that mass incarceration in the United States had, in fact, emerged as a stunningly comprehensive and well-disguised system of racialized social control that functions in a manner strikingly similar to Jim Crow.

Michelle Alexander, *The New Jim Crow* (New York: The New Press, 2010), pp. 1–4.

Reading 17-2   Are Prisons Obsolete? | Angela Y. Davis

Study Questions

As you read the excerpt, please consider the following questions:

1. What does Davis mean by "the prison industrial complex"?

2. What does Davis think decarceration would look like?

3. What might Davis mean when she says that punishment does not necessarily follow from crime?

If jails and prisons are to be abolished, then what will replace them? This is the puzzling question that often interrupts further consideration of the prospects for abolition.

It is true that if we focus myopically on the existing system . . . it is very hard to imagine a structurally similar system capable of handling such a vast population of lawbreakers. If, however, we shift our attention from the prison, perceived as an isolated institution, to the set of relationships that comprise the prison industrial complex, it may be easier to think about alternatives. In other words, a more complicated framework may yield more options than if we simply attempt to discover a single substitute for the prison system. The first step, then, would be to let go of the desire to discover one single alternative system of punishment that would occupy the same footprint as the prison system.

Since the 1980s, the prison system has become increasingly ensconced in the economic, political and ideological life of the United States and the transnational trafficking in U.S. commodities, culture, and ideas. Thus, the prison industrial complex is much more than the sum of all the jails and prisons in this country. It is a set of symbiotic relationships among correctional communities, transnational corporations, media conglomerates, guards' unions, and legislative and court agendas. If it is true that the contemporary meaning of punishment is fashioned through these relationships, then the most effective abolitionist strategies will contest these relationships and propose alternatives that pull them apart....

An abolitionist approach ... would require us to imagine a constellation of alternative strategies and institutions, with the ultimate aim of removing the prison from the social and ideological landscapes of our society. In other words, we would not be looking for prisonlike substitutes for the prison, such as house arrest safeguarded by electronic surveillance bracelets. Rather, positing decarceration as our overarching strategy, we would try to envision a continuum of alternatives to imprisonment—demilitarization of schools, revitalization of education at all levels, a health system that provides free physical and mental care to all, and a justice system based on reparation and reconciliation rather than retribution and vengeance....

To reiterate, rather than try to imagine one single alternative to the existing system of incarceration, we might envision an array of alternatives that will require radical transformations of many aspects of our society. Alternatives that fail to address racism, male dominance, homophobia, class bias, and other structures of domination will not, in the final analysis, lead to decarceration and will not advance the goal of abolition....

... Recognize that "punishment" does not follow from "crime" in the neat and logical sequence offered by discourses that insist on the justice of imprisonment, but rather punishment—primarily through imprisonment (and sometimes death)—is linked to the agendas of politicians, the profit drive of corporations, and media representations of crime.

Angela Y. Davis, "Alternatives to the Prison Industrial Complex" (editor's title, originally excerpted and reprinted from "Imprisonment and Reform" and "Abolitionist Alternatives") from *Are Prisons Obsolete?* (New York: Seven Stories Press, 2003).

Reading 17-3   Speech in Favor of Capital Punishment (1868) | John Stuart Mill

Study Questions

As you read the excerpt, please consider the following questions:

1. Why does Mill suggest that capital punishment is less cruel than other punishments?
2. Why does Mill claim that we can't judge whether the death penalty fails to work?
3. What does Mill mean by suggesting that the purpose of penal justice is to deter?

When there has been brought home to any one, by conclusive evidence, the greatest crime known to the law; and when the attendant circumstances suggest no palliation of the guilt, no hope that the culprit may even yet not be unworthy to live among mankind, nothing to make it probable that the crime was an exception to his general character rather than a consequence of it, then I confess it appears to me that to deprive the criminal of the life of which he has proved himself to be unworthy—solemnly to blot him out from the fellowship of mankind and from the catalogue of the living—is the most appropriate as it is certainly the most impressive, mode in which society can attach to so great a crime the penal consequences which for the security of life it is indispensable to annex to it. I defend this penalty, when confined to atrocious cases, on the very ground on which it is commonly attached—on that of humanity to the criminal; as beyond comparison the least cruel mode in which it is possible adequately to deter from the crime. If, in our horror of inflicting death, we endeavor to devise some punishment for the living criminal which shall act on the human mind with a deterrent force at all comparable to that of death, we are driven to inflictions less severe indeed in appearance, and therefore less efficacious, but far more cruel in reality. Few, I think, would venture to propose, as a punishment for aggravated murder, less than imprisonment with hard labor for life; that is the fate to which a murderer would be consigned by the mercy which shrinks from putting him to death. But has it been sufficiently considered what sort of a mercy this is, and what kind of life it leaves to him? If, indeed, the punishment is not really inflicted—if it becomes the sham which a few years ago such punishments were rapidly becoming— then, indeed, its adoption would be almost tantamount to giving up the attempt to repress murder altogether. But if it really is what it professes to be, and if it is realized in all its rigour by the popular imagination, as it very probably would not be, but as it must be if it is to be efficacious, it will be so shocking that when the memory of the crime is no longer fresh, there will be almost insuperable difficulty in executing it. What comparison can there really be, in point of severity, between consigning a man to the short pang of a rapid death, and immuring him in a living tomb, there to linger out what may be a long life in the hardest and most monotonous toil, without any of its alleviations or rewards— debarred from all pleasant sights and sounds, and cut off from all earthly hope, except a slight mitigation of bodily restraint, or a small improvement of diet? Yet even such a lot as this, because there is no one moment at which the suffering is of terrifying intensity, and, above all, because it does not contain the element, so imposing to the imagination, of the unknown, is universally reputed a milder punishment than death—stands

in all codes as a mitigation of the capital penalty, and is thankfully accepted as such. For it is characteristic of all punishments which depend on duration for their efficacy—all, therefore, which are not corporal or pecuniary—that they are more rigorous than they seem; while it is, on the contrary, one of the strongest recommendations a punishment can have, that it should seem more rigorous than it is; for its practical power depends far less on what it is than on what it seems. There is not, I should think, any human infliction which makes an impression on the imagination so entirely out of proportion to its real severity as the punishment of death. The punishment must be mild indeed which does not add more to the sum of human misery than is necessarily or directly added by the execution of a criminal. As my hon. Friend the Member for Northampton (Mr. Gilpin) has himself remarked, the most that human laws can do to anyone in the matter of death is to hasten it; the man would have died at any rate; not so very much later, and on the average, I fear, with a considerably greater amount of bodily suffering. Society is asked, then, to denude itself of an instrument of punishment which, in the grave cases to which alone it is suitable, effects its purposes at a less cost of human suffering than any other; which, while it inspires more terror, is less cruel in actual fact than any punishment that we should think of substituting for it. My hon. Friend says that it does not inspire terror, and that experience proves it to be a failure. But the influence of a punishment is not to be estimated by its effect on hardened criminals. Those whose habitual way of life keeps them, so to speak, at all times within sight of the gallows, do grow to care less about it; as, to compare good things with bad, an old soldier is not much affected by the chance of dying in battle. I can afford to admit all that is often said about the indifference of professional criminals to the gallows. Though of that indifference one-third is probably bravado and another third confidence that they shall have the luck to escape, it is quite probable that the remaining third is real. But the efficacy of a punishment which acts principally through the imagination, is chiefly to be measured by the impression it makes on those who are still innocent; by the horror with which it surrounds the first promptings of guilt; the restraining influence it exercises over the beginning of the thought which, if indulged, would become a temptation; the check which it exerts over the graded declension towards the state–never suddenly attained—in which crime no longer revolts, and punishment no longer terrifies. As for what is called the failure of death punishment, who is able to judge of that? We partly know who those are whom it has not deterred; but who is there who knows whom it has deterred, or how many human beings it has saved who would have lived to be murderers if that awful association had not been thrown round the idea of murder from their earliest infancy? Let us not forget that the most imposing fact loses its power over the imagination if it is made too cheap. When a punishment fit only for the most atrocious crimes is lavished on small offences until human feeling recoils from it, then, indeed, it ceases to intimidate, because it ceases to be believed in. The failure of capital punishment in cases of theft is easily accounted for; the thief did not believe that it would be inflicted. He had learnt by experience that jurors would perjure themselves rather than find him guilty; that Judges would seize any excuse for not sentencing him to death, or for recommending him to mercy; and that if neither jurors nor Judges were merciful, there were still hopes from an authority above both.

When things had come to this pass it was high time to give up the vain attempt. When it is impossible to inflict a punishment, or when its infliction becomes a public scandal, the idle threat cannot too soon disappear from the statute book. And in the case of the host of offences which were formerly capital, I heartily rejoice that it did become impracticable to execute the law. If the same state of public feeling comes to exist in the case of murder; if the time comes when jurors refuse to find a murderer guilty; when Judges will not sentence him to death, or will recommend him to mercy; or when, if juries and Judges do not flinch from their duty, Home Secretaries, under pressure of deputations and memorials, shrink from theirs, and the threat becomes, as it became in the other cases, a mere *brutum fulmen* [futile threat]; then, indeed, it may become necessary to do in this case what has been done in those–to abrogate the penalty. That time may come—my hon. Friend thinks that it has nearly come. I hardly know whether he lamented it or boasted of it; but he and his Friends are entitled to the boast; for if it comes it will be their

doing, and they will have gained what I cannot but call a fatal victory, for they will have achieved it by bringing about, if they will forgive me for saying so, an enervation, an effeminacy, in the general mind of the country. For what else than effeminacy is it to be so much more shocked by taking a man's life than by depriving him of all that makes life desirable or valuable? Is death, then, the greatest of all earthly ills? *Usque adeone mori miserum est* [is it so wretched then to die]? Is it, indeed, so dreadful a thing to die? Has it not been from of old one chief part of a manly education to make us despise death—teaching us to account it, if an evil at all, by no means high in the list of evils; at all events, as an inevitable one, and to hold, as it were, our lives in our hands, ready to be given or risked at any moment, for a sufficiently worthy object? I am sure that my hon. Friends know all this as well, and have as much of all these feelings as any of the rest of us; possibly more. But I cannot think that this is likely to be the effect of their teaching on the general mind. I cannot think that the cultivating of a peculiar sensitiveness of conscience on this one point, over and above what results from the general cultivation of the moral sentiments, is permanently consistent with assigning in our own minds to the fact of death no more than the degree of relative importance which belongs to it among the other incidents of our humanity.

The men of old cared too little about death, and gave their own lives or took those of others with equal recklessness. Our danger is of the opposite kind, lest we should be so much shocked by death, in general and in the abstract, as to care too much about it in individual cases, both those of other people and our own, which call for its being risked. And I am not putting things at the worst, for it is proved by the experience of other countries that horror of the executioner by no means necessarily implies horror of the assassin. The stronghold, as we all know, of hired assassination in the 18th century was Italy; yet it is said that in some of the Italian populations the infliction of death by sentence of law was in the highest degree offensive and revolting to popular feeling.

Much has been said of the sanctity of human life, and the absurdity of supposing that we can teach respect for life by ourselves destroying it. But I am surprised at the employment of this argument, for it is one which might be brought against any punishment whatever. It is not human life only, not human life as such, that ought to be sacred to us, but human feelings. The human capacity of suffering is what we should cause to be respected, not the mere capacity of existing. And we may imagine somebody asking how we can teach people not to inflict suffering by ourselves inflicting it? But to this I should answer—all of us would answer—that to deter by suffering from inflicting suffering is not only possible, but the very purpose of penal justice. Does fining a criminal show want of respect for property, or imprisoning him, for personal freedom? Just as unreasonable is it to think that to take the life of a man who has taken that of another is to show want of regard for human life. We show, on the contrary, most emphatically our regard for it, by the adoption of a rule that he who violates that right in another forfeits it for himself, and that while no other crime that he can commit deprives him of his right to live, this shall. There is one argument against capital punishment, even in extreme cases, which I cannot deny to have weight—on which my hon. Friend justly laid great stress, and which never can be entirely got rid of. It is this—that if by an error of justice an innocent person is put to death, the mistake can never be corrected; all compensation, all reparation for the wrong is impossible. This would be indeed a serious objection if these miserable mistakes—among the most tragical occurrences in the whole round of human affairs—could not be made extremely rare. The argument is invincible where the mode of criminal procedure is dangerous to the innocent, or where the Courts of Justice are not trusted. And this probably is the reason why the objection to an irreparable punishment began (as I believe it did) earlier, and is more intense and more widely diffused, in some parts of the Continent of Europe than it is here. There are on the Continent great and enlightened countries, in which the criminal procedure is not so favorable to innocence, does not afford the same security against erroneous conviction, as it does among us; countries where the Courts of Justice seem to think they fail in their duty unless they find somebody guilty; and in their really laudable desire to hunt guilt from its hiding places, expose themselves to a serious danger of condemning the innocent. If our own

procedure and Courts of Justice afforded ground for similar apprehension, I should be the first to join in withdrawing the power of inflicting irreparable punishment from such tribunals.

But we all know that the defects of our procedure are the very opposite. Our rules of evidence are even too favorable to the prisoner; and juries and Judges carry out the maxim, "It is better that ten guilty should escape than that one innocent person should suffer," not only to the letter, but beyond the letter. Judges are most anxious to point out, and juries to allow for, the barest possibility of the prisoner's innocence. No human judgment is infallible; such sad cases as my hon. Friend cited will sometimes occur; but in so grave a case as that of murder, the accused, in our system, has always the benefit of the merest shadow of a doubt. And this suggests another consideration very germane to the question. The very fact that death punishment is more shocking than any other to the imagination, necessarily renders the Courts of Justice more scrupulous in requiring the fullest evidence of guilt. Even that which is the greatest objection to capital punishment, the impossibility of correcting an error once committed, must make, and does make, juries and Judges more careful in forming their opinion, and more jealous in their scrutiny of the evidence. If the substitution of penal servitude for death in cases of murder should cause any declaration in this conscientious scrupulosity, there would be a great evil to set against the real, but I hope rare, advantage of being able to make reparation to a condemned person who was afterwards discovered to be innocent. In order that the possibility of correction may be kept open wherever the chance of this sad contingency is more than infinitesimal, it is quite right that the Judge should recommend to the Crown a commutation of the sentence, not solely when the proof of guilt is open to the smallest suspicion, but whenever there remains anything unexplained and mysterious in the case, raising a desire for more light, or making it likely that further information may at some future time be obtained. I would also suggest that whenever the sentence is commuted the grounds of the commutation should, in some authentic form, be made known to the public. Thus much I willingly concede to my hon. Friend; but on the question of total abolition I am inclined to hope that the feeling of the country is not with him, and that the limitation of death punishment to the cases referred to in the Bill of last year will be generally considered sufficient. The mania which existed a short time ago for paring down all our punishments seems to have reached its limits, and not before it was time.

We were in danger of being left without any effectual punishment, except for small of offences. What was formerly our chief secondary punishment—transportation—before it was abolished, had become almost a reward. Penal servitude, the substitute for it, was becoming, to the classes who were principally subject to it, almost nominal, so comfortable did we make our prisons, and so easy had it become to get quickly out of them. Flogging—a most objectionable punishment in ordinary cases, but a particularly appropriate one for crimes of brutality, especially crimes against women—we would not hear of, except, to be sure, in the case of garrotters, for whose peculiar benefit we reestablished it in a hurry, immediately after a Member of Parliament

had been garrotted. With this exception, offences, even of an atrocious kind, against the person, as my hon. and learned Friend the Member for Oxford (Mr. Neate) well remarked, not only were, but still are, visited with penalties so ludicrously inadequate, as to be almost an encouragement to the crime. I think, Sir, that in the case of most offences, except those against property, there is more need of strengthening our punishments than of weakening them; and that severer sentences, with an apportionment of them to the different kinds of offences which shall approve itself better than at present to the moral sentiments of the community, are the kind of reform of which our penal system now stands in need. I shall therefore vote against the Amendment.

John Stuart Mill, *The Collected Works of John Stuart Mill, Volume XXVIII - Public and Parliamentary Speeches Part I November 1850–November 1868*, ed. John M. Robson and Bruce L. Kinzer (Toronto: University of Toronto Press, London: Routledge and Kegan Paul, 1988). http://oll.libertyfund.org /titles/262#lf0223-28_label_1257.

Reading 17-4   A Theory of Just Execution | Lloyd Steffen

Study Questions

As you read the excerpt, please consider the following questions:

1. What does Steffen mean when he suggests that the state should not ordinarily kill its own citizens?

2. What are the nine criteria that Steffen outlines for the justification of the death penalty?

3. Why do you think Steffen concludes that current execution practice does not live up to the standards of the theory?

Is capital punishment a justifiable use of lethal force against a citizen? Could it be an exception to the moral presumption that ordinarily states ought not to kill their citizens?

To answer this question, let us construct a theory of just execution on the *model* of just war. Let us say that in order for the moral presumption against capital punishment to be lifted, various criteria would have to be met, The tests or criteria that would constrain the state in the interests of justice yet conceivably permit a use of lethal force would be nine in number:

1. The execution power must be legitimately authorized.
2. Just cause for the use of the death penalty must be established.

3. The motivation for applying lethal punishment must be justice, not vengeance.
4. Executions must be administered fairly, without accidental features such as race, religion, class, or sex affecting administration of the death penalty.
5. The death penalty is to be used as an expression of cherished values, and it must not subvert the goods of life but promote and advance the value of life.
6. Executions ought not to be cruel.
7. Execution ought to be a last resort, with no other response to the offender except execution adequately serving the interests of justice.

8. Execution ought to restore a value equilibrium distorted and upset by the wrongdoing committed by the person on whom execution is visited.
9. Execution should be a response proportionate to the offense committed.

This natural law-based theory of just execution says this: if all nine of these criteria are satisfied, the presumption against the state using capital punishment as a legitimate mode of lethal force against a citizen can be lifted, and an execution can go forward as a morally justifiable act.

My own examination of the death penalty has led me to conclude that given the strict requirements of the theory, no execution in America as part of the execution system can possibly meet all of the criteria, so no execution is morally justified. What is significant about this statement is that it represents a morally moderate conclusion, since one can oppose capital punishment yet still affirm that there are situations where the state can act to kill a citizen and do so justifiably. The point is that execution does not happen to be a form of state killing that meets the test of moral justification. Just execution theory convinces me that where capital punishment is concerned, the presumption against the state killing its own citizens should remain in place and stay undisturbed.

If the practice of execution is evaluated in light of the moral guidelines of just execution theory, that theory will itself contribute to sounding the death knell of capital punishment. The practice will be exposed as unjust and unjustifiable, for the execution practice will necessarily fail to meet the stringent demands of reason and justice.

Lloyd Steffen, *Ethics and Experience* (Lanham, MD: Rowman and Littlefield, 2012).

Review Exercises

1. What essential characteristics of legal punishment distinguish it from other types of punishment?
2. What is the significance of the idea of decarceration, and what is the goal of critics of mass incarceration?
3. What is the difference between the mechanisms of deterrence and prevention? Given their meanings, does the death penalty prevent murders? Deter would-be killers? How?
4. If legal punishment works as a deterrent for murder, how does it work? For whom would it work? How might the death penalty be constructed so it has a deterrent effect?
5. How do the retributivist arguments differ from the deterrence arguments with regard to the death penalty?
6. Explain the idea of restorative justice and the possibility of alternatives to incarceration.
7. What is the *lex talionis* view of punishment? How does it differ from the proportional view?
8. Discuss the arguments for and against the identification of retributivism with revenge.
9. Why is the notion of responsibility critical to the retributivist view of legal punishment? How does the insanity defense fit in here?
10. What is the significance of racial disparities in thinking about the system of punishment?

Discussion Cases

1. Imprisonment. Steven's mother was imprisoned for drug possession with intent to distribute when he was just a baby. Steven grew up visiting his mother in prison. He has since become politically active and has been advocating on campus for alternatives to incarceration. Steven asks an acquaintance from his philosophy class, Janelle, to sign a petition that aims to provide more state funding for rehabilitation and drug treatment. Janelle is opposed to this. She says, "I have no sympathy for criminals. They get what they deserve." Steven replies, "But consider my mom's case. She's not really a bad person. She had a drug addiction problem, and she sold drugs to support her own habit. Her addiction could have been treated by rehab. But she ended up in prison, which meant pretty hard times for me and my sisters." "Well, she should have thought about that before she committed the crime," Janelle says. "If we start letting the drug dealers out of prison, all hell will break loose." Steven responds, "Well, growing up with a mom in prison was pretty much hell for me. And now that she's out of prison, she's having a hard time getting a job and an apartment. She feels like it's harder than ever to make ends meet, and I worry she's going to turn back to drugs or even dealing. How did her imprisonment help her or society?"

Whose side are you on? Is prison an appropriate punishment for nonviolent drug crimes? Does it matter whether a criminal has a family that is impacted by imprisonment? Why or why not?

2. Doctors and Execution. Dr. Kaur has been asked to serve as a consultant for the state as it is revising its protocol for use of lethal injection in executions. Dr. Kaur is not personally opposed to the death penalty, but she knows that the American Medical Association and other doctors' groups object to the involvement of doctors in executions.

These organizations argue that doctors take an oath to preserve life and thus should not be accessories to the taking of life. But Dr. Kaur thinks it is important to find humane ways to execute people. And she figures that it would be better if doctors, who understand how the lethal injection protocol works, were involved in the process. She agrees to work with the state as it reviews and revises its lethal injection protocol.

Is Dr. Kaur doing the right thing? Should doctors be involved in finding humane ways to execute convicted criminals? Why or why not?

3. Death Penalty Cases. Suppose you are a member of a congressional committee that is determining the types of crime that can be punishable by death. What kinds of cases, if any, would you put on the list? The killing and sexual assault of a minor? War crimes? Killings of police officers or public figures? Multiple murderers? Mob hits or other cases in which someone gives an order to kill but does not carry it out themselves? Others? What about the premeditated killing of a physically abusive spouse?

Why would you pick out just those crimes on your list as appropriately punished by death or as the worst crimes? What ethical values can you cite to justify your choices?

Knowledge Check Answer Key

1. **d.** It is false that the death penalty is illegal under U.S. federal law.

2. **c.** Desert is the most basic concern of retributivist theories of punishment.

3. **a.** Deterrence is the idea is most typically associated with utilitarian thinking about punishment.

4. **b.** Restorative justice emphasizes healing a broken community by reconciling victims and offenders.

18 Peace, Violence, and War

18.1 Explain the difference between positive and negative peace.

18.2 Describe the basic idea of realism.

18.3 Articulate arguments for and against pacifism and nonviolence.

18.4 Explain the distinction made in just war theory between *jus ad bellum* and *jus in bello*, as well as key terms such as *just cause, legitimate authority, discrimination*, and *noncombatant immunity*.

18.5 Evaluate current issues including the use of drones and targeted assassination, and the morality of terrorism and torture.

18.6 Explain the history and concept of war crimes and crimes against humanity and the problem of victor's justice.

18.7 Defend a thesis about the ethics of war, the idea of peace, and the problem of violence.

War in Ukraine

In February 2022, Russian troops crossed the border into Ukraine. The Russian invasion of 2022 followed up on a previous Russian attack in the Crimean Peninsula in 2014. Russia had offered a variety of justifications for these attacks: an effort to "de-Nazify" Ukraine, the need for Ukraine to remain neutral, historic claims about Ukraine belonging to Russia, and so on. Most of the world rejected these justifications, and the Russian invasion was widely condemned as a blatant act of aggres-

SOPA Images/Getty Images

sion. The United Nations General Assembly issued a proclamation deploring Russian aggression and demanding the immediate Russian withdrawal from Ukraine.[1] The United States accused Russian forces of committing war crimes, including deliberately destroying civilian targets.[2] And the International Criminal Court (ICC) began collecting testimony and investigating allegations of war crimes.[3] In response, European nations and the United States began supplying Ukraine with weapons and military aid. There were serious fears of escalation, as Russia had threatened to employ nuclear weapons.

The invasion of Ukraine prompted renewed conversations about the question of whether and when war can be justified. Pacifists condemn the folly of war and wonder why human beings continue to engage in warfare. They may see the war in Ukraine as the latest example of the general problem of war. But defenders of the just war theory argue that war can be justified, while also establishing moral guidelines that condemn war crimes. A third option in thinking about war is known as realism, which says that morality simply does not apply in thinking about war, since war is a political and historical occurrence based on power and domination. These points of view—pacifism, just war, and realism—can be employed in evaluating the Russian invasion and other wars.

What Do You Think?

1. What is the best moral response to wars such as Russia's invasion of Ukraine?

2. Did Russia commit war crimes (and what counts as a war crime)?

3. How can war crimes be prosecuted and punished?

4. How can we prevent future wars?

Introduction

18.1   Explain the difference between positive and negative peace.

The war in Ukraine is the latest example of traditional warfare involving nation-states and large troop formations engaged in pitched battles. This kind of warfare existed in the ancient world and became more and more destructive with the creation of mechanized weapons in the past couple of centuries. But violence is a more general phenomenon that involves other kinds of actions that are less dramatic than wars between nations. This includes domestic violence, criminality, terrorism, and targeted attacks. As we shall see in the "Current Issues" section of this chapter, there are a number of complexities to consider in thinking about all that is involved in Peace, Violence and War.

A significant question is "what counts as violence?" It seems fairly clear that mechanized warfare involving bombs, tanks, and artillery is violent. But what about cyberattacks? Are they violent? Such attacks can harm people, but a cyberattack on a computer network seems less violent than dropping a bomb. There is a continuum here that connects war to other forms of violence. And what about nonviolence? Some nonviolent tactics may seem harmful and coercive. Strikes, embargoes, and boycotts can harm people after all; and they intend

to force a change in policy. But are they violent? A definition of violence would seem to include the idea that violence is harmful. But are all harmful actions violent? Consider, for example, the moral question of spanking children—is that a kind of violence, or is it a justifiable form of punishment? As you will see, some of what we discuss here will overlap with issues discussed in the chapter on punishment and the death penalty. Important considerations here, as in that chapter, involve questions about the intentions guiding our actions and the consequences produced by them.

A related question is "what counts as peace?" Does peace require that we live in absolute harmony without disagreement? The idea of harmony—what we might call **positive peace**—is an unlikely outcome in the human world. Positive peace can be contrasted with **negative peace**, in which there is no overt or direct violence—no punching, shooting, or killing. But negative peace may be lacking. Is it really peaceful when there is no overt or direct violence—no punching, shooting, or killing—but there is inequality, poverty, oppression, and despair? Scholars of peace have appealed to the idea of **structural violence** to describe conditions in which there is inequality and oppression, despite the lack of any direct or overt violence. This connects to ideas such as structural racism, which we discussed in Chapter 13. But some critics claim that structural violence is only a metaphor and that there is an important difference between direct violence—killing, shooting, punching—and the indirect or structural violence of inequality, poverty, racism, and the like.[4]

As we begin, it is important to acknowledge that people disagree about these issues and that there are conceptual complexities that require careful philosophical attention. There are also questions to consider about what is effective. We should note that the question of whether violence or nonviolence can be effective is an empirical matter that requires substantial research. The issue of effectiveness is also comparative: it asks whether violence is more effective than nonviolence (and vice versa). The question of effectiveness is especially vexing with regard to large-scale violence and war, since this comparative judgment asks us to imagine what philosophers call "counterfactual" historical circumstances. What would have happened, for example, if Hitler had been assassinated in 1939? Would that minimal use of violence have prevented the horrors of the Holocaust and the Second World War? And if so, could we say, in general, that some minimal amount of violence can be justified if it is used to prevent further and worse violence? Of course, philosophers will ask "how would we know?" with regard to these kinds of counterfactual comparisons. And some non-consequentialist approaches to ethics are simply not interested in questions of effectiveness.

Moral Approaches to War and Peace

Most people assume that there is a right to use violence in self-defense. And many also think that we are *permitted* (some may say *required*) to use violence in defense of innocent children. The natural law tradition maintains that individuals have a right to life and liberty—and that violence can be employed to defend life and liberty against those who threaten it, including the life and liberty of defenseless and innocent others. A consequentialist argument could also be used here. More happiness will be produced for more people when such threats are eliminated. For a strict consequentialist, if the goal is to eliminate threats, the means employed are irrelevant. If war or other forms of violence work to produce good outcomes, they can be used as a tool to defend social welfare.

In this chapter, we discuss three alternative approaches to the justification of violence. One maintains

that violence is always wrong—this is **pacifism**. Another approach, often called **realism**, maintains that there are no *moral* limits on violence in warfare, even though there may be *pragmatic* or *strategic* reasons to limit violence. In the middle between these two extremes is an idea known as **just war theory**, which holds that violence can be justified when it is employed in limited and focused ways. The just war theory is grounded on a fundamental claim about the justification of violence in self-defense, and it extends this to a consideration of violence used in defense of others. While the just war theory is not directly applicable to the issue of domestic law enforcement, there are clear parallels between the idea that war can be justified and the idea that violence can be employed by armed guards to defend people against domestic criminals and terrorists. If we have a right to use violence to defend ourselves against those who would do violence to us, we can also delegate defense to others—the police or the army. Furthermore, we might claim that while we are entitled to defend ourselves against violence, we are also entitled (or even obliged) to defend innocent and defenseless others from those who would do them harm. Realists claim that in such circumstances, anything goes. We are entitled to pursue our own interests and defense in whatever way works. Pacifists have a difficult choice to make about the right to use violence

Figure 18-1 Violence and war continue to afflict us, while raising complicated moral questions.

Eric J. Tilford/ZUMAPRESS/Newscom

Table 18-1 Outline of Moral Approaches to War

	Pacifism	Just War	Realism
Thesis	War is never justified.	War can be justified.	Moral judgment does not apply to war.
Corollaries and Implications	Creative and active *nonviolence* should be employed.	War should be limited by the moral concerns of *jus ad bellum* and *jus in bello*; violations of these limits are "war crimes."	We should do what is necessary in war to achieve victory and maximize our interests; there can be no crimes in war.
Connections with Moral Theory	*Deontological* prohibition against killing; or *consequentialist* claim that war causes more harm than good and that nonviolence can produce good outcomes.	Combination of *deontological* concerns (e.g., right intention, noncombatant immunity) and *consequentialist* concerns (proportionality); connected with natural law tradition and need for defense of life, liberty, and other rights.	*Consequentialist* concern with victory can be focused on national self-interest or on the need for balance of power and international stability; tends to focus on cost–benefit analysis and pragmatic or strategic concerns.
Relevant Authors	Mohandas K. Gandhi; Jane Addams; Martin Luther King Jr.; Andrew Fitz-Gibbon; James Lawson	Thomas Aquinas; Michael Walzer; Larry May	Thucydides

in self-defense. But they tend to maintain that nonviolent alternatives should be developed and employed in a sustained and deliberate fashion.

As we mentioned above, the discussion of the justification of violence depends on the question of what violence is. Violence is generally thought of as the use of physical force to cause injury to another. Physical assaults, shooting, and bombing are examples. However, we typically do not say that someone who pushed another out of the way of an oncoming car had been violent or acted violently. This is because violence also implies infringement of another person's rights or autonomy in some way, as well as the intent to do harm. Violence also has the sense of something intense or extreme. A small injury to another may not be considered an act of violence. Whether some sports—for example, football—can be considered violent games is something to think about. But it seems clear that the destruction and harm of war is violent. The three moral approaches to thinking about the justification of

violence—realism, pacifism, and the just war theory—are primarily focused on the morality of war, which may be defined as sustained and organized political violence. But the arguments presented here can be expanded and applied to the justification of other sorts of violence (e.g., as Lloyd Steffen did in his discussion of the death penalty in Chapter 17). To get a better sense of these implications, let's turn to a more detailed exposition of realism, pacifism, and just war theory.

Realism

18.2 Describe the basic idea of realism.

Realism is the idea that in the "real world" of social and political life, violence is one tool among others to be employed strategically to get things done. Realists tend to be consequentialists, who are primarily focused on outcomes and results—and who are not as concerned with the morality of the means employed to achieve such results. Realism is often characterized as holding an "anything goes" approach to the question of violence. The idea of realism has roots in the thinking of Thucydides, the ancient Greek historian of the Peloponnesian War. In his account of a battle between the Athenians and the inhabitants of the island of Melos, Thucydides describes an attempted negotiation prior to the battle. The Athenians argue that since they have the more powerful military, the Melians ought to surrender, since it is useless for them to fight. The Athenians explain that the stronger party does whatever it can get away with, while the weaker party is prudent to acquiesce. The Athenians go on to say that the strong sometimes have to use violence to establish their supremacy and as a warning against those who might challenge them. The Melians do not submit to the Athenian threat. The Athenians attack, killing or enslaving all of the inhabitants of the island of Melos. One moral of this story is that it is better to be strong than to be weak. Another takeaway is that there may be no limits in war. From this perspective, war is understood as an existential struggle for supremacy. Perhaps it is possible to achieve a balance of power between equal powers. But if another power is threatening you, the realist would argue that in a life-or-death struggle it is necessary to do whatever it takes to defend against the threat of annihilation. Realists are opposed to the idea that there are inherent or intrinsic moral limits on the justification of violence. Indeed, they may argue that adherence to limitations on violence can make a nation look weak and ineffectual and produce more harm than good.

Realism is sometimes related to "militarism," a social and ethical system that celebrates martial power and military might. Some militarists argue that the highest glory is to be found in military adventures—an idea with a deep history that goes back to Achilles, the warrior hero in Homer's *Iliad*. Achilles and other heroes in warrior cultures view warfare as a test of manhood, which produces virtues such as loyalty, courage, and steadfastness (see Chapter 8's discussion of virtue). Some continue to celebrate this spirit of masculine sacrifice and the glory of military service. But in modern culture, we have also expanded the definition of service and sacrifice to include gender-neutral virtues: it is not manhood that is tested but dedication and valor. Indeed,

in the American military, women have been active participants for decades, and a recent policy change allows women to serve in combat.

Critics of militarism argue that there should be nonviolent ways to produce the same sorts of virtues. In his essay "The Moral Equivalent of War," American pragmatist philosopher William James called for a substitute for war. He wanted to find a way to develop virtues such as heroism and loyalty without the destruction of armed conflict.[5] But James was generally an opponent of war—especially the expansive American war in the Philippine islands. He and other philosophers—including the American feminist and pacifist author Jane Addams—were actively involved in the antiwar movement during the early part of the twentieth century.

Realists generally deny that moral ideas can be applied in warfare or that moral concerns should inhibit us from doing what is necessary to achieve victory. If we must bomb civilians or use torture to win a war, then that is what we must do. But realists are not simply bloodthirsty. They might agree that there are good pragmatic reasons to limit the use of violence. Violence can provoke a backlash (as enemies fight harder and unite against a dominant power). For realists, the central question is about what works. If terror bombing works, then it should be used, but if it does not work, it should be avoided. Realists also have to consider the costs and benefits of warfare. War can be expensive. Realists do not advocate war at any cost. Instead, realists want to be strategic about the use of violence. It is imprudent to get involved in battles that cannot be won or that are so costly that they leave us in a weakened state. Note here that realism is focused on the question of prudence, strategy, and pragmatism—it is a consequentialist approach that is not concerned with moral questions about the means employed. From a utilitarian perspective, war may be employed as a way of pursuing the greatest happiness for the greatest number of those living within a polity. (Note that such a use of the utilitarian calculus ignores suffering on the other side.) Realism may also be criticized as being amoral, as when it simply denies that morality applies in the context of war. This version of realism will hold that "all's fair in love and war" or that "war is hell"—both clichés point in the direction of the realist idea that in war there is no morality at all.

Pacifism

18.3   Articulate arguments for and against pacifism and nonviolence.

Pacifism lies on the opposite end of the spectrum from realism. While extreme realists argue that there are no moral limits in warfare, extreme pacifists argue that war is always wrong. Pacifism is often grounded in a deontological claim that focuses on the morality of killing. Deontological pacifists will maintain that there is an absolute moral rule against killing. Pacifism is also grounded in a more positive commitment to active nonviolence. Some forms of pacifism extend the idea of nonviolence in a very general way that condemns violence done to sentient beings in general, including nonhuman animals. Other forms of pacifism are narrowly focused on a condemnation of war as the most horrible form of violence, which must be opposed. Not all pacifists oppose the use of all types of force. After all, there are nonphysical means of exerting force, and even nonviolent social protest is a way of mobilizing social force. One can think of there being degrees of pacifism—that is, in terms of the degree and type of force thought acceptable. Some pacifists may reluctantly allow the use of physical and even lethal physical force when it is absolutely necessary, such as to defend oneself.

Pacifists generally maintain that nonviolent alternatives to violence are preferable and should be actively pursued in a creative and sustained fashion. As mentioned above, William James and Jane Addams were important American thinkers who were opposed to war. Jane Addams helped found the Women's Peace Party as part of her opposition to World War I (the organization evolved into the Women's International League for Peace and Freedom, which is still active today). Addams was an advocate for women's rights who also devoted herself to working on behalf of immigrants and the poor. She explained in 1917 (during the First World War) that pacifism is not passive or isolationist. Rather, Addams's work shows that pacifism includes an active commitment to create a more just international order. She said,

With visions of international justice filling our minds, pacifists are always a little startled when those who insist that justice can only be established by war accuse us of caring for peace, irrespective of justice. Many of the pacifists in their individual and corporate capacity have long striven for social and political justice with a fervor perhaps equal to that employed by the advocates of force, and we realize that a sense of justice has become the keynote to the best political and social activity in this generation. Although this ruling passion for juster relations between man and man, group and group, or between nation and nation, is not without its sterner aspects, among those who dream of a wider social justice throughout the world there has developed a conviction that justice between men or between nations can be achieved only through understanding and fellowship, and that a finely tempered sense of justice, which alone is of any service in modern civilization, cannot be secured in the storm and stress of war.[6]

Addams was influenced by Leo Tolstoy, the Russian novelist who also had an influence on Mohandas K. Gandhi, the great Indian proponent of nonviolent

Figure 18-2 Jane Addams (1860–1935) was an important peace activist.

Library of Congress Prints and Photographs Division Washington, D.C. [LC-US262-13484]

protest. Gandhi put his commitment to nonviolence to work in his effort to force the British out of India. He called his method of nonviolent protest *satyagraha*, which means "love force" or "truth force." This method was adopted by Martin Luther King Jr., James Lawson, and others working in the American Civil Rights Movement of the 1950s and '60s. Gandhi, King, and Lawson were actively engaged in trying to change the world by using nonviolent social protest, including nonviolent civil disobedience. While King is best known as a civil rights activist, he was also a critic of war. He opposed the Vietnam War, for example, arguing that using war to settle differences is neither just nor wise.[7]

The reasons given in support of pacifism vary. Jane Addams based her opposition to war in her deep commitment to justice, her concern for international solidarity, and her sense that war often causes the most suffering for the poor and the dispossessed. She also thought there was a connection between pacifism and the empowerment of women, since it was mothers and wives who were asked to sacrifice their sons and husbands in the war effort. She explained that women often experienced a call "to defend those at the bottom of society who, irrespective of the victory or defeat of any army, are ever oppressed and overburdened." She continued: "The suffering mothers of the disinherited feel the stirring of the old impulse to protect and cherish their unfortunate children, and women's haunting memories instinctively challenge war as the implacable enemy of their age-long undertaking."[8]

Addams's arguments against war are grounded in claims about ethics, justice, and feminism. They are not connected to any specific religious argument. Others ground pacifism and their commitment to nonviolence in religious claims. Gandhi was dedicated to the idea of *ahimsa* (Sanskrit for nonviolence), which is a common value in South Asian traditions such as Hinduism, Buddhism, and Jainism. In a text from 1916, Gandhi explain his understanding of *ahimsa* as follows:

Literally speaking, *ahimsa* means non-killing. But to me it has a world of meaning and takes me into realms much higher, infinitely higher, than the realm to which I would go, if I merely understood by *ahimsa* non-killing. *Ahimsa* really means that you may not offend anybody, you may not harbor an uncharitable thought even in connection with one who may consider himself to be your enemy. Pray notice the guarded nature of this thought; I do not say "whom you consider to be your enemy," but "who may consider himself to be your enemy." For one who follows the doctrine of ahimsa, there is no room for an enemy; he denies the existence of an enemy. But there are people who consider themselves to be his enemies, and he cannot help that circumstance. So, it is held that we may not harbor an evil thought even in connection with such persons. If we return blow for blow, we depart from the doctrine of *ahimsa*.[9]

King developed his ideas about nonviolence from reading Gandhi. But as a Baptist minister, he also adopted a pacifist interpretation of the Christian Gospels, an interpretation that is shared by such groups as Mennonites and Quakers. These Christians view Jesus as a pacifist who maintained (in the Sermon on the Mount found in the Gospel of Matthew 5, e.g.,) that peacemakers are blessed, that one should not return evil for evil, and that we should love even our enemies.

King worked closely with James Lawson, another African American Christian leader, who helped to train civil rights protestors in the techniques of nonviolent protest. In the 1950s, Lawson went to prison as a conscientious objector during the Korean War. During the 1960s, he led the movement of sit-ins at segregated lunch counters. And he helped draft the founding document of the Student Nonviolent Coordinating Committee (SNCC), which stated:

Nonviolence as it grows from the Judeo-Christian tradition seeks a social order of justice permeated by love. Integration of human endeavor represents the crucial first step towards such a society. Through nonviolence, courage displaces fear; love transforms hate. Acceptance dissipates prejudice; hope ends despair. Peace dominates war; faith reconciles doubt. Mutual regard cancels enmity. Justice for all overcomes injustice. The redemptive community supersedes systems of gross social immorality.[10]

Lawson has continued to work, organizing nonviolent social movements. And he has offered a positive assessment of the nonviolent work of the Black Lives Matter movement (see reading excerpt from Lawson).

Nonreligious arguments for pacifism may be derived more generally from consequentialist considerations. Consequentialist pacifists believe that nonviolent means work better than violence to produce social goods. Violence does more harm than good, they argue, because violence begets violence. How can we determine whether or not this is true? We can look to see whether historical examples support the generalization. We also can inquire whether this may result from something in human nature. Are we overly prone to violence and bloodlust? Are we able to restrain ourselves when we turn to war? Our judgments will then depend on adequate factual assessments. We should note that it is difficult to weigh the benefits and costs of war—because we would have to engage in counterfactual speculation, asking what would have happened if we had (or had not) gone to war. War does cause substantial damage; however, it is an open question whether the damage of war is worse than the damage that would result if we did not use war to respond to aggressive dictators or genocidal regimes.

Most pacifists argue that killing is wrong. But critics of this view contend that if killing is wrong, there may be times when we need to kill to prevent killing from occurring. Consider, for example, whether it is justifiable to kill those who threaten the innocent. Should an exception to the rule against killing be made to prevent such killing? Would it be acceptable to kill in self-defense? Or in defense of innocent children, such as the children killed during attacks on schools? Or in defense of those who are being slaughtered by genocidal or racist governments? Pacifists must address the criticism that it seems inconsistent to hold that life is of the highest value and yet not be willing to use force to defend it. One way they might address this objection is to clarify that pacifism is not passive—pacifists do not advocate doing nothing in response to atrocity. Rather, they can be committed to active, creative, and sustained efforts to help people and defend the innocent, so long as such efforts do not involve killing. Pacifists also argue that the problem of war is that innocent people are accidentally killed even by the "good guys" and that it is very difficult to focus the destructive power of war in a way that does not harm the innocent.

Just War Theory

18.4 Explain the distinction made in just war theory between *jus ad bellum* and *jus in bello*, as well as key terms such as *just cause, legitimate authority, discrimination*, and *noncombatant immunity*.

Intermediate between pacifism and realism is the idea that the use of force, including military force, is justified in limited and specific circumstances. The just war theory attempts to clarify when it is justifiable to resort to the use of lethal force. The just war approach is more or less the mainstream theory of the American military and political system. While some critics may argue that American military strategy includes a realist element—that the United States is engaged in asserting force and displaying strength around the globe—the rhetoric used to explain American military power is generally grounded in just war language. President Barack Obama defended this idea when he delivered his Nobel Peace Prize acceptance speech. According to Obama, philosophers and theologians developed the just war idea over time as they attempted to find moral language to criticize and limit the destructive power of war. "The concept of a 'just war' emerged, suggesting that war is justified only when certain conditions were met: if it is waged as a last resort or in self-defense; if the force used is proportional; and if, whenever possible, civilians are spared from violence."[11]

As Obama noted, the just war theory is not new. Indeed, it has a long history. Its origins can be traced to the writings of Augustine, one of the ancient fathers of the Catholic Church. Augustine wanted to reconcile traditional Christian views about the immorality of violence with the necessity of defending the Roman Empire from invading forces.[12] He asked what one should do if one sees an individual attacking an innocent, defenseless victim. His response was that one should intervene and do whatever is necessary (but only so much as was necessary) to protect the victim, even up to the point of killing the aggressor. Further developments of the theory were provided by Thomas Aquinas, who provides a natural law justification of the violence used in self-defense. Medieval codes of chivalry also have something in common with just war ideas. But the theory gets its most systematic exposition in the work of early modern theologians and jurists such as Francisco de Vitoria, Francisco Suárez, and Hugo Grotius. We discussed Vitoria in Chapter 7 in association with the natural law theory. In the sixteenth century, Vitoria applied just war concepts and other natural law principles to the question of whether a war against the Indigenous people of the Americas would be justified. He argued that "the law of peoples" required that the Native Americans should treat the Spanish with hospitality. But if the Spanish were attacked, they had the right to fight in defense. Some critics see this as a hypocritical and self-serving, although the idea of fighting in self-defense is regarded as a fundamental principle. This principle and the just war theory were further elucidated by Suárez, another Spanish thinker who was active in the sixteenth and seventeenth centuries. Suárez explained that war is not evil or forbidden. He claimed that war is not opposed to peace; rather, war is opposed to an unjust peace. And he further explained that war is not opposed to the Christian idea of love. He wrote, "war is not opposed to the love of one's enemies; for whoever wages war honorably hates, not individuals, but the actions which he justly punishes."[13] Grotius was a Dutch author of the seventeenth century, who argued that war was justified in a system of international law, as a way of restoring and preserving justice—and peace. As Grotius stated at the beginning of his book *The Rights of War and Peace*, "war is undertaken for the sake of peace . . . and war itself will lead us to peace as its proper end."[14] These basic ideas about justice in war have been refined by more contemporary thinkers. In more recent times, just war ideas have been instituted in international law, which asserts the right of a nation to defend itself against aggression while also calling for protections for civilians and prisoners of war. These ideas can be found in international conventions, as well as in the Charter of the United Nations and other treaties signed by world powers.

There is general agreement that just war theory includes two basic areas: principles that would have to be satisfied for a nation to be justified in using military force, or initiating a war; and principles governing the conduct of the military action or war itself. These have

been given the Latin names of *jus ad bellum* (the justness of going to war) and *jus in bello* (justness in war).

Jus Ad Bellum

The most important question of the just war theory is whether there is a justification for taking up arms. This is a primary focus of *jus ad bellum*. The question of the justification of war (just cause) is connected to a number of other considerations including who has the right to declare war, whether war is a proportionate response, whether nonviolence might be effective, and what kinds of intentions guide the resort to war. We discuss these briefly here.

Just Cause To use force against another nation, there must be a serious reason to justify it. Defense of one's territory against an invader is a prime example of a just cause for war. Nations have the right to defend themselves against aggression. In this regard, most just war theorists will consider the Ukrainian response to the Russian invasion as a clear case of justified war. Michael Walzer, an important defender of just war theory, wrote soon after the Russian invasion, "Russia's invasion of Ukraine is illegal under international law, and it is unjust according to every version of just war theory."[15] The Ukrainian response to Russian aggression is thus justified as a response to aggression.

The just cause idea does not permit war for minor wrongs or to respond to an insult. But what about wars that are engaged in order to defend human rights or protect civilians against ethnic cleansing or genocide? A newly developing concept of just cause includes the idea of intervening to prevent another nation from harming its own population. This idea is known as humanitarian intervention—the idea of using limited military force for humanitarian purposes. The United Nations has expanded the idea recently under the concept of a "responsibility to protect" (sometimes called "R2P"). The R2P idea holds that the international community has a responsibility to intervene to protect people from their own government and to prevent war crimes and crimes against humanity (which we discuss in more detail later in this chapter).

Other causes for war have been proposed. Could war be employed to prevent the spread of communism, to rid another country of a despotic leader, to prevent a nation from obtaining nuclear weapons, or to protect the world's oil supply? These may be viewed as cases of self-defense, using a broad definition of what is in a nation's vital interest. But the just war theory in general attempts to limit the causes of war.

One contentious issue related to just cause is the justification of preventive and preemptive strikes. If a neighboring nation is about to invade one's territory, preemptive defense against threatened aggression would seem to be a just response. A nation need not wait to be attacked when it knows an invasion is impending. The principle of "only if attacked first" may be too strict. Traditionally, preemptive attacks were thought to be justified if an attack was *imminent*. However, in the age of terrorists with weapons of mass destruction or states that possess these weapons, some have argued that to wait until an attack is imminent is to wait too long. This logic has been employed to justify a variety of attacks. For example, Israel has attacked weapons sites in Iraq (in 1981) and in Syria in more recent years in an effort to prevent its enemies from developing deadly weapons. The 2003 U.S. invasion of Iraq was justified as an attempt to prevent Iraq from using, developing, and disseminating weapons of mass destruction. While some just war theorists supported this invasion, others argued that preventive war was an immoral use of war.[16] The danger of preventive war is that it can cause an escalation in violence, as each side may feel justified in attacking first.

Legitimate Authority If we assume that we can agree on the question of what counts as a just cause for war, another concern is the question of who has the authority to declare war. Traditionally, it was thought to be the sovereign power that had the right to declare war. In the world of kings and queens, it was the monarch who declared war. In democracies, however, we presume that the power to declare war rests in the hands of the duly elected government. In the United States, there has been some concern about where the power to declare war resides: in Congress or in the president. The Constitution (Article I, Section 8, Clause 11) stipulates that the power to declare war rests in the hands of the Congress. However, in recent decades, the president has sent military forces into battle without explicit declarations of war. Leaving aside this constitutional question,

we might wonder whether it makes sense for the civilian leadership to declare war. Wouldn't it be wiser to let the military decide when and where to fight? After all, soldiers are the experts in war. However, civilian control of the military is a central idea for democratic nations, which believe that warfare must be approved by the people through duly elected representatives. This can lead to a difficulty, however, as military priorities may conflict with the concerns of the civilian leadership.

The issue of legitimate authority points toward other problems. Who has a claim to legitimate authority in a civil war or a revolution? That's a difficult question to answer. Another problem has to do with the development of international institutions such as the United Nations. Should the United States defer to the judgments of the UN Security Council about wars and interventions? Or do the United States and other nations have the right to "go it alone" when it comes to war? In 2004, the secretary-general of the United Nations, Kofi Annan, declared that the United States had violated the UN Charter by going to war against Iraq and that the war was illegal.[17] But the United States maintained that it had a moral right to go to war without UN approval. The issue of legitimate authority remains an important concern for thinking about the justification of war.

Proportionality Not only must the cause be just, according to the theory, but also the probable good to be produced by the intervention must outweigh the likely evil that the war will cause. Before engaging in warfare, we should consider the probable costs and benefits and compare them with the probable costs and benefits of doing something else or of doing nothing. Involved in this utilitarian calculation are two elements: one assesses the likely costs and benefits, and the other weighs their relative value. The first requires historical and empirical information, whereas the second involves ethical evaluations. In making such evaluations, we might well compare lives that are likely to be saved with lives lost, for example. But how do we compare the value of freedom and self-determination, or a way of life with the value of a life itself? How do we factor in the long-term impacts of war, including the possibility of post-traumatic stress for soldiers and civilians? Moreover, there is the difficulty of assessing costs and benefits with regard to a complex and chaotic activity such as fighting a war.

Last Resort The just war theory holds that war should be a last resort. Military interventions are extremely costly in terms of suffering, loss of life, and other destruction, so other means must be considered first. They need not all be tried first, for some will be judged useless beforehand. However, nonviolent means should be attempted, at least those that are judged to have a chance of achieving the goal specified by the just cause. Negotiations, threats, and boycotts are examples of such means. When is enough finally enough? When have these measures been given sufficient trial? There is always something more that could be tried. This is a matter of prudential judgment and therefore always uncertain.[18]

Right Intention Military action should be directed to the goal set by the cause and to the eventual goal of peace. Thus, wars fought to satisfy hatred and bloodlust or to obtain wealth are unjustified. The focus on intentions is a deontological element in the *jus ad bellum* consideration. Recall that Kant's deontological theory focused on the intention behind an act (what Kant called the "good will" and the nature of the maxims of action). In thinking about going to war, this principle would remind us that we ought to intend good things even as we employ violent means. The right intention principle seems to imply that there should be no gratuitous cruelty such as would follow from malicious intentions. This moves us into discussion of the conduct of a war, the second area covered by the principles of just war theory.

Jus In Bello

Even if a war were fought for a just cause and by a legitimate authority, with the prospect of achieving more good than harm, as a last resort only, and with the proper intention, it still would not be fully just if it were not conducted justly or in accordance with certain principles or moral guidelines. The *jus in bello* part of the just war theory consists of several principles.

Proportionality The principle of proportionality stipulates that in the conduct of the conflict, violence should be focused on limited objectives. No more force than necessary should be used. And the force or means used should be proportionate to the importance of the particular objective for the cause as a whole. This principle is obviously similar to the principle of proportionality discussed previously in thinking about *jus ad bellum*; however, within the *jus in bello* consideration of proportionality, the cost–benefit analysis is focused on limited war aims and not on the question of the war itself.

Discrimination Just warriors should not intentionally attack noncombatants and nonmilitary targets. While this principle sounds straightforward, there are complex issues to sort out in terms of what counts as a nonmilitary target or who is a noncombatant. Are roads, bridges, and hospitals that are used in the war effort military targets? The general consensus is that the roads and bridges are targets if they contribute directly and in significant ways to the military effort, but that hospitals are not legitimate targets. The principle to be used in making this distinction is the same for the people as for the things. Those people who contribute directly are combatants, and those who do not are not combatants. There is some vagueness here. Is a soldier at home on leave a legitimate target? One writer suggests that persons who are engaged in doing what they do ordinarily as persons are noncombatants, while those who perform their functions specifically for the war effort are combatants.[19] Thus, those who grow and provide food would be noncombatants, whereas those who make or transport the military equipment would be combatants.

Note, too, that although we also hear the term *innocent civilians* in such discussions, it is noncombatants who are supposed to be out of the fight and not people who are judged on some grounds to be "innocent" in a deeper moral sense. Soldiers fighting unwillingly might be thought to be innocent but are nevertheless combatants. Those behind the lines spending time verbally supporting the cause are not totally innocent, yet they are noncombatants. The danger of using the term *innocents* in place of *noncombatants* is that it also allows some to say that no one living in a certain country is immune because they are all supporters of their country and so not innocent. However, this is contrary to the traditional understanding of the principle of discrimination.

One way of describing the discrimination principle is to say that noncombatants should have immunity from harm. The idea of *noncombatant immunity* says that noncombatants should not be intentionally harmed. Combatants are not immune because they are a threat. Thus, when someone is not or is no longer a threat, as when they have surrendered or are incapacitated by injury, they are not to be regarded as legitimate targets. The discrimination principle does not require that no noncombatants be injured or killed, but only that they not be the direct targets of attack. Although directly targeting and killing civilians may have a positive effect on a desired outcome, this would not be justified. The principle of discrimination is a deontological principle that stipulates a duty not to deliberately target noncombatants.

Nonetheless, some noncombatants are harmed in modern warfare—as bombs go astray and battles rage within cities. Noncombatant harms can be permitted by application of the *principle of double effect*. Noncombatant harms can be permitted if they are the foreseen but unintended and accidental result of a legitimate war aim. Not only must the noncombatants not be directly targeted but also the number of them likely to be injured when a target is attacked must not be disproportionately great compared to the significance of the target. Thus if a bomb goes astray and kills some children, this could be permitted by the principle of double effect if the intended target was a legitimate one, if the numbers harmed were minimal, and if the death of the children was not directly intended. In such a case, these children would be described as *collateral damage*, that is, as harms that are accidental and unintended.

Intrinsically Evil Means A final concern of *jus in bello* is a strictly deontological prohibition on the use of means that are viewed as being evil in themselves (or *mala in se*, as this is expressed in Latin). One obvious inherently evil act is rape. Rape has long been a weapon of war, employed by conquering armies as a way of degrading and terrorizing a conquered people. But just warriors ought not engage in rape. We should also prohibit slavery as a

► **Knowledge Check**   Answers appear at the end of the chapter.

1. What best explains the difference between positive and negative peace?

    a. Positive peace is focused on supporting war, while negative peace opposes war.

    b. Positive peace involves social harmony, while negative peace is the absence of overt violence.

    c. Positive peace creates structural violence, while negative peace is critical of structural violence.

    d. Positive peace exists when there is no war, while negative peace can exist within war.

2. What is *satyagraha*?

    a. This is a synonym for positive peace, used by Tolstoy in his novels.

    b. This is the Greek word used by Thucydides in describing the power of the Athenians.

    c. It is a concept employed by just war theorists in discussing noncombatant immunity.

    d. It means love force and is a method of nonviolent protest.

3. Which of the following is NOT a concern of *jus ad bellum*?

    a. Ensuring there is a just cause for war

    b. Only using force as a last resort

    c. Making sure that war is fought with the right intention

    d. Using war to produce a just and lasting peace

4. How is the idea of "double effect" employed in thinking about *jus in bello*?

    a. It is used to allow for collateral damage.

    b. It is employed to condemn the use of intrinsically evil actions.

    c. It is used to help calculate a judgment about proportionality.

    d. It is employed by legitimate authorities to justify their power.

means of warfare—for example, forcing captured enemies to engage in hard labor or using them as human shields. We might also think that the use of poisons—including poison gas—is intrinsically wrong. And most just war accounts maintain that torture is intrinsically wrong, although (as we shall see) in recent years there has been an open debate about the morality of torture in American war-making. To say that these things are wrong in themselves creates a deontological prohibition on such weapons and actions: just warriors may not use such weapons even if they might work to produce good outcomes.

According to just war theory, then, for a war or military intervention to be justified, certain conditions for going to war must be satisfied, and the conduct in the war must follow certain principles or moral guidelines. We could say that if any of the principles are violated, a war is unjust; or we could say that it was unjust in this regard but not in some other aspects. Just war ideas have become part of national and international law, including the U.S. Army Rules for Land Warfare and the UN Charter. Its principles appeal to common human reason and both consequentialist and non-consequentialist concerns.

Realists maintain that the moral limits imposed by the just war theory can get in the way of victory and the goal of establishing power and supremacy. Pacifists maintain that the just war theory is too permissive. They might reject, for example, the way that the doctrine of double effect allows noncombatants to be harmed. To evaluate realism, pacifism, and the just war theory, you must think about how you evaluate the various consequentialist and deontological principles and ideas appealed to by each approach.

Current Issues

18.5 Evaluate current issues including the use of drones and targeted assassination, and the morality of terrorism and torture.

Terrorism, Mass Shootings, and the War on Terrorism

The moral perspectives discussed above might be applied to the issue of terrorism as follows. Terrorism would be condemned by pacifists, along with other acts

of killing. Just war theory would condemn terrorism that deliberately kills noncombatants as violating the *jus in bello* principle of discrimination. Realists may argue that terrorism is acceptable if it works as a strategy.

We can describe an act of violence as terrorism when this violent act causes or intends to cause widespread terror. Usually, this terrifying act has a political goal (although there may be nihilistic terrorists who blow up things just for fun). Some maintain that terrorism is a politically loaded term, employed to denigrate one's enemies. Some say that one person's terrorist is another person's freedom fighter. But the common element in a definition of terrorism is the use of attacks on noncombatants. The first known use of the term *terrorism* was during the French Revolution for those who, like Maximilien Robespierre, used violence *on behalf* of a state. Only later was the term used to categorize violence *against* a state. The U.S. Code of Justice (Title 22, section 2656f(d)) defines terrorism as "premeditated, politically motivated violence perpetrated against noncombatant targets by subnational groups or clandestine agents, usually intended to influence an audience." The FBI defines terrorism as "the unlawful use of force or violence against persons or property to intimidate or coerce a government, the civilian population, or any segment thereof, in furtherance of political or social objectives."[20]

By combining these definitions, we see that terrorism is, first of all, a particular kind of violence with particular aims and goals. The more immediate goal is to create fear. This is why civilians simply going about their daily routines are targeted at random. The more distant goals vary. Terrorists may use such violence to achieve some political goal such as independence from a larger national unit or to fight back against occupying armies or to protest against particular injustices. A terrorist may be motivated by religious or political ideology. Although after the terrorist attacks of September 11, 2001, public attention was often focused on Islamic militants employing terror tactics, it is important to note that terrorism can be employed by people from a variety of religions, and it can be used by secularly minded political groups. Christians have employed terror tactics (as in the struggles in Northern Ireland or the anti-apartheid violence in South Africa). And Marxist revolutionaries have employed terrorism in pursuit of their goals. One could argue that the Ku Klux Klan used terrorism to subjugate the Black population in the American South. And Black militants in the 1960s advocated terrorism against White supremacy. One could argue that Native Americans used terrorism against the White settlers of the American West. And one could argue that colonial powers used terror tactics against Indigenous communities. And so on. Any time there is an attempt to manipulate a political situation by applying indiscriminate force, it is possible that there is terrorism. We might even suspect that the use of firebombing and atomic bombing during the Second World War was a sort of terrorism—terror bombing that aimed to force the enemy to surrender by indiscriminately bombing civilian population centers.

Terrorists seem to lack the ability to empathize with the innocent victims of their attacks. Terrorists may demonize entire nations and peoples, killing out of hatred. But they may also be engaged in a consequentialist calculation that has much in common with the thinking of realism. From a realist perspective, there is nothing inherently wrong with targeting innocent civilians for attack. And if one is on the losing end of a military conflict, it might be necessary to resort to terror attacks as a way of continuing the fight. Those who resort to terror may be motivated by political or religious ideology. But they may also feel they have no other way to influence the state of affairs than to resort to terrorism.

In evaluating terrorism, we might reject it outright as a form of unjustified killing. From this standpoint, terrorism is like murder—by definition wrong. Terrorism would be condemned in this way by pacifists, who maintain that all violence is wrong. Pacifists would also consider a war against terrorism wrong, since they believe that war is wrong. They may also view terrorism as an example of what is wrong with war and violence—it tends to spread to the deliberate targeting of noncombatants. Moreover, they might point out that terrorism produces backlash and escalation, which only tends to beget more violence.

Could there be an ethical justification of terrorism? The reasoning that supports terrorism is most often basically consequentialist. This is connected with the realist approach to the justification of violence, which holds that the end justifies the means. If one supported this type of reasoning, one would want to know whether, in fact, the benefits outweighed the harm and suffering caused by the means. One could do empirical studies to see whether terrorism actually produces desired outcomes. Did the terror bombing of Japan during World War II result in the surrender of the Japanese? Did the September 11 attacks bring down the U.S. government or change its international behavior? Did terror attacks on American military forces in Iraq and Afghanistan lead Americans to retreat? These sorts of questions point to the primary realist concern, which is the prudential and strategic application of power.

One might, however, question the consequentialist nature of realist reasoning by appealing to the just war theory's ideas about noncombatant immunity and discrimination. Indiscriminate violence can be rejected on realist grounds as simply being an inefficient use of power and resources. But in the just war tradition, the principle of discrimination is a non-consequentialist or deontological prohibition. Noncombatants cannot be intentionally or directly targeted, their deaths being used to send a message to others (no matter the importance of justification of the cause for which we are fighting). International law also condemns terrorism. The Geneva convention, including the fourth (adopted in 1949), enunciated principles that aim to protect civilian populations from the worst effects of war. These conventions hold that civilians should not be directly attacked. From the standpoint of international law and the just war theory, terrorism is a war crime.

As mentioned, terrorism became a topic of public concern after September 11, 2001. On that day, Al-Qaeda terrorists crashed loaded passenger jets into the World Trade Center in New York, the Pentagon in Washington, D.C., and a field near Shanksville, Pennsylvania, killing nearly three thousand people. The U.S. administration of President George W. Bush came to call its response to these attacks "the war on terrorism." This war began as the United States and its allies invaded Afghanistan in late 2001, in an unsuccessful effort to capture or kill the leadership of the Al-Qaeda terrorist group, including Osama bin Laden. Afghanistan was viewed by most of the international community both as a failed state being ruled by an extremist religious faction—the

Taliban—and as the haven from which Al-Qaeda masterminded the September 11 attacks. Within two years, another front in the war on terrorism opened in Iraq, as the United States invaded the country in March 2003. Although Iraq had nothing to do with the September 11 terrorist attacks, President George W. Bush argued that the leader of Iraq, Saddam Hussein, was a malicious dictator who was a threat to stability in the region, that he had used chemical weapons against his own people, and—quite controversially—that he was currently stockpiling other weapons of mass destruction, or WMDs. After the U.S. invasion of Iraq, no such weapons were ever found, but the country did descend into a bloody and destructive civil war, which has continued to destabilize the region. During the past twenty years, the war on terror led to other American military attacks in a number of other countries including Libya, Yemen, Syria, and Pakistan. These attacks were often fought by drone aircraft and special operations forces, which target specific terrorists or terrorist groups.

In addition to hunting down and killing terrorist targets, American forces were employed on the ground in Afghanistan in an effort at nation-building and were engaged in ongoing hostilities with local fighters affiliated with the Taliban, the group that had ruled Afghanistan prior to the American invasion in 2001. In 2021, on the twentieth anniversary of the September 11 attacks, the United States withdrew its troops from Afghanistan. The Taliban swept quickly back into power. Critics of war argued that this return to the *status quo ante* (the state of affairs before the war) showed the futility of war and of using military power to force regime change and build democracy. But defenders of the war in Afghanistan saw the U.S. withdrawal as a failure of nerve in what they viewed as a historically necessary and morally justified use of military force.

Terrorism remains an issue of grave concern throughout the world. But is war the answer? The casualties in the war on terrorism are significant. The Costs of War project at Brown University estimates that more than nine hundred thousand people have been killed by direct violence in wars in Iraq, Afghanistan, Syria, and Pakistan.[21] This total includes civilians and armed forces. Many more have died from indirect harms related to war, including malnutrition and degraded infrastructure. For example, thirty-eight million people were displaced by these wars.

In the aftermath of 9/11, the global struggle against terrorism focused on attacks carried out by international terrorists and their sympathizers who were intent on inflicting damage against American and European targets. But in recent years, Americans have become increasingly aware of so-called "homegrown" or domestic terrorists, who are often motivated by racism or by anti-government sentiment. A variety of attacks against innocent civilians have occurred in the United States and elsewhere. Something like this occurred in the Oklahoma City bombing of 1994, which was an attack on a federal building. In the decades since then, bombings and shootings have afflicted cities and schools across the United States and elsewhere. Sometimes this is targeted violence motivated by anti-Semitic, racist, or homophobic ideology. Other times, the violence of mass shootings seems to be random and focused on soft targets such as schools. The phenomenon of school shootings is especially disturbing, as mass murder is committed against vulnerable schoolchildren and their teachers.

Some claim that it is difficult to define terrorism, pointing out that one person's "freedom fighter" is another person's "terrorist." But terrorism is generally agreed to involve violent acts that deliberately intend to inflict harm on those who do not deserve to be harmed. According to that definition, school shootings can be described as terrorism. These acts may not be politically motivated, but they certainly inflict harm on the innocent. Most would agree that violence of this sort is wrong. And many would also agree that the police and the military are justified in using violent force to kill those who kill children.

But pacifists argue that there is a significant risk of escalation, such as occurred during the war on terrorism. The moral conversation prompted by terrorism, mass shootings, and the like continues. Some argue that gun control should be part of the solution domestically. Pacifists would likely be sympathetic to the idea of beating swords into ploughshares and aiming toward a general disarmament. They might also be interested in nonviolent prevention of hate and violence—such as could happen through better psychological care, education, and the development of more human values. But on the other side, realists warn that violence has always been part of human nature. They might suggest that the best solution is to harden soft targets, perhaps by arming teachers. Realists might also argue that we need to be more proactive in searching out, capturing, punishing, and killing terrorists. The just war theory will caution that in pursuing terrorists, we ought not risk becoming terrorists ourselves. In the background of this conversation is the cautionary tale of the United States' twenty-year-long war on terrorism and the ongoing problem of mass shootings and terrorist violence.

Targeted Killing and Drones

Terrorists are not necessarily part of any recognized state. Often they are loosely affiliated, acting alone or organized in small cells. They may be motivated by radical ideology read online or viewed in videos. And terrorists do not declare war or put on uniforms that distinguish them as combatants. For these reasons, some argue that the weapons and rules of traditional just war theory may not apply. Others contend that terrorists are simply criminals and that domestic and international law enforcement should be employed to bring them to justice.

Should terrorists be viewed as criminals, who ought to be captured if possible and put on trial so that they might be punished? Or are terrorists *enemy combatants* who may be killed or captured without a trial and held as prisoners of war until an eventual peace treaty is concluded? Or are terrorists *unlawful combatants* whose actions and ideology put them outside of the established moral and legal framework for dealing with enemy combatants? The term *unlawful combatant* has been employed by the United States to indicate that the normal rules for dealing with criminals and enemy fighters do not apply to those suspected of terrorism. For example, American policy is that terrorist suspects can be killed without trial. And when captured, terrorism suspects have been held without trial in extraterritorial prisons such as the American prison at Guantanamo Bay in Cuba (discussed in Chapter 7). Terror suspects have been tortured. And Americans have engaged in targeted killing of terrorists, hunting them down in foreign lands (often in violation of the sovereignty of foreign nations).

The most famous case of targeted killing is that of Osama bin Laden. Osama bin Laden was the leader of Al Qaeda at the time of the September 11 attacks. He was killed by an American military attack on his compound in Abbottabad, Pakistan, on May 2, 2011. The operation that killed him was in violation of Pakistani sovereignty. When he was killed, he was accompanied by his wives and children. He was not actively engaged in military operations. Some claim that he was unarmed. A book by one of the Navy SEALs involved in the raid maintained that bin Laden was shot in the head as he peered down a dark hallway and again in the chest as he lay convulsing in a pool of his own blood.[22] The SEALs feared he could have had a booby trap or suicide vest at his disposal. President Obama explained in a speech to the nation celebrating the death of bin Laden that there was a firefight, which led to him being killed.

Whether bin Laden posed an active threat to the Navy SEAL team that attacked him or not, Obama and others maintained that killing him was justified. Obama explained that bin Laden was responsible for killing Americans, characterizing him also as "a mass murderer of Muslims." Obama concluded, "[H]is demise should be welcomed by all who believe in peace and human dignity."[23] Eric Holder, the attorney general of the United States at the time, further stated, "The operation against bin Laden was justified as an act of national self-defense. It's lawful to target an enemy commander in the field."[24] Critics objected that the killing was a violation of international law and that Americans had an obligation to work to try to extradite bin Laden and put him on trial. Critics might also object to Holder's claim that bin Laden was a "commander in the field." Is a terrorist who is resting at home in the middle of the night a commander in the field?

A similar case occurred in 2020 with the assassination of Iranian general Qasem Soleimani by an American drone at an airbase in Iraq. In a press release, the U.S. Defense Department justified this attack by claiming that General Soleimani was the head of an Iranian unit designated as a terrorist organization, the Islamic Revolutionary Guard Corps-Quds Force; and stating that "General Soleimani and his Quds Force were responsible for the deaths of hundreds of American and coalition service members and the wounding of thousands more."[25] Critics argued that the killing of Soleimani was illegal and immoral. A special rapporteur for the United Nations, Agnes Callamard, noted that this was the first known case of one nation using a drone attack to kill a high-ranking official of another nation. She warned that there were risks of escalation as powerful states that possess drones may act with impunity to kill members of foreign governments.[26] In the summer of 2022, American forces were involved in another highly publicized drone killing in Afghanistan. President Biden authorized a drone attack that killed Ayman al-Zawahiri, an Al-Qaeda leader whom Biden said was "deeply involved in planning 9/11" and whom he described as a "mastermind of attacks against Americans."[27] The Taliban regime in Afghanistan condemned the attack as a violation of international law.[28]

The question here is whether it is morally and legal permissible to employ targeted killing as a method of warfare. The larger question from the standpoint of the just war theory is whether it is permissible to target an enemy commander or other soldier who is not actively engaged in fighting. The just war idea of discrimination encourages us to distinguish between soldiers who are actively fighting and those who are in hospitals, on leave, or engaged in nonlethal support operations. One reason to avoid targeting soldiers behind the lines is to keep violence contained on the battlefield. But some may argue that this convenient distinction between combatants who are fighting and soldiers on leave does not hold in a war on terrorism where there are no specified fields of battle and where terrorists themselves refuse to adhere to the distinction between combatants and noncombatants. A realist would have no problem with targeting a terrorist mastermind, a general, or a political leader, except for pragmatic concerns about potential blowback from such attacks. The just war theory may also permit assassinations of terrorist masterminds and political leaders if such attacks are discriminate and proportional. It seems clear, for example, that less violence is involved in a targeted killing than in a full-fledged invasion and that the violence of targeted killing is usually focused in a way that seeks to minimize collateral damage. One concern, however, is that employing targeted assassination opens the door for similar attacks

coming from the other side. Could Al-Qaeda or Iran make similar arguments in attempting to justify attacks on American political or military leaders? The presumption here is that the "good guys"—those who fight justly and who have a just cause—are permitted to employ targeted killing, while the "bad guys" are not.

The issue of targeted killing has become more pressing because of the use of unmanned drones. Drone aircraft, piloted by remote control, can attack terrorist suspects around the world, easily crossing borders. Drones have been used to attack targets in a variety of countries. One advantage of drones is that they are more precise than other sorts of bombing, allowing for more discriminate and proportional killing. It is possible that pacifists and opponents of war may be sympathetic to the idea of minimizing harm, avoiding all-out war, and developing more precise weapons. But pacifists may also worry that drones make violence more likely—and may lead to escalation. And despite claims of precision, civilian noncombatants have been killed by the use of drones. One estimate from the Bureau of Investigative Journalism claims the United States has killed between 8,500 and 16,900 people in Yemen, Afghanistan, Somalia, Pakistan, and elsewhere with drone strikes (between 2010 and 2020), including 900 to 2,200 civilians.[29] Such killing may be defensible on just war grounds, with civilian death justified as collateral damage. But the civilian death toll is still morally troubling. In April 2016, President Obama admitted the difficulty, saying of the drone war, "It wasn't as precise as it should have been, and there's no doubt civilians were killed that shouldn't have been. . . . We have to take responsibility where we're not acting appropriately, or just made mistakes."[30]

Another advantage of using drones is that they are cheaper than manned aircraft. And they do not put pilots at risk. However, they return us to the problem of who counts as a combatant. Would the remote-control drone pilots, who fly these drones from facilities based in the United States and who thus never come near the battlefield, be considered "combatants"? One worry along these lines is that remote-control piloting of drones extends our idea of what counts as "the battlefield" in a way that undermines the just war effort to constrain violence to a confined space of battle.

Defenders of drones argue that they are an essential response to terrorism. The war on terrorism is not a traditional war, with armies fighting each other on clearly marked battlefields. Terrorists do not wear uniforms. Indeed, they try to blend into the local populace. And they employ mundane objects and camouflaged devices as part of their weaponry: car bombs, suicide vests, and most notoriously, commercial jet airliners. Perhaps the rules have changed for a war on terrorism, which leads to a changed evaluation of the use of targeted killing. And since terrorists plan their operations in cities and villages around the globe, it might be necessary to use drones to cross borders and kill terrorists where they are doing their planning.

Another problem arises when we think about the justification of targeted killing of terrorists—whether by drones or by other means—and that is the question of preventive violence. We might think that the killings of Osama bin Laden, General Soleimani, or Ayman al-Zawahiri were justifiable because these men were responsible for terrorist attacks in the past. But the drone and targeted killing policy of the United States also allows for targeted killing of terrorists who have not themselves committed terrorism and who may not be an imminent threat. A Justice Department memo from 2013 outlined the justification of targeted killing, explaining that the policy "does not require the United States to have clear evidence that a specific attack on U.S. persons and interests will take place in the immediate future."[31] In other words, it may be enough to be thinking about terrorism to be liable for targeted killing. Such an idea might make sense from a standpoint that advocates preventive warfare. If the U.S. invasion of Iraq was justified as a war aiming to prevent Iraq from obtaining or using weapons of mass destruction to terrorize the world, couldn't a drone attack on a terrorist in Yemen be justified by the same logic? A defender of the drone program will argue that it is better to prevent terrorist attacks before they happen. But a critic will argue that it is a disproportionate escalation of hostilities.

The discussion of drones has become even more contentious due to the government policy of allowing targeted killing of American citizens. The Department of Justice memo mentioned earlier was used to justify the killing of American citizens who are actively involved in Al-Qaeda and who are residing in foreign countries. This policy was employed in the killing of four Americans in Yemen and Pakistan in 2011.[32] Among those killed was a radical Muslim cleric, Anwar al-Awlaki, who was born in New Mexico and attended college in Colorado. He was killed along with his son and another American associate. The U.S. government claims that al-Awlaki was actively involved in planning terrorist operations against the United States and thus that his killing was justified. Such a justification might appeal to just war ideas about the killing of aggressive combatants. Or targeted killing might be justified by realists as part of the struggle for supremacy in the world of power and politics. Critics have argued that it is illegal for the government to execute American citizens without attempting to capture them and put them on trial, perhaps maintaining that domestic and international law enforcement standards should be employed. But President Obama defended the drone program by maintaining that it was part of a just war against terrorism, which is discriminate and proportional in its approach to targeted killing.[33] President Trump made the point more forcefully when he defended the killing of General Soleimani. He said, "To terrorists who harm or intend to harm any American, we will find you; we will eliminate you."[34]

Weapons of Mass Destruction

One of the central concerns of the war on terrorism is the issue of weapons of mass destruction. Recall that the proliferation of weapons of mass destruction was a primary reason given by George W. Bush as a cause for the invasion of Iraq in 2003. The Bush administration

Figure 18-3 Weapons of mass destruction create unique moral concerns.

maintained that the invasion was necessary to prevent Saddam Hussein from obtaining weapons of mass destruction, especially nuclear weapons. The issue of weapons of mass destruction remains a concern with regard to Iran and North Korea. International sanctions against Iran were directed against that country's nuclear program. And the Korean peninsula remains tense due to North Korea's nuclear capabilities. In 2013, there was evidence that the Syrian government had used chemical weapons against rebels. This was widely condemned by the international community, leading to a change in the U.S. policy toward the civil war in Syria. And during the summer of 2022 (when this book was being revised), there was concern that Russia might employ weapons of mass destruction in its war in Ukraine.

The category of weapons of mass destruction usually includes biological, chemical, and nuclear weapons. Biological weapons are living microorganisms that can be used as weapons to maim, incapacitate, and kill. Among these weapons is anthrax, which infects either the skin or the lungs. Breathing only a small amount of anthrax causes death in 80 to 90 percent of cases. Smallpox, cholera, and bubonic or pneumonic plague are other biological agents that might be used. Genetic engineering may also be used to make more virulent strains. There have been no proven usages of biological weapons in modern wars. One hundred sixty-three states have ratified the Biological Weapons Convention (1975), which prohibits the production, stockpiling, and use of such agents as weapons.

Chemical weapons include blister agents such as mustard gas, which is relatively easy and cheap to produce. It produces painful blisters, and it incapacitates rather than kills. Iraq used mustard gas in its 1980 to 1988 war with Iran as well as some type of chemical weapon on the Kurdish inhabitants of Halabja in 1988. Through low-level repeated airdrops, as many as five thousand defenseless people in that town were killed. Phosgene is a choking agent, and hydrogen cyanide "prevents transfer of oxygen to the tissues." Large quantities of the latter, however, would be needed to produce significant effects.[35] Hydrogen cyanide is a deadly poison gas, as is evidenced by its use in executions in the gas chamber. Sarin is called a nerve "gas," but it is actually a liquid. It affects the central nervous system and is highly toxic. In 1995, the Japanese cult group Aum Shinrikyo deployed

sarin in the Tokyo subway. It sickened thousands and killed twelve people. Sarin is the gas employed in attacks in Syria that killed more than one thousand people. Chemical weapons were also used in both world wars. For example, in World War I, the Germans used mustard gas and chlorine, and the French used phosgene. Although it might not be usually classified as the use of a chemical weapon, in 1945 American B-29 bombers "dropped 1665 tons of napalm-filled bombs on Tokyo, leaving almost nothing standing over 16 square miles." One hundred thousand people were killed in this raid, not from napalm directly but from the fires that it caused.[36] One hundred and eighty-eight nations are party to the Chemical Weapons Convention (1994). Because chemical weapons can be made by private groups in small labs, however, verifying international compliance with the convention is highly problematic.

Nuclear weapons, including both fission and fusion bombs, are the deadliest weapons. They produce powerful explosions and leave radiation behind that causes ongoing damage. The effects were well demonstrated by the U.S. bombings of Hiroshima and Nagasaki in August 1945. It is estimated that 150,000 people perished in these two attacks and their immediate aftermath, with an eventual total of nearly three hundred thousand deaths caused by these bombs (as survivors died of subsequent maladies attributed to the bombing).[37] Among the casualties at Hiroshima were American citizens—including American prisoners of war and Japanese Americans who were unable to escape from Japan once the war began. Some three thousand Japanese Americans were in Hiroshima when the bomb was dropped; eight hundred to one thousand survived and returned to the United States.[38]

Since the bombings of Hiroshima and Nagasaki, no other nation has ever employed nuclear weapons in wartime. Perhaps we learned a moral lesson from the sheer destructive power of these bombings. But for many decades after World War II, many countries continued to stockpile weapons. The world's nuclear arsenals grew to include unimaginable destructive power throughout the Cold War. Recognizing that nuclear weapons were pointing toward the nihilistic conclusion of mutually assured destruction, the nuclear powers have attempted to limit nuclear arsenals. There have been many nuclear weapons treaties designed to limit nuclear stockpiles and prevent proliferation. Nations known to have nuclear weapons now include

China, France, India, Israel, North Korea, Pakistan, Russia, the United Kingdom, and the United States.

Although some dream of complete disarmament, we are far from a nuclear-free world. And despite the fact that some progress has been made with regard to reducing nuclear stockpiles, this work has been jeopardized by the Russian-Ukrainian war. In 2010, in a treaty known as "New START," the United States and Russia agreed to limit the number of nuclear warheads in their arsenals.[39] In 2021, the two countries agreed to extend this treaty through 2026.[40] However in February of 2023, a year after the Russian invasion of Ukraine, Russia announced it was "suspending" its participation with this treaty.[41] Russia also announced that it might begin testing its nuclear weapons as well, despite the fact that a nuclear test ban treaty has been in place since the 1990's. Arms control experts worried that this nuclear saber-rattling could have the effect of re-kindling the world's nuclear arms race.[42]

The global community continues to be concerned about nuclear proliferation. There is a worrisome global black market in nuclear materials and know-how. These weapons are difficult but not impossible to make. And many fear so-called "loose nukes," nuclear weapons that are not carefully guarded (e.g., in the former Soviet Union) and that could be sold on the black market to terrorists. There was an attempt to confine possession of nuclear weapons to the original nuclear powers: the United States, the United Kingdom, France, the Soviet Union (now Russia), and China. But in recent decades, nuclear weaponry has been developed by Israel and India, with Pakistan joining the nuclear club in 1998. North Korea successfully detonated a nuclear device in 2006 and claimed to have tested a hydrogen bomb in early 2016, an act that provoked outrage in the international community. Other states have agreed not to pursue nuclear weapons by signing on to the Nuclear Non-Proliferation Treaty. At least one state has voluntarily given up its nuclear weapons: South Africa dismantled them in the 1990s.

In calling these nuclear, chemical, and biological devices *weapons of mass destruction*, we imply that they are of a different order of magnitude than the usual means of modern warfare. It is clear why nuclear weapons are labeled in this way, but it is not so clear why the others are. Even when used somewhat extensively in World War I, "fewer than 1 percent of battle deaths" during that war were caused by gas, and only "2 percent of those gassed during the war died, compared with 24 percent of those struck by bullets, artillery shells, or shrapnel."[43] For gas to work well, there can be no wind or sun, and it must be delivered by an aircraft flying at very low altitude. If delivered by bombs, the weapons would be incinerated before they could become effective. Today's gas masks and antibiotics and other preventives and treatments lessen the lethality of such weapons even more. In 1971, smallpox accidentally got loose in Kazakhstan but killed only three people; and in 1979, a large amount of anthrax was released through the explosion of a Soviet plant, but only sixty-eight people were killed.[44] There have been subsequent scares with regard to chemical and biological agents. In 2001, Americans were frightened by anthrax scares, as suspicious white powder was sent by the mail. In 2013, federal authorities arrested domestic terrorists who sent letters laced with the poison ricin through the mail to judges and politicians, including one to the president. Ricin is made from castor beans and is quite deadly: a dose about the size of a grain of salt can cause death.

Realists would have no moral problem with weapons of mass destruction, provided that they work. One concern is that such weapons are difficult to use without harming your own soldiers. The wind can blow chemical and biological weapons in the wrong direction, and nuclear weapons leave deadly radiation that can harm one's own troops. On the other hand, just war theorists may argue that weapons of mass destruction are *mala in se* or evil in themselves (and so prohibited). But we need not appeal to intrinsic qualities of the weapons to form a moral critique of weapons of mass destruction. Principles from the just war theory that are used to evaluate terrorism and other warfare can be employed to evaluate the use of weapons of mass destruction. The principle of discrimination tells us that it is morally wrong to deliberately target innocent civilians with firebombs, nuclear bombs, or chemical weapons. And massive destruction caused by these weapons might fail the proportionality test as well. One wonders, however, whether ordinary bombs and bullets that explode and kill many more people than biological or chemical weapons are less objectionable. During the Second

World War, more civilians were killed by conventional bombs than were killed by atomic bombs. And land mines continue to be a cause of harm—left behind in battlefields to harm civilians after conflicts end. Nevertheless, people seem to fear biological and chemical weapons more than conventional weapons. Possibly it is the thought of being killed by something invisible—radiation sickness or poison gas—that makes them so feared and is behind the desire to call them weapons of mass destruction, with the implication that they are morally abhorrent and are intrinsically evil.

Torture

Torture is typically viewed by just war theorists as an intrinsically evil means that should not be employed in warfare. Indeed, it is viewed as a criminal activity, outlawed by the Geneva convention and by other international treaties such as the UN Convention against Torture. But some have argued that torture could be justified. During the American "war on terrorism," some U.S. government officials sought to justify techniques that have traditionally been viewed as torture by calling them "enhanced interrogation methods" and by offering consequentialist justifications of the usefulness of torture. In congressional testimony in February 2007, the director of the CIA, Michael Hayden, admitted that the United States has used waterboarding on prisoners. Waterboarding is a technique in which a prisoner's head is strapped to a board with their face drenched in water to produce a sensation of drowning. The CIA admitted that it used waterboarding on one particular terror suspect, Khalid Shaikh Mohammed, 183 times; another suspect was waterboarded 83 times.[45] These prisoners were subjected to other so-called "enhanced interrogation techniques": they were kept disoriented, naked, and cold. We have learned that prisoners were slammed against walls, given suppositories, prevented from sleeping, and kept in stress positions. The Red Cross concluded that this treatment was torture and that it was cruel, inhuman, and degrading.[46]

But the government under George W. Bush argued that this use of torture was justified. Former Vice President Dick Cheney explained,

No moral value held dear by the American people obliges public servants to sacrifice innocent lives to spare a captured terrorist from unpleasant things. And when an entire population is targeted by a terror network, nothing is more consistent with American values than to stop them. The interrogations were used on hardened terrorists after other efforts had failed. They were legal, essential, justified, successful, and the right thing to do.[47]

Cheney's justification of torture is a straightforwardly utilitarian justification: it works to prevent terrorism and should not be prohibited by a "moral value." The Bush administration's legal staff provided legal and moral justifications of torture. The Office of Legal Counsel in the Justice Department issued a number of memos suggesting that certain methods of trying to extract information from prisoners suspected of terrorism were not torture. The author of a number of these memos, John Yoo, argued that "inflicting physical pain does not count as torture unless the interrogator specifically intends the pain to reach the level associated with organ failure or death."[48] This definition was given to allow certain enhanced interrogation techniques while avoiding the legal prohibition on torture. According to this definition, waterboarding—simulated drowning—does not count as torture. Critics complained loudly that waterboarding was indeed torture and that this was not consistent with American law or international law and that the use of torture was contrary to American values.[49] For example, the U.S. Uniform Code of Military Justice makes "cruelty, oppression, or maltreatment of prisoners a crime."[50] Senator John McCain—who was himself tortured as a prisoner of war in Vietnam—spoke out against torture. And when Barack Obama became president, he banned the use of these "enhanced interrogation methods." But when he became president, Donald Trump expressed an interest in bringing back waterboarding, claiming that it "works" and that the United States needed to "fight fire with fire." He complained that terrorists were "chopping off people's heads" but that if the United States did not resume the use of torture, "we're not playing on an even field."[51]

Pacifists condemn torture as another example of unjustified violence. They may also point out that this episode from recent history indicates the ugly logic of war—that we can end up betraying our own values in the name of victory and power—and that this shows us why war is a corrupting and immoral force. Realists may nod in agreement with Dick Cheney's consequentialist justification of torture. And they may agree with Donald Trump that if terrorists are using torture, we should "fight fire with fire." Realists are not opposed to using supposedly immoral means to achieve other goals. Indeed, realists may also add that our enemies are not opposed to using torture and to employing other cruel techniques, including beheading prisoners. Realists may argue that the best way to fight cruelty is to employ cruelty in return. Just war theorists will not agree to that line of reasoning. Instead, they may argue that torture ought to be considered as one of those actions that are evil in themselves and that are prohibited by principles of *jus in bello*. They may argue that even if torture works, there are some things we simply ought not do in pursuit of justified causes. As President Biden explained in commemorating the International Day in Support of Victims of Torture:

> We know that torture is an ineffective method for gaining reliable intelligence. We know that it is prohibited universally, and violates U.S. and international law. We know that it spurs terrorist recruitment and violent extremism. And we know that it compromises our moral standing in the world. . . . Torture, wherever it occurs, is a stain on our moral conscience. We all must redouble our efforts to end such inhumane practice for good.[52]

At issue in the moral evaluation of torture is the consequentialist question of whether it works, as well as the deontological question of whether it is, as Biden put it, an inhumane practice that puts a stain on the moral conscience of those who use it.

War Crimes and Universal Human Rights

18.6 Explain the history and concept of war crimes and crimes against humanity and the problem of victor's justice.

One of the difficulties of thinking about the morality of war is that, as the realists may insist, there is no international authority that could regulate behavior in war. Realists argue that victors dispense so-called "victor's justice." Usually the term *victor's justice* is thought of as an accusation of unilateral and hypocritical judgment, as the victors punish the losers while failing to prosecute or condemn their own unjust or immoral actions. Consider, for example, a scene from the 2003 documentary *The Fog of War* in which former defense secretary Robert S. McNamara is interviewed about his participation in the bombing of Japan during World War II. McNamara worked with General Curtis LeMay to coordinate the bombing. In addition to the atomic bomb attacks mentioned previously, American planes dropped incendiary bombs on a large number of Japanese cities, causing massive damage and killing millions. As McNamara reflects on this in the film, he acknowledges that the bombing would have been viewed as a war crime if the Americans had lost. He said that LeMay suggested, "If we had lost the war, we'd all have been prosecuted as war criminals." McNamara continued, "And I think he's right. He . . . and, I'd say, I . . . were behaving as war criminals. LeMay recognized that what he was doing would be thought immoral if his side had lost. But what makes it immoral if you lose and not immoral if you win?"[53] The realist will argue that this shows us that moral judgments do not apply in wartime and that the goal is to win so that one can be the victor dispensing victor's justice.

On the other hand, there is a growing consensus in the international community that moral judgment should apply to behavior in war. International agreements, treaties, and institutions have developed in the past centuries that aim to limit warfare and prosecute immoral actions done in war. These efforts in international law are grounded in ideas that are closely connected to ideas found in the just war theory—most important, that civilians should not be targeted and that certain actions—rape, for example—are always immoral. Many of the elements of the laws of war and the nature of war crimes have been developed in the various declarations of the Geneva convention and in other international treaties and agreements. For example, the 1984 UN Convention against Torture, which was ratified by the United States, requires that all signatory nations avoid cruel, inhuman, or degrading treatment.[54]

Those who violate these conventions and protocols may be held to be guilty of "war crimes." One important source for the conventions regarding war crimes were the war crimes tribunals conducted after World War II, both the Nuremberg trials and the Tokyo trials. There have been questions about the legal procedures and standards of proof employed in these trials. But in general, they are viewed as examples of the developing moral consensus about the rules of war. The Nuremberg trials established three categories of crimes: *crimes against the peace* (involving aggression and preparation for war), *war crimes* (including murder, maltreatment of prisoners, etc.), and *crimes against humanity* (involving racial, religious, or political persecution of civilians). The last category, *crimes against humanity* included a newly developed concept—that of *genocide*, the deliberate effort to exterminate a people. As is well known, the Nazis were engaged in a genocidal campaign of extermination against Jews, Gypsies, and others. Nazi death camps were employed in an efficient and mechanized effort to annihilate the Jewish people, resulting in the deaths of six million Jews (out of a prior population of nine million Jews in the German-controlled parts of Europe). This event is referred to as the Holocaust. The mass extermination of civilians is a war crime and a crime against humanity.

The idea of a crime against humanity and of war crimes in general can be understood in relation to the natural law and natural rights theories discussed in Chapter 7. Certain actions violate the natural value and dignity of persons, and all human beings should know this based on a common moral sense, no matter what orders they receive. Sometimes crimes against humanity are described as actions that "shock the moral conscience of humankind." The Rome Statute of the International Criminal Court defines crimes against humanity as involving "widespread or systematic attack directed against any civilian population" including among other criminal actions the following kinds of actions: "murder; extermination; enslavement; deportation or forcible transfer of population; imprisonment or other severe deprivation of physical liberty in violation of fundamental rules of international law; torture; rape, sexual slavery, enforced prostitution, forced pregnancy, enforced sterilization, or any other form of sexual violence of comparable gravity."[55]

The important point here is that soldiers cannot be excused for criminal behavior by claiming that they are merely following orders. Principle IV of the Nuremberg trials stipulates, "The fact that a person acted pursuant to order of his Government or of a superior does not relieve him from responsibility under international law, provided a moral choice was in fact possible to him."[56] Moreover, Principle III of the Tribunal stipulated that heads of state and other political leaders were not excused from prosecution. The Nuremberg trials put twenty-two Nazi leaders on trial (Hitler, Himmler, Goebbels, and other Nazi leaders were already dead), resulting in convictions for nineteen of them and death sentences for twelve. While the Nuremberg trials are viewed as an important step in the development of war crimes tribunals and international law, some still worry that they remained examples of victor's justice—since there was no similar accounting for war crimes committed by the Allied powers.[57]

Since Nuremberg, the international community has worked to create a more impartial system for dealing with war crimes and crimes against humanity, including the development of an International Criminal Court in The Hague. But egregious attacks on civilians continue to occur, attacks that are referred to as "ethnic cleansing" or genocide. These attacks have occurred in Kosovo, in Rwanda, in Sudan, in Syria, and elsewhere. The international community condemns such atrocities, but it is often at a loss as to what to do about them. Military intervention is risky, and pacifists will argue for nonviolent responses. A significant problem is whether a war of intervention intended to rescue civilians will produce more harm than good in the long run. Although there is a developing international consensus about war crimes, the world is still not able to agree on strategies for responding to such crimes.

Consider, as an example of this problem, the Russian attack on Ukraine, which we mentioned in the opening vignette of this chapter. The Russian invasion was widely viewed as a criminal act of aggression, and Russia was accused of war crimes including deliberately killing civilians, rape, and torture.[58] But condemnation of these atrocities by the international community was not able to prevent them from happening. And we return to the question of whether a coalition of nations or the international community could use military force to intervene in conflicts and circumstances where war crimes are being committed.

Chapter Summary

18.1 What is the difference between positive and negative peace?

Positive peace envisions a condition of social harmony and justice, not plagued by structural violence. Negative peace is merely the absence of overt or direct violence and may include structural violence.

18.2 What is the basic idea of realism?

Realism is the view that moral judgment does not apply in thinking about war. It is typically connected to a view of history, politics, and war that claims that in the "real" world it is power and strength that matter. Realists typically disagree with the idea that there are any moral limits on warfare, although they may admit that limitations on violence can be strategically useful.

18.3 What are some arguments for and against pacifism and nonviolence?

Pacifists may oppose war on consequentialist grounds, holding that nonviolence tends to produce better outcomes than violence or war. Any discussion of pacifism and nonviolence ought to include some account of nonviolent methods and strategies. This includes the use of nonviolence in the campaigns led by Gandhi in India or by King and Lawson in the United States. Pacifists may also oppose war on deontological grounds by claiming that killing is wrong or that nonviolence is a morally superior method. Opponents of pacifism may dispute the consequentialist claim that war always produces worse outcomes. These opponents would also need to consider arguments about the limitations of nonviolent methods. Opponents of pacifism may also claim that killing and war can be justified, especially in the case of self-defense and in cases that use violence in order to prevent violence.

18.4 How can we explain the distinction made in just war theory between *jus ad bellum* and *jus in bello*, as well as key terms such as *just cause, legitimate authority, discrimination*, and *noncombatant immunity*?

Jus ad bellum is concerned with justice in going to war. Typically, the idea of *jus ad bellum* includes the claim that there ought to be a just cause for war and that those engaging in war are authorized to go to war. Among the just causes for war is the idea of a justified response to aggression and the idea that just warriors may fight in order to protect those who are being oppressed by their governments. The concerns of *jus in bello* focus on issues that arise within war. This includes the need to discriminate between those who can be legitimately targeted and those who may not. Noncombatant immunity is the idea that noncombatants are not legitimate targets of direct attack.

18.5 How would the moral theories discussed here evaluate current issues including the use of drones and targeted assassination, and the morality of terrorism and torture?

An evaluation of these issues should begin by clarifying a standpoint in the morality of war, either in terms of realism, pacifism, or just war theory. Realists typically only ask whether these activities work and are useful. From a realist perspective, drones, targeted assassination, torture, even terrorism can be justified if they are useful. Such an evaluation depends on an empirical evaluation that involves a kind of cost–benefit analysis. Pacifists generally oppose these uses of violence. Pacifists may be sympathetic to the idea of finding ways to minimize violence with precision weapons, but they typically argue that drones and assassination run the risk of escalation. Just war theorists will likely be more sympathetic to the use of drones and targeted assassination, as a kind of minimal use of justified violence that avoids escalation and collateral damage. But just war theorists may be worried about the way that drones and targeted assassination lead to violence occurring away from the battlefield. In general, pacifists and just war theorists agree that terrorism and torture are wrong. The pacifist argument against these actions follows from the pacifist rejection of violence in general. Terrorism is condemned by just war theory as an illegitimate attack on noncombatants, while torture is often included among a list of actions that are viewed as *mala in se* or evil in themselves.

18.6 What is the history and concept of war crimes and crimes against humanity? And what is the problem of victor's justice?

War crimes have been defined by international law through the use of war crimes tribunals, which build on ideas that are familiar from the just war tradition and from treaties and other legal documents. These crimes include crimes against the peace (i.e., aggression) and war crimes (e.g., torturing prisoners or using rape as a weapon). A related set of crimes known as crimes against humanity include genocide and ethnic cleansing. One problem in thinking about war crimes involves a one-sided application of the concept. The idea of victor's justice expresses the worry that the victors in a war will accuse those they've defeated of war crimes. To remedy this problem, we need a more universal concept of war crimes and an impartial application and enforcement of the idea.

18.7 Defend a thesis about the ethics of war, the idea of peace, and the problem of violence.

To defend a thesis about war, peace, and violence, we would need to provide definitions of these ideas. This includes thinking about the difference between positive and negative peace. It also involves thinking about what counts as violence and what qualifies as nonviolence. A philosophical approach to this problem would also need to consider what counts as war—and whether, for example, targeted assassination is a war or something less than war. After clarifying these concepts, such a thesis would need to evaluate realism, pacifism, and just war theory while also defining these ideas. This evaluation ought to make use of basic concepts of moral theory such as the difference between consequentialist and non-consequentialist approaches. This might include a discussion of the right of self-defense, the morality of defending others, and the value of a prohibition against killing. This evaluation also ought to include some comparative evaluation of the efficacy of violent and nonviolent methods.

Primary Source Readings

In the readings in this chapter, we have selections representing pacifism and just war theory. First, we will read an excerpt by Andrew Fitz-Gibbon, who considers the difference between a comprehensive commitment to nonviolence and a more pragmatic or strategic use of nonviolence. Following this essay, we have a short excerpt from civil rights leader James Lawson, which discusses nonviolence in the context of recent social justice protests including Black Lives Matters protests. Next, we have an excerpt from an essay by Michael Walzer, a leading exponent of the just war theory, which evaluates some key elements of the theory. These readings conclude with a short excerpt by Larry May, another leading defender of the just war theory, that considers the idea of war crimes.

Reading 18-1   Selective and Comprehensive Nonviolence | Andrew Fitz-Gibbon

Study Questions

1. What is the difference between nonviolence as a "good" and as a strategy or tool?
2. What are some of the successful uses of nonviolence discussed by Fitz-Gibbon?
3. What might Fitz-Gibbon mean when he suggests that "comprehensive nonviolentists" will practice nonviolence in all aspects of personal, social, and political life?

Despite the predominance of war in political affairs, peace and nonviolence were central ideas behind much political activism in the twentieth century. M. K. Gandhi was the first to use techniques of nonviolent resistance, first in South Africa and then in India. For Gandhi, nonviolent protest required as much courage as warfare ...

Gandhi and King held in creative tension of the notions that nonviolence was a "good," an end in itself—something akin to love or truth—with the notion of nonviolent resistance as a political strategy. In other words, nonviolence was not merely a political technique, but the outworking of a deeper metaphysics.

Since King, nonviolence as a political tool has been developed most especially by Gene Sharp (1973a-c, 2005). Sharp analyzed different techniques for using nonviolent protest as a means of achieving political ends. He suggested 198 different methods of nonviolent action in order to bring about social change. Peter Ackerman and Jack Duvall (2000) built on the pioneering work of Sharp. Ackerman and Duvall analyzed 12 different movements in the twentieth century which accomplished social and political change by direct nonviolent action. On close analysis, many of the movements were not as clearly nonviolent as Ackerman and Duvall suggest. Such change is accomplished by seizing the initiative to control a conflict to make the opposition give-in to demands against their will. In practice, nonviolent direct action is far from "peaceful." Nonetheless, their conclusion is persuasive: nonviolent direct action is a powerful means of social and political change. Their organization, the International Center on Nonviolent Conflict, through its publications and DVDs was influential in the overthrow of Serbian leader Slobodan Milosevic in 2000, and Ukrainian leader Viktor Yanukovych in 2004–2005. Their techniques were extensively used in the Arab Spring revolutions of 2010–2011 (see Gan, 2013, 70).

However, some on the Left criticize nonviolent direct action as politically ineffective and not going far

enough ... Yet, in Eastern Europe, it was just such liberalism that the masses pursued as Soviet Communism faded.

Those who see nonviolence as more than a socio-political strategy also have criticized the direction that Sharp, Ackerman, and Duvall have taken. Barry L. Gan notes a distinction between "selective nonviolence" and "comprehensive nonviolence" (2013, 73 ff). Selective nonviolence rejects the use of violence for pragmatic reasons in order to accomplish a political aim. The "good" is not nonviolence itself, but rather the political goal. If violence could achieve the goal more effectively and quickly, then violence would be used. However, some selective nonviolentists consider nonviolence as always a better strategy than violence, and so make no resort to violent tactics. Nonetheless, nonviolence is still considered merely a tool to use toward some other goal. Comprehensive nonviolence is the rejection of violence in all its forms; nonviolence being considered a good in itself. A comprehensive nonviolentist will attempt to practice nonviolence in all aspects of personal, social, and political life. Comprehensive nonviolentists reject some of the techniques suggested by Sharp as being inherently violent.

Andrew Fitz-Gibbon, "Peace," in *The Bloomsbury Companion to Political Philosophy*, ed. Andrew Fiala (London: Bloomsbury Publishing, 2015).

Ackerman, P., and Duvall, J. (2000), *A Force More Powerful: A Century of Nonviolent Conflict*. Palgrave: New York.

Sharp, G. (1973a), *The Politics of Nonviolent Action: Part One Power and Struggle*. Boston, MA: Porter Sargent.

—(1973b), *The Politics of Nonviolent Action: Part Two The Methods of Nonviolent Action*. Boston, MA: Porter Sargent.

—(1973c), *The Politics of Nonviolent Action: Part Three The Dynamics of Nonviolent Action*. Boston, MA: Porter Sargent.

—(2005), *Waging Nonviolent Struggle: 20th Century Practice and 21st Century Potential*. Boston, MA: Porter Sargent.

Gan, B. L. (2013), *Violence and Nonviolence: An Introduction*. Lanham: Rowman & Littlefield.

Reading 18-2   The Power of Nonviolence in the Fight for Racial Justice | James Lawson

Study Questions

1. What are the three nonviolent movements that Lawson identifies?
2. What does Lawson suggest about the nonviolent nature of Black Lives Matter protests?
3. Why do you think Lawson warns that nonviolence is "the only way" to make progress?

Multitudes of Americans do not understand that our present freedoms represent the consequences of three essentially nonviolent movements of the 20th century: the push by women for the right to vote especially the period between 1910 and 1820; the labor movement in the workers strikes from the 1930s to the 1960s; and then what the late congressman John Lewis has called the non-violent movement of America, which others have termed the civil rights movement from 1953 to 1973.

In all three of these major movements, you see millions and millions of people struggling to shape a more democratic society, but the opposition to that today still comes from racism, sexism, and the violence of plantation capitalism. The slow climb in the quality of life for millions of people is not a result of plantation capitalism and big business. The power structures have not done this.... It has come about because we the people have done the work to organize.

We have recently experienced perhaps the largest, most creative non-violent movements that have captured the imagination of the human family. The general term for that campaign is Black Lives Matter, and it has resulted in millions of people in the streets and peaceful marches and largely peaceful demonstrations.

In this moment, we need to understand nonviolence more than ever. In the early part of the 20th century, Gandhi proceeded to experiment with nonviolent struggle and also drew from the religion of Jainism. Nonviolence is a philosophy and a methodology he called "satyagraha," putting together the Indian word *satya*, meaning primarily truth, God, soul, spirit, or love, with *graha*, meaning strength, power, or force. We also call it soul force.

In contrast to non-violence ... violent structures of inequity and injustice ... will turn our planet into a hothouse and then into an ice-cold Mars. Military violence, domestic violence, the continued lynching of people in the prison systems by the police—that system of violence is causing our society to sink into greater and greater chaos, turmoil, confusion, animosity, and division. The contemporary world has too much violent rhetoric and violent means and weaponry. Either the nations and the peoples of the world will pick up nonviolent struggle, or the current way in which the world moves will conclude with a massive suicide of the human race and life as we know it on this planet earth.

Human life as we know it is such a powerful mysterious stream of energies and powers, and I submit that nonviolence is the only way to make progress for the well-being of the human family. It is the only way we the people of the United States can proceed to make equality, liberty, justice, and the beloved community a reality at every crossroads, every rural and urban area of this country in the world. There are never any guarantees, but it is important to act as if it were possible to radically transform the world.

James M. Lawson Jr., *Revolutionary Nonviolence: Organizing for Freedom* (Berkeley: University of California Press, 2022).

Reading 18-3   The Triumph of Just War Theory (and the Dangers of Success) | Michael Walzer

Study Questions

1. Why do you suppose justice has become "one of the tests" for thinking about military strategies and tactics?
2. Walzer suggests that a pacifist interpretation of just war theory is a "bad argument"—why?
3. What does Walzer mean when he says that just war theory is a tool to be used by those who expect to use power and force?

Perhaps naively, I am inclined to say that justice has become, in all Western countries, one of the tests that any proposed military strategy or tactic has to meet—only one of the tests and not the most important one, but this still gives just war theory a place and standing that it never had before. It is easier now than it ever was to imagine a general saying, "No, we can't do that; it would cause too many civilian deaths; we have to find another way."

For many years, we have used the theory of just war to criticize American military actions, and now it has been taken over by the generals and is being used to explain and justify those actions. Obviously, we must resist. The easiest way to resist is to make noncombatant immunity into a stronger and stronger rule, until it is something like an absolute rule: all killing of civilians is (something close to) murder; therefore any war that leads to the killing of civilians is unjust; therefore every war is unjust. So pacifism reemerges from the very heart of the theory that was originally meant to replace it. . . .

Since I believe that war is still, sometimes, necessary, this seems to me a bad argument and, more generally, a bad response to the triumph of just war theory. It sustains the critical role of the theory vis-à-vis war generally, but it denies the theory the critical role it has always claimed, which is internal to the business of war

and requires critics to attend closely to what soldiers try to do and what they try not to do. The refusal to make distinctions of this kind, to pay attention to strategic and tactical choices, suggests a doctrine of radical suspicion. This is the radicalism of people who do not expect to exercise power or use force, ever, and who are not prepared to make the judgments that this exercise and use require. By contrast, just war theory, even when it demands a strong critique of particular acts of war, is the doctrine of people who do expect to exercise power and use force. We might think of it as a doctrine of radical responsibility, because it holds political and military leaders responsible, first of all, for the well-being of their own people, but also for the well-being of innocent men and women on the other side. Its proponents set themselves against those who will not think realistically about the defense of the country they live in and also against those who refuse to recognize the humanity of their opponents. They insist that there are things that it is morally impermissible to do even to the enemy. They also insist, however, that fighting itself cannot be morally impermissible. A just war is meant to be, and has to be, a war that it is possible to fight.

Michael Walzer, "The Triumph of Just War Theory (and the Dangers of Success)," *Social Research* 69: 4 (Winter 2002): 925–933.

Reading 18-4   War Crimes and Just Wars | Larry May

Study Questions

1. What is the apparent paradox that May introduces here?
2. What is the role of values such as compassion, mercy, and honor in thinking about the duties of soldiers?
3. How does May explain the difference between crimes against peace and war crimes?

War crimes are crimes committed during armed conflict. In this book, I argue that the best way to understand war crimes is as crimes against humaneness. By this I mean that war crimes are not best understood as crimes against the whole of humanity or as crimes of aggression or even primarily as crimes against justice, but that they are violations of the principle requiring that soldiers act humanely, that is with mercy and compassion, even as these same soldiers are allowed to kill enemy soldiers. The apparent paradox of this remark illustrates the conceptual problems of understanding, and normatively grounding, the idea of war crimes and of international prosecutions for such crimes.

The book tries to make sense of one of the ideas embedded in contemporary international law, namely that there are severe restrictions on how soldiers can fight in war, even if they fight with just cause and their opponents have committed atrocities. Humanitarian considerations of mercy and compassion count morally in war, and often these considerations are not reducible to considerations of justice. There are two reasons for thinking this. First, sometimes humanitarian considerations become duties because one has rendered another person completely dependent on one, by taking that person prisoner for instance, and that then create fiduciary or stewardship duties toward the one rendered dependent and vulnerable. Second, even if humanitarian considerations are not duties of soldiers, they must be adhered to if soldiers are to fight with honor. This is because soldiers, to be more than mere killers, must restrain themselves according to higher than normal standards of behavior. Honor is the key component in the way the military academies have trained soldiers for hundreds of years....

The close relation between Just War theory and the international law of war crimes is accepted by many scholars but not well explained. One explanation for this close relation is simply that the major categories of both Just War theory and international criminal law overlap. In Just War theory, there are two important questions: Was the decision to wage war morally justified (*jus ad bellum*), and were the tactics employed in war morally justified (*jus in bello*)? This Just War division is reflected in international criminal law's distinction between crimes against peace and war crimes. The decision to wage war in an aggressive manner is subject to prosecution as a crime against peace. The use of inhumane tactics during war is subject to prosecution as a war crime. Indeed, it is sometimes said in international law that crimes against peace are *jus ad bellum* violations and war crimes are *jus in bello* violations.

Larry May, *War Crimes and Just War* (Cambridge, UK: Cambridge University Press, 2007).

Review Exercises

1. Why is the just war theory considered a middle path between realism and pacifism?

2. What arguments can be made in defense of pacifism?

3. What kinds of nonviolent strategies might be employed in social protest movements?

4. Why might someone suggest that war can be used in pursuit of peace or justice?

5. List and explain the basic principles of *jus ad bellum* and *jus in bello*. Apply these principles to a recent war.

6. How might just war principles be applied to issues such as targeted assassination and war crimes?

7. Can terrorism or torture be justified? On what grounds? What would pacifists, just war theorists, and realists each say?

8. How does the principle of double effect apply in just war thinking?

9. What counts as a "war crime" or a "crime against humanity"? And what is the problem of victor's justice?

10. How might the concepts of this chapter be used to evaluate some current issues involving peace, nonviolent protest, and violence: for example, social justice protests, school shootings, structural violence, or domestic violence?

Discussion Cases

1. Military Service. Although military service is no longer compulsory in the United States, American males age eighteen to twenty-five have to register with the Selective Service. If a young man does not register, he may be denied benefits and employment opportunities. James recently turned eighteen. He is opposed to war and is considering not signing up. He is explaining this to his parents. James says, "Look, I don't want to support a system that fights unjust wars and I won't fight in one. So I'm not going to sign up." James's father is a military veteran. He responds, "We've all got a duty to serve our country, whether just or unjust. And anyway, you're wrong to claim we fight unjust wars. Our military fights justly. Do your duty and register." James's brother has a different opinion. He says, "Your moral principles don't apply in war. There are no just or unjust wars. There are only winners and losers. It's better to be on the winning side. You should register because you want the benefits and don't want to get busted."

Whom do you agree with here: James, his father, or his brother? Should a person register to fight if he doesn't believe in the justice of the wars that are being fought? How should moral principles apply in this case?

2. Terrorism. Marta has expressed sympathy for rebels fighting in country X. These rebels have been fighting against an unjust and malicious regime. The regime has killed innocent civilians and has an awful record of human rights violations. The rebellion started as a nonviolent protest in the streets, but now the rebels have taken up arms and are actively fighting government forces. They have begun to employ terror tactics, exploding car bombs in the city center in the capital. Marta supports the rebel cause and has even bought a T-shirt with a slogan from the rebel campaign on it. Marta's roommate, Andrea, is appalled. Andrea tells her, "How can you wear a T-shirt celebrating terrorists? They kill innocent people. Even if their cause is just, the rebels have crossed the line. They're murderers. All terrorists are simply murderers."

Marta replies, "That's easy for you to say because you're not suffering under a repressive government. The rebels are justified in doing whatever it takes to bring down the government. The government forces are ruthless and strong—the rebels have to use terrorism: it's their only tool."

Whom do you agree with: Marta or Andrea? Is terrorism justified as a tool of last resort? Or is terrorism always murder? Explain your answer, making use of concepts employed in discussions of realism, just war theory, and pacifism.

3. Military Intervention. The ruler of country Z has a terrible record of human rights violations. He has ordered the slaughter of civilians and has threatened to invade neighboring states. He has been working with known arms dealers to develop his military capacity. And he has worked to spread his influence by supporting insurgent fighters and terrorist groups in other countries. Three students are debating this case and what the United States should do in response. Roxanne is a realist. She argues that the United States should attack country Z with massive force as soon as possible with the goal of decapitating the regime. "That's what we did in Japan during World War II. And now Japan is a peaceful and stable ally." Patrick is a pacifist. He disagrees. "You know that we dropped atomic weapons on Japan and firebombed cities. It was immoral to do that. The end doesn't justify the means. We have to find nonviolent alternatives to deal with Z." Justin advocates limited use of military force. He says, "The just war tradition might allow for preemptive force and may allow for limited war in defense of human rights. But we have to be careful not to kill civilians." Roxanne shakes her head. "Sorry, but you can't win a war without killing civilians. And the faster you win, the better for everyone." Patrick sighs. "Have we even tried all of the nonviolent alternatives?" Justin shrugs. "If we go to war, it can only be a last resort. But, Roxanne, you can't just kill the innocent. You've got to win hearts and minds, as well."

Whom do you agree with in this debate? Why? What do you suggest we do about brutal dictators and aggressive regimes?

Knowledge Check Answer Key

1. **b.** Positive peace involves social harmony, while negative peace is the absence of overt violence.

2. **d.** *Satyagraha* means love force and is a method of nonviolent protest.

3. **d.** Using war to produce a just and lasting peace is not a concern of *jus ad bellum*.

4. **a.** The idea of the "double effect" is used to allow for collateral damage when thinking about *jus in bello*.

19 Environmental Ethics

Learning Outcomes

After reading this chapter, you should be able to:

19.1 Explain the difference between anthropocentric and non-anthropocentric (ecocentric or biocentric) approaches in terms of environmental ethics.

19.2 Clarify the difference between intrinsic value and instrumental value.

19.3 Explain how cost–benefit analysis applies in thinking about environmental issues.

19.4 Apply the concept of environmental justice to some concrete issues.

19.5 Analyze differences and similarities between ecofeminism and deep ecology.

19.6 Evaluate current environmental challenges, including issues related to climate change, pollution, wilderness preservation, and native lands.

19.7 Defend a thesis with regard to environmental issues and the value of nonhuman nature.

The Costs of Climate Change

Climate change is costly. According to one estimate, prepared by the U.S. Office of Management and Budget in 2022, the cost of environmental disasters related to climate change was approximately $120 billion per year during each of the prior five years.[1] These costs included responses to floods, droughts, wildfires, crop failures, and storms—each of which may be exacerbated by global warming. The Federal Budget Office warns that these costs will continue to increase as the climate warms. They estimate that

David Grossman/Alamy

by the end of this century, this could cost the United States $2 trillion per year. Scientists are still trying to figure out exactly how much the warming atmosphere will contribute to more intense storms, rising sea levels, and increased risk of drought, flood, and fire.[2] But there is no doubt that climate change is costly and will continue to be so. These economic costs are, of course, only part of the picture. A warming climate will also cause ecosystems to fail and species to go extinct on land and in the oceans. This includes the possibility of what some are warning may be the sixth mass extinction event in the history of the Earth.[3]

And yet today we continue to enjoy the benefits of a global economy that runs on fossil fuels. This economy provides us with goods that we enjoy—including food and consumer goods that are shipped around the world, advanced heating and cooling systems, and the convenience of cars and airplanes. This economy runs on fossil fuels, which add climate-changing gases like carbon dioxide to the atmosphere. In 2022, the Intergovernmental Panel on Climate Change stated bluntly that "limiting global warming will require major transitions in the energy sector."[4] But such a transition will also be costly and may cause disruptions and inconveniences, as shipping, transportation, and other sectors of the economy shift away from fossil fuels in order to reduce carbon emissions. There is a fundamental conflict here between the conveniences and habits of the present generation and the costs that will be borne by future generations, who will inherit a warmer world.

What Do You Think?

1. Do present generations have a duty to reduce carbon emissions for the benefit of future generations?

2. Are you concerned about the damage that a changing climate might inflict on nonhuman nature, including the risk of mass extinctions?

3. What kinds of things should people (including yourself) do to prevent and mitigate the risk of climate change?

4. Is individual action enough or do we also need a systematic and structural approach to climate change? And what kinds of ethical ideas might help to support structural change at the international level?

Introduction

19.1 Explain the difference between anthropocentric and non-anthropocentric (ecocentric or biocentric) approaches in terms of environmental ethics.

Between 2015 and 2021, six different wildfires threatened the giant sequoia trees of California's Sierra Nevada. These ancient trees are among the largest and oldest living things on Earth. They grow in a narrow ecosystem, at elevations between 5,000 and 7,000 feet in the mountains of California. The oldest of these trees are over three thousand years old. During the fires that burned through the California mountains in recent years, the groves of giant sequoias were devastated. The National Park Service estimates that between twenty-two hundred and thirty-five hundred giant trees were killed by fire.[5] Sequoias live in an ecosystem that has always been regularly burned by wildfire. As a result, they are adapted to a world of fire. Fire helps their seeds germinate and clears the underbrush so the saplings can grow. The bark of the sequoia is thick and the tree's canopy is high above the undergrowth, which helps these trees resist fire. But as the National Park Service explains, in the 1860s, the typical pattern of forest fires was altered, as American settlers drove out native tribes, brought in sheep that ate the undergrowth, and eventually began suppressing wildfires. This led to a changed forest ecosystem. And then in the past couple of decades, a long-lasting drought afflicted the American West along with a warming climate. This left the sequoia forests vulnerable to increasingly intense fires.

Some may suggest that this is just the way nature works. There are long cycles of warming and cooling, rain, snow, drought, and fire. These cycles include the rise and fall of plant and animal species. Some may shrug, thinking there is not much we can do about forest fires and the death of these giant trees. But others may feel that something precious is lost when a three-thousand-year-old tree dies. Some may mourn the loss of these trees. And many will wonder whether human beings have an obligation to repair the damage we have done to the ecosystem, while also taking action to better manage and preserve these ancient forests.

The issues discussed here are concerns of what philosophers call "environmental ethics." Environmental ethics asks us to consider moral questions that arise in thinking about our relationship with the nonhuman world. These questions sometimes focus on the value of nonhuman objects such as trees and forests—and our obligations to them. But environmental ethicists also ask questions about how we ought to manage environmental issues in light of their impacts on human beings. Ethicists often use the term "environmental justice" when discussing questions about the impact of environmental issues on human beings and on future generations.

To make this clear, in addition to thinking about the value of trees like the giant sequoia, we should also consider the way that wildfire harms human beings. Fires in California during the last decade have killed hundreds of human beings, including firefighters. They have also caused billions of dollars in property damage. In 2017, a fire in the California wine country killed forty-four people.[6] A year later, the Camp Fire in Northern California killed eighty-five people.[7] And while California fires occupy the headlines in the United States, similar stories occur across the globe. In 2017, a wildfire killed more than sixty people in Portugal.[8] In 2018, a fire killed more than one hundred people in Greece.[9] And on it goes. The good news is that modern technologies make it easier for human beings to predict the course of deadly forest fires and escape their wrath. The deadliest fires in modern history occurred in the nineteenth century. The Peshtigo Fire, which burned across northern Wisconsin in 1871, killed as many as twenty-five hundred people.[10] The bad news is that as the climate changes and human population grows, it is likely that we will continue to confront deadly wildfires.

If the focus of our concern is on the people who are harmed by an environmental impact, we would say that our focus is **anthropocentric**, which means human-centered. As should be obvious, the concerns of environmental justice are anthropocentric. But we might also be concerned with damage to the nonhuman world. In that case, we would say that our concerns are **non-anthropocentric.** If, for example, we believe that sequoia trees have value apart from our interest in them, our concerns are non-anthropocentric. Environmental ethicists sometimes also describe non-anthropocentrism using terms such as **biocentrism** and **ecocentrism**. Biocentrism focuses on the value of living things (i.e., animals and even plants), while ecocentrism is broader and is concerned with large ecosystems and

even with nonliving things (e.g., glaciers, watersheds, or maybe even the Earth itself).

There have always been wildfires, just as there have always been deadly storms, floods, droughts, and hurricanes. But as we saw in our discussion of wildfire, human activity causes changes in this natural phenomenon. Something similar likely holds true for hurricanes and other storms. A 2022 report from NASA concludes that a changing climate will cause hurricanes to become more intense and more destructive.[11] This is due to warmer oceans, higher temperatures, and rising sea levels caused by climate change.

At issue here is a question of the value of nature and our place within it. Is the natural world something to be revered and cherished? Or is Mother Nature to be feared and dominated? What sorts of impacts should human beings have on the environment? When environmental disasters occur, how should we respond? And what should we do to mitigate future disasters?

These sorts of questions must be confronted as the human population continues to expand. Earth's human population is approaching 8 billion people.[12] The human population is expected to increase through this century—up to 9.7 billion by 2050 and around 11 billion by the end of the century.[13] At the same time, standards of living are increasing, which creates greater demand for energy, more pollution, and related environmental impacts. The United Nations published a "Global Environmental Outlook" report in 2019 that offered a dire warning about the future. Among the conclusions of the report was the following:

> Unsustainable production and consumption patterns and trends and inequality, when combined with increases in the use of resources that are driven by population growth, put at risk the healthy planet needed to attain sustainable development. Those trends are leading to a deterioration in planetary health at unprecedented rates, with increasingly serious consequences, in particular for poorer people and regions.[14]

Among the issues indicated as problems in the report are climate change, loss of biodiversity (including the loss of pollinators and coral reefs), water pollution and depletion, and high urban air pollution.[15]

The air pollution problem is particularly severe in developing countries. And this leads to a question of environmental justice. Often the air pollution found in developing countries is the result of producing goods that will be consumed by those in the developed world. Consider, for example, the level of particulate matter (PM 2.5) found in the air. This causes the air to be hazy and is damaging to the lungs when breathed. The UN Report states, "Asia had the highest absolute number of deaths in 2016 attributable to PM 2.5 exposure, due to its large populations and high levels of industrial activity. However, PM 2.5 exposures have begun to decline in China but are increasing in parts of South Asia. Asian countries also bear the largest burden of air pollution caused by the production of goods consumed in other regions of the world, primarily Western Europe and North America."[16] If we wonder whether this is fair, we are asking a question about environmental justice.

Even in the United States, air pollution remains a problem. California's Central Valley has some of the worst air pollution in the country (including significant levels of PM 2.5). The Central Valley is the agricultural powerhouse of California, which means that there is a large population of farmworkers—a poor and often immigrant labor force. This region also has a high number of children with asthma and other respiratory problems. Studies in the Central Valley show that air pollution rates are correlated with asthma attacks, heart attacks, and emergency room visits for pneumonia and bronchitis.[17] These rates are higher than in areas of coastal California, which leads us again to ask questions about environmental justice. Is it fair that the farmworkers who produce food for those who live on the coast suffer from the adverse effects of air pollution?

We can see from the examples discussed here—climate change, wildfire management, hurricane impacts, and air pollution—that there are a variety of important environmental issues. Some may argue that these issues are properly a subset of other ethical concerns. For example, some may view environmental justice in connection to issues concerning social justice, economic inequality, and global justice (as discussed in Chapters 14 and 16). Others may deny that we can have ethical obligations to something as abstract as "the

Figure 19-1 Environmental disasters such as hurricanes can cause significant damage.

environment." Others will argue that we do have obligations to the environment, as well as to animal species (we will discuss obligations to animals in more detail in Chapter 17). Regardless, most would agree that we ought to be concerned about the negative impacts that environmental problems cause for people, especially the vulnerable poor communities that are often most adversely affected by pollution and natural disasters. We may also have obligations to future generations: to leave a livable world to our children and grandchildren.

The Environment and Its Value

19.2 Clarify the difference between intrinsic value and instrumental value.

The word *environment* comes from *environs*, which means "in circuit" or "turning around in" in Old French.[18] From this comes the common meaning of environment as surroundings, which has a spatial meaning: the surrounding environment is the area around us. However, we have also come to use the term more broadly to refer to what goes on in that space—that is, the climate and other factors that act on living organisms or individuals inhabiting the space. We can think of the environment as a systematic collection of materials with various physical and chemical interactions. Or we can think of it in a more organic way, giving attention to the many ways in which individual life forms are interdependent in their very nature. From the latter viewpoint, we cannot even think of an individual as an isolated atomic thing because its environment is a fundamental part of itself. From this point of view, the environment stands in relation to the beings within it—not externally, but internally.

What does it mean for people to value the environment? Certainly, most people realize the important effects that their environment has on them. Those things that produce benefit are good; those that cause harm are bad. Most of the time, it is a mixture of both. Growth is generally good, and poison is bad. But where does this positive or negative value come from? Is "badness" somehow there in the poison? Is "goodness" contained in the idea of growth? This is a considerably difficult metaphysical and moral problem. Does a thing have value in the same sense that it has hair or weight? This does not seem to be so because a thing's value does not seem to be something it possesses. When we value something, we have a positive response toward it. One way to explain this is to think that the value of things is a matter of our preferences or desires. But we also want to know whether we *should* prefer or desire them. Is there something about the things that we value—some attributes that they have, for example—that provide a legitimate basis for our valuing them? In answering this question, we should bear in mind our earlier discussions (in the first half of this book) of the objectivity of values and the relation between the facts of nature and value judgments. Is it possible to derive an "ought" with regard to the environment? Is there a natural state of affairs that we ought to value? Or are our environmental values merely tastes or preferences?

One distinction about value plays a particularly significant role in environmental ethics: that between intrinsic and instrumental value. Things have **intrinsic value**, sometimes referred to as **inherent value**, when they have value or worth in themselves. We value things that have intrinsic value for their own sake and not for what we can get or do with them. Something has **instrumental value** if it is valued because of its usefulness for some other purpose and for someone. Some environmentalists believe that trees, for example, have only instrumental and not intrinsic value.

They think that trees are valuable because of their usefulness to us. Those who think this way may point out, for example, that trees provide us with wood and pulp. This kind of instrumental value is fairly obvious. But trees also help to convert carbon dioxide in the air into oxygen, through the process of photosynthesis. They also provide humans with canopied forests to enjoy and explore. In urban areas, trees can also help to reduce the temperature of urban heat islands. Some environmental ethicists use the term "**ecosystem services**" to explain these kinds of instrumental value. In a sense, the idea of ecosystem services asks us to consider what the ecosystem does for us—what it provides us. This is understood not only in economic terms (as in the price of wood or pulp) but also in terms of other kinds of value, including aesthetic values, health values, and so on. Other environmentalists believe that plants and ecosystems have value in themselves. This idea might hold that a three-thousand-year-old sequoia is valuable, not because of *what it does for us* but, rather, because of *what it is*. From this perspective, the tree is simply valuable, without reference to its usefulness for us. It is easy to see that the distinction between instrumental value and intrinsic value maps fairly well onto the distinction between anthropocentrism and non-anthropocentrism. Those who focus on instrumental value tend to take an anthropocentric approach, while those who claim that animals, trees, or ecosystems have intrinsic value tend toward a non-anthropocentric view. Somewhere between these two divergent approaches to environmental ethics we might find a moderate or centrist position that combines elements of each, in what we might call a mixed view (see Table 19-1).

Another term sometimes used in discussions about environmental ethics is *prima facie value*. (As we saw in our discussion of W. D. Ross's concept of *prima facie duties* in Chapters 3 and 7, *prima facie* means "at first glance" or "at first sight.") Something has prima facie value if it has the kind of value that can be overcome by other interests or values. For example, we might think that a rainforest has some sort of prima facie value but that if the local population needed more land on which to cultivate food, people might be justified in cutting some of the trees to make room for crops.

Table 19-1 Outline of Moral Approaches to Environmental Ethics

	Non-Anthropocentrism	Moderate or Mixed View	Anthropocentrism
Thesis	Biocentric or ecocentric focus of deep ecology or ecofeminism	Balancing human and nonhuman interests	Environmental issues must be resolved in terms of human interests
Corollaries and Implications	Nonhuman entities (species, ecosystems, etc.) have intrinsic value that cannot be reduced to human interests; focus on wilderness preservation; ecofeminist critique of other forms of domination	Recognizes intrinsic and instrumental value of nonhuman beings; sustainable development and environmental justice balance human needs with respect for nature	Human profit, health, and happiness are primary; denies intrinsic value of nonhuman beings (they only have instrumental value); environmental justice for humans only
Connections with Moral Theory	Deontological focus on duties generated by intrinsic value of nature and respect for nature; consequentialist analysis extended to include consequences for nonhuman beings	Deontological concern for nonhuman beings in connection with respect for human interests; consequentialist analysis may balance human and nonhuman concerns	Deontological and consequentialist concern is focused only on human beings; duties to nature are indirectly based in respect for human property rights or preventing human suffering
Relevant Authors/ Examples	Bill Devall and George Sessions; Vandana Shiva; Winona LaDuke	Ramachandra Guha	William Baxter

Anthropocentrism

The terms **anthropocentrism** and **anthropocentric** refer to a human-centered perspective. A perspective is anthropocentric if it holds that humans alone have intrinsic worth or value. According to the anthropocentric perspective, things are good to the extent that they promote the interests of human beings. Thus, for example, some people believe that animals are valuable only insofar as they promote the interests of humans or are useful to us in one or more of a variety of ways. (More discussion of this is found in Chapter 17 on animal ethics.) For example, animals provide nutritional, medical, protective, emotional, and aesthetic benefits for us. People who hold an anthropocentric view also may believe that it is bad to cause animals needless pain, but if their

pain is necessary to ensure some important human good, it is justified. We do obtain useful products from the natural world. For example, Taxol is a drug synthesized from the bark of the Pacific yew tree and is useful in treating ovarian and breast cancers. In the most basic and general sense, nature provides us with our food, shelter, and clothing.

According to an anthropocentric perspective, the environment or nature has no value in itself. Instead, its value is measured by how it affects human beings. Wilderness areas are instrumentally valuable to us as sources of recreation and relaxation, and they provide natural resources to meet our physical needs, such as lumber for housing and fuel. Estuaries, grasslands, and ancient forests also purify our air and clean our water.

As mentioned earlier, we can describe these kinds of useful products of the environment as ecosystem services.

Sometimes anthropocentric values conflict. For instance, we cannot both preserve old-growth forests for their beauty or historical interest and also use them for lumber. Therefore, we need to think about the relative value of aesthetic experiences and historical appreciation as compared with cheaper housing, lumbering jobs, and the impact of lumbering on erosion, climate change, forest fire risks, and so on. Consider the value of three-thousand-year-old sequoia trees. Touching one of these giants today connects us to the beginning of the Common Era. We can imagine all of the major events in history that have occurred during the life of this tree and, in doing so, gain a greater appreciation of the reality of those events and their connection to us and the world as we experience it. How would the value of this experience compare with the value of the tree's wood on the lumber market? Cost–benefit analyses present one method for making such comparisons.

Cost–Benefit Analysis

19.3   Explain how cost–benefit analysis applies in thinking about environmental issues.

Because many environmental issues appeal to diverse values and involve competing interests, we can use a technique known as *cost–benefit analysis* to help us think about how to approach any given environmental problem. If we have a choice between various actions or policies, we need to assess and compare the various harms (or costs) and benefits that each entails in order to know which is the better action or policy. Using this method, we should choose the option that has the greater net balance of *benefits* over harms (or *costs*). This is connected to utilitarian reasoning. For example, suppose we are considering whether to hold industrial polluters to stricter emissions standards. If emissions were reduced, acid rain and global warming would be curtailed. These are important benefits. However, this would also create increased costs for the polluting companies, their employees, and those who buy their products or use their services. We should consider whether the benefits would be worth those costs. We would also need to assess the relative costs and benefits of alternative policies designed to address acid rain and global warming.

Involved in such analyses are two distinct elements. One is an assessment or description of these factual matters as far as they can be known. What exactly are the likely effects of doing this or that? The other is evaluation, or the establishment of relative values. In cost–benefit analyses, the value is generally defined in anthropocentric terms. But we still need to clarify which values matter most—clean air, economic development, and so forth. In addition, if we have a fixed amount of money or resources to expend on an environmental project, we know that this money or these resources will not be available for projects elsewhere. Thus, every expenditure will have a certain *opportunity cost*. In being willing to pay for the environmental project, we will have some sense of its importance in comparison with other things that we will not then be able to do or have. However, if we value something else just as much or more than cleaner air or water, for example, we will not be willing to pay for the cleaner air or water.

In making such evaluations, we may know what monetary costs will be added to a particular forest product, such as lumber, if limits on logging were enacted. However, we are less sure about how we should value a tree that is three thousand years old. How do we measure the historical appreciation or the aesthetic value of the tree (or the animals that live in the tree)? How do we measure the recreational value of the wilderness? What is beauty or the life of a tree worth? The value of these "intangibles" is difficult to measure because measuring implies that we use a standard means of evaluation. Only if we have such a standard can we compare, say, the value of a breathtaking view to that of a dam about to be built on the site. Sometimes, we use monetary valuations, even for such intangibles as human lives or life years. For example, in insurance and other contexts, people attempt to give some measure of the value of a life.[19] Doing so is sometimes necessary, but it is obviously also problematic.

The idea of ecosystem services can be useful in thinking about cost–benefit analyses. One of the factors that ought to be included in an environmental decision from an anthropocentric vantage point is the value of these ecosystem services. This kind of issue arises, for example, in thinking about mitigation, restoration, and prevention projects. For example, there are costs that must be considered in restoring a habitat—say a wetland, a forest, or a prairie. But these costs may be offset by the ecosystem services provided by the restored resource. This is difficult to measure, of course. But the concept of ecosystem service may be useful for those who propose such projects. In addition to focusing on the intrinsic value of a wetland, say, an anthropocentric argument in favor of restoring that wetland might also include an analysis of the kinds of services provided by the wetland. This could include abstract arguments about the value of biodiversity. But it might also include concrete accounts of how restored wetlands help to support hunting and fishing, and how wetlands can protect urban areas from flooding during storms.

Environmental Justice

19.4   Apply the concept of environmental justice to some concrete issues.

Another anthropocentric concern is how environmental costs are distributed across human populations. As mentioned above, this is connected to the issues of social justice and economic justice. An important question from the standpoint of environmental justice is how environmental policies and projects impact people in different ways, including in particular, how underserved, marginalized, and low-income communities of people are affected by environmental problems. This may include the question of "environmental racism," which is concerned with how unjust environmental policies impact different racial groups unequally. This can reflect racial injustices in society and can also contribute to further disadvantages for oppressed people. Another question related to environmental justice is how our activities will affect future generations. Do we have an obligation to leave them a clean environment? It is difficult to figure out what justice requires for future generations. But the more pressing issue is the distribution of benefits and harms for actual persons living in the present in a world in which racism, classism, sexism, and intolerance undermine just distributions.

Environmental justice is a mainstream idea, which the U.S. Environmental Protection Agency defines as "the fair treatment and meaningful involvement of all people regardless of race, color, national origin, or income with respect to the development, implementation, and enforcement of environmental laws, regulations, and policies."[20] It may seem odd that we would need to emphasize that environmental issues should contain an element of social justice and equity, if we think that environmental issues are about "the environment" and not about people. But in reality, people in underserved and low-income communities end up suffering most from environmental degradation. For example, consider the fact that affluent nations with established and efficient infrastructure will be able to respond to the changing climate in ways that poorer nations will not. People whose income is below the federal poverty level tend to live closer to polluted lands and toxic waste dumps because more affluent people can move away and can use their resources to fight against pollution in the areas where they live. This is a concern not only in the United States, where poor people suffer most from the effects of pollution, but also across the globe. Environmental regulations are often nonexistent or are loosely enforced in developing countries.

One notorious case that frequently comes up in discussions of environmental justice is the gas leak at the Union Carbide plant in Bhopal, India, in 1984. More than 3,000 people died within the first days of the poisonous gas leak. The final death toll is estimated to be at least 15,000, with the health of more than 600,000 people affected.[21] Amnesty International puts the death toll higher: 22,000 killed with at least 150,000 still battling diseases of the lungs or liver that are attributed to the toxic waste.[22] In addition to the human casualties, the disaster left behind polluted land and water, which is still not cleaned up. The local managers responsible for the disaster received minor fines and punishments after being found guilty of criminal negligence in the case. However, the former chairman of Union Carbide, Warren Anderson, never received any punishment. In 2012, an American court dismissed a lawsuit filed by Bhopal residents against Anderson and Dow Chemical, which owns Union Carbide. The dismissal protected Anderson and the company from claims for environmental remediation at the disaster site.[23] This case is remarkable because of the numbers affected and the relatively minor punishments meted out to responsible parties, and because it pushes our understanding of what counts as "the environment." Often we think of environmentalism as focused on wild natural settings, but the air and water of urban landscapes are also part of the environment. The Bhopal case reminds us that pollution can cause death and that it is often people who live in poverty who suffer the most from the impacts of industrial accidents.[24]

There are a variety of issues that come under the rubric of environmental justice, including where waste dumps are located, whether farmworkers and farming communities are properly protected from the effects of fertilizers and pesticides, how uranium is mined, how hunting and fishing are regulated and enforced, who pays for environmental remediation efforts, and who guarantees that polluters are punished. These concerns are connected to other social justice concerns and are entirely anthropocentric. This has led some to complain that the focus on environmental justice is a distraction from the larger concern for the value of ecosystems in themselves, apart from human interests. One scholar of environmentalism, Kevin DeLuca, laments this anthropocentric focus, concluding, "Abandoning wilderness-centered environmentalism is a disastrous error. The finest moments of environmentalism often involve humans exceeding self-concern and caring for wilderness and other species because of their intrinsic being."[25] This claim points us to the ecocentric or biocentric approach to environmental ethics.

Ecocentrism

According to the anthropocentric perspective, environmental concerns ought to be directed to the betterment of people, who alone have intrinsic value. In contrast with this view are **ecocentrism** and **biocentrism.** As mentioned above, ecocentrism is broadly concerned with the value of nonhuman entities and systems, while biocentrism focuses a bit more closely on living things. In either case, the basic standpoint is non-anthropocentric. The idea of ecocentrism is that it is not just humans who have intrinsic worth or value but also such things as plants, animals, and ecosystems. There are variations within this perspective, with some theorists holding that

individual life forms have such intrinsic worth and others stressing that it is whole systems or ecosystems that have such value. In this view, ethical questions related to the environment involve determining what is in the best interests of these life forms, or what furthers or contributes to (or is a satisfactory fit with) some ecosystem.

Ecocentrists are critical of anthropocentrists. Why, they ask, do only humans have intrinsic value while everything else has merely instrumental value for us? Some fault the Judeo-Christian tradition for this view. In particular, they single out the biblical mandate to "subdue" the Earth and "have dominion over the fish of the sea and over the birds of the air and every living thing that moves upon the Earth" as being responsible for this instrumentalist view of nature and other living things.[26] Others argue that anthropocentrism is a reductionist perspective. According to this view, all of nature is reduced to the level of "thing-hood." The seventeenth-century French philosopher René Descartes is sometimes cited as a source of this reductionist point of view because of his belief that the essential element of humanity is the ability to think ("I think, therefore I am," etc.) and his belief that animals are mere biological machines.[27] Early evolutionary accounts also sometimes depicted humans as the pinnacle of evolution or the highest or last link in some great chain of being. We can ask ourselves whether we place too high a value on human beings and our powers of reason and intelligence. Ecocentrists criticize the view that we ought to seek to understand nature so that we can have power over it because it implies that our primary relation to nature is one of domination.

Ecocentrists hold that we ought rather to regard nature with admiration and respect because nature and natural beings have intrinsic value. Let us return to our example of the three-thousand-year-old sequoia tree. You may have seen pictures of trees large enough for tunnels to be cut through, allowing cars to pass. In the 1880s, such a tunnel was cut through a giant sequoia near Wawona, California, on the south end of what is now Yosemite National Park. Tourists enjoyed driving through the tunnel. However, some people claimed that this was a mutilation of and an insult to this majestic tree. They said that the tree itself had a kind of integrity, intrinsic value, and dignity that should not be invaded lightly. Another way to put it would be to say that the tree itself had moral standing.[28] What we do to the tree itself matters morally, they insisted.

On what account could trees be thought to have this kind of moral standing? All organisms, it might be argued, are self-maintaining systems.[29] Because they are organized systems or integrated living wholes, organisms are thought to have intrinsic value and even moral standing. The value may be only prima facie, but nevertheless, they have their own value in themselves and are not just to be valued in terms of their usefulness to people. According to this perspective, the giant sequoias of Wawona should not merely be thought of in terms of their tourist value.

Further, there are things that can be good and bad for the trees themselves. For example, the tunnel in the Wawona tree eventually weakened the tree, and it fell during a snowstorm in 1968. Although trees are not **moral agents**—beings that act responsibly for moral reasons—they may still be thought of as moral patients. A **moral patient** is any being for which what we do to it matters, in itself. A moral patient is any being toward whom we can have *direct duties*, rather than simply *indirect duties*. If a tree is a moral patient, we ought to behave in a certain way toward it for its sake, and not just indirectly for the sake of how it will eventually affect us. Ecocentrists may argue that there are things that are in the best interests of trees, even if the trees take no conscious interest in them.

In addition to those who argue that all life forms have intrinsic value, there are others who take an even broader and more holistic approach that focuses on the value of ecosystems. An *ecosystem* is an integrated system of interacting and interdependent parts within a circumscribed locale. They are loosely structured wholes. The boundary changes and some members come and go. Sometimes, there is competition within the whole—as in the relation between predators and prey in a given habitat. Sometimes there is *symbiosis*, with each part living in cooperative community with the other parts—as in the relationship between flowers and the bees that pollinate them. The need to survive pushes various creatures to be creative in their struggle for an adaptive fit. There is a unity to the whole, but it is loose and decentralized. Why is this unity to be thought of as having value in itself?

One answer is provided by the environmental philosopher Aldo Leopold. In the 1940s, he wrote in his famous essay "The Land Ethic" that we should think about the land as "a fountain of energy flowing through a circuit of soils, plants, and animals."[30] Look at any environment supporting life on our planet and you will find a *system* of life, intricately interwoven and interdependent elements that function as a whole. Such a system is organized in the form of a *biotic pyramid*, with myriad smaller organisms at the bottom and gradually fewer and more complex organisms at the top. Plants depend on the earth, insects depend on the plants, and other animals depend on the insects. Leopold did not think it amiss to speak about the whole system as being healthy or unhealthy. If the soil is washed away or abnormally flooded, the whole system suffers or is sick. In this system, individual organisms feed off one another. Some elements come and others go. It is the whole that continues. Leopold also believed that a particular type of ethics follows from this view of nature—a biocentric or ecocentric ethics. He believed that "a thing is right when it tends to preserve the integrity, stability, and beauty of the biotic community. It is wrong when it tends to do otherwise."[31] The system has a certain *integrity* because it is a unity of interdependent elements that combine to make a whole with a unique character. It has a certain *stability*, not because it does not change, but because it changes only gradually. Finally, it has a particular *beauty*. Here beauty is a matter of harmony, well-ordered form, or unity in diversity.[32] When envisioned on a larger scale, the entire Earth system may then be regarded as one system with a certain integrity, stability, and beauty. Morality becomes a matter of preserving this system or doing only what befits it.

The kind of regard for nature that is manifest in biocentric and ecocentric points of view is not limited to contemporary philosophers. One source of this way of thinking can be traced to certain forms of European and American Romanticism, which imbued nature with spiritual value. The transcendentalists Ralph Waldo Emerson and Henry David Thoreau fall into this category. Transcendentalism was a movement of romantic idealism that arose in the United States in the mid-nineteenth century. Rather than regarding nature as foreign or alien, Emerson and Thoreau thought of it as a friend or kindred spirit. Acting on such a viewpoint, Thoreau retreated to Walden Pond to live life to its fullest and commune with nature. He wanted to know its moods and changes and all its phenomena. Although Thoreau and Emerson read the "lessons" of nature, they also read broadly the texts of European and Asian thinkers. Some have characterized aspects of their nature theory as idealism, the view that all is idea or spirit; others characterize it as pantheism, the doctrine that holds that God is present in the whole of nature. The transcendentalists influenced John Muir, the founder of the Sierra Club. Muir held a similar view of the majesty, sacredness, and spiritual value of nature.[33] He transformed his love of nature into practical action, successfully petitioning Congress for passage of a national parks bill that established Yosemite and Sequoia National Parks.

We should pause here to point out the need for a critical reinterpretation of John Muir and the early years of the American conservation movement. The conservationists of the nineteenth century was established at the same time that native peoples were being driven off the land in the American West, and while slaves were working the land in the American South. Muir had racist views of Black and Native American people that were typical of White men of his era, and that we can no longer countenance today. Indeed, the Sierra Club, which Muir founded, has taken steps to distance itself from Muir's racism.[34] We should also note that the "wilderness" that Muir celebrated had once been occupied by native peoples. Yosemite Valley and the surrounding lands that became Yosemite National Park, for example, was once home to Indigenous Miwok people, which includes the tribe known as the Ahwahneechee.[35] These native peoples were forcibly removed from the area in the 1850s. It was after that that Muir helped convince President Theodore Roosevelt to make the area a national park in 1890; and it was in 1892 that Muir founded the Sierra Club in Yosemite.[36] It is important to acknowledge that the idea of preserving a unique natural wonder like Yosemite only came to fruition after the native peoples were removed. This process of reevaluating the early heroes of environmentalism has led some to question Aldo Leopold's land ethic, although Leopold's approach was not focused on an empty wilderness but instead was more sensitive to the

way that the land depended on the people who inhabit it.[37] Another important moment in this reassessment involves another bastion of the early American conservation movement, James Audubon, the namesake of the Audubon Society. The Audubon Society aims to preserve birds and the forest and other places that provide habitat for birds. But James John Audubon owned slaves.[38] In 2021, an article was published in *Audubon Magazine*, written by J. Drew Lanham, a Black man and a bird lover. In trying to come to terms with Audubon's racism, Lanham points out that it is important to note this glaring blind spot within the American conservation movement—and that in the twenty-first century, we should work to overcome this legacy.[39]

One important issue here is the question of how human beings imagine nature—and what we bring with us in imagining nature. Do we look beyond human suffering and seek to escape from injustice by retreating into the wilderness? Thoreau, for example, retreated to Walden Pond to contemplate nature and read Chinese philosophy. But he also remained engaged with the suffering and injustices of the political world. He engaged in civil disobedience in his protest against war and slavery. But we should note that Audubon and Muir were not as engaged with the problem of human injustice. This does not mean that the nature idealism of Muir can simply be dismissed. But it does remind us that we must look out for our own blind spots, as we consider the question of environmental ethics and issues of environmental justice. It also means that we should listen to other voices who articulate an ecocentric point of view, including especially those who were oppressed and dispossessed by those early advocates of the conservation movement.

One important source for such a worldview is the wisdom of Indigenous traditions. For example, Native American views on nature provide a fertile source of biocentric thinking. For instance, Eagle Man, an Oglala Sioux writer, emphasizes the unity of all living things. All come from tiny seeds, and so all are brothers and sisters. The seeds come from Mother Earth and depend on her for sustenance. We owe her respect, for she comes from the "Great Spirit Above."[40] This idea of "Mother Earth" as a source and focal point has also been articulated by Native American author and activist Winona LaDuke. In the 1990s, a group of Indigenous women met in China and offered a declaration of solidarity with Mother Earth. That declaration incorporated ideas expressed by Winona LaDuke:

> The Earth is our mother. From her we get our life, and our ability to live. It is our responsibility to care for our Mother, and in caring for our Mother, we care for ourselves. Women, all females are a manifestation of Mother Earth in human form. We are her daughters, and in my cultural instructions we are to care for her. I am taught to live in respect for Mother Earth. . . . One hundred years ago, one of our great leaders, Chief Seattle, stated, "What befalls the Earth befalls the people of the Earth." And that is the reality today, and the situation of the status of women, and the status of indigenous women and indigenous peoples.[41]

LaDuke is a well-known advocate for the rights of native peoples who has also been engaged in electoral politics. In the 1990s, she was the Green Party's candidate for vice president, on the ticket with Ralph Nader. In the speech quoted above, she continues by pointing out that Indigenous peoples are not represented at the United Nations. She argues that environmental problems are linked to the exploitation and oppression of Indigenous people. Her vision of nature is not one that is devoid of people. Rather, it is one in which people live in harmony with the land.

Romantic and idealistic ideas provide a stark contrast to anthropocentric views of a reductionist type. However, they also raise many questions. For example, we can ask the transcendentalist how nature can be spirit or god in more than a metaphorical sense. And we can ask proponents of views such as Aldo Leopold's why is it that nature is good? Nature can be cruel, at least from the point of view of certain animals, and even from our own viewpoint as we suffer the damaging results of typhoons or volcanic eruptions. And, more abstractly, on what basis can we argue that whatever exists is good—especially in a world that contains predation, natural disasters, and the social disasters of racism, slavery, genocide, and environmental injustice?

Deep Ecology

Another variant of ecocentrism is the deep ecology movement. Members of this movement distinguish themselves from mainstream environmentalism, which they call "shallow ecology" and criticize as fundamentally anthropocentric. The term *deep ecology* was first used by Arne Naess, a Norwegian philosopher and environmentalist.[42] Deep ecologists take a holistic view of nature and believe that we should look more deeply to find the root causes of environmental degradation. The idea is that our environmental problems are deeply rooted in the Western psyche, and radical changes of viewpoint are necessary if we are to solve these problems. Western reductionism, individualism, and consumerism are said to be the causes of our environmental problems. The solution is to rethink and reformulate certain metaphysical beliefs about whether all reality is reducible to atoms in motion. It is also to rethink what it is to be an individual. Are individuals separate and independent beings? Or are they interrelated parts of a whole?

According to deep ecologists, solving our environmental problems requires a change in our views about what is a good quality of life. The good life, deep ecologists assert, is not one that stresses the possession of things and the search for satisfaction of wants and desires. Instead, a good life is one that is lived simply, in communion with one's local ecosystem. Arne Naess lived his message. He retreated to a cabin in the mountains of Norway, which he built with his own hands. He lived a modest life until his death at age ninety-six in 2009.

In addition to describing the need for radical changes in our basic outlook on life, the deep ecologist platform also holds that any intrusion into nature to change it requires justification. If we intervene to change nature, we must show that a vital need of ours is at stake.[43] We should be cautious in our actions because the results of our actions may be far-reaching and harmful. And we should view nature *as it is* as good, right, and well balanced. Deep ecology also includes the belief that the flourishing of nonhuman life requires a "substantial decrease in the human population."[44] George Sessions argues that "humanity must drastically scale down its industrial activities on Earth, change its consumption lifestyles, stabilize," and "reduce the size of the human population by humane means."[45]

Some critics maintain that deep ecologists are misanthropic because of their interest in reducing the human population or suggest that they are advocating totalitarian methods for achieving a reduction in human population. Some go so far as to malign deep ecology as "eco-fascism," equating it with fascist plans to create an ecological utopia through population control. Others worry that there may be implicit eugenic and imperialistic agendas when affluent Americans and Europeans advocate population control (see the Ramachandra Guha reading at the end of this chapter). This critique might be linked to our prior discussion of the way that Muir and an earlier generation of ecologists valued a vision of nature that had been emptied of native people. However, deep ecologists would reply that they recognize that population reduction can be achieved only through humane methods such as the empowerment of women and making contraception available.

The members of the deep ecology movement have been quite politically active. Their creed contains the belief that people are responsible for Earth. Beliefs such as this often provide a basis for the tactics of groups such as Earth First! Some radicals advocate direct action to protect the environment, including various forms of "ecosabotage"—for example, spiking trees to prevent logging and cutting power lines.[46] It is important to note that Arne Naess, himself, was interested in nonviolence. He wrote extensively about Gandhi's nonviolent methods, and he conceived his commitment to the environment in conjunction with Gandhian ideas about the interconnectedness of life. And he employed nonviolent methods in his own protests—such as chaining himself to a boulder to protest a project aimed at building a dam on a river.

Some critics of deep ecology have worried about aggressive forms of environmental protest that they call "ecoterrorism."[47] Of course, there are important distinctions to be made between nonviolent protest, civil disobedience, and more violent forms of protest. Nonetheless, deep ecologists maintain that the stakes are high and that action should be taken to change the status quo—even if this action is only at the level of personal lifestyle choices. On a philosophical level, the view

---

▶ **Knowledge Check**   Answers appear at the end of the chapter.

1. Anthropocentric approaches to environmental ethics are concerned with which of the following?

   a. Cost–benefit analysis involving human concerns

   b. Preserving the intrinsic value of nature

   c. Saving the earth by reducing human population

   d. Ending human domination over the natural world

2. A concern for "environmental racism" is properly understood as connected with _____?

   a. Biocentrism

   b. Ecocentrism

   c. The "land ethic"

   d. Environmental justice

3. How might we describe an account that insists that trees are valuable only because they provide wood and pulp for us to use?

   a. This account is focused on the intrinsic value of trees.

   b. This account is concerned with the instrumental value of trees.

   c. This account is interested in the question of environmental justice.

   d. This account is a form of biocentrism.

4. Which of the following is NOT primarily a concern of ecocentric thinkers?

   a. Preserving wildlands because of the ecosystem services they provide for human beings

   b. A holistic approach to the environment that emphasizes the integrity of the biotic community, including soils and ecosystems

   c. The belief that the natural world is a moral patient deserving moral concern and respect

   d. The idea that natural systems have a kind of beauty and goodness that cannot be understood merely as an instrumental value

that all incursions into nature can be justified only by our vital needs seems to run counter to our intuitions. The implication here is that we must not build a golf course or a house patio because these would change the Earth and its vegetation, and the need to play golf or sit on a patio is hardly vital. Do natural things have as much value as people and their interests? The view that nature itself has a "good of its own" or that the whole system has value in itself raises complex metaphysical and psychological questions. However we may feel about these issues, deep ecologists provide a valuable service by calling our attention to the possible deep philosophical roots and causes of some of our environmental problems.

Ecofeminism

19.5 Analyze differences and similarities between ecofeminism and deep ecology.

Another variant of ecological ethics is called *ecofeminism* or *ecological feminism*.[48] It may be seen as part of a broader movement that locates the source of environmental problems not in metaphysics or worldviews, as deep ecologists do, but in social practices. *Social ecology*, as this wider movement is called, holds that we should look to particular social patterns and structures to discover what is wrong with our relationship to the environment. Ecofeminists believe that the problem lies in a male-centered view of nature, in which human domination over nature mirrors male domination over women. According to Karen Warren, a philosopher and environmental activist, ecofeminism is "the position that there are important connections . . . between the domination of women and the domination of nature, an understanding of which is crucial to both feminism and environmental ethics."[49]
Deep ecology and ecofeminism both offer radical critiques of mainstream worldviews. But deep ecologists and ecofeminists do not necessarily agree. The deep ecologists may criticize ecofeminists for concentrating insufficiently on the environment, and ecofeminists may accuse deep ecologists of the very male-centered view that they believe is the source of our environmental problems.

A variety of ecofeminist views are espoused by diverse groups of feminists.[50] One version celebrates the ways that women differ from men. This view is espoused by those who hold that women—because of their female experience or nature—tend to value organic, non-oppressive relationships. They stress caring and emotion, and they seek to replace conflict and assertion of rights with cooperation and community. This idea has obvious connections with the work of those interested in the feminist ethics of care (as discussed in Chapter 9). From this perspective, a "feminine" ethic should guide our relationship to nature. Rather than use nature in an instrumentalist fashion that views the natural world as a resource to be managed, used, and exploited, they urge that we should cooperate with nature. We should manifest a caring and benevolent regard for nature, just as we do for other human beings. One version of this view would have us think of nature itself as in some way divine. Rather than think of God as a distant creator who transcends nature, these religiously oriented ecofeminists think of God as a being *within* nature. Some also refer to this God as "Mother Nature" or "Gaia," after the name of a Greek goddess.[51]

Another version of ecofeminism rejects the dualism often found in the Western philosophical tradition. This approach holds that the Western tradition promotes the devaluing and domination of both women and nature. Rather than divide reality into contrasting elements—the active and passive, the rational and emotional, the dominant and subservient—they encourage us to recognize the diversity within nature and among people. They would similarly support a variety of ways of relating to nature. Thus, they believe that even though science that proceeds from a male-oriented desire to control nature has made advances and continues to do so, its very orientation causes it to miss important aspects of nature. If, instead, we also have a feeling for nature and a listening attitude, we might be better able to know what actually is there. They also believe that we humans should see ourselves as part of the community of nature, not as distinct, nonnatural beings functioning in a world that is thought to be alien to us. Some versions of ecofeminism emphasize the way that women understand their bodies and their reproductive power, maintaining that women have a closer relationship with the body and thus with the natural world. Others view feminine categories as socially constructed, albeit in a way that emphasizes the female connection with nature (and the male as liberated from, and thus able to dominate, nature).

Ecofeminism is also often connected to a critique of colonialism, racism, and other forms of domination involving class, ethnicity, and gender. We mentioned previously Winona LaDuke's emphasis on the exclusion of Indigenous voices and her idea of women as a manifestation of Mother Earth. But LaDuke, and other Native American women, has been reluctant to embrace the idea of ecofeminism, seeing their advocacy on behalf of Indigenous people and the environment as more important than the focus on gender. In discussing this, Noël Sturgeon warns that there is the risk of cultural appropriation and "othering" when ecofeminists view Indigenous women as having special knowledge without actively engaging the concerns of those women. As Sturgeon says, "much of the ecofeminist discourse about Native American women silences their voices even while idealizing them."[52]

One famous proponent of ecofeminism, Vandana Shiva, weaves these ideas together in advocating for her vision of what she calls "Earth Democracy." Shiva writes that in the prevailing worldview, "Nature, women and non-white people merely provide 'raw' material." She continues, "The devaluation of contributions from women and nature goes hand-in-hand with the value assigned to acts of colonization as acts of development and improvement."[53] While Shiva is considered among the leading figures in ecofeminism, her views have also been subject to considerable critique. She has, among other things, argued against advanced biotechnologies (such as GMOs). Her argument against biotechnology fits within her general critique of "Western" science, corporations, and technology. But critics have complained that a knee-jerk reaction against biotechnology is neither scientifically supportable nor good for people who need inexpensive nutritious food.[54]

Building on ideas found in the first generation of ecofeminism, in more recent years, new voices have endeavored to point out that hierarchy and domination occur in a variety of contexts—and that ecological problems need to be addressed from a vantage point that is broad, global, and intersectional. Leah Thomas is an emerging leader in the field of what is coming to be known as "intersectional environmentalism." She has argued that mainstream environmentalism often lacks voices from marginalized communities. She writes:

> The lack of representation of Black, Brown, Indigenous, Asian, low-income, LGBTQ+, disabled, and other marginalized voices has led to an ineffective form of mainstream environmentalism that doesn't truly stand for the liberation of people and the planet.... Social injustice and environmental injustice are fueled by the same flame: the undervaluing, commodification, and exploitation of all forms of life and natural resources, from the smallest blade of grass to those living in poverty and oppressed people worldwide.[55]

Figure 19-2 Vandana Shiva is a proponent of ecofeminism.

Awakening/Corbis Entertainment/Getty Images

It is sometimes difficult to conceive the practical upshots of ecocentrism, ecological feminism, and deep ecology. We noted previously that Naess and the deep ecologists emphasize living simply and in connection with the local environment. Ecofeminists might add that a sense of justice and equality also requires that we attend to the ways in which environmental destruction impacts women and the way that male-dominant gender roles tend to reinforce exploitation and domination of nature. Ecofeminism and deep ecology both pose a serious challenge to the status quo and its anthropocentric and dominating approach to the natural world.

Ethical anthropocentrists will advocate wise and judicious use of nature, one that does not destroy the very nature that we value and on which we depend. But non-anthropocentrists maintain that we must care for and about nature for its own sake and not just in terms of what it can do for us. This debate is about the very place of human beings within the natural world.

Current Issues

19.6 Evaluate current environmental challenges, including issues related to climate change, pollution, and wilderness preservation and native lands.

We can now take these anthropocentric and ecocentric theories and examine how they might apply to environmental issues confronting us today. We will consider the following problems: climate change, waste disposal and pollution, and wilderness preservation. We will also consider international environmental conventions as a possible means of addressing global environmental issues.

Climate Change

The great majority of scientists now agree that our modern industrial society has created a potentially deadly phenomenon known as the *greenhouse effect*, *global warming*, or *climate change*. There is no denying that the global climate is changing, as the level of carbon dioxide in the atmosphere has increased during the past century. In the summer of 2022, NASA reported that global CO_2 concentration was now at about 420 ppm.[56]

This level of CO_2 concentration had not been seen on Earth since the Pliocene epoch, 2.5 million years ago, when Earth was three degrees Centigrade warmer than it is today and when sea levels were 5 meters higher (that's over 16 feet).[57] Coastlines are crumbling as the climate changes and sea levels rise.[58] There is substantial, albeit complicated, evidence that storms are increasing in severity as a result of climate change heating up the oceans.[59] And there is no question that the Arctic ice cap is melting, with ever-larger swaths of ice disappearing during the summer months. In the summer of 2012, the seasonal Arctic melt reached a surprising new level, with the ice covering only about 24 percent of the Arctic Ocean. In the 1970s, coverage during this season was around 50 percent.[60] NASA indicates that Artic sea ice has declined 13 percent per decade since the 1970s.[61] According to a 2020 paper that used various models to predict future Arctic sea ice variations, most simulations predict that the Arctic Ocean would be "practically sea-ice free" by 2050.[62] Melting Arctic ice is not only a *sign* of climate change, it is also a *contributor* to the process. The white Arctic ice reflects the sun, so the more ice there is, the more heat is reflected without being absorbed by the ocean. As the ice melts, however, the dark blue water of the ocean absorbs the solar rays no longer being reflected by the ice, which, in turn, warms the nearby air. The warmer air melts more ice, and so on, creating a feedback loop.

The Arctic ice cap is not the only significant melting process associated with climate change. The ice that covers Antarctica and Greenland has also been melting at an alarming rate and slipping into the sea. NASA reports that since 2002, Greenland has been losing 274 billion metric tons of ice per year, while Antarctica has been losing 152 billion metric tons per year.[63] According to the National Snow and Ice Data Center, the ice sheets in Greenland and Antarctica contain more than 99 percent of the earth's fresh water. If Greenland's ice melted, it could raise sea level by 20 feet; if the Antarctic ice melted, the sea level would rise by 200 feet.[64] While most experts think it is unlikely that a massive rise in sea level will happen in the foreseeable future, some experts warn that sea levels could rise by up to 2 feet or more by 2100.[65] A report published in 2022 by the National Oceanographic and Atmospheric

Administration predicts that if we "significantly reduce" greenhouse gas emissions by 2100, sea-level rise will be limited to 2 feet; but if we do not reduce emissions, sea level could rise by 7 feet by the end of the century.[66] Climate change has also caused the oceans to become more acidic as carbon dioxide is absorbed into the oceans. This process has already had negative impacts on delicate marine life, such as the oysters of the Pacific Northwest: oyster shells don't form properly in more acidic water.[67] There will be adverse impacts on fish and corals as the oceans become more acidic.

Melting Arctic ice may also change patterns of ocean currents that have been stable for the past ten thousand years. For example, the Gulf Stream pulls warm water north from near the equator and into the North Atlantic, where some of it evaporates. As the water evaporates, the ocean becomes saltier and heavier and the denser water sinks, cooling and starting a return path to the south. Changing temperatures could alter this process. Shifts in the Gulf Stream could cause weather and climatic changes in Europe and North America, although scientists disagree about what these impacts might be. Some warn that Europe would cool if the Gulf Stream shifted, but others think this is unlikely.[68] While this dispute is an indication of the difficulty of making predictions about climate change, the vast majority of scientists agree that the atmosphere and the oceans are changing.[69]

Climate change may produce hundreds of millions of environmental refugees, which is an environmental justice concern. Those refugees may be displaced by rising tides, storm damage, and changes in agricultural production. Residents of low-lying islands—such as the Marshall Islands, Kiribati, the Maldives, and the Seychelles—and low, flood-prone countries—such as Bangladesh—may be dislocated as sea levels rise and river floods become harder to control.[70]

Some skeptics dispute whether the changes are entirely man-made, but the vast majority of experts believe that one of the major causes of climate change is the burning of fossil fuels, which are the primary energy source for modern societies. The resulting gases—carbon dioxide, methane, fluorocarbons, and nitrous oxide, among others—are released into the atmosphere. There, these gases combine with water vapor and prevent the sun's infrared rays from radiating back into space. The trapped solar radiation contributes to increased air temperature. In this way, the gases function in much the same way as the glass panes of a greenhouse. Newly released gases will remain in the atmosphere for thirty to a hundred years; since greenhouse gas emissions continue to rise, their buildup in the atmosphere is expected to increase over time. Automobile exhaust, along with industrial power plants and agricultural operations, produce most of the gases that lead to climate change. Deforestation also contributes to the warming because there are fewer trees and other plant life to absorb carbon dioxide before it reaches the atmosphere.

According to the EPA, carbon dioxide accounted for 79 percent of U.S. greenhouse gas emissions in 2020.[71] Carbon dioxide (CO_2) is emitted when fossil fuels are burned to produce electricity or to fuel cars and other forms of transportation. CO_2 is also produced as a by-product of industrial processes and, along with methane, as a result of animal agriculture. Scientists have warned that global emissions should be limited and reduced. When civilization originally developed, the atmosphere contained about 275 ppm of CO_2. Some environmental activists argue that we ought to limit global CO_2 levels to 350 parts per million.[72] But as we have seen, we passed the 350 ppm threshold, with recent measurements putting the concentration of CO_2 at around 420 ppm and growing. And emissions continue to increase. In order to slow and stop climate change, human beings need to limit the emission of CO_2 and also find ways to capture and sequester CO_2 that is already in the atmosphere. But the nations of the world don't seem to be acting fast enough. In April 2022, in response to a dire report from the Intergovernmental Panel on Climate Change, Antonio Guterres, the secretary-general of the United Nations, said, "we are on a fast track to climate disaster" unless we find a way to limit the use of fossil fuels.[73]

Although the bulk of greenhouse gases emitted since the start of the Industrial Revolution have come from Europe, the United States, and other developed regions, recent increases in carbon dioxide levels are often attributed to growth in the developing world, especially in China.[74] According to the EPA (based on 2014 data), the main CO_2 producers as a share of the world's total CO_2 emitted are China (30 percent), the United States

(15 percent), the European Union (9 percent), and India (7 percent).[75]

Climate changes have occurred throughout Earth's history, and while they have usually been gradual, that has not always been the case. Sixty-five million years ago, the dinosaurs are thought to have been wiped out by a dramatic and rapid change in climate caused by a giant meteorite that hit Earth near Mexico's Yucatán Peninsula. The meteorite may have put so much dust into the air that it blocked much of the sun's light, causing temperatures to drop and plants to die—which, in turn, brought about the demise of the dinosaurs. Within the time span of human existence, climate changes have usually occurred over several generations, allowing people to adapt. If these changes occur rapidly, however, such adaptation becomes more difficult. For example, food supplies could be severely stressed. Reduced land fertility could also pose a threat to international security. If crop yields decrease and water shortages increase, peoples and nations suffering severe shortages may resort to violence. These people may migrate to urban "slums," causing overcrowding, widespread poverty, and infrastructure breakdown.[76] All of the issues listed above are anthropocentric concerns—they are focused on how climate change may impact human beings. These issues might also be supplemented with a more ecocentric focus on the species and ecosystems that may be disrupted by climate change.

How do we know that present-day global warming is not just part of a natural pattern? Scientists have determined that recent temperatures and the increased levels of carbon dioxide in the atmosphere are dramatically greater than anything that has occurred in the past. Scientists have drilled deep into the ice and brought up cylindrical *ice cores* that have markings similar to the rings inside of trees. They can read the age of the ice cores and analyze the chemicals and air bubbles in them to determine the average temperature of each year, as well as the carbon dioxide levels during each year. Samples as old as six hundred thousand years have been obtained, and from these samples, scientists know that the temperature and greenhouse gases have increased with unprecedented speed in the past decades. From this, they can also predict how temperatures will continue to rise unless emissions are controlled.[77]

Scientists still disagree about how much Earth will warm, how quickly it will happen, and how different regions will be affected. However, evidence is now accumulating for the acceleration of this effect in the form of receding glaciers, rising sea levels, and the spreading of plant and animal species farther north and to higher altitudes that were previously too cold to support such life. Some European butterfly and bird species have moved their habitats northward of their previous ranges. Unfortunately, some studies show that not all species are able to keep pace with rapidly changing climate zones.[78] Butterfly populations have declined as a result of the changing climate.[79] Bird populations are threatened when their preferred habitats change as a result of changing climate.[80] When we consider the problem of animals unable to adapt quickly enough to the planet's changing climate zones, should we focus on the intrinsic value of butterflies and birds, or should we focus on what this may portend for human beings as global temperatures continue to rise?

Further evidence of an accelerated global warming can be seen in the melting of mountain glaciers.[81] While some ecocentrists may argue that mountain glaciers have a kind of intrinsic value, the loss will also have a practical impact on human communities that depend on glaciers for their water supply. The melting of mountain glaciers can also produce more severe flooding during the rainy season, along with less regular flows of water during the rest of the year.[82]

Some people may benefit from climate change—say, those living in northern latitudes. But it is most likely that changing crop yields and lost coastlines will have negative impacts on billions of human beings. Returning us to the concerns of environmental justice, it is important to note that those who are historically most responsible for climate-changing emissions are the least likely to be harmed. Affluent people living in developed countries will be able to adapt and respond to climate change, while poor people in developing countries are most likely to be harmed. Moreover, the cost to future generations must also be considered. How much we worry about the impact on our descendants will depend on the expected severity of the effects. Those who calculate the costs and benefits must also factor in the uncertainties that are involved.

What can be done about global warming? And is it too late? Scientists generally believe that we may still have time to prevent radical climate change. But they tend to agree that we need to reduce the emission of greenhouse gases now. And some warn that we may be too late. James Hansen, the former head of the NASA Goddard Institute for Space Studies, has sounded a significant alarm. In 2012, Hansen warned that disintegrating ice sheets would accelerate climate change. As a result, "Sea levels would rise and destroy coastal cities. Global temperatures would become intolerable. Twenty to fifty percent of the planet's species would be driven to extinction. Civilization would be at risk."[83] Hansen's argument is ultimately anthropocentric: he means *human* civilization is at risk. In 2016, Hansen and other climate scientists updated this warning, arguing that melting ice would cause a rapid sea-level rise of up to several meters. This could inundate all coastal cities by the end of this century. Hansen states, "That would mean the loss of all coastal cities, most of the world's largest cities, and all of their history."[84] Because Hansen views the risk as so great and the consequences so dire, he opposes new fossil fuel projects that would ultimately lead to more CO_2 emissions—including the development of tar sands in Canada and new pipelines to transport crude oil. From Hansen's perspective, remaining fossil fuel reserves should stay buried in the ground, no matter how profitable or useful they may prove in the short term.

Among the means of reducing greenhouse gases are better mileage standards for cars and expanded public transportation options. Other methods include alternative sources of power, such as wind, solar, and nuclear. European countries have taken the lead in this effort. For example, Germany has made a commitment to abandon fossil fuels by 2050 and, in recent years, has made great strides toward replacing its fossil fuel infrastructure with renewable energy sources.[85] According to Stanford professor Mark Z. Jacobson: "It's absolutely not true that we need natural gas, coal, or oil—we think it's a myth. . . . You could power America with renewables from a technical and economic standpoint. The biggest obstacles are social and political—what you need is the will to do it."[86] Opponents of alternative energy sources argue that the economic costs would be prohibitive and would place great burdens on taxpayers. Whether or

not this is true, the position points to a different set of values and a different assessment of costs and benefits. One way of describing this difference is to locate it in a dispute about short-term vs. long-term interests.

Instead of, or in addition to, greater fuel efficiency standards and alternative energy sources, some suggest imposing a carbon tax on people and companies that burn fossil fuels. This tax could be used, for example, to reimburse or give tax credits to homeowners who use solar cells or energy-efficient appliances; the tax could also be used to fund research into possible means of capturing carbon dioxide and preventing it from being released into the atmosphere. A small tax could yield some \$50 billion for such purposes. Former vice president Al Gore once proposed that such a tax be used in place of payroll taxes for Social Security and Medicare.[87]

Other proposed solutions to climate change involve so-called "geo-engineering" projects that could either remove CO_2 from the atmosphere or that could help to cool the planet. Some of this is fairly simple, involving known technologies. One solution involves planting trees. A bit more complicated, perhaps, is the idea of installing "cool pavement" in cities, which can lower temperatures in urban heat islands.[88] More elaborate technological solutions include proposals to remove carbon from the atmosphere and store it underground, as well as proposals to protect Earth from the sun—either by building shades in space or by stimulating volcanoes to produce ash, which would reflect sunlight. These geo-engineering solutions aim to fix the problem without addressing the underlying issues of consumption and pollution. From the standpoint of deep ecology, such an approach looks like another example of human hubris. But proponents of geo-engineering argue that it is too late to halt climate change by returning to the sort of simple, eco-friendly living espoused by deep ecologists. Furthermore, as the climate continues to change, environmental justice concerns will point in the direction of plans to mitigate the damage that climate change will create for vulnerable human populations.

Waste Disposal and Pollution

Another issue of environmental concern is waste disposal and pollution. Like global warming, the negative impacts of these problems on humans and animals are far-reaching. Humans produce tons of garbage each year that must be put somewhere. Just how much garbage is there? According to the U.S. EPA, based on 2018 data, Americans generated about 292 million tons of trash that year; this included 69 million tons of waste that was recycled and 25 million tons that was composted, which amounts to a 32 percent recycling and composting rate.[89] According to the World Bank, waste disposal problems will continue to grow as populations grow globally. "In 2020, the world was estimated to generate 2.24 billion tons of solid waste. . . . With rapid population growth and urbanization, annual waste generation is expected to increase by 73 percent from 2020 levels to 3.88 billion tons in 2050."[90] This remains a significant concern for the developing world, pointing to an issue of environmental justice. The World Bank concludes:

> Compared to those in developed nations, residents in developing countries, especially the urban poor, are more severely impacted by unsustainably managed waste. In low-income countries, over 90% of waste is often disposed in unregulated dumps or openly burned. These practices create serious health, safety, and environmental consequences.[91]

Typical American trash includes a variety of disposable items. As most Americans are aware, plastic straws, utensils, and shopping bags are an environmental concern. These single-use items do not biodegrade, or break down, in landfills. Instead, they break into small pieces that contaminate the soil and water. Cities, states, and countries have taken action or considered taking action to ban plastic bags, utensils, and straws. The city of Seattle was one of the first to ban straws and utensils. The "Straw-less in Seattle" campaign was part of the city's effort to reduce waste. Proponents of these sorts of regulations argue that plastic bags make up a majority of marine debris and cost millions of dollars to dispose of properly. But some critics pointed out that paper bags are not really that much better—since they take up more space in landfills.[92] Many say the preferred option is reusable cloth bags; however, some maintain that reusable cloth shopping bags are unsanitary and spread disease, citing a study that showed that foodborne illness increased in San Francisco after the city banned plastic bags in 2007.[93] Despite the concerns, many communities have slowly transitioned to reusable cloth bags, reusable straws, and nonplastic utensils made from biodegradable materials. Related to this is the issue of disposable cups and other food service items. Consider, for example, the iconic disposable Starbucks cup. The company churns through seven billion of those per year at stores across the globe.[94] In 2022, Starbucks announced it was aiming to reduce its waste and carbon emissions by, among other things, encouraging customers to use reusable cups. This plan is already moving quickly in South Korea, where Starbucks plans to discontinue offering disposable cups by 2025.[95]

So-called e-waste is also a major problem. This includes outdated cellphones, computers, TVs, and printers. Over fifty million tons of this waste is discarded globally per year, with two countries—China and the United States—accounting for a significant proportion of the world's electronic waste.[96] Such items contain huge amounts of toxins: beryllium, cadmium, chromium, lead, mercury, and so on. Some electronics companies are working hard to find less harmful ways to deal with electronic waste. But too often, there are environmental justice issues involved, as electronic waste is commonly sent to countries in Africa and Asia, where it is dumped, often at the expense of local populations and pollution of the local environment.[97] Studies indicate that people living near an electronic waste dump in China face elevated cancer risks as a result of exposure to hazardous chemicals. Residents were melting down scavenged electronic products in their homes and backyards in order to extract precious metals concealed within those products, with health hazards resulting from exposure to toxic fumes produced during this process.[98]

One obvious solution to the e-waste problem is recycling. Indeed, the solution to the problem of waste disposal, in general, is recycling. For example, recycled bottles and cans can be turned into reusable metal and glass, as well as roads, bike parts, and even carpets.[99] Americans use more than eighty billion aluminum beverage cans every year, recycling over sixty billion of them.[100] The energy used to recycle aluminum is 95 percent less than the cost of manufacturing cans from virgin materials. The world only recycles about half of the aluminum cans used every year. But, according to environmental reporter Larry West, "Recycling aluminum saves 90% to 95% of the energy needed to make aluminum from bauxite ore." And: "All in all, the energy it takes to replace all of the aluminum cans wasted every year in the United States alone is equivalent to 16 million barrels of oil, enough to keep a million cars on the road for a year."[101]

Recycling, in fact, is tackling a wide variety of problems related to waste disposal and pollution. One promising idea is to find ways to convert food and plant waste into fuel. Organic material converted to fuel is known as *biomass fuel* or *biofuel*. Methane gas can be collected from landfills. And plants can be converted directly into usable forms of energy—such as corn that is converted into ethanol. Biomass fuels can be produced in ways that contribute to pollution and to climate change, but when done right—using waste products, rather than growing plants only for fuel consumption—they could hold one of the keys to a sustainable future. Another promising idea is to use switchgrass—a common grass native to North America—to produce biofuels in the form of pellets that can be burned in stoves or in the form of ethanol, which can run combustion engines.[102]

While the use of recycling and the development of biomass fuels offer solutions to the problem of waste and pollution, these approaches remain firmly within the anthropocentric approach that emphasizes minimizing costs and maximizing benefits for human beings. A simpler solution, and one that is espoused by advocates of ecocentrism, would be to cut down on consumption in general. From this perspective, it is not enough to recycle or to drive a biofuel vehicle—since recycling itself uses resources and energy and the biofuel vehicle still contributes its share of pollution. A more ecocentric approach would encourage people to ask, for example, whether it is necessary to use aluminum cans at all (not just whether it is necessary to recycle them) or whether it is possible to cut down on driving. The anthropocentric approach is not necessarily opposed to cutting down on consumption; however, it is in favor of finding ways to maximize our ability to consume while minimizing the ecological impact of consumption.

Wilderness Preservation and Native Lands

The use and preservation of the planet's wild and undeveloped areas is an issue of enduring ethical concern. According to the University of Montana's Wilderness.net information site, in 2015, the United States had 765 designated wilderness areas, encompassing over 109 million acres in forty-four states and Puerto Rico. That means that about 5 percent of the United States is protected as wilderness—an area slightly larger than the state of California. Much of this wilderness is in Alaska. Within the lower forty-eight states, about 2.7 percent of land is preserved as wilderness—an area about the size of Minnesota.[103] If these wilderness areas were not set aside and protected, their natural resources—including oil reserves, minerals, and forests—would almost certainly be developed. But we also value these wilderness areas for our own recreation, including fishing and hunting, as well as for the habitats they provide to various animal species.

One example of the controversy over protecting wilderness is the question of drilling for oil in Alaska's Arctic National Wildlife Refuge. The refuge was the last part of Alaska's Arctic coastline not open for oil production; its ecosystem includes a number of birds and animals in a tundra area, and is home to Indigenous peoples, the Gwich'in and Iñupiat people. The refuge was opened for oil leases during the Trump administration and canceled by the Biden administration. We might have an ecocentric concern for protecting this fragile ecosystem. Opponents of oil development in the refuge argue that such development would hurt the ecosystem. It might also have a negative impact on the humans who hunt the animals that live there—a concern for those who are interested in environmental justice. But environmental justice concerns also point in the other direction: some Indigenous peoples argue that they should be able to benefit from revenue that could be generated by exploiting the oil resource; that argument was made by Indigenous people in Alaska who opposed Biden's decision to stop oil drilling there.[104] In general, those who argue in favor of drilling point out that the refuge contains large oil deposits that could benefit the economy. As the price of gasoline and other petroleum products goes up, we are looking for new, unexplored oil reserves—the refuge is just such a site, they argue. Advocates of drilling maintain that efforts to protect sensitive wilderness areas are preventing necessary economic development. Opponents argue that oil development would create unacceptable environmental costs, accelerating climate change and harming animals and natural ecosystems.

Related issues include the construction of oil pipelines and the use of *fracking*, a process for oil and gas extraction that uses hydraulic fracturing (or "fracking") of subterranean rock formations to release gas and oil. The procedure allows extractors to reach reserves that are inaccessible through other drilling technologies. Opponents of fracking contend that the chemicals used in the process are hazardous and can migrate and contaminate groundwater. Opponents have also argued that fracking can cause earthquakes, even in seismically stable regions. Defenders of the process say that such risks are negligible and that the benefits of recovering more fossil fuels outweigh the risks.

The means of extraction isn't the only controversial issue related to oil and gas development. Also a subject of intense debate is the way these resources are transported to market. One contentious project was the Keystone XL Pipeline, which aimed to deliver petroleum products from Alberta, Canada, to the United States. The controversy about the project spanned across the Obama, Trump, and Biden administrations—with Biden canceling the project. The pipeline would have carried petroleum from the tar sands of Alberta to the Gulf Coast. The route for the proposed pipeline was changed to avoid sensitive environmental areas, such as the Sand Hills of Nebraska, but environmentalists argued that these modifications were insufficient. A similarly contested development project was the Dakota Access Pipeline, which was intended to ship oil out of North Dakota. Members of the Standing Rock Tribe protested this project, claiming that it would disrupt ancestral lands and damage the tribe's water supply. The resulting protests generated international interest in a standoff involving conflicting ideas about environmental justice, respect for Indigenous peoples, and the world's need for oil. The Trump administration pushed the project through, but the Biden administration called for a new review of the pipeline's environmental impact.

Environmentalists were generally opposed to these petroleum projects. Development of the tar sands of Alberta, they contend, would also cause large-scale destruction of forests and other ecosystems involved in the process. They argue that instead of producing more fossil fuels in wild places, the burning of which contributes to climate change, we should be investing in alternative energy sources.[105] The extraction of oil from tar sands is costly and dirty.[106] But, on the other hand, the demand for oil continues to rise: the development of tar sand deposits and fracking is driven by the market demand for petroleum products. If we want to continue driving gasoline-fueled cars the way we do, we might need that oil. At the same time, advocates of environmental justice were concerned about the rights of Indigenous peoples who would be affected by these projects.

Forests and wilderness areas are valuable for many reasons. They can provide beneficial new technologies—such as cures for diseases derived from wild species of plants and animals. Forests also provide habitats for wildlife, including threatened species. They provide us with leisure and relaxation, and with recreational opportunities such as white-water rafting, fishing, hiking, and skiing. They also provide aesthetic and religious experiences, and a chance to commune with the wider world of nature. But questions remain. Are we preserving wilderness for its own sake? Should wilderness areas be viewed as resource reserves, which ought to be developed when we need them? And what about the rights and interests of Indigenous people whose lands are affected by development projects?

International Environmental Conventions

Because of widespread concerns about these and other environmental issues, many international meetings and conventions have been held over the past several decades. Issues like global warming, biodiversity, and natural resource protection have been on the radar of international groups for many decades. As early as the 1990s, international organizations were calling for the reduction of greenhouse gases. The United States and other nations agreed in 1997, under a plan known as the Kyoto Protocol, to restrict greenhouse gas emissions to "at least 5 percent below levels measured in 1990" by the year 2012.[107] The protocol also allowed the thirty-five industrialized countries that were covered by it to "earn credits toward their treaty targets by investing in emissions cleanups outside their borders," a so-called *cap-and-trade* system.[108] Developing countries, such as India and China, were exempt from the controls so as to give them a better chance to catch up economically with more developed nations. Although the United States helped develop this agreement, Congress refused to pass it, and President George W. Bush pulled out of the agreement when he took office in 2001, holding that it was flawed and would hurt the U.S. economy.

The Kyoto Protocol did not achieve its goals. Developed countries did not meet their lowered emissions targets. And from its inception, a significant problem for the Kyoto Protocol was the exemption for developing countries. China and India continued to grow their carbon footprints, along with the United States and other nations. In 2011, Canada officially rejected the Kyoto Protocol, arguing that it was not working to impose limits on the two largest producers of greenhouse gases, the United States and China, and that there was no way to meet the Kyoto targets without serious economic dislocation in Canada.[109] Nevertheless, international negotiations to reduce greenhouse gas emissions continue. An important round of climate talks took place in 2015 in Paris, where the international community agreed to work to keep climate change below 2°C. And once again, the United States refused to play along: in 2017, President Trump announced the United States would withdraw from the Paris agreement, claiming it was a bad deal for the American economy.[110] In 2021, the Biden administration announced it would rejoin the agreement.[111] But in the summer of 2022, the U.S. Supreme Court issued a ruling that made it more difficult for Washington to regulate carbon pollution.[112]

This apparent failure of the international community to craft a practical response to the problem of global warming has led some to become outraged and others to despair. Among the more famous voices engaged in this debate is Greta Thunberg, a young Swedish activist who emerged onto the international stage in 2018. She had staged a climate-oriented strike at her school, and later at the Swedish parliament. Thunberg accused the adults of the world of incompetence and inaction. In a speech at the United Nations in 2019, she said, "You say you

love your children above all else, and yet you are stealing their future in front of their very eyes."[113] In an essay she published in 2021, she accused the leaders of the world of "decades of blah, blah, blah."[114] She implored world leaders to stop stalling and take action on climate change.

There is a major divide between those who want radical action to fix environmental problems and politicians and business leaders, who advocate a more cautious approach. At issue here is a substantial difference of opinion about fundamental values. On the one hand, people value the success of short-term business ventures and the need for quick and easy access to natural resources. On the other hand, long-term environmental sustainability is also important to human well-being—not to mention the well-being of animals, plants, and ecosystems. What is the extent of our obligation to curb emissions and preserve forests and other wilderness areas, especially in light of the fact that these efforts often have a negative effect on other human interests, such as the ability of many people to make a living?

Global Justice and The Tragedy of the Commons

The preservation of the environment is a global issue. Although many problems are specific to certain areas of the world, others, such as global warming, are shared in common. As we have noted, poor people in developing countries may be the most negatively impacted by climate change. However, just as in the developed world, many

Figure 19-3 Greta Thunberg has become a prominent voice in the environmental community.

in developing countries are more concerned with economic growth and development than they are with the
environment. In fact, some people in poor nations even
view the environmentalist movement as an example of
Western elitism (see the Ramachandra Guha reading that
follows). Only wealthy Westerners, they suggest, can
afford to preserve unchanged an environment or wilderness that impoverished people need to use and change in
order to survive. From this perspective, poor people who
are struggling to survive should not be asked to curtail
their own development while citizens of affluent nations
enjoy goods unobtainable in the developing countries.

The concern for environmental justice, which we discussed previously, will tell us that we ought to consider
social justice concerns as we deal with environmental
issues. Is it fair that those in affluent nations are able
to live comfortable lives while generating a disproportionately large share of waste and pollution? And what
about the rights, needs, and interests of Indigenous
people whose lives and lands intersect with resources
desired by the global economy? Most environmentalists agree that a sustainable solution to current environmental crises will have to deal with remaining social
inequalities across the globe. As we've seen, international agreements regulating greenhouse gases contain
variances that attempt to accommodate the inequalities
between developed and developing countries.

While alternative fuels, recycling, and other environmentally friendly technologies seem to offer promising
solutions to our environmental problems, they do not
address the problem of inequality and egoistic rationality. Those in the poorer parts of the world want to
have the goods that those in the affluent nations have.
And those in affluent countries do not want to give up
their current standard of living. However, there are not
enough resources available for everyone to enjoy the
standard of living of an average American. One solution is to find ways for those in developing regions
to raise living standards in ways that create minimal
impact on the environment; economic growth that is
environmentally sustainable is referred to as *sustainable development*. But those in the affluent countries
cannot reasonably expect poorer nations to do their part
for the environment while the affluent countries fail to
control their own growth and consumption. It might be

necessary, in the name of global environmental justice,
for affluent countries to radically scale back their level of
consumption. Paul and Anne Ehrlich, influential demog-
raphers who have been warning about overpopulation
for decades, state: "if we fail to bring population growth
and over-consumption under control, then we will
inhabit a planet where life becomes increasingly unten-
able."[115] The problem is not only that the human population is approaching eight billion but also that everyone
wants to consume as much as the average American.

Who has a right to consume the world's resources?
Issues surrounding resource consumption and allocation may make it impossible to create a stable system
of global environmental justice. One concern is based
on claims about property rights and capitalism. According to this perspective, landowners have a natural right
to develop the resources they possess. To maintain that
certain landowners (or countries) should not develop
their land or resources appears to be a violation of basic
property rights. Furthermore, there is no guarantee that
common areas not owned by anyone—the so-called
"commons"—will be adequately protected. The oceans
and the atmosphere are vast commons. Since they
belong to no one, they are easy prey for exploitation,
and they are also used as vast sinks into which we flush
our waste. The American ecologist Garrett Hardin warns
that self-interested individuals will take advantage of
unprotected common areas, according to a concept that
he calls "the tragedy of the commons." (For more on
Hardin, see Chapter 20.) He also points out the ethical challenge of global environmental justice in his discussion of what he calls "life-boat ethics." According to
Hardin, we should imagine that we are each floating in
an isolated lifeboat, competing with one another to survive. Our lifeboats have a limited carrying capacity, so
our obligation is to take care of ourselves first—to manage our own resources. Hardin's perspective leaves us
with a world of isolated nation-states, each struggling to
survive as the growing human population continues to
strain the earth's limited resources. Moreover, his tragic
conclusion is that if this is the way we conceive the
world, we may not be able to fend off the collapse of
the commons, since each of us will try to exploit what's
left for our own benefit.[116] This is a form of the prisoner's dilemma that results from egoism (as discussed

in Chapter 4): as each pursues their own self-interest in a world of self-interested people, we may soon end up with unwanted outcomes.[117] From this perspective, which is firmly anthropocentric and even egocentric, the most rational short-term strategy may be to find ways to exploit the environment and enrich oneself before the true impact of the environmental crisis is upon us, to build up our reserves so that we can ride out the coming environmental storm.

This sort of short-term and self-interested reasoning is criticized by both anthropocentric and ecocentric environmentalists. Ecocentrists maintain that we have an obligation to the ecosystem not to overexploit it. Anthropocentrists point out that we have a humanitarian obligation to help others who are suffering, as well as a duty to future generations to make sure we don't destroy the commons and overexploit the ecosystem. Both note that short-term self-interest can lead to disastrous consequences, as evidenced by "collapsed" or failed societies such as the Rapa Nui on Easter Island and the Maya in the Yucatán.[118] In each case, unsustainable growth led to the downfall of an entire civilization. Societies that collapse do so because they are unable to restrain their own development and unable to focus on the long-term sustainability of their practices. It may be that this is simply part of the natural cycle of life. Organisms grow, reproduce, and consume until they outstrip their resource base. When the resource base is overexploited, the population dies back. But the stakes are quite high now that environmental impacts have created truly global problems. And those who suffer the most from environmental degradation will be the most vulnerable among us. An environmental justice perspective tells us that we have an obligation to protect those vulnerable people.

We have seen in this chapter that there are a variety of environmental problems confronting us today, from urban pollution to climate change. Some may view these problems from an anthropocentric perspective, focused on cost–benefit analysis or a concern for environmental justice. Others will point toward a deeper set of ecocentric concerns that emphasize the intrinsic value of wilderness and natural systems. The ethical issues to be considered here are complex, as are the causes and possible solutions to environmental challenges.

Chapter Summary

19.1 What explains the difference between anthropocentric and non-anthropocentric (ecocentric or biocentric) approaches about environmental ethics?

Anthropocentric approaches are human-oriented. From this perspective, the focal point is human rights, needs, and interests, involving cost-benefit analysis and some forms of environmental justice. Non-anthropocentric approaches are interested in thinking about environmental issues from a perspective that does not privilege human rights, needs, and interests. Biocentrism focuses on the value of living things such as plants, fish, and animals. Ecocentrism adopts an even wider viewpoint, considering the value of ecosystems, watersheds, and the planet as a whole.

19.2 What is the difference between intrinsic value and instrumental value?

The idea of instrumental value locates the value of something in its usefulness. Typically this is understood anthropocentrically, as the value of a thing for human purposes. For example, a tree is instrumentally valuable as a source of wood and pulp. Intrinsic value locates value in objects apart from their usefulness. A focus on intrinsic value is often connected to a non-anthropocentric understanding of the value of nonhuman things and the natural world. For example, to say that a tree has intrinsic value is to say that it has a kind of dignity or worth in itself, apart from its potential uses.

19.3 Explain how cost–benefit analysis applies in thinking about environmental issues.

Cost–benefit analysis is usually connected to an anthropocentric and utilitarian approach to environmental ethics. Human activities include environmental costs that must be correlated with proposed benefits. Sometimes this includes the idea of ecosystem services, which are the benefits provided by healthy ecosystems.

19.4 How can we apply the concept of environmental justice to some concrete issues?

Environmental justice is typically understood as an anthropocentric concern for how environmental harms and benefits are distributed across human populations. Environmental justice is concerned, for example, with the question of whether adverse environmental impacts (e.g., pollution) are more likely to harm poor and marginalized people than affluent people. Environmental justice often includes consideration for Indigenous people who are impacted by development projects such as oil pipelines. In thinking about pollution, climate change, or wilderness preservation, the concerns of environmental justice ask us to attend to the needs of human beings who are impoverished, marginalized, or disenfranchised.

19.5 How can we analyze differences and similarities between ecofeminism and deep ecology?

Ecofeminism offers a critical perspective on the ways that domination of nature is connected to domination of women. Ecofeminism is often critical of colonialism and economies that exploit the land. Deep ecology is also critical of exploitative uses of nature. But it tends to focus its attention on a metaphysical critique of the idea that human beings are distinct or separate from nature. Both offer radical critiques of mainstream worldviews.

19.6 Evaluate current environmental challenges, including issues related to climate change, pollution, and wilderness preservation and native lands.

Climate change is a significant challenge resulting from burning fossil fuels. There are international protocols aiming to reduce fossil fuel consumption. But this will require trade-offs that will need to be evaluated using cost–benefit analysis. This evaluation becomes difficult when we attempt to think about the needs and interests of future generations in comparison with the present. Pollution includes air pollution, solid waste pollution, and e-waste. The problem of pollution asks us to consider reducing the demand for raw materials and recycling when possible. Wilderness preservation remains a contentious issue involving conflicts between those who want to develop natural resources for human usages and those who think these resources should be preserved. Often the discussion of wilderness preservation asks us to consider the concerns of environmental justice, including the question of the needs, rights, and interests of Indigenous peoples.

19.7 What kind of thesis might you defend with regard to environmental issues and the value of nonhuman nature?

To defend a thesis about environmental ethics, students ought to consider what they think about the difference between anthropocentrism and non-anthropocentrism. To think about this requires you to consider the question of whether there are intrinsic values in nature or whether the world is a resource for us to use instrumentally. Students may want to decide whether they agree with the perspective of Aldo Leopold's land ethic, whether they are concerned with the problems identified from the environmental justice standpoint, whether they think the ecofeminist critique has any merit, and whether they agree with the radical vantage point of deep ecology. These various environmental perspectives will need to be applied to cases and issues in a way that is sensitive to the facts and the science that helps explain challenges such as climate change, pollutions, and wilderness preservation.

Primary Source Readings

The first reading for this chapter is a short excerpt from William Baxter, who argues that anthropocentrism is the only possible approach to environmental questions and concludes that we should accept an "optimal" pollution level for human beings. In the second reading, Bill Devall and George Sessions explain the key elements of the non-anthropocentric approach of deep ecology. Next, Ramachandra Guha raises questions about deep ecology from the perspectives of the developing world and Indian and German environmentalism. The last reading is a short excerpt from a column written by Greta Thunberg, who condemns decades of inaction by the world's leaders in dealing with the crisis of climate change.

Reading 19-1   People or Penguins: The Case for Optimal Pollution | William F. Baxter

Study Questions

As you read the excerpt, please consider the following questions:

1. What are the four criteria or goals that Baxter suggests? In what ways are these people-oriented criteria?

2. Does he believe that people-oriented criteria will necessarily be bad for the penguins or other elements of our environment? Why or why not?

3. Why does he believe there is no right level of pollution?

My criteria are oriented to people, not penguins. Damage to penguins, or sugar pines, or geological marvels is, without more, simply irrelevant.... Penguins are important because people enjoy seeing them walk about rocks; and furthermore, the well-being of people would be less impaired by halting use of DDT than by giving up penguins. In short, my observations about environmental problems will be people-oriented, as are my criteria. I have no interest in preserving penguins for their own sake.

It may be said by way of objection to this position, that it is very selfish of people to act as if each person represented one unit of importance and nothing else was of any importance. It is undeniably selfish. Nevertheless I think it is the only tenable starting place for analysis for several reasons. First, no other position corresponds to the way most people really think and act—i.e., corresponds to reality.

Second, this attitude does not portend any massive destruction of nonhuman flora and fauna, for people depend on them in many obvious ways, and they will be preserved because and to the degree that humans do depend on them.

Third, what is good for humans is, in many respects, good for penguins and pine trees—clean air, for example. So that humans are, in these respects, surrogates for plant and animal life.

Fourth, I do not know how we could administer any other system....

I reject the proposition that we *ought* to respect the "balance of nature" or to "preserve the environment" unless the reason for doing so, express or implied, is the benefit of man.

I reject the idea that there is a "right" or "morally correct" state of nature to which we should return. The word "nature" has no normative connotation. Was it "right" or "wrong" for the earth's crust to heave in contortion and create mountains and seas? Was it "right" for the first amphibian to crawl up out of the primordial ooze? Was it "wrong" for plants to reproduce themselves and alter the atmospheric composition in favor of oxygen? For animals to alter the atmosphere in favor of carbon dioxide both by breathing oxygen and eating plants? No answers can be given to these questions because they are meaningless questions....

... It follows that there is no normative definition of clean air or pure water—hence no definition of polluted air—or of pollution—except by reference to the needs of man. The "right" composition of the atmosphere is one which has some dust in it and some lead in it and some hydrogen sulfide in it—just those amounts that attend a sensibly organized society thoughtfully and knowledgeably pursuing the greatest possible satisfaction for its human members.

The first and most fundamental step toward solution of our environmental problems is a clear recognition that our objective is not pure air or water but rather some optimal state of pollution.

William F. Baxter, *People or Penguins: The Case for Optimal Pollution* (New York: Columbia University Press, 1974).

Reading 19-2 Deep Ecology | Bill Devall and George Sessions

Study Questions

As you read the excerpt, please consider the following questions:

1. How do the authors describe the alternative presented by deep ecology?
2. How do the authors contrast the view of deep ecology with what they describe as the dominant worldview?
3. Explain briefly each of the eight basic principles of the platform of the deep ecology movement.

Reform Environmentalism

Environmentalism is frequently seen as the attempt to work only within the confines of conventional political processes of industrialized nations to alleviate or mitigate some of the worst forms of air and water pollution, destruction of indigenous wildlife, and some of the most short-sighted development schemes.

One scenario for the environmental movement is to continue with attempts at reforming some natural resource policies. For example, ecoactivists can appeal administrative decisions to lease massive areas of public domain lands in the United States for mineral development, or oil and gas development. They can comment on draft Environmental Impact Reports; appeal to politicians to protect the scenic values of the nation; and call attention to the massive problems of toxic wastes, air and water pollution, and soil erosion. These political and educational activities call to the need for healthy ecosystems.

However, environmentalism in this scenario tends to be very technical and oriented only to short-term public policy issues of resource allocation. Attempts are made to reform only some of the worst land use practices without challenging, questioning or changing the basic assumptions of economic growth and development. Environmentalists who follow this scenario will easily be labeled as "just another special issues group." In order to play the game of politics, they will be required to compromise on every piece of legislation in which they are interested.[1]

Generally, this business-as-usual scenario builds on legislative achievements such as the National Environmental Policy Act (NEPA) and the Endangered Species Act in the United States, and reform legislation on pollution and other environmental issues enacted in most industrialized nations.

This work is valuable. The building of proposed dams, for example, can be stopped by using economic arguments to show their economic liabilities. However, this approach has certain costs. One perceptive critic of this approach, Peter Berg, directs an organization seeking decentralist, local approaches to environmental problems. He says this approach "is like running a battlefield aid station in a war against a killing machine that operates beyond reach and that shifts its ground after each seeming defeat."[2] Reformist activists often feel trapped in the very political system they criticize. If they don't use the language of resource economists—language which converts ecology into "input-output models," forests into "commodity production systems," and which uses the metaphor of human economy in referring to Nature—then they are labeled as sentimental, irrational, or unrealistic.

Murray Bookchin, author of *The Ecology of Freedom* (1982) and *Post-Scarcity Anarchism* (1970), says the choice is clear. The environmental/ecology movement can "become institutionalized as an appendage of the very system whose structure and methods it professes to oppose," or it can follow the minority tradition. The minority tradition focuses on personal growth within a small community and selects a path to cultivating ecological consciousness while protecting the ecological integrity of the place.[3]

Deep Ecology and Cultivating Ecological Consciousness

In contrast to the preceding scenarios, deep ecology presents a powerful alternative.

Bill Devall and George Sessions, *Deep Ecology: Living as if Nature Mattered* (Salt Lake City, UT: Peregrine, 1985). Reprinted by permission.

Deep ecology is emerging as a way of developing a new balance and harmony between individuals, communities, and all of Nature. It can potentially satisfy our deepest yearnings: faith and trust in our most basic intuitions; courage to take direct action; joyous confidence to dance with the sensuous harmonies discovered through spontaneous, playful intercourse with the rhythms of our bodies, the rhythms of flowing water, changes in the weather and seasons, and the overall processes of life on Earth. We invite you to explore the vision that deep ecology offers.

The deep ecology movement involves working on ourselves, what poet-philosopher Gary Snyder calls "the real work," the work of really looking at ourselves, of becoming more real.

This is the work we call cultivating ecological consciousness. This process involves becoming more aware of the actuality of rocks, wolves, trees, and rivers—the cultivation of the insight that everything is connected. Cultivating ecological consciousness is a process of learning to appreciate silence and solitude and rediscovering how to listen. It is learning how to be more receptive, trusting, holistic in perception, and is grounded in a vision of nonexploitive science and technology.

This process involves being honest with ourselves and seeking clarity in our intuitions, then acting from clear principles. It results in taking charge of our actions, taking responsibility, practicing self-discipline and working honestly within our community. It is simple but not easy work. Henry David Thoreau, nineteenth-century naturalist and writer, admonishes us, "Let your life be a friction against the machine."

Cultivating ecological consciousness is correlated with the cultivation of conscience. Cultural historian Theodore Roszak suggests in *Person/Planet* (1978), "Conscience and consciousness, how instructive the overlapping similarity of those two words is. From the new consciousness we are gaining of ourselves as persons perhaps we will yet create a new conscience, one whose ethical sensitivity is at least tuned to a significant good, a significant evil."[4]

We believe that humans have a vital need to cultivate ecological consciousness and that this need is related to the needs of the planet. At the same time, humans need direct contact with untrammeled wilderness, places undomesticated for narrow human purposes.

Many people sense the needs of the planet and the need for wilderness preservation. But they often feel depressed or angry, impotent and under stress. They feel they must rely on "the other guy," the "experts." Even in the environmental movement, many people feel that only the professional staff of these organizations can make decisions because they are experts on some technical scientific matters or experts on the complex, convoluted political process. But we need not be technical experts in order to cultivate ecological consciousness. Cultivating ecological consciousness, as Thoreau said, requires that "we front up to the facts and determine to live our lives deliberately, or not at all." We believe that people can clarify their own intuitions and act from deep principles.

Deep ecology is a process of ever-deeper questioning of ourselves, the assumptions of the dominant worldview in our culture, and the meaning and truth of our reality. We cannot change consciousness by only listening to others, we must involve ourselves. We must take direct action.

Organizations which work only in a conventional way on political issues and only in conventional politics will more or less unavoidably neglect the deepest philosophical-spiritual issues. But late industrial society is at a turning point, and the social and personal changes which are necessary may be aided by the flow of history....

The trick is to trick ourselves into reenchantment. As Watts says, "In the life of spontaneity, human consciousness shifts from the attitude of strained, willful attention to *koan*, the attitude of open attention or contemplation." This is a key element in developing ecological consciousness. This attitude forms the basis of a more "feminine" and receptive approach to love, an attitude which for that very reason is more considerate of women.[5]

In some Eastern traditions, the student is presented with a *koan*, a simple story or statement which may sound paradoxical or nonsensical on the surface but as the student turns and turns it in his or her mind, authentic understanding emerges. This direct action of turning and turning, seeing from different perspectives and from different depths, is required for the cultivation of consciousness. The *koan*-like phrase for deep ecology, suggested by prominent Norwegian philosopher Arne Naess, is: "simple in means, rich in ends."

Cultivating ecological consciousness based on this phrase requires the interior work of which we have been speaking, but also a radically different tempo of external actions, at least radically different from that experienced by millions and millions of people living "life in the fast lane" in contemporary metropolises. As Theodore Roszak concludes, "Things move slower; they stabilize at a simpler level. But none of this is experienced as a loss or a sacrifice. Instead, it is seen as a liberation from waste and busywork, from excessive appetite and anxious competition that allows one to get on with the essential business of life, which is to work out one's salvation with diligence."[6]

… Quiet people, those working on the "real work," quite literally turn down the volume of noise in their lives. Gary Snyder suggests that, "The real work is what we really do. And what our lives are. And if we can live the work we have to do, knowing that we are real, and that the world is real, then it becomes right. And that's the real work: to make the world as real as it is and to find ourselves as real as we are within it."[7]

Engaging in this process, Arne Naess concludes, people "… will necessarily come to the conclusion that it is not lack of energy consumption that makes them unhappy."[8]

One metaphor for what we are talking about is found in the Eastern Taoist image, the *organic* self. Taoism tells us there is a way of unfolding which is inherent in all things. In the natural social order, people refrain from dominating others. Indeed, the ironic truth is that the more one attempts to control other people and control nonhuman Nature, the more disorder results, and the greater the degree of chaos. For the Taoist, spontaneity is not the opposite of order but identical with it because it flows from the unfolding of the inherent order. Life is not narrow, mean, brutish, and destructive. People do not engage in the seemingly inevitable conflict over scarce material goods. People have fewer desires and simple pleasures. In Taoism, the law is not required for justice; rather, the community of persons working for universal self-realization follows the flow of energy.[9]

To study the Way is to study the self.

To study the self is to forget the self.

To forget the self is to be enlightened by all things.

To be enlightened by all things is to remove the barriers between one's self and others.

—Dogen

As with many other Eastern traditions, the Taoist way of life is based on compassion, respect, and love for all things. This compassion arises from self-love, but self as part of the larger *Self*, not egotistical self-love.

Deep Ecology

The term *deep ecology* was coined by Arne Naess in his 1973 article, "The Shallow and the Deep, Long-Range Ecology Movements."[10] Naess was attempting to describe the deeper, more spiritual approach to Nature exemplified in the writings of Aldo Leopold and Rachel Carson. He thought that this deeper approach resulted from a more sensitive openness to ourselves and nonhuman life around us. The essence of deep ecology is to keep asking more searching questions about human life, society, and Nature as in the Western philosophical tradition of Socrates. As examples of this deep questioning, Naess points out "that we ask why and how, where others do not. For instance, ecology as a science does not ask what kind of a society would be the best for maintaining a particular ecosystem—that is considered a question for value theory, for politics, for ethics." Thus, deep ecology goes beyond the so-called factual scientific level to the level of self and Earth wisdom.

Deep ecology goes beyond a limited piecemeal shallow approach to environmental problems and attempts to articulate a comprehensive religious and philosophical worldview. The foundations of deep ecology are the basic intuitions and experiencing of ourselves and Nature which comprise ecological consciousness. Certain outlooks on politics and public policy flow naturally from this consciousness. And in the context of this book, we discuss the minority tradition as the type of community most conducive both to cultivating ecological consciousness and to asking the basic questions of values and ethics addressed in these pages.

Many of these questions are perennial philosophical and religious questions faced by humans in all cultures over the ages. What does it mean to be a unique human individual? How can the individual self-maintain and increase its uniqueness while also being an inseparable aspect of the whole system wherein there are no sharp breaks between self and the *other*? An ecological perspective, in this deeper sense, results in what Theodore Roszak calls "an awakening of wholes greater than the sum of their parts. In spirit, the discipline is contemplative and therapeutic."[11]

Ecological consciousness and deep ecology are in sharp contrast with the dominant worldview of technocratic-industrial societies which regards humans as isolated and fundamentally separate from the rest of Nature, as superior to, and in charge of, the rest of creation. But the view of humans as separate and superior to the rest of Nature is only part of larger cultural patterns. For thousands of years, Western culture has become increasingly obsessed with the idea of *dominance*: with dominance of humans over nonhuman Nature, masculine over the feminine, wealthy and powerful over the poor, with the dominance of the West over non-Western cultures. Deep ecological consciousness allows us to see through these erroneous and dangerous illusions.

For deep ecology, the study of our place in the Earth household includes the study of ourselves as part of the organic whole. Going beyond a narrowly materialist scientific understanding of reality, the spiritual and the material aspects of reality fuse together. While the leading intellectuals of the dominant worldview have tended to view religion as "just superstition," and have looked upon ancient spiritual practice and enlightenment, such as found in Zen Buddhism, as essentially subjective, the search for deep ecological consciousness is the search for a more objective consciousness and state of being through an active deep questioning and meditative process and way of life.

Many people have asked these deeper questions and cultivated ecological consciousness within the context of different spiritual traditions—Christianity, Taoism, Buddhism, and Native American rituals, for example. While differing greatly in other regards, many in these traditions agree with the basic principles of deep ecology.

Warwick Fox, an Australian philosopher, has succinctly expressed the central intuition of deep ecology: "It is the idea that we can make no firm ontological divide in the field of existence: That there is no bifurcation in reality between the human and the non-human realms ... to the extent that we perceive boundaries, we fall short of deep ecological consciousness."[12]

From this most basic insight or characteristic of deep ecological consciousness, Arne Naess has developed two ultimate norms or intuitions which are themselves not derivable from other principles or intuitions. They are arrived at by the deep questioning process and reveal the importance of moving to the philosophical and religious level of wisdom. They cannot be validated, of course, by the methodology of modern science based on its usual mechanistic assumptions and its very narrow definition of data. These ultimate norms are *self-realization* and *biocentric equality*.

Self-Realization

In keeping with the spiritual traditions of many of the world's religions, the deep ecology norm of self-realization goes beyond the modern Western self which is defined as an isolated ego striving primarily for hedonistic gratification or for a narrow sense of individual salvation in this life or the next. This socially programmed sense of the narrow self or social self dislocates us, and leaves us prey to whatever fad or fashion is prevalent in our society or social reference group. We are thus robbed of beginning the search for our unique spiritual/biological personhood. Spiritual growth, or unfolding, begins when we cease to understand or see ourselves as isolated and narrow competing egos and begin to identify with other humans from our family and friends to, eventually, our species. But the deep ecology sense of self requires a further maturity and growth, an identification which goes beyond humanity to include the nonhuman world. We must see beyond our narrow contemporary cultural assumptions and values, and the conventional wisdom of our time and place, and this is best achieved by the meditative deep questioning process. Only in this way can we hope to attain full mature personhood and uniqueness.

A nurturing nondominating society can help in the "real work" of becoming a whole person. The "real work" can be summarized symbolically as the realization of "self-in-Self" where "Self" stands for organic wholeness. This process of the full unfolding of the self can also be summarized by the phrase, "No one is saved until we are all saved," where the phrase "one" includes not only me, an individual human, but all humans, whales, grizzly bears, whole rain forest ecosystems, mountains and rivers, the tiniest microbes in the soil, and so on.

Biocentric Equality

The intuition of biocentric equality is that all things in the biosphere have an equal right to live and blossom and to reach their own individual forms of unfolding and self-realization within the larger Self-realization. This basic intuition is that all organisms and entities in the ecosphere, as parts of the interrelated whole, are equal in intrinsic worth. Naess suggests that biocentric equality as an intuition is true in principle, although in the process of living, all species use each other as food, shelter, etc. Mutual predation is a biological fact of life, and many of the world's religions have struggled with the spiritual implications of this. Some animal liberationists who attempt to side-step this problem by advocating vegetarianism are forced to say that the entire plant kingdom including rain forests have no right to their own existence. This evasion flies in the face of the basic intuition of equality.[13] Aldo Leopold expressed this intuition when he said humans are "plain citizens" of the biotic community, not lord and master over all other species.

Biocentric equality is intimately related to the all-inclusive Self-realization in the sense that if we harm the rest of Nature then we are harming ourselves. There are no boundaries and everything is interrelated. But insofar as we perceive things as individual organisms or entities, the insight draws us to respect all human and nonhuman individuals in their own right as parts of the whole without feeling the need to set up hierarchies of species with humans at the top.

The practical implications of this intuition or norm suggest that we should live with minimum rather than maximum impact on other species and on the Earth in general. Thus we see another aspect of our guiding principle: "simple in means, rich in ends." ...

Dominant Worldview	Deep Ecology
• Dominance over Nature	• Harmony with Nature
• Natural environment as resource for humans	• All nature has intrinsic worth/biospecies equality
• Material/economic growth for growing human population	• Elegantly simple material needs (material goals serving the larger goal of self-realization)
• Belief in ample resource reserves	• Earth "supplies" limited
• High technological progress and solutions	• Appropriate technology; nondominating science
• Consumerism	• Doing with enough/ recycling
• National/centralized community	• Minority tradition/ bioregion

A fuller discussion of the biocentric norm as it unfolds itself in practice begins with the realization that we, as individual humans, and as communities of humans, have vital needs which go beyond such basics as food, water, and shelter to include love, play, creative expression, intimate relationships with a particular landscape (or Nature taken in its entirety) as well as intimate relationships with other humans, and the vital need for spiritual growth, for becoming a mature human being.

Our vital material needs are probably more simple than many realize. In technocratic-industrial societies there is overwhelming propaganda and advertising which encourages false needs and destructive desires designed to foster increased production and consumption of goods. Most of this actually diverts us from facing reality in an objective way and from beginning the "real work" of spiritual growth and maturity.

Many people who do not see themselves as supporters of deep ecology nevertheless recognize an overriding vital human need for a healthy and high-quality natural environment for humans, if not for all life, with minimum intrusion of toxic waste, nuclear radiation from human enterprises, minimum acid rain and smog, and enough free flowing wilderness so humans can get in touch with their sources, the natural rhythms and the flow of time and place.

Drawing from the minority tradition and from the wisdom of many who have offered the insight of interconnectedness, we recognize that deep ecologists can offer suggestions for gaining maturity and encouraging the processes of harmony with Nature, but that there is no grand solution which is guaranteed to save us from ourselves.

The ultimate norms of deep ecology suggest a view of the nature of reality and our place as an individual (many in the one) in the larger scheme of things. They cannot be fully grasped intellectually but are ultimately experiential. . . .

As a brief summary of our position thus far, the table on page 570 summarizes the contrast between the dominant worldview and deep ecology.

Basic Principles of Deep Ecology

In April 1984, during the advent of spring and John Muir's birthday, George Sessions and Arne Naess summarized fifteen years of thinking on the principles of deep ecology while camping in Death Valley, California. In this great and special place, they articulated these principles in a literal, somewhat neutral way, hoping that they would be understood and accepted by persons coming from different philosophical and religious positions.

Readers are encouraged to elaborate their own versions of deep ecology, clarify key concepts and think through the consequences of acting from these principles.

Basic Principles

1. The well-being and flourishing of human and non-human Life on Earth have value in themselves (synonyms: intrinsic value, inherent value). These values are independent of the usefulness of the nonhuman world for human purposes.

2. Richness and diversity of life forms contribute to the realization of these values and are also values in themselves.

3. Humans have no right to reduce this richness and diversity except to satisfy *vital* needs.

4. The flourishing of human life and cultures is compatible with a substantial decrease of the human population. The flourishing of nonhuman life requires such a decrease.

5. Present human interference with the nonhuman world is excessive, and the situation is rapidly worsening.

6. Policies must therefore be changed. These policies affect basic economic, technological, and ideological structures. The resulting state of affairs will be deeply different from the present.

7. The ideological change is mainly that of appreciating *life quality* (dwelling in situations of inherent value) rather than adhering to an increasingly higher standard of living. There will be a profound awareness of the difference between the big and the great.

8. Those who subscribe to the foregoing points have an obligation directly or indirectly to try to implement the necessary changes.

Notes

1. The most informative recent book on reformist environmentalism in the context of British society is Philip Lowe and Jane Goyder's *Environmental Groups in Politics* (London: George Allen, 1983). Sociological explanations of the environmental movement in North America are found in Craig R. Humphrey and Frederick R. Butell's *Environment, Energy and Society* (Belmont, CA: Wadsworth, 1983); Allan Schnaiberg's *The Environment: From Surplus to Scarcity* (New York: Oxford, 1980); Lester Milbrath's *Environmentalists* (Albany: State University of New York Press, 1984); "Sociology of the Environment," *Sociological Inquiry 53* (Spring 1983); Jonathon Porritt, *Green: The Politics of Ecology Explained* (New York: Basil Blackwell, 1985).

2. Peter Berg, editorial, *Raise the Stakes* (Fall 1983).

3. Murray Bookchin, "Open Letter to the Ecology Movement," *Rain* (April 1980), as well as other publications.

4. Theodore Roszak, *Person/Planet* (Garden City, NY: Doubleday, 1978), p. 99.

5. _____. *Nature, Man and Woman* (New York: Vintage, 1970), p. 178.

6. Roszak, p. 296.

7. Gary Snyder, *The Real Work* (New York: New Directions, 1980), p. 81.

8. Stephen Bodian, "Simple in Means, Rich in Ends: A Conversation with Arne Naess," *Ten Directions* (California: Institute for Transcultural Studies, Zen Center of Los Angeles, Summer/Fall 1982).

9. Po-Keung Ip, "Taoism and the Foundations of Environmental Ethics," *Environmental Ethics 5* (Winter 1983), pp. 335–344.

10. Arne Naess, "The Shallow and The Deep, Long-Range Ecology Movements: A Summary," *Inquiry 16* (Oslo, 1973), pp. 95–100.

11. Theodore Roszak, *Where the Wasteland Ends* (New York: Anchor, 1972).

12. Warwick Fox, "Deep Ecology: A New Philosophy of Our Time?" *The Ecologist*, v. 14, 506, 1984, pp. 194–200. Arne

Naess replies, "Intuition, Intrinsic Value and Deep Ecology," *The Ecologist*, v. 14, 5–6, 1984, pp. 201–204.

13. Tom Regan, *The Case for Animal Rights* (New York: Random House, 1983). For excellent critiques of the animal rights movement, see John Rodman, "The Liberation of Nature?" *Inquiry 20* (Oslo, 1977). J. Baird Callicott, "Animal Liberation," *Environmental Ethics* 2, 4 (1980); see also John Rodman, "Four Forms of Ecological Consciousness Reconsidered" in T. Attig and D. Scherer (Eds.), *Ethics and the Environment* (Englewood Cliffs, NJ: Prentice Hall, 1983).

Reading 19-3   Radical American Environmentalism and Wilderness Preservation: A Third World Critique | Ramachandra Guha

Study Questions

As you read the excerpt, please consider the following questions:

1. Why does Guha think the emphasis on wilderness preservation is harmful?

2. What problems does he have with the invocation of Eastern religions?

3. How does he believe that elements of deep ecology favor the rich and urban elite in developing counties?

The respected radical journalist Kirkpatrick Sale recently celebrated "the passion of a new and growing movement that has become disenchanted with the environmental establishment and has in recent years mounted a serious and sweeping attack on it—style, substance, systems, sensibilities and all."[1] The vision of those whom Sale calls the "New Ecologists"—and what I refer to in this article as deep ecology—is a compelling one. Decrying the narrowly economic goals of mainstream environmentalism, this new movement aims at nothing less than a philosophical and cultural revolution in human attitudes toward nature. In contrast to the conventional lobbying efforts of environmental professionals based in Washington, it proposes a militant defence of "Mother Earth," an unflinching opposition to human attacks on undisturbed wilderness. With their goals ranging from the spiritual to the political, the adherents of deep ecology span a wide spectrum of the American environmental movement....

In this article I develop a critique of deep ecology from the perspective of a sympathetic outsider.... I speak admittedly as a partisan, but of the environmental movement in India, a country with an ecological diversity comparable to the U.S., but with a radically dissimilar cultural and social history.... Specifically, I examine the cultural rootedness of a philosophy that likes to present itself in universalistic terms. I make two main arguments: first, that deep ecology is uniquely American, and despite superficial similarities in rhetorical style, the social and political goals of radical environmentalism in other cultural contexts (e.g., West Germany and India) are quite different; second, that the social consequences of putting deep ecology into practice on a worldwide basis (what its practitioners are aiming for) are very grave indeed.

The Tenets of Deep Ecology

... Adherents of the deep ecological perspective in [America], while arguing intensely among themselves over its political and philosophical implications, share

Ramachandra Guha, "Radical American Environmentalism and Wilderness Preservation: A Third World Critique." *Environmental Ethics* 11: 1 (Spring 1989). Reprinted with permission from the author.

some fundamental premises about human-nature interactions. As I see it, the defining characteristics of deep ecology are fourfold:

First, deep ecology argues that the environmental movement must shift from an "anthropocentric" to a "biocentric" perspective. In many respects, an acceptance of the primacy of this distinction constitutes the litmus test of deep ecology. A considerable effort is expended by deep ecologists in showing that the dominant motif in Western philosophy has been anthropocentric—i.e., the belief that man and his works are the center of the universe—and conversely, in identifying those lonely thinkers (Leopold, Thoreau, Muir, Aldous Huxley, Santayana, etc.) who, in assigning man a more humble place in the natural order, anticipated deep ecological thinking. In the political realm, meanwhile, establishment environmentalism (shallow ecology) is chided for casting its arguments in human-centered terms. Preserving nature, the deep ecologists say, has an intrinsic worth quite apart from any benefits preservation may convey to future human generations. The anthropocentric-biocentric distinction is accepted as axiomatic by deep ecologists, it structures their discourse, and much of the present discussions remains mired within it.

The second characteristic of deep ecology is its focus on the preservation of unspoilt wilderness—and the restoration of degraded areas to a more pristine condition—to the relative (and sometimes absolute) neglect of other issues on the environmental agenda.... Morally, [this] is an imperative that follows from the biocentric perspective; other species of plants and animals, and nature itself, have an intrinsic right to exist.... The preservation of wilderness also turns on a scientific argument—viz., the value of biological diversity in stabilizing ecological regimes and in retaining a gene pool for future generations. Truly radical policy proposals have been put forward by deep ecologists on the basis of these arguments. The influential poet Gary Snyder, for example, would like to see a 90 percent reduction in human populations to allow a restoration of pristine environments, while others have argued forcefully that a large portion of the globe must be immediately cordoned off from human beings.

Third, there is a widespread invocation of Eastern spiritual traditions as forerunners of deep ecology. Deep ecology, it is suggested, was practiced both by major religious traditions and at a more popular level by "primal" peoples in non-Western settings. This complements the search for an authentic lineage in Western thought. At one level, the task is to recover those dissenting voices within the Judeo-Christian tradition; at another, to suggest that religious traditions in other cultures are, in contrast, dominantly if not exclusively "biocentric" in their orientation. This coupling of (ancient) Eastern and (modern) ecological wisdom seemingly helps consolidate the claim that deep ecology is a philosophy of universal significance.

Fourth, deep ecologists, whatever their internal differences, share the belief that they are the "leading edge" of the environmental movement. As the polarity of the shallow/deep and anthropocentric/biocentric distinctions makes clear, they see themselves as the spiritual, philosophical, and political vanguard of American and world environmentalism.

Toward a Critique

Although I analyze each of these tenets independently, it is important to recognize, as deep ecologists are fond of remarking in reference to nature, the interconnectedness and unity of these individual themes.

1. Insofar as it has begun to act as a check on man's arrogance and ecological hubris, the transition from an anthropocentric (human-centered) to a biocentric (humans as only one element in the ecosystem) view in both religious and scientific traditions is only to be welcomed. What is unacceptable are the radical conclusions drawn by deep ecology, in particular, that intervention in nature should be guided primarily by the need to preserve biotic integrity rather than by the needs of humans. The latter for deep ecologists is anthropocentric, the former biocentric. This dichotomy is, however, of very little use in understanding the dynamics of environmental degradation. The two fundamental ecological problems facing the globe are (i) overconsumption by the industrialized world and by urban elites in the Third World and (ii) growing militarization, both in a short-term sense (i.e., ongoing regional wars) and in a long-term sense (i.e., the arms race and the prospect of nuclear annihilation). Neither of these problems has any tangible connection to the anthropocentric-biocentric distinction. Indeed, the

agents of these processes would barely comprehend this philosophical dichotomy. The proximate causes of the ecologically wasteful characteristics of industrial society and of militarization are far more mundane: at an aggregate level, the dialectic of economic and political structures, and at a micro-level, the life-style choices of individuals. These causes cannot be reduced, whatever the level of analysis, to a deeper anthropocentric attitude toward nature; on the contrary, by constituting a grave threat to human survival, the ecological degradation they cause does not even serve the best interests of human beings! If my identification of the major dangers to the integrity of the natural world is correct, invoking the bogy of anthropocentricism is at best irrelevant and at worst a dangerous obfuscation.

2. If the above dichotomy is irrelevant, the emphasis on wilderness is positively harmful when applied to the Third World. If in the U.S. the preservationist/utilitarian division is seen as mirroring the conflict between "people" and "interests," in countries such as India the situation is very nearly the reverse. Because India is a long settled and densely populated country in which agrarian populations have a finely balanced relationship with nature, the setting aside of wilderness areas has resulted in a direct transfer of resources from the poor to the rich. Thus, Project Tiger, a network of parks hailed by the international conservation community as an outstanding success, sharply posits the interests of the tiger against those of poor peasants living in and around the reserve. The designation of tiger reserves was made possible only by the physical displacement of existing villages and their inhabitants; their management requires the continuing exclusion of peasants and livestock. The initial impetus for setting up parks for the tiger and other large mammals such as the rhinoceros and elephant came from two social groups, first, a class of ex-hunters turned conservationists belonging mostly to the declining Indian feudal elite and second, representatives of international agencies, such as the World Wildlife Fund (WWF) and the International Union for the Conservation of Nature and Natural Resources (IUCN), seeking to transplant the American system of national parks onto Indian soil. In no case have the needs of the local population been taken into account, and as in many parts of Africa, the designated wildlands

are managed primarily for the benefit of rich tourists. Until very recently, wildlands preservation has been identified with environmentalism by the state and the conservation elite; in consequence, environmental problems that impinge far more directly on the lives of the poor—e.g., fuel, fodder, water shortages, soil erosion, and air and water pollution—have not been adequately addressed.

Deep ecology provides, perhaps unwittingly, a justification for the continuation of such narrow and inequitable conservation practices under a newly acquired radical guise. Increasingly, the international conservation elite is using the philosophical, moral, and scientific arguments used by deep ecologists in advancing their wilderness crusade. A striking but by no means atypical example is the recent plea by a prominent American biologist for the takeover of large portions of the globe by the author and his scientific colleagues. Writing in a prestigious scientific forum, the *Annual Review of Ecology and Systematics*, Daniel Janzen argues that only biologists have the competence to decide how the tropical landscape should be used. . . . Janzen exhorts his colleagues to advance their territorial claims on the tropical world more forcefully, warning that the very existence of these areas is at stake: "if biologists want a tropics in which to biologize, they are going to have to buy it with care, energy, effort, strategy, tactics, time, and cash."[2]

This frankly imperialist manifesto highlights the multiple dangers of the preoccupation with wilderness preservation that is characteristic of deep ecology. As I have suggested, it seriously compounds the neglect by the American movement of far more pressing environmental problems within the Third World. But perhaps more importantly, and in a more insidious fashion, it also provides an impetus to the imperialist yearning of Western biologists and their financial sponsors, organizations such as the WWF and IUCN. The wholesale transfer of a movement culturally rooted in American conservation history can only result in the social uprooting of human populations in other parts of the globe.

3. I come now to the persistent invocation of Eastern philosophies as antecedent in point of time but convergent in their structure with deep ecology. Complex and internally differentiated religious traditions—Hinduism, Buddhism, and Taoism—are lumped together as holding

a view of nature believed to be quintessentially bio-centric. Individual philosophers such as the Taoist Lao Tzu are identified as being forerunners of deep ecology. Even an intensely political, pragmatic, and Christian-influenced thinker such as Gandhi has been accorded a wholly undeserved place in the deep ecological pan-theon. Thus, the Zen teacher Robert Aitken Roshi makes the strange claim that Gandhi's thought was not human-centered and that he practiced an embryonic form of deep ecology which is "traditionally Eastern and is found with differing emphasis in Hinduism, Taoism and in Theravada and Mahayana Buddhism."[3] Moving away from the realm of high philosophy and scriptural religion, deep ecologists make the further claim that at the level of material and spiritual practice "primal" peoples subordinated themselves to the integrity of the biotic universe they inhabited.

I have indicated that this appropriation of Eastern traditions is in part dictated by the need to construct an authentic lineage and in part a desire to present deep ecology as a universalistic philosophy.... As it stands, [this reading] does considerable violence to the histori-cal record. Throughout most recorded history the char-acteristic form of human activity in the "East" has been a finely tuned but nonetheless conscious and dynamic manipulation of nature. Although mystics such as Lao Tzu did reflect on the spiritual essence of human relations with nature, it must be recognized that such ascetics and their reflections were supported by a soci-ety of cultivators whose relationship with nature was a far more *active* one. Many agricultural communities do have a sophisticated knowledge of the natural envi-ronment that may equal (and sometimes surpass) codi-fied "scientific" knowledge; yet, the elaboration of such traditional ecological knowledge (in both material and spiritual contexts) can hardly be said to rest on a mys-tical affinity with nature of a deep ecological kind....

In a brilliant article, the Chicago historian Ronald Inden points out that this romantic and essentially pos-itive view of the East is a mirror image of the scien-tific and essentially pejorative view normally upheld by Western scholars of the Orient. In either case, the East constitutes the Other, a body wholly separate and alien from the West; it is defined by a uniquely spiritual and nonrational "essence," even if this essence is valorized

quite differently by the two schools. Eastern man exhibits a spiritual dependence with respect to nature—on the one hand, this is symptomatic of his prescientific and backward self, on the other, of his ecological wis-dom and deep ecological consciousness. Both views are monolithic, simplistic, and have the characteristic effect—intended in one case, perhaps unintended in the other—of denying agency and reason to the East and making it the privileged orbit of Western thinkers....

4. How radical, finally, are the deep ecologists? ... To my mind, deep ecology is best viewed as a radical trend within the wilderness preservation movement. Although advancing philosophical rather than aesthetic arguments and encouraging political militancy rather than negotiation, its practical emphasis—viz., preser-vation of unspoilt nature—is virtually identical. For the mainstream movement, the function of wilderness is to provide a temporary antidote to modern civilization. As a special institution within an industrialized society, the national park "provides an opportunity for respite, con-trast, contemplation, and affirmation of values for those who live most of their lives in the workaday world."[4] Indeed, the rapid increase in visitations to the national parks in postwar America is a direct consequence of economic expansion....

Here, the enjoyment of nature is an integral part of the consumer society. The private automobile (and the life style it has spawned) is in many respects the ultimate ecological villain, and an untouched wilder-ness the prototype of ecological harmony; yet, for most Americans it is perfectly consistent to drive a thousand miles to spend a holiday in a national park. They pos-sess a vast, beautiful, and sparsely populated continent and are also able to draw upon the natural resources of large portions of the globe by virtue of their economic and political dominance. In consequence, America can simultaneously enjoy the material benefits of an expanding economy and the aesthetic benefits of unspoilt nature. The two poles of "wilderness" and "civilization" mutually coexist in an internally coherent whole, and philosophers of both poles are assigned a prominent place in this culture. Paradoxically as it may seem, it is no accident that Star Wars technology and deep ecology both find their fullest expression in that leading sector of Western civilization, California.

Deep ecology runs parallel to the consumer society without seriously questioning its ecological and socio-political basis.... The archetypal concerns of radical environmentalists in other cultural contexts are in fact quite different. The German Greens, for example, have elaborated a devastating critique of industrial society which turns on the acceptance of environmental limits to growth. Pointing to the intimate links between industrialization, militarization, and conquest, the Greens argue that economic growth in the West has historically rested on the economic and ecological exploitation of the Third World.

[Hence] the roots of global ecological problems lie in the disproportionate share of resources consumed by the industrialized countries as a whole *and* the urban elite within the Third World. Since it is impossible to reproduce an industrial monoculture worldwide, the ecological movement in the West must begin by cleaning up its own act.... The expansionist character of modern Western man will have to give way to an ethic of renunciation and self-limitation, in which spiritual and communal values play an increasing role in sustaining social life....

Many elements of the Green program find a strong resonance in countries such as India, where a history of Western colonialism and industrial development has benefited only a tiny elite while exacting tremendous social and environmental costs. The ecological battles presently being fought in India have as their epicenter the conflict over nature between the subsistence and largely rural sector and the vastly more powerful commercial-industrial sector. Perhaps the most celebrated of these battles concerns the Chipko (Hug the Tree) movement, a peasant movement against deforestation in the Himalayan foothills. Chipko is only one of several movements that have sharply questioned the nonsustainable demand being placed on the land and vegetative base by urban centers and industry. These include opposition to large dams by displaced peasants, the conflict between small artisan fishing and large-scale trawler fishing for export, the countrywide movements against commercial forest operations, and opposition to industrial pollution among downstream agricultural and fishing communities.

Two features distinguish these environmental movements from their Western counterparts. First, for the sections of society most critically affected by environmental degradation—poor and landless peasants, women, and tribals—it is a question of sheer survival, not of enhancing the quality of life. Second, and as a consequence, the environmental solutions they articulate deeply involve questions of equity as well as economic and political redistribution. Highlighting these differences, a leading Indian environmentalist stresses that "environmental protection per se is of least concern to most of these groups. Their main concern is about the use of the environment and who should benefit from it." They seek to wrest control of nature away from the state and the industrial sector and place it in the hands of rural communities who live within that environment but are increasingly denied access to it. These communities have far more basic needs, their demands on the environment are far less intense, and they can draw upon a reservoir of cooperative social institutions and local ecological knowledge in managing the "commons"—forests, grasslands, and the waters—on a sustainable basis. If colonial and capitalist expansion has both accentuated social inequalities and signaled a precipitous fall in ecological wisdom, an alternate ecology must rest on an alternate society and polity as well.

This brief overview of German and Indian environmentalism has some major implications for deep ecology. Both German and Indian environmental traditions allow for a greater integration of ecological concerns with livelihood and work. They also place a greater emphasis on equity and social justice (both within individual countries and on a global scale) on the grounds that in the absence of social regeneration, environmental regeneration has very little chance of succeeding, Finally, and perhaps most significantly, they have escaped the preoccupation with wilderness preservation so characteristic of American cultural and environmental history.

A Homily

In 1958, the economist J. K. Galbraith referred to overconsumption as the unasked question of the American conservation movement. There is a marked selectivity, he wrote, "in the conservationist's approach to materials consumption. If we are concerned about our great appetite for materials, it is plausible to seek to increase the supply, to decrease waste, to make better use of the stocks available, and to develop substitutes. But what of the appetite itself? Surely this is the ultimate source of the problem. If it continues its geometric course, will it not one day have to be restrained? Yet in the literature of the resource problem this is the forbidden question. Over it hangs a nearly total silence."[5]

The consumer economy and society have expanded tremendously in the three decades since Galbraith penned these words; yet his criticisms are nearly as valid today. I have said "nearly," for there are some hopeful signs. Within the environmental movement several dispersed groups are working to develop ecologically benign technologies and to encourage less wasteful life styles. Moreover,

outside the self-defined boundaries of American environmentalism, opposition to the permanent war economy is being carried on by a peace movement that has a distinguished history and impeccable moral and political credentials ... A truly radical ecology in the American context ought to work toward a synthesis of the appropriate technology, alternate life style, and peace movements. By making the (largely spurious) anthropocentric-biocentric distinction central to the debate, deep ecologists may have appropriated the moral high ground, but they are at the same time doing a serious disservice to American and global environmentalism.

Notes

1. Kirkpatrick Sale, "The Forest for the Trees: Can Today's Environmentalists Tell the Difference," *Mother Jones* 11, No. 8 (November 1986): 26.

2. Daniel Janzen, "The Future of Tropical Ecology," *Annual Review of Ecology and Systematics* 17 (1986): 305–306; emphasis added.

3. Robert Aitken Roshi, "Gandhi, Dogen, and Deep Ecology," reprinted as appendix C in Bill Devall and George

Sessions, *Deep Ecology: Living as if Nature Mattered* (Salt Lake City: Peregrine Smith Books, 1985).

4. Joseph Sax, *Mountains Without Handrails: Reflections on the National Parks* (Ann Arbor: University of Michigan Press, 1980), 42.

5. John Kenneth Galbraith, "How Much Should a Country Consume?" in Henry Jarrett, ed., *Perspectives on Conservation* (Baltimore: Johns Hopkins Press, 1958), pp. 91–92.

Reading 19-4   There Are No Climate Leaders Yet | Greta Thunberg

Study Questions

As you read the excerpt, please consider the following questions:

1. What does Thunberg mean by "greenwash" and "blah, blah, blah"?

2. Is Thunberg correct in linking the climate issue to the larger sustainability crisis? How does that connect to the issues of environmental justice that we discussed in this chapter?

3. Are there reasons to be hopeful? And how is that connected to the need for leadership?

The UN secretary general, António Guterres, called the recent IPCC report on the climate crisis a "code red" for humanity. "We are at the verge of the abyss," he said.

You might think those words would sound some kind of alarm in our society. But, like so many times before, this didn't happen. The denial of the climate and ecological crisis runs so deep that hardly anyone

takes real notice any more. Since no one treats the crisis like a crisis, the existential warnings keep on drowning in a steady tide of greenwash and everyday media news flow.

And yet there is still hope, but hope all starts with honesty.

Because science doesn't lie. The facts are crystal clear, but we just refuse to accept them. We refuse to acknowledge that we now have to choose between saving the living planet or saving our unsustainable way of life. Because we want both. We demand both.

But the undeniable truth is that we have left it too late for that. And no matter how uncomfortable that reality may seem, this is exactly what our leaders have chosen for us with their decades of inaction. Their decades of blah, blah, blah. . . .

Science doesn't lie, nor does it tell us what to do. But it does give us a picture of what needs to be done. We are of course free to ignore that picture and remain in denial. Or to go on hiding behind clever accounting, loopholes and incomplete statistics. As if the atmosphere would care about our frameworks. As if we could argue with the laws of physics. . . .

The climate and ecological emergency is, of course, only a symptom of a much larger sustainability crisis. A social crisis. A crisis of inequality that dates back to colonialism and beyond. A crisis based on the idea that some people are worth more than others and therefore have the right to exploit and steal other people's land and resources. It's all interconnected. It's a sustainability crisis that everyone would benefit from tackling. But it's naive to think that we could solve this crisis without confronting the roots of it.

Things may look very dark and hopeless, and given the torrent of reports and escalating incidents, the feeling of despair is more than understandable. But we need to remind ourselves that we can still turn this around. It's entirely possible if we are prepared to change.

Hope is all around us. Because all it would really take is one—one world leader or one high-income nation or one major TV station or leading newspaper who decides to be honest, to truly treat the climate crisis as the crisis that it is. One leader who counts all the numbers—and then takes brave action to reduce emissions at the pace and scale the science demands. Then everything could be set in motion towards action, hope, purpose and meaning.

The clock is ticking. Summits keep happening. Emissions keep growing. Who will that leader be?

Greta Thunberg, "There Are No Real Climate Leaders Yet – Who Will Step Up at Cop26?" *The Guardian*, October 21, 2021. https://www.theguardian.com/commentisfree/2021/oct/21/climate-leaders-cop26-uk-climate-crisis-glasgow.

Review Exercises

1. What is the difference between intrinsic and instrumental value? Give an example of each.

2. What is anthropocentrism? How is it different from ecocentrism?

3. How do cost–benefit analyses function in environmental arguments? Give an example of an environmental problem today and how cost–benefit analysis could be used to analyze it.

4. Explain how the concept of environmental justice can be used to provide a critical analysis of the impact of pollution.

5. What is Aldo Leopold's basic principle for determining what is right and wrong in environmental matters?

6. Analyze the critical perspective of Indigenous people and controversies about racism in the conservation movement.

7. What is deep ecology? According to this view, what are the root causes of our environmental problems?

8. Explain how ecofeminism could be used to analyze a problem such as the adverse impacts of pollution on poor people.

9. What is the problem of the tragedy of the commons, and how is it connected to capitalism and the idea of property rights?

10. How are conflicts in environmental ethics connected to the question of global justice?

Discussion Cases

1. Climate Change. Carla and Remi are debating climate change. Carla believes that it is nothing to worry about. "Even if the scientists could ever really establish that burning fossil fuels causes climate change, there's no need to worry. Scientists will find ways to fix the problem. And we can always move to higher ground or just move north, where it's cooler." Remi laughs out loud. "Ha! That's easy for you to say," Remi replies. "Americans will probably be able to survive the changing climate. But people in other parts of the world are really going to suffer. And anyway, it's not just about the humans. We should also be concerned about the value of natural things like glaciers and forests." Carla shakes her head. "I don't really get you environmentalists. First, you say that poor people will suffer. Then, you say that glaciers and forests will suffer. But aren't people more important than glaciers? And if we had to melt all the glaciers to provide drinking water for poor people, wouldn't that be the right thing to do?"

Whom do you agree with here? Explain your answer with reference to philosophical concepts such as anthropocentrism and ecocentrism.

2. Preserving the Trees. XYZ Timber Company has been logging forests in the Pacific Northwest for decades. It has done moderately well in replanting areas it has logged, but it has also been logging in areas where some trees are hundreds of years old. Now, the company plans to build roads into a similar area of the forest and cut down similarly ancient trees. An environmental group, Trees First, is determined to prevent this. Its members have blocked the roads that have been put in by the timber company and have also engaged in the practice known as *tree spiking*—in which iron spikes are driven into trees to discourage the use of power saws. Loggers are outraged because tree spiking can make logging extremely dangerous. When a saw hits these spikes, it becomes uncontrollable, and loggers can be seriously injured.

Forest rangers have been marking trees found to be spiked and have noted that some spikes are not visible and will present a hidden danger for years to come. People from Trees First insist that this is the only way to prevent the shortsighted destruction of old-growth forests. They argue that XYZ Timber Company has too much political power and has ignored public protests against their logging practices. The only way to get the company's attention, they say, is to put their employees at risk.

What is your assessment of the actions of the XZY Timber Company and the actions of Trees First? Is it ever justifiable to use extreme protest methods such as tree spiking that put lives at risk? Why or why not?

3. Sustainable Development. The people of the Amazon River basin, who live in rural poverty, have begun burning and clearing large sections of the forest. They are doing so to create farmland in order to earn a living for themselves and their families. But the burning and deforestation destroy ecosystems of rare plants and animals and contribute to global warming. As a result, representatives from environmental groups in the United States and other wealthy countries have traveled to the region seeking to persuade the locals to cease this practice and pursue a more sustainable livelihood based on ecotourism. The people of the Amazon River basin are offended by these proposals. They point out that North Americans already have destroyed much of their own forests and become prosperous. "Who are you to criticize us?" they ask. "It is a luxury to worry about what the weather will be like a hundred years from now. We have to worry about what we will eat tomorrow."

Whose position do you find more persuasive here—the environmentalists or the people of the Amazon River basin? How would you balance global concerns about deforestation and global warming against the subsistence needs of cultures in environmentally sensitive areas?

Knowledge Check Answer Key

1. **a.** Anthropocentric approaches to environmental ethics are concerned with cost–benefit involving human concerns.

2. **d.** A concern for "environmental racism" is connected with environmental justice.

3. **b.** Insistence that trees are valuable only because they provide wood and pulp for humans to use is an example of instrumental value.

4. **a.** Ecosystems services are not a primary concern of ecocentric thinkers.

20 Animal Ethics—and Beyond

Learning Outcomes

After reading this chapter, you should be able to:

20.1 Explain the difference between anthropocentric and non-anthropocentric views of animal ethics.

20.2 Explain the importance of sentience and equal consideration in thinking about animal ethics.

20.3 Define speciesism and articulate criticisms of this idea.

20.4 Explain the difference between a concern for animal welfare and a concern for animal rights.

20.5 Evaluate current issues in animal ethics including hunting, vegetarianism, animal research, and endangered species protection.

20.6 Articulate some connections between animal ethics and other topics involving nonhuman beings.

20.7 Defend a thesis with regard to animal ethics.

Hunting and Eating

What kind of meat, if any, is best to eat? Is it better to hunt your own meat or to eat meat that is grown on a factory farm? Of course, vegans and vegetarians don't eat meat. The vegetarian argument typically rests on the claim that intensive modern agriculture—what critics call "factory farms"—creates conditions in which animals live miserable lives until they are cruelly killed. Defenders of hunting may claim that hunting at least allows animals to live natural lives until they are killed, unlike the animals that are raised on factory farms. But defend-

iStock.com/EvanTravels

ers of intensive modern animal agriculture point out that in efficient modern slaughterhouses, anti-cruelty regulations seek to ensure that animals die quickly and with a minimum of pain. Good hunters also try to minimize the cruelty of the kill. But in the unpredictable world of the wild, animals can be injured or maimed before they are eventually killed.

Another option is so-called "free-range" meat, which comes from farm animals that are allowed to live somewhat natural lives before they are slaughtered. Some consumers are willing to pay extra to guarantee that the creatures whose meat they eat are raised in humane conditions. But defenders of intensive animal agriculture argue that there is no way to supply enough free-range products to consumers in a world with an ever-expanding appetite for meat. The vegetarian replies in turn that rather than seeking to increase the supply of meat, it would be better if people ate less meat or even stopped eating meat altogether.

What Do You Think?

1. Is hunting or "free-range" meat preferable to the meat produced by factory farming? Why?
2. What ethical rules and regulations ought to govern hunting and animal agriculture?
3. Are the vegans and vegetarians right that it would be better to eat less meat or to stop eating meat entirely?
4. What kinds of animals is it acceptable to hunt, to farm, and to eat?

Introduction

20.1 Explain the difference between anthropocentric and non-anthropocentric views of animal ethics.

What kinds of animals we should eat or hunt is a central question for animal ethics. Like "environmental ethics" (discussed in Chapter 19), animal ethics is concerned with the difference between anthropocentrism and non-anthropocentrism. At issue here are fundamental concerns about the ontological and moral status of nonhuman things. This issue asks us to consider fundamental questions about being human and the extent to which we are similar to or different from nonhuman animals. Human beings are animals, after all. But we are also the only animals that raise questions about the morality of killing other animals. Does this make us superior to nonhuman animals, or does it give us a greater responsibility? **Anthropocentric** (or human-centered) answers to these questions will maintain that humans are superior or that human concerns matter most. **Non-anthropocentric** answers reject such claims, maintaining that we also ought to consider things from a standpoint that takes the interests and welfare of nonhuman animals seriously.

These issues eventually lead us to consider the ontological and moral status of other nonhuman things. We have touched on this question in a variety of ways throughout this book. It is connected to our thinking about the ontological and moral status of human fetuses. It is connected to what we think about

brain-dead human bodies. It is also connected to what we think about ecosystems. And, as we'll see toward the end of the present chapter, these issues also ask us to think about the moral status of some hypothetical other beings, including extraterrestrial life-forms and artificial intelligence. These last concerns may seem bizarre, but a key question in animal ethics has to do with the value of nonhuman sentience, suffering, and consciousness. If we were to encounter intelligent extraterrestrial life or to develop an advanced AI that was sentient, we might be able to use our understanding of animal ethics to guide our thinking about these far-out examples.

It seems that as our technology advances, new moral problems arise. The ethical problem of factory farming is created by the technologies that make intensive animal agriculture possible, including advances in shipping, waste removal, disease prevention, and the mechanization of the slaughterhouse. But new technologies also may provide us with solutions to old moral problems. What would vegetarians think, for example, if we could develop an alternative to meat that was grown in a test tube?

Moral Approaches to Animal Ethics

The ethical questions raised by animals are all around us. The moral question of which animals we eat (or do not eat) is something we confront three times a day as we make choices about food. We also likely consume products tested on animals every day. We may occasionally go to zoos, circuses, and rodeos. Some of us own pets or raise domesticated animals. Our lives are intertwined with the lives of animals, both wild and domesticated. The U.S. legal system contains extensive regulations for animal care and to prevent cruelty to animals, and we generally see ourselves as caring about their proper treatment. However, we do not often reflect explicitly on the question of the moral status of animals. We are often unclear about the underlying reasons for what we see as acceptable or unacceptable ways of treating them.

One way to get a clearer sense of these reasons is to consider the different ways in which we might value animals. For example, some people find pleasure in animals as pets or companions. Others have an economic interest in them, raising and selling them as commodities. Animals are sources of food and clothing. We benefit from them when they are used in experiments to test the safety and effectiveness of drugs, detergents, and cosmetics. Some people enjoy fishing and hunting. Even ecotourism depends on animals, as people travel to appreciate and photograph animals in their natural habitats. Animals are also sources of pleasure and wonder because of their variety, beauty, and strength.

This suggests the wide range of reasons that animals may be viewed as having value. The most obvious is that animals satisfy human needs: they feed us, clothe us, work for us, and allow some of us to make money. A perspective that focuses on human need and satisfaction is *anthropocentric*. Such a perspective typically views animals as having instrumental value (as opposed to intrinsic value), as we discussed in Chapter 19. It is possible to develop a theory of animal welfare from within anthropocentric concerns. Many farmers, horse racers, and pet owners say they get more out of their animals when they treat them well. Thus, concern for the health and welfare of animals allows us to profit from them. In this view, there is more profit in humane animal treatment than in cruel treatment (although critics of modern industrial farming may disagree). Those who manage herds of wildlife and those who raise and kill animals for human consumption view animals as commodities to be managed and controlled.

A further anthropocentric position is that learning to care for animals and treat them well is a natural and normal part of human experience that humans developed among other animals and in specific relation to them. From a virtue ethics standpoint, one could argue that there are important virtues developed in properly relating to animals. The ethics of hunting (which we will discuss in more detail later) may be described in virtue ethics terms: virtuous hunters allow for fair chase, kill in moderation, and kill cleanly and without cruelty. A similar idea can be found in the writing of Immanuel Kant.

Kant did not think that animals had any value in themselves, since nonhuman animals are not rational beings. But Kant thought that cruelty to animals was a breeding ground for callousness and indifference to suffering, which tended to make human beings treat each other more cruelly.[1] From this perspective, moral duties to animals are only *indirect*: the treatment of animals matters in terms of its impact, or potential impact, on other humans. We might also recall here that animals are often considered to be property—and that damaging another person's pets or livestock is frequently viewed as a property crime.

A different approach to animal ethics focuses on non-anthropocentric accounts of the value of animals. Such approaches ask about what is in the interest of the animals themselves, apart from human interests. One non-anthropocentric approach focuses on nonhuman animals as *sentient* creatures, which means that they can feel pleasure and pain just as we do. Indeed, many animals, especially the primates that are genetically closest to us, display striking similarities to human beings in their emotions, communication, relationships, and social groups. In this view, we may be obliged to ask whether we are ever justified in causing them physical or psychological suffering, or killing them. A second approach focuses on nonhuman animals as individuals who have interests and rights. Those who focus on animal sentience and welfare tend to operate within consequentialist or utilitarian terms, while those who focus on animal rights more typically appeal to non-consequentialist or deontological theories of value, perhaps even arguing that animals have intrinsic value. From the sentience/welfare perspective, we may have to balance the interests of different sentient beings according to some version of the utilitarian calculus: perhaps some nonhuman animals could be killed or used in a cruelty-free fashion for the well-being of a greater number of human animals. But from the animal rights perspective, there is a positive duty to respect the rights of animals—and, more controversially, there may be an active duty to prevent them from being harmed.

Sentience, Equal Consideration, and Animal Welfare

20.2 Explain the importance of sentience and equal consideration in thinking about animal ethics.

According to some philosophers, sentience is the key to the ethical status of animals. If animals have the capacity to feel and sense, it makes sense to talk about their welfare or well-being, and we should take their sentience into account. This tradition dates back at least to the utilitarian Jeremy Bentham, who wrote in 1789 that to know the ethical status of animals, we need only ask if they can suffer.

> The day may come when the rest of the animal creation may acquire those rights which never could have been withholden from them but by the hand of tyranny. . . . But a full-grown horse or dog is beyond comparison a more rational, as well as a more conversable animal, than an infant of a day or a week or even a month, old. But suppose they were otherwise, what would it avail? The question is not, Can they reason? nor Can they talk? but, Can they suffer?[2]

Figure 20-1 Are animals sentient? Are they worthy of moral consideration?

skynesher/E+/Getty Images

Besides feeling pleasure and pain, many animals—especially highly social mammals—seem to experience other types of emotions, such as fear, grief, and anger. While philosopher René Descartes thought that animals were mere machines devoid of an inner sense or consciousness, the welfare approach views animals as sentient, suffering beings. The assumption of sentience is one of the reasons we have laws that protect animals from cruelty. However, what counts as cruelty is disputed. For example, many people disagree about whether caging certain animals is cruel.

People also disagree about the reasons we shouldn't be cruel to animals. Some believe—as Kant did—that animal cruelty is wrong because of the effect of cruelty on those who are cruel. They argue that if one is cruel to a sentient animal, one is more likely to be cruel to people as well. We might also note that those who witness cruelty to animals may be affected by it. They may suffer from seeing an animal suffer, as Gandhi reported previously, after seeing a lamb slaughtered (we will discuss Gandhi's thinking in more detail in a moment).

However, unless one believes that human suffering is the only suffering that matters morally, then the most obvious reason not to be cruel to animals is that the suffering of the animals is bad for *them*. Whether or not something is cruel to an animal might be determined by the extent of the pain and the purpose for which it is caused. We might speak of some veterinary medical procedures as causing "necessary" pain to heal a sick animal, but cruel farming practices might be said to cause animals "unnecessary" pain. Not all pain is bad, even for humans. Pain often tells us of some health problem that can be fixed. The badness of suffering also may be only prima facie bad. The suffering may be worth it—that is, overcome by the good end it will achieve. Doing difficult things is sometimes painful, but we think it is sometimes worth the pain. In these cases, we experience not only the pain but also the benefit. In the case of animals, however, they often experience the pain of, say, an experiment performed on them without understanding it or enjoying its potential benefit. Is this ever justified?

In discussions of animal sentience, we also have to ask whether animals have different capacities to feel pain. Nonhuman animals with more developed and complex nervous systems and brains will likely have more capacity to feel pain as well as pleasure of various sorts. To fully decide this question, we would need to think carefully about the physiology of various animals. For example, it might be that horses have thick skin, so kicking a horse with spurs may not hurt the horse the way it would hurt a human.

One significant point of emphasis for the discussion of sentient animals and their welfare is the question of what sorts of experiences are normal and good for animals. For example, the pain of childbirth in humans is frequently considered part of a productive and joyful activity. But defenders of animal welfare argue that much of the pain and suffering animals are subjected to—especially in intensive animal agriculture—does not produce any benefit for the animals. Indeed, some contend that the process of intensive animal agriculture as a whole is wrong because it continuously violates the normal functioning of the animals. This happens, for example, when animals are kept confined in small spaces, packed together in intensive feeding operations, and when their bodies are altered. Intensive animal agriculture involves cropping chickens' beaks, removing cattle's horns, confining veal calves and feeding them a diet that makes them anemic, and force-feeding geese a diet that sickens them in order to produce foie gras. These operations do not respect what philosopher Martha Nussbaum calls "the dignity of the species." Nussbaum claims that sentient animals should be given the opportunity to live according to the natural dignity of their species. Nussbaum concludes: "No sentient animal should be cut off from the chance for a flourishing life, a life with the type of dignity relevant to that species...all sentient animals should enjoy certain positive opportunities to flourish."[3] Of course, there is an open and complex question about what it means for an animal to flourish. Should domesticated cats and dogs be allowed to reproduce unchecked; in other words, do spaying and neutering prevent them from flourishing? If we don't spay and neuter our pets, how will we deal with overpopulation? Further, should animals be allowed to roam freely, or is it permissible to confine them? And so on. The question of what counts as living according to the natural dignity of a species remains open to debate.

In the wild, it is a fact of life that animals feed on and cause pain to one another. Predation prevails. Carnivores kill for food. The fawn is eaten by the cougar. Natural processes such as floods, fires, droughts, and volcanic eruptions also contribute to animal suffering and death. If animal suffering is important, are we ethically obligated to lessen it in cases where we could do so? For example, in 1986, the Hubbard Glacier in Alaska began to move, and in a few weeks, it had sealed off a fjord. As freshwater runoff poured into the enclosed water, its salinity decreased, threatening the lives of porpoises and harbor seals that were trapped inside by the closure. Some people wanted to rescue the animals, while others held that this was a natural event that should be allowed to run its course.[4]

We tend to think we have a greater obligation not to *cause* pain or harm than we do to *relieve* it. In special cases, however, we may have a duty to relieve pain or prevent the harm. A lifeguard may have an obligation to rescue a drowning swimmer that the ordinary bystander does not. A parent has more obligation to prevent harm to their child than a stranger does. In the case of nonhuman animals, do we have similar obligations to prevent harm? Do we feel constrained to prevent the pain and deaths of animals in the wild? In general, it would seem that although we may choose to do so out of sympathy, we may not be obligated to do so. At least the obligation to prevent harm seems less stringent than the obligation not to cause a similar harm. But if there is this moral difference between preventing and causing harm, then while we may be justified in *allowing* animals in the wild to die or suffer pain, it does not follow that we are justified in *causing* similar pain or harm to them. Just because nature is cruel does not necessarily give us the right to be so.

Speciesism

20.3 Define speciesism and articulate criticisms of this idea.

The animal welfare focus is most closely associated with the work of the influential ethicist Peter Singer, whose 1975 book *Animal Liberation* is excerpted as a reading for this chapter. Singer maintains that since animals are sentient, their interests should be given equal consideration to those of humans. Singer does not mean that animals should be treated as exactly equal to humans but, rather, that animal interests should be taken into account. Animals may have different interests than we do, but that does not mean that their interests may be ignored. Philosopher David DeGrazia has explained the idea of equal consideration as follows: "equal consideration, whether for humans or animals, means in some way giving equal moral weight to the relevantly similar interests of different individuals."[5] DeGrazia goes on to explain that if we don't consider relevantly similar interests equally, we are guilty of creating a differential hierarchy of moral status that is elitist and resembles caste systems or aristocracies.

Singer rejects such an elitist or hierarchical account of animal interests as the result of a self-interested and arbitrary way of drawing moral lines. Singer maintains that not giving equal consideration to the interests of animals is **speciesism**, an objectionable attitude similar to racism or sexism. Speciesism is objectionable because it involves treating animals badly simply because they are members of a different species and giving preference to members of our own species simply because we are human beings.[6] But on what grounds is this objectionable? According to Singer, having interests is connected to the ability to feel pleasure and pain, because pleasure is derived from the satisfaction of interests. Thus, from Singer's standpoint, animal interests should be considered because there is no non-speciesist way to draw the line between animal interests and human interests. Both humans and animals seek pleasure and avoid pain; valuing human pleasure over animal pleasure, for example, is arbitrary and unjustifiable. (Animals are different from plants in this regard. Plants have things that are *in their interest* even though they do not *have interests*.) Singer concludes that among animals that have relevantly similar interests, these interests should be given equal consideration. Not everyone accepts this idea, of course. In one of the readings for this chapter, Bonnie Steinbock argues that it is appropriate to give preference to the interests of humans. Her argument focuses on specific mental capacities that human beings have, which she views as superior to the mere sentience of nonhuman animals. She writes, "certain capacities, which seem to be unique to human beings, entitle their possessors to a privileged position in the moral community."[7] Among those capacities may be the ability to think about morality and to act on moral responsibility—which seems to involve more than the bare ability to experience pleasure and pain and to have interests.

Animal Rights

20.4 Explain the difference between a concern for animal welfare and a concern for animal rights.

It is one thing to say that the suffering of a nonhuman animal is a bad thing in itself. It is another to say that nonhuman animals have a *right* not to be caused to suffer or feel pain. To consider the question of animal rights, we need to first review our discussions about what a right is and what it means to have a right. A *right* is generally defined as a strong and *legitimate claim* that can be made by a claimant against someone. Rights claims are often grounded in ideas about what is natural or fitting, as we saw in our discussion on natural law and natural rights in Chapter 7. Thus, if I claim a right to freedom of speech, I am asserting my legitimate claim against anyone who would prevent me from speaking out, and I am claiming that there is something about me as a human being that makes my freedom of speech essential. A person can claim a right to have or be given something (a positive right) as well as a right not to be prevented from doing something (a negative right). Legal rights are claims that the law recognizes and enforces. However, we also hold that there are moral rights—in other words, things we can rightly claim, even if the law does not enforce the claim.

Just who can legitimately claim a moral right to something, and on what grounds? One might think that to be the kind of being who can have rights, one must be able to claim them and understand them. If this were so, the cat who is left money in a will would not have a right to it because the cat does not understand that it has such a right and could not claim that its rights have been violated if the money is withheld. But if the capacity to understand or claim a right is the only thing that matters, we might have to conclude that human infants have no rights—to inherit money or be protected from abuse and neglect—because they cannot understand or claim them. But we generally think that infants have a right to care from their parents, even if they do not understand this right and cannot claim it. We make similar claims for the rights of individuals with developmental disabilities who are also often unable to claim or understand their rights. One might think that only **moral agents**—those beings who can make and act on moral judgments—have rights. According to this view, a person only has rights if they are a full member of the moral community, with duties and responsibilities. On the other hand, it is not unreasonable to think that this is too stringent a requirement. Perhaps it is sufficient for one to be a moral patient in order to be the type of being who can have rights. A **moral patient** is an object of moral concern, the kind of being who matters morally. Moral patients have rights, but they do not have correlated responsibilities. Thus, children have rights but are not considered to be full moral agents; we ought not harm them, but they are viewed as less than fully responsible. As we considered in Chapter 19, some may think that trees could be considered as moral patients. But does it make sense to say that trees have rights? If this does not seem to be correct, what other reasons can be given for why a being might have rights?

We could argue that it is just because they can feel pain that sentient beings have a *right not to suffer*, or at least not to suffer needlessly. This would mean that others have a *duty* with regard to this claim. However, we may have duties not to needlessly hurt animals, even if they don't have the *right* to be treated in ways that never cause them pain. We have many duties that are not directly a matter of respecting anyone's rights. For example, I may have a duty not to purchase and then destroy a famous and architecturally important building—but not because the building has a right to exist. Thus, from the fact that we have duties to animals—not to make them suffer needlessly, for example—we cannot necessarily conclude that they have rights. If we want to argue for this view, we would need to make

a clearer connection between duties and rights or we would need to show why some particular duties also imply rights. Not all duties are a function of rights, as I might have a duty to develop my talents, even though no one has a right that I do so. However, having a right seems to entail that someone has a duty to protect that right.

As we have seen, some philosophers have pointed to the fact that animals have *interests* as a basis for asserting that they have rights. To have an interest in something is usually thought to require consciousness of that thing as well as desire for it. A being that has a capacity for conscious desire is a being that can have rights, according to this position. Thus, the philosopher Joel Feinberg says that it is because nonhuman animals have "conscious wishes, desires, and hopes . . . urges and impulses" that they are the kind of beings who can have rights.[8] It is these psychological capacities that make animals capable of having rights to certain treatment, according to this view. Similarly, Tom Regan argues that nonhuman animals have rights, just as we do, because they are what he calls the "subject of a life."[9] This idea is similar to Feinberg's because it states that because animals have an inner life, which includes conscious desires and wants, they have the status of rights possessors. Nonhuman animals differ among themselves in their capacity to have these various psychological experiences, and it probably parallels the development and complexity of their nervous systems. A dog may be able to experience fear, but, most likely, the flea on its ear does not. In more ambiguous cases, however, drawing such distinctions may prove difficult in practice, when we would have to determine the character of a particular animal's inner life. The more serious challenge for such views is to support the more basic claim that inner psychic states are a moral foundation for rights.

We noted previously that Peter Singer maintains that because the interests of animals are similar to ours, they ought to be given equal weight. This does not mean, in his view, that they have a *right* to whatever we have a right to. It would make no sense to say that a pig has a right to vote because it has no interest in voting and lacks the capacity to vote. However, according to

Singer, it would make sense to say that we ought to give equal consideration to the pig's suffering. Pigs shouldn't be made to suffer needlessly to satisfy human whims. But Singer is reluctant to say that animals have rights. As a utilitarian, he avoids speaking of rights (you might recall from Chapter 7 that the utilitarian Jeremy Bentham described rights as "nonsense on stilts"). This can lead to some confusion. For example, Singer has explained that the "animal rights movement" does not need the concept of rights.[10] The point here is that the phrase "animal rights" is sometimes used in popular parlance as an umbrella term that encompasses a variety of philosophical perspectives, including both utilitarian and non-consequentialist positions.

Others argue that animals need not be treated as equal to humans and that their interests should not be given equal weight with ours. It is because of the difference in species' *abilities* and *potentialities* that animals are a lesser form of being, according to these views. (The Bonnie Steinbock reading for this chapter presents such a view.) However, this does not mean that animals' interests should be disregarded. It may mean that peripheral or minor interests of human beings should not override more serious interests of animals. It is one thing to say that animals may be used, if necessary, for experiments that will save the lives of human beings, but it is quite another to say that they may be harmed in testing cosmetics or other things that are not necessary for human life. Whether this position would provide a sufficient basis for vegetarianism might depend on the importance of animal protein to human health, for example, and whether animals could be raised humanely for food.

Abolition or Reform

We have, so far, outlined a variety of ways of thinking about animal ethics in a continuum that extends from an anthropocentric focus toward the non-anthropocentric concerns of animal welfare and animal rights theories. This continuum is summarized in Table 20-1. But before concluding this overview of moral approaches to the topic, let's consider a question of the intensity or degree of commitment found in various forms of animal ethics. At issue here is the question of the difference between abolition and reform. This question holds for a variety of other topics. Some critics of criminal justice have called for prisons to be abolished, for example, while others call only for reform (as we discussed in Chapter 17). A similar divide is found in discussions of animal ethics.

Some theorists and activists have called for the abolition of meat eating, animal agriculture, and animal testing. Tom Regan and others who argue in defense of animal rights typically reach such a conclusion. A contemporary author who has argued vigorously in favor of abolitionism is philosopher and author Gary Francione. Francione is the author of a number of books and articles, as well as a website that argues for abolition and veganism (https://www.abolitionistapproach.com/). Francione has argued that if one grants that animals matter morally, one must become a vegan and one must be committed to the project of abolishing animal agriculture and other institutions that exploit animals. As he explains, "if nonhumans are persons and have a right not to be used as property, we must abolish our institutionalized exploitation of them."[11] From the standpoint of abolitionism, gradual reforms—making animal agriculture less cruel and more "humane"—is inadequate. In response, others have argued in defense of reform. Peter Singer, for example, has seemed to offer reformist arguments that applaud the gradual improvement of animal agriculture and animal experimentation. He has, for instance, praised companies such as Whole Foods that are working to reform animal agriculture, saying that instead of boycotting meat and meat-producers and sellers, it might be better to work toward a situation in which meat will be "as compassionately produced as possible."[12] This reformist spirit has been criticized by Francione and other abolitionists who think there is no possible way for meat to be produced compassionately.[13]

The reformist approach fits best with a kind of utilitarianism that is interested in making improvements that involve trade-offs and a kind of cost–benefit analysis. Abolitionism tends to hold that those kinds of trade-offs and gradual improvements are not morally justifiable, since the very idea of exploiting and killing animals is wrong. A number of authors have continued to debate

Table 20-1   Outline of Moral Approaches to Animal Ethics

	Animal Rights	Animal Welfare	Anthropocentrism
Thesis	Nonhuman animals have rights that generate duties.	The interests of nonhuman animals ought to be taken into account.	Human beings are the only objects of moral concern.
Corollaries and Implications	The claim that nonhuman animals have inherent value results in radical/abolitionist criticism of animal experimentation and animal agriculture; to claim that only human beings have rights is speciesism	The claim that animal welfare—suffering, harm, flourishing, and enjoyment—ought to be taken into account results in substantial critique of animal agriculture and animal experimentation; to deny the importance of animal suffering or flourishing is speciesism	This view defends animal agriculture and experimentation in the name of human interests; cruelty to animals is condemned based on its tendency to debase human beings; rejects the accusation of speciesism and defends human interests as more important than those of animals
Connections with Moral Theory	Deontological approach focuses on the rights of animals and corollary duties not to harm or use them.	Consequentialism focuses on harms, interests, and preferences of nonhuman animals in comparison with human interests.	Consequentialism focuses only on human interests, harms, and benefits; deontological respect for rights only applies to human beings.
Relevant Authors/Examples	Tom Regan; Gary Francione	Peter Singer; Jeremy Bentham	Immanuel Kant; Bonnie Steinbock

this question in relation to the challenge of factory farming and with regard to animal experimentation and other concerns of animal use and exploitation, including circuses, zoos, horse racing, hunting, and so on. Bob Fischer has offered an interesting conclusion with regard to the question of meat eating. The subtitle of Fischer's recent book on the topic explains his point of view: *The Ethics of Eating Animals: Usually Bad, Sometimes Wrong, and Often Permissible*.[14] Fischer considers a number of interesting questions in presenting his argument, including whether it would be permissible to eat "roadkill," insects, and other animals not usually considered in this conversation. He also asks us to consider whether drastic calls for abolition may also include racist and classist assumptions. Issues to consider here include the value of meat eating and

animal use in different cultures, the way that labor in animal industries is typically low-paying and undertaken by people from certain racial or ethnic groups, and worries about the cost of food and the potential expense of a vegan diet. An abolitionist may argue in response that these social issues will be addressed as the process of abolition unfolds.

Finally, it is worth noting here that abolitionism is a project of the future—and that there are billions of animals who suffer every year when they are used in animal agriculture, animal experiments, and in other industries that exploit animals. One substantial argument in favor of reform is that gradual improvement in the conditions in which animals live and die can have significant and concrete positive impact on the lives of animals in the present.[15]

Current Issues

20.5 Evaluate current issues in animal ethics including hunting, vegetarianism, animal research, and endangered species protection.

Hunting and Harvesting Wild Animals

Gray wolves were once hunted to the brink of extinction in the United States. By 1970, only two states—Alaska and Minnesota—still had viable gray wolf populations. During the 1970s, various subspecies of gray wolf were given protection from hunting under the Endangered Species Act. For some subspecies—the Texas wolf, for example—it was too late. The Texas wolf and other subspecies have disappeared forever. By 1978, all gray wolf subspecies in the lower forty-eight states were protected against hunting.[16] In 1995, wolves captured in Canada were reintroduced to the western United States in an effort to regenerate the U.S. wolf population. Western ranchers feared that these wolves would prey on their livestock, and in some places, they were permitted to shoot wolves that had killed their sheep or cattle. By 2009, the population of wolves had grown large enough that the U.S. Fish and Wildlife Service removed the gray

---

▶ **Knowledge Check**   Answers appear at the end of the chapter.

1. Which of the following is an *anthropocentric* reason for opposing animal cruelty?

   a. Animals suffer under cruel conditions, and their suffering matters morally.

   b. Domesticated animals belong to someone, and cruelty toward those animals violates the owner's property rights.

   c. Animals have interests and rights; cruelty is wrong because it harms those interests and violates those rights.

   d. Farm animals are derived from wild species, and it is cruel to alter a species through breeding and genetic engineering.

2. How might we describe the following concern: "Animals suffer and their suffering matters"?

   a. It is focused on sentience.

   b. It is focused on animal rights.

   c. It is anthropocentric.

   d. It is ethnocentric.

3. What is speciesism?

   a. It is the theory that species have evolved over time from other species via natural selection.

   b. It is a theory about the beauty and integrity of the human species.

   c. It is a concept used to describe the way that animals are grouped together according to shared genetic makeup.

   d. It is an idea used to describe the unjustified preference for members of your own species.

4. Which is true of the animal rights perspective?

   a. It is concerned with reforming farming and other practices in order to improve the lives of animals.

   b. It is the idea that the value of an animal is understood in relation to human property rights.

   c. It maintains that individual animals have a kind of dignity and value that should protect them from harm.

   d. It wants to make sure that current practices such as factory farming and animal experimentation serve important human interests.

wolf from the list of endangered species. This move prompted some states to legalize wolf hunting. Controversially, this included wolf hunting near Yellowstone National Park—a practice that raised objections because the national parks are supposed to protect animals from hunting. In subsequent years, wolf hunting has resumed in Wyoming, Wisconsin, Minnesota, Idaho, and Montana. Thousands of wolves have been killed in the past couple of decades, including five hundred wolves that were killed in the 2021–2022 hunting season in Montana, Wyoming, and Idaho.[17] Naturalists have been outraged, but lawmakers have called for hunters to harvest more wolves with the goal of shrinking the wolf population in the Northern Rockies.

Opponents of wolf hunts criticize the language used to describe these hunts, complaining that it is a euphemism to use the word "harvest" to describe such killing. This points to the question of whether a wolf is a creature with a right to life or something more like a crop to be managed and harvested. Some view wolves as noble symbols of a vanishing wilderness. Others see them as animals very similar to the dogs we keep as pets. Still others view wolves as dangerous predators that pose a risk to sheep and other herd animals. Such perspectives reflect different answers to the question, What is the value of a wolf—or any other animal?

Is there a humane way to kill a wolf or another nonhuman animal? During wolf harvests, the animals may be shot or trapped. Animal welfare advocates have been especially critical of using leg traps to kill wolves. One antitrapping group, Footloose Montana, argues that trapping is cruel because it causes excessive suffering and is not in line with the "fair chase" ethos of hunting.[18] Leg traps are intended to hold the wolf until the hunter arrives to finally kill it. Trappers insist that they check their traps often and kill the animals quickly. But some animals are caught in traps for long periods of time. Some die of hypothermia. Others chew off their own legs or are attacked by other predators. Another problem with trapping is that it is indiscriminate. A 2012 report about a trapping program employed by the Wildlife Services in California indicated that traps in California had killed fifty thousand unintended animals since 2000, including protected species such as bald eagles and more than one thousand dogs.[19] A 2016 report claims, "In 2014, Wildlife Services killed 322 wolves, 61,702 coyotes, 2,930 foxes, 580 black bears, 796 bobcats, five golden eagles, and three bald eagles."[20] The report stated that the animals

Figure 20-2 Wolf hunting raises moral questions about animal ethics.

ITAR-TASS Photo Agency/Alamy Stock Photo

were trapped or poisoned. Poison is a common way of dealing with household pests such as rats and mice—along with sticky traps and glue boards. Critics complain that these are inhumane ways of killing pest animals: poison causes internal hemorrhaging and dehydration, while glue boards keep animals immobile until they succumb to dehydration and starvation. For this reason, some argue that snap traps—the old fashioned mousetrap—are the most humane way to kill mice and rats because the trap kills instantly. Others worry that there is no humane way to kill an animal.

A further question is whether trapping and poisoning lives up to the standards of "fair chase." The idea of fair chase in hunting ethics is that the animal should stand some chance and the hunter requires some skill and good luck. According to one definition, fair chase involves a balance between the hunter and the hunted animal "that allows hunters to occasionally succeed, while animals generally avoid being taken."[21] The concept of fair chase might be used to criticize the practice of "rigged" hunting, in which companies obtain "trophy" animals and confine them in certain ways so that hunters have a much better chance at a kill. Such companies often buy their animals from dubious suppliers, including exotic animal auctions, and their hunts have been known to include "zebras, camels, ostriches, kangaroos, and lion cubs."[22] Other problematic forms of hunting include the use of bait to attract animals to be shot. For example, the practice of baiting bears is banned in eighteen of the twenty-eight states in which bear hunting is legal. Defenders of bear baiting argue that it helps to maintain the population of bears. But when the issue was being debated in the Midwest a couple of decades ago, the governor of Minnesota, Jesse Ventura, said of bear baiting, "that ain't sport, that's an assassination."[23] However, the state of Alaska allows and even promotes bear baiting, publishing a bear baiters "code of ethics."[24]

The question of hunting ethics burst into public consciousness with the killing of Cecil the Lion in Zimbabwe in 2015. Cecil was an iconic lion—a local favorite who inhabited the Hwange National Park, where he was protected against hunting. According to media reports, Cecil was lured out of the park with bait and then shot with a bow and arrow by a dentist from Minnesota, who reportedly paid $50,000 for the opportunity. Some reports

maintained that Cecil was not killed by the arrow—and that he survived for forty hours, while the hunters tracked him down and finally killed him with a gunshot. Across the globe, there was outraged reaction to the fact that a protected lion was killed for sport and without regard for fair chase hunting ethics.[25] In response to the outrage, the U.S. Fish and Wildlife Service announced that it would list the African lion as an endangered species, which would prevent lion trophies from being imported into the United States.[26]

In addition to baiting animals and luring them out of protected areas, other controversial practices include hunting wolves and other animals from helicopters or small planes, such as occurs in Alaska. According to one report, aerial wolf hunts in Alaska kill several hundred wolves every winter.[27] This practice is not only a matter of sport hunting but also a way of balancing predator and prey populations—which is the only legal reason for such hunts under federal law. Critics of airborne hunting consider it cruel and inhumane because the plane or helicopter is used to chase animals across the snow until they are exhausted and because shots fired from the air rarely result in a clean kill.[28] In 2008, when the former governor of Alaska, Sarah Palin, was a candidate for vice president of the United States, aerial wolf hunting in Alaska became a political issue, since Governor Palin had championed the program of shooting wolves from the air, which she argued helped to eliminate predatory wolves in order to protect herds of moose and caribou.[29]

The debate over hunting points toward several complex ethical questions. Should we be concerned for the welfare of wild animals and endangered species? Do such animals have a right to live their lives free from human interference? Is it acceptable to "harvest" them as long as we kill them humanely? Is hunting part of an ancient predator–prey dynamic that defines the rest of the natural world, or do humans have greater moral responsibilities than other animals? How and why should human beings care about the well-being of individual animals or animal species, or about ecosystems that include both predators and prey animals?

It is clear that different approaches to animal ethics view this issue differently. An anthropocentric approach to animal ethics would likely support hunting as a legitimate human pastime, especially if hunting is used for food, to protect human beings from aggressive animals, and to protect domestic animals. Hunters—and fishermen—often maintain that they love and respect the animals they hunt. And things get even more complicated as hunting is sometimes done in the company of working animals such as the dogs that stir up and retrieve birds. It is worth noting that hunters love the dogs they hunt with. Within the anthropocentric approach, we might properly find debates about bear baiting and aerial shooting. These debates may consider the well-being of the animals hunted, but they are often about the kinds of virtues that should exhibited by hunters. A similar sort of anthropocentric consideration is found in thinking about the ethics of fishing. People who fish are restricted by licensing and other regulations that govern what kinds of fish can be caught and when. Those regulations are typically focused on the well-being of the fish population. But this focus is anthropocentric: it aims to preserve the fishery for future fishermen or fisherwomen. Non-anthropocentric critics of hunting and fishing may argue that there is something morally wrong with hunting or fishing. This argument would be based on some claim about the welfare or even the rights of the animals involved.

There are also cultural and historical claims made about the importance of hunting and fishing for human communities. Those claims would also be anthropocentric, focused on human concerns. Indigenous people may claim that hunting is an essential part of their cultural heritage. In the Pacific Northwest, for example, the Makah tribe has applied for permission to resume hunting gray whales. But those whales are protected by the Marine Mammals Protection Act. In its application for permission to resume hunting whales, the tribe pointed out that it has a fifteen hundred years' tradition of whaling and that whaling both serves subsistence needs (as a source of food) and is part of the tribe's effort to restore and preserve its culture.[30] But advocates for the whales are opposed to the idea. The Sea Shepherd organization has stated that they oppose the intentional killing of whales, "no matter the circumstances." As they say, their "opposition to whaling is categorical and uncompromising."[31] The Sea Shepherd organization has a long history of documenting and lobbying against the killing of whales, dolphins, and other sea life. Paul Watson, the president of Sea Shepherd, has explained that his concern is biocentric and not anthropocentric. He wrote in an essay in 2019, "We must shake off the anthropocentric mindset and embrace a biocentric understanding of the natural world."[32] Watson suggests in the same essay that we can learn biocentrism from Indigenous people. But the Makah tribe maintains that their view of nature includes whale hunting as part of their understanding of the interconnected nature of the world. Charlotte Coté, a member of a related tribe, the Nuu-chah-nulth, who is also a professor at the University of Washington, has explained that the philosophy of her people is that "everything is one," which she explains as "an understanding that everything in life is connected."[33] But should whale hunting be part of this interconnected whole? The case of the Makah tribe was still being litigated as this chapter was being written in 2022.

Moral Vegetarianism

There are a variety of concrete issues that arise in discussing animals and their welfare. In addition to hunting, the most obvious issue is whether we ought to raise and kill animals for food. The discussion of hunting overlaps with discussions of eating animals. Although wolves are not hunted for their meat, harvesting wolves is intended to protect domesticated animals such as cattle and sheep and to protect wild herds of elk, caribou, moose, and deer, which are hunted for their meat. This raises the interesting question about which animals we eat and which animals we don't, and evokes the philosophical issue of cultural relativism (as discussed in Chapter 3). Some cultures eat dogs; others don't. Some cultures eat pigs; others don't. Do these differences reflect moral truths of some kind, or mere cultural conventions and taboos?

Some cultures and individuals don't eat animals at all. The ancient Greek philosopher Pythagoras and his followers were vegetarians, as are some Hindus, Buddhists, and Jains in varying degrees. The nineteenth-century Russian novelist Leo Tolstoy was a vegetarian. Tolstoy maintained that those who are "really and seriously seeking to live a good life" will abstain from animal food because "its use is simply immoral, as it involves the performance of an act which is contrary to moral feeling—killing."[34] Tolstoy's ideas had an influence on Mohandas Gandhi (discussed in Chapter 2), whose vegetarianism was also connected to his Hindu religion and culture. In his autobiography, Gandhi describes witnessing a ceremonial sacrifice of a lamb. When a friend explained to him that a lamb does not feel anything while being slaughtered, Gandhi replied that if the lamb could speak, it would tell a different tale. Gandhi concludes,

> To my mind the life of a lamb is no less precious than that of a human being. I should be unwilling to take the life of a lamb for the sake of the human body. I hold that, the more helpless a creature, the more entitled it is to protection by man from the cruelty of man.[35]

There are degrees of vegetarianism. All vegetarians avoid eating animals, although some may eat eggs, dairy products, or even fish. Vegans avoid consuming both animals and animal products, including eggs, dairy, and, in some cases, honey. Some people observe vegetarian diets for health reasons—because of a food allergy or in an effort to follow a high-fiber, low-fat diet. But many vegetarians avoid eating animals for ethical reasons. The deep ethical question is whether there are good moral reasons to avoid meat and animal products or whether the consumption of animals is morally justified. As noted above, there are degrees of criticism of meat eating. Some vegans argue for the abolition of animal agriculture. But others—both meat eaters and ethical vegetarians—focus more on reforming animal agriculture, minimizing meat consumption, and seeking to produce meat in humane and compassionate ways.

Most meat eaters think there is nothing wrong with consuming animals and animal products. Meat eating is deeply rooted in custom and tradition. One traditional idea holds that animals are given to us by God for our use. A related idea maintains that there is a hierarchy of beings, with humans at the top, and this entitles us to use the animals below us. Others assume that animals do not feel pain when they are slaughtered, or that animals are not moral "persons" because they do not have the sort of consciousness that would give them an interest in living. (You might want to compare such positions to other cases where moral status is in question, such as human fetuses or adults who are in a permanent vegetative state because of an illness or accident.) Another argument holds that vegetarianism is *supererogatory*: that it might be admirable to abstain from eating animals but that there is no duty to do

so.[36] Still others argue that the morality of eating meat depends on the way the meat is raised—whether it is produced on industrial farms or in a "cruelty-free" manner (including free-range or cage-free animals). This issue has even shown up on state ballots: in California in 2008, voters approved the Prevention of Farm Animal Cruelty Act, which aimed to prevent cruelty in the treatment of veal calves, pigs, and chickens. The law went into effect in 2015, allowing farmers time to update their methods. In 2018, voters in California approved an update to the law, the Prevention of Cruelty to Farm Animals Act, which closed loopholes in the original law by preventing eggs, veal, and other animal products that were unethically sourced from being imported into the state. That led to lawsuits from pork producers who claimed that the law violated the interstate commerce clause of the U.S. Constitution.[37] Litigation is ongoing. Similar laws have been established in several other states, such as Arizona and Colorado, as well as in the European Union.[38]

A strictly utilitarian account of animal ethics would be focused on whether causing animal suffering can be justified by some account of the greater good. If we are primarily focused on human good, we might say that animal suffering is outweighed by the human interest in nutritious and delicious meat and other animal products. Another utilitarian argument might point out that by raising animals for food and clothing, we produce animals that otherwise would never have been born—so even though these animals are used and killed, they enjoy pleasures while alive that they would not have enjoyed if not for animal agriculture. Unless their lives involve a greater amount of pain than pleasure, we may have done these animals a favor by raising them.

But critics of industrialized agriculture argue that "factory farms" produce animals that live miserable lives and are then killed for human purposes. While such farms are not intentionally cruel, they employ practices that would certainly appear to be cruel if viewed from the perspective of the animals. Animals are branded, force-fed, and confined, frequently without enough space to exercise or even turn around. They are kept in close proximity to other animals, which makes them susceptible to infectious diseases—and prompts industrial farms to pump them full of antibiotics.

Industrialized agriculture also uses breeding technologies, including genetic engineering and cloning, which aim to maximize meat production. For example, these processes create animals that are bred to be large, and then they are fed so much that eventually they cannot stand up. Chickens packed into close quarters often have their beaks and claws removed to prevent injury to themselves and other chickens. And some animals—for example, veal cattle or geese raised for foie gras—are kept in cages that prevent almost all movement and force-fed in ways that negatively impact their health. Tasty veal comes from anemic calves, and delicious foie gras comes from diseased goose liver.

Animals are crowded into trucks and transported for slaughter in ways that often result in significant stress, with thousands of animals dying on the way.[39] In the slaughterhouses, there are assembly-line processes by which animals are stunned and killed. Some animals are severely injured before they are slaughtered. Animal welfare advocates have posted videos of "downer cattle" (cattle who can't or won't walk under their own power to the slaughterhouse) who are dragged or forklifted into the killing line. Federal law requires that mammals be stunned before killing. But in some cases, there may be a problem in properly stunning the animals. Peter Singer and Jim Mason conclude, "it is probable that anyone who eats meat will, unknowingly, from time to time be eating meat that comes from an animal who died an agonizing death."[40] There are legal and ethical standards that regulate the meat production industry. But the industrial meat production process is focused on speed and efficiency. This is necessary because of the great demand for meat among the general public. In the United States in 2017, the meat and poultry industry processed 100 billion pounds of meat. This included 9 billion chickens, 32.2 million cattle and calves, 241.7 million turkeys, 2.2 million sheep and lambs, and 121 million hogs.[41]

The appetite for meat is growing worldwide, with the global demand increasing every year. One estimate suggests that by 2050, global meat demand will reach 570 million tons, which would be twice the rate of consumption that existed in 2008.[42] There will likely be substantial environmental costs from more extensive meat production, and many argue on environmental grounds that we ought to curtail meat consumption. But defenders of industrial agriculture argue that if we want to feed a human population of seven billion and counting, we need intensified agricultural procedures. Indeed, if the demand for meat continues to grow, we will need to develop even more efficient and productive ways of raising animals for meat: the global population cannot be fed on meat from free-range farms.

Vegetarian critics of factory farming and the growing appetite for meat argue that there are nutritious and delicious alternatives to meat. They also point out that animal agriculture is hard on the environment. The animals that we consume eat grains, require fresh water, and produce waste. Vegetarians argue that it would be more efficient and less wasteful to feed the growing human population if we ate lower on the food chain. This would leave a smaller ecological footprint and make more grain and other food available to fight human hunger around the world.[43]

Vegetarianism is also connected with other political and moral ideas. Some feminists argue that meat eating is connected to male dominance and the oppression of women; other feminists contend that the idea of care ethics should encompass care for animals.[44] Vegetarians often cite medical studies that indicate eating meat is not necessary for human health. This is especially true in much of the developed world, where nutritious alternatives are easily found in the typical supermarket. If meat eating is not necessary for human health, meat becomes a luxury good. And then we may ask whether it is morally justified to cause animal suffering in support of a human indulgence. Building on this kind of argument, some vegans, such as Gary Francione, whom we discussed above, argue that we ought to abolish meat production entirely. On the other hand, many argue that human interests matter more than animal interests and that eating meat is easily justified by appealing to basic human interests.

Given the ecological pressures created by growing demand for meat, as well as concerns for animal suffering, many are arguing that we should eat less meat and even consider producing meat that is grown in test tubes—called variously in vitro meat, cultured meat, or cultivated meat. Peter Singer has argued that if we could produce nutritious, tasty, and affordable meat in test tubes, we ought to do so. He maintains that this would reduce animal suffering while also reducing the environmental harms caused by meat production. As Singer concluded:

> Some vegetarians and vegans may object to in vitro meat, because they don't see the need for meat at all. That's fine for them, and of course they are free to remain vegetarians and vegans, and choose not to eat in vitro meat. My own view is that being a vegetarian or vegan is not an end in itself, but a means toward reducing both human and animal suffering, and leaving a habitable planet to future generations. I haven't eaten meat for 40 years, but if in vitro meat becomes commercially available, I will be pleased to try it.[45]

At this point, in vitro meat is not currently widely available. But an incipient "cultured meat" industry is growing. As might be expected, not everyone is in favor of this. Gary Francione, the vegan author discussed above, has argued against cultured meat based on the fact that in order to grow meat in vitro, animal products are needed (basically a medium of animal blood and hormones is required to begin with—typically fetal blood). Francione contends that even cultured meat still requires some animals to be killed as part of the process.[46] But new processes are being developed that could produce meat without the use of animal inputs.[47]

iStockphoto.com/SensorSpot

Figure 20-3 Chicks being processed on a conveyor belt in an industrial agriculture operation.

Animal Experimentation

Another issue is the use of animals in scientific and industrial research. Some animal rights advocates claim that it is cruel and unnecessary to use animals in scientific and industrial research. Defenders of animal experimentation argue that most of the gains we have made in terms of modern medicine and in safety for modern industrial products are the results of experiments performed on animals.

Animal research has a long history. In the third century BCE in Alexandria, Egypt, animals were used to study bodily functions.[48] Aristotle cut open animals to learn about their structure and development. The Roman physician Galen used certain animals to show that veins do not carry air but blood. And in 1622, William Harvey used animals to exhibit the circulation of the blood. Animals were used in 1846 to show the effects of anesthesia and in 1878 to demonstrate the relationship between bacteria and disease.[49]

In the twentieth century, research with animals made many advances in medicine possible, from cures for infectious diseases and the development of immunization techniques and antibiotics, to the development of surgical procedures. For example, in 1921, an Ontario doctor and his assistant severed the connection between the pancreases and digestive systems of dogs in order to find the substance that controlled diabetes. In so doing, they isolated insulin and thus opened the possibility for treating the millions of people who have that disease.[50] During the development of a polio vaccine, hundreds of primates were killed, but as a result of these experiments, today polio is almost eradicated in the developed world. In 1952, there were fifty-eight thousand cases of this crippling disease in the United States, and in 1984, there were just four. Now, the disease has been virtually eliminated (despite reports in the early 2020's of a few new cases across the globe).[51] AIDS researchers have used monkeys to test vaccines against HIV, and animal research has been an important part of the study of human paralysis. In 2000, "researchers at the University of Massachusetts Medical School [took] immature cells from the spinal cords of adult rats, induced them to grow, and then implanted them in the gap of the severed spinal cords of paralyzed rats."[52] Soon, the rats were able to move, stand, and walk. This research has given hope to the hundreds of thousands of people in the United States and around the world who suffer from spinal-cord damage. It is part of a growing field of tissue engineering in which scientists grow living tissue to replace damaged parts of the human body (see further discussion of biotechnologies in Chapter 12).

Today, laboratory researchers are using leopard frogs to test the pain-killing capacity of morphine, codeine, and Demerol. Japanese medaka fish are being used as a model to determine the cancer-causing properties of substances that are released into rivers and lakes. And research using the giant Israeli scorpion has found a way to use the scorpion venom to treat brain tumors, called gliomas.[53] Other promising research creates genetically modified animals to use as drug-producing machines. For example, scientists have spliced human genes into the DNA of goats, sheep, and pigs. These mammals then secrete therapeutic proteins in their milk, which can be used to treat hemophilia and cystic fibrosis.[54] Animal models have proved to be useful in the production of vaccines for COVID-19 and for studying the effects of the disease and potential treatments. This research has included mice who have been genetically engineered to be susceptible to the disease, as well as hamsters, ferrets, cats, and monkeys.[55]

Opposition to animal research dates back to at least the nineteenth century. *Anti-vivisectionists* campaigned against dissecting live animals and other common practices that inflicted pain on animals. In 1876, the British Parliament passed the first animal welfare act, the Cruelty to Animals Act. A few states in the United States passed anti-cruelty laws in the nineteenth and early twentieth centuries, but it was not until 1966 that the United States instituted a federal law regulating animal research. The Animal Welfare Act of 1966 (AWA) came about, in part, in response to a national outcry over a family dog, Pepper, that had become a stray and ended up being euthanized in a hospital after being subjected to a laboratory experiment. The AWA set minimum standards for handling cats, dogs, nonhuman primates, rabbits, hamsters, and guinea pigs. It also sought to regulate the use of dogs and cats so that pets like Pepper did not end up in lab experiments.[56] In a 1976 amendment, Congress exempted rats, mice, birds, horses, and farm animals from the protections of the AWA because of problems with enforcement and funding.[57] Such exclusions were reinforced in 2002 in an amendment to the annual farm bill, and subsequent efforts to revoke it have failed in Congress. So, while the Animal Welfare Act requires careful treatment of some animals used in research, such as dogs, it does not cover the vast majority of laboratory animals. It is estimated that 95 percent of animals used in laboratory research are mice, rats, and birds, all of which the AWA does not cover.[58] While the AWA has been effective in limiting animal cruelty, critics contend that it leaves much to be desired, since it fails to regulate the treatment of farm animals.[59]

There is an ongoing dispute about how many animals are actually used in research in a given year. Humane Society estimates the total number in the United States at fifty million.[60] Another recent estimate published in 2021 suggests that 111 million mice and rats are used in American labs, but that number has been disputed.[61] The problem is that there is no standard reporting procedure or regular accounting of lab animals used, since these animals are not covered by the Animal Welfare Act.[62] Opponents of animal research argue that whatever the actual number, this is too much cruelty in the name of research. Groups like People for the Ethical Treatment of Animals (PETA), the American Society for the Prevention of Cruelty to Animals (ASPCA), and the Humane Society continue to question the need for animal research and argue that alternatives are being neglected. Johns Hopkins University's Center for Alternatives to Animal Testing maintains that "the best science is humane science."[63]

The AWA requires laboratories to report the number of animals used—again with a specific focus only on certain species. On university campuses, animal use is monitored by the Institutional Animal Care and Use Committees (IACUCs). If you do scientific research involving animals as a student, you may have to learn how to prepare a protocol for approval by an IACUC. According to the U.S. Department of Agriculture—which also monitors the use of animals in research—in 2018, there were more than eighteen thousand cats, more than fifty-nine thousand dogs, and more than seventy thousand primates being used in animal research in the United States.[64] Not all of these animals were subjected to painful intervention: they were used

in a variety of experiments involving different levels of pain and experimental treatment. One particularly controversial type of medical research involves chimpanzees, an intelligent species of ape that is a close relative of human beings. In 2013, the National Institutes of Health announced that it was going to end chimpanzee research, in part, as a result of ethical concerns.[65] The Humane Society and PETA applauded this move. The NIH had planned to keep fifty chimpanzees in reserve in case they were needed for future research. But in late 2015, they announced that even this reserve cohort of chimpanzees would be retired.[66]

A basic question here is whether we are justified in using nonhuman animals for research that may benefit human beings (and that may also benefit animals, as in veterinary research). A utilitarian approach that focused only on human interests and concerns would claim that if human beings benefit, such research is justified. A broader utilitarian position that takes animal suffering into account would explore the question of whether the benefits of animal research outweigh the harms of such research on the animals involved.

While opponents of animal research criticize the large numbers of animals used in research, defenders of animal research point out that these numbers are best interpreted in comparison with other uses of animals. The advocacy group Speaking of Research makes such an argument in comparing the relatively small numbers of animals used in research to the much larger number of animals consumed as food.[67] Of course, as we've noted above, these comparisons are difficult to make because there are disagreements about the numbers of mice and rats used in research. Nonetheless, it is worth thinking about some sort of rough comparison that takes into account the benefits produced by animal research in comparison with the value of animal agriculture. In making that kind of comparative evaluation, we are likely thinking about some sort of utilitarian analysis involving a kind of cost–benefit analysis.

One important moral question is whether the use of animals is really *necessary* to facilitate the medical advances of the past two centuries. Even if it was once necessary, is the use of animals still necessary in today's medical research, given dramatic technological advances? Animal rights activists argue that other sources of information can now be used, including population studies or epidemiology, monitoring of human patients, noninvasive medical imaging devices, autopsies, tissue and cell cultures, in vitro tests, and computer models. Activists also argue that the use of animals as experimental subjects has sometimes actually delayed the use of effective treatment. One example cited in this regard is the development of penicillin for the treatment of bacterial infections. When Alexander Fleming tested penicillin on infected rabbits, it proved ineffective, and thus, he put it aside for a decade, not knowing that rabbits—unlike humans—excrete penicillin in their urine.[68]

The scientific and ethics communities have come to embrace an idea known as "the 3 R's" of animal research: reduce, replace, and refine. The basic idea is that scientists should reduce the use of animals in experimentation, find scientifically valid ways of replacing animals, and seek to refine experimental procedures in ways that are less cruel and more compassionate. David DeGrazia has argued that we must go further and ask whether a scientific project involving animals is really necessary to begin with, while also seeking to ensure that lab animals are living the "best life possible" in the laboratory setting.[69]

Some opponents of animal research argue that those who hold we can use animals in experimentation are inconsistent because they claim both that animals are sufficiently different from humans to be ethically used in experiments, and that they are sufficiently like humans to make the experimental results apply to us. Proponents of animal research answer this criticism by pointing out that mice, although quite different from humans, make very good models for the study of human health, simply because we share so many genes with them.[70] Furthermore, they contend, cell culture and computer studies are insufficient. If we moved directly from these cell or computer studies to the use of these drugs or treatments in humans, we would put patients at risk. Take the case of the drug thalidomide, an anti-nausea drug that was insufficiently tested on animals and ended up causing more than ten thousand babies to be born with birth defects when it was prescribed to pregnant women in the 1950s.

Whether using animals is necessary for various medical advances or whether other kinds of studies can be substituted is an empirical matter. However, most likely, some animal research is redundant or simply unnecessary, and other methods could serve just as well or better. For example, longitudinal human epidemiological studies provide better and more reliable data than many animal studies—even though human epidemiological studies are harder and more costly to conduct.

A primary ethical concern about the use of nonhuman animals in research involves the extent to which pain is inflicted on these experimental subjects. Sometimes, pain is a necessary part of the experiment, such as in pain studies in which the purpose is to find better ways to relieve pain in humans. Those who oppose animal research cite other examples of cruelty to animal subjects. It is not only the physical pain of the experiments they point to but also psychological pains, such as those that stem from being caged for long periods of time. This is especially true, they argue, for intelligent social animals.

There are at least three positions on the use of nonhuman animals in research. One opposes all use of animals. This would be a kind of abolitionist perspective that would come, for example, from a commitment to animal rights. At the other end of the spectrum is the anthropocentric position that nonhuman animals have no rights or moral standing and thus can be used as we choose. In the middle is the belief that animals have some moral status and thus limits and restrictions should be placed on conducting research with these creatures. But even many who support animal rights might agree that the use of animals in experimentation can sometimes be ethically justified. In this view, animal research may be justified if it does, in fact, help us develop significant medical advances, if it provides information that cannot be obtained in any other way, and if experiments are conducted with as little discomfort for the animals as possible. The ethical status of animal experiments for other less vital purposes, such as cosmetics development, is an even more controversial issue.

Endangered Species

International efforts to protect animals often aim to prevent them from going extinct or losing their natural habitats. International conferences, such as the

United Nations Convention on International Trade in Endangered Species, held in November 2002, in Santiago, Chile, try to address these problems. Among the issues discussed in Santiago was whether certain African nations should be allowed to sell elephant ivory, which they had stockpiled in the decades before elephants became a legally protected species. The United States prohibits imports of ivory through laws that include the African Elephant Conservation Act of 1989. But ivory remains in demand in various parts of the world, fueled by the illegal hunting, or *poaching*, of elephants. According to a 2016 report from the Center for Biological Diversity, elephant populations are declining in Africa. Forty years ago, there were an estimated one million elephants in the wild—with as many as five million specimens a century ago. Today, there are fewer than one hundred thousand forest elephants and fewer than four hundred thousand savannah elephants left in Africa.[71] In the United States, there is a movement to classify these African elephants as endangered species, which would strengthen protections for them. But this movement came up against opposition from the Trump administration, which reversed a ban on importing elephant trophies and ivory.[72] Lawsuits and legal wrangling followed. And in 2022, the Biden administration lost a lawsuit and agreed to allow some elephant trophies to be imported.[73] Proponents of trophy hunting argue that hunters who travel to Africa to kill elephants obtain expensive permits and pay top dollar for guides and travel—and that this money can help to protect and conserve the elephant population. Critics argue that killing some members of an endangered species in order to protect the species seems hypocritical and contradictory. And beyond that, elephant lovers claim that elephants are unique and special animals, with long memories and complicated social lives, who deserve protection for their own sake.

With elephants in mind, we might note that the Ringling Bros. and Barnum & Bailey circus retired its elephants in 2016. Critics had complained that the elephants—and other animals used in circuses—are abused, that they are manipulated by electric prods and metal hooks, beaten, and kept in unhealthy conditions. Circus trainers denied the accusations. The circus elephants used are typically Asian elephants, which are endangered in the wild. These elephants live long lives (up to sixty-five years) in social groups and families. Critics contend that making animals perform in the circus is abusive and unnatural, and that using endangered species in the circus violates the idea of protecting the species. In its defense, Ringling Bros. had planned to keep its retired elephants at a facility in Florida, where it planned to breed them.[74] But after further pushback from activists who claimed that the breeding facility was still cruel, the elephants have been sent to a wildlife sanctuary in Florida, where they are free to roam, swim, and socialize in a more natural habitat.[75]

One final case regarding elephants is worth considering: the case of Happy the elephant. Happy is an Asian elephant who has lived in the Bronx Zoo for forty-five years. In 2018, an animal rights advocacy group, the Nonhuman Rights Project, sued the Bronx Zoo, seeking a writ of habeas corpus on behalf of Happy (this is a legal way of challenging illegal confinement). They argued that Happy was a "legal person" entitled to fundamental rights, including "bodily integrity and bodily liberty."[76] They argued that Happy should be relocated to an appropriate elephant sanctuary. The New York Court of Appeals ruled on the case in June 2022, arguing nonhuman animals do not have the right to seek a writ of habeas corpus. As the court stated, "the great writ protects the right to liberty of humans because they are humans with certain fundamental liberty rights recognized by law."[77] In addition to making a fundamental claim about the *human* focus of rights, the court also declared that to extend the idea of rights and personhood to nonhuman animals "would have significant implications for the interactions of humans and animals in all facets of life, including risking the disruption of property rights, the agricultural industry (among others), and medical research efforts."[78] Despite the fact that the court ruled against them, the Nonhuman Rights Project declared that they had made a step in the direction of establishing legal rights for nonhuman animals, since this was the first time in history that an appellate court had seriously considered the question.[79]

While the court denied the claim that nonhuman animals have rights, the government nonetheless does protect animals. In the United States, the protection of

Anup Shah/Nature Picture Library/Alamy

Figure 20-4 Elephants have recently been a subject of moral and legal disputes.

wild animals is handled by a patchwork of laws and agencies. For example, the Marine Mammal Protection Act of 1972 "establishe[d] a moratorium on the taking and importation of marine mammals, including parts and products." The Department of the Interior is charged with enforcing the management and protection of sea otters, walruses, polar bears, dugong, and manatees. The 1973 Endangered Species Act protects species that are threatened with extinction and those that the secretaries of the interior or commerce place on a list of endangered species. As we saw above, this has been a successful endeavor in the case of the gray wolf, which has increased to a self-sustaining population in the United States.

But the news is not good for other species. In the United States, as of July 2022, 733 animal species are listed as either endangered or threatened. This includes 96 mammalian species, such as bears, foxes, manatees, ocelots, otters, panthers, rats, and whales.[80] The International Union for Conservation of Nature (IUCN) produces a "red list" of animal and plant species that are endangered around the world. In the summer of 2022, they reported that some forty thousand species are threatened with extinction.[81] Some species, such as the Sumatran rhino, are on the verge of extinction—with fewer than thirty living specimens left as of 2019.[82]

Others have gone extinct in recent memory: the last male member of the species of northern white rhino died in Kenya in 2018. Two females of this species remain alive as of 2022; the younger of the pair, Fatu, is being used in a creative breeding program that aims to resurrect the species.[83] On the other hand, there has been some good news. After many years of conservation efforts, the mountain gorillas in Eastern Africa are making a comeback. When the renowned primatologist Dian Fossey arrived in Rwanda in 1967, there were only 240 gorillas left in the wild. In 2016, there were 880 gorillas, with more than 1,000 in 2018.[84] Those are still small numbers, but it provides evidence that species can be preserved with concerted human effort to protect habitat and curb poaching.

Some of the successes are due to the fact that there are more protected areas in the world, including wildlife refuges and reserves. Destruction of animal habitat may be the most potent threat to animal species. Although animals can often adapt to gradual changes in their environment, rapid change often makes such adjustment impossible. Many human activities—such as cutting down trees, damming rivers, mining, drilling, and pipeline building—can cause such rapid change. Another cause of species loss is when humans introduce non-native species into an environment, thus upsetting a delicate ecological balance. Overexploitation of animal populations is also a source of extinction. For example, many species of sharks are being fished into extinction by fishermen—who only want their fins for the Asian delicacy shark-fin soup.[85] The commercial fishing industry threatens not only the species it harvests for food but also other species caught as "by-catch." Whales, dolphins, and other marine mammals are also threatened by commercial fishing operations. Marine mammals caught in gill nets drown, trapped under water, unable to reach the surface to breathe. According to a 2014 report from National Public Radio, 650,000 marine mammals are killed every year in commercial fishing operations, including 300,000 dolphins and whales and 350,000 seals and sea lions.[86] This so-called by-catch, accidental entrapment in fishing nets intended to catch other fish, could be remedied by the use of other fishing technologies.

Some point out that species go extinct naturally without human intervention. Through the course of evolution, the species that have been lost have been replaced at a higher rate than they have disappeared, which helps explain the wondrous diversity of our planet's species. But the rate of replacement may no longer be able to keep up because of the accelerated pace of species loss. Those who are concerned about the global ecosystem worry about this loss of biodiversity—both because they value different species for their own sake as having intrinsic value (as we discussed in Chapter 16) and because they see biodiversity as good for the larger ecosystem and thus good for human beings.

While some hold that individual animals have rights or a particular moral status, others believe it is animal species that we ought to protect, not individual animals. It may seem obvious that we have good anthropocentric reasons for preserving animal as well as plant species. We have aesthetic interests in a variety of different life-forms. Naturalists, hikers, hunters, and bird-watchers know the thrill of being able to observe rare species. The diversity and strangeness of nature are themselves objects of wonder. We also have nutritional and health interests in preserving species. Some species may now seem to have no value for humans, but examples such as the medaka fish and the giant Israeli scorpion, discussed previously, should remind us how important seemingly "minor" species can prove to be for human needs. Loss of species leaves us genetically poorer and more ignorant about the natural systems to which we belong. Animals tell us about ourselves, our history, and how natural systems work or could work. "Destroying species is like tearing pages out of an unread book, written in a language humans hardly know how to read, about the place where they live," writes environmental ethicist Holmes Rolston.[87] If we destroy the mouse lemur, for example, we destroy the modern animal that is closest to the primates from which our own human line evolved.[88]

However, when we ask whether animal species have *moral standing* or *intrinsic value* or even *rights*, we run into puzzling issues. An animal species is not an individual. It is a collection and, in itself, cannot have the kind of interests or desires that may be the basis for the moral standing or rights of individual animals. Thus, according to philosopher Nicholas Rescher, "moral obligation is... always interest-oriented. But only individuals can be said to have interests; one only has moral obligations to particular individuals or particular groups thereof."[89] If we can have duties to a group of individuals and a species is a group, we may have duties to species. Still, this does not imply that the species has rights.

Some people challenge the very notion of species and question whether a species is identical to the individuals it includes. Consider just what we might mean by a *species*. Is it not a concept constructed by humans as a way of grouping and comparing organisms? Charles Darwin wrote, "I look at the term species, as one arbitrarily given for the sake of convenience to a set of individuals closely resembling each other."[90] If a species is but a class or category of things, it does not actually exist as an individual thing. If it does not exist, how could it be said to have interests or rights? However, consider the following possibility, suggested by Holmes Rolston: "A species is a living historical form (Latin *species*), propagated in individual organisms, that flows dynamically over generations."[91] As such, species are units of evolution that exist in time and space. According to Rolston, "a species is a coherent, ongoing form of life expressed in organisms, encoded in gene flow, and shaped by the environment."[92] If we think of species in this way, it may be intelligible to speak of our having duties to an animal species, as forms of life that span millions of years through their genetic legacies. Our duties, then, would be to a dynamic continuum, a living environmental process, and extinction would be wrong because it ends a "lifeline" or a "unique story." Or, finally, as Rolston writes, "A duty to a species is more like being responsible to a cause than to a person. It is commitment to an *idea*."[93] Although Rolston's explanation of the nature of species and his arguments for the view that we have duties to them are often metaphorical ("story," "lifeline"), nevertheless, his reasoning is intriguing. It also raises metaphysical and ontological questions: What kinds of beings exist or have worth?

Those who support animal rights as the rights of individual animals to certain treatment do not always agree in concrete cases with those who believe that it is species that ought to be protected. Suppose, for example, that a certain population of deer is threatened because its numbers have outstripped the food supply and the deer are starving to death. In some such cases, wildlife officials have sought to thin herds by euthanizing animals or allowing for limited hunting. It is thought to be for the sake of the herd that these animals are killed. Those who seek to protect species of animals may endorse such "thinning" if it does, in fact, help preserve the species. But animal rights activists might criticize such an approach and argue that ways should be found to save each of the deer. The animal rights scholar Tom Regan has referred to such holistic claims about animals and ecosystems as a sort of "environmental fascism."[94] By using this phrase, Regan means to connect the idea of controlling animal populations to the policies of fascist governments such as Nazi Germany. If individual animals are thought to have rights, it would be wrong to cull them for the well-being of the whole.

Other Nonhumans

20.6 Articulate some connections between animal ethics and other topics involving nonhuman beings.

As we conclude this chapter—and this book—let's consider another possible ethical frontier: the question of how we ought to behave toward other nonhuman beings, such as extraterrestrial life-forms or sentient artificial intelligence (what some call "digital minds"). This may seem like a far-out and speculative question, best left to science fiction. But there was a public debate about whether a Google AI system was sentient and had a "soul," in the summer of 2022.[95] And astronomers have discovered nearly five thousand "exoplanets" in our galaxy (planets that exist outside of our solar system); and some are searching for worlds that could be inhabitable by alien life-forms.[96]

Philosophers have long been interested in these sorts of questions. One interesting source is Immanuel Kant, who speculated in the late eighteenth century about the possibility of extraterrestrial intelligence. In his *Anthropology* lectures, he stated that in order to fully understand humanity, which he defines as a "terrestrial rational being," we would need to compare humanity to some "non-terrestrial rational being."[97] Kant had speculated about extraterrestrial life since he was a young man, writing about it in 1755 in an essay entitled "Universal Natural History and Theory of the Heavens."[98] Kant's speculation invites us to reconsider the categorical imperative and the idea of respect for rational beings (as discussed in Chapter 6). The moral law commands us to respect rational beings because they have a kind of dignity and worth that is deserving of moral respect. Rational beings are also the kinds of beings that are subject to the moral law, since they are able to understand and limit their autonomy according to the idea of law. With this in mind, it is possible to imagine that extraterrestrial life-forms that are rational in the Kantian sense might count as "persons" who are deserving of moral respect. The same would likely hold for intelligent machines that exhibited the same form of rationality.

Another approach to this topic would emphasize sentience understood here as the ability to suffer and experience pain and pleasure. This is typically the focal point of utilitarian theories. If we were to encounter sentient alien life-forms, a utilitarian might argue that we should take their suffering into account. Again, something similar would appear to hold for sentient artificial intelligences. Utilitarian philosophers such as Bentham were willing to include nonhuman animals in their utilitarian calculation. Perhaps they would be willing to consider extraterrestrials as well. An important utilitarian philosopher, J. J. C. Smart, provided this sort of argument forty years ago in considering how our circle of concern and benevolence has gradually expanded. Smart wrote,

> The increased attention to the sufferings of animals is one of the most notable examples of progress in ethics over the last hundred years or so. We should, of course, be equally mindful of extra-terrestrial consciousnesses, should we come across any such and have to interact with them....
>
> Thus concern for family, tribe and nation gets extended to a concern for all humanity, to all sentient beings on earth, including the non-human animals, and finally perhaps to all sentient beings, including extra-terrestrial ones, if we should ever come across them.[99]

There are many questions about extraterrestrial life, and AI that need to be considered in much more detail than we can provide here. One of these that's worth noting in passing is the issue of whether we can program artificial systems to make ethical decisions. This is a crucial question for self-driving vehicles, for example, which may need to "make decisions" involving morally complex trade-offs. For example, should a self-driving vehicle swerve to avoid a dog but thereby cause an accident that harms human beings? That's a matter for a different book, perhaps. For our purposes, in the present chapter, let's consider a fundamental issue that connects with the question of animal ethics. This is the question of how we would know that an AI system or extraterrestrial life-form was rational or sentient. This points to issues that are both metaphysical and epistemological. And note that the same metaphysical and epistemological issues will arise in thinking about the experience of nonhuman animals. Some simply declare that only human beings are rational or sentient or of moral worth—basing this declaration on a fundamental metaphysical claim about the structure of the universe. Religious people might dogmatically state, for example, that only human beings have souls. But a different approach would look to behaviors and external signs of sentience, consciousness, and rationality. One famous example of this is the "Turing test," named after the mathematician and computer scientist Alan Turing.[100] The gist of this is that we should evaluate the "intelligence" of a machine based on its ability to imitate the linguistic behavior of a human being. If a machine is able to converse with us in natural language and we can't tell the difference between the machine's responses and the responses of some other human being, then for all we know the machine is intelligent (or in Turing's language that it can "think"). There are deep questions that arise here, including how we would know whether the computer is merely "imitating" human intelligence or is "actually" a rational being—and whether that distinction between imitation and actuality really matters.

Philosophers have spent decades debating these kinds of questions. One of the criticisms made of the Turing test is that it is anthropocentric. The Turing test assumes that human linguistic behavior is the key to intelligence. We can see that this is a problem in thinking about non-human animals. Octopuses, whales, and chimpanzees seem to exhibit intelligence of various sorts. But this nonhuman intelligence does not readily lend itself to a kind of Turing test proof. Of course, we might note in response that the Turing test is not supposed to account for all kinds of intelligence. Nor is it about mere sentience, the ability to feel pain or pleasure. An advanced machine may be able to communicate with us and pass the Turing test; but can the machine suffer—and how would we even know what machine suffering would be like? In this regard, isn't the suffering of an animal such as a chimpanzee much easier to discern, since the chimp shares much with us in terms of its basic physiology?

Here we find ourselves thinking about what matters in pondering our moral regard for the nonhuman and how we might know or measure it. Are octopuses, whales, and chimpanzees sentient or intelligent? How would we know? And does their sentience or intelligence matter for our moral regard for them? Extrapolating from this, we might wonder what we should think about alien life or artificial intelligence systems—if we should ever encounter them. These entities would be as different from us as octopuses and whales are. We might also speculate further and consider how our moral self-understanding would evolve if we were to encounter such alien forms of intelligence and life. How might such a discovery change our understanding of how we ought to behave with regard to the nonhuman life-forms that we share this planet with? And so the question of "other nonhumans" returns us to the question of what sorts of beings are moral patients and what sorts of obligations and responsibilities we have to those beings.

Chapter Summary

20.1 What is the difference between anthropocentric and non-anthropocentric views of animal ethics?

Anthropocentric views of animal ethics are focused on human needs and interests. For example, an anthropocentric account might be interested in the value of animals for human uses—as in hunting, meat eating, or entertainment. Non-anthropocentric approaches are not merely concerned with human needs and interests but with the well-being (and maybe even the rights) of animals as things that have value in themselves apart from human uses.

20.2 What is the significance of sentience and equal consideration in thinking about animal ethics?

One non-anthropocentric approach to animal ethics focuses on animal welfare and is concerned with equal consideration for sentient beings. Sentience is the ability to suffer and feel pain or pleasure. Some defenders of animal welfare argue that if a being suffers, its suffering matters morally and ought to be taken into account. This does not mean that sentient animals should be treated as exactly equal to human beings. Rather, it means that we ought to give equal consideration for the suffering of sentient animals. This idea is typical of those types of animal welfare theories that grow out of utilitarianism, with a source in Jeremy Bentham's thinking.

20.3 How can we define and criticize the idea of speciesism?

"Speciesism" is a term coined by Peter Singer, intending it pejoratively: according to Singer, it is wrong to be a speciesist. The reason for this is that speciesists give unjustifiable preference to members of their own species, and thus fail to give equal consideration to members of other species. The idea could be criticized by defenders of anthropocentrism who claim that it is not wrong for us to give preference to members of the human species.

20.4 What is the difference between a concern for animal welfare and a concern for animal rights?

The idea of animal welfare typically develops out of a non-anthropocentric utilitarianism that takes animal suffering seriously. But one can give animal suffering equal consideration without claiming that animals have rights. The animal rights perspective makes a relatively stronger claim about animals that is grounded in the idea that thy have basic rights because they have needs and interests, and exist as "subjects of a life," as Tom Regan put it. Animal welfare approaches can offer significant criticisms of factory farming and other practices. But as a utilitarian theory, animal welfare may also be open to the idea of reforming and improving these practices in a world that involves trade-offs and complex cost–benefit analyses. Animal rights theories tend to reject reformism in favor of outright abolition of practices such as meat production, which they claim violate the rights of animals.

20.5 How might we evaluate current issues in animal ethics including hunting, vegetarianism, animal research, and endangered species protection?

Anthropocentric arguments can be mounted for each of these topics, with its advocates defending hunting, meat eating, and animal research based on the idea that human beings are entitled to use animals because we are somehow superior to them. This does not mean that anthropocentrists support outright cruelty in these practices. In hunting, for example, an anthropocentric approach may still support the idea of "fair chase"; and anthropocentrists might also argue that vegetarianism is good for human health or that it is good for the ecosystem (and thus for human beings who will benefit from a healthy ecosystem). Non-anthropocentrists who are sympathetic to either animal welfare or animal rights thinking typically offer stronger criticisms of practices that harm animals. The animal rights perspective typically pushes in the direction of veganism and abolitionism with regard to hunting, animal research, circuses, rodeos, and so on. An animal welfare approach will also be critical of such practices, typically calling for reform and improvement (in addition to, or in place of, abolition). With regard to endangered species, one important question is about the relative value of individual animals and an entire species. The issue here is about the proper focal point of moral concern—and whether that focal point is found in the concrete life and experience of an individual animal or in the value of something as abstract as a species.

20.6 What are some connections between animal ethics and other topics involving nonhuman beings?

The other topics discussed in this chapter were extraterrestrial life and artificial intelligence. These topics involve questions of who is a moral patient and what the criteria are for moral concern. If extraterrestrial life were rational and/or sentient, then it might be worthy of moral regard. The same is true of artificial intelligences. There are difficulties in knowing whether an alien or a computer is sentient, intelligent, or rational. These difficulties parallel similar difficulties in knowing and evaluating the consciousness and experience of nonhuman terrestrial animals.

20.7 Defend a thesis with regard to animal ethics.

To defend a thesis about animal ethics, students must determine whether they agree with anthropocentrism or with a non-anthropocentric point of view such as the animal welfare or animal rights ideas. They must also decide whether they are interested in reforming the way we treat animals or abolishing objectionable practices. In addition, students must decide what they think about the moral importance of sentience and rationality, as found in nonhuman life. This general thesis about animal ethics can then be applied to specific cases in ways that are sensitive to the complexity of these cases—and that reflect an understanding of how human uses of nonhuman animals have evolved and developed.

Primary Source Readings

In this chapter, we have raised many questions about animal ethics, including questions about the ethics of hunting, vegetarianism, the use of animals in research, and the moral status or rights of animals as individuals and as species. This chapter's readings present different ideas about whether human beings and nonhuman animals deserve to be given equal consideration. The first reading is from Peter Singer, one of the most important authors writing about animal welfare and what he calls "speciesism." His 1975 book *Animal Liberation* is a foundational text for those concerned with animal ethics. The second reading, from animal rights defender Tom Regan, argues that animals have inherent value and that animal experimentation and animal agriculture ought to be abolished. The third reading, from bioethicist Bonnie Steinbock, argues for a more anthropocentric idea of value. She contends that it is not wrong to prefer the interests of humans over the interests of animals. We conclude with a short excerpt from an essay about animals, aliens, and AI published by Michael Dorf, where the author reminds us of the connections among these three topics.

Reading 20-1   All Animals are Equal | Peter Singer

Study Questions

As you read the excerpt, please consider the following questions:

1. Does equal consideration imply identical treatment? Why or why not, according to Singer?

2. What is *speciesism*? Do you agree with Singer's claim about how speciesism connects with racism and sexism?

3. Why does Singer prefer the principle of equal consideration of interests to concerns about whether or not certain beings have rights?

The extension of the basic principle of equality from one group to another does not imply that we must treat both groups in exactly the same way, or grant exactly the same rights to both groups. Whether we should do so will depend on the nature of the members of the two groups. The basic principle of equality does not require equal or identical treatment; it requires equal consideration. Equal consideration for different beings may lead to different treatment and different rights....

It is on this basis that the case against racism and the case against sexism must both ultimately rest; and it is in accordance with this principle that the attitude that we may call "speciesism," by analogy with racism, must also be condemned. Speciesism—the word is not an attractive one, but I can think of no better term—is prejudice or attitude of bias in favor of the interests of members of one's own species and against those of members of other species.... If possessing a higher degree of intelligence does not entitle one human to use another for his or her own ends, how can it entitle humans to exploit nonhumans for the same purpose? ...

The real weight of the moral argument does not rest on the assertion of the existence of the right, for this in turn has to be justified on the basis of the possibilities for suffering and happiness. In this way we can argue for equality for animals without getting embroiled in philosophical controversies about the ultimate nature of rights.

In misguided attempts to refute the arguments of this book, some philosophers have gone to much trouble developing arguments to show that animals do not have rights. They have claimed that to have rights a being must be autonomous, or must be a member of a community, or must have the ability to respect the rights of others, or must possess a sense of justice. These claims are irrelevant to the case for Animal Liberation. The language of rights is a convenient political shorthand....

If a being suffers there can be no moral justification for refusing to take that suffering into consideration. No matter what the nature of the being, the principle of equality requires that its suffering be counted equally with the like suffering—insofar as rough comparisons can be made—of any other being. If a being is not capable of suffering, or of experiencing enjoyment or happiness, there is nothing to be taken into account. So the limit of sentience (using the term as a convenient if not strictly accurate shorthand for the capacity to suffer and/or experience enjoyment) is the only defensible boundary of concern for the interests of others. To mark this boundary by some other characteristic like intelligence or rationality would be to mark it in an arbitrary manner.

Peter Singer, *Animal Liberation*, 2nd ed. (New York: New York Review, 1990).

Reading 20-2 The Case for Animal Rights | Tom Regan

Study Questions

As you read the excerpt, please consider the following questions:

1. What is the basic similarity between human and nonhuman beings that is the focus of Regan's account?

2. How does Regan understand the inherent value of nonhuman animals?

3. How does his view of the equality of inherent value lead to an abolitionist conclusion with regard to animal experimentation and commercial animal agriculture?

Animals, it is true, lack many of the abilities humans possess. They can't read, do higher mathematics, build a bookcase or make baba ghanoush. Neither can many human beings, however, and yet we don't (and shouldn't) say that they (these humans) therefore have less inherent value, less of a right to be treated with respect, than do others. It is the similarities between those human beings who most clearly, most non-controversially have such value...not our differences, that matter most. And the really crucial, the basic similarity is simply this: we are each of us the experiencing subject of a life, a conscious creature having an individual welfare that has importance to us whatever our usefulness to others. We want and prefer things, believe and feel things, recall and expect things. And all these dimensions of our life, including our pleasure and pain, our enjoyment and suffering, our satisfaction and frustration, our continued existence or our untimely death—all make a difference to the quality of our life as lived, as experienced, by us as individuals. As the same is true of those animals that concern us (the ones that are eaten and trapped, for example), they too must be viewed as the experiencing subjects of a life, with inherent value of their own.

Some there are who resist the idea that animals have inherent value. "Only humans have such value," they profess. How might this narrow view be defended? Shall we say that only humans have the requisite intelligence, or autonomy, or reason? But there are many, many humans who fail to meet these standards and yet are reasonably viewed as having value above and beyond their usefulness to others. Shall we claim that only humans belong to the right species, the species Homo sapiens? But this is blatant speciesism....

Well, perhaps some will say that animals have some inherent value, only less than we have. Once again, however, attempts to defend this view can be shown to lack rational justification. What could be the basis of our having more inherent value than animals? Their lack of reason, or autonomy, or intellect? Only if we are willing to make the same judgment in the case of humans who are similarly deficient. But it is not true that such humans—the retarded child, for example, or the mentally deranged—have less inherent value than you or I. Neither, then, can we rationally sustain the view that animals like them in being the experiencing subjects of a life have less inherent value. All who have inherent value have it equally, whether they be human animals or not....

Having set out the broad outlines of the rights view, I can now say why its implications for farming and science, among other fields, are both clear and uncompromising. In the case of the use of animals in science, the rights view is categorically abolitionist....

As for commercial animal agriculture, the rights view takes a similar abolitionist position.

In Peter Singer, ed., *In Defense of Animals* (New York: Basil Blackwell, 1985).

Study Questions

As you read the excerpt, please consider the following questions:

1. Is Steinbock right in claiming that there are morally relevant differences between human beings and nonhuman animals?

2. What is the point of Steinbock's claim about choosing to feed a hungry child before feeding your hungry dog?

3. How does Steinbock argue for the justification of some animal experimentation?

We do not subject animals to different moral treatment simply because they have fur and feathers, but because they are in fact different from human beings in ways that could be morally relevant. It is false that women are incapable of being benefited by education, and therefore that claim cannot serve to justify preventing them from attending school. But this is not false of cows and dogs, even chimpanzees....Feeding starving children before feeding starving dogs is just like a Catholic charity's feeding hungry Catholics before feeding hungry non-Catholics. It is simply a matter of taking care of one's own, something which is usually morally permissible. But whereas we would admire the Catholic agency which did not discriminate, but fed all children, first come, first served, we would feel quite differently about someone who has this policy for dogs and children....I might feel much more love for my dog than for a strange child—and yet I might feel morally obliged to feed the child before I fed my dog. If I gave in to the feelings of love and fed my dog and let the child go hungry, I would probably feel guilty....Human beings have a different moral status from members of other species because of certain capacities which are characteristic of being human. We may not all be equal in these capacities, but all human beings possess them to some measure, and nonhuman animals do not. For example, human beings are normally held to be responsible for what they do. In recognizing that someone is responsible for his or her actions, you accord that person a respect which is reserved for those possessed of moral autonomy, or capable of achieving such autonomy. Secondly, human beings can be expected to reciprocate in a way that nonhuman animals cannot....

...Certain capacities, which seem to be unique to human beings, entitle their possessors to a privileged position in the moral community. Both rats and human beings dislike pain, and so we have a *prima facie* reason not to inflict pain on either. But if we can free human beings from crippling diseases, pain and death through experimentation which involves making animals suffer, and if this is the only way to achieve such results, then I think that such experimentation is justified because human lives are more valuable than animals' lives....

My point is not that the lack of the sorts of capacities I have been discussing gives us a justification for treating animals just as we like, but rather that it is these differences between human beings and nonhuman animals which provide a rational basis for different moral treatment and consideration....It is certainly not wrong of us to extend special care to members of our own species, motivated by feelings of sympathy, protectiveness, etc. If this is speciesism, it is stripped of its tone of moral condemnation.

Bonnie Steinbock, "Speciesism and the Idea of Equality." *Philosophy* 53: 204 (April 1978), pp. 247–256.

Reading 20-4   Do Androids Dream of Animal Rights? | Michael C. Dorf

Study Questions

1. Is Dorf right to suggest that we sometimes forget that our machines are not really sentient or alive?

2. Is Phillip K. Dick's proposal regarding the importance of "empathy" worth considering? And what might that tell us about AI or about nonhuman animals?

3. Why does Dorf suggest that thinking about E.T. and AI can help us think more clearly about nonhuman animals? Do you agree?

What does the renewed serious and pop-culture focus on the future of AI tell us about the present? Partly, it might simply reflect the fact that while true AI remains a long way off, capacities like voice recognition and artificial speech have improved to the point that one can sometimes forget that our machines are simply executing programs. It is now easier than ever before to imagine a future AI.

Yet exploring the nature of the AI debate reveals something unexpected. Its terms have important implications for how we think about beings who exist in the here and now: non-human animals.

. . .

Whether someone should be treated with dignity—be treated as someone rather than something—should not depend on whether that someone happens to be a member of the species homo sapiens.

The connection between rights for robots and rights for animals has not been lost on science fiction writers. For example, the 1968 Philip K. Dick novel, *Do Androids Dream of Electric Sheep?* (on which the film *Blade Runner* was based) poses the question of what it means to be human in a conflict between humans and androids playing out on a ruined planet Earth. The humans in charge believe that the key is the ability to feel empathy—an ability that the book's androids lack. Strikingly, a test to determine whether a subject is an android looks at the subject's reaction to being told that she has received a calfskin wallet as a birthday present. The right reaction, the one felt by empathic humans but not by the unfeeling androids, is one of horror and disgust at the prospect of the killing and exploitation of a baby cow.

Express animal rights themes can be found in other popular science fiction as well. E.T. tells the story of an extraterrestrial rather than of a robot, but aliens and robots occupy roughly the same fraught territory in science fiction. Notably, under the mysterious but benign telepathic influence of the angelic E.T., Elliott and his fellow students release the frogs destined to be killed in his science class. The ability to empathize with one set of others—whether aliens or sentient robots—is connected to the ability to empathize with others more generally, whether they are people of a different race or religion, or sentient animals of a different species.

. . .

Is true artificial sentience possible? That is a scientific and technological question to which we do not yet have the answer. But we already have abundant evidence of the reality of non-human sentience among our fellow Earthlings. If and when we create artificial sentience, we should accord the resulting mechanical beings respect. In the meantime, I would suggest that anxieties about the status of those hypothetical beings reflect projected guilt over our hideous disregard for the interests of the billions of sentient animals we exploit, torture, and kill in the here and now.

Michael C. Dorf, "Do Androids Dream of Animal Rights?" *Verdict*, December 15, 2015. https://verdict.justia.com/2015/12/30/do-androids-dream-of-animal-rights (accessed February 27, 2023).

Review Exercises

1. In your view, is it acceptable to hunt animals? If yes, then which animals: bears, wolves, elephants, or whales? Does the method matter? Is trapping or aerial hunting acceptable? Justify your answers using concepts from this chapter.

2. What counts as cruelty to animals? What's wrong with cruelty to animals?

3. What do you think about the fact that certain cultures practice hunting and fishing? Does cultural heritage matter in thinking about hunting whales, dolphins, and other animals?

4. List some anthropocentric reasons for protecting individual animals and/or endangered animal species.

5. Do animals have interests, feel pleasure, and experience pain? Are these interests, pains, and pleasures worth "equal consideration"? Is it "speciesist" to ignore or downplay animal experience?

6. What is the meaning of the term *rights*? Does it make sense to apply this term to animals? Why or why not?

7. Evaluate moral arguments in defense of vegetarianism. Are these arguments persuasive?

8. Do animal *species* have moral standing of some sort, or is the value of an animal found in its individual life? And how might that question guide our thinking about hunting and endangered species?

9. What reasons do supporters give for using nonhuman animals in experimental research? What objections to this practice do their opponents raise? Be sure your answer makes reference to issues such as the extent and purpose of pain.

10. Describe and defend your thinking about the general value of nonhuman beings—including nonhuman animals and even extraterrestrial life and sentient computers. What are your basic criteria for thinking that a being is a "moral patient"?

Discussion Cases

1. Animal Experimentation. Antonio wants to become a doctor and is pursuing a premed major. He has dissected frogs and worms in some of his biology classes. He knows that animal research has produced good outcomes for human beings, including antibiotics and other cures for diseases. Antonio's roommate, Joseph, is a vegetarian who is opposed to all animal research. One night, as Joseph is cooking some tofu, he says, "Look, Antonio, there are all kinds of healthy alternatives to eating meat. There are also alternatives to using animals in research. You can now use computer models to accomplish most of the same outcomes." Antonio disagrees. "Maybe vegetarian food can be nutritious. But even if there were other ways to do medical research, I'd want to be sure that a drug or treatment really worked on an animal before I used it on a human being."

Whose position is closest to your own? Which ways of treating animals do you find acceptable, and which do you find unacceptable? Is animal experimentation ever justified? If so, on what grounds? What about eating meat?

2. People versus the Gorilla. Many of the world's few remaining mountain gorillas are located in the thirty-thousand-acre Parc des Volcans in the small African country of Rwanda. Rwanda has the highest population density in Africa. Most people there live on small farms. To this population, the Parc des Volcans represents valuable land that could be used for farming to feed an expanding human population. Opening the park to development could support thirty-six thousand people on subsistence farms. But it would have an adverse impact on the gorilla population.

Should the park be maintained as a way to preserve the gorillas, or should it be given to the people for farming? To what extent, if any, do humans have an obligation to look for new and creative ways to meet their own needs in order to protect the interests of animals?

3. What Is Wildlife Worth? In a number of states, bridges and tunnels have been built that allow wildlife to cross busy highways. These wildlife crossings can help to reduce the risk of cars crashing into animals. They can also have a positive impact on animal populations. Highways can separate populations of wildlife, causing inbreeding, which can exacerbate the well-being of those populations. Significant investment has been made on wildlife crossings in a variety of states from Florida to Montana to California. These crossing help bears, cougars, panthers, alligators, raccoons, and other animals move through the landscape. But they are not cost-free. An ambitious wildlife crossing is planned for the freeway north of Los Angeles. It will be the world's largest, spanning ten lanes of freeway.[101] The crossing will cost $90 million, involving a combination of private donations and public funds. It will allow cougars, coyotes, and other animals to move across the freeway and access the Santa Monica Mountains.

What do you think about the idea of spending state (or private) funds on building wildlife crossings? Is this a good use of funds?

Knowledge Check Answer Key

1. **b.** The anthropocentric answer is "Domesticated animals belong to someone, and cruelty toward those animals violates the owner's property rights."

2. **a.** The statement "Animals suffer and their suffering matters" is focused on sentience.

3. **d.** Speciesism is an idea used to describe the unjustified preference for members of your own species.

4. **c.** The animal rights perspective maintains that individual animals have a kind of dignity and value that should protect them from harm.

Endnotes

Chapter 1

1. Alfred North Whitehead, *Process and Reality* (New York: Macmillan, 1929), p. 4.

2. E. O. Wilson, *Sociobiology: The New Synthesis* (Cambridge, MA: Harvard University Press, 1975).

3. E. O. Wilson, *On Human Nature* (Cambridge, MA: Harvard University Press, 1978), p. 2.

4. See Richard Dawkins, *The Selfish Gene* (Oxford: Oxford University Press, 1989).

5. See Frans de Waal, *Good Natured: The Origins of Right and Wrong in Humans and Other Animals* (Cambridge, MA: Harvard University Press, 1996). Also see Morton Hunt, *The Compassionate Beast: What Science Is Discovering about the Human Side of Humankind* (New York: William Morrow, 1990).

6. G. E. Moore, *Principia Ethics* (Buffalo, NY: Prometheus, 1903).

7. W. D. Ross, *Foundations of Ethics* (Oxford: Clarendon Press, 1939), pp. 144–45.

8. Michael Ruse, *Sociobiology: Sense or Nonsense?* (New York: Springer, 1985), p. 237.

9. Richard Dawkins, *The Selfish Gene*, 30th Anniversary Edition (Oxford: Oxford University Press, 2006), p. xxi.

10. Amia Srinivasan, "Feminism and Metaethics," in Tristram McPherson and David Plunkett, eds., *The Routledge Handbook of Metaethics* (New York: Routledge, 2017), p. 596.

11. Charles Mills, "Ideal Theory as Ideology." *Hypatia* 20: 3 (Summer 2005), pp. 165–84.

12. Charles Mills, *The Racial Contract* (Ithaca, NY: Cornell University Press, 1999).

13. Naomi Zack, *The Ethics and Mores of Race : Equality after the History of Philosophy, with a New Preface* (Lanham, MD: Rowman & Littlefield, 2015).

Chapter 2

1. http://www.un.org/en/documents/udhr/

2. Eleanor Roosevelt, "The Struggle for Human Rights" (1948), at https://erpapers.columbian.gwu.edu/struggle-human-rights-1948 (accessed November 22, 2022).

3. https://www.uscirf.gov/publication/2022-annual-report (accessed November 22, 2022).

4. Trump interview on CNN with Anderson Cooper March 20, 2016; https://www.cnn.com/videos/politics/2016/03/10/donald-trump-islam-intv-ac-cooper-sot.cnn (accessed November 22, 2022).

5. Immanuel Kant, "An Answer to the Question: 'What Is Enlightenment?'" in *Kant: Political Writings* (Cambridge: Cambridge University Press, 1991), p. 54.

6. https://survey2020.philpeople.org/survey/results/all

7. https://www.pewresearch.org/religion/2021/12/14/about-three-in-ten-u-s-adults-are-now-religiously-unaffiliated/

8. Although this claim is often attributed to Dostoevsky, it is not directly stated by any one of his characters. Nonetheless, it is the basic idea of his atheist characters: Ivan Karamazov in *The Brothers Karamazov* and Kirilov and Stavrogin in *The Devils*.

9. John Hick, *An Interpretation of Religion: Human Responses to the Transcendent*, 2nd ed. (New Haven, CT: Yale University Press, 2005), p. xl.

10. Hick, *An Interpretation of Religion*, p. 316.

11. Dalai Lama, *Kindness, Clarity, and Insight* (Ithaca, NY: Snow Lion Publications, 2006), p. 58.

12. Parliament of the World's Religions, *Towards a Global Ethic*, p. 2: https://parliamentofreligions.org/global-ethic/towards-a-global-ethic-an-initial-declaration/ (accessed December 5, 2022).

13. Stephen Prothero, *God Is Not One: The Eight Rival Religions That Run the World—And Why Their Differences Matter* (New York: HarperCollins, 2010), p. 2.

14. Suzanne J. Crawford, et al., *American Indian Religious Traditions: An Encyclopedia* (Santa Barbara, CA: ABC-CLIO, 2005), vol. 1, pp. 344–50.

15. Sam Harris, *Free Will* (New York: Free Press, 2012), p. 1.

16. Prothero, *God Is Not One*, p. 2.

17. Craig Calhoun, Mark Juergensmeyer, and Jonathan VanAntwerpen, *Rethinking Secularism* (New York: Oxford University Press, 2011), p. 10.

18. Paul Kurtz, "Neo-Humanist Statement of Secular Principles and Values," https://kurtz.institute/neo-humanist-statement (accessed December 5, 2022).

19. Jürgen Habermas, "Struggles for Recognition in the Democratic Constitutional State," in *Multiculturalism: Examining the Politics of Recognition,* ed. Amy Gutmann (Princeton, NJ: Princeton University Press, 1994), pp. 132–33.

20. Jürgen Habermas, "Struggles for Recognition," p. 133.

21. José Casanova, "Public Religions Revisited," in *Religion: Beyond a Concept,* ed. Hent de Vries (New York: Fordham University Press, 2007), p. 119.

22. See Enrique Dussel, *Beyond Philosophy: Ethics, History, Marxism, and Liberation Theology* (Lanham, MD: Rowman & Littlefield, 2003).

Chapter 3

1. Anne Fadiman, *The Spirit Catches You and You Fall Down: A Hmong Child, Her American Doctors, and the Collision of Two Cultures* (New York: Farrar, Straus and Giroux, 1998).

2. Ruth Benedict, "Anthropology and the Abnormal," *Journal of General Psychology* 10 (1934), pp. 60–70.

3. Gilbert Harman, *The Nature of Morality: An Introduction to Ethics* (New York: Oxford University Press, 1977), p. 11.

4. Friedrich Nietzsche, *The Will to Power* (New York: Random House, 1968), no. 481, p. 267.

5. Martha C. Nussbaum, *Women and Human Development* (Cambridge, UK: Cambridge University Press, 2001), p. 105.

6. Ibid., p. 106.

7. Ibid., pp. 78–80.

8. Alain Locke, "Cultural Relativism and Ideological Peace," in *The Works of Alain Locke,* ed. Charles Molesworth (Oxford, UK: Oxford University Press, 2012), p. 548.

9. Ibid.

10. Alain Locke, "Pluralism and Intellectual Democracy," in *The Works of Alain Locke,* ed. Charles Molesworth (Oxford, UK: Oxford University Press, 2012), pp. 565–66.

11. These are not necessarily complete and coherent arguments for relativism. Rather, they are more popular versions of why people generally are inclined to what they believe is relativism.

12. Susan Moller Okin, "Feminism and Multiculturalism: Some Tensions." *Ethics* 108: 4 (July 1998), p. 665.

13. Richard Rorty, "Pragmatism, Relativism, and Irrationalism," *Proceedings and Addresses of the American Philosophical Association* 53: 6 (1980), p. 727.

14. G. E. Moore, *Principia Ethica* (Cambridge, UK: Cambridge University Press, 1903).

15. Bruce W. Brower, "Dispositional Ethical Realism," *Ethics* 103: 2 (January 1993), pp. 221–49.

16. John Lachs, "Relativism and Its Benefits" *Soundings* 56: 3 (Fall 1973), p. 319.

17. W. D. Ross, *The Right and the Good* (Oxford, UK: Oxford University Press, 1930), Chapter 1.

Chapter 4

1. Paul Kurtz, *Multi-Secularism: A New Agenda* (New Brunswick, NJ: Transaction Publishing, 2010), p. 38.

2. "The New Age of Ayn Rand: How She Won Over Trump and Silicon Valley." *The Guardian*, April 10, 2017; https://www.theguardian.com/books/2017/apr/10/new-age-ayn-rand-conquered-trump-white-house-silicon-valley.

3. Ibid.

4. Stephen Prothero, "You Can't Reconcile Ayn Rand and Jesus," *USA Today*, June 5, 2011. http://usatoday30.usatoday.com/news/opinion/forum/2011-06-05-Ayn-Rand-and-Jesus-dont-mix_n.htm (accessed November 27, 2022).

5. Ayn Rand, "The Objectivist Ethics." https://courses.aynrand.org/works/the-objectivist-ethics/ (accessed November 27, 2022).

6. Alan Gewirth, *Reason and Morality* (Chicago: University of Chicago Press, 1981), p. 85.

7. Kurt Baier, *The Rational and the Moral Order* (Open Court, 1995), p. 159. Also see James P. Sterba, "Morality and Self-Interest." *Philosophy and Phenomenological Research* 59: 2 (June 1999).

8. Tenzin Gyatso, "Compassion and the Individual," THE OFFICE OF HIS HOLINESS THE DALAI LAMA. https://www.dalailama.com/messages/compassion-and-human-values/compassion

9. For a discussion of "weakness of will," see Gwynneth Matthews, "Moral Weakness," *Mind* 299 (July 1966), pp. 405–19; Donald Davidson, "How Is Weakness of the Will Possible?" in *Moral Concepts*, ed. Joel Feinberg (New York: Oxford University Press, 1970), pp. 93–113.

10. From the *Springfield Monitor* (ca. 1928), cited in Louis Pojman, *Ethics* (Belmont, CA: Wadsworth, 1990), p. 41.

11. Henry Sidgwick, *The Methods of Ethics* (London: MacMillan and Co., 1884), p. 47.

12. Thomas Hobbes, *Leviathan*, in *The English Works of Thomas Hobbes*, ed. Sir William Molesworth (London: John Bohn, 1839), pp. 2:38–41, 85.

13. Ibid., Chapter 14.

14. Tom Scanlon, *What We Owe Each Other* (Cambridge, MA: Harvard University Press, 1998); David Gauthier, *Morals by Agreement* (Oxford, UK: Oxford University Press, 1987); John Rawls, *A Theory of Justice* (Cambridge, MA: Harvard University Press, 1971).

15. See Adam Smith, *The Wealth of Nations* (New York: Edwin Cannan, 1904).

16. See the communitarian views in Robert Bellah, *Habits of the Heart* (Berkeley: University of California Press, 1985); and Amitai Etzioni, *The Spirit of Community: Rights, Responsibilities, and the Communitarian Agenda* (New York: Crown, 1993).

17. Virginia Held, *The Ethics of Care: Personal, Political, and Global* (Oxford, UK: Oxford University Press, 2006), p. 21.

18. Lisa Tessman, *Moral Failure: On the Impossible Demands of Morality* (Oxford, UK: Oxford University Press, 2015), p. 231.

19. Held, *The Ethics of Care*, p. 96.

20. Benjamin Franklin, "Poor Richard's Almanac," in *American Philosophy: A Historical Anthology*, ed. Barbara MacKinnon (New York: State University of New York Press, 1985), pp. 46–47.

21. Thomas Aquinas, *Summa Theologica*, I–II, p. 94.2.

Chapter 5

1. United Nations Department of Economic and Social Affairs, https://population.un.org/wpp/Publications/Files/WPP2019_10KeyFindings.pdf (accessed November 28, 2022).

2. United Nations, Sustainable Development Goals: Goal 12: Ensure Sustainable Consumption and Production Patterns, http://www.un.org/sustainabledevelopment/sustainable-consumption-production/ (accessed November 28, 2022).

3. Office of the United Nations High Commissioner for Human Rights, "Convention Against Torture and Other Cruel, Inhuman, or Degrading Treatment or Punishment," https://www.ohchr.org/en/instruments-mechanisms/instruments/declaration-protection-all-persons-being-subjected-torture-and#:~:text=For%20the%20purpose%20of%20this,him%20for%20an%20act%20he, accessed December 23, 2022.

4. Scott Shane, "Waterboarding Used 266 Times on 2 Suspects." *New York Times,* April 19, 2009. http://www.nytimes.com/2009/04/20/world/20detain.html?_r50

5. Chris McGreal, "Dick Cheney Defends Use of Torture on Al-Qaida Leaders." *Guardian*, September 9, 2011. http://www.guardian.co.uk/world/2011/sep/09/dick-cheney-defends-torture-al-qaida

6. *San Francisco Examiner*, February 2, 1993, p. A4; *San Francisco Chronicle*, May 5, 2007, p. A5.

7. Peter Singer, *Writings on an Ethical Life* (New York: HarperCollins, 2001), p. 16.

8. John Stuart Mill, *Utilitarianism*, ed. Oskar Priest (Indianapolis: Bobbs-Merrill, 1957), p. 20.

9. Mark Tunick, "Tolerant Imperialism: John Stuart Mill's Defense of British Rule in India." *The Review of Politics* 68: 4 (2006), pp. 586–611.

10. John Stuart Mill, "The Negro Question," in *The Collected Works of John Stuart Mill, Volume XXI - Essays on Equality, Law, and Education* (Toronto: University of Toronto Press, 1984), p. 672.

11. Ibid.

12. Mill, *Utilitarianism*, p. 24.

13. "Golden Gate Bridge Suicide Barrier Delays Add $2.3 Million to Cost." *San Jose Mercury News*, March 26, 2022. https://www.mercurynews.com/2022/03/26/golden-gate-bridge-suicide-barrier-delays-to-cost-23m-2/ (accessed June 5, 2022).

14. Jeremy Bentham, *An Introduction to the Principles of Morals and Legislation* (New York: Oxford University Press, 1879), p. 1.

15. Mill, *Utilitarianism*, p. 22.

16. These elements for calculation of the greatest amount of happiness are from Bentham's *Principles of Morals and Legislation*.

17. Bentham, *Principles of Morals and Legislation*.

18. Mill, *Utilitarianism*, p. 14.

19. Note that this is an empiricist argument. It is based on an appeal to purported facts. People's actual preferences for intellectual pleasures (if true) are the only source we have for believing them to be more valuable.

20. J. J. C. Smart and Bernard Williams, *Utilitarianism: For and Against* (New York: Cambridge University Press, 1973). Also see Samuel Scheffler, *The Rejection of Consequentialism* (New York: Oxford University Press, 1984). In *The Limits of Morality* (New York: Oxford University Press, 1989), Shelly Kagan distinguishes the universalist element of utilitarianism—its demand that I treat all equally—from the maximizing element—that I must bring about the most good possible. The first element makes utilitarianism too demanding, whereas the second allows us to do anything as long as it maximizes happiness overall.

21. Philippa Foot, "The Problem of Abortion and the Doctrine of Double Effect," in *Virtues and Vices* (Oxford: Basil Blackwell, 1978); and Judith Jarvis Thomson, "Killing, Letting Die, and the Trolley Problem," *The Monist* (1976), pp. 204–17.

22. See, for example, work done by Joshua Greene and the Moral Cognition Lab at Harvard University, https://www.joshua-greene.net/research/moral-cognition, accessed December 23, 2022.

23. C. David Navarrete, Melissa M. McDonald, Michael L. Mott, and Benjamin Asher, "Virtual Morality: Emotion and Action in a Simulated Three-Dimensional 'Trolley Problem.'" *Emotion* 12: 2 (April 2012), pp. 364–70.

24. Katja Wiech, Guy Kahane, Nicholas Shackel, Miguel Farias, Julian Savulescu, and Irene Tracey, "Cold or Calculating? Reduced Activity in the Subgenual Cingulate Cortex Reflects Decreased Emotional Aversion to Harming in Counterintuitive Utilitarian Judgment." *Cognition* 126: 3 (March 2013), pp. 364–72.

25. Daniel M. Bartels and David A. Pizarro, "The Mismeasure of Morals: Antisocial Personality Traits Predict Utilitarian Responses to Moral Dilemmas." *Cognition* 121: 1 (October 2011), pp. 154–61.

26. See, for example, the explanation of this difference in J. J. C. Smart, "Extreme and Restricted Utilitarianism." *Philosophical Quarterly* (1956).

27. Richard Brandt, "Some Merits of One Form of Rule Utilitarianism," in *Morality and the Language of Conduct*, ed. H. N. Castaneda and George Nakhnikian (Detroit: Wayne State University Press, 1970), pp. 282–307.

28. This explanation is given by Mary Warnock in her Introduction to the Fontana edition (1964) of Mill's *Utilitarianism*.

Chapter 6

1. John Rawls, *A Theory of Justice*, Revised Edition (Cambridge, MA: Harvard University Press, 1999), p. 333.

2. Jeremy Bentham, *Deontology or the Science of Morality* (Edinburgh: William Tait, 1834), vol. 1, Chapter 2.

3. Immanuel Kant, *Critique of Practical Reason*, in *Practical Philosophy* (Cambridge, UK: Cambridge University Press, 1999), 5: 130, p. 244.

4. See, for example: Pauline Kleingeld, "The Problematic Status of Gender-Neutral Language in the History of Philosophy: The Case of Kant." *Philosophical Forum* 25 (1993), pp. 134–50; Mari Mikkola, "Kant on Moral Agency and Women's Nature." *Kantian Review* 16: 1 (2011), pp. 89–111; Huaping Lu-Adler, "Kant and Slavery—Or Why He Never Became a Racial Egalitarian." *Critical Philosophy of Race* (forthcoming), preprint at PhilArchive: https://philarchive.org/archive/LUAKASv1 (accessed December 4, 2022).

5. Immanuel Kant, *The Conflict of the Faculties*, in *Religion and Rational Theology*, ed. A. W. Wood and G. di Giovanni (Cambridge, UK: Cambridge University Press, 1996), p. 283.

6. Epictetus, *The Discourses*, 3.7 (Internet Classics Archive: http://classics.mit.edu//Epictetus/discourses.html).

7. Marcus Aurelius, *The Meditations* (Internet Classics Archive: http://classics.mit.edu//Antoninus/meditations.html), bk. 8.

8. Aurelius, *Meditations*, bk. 7.

9. Kant, *Critique of Practical Reason* 5: 127, p. 242. Also see J. B. Schneewind, "Kant and Stoic Ethics," in *Essays on the History of Moral Philosophy* (Oxford, UK: Oxford University Press, 2009).

10. See Luigi Caranti, "Kant's Theory of Human Rights," in *Routledge Handbook of Human Rights*, Thomas Cushman, ed. (New York: Routledge, 2011).

11. Immanuel Kant, *Critique of Pure Reason*, trans. Norman Kemp Smith (New York: St. Martin's, 1965), p. 635.

12. We will not distinguish here *motive* and *intention*, although the former usually signifies that out of which we act (an impetus or push) and the latter that for which we act (an aim or objective).

13. Kant, *Fundamental Principles of the Metaphysics of Morals*, trans. Abbott (Project Gutenberg: http://www.gutenberg.org/cache/epub/5682/pg5682.html), second section.

14. See also the criticism of Kantian theories of justice in the treatment of gender and justice in Susan Moller Okin, *Justice, Gender, and the Family* (New York: Basic Books, 1989), pp. 3–22; Marilyn Friedman, "The Social Self and the Partiality Debates," in *Feminist Ethics*, ed. Claudia Card (Lawrence: University of Kansas Press, 1991).

15. For discussion, see: Pauline Kleingeld, "On Dealing with Kant's Sexism and Racism." *Society for German Idealism and Romanticism Review* 2: 2 (2019), pp. 3–22; essays in *Kant and Colonialism: Historical and Critical Perspectives*, eds. Katrin Flikschuh and Lea Ypi (Oxford, UK: Oxford University Press, 2014); Pauline Kleingeld, "Kant's Second Thoughts on Race." *The Philosophical Quarterly* 57: 229 (2007), pp. 573–92.

16. Charles W. Mills, "Black Radical Kantianism." *Res Philosophica*, 95: 1 (2018), pp. 1–33.

17. Ibid.

18. W. D. Ross, *The Right and the Good* (Oxford, UK: Oxford University Press, 1930).

19. Immanuel Kant, "What Is Enlightenment?" in *Kant, Political Writings*, Hans Reiss, ed. (Cambridge, UK: Cambridge University Press, 1970), pp. 54–60.

20. For further discussion, see Andrew Fiala, *Public War, Private Conscience: The Ethics of Political Violence* (London: Continuum, 2010).

Chapter 7

1. "UNHCR: A Record 100 Million People Forcibly Displaced Worldwide." UN Human Rights Commission press release, May 23, 2022. https://news.un.org/en/story/2022/05/1118772

2. Adam Isacson, "A Tragic Milestone: 20,000 Migrants Deported to Haiti since Biden Inauguration," February 2022. https://www.wola.org/analysis/a-tragic-milestone-20000th-migrant-deported-to-haiti-since-biden-inauguration/.

3. Thomas Jefferson, "The Declaration of Independence," in *Basic Writings of Thomas Jefferson*, ed. Philip S. Foner (New York: Wiley, 1944), p. 551.

4. John Locke, *Two Treatises of Government* (London, 1690), ed. Peter Laslett (Cambridge, UK: Cambridge University Press, 1960).

5. Human Rights Watch, "High Cost of Guantanamo's 'Forever Prisoners,'" May 4, 2022. https://www.hrw.org/news/2022/05/04/high-cost-guantanamos-forever-prisoners; see also: The Guantanamo Docket at *New York Times*, http://projects.nytimes.com/guantanamo/detainees

6. "Is Force-Feeding Torture?" *New York Times*, May 31, 2013. http://www.nytimes.com/2013/06/01/opinion/nocera-is-force-feeding-torture.html

7. Henry David Thoreau, "Civil Disobedience," in *Miscellanies* (Boston: Houghton Mifflin, 1983), pp. 136–37.

8. Cicero, *Republic*, in *Cicero's Tusculan Disputations. Also, Treatises on the Nature of the Gods, and on the Commonwealth*, bk. 3 at 22 (Project Gutenberg), http://www.gutenberg.org/files/14988/14988-h/14988-h.htm

9. Thomas Aquinas, *Summa Theologica*, in *Basic Writings of Saint Thomas Aquinas*, ed. Anton Pegis (New York: Random House, 1948).

10. Aquinas, *Summa Theologica*, Q.91 a.4. Aquinas is quoting Cicero's *Rhetoric*.

11. This is an incomplete presentation of the moral philosophy of Thomas Aquinas. We should also note that he was as much a theologian as a philosopher, if not more so. True and complete happiness, he believed, would be achieved only in knowledge or contemplation of God.

12. Hugo Grotius, *On the Rights of War and Peace* (Cambridge, UK: Cambridge University Press, 1854), vol. 1, p. xxvii.

13. Hugo Grotius, *On the Rights of War and Peace* (Oxford: Clarendon Press, 1925), vol. 2, p. 201.

14. Henry Veatch, "Natural Law: Dead or Alive?" at Liberty Fund, http://oll.libertyfund.org/index.php?Itemid=259&id=168&option=com_content&task=view#anchor249499 (originally published 1978).

15. Ralph M. McInerny, *Ethica Thomistica: The Moral Philosophy of Thomas Aquinas*. (Washington, DC: Catholic University of America Press, 1997), p. 56.

16. Germain Grisez, Joseph Boyle, and John Finnis, "Practical Principles, Moral Truth, and Ultimate Ends," *American Journal of Jurisprudence* 32 (1987), p. 106.

17. Larry Arnhart, *Darwinian Natural Right: The Biological Ethics of Human Nature* (Albany: State University of New York Press, 1998), p. 7.

18. John Finnis, *Natural Law and Natural Rights* (Oxford, UK: Oxford University Press, 2011), p. 31.

19. Voltaire, *Oeuvres*, XXV, p. 39; XI, p. 443, quoted in Carl L. Becker, *The Heavenly City of the Eighteenth-Century Philosophers* (New Haven, CT: Yale University Press, 2003), p. 52; Becker's translation.

20. Thomas Jefferson, Declaration of Independence.

21. John Locke, *Two Treatises of Government* (London, 1690), ed. Peter Laslett (Cambridge, UK: Cambridge University Press, 1960), Chapter 2, p. 271.

22. Jeremy Bentham, *Anarchical Fallacies*, in *The Works of Jeremy Bentham* (Edinburgh: William Tait, 1843), p. 501.

23. Alasdair MacIntyre, *After Virtue*, 3rd ed. (Notre Dame, IN: Notre Dame University Press, 2007), 69.

24. Ibid.

25. On negative or liberty rights, see, for example, the work of Robert Nozick, *State, Anarchy and Utopia* (New York: Basic Books, 1974). See further discussion on welfare and liberty rights in Chapter 14 of this book, "Economic Justice."

26. John Stuart Mill, *Utilitarianism*, in Mill, *On Liberty and Utilitarianism* (New York: Random House, 1993), p. 222.

27. The term *pragmatic* concerns what "works." Thus, to accept something on pragmatic grounds means to accept it because it works for us in some way. For Walter Lippmann's views, see *Essays in the Public Philosophy* (Boston: Little, Brown, 1955).

28. See, for example: Brian Smith, "One Body of People: Locke on Punishment, Native Land Rights, and the Protestant Evangelism of North America." *Locke Studies* 18: 1 (2018), pp. 1–40; Nagamitsu Miura, *John Locke and the Native Americans* (Newcastle, UK: Cambridge Scholars Publishing, 2013); James Farr, "Locke, Natural Law, and New World Slavery." *Political Theory* 36: 4 (2008), pp. 495–522.

29. See Lina Mann, "The Enslaved Household of President Thomas Jefferson." (White House Historical Association, 2019): https://www.whitehousehistory.org/slavery-in-the-thomas-jefferson-white-house.

30. See Francisco de Vitoria, *De Indis* and *De Jure Belli* (On the Indians and On the Law of War) in *Vitoria, Political Writings* (Cambridge:, UK Cambridge University Press, 1991). Antony Anghie has remarked that "Vitoria's scheme finally endorses and legitimizes endless Spanish incursions into Indian society." Antony Anghie, *Imperialism, Sovereignty and the Making of International Law* (Cambridge, UK: Cambridge University Press, 2004), p. 21.

31. Lysander Spooner, *The Unconstitutionality of Slavery* (Boston: Bela Marsh, 1860/1845), p. 43.

32. Frederick Douglass, "What to the Slave Is the Fourth of July?" (1852) at Blackpast.org: https://www.blackpast.org/african-american-history/speeches-african-american-history/1852-frederick-douglass-what-slave-fourth-july/ (accessed September 12, 2022).

33. Mary Wollstonecraft, *A Vindication of the Rights of Woman* (London: J. Johnson, 1792—online version at https://oll.libertyfund.org/title/wollstonecraft-a-vindication-of-the-rights-of-woman), Chapter V.

34. Richard Rorty, *Contingency, Irony, Solidarity* (Cambridge, UK: Cambridge University Press, 1989), p. 175.

35. Craig Boyd, *A Shared Morality: A Narrative Defense of Natural Law Ethics* (Grand Rapids, MI: Brazos Press, 2007), p. 183.

Chapter 8

1. Ted Cruz on Twitter, October 13, 2021: https://twitter.com/tedcruz/status/1448344091989774342

2. Data on mortality rates during COVID are available on Johns Hopkins University Coronavirus Resource Center: https://coronavirus.jhu.edu/data/mortality

3. Sanja Ivic, "Vietnam's Response to the COVID-19 Outbreak." *Asian Bioethics Review* 12, pp. 341–347 (2020). https://doi.org/10.1007/s41649-020-00134-2; Robert E. Allinson, "The Primacy of Duty and Its Efficacy in Combating COVID-19." *Public Health Ethics* 13: 2 (July 2020), pp. 179–189. https://doi.org/10.1093/phe/phaa029; Jana S. Rošker, "Chinese Philosophy of Life, Relational Ethics and the COVID-19 Pandemic. *Asian Philosophy* 31: 1 (2021), pp. 64–77, doi: 10.1080/09552367.2020.1863624

4. Jon Krakauer, *Where Men Win Glory: The Odyssey of Pat Tillman* (New York: Doubleday, 2009).

5. John McCain, *Character Is Destiny* (New York: Random House, 2007).

6. Susan Wolf, "Moral Saints," *The Journal of Philosophy* 89: 8 (August 1982), p. 419.

7. W. T. Jones, *A History of Western Philosophy: The Classical Mind*, 2nd ed. (New York: Harcourt, Brace & World, 1969), pp. 214–216.

8. This was asserted by the neo-Platonist Porphyry (ca. 232 CE). However, others believe that the work got its name because it was edited by Nicomachus. See Alasdair MacIntyre, *After Virtue* (Notre Dame, IN: Notre Dame University Press, 1984), p. 147.

9. Milton Gonsalves, *Fagothey's Right and Reason*, 9th ed. (Columbus, OH: Merrill, 1989), p. 201.

10. Jones, *A History of Western Philosophy*, p. 233.

11. Aristotle, *Politics*, 1254b in *Aristotle in 23 Volumes*, Vol. 21, trans. H. Rackham (Cambridge, MA: Harvard University Press; London: William Heinemann, 1944); at Perseus: http://www.perseus.tufts.edu/hopper/text?doc=Perseus:text:1999.01.0058.

12. Aristotle, *Politics*, 1255a in *Aristotle in 23 Volumes*, Vol. 21.

13. *Colossians*, 3: 18–22; *Ephesians* 6: 1–5.

14. Lisa Tessman, *Burdened Virtues: Virtue Ethics for Liberatory Struggles* (Oxford, UK: Oxford University Press, 2005), p. 7.

15. Tessman, *Burdened Virtues*, p. 7

16. Also see, for example: Cynthia A. Freeland, ed., *Feminist Interpretations of Aristotle* (University Park, PA: Pennsylvania State University Press, 1998).

17. Confucius, *Analects*, in *The Chinese Classics—Volume 1: Confucian Analects*, bk. 1, Chapter 6, trans. James Legge (Project Gutenberg), http://www.gutenberg.org/files/4094/4094-h/4094-h.htm (accessed December 5, 2022).

18. Sunil Sehgal, ed., *Encyclopedia of Hinduism* (New Delhi: Sarup and Sons, 1999), p. 2:364.

19. Vensus A. George, *Paths to the Divine: Ancient and Indian* (Washington, DC: CRVP Press, 2008), p. 205.

20. Peter Harvey, *Buddhism: Teachings, History and Practices* (Cambridge, UK: Cambridge University Press, 1990), pp. 68–69.

21. See, for example, the collection of articles in Christina Hoff Sommers, *Vice and Virtue in Everyday Life* (New York: Harcourt Brace Jovanovich, 1985).

22. Philippa Foot, *Virtues and Vices* (Oxford, UK: Oxford University Press, 2002).

23. Alasdair MacIntyre, "The Virtue in Heroic Societies" and "The Virtues at Athens," in *After Virtue* (Notre Dame, IN: Notre Dame University Press, 1984), pp. 121–45.

24. Alasdair MacIntyre, "Incommensurability, Truth, and the Conversation between Confucians and Aristotelians about the Virtues" in E. Deutsch, ed., *Culture and Modernity: East-West Philosophic Perspectives* (Honolulu: University of Hawaii Press, 1991).

25. Foot, *Virtues and Vices*, p. 10.

26. Foot, *Virtues and Vices*, 15.

27. Kant, "Doctrine of Virtue," in *Metaphysics of Morals*, trans. Mary Gregor (Cambridge, UK: Cambridge University Press, 1996), pp. 184–85.

Chapter 9

1. Jessie Yeung et al., "Iranian Women Burn Their Hijabs as Hundreds Protest Death of Mahsa Amini." CNN, September 21, 2022. https://www.cnn.com/2022/09/21/middleeast/iran-mahsa-amini-death-widespread-protests-intl-hnk (accessed January 31, 2023).

2. Alex Hardie and Hande Atay Alam, "As Many as 14,000 Arrested in Iran over Last Six Weeks, United Nations Says." CNN, November 3, 2022. https://www.cnn.com/2022/11/03/middleeast/iran-protests-arrests-united-nations-intl (accessed January 31, 2023).

3. C. Mandler, "U.S. Judge Approves $24 Million Equal Pay Settlement for U.S. Women's Soccer Team." CBS News, August 15, 2022. https://www.cbsnews.com/news/judge-approves-24-million-equal-pay-deal-us-womens-soccer-team/ (accessed January 31, 2023).

4. See John Reilly, "LGBTQ Groups Condemn Brittney Griner's Sentence." *Metro Weekly*, August 2022. https://www.metroweekly.com/2022/08/lgbtq-groups-condemn-brittney-griners-sentence/ (accessed January 31, 2023); and Rod Dreher, "Is Brittney Griner Worth It?" *American Conservative*, August 2, 2022. https://www.theamericanconservative.com/is-brittney-griner-worth-it/ (accessed January 31, 2023).

5. Noëlle McAfee, "Feminist Philosophy." *Stanford Encyclopedia of Philosophy Archive* (Fall 2018 Edition). https://plato.stanford.edu/archives/fall2018/entries/feminist-philosophy/ (accessed January 31, 2023).

6. Simone de Beauvoir, *The Second Sex*, trans. H. M. Parshley (New York: Knopf, 1953), p. 273.

7. See Emi Koyama, "The Transfeminist Manifesto," in *The Feminist Theory Reader: Local and Global Perspectives*, 4th ed., eds. Carole R. McCann and Seung-kyung Kim (New York: Routledge, 2017).

8. See Jane Ribbens McCarthy, "Caring After Death: Issues of Embodiment and Relationality," in *Critical Approaches to Care: Understanding Caring Relations, Identities and Cultures*, eds Chrissie Rogers and Susie Weller (New York: Routledge, 2012).

9. Virginia Held, *The Ethics of Care: Personal, Political, and Global* (Oxford, UK: Oxford University Press, 2026), p. 10.

10. Carol Gilligan, "Concepts of the Self and of Morality," *Harvard Educational Review* 47: 4 (November 1977), pp. 481–517.

11. This is a summary of a question that was posed by researchers for Lawrence Kohlberg. In Carol Gilligan, *In a Different Voice* (Cambridge, MA: Harvard University Press, 1982), pp. 28, 173.

12. Gilligan, *In a Different Voice.*

13. We use the term *sex* to refer to the biological male or female. The term *gender* includes psychological feminine and masculine traits as well as social roles assigned to the two sexes.

14. From Carol Gilligan, "Moral Orientation and Moral Development," in *Women and Moral Theory*, ed. Eva Feder Kittay and Diana T. Meyers (Totowa, NJ: Rowman & Littlefield, 1987), p. 23.

15. Gilligan, "Moral Orientation and Moral Development."

16. Nel Noddings, *Caring: A Feminine Approach to Ethics and Moral Education* (Berkeley: University of California Press, 1984).

17. Lawrence Kohlberg, *The Psychology of Moral Development* (San Francisco: Harper & Row, 1984).

18. Gilligan, "Moral Orientation and Moral Development," p. 22.

19. Cited in Gilligan, "Moral Orientation and Moral Development."

20. See also Nancy Chodorow, *The Reproduction of Mothering* (Berkeley: University of California Press, 1978).

21. See, for example, Gilligan, "Adolescent Development Reconsidered," in *Mapping the Moral Domain*, ed. Carol Gilligan, Janie Victoria Ward, and Jill McLean Taylor (Cambridge, MA: Harvard University Press, 1988).

22. Gilligan, "Moral Orientation and Moral Development," pp. 22–23. Emphasis added.

23. Gilligan, "Moral Orientation and Moral Development," p. 25.

24. Catherine G. Greeno and Eleanor E. Maccoby, "How Different Is the 'Different Voice'?" in "On *In a Different Voice*: An Interdisciplinary Forum," *Signs: Journal of Women in Culture and Society* 11: 2 (Winter 1986), pp. 211–20.

25. See, for example, Caroline Whitbeck, "The Maternal Instinct," in *Mothering: Essays in Feminist Theory*, ed. Joyce Trebilcot (Totowa, NJ: Rowman & Allanheld, 1984).

26. See, for example, Sara Ruddick, *Maternal Thinking: Toward a Politics of Peace* (Boston: Beacon, 1989).

27. Ruddick, *Maternal Thinking*, p. 214.

28. See Alison Stone, "Essentialism and Anti-Essentialism in Feminist Philosophy." *Journal of Moral Philosophy* 1: 2 (2004), pp. 135–53.

29. Catharine MacKinnon, *Feminism Unmodified* (Cambridge: Harvard University Press, 1987), 39.

30. Amanda Cawston and Alfred Archer, "Rehabilitating Self-Sacrifice: Care Ethics and the Politics of Resistance." *International Journal of Philosophical Studies* 26: 3 (2018), pp. 456–77,

31. Michael Slote, *The Ethics of Care and Empathy* (New York: Routledge, 2007), p. 9, footnote no. 7.

32. Mary Wollstonecraft, *A Vindication of the Rights of Women* (New York: Penguin Books, 2006), p. 91.

33. Elizabeth Cady Stanton, "Address Delivered at Seneca Falls, July 19, 1848," in *Elizabeth Cady Stanton and Susan B. Anthony Reader*, ed. Ellen Carol Dubois (Boston: Northeastern University Press, 1992), 31.

34. Frederick Douglass, July 28, 1848, in *Women's Suffrage in America*, eds. Elizabeth Frost-Knappman and Kathryn Cullen-DuPont (New York: Facts on File, 2005), pp. 78–9.

35. Harriet Taylor Mill, "The Enfranchisement of Women," in *The Complete Works of Harriet Taylor Mill* (Bloomington: Indiana University Press, 1998), 51.

36. United Nations Declaration of Human Rights, https://www.un.org/en/about-us/universal-declaration-of-human-rights (accessed January 31, 2023).

37. de Beauvoir, *The Second Sex.*

38. Betty Friedan, *The Feminine Mystique* (New York: Norton, 2001), p. 508.

39. bell hooks, *Ain't I a Woman: Black Women and Feminism* (New York: Routledge, 2015), 13.

40. bell hooks, *Feminist Theory from Margin to Center* (Boston: South End Press, 1984), 39.

41. Martha C. Nussbaum, *Women and Human Development: The Capabilities Approach* (Cambridge, UK: Cambridge University Press, 2001), p. 7.

42. This terminology is from Rosemarie Tong's *Feminine and Feminist Ethics* (Belmont, CA: Wadsworth, 1993). As a source of the terminology, Tong also cites Betty A. Sichel, "Different Strains and Strands: Feminist Contributions to Ethical Theory," *Newsletter on Feminism* 90: 2 (Winter 1991), p. 90; and Susan Sherwin, *No Longer Patient: Feminist Ethics and Health Care* (Philadelphia: Temple University Press, 1992), p. 42.

43. Aristotle, *Politics*, as quoted in "Theories of Sex Difference," by Caroline Whitbeck in *Women and Moral Theory*, p. 35.

44. Jean-Jacques Rousseau, *Emile*, trans. Allan Bloom (New York: Basic Books, 1979). Also see Nancy Tuana, *Woman and the History of Philosophy* (New York: Paragon House, 1992).

45. Susan Moller Okin, "Gender, the Public and the Private," in *Political Theory Today*, ed. David Held (Stanford, CA: Stanford University Press, 1991), p. 77.

46. Okin, "Gender, the Public and the Private."

47. Gilligan, "Moral Orientation and Moral Development," p. 32.

48. "Malala Yousafzai Tells Emma Watson: I'm a Feminist Thanks to You." *The Guardian*, November 5, 2015. http://www.theguardian.com/world/2015/nov/05/malala-yousafzai-tells-emma-watson-im-a-feminist-thanks-to-you (accessed February 1, 2023).

49. "More Than 2,000 Women Murdered by Men in One Year, New Violence Policy Center Study Finds." https://vpc.org/press/more-than-2000-women-murdered-by-men-in-one-year-new-violence-policy-center-study-finds/ (accessed January 31, 2023).

50. "Missing and Murdered Indigenous People Crisis." https://www.bia.gov/service/mmu/missing-and-murdered-indigenous-people-crisis (accessed January 31, 2023).

51. "1 Is Too Many." https://obamawhitehouse.archives.gov/1is2many (accessed February 1, 2023).

52. Andrea Dworkin, *Pornography: Men Possessing Women* (New York: Perigee Books, 1981).

53. Naomi Wolf, *The Beauty Myth: How Images of Beauty Are Used against Women* (New York: Harper Perennial, 2002); Cressida J. Heyes and Meredith Jones, *Cosmetic Surgery: A Feminist Primer* (New York: Ashgate, 2009).

54. Wolf, *The Beauty Myth*, p. 5.

55. Wendy McElroy, *XXX: A Woman's Right to Pornography* (New York: St. Martin's Press, 1995).

56. Nicholas D. Kristof and Sheryl WuDunn, *Half the Sky: Turning Oppression into Opportunity for Women Worldwide* (New York: Vintage, 2010), p. xvii.

57. Robert Paul Churchill, *Women in the Crossfire* (Oxford: Oxford University Press, 2018), x.

58. United Nations, "Killings of Women and Girls by Their Intimate Partner or Other Family Members: Global Estimates 2020." https://www.unodc.org/documents/data-and-analysis/statistics/crime/UN_BriefFem_251121.pdf (accessed January 31, 2023).

59. Human Rights Campaign, "Fatal Violence against the Transgender and Gender Non-Conforming Community in 2022." https://www.hrc.org/resources/fatal-violence-against-the-transgender-and-gender-non-conforming-community-in-2022 (accessed January 31, 2023).

60. World Economic Forum, *Global Gender Gap Report 2022: Key Findings* https://www.weforum.org/reports/global-gender-gap-report-2022/digest (accessed January 31, 2023).

61. World Economic Forum, *Global Gender Gap Report 2022*, https://www3.weforum.org/docs/WEF_GGGR_2022.pdf (accessed January 31, 2023).

62. U.S. Census, "Equal Pay Day: March 15, 2022." https://www.census.gov/newsroom/stories/equal-pay-day.html (accessed January 31, 2023).

63. Brookings Institution, "Boys Left Behind: Education Gender Gaps across the US," October 12, 2022. https://www.brookings.edu/blog/up-front/2022/10/12/boys-left-behind-education-gender-gaps-across-the-us/ (accessed January 31, 2023).

Chapter 10

1. See Centers for Disease Control and Prevention Museum, COVID-19 Timeline, https://www.cdc.gov/museum/timeline/covid19.html (accessed December 14, 2022).

2. World Health Organization, https://covid19.who.int/ (accessed December 14, 2022).

3. See Centers for Disease Control and Prevention Museum, COVID-19 Timeline, https://www.cdc.gov/museum/timeline/covid19.html (accessed December 14, 2022).

4. Selena Simmons-Duffin, "This Is How Many Lives Could Have Been Saved with COVID Vaccinations in Each State." NPR, https://www.npr.org/sections/health-shots/2022/05/13/1098071284/this-is-how-many-lives-could-have-been-saved-with-covid-vaccinations-in-each-sta (accessed December 14, 2022); also see: https://globalepidemics.org/vaccinations/ (accessed December 14, 2022).

5. Constitution of the World Health Organization (adopted 1946), https://apps.who.int/gb/bd/PDF/bd47/EN/constitution-en.pdf?ua=1 (accessed December 14, 2022).

6. Jonathan Metzl, "Why Against Health?," in *Against Health: How Health Became the New Morality*, eds. Jonathan M. Metzl and Anna Kirkland (New York: New York University Press, 2010), pp. 1–2.

7. Kathleen Lebesco, "Fat Panic and the New Morality," in *Against Health: How Health Became the New Morality*, eds. Jonathan M. Metzl and Anna Kirkland (New York: New York University Press, 2010).

8. Osamu Muramoto and Walter G. Englert, "Socrates and Temporal Lobe Epilepsy: A Pathographic Diagnosis 2,400 Years Later." *Epilepsia* 47 (2006), pp. 652–654. Also see

M. Bou Nasif, et al., "Epilepsy—from Mysticism to Science." *Revue Neurologique* 177: 9 (2021), pp. 1047–1058.

9. APA, "Position Statement on Conversion Therapy and LGBTQ Patients" (2018). https://www.psychiatry.org /getattachment/3d23f2f4-1497-4537-b4de-fe32fe8761bf /Position-Conversion-Therapy.pdf (accessed December 14, 2022).

10. Governor Doug Ducey, March 30, 2022. https://azgovernor. gov/sites/default/files/sb1138_sb1165_signing_letter.pdf (accessed December 14, 2022).

11. Human Rights Campaign, "Human Rights Campaign Condemns Gov. Doug Ducey for Signing Anti-Transgender Bills, Putting the Well-Being of Youth At Risk," March 30, 2022. https://www.hrc.org/press-releases /breaking-human-rights-campaign-condemns-gov-doug -ducey-for-signing-anti-transgender-bills-putting-the-well -being-of-youth-at-risk (accessed December 14, 2022).

12. See T. A. Cavanaugh, *Hippocrates' Oath and Asclepius' Snake: The Birth of a Medical Profession* (Oxford, UK: Oxford University Press, 2017).

13. Plato, *Protagoras*, 313e, in *Plato, Complete Works* (Indianapolis, IN: Hackett Publishing, 1997).

14. Plato, *Theaetetus*, 148e, in Ibid.

15. "The Belmont Report," 1979, at Health and Human Services website. https://www.hhs.gov/ohrp/regulations-and-policy /belmont-report/read-the-belmont-report/index .html#xbasic (accessed December 14, 2022).

16. The Nuremburg Code (1947) at National Holocaust Museum. https://www.ushmm.org/information/exhibitions /online-exhibitions/special-focus/doctors-trial /nuremberg-code (accessed December 14, 2022).

17. World Medical Association Declaration of Helsinki: Ethical Principles for Medical Research Involving Human Subjects (2013). https://www.wma.net/policies-post/wma -declaration-of-helsinki-ethical-principles-for-medical -research-involving-human-subjects/ (accessed December 14, 2022).

18. Tom Beauchamp and James Childress, *Principles of Biomedical Ethics*, 8th ed. (New York: Oxford University Press, 2019).

19. See Walter Johnson and Eleonore Pauwels, "How to Optimize Human Biology: Where Genome Editing and Artificial Intelligence Collide." Wilson Briefs (The Wilson Center), October 2017, https://www.wilsoncenter.org /sites/default/files/media/documents/publication/how _to_optimize_human_biology.pdf (accessed December 14,

2022); also P. Schröder-Bäck, P. Duncan, W. Sherlaw, et al., "Teaching Seven Principles for Public Health Ethics: Towards a Curriculum for a Short Course on Ethics in Public Health Programmes." *BMC Medical Ethics* 15: 73 (2014).

20. Rushworth Kidder, *How Good People Make Tough Choices* (New York: HarperCollins, 2009).

21. See Louise Campbell, "Kant, Autonomy and Bioethics." *Ethics, Medicine and Public Health* 3: 3 (2017), pp. 381–392.

22. See Erich H. Loewy, "In Defense of Paternalism." *Theoretical Medicine and Bioethics* 26 (2005), pp. 445–468.

23. See "I Wish I Was a Little Bit Taller." *GQ*, September 15, 2022, https://www.gq.com/story/leg-lengthening (accessed December 14, 2022).

24. See S. Higgins and A. Wysong, "Cosmetic Surgery and Body Dysmorphic Disorder—An Update." *International Journal of Women's Dermatology*, 4: 1 (2017), pp. 43–48.

25. See Raymond Angelo Belliotti, *Posthumous Harm: Why the Dead Are Still Vulnerable* (Lanham, MD: Rowman and Littlefield, 2013).

26. See William Perez, "The Trouble with Anesthetizing the Dead." *The Linacre Quarterly* 86: 4 (2019), pp. 271–274.

27. CDC, "US Overdose Deaths 2021," May 11, 2022. https:// www.cdc.gov/nchs/pressroom/nchs_press_releases /2022/202205.htm (accessed December 14, 2022).

28. See Beth A. Lown and Michael J. Goldberg, "Do Physicians Have Collective, Not Just Individual, Obligations to Respond to the Opioid Crisis?" *AMA Journal of Ethics* 22: 8 (2020) pp. 668–674.

29. See "The Family That Built an Empire of Pain." *The New Yorker*, October 3, 2017, https://www.newyorker.com /magazine/2017/10/30/the-family-that-built-an-empire -of-pain (accessed December 14, 2022).

30. Alonso, J. Sanchez, "Purdue Pharma Deceptive Research Misconduct: The Importance of the Use of Independent, Transparent, Current Research." *Voices in Bioethics* 7 (2021).

31. CDC, "Advancing Health Equity in Chronic Disease Prevention and Management." https://www.cdc.gov /chronicdisease/healthequity/index.htm (accessed December 14, 2022).

32. "Key Facts on Health and Health Care by Race and Ethnicity." Kaiser Family Foundation, January 26, 2022. https:// www.kff.org/report-section/key-facts-on-health-and -health-care-by-race-and-ethnicity-health-status -outcomes-and-behaviors/ (accessed December 14, 2022).

33. Anita Silvers, "Bedside Justice and Disability: Personalizing Preserving Impartiality," in *Medicine and Social Justice : Essays on the Distribution of Health Care*, Rosamond Rhodes, et al, eds. (Oxford, UK: Oxford University Press, 2002), 235.

34. See Health Resources & Services Administration, "Organ Donations Statistics." https://www.organdonor.gov/learn /organ-donation-statistics (accessed December 14, 2022).

35. Organ Procurement and Transplantation Network, "Ethical Principles in the Allocation of Human Organs," updated June 2015. https://optn.transplant.hrsa.gov /professionals/by-topic/ethical-considerations/ethical -principles-in-the-allocation-of-human-organs/ (accessed December 14, 2022).

36. See D. B. White, M. H. Katz, J. M. Luce, and B. Lo, "Who Should Receive Life Support during a Public Health Emergency? Using Ethical Principles to Improve Allocation Decisions." *Annals of Internal Medicine* 150: 2 (2009), pp. 132–138; Whitney Kerr and Harald Schmidt, "COVID-19 Ventilator Rationing Protocols: Why We Need to Know More about the Views of Those with Most to Lose." *Journal of Medical Ethics* 47 (2021), pp. 133–136.

37. John Harris, *The Value of Life: An Introduction to Medical Ethics* (New York: Taylor & Francis, 1990).

38. Andrew Soergel, "States Competing in 'Global Jungle' for PPE." *U.S. News*, April 7, 2020. https://www.usnews .com/news/best-states/articles/2020-04-07/states -compete-in-global-jungle-for-personal-protective -equipment-amid-coronavirus (accessed December 14, 2022).

39. "COVID Vaccines: Widening Inequality and Millions Vulnerable." *UN News*, September 19, 2021. https://news .un.org/en/story/2021/09/1100192 (accessed December 14, 2022).

40. Constitution of the World Health Organization (adopted 1946), https://apps.who.int/gb/bd/PDF/bd47/EN /constitution-en.pdf?ua=1 (accessed December 14, 2022).

41. "Sanders Highlights Failures of Health Care System and Calls for Medicare for All," Senate speech of September 14, 2022. https://www.sanders.senate.gov/press-releases /prepared-remarks-sanders-highlights-failures-of-health -care-system-and-calls-for-medicare-for-all/ (accessed December 14, 2022).

42. "Remarks by President Trump in State of the Union," February 4, 2022. https://trumpwhitehouse.archives.gov /briefings-statements/remarks-president-trump-state -union-address-3/ (accessed December 14, 2022).

43. Kai Nielsen, "Autonomy, Equality, and a Just Health Care System." *International Journal of Applied Philosophy* 4: 3 (Spring 1989), pp. 39–44.

44. Kai Nielsen, "A Moral Case for Socialism." *Critical Review* 3 :3-4 (1989), pp. 542–553.

45. John David Lewis, "There Is no Right to Healthcare." in *Medical Ethics*, 2nd ed., ed Michael Boylan (New York: Wiley-Blackwell, 2013), pp. 275–282.

46. Norman Daniels, *Just Health: Meeting Health Needs Justly* (Cambridge, UK: Cambridge University Press, 2007), p. 58.

47. Daniels, *Just Health*, p. 58.

48. Norman Daniels, "Is There a Right to Health Care? And If So, What Does It Encompass?" in *A Companion to Bioethics*, 2nd ed., eds. Helga Kuhse and Peter Singer (New York: Wiley-Blackwell, 2009), pp. 362–372.

49. Norman Daniels, "The Ethics of Health Reform: Why We Should Care about Who Is Missing Coverage: Keynote Address." *Connecticut Law Review* 150 (2012). https:// opencommons.uconn.edu/law_review/150 (accessed December 14, 2022).

50. James Childress, et al., "Public Health Ethics: Mapping the Terrain." *Journal of Law, Medicine & Ethics* 30: 2 (2002), pp. 170–178.

51. Greg Bognar, "QALY's, DALY's, and Their Critics," in *The Routledge Companion to Bioethics* eds. John D. Arras, Elizabeth Fenton, and Rebecca Kukla (New York: Routledge, 2015).

52. Anita Silvers, "Bedside Justice and Disability: Personalizing Preserving Impartiality," in *Medicine and Social Justice: Essays on the Distribution of Health Care*, First Edition, eds. Rosamond Rhodes, et al. (Oxford, UK: Oxford University Press, 2002).

53. See Richard Cookson and Paul Dolan, "Principles of Justice in Health Care Rationing." *Journal of Medical Ethics* 26 (2000), pp. 323–329.

54. Phillip R. Reilly, "Eugenics and Involuntary Sterilization: 1907–2015." *Annual Review of Genomics and Human Genetics* 16 (2015), pp. 351–368.

55. Wendy Rogers, "Vulnerability and Bioethics," in *Vulnerability: New Essays in Ethics and Feminist Philosophy*, eds. Catriona Mackenzie, Wendy Rogers, and Susan Dodds (Cambridge, UK: Cambridge University Press, 2014), p. 77.

56. Rogers, "Vulnerability and Bioethics," p. 79.

57. Martha C. Nussbaum, *Frontiers of Justice : Disability, Nationality, Species Membership* (Cambridge, MA: Harvard University Press, 2006), pp. 405–406.

58. Nussbaum, *Frontiers of Justice*, p. 127.

59. See Daniel Engster, "Care Ethics, Dependency, and Vulnerability." *Ethics and Social Welfare* 13: 2 (2019), pp. 100–114; Sarah Clark Miller, "From Vulnerability to Precariousness: Examining the Moral Foundations of Care Ethics." *International Journal of Philosophical Studies* 28: 5 (2020), pp. 644–661; and Angela K. Martin, Angela, Nicolas Tavaglione, and Samia Hurst, "Resolving the Conflict: Clarifying 'Vulnerability' in Health Care Ethics." *Kennedy Institute of Ethics Journal* 24: 1 (2014), pp. 51–72.

60. Nussbaum, *Frontiers of Justice*, p. 98.

61. U.S. Health and Human Services, Guidance on "Long COVID" as a Disability Under the ADA, Section 504, and Section 1557, July 26, 2021. https://www.hhs.gov/civil-rights/for-providers/civil-rights-covid19/guidance-long-covid-disability/index.html#footnote10_0ac8mdc (accessed December 14, 2022).

62. The following is adapted from a newspaper column by Andrew Fiala in *The Fresno Bee*, February 7, 2020. https://www.fresnobee.com/living/liv-columns-blogs/andrew-fiala/article240087318.html (accessed December 14, 2022).

63. George J. Annas, *Worst Case Bioethics: Death, Disaster, and Public Health* (Oxford, UK: Oxford University Press, 2010), pp. 227–228.

64. Rebecca L. Thom, et al., "Inequitable Access to Transplants: Adults with Impaired Decision-Making Capacity." *Transplant International: Official Journal of the European Society for Organ Transplantation* 35 (2022), p. 10084.

65. J. J. Curtis, "Ageism and Kidney Transplantation." *American Journal of Transplantation* 6 (2006), pp. 1264–1266.

66. Helen T. D'Couto, "Forcing My COVID Patients to Die Alone Is Inhumane—and Unnecessary." WBUR Commentary, March 7, 2022. https://www.wbur.org/cognoscenti/2022/03/07/covid-patients-icu-dying-alone-helen-t-dcouto (accessed December 14, 2022); Thana C. de Campos-Rudinsky "On Love, Dying Alone, and Community" *The New Bioethics*, 28:3 (2022), 238–251.

67. Daniela J. Lamas, "You're Dying, I Told My Patient. I Wish I Hadn't." *New York Times*, October 6, 2021. https://www.nytimes.com/2021/10/06/opinion/doctor-patient-death-truth.html (accessed December 14, 2022).

68. "Is Truth the Best Medicine for Dying Patients: Letters." *New York Times*, October 23, 2021. https://www.nytimes.com/2021/10/23/opinion/letters/doctors-patients-death.html (accessed December 14, 2022).

Chapter 11

1. Gretchen E. Ely, "What Ireland's History with Abortion Might Teach Us about a Post-Roe America." *PBS NewsHour*, May 18, 2022. https://www.pbs.org/newshour/health/what-irelands-history-with-abortion-might-teach-us-about-a-post-roe-america (accessed September 7, 2022).

2. Gustavo Solis. "Mexican Abortion Clinics Bracing for Influx of Americans." KPBS, June 30, 2022. https://www.kpbs.org/news/border-immigration/2022/06/30/mexican-abortion-clinics-bracing-influx-americans (accessed September 7, 2022).

3. See Andrew Fiala, "Legal but Rare: Toward a Transformative Critical Theory of Abortion and Unwanted Pregnancy." *International Journal of Applied Philosophy* 33: 2 (Fall 2019), pp. 203–20.

4. NARAL Pro-Choice America, "Abortion Access." https://www.prochoiceamerica.org/issue/abortion-access/ (accessed September 3, 2022).

5. National Right to Life Committee (NRLC), "When Does Life Begin?" http://www.nrlc.org/abortion/wdlb/ (accessed September 3, 2022).

6. CA Legislative Information, PART 1.85. End of Life Option Act [443 - 443.22]. https://leginfo.legislature.ca.gov/faces/codes_displayText.xhtml?lawCode=HSC&division=1.&title=&part=1.85.&chapter=&article= (accessed November 7, 2022).

7. Ronald Dworkin, "Life Is Sacred: That's the Easy Part." *New York Times Magazine*, May 16, 1993. https://www.nytimes.com/1993/05/16/magazine/life-is-sacred-thats-the-easy-part.html (accessed September 6, 2022).

8. "Assisted Suicide: The Philosophers' Brief." *New York Review of Books*, March 27, 1997. https://www.nybooks.com/articles/1997/03/27/assisted-suicide-the-philosophers-brief/ (accessed January 24, 2023).

9. Pope John Paul II, *Evangelium Vitae* (The Gospel of Life). https://www.vatican.va/content/john-paul-ii/en/encyclicals/documents/hf_jp-ii_enc_25031995_evangelium-vitae.html (accessed September 6, 2022).

10. See Andrew Fiala, *What Would Jesus Really Do? The Power and Limits of Jesus's Moral Teachings* (Lanham, MD: Rowman and Littlefield, 2007), Chapters 6 and 7.

11. Dayna Ruttenberg, "My Religion Makes Me Pro-abortion." *The Atlantic*, June 14, 2022. https://www.theatlantic.com /family/archive/2022/06/judaism-abortion-rights -religious-freedom/661264/ (accessed September 12, 2022).

12. Ruttenberg, "My Religion Makes Me Pro-abortion."

13. J. Gay-Williams, "The Wrongfulness of Euthanasia," from *Intervention and Reflection: Basic Issues in Medical Ethics* 7th ed. (Belmont, CA: Thomson/Wadsworth, 2004).

14. Judith Jarvis Thomson, "A Defense of Abortion." *Philosophy and Public Affairs* 1: 1 (Fall 1971), pp. 47–66.

15. In the prescientific era, many people held that the egg provided the entire substance and the sperm only gave it a charge or impetus to grow, or that the sperm was "the little man" and only needed a place to grow and obtain nourishment, which the egg provided. We now know about the contribution of both sperm and ovum to the zygote.

16. This issue has recently arisen with developments in stem cell research and cloning.

17. Bonnie Steinbock, *Life before Birth: The Moral and Legal Status of Embryos and Fetuses,* 2nd ed. (Oxford, UK: Oxford University Press, 2011), pp. 46–50.

18. Amicus Curiae Brief by the American College of Obstetricians and Gynecologists (and other medical organizations) submitted to Dobbs v. Jackson, p. 14: https://www.acog .org/-/media/project/acog/acogorg/files/advocacy/amicus -briefs/2021/20210920-dobbs-v-jwho-amicus-brief .pdf?la=en&hash=717DFDD07A03B93A04490E66835BB8C5 (accessed February 6, 2023).

19. Sheryl Gay Stolberg, "Definition of Fetal Viability Is Focus of Debate in Senate." *New York Times*, May 15, 1997, p. A13.

20. Stolberg, "Definition of Fetal Viability." Also see UC Davis Health News, "Racial, Socioeconomic Disparities Fuel Increased Infant Mortality Rates in California," August 11, 2020. https://health.ucdavis.edu/news/headlines /racial-socioeconomic-disparities-fuel-increased -infant-mortality-rates-in-california/2020/08 (accessed September 8, 2022).

21. Don Marquis, "Why Abortion Is Immoral." *Journal of Philosophy* 86: 4 (1989), p. 191.

22. Marquis, "Why Abortion Is Immoral," p. 192.

23. Mary Anne Warren, "On the Moral and Legal Status of Abortion." *Monist* 57, No. 1 (January 1973), pp. 43–61.

24. Warren, "On the Moral and Legal Status of Abortion."

25. William Breitbart et al., "Depression, Hopelessness, and Desire for Hastened Death in Terminally Ill Patients with Cancer." *Journal of the American Medical Association* 284: 22 (2000), pp. 2907–11.

26. Pope John Paul II, *Evangelium Vitae*, para. 66. https://www .vatican.va/content/john-paul-ii/en/encyclicals/documents /hf_jp-ii_enc_25031995_evangelium-vitae.html (accessed February 6, 2023).

27. Seneca, "On the Proper Time to Slip the Cable," in *Seneca: Letters from a Stoic* (New York: Dover, 2016), 176.

28. Two types of cases are to be distinguished from both persistent vegetative state and coma. One is called *locked-in syndrome*, in which a person may be conscious but unable to respond. The other is *dementia*, or senility, in which the content of consciousness is impaired, as in Alzheimer's disease. Neither the person in a persistent vegetative state or coma nor the person with locked-in syndrome or dementia is considered dead by whole-brain death criteria. We may say the person's life has a diminished value, but they are not legally dead. However, some people argue that because the ability to think is what makes us persons, when someone loses this ability, as in the case of PVS, we ought to consider the person dead. Newborns with little or no upper brain or brain function also then and for the same reason could be considered dead. However, these are living, breathing beings, and it would be difficult to think of them as dead in the sense that we would bury them as they are. Rather than declare them dead, as some people have argued, others believe that it would be more practical and reasonable to judge these cases in terms of the kind of life they are living and to ask whether it would be morally permissible to bring about their deaths or allow them to die.

29. See "What Does It Mean to Die?" *The New Yorker*, February 5, 2018. https://www.newyorker.com /magazine/2018/02/05/what-does-it-mean-to-die (accessed September 7, 2022).

30. Robert Miller, *Problems in Health Care Law*, 9th ed. (Sudbury, MA: Jones and Bartlett Publishers), pp. 768ff.

31. Ad Hoc Committee of the Harvard Medical School to Examine the Definition of Brain Death, "A Definition of Irreversible Coma." *Journal of the American Medical Association* 205 (1968), p. 377.

32. "Marital Rape," Rape, Abuse & Incest National Network. http://www.rainn.org/public-policy/sexual-assault-issues/marital-rape (accessed January 24, 2023).

33. "Why Rape Exceptions in Abortion Bans Are More Complicated in Reality," ABC News, August 19, 2022. https://abcnews.go.com/US/rape-exceptions-abortions-bans-complicated-reality/story?id=88237926 (accessed September 15, 2022).

34. Jeff Cercone, "Could 10-Year-Old Rape Victim Have Gotten Abortion in Ohio? Experts Say Exceptions in Law Are Vague." Politifact, July 21, 2022. https://www.politifact.com/article/2022/jul/21/could-10-year-old-rape-victim-have-gotten-abortion/ (accessed January 24, 2023).

35. Joe Biden Press Briefing, July 8, 2022. https://www.whitehouse.gov/briefing-room/speeches-remarks/2022/07/08/remarks-by-president-biden-on-protecting-access-to-reproductive-health-care-services/ (accessed September 8, 2022).

36. Thomson, "A Defense of Abortion."

37. See the summary of these views in Dworkin, "Feminism and Abortion," *New York Review of Books*, June 10, 1993, https://www.nybooks.com/articles/1993/06/10/feminism-and-abortion/ (accessed February 6, 2023).

38. Catharine A. MacKinnon, *Women's Lives, Men's Laws* (Cambridge, MA: Harvard University Press, 2005), p. 140.

39. Bertha Alvarez Manninen, "The Value of Choice and the Choice to Value: Expanding the Discussion about Fetal Life within Prochoice Advocacy." *Hypatia* 28: 3 (Summer 2013), pp. 663–83.

40. See Rosalind Hursthouse, "Virtue Theory and Abortion." *Philosophy and Public Affairs* 20: 3 (1991).

41. Hursthouse, "Virtue Theory and Abortion," p. 242.

42. Thomson, "A Defense of Abortion," pp. 65–66.

43. Rachel Wong, "We Need to Address Questions of gender in Assisted Dying." The Conversation, October 24, 2017. https://theconversation.com/we-need-to-address-questions-of-gender-in-assisted-dying-85892 (accessed January 24, 2023).

44. U.S. Holocaust Museum, https://encyclopedia.ushmm.org/content/en/article/euthanasia-program (accessed September 8, 2022).

45. Peter Singer, *Practical Ethics*, 3rd ed. (Cambridge: Cambridge University Press, 2011), p. 167.

46. Some donors—including former presidential candidate Steve Forbes—threatened to withdraw funding from Princeton University when Princeton hired Singer to teach ethics. See Debra Galant, "Peter Singer Settles In, and Princeton Looks Deeper; Furor over the Philosopher Fades Though Some Discomfort Lingers." *New York Times*, March 5, 2000. https://www.nytimes.com/2000/03/05/nyregion/peter-singer-settles-princeton-looks-deeper-furor-over-philosopher-fades-though.html (accessed January 24, 2023).

47. Harriet McBryde Johnson, "Unspeakable Conversations." *New York Times Magazine*, February 16, 2003. https://www.nytimes.com/2003/02/16/magazine/unspeakable-conversations.html (accessed January 24, 2023).

48. Tom Shakespeare, *Disability Rights and Wrongs* (New York: Routledge, 2006), Chapter 8.

49. John Kelly, "The Answer Is Not Medically Assisted Suicide–Disabled People Demand Full Civil, Human Rights." *The Quincy Sun* (Quincy, MA), August 18, 2022. https://notdeadyet.org/wp-content/uploads/2022/08/Quincy-Sun-page-John-Kelly-op-ed.pdf (accessed September 6, 2022).

50. Susan A. Cohen, "Abortion and Women of Color: The Bigger Picture." *Guttmacher Policy Review* 11: 3 (Summer 2008). https://www.guttmacher.org/sites/default/files/article_files/gpr110302.pdf (accessed January 24, 2023).

51. Guttmacher Institute, "Induced Abortion in the United States (2019)." https://www.guttmacher.org/fact-sheet/induced-abortion-united-states# (accessed January 24, 2023).

52. Cecilia Lenzen, "Facing Higher Teen Pregnancy and Maternal Mortality Rates, Black Women Will Largely Bear the Brunt of Abortion Limits." *The Texas Tribune*, June 30, 2022. https://www.texastribune.org/2022/06/30/texas-abortion-black-women/ (accessed January 24, 2023).

53. See Shyrissa Dobbins-Harris, "The Myth of Abortion as Black Genocide: Reclaiming Our Reproductive Choice." *National Black Law Journal* 26: 1 (2017), 85–127, https://escholarship.org/content/qt0988p9xp/qt0988p9xp.pdf (accessed September 7, 2022).

54. "Female Infanticide," BBC. https://www.bbc.co.uk/ethics/abortion/medical/infanticide_1.shtml (accessed September 7, 2022).

55. Wei Xing Zhu, Li Lu, and Therese Hesketh, "China's Excess Males, Sex Selective Abortion, and One Child Policy: Analysis of Data from 2005 National Intercensus Survey." *British Medical Journal* (April 9, 2009), p. 388. http://dx.doi.org/10.1136/bmj.b1211 (accessed January 24, 2023).

56. Sneha Barol, "A Problem-and-Solution Mismatch: Son Preference and Sex-Selective Abortion Bans." *Guttmacher Policy Review* 15: 2 (Spring 2012). https://www.guttmacher.org/gpr/2012/05/problem-and-solution-mismatch-son-preference-and-sex-selective-abortion-bans (accessed February 6, 2023).

57. Rowena Mason, "The Abortion of Unwanted Girls Taking Place in the UK." *The Telegraph*, January 10, 2013. http://www.telegraph.co.uk/news/uknews/crime/9794577/The-abortion-of-unwanted-girls-taking-place-in-the-UK.html (accessed January 24, 2023).

58. Ed O'Keefe, "Bill Banning 'Sex-Selective Abortions' Fails in the House." *Washington Post*, May 31, 2012. http://www.washingtonpost.com/blogs/2chambers/post/bill-banning-sex-selective-abortions-fails-in-the-house/2012/05/31/gJQAgCYn4U_blog.html (accessed January 24, 2023).

59. "Abortion Bans in Cases of Sex or Race Selection or Genetic Anomaly." Guttmacher Institute, August 1, 2022. https://www.guttmacher.org/state-policy/explore/abortion-bans-cases-sex-or-race-selection-or-genetic-anomaly (accessed September 7, 2022).

60. U.S. Supreme Court, *Roe v. Wade* (1973).

61. U.S. Supreme Court, *Griswold v. Connecticut* (1965).

62. U.S. Supreme Court, *Casey v. Planned Parenthood* (1992).

63. U.S. Supreme Court, *Dobbs v. Jackson* (2022).

64. U.S. Supreme Court, *Dobbs v. Jackson* (2022).

65. U.S. Supreme Court, *Dobbs v. Jackson* (2022).

66. See John Noonan, *The Morality of Abortion* (Cambridge, MA: Harvard University Press, 1970), p. 18ff.

67. U.S. Supreme Court, *Roe v. Wade* (1973), footnote 22.

68. Dorothy E. McBride, *Abortion in the United States: A Reference Book* (Santa Barbara, CA: ABC-CLIO, 2008), p. 7.

69. "Historical Attitudes to Abortion," BBC Ethics Guide. http://www.bbc.co.uk/ethics/abortion/legal/history_1.shtml (accessed January 24, 2023).

70. U.S. Supreme Court, *Roe v. Wade* (1973).

71. U.S. Supreme Court, *Dobbs v. Jackson* (2022).

72. AHA Amicus Curiae Brief in Dobbs v. Jackson Women's Health Organization (September 2021). https://www.historians.org/news-and-advocacy/aha-advocacy/aha-amicus-curiae-brief-in-dobbs-v-jackson-womens-health-organization-(september-2021) (accessed September 6, 2022).

73. Oregon Public Health Division, *Oregon Death with Dignity Act: 2021 Data Summary*, February 2022, https://www.oregon.gov/oha/PH/PROVIDERPARTNERRESOURCES/EVALUATIONRESEARCH/DEATHWITHDIGNITYACT/Documents/year24.pdf (accessed September 7, 2022).

74. Thomas A. Shannon, ed., *Termination of Life on Request and Assisted Suicide (Review Procedures) Act* in *Death and Dying: A Reader* (Lanham, MD: Rowman & Littlefield, 2004), p. 122.

75. "Netherlands Backs Euthanasia for Terminally Ill Children under-12." BBC, October 14, 2020. https://www.bbc.com/news/world-europe-54538288 (accessed September 7, 2022).

76. Chandrika Narayan, "First Child Dies by Euthanasia in Belgium." CNN, September 17, 2016. https://www.cnn.com/2016/09/17/health/belgium-minor-euthanasia (accessed September 7, 2022).

77. Eduard Verhagen and Pieter J. J. Sauer, "The Groningen Protocol—Euthanasia in Severely Ill Newborns." *New England Journal of Medicine* 352 (March 10, 2005), pp. 959–62.

78. Jim Holt, "Euthanasia for Babies?" *New York Times Magazine*, July 10, 2005. https://www.nytimes.com/2005/07/10/magazine/euthanasia-for-babies.html (accessed January 24, 2023).

79. Regional Euthanasia Review Committees, *Annual Report 2019*, April 2020. https://english.euthanasiecommissie.nl/binaries/euthanasiecommissie-en/documenten/publications/annual-reports/2002/annual-reports/annual-reports/Annual+report+2019.pdf (accessed September 7, 2022).

80. Regional Euthanasia Review Committees, *Annual Report 2019*.

81. Oregon Public Health Division, *Oregon Death with Dignity Act*.

82. See Kathleen Kingsbury, "When Is Sedation Really Euthanasia?" *Time*, March 21, 2008. https://content.time.com/time/health/article/0,8599,1724911,00.html (accessed January 24, 2023); and Molly L. Olsen, Keith M. Swetz, and Paul S. Mueller, "Ethical Decision Making with End-of-Life Care: Palliative Sedation and Withholding or Withdrawing Life-Sustaining Treatments." *Mayo Clinic Proceedings* 85: 10 (October 2010), pp. 949–54. https://www.mayoclinicproceedings.org/article/S0025-6196(11)60237-1/fulltext (accessed January 24, 2023).

83. Denise Grady, "Medical and Ethical Questions Raised on Deaths of Critically Ill Patients." *New York Times*, July 20, 2006. https://www.nytimes.com/2006/07/20/health /medical-and-ethical-questions-raised-on-deaths-of -critically-ill.html (accessed January 24, 2023).

84. Quoted in Susan Okie, "Dr. Pou and the Hurricane— Implications for Patient Care during Disasters" *New England Journal of Medicine*, January 3, 2008. https://www .nejm.org/doi/full/10.1056/nejmp0707917 (accessed September 12, 2022).

85. See, for example, Warren S. Quinn, "Actions, Intentions, and Consequences: The Doctrine of Double Effect." *Philosophy and Public Affairs* 18: 4 (Fall 1989), pp. 334–51.

86. Secretary of Health and Human Services, letter of July 12, 2022, https://www.hhs.gov/sites/default/files /emergency-medical-care-letter-to-health-care-providers .pdf (accessed September 12, 2022).

87. *State of Texas v. Xavier Becerra* (2022). https://www .texasattorneygeneral.gov/sites/default/files/images /executive-management/20220714_1-0_Original%20 Complaint%20Biden%20Admin.pdf (accessed September 12, 2022).

88. Adam Omelianchuk, "Dusting Off Double Effect for the Post-Dobbs Era." Hastings Center Bioethics Forum, August 30, 2022. https://www.thehastingscenter.org /dusting-off-double-effect-for-the-post-dobbs-era/ (accessed September 8, 2022).

89. Philippa Foot, "The Problem of Abortion and the Doctrine of the Double Effect." *Oxford Review* 5 (1967): pp. 5–15. https://philpapers.org/archive/FOOTPO-2.pdf (accessed January 24, 2023).

90. Foot, "The Problem of Abortion."

91. American Association of Pro-Life Obstetricians and Gynecologists, "Premature Delivery Is Not Induced Abortion," (no date). https://aaplog.org/premature -delivery-is-not-induced-abortion/ (accessed September 12, 2022).

Chapter 12

1. "'Designer Baby' Is an Epithet" (video in which He explains his rationale). https://www.youtube.com /watch?v=Qv1svMfaTWU (accessed January 27, 2023).

2. Claire Maldarelli, "Engineering HIV-Resistant Babies May Have Accidentally Changed Their Brains." *Popular Science*, February 22, 2019. https://www.popsci.com/china -gene-edited-twins-more-changes (accessed January 27, 2023).

3. Judy Lin, "Farsighted Engineer Invents Bionic Eye to Help the Blind." *UCLA Today*, March 21, 2013. https://newsroom .ucla.edu/stories/wentai-liu-artificial-retina-244393 (accessed January 27, 2023); Hilary Brueck, "This Bionic Eye Could Help the Blind See—from the Back of Their Head." *Fortune*, January 6, 2016. http://fortune.com/2016/01/06 /bionic-eye-monash/ (accessed January 27, 2023).

4. "Cochlear Implants." Mayo Clinic. https://www.mayoclinic .org/tests-procedures/cochlear-implants/about/pac -20385021 (accessed January 27, 2023).

5. Lakshmi Bangalore, "Yale Scientists Repair Injured Spinal Cords Using Patients' Own Stem Cells." *Yale News*, February 22, 2021. https://news.yale.edu/2021/02/22/yale -scientists-repair-injured-spinal-cords-using-patients -own-stem-cells (accessed January 27, 2023).

6. Leon Kass, "Ageless Bodies, Happy Souls." *The New Atlantis* 1 (Spring 2003). https://www.thenewatlantis.com /publications/ageless-bodies-happy-souls (accessed January 27, 2023).

7. Michael J. Sandel, "The Case against Perfection." *The Atlantic*, April 2004. https://www.theatlantic.com/magazine /archive/2004/04/the-case-against-perfection/302927/ (accessed January 27, 2023).

8. Guy Kahane, "Mastery without Mystery: Why There Is no Promethean Sin in Enhancement." *Journal of Applied Philosophy* 28: 4 (2011), pp. 355–68.

9. Nick Bostrom, "In Defense of Posthuman Dignity." *Bioethics* 19: 3 (2005), p. 211.

10. "Close-up of Richard Jenne, the Last Child Killed by the Head Nurse at the Kaufbeuren-Irsee Euthanasia Facility." United States Holocaust Memorial Museum. https:// collections.ushmm.org/search/catalog/pa10049 (accessed January 27, 2023).

11. Susan B. Levin, *Posthuman Bliss? The Failed Promise of Transhumanism* (Oxford, UK: Oxford University Press, 2021), p. 145.

12. Julian Savulescu and Gary Kahane, "The Moral Obligation to Create Children with the Best Chance of the Best Life." *Bioethics* 23: 5 (2009), pp. 274–290.

13. Savulescu and Kahane, "The Moral Obligation to Create Children," p. 282.

14. Rosemarie Garland-Thomson, "Integrating Disability, Trans-forming Feminist Theory." *NWSA Journal* 14: 3 (2002), p. 21.

15. Rosemarie Garland-Thomson, "How We Got to CRISPR: The Dilemma of Being Human." *Perspectives in Biology and Medicine* 63: 1 (Winter 2020), p. 34.

16. Francis Fukuyama, *Our Posthuman Future: Consequences of the Biotechnology Revolution* (New York: Farrar, Straus, and Giroux, 2002).

17. Bostrom, "In Defense of Posthuman Dignity." *Bioethics* 19: 3 (2005), p. 213.

18. Leon Kass, "The Wisdom of Repugnance," in *Life Liberty & the Defense of Dignity: The Challenge for Bioethics* (San Francisco: Encounter Books, 2002), p. 150.

19. Leon Kass, "Organs for Sale," in *Life Liberty & the Defense of Dignity: The Challenge for Bioethics* (San Francisco: Encounter Books, 2002), p. 179.

20. Abby Phillip, "A Paralyzed Woman Flew an F-35 Fighter Jet in a Simulator—Using Only Her Mind." *Washington Post*, March 3, 2015. https://www.washingtonpost.com/news /speaking-of-science/wp/2015/03/03/a-paralyzed -woman-flew-a-f-35-fighter-jet-in-a-simulator-using-only -her-mind/ (accessed January 27, 2023).

21. "'We Did It!' Brain-Controlled 'Iron Man' Suit Kicks Off World Cup." *NBC News*, June 12, 2014. http://www.nbcnews.com /storyline/world-cup/we-did-it-brain-controlled-iron-man -suit-kicks-world-n129941 (accessed January 27, 2023).

22. NIH, "Cochlear Implants," March 24, 2021, https://www .nidcd.nih.gov/health/cochlear-implants (accessed January 27, 2023).

23. Jerry Adler, "Why Brain-to-Brain Communication Is No Longer Unthinkable." *Smithsonian*, May 2015. http://www .smithsonianmag.com/innovation/why-brain-brain -communication-no-longer-unthinkable-180954948 /?no-ist (accessed January 27, 2023).

24. James Gorman, "In a First, Experiment Links Brains of Two Rats." *New York Times*, February 28, 2013. http://www .nytimes.com/2013/03/01/science/new-research -suggests-two-rat-brains-can-be-linked.html?_r=0. (accessed January 27, 2023).

25. "Man Wriggles Rat's Tail Using Only His Thoughts." NBC News, April 9, 2013 https://www.nbcnews.com/id /wbna5148081, (accessed February 6, 2023).

26. Kelly Servick, "In a First, Brain Implant Lets Man with Complete Paralysis Spell Out Thoughts: 'I Love My Cool Son.'" *Science*, March 22, 2022. https://www.science.org /content/article/first-brain-implant-lets-man-complete -paralysis-spell-out-thoughts-i-love-my-cool-son (accessed January 27, 2023).

27. Stefan Lorenz Sorgner, *We Have Always Been Cyborgs* (Bristol, UK: Bristol University Press, 2022).

28. Sammy Mngqosini, "Ice Skating Set to Gradually Raise Minimum Competition Age from 15 to 17 after Kamila Valieva Doping Scandal." CNN, June 7, 2022, https://www.cnn .com/2022/06/07/sport/kamila-valieva-ice-skating-minimum -age-spt-intl/index.html (accessed January 27, 2023).

29. Rose Eveleth, "Should Oscar Pistorius's Prosthetic Legs Disqualify Him from the Olympics?" *Scientific American*, July 24, 2012 http://www.scientificamerican.com/article.cfm?id= scientists-debate-oscar-pistorius-prosthetic-legs-disqualify -him-olympics (accessed January 27, 2023).

30. "Blade Jumper Puts Tokyo Discontent Aside, Focuses on 'Being the Best.'" *Kyodo News*, August 24, 2021. https://english.kyodonews.net/news/2021/08 /557aece39c83-blade-jumper-puts-olympic-discontent -aside-focuses-on-being-the-best.html (accessed January 22, 2023).

31. Alan Schwarz, "Drowned in a Stream of Prescriptions." *New York Times*, February 2, 2013. http://www.nytimes.com/2013/02/03 /us/concerns-about-adhd-practices-and-amphetamine -addiction.html (accessed January 22, 2023).

32. Will Oremus, "The New Stimulus Package." *Slate*, March 27, 2013. http://www.slate.com/articles/technology /superman/2013/03/adderall_ritalin_vyvanse_do_smart _pills_work_if_you_don_t_have_adhd.2.html (accessed January 22, 2023).

33. Will Oremus, "Spark of Genius." *Slate*, April 1, 2013. http:// www.slate.com/articles/technology/superman/2013/04 /tdcs_and_rtms_is_brain_stimulation_safe_and_effective .html (accessed January 27, 2023).

34. Rachel Wurzman et al., "An Open Letter Concerning Do-It-Yourself Users of Transcranial Direct Current Stimulation." *Annals of Neurology* 80: 1 (2016), pp. 1–4.

35. Juli Fraga, "After IVF, Some Struggle with What to Do with Leftover Embryos." NPR, August 20, 2016. https://www .npr.org/sections/health-shots/2016/08/20/489232868 /after-ivf-some-struggle-with-what-to-do-with-leftover -embryos (accessed January 27, 2023).

36. Teresa Woodard, "Surrogate Mother Who Refused Abortion Launches Effort to Change Laws." WFAA, December 21, 2018. https://www.wfaa.com/article/news/surrogate -mother-who-refused-abortion-launches-effort-to-change -laws/287-624403667 (accessed January 27, 2023).

37. Chhavi Sachdev, "Once the Go-to Place for Surrogacy, India Tightens Control over Its Baby Industry." *The World*,

July 4, 2018. https://theworld.org/stories/2018-07-04/once-go-place-surrogacy-india-tightens-control-over-its-baby-industry (accessed January 27, 2023).

38. Holly Honderich, "Nebraska Grandmother Acts as Surrogate for Gay Son." BBC News, December 2, 2020. https://www.bbc.com/news/world-us-canada-47780124 (accessed January 27, 2023).

39. Danny Lewis, "US Panel Deems 'Three Parent Babies' Ethical to Test." *Smithsonian*, February 8, 2016. http://www.smithsonianmag.com/smart-news/us-panel-deems-three-parent-babies-ethical-test-180958057/?no-ist (accessed January 27, 2023).

40. "Text: Bush Announces Position on Stem Cell Research." *Washington Post*, August 9, 2001. http://www.washingtonpost.com/wp-srv/onpolitics/transcripts/bushtext_080901.htm (accessed January 27, 2023).

41. Bill Weir, "Adult Stem Cells: A Piece of My Heart, from Cells in My Arm." *ABCNews*, January 28, 2013. http://abcnews.go.com/Health/stem-cells-bill-weir-nightline-sees-cells-turned/story?id=18252405 (accessed January 27, 2023).

42. "Nobel Prize in Physiology or Medicine." Nobelprize.org, press release, October 8, 2012. http://www.nobelprize.org/nobel_prizes/medicine/laureates/2012/press.html

43. David Cyranoski, "How Human Embryonic Stem Cells Sparked a Revolution." *Nature*, March 20, 2018, https://www.nature.com/articles/d41586-018-03268-4 (accessed January 27, 2023).

44. *Scientific American*, July 2005, A6–A27.

45. Henry Fountain, "A First: Organs Tailor-Made with Body's Own Cells." *New York Times*, September 15, 2012. https://www.nytimes.com/2012/09/16/health/research/scientists-make-progress-in-tailor-made-organs.html (accessed January 27, 2023).

46. Henry Fountain, "Groundbreaking Surgery for Girl Born without Windpipe." *New York Times*, April 30, 2013. https://www.nytimes.com/2013/04/30/science/groundbreaking-surgery-for-girl-born-without-windpipe.html (accessed January 27, 2023).

47. Henry Fountain, "Young Girl Given Bioengineered Windpipe Dies." *New York Times*, July 7, 2013. http://www.nytimes.com/2013/07/08/science/young-girl-given-bioengineered-windpipe-dies.html (accessed January 27, 2023).

48. Maggie Fox, "Researchers Grow Kidney, Intestine from Stem Cells." *NBC News*, October 8, 2015. http://www.nbcnews.com/health/health-news/researchers-grow-kidney-intestine-stem-cells-n441066 (accessed January 27, 2023).

49. Jessica Hamzelou, "This Company Is About to Grow New Organs in a Person for the First Time." *MIT Tech Review*, August 25, 2022. https://www.technologyreview.com/2022/08/25/1058652/grow-new-organs/ (accessed January 27, 2023).

50. Bangalore, "Yale Scientists Repair Injured Spinal Cords."

51. Linda Rath, "Electrically Stimulated Stem Cells Aid Stroke Recovery in Rodents, Stanford Researchers Find." *Stanford Medicine News*, April 14, 2022. https://med.stanford.edu/news/all-news/2022/04/electrical-stimulation-stem-cells-stroke.html (accessed January 27, 2023).

52. "FDA Warns about Stem Cell Therapies." FDA.gov, September 3, 2019. https://www.fda.gov/consumers/consumer-updates/fda-warns-about-stem-cell-therapies (accessed January 27, 2023).

53. Kass, "Ageless Bodies, Happy Souls."

54. "Final Report of the National Academies' Human Embryonic Stem Cell Research Advisory Committee and 2010 Amendments to the National Academies' Guidelines for Human Embryonic Stem Cell Research." National Academies.org, 2010, Appendix C, p. 23, National Academies Press. http://www.nap.edu/openbook.php?record_id=12923&page=23#p2001b5399970023001 (accessed January 27, 2023).

55. Nicholas Wade, "Group of Scientists Drafts Rules on Ethics for Stem Cell Research." *New York Times*, April 27, 2005. https://www.nytimes.com/2005/04/27/health/group-of-scientists-drafts-rules-on-ethics-for-stem-cell-research.html (accessed January 27, 2023).

56. Gautam Naik, "Scientists Make First Embryo Clones from Adults." *Wall Street Journal*, April 17, 2014. http://www.wsj.com/articles/SB10001424052702303626804579507593658361428 (accessed January 27, 2023).

57. John D. Loike and Alan Kadish, "The Reproductive Technology Advances No One Asked For." *The New Scientist*, June 22, 2022. https://www.the-scientist.com/news-opinion/opinion-the-reproductive-technology-advances-no-one-asked-for-70160 (accessed January 27, 2023).

58. Jason Thompson, "Here, Kitty, Kitty, Kitty, Kitty, Kitty!" *San Francisco Chronicle*, February 24, 2002, D6.

59. *New York Times*, October 8, 2004, A24.

60. Peter Fimrite, "Pet-Cloning Business Closes—Not 'Commercially Viable.'" *San Francisco Chronicle*, October 11, 2006, B9.

61. James Barron, "Biotech Company to Auction Chances to Clone a Dog." *New York Times*, May 21, 2008, A17. https://www.nytimes.com/2008/05/21/us/21dog.html (accessed January 27, 2023).

62. American Anti-Vivisection League, "Animal Cloning," https://aavs.org/our-work/campaigns/animal-cloning/ (accessed February 6, 2023).

63. Nick Collins, "Human Cloning 'within 50 Years.'" *Telegraph*, December 18, 2012. https://www.telegraph.co.uk/news/science/science-news/9753647/Human-cloning-within-50-years.html (accessed January 27, 2023).

64. "Copied Cat Hardly Resembles Original." CNN.com, January 21, 2003.

65. Discussed in Michael J. Sandel, *The Case against Perfection: Ethics in the Age of Genetic Engineering* (Cambridge, MA: Harvard University Press, 2009), Chapter 1.

66. "Couple 'Choose' to Have Deaf Baby." BBC, April 8, 2002. http://news.bbc.co.uk/2/hi/health/1916462.stm (accessed January 27, 2023). Also see Darshak M. Sanghavi, "Wanting Babies Like Themselves, Some Parents Choose Genetic Defects." *New York Times*, December 5, 2006. http://www.nytimes.com/2006/12/05/health/05essa.html (accessed January 27, 2023).

67. Tom Abate, "Genome Discovery Shocks Scientists." *San Francisco Chronicle*, February 11, 2001, A1. https://www.sfgate.com/news/article/Genome-Discovery-Shocks-Scientists-Genetic-2953173.php (accessed January 27, 2023).

68. *New York Times*, October 21, 2004, A23.

69. Nicholas Wade, "In the Genome Race, the Sequel Is Personal." *New York Times*, September 4, 2007. http://www.nytimes.com/2007/09/04/science/04vent.html (accessed January 27, 2023).

70. Tom Abate, "Proofreading the Human Genome." *San Francisco Chronicle*, October 7, 2002, E1; Nicholas Wade, "Gene-Mappers Take New Aim at Diseases." *New York Times*, October, 30, 2002, A21.

71. Wade, "Gene-Mappers."

72. David Nield, "Researchers Identify a Potential 'Thinness' Gene That Stops Mice Putting on Weight." *Science Alert*, May 22, 2020. https://www.sciencealert.com/researchers-find-a-new-thinness-gene-that-could-help-some-people-tackle-weight-gain (accessed January 27, 2023).

73. Nicholas D. Kristof, "Building Better Bodies." *New York Times*, August 25, 2004. http://www.nytimes.com/2004/08/25/opinion/building-better-bodies.html (accessed January 27, 2023).

74. World Anti-Doping Agency, "Gene Doping" https://www.wada-ama.org/en/gene-doping (accessed February 6, 2023).

75. "Genetic Privacy." *Nature*, January 17, 2013. http://www.nature.com/news/genetic-privacy-1.12238 (accessed January 27, 2023).

76. Andrew Pollack, "Panel Sees No Unique Risk from Genetic Engineering." *New York Times*, July 28, 2004, A13. https://www.nytimes.com/2004/07/28/us/panel-sees-no-unique-risk-from-genetic-engineering.html (accessed January 27, 2023).

77. Jane E. Brody, "Facing Biotech Foods without the Fear Factor." *New York Times*, January 11, 2005, D7. https://www.nytimes.com/2005/01/11/health/facing-biotech-foods-without-the-fear-factor.html (accessed January 27, 2023).

78. Pollack, "Panel Sees No Unique Risk."

79. Brody, "Facing Biotech Foods."

80. "GMO Facts." Non-GMO Project, https://www.nongmoproject.org/gmo-facts/understanding-low-and-high-risk/#:~:text=The%20USDA%20estimates%20that%20up,planted%20in%20GMO%20commodity%20crops (accessed January 27, 2023).

81. "GMO Labeling." Whole Foods Market.com https://www.wholefoodsmarket.com/quality-standards/gmo-labeling (accessed January 27, 2023).

82. Tom Philpott, "How GMOs Unleashed a Pesticide Gusher." *Mother Jones*, October 3, 2012. http://www.motherjones.com/tom-philpott/2012/10/how-gmos-ramped-us-pesticide-use (accessed January 27, 2023).

83. See "Genetically Modified Foods: Harmful or Helpful." *ProQuest*. http://www.csa.com/discoveryguides/gmfood/overview.php

84. *New York Times*, January 1, 2005, D7.

85. *New York Times*, January 1, 2005, D7.

86. Bartosz Brzezinski, "Like It or Not, Gene-Edited Crops Are Coming to the EU." *Politico*, October 4, 2022. https://www.politico.eu/article/gene-edited-crop-eu-climate-change-drought-agriculture/ (accessed January 27, 2023).

87. Charles Xu, "Nothing to Sneeze at: the Allergenicity of GMOs" Harvard Blog on GMO's, August 10, 2015 (accessed February 6, 2023).

88. Sean Poulter, "Can GM Food Cause Immunity to Antibiotics?" *Daily Mail* http://www.dailymail.co.uk/health/article-128312/Can-GM-food-cause-immunity-antibiotics.html (accessed January 27, 2023).

89. See www.greennature.com.

90. James Gallagher, "Xenotransplantation: Are Pigs the Future of Organ Transplants?" BBC, March 13, 2022. https://www.bbc.com/news/health-60708120 (accessed January 27, 2023).

91. Benjamin Smood et al., "Genetically-Engineered Pigs as Sources for Clinical Red Blood Cell Transfusion: What Pathobiological Barriers Need to Be Overcome?" *Blood Reviews* 35 (2019), pp. 7–17.

Chapter 13

1. Oral arguments before the U.S. Supreme Court, *Students for Fair Admissions v. University of North Carolina*, October 31, 2022, U.S. Supreme Court No. 21-707 p. 4–5, https://www.supremecourt.gov/oral_arguments/argument_transcripts/2022/21-707_9o6b.pdf (accessed December 12, 2022).

2. Oral Arguments, *Students for Fair Admissions*, p. 69.

3. Oral Arguments, *Students for Fair Admissions*, pp. 69–70. https://www.supremecourt.gov/oral_arguments/argument_transcripts/2022/21-707_9o6b.pdf (accessed December 12, 2022).

4. Kristen Griest, "With Equal Opportunity Comes Equal Responsibility." Modern War Institute, February 25, 2021. https://mwi.usma.edu/with-equal-opportunity-comes-equal-responsibility-lowering-fitness-standards-to-accommodate-women-will-hurt-the-army-and-women/ (accessed December 12, 2022).

5. See Mary Anne Warren, "Secondary Sexism and Quota Hiring." *Philosophy and Public Affairs* 6: 3 (Spring 1977), pp. 240–261.

6. Tanya L. Domi, "Women in Combat: Policy Catches Up with Reality." *New York Times*, February 8, 2013. http://www.nytimes.com/2013/02/09/opinion/women-in-combat-policy-catches-up-with-reality.html?_r=0 (accessed December 12. 2022).

7. Preamble to the Civil Rights Act of 1964. http://www.ourdocuments.gov/doc.php?flash=true&doc=97&page=transcript (accessed December 12, 2022).

8. EEO Policy Statement, U.S. Equal Employment Opportunity Commission, April 2021. https://www.eeoc.gov/eeo-policy-statement (accessed December 12, 2022).

9. See Linda Alcoff, "Critical Philosophy of Race." *Stanford Encyclopedia of Philosophy*, 2021. https://plato.stanford.edu/entries/critical-phil-race/ (accessed December 12, 2022).

10. Cornel West, Foreword to Kimberlé Crenshaw, Neil Cotanda, Gary Peller, and Kendall Thomas, eds., *Critical Race Theory: The Key Writings that Formed the Movement* (New York: The New Press, 1995), p. xi.

11. Rashawn Ray and Alexandra Gibbons, "Why Are States Banning Critical Race Theory." Brookings Institute, November 2021. https://www.brookings.edu/blog/fixgov/2021/07/02/why-are-states-banning-critical-race-theory/ (accessed December 12, 2022).

12. State of Florida, "Governor Ron DeSantis Signs Legislation to Protect Floridians from Discrimination and Woke Indoctrination," April 22, 2022, https://www.flgov.com/2022/04/22/governor-ron-desantis-signs-legislation-to-protect-floridians-from-discrimination-and-woke-indoctrination/ (accessed December 12, 2022).

13. State of Florida, "Governor Ron DeSantis Signs Legislation."

14. See https://www.nytimes.com/interactive/2019/08/14/magazine/1619-america-slavery.html (accessed December 12, 2022); and Nikole Hannah-Jones, *The 1619 Project: A New Origin Story* (New York: Random House, 2021).

15. See https://trumpwhitehouse.archives.gov/wp-content/uploads/2021/01/The-Presidents-Advisory-1776-Commission-Final-Report.pdf (accessed December 12, 2022).

16. See Robert L. Anemone, *Race and Human Diversity: A Bio-cultural Approach*, Second Edition (New York: Routledge, 2019), Chapter 1.

17. L. Luigi Luca Cavalli-Sforza, Paolo Menozzi, and Alberto Piazza, *History and Geography of Human Genes* (Princeton, NJ: Princeton University Press, 1994), p. 19.

18. Rodrigo Perez Ortega, "Human Geneticists Curb Use of the Term 'Race' in Their Papers." *Science*, December 2, 2021. https://www.science.org/content/article/human-geneticists-curb-use-term-race-their-papers (accessed December 12, 2022).

19. Robert Gooding-Williams, "W. E. B. Du Bois." *The Stanford Encyclopedia of Philosophy* (Spring 2020 Edition). https://plato.stanford.edu/archives/spr2020/entries/dubois (accessed December 12, 2022).

20. Kwame Anthony Appiah, "Racisms," in *Anatomy of Racism*, ed. David Goldberg (Minneapolis: University of Minnesota Press, 1990), p. 5.

21. Lucius Outlaw, Jr., "If Not Races, Then What? Toward a Revised Understanding of Bio-Social Groupings." *Graduate Faculty Philosophy Journal* 35: 1–2 (2014), pp. 275–296.

22. Lucius Outlaw, Jr., "Toward a Critical Theory of 'Race,'" in Bernard Boxill, ed. *Race and Racism* (Oxford: Oxford University Press, 2001), p. 69.

23. Ibram X. Kendi, *How to Be an Anti-Racist* (New York: Penguin Random House, 2019), 6.

24. See Sally Haslanger, "Oppressions: Racial and Other," in *Racism in Mind* (Ithaca, NY: Cornell University Press, 2004).

25. National Center for Education Statistics, Fast Facts SAT 2021. https://nces.ed.gov/fastfacts/display.asp?id=171 (accessed December 12, 2022).

26. Ember Smith and Richard V. Reeves, "SAT Math Scores Mirror and Maintain Racial Inequity." Brookings Institute, December 1, 2020. https://www.brookings.edu/blog/up-front/2020/12/01/sat-math-scores-mirror-and-maintain-racial-inequity/ (accessed December 12, 2022).

27. Scott Jaschik, "SAT Scores Down Again, Wealth Up Again." *Inside Higher Ed*, August 29, 2007. http://www.insidehighered.com/news/2007/08/29/sat#ixzz2Rzt6hJJ3 (accessed April 30, 2013).

28. "Admissions without SAT or ACT," *Inside Higher Ed*. March 28, 2022. https://www.insidehighered.com/admissions/article/2022/03/28/cal-state-will-do-admissions-without-sat-or-act#:~:text=By&text=The%20California%20State%20University%20Board,won't%20look%20at%20them (accessed December 12, 2022).

29. See "Are Asian American College Applicants at a Disadvantage? Supreme Court Debate Stirs Fear." *LA Times*, November 4, 2022, https://www.latimes.com/california/story/2022-11-04/supreme-court-debate-on-affirmative-action-capture-asian-american-fears (accessed December 12, 2022).

30. See Rosalind Chou and Joe Feagin, *The Myth of the Model Minority: Asian Americans Facing Racism* (Boulder, CO: Paradigm Publishing, 2008).

31. T. L. Dixon, "Network News and Racial Beliefs: Exploring the Connection between National Television News Exposure and Stereotypical Perceptions of African Americans," *Journal of Communication* 58 (2008), pp. 321–37.

32. T. L. Dixon, "Crime News and Racialized Beliefs: Understanding the Relationship between Local News Viewing and Perceptions of African Americans and Crime." *Journal of Communication* 58 (2008), pp. 106–25.

33. U.S. Census, "Equal Pay Day: March 15, 2022." https://www.census.gov/newsroom/stories/equal-pay-day.html (accessed December 12, 2022).

34. Payscale: "2022 State of the Gender Pay Gap Report." https://www.payscale.com/research-and-insights/gender-pay-gap/ (accessed December 12, 2022).

35. Kimberlé Williams Crenshaw, "The Structural and Political Dimensions of Intersectional Oppression," in Patrick R. Grzanka, ed. *Intersectionality: A Foundations and Frontiers Reader* (Boulder, CO: Westview Press, 2014), p. 17.

36. Crenshaw, "Intersectional Oppression," p. 17.

37. "Black Man Fatally Shot by Akron Police Officers Was Unarmed, Authorities Say." *PBS Newshour*, July 3, 2022. https://www.pbs.org/newshour/nation/black-man-fatally-shot-by-akron-police-officers-was-unarmed-authorities-say (accessed December 12, 2022).

38. Jordan Culver, "Trump Says Violent Minneapolis Protests Dishonor George Floyd's Memory, Twitter Labels 'Shooting' Tweet as 'Glorifying Violence.'" *USA Today*, May 29, 2020. https://www.usatoday.com/story/news/politics/2020/05/28/george-floyd-donald-trump-twitter-jacob-frey-thugs/5281374002/ (accessed December 12, 2022).

39. Max Cohen, "Trump: Black Lives Matter Is a Symbol of Hate." *Politico*, September 1, 2020. https://www.politico.com/news/2020/07/01/trump-black-lives-matter-347051 (accessed December 12, 2022).

40. "Ex-Cops Kueng, Thao Sentenced for Violating George Floyd's Rights." *Politico*, July 2022, https://www.politico.com/news/2022/07/27/alexander-kueng-tou-george-floyd-sentencing-00048196 (accessed December 12, 2022).

41. Thomas Paine, *Rights of Man*, in *Thomas Paine: Collected Writings* (New York: Library of America, 1955, reprinted 2012), p. 465.

42. Executive Order 10925 (1961). https://www.presidency.ucsb.edu/documents/executive-order-10925-establishing-the-presidents-committee-equal-employment-opportunity (accessed January 20, 2023).

43. Bruce P. Lapenson, *Affirmative Action and the Meanings of Merit* (Lanham, MD: University Press of America, 2009), p. 3.

44. Linda Greenhouse, "University of Michigan Ruling Endorses the Value of Campus Diversity." *New York Times*, June 24, 2003, pp. A1, A25.

45. This aspect of the bill confirmed the "disparate impact" notion of the 1971 U.S. Supreme Court ruling in *Griggs v. Duke Power Company*, which required companies to revise their business practices that perpetuated past discrimination. This was weakened by the Court's 1989 ruling in *Wards Cove Packing Co. v. Antonio*, which, among other things, put the burden of proof on the employee to show that the company did not have a good reason for some discriminatory business practice.

46. Equal Opportunity Employment Commission, http://www.eeoc.gov/federal/otherprotections.cfm (accessed December 12, 2022).

47. http://www.lillyledbetter.com/

48. David A. Harris, "Driving While Black: Racial Profiling on Our Nation's Highways." *ACLU*, June 7, 1999. http://www.aclu.org/racial-justice/driving-while-black-racial-profiling-our-nations-highways (accessed December 12, 2022).

49. Donald Tomaskovic-Devey and Patricia Warren, "Explaining and Eliminating Racial Profiling." *American Sociological Association Contexts* (Spring 2009), http://contexts.org/articles/spring-2009/explaining-and-eliminating-racial-profiling/ (accessed December 12, 2022).

50. Harris, "Driving While Black."

51. Bill Weir and Nick Capote, "NYPD's Controversial Stop-and-Frisk Policy: Racial Profiling or 'Proactive Policing'?" ABC's *Nightline*, May 1, 2013, http://abcnews.go.com/US/nypds-controversial-stop-frisk-policy-racial-profiling-proactive/story?id=19084229#.UYLbtSvEo_s (accessed December 12, 2022).

52. "Black New Yorkers Are Twice as Likely to Be Stopped by the Police, Data Shows" *New York Times*, September 23, 2020, https://www.nytimes.com/2020/09/23/nyregion/nypd-arrests-race.html (accessed December 12, 2022).

53. SB 1070. http://www.azleg.gov/legtext/49leg/2r/bills/sb1070s.pdf (accessed December 12, 2022).

54. SB 1070. http://www.azleg.gov/legtext/49leg/2r/bills/sb1070s.pdf (accessed December 12, 2022).

55. Diane McWhorter, "The Strange Career of Juan Crow." *New York Times*, June 16, 2012. http://www.nytimes.com/2012/06/17/opinion/sunday/no-sweet-home-alabama.html (accessed December 12, 2022).

56. Julia Preston, "Immigration Crackdown Also Snares Americans." *New York Times*, December 13, 2011, http://www.nytimes.com/2011/12/14/us/measures-to-capture-illegal-aliens-nab-citizens.html?pagewanted=all (accessed December 12, 2022).

57. Ilya Somin, "End Racial Profiling in Immigration Enforcement." *Reason*, August 6, 2022, https://reason.com/volokh/2022/08/06/end-racial-profiling-in-immigration-enforcement/ (accessed December 12, 2022).

58. Libby Sander, "6 Imams Removed from Flight for Behavior Deemed Suspicious." *New York Times*, November 22, 2006, http://www.nytimes.com/2006/11/22/us/22muslim.html?bl&ex=1164517200&en=24531ca1fa7314e1&ei=5087%0A (accessed December 12, 2022).

59. Amy Gardner, "9 Muslim Passengers Removed from Jet." *Washington Post*, January 2, 2009, http://www.washingtonpost.com/wp-dyn/content/article/2009/01/01/AR2009010101932.html?hpid=topnews (accessed December 12, 2022). Also see Amy Gardner and Spencer S. Hsu, "Airline Apologizes for Booting 9 Muslim Passengers from Flight." *Washington Post*, January 3, 2009, http://www.washingtonpost.com/wp-dyn/content/article/2009/01/02/AR2009010201695.html (accessed December 12, 2022).

60. Sam Harris, "In Defense of Profiling." Sam Harris Blog, April 2012, http://www.samharris.org/blog/item/in-defense-of-profiling (accessed December 12, 2022).

61. Randall Kennedy, "Suspect Policy." *New Republic*, September 13 and 20, 1999, p. 35.

62. Heather MacDonald, "The Myth of Racial Profiling." *City Journal* 11: 2 (Spring 2001). http://www.city-journal.org/html/11_2_the_myth.html (accessed December 12, 2022).

63. U.S. Department of Justice, "Federal Jury Finds Three Men Guilty of Hate Crimes in Connection with the Pursuit and Killing of Ahmaud Arbery," February 22, 2022. https://www.justice.gov/opa/pr/federal-jury-finds-three-men-guilty-hate-crimes-connection-pursuit-and-killing-ahmaud-arbery (accessed December 12, 2022).

64. U.S. Department of Justice, "Federal Jury Finds Three Men Guilty."

65. "Hate Crimes," FBI. https://www.fbi.gov/investigate/civil-rights/hate-crimes (accessed December 12, 2022).

66. "Hate Crimes," National Institute of Justice. http://www.nij.gov/topics/crime/hate-crime/ (accessed December 12, 2022).

67. Brian Levin, "The Long Arc of Justice: Race, Violence and the Emergence of Hate Crime Law," in *Hate Crimes*, ed. Barbara Perry (Westport, CT: Greenwood Publishing, 2008), p. 1:8.

68. "Hate Crime Statistics, 2019," FBI. https://ucr.fbi.gov/hate-crime/2019/topic-pages/incidents-and-offenses (accessed December 12, 2022).

69. "Amish Beard Cutting Case," FBI, February 8, 2013. http://www.fbi.gov/news/stories/2013/february/16-sentenced-in-amish-beard-cutting-case (accessed December 12, 2022).

70. Robert K. Fullinwider, "Affirmative Action and Fairness." *Report from the Institute for Philosophy and Public Policy* 11: 1 (Winter 1991), pp. 10–13.

71. John F. Kain, Daniel M. O'Brien, and Paul A. Jargowsky, *Hopwood and the Top 10 Percent Law: How They Have Affected the College Enrollment Decisions of Texas High School Graduates*. Report for the Texas Schools Project at the University of Texas at Dallas, March 25, 2005, https://citeseerx.ist.psu.edu/document?repid=rep1&type=pdf&doi=bd1caa21bef3170ddb1b4f-c568116723b2ddbf97 (accessed January 20, 2023).

72. "Despite Diversity Efforts, UC Minority Enrollment Down since Prop. 209," KQED, February 24, 2013. https://www.kqed.org/news/57464/despite-diversity-efforts-uc-minority-enrollment-down-since-prop-209 (accessed December 12, 2022).

73. Kevin Carey, "A Detailed Look at the Downside of California's Ban on Affirmative Action." *New York Times*, August 21, 2022. https://www.nytimes.com/2020/08/21/upshot/00up-affirmative-action-california-study.html, (accessed December 12, 2022).

74. https://studentsforfairadmissions.org/ (accessed December 12, 2022).

75. "Remarks on Signing the Bill Providing Restitution for the Wartime Internment of Japanese-American Civilians" August 10, 1988. https://www.reaganlibrary.gov/archives/speech/remarks-signing-bill-providing-restitution-wartime-internment-japanese-american#:~:text=The%20legislation%20that%20I%20am,with%20property%20than%20with%20honor (accessed December 12, 2022).

76. "Reparations Are for Descendants of Black Slaves, Says California Official," NBC News, January 28, 2022. https://www.nbcnews.com/news/nbcblk/reparations-are-descendants-black-slaves-says-california-official-rcna13955 (accessed December 12, 2022).

77. California Truth and Healing Council, https://tribalaffairs.ca.gov/cthc/ (accessed December 12, 2022).

78. "The Pope's Apology to Indigenous People Doesn't Go Far Enough, Canada Says," NPR, July 28, 2022. https://www.npr.org/2022/07/28/1114207125/canada-pope-apology-indigenous (accessed December 12, 2022).

79. "Canada Pledges $40 Billion in Talks over Rampant Abuses of Indigenous Children" NPR, December 14, 2012 (note: that figure is in Canadian dollars). https://www.npr.org/2021/12/14/1064081667/canada-pledges-40-billion-abuses-indigenous-children (accessed December 12, 2022).

80. Stephen Carter, *Reflections of an Affirmative Action Baby* (New York: Basic Books, 1991).

81. Professor Jonathan Leonard, cited in the *San Francisco Examiner*, September 29, 1991.

82. *Time*, May 27, 1991, p. 23.

83. Amy Argetsinger, "Princeton's Former President Challenges 'Bastions of Privilege,'" *San Francisco Chronicle*, April 17, 2004, p. A5.

84. *Ricci v. DeStefano*, 557 U.S. (2009).

Chapter 14

1. Derrick Johnson and Wisdom Cole, "NAACP CEO: Biden's Reported Plan to Cancel Student Debt Isn't Enough" CNN, August 24, 2022. https://www.cnn.com/2022/08/24/perspectives/student-loan-debt-biden-naacp/index.html (accessed December 16, 2022).

2. Quoted in "'Slap in the Face': Republicans Enraged after Biden 'Forgives' Billions in Student Debt," *National Review*, August 24, 2022. https://www.nationalreview.com/news/republicans-enraged-after-biden-forgives-billions-of-dollars-of-student-debt-insulting-hard-working-americans/ (accessed August 24, 2022).

3. Thomas Massaro, *Living Justice: Catholic Social Teaching in Action*, 2nd classroom ed. (Lanham, MD: Rowman & Littlefield, 2011), p. 2.

4. Pope Francis, *Fratelli Tutti* (All Brothers), 2020. https://www.vatican.va/content/francesco/en/encyclicals/documents/papa-francesco_20201003_enciclica-fratelli-tutti.html (accessed August 24, 2022).

5. Pope Francis, *Fratelli Tutti*.

6. Sohail H. Hashmi, "The Problem of Poverty in Islamic Ethics," in *Poverty and Morality: Religious and Secular Perspectives*, eds. William Galston and Peter Hoffenberg (Cambridge, UK: Cambridge University Press, 2010), 197.

7. John Stuart Mill, *Principles of Political Economy with Some of Their Applications to Social Philosophy*, ed. William J. Ashley (originally published 1909; from Library of Economics and Liberty), bk. 2, Chapter 13, sec. 2. http://www.econlib.org/library/Mill/mlP26.html (accessed December 16, 2022).

8. John Stuart Mill, "The Negro Question" (1850), in *The Collected Works of John Stuart Mill, Volume XXI—Essays on Equality, Law, and Education*, ed. John M. Robson (Toronto: University of Toronto Press; London: Routledge and Kegan Paul, 1984). http://oll.libertyfund.org/title/255/21657 (accessed December 16, 2022).

9. John Stuart Mill, *Chapters on Socialism* (1879), in *The Collected Works of John Stuart Mill, Volume V—Essays on Economics and Society Part II*, ed. John M. Robson (Toronto: University of Toronto Press; London: Routledge and Kegan Paul, 1967). http://oll.libertyfund.org/title/232/16747 (accessed March 15, 2016).

10. John Stuart Mill, *Principles of Political Economy*, bk. 5, Chapter 11, sec. 44.

11. Immanuel Kant, *Lectures on Ethics* (Indianapolis: Hackett, 1981), p. 194.

12. Immanuel Kant, *The Metaphysics of Morals* (Cambridge: Cambridge University Press, 2017), p. 110.

13. Kant, *The Metaphysics of Morals*, p. 110.

14. See Kevin E. Dodson, "Kant's Socialism: A Philosophical Reconstruction." *Social Theory and Practice* 29: 4 (2003), pp. 525–538; and Harry van der Linden, *Kantian Ethics and Socialism* (Indianapolis: Hackett Publishing, 1988).

15. See Alexander W. Cappelen and Bertil Tungodden, "Tax Policy and Fair Inequality," in *Taxation: Philosophical Perspectives*, Martin O'Neill and Shepley Orr, eds. (Oxford, UK: Oxford University Press, 2018), pp. 111–123.

16. Tibor R. Machan, "Libertarian Justice: A Natural Rights Approach," in *Liberty and Justice*, Tibor R. Machan, ed. (Stanford, CA: Hoover Institution Press, 2006), p. 111.

17. We associate the saying "From each according to his ability, to each according to his need" with Karl Marx, but it actually originated with the "early French socialists of the Utopian school, and was officially adopted by German socialists in the Gotha Program of 1875." Nicholas Rescher, *Distributive Justice* (Indianapolis: Bobbs-Merrill, 1966), pp. 73–83.

18. James S. Fishkin, *Justice, Equal Opportunity, and the Family* (New Haven, CT: Yale University Press, 1983), p. 4.

19. Bernard Williams, "The Idea of Equality," in *Philosophy, Politics and Society* (second series), ed. Peter Laslett and W. G. Runciman (Oxford, UK: Basil Blackwell, 1962), pp. 110–131.

20. Harry Frankfurt, "Equality as a Moral Ideal." *Ethics* 98 (1987), pp. 21–43.

21. John H. Schaar, "Equality of Opportunity, and Beyond," in *NOMO SIX: Equality*, ed. J. Chapman and R. Pennock (New York: Atherton Press, 1967).

22. Schaar, "Equality of Opportunity."

23. See Thomas Nagel, "Justice," in *What Does It All Mean: A Very Short Introduction to Philosophy* (New York: Oxford University Press, 1987), pp. 76–86.

24. Robert Nozick, *Anarchy, State, and Utopia* (New York: Basic Books, 1977), p. 169.

25. Milton Friedman, *Capitalism and Freedom* (Chicago: University of Chicago Press, 1982), p. 133.

26. Friedman, *Capitalism and Freedom*, p. 133.

27. Stephen Nathanson, "John Stuart Mill on Economic Justice and the Alleviation of Poverty." *Journal of Social Philosophy* 43: 2 (Summer 2012), pp. 161–176.

28. Stephen Holmes, "Welfare and the Liberal Conscience." *Report from the Institute for Philosophy and Public Policy* 15: 1 (Winter 1995), pp. 1–6.

29. Morton White, *The Philosophy of the American Revolution* (New York: Oxford University Press, 1978), p. 161. Italics added by White and editors.

30. Robert B. Reich, "The Other Surplus Option," *New York Times*, August 11, 1999. http://www.nytimes.com/1999/08/11/opinion/the-other-surplus-option.html (accessed December 16, 2022).

31. John Rawls, *A Theory of Justice* (Cambridge, MA: Harvard University Press, 1971).

32. Rawls, *A Theory of Justice*, p. 302.

33. Rawls, *A Theory of Justice*, pp. 100–103.

34. Rawls, *A Theory of Justice*, pp. 100–103.

35. Rawls, *A Theory of Justice*, p. 73.

36. John Rawls, *Political Liberalism*, expanded ed. (New York: Columbia University Press, 2005).

37. Amitai Etzioni, Andrew Volmert, and Elanit Rothschild, *The Communitarian Reader: Beyond the Essentials* (Lanham, MD: Rowman & Littlefield, 2004), p. 21.

38. Amitai Etzioni, *Next: The Road to the Good Society* (New York: Basic Books, 2001), p. 101.

39. Amartya Sen, *Development as Freedom* (Oxford, UK: Oxford University Press, 1999).

40. U.S. Census Bureau, "Income and Poverty in the United States: 2020." https://www.census.gov/library/publications/2021/demo/p60-273.html (accessed December 16, 2022).

41. U.S. Census Bureau, "Poverty Thresholds 2022." https://www.census.gov/data/tables/time-series/demo/income-poverty/historical-poverty-thresholds.html (accessed December 16, 2022).

42. U.S. Census Bureau, "Income and Poverty in the United States: 2020."

43. "HUD 2020 Annual Homeless Assessment," March 18, 2021. https://www.hud.gov/press/press_releases_media_advisories/hud_no_21_041 (accessed December 16, 2022).

44. "World's Billionaires List: The Richest in 2022," March 2022. https://www.forbes.com/billionaires (accessed December 16, 2022).

45. Martin Crutsinger, "Greenspan Talk Doesn't Roil Markets," *The Washington Post*, March 13, 2007. http://www.washingtonpost.com/wp-dyn/content/article/2007/03/13/AR2007031300744.html (accessed January 20, 2023).

46. Dominic Rushe, "The Richest Americans Became 40% Richer during the Pandemic," *The Guardian*, October 5, 2021. https://www.theguardian.com/media/2021/oct/05/richest-americans-became-richer-during-pandemic (accessed December 16, 2022).

47. Chuck Collins, Omar Ocampo, and Sophia Paslaski, "Billionaire Bonanza 2020," Institute for Policy Studies. https://ips-dc.org/billionaire-bonanza-2020/ (accessed December 16, 2022).

48. Derek Saul, "CEOs Made 324 Times More than Their Median Workers in 2021, Union Report Finds" *Forbes*, July 18, 2022. https://www.forbes.com/sites/dereksaul/2022/07/18/ceos-made-324-times-more-than-their-median-workers-in-2021-union-report-finds/?sh=224bfefeac52 (accessed December 16, 2022).

49. Leila Bengali and Mary Daly, "U.S. Economic Mobility: The Dream and the Data," Federal Reserve Bank of San Francisco Economic Letter, 2013. https://www.frbsf.org/economic-research/files/el2013-06.pdf (accessed August 26, 2022.

50. Mark Robert Rank, Lawrence M. Eppard, and Heather E. Bullock, "The United States Is No Longer a Land of Upward Mobility and Opportunity," in *Poorly Understood: What America Gets Wrong about Poverty* (New York: Oxford, 2021), p. 131.

51. U.S. Census Bureau, "Income and Poverty in the United States: 2020."

52. Aditya Aladangady and Akila Forde, "Wealth Inequality and the Racial Wealth Gap," Federal Reserve Notes, October 22, 2021. https://www.federalreserve.gov/econres/notes/feds-notes/wealth-inequality-and-the-racial-wealth-gap-20211022.htm (accessed December 16, 2022).

53. William A. Darity Jr. and A. Kirsten Mullen, *From Here to Equality, 2nd ed.: Reparations for Black Americans in the Twenty-First Century* (Chapel Hill: University of North Carolina Press, 2022). Preface to the 2nd ed.

54. U.S. Census, "Equal Pay Day: March 15, 2022." https://www.census.gov/newsroom/stories/equal-pay-day.html (accessed December 16, 2022).

55. Rawls, *A Theory of Justice*, p. 86.

56. Rawls, *A Theory of Justice*, p. 244.

57. Rawls, *Political Liberalism*, p. lvii.

58. Yang 2020, "The Freedom Dividend." https://2020.yang2020.com/policies/the-freedom-dividend/ (accessed December 16, 2022).

59. U.S. Department of Labor, State Minimum Wage Laws. https://www.dol.gov/agencies/whd/minimum-wage/state (accessed December 16, 2022).

60. Roger Daniels, *Franklin D. Roosevelt: The War Years, 1939–1942* (Champaign: University of Illinois, 2016), p. 265.

61. See the Living Wage Calculator, http://livingwage.mit.edu/ (accessed .August 26, 2022)

62. United States Census Bureau, "U.S. Poverty Rate Is 12.8% but Varies Significantly by Age Groups" https://www.census.gov/library/stories/2022/10/poverty-rate-varies-by-age-groups.html (accessed January 20, 2023).

63. United Nations, "OHCHR and the Human Rights Dimension of Poverty." https://www.ohchr.org/en/poverty (accessed December 16, 2022).

64. Sabrina Tavernise, "Education Gap Grows between Rich and Poor, Studies Say," *New York Times*, February 9, 2012, http://www.nytimes.com/2012/02/10/education/education-gap-grows-between-rich-and-poor-studies-show.html?pagewanted=all&_r=0 (accessed December 16, 2022).

65. Poverty. https://www.healthypeople.gov/2020/topics-objectives/topic/social-determinants-health/interventions-resources/poverty#:~:text=Residents%20of%20impoverished%20neighborhoods%20or,mortality%2C%20and%20lower%20life%20expectancy.&text=Some%20population%20groups%20living%20in,adverse%20health%20outcomes%20than%20others (accessed August 26, 2022).

66. David Himmelstein, Elizabeth Warren, Deborah Thorne, and Steffie Woolhandler, "MarketWatch: Illness and Injury as Contributors to Bankruptcy." *Health Affairs* Web Exclusive, February 2, 2005, W5–62. As cited in T. R. Reid, *The Healing of America: A Global Quest for Better, Cheaper, and Fairer Health Care* (New York: Penguin, 2009).

67. David U. Himmelstein, Robert M. Lawless, Deborah Thorne, Pamela Foohey, and Steffie Woolhandler, "Medical Bankruptcy: Still Common Despite the Affordable Care Act." *American Journal of Public Health* 109: 3 (2019), pp. 431–433.

68. Nina Owcharenko Schaefer, "Repealing Obamacare and Getting Health Care Right." *The Heritage Foundation*, November 9, 2010, http://www.heritage.org/research /reports/2010/11/repealing-obamacare-and-getting -health-care-right (accessed December 16, 2022).

69. Beatrix Hoffman, *Health Care for Some: Rights and Rationing in the United States since 1930* (Chicago: University of Chicago Press, 2012).

70. Hoffman, *Health Care for Some*.

71. Melanie Hanson, "Student Loan Debt vs Other Debts." Education Data Initiative, October 2021. https:// educationdata.org/student-loan-debt-vs-other-debts (accessed December 16, 2022).

72. Hanson, "Student Loan Debt."

Chapter 15

1. Development Initiatives, "0.7% Aid Target Factsheet." https://devinit.org/resources/0-7-aid-target-2/ (accessed February 2, 2023).

2. George Ingram, "What Every American Should Know about US Foreign Aid." Brookings Institution, October 2, 2019. https://www.brookings.edu/opinions/what-every -american-should-know-about-u-s-foreign-aid/ (accessed February 2, 2023).

3. Donor Tracker, "At a Glance: US." https://donortracker.org /donor_profiles/united-states (accessed February 2, 2023).

4. World Bank, *Poverty and Shared Prosperity 2022* (Washington, DC: The World Bank), p. xiii. https:// openknowledge.worldbank.org/bitstream/handle /10986/37739/9781464818936.pdf?sequence= 65&isAllowed=y (accessed February 2, 2023).

5. Ian Goldin and Mike Mariathasan, *The Butterfly Defect: How Globalization Creates Systematic Risks, and What to Do about It* (Princeton, NJ: Princeton University Press, 2014).

6. "Within Our Grasp: A World Free of Poverty—World Bank Group President Jim Yong Kim's Speech at Georgetown University," April 2, 2013. http://www.worldbank.org /en/news/speech/2013/04/02/world-bank-group -president-jim-yong-kims-speech-at-georgetown -university (accessed February 2, 2023).

7. António Guterres, "UN Secretary General's Statement as the World Population Hits 8 Billion," November 14, 2022. https:// www.un.org/africarenewal/magazine/november-2022 /un-secretary-general%E2%80%99s-statement-world -population-hits-8-billion (accessed February 2, 2023).

8. Thomas Pogge, "Are We Violating the Human Rights of the World's Poor?" *Yale Human Rights & Development Journal* 14: 2 (2011), pp. 1–33.

9. Thomas Pogge, *World Poverty and Human Rights* (Cambridge, UK: Polity Press, 2008), pp. 211–12.

10. Kok-Chor Tan, *What Is This Thing Called Global Justice?* (New York: Routledge, 2017), p. 125.

11. Peter Singer, "Famine, Affluence, and Morality." *Philosophy and Public Affairs* 1: 3 (Spring 1972), p. 231.

12. Michael Schur, Foreword to Peter Singer, *The Life You Can Save*, 10th Anniversary ed. (Bainbridge Island, WA: The Life You Can Save, 2019), no page numbers.

13. Dylan Matthews, "Join Wall Street, Save the World." *Washington Post*, May 31, 2013. http://www.washingtonpost .com/blogs/wonkblog/wp/2013/05/31/join-wall-street -save-the-world/ (accessed February 2, 2023).

14. Peter Singer, *The Most Good You Can Do* (New Haven, CT: Yale University Press, 2015), p. 47.

15. Singer, *The Most Good You Can Do*, p. 113.

16. Garrett Hardin, "Living on a Lifeboat." *BioScience* 24: 10 (October 1974), pp. 561–68.

17. Thomas Aquinas, *Summa Theologiae*, trans. by the Fathers of the English Dominican Province, Online ed., II–II, Q 66, Art. 7. http://www.newadvent.org/summa/3066.htm (accessed February 2, 2023).

18. Alan B. Krueger and Jitka Maleckova, "Does Poverty Cause Terrorism?" *New Republic*, June 24, 2002, p. 27.

19. John Rawls, *The Law of Peoples* (Cambridge, MA: Harvard University Press, 2001).

20. Rawls, *The Law of Peoples*, p. 37.

21. Teju Cole, "The White Savior Industrial Complex." *The Atlantic*, March 21, 2012. https://www.theatlantic.com /international/archive/2012/03/the-white-savior -industrial-complex/254843/ (accessed February 2, 2023).

22. Edward Said, *Orientalism* (London: Penguin, 1977).

23. Kwasi Wiredu, "Conceptual Decolonization as an Imperative in Contemporary African Philosophy: Some Personal Reflections." *Rue Descartes* 36 (2002), https://doi.org/10.3917/rdes.036.0053, p. 9.

24. Krushil Watene, "Transforming Global Justice Theorizing: Indigenous Philosophies," in *The Oxford Handbook of Global Justice*, ed. Thom Brooks (Oxford: Oxford University Press, 2020), p. 174.

25. Eddy Souffrant, *Global Development Ethics: A Critique of Global Capitalism* (Lanham, MD: Rowman and Littlefield, 2019), p. 182.

26. Souffrant, *Global Development Ethics*, p. 243.

27. "'White Saviour' Row: David Lammy Denies Snubbing Comic Relief." *The Guardian*, February 28, 2019. https://www.theguardian.com/tv-and-radio/2019/feb/28/david-lammy-stacey-dooley-comic-relief-white-saviour-row-uganda-red-nose-day-film (accessed February 2, 2023).

28. Peter Singer, "Who Needs More White Saviors?" *Project Syndicate*, April 3, 2019. https://www.project-syndicate.org/commentary/white-people-helping-africans-extreme-poverty-by-peter-singer-2019-04 (accessed February 2, 2023).

29. Robert Wright, "Two Years Later, a Thousand Years Ago." *New York Times*, Op-Ed., September 11, 2003. https://www.nytimes.com/2003/09/11/opinion/two-years-later-a-thousand-years-ago.html (accessed February 2, 2023).

30. Thomas L. Friedman, *The World Is Flat: A Brief History of the Twenty-First Century* (New York: Farrar, Straus, and Giroux, 2005), p. 8.

31. Jan Scholte, *Globalization: A Critical Introduction*, 2nd ed. (New York: Palgrave MacMillan, 2005), pp. 15–17.

32. Scholte, *Globalization: A Critical Introduction*.

33. Samuel P. Huntington, *The Clash of Civilizations* (New York: Simon and Schuster, 1996).

34. Michael D. Barr, *Cultural Politics and Asian Values: The Tepid War* (London: Routledge, 2002), Chapter 3.

35. U.S Public Law 116-76. https://www.govinfo.gov/content/pkg/PLAW-116publ76/pdf/PLAW-116publ76.pdf (accessed February 2, 2023).

36. Amartya Sen, *Human Rights and Asian Values* (New York: Carnegie Council on Human Rights, 1997), 31.

37. See essays in Ali Mohammadi, *Islam Encountering Globalization* (London: Routledge, 2002).

38. United Nations Development Programme, "Arab Human Development Report 2022," June 24, 2022, p. 3. https://www.undp.org/arab-states/publications/arab-human-development-report-2022-expanding-opportunities-inclusive-and-resilient-recovery-post-covid-era) (accessed February 2, 2023).

39. World Economic Forum, *Global Gender Gap Report 2021*, March 2021, p. 26. https://www3.weforum.org/docs/WEF_GGGR_2021.pdf (accessed February 2, 2023).

40. See, for example: Siobhán O'Grady, "As Egypt Hosts COP27, Its Most Famous Political Prisoner May Die, Family Warns." *Washington Post*, November 3, 2022. https://www.washingtonpost.com/world/2022/11/03/alaa-prisoner-egypt-cop27/ (accessed February 2, 2023).

41. "Qatar: Six Things You Need to Know about the Hosts of the 2022 FIFA World Cup." Amnesty International, November 16, 2022. https://www.amnesty.org/en/latest/news/2022/11/qatar-six-things-you-need-to-know-about-the-hosts-of-the-2022-fifa-world-cup/ (accessed February 2, 2023).

42. See https://www.bloomberg.com/news/articles/2022-11-18/qatar-said-to-ban-alcohol-sales-in-world-cup-stadiums (accessed February 2, 2023).

43. World Bank, Fact Sheet: An Adjustment to Global Poverty Lines." https://www.worldbank.org/en/news/factsheet/2022/05/02/fact-sheet-an-adjustment-to-global-poverty-lines (accessed February 2, 2023).

44. World Bank, *Poverty and Shared Prosperity 2022*, p. xiii. https://openknowledge.worldbank.org/bitstream/handle/10986/37739/9781464818936.pdf?sequence=65&isAllowed=y (accessed February 2, 2023).

45. Bangladesh minimum wage at https://www.minimum-wage.org/international/bangladesh (accessed February 2, 2023).

46. See https://theconversation.com/years-after-the-rana-plaza-tragedy-bangladeshs-garment-workers-are-still-bottom-of-the-pile-159224 (accessed February 20, 2023).

47. Jeffrey D. Sachs, "The End of Poverty." *Time*, March 6, 2005. https://content.time.com/time/subscriber/article/0,33009,1034738-1,00.html (accessed February 2, 2023).

48. World Health Organization, "Malaria," June 28, 2019. http://www.who.int/features/factfiles/malaria/en/ (accessed February 2, 2023).

49. World Health Organization, World Malaria Report 2021, https://www.who.int/teams/global-malaria-programme/reports/world-malaria-report-2021 (accessed February 20, 2023).

50. Worldometer, "Life Expectancy of the World Population." https://www.worldometers.info/demographics/life-expectancy/ (accessed February 2, 2023).

51. World Bank Open Data, https://data.worldbank.org/ (accessed February 2, 2023).

52. World Bank Open Data, https://data.worldbank.org/.

53. Frantz Fanon, *The Wretched of the Earth* (New York: Grove Press, 1968).

54. Fanon, *The Wretched of the Earth*, p. 96.

55. Dinesh D'Souza, "Two Cheers for Colonialism." *Chronicle of Higher Education*, May 10, 2002. https://www.chronicle.com/article/two-cheers-for-colonialism/ (accessed February 2, 2023).

56. Dinesh D'Souza, *Obama's America: Unmaking the American Dream* (Washington, DC: Regnery Publishing, 2012), 219.

57. D'Souza, "Two Cheers for Colonialism."

58. "United States Summary Information," Environmental Working Group, Farm Subsidies. https://farm.ewg.org/ (accessed February 2, 2023).

59. Gary S. Fields, *Working Hard, Working Poor: A Global Journey* (Oxford, UK: Oxford University Press, 2011), p. 114.

60. See NAFTA, "Renegotiation." Encyclopedia Britannica. https://www.britannica.com/event/North-American-Free-Trade-Agreement/Renegotiation (accessed February 2, 2023).

61. Tim Johnson, "Free Trade: As U.S. Corn Flows South, Mexicans Stop Farming." *McClatchy News*, February 1, 2011. https://account.mcclatchydc.com/paywall/subscriber-only?resume=24609829&intcid=ab_archive (accessed February 2, 2023).

62. Jim Acosta, "U.S., Other Powers Kick Russia out of G8." *CNN*, March 24, 2014. http://www.cnn.com/2014/03/24/politics/obama-europe-trip/ (accessed February 2, 2023).

63. Adrian Morrow, "Toronto Police Were Overwhelmed at G20, Review Reveals." *Globe and Mail*, June 23, 2011. https://www.theglobeandmail.com/news/toronto/toronto-police-were-overwhelmed-at-g20-review-reveals/article584399/ (accessed February 2, 2023).

64. Naomi Klein, interview on PBS, April 21, 2001. http://www.pbs.org/wgbh/commandingheights/shared/minitext/int_naomiklein.html (accessed February 2, 2023).

65. Noam Chomsky, quoted in Jack Lule, *Globalization and Media: Global Village of Babel* (Lanham, MD: Rowman & Littlefield, 2012), p. 11.

66. Joseph E. Stiglitz, *Globalization and Its Discontents* (New York: Norton, 2003), p. 19.

67. Stiglitz, *Globalization and Its Discontents*, pp. 80–81.

68. Jagdish Bhagwati, *In Defense of Globalization* (Oxford, UK: Oxford University Press, 2007); see especially the Afterword.

69. See Rory Horner et al., "How Anti-Globalisation Switched from a Left to a Right-Wing Issue—and Where It Will Go Next," January 25, 2016. https://theconversation.com/how-anti-globalisation-switched-from-a-left-to-a-right-wing-issue-and-where-it-will-go-next-90587; or Stefanie Walter, "The Backlash against Globalization." *Annual Review of Political Science* 24: 1 (2021), pp. 421–42.

70. Loretta Napoleoni, *Rogue Economics* (New York: Seven Stories Press, 2011), p. 195.

71. See Pogge, *World Poverty and Human Rights*, Section 9.2.

72. Jeffrey Sachs, *The End of Poverty: Economic Possibilities for Our Time* (New York: Penguin Press, 2005), Chapter 12.

73. Wright, "Two Years Later."

74. See for example, "The Monterrey Consensus on Financing for Development." https://www.un.org/en/development/desa/population/migration/generalassembly/docs/globalcompact/A_CONF.198_11.pdf (accessed February 2, 2023).

75. Poncie Rutsch, "Guess How Much of Uncle Sam's Money Goes to Foreign Aid. Guess Again!" *NPR*, February 10, 2015. http://www.npr.org/sections/goatsandsoda/2015/02/10/383875581/guess-how-much-of-uncle-sams-money-goes-to-foreign-aid-guess-again (accessed February 2, 2023).

76. Ken Hackett, "Surprise! Americans Want to 'Slash' Foreign Aid—to 10 Times Its Current Size." *Christian Science Monitor*, March 7, 2011. http://www.csmonitor.com/Commentary/Opinion/2011/0307/Surprise!-Americans-want-to-slash-foreign-aid-to-10-times-its-current-size (accessed February 2, 2023).

77. Hackett, "Surprise! Americans Want to 'Slash' Foreign Aid."

78. Donor Tracker, "At a Glance: US."

79. See Borgen Report, "The Most Generous Nations Helping the World's Poor." https://borgenproject.org/most-generous-donor-nations/ (accessed February 2, 2023).

80. Mark Anderson, "UK Passes Bill to Honour Pledge of 0.7% Foreign Aid Target." *The Guardian*, March 9, 2015. http://www.theguardian.com/global-development/2015/mar/09/uk-passes-bill-law-aid-target-percentage-income (accessed February 2, 2023).

81. Thomas Fuller and Keith Bradsher, "Deadly Collapse in Cambodia Renews Safety Concerns." *New York Times*, May 16, 2013 http://www.nytimes.com/2013/05/17 /world/asia/cambodia-factory-ceiling-collapse.html? _r=0 (accessed February 2, 2023).

82. Charles Duhigg and David Barboza, "In China, Human Costs Are Built into an iPad." *New York Times*, January 25, 2012. http://www.nytimes.com/2012/01/26/business /ieconomy-apples-ipad-and-the-human-costs-for -workers-in-china.html?pagewanted=all (accessed February 2, 2023).

83. See "The International Accord for Health and Safety in the Textile and Garment Industry." https://internationalaccord .org/ (accessed February 2, 2023).

84. Clean Clothes Campaign, Brief on Pakistan, November 2022. https://cleanclothes.org/file-repository/deadly -incidents-pakistan-brief-nov-2022.pdf/view (accessed February 2, 2023).

85. Peter Grier, "The Walt Disney Company Pulls Out of Bangladesh: Will That Make Workers Safer?" *Christian Science Monitor*, May 3, 2013. http://www.csmonitor.com /USA/2013/0503/The-Walt-Disney-Company-pulls-out -of-Bangladesh-Will-that-make-workers-safer (accessed February 2, 2023).

86. See Alex Nicholls and Charlotte Opal, *Fair Trade: Market Driven Ethical Consumption* (London: SAGE Publications, 2005).

87. See Peter Griffiths, "Ethical Objections to Fair Trade." *Journal of Business Ethics* 105 (2012), pp. 357–73.

88. José Jorge Mendoza, *The Moral and Political Philosophy of Immigration : Liberty, Security, and Equality* (Lanham, MD: Lexington Books, 2016), p. xii.

89. See "Europe Welcomes Ukrainian Refugees but Others, Less So," February 28, 2022. https://www.npr.org/2022 /02/28/1083423348/europe-welcomes-ukrainian -refugees-but-others-less-so (accessed February 2, 2023).

Chapter 16

1. Rafael Ballester-Arnal, et al., "Pornography Consumption in People of Different Age Groups: An Analysis Based on Gender, Contents, and Consequences." *Sexuality Research and Social Policy* (May 2022).

2. Emma Wood, "Does Ethical Porn Exist?" The Ethics Centre, May 18, 2016. https://ethics.org.au/does-ethical-porn -exist/ (accessed February 19, 2023).

3. H.R. 8404—Respect for Marriage Act. https://www .congress.gov/bill/117th-congress/house-bill/8404 /text (accessed December 21, 2022).

4. Louise Perry, *The Case against the Sexual Revolution* (Cambridge, UK: Polity, 2022), pp. 66–67.

5. This paragraph is based on Raja Halwani, *Philosophy of Love, Sex, and Marriage: An Introduction*, 2nd ed. (New York: Routledge, 2018), pp. 4–5.

6. Aristotle, *The Nicomachean Ethics* Book VIII, Part 3 (Ross Translation at http://classics.mit.edu/Aristotle /nicomachaen.8.viii.html).

7. Camille Paglia, *Sex, Art, and American Culture* (New York: Vintage Books, 1992), p. 113.

8. "The Third Gender and Hijras." Harvard Divinity School, 2018. https://hwpi.harvard.edu/files/rpl/files/gender _hinduism.pdf?m=1597338930 (accessed February 19, 2023).

9. "India Court Recognises Transgender People as Third Gender." BBC News, April 15, 2014. https://www.bbc.com /news/world-asia-india-27031180 (accessed February 19, 2023).

10. "Female Genital Mutilation Fact Sheet." World Health Organization, January 31, 2023. http://www.who.int /mediacentre/factsheets/fs241/en/ (accessed February 19, 2023).

11. James Ciment, "Senegal Outlaws Female Genital Mutilation." *British Medical Journal* 3 (February 6, 1999), p. 348; and Joel E. Frader et al., "Female Genital Mutilation." *Pediatrics* 102: 1 (July 1998), p. 153.

12. Ciment, "Senegal Outlaws Female Genital Mutilation"; Frader et al., "Female Genital Mutilation."

13. Elisabeth Rosenthal, "Genital Cutting Raises by 50% Likelihood Mothers or Their Newborns Will Die, Study Finds." *New York Times*, June 2, 2006, p. A10. http://www.nytimes .com/2006/06/02/world/africa/02mutilation.html?_r=0 (accessed February 19, 2023).

14. "Female Genital Mutilation Fact Sheet," World Health Organization.

15. Heidi E. Fjeld, *The Return of Polyandry: Kinship and Marriage in Central Tibet* (New York: Berghahn Books, 2022).

16. John Stuart Mill, "Letter to Lord Amberley," February 2, 1870, in *The Collected Works of John Stuart Mill*, vol. 17, ed. Francis E. Mineka and Dwight N. Lindley (Toronto: University of Toronto Press; London: Routledge and Kegan Paul, 1972), p. 1525.

17. Jeremy Bentham, *Principles of Penal Law* in *Works of Jeremy Bentham* (Edinburgh: W. Tait, 1838), vol. 1, pt. 2, p. 546.

18. Carol Pateman, "What's Wrong with Prostitution?" Chapter 7 in *The Sexual Contract* (Stanford, CA: Stanford University Press, 1988).

19. Immanuel Kant, *Lectures on Ethics* (Indianapolis: Hackett Publishing, 1981), pp. 169–71.

20. Immanuel Kant, "On Defiling Oneself by Lust," in *The Metaphysics of Morals* in *Kant, Practical Philosophy* (Cambridge, UK: Cambridge University Press, 1999), pp. 548–49.

21. Kant, *Metaphysics of Morals*, pp. 427–28.

22. Kant, *Metaphysics of Morals*, pp. 497–98.

23. Onora O'Neill, "Between Consenting Adults." *Philosophy & Public Affairs* 14: 3 (1985), p. 272.

24. Finnis, "Law, Morality, and "Sexual Orientation," p. 1064.

25. Jessica Flanigan, "The Case for Decriminalizing Sex Work," in *The Routledge Handbook of Philosophy of Sex and Sexuality*, eds. Lori Watson, Clare Chambers, and Brian D. Earp (New York: Routledge, 2022), pp. 534–35.

26. Carole Pateman, *The Sexual Contract*, preface to the 30th anniversary ed. (Cambridge, UK: Polity Press, 2018),. p. xi.

27. "262 Celebrities, Politicians, CEOs, and Others Who Have Been Accused of Sexual Misconduct since April 2017." Vox. https://www.vox.com/a/sexual-harassment-assault -allegations-list, updated through July 16, 2021 (accessed February 19, 2023).

28. Samantha Granville, "Harvey Weinstein Found Guilty in Second Sex Crimes Trial." BBC News, December 20, 2022. https://www.bbc.com/news/world-us-canada-63867784 (accessed February 19, 2023).

29. "Donald Trump: Taped Comments about Women." New York Times, October 8, 2016. https://www.nytimes .com/2016/10/08/us/donald-trump-tape-transcript.html (accessed February 19, 2023).

30. Susan Chira, "Numbers Hint at Why #MeToo Took Off: The Sheer Number Who Can Say Me Too." *New York Times*, February 21, 2018, https://www.nytimes.com/2018/02 /21/upshot/pervasive-sexual-harassment-why-me-too -took-off-poll.html (accessed February 19, 2023).

31. "Fast Facts: Preventing Sexual Violence." CDC. https:// www.cdc.gov/violenceprevention/sexualviolence /fastfact.html (accessed February 19, 2023).

32. Susan Brownmiller, *Against Our Will: Men, Women, and Rape* (New York: Ballantine Books, 1993, originally published in 1975), p. 391.

33. "Perpetrators of Sexual Violence: Statistics." Rape, Abuse, and Incest National Network (RAINN). https://www.rainn .org/statistics/perpetrators-sexual-violence (accessed February 19, 2023).

34. "Scope of the Problem: Statistics." Rape, Abuse, and Incest National Network (RAINN). https://www.rainn.org /statistics/scope-problem (accessed February 19, 2023).

35. Sarah Johnson, "'Marry Your Rapist' Laws in 20 Countries Still Allow Perpetrators to Escape Justice." *The Guardian*, April 14, 2021. https://www.theguardian.com/global -development/2021/apr/14/marry-your-rapist-laws-in -20-countries-still-allow-perpetrators-to-escape-justice (accessed February 19, 2023).

36. "Intimate Partner Sexual Violence." Rape, Abuse, and Incest National Network. https://www.rainn.org/articles /intimate-partner-sexual-violence (accessed February 19, 2023).

37. Manveena Suri and Jack Bantock, "Landmark Indian Court Ruling Says Rape Includes Marital Rape and Extends Abortion Rights to 24 Weeks." CNN, September 29, 2022. https://www.cnn.com/2022/09/29/asia/india-supreme -court-marital-rape-abortion-intl/index.html (accessed February 19, 2023).

38. Wikipedia, "Marital Rape Laws by Country." https://en .wikipedia.org/wiki/Marital_rape_laws_by_country (accessed February 19, 2023).

39. "Campus Sexual Violence: Statistics." Rape, Abuse, and Incest National Network. https://www.rainn.org/statistics /campus-sexual-violence (accessed February 19, 2023).

40. U.S Supreme Court, *Obergefell v. Hodges*, Decided June 26, 2015.

41. Abby Ohlheiser, "Kentucky Clerk Kim Davis on Gay Marriage Licenses." *Washington Post*, September 1, 2015. https://www.washingtonpost.com/news/acts-of-faith /wp/2015/09/01/kentucky-clerk-kim-davis-on-gay -marriage-licenses-it-is-a-heaven-or-hell-decision/ (accessed February 19, 2023).

42. Justice Thomas concurring, *Dobbs v. Jackson* (2022), p. 3. https://www.supremecourt.gov/opinions /21pdf/19-1392_6j37.pdf (accessed February 19, 2023).

43. President Joe Biden Signing Statement, White House, December 13, 2022. https://www.whitehouse.gov /briefing-room/speeches-remarks/2022/12/13/remarks -by-president-biden-and-vice-president-harris-at-signing -of-h-r-8404-the-respect-for-marriage-act/ (accessed February 19, 2023).

44. Justice A. Scalia dissent, *Lawrence v. Texas* (02–102) 539 U.S. 558 (2003), no page numbers. https://www.law.cornell.edu/supct/html/02-102.ZD.html (accessed February 19, 2023).

45. Defense of Marriage Act, http://www.gpo.gov/fdsys/pkg/BILLS-104hr3396enr/pdf/BILLS-104hr3396enr.pdf (accessed February 19, 2023).

46. Lindsay Wise, "In Federal Gay-Marriage Case, More Than 1,100 Benefits at Stake." *McClatchy News*, March 27, 2013. https://www.mcclatchydc.com/news/nation-world/national/article24747409.html (accessed February 19, 2023).

47. *United States v. Windsor* 570 U.S. ___ (2013), pp. 25–26.

48. Thom Shanker, "Partners of Gays in Service Are Granted Some Benefits." *New York Times*, February 11, 2013. http://www.nytimes.com/2013/02/12/us/partners-of-gay-military-personnel-are-granted-benefits.html (accessed February 19, 2023).

49. David Masci, Elizabeth Podrebarac Sciupac, and Michael Lipka, "Same-Sex Marriage around the World." Pew Research Center, October 28, 2019. https://www.pewresearch.org/religion/fact-sheet/gay-marriage-around-the-world/ (accessed February 19, 2023).

50. "Map of Countries That Criminalise LGBT People." Human Dignity Trust. https://www.humandignitytrust.org/lgbt-the-law/map-of-criminalisation/ (accessed February 19, 2023).

51. "Map of Countries that Criminalise LGBT People."

52. Mark Regnerus, "How Different Are the Adult Children of Parents Who Have Same-Sex Relationships? Findings from the New Family Structures Study." *Social Science Research* 41 (2012), p. 752.

53. "Brief Amicus Curiae of the United States Conference of Catholic Bishops in Support of Petitioners and Supporting Reversal"—re *Hollingsworth v. Perry*, January 29, 2013. http://www.usccb.org/about/general-counsel/amicus-briefs/upload/hollingsworth-v-perry.pdf (accessed February 19, 2023).

54. Tom Bartlett, "Controversial Gay-Parenting Study Is Severely Flawed, Journal's Audit Finds." *Chronicle of Higher Education*, July 26, 2012. https://www.chronicle.com/blogs/percolator/controversial-gay-parenting-study-is-severely-flawed-journals-audit-finds (accessed February 19, 2023).

55. "Brief of Amicus Curiae American Sociological Association in Support of Respondent Kristin M. Perry and Respondent Edith Schlain Windsor"—re *Hollingsworth v. Perry*.

http://www.asanet.org/documents/ASA/pdfs/12-144_307_Amicus_%20(C_%20Gottlieb)_ASA_Same-Sex_Marriage.pdf (accessed February 19, 2023).

56. See Richard Fry and Kim Parker, "Rising Share of U.S. Adults Are Living without a Spouse or Partner." Pew Research Center, October 5, 2021, https://www.pewresearch.org/social-trends/2021/10/05/rising-share-of-u-s-adults-are-living-without-a-spouse-or-partner/ (accessed February 19, 2023).

57. Derek Thompson, "The Decline of Marriage and the Rise of Unwed Mothers: An Economic Mystery." *Atlantic*, March 18, 2013. http://www.theatlantic.com/business/archive/2013/03/the-decline-of-marriage-and-the-rise-of-unwed-mothers-an-economic-mystery/274111/ (accessed February 19, 2023).

58. See Andrew Fiala, *What Would Jesus Really Do?* (Lanham, MD: Rowman & Littlefield, 2007), chapter 9.

59. *Defense of Marriage Act*. http://www.gpo.gov/fdsys/pkg/CRPT-104hrpt664/pdf/CRPT-104hrpt664.pdf (accessed February 19, 2023).

60. *Obergefell v. Hodges* (2015), p. 4; at https://www.supremecourt.gov/opinions/14pdf/14-556_3204.pdf (accessed February 19, 2023).

61. John Roberts dissent in *Obergefell v. Hodges* (2015), p. 20; at https://www.supremecourt.gov/opinions/14pdf/14-556_3204.pdf (accessed February 19, 2023).

62. John Corvino and Maggie Gallagher, *Debating Same-Sex Marriage* (New York: Oxford University Press, 2012), p. 83.

63. Corvino and Gallagher, *Debating Same-Sex*, p. 21.

64. Talia Bettcher, "Feminist Perspectives on Trans Issues," in *The Stanford Encyclopedia of Philosophy* ed. Edward N. Zalta (2020). https://plato.stanford.edu/archives/fall2020/entries/feminism-trans/ (accessed February 19, 2023).

65. The Human Rights Campaign, "Glossary of Terms." https://www.hrc.org/resources/glossary-of-terms (accessed February 19, 2023).

66. Congregation for Catholic Education, "Male and Female He Created Them," 2019. http://www.educatio.va/content/dam/cec/Documenti/19_0997_INGLESE.pdf (accessed February 19, 2023).

67. "It's Intersex Awareness Day." Amnesty International, October 26, 2018. https://www.amnesty.org/en/latest/news/2018/10/its-intersex-awareness-day-here-are-5-myths-we-need-to-shatter/ (accessed February 19, 2023).

68. See Human Rights Campaign, "Mapping the Intersex Exceptions." https://www.hrw.org/feature/2022/10/26 /mapping-the-intersex-exceptions (accessed February 19, 2023).

69. Kailyn Brown, "Martina Navratilova Says 'Put An asterisk' Next to Transgender Swimmer Lia Thomas." *Los Angeles Magazine*, March 18, 2022. https://www.lamag.com /citythinkblog/martina-navratilova-on-trasgender -swinner-lia-thomas/ (accessed February 19, 2023).

70. J. K. Rowling, "J. K. Rowling Writes about Her Reasons for Speaking Out on Sex and Gender Issues," June 10, 2020. https://www.jkrowling.com/opinions/j-k-rowling-writes -about-her-reasons-for-speaking-out-on-sex-and-gender -issues/ (accessed February 19, 2023).

71. Laurel Powell, "2021 Becomes Deadliest Year on Record for Transgender and Non-Binary People." Human Rights Campaign, November 9, 2021. https://www.hrc.org/press -releases/2021-becomes-deadliest-year-on-record-for -transgender-and-non-binary-people (accessed February 19, 2023).

72. Samuel Alito dissent in *Bostock v. Clayton County* (2020), p. 45. https://www.supremecourt.gov /opinions/19pdf/17-1618_hfci.pdf (accessed February 19, 2023).

73. Loren Cannon, *The Politicization of Trans Identity* (Lanham, MD: Lexington Books, 2022), p. 193.

74. "New Data Show That STDs Remain Far Too High," Centers for Disease Control, 2020. https://www.cdc.gov/std /statistics/2020/default.htm (accessed February 19, 2023).

75. Ben Quinn, "Pope Signals Shift away from Catholic Church's Prohibition of Condoms." *The Guardian*, November 20, 2010. http://www.theguardian.com/world/2010/nov/20 /pope-benedict-catholic-church-condoms (accessed February 19, 2023).

76. California Department of Education, "FAQ for Sexual Education, HIV/AIDS, and STDs." https://www.cde.ca.gov/ls /he/se/faq.asp#accordionfaq (accessed February 19, 2023).

77. Sarah Kliff, "Under Obama Administration, Abstinence-Only Education Finds Surprising New Foothold." *Washington Post*, May 8, 2012, http:// www.washingtonpost.com/blogs/wonkblog/post /under-obama-administration-abstinence-only -education-finds-surprising-new-foothold/2012/05/08 /gIQA8fcwAU_blog.html (accessed February 19, 2023); also see Christopher Trenholm, et al., *Impacts of Four Title V, Section 510 Abstinence Education Program.*

Mathematica Policy Research for Department of Health and Human Services, April 12, 2007. https://aspe.hhs.gov /reports/impacts-four-title-v-section-510-abstinence -education-programs-1 (accessed February 19, 2023).

78. "Sex Ed Can Help Prevent Teen Pregnancy." *Washington Post*, March 24, 2008. http://www.washingtonpost.com /wp-dyn/content/article/2008/03/24/AR2008032401515. html (accessed February 19, 2023).

Chapter 17

1. "President Donald J. Trump Is Committed to Building on the Successes of the First Step Act." White House Archive, April 1, 2019. https://trumpwhitehouse.archives.gov /briefings-statements/president-donald-j-trump -committed-building-successes-first-step-act/ (accessed February 21, 2023).

2. Linda Bordoni, "Pope Francis: 'Death Penalty Inadmissible.'" *Vatican News*, August 2, 2018. https://www.vaticannews .va/en/pope/news/2018-08/pope-francis-cdf-ccc-death -penalty-revision-ladaria.html (accessed February 21, 2023).

3. "European and World Day against the Death Penalty, 10 October 2021: Joint Statement by the High Representative on Behalf of the European Union and the Secretary-General on Behalf of the Council of Europe," October 8, 2021. https://www.consilium .europa.eu/en/press/press-releases/2021/10/08 /european-and-world-day-against-the-death-penalty -joint-statement-by-the-high-representative-on-behalf -of-the-european-union-and-the-secretary-general-on -behalf-of-the-council-of-europe/ (accessed February 21, 2023).

4. Amnesty International, "Death Sentences and Executions 2021," May 24, 2022. https://www.amnesty.org/en /documents/act50/5418/2022/en/ (accessed February 21, 2023).

5. Death Penalty Information Center, "On 20th Anniversary of Atkins v. Virginia," June 22, 2022. https:// deathpenaltyinfo.org/news/on-20th-anniversary-of -atkins-v-virginia-supreme-court-denies-petition-to -review-procedural-loophole-permitting-execution-of -intellectually-disabled-prisoners (accessed February 21, 2023).

6. Death Penalty Information Center. "State by State." https://deathpenaltyinfo.org/state-and-federal -info/state-by-state (accessed February 21, 2023).

7. Rachel Ramirez, "High Rate of Executions during Trump's Last Weeks in Office Explained." Vox, December 11, 2020. https://www.vox.com/21736993/trump-federal -execution-december (accessed February 21, 2023).

8. See Ames Grawert and Noah Kim, "Myths and Realities: Understanding Recent Trends in Violent Crime." Brennan Center for Justice, July 12, 2022. https://www.brennancenter .org/our-work/research-reports/myths-and-realities -understanding-recent-trends-violent-crime (accessed February 21, 2023).

9. David Frum, "The Coming Democratic Crack-Up." *The Atlantic*, September 21, 2015. http://www.theatlantic. com/politics/archive/2015/09/the-democrats-looming -dilemma/406426/ (accessed February 21, 2023).

10. Steven D. Levitt, "Understanding Why Crime Fell in the 1990s: Four Factors That Explain the Decline and Six That Do Not." *Journal of Economic Perspectives* 18: 1 (2004), pp. 163–90. Also see John J. Donohue and Steven D. Levitt, "The Impact of Legalized Abortion on Crime over the Last Two Decades." *American Law and Economics Review* 22: 2 (Fall 2020), pp. 241–302.

11. Kevin Drum, "Lead: America's Real Criminal Element." *Mother Jones*, January/February 2013. http://www .motherjones.com/environment/2013/01/lead-crime -link-gasoline (accessed February 21, 2023); also see Jennifer L. Doleac, "New Evidence That Lead Exposure Increases Crime." Brookings, June 1, 2017. https://www .brookings.edu/blog/up-front/2017/06/01/new -evidence-that-lead-exposure-increases-crime/ (accessed February 21, 2023).

12. See Richard Brandt, *Ethical Theory* (Englewood Cliffs, NJ: Prentice Hall, 1959).

13. Thomas Szasz, *The Myth of Mental Illness* (New York: Harper & Row, 1961).

14. Rachel Aviv, "The Science of Sex Abuse." *New Yorker*, January 6, 2013. http://www.newyorker.com /magazine/2013/01/14/the-science-of-sex-abuse (accessed February 21, 2023).

15. Hennessey Haynes, "Reoffending and Restorative Justice," in *Handbook of Restorative Justice*, eds. Gerry Johnstone and Daniel Van Ness (London: Willan Publishing, 2007), p. 432 ff.

16. Patricia Leigh Brown, "Opening Up, Students Transform a Vicious Circle." *New York Times*, April 4, 2013. http://www .nytimes.com/2013/04/04/education/restorative-justice -programs-take-root-in-schools.html?pagewanted=all (accessed February 21, 2023).

17. See Laura Magnani and Harmon L. Wray, *Beyond Prisons: A New Interfaith Paradigm for Our Failed Prison System* (Minneapolis: Fortress Press, 2006).

18. See Trudy Conway, David McCarthy, and Vicki Schieber, eds., *Where Justice and Mercy Meet* (Collegeville, MN: Liturgical Press, 2013).

19. "Responsibility, Rehabilitation, and Restoration: A Catholic Perspective on Crime and Criminal Justice," U.S. Conference of Catholic Bishops, 2000. http:// www.usccb.org/issues-and-action/human-life-and -dignity/criminal-justice-restorative-justice/ crime-and-criminal-justice.cfm (accessed February 21, 2023).

20. "Responsibility, Rehabilitation, and Restoration."

21. United Nations, *Handbook on Restorative Justice Programs*, 2nd ed. (Vienna: United Nations, 2020), p. 3.

22. Lyn S. Graybill, *Truth and Reconciliation in South Africa* (London: Lynne Rienner Publishing, 2002), p. 8; "Truth and Reconciliation Commission (TRC)," South African History Online. https://www.sahistory.org.za/article /truth-and-reconciliation-commission-trc-0 (accessed February 21, 2023).

23. *Truth and Reconciliation Commission of South Africa Report* (1998), vol. 1, para. 36, p. 9. http://www.justice.gov.za/trc /report/ (accessed February 21, 2023).

24. Rich Kluckow and Zhen Zeng, "Correctional Populations in the United States, 2020." Bureau of Justice Statistics, March 2022. https://bjs.ojp.gov/content/pub/pdf/cpus20st.pdf (accessed February 21, 2023).

25. Bureau of Justice Statistics, "Total Correctional Population." http://www.bjs.gov/index.cfm?ty=kfdetail&iid=487 (accessed February 21, 2023); also see E. Ann Carson, "Prisoners in 2014." U.S. Department of Justice, September 2015. http://www.bjs.gov/content/pub/pdf/p14.pdf (accessed February 21, 2023); and Danielle Kaeble, Lauren Glaze, Anastasios Tsoutis, and Todd Minton, "Correctional Populations in the United States, 2014." U.S. Department of Justice, Revised January 21, 2016. http://www.bjs.gov /content/pub/pdf/cpus14.pdf (accessed February 21, 2023).

26. Bureau of Justice Statistics, "Correctional Populations in the United States, 2020."

27. Bureau of Justice Statistics, "Correctional Populations in the United States, 2020."

28. Bureau of Justice Statistics, "Correctional Populations in the United States, 2020."

29. Helen Fair and Roy Walmsley, "World Prison Population List." Institute for Crime & Justice Policy Research, World Prison Brief, 13th ed. https://www.prisonstudies.org/sites/default/files/resources/downloads/world_prison_population_list_13th_edition.pdf (accessed February 21, 2023).

30. Jim Webb, "Why We Must Fix Our Prisons." *San Francisco Chronicle*, March 29, 2009, p. 4; also see Associated Press, "Nation's Inmate Population Increased 2.3 Percent Last Year." *New York Times*, April 25, 2005, p. A14.

31. "U.S. Inmate Count Far Exceeds Those of Other Nations." *New York Times*, April 23, 2008, pp. A1, A14.

32. Jason DeParle, "The American Prison Nightmare." *New York Review of Books*, April 12, 2007, pp. 33, 36. http://www.nybooks.com/articles/2007/04/12/the-american-prison-nightmare/ (accessed February 21, 2023).

33. Kristin Samuelson, "High Incarceration Rates Fuel COVID-19 Spread and Undermine U.S. Public Safety." *Northwestern University News*, September 2, 2021. https://news.northwestern.edu/stories/2021/september/incarceration-covid-19-spread-public-safety/ (accessed February 21, 2023).

34. See "No Escape: The Trauma of Witnessing Violence in Prison." Prison Policy Initiative, December 2020. https://www.prisonpolicy.org/blog/2020/12/02/witnessing-prison-violence/ (accessed February 21, 2023). Also see a report on prisons from 2006 that warned that the experience of prisoners is too often marked by "rape, gang violence, abuse by officers, infectious disease, and never-ending solitary confinement": John J. Gibbons and Nicholas de B. Katzenbach, *Confronting Confinement* (New York: Vera Institute of Justice, 2006), p. iii.

35. "US: Injustices Filling the Prisons." Human Rights Watch, January 31, 2013. http://www.hrw.org/news/2013/01/31/us-injustices-filling-prisons (accessed February 21, 2023).

36. "Annual Determination of Average Cost of Incarceration Fee (COIF)." Federal Register, September 1, 2021. https://www.federalregister.gov/documents/2021/09/01/2021-18800/annual-determination-of-average-cost-of-incarceration-fee-coif (accessed February 21, 2023).

37. National Institute of Corrections, "Hawaii 2019." https://nicic.gov/state-statistics/2019/hawaii-2019 (accessed February 21, 2023).

38. California Legislative Analyst Office, "How Much Does It Cost to Incarcerate an Inmate?" https://lao.ca.gov/policyareas/cj/6_cj_inmatecost (accessed February 21, 2023).

39. California Legislative Analyst Office, "The 2022–23 Budget: Governor's Proposals for CDCR Operations." https://lao.ca.gov/Publications/Report/4517#l (accessed February 21, 2023).

40. Prerna Anand, "Winners and Losers: Corrections and Higher Education in California." *California Common Sense,* September 5, 2012. http://www.cacs.org/ca/article/44 (accessed February 21, 2023).

41. Ted Andersen, "Worst in Nation: Calif. Spends 6 Times More on Prisoners than on Students, Says Report." SF GATE, October 26, 2018. https://www.sfgate.com/bayarea/article/Calif-spends-6-times-more-on-prisoners-than-13339911.php (accessed February 21, 2023).

42. Jennifer Steinhauer, "Schwarzenegger Seeks Shift from Prisons to Schools." *New York Times,* January 6, 2010. http://www.nytimes.com/2010/01/07/us/07calif.html (accessed February 21, 2023).

43. Bureau of Justice Statistics, "Prisoners in 2020," December 2021. https://bjs.ojp.gov/content/pub/pdf/p20st.pdf (accessed February 21, 2023).

44. Bureau of Justice Statistics, "Prisoners in 2020."

45. Bureau of Justice Statistics, "Prisoners in 2020."

46. Calculating percentages based on E. Ann Carson, "Prisoners in 2020—Statistical Tables." Bureau of Justice Statistics, December 2021. https://bjs.ojp.gov/content/pub/pdf/p20st.pdf (accessed February 21, 2023).

47. Glenn Kessler, "The Stale Statistic that One in Three Black Males 'Born Today' Will End Up in Jail." *Washington Post*, June 16, 2015. https://www.washingtonpost.com/news/fact-checker/wp/2015/06/16/the-stale-statistic-that-one-in-three-black-males-has-a-chance-of-ending-up-in-jail/ (accessed February 21, 2023).

48. Michelle Alexander, *The New Jim Crow* (New York: The New Press, 2010), p. 179.

49. Michelle Alexander, *The New Jim Crow*, p. 180.

50. Clark Neily, "Prisons Are Packed because Prosecutors Are Coercing Plea Deals." NBC News, August 8, 2019. https://www.nbcnews.com/think/opinion/prisons-are-packed-because-prosecutors-are-coercing-plea-deals-yes-ncna1034201 (accessed February 21, 2023).

51. Carlos Berdejó, "Criminalizing Race: Racial Disparities in Plea-Bargaining." *Boston College Law Review* 59: 4 (2018).

52. Curtis Bunn, "Black People Are Still Killed by Police at a Higher Rate than Other Groups." NBC News, March 3, 2022. https://www.nbcnews.com/news/nbcblk/report-black-people-are-still-killed-police-higher-rate-groups-rcna17169 (accessed February 21, 2023).

53. For substantial discussion, see Samuel Walker, Cassia Spohn, and Miriam DeLone, *The Color of Justice: Race, Ethnicity, and Crime in America*, 6th ed. (Boston: Cengage, 2018).

54. DeParle, "The American Prison Nightmare."

55. Michelle Alexander, *The New Jim Crow*, p. 17.

56. John H. Langbein interview, *Frontline*, PBS, January 16, 2004. http://www.pbs.org/wgbh/pages/frontline/shows /plea/interviews/langbein.html (accessed February 21, 2023).

57. Sara Wakefield and Christopher Uggen, "Incarceration and Stratification." *Annual Review of Sociology* 36 (2010), pp. 387–406.

58. Stan Alcorn, "'Check Yes or No': The Hurdles of Job Hunting with a Criminal Past." NPR's *All Things Considered*, January 31, 2013. http://www.npr.org/2013/01/31 /170766202/-check-yes-or-no-the-hurdles-of-employment -with-criminal-past (accessed February 21, 2023).

59. See Ed Chung, Maritza Perez, and Lea Hunter, "Rethinking Federal Marijuana Policy." Center for American Progress, May 1, 2018. https://www.americanprogress.org/article /rethinking-federal-marijuana-policy/ (accessed February 21, 2023).

60. Amnesty International, "Death Sentences and Executions 2021." https://www.amnesty.org/en/documents /act50/5418/2022/en/ (accessed February 21, 2023).

61. Amnesty International, "Death Sentences and Executions 2021," pp. 26–27.

62. "Introduction to the Death Penalty," Death Penalty Information Center. http://www.deathpenaltyinfo.org/part-i -history-death-penalty (accessed February 21, 2023).

63. *Gregg v. Georgia*, 428 U.S. 153 (1976) at III.c.

64. Maura Dolan and Joseph Serna, "Federal Appeals Court Upholds California's Death Penalty." *Los Angeles Times*, November 12, 2015. http://www.latimes.com/local /lanow/la-me-ln-court-upholds-california-death-penalty -20151112-story.html

65. "California Governor Gavin Newsom Orders Dismantling of State's Death Row." Death Penalty Information Center, February 1, 2022, https://deathpenaltyinfo.org/news /california-governor-gavin-newsom-orders-dismantling -of-californias-death-row (accessed February 21, 2023).

66. Death Penalty Information Center, "Facts about the Death Penalty," updated July 29, 2022. http://www .deathpenaltyinfo.org/documents/FactSheet.pdf (accessed February 21, 2023).

67. Death Penalty Information Center, "Facts about the Death Penalty."

68. Mike Farrell, "Death Penalty Thrives in Climate of Fear." *San Francisco Chronicle*, February 24, 2002, p. D3.

69. Death Penalty Information Center, "Facts about the Death Penalty."

70. Innocence Project, "Exonerate the Innocent." https:// innocenceproject.org/exonerate/ (accessed February 21, 2023).

71. Innocence Project, "Exonerate the Innocent."

72. Margaret Carlson, "Death, Be Not Proud." *Time*, February 13, 2000, p. 38. http://content.time.com/time/magazine /article/0,9171,39180,00.html (accessed February 21, 2023).

73. Amnesty International, "Death Penalty and Race," May 18, 2017. http://www.amnestyusa.org/our-work/issues /death-penalty/us-death-penalty-facts/death-penalty -and-race (accessed February 21, 2023).

74. Death Penalty Information Center, "Research on the Death Penalty." http://www.deathpenaltyinfo.org/research -death-penalty (accessed February 21, 2023).

75. Death Penalty Information Center, "Facts about the Death Penalty."

76. U.S. Census Bureau, "Quick Facts." https://www.census .gov/quickfacts/fact/table/US/PST045221 (accessed February 21, 2023).

77. Death Penalty Information Center, "Facts about the Death Penalty."

78. See "Equal Justice Initiative Report on Racial Discrimination in Jury Selection." Death Penalty Information, August 3, 2021. https://deathpenaltyinfo.org/news/equal-justice -initiative-releases-report-on-racial-discrimination-in -jury-selection (accessed February 21, 2023).

79. "Former Georgia Death Row Prisoner Johnny Lee Gates Released after 43 Years in Prison." American Bar Association, July 23, 2020, https://www.americanbar.org /groups/committees/death_penalty_representation /project_press/2020/summer/johnny-lee-gates-released/ (accessed February 21, 2023).

80. Angela Y. Davis, *Abolition Democracy: Beyond Empire, Prisons, and Torture* (New York: Seven Stories Press, 2005).

81. Lincoln Caplan, "Disgracing 'the Quintessential System of Justice.'" *New York Times*, April 26, 2013. http://takingnote .blogs.nytimes.com/2013/04/26/disgracing-the -quintessential-system-of-justice/ (accessed February 21, 2023).

82. See, for example, Claudia Wallis, "Too Young to Die." *Time*, March 14, 2005, p. 40. http://content.time.com/time /magazine/article/0,9171,1034712,00.html (accessed February 21, 2023).

83. Richard C. Dieter, "Smart on Crime: Reconsidering the Death Penalty in a Time of Economic Crisis." Death Penalty Information Center, October 2009. http://www .deathpenaltyinfo.org/documents/CostsRptFinal.pdf (accessed February 21, 2023).

84. "Death Penalty Report." California Committee on the Revision of the Penal Code, November 2021, p. 31. http:// www.clrc.ca.gov/CRPC/Pub/Reports/CRPC_DPR.pdf (accessed February 21, 2023).

85. "Death Penalty Report." California Committee on the Revision of the Penal Code.

86. John Stuart Mill, "Speech in Defense of Capital Punishment," vol. 28 in *The Collected Works of John Stuart Mill*, eds. John M. Robson and Bruce L. Kinzer (Toronto: University of Toronto Press, 1988), pp. 305–10.

87. See Hugo Bedau, "Capital Punishment and Retributive Justice," in *Matters of Life and Death*, ed. Tom Regan (New York: Random House, 1980), pp. 148–82.

88. It dropped from 3.09 people per 100,000 residents in 1975 to 2.74 per 100,000 in 1983. "Amnesty International and the Death Penalty," Amnesty International USA, *Newsletter* (Spring 1987).

89. See Hugo Bedau, *The Death Penalty in America* (Chicago: Aldine, 1967), in particular Chapter 6, "The Question of Deterrence."

90. Death Penalty Information Center, "States With No Death Penalty Share Lower Homicide Rates" https://death-penaltyinfo.org/stories/states-with-no-death-penalty -share-lower-homicide-rates (accessed March 3, 2023).

91. Roy D. Adler and Michael Summers, "Capital Punishment Works." *Wall Street Journal*, November 2, 2007. http://www .wsj.com/articles/SB119397079767680173 (accessed February 21, 2023).

92. Gebhard Kirchgässner, "Econometric Estimates of Deterrence of the Death Penalty: Facts or Ideology?" *Kyklos* 64: 3 (July 18, 2011), pp. 468–69.

93. Daniel S. Nagin and John V. Pepper, eds., *Deterrence and the Death Penalty* (Washington, DC: National Academies Press, 2012), p. 2.

94. Immanuel Kant, *The Philosophy of Law* (Edinburgh: T&T Clark, 1887), part 2, sec. 49.E.

95. Jeffrey Reiman, "Justice, Civilization, and the Death Penalty: Answering Van den Haag." *Philosophy and Public Affairs* 14: 2 (1985), pp. 119–34.

96. Mohandas K. Gandhi, "From Europe" (Sept. 10, 1925) in *Gandhi Collected Works* (New Delhi: Publications Division Government of India, various dates), vol. 33 (September 25, 1925–February 10, 1926), p. 72.

97. Mohandas K. Gandhi, "From Europe," p. 73.

98. See Andrew Fiala, *What Would Jesus Really Do?* (Lanham, MD: Rowman & Littlefield, 2006), especially Chapter 8.

99. Conway et al., *Where Justice and Mercy Meet*.

100. Donald Kraybill, Steven Nolt, and David Weaver-Zercher, *Amish Grace: How Forgiveness Transcended Tragedy* (San Francisco: John Wiley and Sons/Jossey-Bass, 2007). See Andrew Fiala, "Radical Forgiveness and Human Justice." *Heythrop Journal* 53: 3 (May 2012), pp. 494–506.

101. Associated Press, "Mother of Gunman Who Killed Five Amish Girls in 2006 Cares for Survivor of Son's Massacre," December 9, 2013. http://www.nydailynews.com/news /national/mother-amish-killer-cares-survivor-son-massacre -article-1.1542337 (accessed February 21, 2023).

102. Paul Tullis, "Can Forgiveness Play a Role in Criminal Justice?" *New York Times*, January 4, 2013. http://www.nytimes .com/2013/01/06/magazine/can-forgiveness-play-a-role -in-criminal-justice.html (accessed February 21, 2023).

103. "Uproar over Bloody Electrocution," *San Francisco Chronicle*, July 9, 1999, p. A7. http://www.sfgate.com/news /article/Uproar-Over-Bloody-Electrocution-Florida -2919750.php (accessed February 21, 2023); Associated Press, "An Execution Causes Bleeding." *New York Times*, July 8, 1999, p. A10. http://www.nytimes .com/1999/07/09/us/an-execution-causes-bleeding. html (accessed February 22, 2023).

104. See Adam Liptak, "Critics Say Execution Drug May Hide Suffering." *New York Times*, October 7, 2003, pp. A1, A18. http://www.nytimes.com/2003/10/07/us/critics-say -execution-drug-may-hide-suffering.html (accessed February 22, 2023).

105. Michael L. Radelet, "Botched Executions." Death Penalty Information Center. http://www.deathpenaltyinfo.org /some-examples-post-furman-botched-executions (accessed February 22, 2023).

106. Reuters, "Drugs for Lethal Injection Aren't Reliable, Study Finds." *New York Times*, April 24, 2007. http://www .nytimes.com/2007/04/24/us/24injection.html (accessed February 21, 2023).

107. Makiko Kitamura and Adi Narayan, "Europe Pushes to Keep Lethal Injection Drugs from U.S. Prisons." *Bloomberg Business Week*, February 7, 2013. http://www .businessweek.com/articles/2013-02-07/europe-pushes -to-keep-lethal-injection-drugs-from-u-dot-s-dot -prisons (accessed February 21, 2023).

Chapter 18

1. Declaration of the United Nations General Assembly, March 1, 2022. https://new-york-un.diplo.de/blob /2515116/4685bdecc4ff06d9a0c6977086f8d7f8 /220302-unga-resolution-aggression-against-ukraine -data.pdf (accessed February 22, 2023).

2. U.S. State Department, "War Crimes by Russia's Forces in Ukraine," March 23, 2022. https://www.state.gov /war-crimes-by-russias-forces-in-ukraine/ (accessed February 22, 2023).

3. Loveday Morris, "An 'Unprecedented' Effort to Document War Crimes in Ukraine." *Washington Post*, May 29, 2022. https://www.washingtonpost.com/world/2022/05/28 /ukraine-war-crimes-investigations/ (accessed February 22, 2023).

4. See Kenneth E. Boulding, "Twelve Friendly Quarrels with Johan Galtung." *Journal of Peace Research* 14: 1 (1977), pp. 75–86.

5. William James, "The Moral Equivalent of War." *Popular Science Monthly*, October 1910.

6. Jane Addams, "Patriotism and Pacifists in Wartime," in *Jane Addams's Essays and Speeches on Peace* (London: Continuum, 2005), p. 163.

7. Martin Luther King Jr., "Beyond Vietnam" (speech from April 4, 1967) at Martin Luther King Papers Project (Stanford). https://kinginstitute.stanford.edu/encyclopedia /beyond-vietnam (accessed February 22, 2023).

8. Jane Addams, *The Long Road of Women's Memory* (New York: Macmillan, 1916), p. 140.

9. Mohandas K. Gandhi, "Doctrine of Ahimsa," in 1916 Speech on Ashram Vows to YMCA of Madras, in *Gandhi Collected Works* (New Delhi: Publications Division Government of India, various dates), vol. 15 (May 21, 1915–August 31, 1966), p. 168.

10. Statement of Purpose of the Student Nonviolent Coordinating Committee, 1960, National Humanities Center. http://nationalhumanitiescenter.org/pds/maai3/protest /text2/snccstatementofpurpose.pdf (accessed February 22, 2023).

11. "Remarks by the President at the Acceptance of the Nobel Peace Prize," The White House, press release, December 10, 2009. https://obamawhitehouse.archives.gov/the-press -office/remarks-president-acceptance-nobel-peace-prize (accessed February 22, 2023).

12. Robert W. Tucker, *The Just War* (Baltimore: Johns Hopkins University Press, 1960), p. 1.

13. Francisco Suárez, "On War," in Francisco Suárez, *Selections from Three Works* (Liberty Fund, 2015), sec. 1. https:// oll.libertyfund.org/title/selections-from-three-works (accessed February 22, 2023).

14. Hugo Grotius, *The Rights of War and Peace* (New York: M. Walter Dunne, 1901), Book 1, Chapter 1, at Liberty Fund. https://oll.libertyfund.org/title/grotius-the-rights-of -war-and-peace-1901-ed?html=true#Grotius_0138 _127 (accessed February 22, 2023).

15. Michael Walzer, "The Just War of the Ukrainians." *Wall Street Journal*, March 26, 2022.

16. See Andrew Fiala, *The Just War Myth* (Lanham, MD: Rowman & Littlefield, 2008), Chapter 6.

17. "Lessons of Iraq War Underscore Importance of UN Charter—Annan." *UN News Centre*, September 16, 2004. https://news.un.org/en/story/2004/09/115352 (accessed February 22, 2023).

18. We might consider this particular principle as what is called a regulative rather than a substantive principle. Instead of telling us when something is enough or the last thing we should try, it can be used to prod us to go somewhat further than we otherwise would.

19. James Childress, "Just-War Theories." *Theological Studies* (1978), pp. 427–45.

20. Both definitions found at "Terrorism," National Institute of Justice, September 12, 2011. https://nij.ojp.gov/topics /crimes/domestic-radicalization-and-terrorism (accessed February 22, 2023).

21. Costs of War, "Summary of Findings." https://watson. brown.edu/costsofwar/papers/summary (accessed February 22, 2023).

22. Mark Owen, *No Easy Day: The Firsthand Account of the Mission That Killed Osama Bin Laden* (New York: Dutton, 2012).

23. "Remarks by the President on Osama Bin Laden," The White House, press release, May 2, 2011. https:// obamawhitehouse.archives.gov/the-press-office/2011 /05/02/remarks-president-osama-bin-laden (accessed February 22, 2023).

24. Erik Kirschbaum and Jonathan Thatcher, "Concerns Raised over Shooting of Unarmed bin Laden." *Reuters*, May 4, 2011. https://www.reuters.com/article/us-binladen-legitimacy /concerns-raised-over-shooting-of-unarmed-bin-laden -idUSTRE74371H20110504 (accessed February 22, 2023).

25. Statement by the Department of Defense, January 2, 2020. https://www.defense.gov/News/Releases/Release /Article/2049534/statement-by-the-department-of -defense/ (accessed February 22, 2023).

26. "All Drone Strikes 'in Self-Defence' Should Go Before Security Council, Argues Independent Rights Expert." *UN News*, January 9, 2020. https://news.un.org/en /story/2020/07/1068041 (accessed February 22, 2023).

27. "Remarks by President Biden on a Successful Counterterrorism Operation in Afghanistan." White House statement, August 1, 2022. https://www.whitehouse .gov/briefing-room/speeches-remarks/2022/08/01 /remarks-by-president-biden-on-a-successful -counterterrorism-operation-in-afghanistan/ (accessed February 22, 2023).

28. Kevin Liptak et al., "US Kills al Qaeda Leader Ayman al-Zawahiri in Drone Strike in Afghanistan." CNN, August 2, 2022. https://www.cnn.com/2022/08/01/politics /joe-biden-counter-terrorism/index.html (accessed February 22, 2023).

29. "Drone Warfare." Bureau of Investigative Journalism, https://www.thebureauinvestigates.com/projects /drone-war (accessed February 22, 2023).

30. Nicole Gaouette, "Obama: 'No Doubt' U.S. Drones Have Killed Civilians." *CNN*, April 1, 2016. http://www.cnn .com/2016/04/01/politics/obama-isis-drone-strikes-iran/ (accessed February 22, 2023).

31. "Department of Justice White Paper on Lethal Operations Against Al-Qa'ida Leaders" from 2013 at International Committee of the Red Cross, https://casebook.icrc.org /case-study/us-lethal-operations-against-al-qaida-leaders (accessed March 3, 2023).

32. Charlie Savage and Peter Baker, "Obama, in a Shift, to Limit Targets of Drone Strikes." *New York Times*, May 22, 2013. http://www.nytimes.com/2013/05/23/us/us-acknowledges -killing-4-americans-in-drone-strikes.html? (accessed February 22, 2023).

33. "Obama Speech on Drone Policy." *New York Times*. May 23, 2013. http://www.nytimes.com/2013/05/24/us/politics /transcript-of-obamas-speech-on-drone-policy.html (accessed February 22, 2023).

34. Elena Moore and Roberta Rampton, "Timeline: How The U.S. Came to Strike and Kill a Top Iranian General." NPR, January 4, 2020. https://www.npr.org/2020/01/04 /793364307/timeline-how-the-u-s-came-to-strike-and-kill -a-top-iranian-general (accessed February 22, 2023).

35. Federation of American Scientists, "Introduction to Chemical Weapons." https://programs.fas.org/bio /chemweapons/introduction.html (accessed February 22, 2023).

36. Howard W. French, "Tokyo Journal; 100,000 People Perished, but Who Remembers?" *New York Times*, March 14, 2002, p. A4. https://www.nytimes.com/2002/03/14 /world/tokyo-journal-100000-people-perished-but-who -remembers.html (accessed February 22, 2023).

37. John W. Dower, "The Bombed: Hiroshimas and Nagasakis in Japanese Memory," in *Hiroshima in History and Memory*, ed. Michael J. Hogan (Cambridge, UK: Cambridge University Press, 1996).

38. Rinjiro Sodei, *Were We the Enemy? American Survivors of Hiroshima* (Boulder, CO: Westview Press, 1998).

39. U.S. State Department, "New START Treaty." http://www .state.gov/t/avc/newstart/index.htm (accessed February 22, 2023).

40. U.S. State Department, "New START Treaty."

41. Rose Gottemoeller and Marshall L. Brown, Jr., "Legal aspects of Russia's New START suspension provide opportunities for US policy makers" *Bulletin of Atomic Scientists*, March 2, 2023, https://thebulletin.org/2023/03/legal-aspects-of -russias-new-start-suspension-provide-opportunities -for-us-policy-makers/ (accessed March 3, 2023).

42. Marion Messmer, "The other nuclear threat you might have missed from Putin's speech" CNN, March 2, 2023, https://www.cnn.com/2023/03/02/opinions/russia -nuclear-test-putin-messmer/index.html (accessed March 3, 2023).

43. Gregg Easterbrook, "Term Limits: The Meaninglessness of 'WMD.'" *New Republic*, October 7, 2002, 23.

44. Easterbrook, "Term Limits: The Meaninglessness of 'WMD.'"

45. Scott Shane, "Waterboarding Used 266 Times on 2 Suspects." *New York Times*, April 19, 2009. http://www .nytimes.com/2009/04/20/world/20detain.html (accessed February 22, 2023).

46. Mark Danner, "US Torture: Voices from the Black Sites." *New York Review of Books*, April 9, 2009. http://www.nybooks .com/articles/22530 (accessed February 22, 2023).

47. Dick Cheney speaking on *The McLaughlin Group*, May 22, 2009. https://www.npr.org/templates/story/story .php?storyId=104396780 (accessed February 24, 2023)

48. David Luban, "The Defense of Torture." *New York Review of Books*, March 15, 2007, pp. 37–40.

49. Luban, "The Defense of Torture."

50. Uniform Code of Military Justice Sec. 893, Art. 93. https:// www.law.cornell.edu/uscode/text/10/893 (accessed March 3, 2023).

51. Arlette Saenz, "President Trump Tells ABC News' David Muir He 'Absolutely' Thinks Waterboarding Works." ABC News, January 5, 2017. https://abcnews.go.com/Politics /president-trump-tells-abc-news-david-muir-absolutely /story?id=45045055 (accessed February 22, 2023).

52. Statement by President Joseph R. Biden, Jr. on International Day in Support of Victims of Torture June 26, 2021. https://www.whitehouse.gov/briefing-room /statements-releases/2021/06/26/statement-by -president-joseph-r-biden-jr-on-international-day-in -support-of-victims-of-torture/ (accessed February 22, 2023).

53. Errol Morris, *The Fog of War*: Transcript. http://www .errolmorris.com/film/fow_transcript.html (accessed February 22, 2023).

54. "UN Convention against Torture and Other Cruel, Inhuman or Degrading Treatment or Punishment (December 1984)," Audiovisual Library of International Law. https://legal. un.org/avl/ha/catcidtp/catcidtp.html (accessed February 22, 2023).

55. "Crimes against Humanity" United Nations. https://www .un.org/en/genocideprevention/crimes-against-humanity .shtml (accessed February 22, 2023).

56. "Principles of the International Law Recognized in the Charter of the Nüremberg Tribunal and the Judgment of the Tribunal, 1950," Principle IV, at International Committee of the Red Cross. http://www.icrc.org/applic/ihl/ihl .nsf/ART/390-550004?OpenDocument (accessed February 22, 2023).

57. See Michael Biddiss, "Victors' Justice? The Nuremberg Tribunal." *History Today* 45: 5 (May 5, 1995). http://www .historytoday.com/michael-biddiss/victors-justice -nuremberg-tribunal (accessed February 22, 2023).

58. "Ukraine: High Commissioner Updates Human Rights Council." United Nations, July 5, 2022. https://www.ohchr .org/en/statements/2022/07/ukraine-high-commissioner -updates-human-rights-council (accessed February 22, 2023).

Chapter 19

1. Candace Vahlsing, "Quantifying Risks to the Federal Budget from Climate Change." The White House, April 4, 2022. https://www.whitehouse.gov/omb /briefing-room/2022/04/04/quantifying-risks-to-the -federal-budget-from-climate-change/ (accessed February 26, 2023).

2. For a useful website with details about climate data and climate change impacts, see https://climate.nasa.gov/ (accessed February 26, 2023).

3. See Elizabeth Kolbert, *The Sixth Extinction* (New York: Henry Holt, 2014); also see Gerardo Ceballos, Paul R. Ehrlich, and Peter H. Raven, "Vertebrates on the Brink as Indicators of Biological Annihilation and the Sixth Mass Extinction." *Proceedings of the National Academy of Sciences* 117: 24 (June 2020), pp. 13596–13602.

4. Intergovernmental Panel on Climate Change, Press Release for 6th Climate Report: "The Evidence Is Clear: The Time for Action Is Now," April 2022. https://www.ipcc .ch/2022/04/04/ipcc-ar6-wgiii-pressrelease/ (accessed February 26, 2023).

5. National Park Service, "Wildfires Kill Unprecedented Numbers of Large Sequoia Trees," National Park Service, 2022. https://www.nps.gov/articles/000/wildfires-kill -unprecedented-numbers-of-large-sequoia-trees.htm (accessed February 26, 2023).

6. Alex Emslie, "October Fires' 44th Victim: A Creative, Globetrotting Engineer with 'the Kindest Heart.'" KQED, November 28, 2017. https://www.kqed.org/news/11633757 /october-fires-44th-victim-a-creative-globetrotting -engineer-with-the-kindest-heart (accessed February 26, 2023).

7. Tara Law, "88 Confirmed Dead in California's Camp Fire as Search for Victims Ends." *Time Magazine*, November 30, 2018. https://time.com/5468345/search-camp-fire -california/ (accessed February 26, 2023).

8. Raphael Minder, "Portugal Fires Kill More than 60, Including Drivers Trapped in Cars." *New York Times* June 18, 2017. https://www.nytimes.com/2017/06/18/world/europe /portugal-pedrogao-grande-forest-fires.html (accessed February 26, 2023).

9. Helena Smith, "'In My Nightmares I'm Always in the Sea': A Year On from the Greek Fires." *The Guardian*, July 20, 2019. https://www.theguardian.com/world/2019/jul/20 /greek-fires-one-year-on-103-dead-survivors-and -rescuers-look-back (accessed February 26, 2023).

10. Erin Blakemore, "Why America's Deadliest Wildfire Was Largely Forgotten." History.com, July 29, 2021. https://www.history.com/news/peshtigo-fire-america-deadliest-wildfire (accessed February 26, 2023).

11. Angela Colbert, "A Force of Nature: Hurricanes in a Changing Climate." NASA, June 21, 2022. https://climate.nasa.gov/news/3184/a-force-of-nature-hurricanes-in-a-changing-climate/ (accessed February 26, 2023).

12. Worldometers, "Population FAQ." http://www.worldometers.info/ (accessed February 26, 2023).

13. United Nations, "Global Issues: Population." https://www.un.org/en/global-issues/population (accessed February 26, 2023).

14. UN Environment, "Global Environmental Outlook 6," March 4, 2019. https://www.unep.org/resources/global-environment-outlook-6 (accessed February 26, 2023).

15. United Nations Environment Programme, *Global Environment Outlook GEO-6: Healthy Planet, Healthy People.* https://wedocs.unep.org/handle/20.500.11822/27539 (accessed February 26, 2023).

16. UN Environment Programme, *Global Environment Outlook GEO-6*, p. 126.

17. Central Valley Health Policy Institute, "The Impacts of Short-Term Changes in Air Quality on Emergency Room and Hospital Use in California's San Joaquin Valley." http://www.fresnostate.edu/chhs/cvhpi/documents/snapshot.pdf (accessed February 26, 2023).

18. Ernest Weekley, *An Etymological Dictionary of Modern English* (New York: Dover, 1967), pp. 516, 518.

19. Safety regulation needs to make use of such monetary equivalencies, for how else do we decide how safe is safe enough? There is no such thing as perfect safety, for that would mean no risk. Thus, we end up judging that we ought to pay so much to make things just so much safer but no more. The implication is that the increased life years or value of the lives to be saved by stricter regulation is of so much but no more than this much value. See Barbara MacKinnon, "Pricing Human Life." *Science, Technology and Human Values* 11: 2 (Spring 1986), pp. 29–39.

20. United States Environmental Protection Agency, "Environmental Justice." http://www.epa.gov/environmentaljustice/ (accessed February 26, 2023).

21. Andrew North, "Legacy of Bhopal Disaster Poisons Olympics." *BBC News*, May 30, 2012. http://www.bbc.co.uk/news/world-asia-18254334 (accessed February 26, 2023).

22. "28 Years Later, Women in Bhopal Still Waiting for Justice," Amnesty International, December 3, 2012. http://www.amnestyusa.org/news/news-item/28-years-later-women-in-bhopal-still-waiting-for-justice (accessed February 26, 2023).

23. Bob Van Voris and Patricia Hurtado, "Union Carbide Wins Dismissal of Suit over Bhopal Plant." *Bloomberg*, June 28, 2012. http://www.bloomberg.com/news/2012-06-27/union-carbide-wins-dismissal-of-suit-over-bhopal-plant.html (accessed February 26, 2023).

24. See Kristin Shrader-Frechette, *Environmental Justice: Creating Equity, Reclaiming Democracy* (Oxford, UK: Oxford University Press, 2002), p. 10.

25. Kevin DeLuca, "A Wilderness Environmentalism Manifesto: Contesting the Infinite Self-Absorption of Humans," in *Environmental Justice and Environmentalism: The Social Justice Challenge to the Environmental Movement*, eds. Ronald D. Sandler and Phaedra C. Pezzullo (Cambridge, MA: MIT Press, 2007), p. 49.

26. Genesis 1:26–29. Others cite St. Francis of Assisi as an example of the Christian with a respectful regard for nature.

27. René Descartes, *Meditations on First Philosophy* (Indianapolis, IN: Hackett, 1993). However, it might be pointed out that for Descartes this was not so much a metaphysical point as an epistemological one; that is, he was concerned with finding some sure starting point for knowledge and found at least that he was sure that he was thinking even when he was doubting the existence of everything else.

28. See Christopher Stone, *Do Trees Have Standing? Toward Legal Rights for Natural Objects* (Los Altos, CA: William Kaufmann, 1974).

29. Holmes Rolston III, *Environmental Ethics: Duties to and Values in the Natural World* (Philadelphia: Temple University Press, 1988), p. 97.

30. Aldo Leopold, "The Land Ethic," in *Sand County Almanac* (New York: Oxford University Press, 1949).

31. Leopold, "The Land Ethic," p. 262.

32. See John Hospers, *Understanding the Arts* (Englewood Cliffs, NJ: Prentice Hall, 1982).

33. See Stephen R. Fox, *The American Conservation Movement: John Muir and His Legacy* (Madison: University of Wisconsin Press, 1981), p. 5.

34. See Michelle Nijhuis, "Don't Cancel John Muir: But Don't Excuse Him Either." *The Atlantic* April, 21, 2021. https://www.theatlantic.com/ideas/archive/2021/04/conservation-movements-complicated-history/618556/ (accessed February 26, 2023).

35. Jake Bullinger, "Yosemite Finally Reckons with Its Discriminatory Past." Outside, August 23, 2018. https://www.outsideonline.com/outdoor-adventure/environment/yosemite-national-park-native-american-village-miwuk/ (accessed February 26, 2023).

36. "Who Was John Muir?" at Sierra Club website. https://vault.sierraclub.org/john_muir_exhibit/about/ (accessed February 26, 2023).

37. Curt D. Meine, "In a Time of Social and Environmental Crisis, Aldo Leopold's Call for a 'Land Ethic' Is Still Relevant." *The Conversation*, January 5, 2021. https://theconversation.com/in-a-time-of-social-and-environmental-crisis-aldo-leopolds-call-for-a-land-ethic-is-still-relevant-147968 (accessed February 26, 2023).

38. J. Drew Lanham, "What Do We Do about John James Audubon?" *Audubon Magazine*, Spring 2021. https://www.audubon.org/magazine/spring-2021/what-do-we-do-about-john-james-audubon (accessed February 26, 2023).

39. J. Drew Lanham, "What Do We Do About John James Audubon?"

40. Ed McGaa (Eagle Man), "We Are All Related," in *Mother Earth Spirituality: Native American Paths to Healing Ourselves and Our World* (San Francisco: Harper & Row, 1990), pp. 203–9.

41. Winona LaDuke, "Mother of Our Nations: Indigenous Women Address the World," September 1995, in *The Winona LaDuke Reader* (Stillwater, MN: Voyageur Press, 2002), pp. 211–12.

42. Arne Naess, *Ecology, Community, and Lifestyle*, trans. David Rothenberg (Cambridge, UK: Cambridge University Press, 1989).

43. Paul Taylor, *Respect for Nature* (Princeton, NJ: Princeton University Press, 1986).

44. Naess, *Ecology, Community, and Lifestyle*.

45. George Sessions, ed., *Deep Ecology for the 21st Century: Readings on the Philosophy and Practice of the New Environmentalism* (Boston: Shambhala Publications, 1995), p. xxi.

46. On the tactics of ecosabotage, see Bill Devall, *Simple in Means, Rich in Ends: Practicing Deep Ecology* (Layton, UT: Gibbs Smith, 1988).

47. See Michael Martin, "Ecosabotage and Civil Disobedience." *Environmental Ethics* 12: 4 (Winter 1990), pp. 291–310.

48. According to Joseph des Jardins, the term *ecofeminism* was first used by Françoise d'Eaubonne in 1974 in her work *Le Feminisme ou la Mort* (Paris: Pierre Horay, 1974).

See des Jardins, *Environmental Ethics*, 5th edition (Boston: Wadsworth Cengage Learning, 2013), p. 221.

49. Karen J. Warren, "The Power and Promise of Ecological Feminism," *Environmental Ethics* 9 (Spring 1987), pp. 3–20.

50. See the distinctions made by Alison Jaggar between liberal (egalitarian) feminism, Marxist feminism, socialist feminism, and radical feminism. *Feminist Politics and Human Nature* (Totowa, NJ: Rowman & Allanheld, 1983).

51. See Carol Christ, *Laughter of Aphrodite: Reflections on a Journey to the Goddess* (San Francisco, CA: Harper & Row, 1987).

52. Noël Sturgeon, "The Nature of Race: Discourses of Racial Difference in Ecofeminism," in *Ecofeminism: Women, Culture, Nature*, ed. Karen Warren (Bloomington: Indiana University Press, 1997), p. 269.

53. Vandana Shiva, "Reductionism and Regeneration," in *Ecofeminism*, eds. Vandana Shiva and Maria Mies (New York: Zed Books, 2014), p. 25.

54. See Michael Specter, "Seeds of Doubt." *The New Yorker*, August 18, 2014.

55. Leah Thomas, *The Intersectional Environmentalist: How to Dismantle Systems of Oppression to Protect People + Planet* (New York: Little Brown, 2022), pp. 4–5.

56. NASA, "Global Climate Change: Vital Signs of the Planet." https://gpm.nasa.gov/education/websites/global-climate-change-vital-signs-planet (accessed February 26, 2023).

57. David Biello, "400 PPM: Carbon Dioxide in the Atmosphere Reaches Prehistoric Levels." *Scientific American*, May 9, 2013. http://blogs.scientificamerican.com/observations/2013/05/09/400-ppm-carbon-dioxide-in-the-atmosphere-reaches-prehistoric-levels/ (accessed February 26, 2023).

58. Elisabeth Rosenthal, "As the Climate Changes, Bits of England's Coast Crumble." *New York Times*, May 4, 2007. http://www.nytimes.com/2007/05/04/world/europe/04erode.html?_r=0 (accessed February 26, 2023).

59. John McQuaid, "Hurricanes and Climate Change." Nova, November 14, 2012. http://www.pbs.org/wgbh/nova/earth/hurricanes-climate.html (accessed February 26, 2023).

60. Justin Gillis, "Ending Its Summer Melt, Arctic Sea Ice Sets a New Low That Leads to Warnings." *New York Times*, September 19, 2012. http://www.nytimes.com/2012/09/20/science/earth/arctic-sea-ice-stops-melting-but-new-record-low-is-set.html (accessed February 26, 2023).

61. NASA, "Global Climate Change."

62. Dirk Notz and SIMIP Community, "Arctic Sea Ice in CMIP6." *Geophysical Research Letters* 47: 10 (May 28, 2020). https://doi.org/10.1029/2019GL086749 (accessed February 26, 2023).

63. NASA, "Global Climate Change: Vital Signs of the Planet: Ice Sheets." https://climate.nasa.gov/vital-signs/ice-sheets/ (accessed February 26, 2023).

64. "Quick Facts on Ice Sheets." https://nsidc.org/cryosphere/quickfacts/icesheets.html (accessed February 26, 2023).

65. Rebecca Lindsey, "Climate Change: Global Sea Level." Climate.gov, April 19, 2022. https://www.climate.gov/news-features/understanding-climate/climate-change-global-sea-level (accessed February 26, 2023).

66. Lindsey, "Climate Change: Global Sea Level."

67. Dan Vergano, "How Climate Change Threatens the Seas." *USA Today*, March 28, 2013. http://www.usatoday.com/story/news/nation/2013/03/27/climate-change-seas/2024759/ (accessed February 26, 2023).

68. Stephen C. Riser and M. Susan Lozier, "New Simulations Question the Gulf Stream's Role in Tempering Europe's Winters." *Scientific American*, February 1, 2013. http://www.scientificamerican.com/article.cfm?id=new-simulations-question-gulf-stream-role-tempering-europes-winters&page=2 (accessed February 26, 2023).; also see Kara Norton, "A Major Atlantic Current Is at a Critical Transition Point." NOVA, February 17, 2022. https://www.pbs.org/wgbh/nova/article/amoc-shutdown-gulf-stream-climate/ (accessed February 26, 2023).

69. Al Gore, *An Inconvenient Truth* (New York: Rodale, 2006), pp. 148–51.

70. Randy Astaiza, "11 Islands That Will Vanish When Sea Levels Rise." *Business Insider*, October 12, 2012. http://www.businessinsider.com/islands-threatened-by-climate-change-2012-10 (accessed February 26, 2023).

71. United States Environmental Protection Agency, "Overview of Greenhouse Gases" (2020). https://www3.epa.gov/climatechange/ghgemissions/gases.html (accessed February 26, 2023).

72. See https://350.org (accessed February 26, 2023).

73. United Nations, Secretary-General's Video Message on the Launch of the Third IPCC Report, April 4, 2022. https://www.un.org/sg/en/content/sg/statement/2022-04-04/secretary-generals-video-message-the-launch-of-the-third-ipcc-report-scroll-down-for-languages (accessed February 26, 2023).

74. Seth Borenstein, "U.S. Scientists Report Big Jump in Heat-Trapping CO2." *AP News*, March 5, 2013. https://www.yahoo.com/news/us-scientists-report-big-jump-183612249.html (accessed February 26, 2023).

75. United States Environmental Protection Agency, "Global Greenhouse Gas Emissions Data" (2014). https://www3.epa.gov/climatechange/ghgemissions/global.html (accessed February 26, 2023).

76. Thomas Homer-Dixon, "Terror in the Weather Forecast." *New York Times*, April 24, 2007, p. A25. http://www.nytimes.com/2007/04/24/opinion/24homer-dixon.html (accessed February 26, 2023); Celia W. Dugger, "Need for Water Could Double in 50 Years, U.N. Study Finds," *New York Times*, August 22, 2006, p. A12. http://www.nytimes.com/2006/08/22/world/22water.html (accessed February 26, 2023); Jane Kay, "Report Predicts Climate Calamity." *San Francisco Chronicle*, May 7, 2007, p. A1. http://www.sfgate.com/green/article/Report-predicts-climate-calamity-All-continents-2604480.php (accessed February 26, 2023).

77. Gore, *An Inconvenient Truth*, pp. 60–67.

78. Wageningen University and Research Centre, "Butterflies and Birds Unable to Keep Pace with Climate Change in Europe." *Science Daily*, January 18, 2012. http://www.sciencedaily.com/releases/2012/01/120118111742.htm (accessed February 26, 2023).

79. Alex Fox, "Climate Change Lays Waste to Butterflies Across American West." *Smithsonian*, March 2021. https://www.smithsonianmag.com/smart-news/climate-change-lays-waste-butterflies-across-american-west-180977192/ (accessed February 26, 2023).

80. American Bird Conservancy, "Climate Change." https://abcbirds.org/threat/climate-change/ (accessed February 26, 2023).

81. Gore, *An Inconvenient Truth*; Appenzeller, "The Big Thaw."

82. United Nations Environment Programme, *High Mountain Glaciers and Climate Change* (2010). https://wedocs.unep.org/handle/20.500.11822/8101 (accessed February 26, 2023).

83. James Hansen, "Game Over for the Climate." *New York Times*, May 9, 2012. http://www.nytimes.com/2012/05/10/opinion/game-over-for-the-climate.html (accessed February 26, 2023).

84. Graham Readfearn, "Has Veteran Climate Scientist James Hansen Foretold the 'Loss of All Coastal Cities' with Latest Study?" *The Guardian*, March 24, 2016. http://www.theguardian.com/environment/planet-oz/2016/mar/24/has-veteran-climate-scientist-james-hansen-foretold-the-loss-of-all-coastal-cities-with-latest-study (accessed February 26, 2023).

85. Elisabeth Ponsot, "Will Germany Banish Fossil Fuels before the US?" *Mother Jones*, January 23, 2013. http://www.motherjones.com/environment/2013/01/video-germany-will-banish-fossil-fuels-renewable-energy (accessed February 26, 2023).

86. Quoted in Elisabeth Rosenthal, "Life after Oil and Gas." *New York Times*, March 23, 2013. http://www.nytimes.com/2013/03/24/sunday-review/life-after-oil-and-gas.html?ref=opinion (accessed February 26, 2023).

87. Michael Riordan, "Time for a Carbon Tax?" *San Francisco Chronicle*, March 23, 2007, p. B11.

88. Andrew Logan, "Countering Climate Change with Cool Pavement." *MIT News*, August 22, 2021. https://news.mit.edu/2021/countering-climate-change-cool-pavements-0822 (accessed February 26, 2023).

89. United States Environmental Protection Agency, "Advancing Sustainable Materials Management: 2018 Fact Sheet." https://www.epa.gov/sites/default/files/2021-01/documents/2018_ff_fact_sheet_dec_2020_fnl_508.pdf (accessed February 26, 2023).

90. World Bank, "Solid Waste Management," February 11, 2022. https://www.worldbank.org/en/topic/urbandevelopment/brief/solid-waste-management (accessed February 26, 2023).

91. World Bank, "Solid Waste Management."

92. Jon Brooks, "Are Paper Bags Really That Much Better than Plastic?" *KQED*, June 5, 2013. https://www.kqed.org/news/98782/are-paper-bags-really-that-much-better-than-plastic-2 (accessed February 26, 2023).

93. Jonathan Klick and Joshua D. Wright, "Grocery Bag Bans and Foodborne Illness." University of Pennsylvania, Institute for Law & Economics research paper no. 13-2, November 2, 2012. http://ssrn.com/abstract=2196481 (accessed February 26, 2023).

94. Amelia Lucas, "Starbucks Unveils New Plans to Eliminate Single-Use Cups, Encourage Reusable Mugs." CNBC, March 15, 2022. https://www.cnbc.com/2022/03/15/starbucks-unveils-new-plans-to-eliminate-single-use-cups-encourage-reusable-mugs.html (accessed February 26, 2023).

95. Lucas, "Starbucks Unveils New Plans."

96. Statista, Global E-Waste—Statistics & Facts (2021). https://www.statista.com/topics/3409/electronic-waste-worldwide/ (accessed February 26, 2023).

97. "Ghana: Digital Dumping Ground." *PBS's Frontline*, January 23, 2009. http://www.pbs.org/frontlineworld/stories/ghana804/video/video_index.html (accessed February 26, 2023).

98. Oregon State University, "Residents Near Chinese E-Waste Site Face Greater Cancer Risk." *Science Daily*, January 23, 2013. http://www.sciencedaily.com/releases/2013/01/130123101615.htm (accessed February 26, 2023).

99. *Sierra Club Magazine*, November–December 2005, pp. 42–47.

100. A Recycling Revolution, "Aluminum Recycling Facts." http://www.recycling-revolution.com/recycling-facts.html (accessed February 26, 2023).

101. Larry West, "The Benefits of Aluminum Recycling" Tree-Hugger, July 24, 2019, https://www.treehugger.com/the-benefits-of-aluminum-recycling-1204138 (accessed March 3, 2023).

102. National Resources Defense Council, "Biomass Energy and Cellulosic Ethanol." http://www.nrdc.org/energy/renewables/biomass.asp (accessed February 26, 2023).

103. "Fast Facts," Wilderness.net. http://www.wilderness.net/NWPS/fastfacts (accessed February 26, 2023).

104. Ben Hoyle, "Indigenous Alaskans Infuriated by Biden's Decision to Halt Oil Drilling." *The Times*, July 29, 2021. https://www.thetimes.co.uk/article/indigenous-alaskans-infuriated-by-bidens-decision-to-halt-oil-drilling-qc2q8cxqp (accessed February 26, 2023).

105. See "When to Say No." *New York Times*, March 10, 2013. https://www.nytimes.com/2013/03/11/opinion/when-to-say-no-to-the-keystone-xl.html (accessed February 26, 2023).

106. NRDC, "Tar Sands Invasion: How Dirty and Expensive Oil from Canada Threatens America's New Energy Economy," May 2010. https://www.nrdc.org/sites/default/files/TarSandsInvasion.pdf (accessed February 26, 2023).

107. Larry Rohter and Andrew C. Revkin, "Cheers, and Concern, for New Climate Pact." *New York Times*, December 13, 2004. http://www.nytimes.com/2004/12/13/world/americas/cheers-and-concern-for-new-climate-pact.html (accessed February 26, 2023).

108. Rohter and Revkin, "Cheers, and Concern, for New Climate Pact."

109. Ian Austen, "Canada Announces Exit from Kyoto Climate Treaty." *New York Times*, December 12, 2011. http://www.nytimes.com/2011/12/13/science/earth/canada-leaving-kyoto-protocol-on-climate-change.html (accessed February 26, 2023).

110. Jim Daley, "U.S. Exits Paris Climate Accord after Trump Stalls Global Warming Action for Four Years." *Scientific American*, November 4, 2020, https://www.scientificamerican.com/article/u-s-exits-paris-climate-accord-after-trump-stalls-global-warming-action-for-four-years/ (accessed February 26, 2023).

111. H. J. Mai, "U.S. Officially Rejoins Paris Agreement on Climate Change." NPR, February 19, 2021. https://www.npr.org/2021/02/19/969387323/u-s-officially-rejoins-paris-agreement-on-climate-change (accessed February 26, 2023).

112. Michelle Nichols and Kate Abnett, "Supreme Court Ruling Casts Cloud over U.S. Leadership in Global Climate Fight." Reuters, June 30, 2022. https://www.reuters.com/business/environment/us-emissions-ruling-setback-climate-fight-un-says-2022-06-30/ (accessed February 26, 2023).

113. "You Are Stealing Our Future: Greta Thunberg, 15, Condemns the World's Inaction on Climate Change." *Democracy Now*, December 13, 2018, https://www.democracynow.org/2018/12/13/you_are_stealing_our_future_greta (accessed February 26, 2023).

114. Greta Thunberg, "There Are No Real Climate Leaders Yet—Who Will Step Up at Cop26?" *The Guardian*, October 21, 2021. https://www.theguardian.com/commentisfree/2021/oct/21/climate-leaders-cop26-uk-climate-crisis-glasgow (accessed February 26, 2023).

115. Paul and Anne Ehrlich, "Too Many People, Too Much Consumption." *Environment 360*, August 4, 2008. http://e360.yale.edu/feature/too_many_people_too_much_consumption/2041/ (accessed February 26, 2023).

116. Garrett Hardin, "The Tragedy of the Commons." *Science* 162 (1968), pp. 1243–48; also see Garrett Hardin, "Lifeboat Ethics: The Case against Helping the Poor." *Psychology Today*, September 1974.

117. See Andrew Fiala, "Nero's Fiddle: On Hope and Despair and the Ecological Crisis." *Ethics and the Environment* 15: 1 (Spring 2010).

118. Jared Diamond, *Collapse: How Societies Choose to Fail or Succeed* (New York: Viking Press, 2005).

Chapter 20

1. See Immanuel Kant, "Duties to Animals and Spirits," in *Lectures on Ethics* (Cambridge, UK: Cambridge University Press, 1997); and see Tom Regan's discussion in *The Case for Animal Rights* (Berkeley: University of California Press, 1983).

2. Jeremy Bentham, *Introduction to the Principles of Morals and Legislation* (London: Clarendon Press, 1823), Chapter 17, footnote.

3. Martha C. Nussbaum, *Frontiers of Justice: Disability, Nationality, Species Membership* (Cambridge, MA: Harvard University Press, 2006), p. 351.

4. Reported by Holmes Rolston III in *Environmental Ethics: Duties to and Values in the Natural World* (Philadelphia: Temple University Press, 1988), p. 50.

5. David DeGrazia, *Taking Animals Seriously: Mental Life and Moral Status* (Cambridge: Cambridge University Press, 1996), p. 46.

6. Peter Singer, *Animal Liberation: A New Ethic for Our Treatment of Animals* (New York: Random House, 1975). Singer was not the first to use the term *speciesism*. Richard Ryder also used it in his work *Victims of Science: The Use of Animals in Research* (London: Davis-Poynter, 1975).

7. Bonnie Steinbock, "Speciesism and the Idea of Equality." *Philosophy* 53: 204 (April 1978), p. 253.

8. Joel Feinberg, "The Rights of Animals and Unborn Generations," in *Animal Rights and Human Obligations*, eds. Tom Regan and Peter Singer (Englewood Cliffs, NJ: Prentice Hall, 1976), p. 195.

9. Regan, *The Case for Animal Rights*.

10. Peter Singer, "Animal Liberation at 30." *New York Review of Books*, May 15, 2003. http://www.nybooks.com/articles/archives/2003/may/15/animal-liberation-at-30/?pagination=false#fn5-501709338 (accessed February 28, 2023).

11. Gary L. Francione, *Why Veganism Matters: The Moral Value of Animals* (New York: Columbia University Press, 2021), 11.

12. "Singer Says: The Satya Interview with Peter Singer." *Satya*, October 2006. http://www.satyamag.com/oct06/singer.html (accessed February 28, 2023).

13. Francione's critique of Singer is found at https://www.abolitionistapproach.com/mcdonalds-cage-free-eggs-peter-mcsinger-and-the-mcanimal-movement/ (accessed February 28, 2023).

14. Bob Fischer, *The Ethics of Eating Animals: Usually Bad, Sometimes Wrong, and Often Permissible* (New York: Routledge, 2020).

15. See Paul B. Thompson, "Philosophical Ethics and the Improvement of Farmed Animal Lives." *Animal Frontiers* 10: 1 (January 20, 2020), pp. 21–28.

16. Peter Steinhart, The Company of Wolves (New York: Random House, 1996), Chapter 7.

17. Virginia Morell, "Massive Wolf Kill Disrupts Long-Running Study of Yellowstone Park Packs: Hunters Have Killed More than 500 Wolves in Montana, Idaho, and Wyoming in Recent Months." *Science*, January 31, 2022. https://www.science.org/content/article/massive-wolf-kill-disrupts-long-running-study-yellowstone-park-packs# (accessed February 28, 2023).

18. Footloose Montana, "Trapping Is Very Different than Hunting." https://www.footloosemontana.org/trapping-is-not-hunting.html (accessed February 28, 2023).

19. Ken Cole, "The Killing Agency: Wildlife Services' Brutal Methods Leave a Trail of Animal Death." *Sacramento Bee*, April 29, 2012. http://www.sacbee.com/news/investigations/wildlife-investigation/article2574599.html (accessed February 28, 2023).

20. Christopher Ketcham, "The Rogue Agency." *Harper's Magazine*, March 2016. https://harpers.org/archive/2016/03/the-rogue-agency/ (accessed February 28, 2023).

21. Jim Posewitz, *Beyond Fair Chase* (Guilford, CT: Globe Pequot, 1994), p. 57.

22. Wayne Pacelle, "Stacking the Hunt." *New York Times*, December 9, 2003. http://www.nytimes.com/2003/12/09/opinion/09PACE.html (accessed February 28, 2023).

23. "Congress to Consider Banning Bear Baiting on Federal Land." *Brainerd Dispatch*, January 3, 2003. https://www.brainerddispatch.com/sports/congress-to-consider-banning-bear-baiting-on-federal-land (accessed February 28, 2023).

24. Alaska Department of Fish and Game, "Online Bear Baiting Clinic: Ethics and Responsibilities." http://www.adfg.alaska.gov/index.cfm?adfg=bearbaiting.ethics (accessed February 28, 2023).

25. Michael E. Miller, "Did Walter Palmer Give Cecil the Lion a 'Fair Chase'? We Asked a Hunter/Philosopher." *Washington Post*, July 31, 2015. https://www.washingtonpost.com/news/morning-mix/wp/2015/07/31/did-walter-palmer-give-cecil-the-lion-a-fair-chase-we-asked-a-hunterphilosopher/ (accessed February 28, 2023).

26. Erica Goode, "After Cecil Furor, U.S. Aims to Protect Lions through Endangered Species Act." *New York Times*, December 20, 2015. http://www.nytimes.com/2015/12/21/science/us-to-protect-african-lions-under-endangered-species-act.html (accessed February 28, 2023).

27. Defenders of Wildlife, Protect America's Wildlife (PAW) Act, *Aerial Hunting FAQs*. http://www.defenders.org/sites/default/files/publications/aerial_hunting_q_and_a.pdf (accessed February 28, 2023).

28. Defenders of Wildlife, Protect America's Wildlife (PAW) Act.

29. John Frank, "Palin Supports Aerial Hunting of Wolves and Other Wildlife." Politifact, October 1, 2008. https://www.politifact.com/factchecks/2008/oct/01/defenders-wildlife-action-fund-defenders-wildlife-/palin-supports-aerial-shooting-for-a-reason/ (accessed February 28, 2023).

30. See documentation provided at "Makah Tribal Whale Hunt," NOAA Fisheries. https://www.fisheries.noaa.gov/west-coast/marine-mammal-protection/makah-tribal-whale-hunt (accessed February 28, 2023).

31. "For the Whales: Sea Shepherd on Makah Tribe's Request to Hunt Whales." Sea Shepherd, November 6, 2019. https://seashepherd.org/2019/11/06/for-the-whales-sea-shepherd-on-makahs-tribe-request-to-hunt-whales/ (accessed February 28, 2023).

32. Paul Watson, "The Laws of Ecology, for the Survival of the Human Species." Lifegate, December 13, 2019. https://www.lifegate.com/paul-watson-laws-of-ecology (accessed February 28, 2023).

33. Charlotte Coté, *Spirits of Our Whaling Ancestors: Revitalizing Makah and Nuu-chah-nulth* (Seattle: University of Washington Press, 2010), p. 42.

34. Leo Tolstoy, "The First Step," in *Cultural Encyclopedia of Vegetarianism*, ed. Margaret Puskar-Pasewicz (Santa Barbara, CA: ABC-CLIO), p. 248.

35. Mohandas K. Gandhi, *An Autobiography: The Story of My Experiments with Truth* (Boston: Beacon Press, 1993), p. 235.

36. Michael Martin, "A Critique of Moral Vegetarianism," *Reason Papers* 3 (Fall 1976), pp. 13–43.

37. Kenny Torrella, "The Fight over Cage-Free Eggs and Bacon in California, Explained." Vox, August 10, 2021. https://www.vox.com/future-perfect/22576044/prop-12-california-eggs-pork-bacon-veal-animal-welfare-law-gestation-crates-battery-cages (accessed February 28, 2023).

38. See Coalition to Ban the Crates, "State Laws Banning the Extreme Confinement of Mother Pigs and Veal Crates"; and Antonia Noori Farzan and Quentin Ariès, "Europe Weighs Banning Cages for Farm Animals." *Washington Post*, June 1, 2021. https://www.washingtonpost.com/world/2021/07/01/europe-cages-farming/ (accessed February 28, 2023).

39. See Erik Marcus, *Meat Market: Animals, Ethics, and Money* (Boston: Brio Press, 2005), p. 33.

40. See Peter Singer and Jim Mason, *The Ethics of What We Eat: Why Our Food Choices Matter* (New York: Rodale, 2006), pp. 67–68.

41. North American Meat Institute, "The United States Meat Industry at a Glance." https://www.meatinstitute.org//index.php/d/sp/i/47465/pid/47465?ht=d/sp/i/47465/pid/47465 (accessed February 28, 2023).

42. "Globally, We Consume around 350 Million Tons of Meat a Year," The World Counts. https://www.theworldcounts.com/challenges/consumption/foods-and-beverages/world-consumption-of-meat (accessed February 28, 2023). For prior predictions, see Steinfeld et al., "Livestock in a Changing Landscape." United Nations Educational, Scientific, and Cultural Organization, April 2008. http://unesdoc.unesco.org/images/0015/001591/159194e.pdf (accessed February 28, 2023).

43. See James Rachels, "Vegetarianism and 'the Other Weight Problem,'" in *World Hunger and Moral Obligation*, eds. William Aiken and Hugh LaFollette (Englewood Cliffs, NJ: Prentice Hall, 1977).

44. See Carol J. Adams, *The Sexual Politics of Meat: A Feminist-Vegetarian Critical Theory* (New York: Continuum, 1990); or Josephine Donovan and Carol J. Adams, eds., *The Feminist Care Tradition in Animal Ethics: A Reader* (New York: Columbia University Press, 2007).

45. Peter Singer, *Ethics in the Real World: 82 Brief Essays on Things That Matter* (Princeton, NJ: Princeton University Press, 2016), p. 62.

46. Gary L. Francione, "Should Animal Rights Advocates Promote 'In-Vitro' or 'Cultured' Meat?" Animal Rights: The Abolitionist Approach, August 8, 2018. https://www.abolitionistapproach.com/should-animal-rights-advocates-promote-in-vitro-or-cultured-meat/ (accessed February 28, 2023).

47. Matt Reynolds, "The Clean Meat Industry Is Racing to Ditch Its Reliance on Foetal Blood." *Wired*, March 20, 2018. https://www.wired.co.uk/article/scaling-clean-meat-serum-just-finless-foods-mosa-meat (accessed February 28, 2023).

48. Jerod M. Loeb, William R. Hendee, Steven J. Smith, and M. Roy Schwarz, "Human vs. Animal Rights: In Defense of Animal Research." *Journal of the American Medical Association* 262: 19 (November 17, 1989), pp. 2716–20.

49. Loeb et al., "Human vs. Animal Rights."

50. John F. Lauerman, "Animal Research." *Harvard Magazine* (January–February 1999), pp. 49–57.

51. "Everything You Need to Know about Polio in the U.S." Scientific American September 22, 2022, https://www.scientificamerican.com/article/everything-you-need-to-know-about-polio-in-the-u-s/#:~:text=Wild%20poliovirus%20causes%20polio%20unrelated,country%20at%20all%20since%201993 (accessed March 3, 2023).

52. Holcomb B. Noble, "Rat Studies Raise Hope of Conquering Paralysis." *New York Times*. January 25, 2000, p. D7. http://www.nytimes.com/2000/01/25/health/rat-studies-raise-hope-of-conquering-paralysis.html (accessed February 28, 2023).

53. Health Physics Society, "Radioactive Scorpion Venom for Fighting Cancer." *Science Daily*, June 27, 2006. http://www.sciencedaily.com/releases/2006/06/060627174755.htm (accessed February 28, 2023).

54. Tom Abate, "Biotech Firms Transforming Animals into Drug-Producing Machines." *San Francisco Chronicle*, January 17, 2000, p. B1. http://www.sfgate.com/business/article/Biotech-Firms-Transforming-Animals-Into-2783363.php (accessed February 28, 2023).

55. Simon Makin, "From Hamsters to Baboons: The Animals Helping Scientists Understand the Coronavirus." *Scientific American*, May 14, 2020. https://www.scientificamerican.com/article/from-hamsters-to-baboons-the-animals-helping-scientists-understand-the-coronavirus/ (accessed February 28, 2023).

56. U.S. Department of Agriculture, "Legislative History of the Animal Welfare Act," updated June 2014. https://sgp.fas.org/crs/misc/R47180.pdf (accessed February 28, 2023).

57. Lauerman, "Animal Research," p. 51.

58. People for the Ethical Treatment of Animals (PETA), "Rats, Mice, and Birds Deserve Protection under the Animal Welfare Act." http://www.peta.org/features/unc-awa.aspx (accessed February 28, 2023).

59. "The Animal Welfare Act," The Humane League, Jan. 20, 2022, https://thehumaneleague.org/article/animal-welfare-act (accessed February 28, 2023).

60. The Humane Society of the United States, https://www
.humanesociety.org/all-our-fights/taking-suffering-out
-science (accessed February 28, 2023).

61. Larry Carbone, "Estimating mouse and rat use in American
laboratories by extrapolation from Animal Welfare Act-
regulated species." *Scientific Reports* 11, 493 (2021).

62. "How many mice and rats are used in U.S. labs? Controversial study says more than 100 million" Science, January 12,
2021, https://www.science.org/content/article/how-many
-mice-and-rats-are-used-us-labs-controversial-study-says
-more-100-million (accessed February 28, 2023).

63. John Hopkins University, Center for Alternatives to Animal
Testing. http://caat.jhsph.edu/ (accessed February 28, 2023).

64. U.S. Department of Agriculture, Animal and Plant Health
Inspection Service, *Annual Report Animal Usage by Fiscal
Year* (2018). https://www.aphis.usda.gov/animal_welfare
/downloads/Annual-Report-Summaries-State-Pain-FY18.
pdf (accessed February 28, 2023).

65. James Gorman, "Agency Moves to Retire Most Research
Chimps," *The New York Times*, January 22, 2013. http://
www.nytimes.com/2013/01/23/science/nih-moves-to
-retire-most-chimps-used-in-research.html?_r=0
(accessed February 28, 2023).

66. Jocelyn Kaiser, "NIH to End All Support for Chimpanzee
Research." *Science*, November 18, 2015. http://www
.sciencemag.org/news/2015/11/nih-end-all-support
-chimpanzee-research (accessed February 28, 2023).

67. Speaking of Research, "US Statistics." http://
speakingofresearch.com/facts/statistics/ (accessed
February 28, 2023).

68. See C. Ray Greek and Jane Swingle Greek, *Sacred Cows
and Golden Geese: The Human Cost of Experiments on
Animals* (London: Continuum, 2001), pp.73–7.

69. "Is it time to replace one of the cornerstones of animal
research?" *Science*, January 25, 2020. https://www.science
.org/content/article/it-time-replace-one-cornerstones
-animal-research? (accessed February 28, 2023).

70. Lauerman, "Animal Research."

71. Center for Biological Diversity, "Africa's Two Elephant
Species Move Closer to Endangered Species Protection,"
March 15, 2016. https://www.biologicaldiversity.org
/news/press_releases/2016/african-elephants-03-15-2016
.html (accessed February 28, 2023).

72. Colin Dwyer, "Trump Administration Quietly Decides
Again to Allow Elephant Trophy Hunting." NPR,
March 6, 2018. https://www.npr.org/sections/thetwo
-way/2018/03/06/591209422/trump-administration
-quietly-decides-again-to-allow-elephant-trophy-imports
(accessed February 28, 2023).

73. Miranda Green, "U.S. Allows Hunters to Import Some
Elephant Trophies from Africa." *New York Times*, April 1,
2022. https://www.nytimes.com/2022/04/01/science
/elephant-trophies-hunting.html (accessed February 28,
2023).

74. Susan Ager, "As Ringling Ends Circus, See Where Its Elephants Retired." *National Geographic*, September 17,
2015. https://www.nationalgeographic.com/animals
/article/150916-ringling-circus-elephants-florida-center
(accessed February 28, 2023).

75. Cathy Free, "Former Circus Elephants Just Arrived at a
New Sanctuary. They Are Swimming and Grazing on Fruit
Buffets." *Washington Post*, May 13, 2021. https://www
.washingtonpost.com/lifestyle/2021/05/13/circus
-elephant-ringling-sanctuary/ (accessed February 28, 2023).

76. *Nonhuman Rights Project, Inc. v. Breheny*, June 14, 2022.
https://www.nycourts.gov/ctapps/Decisions/2022/
Jun22/52opn22-Decision.pdf (accessed February 28, 2023).

77. *Nonhuman Rights Project, Inc. v. Breheny*.

78. *Nonhuman Rights Project, Inc. v. Breheny*.

79. "Statement on New York Court of Appeals Decision in
Historical Elephant Rights Case," June 14, 2022. https://
www.nonhumanrights.org/media-center/statement
-court-of-appeals-decision/ (accessed February 28,
2023).

80. U.S. Fish and Wildlife Service, Environmental Conservation
Online System, "Listed Species Summary." https://ecos.fws
.gov/ecp/report/boxscore (accessed February 28, 2023).

81. IUCN, "The IUCN Red List of Threatened Species." http://
cmsdocs.s3.amazonaws.com/IUCN_Red_List_Brochure
_2014_LOW.PDF (accessed February 28, 2023).

82. IUCN, "Sumatran Rhino Likely To Go Extinct Unless Action
Is Taken Urgently, Warns IUCN," September 22, 2015.
http://www.iucn.org/media/news_releases/?21904
/Sumatran-Rhino-likely-to-go-extinct-unless-action-is
-taken-urgently-warns-IUCN (accessed February 28, 2023).

83. Carolyn Cowan, "One of World's Last Two Northern White
Rhinos Withdrawn from Breeding Program." Mongabay,
November 1, 2021. https://news.mongabay.com/2021/11
/one-of-worlds-last-two-northern-white-rhinos-withdrawn
-from-breeding-program/ (accessed February 28, 2023).

84. Drew Kann, "Endangered Mountain Gorillas Making a Comeback." *CNN*, March 29, 2016. http://www.cnn .com/2016/03/29/us/iyw-dian-fossey-gorilla-fund/index .html (accessed February 28, 2023); "East Africa's Mountain Gorilla Population."

85. Juliet Eilperin, "Fishing Is Pushing Sharks Closer to Extinction." *Washington Post*, March 1, 2013. https://www .washingtonpost.com/national/health-science/fishing-is -pushing-sharks-closer-to-extinction/2013/03/01 /8dd88eac-81e4-11e2-8074-b26a871b165a_story.html (accessed February 28, 2023).

86. Richard Harris, "Whales, Dolphins Are Collateral Damage in Our Taste for Seafood." *NPR*, January 8, 2014. http:// www.npr.org/sections/thesalt/2014/01/07/260555381 /thousands-of-whales-dolphins-killed-to-satisfy-our -seafood-appetite (accessed February 28, 2023).

87. Rolston III, *Environmental Ethics*, p. 129.

88. Rolston III, *Environmental Ethics*.

89. Nicholas Rescher, "Why Save Endangered Species?," in *Unpopular Essays on Technological Progress* (Pittsburgh, PA: University of Pittsburgh Press, 1980), p. 83. A similar point is made by Tom Regan, *The Case for Animal Rights*, p. 359; and Joel Feinberg, "Rights of Animals and Unborn Generations," pp. 55–56.

90. Charles Darwin, *The Origin of Species* (Baltimore: Penguin, 1968), p. 108.

91. Rolston III, *Environmental Ethics*, p. 135.

92. Rolston III, *Environmental Ethics*, p. 136.

93. Rolston III, *Environmental Ethics*, p. 145.

94. Regan, *The Case for Animal Rights*, pp. 361–62.

95. See Bobby Allyn, "The Google Engineer Who Sees Company's AI as 'Sentient' Thinks a Chatbot Has a Soul." NPR, June 16, 2022. https://www.npr.org/2022/06/16/1105552435 /google-ai-sentient (accessed February 28, 2023). Also see "How a Google Employee Fell for the Eliza Effect." *The Atlantic*, June 21, 2022. https://www.theatlantic.com /ideas/archive/2022/06/google-lamda-chatbot -sentient-ai/661322/ (accessed February 28, 2023).

96. NASA, "The Search for Life." https://exoplanets.nasa.gov /search-for-life/can-we-find-life/ (accessed February 28, 2023).

97. Immanuel Kant, *Anthropology from a Pragmatic Point of View* (Cambridge, UK: Cambridge University Press, 2006), p. 225. For discussion, see Peter Szendy, "Kant in the Land of Extraterrestrials," in *Kant in the Land of Extraterrestrials: Cosmopolitical Philosofictions* (New York: Fordham University Press, 2013), pp 45–80.

98. Immanuel Kant, "Universal Natural History and Theory of the Heavens," in *Kant: Natural Science* (Cambridge, UK: Cambridge University Press, 2012). For discussion, see Szendy, *Kant in the Land of Extraterrestrials*.

99. J. J. C. Smart, "Ethics and Science." *Philosophy* 56: 218 (October 1981), pp. 450 and 462.

100. Alan Turing, "Computing Machinery and Intelligence." *Mind* LIX (236), pp. 433–460.

101. Associated Press, "Construction Breaks Ground on Largest Urban Wildlife Crossing, Set to Stretch over US 101," April 23, 2022. https://www.usatoday.com/story/news /nation/2022/04/23/ca-construction-largest-urban -wildlife-crossing/7422557001/ (accessed February 28, 2023).

Glossary

A

Absolutism metaethical idea that there are eternal and unchanging values and rules (versus *relativism*).

Act utilitarianism utilitarian theory that focuses on judging whether individual acts create the greatest happiness for the greatest number (compare: *rule utilitarianism*).

Active euthanasia actively killing someone for the benefit of the one being killed (versus *passive euthanasia*).

Actuality ontological consideration focused on what a thing is at the present moment (versus what it has the potential to become); often employed in discussions of the ethics of abortion; see also *ontological status* and *potentiality*.

Ad hominem a phrase meaning "to the person"; ad hominem arguments are (usually) fallacious arguments that attack a person rather than the person's idea or logical reasoning.

Advance directive a health care directive that stipulates in advance what sort of care a patient wants or does not want in case of incapacity; see also *living will* and *durable power of attorney*.

Aesthetics the study of beauty and taste.

Affirmative action social programs that take positive steps to remedy past injustice and inequality (usually racial); for example: *preferential treatment*; criticized as *reverse discrimination*.

Ahimsa term meaning nonviolence; associated with South Asian traditions such as Hinduism and Buddhism.

Akrasia see *weakness of will*.

Altruism behavior that is oriented toward the well-being of others (versus egoism); see also *pro-social behavior*.

Animal rights idea that individual animals have an interest in their lives and a corresponding right not to suffer or be killed (associated with Regan); see also *animal welfare*.

Animal welfare idea that animal suffering matters and that we should not cause unnecessary harm to animals (associated with *utilitarianism* and Singer); see also *animal rights*.

Anthropocentrism approach to environmental ethics (and *animal welfare*) that maintains that human interests alone are the proper focal point (versus *biocentrism* and *ecocentrism*).

Arguments from analogy arguments based upon a comparison between items; relevant similarities among things are intended to incline us to accept conclusions about these things that are also relevantly similar.

Asceticism a theory or worldview that is focused on discipline and control, often including denial and control of physical pleasure and sex.

Autonomy self-determination, self-control, independence, and freedom of action.

B

Begging the question a fallacious argument in which the conclusion is assumed in the premises (also called a *circular argument*).

Biocentrism approach to environmental ethics that is focused on the value of biotic systems and all life (versus *anthropocentrism*); see also *ecocentrism*.

Bio-conservatism idea that we should not be "playing God" with regard to biotechnologies, sometimes based upon repugnance toward new technologies (associated with Kass).

Bioengineering projects aiming to develop mechanical supplements for biological systems, which can be used for therapy or enhancement.

Bioethics the application of ethical reasoning to topics involving life and living things.

Biotechnology interventions and manipulations of biological systems and organisms through the use of technological means including genetic engineering, cloning, the use of drugs, surgeries, and so on.

Biotic pyramid the interrelated food chains that unite plants, grazing animals, prey animals, predators, and human beings (associated with Leopold's *land ethic*).

C

Capitalism a social and economic system based on private property and freedom to make profit; see also *laissez-faire capitalism* (versus *socialism* and *communism*).

Cardinal virtues primary virtues; the four cardinal virtues in the ancient Greek tradition are justice, wisdom, moderation, and courage.

Care ethics ethical theory that emphasizes nurturing relationships, while downplaying autonomy and individualism (associated with Noddings).

Casuistry an approach to ethical reasoning that focuses on cases and case studies.

Categorical imperative Kantian idea about the universal form of the moral law, which is not based on hypothetical or conditional interests; Kant's

formulation: "act only according to that maxim, whereby you can will that it should also be a universal law" (versus *hypothetical imperative*).

Circular argument a fallacious argument that assumes what it seeks to prove (also called *begging the question*).

Cisgender someone who identifies with the sexual/gender identity they were assigned at birth or with traditional gender roles (as opposed to *transgender*).

Civil disobedience breaking a law in a civil manner that retains fidelity to the system of justice and accepts punishment as an act of protest.

Civil union a legally recognized relationship between same-sex partners, similar but not identical to marriage (also called *civil partnership* or *domestic partnership*).

Collateral damage term used in just war ethics to describe unintended noncombatant harm that is justified by application of the *principle of double effect*; see also *noncombatant immunity*.

Communism a social and economic system focused on communal ownership of the means of production, radical equality, and the abolition of social classes; see also *socialism* (versus *capitalism*).

Communitarianism a theory of society that emphasizes communal belonging and is critical of the individualistic focus of *liberalism* and *libertarianism*.

Compassion literally "suffering with" another, compassion is an

emotion (or virtue) that is oriented toward alleviating the suffering of others.

Consequentialism normative theories that focus on the consequences of actions; examples include *egoism*, *altruism*, *utilitarianism* (versus *non-consequentialism*).

Contractarianism normative theory that holds that moral norms arise from a contract or agreement between rational parties (associated with Hobbes and Rawls); see also *reciprocal altruism*.

Cosmopolitanism idea that there are (or ought to be) universal norms that unite people across the globe.

Criminal justice justice that is focused on punishment and correction (versus *social justice*); see also *retributive justice, deterrence, restorative justice*.

Cultural competence the ability or capacity to understand and respond to cultural differences.

Cultural relativism a descriptive claim about the fact that values differ depending on cultural context.

D

Decarceration the idea of eliminating prisons or radically reducing the role of incarceration in punishment.

Deep ecology extreme ecocentric idea in environmental ethics that emphasizes human belonging to nature and the intrinsic value of natural things (associated with Devall and Sessions).

Deontological ethics normative theory that morality ought to be focused on duties and adherence to rules and imperatives (associated with Kant).

Descriptive claims propositions that state true or false claims about facts in the world.

Descriptive egoism (defined under egoism).

Descriptive relativism descriptive claim that values differ depending upon culture and perspective.

Deterrence a focal point for consequentialist approaches to *criminal justice*, which is concerned with deterring criminals from committing crime (versus *retributive justice* and *restorative justice*).

Discrimination (in just war) principle of the just war theory that stipulates that just warriors should target only combatants and protect noncombatants; see also *noncombatant immunity*.

Discrimination (as injustice) to treat someone unfairly and unequally based upon racial, ethnic, gender, or other identity claims (not to be confused with discrimination in just war theory).

Distributive justice a theory of justice concerned with the fair distribution of benefits and harms within society (versus *retributive justice* and *procedural justice*).

Divine command theory idea that ethical norms are ultimately based upon the authoritative decrees of God.

Double effect the principle or doctrine of double effect is the idea in deontological ethics that holds that if the intention behind an action is

morally appropriate, unintended (but foreseen and accidental) negative effects may be permissible.

Durable power of attorney used to appoint or empower someone to make health care decisions for you in the case of incapacity; see also *advance directive* and *living will*.

E

Ecocentrism approach to environmental ethics that is focused on the value of the ecosystem as a whole and not merely on its relation to human beings (versus *anthropocentrism*); see also *biocentrism*.

Ecofeminism a critical version of environmental ethics that emphasizes the way that patriarchal systems have abused nature and a more productive feminine connection with nature.

Ecosystem a concept used in environmental ethics that refers to the broad integrated, coordinated, and organized whole, including plants, animals, and human beings.

Ecosystem services an anthropocentric understanding of the way that natural systems support human needs and interests.

Egoism normative or *ethical egoism* claims that we ought to pursue our own self-interest; *descriptive egoism* (also called *psychological egoism*) maintains that as a matter of fact we can pursue only our own self-interest (versus *altruism*).

Embryonic stem cells cells removed from a developing embryo, which can develop into multiple tissues; controversial because the embryo is destroyed to harvest them.

Emotivism metaethical idea that ethical propositions express emotional states (associated with Stevenson).

Empathy the ability or capacity to understand the feelings of another.

Enhancement an intervention that goes beyond natural/normal function and creates superior performance, employed in discussions of biotechnology (versus therapy).

Enlightenment period of fertile development of Western culture and philosophy, during the seventeenth and eighteenth centuries.

Environmental ethics field of ethical inquiry that is concerned with the question of the value of ecosystems, the natural environment, and the distribution of benefits and harms in relation to the environment.

Environmental justice a concern in environmental ethics that is focused on the fair distribution of harms and benefits to human beings in relation to environment impacts such as pollution (related to *distributive justice* and *social justice*).

Epicureanism theory of Epicurus, which holds that pleasure and happiness are primary (also called *hedonism*).

Epistemology theory of knowledge.

Ethical egoism see *egoism*.

Ethnocentrism the tendency to judge or understand things from a biased perspective grounded in one's own culture.

Eudaimonia Greek term for human flourishing and happiness that is more than simply pleasure; associated with Aristotle and *virtue ethics*.

Eugenics goal of producing genetically superior offspring, either through genetic screening or through more forceful interventions including forced sterilization.

Eurocentrism attitude or practice of interpreting the world from a perspective that focuses primarily on European interests, values, and history.

Euthanasia literally good death; also called mercy killing; forms include *active, passive, voluntary, involuntary*, and *nonvoluntary*.

Exoneration to be found innocent of a crime for which one was previously convicted and found guilty.

Extraordinary measures in discussion of end of life care and euthanasia, extraordinary measures are medical interventions that are not proven to be reasonably beneficial—may include, for example, experimental treatments or risky interventions (versus *ordinary measures*).

F

Fair chase idea in hunting ethics that the animal should stand some chance and the hunter requires some skill and good luck.

Female genital mutilation removal of parts of the female genitals (includes a variety of procedures); also called *female circumcision*.

Feminism intellectual commitment and a political movement that seeks justice for women and the end of sexism in all forms.

Feminist ethics a critical theory of ethics that rejects male-dominant

ideas, can include "feminine" ethics emphasizing community and caregiving (associated with Noddings).

Fundamentalism idea that truth is grounded in religious texts, traditions, and prophets.

G

Gay marriage marriage of homosexual couples, also called same-sex marriage; see also *civil union*.

Genetic screening process of choosing embryos based on their genetic assets prior to implantation; can include efforts to modify genes to eliminate disease or produce enhanced capacities.

Genetically modified organisms plants or animals that have been genetically altered by scientists in an effort to improve the stock and increase yield.

Global justice concern for distributive justice, environmental justice, and social justice across the globe.

Globalization process of increasing integration of global markets and ideas, by way of growing international cooperation and international business.

Golden Mean idea associated with virtue ethics that virtue is found in the middle between excess and deficiency.

Golden Rule idea that one ought to love one's neighbor as oneself or do unto others as we would have them do unto us.

Greatest happiness principle utilitarian idea that we ought to work to achieve the greatest happiness for the

greatest number of people; see also *principle of utility*.

H

Hate crime a crime that is accompanied by bias (racial, religious, gender, sexuality) against the individual who is the victim of the crime.

Health equity a concern for fairness and equal opportunity in health and health care.

Hedonism theory that holds that pleasure is the highest good; as a normative theory tells us we ought to pursue pleasure; see also *Epicureanism*.

Hippocratic Oath medical ethics pledge rooted in ancient Greek tradition; primary tenet is to do no harm.

Human rights rights that are basic to human beings, often described in universal terms that transcend national and cultural differences; see also *rights, natural rights*.

Humanism orientation to human concerns and interests (as opposed to theistic or religious orientation); see also *secular ethics*.

Hume's law the claim (derived from David Hume's thinking) that it is illegitimate to derive an "ought" from an "is"; see also *naturalistic fallacy*.

Hypothetical imperative Kantian idea of a conditional rule that governs prudential behaviors and skilled activities aimed at procuring or producing some conditional good (versus *categorical imperative*).

I

Implicit bias unconscious prejudices and attitudes, based upon stereotypical ideas, which affect our judgments and behaviors without conscious awareness.

Imperfect/meritorious duties Kantian idea about duties of virtue that are admirable and praiseworthy but not always necessary (versus *perfect/necessary duties*).

In vitro fertilization a process by which egg and sperm are united outside of the uterus, the consequent embryo is implanted into the uterus—a way to create pregnancy for infertile couples.

Individual relativism idea that ethical claims are relative to an individual's values and perspectives; see also *subjectivism*.

Inherent worth/value value residing by nature in something and without reference to any other value or good; see also *intrinsic value*.

Institutional racism see *structural racism*.

Instrumental value/goods things that are useful or good as tools or as means toward some other good (versus *intrinsic goods*).

Intersectionality an approach to social philosophy that emphasizes how various form of identity, discrimination, and oppression intersect in different ways in diverse cases.

Intrinsic value/goods things that have value in themselves and not merely as tools or means (versus *instrumental goods*); see also *inherent worth*.

Intrinsically evil means concept in just war theory that rules out some weapons and methods of war

as being evil in themselves (or mala in se).

Intuitionism metaethical idea that ethical truths are objective and irreducible and can be known by faculty of intuition (associated with Moore).

Involuntary euthanasia euthanasia that is done against an individual's will (versus *voluntary euthanasia* and *nonvoluntary euthanasia*).

J

Jus ad bellum just war concern for ethical issues arising in deciding to go to war, including *just cause*, *legitimate authority*, and *proportionality*.

Jus in bello just war concern for ethical issues arising within warfare, including *proportionality*, *discrimination*, and prohibition on *intrinsically evil means*.

Just cause concern of jus ad bellum, which holds that a war is justified only if there is a just cause, including defending the innocent or repelling aggression.

Just war theory a theory about the justification of war that maintains that war should be limited by moral concerns; see also *jus ad bellum* and *jus in bello*.

K

Kingdom of ends Kantian ideal of rational, moral society in which persons are respected as ends in themselves.

L

Laissez-faire capitalism form of economic and social organization that

emphasizes leaving the market alone to regulate itself.

Land ethic an ecocentric idea in environmental ethics that views the land as a whole and claims that good actions contribute to the well-being of the whole (associated with Leopold).

Law of peoples idea of international law that transcends national borders.

Legitimate authority concern of jus ad bellum that holds that a war is justified only if the entity declaring war holds power legitimately.

Lex talionis an idea of *retributive justice* that is focused on equivalence or proportionality between the crime and the punishment, often described as "eye for an eye" justice.

LGBT acronym standing for "lesbian, gay, bisexual, and transgendered" (can be extended to include other sexual identities, sometimes abbreviated as LGBT+.

Liberalism a political theory that emphasizes a combination of concern for liberty and concern for social justice and distributive justice (associated with Rawls) (versus *libertarianism* and *socialism*).

Libertarianism a political theory about both the importance of liberty in human life and the limited role of government (associated with Rand) (versus *liberalism* and *socialism*).

Libertinism the quality or state of being a libertine, someone focused on sexual freedom and hedonism.

Liberty rights see *negative rights*.

Living wage a minimum wage standard indexed to the cost of living (versus *minimum wage*).

Living will a form of advance health care directive; see also *advance directive* and *durable power of attorney*.

M

Metaethical relativism metaethical claim that there are no objective or nonrelative values that could mediate disputes about ethics.

Metaethics study of moral concepts and the logic of ethical language.

Metaphysics the study of ultimate reality including the meaning and purpose of things.

Minimum wage legally mandated minimum hourly wage for labor (versus *living wage*).

Modernization theory of development that emphasizes increased secularization, spread of capitalism, and liberalization of economics and politics.

Moral agent a being who is able to express ethical concern and take responsibility for behaviors, attitudes, and actions (versus *moral patient*)

Moral patient an object of ethical concern, a recipient of moral concern, or a being that is viewed as having value (versus *moral agent*).

Moral pluralism see *value pluralism*.

Moral realism idea that there are ethical facts and that moral judgments can be said to be true or false; see also *objectivism*.

N

Natural law a theory of law that is grounded in claims about nature; natural law ethics is a normative theory

that holds that reason can discover objective ethical norms by examining natural human functions (associated with Aquinas).

Natural rights rights or entitlements that we have by nature, which are not created by positive laws and which create a limit to legal intervention; see also *rights*, *human rights*.

Naturalistic fallacy argument that inappropriately derives normative claims from descriptive claims (associated with Moore); see also *Hume's law*.

Negative peace a conception of peace focused on the lack of actual, physical violence (as contrasted with positive peace).

Negative rights rights of noninterference and prevention of harm, often called *liberty rights* (as opposed to *welfare rights* and *positive rights*).

Nepotism showing favoritism toward one's relatives.

Nihilism literally "nothing-ism," in ethics the idea that there are no objectively true values.

Non-anthropocentric the opposite of a human-centered (anthropocentric) worldview; related to claims about intrinsic value, biocentrism, or ecocentrism.

Noncombatant immunity idea in just war theory that noncombatants should not be deliberately targeted; see also *collateral damage*.

Non-consequentialism normative theories that do not focus on consequences of actions but instead on intentions, rules, or principles;

examples include deontology, divine command, and natural law (versus *consequentialism*).

Nonvoluntary euthanasia euthanasia that is done when the patient is incapacitated and unable to express her wishes or give consent (versus *voluntary euthanasia* and *involuntary euthanasia*).

Normative ethics study of prescriptive accounts of how we ought to behave.

Normative judgments evaluative or prescriptive claims about what is good, evil, just, and the like.

O

Objectivism metaethical idea that ethical propositions refer to objective facts (versus *subjectivism*); see also *moral realism*.

Ontological status related to a theory of being (ontology); questions about the moral status of things (fetuses, ecosystems, etc.) depend upon deciding what sorts of beings these things are; see also *actuality* and *potentiality*.

Ontology theory of being or beings; an account of what exists or about the sort of being a thing is.

Ordinary measures in discussions of end of life care and euthanasia, ordinary measures are those medical interventions that are proven to be reasonably beneficial in most cases (vs. *extraordinary measures*).

Original position idea used in John Rawls's theory of justice that asks us to imagine ourselves as original or founding parties to the social contract; see also *veil of ignorance*.

Original sin Christian idea that human beings inherit a tendency to do evil from the original sin of Adam and Eve.

P

Pacifism commitment to nonviolence and opposition to war (associated with Gandhi and King).

Palliative care health care that is aimed at pain management and dealing with suffering.

Palliative sedation sedation employed to provide pain management at the end of life (related to *terminal sedation*).

Paradox of hedonism problem for hedonism: when pursuing pleasure directly, we fail to obtain it; but pleasure occurs when we do not directly pursue it.

Paradox of toleration problem of whether one should tolerate those who are intolerant or who reject the idea of toleration.

Passive euthanasia allowing someone to die ("letting die") for the benefit of the one who is dying (versus *active euthanasia*).

Paternalism the idea that a state or some other authority ought to behave as a "father" who establishes rules that limit an individual's liberty out of concern for that person's overall good.

Perfect/necessary duties Kantian idea about duties of justice that we

always ought to do or that we always ought to avoid (versus *imperfect/ meritorious duties*).

Persistent vegetative state (PVS) a condition of permanent brain damage, characterized by lack of awareness and loss of higher brain functions; patient remains alive but has lost cognitive function; see also *whole brain death*.

Perspectivism relativist idea that there are only perspectives and interpretations, which cannot be reduced to a fundamental fact of the world.

Physician-assisted suicide closely related to euthanasia; doctors prescribe lethal medication but patients take the medication, killing themselves.

Pluralism the claim that there is more than one value or good.

Positive peace a conception of peace that emphasizes wholeness, harmony, and flourishing—and not merely the absence of violence (as contrasted with negative peace).

Positive rights rights of entitlement to basic subsistence and other means of living sometimes called *welfare rights* (as opposed to *liberty rights* and *negative rights*).

Post-structuralism a philosophical movement of the late twentieth century that emphasizes the social construction of categories of thought.

Potentiality ontological consideration focused on what a thing has the potential to become; often employed in discussions of the ethics of abortion; see also *ontological status* and *actuality*.

Precautionary principle an idea used in environmental ethics and in thinking about biotechnology that emphasizes avoiding risk when considering innovations.

Preferential treatment a form of affirmative action that intends to give preference to members of groups who were previously unjustly discriminated against; see *affirmative action*.

Premises the reasons given in an argument that provide support for the argument's conclusion.

Prima facie term meaning "on the face of it" or "at first glance."

Prima facie duties pluralist idea that there are several duties, each of which is valuable but which can end up in conflict (associated with Ross).

Principle of equality idea that we should treat equal things in equal ways and that we ought to treat different things in unequal ways.

Principle of utility utilitarian idea that what matters is the pleasure produced by an action, especially the pleasure produced for the greatest number of people; see also *greatest happiness principle*.

Prisoner's dilemma problem for rational self-interest and social contract: self-interested parties who do not trust one another will be unable to cooperate and thus will end up with less than optimal outcomes.

Problem of evil argument against the existence of God that claims that a good God would not permit evil but since evil exists, God must not exist (versus *theodicy*).

Procedural justice a theory of justice focused on the fairness of the procedures used to distribute benefits and harms (versus *distributive justice*).

Proportionality concern of just war theory that maintains that war should be a proportional last resort and that limited and proportional means should be employed during the course of war.

Pro-social behavior behaviors that intend to help others (versus antisocial behavior).

Psychological egoism (defined under *egoism*).

Q

Quarantine a restriction on human interaction based on worries about contagion.

Queer theory a post-structuralist approach to thinking about gender and sexuality that maintains that sex and gender roles are socially constructed (associated with Butler).

Quickening the point in pregnancy at which the mother is able to detect movement of the fetus; sometimes viewed as the time when the fetus attains moral status.

R

Racial profiling law enforcement technique that targets individuals based upon suspicion resulting from the individual's racial or ethnic identity.

Racialism idea that there are firm biological distinctions between human beings based on racial categories (critiqued by Appiah).

Racism unjust use of racial or ethnic categories to classify individuals and distribute social benefits and harms.

Realism view on ethics of war that maintains that limits on warfare are merely pragmatic or prudential and that the goal is strength and victory.

Reciprocal altruism idea that altruistic behavior is traded with others in a mutually beneficial exchange; see also *contractarianism*.

Regenerative medicine an approach to medical therapy that aims to regrow damaged tissues and organs using stem cells—both embryonic stem cells and other forms of stem cells.

Relativism a variety of claims that deny the objectivity of values including: *descriptive relativism*, *individual relativism* (or *subjectivism*), *metaethical relativism*, and *social or cultural relativism*.

Relativism, social *or* **cultural** idea that ethical claims are relative to a social or cultural matrix.

Religious pluralism idea that diverse religions provide multiple paths toward a common truth (associated with Gandhi).

Reproductive cloning a cloning procedure that aims to develop an individual organism as a substitute for ordinary reproduction (versus *therapeutic cloning*).

Restorative justice an approach to *criminal justice* that seeks to make criminals take responsibility and make amends, while restoring the community that they have broken (versus *retributive justice* and *deterrence*).

Retributive justice a theory of *criminal justice* that focuses on giving criminals what they deserve and forcing them to pay back what they owe to victims or to society (versus *restorative justice* and *deterrence*); see also *lex talionis*.

Reverse discrimination an idea used to criticize affirmative action that claims that actions aiming to help those who were previously discriminated against result in discrimination against those who were the beneficiaries of past discrimination.

Rights basic entitlements that ordinarily cannot be taken away or overridden; can be positive entitlements (*positive rights*) or negative protections (*negative rights*) (associated with Locke); see also *natural rights* and *human rights*.

Rule utilitarianism utilitarian theory that focuses on postulating general rules that will tend to produce the greatest happiness for the greatest number (versus *act utilitarianism*).

S

Secular ethics approach to ethics that locates ethical norms in nonreligious principles acceptable to people from a variety of religions (versus *divine command theory*); see also *humanism*.

Secularization movement away from religious culture and toward a nonreligious public sphere; see also *modernization*.

Sentience the ability to feel, perceive, and be conscious of the world, used in discussions of animal welfare and abortion in considering the moral status of animals and fetuses.

Sex trafficking trading sex for money; also called prostitution.

Sexting sending and receiving sexually explicit messages via cell phones.

Sex-selective abortion abortion performed for the purpose of selecting the gender of the baby.

Skepticism questioning and doubting attitude.

Social contract theory idea that social norms and political agreement are derived from a mutually beneficial contract to which the parties would consent (associated with Hobbes, Locke, and Rawls).

Social Darwinism idea of applying Darwinian evolution to society as a way of improving the genetic stock of humanity (widely repudiated as immoral).

Social justice an approach to justice that is concerned with the fair distribution of goods in society, often associated with natural law theories (versus *criminal justice*).

Socialism a social and economic system focused on developing shared social assets and a social safety net; see also *communism* (versus *capitalism*).

Sociobiology a field of study that applies evolutionary and comparative biology to understanding social phenomena, including ethical behaviors.

Sound argument a valid argument with true premises.

Speciesism a pejorative term used to describe anthropocentrists, who maintain that human beings are superior to nonhuman animals (associated with Singer).

Stem cell research a promising line of research that could help to regenerate damaged tissues; controversial when it employs human *embryonic stem cells*.

Stoicism theory of ancient Stoic philosophers, which holds that obedience to natural law and duty is essential (despite pain).

Straw man argument fallacious argument that describes an opponent's position in such a way as to easily dismiss it.

Structural racism idea that social structures are constituted in ways that create disparate racial outcomes (also called *institutional racism*).

Structural violence violence that is present in oppressive or unjust social structures, even despite the lack of overt physical violence.

Subjectivism metaethical idea that ethical propositions refer to subjective dispositions or values (versus *objectivism*); see also *individual relativism, descriptive relativism, metaethical relativism*.

Supererogatory a term used to describe actions that go above and beyond the call of duty.

T

Teleological adjective used to describe ideas and theories that are focused on goals, purposes, or outcomes (related to *consequentialism*).

Terminal sedation use of sedatives in palliative care that aims to reduce suffering at the end of life but may also contribute to death and be considered as part of euthanasia.

Theodicy theoretical explanation of why a good God would permit evil; response to the *problem of evil*.

Therapeutic cloning a cloning procedure that is used to grow stem cells or tissues that could be used for organ donation or regenerative medicine (versus *reproductive cloning*).

Therapy an intervention employed to return something to natural/normal function, employed in discussions of biotechnology (versus *enhancement*).

Toleration attitude of forbearance or permissiveness for attitudes or behaviors that are disapproved; an open and nonjudgmental attitude.

Totipotent term describing the ability of embryonic stem cells to develop into any kind of tissue; see also *stem cell research*.

Tragedy of the commons worry about degradation of common resources when no one owns them, associated with concerns for environmental degradation (associated with Hardin).

Transgender persons who do not feel comfortable with or who do not identify with the traditional sex/gender roles assigned to them (see *cisgender*).

Transhumanism a movement aiming to improve human abilities, extend human life span, and increase cognitive capacity; sometimes referred to as *post-humanism* (associated with Bostrom).

U

Utilitarianism normative theory that we ought to concern ourselves with the greatest happiness for the greatest number of people (associated with Bentham and Mill).

V

Valid argument an argument in which the conclusion necessarily follows from the premises.

Value pluralism the metaethical idea that there is more than one objective value (associated with Ross); see also *prima facie duties*.

Vegetarianism commitment to avoiding eating meat including veganism, which avoids consuming any animal product including eggs, milk, and leather.

Veil of ignorance idea used in John Rawls's version of the social contract that asks us to ignore concrete facts about our own situation as we imagine the ideal social contract.

Viability the point at which a fetus might live outside of the womb if delivered early; sometimes used as a criteria for determining the permissibility (or not) of abortion.

Virtue ethics normative theory that maintains that the focus of morality is habits, dispositions, and character traits (associated with Aristotle).

Voluntary euthanasia euthanasia that is done with the consent of the one being killed or dying (versus *involuntary euthanasia* and *nonvoluntary euthanasia*).

W

Weakness of will problem in moral psychology: we sometimes will things that we know are not in our own self-interest or are unable to do things we know are good (also called *akrasia*).

Welfare rights see *positive rights*.

Whole brain death legal criteria for death focused not on respiration and heartbeat but on the presence of brain activity; see also *persistent vegetative state*.

Index